Modern Family Law

ASPEN CASEBOOK SERIES

Modern Family Law

Cases and Materials

Sixth Edition

D. Kelly Weisberg
Professor of Law
Hastings College of the Law
University of California

Susan Frelich Appleton
Lemma Barkeloo & Phoebe Couzins Professor of Law
Washington University School of Law

Wolters Kluwer

Published by Wolters Kluwer in New York.

Wolters Kluwer Legal & Regulatory Solutions U.S. serves customers worldwide with CCH, Aspen Publishers, and Kluwer Law International products. (www.WKLegaledu.com)

To contact Customer Service, e-mail customer.service@wolterskluwer.com, call 1–800-234–1660, fax 1–800-901–9075, or mail correspondence to:

Wolters Kluwer
Attn: Order Department
PO Box 990
Frederick, MD 21705

Printed in the United States of America.

2 3 4 5 6 7 8 9 0

ISBN: 978-1-4548-7005-0

Library of Congress Cataloging-in-Publication Data

Names: Weisberg, D. Kelly, author. | Appleton, Susan Frelich, 1948- author.
Title: Modern family law : cases and materials / D. Kelly Weisberg, Susan Frelich Appleton.
Description: Sixth edition. | New York : Wolters Kluwer, 2016. | Includes bibliographical references and index.
Identifiers: LCCN 2015040321 | ISBN 9781454870050 (alk. paper)
Subjects: LCSH: Domestic relations—United States—Cases.
Classification: LCC KF505 .W453 2016 | DDC 346.7301/5—dc23
LC record available at http://lccn.loc.gov/2015040321

SUSTAINABLE FORESTRY INITIATIVE
Certified Chain of Custody
Promoting Sustainable Forestry
www.sfiprogram.org
SFI-01042

SFI label applies to the text stock

About Wolters Kluwer Legal & Regulatory Solutions U.S.

Wolters Kluwer Legal & Regulatory Solutions U.S. delivers expert content and solutions in the areas of law, corporate compliance, health compliance, reimbursement, and legal education. Its practical solutions help customers successfully navigate the demands of a changing environment to drive their daily activities, enhance decision quality and inspire confident outcomes.

Serving customers worldwide, its legal and regulatory solutions portfolio includes products under the Aspen Publishers, CCH Incorporated, Kluwer Law International, ftwilliam.com and MediRegs names. They are regarded as exceptional and trusted resources for general legal and practice-specific knowledge, compliance and risk management, dynamic workflow solutions, and expert commentary.

Dedicated to
our families

■ SUMMARY OF CONTENTS

■ CONTENTS

II. Getting Married 105

IX. Parentage: Formation, Consequences, and Limits of the Parent-Child Relationship 797

PREFACE

The theme of this book—the conflict between respect for privacy and deference to state authority—offers a lens for examining family law today. Each chapter of this book uses this lens to explore the actual and appropriate role of the state in family decisionmaking. Chapter I considers the constitutional underpinnings of a right to privacy for the family and its members. Chapters II and III address the state's regulation of marriage before and after celebration. Intimate partner violence provides the focus of Chapter IV. Chapter V identifies the extent to which the legal system treats members of nontraditional families differently from, or similarly to, members of traditional families. Chapters VI and VII cover state regulation of divorce, including financial consequences, and Chapter VIII examines the state's role in child custody. Chapter IX explores the state's creation of the parent-child relationship as well as the consequences and limits of legal parentage.

Modern Family Law provides valuable interdisciplinary perspectives on family law. The field of family law has been heavily influenced by work in history, psychology, sociology, social work, medicine, anthropology, and philosophy. Many of our excerpts, as well as the Notes and Questions, incorporate these different perspectives in an attempt to shed new light on the nature of legal regulation of the family.

In addition, this book reflects an awareness of the impact that legal rules have on persons' lives. The law affects individuals in profound ways that legal abstractions cannot capture. The book attempts to reveal (through presentation of sociological and psychological research as well as narratives) the subjective experiences of family members when confronted with various socio-legal problems. The book emphasizes that family law is not just analyzed and applied—it is experienced.

Changes in the Sixth Edition

This major revision incorporates the latest legal developments on virtually every topic addressed in previous editions. It reflects not only the significant impact of nationwide marriage equality but also other contemporary developments, such as the retreat from marriage, economic inequalities among families, and new disputes engendered by assisted reproductive technologies. So much new material now exists on the topic of intimate partner violence that this edition includes a separate chapter devoted to that subject. Significant new state and federal legislation and case law update earlier materials throughout the book. In fact, the book includes more than a dozen new principal cases and a similar number of new problems.

New principal cases focus on issues of the constitutionality of a state ban on same-sex marriage; a constitutional challenge to the federal Defense of Marriage Act; the constitutionality of a state law on polygamy; spousal liability for the negligent transmission of sexual transmissible disease; teen dating violence; marital rape; the First Amendment defense to threats to kill a spouse; the rights of same-sex partners at dissolution; the child's right of representation in custody disputes; the effect of "living apart together" on postdissolution spousal support; the application of the Indian Child Welfare Act's special requirements to a noncustodial birth father in a challenged adoption; parentage contests for children conceived through assisted reproduction by same-sex couples and unmarried women; the disposition of frozen embryos; and the responsibilities of a former husband who learns he is not the biological father of a child born during his marriage. This edition devotes considerable attention to recent U.S. Supreme Court opinions on marriage equality (United States v. Windsor and Obergefell v. Hodges) and explores the impact of the marriage equality movement on the entire field of family law.

The book provides expanded coverage of the full range of topics that affect nontraditional families, including legal issues regarding sexual activity and intimacy, same-sex marriage, and parental rights and responsibilities. Considerable new material focuses on the rights (state, federal, international) of same-sex partners in the areas of contract enforcement; divorce; postdissolution support and property (including pension rights); inheritance law; immigration law; discrimination based on sexual orientation and gender identity in housing, employment, and health benefits; name change disputes; criminal and tort law; military service; child custody; parentage; adoption; and assisted reproduction.

Treatment of domestic violence has been expanded significantly and now occupies a separate chapter. Coverage is enhanced by the inclusion of new material on teen dating violence; the role of influential factors in intimate partner violence (such as gender, sexual orientation, disability, mental illness, race and ethnicity, immigration status, and social class); sexual assault in intimate relationships; interference with reproductive decisionmaking; elder abuse; threats to kill posted on social media; non-fatal strangulation; and stalking. In addition, the book adds new material on the dynamics and types of abuse; protection orders; duties of law enforcement; firearm restrictions; cybercrimes; evidentiary issues; intraspousal property crimes; housing and employment discrimination against victims; tort remedies; the role of intimate partner violence in custody decisionmaking; exposure of children to domestic violence; failure to protect; supervised visitation; protections in the Violence Against Women Act (VAWA), Affordable Care Act (ACA), and Family and Medical Leave Act (FMLA); and protection of battered immigrant spouses' rights. Provisions of the recently enacted Violence Against Women Reauthorization Act of 2013 (VAWA 2013) are addressed in depth.

This new edition continues to emphasize excerpts that bring the law to life, such as: women's experiences in abortion decisionmaking; the practice of online dating; the motivations of women who marry murderers; participants in gay and lesbian marriage ceremonies; experiences of persons in polygamous unions; changes in marriage over time; gender-based division of labor for childcare and housework; the effects of paternal leave on later father involvement in childrearing; same-sex partners' experiences of dissolution and discrimination; the effects of adultery on the decision to divorce and on postdivorce adjustment; the effect of divorce on children; the role of intimate partner violence in custody decisionmaking; the difficulties of enforcing child support obligations in the face of poverty; and personal perspectives on intercountry adoption and gamete donation. To continue the emphasis on the human interest aspects of case law, we have added a considerable number of new epilogues to the principal cases. We have included commentaries by lawyers, judges, and litigants (including a personal communication from Jim Obergefell). In addition, we have included photographs that evoke student interest.

This Sixth Edition continues to highlight empirical research and the influence of gender, sexualities, race, and class on family law issues. It incorporates empirical data on such topics as: pregnancy, abortion, and birth rates; teen sexual activity; the impact of access to physician-assisted suicide; online dating; attitudes about interracial marriage and same-sex marriage; research on marital satisfaction; division of labor between the sexes; married women's retention of their birth surnames; same-sex couples' and transgender persons' difficulties in name changes; same-sex parents' rights to be entered on children's birth and death certificates; romance in the workplace; pregnancy discrimination; effects of paternal leave on later father involvement in childrearing; pro se representation; recent national statistics on domestic violence; the frequency, prevalence, and severity of sexual assault and stalking in intimate partner relationships; the return of the extended family; census data on nontraditional families (opposite-sex and same-sex couples); dissolution rate of same-sex relationships; relocation of children; child support enforcement; children who are exposed to domestic violence; supervised visitation; adoption trends and practices; and developmental outcomes for children raised by same-sex parents.

Like earlier editions, this revision gives instructors considerable flexibility in designing family law courses of varying lengths and emphases. The editors have taught two-, three-, and four-unit courses based on these materials. The book can be adapted easily for shorter or longer courses. (The Teacher's Manual accompanying the book provides further pedagogical suggestions and sample syllabi.) For the problem-oriented instructor and student, the book includes many questions and problems, often derived from actual cases or current events.

Editorial Matters

Cases and excerpts have all been edited, often quite extensively. Most deletions are indicated by ellipses, with some exceptions. Some concurring and dissenting opinions have been eliminated; citations have been modified or eliminated; some footnotes and references have been omitted; and paragraphs have been modified, and sometimes combined, to save space and to make the selections more coherent. Brackets are used at times to indicate substantial deletions. Original footnotes in cases and excerpts are reprinted nonconsecutively throughout the book. The editors' textual footnotes are numbered consecutively and appear in brackets to differentiate them from original footnotes. We have followed A Uniform System of Citation except when that style conflicts with the publisher's style.

D. Kelly Weisberg
Susan Frelich Appleton

January 2016

INTRODUCTION

Family law explores the legal regulation of the family and its members. These members include husband, wife, parent, and child, as well as "significant others" whose relationships increasingly push family law beyond its traditional scope.

Family law today reflects a fundamental tension between respect for family privacy and deference to state authority. This conflict forms the overarching theme of this book. Specifically, the book explores the issue: How does the law allocate responsibility for decisionmaking about private family matters? A respect for privacy gives consideration to families' and individual family members' decisional autonomy on matters that intimately affect them.

Conversely, deference to state authority recognizes that the state has important interests (such as protection of vulnerable family members, financial support for dependent individuals, and dispute resolution) that may precipitate intervention in the family. Such concerns necessarily raise questions about the actual, as well as the appropriate, relationship of the state to the family.

Because the state accords legal protection to the family and family members, even basic definitions—what constitutes a "family" and who is a "family member"—are contested. Thus, a central issue explored throughout the book is: Which personal relationships qualify for legal protection and for what purposes?

Family law is a field in transition. Change is apparent in the evolving roles and responsibilities of family members, the definitions of a family, the shrinking social safety net, and the nature of legal regulation of the family and its members. The dynamic character of the field results, in part, from societal influences on family law. Over the past several decades, social developments have prompted significant changes in the field, including:

(1) the women's movement, which has led to changes in gender roles as well as public policy;
(2) the children's rights movement, which has recognized children's increased role in decisionmaking;
(3) changing sexual mores, which have resulted in the decreasing influence of morality;
(4) disillusionment with the traditional family, which has contributed to the growth of alternative family forms;
(5) the increasing visibility and acceptance of sexual minorities;
(6) dissatisfaction with traditional dispute resolution processes, which has given rise to alternative forms of dispute resolution;
(7) developments in reproductive technology, which have altered traditional methods of family formation; and
(8) the rise of the "culture wars" in the political arena, where matters of family law have become a key battleground.

All of these developments are challenging established conceptions of the family and parenthood.

Family law also reflects several important legal trends:

(1) the federalization of family law (that is, the increasing congressional role in family policy);
(2) the constitutionalization of family law (that is, the growing recognition of the constitutional dimensions of the regulation of intimate relationships); and
(3) the movement toward uniformity of state law.

These factors partly explain the changing role of the state in the contemporary regulation of the family.

Family law formerly was the exclusive domain of the states. Each state formulated and applied its own legal rules and procedures. In the past several decades, however, Congress has enacted legislation on many issues of family life—child support, child custody, child abuse and neglect, foster care, adoption, and parental leaves, to name a few. In addition, beginning in the 1960s, the Supreme Court handed down a number of decisions that limit state regulation of the family. One of the most significant developments is the Court's recognition and expansion of the notion of privacy.

Because family law primarily has been a matter of state regulation, legal regulations applicable to the family vary across the country. In an effort to bring uniformity to the field, the Uniform Law Commission has promulgated important model statutes (addressing marriage and divorce, premarital agreements, marital property, paternity establishment, child custody jurisdiction, spousal and child support, adoption, and the parentage of children born of new reproductive technologies). Another unifying influence has been the American Law Institute (ALI), which has proposed a reconceptualization of many aspects of family dissolution, clarifying the underlying principles and making policy recommendations to guide the states.

In the midst of so many societal changes and legal developments, family law has become an active theoretical site, generating fresh thinking about the field and its purposes. Some scholars understand family law as a system designed to privatize dependency, while others insist that family law today simply reflects modern family life. Some critiques challenge family law's conventional boundaries by urging consideration of previously excluded relationships, such as friendships and other care networks. Others seek to decenter marriage (or sex), and still others seek to incorporate welfare law in family law and to make more salient the consequences of economic and racial inequalities among families. Substantive gender equality (as distinguished from formal equality) remains important unfinished business on many theorists' agendas. Ongoing conversations consider whether family law should constitute a distinct field with its own exceptional rules or whether otherwise applicable legal principles should govern regardless of family relationships. Although we use the lens of privacy versus state intervention to examine family law, these alternative perspectives offer illuminating contrasts, and we refer to them when relevant throughout this book.

Today's family law classes offer the challenge and excitement of exploring this rapidly changing legal and theoretical landscape.

■ ACKNOWLEDGMENTS

The authors would like to thank the many individuals who contributed to this project. Colleagues at several institutions provided valuable reviews and suggestions, including Anita Bernstein, Laura Rosenbury, Elizabeth Sepper, and Peter Wiedenbeck. We also gratefully acknowledge the support of Dean Nancy Staudt and Academic Dean Beth Hillman. Several persons skillfully helped with manuscript preparation and administrative tasks, especially Beverly Owens and Divina Morgan. We appreciate the aid of librarians Lena Fish, Mark Kloempken, Kathie Molyneux, and Tony Pelczynski. We also recognize with special thanks the diligent research of the following students and former students: Megan Banta, Tessa Reinhard Castner (who also served as liaison to Jim Obergefell), Rachel Cocalis, Laura Gildengorin, Susannah Porter Lake, and George Morris. Finally, we extend our appreciation to The Froebe Group staff, especially Troy Froebe, Carianne King, Geoffrey Lokke (for his invaluable assistance with copyright permissions), and Cindy Uh, as well as the anonymous reviewers who offered such valuable suggestions. John Devins of Aspen Law & Business deserves our special thanks for shepherding the book through so many editions with such inestimable commitment, enthusiasm, and grace.

The authors would like to thank the following copyright holders for permission to excerpt their materials:

American Law Institute, Principles of the Law of Family Dissolution: Analysis and Recommendations §4.12, cmt. a; §5.04 & cmt. a. (2002). Reprinted with permission of the American Law Institute.

Anderson, Jack, Adventures Among the Polygamists, 1 Investigative Rep. Mag. 4-42 (Jan. 1982). Reprinted with permission.

Bailey, Beth L. From Front Porch to Back Seat: Courtship in Twentieth-Century America. pp. 19-22. © 1988, 1989 The Johns Hopkins University Press. Reprinted with permission of The Johns Hopkins University Press.

Bellafante, Ginia, Even in Gay Circles, the Women Want the Ring, N.Y. Times, May 8, 2005, §6 (Magazine), at 91. Reprinted with permission.

Bernard, Jessie, The Future of Marriage 16-18, 26-28, 40-41, 49-50 (1982). Reprinted with permission.

———, The Good-Provider Role: Its Rise and Fall, 36 Am. Psychol. 2-10 (Jan. 1981). Reprinted with permission.

Bohannon, Paul, The Six Stations of Divorce, in Divorce and After 29-32 (Paul Bohannon ed., 1970). Reprinted with permission by the publisher.

Bonavoglia, Angela, Kathy's Day in Court, Ms., Apr. 1988, at 46-49. Reprinted with permission by the author.

Bradsher, Keith, Ditching Your Betrothed May Cost You: Wedding Rings, Gowns, Cakes and Deposits Add Up, S.F. Chron., Mar. 20, 1990, at B5. Reprinted with permission.

Callahan, Sidney, Abortion and the Sexual Agenda, 113 Commonweal 232, 232-236 (1986). Reprinted with permission.

Caplow, Theodore, et al., The Quality of Marriage in Middletown: 1924-1976, in Middletown Families: Fifty Years of Change and Continuity 116-118, 120-121, 124-125, 126, 127, 135 (1982). Reprinted with permission by the publisher.

Cole, Harriette, Jumping the Broom: The African-American Wedding Planner 16-18 (1993). Reprinted with permission by the publisher.

Conde, Carlos H., Philippines Stands All But Alone in Banning Divorce, N.Y. Times, June 18, 2011. Reprinted with permission.

Coplan, Jill Hamburg, When a Woman Loves a Woman, NYU Alumni Mag. (Fall 2011) at 38. Reprinted with permission by the New York University Alumni Magazine.

Davis, Peggy Cooper, Moore v. East Cleveland: Constructing the Suburban Family, in Family Law Stories 77, 88-89 (Carol Sanger ed., 2008). Reprinted with permission by the publisher.

Demos, John, A Little Commonwealth (1999) pp. 152, 154-155, 157-162. © 1971 by Oxford University Press, Inc. By permission of Oxford University Press, USA.

Egan, Jennifer, Love in the Time of No Time, N.Y. Times, Nov. 23, 2003, §6 (Magazine), at 66. http://www.nytimes.com/2003/11/23/magazine/love-in-the-time-of-no-time.html?pagewanted=all&src=pm. Reprinted with permission by the author.

Friedman, Lawrence M., A History of American Law 141-142, 142-144, 378-381 (3d ed. 2005). Reprinted with permission by the publisher.

Garrow, David J., Toward a More Perfect Union, N.Y. Times, May 9, 2004, §6 (Magazine), at 52. Reprinted with permission by the author.

Gelles, Richard J. & Murray A. Straus, Intimate Violence 84, 88-96 (1988). Reprinted with permission by the publisher.

Goldstein, Dana, Conjugal Visits, Marshall Project (Feb. 11, 2015). Reprinted with permission.

Greenberg, Judith G., Domestic Violence and the Danger of Joint Custody Presumptions, 25 N. Ill. U. L. Rev. 403, 407-413 (2005). Reprinted with permission by the Northern Illinois University Law Review.

Grossberg, Michael, Governing the Hearth: Law and the Family in Nineteenth-Century America 156-157, 175-177, 189-193 (1985). Reprinted with permission by the publisher.

Halem, Lynne Carol, Divorce Reform: Changing Legal and Social Perspectives 181-183, 269-277 (1980). Reprinted with permission by the publisher.

Hall, Julie H. & Frank D. Fincham, Relationship Dissolution Following Infidelity, in Handbook of Divorce and Relationship Dissolution 153, 154, 156, 157-158, 159-160 (Mark A. Fine & John H. Harvey eds., 2006). Reprinted with permission by the publisher.

Hamilton, Vivian, Mistaking Marriage for Social Policy, 11 Va. J. Soc. Pol'y & L. 307, 355-360, 368-370 (2004). Reprinted with permission by the author.

Hetherington, E. Mavis, Marriage and Divorce American Style, Am. Prospect Online, Apr. 7, 2002. Reprinted with permission by American Prospect Online and the author.

Hochschild, Arlie and Ann Machung, The Second Shift: Working Families and the Revolution at Home 4, 7-10 (rev. ed., 2012). Reprinted with permission.

Isenberg, Sheila, Women Who Love Men Who Kill 34-35, 223-236 (2000). Reprinted with permission by the Kaplan Agency.

Joseph, Elizabeth, My Husband's Nine Wives, N.Y. Times, May 23, 1991, at A15. Reprinted with permission by the author.

Jurow, Judge George L., Reflections on the Legacy of In re Rebecca B., May 12, 2015. Reprinted with permission.

Kershaw, Sarah, In Some Adoptions, Love Doesn't Conquer All, N.Y. Times, Apr. 18, 2010, at ST1. Reprinted with permission.

Krause, Harry D., Child Support Reassessed: Limits of Private Responsibility and the Public Interest, in Divorce Reform at the Crossroads 166, 178-180 (Stephen D. Sugarman & Herma Hill Kay eds., 1990). Reprinted with permission.

Kressel, Kenneth, et al., Professional Intervention in Divorce: The Views of Lawyers, Psychotherapists, and Clergy, in Divorce and Separation 246, 250-255 (George Levinger & Oliver C. Moles eds., 1979). Reprinted with permission by the publisher.

LaFleur, Jo Carol, "Go Home and Have Your Baby," in The Courage of Their Convictions 320-328 (Peter Irons ed., 1988). Reprinted with permission by the publisher.

Leland, John, Beyond the Slogans: Inside an Abortion Clinic, N.Y. Times, Sept. 18, 2005, §1, at 1. Reprinted with permission.

Luker, Kristin, Abortion and the Politics of Motherhood 20-29 (1984). Reprinted with permission by the publisher.

Marquardt, Elizabeth, Between Two Worlds: The Inner Lives of Children of Divorce 21-22, 30-31 (2005). Reprinted with permission by the publisher and the Carol Mann Agency.

Mauro, Tony, A "Cultural Milestone" at the High Court: *Lawrence* Gay Attorneys Turned Out in Force to Witness *Lawrence* Arguments, Tex. Law., Mar. 31, 2004, at 11. Reprinted with permission.

Meier, Joan S., Domestic Violence, Child Custody, and Child Protection: Understanding Judicial Resistance and Imagining the Solutions, 11 Am. U. J. Gender Soc. Pol'y & L. 657, 705-707 (2003). Reprinted with permission of the American University Journal of Gender and Society

Mnookin, Robert H., Child-Custody Adjudication: Judicial Functions in the Face of Indeterminacy, 39 Law & Contemp. Probs. 226, 233-237, 255-256, 261-264, 289-291 (1975). Reprinted with permission by the author.

National Marriage Project, Social Indicators of Marital Health & Well-Being: Trends of the Past Five Decades: Marriage in The State of Our Unions: Marriage in America 62 (2012). Reprinted with permission.

National Partnership for Women & Families, Dads Expect Better 2-4 (June 2012), http://www.nationalpartnership.org/site/DocServer/Dads_Expect_Better_June_2012.pdf?docID=10581. Reprinted with permission by the National Partnership for Women & Families.

Obergefell, Jim, The Legacy of Obergefell v. Hodges, personal communication, July 28, 2015. Reprinted with permission.

Okin, Susan Moller, Justice, Gender, and the Family 122-123 (1989). Reprinted with permission by the publisher.

Papke, David Ray, State v. Oakley, Deadbeat Dads, and American Poverty, 26 W. New Eng. L. Rev. 9, 10-15 (2004). Reprinted with permission by the author.

Parkman, Allen M., Good Intentions Gone Awry: No-Fault Divorce and the American Family 72-75, 79-81 (2000). Reprinted with permission by the publisher.

Pearson, Jessica, & Nancy Thoennes, The Denial of Visitation Rights: A Preliminary Look at its Incidence, Correlates, Antecedents and Consequences, 10 Law & Pol'y 363, 375-379 (1988). Reprinted with permission by Law & Policy, John Wiley & Sons.

Pratt, Robert A., Crossing the Color Line: A Historical Assessment and Personal Narrative of Loving v. Virginia, 41 How. L.J. 229, 234-244 (1998). Reprinted with permission by the Howard Law Journal.

Presser, Stephen B., The Historical Background of the American Law of Adoption, 11 J. Fam. L. 443, 446-489 (1971). Reprinted with permission by the author.

Reinert, Patty, Pair Proud They Could Get Sodomy Law Thrown Out, Hous. Chron., Apr. 25, 2004, at A1. Reprinted with permission.

Rhode, Deborah L. & Martha Minow, Reforming the Questions, Questioning the Reforms: Feminist Perspectives on Divorce Law, in Divorce Reform at the Crossroads 191-199, 209-210 (Stephen D. Sugarman & Herma Hill Kay eds., 1990). Reprinted with permission.

Riessman, Catherine K., Divorce Talk: Women and Men Make Sense of Personal Relationships 65-72 (1990). Reprinted with permission by the publisher.

Roraback, Catherine G., Griswold v. Connecticut: A Brief Case History, 16 Ohio N.U. L. Rev. 395, 395-401 (1989). Reprinted with permission by the Ohio Northern University Law Review.

Rosenwald, Michael S., How Jim Obergefell Became the Face of the Supreme Court Gay Marriage Case, Wash. Post, Apr. 6, 2015. Reprinted with permission.

Scott, Elizabeth S. & Robert Emery, Child Custody Dispute Resolution: The Adversarial System and Divorce Mediation, in Psychology and Child Custody Determinations: Knowledge, Roles and Expertise 23-27, 39-42, 45-51 (Lois A. Weithorn ed., 1987). Reprinted with permission by the publisher.

Shahar, Robin, postscript, personal communication, Jul. 8, 2015. Reprinted with permission.

Social Trends Institute, Global Family Structure (2011). Reprinted with permission.

Spector, Robert G., The Do's and Don'ts When One Lawyer Represents Both Parties, Fam. Advoc. (Spring 1991), at 16-18. Reprinted with permission of the author.

Sugarman, Stephen D., Dividing Financial Interests on Divorce, in Divorce Reform at the Crossroads 130, 136-141 (Stephen D. Sugarman & Herma Hill Kay eds., 1990). Reprinted with permission.

Thomson, Judith Jarvis, A Defense of Abortion, 1 Phil. & Pub. Aff. 47-63 (1971). Reprinted with permission by Philosophy & Public Affairs and the author.

"Uniform Child Custody Jurisdiction & Enforcement Act (UCCJEA), Uniform Marriage and Divorce Act (UMDA), Uniform Parentage Act (UPA), Uniform Premarital Agreement Act (UPAA)."

Walker, Lenore, Terrifying Love: Why Battered Women Kill and How Society Responds 23-41 (1989). Reprinted with permission by the publisher.

Websdale, Neil, Assessing Risk in Domestic Violence Cases in Encyclopedia of Domestic Violence 38, 38-40 (Nicky Ali Jackson ed. 2007). Reprinted with permission.

Weddington, Sarah A., Question of Choice: 40th Anniversary Edition Revised and Updated (2013). Reprinted with permission by the author.

Weisberg, D. Kelly, Barred from the Bar: Women and Legal Education in the United States: 1870-1890, 28 J. Legal Educ. 485, 488-493 (1977). Copyright © 1977 Association of American Law Schools.

Weisberg, D. Kelly, Professional Women and the Professionalization of Motherhood: Marcia Clark's Double Bind, 6 Hastings Women's L.J. 295, 312-319, 321-322 (1995). Reprinted with permission by the Hastings Women's Law Journal.

Wilcox, W. Bradford, Marriage in Decline: No Big Deal? Institute of Family Studies, Apr. 1, 2015. Reprinted with permission.

Williams, Joan, Is Coverture Dead? Beyond a New Theory of Alimony, 82 Geo. L.J. 2227, 2267-2272, 2274-2275 (1994). Reprinted with permission by the George Washington Law Review and the author.

Williams, Wendy W., Equality's Riddle: Pregnancy and the Equal Treatment/Special Treatment Debate, 13 N.Y.U. Rev. L. & Soc. Change 325, 333-349 (1984-1985). Reprinted with permission by the New York University Review of Law & Social Change and the author.

Wolfer, Judith A., Top Ten Myths About Domestic Violence, 42 Md. Bar J. 38, 38-41 (2009). Reprinted with permission.

Woo, Elaine, Marc Christian MacGinnis Dies at 56; Rock Hudson's Ex-Lover, L.A. Times, Dec. 5, 2009, http://articles.latimes.com/2009/dec/05/local/la-me-marc-christian5-2009dec05. Reprinted with permission.

Wooten, Colton, A Father's Day Plea to Sperm Donors, N.Y. Times, June 19, 2011, at WK9 (op ed). Reprinted with permission.

Zuccardy, Jill M., Nicholson v. Williams: The Case, 82 Denv. U. L. Rev. 655, 657-660, 663-665, 667, 669 (2005). Reprinted with permission.

Images

Abuse, photograph. Reproduced by permission of iStock by Getty Images.

Baird, William, photograph. Reproduced by permission of Peter Simon.

Brown, Dusten and daughter Veronica, photograph. Reproduced by permission of Getty Images.

Brown, Kody, and wives Meri, Janelle, Christine, and Robyn, photograph. © Corbis. Reproduced by permission of Corbis.

Brown, Pat, California governor, photograph. © Corbis. Reproduced by permission of Corbis.

Bonauto, Mary, attorney, photograph. Reproduced by permission of the Gay & Lesbian Advocates & Defenders (GLAD).

Capobianco, Melanie and Matt, photograph. (c) Corbis. Reproduced by permission of Corbis.

Child custody, photograph. Reproduced by permission of Fotolia.com.

Cruzan, Nancy, gravestone, photograph. Reproduced by permission of Wellcome Library, London.

DeBoer, April, Jayne Rowse, and children, photograph. Corbis. Reproduced by permission of Corbis.

Elonis, Anthony, photograph. Courtesy of Facebook.

Garland, Lillian, photograph. Reproduced by permission of Getty Images.

Gonzales, Elian, and Fidel Castro, photograph. © Corbis. Reproduced by permission of Corbis.

Gonzales, Jessica, photograph. Reproduced by permission of the Associated Press.

Griswold, Estelle, photograph. © Corbis. Reproduced by permission of Corbis.

Hudson, Rock, photograph. © Corbis. Reproduced by permission of Corbis.

Ketubah, photograph. Reproduced by permission of Yale University.
Kowalski, Sharon, photograph. Reproduced by permission of Sophia Hantzes.
Lawrence, John & Tyron Garner, photograph. © Corbis. Reproduced by permission of Corbis.
Loving, Mildred and Richard, photograph. © Corbis. Reproduced by permission of Corbis.
MacGinnis, Marc Christian, photograph. © Corbis. Reproduced by permission of Corbis.
Marvin, Lee and Michelle Triola, photography. © Corbis. Reproduced by permission of Corbis.
Nesset-Sale, Jo Carol (LaFleur), photograph. Reproduced by permission of Jo Carol (LaFleur) Nesset-Sale.
Obergefell, Jim and John Arthur, photograph. Reproduced by permission.
Online dating, photograph. Reproduced by permission of Getty Images.
Patric, Jason and family, photograph. Reproduced by permission of FameFlynet, Inc.
Piscopo, Joe, photograph. © Corbis. Reproduced by permission of Corbis.
Principles of the Law of Family Dissolution, front cover, photograph. Reproduced by permission of the American Law Institute.
Savelyev, Artyom, photograph. Reproduced by permission of Associated Press.
Shanks, Randall, photograph. Reproduced by permission.
Shahar, Robin, photograph. Reproduced by permission of Robin Shahar.
Spyer, Thea, photograph. © Corbis. Reproduced by permission of Corbis.
Stern, Elizabeth & William, photograph. © Corbis. Reproduced by permission of Corbis.
Troxel, Jennifer & Gary, photograph. Reproduced by permission of Associated Press and USA Today.
von Stade, Frederica, photograph. Reproduced by permission of Getty Images.
Wallerstein, Judith, photograph. Reproduced by permission of the New York Times and Redux Pictures.
Weddington, Sarah, photograph. © Corbis. Reproduced by permission of Corbis and Sarah Weddington.
Whitehead, Mary Beth, photograph. © Corbis. Reproduced by permission of Corbis.
Wife beating, photograph. © Corbis. Reproduced by permission of Corbis.
Woman juggling clocks, photograph. Reproduced by permission of Fotolia.com.

Modern Family Law

I

Private Family Choices: Constitutional Protection for the Family and Its Members

Family law portrays family life as private. Indeed, the Supreme Court has written often about "the private realm of family life which the state cannot enter." What is the source of this limitation on state authority? Whom does it protect—family units or individual family members? What room does it leave for laws governing the family and other forms of regulation? What role does it envision for the state? And what does "family" mean, anyhow?

This chapter explores these questions. It begins with the development of the Supreme Court's privacy doctrine. It then considers controversies that sometimes pit family members against one another. Throughout, the cases, narratives, and other excerpts center on some of today's most divisive legal issues: contraception, parental authority, abortion, sexual freedom, and end-of-life choices. Emphasizing such contested matters, this chapter provides a lens through which to examine the outer limits of the state's power to regulate personal and family decisionmaking.

A. Evolution of the Right to Privacy

1. The Birth of Privacy

a. Meanings of Privacy

GRISWOLD v. CONNECTICUT

381 U.S. 479 (1965)

Mr. Justice DOUGLAS delivered the opinion of the Court.

Appellant Griswold is Executive Director of the Planned Parenthood League of Connecticut. Appellant Buxton is a licensed physician and a professor at the Yale Medical School who served as Medical Director for the League at its Center in New Haven. [Appellants were arrested and charged with giving information, instruction, and medical advice to married persons on means of preventing conception.]

The [statute] whose constitutionality is involved . . . provides:

> Any person who uses any drug, medicinal article, or instrument for the purpose of preventing conception shall be fined not less than fifty dollars or imprisoned not less than sixty days nor more than one year or be both fined and imprisoned. . . .

The appellants were found guilty as accessories and fined $100 each, against the claim that the accessory statute as so applied violated the Fourteenth Amendment. . . . We think that appellants have standing to raise the constitutional rights of the married people with whom they had a professional relationship. . . .

Coming to the merits, we are met with a wide range of questions that implicate the Due Process Clause of the Fourteenth Amendment. Overtones of some arguments suggest that Lochner v. New York, 198 U.S. 45 [(1905)], should be our guide. But we decline that invitation. We do not sit as a super-legislature to determine the wisdom, need, and propriety of laws that touch economic problems, business affairs, or social conditions. This law, however, operates directly on an intimate relation of husband and wife and their physician's role in one aspect of that relation.

The association of people is not mentioned in the Constitution nor in the Bill of Rights. The right to educate a child in a school of the parents' choice—whether public or private or parochial—is also not mentioned. Nor is the right to study any particular subject or any foreign language. Yet the First Amendment has been construed to include certain of those rights.

By Pierce v. Society of Sisters, [268 U.S. 510 (1925),] the right to educate one's children as one chooses is made applicable to the States by the force of the First and Fourteenth Amendments. By Meyer v. Nebraska, [262 U.S. 390 (1923),] the same dignity is given the right to study the German language in a private school. . . .

In NAACP v. Alabama, 357 U.S. 449, 462 [(1958),] we protected the "freedom to associate and privacy in one's associations," noting that freedom of association was a peripheral First Amendment right. . . . In other words, the First Amendment has a penumbra where privacy is protected from governmental intrusion. . . . Association . . . is a form of expression of opinion; and while it is not expressly included in the First Amendment, its existence is necessary in making the express guarantees fully meaningful.

The foregoing cases suggest that specific guarantees in the Bill of Rights have penumbras, formed by emanations from those guarantees that help give them life and substance. See Poe v. Ullman, 367 U.S. 497, 516-522 [(1961)] (dissenting opinion). Various guarantees create zones of privacy. The right of association contained in the penumbra of the First Amendment is one, as we have seen. The Third Amendment in its prohibition against the quartering of soldiers "in any house" in time of peace without the consent of the owner is another facet of that privacy. The Fourth Amendment explicitly affirms the "right of the people to be secure in their persons, houses, papers, and effects, against unreasonable searches and seizures." The Fifth Amendment in its Self-Incrimination Clause enables the citizen to create a zone of privacy which government may not force him to surrender to his detriment. The Ninth Amendment provides: "The enumeration in the Constitution, of certain rights, shall not be construed to deny or disparage others retained by the people." . . . We have had many controversies over these penumbral rights of "privacy and repose." See, e.g., Skinner v. Oklahoma, 316 U.S. 535, 541 [(1942)]. . . .

The present case, then, concerns a relationship lying within the zone of privacy created by several fundamental constitutional guarantees. And it concerns a law which, in forbidding the use of contraceptives rather than regulating their manufacture or sale, seeks to achieve its goals by means having a maximum destructive impact upon that relationship. Such a law cannot stand in light of the familiar principle, so often applied by this Court, that a "governmental purpose to control or prevent activities constitutionally subject to state regulation may not be achieved by means which sweep unnecessarily broadly and thereby invade the area of protected freedoms." NAACP v. Alabama, 377 U.S. 288, 307 [(1964)]. Would we allow the police to search the sacred precincts of marital bedrooms for telltale signs of the use of contraceptives? The very idea is repulsive to the notions of privacy surrounding the marriage relationship.

We deal with a right of privacy older than the Bill of Rights—older than our political parties, older than our school system. Marriage is a coming together for better or for worse, hopefully enduring, and intimate to the degree of being sacred. It is an association that promotes a way of life, not causes; a harmony in living, not political faiths; a bilateral loyalty, not commercial or social projects. Yet it is an association for as noble a purpose as any involved in our prior decisions. Reversed.

Mr. Justice Goldberg, whom The Chief Justice and Mr. Justice Brennan join, concurring.

I agree with the Court that Connecticut's birth-control law unconstitutionally intrudes upon the right of marital privacy. . . . I add these words to emphasize the relevance of [the Ninth] Amendment to the Court's holding. . . . The Amendment is almost entirely the work of James Madison. . . . It was proffered to quiet expressed fears that a bill of specifically enumerated rights could not be sufficiently broad to cover all essential rights and that the specific mention of certain rights would be interpreted as a denial that others were protected. . . .

. . . To hold that a right so basic and fundamental and so deep-rooted in our society as the right of privacy in marriage may be infringed because that right is not guaranteed in so many words by the first eight amendments to the Constitution is to ignore the Ninth Amendment and to give it no effect whatsoever. [T]he Ninth Amendment simply lends strong support to the view that the "liberty" protected by the Fifth and Fourteenth Amendments from infringement by the Federal Government or the States is not restricted to rights specifically mentioned in the first eight amendments. . . .

Mr. Justice HARLAN, concurring in the judgment. . . .

In my view, the proper constitutional inquiry in this case is whether this Connecticut statute infringes the Due Process Clause of the Fourteenth Amendment because the enactment violates basic values "implicit in the concept of ordered liberty," Palko v. Connecticut, 302 U.S. 319, 325 [(1937)]. For reasons stated at length in my dissenting opinion in Poe v. Ullman, [367 U.S. 497, 522 (1961)], I believe that it does. . . .

. . . Judicial self-restraint will . . . be achieved in this area, as in other constitutional areas, only by continual insistence upon respect for the teachings of history, solid recognition of the basic values that underlie our society, and wise appreciation of the great roles that the doctrines of federalism and separation of powers have played in establishing and preserving American freedoms. . . .

[In a separate concurring opinion, Justice White agrees that the statute violates the liberty protected by the Due Process Clause, questioning how the statutory ban serves the state's asserted interest in deterring illicit sexual relationships.]

Mr. Justice BLACK, with whom Mr. Justice STEWART joins, dissenting. . . .

The Court talks about a constitutional "right of privacy" as though there is some constitutional provision or provisions forbidding any law ever to be passed which might abridge the "privacy" of individuals. But there is not. . . . I like my privacy as well as the next one, but I am nevertheless compelled to admit that government has a right to invade it unless prohibited by some specific constitutional provision. . . .

My Brother Goldberg has adopted the recent discovery[12] that the Ninth Amendment as well as the Due Process Clause can be used by this Court as authority to strike down all state legislation which this Court thinks violates "fundamental principles of liberty and justice," or is contrary to the "traditions and [collective] conscience of our people." He also states, without proof satisfactory to me, that in making decisions on this basis, judges will not consider "their personal

---

12. See Patterson, The Forgotten Ninth Amendment (1955). . . . In Redlich, Are There "Certain Rights . . . Retained by the People"?, 37 N.Y.U. L. Rev. 787 [(1962)], Professor Redlich, in advocating reliance on the Ninth and Tenth Amendments to invalidate the Connecticut law before us, frankly states:

> But for one who feels that the marriage relationship should be beyond the reach of a state law forbidding the use of contraceptives, the birth control case poses a troublesome and challenging problem of constitutional interpretation. He may find himself saying, "The law is unconstitutional—but why?" There are two possible paths to travel in finding the answer. One is to revert to a frankly flexible due process concept even on matters that do not involve specific constitutional prohibitions. The other is to attempt to evolve a new constitutional framework within which to meet this and similar problems which are likely to arise.

Id., at 798.

and private notions." One may ask how they can avoid considering them. Our Court certainly has no machinery with which to take a Gallup Poll. And the scientific miracles of this age have not yet produced a gadget which the Court can use to determine what traditions are rooted in the "[collective] conscience of our people." . . .

Mr. Justice STEWART, whom Mr. Justice BLACK joins, dissenting.

. . . I think this is an uncommonly silly law. As a practical matter, the law is obviously unenforceable, except in the oblique context of the present case. As a philosophical matter, I believe the use of contraceptives in the relationship of marriage should be left to personal and private choice, based upon each individual's moral, ethical, and religious beliefs. As a matter of social policy, I think professional counsel about methods of birth control should be available to all, so that each individual's choice can be meaningfully made. But we are not asked in this case to say whether we think this law is unwise, or even asinine. We are asked to hold that it violates the United States Constitution. And that I cannot do. . . . With all deference, I can find no such general right of privacy in the Bill of Rights, in any other part of the Constitution, or in any case ever before decided by this Court.

At the oral argument in this case, we were told that the Connecticut law does not "conform to current community standards." But it is not the function of this Court to decide cases on the basis of community standards. . . . If, as I should surely hope, the law before us does not reflect the standards of the people of Connecticut, the people of Connecticut can freely exercise their true Ninth and Tenth Amendment rights to persuade their elected representatives to repeal it. That is the constitutional way to take this law off the books.

Michael Grossberg, Governing the Hearth: Law and the Family in Nineteenth-Century America

156-157, 175-177, 189-193 (1985)

At the heart of the nineteenth-century controversy over family limitation lay the quiet determination of American mothers and fathers to reduce the number of children they reared. They initiated what historical demographers now designate the "demographic transition": a reduction in family size that characterized most Western nations. In America, white female fertility, the critical measure of family size, declined in each decade of the century, falling from 7.04 in 1800 to 3.56 a hundred years later. . . .

Although the exact sources [of this transition] remain uncertain, some characteristics of the republican household offer clues. . . . These include the child-centered nature of the republican home in which numerous offspring seemed to inhibit proper child care; the rise of what historian Daniel Scott Smith terms "domestic feminism," or the determination of women to assert their individuality and household authority by regulating pregnancy and marital sexuality; the economic incentives of market capitalism in which large families seemed a burden and in which moderation and self-control became prized virtues; the companionate nature of republican matrimony, which fostered the separation of sexual pleasure from protection; and the emerging American insistence on overcoming what had previously been considered natural forces beyond human control. . . .

Though it is difficult to pierce the privacy surrounding family limitation, at the beginning of the nineteenth century, husbands and wives apparently still relied on age-old methods of birth control such as delayed marriage, breast feeding, and abstinence (as well as *coitus interruptus* and other active contraceptive practices). . . .

Although statutes prohibiting various forms of abortion had been on the books since the 1820s, there were few explicit restrictions on contraception until the 1870s. But federal and state acts labeling both abortion and contraception obscene capped the growing determination of family savers to ban all forms of family limitation. [For example, although] he sympathized with women's fears about childbirth and rearing large families, [Augustus] Gardner confidently insisted that efforts made "to avoid propagation, are ten thousand-fold more disastrous to the health and constitution, to say nothing of the demoralization of mind and heart. . . ." Gardner [and his followers] looked to the criminal law for relief.

Self-appointed purity campaigners led the drive against contraception. New Yorkers created the first purity society in 1872, the New York Society for the Suppression of Vice. [T]he society's point man for purity reform was a little known ex-dry goods salesman, Anthony Comstock. The son of devout Connecticut parents, he tried unsuccessfully to make his fortune as a businessman in New York City. The flagrant vices he encountered in the city shocked him into a highly publicized vigilante campaign. It culminated in his appointment as the antivice society's chief agent, thus launching his career as late nineteenth-century America's self-avowed savior of public morals.

Comstock regarded the feeble statutes then on the books as the weakest link in his war on vice. . . . In 1872 he convinced the antivice society to send him to Washington to press for a rigorous national statute. [There] the vice crusader succeeded beyond his wildest expectations. Armed with a display case of vice paraphernalia and vivid tales of his fights with the panderers of obscenity, Comstock enlisted the aid of Vice President Henry Wilson and Supreme Court Justice William Strong to draft a new obscenity law. The bill passed with little debate and became law on 1 March 1873. [It became known as the "Comstock law."]

The act's primary purpose was to ban the circulation and importation of obscene materials through the national mails. Specifically included on the list of banned goods was every article designed, adapted, or intended "for preventing conception or producing abortion, or for indecent or immoral use; and every article, instrument, substance, drug, medicine, or thing which is advertised or described in a manner calculated to lead another to use or apply it for preventing conception or producing abortion, or for any indecent or immoral purpose. . . ." The act set punishment at a $5,000 fine, one to ten years at hard labor, or both. . . .

[P]urity crusaders also prodded state legislators into action. Antivice societies, and after 1885 the Social Purity Alliance, succeeded in persuading twenty-two legislatures to enact general obscenity laws and another twenty-four to specifically ban birth control and abortion. [Courts upheld convictions under these laws.]

Let loose by Congress, state legislatures, and the courts, vice hunters prowled the nation sniffing out their prey. Posing as customers or using decoy letters, federal agents and local societies purchased proscribed items and then arrested sellers. . . . Comstock in fact caught his most famous victim with a birth-control ploy. Having been warned not to tangle with the infamous Madame Restell, he took her capture as a personal challenge. In the guise of an impoverished father, Comstock pleaded for contraceptive information because his meager finances could support no more children. When she obliged, he arrested her. Faced with the almost certain prospect of jail at the age of 67, Restell slit her throat with a carving knife. Comstock experienced no remorse: "a bloody end to a bloody life."

. . . Congress strengthened the federal ban in 1908. By the 1930s eight states specifically prohibited the flow of contraceptive information while the rest acted through broadened obscenity laws. Contraception remained a taboo subject, even though, much like prohibition, the statutes expressed a moral standard clearly at odds with actual practices. . . . Birth control, no matter how essential family limitation had become to the republican family, still violated the nation's code of proper domestic behavior. Fears aroused by the immigration of seemingly fecund non-Protestant women, charges of race suicide leveled against non-immigrant mothers who regulated their child bearing, and the ever-present concern over changes in gender responsibilities reinvigorated the stigma attached to the practice.

The constitutionality of the ban was also impenetrable. [Judicial cases] demonstrated the formidable opposition facing birth-control advocates. . . . Birth control continued to be an obscene subject banished from polite society. . . .

Catherine G. Roraback, Griswold v. Connecticut: A Brief Case History

16 Ohio N.U. L. Rev. 395, 395-401 (1989)

Estelle Griswold (left) and Planned Parenthood colleague Cornelia Jahncke celebrate the Supreme Court victory.

The [Connecticut] ban on the use of contraceptives had been on the statute books of this state for some *eighty-six* years. Many other jurisdictions had similar laws, but by the late 1950's these laws had been either repealed or their impact minimized by judicial interpretation. In 1958 only Connecticut had an absolute ban on contraceptive devices, one without an exception even for situations where the life of the mother might be endangered by a pregnancy. [T]here were regular attempts to obtain legislative repeal of the statute. In each biennial session of the General Assembly a repealer bill was introduced, vociferous and vituperative hearings were held, and the bill was eventually voted down. . . .

[I]t is hard to remember the attitudes toward birth control in the 1950's. The statutory prohibition on the use of contraceptives even by married persons was accepted by many as a legitimate exercise of the police powers of the state. That is not to say that private doctors did not provide such advice and services to their private patients, nor that patients able to afford private medical care did not obtain contraceptive advice. However, even that private care was often circumspect and clandestine, and some private physicians refused to provide these services at all. Certainly these services were not available to unmarried persons.

Although contraceptives were available for purchase in drugstores throughout the state, that availability was usually "under-the-counter." Druggists also sold such items on prescription of a private physician. The activities of the state Planned Parenthood League were limited to educational and legislative programs and a referral service to clinics in neighboring New York and Rhode Island, with transportation furnished by volunteers to enable the women to take advantage of the out-of-state services.

But no medical source of contraceptive advice or services was available in this state to those dependent on publicly provided health care. It was the physicians and medical personnel operating in public clinics who were subjected to public scrutiny and threat of prosecution. And because it was here that these statutes impacted, it was the poor people of this state who were deprived of medically supervised contraceptive advice and services. [After 1940, when nine Planned Parenthood clinics were closed, no public or private facility provided free birth control.]

In 1957, Estelle Griswold, a dynamic, vivacious woman, had only recently become the executive director of the Planned Parenthood League of Connecticut. She found herself frustrated by the legal situation in Connecticut and her inability to organize Planned Parenthood clinics in the state.

In the course of preparations that year for the biennial legislative hearing on repeal of the anti-birth-control statute, she arranged for C. Lee Buxton to testify. Buxton had only recently come to New Haven as professor and chairman of the Department of Obstetrics and Gynecology at the Yale University School of Medicine. . . . He felt deeply that the statute banning the use of contraceptive devices and the accessory statute preventing him from giving what he felt to be the advice and care his patients deserved were gross invasions of his patients' rights, and highly improper impediments on his ability to practice his profession.

It was at this point, as legend has it, that Estelle invited both Lee Buxton and Fowler Harper to her home one day in the fall of 1957 and introduced them over cocktails. Fowler, then a professor at the Yale Law School, taught—among other subjects—family law. He was a social activist, involved in the community, always ready to take on a cause and to use his full energies and legal skills to cure an inequity. . . . He most certainly reacted with verve and gusto as Lee spoke of his frustrations about the Connecticut law banning the use of contraceptives and his inability to properly serve his patients. And, the legend holds, it was from this conversation that the litigation which culminated in *Griswold* originated. . . .

[The chosen strategy was for Dr. Buxton and some of his married patients to seek in state court a declaratory judgment that the statute was unconstitutional or should not apply when pregnancy threatened a woman's life or health.] One of the patients bringing suit was Jane Doe, a young twenty-five-year-old housewife. . . . While hospitalized [for pregnancy complications] she had suffered a stroke, her pregnancy could not be aborted, and she had had to continue the pregnancy until at term she had a stillbirth. As a result she was permanently paralyzed on her right side, her speech was impaired and she had residual kidney damage. It was Dr. Buxton's opinion that she would not survive another pregnancy.

The other plaintiff-patients were two married couples. One, the Poes, had had three abnormal children, none of whom had survived more than ten weeks. They sought contraceptive advice because they did not feel they could emotionally survive the birth of another such child. The other couple, the Hoes, had conflicting blood groupings and were considered unlikely to have a normal child born to them.

When these suits were begun in May of 1958, there was . . . no discussion of rights of privacy. . . . The due process arguments in the briefs filed in the Connecticut courts stressed rights to life and liberty, to health, to happy marital relationships, free of governmental intrusion. But the obverse of that phrase—privacy—was not used. . . .

It was in the due process arguments presented on the appeal [by the law's challengers] to the United States Supreme Court in this case that the first specific mention of "privacy" occurred in this litigation. However, the Supreme Court never reached this or any of the other substantive arguments raised on this appeal. Rather, it held [in Poe v. Ullman, 367 U.S. 497 (1961),] that there was no controversy before the Court, that there had been an absence of any prosecutions under the statutes, and that therefore Dr. Buxton and his patients faced no realistic threat of prosecution.

In Connecticut the implications of this disconcerting outcome were pondered. . . . After much consultation and discussion, it was finally decided that the Planned Parenthood League of Connecticut would open one facility in New Haven, and that if no prosecution ensued, it would expand such services to other cities. Thus on November 1, 1961, the Planned Parenthood League of Connecticut opened the first birth control clinic in [Connecticut] since 1940, with Estelle T. Griswold as its director and C. Lee Buxton as its medical director. [Ten days later, they were arrested and charged with aiding and abetting] certain married women to "use a drug, medicinal article and instrument, for the purpose of preventing conception." The clinic closed its doors. . . .

From the beginning of this prosecution, the defense attacked the statutory contraceptive ban, repeating in depth all of the prior arguments as to the unconstitutionality of the statute but adding now, specifically the infringement which it imposed on the patient's right to privacy. In doing so we drew on the development of that right as it had been expounded at length in the two dissenting opinions in *Poe*. Mr. Justice Douglas's dissent found such a right in "the totality of the constitutional scheme under which we live," [367 U.S. at 521,] while Mr. Justice Harlan found its protection in the due process protections of the fourteenth amendment [id. at 540].

Notes and Questions

1. Sources. What are the constitutional sources of the right to privacy, according to *Griswold*? According to the concurring opinions? Explain the majority's difficulty in identifying the source of this right. On what basis do the dissenters disagree?

2. State intrusion. What aspect of the statute disturbs the majority? If Connecticut had sought to prevent use of contraceptives by, say, banning the manufacture or sale of such materials, what result? How significant is the fact that Connecticut prohibited couples' behavior with regard to contraceptive use, as distinguished from some other sex-related activity? What of possession of pornography, for example? Compare Stanley v. Georgia, 394 U.S. 557 (1969), with Osborne v. Ohio, 495 U.S. 103 (1990). Access to sex toys? Compare Reliable Consultants, Inc. v. Earle, 517 F.3d 738, 744 (5th Cir. 2008), with 1568 Montgomery Highway, Inc. v. City of Hoover, 45 So. 3d 319, 340 (Ala. 2010).

3. Role of marriage? How critical is the marital status of the contraceptive users? To whom does the right to privacy belong, according to *Griswold*? Each spouse? The marital unit? See Martha Albertson Fineman, What Place for Family Privacy?, 67 Geo. Wash. L. Rev. 1207, 1212 (1999) (*Griswold* shows that the "idea of the entity of the family as something 'private' predates, and is analytically separate from, the constitutional idea of individual privacy"). Suppose the spouses disagree. May the state resolve the disagreement?

4. State interests. Why did Connecticut enact this legislation? What do the excerpts by historian Michael Grossberg and attorney Catherine Roraback (counsel to Planned Parenthood League of Connecticut during *Griswold*) suggest? See also Andrea Tone, Devices and Desires: A History of Contraceptives in America (2001). What role do the state's reasons play in *Griswold*?

5. Privacy's origins. In an omitted footnote, Justice Black's dissent claims that the concept of a "right to privacy" originated in an 1890 article by Samuel Warren and his then-law partner Louis Brandeis, The Right to Privacy, 4 Harv. L. Rev. 193 (1890). Reportedly written in response to press coverage of the wedding of Warren's socialite daughter, the article sought a basis in tort law for the protection of privacy from threats posed by the new technologies of photography and broadcasting. As a Supreme Court Justice, Brandeis later cited the Constitution for "the right to be let alone." See, e.g., Olmstead v. United States, 277 U.S. 438, 478 (1928) (dissenting opinion) (recognizing Fourth Amendment protection against governmental wiretapping). See also Katz v. United States, 389 U.S. 347, 353 (1967) (adopting Brandeis's reasoning). Justice Goldberg's concurrence in *Griswold* invokes Brandeis's understanding.

How closely does the *Griswold* majority's concept of privacy resemble that of Warren and Brandeis? Does *Griswold*'s notion of privacy protect the right not to have information made public? The right to be let alone? The right to self-determination? For a contemporary taxonomy, see generally Daniel J. Solove, Understanding Privacy 101-170 (2008).

6. Privacy and technology. Given Warren's and Brandeis's fears about new technology, how should their proposed right evolve in response to still newer developments? See, e.g., Lori Andrews, I Know Who You Are and I Saw What You Did: Social Networks and the Death of Privacy (2012); Theresa M. Payton & Theodore Claypoole, Privacy in the Age of Big Data (2014).

7. Birth control movement. The radical birth control movement in the United States emerged as part of the Socialist Party's agenda in the early 1900s. Activist Margaret Sanger's role in the movement grew out of her encounter as a visiting nurse with a poor woman who died because she could not avoid another pregnancy. But Sanger also appreciated the broader implications of birth control, as explained below:

> Most American socialists at this time, primarily oriented to class relations, saw birth control . . . in terms of economics. They were concerned to help raise the standard of living of workers and thus increase their freedom to take political control over their own lives. Measured against this goal, birth control was at most an ameliorative reform. Seen in terms of sexual politics, however, birth control was revolutionary because it could free women entirely from the major burden that differentiated them from men and made them dependent on men. Sanger gained this perspective in Europe from the sexual liberation theorists such as Havelock Ellis. . . . His idealism about the potential beauty and expressiveness of human sexuality and his rage at the damage caused by sexual repression fired Sanger with a sense of the overwhelming importance, urgency, and profundity of the issue of birth control. . . .[1]

Sanger founded the American Birth Control League, which later became Planned Parenthood. See generally Jonathan Eig, The Birth of the Pill: How Four Crusaders Reinvented Sex and Launched a Revolution (2014).

8. Birth control and race. Grossberg recounts how fears of "race suicide" (that is, a declining birth rate among whites at a time of growing immigration) supported birth control restrictions. In contrast to their white counterparts' focus on access to birth control, women of color embraced a larger agenda. African-American women's understanding of reproductive rights was shaped by the history of sexual exploitation during slavery, sterilization abuse, and societal inattention to high maternal and infant mortality rates; many supported birth control and abortion rights, despite Black Nationalist organizations' condemnation in the 1970s of such measures as tools for genocide. Puerto Rican activists' advocacy for women's autonomy and state-supported health care stemmed from U.S.-sponsored sterilization there and harm suffered by some Puerto Rican participants in clinical trials for the birth control pill. Native American women also worked for contraception as part of a wider mission to improve health care. See Jennifer Nelson, Women of Color and the Reproductive Rights Movement 19, 186 (2003); Dorothy Roberts, Killing the Black Body: Race, Reproduction, and the Meaning of Liberty 22-55 (1999); Jael Silliman et al., Undivided Rights: Women of Color Organize for Reproductive Justice 143 (2004).

---

[1]. Linda Gordon, The Moral Property of Women: A History of Birth Control Politics in America 145 (2002).

EISENSTADT v. BAIRD

405 U.S. 438 (1972)

Activist William Baird speaks to the press after his birth control lecture at Boston University.

Mr. Justice BRENNAN delivered the opinion of the Court.

Appellee William Baird was convicted at a bench trial in the Massachusetts Superior Court under Massachusetts General Laws Ann., c. 272, §21, first, for exhibiting contraceptive articles in the course of delivering a lecture on contraception to a group of students at Boston University and, second, for giving a young woman a package of Emko vaginal foam at the close of his address. The Massachusetts Supreme Judicial Court unanimously set aside the conviction for exhibiting contraceptives on the ground that it violated Baird's First Amendment rights, but by a four-to-three vote sustained the conviction for giving away the foam. Commonwealth v. Baird, 355 Mass. 746, 247 N.E.2d 574 (1969). . . .

Massachusetts General Laws Ann., c. 272, §21 [provides] a maximum five-year term of imprisonment for "whoever . . . gives away . . . any drug, medicine, instrument, or article whatever for the prevention of conception," except as authorized in §21A. . . . As interpreted by the State Supreme Judicial Court, these provisions make it a felony for anyone, other than a registered physician or pharmacist acting in accordance with the terms of §21A, to dispense any article with the intention that it be used for the prevention of conception. [M]arried persons may obtain contraceptives to prevent pregnancy, but only from doctors or druggists on prescription; . . . single persons may not obtain contraceptives from anyone to prevent pregnancy. . . .

The question for our determination in this case is whether there is some ground of difference that rationally explains the different treatment accorded married and unmarried persons under Massachusetts General Laws Ann., c. 272, §§21 and 21A.[7] . . .

First. [W]e cannot agree that the deterrence of premarital sex may reasonably be regarded as the purpose of the Massachusetts law.

It would be plainly unreasonable to assume that Massachusetts has prescribed pregnancy and the birth of an unwanted child as punishment for fornication, which is a misdemeanor under Massachusetts General Laws Ann., c. 272, §18. Aside from the scheme of values that assumption would attribute to the State, it is abundantly clear that the effect of the ban on distribution of contraceptives to unmarried persons has at best a marginal relation to the proffered objective. . . . Like Connecticut's laws [in *Griswold*], §§21 and 21A do not at all regulate the distribution of contraceptives when they are to be used to prevent, not pregnancy,

---

7. Of course, if we were to conclude that the Massachusetts statute impinges upon fundamental freedoms under *Griswold*, the statutory classification would have to be not merely *rationally* related to a valid public purpose but *necessary* to the achievement of a *compelling* state interest. E.g., Loving v. Virginia, 388 U.S. 1 (1967). But . . . we do not have to address the statute's validity under that test because the law fails to satisfy even the more lenient equal protection standard.

but the spread of disease. Nor, in making contraceptives available to married persons without regard to their intended use, does Massachusetts attempt to deter married persons from engaging in illicit sexual relations with unmarried persons. Even on the assumption that the fear of pregnancy operates as a deterrent to fornication, the Massachusetts statute is thus so riddled with exceptions that deterrence of premarital sex cannot reasonably be regarded as its aim. . . .

Second. . . . If health were the rationale of §21A, the statute would be both discriminatory and overbroad. . . . The Court of Appeals [stated]: "If the prohibition [on distribution to unmarried persons] . . . is to be taken to mean that the same physician who can prescribe for married patients does not have sufficient skill to protect the health of patients who lack a marriage certificate, or who may be currently divorced, it is illogical to the point of irrationality." 429 F.2d, at 1401. Furthermore, we must join the Court of Appeals in noting that not all contraceptives are potentially dangerous. . . ." If [health] was the Legislature's goal, §21 is not required" in view of the federal and state laws *already* regulating the distribution of harmful drugs. . . .

Third. If the Massachusetts statute cannot be upheld as a deterrent to fornication or as a health measure, may it, nevertheless, be sustained simply as a prohibition on contraception? . . . We need not and do not, however, decide that important question in this case because, whatever the rights of the individual to access to contraceptives may be, the rights must be the same for the unmarried and the married alike.

If under *Griswold* the distribution of contraceptives to married persons cannot be prohibited, a ban on distribution to unmarried persons would be equally impermissible. It is true that in *Griswold* the right of privacy in question inhered in the marital relationship. Yet the marital couple is not an independent entity with a mind and heart of its own, but an association of two individuals, each with a separate intellectual and emotional makeup. If the right of privacy means anything, it is the right of the *individual*, married or single, to be free from unwarranted governmental intrusion into matters so fundamentally affecting a person as the decision whether to bear or beget a child. See Stanley v. Georgia, 394 U.S. 557 (1969). See also Skinner v. Oklahoma ex rel. Williamson, 316 U.S. 535 (1942); Jacobson v. Massachusetts, 197 U.S. 11, 29 (1905).

On the other hand, if *Griswold* is no bar to a prohibition on the distribution of contraceptives, the State could not, consistently with the Equal Protection Clause, outlaw distribution to unmarried but not married persons. In each case the evil, as perceived by the State, would be identical, and the underinclusion would be invidious.

. . . We hold that by providing dissimilar treatment for married and unmarried persons who are similarly situated, Massachusetts General Laws Ann., c. 272, §§21 and 21A, violate the Equal Protection Clause. The judgment of the Court of Appeals is affirmed.

Notes and Questions

1. Beyond *Griswold*. How does *Eisenstadt* resolve the issues left open in *Griswold*: the *distribution* of contraceptives to *unmarried* individuals?

2. Privacy's meaning. How does *Eisenstadt* define "privacy"? How does the meaning of "privacy" articulated in *Eisenstadt* differ from that in *Griswold*?

3. Whose privacy? How does *Eisenstadt* answer the question whether the right to privacy belongs to the family unit or each member of the family? Does it indicate how to resolve conflicts between family members over "private" matters? What would a relational understanding of privacy and autonomy entail? See Jennifer Nedelsky, Law's Relations: A Relational Theory of Self, Autonomy, and Law (2011).

4. The equal protection basis. Why does the Court rely on the Equal Protection Clause instead of the constitutional provisions invoked in *Griswold*? Does *Eisenstadt*'s approach provide a firmer basis for the right to privacy? To what extent does *Eisenstadt* implicitly reflect concerns about gender equality?

5. State interests: privacy versus privatization. Why did Massachusetts enact the challenged law? How does the Court address the state's interests? What does the Massachusetts law contribute to the understanding of family law as part of a systematic effort to channel sexual activity into marriage? See generally, e.g., Richard A. Posner, Sex and Reason 243-266 (1992).

Consistent with this view, several commentators see family law as regulation aimed at keeping dependency private (the privatization of dependency). See, e.g., Martha Albertson Fineman, The Autonomy Myth: A Theory of Dependency (2004); Anne L. Alstott, Private Tragedies? Family Law as Social Insurance, 4 Harv. L. & Pol'y Rev. 3 (2010). Does this theory help explain the state intrusion experienced by the poor, whom critics say often must bargain away their family privacy for state assistance? See, e.g., Khiara M. Bridges, Privacy Rights and Public Families, 34 Harv. J.L. & Gender 113, 171 (2011) (positing the privacy right as a function of class).

6. Scope of protection. States routinely create legal distinctions based on marriage, awarding family benefits only to married couples. The Supreme Court emphasized marriage's unique material and psychic advantages when holding that the Constitution requires equal access for same-sex couples. Obergefell v. Hodges, 135 S. Ct. 2584, 2601 (2015) (reprinted in Chapter II). How do you reconcile the Court's assumptions in *Obergefell* with *Eisenstadt*'s rejection of discrimination based on marital status? Note that both cases consider equality across (rather than within) families. See also Clare Huntington, Postmarital Family Law: A Legal Structure for Nonmarital Families, 67 Stan. L. Rev. 167 (2015) (noting how family law assumes marriage and overlooks nonmarital families).

7. Distribution. The Court subsequently addressed the substantive issue avoided in *Eisenstadt*. Carey v. Population Services International, 431 U.S. 678 (1977), struck down a statute barring distribution of all contraceptives except by licensed pharmacists. The majority explained that such limitations on access to contraceptives impose burdens similar to limitations on use; hence, both must satisfy the compelling state interest test.

8. "The pill." Why did contraception become a constitutional issue at this time in history? The birth control pill, approved by the Food and Drug Administration (FDA) in 1960, quickly came to symbolize the sexual revolution and "women's liberation." See generally Elaine Tyler May, America and the Pill: A

History of Promise, Peril, and Liberation (2010). To date, no male contraceptive "pill" is available, and critics have dubbed contemporary legislative and political efforts to restrict access to contraception part of a "war on women" and a revival of attitudes from the Comstock era. See Priscilla J. Smith, Contraceptive Comstockery: Reasoning from Immorality to Illness in the Twenty-First Century, 47 Conn. L. Rev. 971 (2015).

9. Campus sex. Baird's distribution of birth control in a university setting occurred during the sexual revolution and the resurgence of popular feminism. Conversations about college students' sexual practices now focus on "hooking up" and sexual assault. See Paula England et al., Hooking up and Forming Romantic Relationships on Today's College Campuses, in The Gendered Society Reader 531 (Michael S. Kimmel & Amy Aronson eds., 3d ed. 2008); Deborah Tuerkheimer, Rape On and Off Campus, 65 Emory L.J. 1 (2015). How might *Eisenstadt* have contributed to these developments?

10. Birth control and class. Roraback, supra, notes that criminal prohibitions disproportionately affected clients of public family-planning clinics. How might *Griswold* and *Eisenstadt* operate to reduce poverty? See Cary Franklin, *Griswold* and the Public Dimension of the Right to Privacy, 124 Yale L.J. F. 332 (2015). Note that even before *Eisenstadt* Congress enacted the Family Planning and Population Research Act of 1970, which encouraged, inter alia, the development of accessible family planning services. 42 U.S.C. §300.

Contemporary studies document a class divide in contraceptive use and marriage, with lower rates for both among the economically vulnerable. What are the implications for *Eisenstadt*'s commitment to equality and for family law more generally? See generally June Carbone & Naomi Cahn, Marriage Markets: How Inequality Is Remaking the American Family (2014); Isabel V. Sawhill, Generation Unbound: Drifting into Sex and Parenthood Without Marriage (2014).

NOTE: THE CONTRACEPTIVE MANDATE AND THE *HOBBY LOBBY* CASE

The Affordable Care Act (ACA), which Congress enacted in 2010, requires large employers to furnish group health insurance for their employees. Per regulations, coverage must provide women with free preventive care and screenings, including prescription contraceptive methods, sterilization procedures, and patient education and counseling. This "contraceptive mandate" recognizes that women pay more for preventive care, that cost barriers thwart their access to contraception, and that access problems result in unintended pregnancies, with personal and economic effects.

Regulations offered exemptions to religious employers (such as churches) and accommodations for nonprofit employers with religious objections, but not for-profit corporations. In Burwell v. Hobby Lobby Stores, Inc., 134 S. Ct. 2751 (2014), for-profit corporations raised religious objections to covering certain contraceptive methods that they contended operated as abortifacients. Suing under the Religious Freedom Restoration Act (RFRA), they argued that the mandate (1) substantially burdens the practice of their faith; (2) does not advance a compelling interest; and (3) does not represent the least restrictive means of pursuing the government's objective of supplying these products to women.

A closely divided Court sided with the challengers. The majority reasoned that these closely held corporations, "family businesses," could exercise religion and that less restrictive means than the mandate could advance the government's interests in public health and gender equality, which were assumed to be compelling. In particular, the majority cited as alternative means government funding or the accommodations provided for nonprofit employers with religious objections, which can self-certify such objections to require the insurer to provide the contraceptive coverage.

The majority thus assumed that the employees in question would have access to contraception without cost, and it disclaimed any implications for religion-based objections to other types of health care or employee benefits (such as those triggered by same-sex marriage). In dissent, Justice Ginsburg challenged the majority's analysis, taking special aim at the exceptional, unfavorable treatment of birth control, which is essential to women's ability "to participate equally in the economic and social life of the Nation." Id. at 2787 (Ginsburg, J., dissenting).

For commentary suggesting implications for family law, compare, e.g., Helen M. Alvaré, No Compelling Interest: The "Birth Control" Mandate and Religious Freedom, 58 Vill. L. Rev. 379 (2013), with Elizabeth Sepper, Gendering Corporate Conscience, 38 Harv. J.L. & Gender 193 (2015). On the mandate's apparent economic benefits for women, see Nora V. Becker & Daniel Polsky, Women Saw Large Decrease in Out-of-Pocket Spending for Contraceptives After ACA Mandate Removed Cost Sharing, 34 Health Affairs 1204 (2015). The Supreme Court will review challenges to the accommodation for nonprofit employers. Zubik v. Burwell, 2015 WL 2473206 (2015).

Problems

1. Suppose that a "grandfathered" employer (exempt from the ACA mandate because of a preexisting plan) provides employees with comprehensive prescription drug coverage that includes Viagra, which allows sexual intercourse for some men, but not contraceptives, which accomplish a similar objective for some women. Would such action violate laws that prohibit sex-based discrimination in the workplace (Title VII and the Pregnancy Discrimination Act)? See Standridge v. Union Pac. R.R. Co., 479 F.3d 936 (8th Cir. 2007). Would excluding both Viagra and contraceptives from the plan eliminate any discrimination? See Erickson v. Bartell Drug Co., 141 F. Supp. 2d 1266 (W.D. Wash. 2001); Sylvia A. Law, Sex Discrimination and Insurance for Contraception, 73 Wash. L. Rev. 363 (1998).

2. Suppose that owners/operators of a for-profit corporation to which the mandate applies assert religious objections to nonmarital sex and thus to providing coverage of all forms of contraception for *unmarried* employees. Would this employer be entitled to relief, as you understand *Hobby Lobby*? What additional information would you need to answer the question? On the repercussions of such "complicity-based conscience claims," see Douglas NeJaime & Reva B. Siegel, Conscience Wars: Complicity-Based Conscience Claims in Religion and Politics, 124 Yale L.J. 2516 (2015).

Suppose that an *employee* asserts religious objections to employer-provided contraception coverage for him and his family, including his three teenage daughters. Would this employee be entitled to relief from a portion of his employer's standard plan? Suppose that the employer is the state. See Wieland v. U.S. Dept. of Health & Human Servs., 978 F. Supp. 2d 1008 (E.D. Mo. 2013), *rev'd & remanded,* 793 F.3d 949 (8th Cir. 2015).

b. Roots of Privacy

Griswold and *Eisenstadt* break new ground in explicitly recognizing a constitutional right to privacy. Yet some 40 years earlier, the Supreme Court expressed an understanding of the family that established a foothold for this right, as the cases below reveal.

MEYER v. NEBRASKA

262 U.S. 390 (1923)

Mr. Justice McReynolds delivered the opinion of the Court.

Plaintiff in error was tried and convicted . . . under an information which charged that on May 25, 1920, while an instructor in Zion Parochial School he unlawfully taught the subject of reading in the German language to Raymond Parpart, a child of 10 years, who had not attained and successfully passed the eighth grade. [A Nebraska statute prohibited any person from teaching languages other than English, except to pupils who had successfully completed the eighth grade, and classified a violation as a misdemeanor, punishable by a fine and/or imprisonment. The state supreme court affirmed the conviction.]

The problem for our determination is whether the statute as construed and applied unreasonably infringes the liberty guaranteed to the plaintiff in error by the Fourteenth Amendment: "No state . . . shall deprive any person of life, liberty or property without due process of law."

While this court has not attempted to define with exactness the liberty thus guaranteed, [w]ithout doubt, it denotes not merely freedom from bodily restraint but also the right of the individual to contract, to engage in any of the common occupations of life, to acquire useful knowledge, to marry, establish a home and bring up children, to worship God according to the dictates of his own conscience, and generally to enjoy those privileges long recognized at common law as essential to the orderly pursuit of happiness by free men. The established doctrine is that this liberty may not be interfered with, under the guise of protecting the public interest, by legislative action which is arbitrary or without reasonable relation to some purpose within the competency of the state to effect. Determination by the Legislature of what constitutes proper exercise of police power is not final or conclusive but is subject to supervision by the courts.

The American people have always regarded education and acquisition of knowledge as matters of supreme importance which should be diligently promoted. . . . Corresponding to the right of control, it is the natural duty of the parent to give his children education suitable to their station in life; and nearly all the states, including Nebraska, enforce this obligation by compulsory laws.

Practically, education of the young is only possible in schools conducted by especially qualified persons who devote themselves thereto. The calling always has been regarded as useful and honorable, essential, indeed, to the public welfare. Mere knowledge of the German language cannot reasonably be regarded as harmful. . . . Plaintiff in error taught this language in school as part of his occupation. His right thus to teach and the right of parents to engage him so to instruct their children, we think, are within the liberty of the Amendment. . . . Evidently the Legislature has attempted materially to interfere with the calling of modern language teachers, with the opportunities of pupils to acquire knowledge, and with the power of parents to control the education of their own.

It is said the purpose of the legislation was to promote civic development by inhibiting training and education of the immature in foreign tongues and ideals before they could learn English and acquire American ideals, and "that the English language should be and become the mother tongue of all children reared in this state." It is also affirmed that the foreign born population is very large, that certain communities commonly use foreign words, follow foreign leaders, move in a foreign atmosphere, and that the children are thereby hindered from becoming citizens of the most useful type and the public safety is imperiled.

That the state may do much, go very far, indeed, in order to improve the quality of its citizens, physically, mentally and morally, is clear; but the individual has certain fundamental rights which must be respected. The protection of the Constitution extends to all, to those who speak other languages as well as to those born with English on the tongue. Perhaps it would be highly advantageous if all had ready understanding of our ordinary speech, but this cannot be coerced by methods which conflict with the Constitution—a desirable end cannot be promoted by prohibited means. . . . No emergency has arisen which renders knowledge by a child of some language other than English so clearly harmful as to justify its inhibition with the consequent infringement of rights long freely enjoyed. We are constrained to conclude that the statute as applied is arbitrary and without reasonable relation to any end within the competency of the state.

As the statute undertakes to interfere only with teaching which involves a modern language, leaving complete freedom as to other matters, there seems no adequate foundation for the suggestion that the purpose was to protect the child's health by limiting his mental activities. It is well known that proficiency in a foreign language seldom comes to one not instructed at an early age, and experience shows that this is not injurious to the health, morals or understanding of the ordinary child. [Reversed.]

PIERCE v. SOCIETY OF SISTERS

268 U.S. 510 (1925)

Mr. Justice McReynolds delivered the opinion of the Court. . . .

[The Compulsory Education Act, effective September 1, 1926,] requires every parent, guardian, or other person having control or charge or custody of a child between 8 and 16 years to send him "to a public school for the period of time a public school shall be held during the current year" in the district where the child resides; and failure so to do is declared a misdemeanor. . . . The manifest purpose is to compel general attendance at public schools by normal children, between 8 and

16, who have not completed the eighth grade. And without doubt enforcement of the statute would seriously impair, perhaps destroy, the profitable features of appellees' business and greatly diminish the value of their property.

Appellee, the Society of Sisters, is an Oregon corporation, organized in 1880, with power to care for orphans, educate and instruct the youth, establish and maintain academies or schools, and acquire necessary real and personal property. . . . The Compulsory Education Act of 1922 has already caused the withdrawal from its schools of children who would otherwise continue, and their income has steadily declined. The appellants, public officers, have proclaimed their purpose strictly to enforce the statute.

[T]he Society's bill alleges that the enactment conflicts with the right of parents to choose schools where their children will receive appropriate mental and religious training, the right of the child to influence the parents' choice of a school, the right of schools and teachers therein to engage in a useful business or profession, and is accordingly repugnant to the Constitution and void. And, further, that unless enforcement of the measure is enjoined the corporation's business and property will suffer irreparable injury. [Similarly, appellee Hill Military Academy, an elementary, college preparatory, and military training school for boys, alleges a violation of its Fourteenth Amendment rights and seeks an injunction.]

[The court below ruled for appellees, based on the Fourteenth Amendment's guarantee against the deprivation of property without due process of law and the liberty of parents and guardians to direct the education of children by selecting reputable teachers and places; it determined that appellees' schools were not unfit or harmful to the public.]

No question is raised concerning the power of the state reasonably to regulate all schools, to inspect, supervise, and examine them, their teachers, and pupils; to require that all children of proper age attend some school, that teachers shall be of good moral character and patriotic disposition, that certain studies plainly essential to good citizenship must be taught, and that nothing be taught which is manifestly inimical to the public welfare.

The inevitable practical result of enforcing the act under consideration would be destruction of appellees' primary schools, and perhaps all other private primary schools for normal children within the state of Oregon. Appellees are engaged in a kind of undertaking not inherently harmful, but long regarded as useful and meritorious. [T]here are no peculiar circumstances or present emergencies which demand extraordinary measures relative to primary education.

Under the doctrine of Meyer v. Nebraska, 262 U.S. 390 [(1923)], we think it entirely plain that the Act of 1922 unreasonably interferes with the liberty of parents and guardians to direct the upbringing and education of children under their control. As often heretofore pointed out, rights guaranteed by the Constitution may not be abridged by legislation which has no reasonable relation to some purpose within the competency of the state. The fundamental theory of liberty upon which all governments in this Union repose excludes any general power of the state to standardize its children by forcing them to accept instruction from public teachers only. The child is not the mere creature of the state; those who nurture him and direct his destiny have the right, coupled with the high duty, to recognize and prepare him for additional obligations. . . .

The decrees below [restraining enforcement of the Act] are affirmed.

Notes and Questions on *Meyer* and *Pierce*

1. Substantive due process. *Meyer* and *Pierce* establish the foundation for the right to privacy. Why? Whose interests does each case vindicate? What is the connection between privacy and the professional and proprietary interests (of teachers and schools) protected by the Court? Although neither case mentions "privacy," *Griswold*, the first case to articulate a constitutional right to privacy, relies on both these precedents.

Despite holdings addressing the economic claims raised by a school teacher and private schools, respectively, *Meyer* and *Pierce* include dicta establishing parental autonomy—the freedom of parents to control the upbringing of their children. Through such dicta, these cases extend substantive due process, found in the constitutional protection of personal "liberty," to limit the authority of government to interfere in certain family matters. On what basis do the Justices decide what "liberty" encompasses?

The broad liberal principles of family autonomy in the face of government intervention, found in *Meyer* and *Pierce*, survived the Court's subsequent repudiation of economic substantive due process. Indeed, these cases, along with *Griswold*, form the basis of a revived substantive due process that now protects "a loose amalgam of personal liberties relating to family life."[2]

2. Whose privacy? Does the nascent interest in privacy recognized in *Meyer* and *Pierce* belong to the family unit or to individual family members? Do these precedents help answer similar questions posed about *Griswold* and *Eisenstadt*? What common features are shared by the two contexts, birth control and childrearing? What distinguishes them?

3. Slavery, families, and pluralism. Professor Peggy Davis emphasizes how *Meyer* and *Pierce*, rooted in antislavery traditions that originally produced the Fourteenth Amendment, promote pluralism. Slavery ignored family relationships, prohibiting slave parents from teaching chosen moral values to their children. By contrast, the autonomy recognized by *Meyer* and *Pierce* allows families room to make their own choices and embrace their own values:

> To think of family liberty as a guarantee offered in response to slavery's denials of natal connection is to understand it, not as an end in itself, but as a means to full personhood. People are not meant to be socialized to uniform, externally imposed values. People are to be able to form families and other intimate communities within which children might be differently socialized and from which adults would bring different values to the democratic process. This reconstructed Constitution gives coherence and legitimacy to the themes of autonomy and social function sounded in *Meyer, Pierce* [and later cases]. The idea of civil freedom that grows out of the history of slavery, antislavery, and Reconstruction entails more than the right to continue one's genetic kind in private. It also entails a right of family that derives from a human right of intellectual and moral autonomy. . . . For parents and other guardians, civil freedom brings a right to choose and propagate *values*. For children, civil freedom brings nothing less than the right to grow

[2]. David D. Meyer, Self-Definition in the Constitution of Faith and Family, 86 Minn. L. Rev. 791, 804-805 (2002).

to moral autonomy, because the child-citizen, like the child-slave, flowers to moral independence only under authority that is flexible in ways that states and masters cannot manage, and temporary in ways that states and masters cannot tolerate.[3]

4. State interests. What reasons prompted enactment of the laws struck down in *Meyer* and *Pierce*? What standard of review does the Court use to assess the state interests? Why does the Court find no "emergency" in either case?

5. History. Professor Barbara Woodhouse explains that the Nebraska law in *Meyer* stemmed from post-World War I anti-German bias. At the time, 16 states had similar English-only laws. By contrast, the Oregon law challenged in *Pierce,* reflecting the movement for universal free public education, was influenced by egalitarian Populist notions, as well as anti-Catholic and anti-immigrant sentiments, common in the 1890s.[4] Contemporary efforts to make English the "official language" of the United States have sparked renewed relevance for *Meyer*. See, e.g., Scott J. Bent, Note, "If You Want to Speak Spanish, Go Back to Mexico"?: A First Amendment Analysis of English-Only Rules in Public Schools, 73 Ohio St. L.J. 343 (2012).

6. Additional sources.

a. Procreative freedom. Roots of privacy can be found in Skinner v. Oklahoma, 316 U.S. 535 (1942), which invalidated as a denial of equal protection a statute punishing some criminals with sterilization. The Court applied "strict scrutiny" because the statute "involves one of the basic civil rights of man" and inflicts permanent deprivation of "a basic liberty." Id. at 541. But see Ariela R. Dubler, Sexing *Skinner*: History and the Politics of the Right to Marry, 110 Colum. L. Rev. 1348 (2010) (showing how *Skinner* reflected concerns about unrestrained, nonprocreative sexual activities).

This respect for procreative freedom contrasts with the Court's earlier approach in Buck v. Bell, 274 U.S. 200 (1927), upholding compulsory sterilization for an inmate of the State Colony for Epileptics and Feeble Minded, citing protection of the public welfare, and saying "[t]hree generations of imbeciles are enough." Id. at 207. *Buck*, which many regard as the culmination of this country's attraction to the eugenics movement, has generated considerable criticism.[5] Does *Buck*'s approach survive *Griswold* and *Eisenstadt*? Does state interference with the ability to procreate evoke the same analysis as interference with the ability to avoid procreation? In an omitted portion of Justice Goldberg's concurrence in *Griswold*, he observes that the dissenters' refusal to invalidate the birth control prohibition would compel them to uphold "a law requiring compulsory birth control." 381 U.S. at 497. Would it?

---

[3]. Peggy Cooper Davis, Contested Images of Family Values: The Role of the State, 107 Harv. L. Rev. 1348, 1363, 1371-1372 (1994).

[4]. Barbara Bennett Woodhouse, "Who Owns the Child?": *Meyer* and *Pierce* and the Child as Property, 33 Wm. & Mary L. Rev. 995, 1004, 1017-1018 (1992).

[5]. Eugenicists sought to improve the human race by curbing reproduction by criminals, the insane, and other "degenerates." See, e.g., Gordon, supra note [1], at 190-203. For critical commentary, see, e.g., Paul A. Lombardo, Three Generations, No Imbeciles: Eugenics, the Supreme Court, and Buck v. Bell (2008); Dorothy Roberts, Killing the Black Body: Race, Reproduction, and the Meaning of Liberty 69-72 (1999).

b. Control of the body. Union Pacific Railway Co. v. Botsford, 141 U.S. 250 (1891), also provided an underpinning of the right to privacy. In a dispute about a physical examination in a personal injury case, the Court said: "The right to one's person may be said to be a right of complete immunity: to be let alone." Id. at 251 (quoting Cooley on Torts, 29).

Which approach provides stronger support for the privacy articulated in *Griswold* and *Eisenstadt*: the special concern for control over one's body in *Botsford*? Or the protection for parental autonomy in *Meyer* and *Pierce*?

7. New applications. *Meyer* and *Pierce* proved pivotal precedents when the Supreme Court struck down the application of a broad third-party visitation statute in Troxel v. Granville, 530 U.S. 57 (2000) (reprinted in Chapter VIII). Although the case sharply divided the Court, several of the Justices took the opportunity both to reaffirm parents' fundamental liberty interest in childrearing and also to note the changing nature of the American family. 530 U.S. at 63-64, 85, 90, 98 (opinions of O'Connor, Stevens, and Kennedy, JJ.). What is a "family" for purposes of understanding the rights articulated in *Meyer* and *Pierce*? (Chapter V explores such questions.)

Do *Meyer* and *Pierce* apply to a "family business," such as those that successfully sued in *Hobby Lobby* (noted supra)? Does *Hobby Lobby* suggest protection for business owners' transmission of their values as they make choices for their for-profit corporations and employees, similar to the way that parents transmit their values through their (constitutionally protected) childrearing choices?

2. The Growth of Privacy

a. Abortion as a Private Choice

ROE v. WADE

410 U.S. 113 (1973)

Mr. Justice BLACKMUN delivered the opinion of the Court. . . .

The Texas statutes that concern us here . . . make it a crime to "procure an abortion," as therein defined, or to attempt one, except with respect to "an abortion procured or attempted by medical advice for the purpose of saving the life of the mother." Similar statutes are in existence in a majority of the States. . . .

[Jane Roe sued for a declaratory judgment that the Texas criminal abortion statutes were unconstitutional on their face and an injunction restraining their enforcement.] Roe alleged that she was unmarried and pregnant; that she wished to terminate her pregnancy by an abortion "performed by a competent, licensed physician, under safe, clinical conditions"; that she was unable to get a "legal" abortion in Texas because her life did not appear to be threatened by the continuation of her pregnancy; and that she could not afford to travel to another jurisdiction in order to secure a legal abortion under safe conditions. She claimed that the Texas statutes were unconstitutionally vague and that they abridged her right of personal privacy, protected by the First, Fourth, Fifth, Ninth, and Fourteenth Amendments. By an amendment to her complaint Roe purported to sue "on behalf of herself and all other women" similarly situated. [The district court held that the Ninth and Fourteenth Amendments protected the fundamental right to choose to have children and that the Texas statutes were unconstitutionally vague.]

The principal thrust of appellant's attack on the Texas statutes is that they improperly invade a right, said to be possessed by the pregnant woman, to choose to terminate her pregnancy. Appellant would discover this right in the concept of personal "liberty" embodied in the Fourteenth Amendment's Due Process Clause; or in personal marital, familial, and sexual privacy said to be protected by the Bill of Rights or its penumbras, see Griswold v. Connecticut, 381 U.S. 479 (1965); Eisenstadt v. Baird, 405 U.S. 438 (1972); id., at 460 (White, J., concurring in result); or among those rights reserved to the people by the Ninth Amendment, Griswold v. Connecticut, 381 U.S., at 486 (Goldberg J., concurring). Before addressing this claim, we feel it desirable briefly to survey, in several aspects, the history of abortion, for such insight as that history may afford us, and then to examine the state purposes and interests behind the criminal abortion laws.

VI

It perhaps is not generally appreciated that the restrictive criminal abortion laws in effect in a majority of States today are of relatively recent vintage. Those laws, generally proscribing abortion or its attempt at any time during pregnancy except when necessary to preserve the pregnant woman's life, are not of ancient or even of common-law origin. Instead, they derive from statutory changes effected, for the most part, in the latter half of the 19th century. . . .

[A]t common law, abortion performed before "quickening"—the first recognizable movement of the fetus in utero, appearing usually from the 16th to the 18th week of pregnancy— was not an indictable offense. The absence of a common-law crime for prequickening abortion appears to have developed from a confluence of earlier philosophical, theological, and civil and canon law concepts of when life begins. . . .

. . . In a frequently cited passage, Coke took the position that abortion of a woman "quick with childe" is "a great misprision, and no murder." . . . A recent review of the common-law precedents argues, however, that those precedents contradict Coke and that even postquickening abortion was never established as a common-law crime. This is of some importance because while most American courts ruled, in holding or dictum, that abortion of an unquickened fetus was not criminal under their received common law, others followed Coke in stating that abortion of a quick fetus was a "misprision," a term they translated to mean "misdemeanor." That their reliance on Coke on this aspect of the law was uncritical and, apparently in all the reported cases, dictum (due probably to the paucity of common-law prosecutions for postquickening abortion), makes it now appear doubtful that abortion was ever firmly established as a common-law crime even with respect to the destruction of a quick fetus.

. . . England's first criminal abortion statute, Lord Ellenborough's Act, 43 Geo. 3, c. 58, came in 1803. It made abortion of a quick fetus, §1, a capital crime, but in §2 it provided lesser penalties for the felony of abortion before quickening, and thus preserved the "quickening" distinction. . . .

. . . In this country, the law in effect in all but a few States until mid-19th century was the preexisting English common law. Connecticut, the first State to enact abortion legislation, adopted in 1821 that part of Lord Ellenborough's Act that related to a woman "quick with child." The death penalty was not imposed. Abortion before quickening was made a crime in that State only in 1860. In 1828, New York enacted legislation that, in two respects, was to serve as a model for early anti-abortion statutes. First, while barring destruction of an unquickened fetus as well as a quick fetus, it made the former only a misdemeanor, but the latter second-degree manslaughter. Second, it incorporated a concept of therapeutic abortion [necessary to save the life of the woman]. By 1840, when Texas had received the common law, only eight American States had statutes dealing with abortion. . . .

Gradually, in the middle and late 19th century the quickening distinction disappeared from the statutory law of most States and the degree of the offense and the penalties were increased. By the end of the 1950's, a large majority of the jurisdictions banned abortion, however and whenever performed, unless done to save or preserve the life of the mother. The exceptions, Alabama and the District of Columbia, permitted abortion to preserve the mother's health. . . . In the past several years, however, a trend toward liberalization of abortion statutes has resulted in adoption, by about one-third of the States, of less stringent laws, most of them patterned after the ALI Model Penal Code, §230.3. . . .

It is thus apparent that at common law, at the time of the adoption of our Constitution, and throughout the major portion of the 19th century, abortion was viewed with less disfavor than under most American statutes currently in effect. Phrasing it another way, a woman enjoyed a substantially broader right to terminate a pregnancy than she does in most States today. [The opinion then noted that the American Medical Association, American Public Health Association, and American Bar Association all supported liberalizing abortion laws.]

VII

Three reasons have been advanced to explain historically the enactment of criminal abortion laws in the 19th century and to justify their continued existence.

It has been argued occasionally that these laws were the product of a Victorian social concern to discourage illicit sexual conduct. Texas, however, does not advance this justification in the present case, and it appears that no court or commentator has taken the argument seriously. . . .

A second reason is concerned with abortion as a medical procedure. When most criminal abortion laws were first enacted, the procedure was a hazardous one for the woman. . . . Thus, it has been argued that a State's real concern in enacting a criminal abortion law was to protect the pregnant woman, that is, to restrain her from submitting to a procedure that placed her life in serious jeopardy.

Modern medical techniques have altered this situation. Appellants and various amici refer to medical data indicating that abortion in early pregnancy, that is, prior to the end of the first trimester, although not without its risk, is now relatively safe. Mortality rates for women undergoing early abortions, where the procedure is legal, appear to be as low as or lower than the rates for normal childbirth. Consequently, any interest of the State in protecting the woman from an inherently hazardous procedure, except when it would be equally dangerous for her to forgo it, has largely disappeared. Of course, important state interests in the areas of health and medical standards do remain. The State has a legitimate interest in seeing to it that abortion, like any other medical procedure, is performed under circumstances that insure maximum safety for the patient. . . . The prevalence of high mortality rates at illegal "abortion mills" strengthens, rather than weakens, the State's interest in regulating the conditions under which abortions are performed. Moreover, the risk to the woman increases as her pregnancy continues. Thus, the State retains a definite interest in protecting the woman's own health and safety when an abortion is proposed at a late stage of pregnancy.

The third reason is the State's interest—some phrase it in terms of duty—in protecting prenatal life. Some of the argument for this justification rests on the theory that a new human life is present from the moment of conception. The State's interest and general obligation to protect life then extends, it is argued, to prenatal life. Only when the life of the pregnant mother herself is at stake, balanced against the life she carries within her, should the interest of the embryo or fetus not prevail. . . . In assessing the State's interest, recognition may be given to the . . . claim that as long as at least *potential* life is involved, the State may assert interests beyond the protection of the pregnant woman alone.

Parties challenging state abortion laws have sharply disputed in some courts the contention that a purpose of these laws, when enacted, was to protect prenatal life. Pointing to the absence of legislative history to support the contention, they claim that most state laws were designed solely to protect the woman. Proponents of this view point out that in many States, including Texas, by statute or judicial interpretation, the pregnant woman herself could not be prosecuted for self-abortion or for cooperating in an abortion performed upon her by another. They claim that adoption of the "quickening" distinction through received common law and state statutes tacitly recognizes the greater health hazards inherent in late abortion and impliedly repudiates the theory that life begins at conception.

It is with these interests, and the weight to be attached to them, that this case is concerned.

VIII

The Constitution does not explicitly mention any right of privacy. In a line of decisions, however, going back perhaps as far as Union Pacific R. Co. v. Botsford, 141 U.S. 250, 251 (1891), the Court has recognized that a right of personal privacy, or a guarantee of certain areas or zones of privacy, does exist under the Constitution. In varying contexts, the Court or individual Justices have, indeed, found at least the roots of that right in the First Amendment, Stanley v. Georgia, 394 U.S. 557, 564 (1969); in the Fourth and Fifth Amendments; in the penumbras of the Bill of Rights, Griswold v. Connecticut, 381 U.S., at 484-485; in the Ninth Amendment, id., at 486 (Goldberg, J., concurring); or in the concept of liberty guaranteed by the first section of the Fourteenth Amendment, see Meyer v. Nebraska, 262 U.S. 390, 399 (1923). These decisions make it clear that only personal rights that can be deemed "fundamental" or "implicit in the concept of ordered liberty," are included in this guarantee of personal privacy. They also make it clear that the right has some extension to activities relating to marriage, procreation, contraception, family relationships, and child rearing and education [citing *Meyer, Pierce, Eisenstadt, Skinner,* and Loving v. Virginia, 388 U.S. 1 (1967)].

This right of privacy, whether it be founded in the Fourteenth Amendment's concept of personal liberty and restrictions upon state action, as we feel it is, or, as the District Court determined, in the Ninth Amendment's reservation of rights to the people, is broad enough to encompass a woman's decision whether or not to terminate her pregnancy. The detriment that the State would impose upon the pregnant woman by denying this choice altogether is apparent. Specific and direct harm medically diagnosable even in early pregnancy may be involved. Maternity, or additional offspring, may force upon the woman a distressful life and future. Psychological harm may be imminent. Mental and physical health may be taxed by child care. There is also the distress, for all concerned, associated with the unwanted child, and there is the problem of bringing a child into a family already unable, psychologically and otherwise, to care for it. In other cases, as in this one, the additional difficulties and continuing stigma of unwed motherhood may be involved. All these are factors the woman and her responsible physician necessarily will consider in consultation.

On the basis of elements such as these, appellant and some amici argue that the woman's right is absolute and that she is entitled to terminate her pregnancy at whatever time, in whatever way, and for whatever reason she alone chooses. With this we do not agree. Appellant's arguments that Texas either has no valid interest at all in regulating the abortion decision, or no interest strong enough to support any limitation upon the woman's sole determination, are unpersuasive. The Court's decisions recognizing a right of privacy also acknowledge that some state regulation in areas protected by that right is appropriate. As noted above, a State may properly assert important interests in safeguarding health, in maintaining medical standards, and in protecting potential life. At some point in pregnancy, these respective interests become sufficiently compelling to sustain regulation of the factors that govern the abortion decision. The privacy right involved, therefore, cannot be said to be absolute. In fact, it is not clear to us that the claim asserted by some amici that one has an unlimited right to do with one's body as one pleases bears a close relationship to the right of privacy previously articulated in the Court's decisions. The Court has refused to recognize an unlimited right of this kind in the past. Jacobson v. Massachusetts, 197 U.S. 11 (1905) (vaccination); Buck v. Bell, 274 U.S. 200 (1927) (sterilization).

We therefore conclude that the right of personal privacy includes the abortion decision, but that this right is not unqualified and must be considered against important state interests in regulation. . . . Where certain "fundamental rights" are involved, the Court has held that regulation limiting these rights may be justified only by a "compelling state interest," and that legislative enactments must be narrowly drawn to express only the legitimate state interests at stake. . . .

IX . . .

The appellee and certain amici argue that the fetus is a "person" within the language and meaning of the Fourteenth Amendment. In support of this, they outline at length and in detail the well-known facts of fetal development. If this suggestion of personhood is established, the appellant's case, of course, collapses, for the fetus' right to life would then be guaranteed specifically by the Amendment. . . .

The Constitution does not define "person" in so many words. Section 1 of the Fourteenth Amendment contains three references to "person." The first, in defining "citizens," speaks of "persons born or naturalized in the United States." The word also appears both in the Due Process Clause and in the Equal Protection Clause. "Person" is used in other places in the Constitution. . . . But in nearly all these instances, the use of the word is such that it has application only postnatally. None indicates, with any assurance, that it has any possible prenatal application.[54] All this, together with our observation, supra, that throughout the major portion of the 19th century prevailing legal abortion practices were far freer than they are today, persuades us that the word "person," as used in the Fourteenth Amendment, does not include the unborn. . . .

The pregnant woman cannot be isolated in her privacy. She carries an embryo and, later, a fetus. . . . The situation therefore is inherently different from marital intimacy, or bedroom possession of obscene material, or marriage, or procreation, or education, with which *Eisenstadt* and *Griswold, Stanley, Loving, Skinner* and *Pierce* and *Meyer* were respectively concerned. As we have intimated above, it is reasonable and appropriate for a State to decide that at some point in time another interest, that of health of the mother or that of potential human life, becomes significantly involved. The woman's privacy is no longer sole and any right of privacy she possesses must be measured accordingly.

Texas urges that, apart from the Fourteenth Amendment, life begins at conception and is present throughout pregnancy, and that, therefore, the State has a compelling interest in protecting that life from and after conception. We need not resolve the difficult question of when life begins. When those trained in the respective disciplines of medicine, philosophy, and theology are unable to arrive at any consensus, the judiciary, at this point in the development of man's knowledge, is not in a position to speculate as to the answer.

It should be sufficient to note briefly the wide divergence of thinking on this most sensitive and difficult question. There has always been strong support for the view that life does not begin until live birth [citing the Stoics and the Jewish and Protestant communities]. As we have noted, the common law found

---

54. When Texas urges that a fetus is entitled to Fourteenth Amendment protection as a person, it faces a dilemma. Neither in Texas nor in any other State are all abortions prohibited. Despite broad proscription, [a therapeutic] exception always exists. . . . But if the fetus is a person who is not to be deprived of life without due process of law, and if the mother's condition is the sole determinant, does not the Texas exception appear to be out of line with the Amendment's command? There are other inconsistencies between Fourteenth Amendment status and the typical abortion statute. It has already been pointed out that in Texas the woman is not a principal or an accomplice with respect to an abortion upon her. If the fetus is a person, why is the woman not a principal or an accomplice? Further, the penalty for criminal abortion . . . is significantly less than the maximum penalty for murder. . . . If the fetus is a person, may the penalties be different?

greater significance in quickening. Physicians and their scientific colleagues have regarded that event with less interest and have tended to focus either upon conception, upon live birth, or upon the interim point at which the fetus becomes "viable," that is, potentially able to live outside the mother's womb, albeit with artificial aid. Viability is usually placed at about seven months (28 weeks) but may occur earlier, even at 24 weeks. [T]he existence of life from the moment of conception [is] the official belief of the Catholic Church. [T]his is a view strongly held by many non-Catholics as well, and by many physicians. Substantial problems for precise definition of this view are posed, however, by new embryological data that purport to indicate that conception is a "process" over time, rather than an event, and by new medical techniques such as menstrual extraction, the "morning-after" pill, implantation of embryos, artificial insemination, and even artificial wombs.

In areas other than criminal abortion, the law has been reluctant to endorse any theory that life, as we recognize it, begins before live birth or to accord legal rights to the unborn except in narrowly defined situations and except when the rights are contingent upon live birth [citing tort and property law]. In short, the unborn have never been recognized in the law as persons in the whole sense.

X

In view of all this, we do not agree that, by adopting one theory of life, Texas may override the rights of the pregnant woman that are at stake. We repeat, however, that the State does have an important and legitimate interest in preserving and protecting the health of the pregnant woman, whether she be a resident of the State or a non-resident who seeks medical consultation and treatment there, and that it has still another important and legitimate interest in protecting the potentiality of human life. These interests are separate and distinct. Each grows in substantiality as the woman approaches term and, at a point during pregnancy, each becomes "compelling."

With respect to the State's important and legitimate interest in the health of the mother, the "compelling" point, in the light of present medical knowledge, is at approximately the end of the first trimester. This is so because of the now-established medical fact . . . that until the end of the first trimester mortality in abortion may be less than mortality in normal childbirth. It follows that, from and after this point, a State may regulate the abortion procedure to the extent that the regulation reasonably relates to the preservation and protection of maternal health [for example, by requiring licensure of abortion providers or certain facilities].

This means, on the other hand, that, for the period of pregnancy prior to this "compelling" point, the attending physician, in consultation with his patient, is free to determine, without regulation by the State, that, in his medical judgment, the patient's pregnancy should be terminated. If that decision is reached, the judgment may be effectuated by an abortion free of interference by the State.

With respect to the State's important and legitimate interest in potential life, the "compelling" point is at viability. This is so because the fetus then presumably has the capability of meaningful life outside the mother's womb. State regulation protective of fetal life after viability thus has both logical and biological justifications. If the State is interested in protecting fetal life after viability, it may go so far as to proscribe abortion during that period, except when it is necessary to preserve the life or health of the mother. . . .

XI

To summarize and to repeat:

1. A state criminal abortion statute of the current Texas type, that excepts from criminality only a *life-saving* procedure on behalf of the mother, without regard to pregnancy stage and without recognition of the other interests involved, is violative of the Due Process Clause of the Fourteenth Amendment.

(a) For the stage prior to approximately the end of the first trimester, the abortion decision and its effectuation must be left to the medical judgment of the pregnant woman's attending physician.

(b) For the stage subsequent to approximately the end of the first trimester, the State, in promoting its interest in the health of the mother, may, if it chooses, regulate the abortion procedure in ways that are reasonably related to maternal health.

(c) For the stage subsequent to viability, the State in promoting its interest in the potentiality of human life may, if it chooses, regulate, and even proscribe, abortion except where it is necessary, in appropriate medical judgment, for the preservation of the life or health of the mother. . . .

This holding, we feel, is consistent with the relative weights of the respective interests involved, with the lessons and examples of medical and legal history, with the lenity of the common law, and with the demands of the profound problems of the present day. The decision leaves the State free to place increasing restrictions on abortion as the period of pregnancy lengthens, so long as those restrictions are tailored to the recognized state interests. The decision vindicates the right of the physician to administer medical treatment according to his professional judgment up to the points where important state interests provide compelling justifications for intervention. Up to those points, the abortion decision in all its aspects is inherently, and primarily, a medical decision, and basic responsibility for it must rest with the physician. . . .

Mr. Justice REHNQUIST, dissenting. . . .

. . . I have difficulty in concluding, as the Court does, that the right of "privacy" is involved in this case. Texas, by the statute here challenged, bars the performance of a medical abortion by a licensed physician on a plaintiff such as Roe. A transaction resulting in an operation such as this is not "private" in the ordinary usage of that word. Nor is the "privacy" that the Court finds here even a distant relative of the freedom from searches and seizures protected by the Fourth Amendment to the Constitution, which the Court has referred to as embodying a right to privacy. Katz v. United States, 389 U.S. 347 (1967).

The fact that a majority of the States reflecting, after all, the majority sentiment in those States, have had restrictions on abortions for at least a century is a strong indication, it seems to me, that the asserted right to an abortion is not "so rooted in the traditions and conscience of our people as to be ranked as fundamental," Snyder v. Massachusetts, 291 U.S. 97, 105 (1934). . . . To reach its result, the Court necessarily has had to find within the scope of the Fourteenth Amendment a right that was apparently completely unknown to the drafters of the Amendment. [T]he drafters did not intend to have the Fourteenth Amendment withdraw from the States the power to legislate with respect to this matter. . . .

Sarah Weddington, A Question of Choice: Roe v. Wade 40th Anniversary Edition Revised and Updated[6]

14-16, 39-43, 49-62 (2013)

Attorney Sarah Weddington, after becoming White House Advisor on Women's Issues, 1979

My mouth goes dry as I put myself back in those days in Austin [Texas, in 1967] when my period was late. I was in my third year of law school, going to school full-time and supporting myself by working several jobs. I was seriously dating Ron Weddington, who was finishing his undergraduate degree after returning from the army; he was planning to start law school the following summer. . . .

[Once pregnancy was confirmed, we] began to go over the possibilities. Abortion was one, but we were worried about the risks of an illegal procedure. . . . If we decided on abortion, the next problem was: Where to go? There were no ads in the phone books or newspapers; this was all undercover. You had to find someone who knew a name, a place—and I refused to tell anyone my situation. . . . Ron [heard] about a doctor in Piedras Negras, across [the Mexican border]. The doctor had some medical experience in the United States, spoke excellent English, and performed abortions. Abortion was illegal in Mexico, but the woman Ron spoke to told him [that] several women she knew had been to this doctor, and everything had turned out fine. He charged $400—cash only. [Ron made the necessary arrangements, obtained a powerful painkiller, and got the name of someone who might help in case of medical trouble.]

I was grateful that at least the inside of the building was clean. I could not read what appeared to be a medical diploma on the wall, but it made me feel better. . . . I was one of the lucky ones. [W]hen I felt the anesthesia taking effect, my last thoughts were: I hope I don't die, and I pray that no one ever finds out about this. . . .

Roe v. Wade started at a garage sale, amid paltry castoffs. [Weddington and her friends were raising money for an abortion referral project.] The referral project volunteers were worried about being involved in covert activity. . . . While we sorted our prized junk at the garage sale, Judy [Smith] posed the primary questions that the volunteers wanted answered: Could they be prosecuted and/or convicted as accomplices to the crime of abortion simply for referring women? Would it make any legal difference if they sent women only to places where abortion was legal? . . . The [Texas] statute made it a crime to "furnish

[6]. Sarah Weddington is the attorney who represented Jane Roe in Roe v. Wade.

the means for procuring an abortion," but I didn't know whether that applied only to drugs and instruments, not information. I knew Texas also had a general accomplice statute that applied to a variety of crimes.

[I began spending time in the University of Texas] law library, meeting with project volunteers, spending more time in the library, and talking to law professors, law students, and other lawyers. [One day] Judy announced that she wanted a lawsuit filed to challenge the constitutionality of the Texas anti-abortion statute. . . .

[I] had not focused on the possibility of *our* filing a lawsuit. After all, my total legal experience consisted of a few uncontested divorces for friends, ten or twelve uncomplicated wills for people with little property, one adoption for relatives, and a few miscellaneous matters. . . . The idea of challenging the Texas abortion law in federal court was overwhelming [but] I was the best free legal help available [and I wanted to help others avoid what we had gone through]. [P]erhaps my inexperience was a plus. I did not fully appreciate that the odds were stacked against our endeavor. . . .

[Weddington asked former classmate Linda Coffee, who was familiar with federal litigation, to help.] [O]ur constant worry was about the right plaintiffs. . . . Then a woman went to Dallas lawyer Henry McCluskey, a friend of Linda's who knew of the proposed lawsuit. . . . She had had a rough life: She already had one child and did not want another. Her mother had taken her daughter away from her and she seldom got to see her. She had never finished the tenth grade, was working as a waitress, and knew she would lose her job if the pregnancy continued. She could barely support herself, much less a child. . . .

. . . She had found an illegal place in Dallas, she admitted, but she didn't like the looks of it. She had no money to travel to another state. As the conversation continued [in our meeting at a Dallas pizza parlor, this woman] asked if it would help if she had been raped. We said no; the Texas law had no exception for rape. It was just as illegal for a doctor to do an abortion for someone who had been raped as it was in any other situation. I did ask, "Were there any witnesses? Was there a police report? Is there any way that we could prove a rape occurred?" Her answer in each instance was no.

Neither Linda nor I questioned her further about how she had gotten pregnant. I was not going to allege something in the complaint that I could not back up with proof. Also, we did not want the Texas law changed only to allow abortion in cases of rape. We wanted a decision that abortion was covered by the right of privacy. After all, the women coming to the referral project were there as a result of a wide variety of circumstances. . . .

We still had to name our plaintiffs [who would use pseudonyms to protect their privacy]. We picked names that rhymed. I liked "Jane Roe."[7] To me the name represented all women, not just one. . . . We filed . . . against Henry Wade,

---

[7]. Norma McCorvey (who was "Jane Roe" in Roe v. Wade) subsequently announced that she had joined the pro-life movement, saying that she had "always been pro-life [but] just didn't know it" and that she had been exploited by abortion rights groups. See "Jane Roe" Joins Anti-Abortion Group, N.Y. Times, Aug. 11, 1995, at A12. Years later, she filed a motion for relief from judgment, seeking to revisit *Roe*, but the case was deemed moot. McCorvey v. Hill, 385 F.3d 846 (5th Cir. 2004), *cert. denied*, 543 U.S. 1154 (2005). See also Norma McCorvey with Andy Meisler, I Am Roe: My Life, Roe v. Wade and Freedom of Choice (1994).

the elected district attorney of Dallas County, the official responsible for law enforcement in that county. We wanted the court to tell Wade's office to leave doctors alone. [The case] became known as *Roe v. Wade*. . . .

Brief for the Amici Curiae Women Who Have Had Abortions and Friends of Amici Curiae in Support of Appellees, Webster v. Reproductive Health Services

492 U.S. 490 (1989) (No. 88-605)

Friends Letter—172, At C29-30

When I was six years old, I was forced to endure a 40-mile trip to what was referred to as "Feather Annie's." I stayed in the car with my father and two brothers while my 41-year-old mother went inside the private residence. My father's serious attitude instilled fear and insecurity in my older brother and I. When my mother returned to the car she was crying. She repeated the words "I'm afraid I'll die—I'm afraid someone will find out I came here and I'll get her (referring to the woman who performed the abortion) in trouble with the law. I'm glad it's over, but I'm afraid—if I die, what will happen to the children?" It was an awful experience for a child who was too young to understand. All the way home she cried and repeated over and over her fear of dying. I do not remember . . . her expressing any regret, she expressed her relief that it was over. Her fears became contagious and needless to say it was traumatic for me and my older brother (one brother was less than 2 years old). Many years later when my brother and I recalled that day, we agreed that the only crime committed was by a society that forced a woman to have to submit herself to fear and agony of that magnitude. Our mother survived and imbued in us forever was our sympathy for her on that day. After all, she had already born six children, she was in poor health, and my father was unemployed in that year of 1936.

My mother told me that it was a terrible tragedy that the little 2 year old neighbor girl's mother died suddenly. When I became old enough to understand I found out that it was no secret, in the small town we lived in, that the young mother had died from a self-induced abortion. As a very young child I was terribly disturbed over the fact that this dear cute little girl had no mother for the reason that her mother had died because she didn't want to have another baby. I felt sad that such a thing could happen, it was hard for me to accept that "Jane's" pretty young mother had to die. I saw sadness in Jane's face and unhappiness was apparent in her father's behavior. I cannot justify a law that allowed such unfortunate circumstances to happen.

In the 1950's my sister lost a good friend who had an illegal abortion. The 28-year old woman who died had five small children. Her unplanned and unwanted pregnancy was more than she was able to handle and her untimely death was the result of not having a choice of a safe and legal abortion. A law with the potential effect of depriving a loving husband and five small children of the presence of a young wife and mother is a disgrace in a compassionate society.

As these excerpts reveal, abortion was a dangerous procedure before legalization. In fact, abortion was the leading cause of maternal deaths in some locales. See generally Leslie J. Reagan, When Abortion Was a Crime: Women, Medicine, and Law in the United States, 1867-1973 (1997).

Notes and Questions

1. ***Roe's* right.** What is the nature of the right recognized by Roe v. Wade? Its parameters? Where in the Constitution does *Roe* situate this right? How does this approach compare with that of *Griswold*? Why is the right to terminate a pregnancy not absolute? Why is it "fundamental" (thereby evoking the compelling state interest test)? Over the years, *Roe*'s recognition of an abortion right has become a prominent illustration of so-called judicial activism. See, e.g., J. Harvie Wilkinson III, Of Guns, Abortion, and the Unraveling Rule of Law, 95 Va. L. Rev. 253 (2009). Supporters of reproductive freedom also note the costs of constitutionalizing abortion, instead of pressing for legislative and political change.[8]

2. ***Roe's* precedents.** Does the protection of childrearing and education in *Meyer* and *Pierce* support *Roe*'s holding? Does the right to privacy in *Roe* come from *Griswold*? See Whalen v. Roe, 429 U.S. 589, 598-599 (1977) (post-*Roe* case attributing to *Griswold* two meanings of "privacy"). Does the definition of the right to privacy in *Eisenstadt* necessarily include abortion freedom? Historical accounts attribute Justice Brennan's choice of the "*bear* or beget" language in *Eisenstadt* to his anticipation of the abortion cases.[9]

3. **Abortion restrictions.** Two types of statutory restrictions were common in the *Roe* era. One type, like the Texas statute, prohibited abortion except to save the life of the mother. A newer type, modeled on the American Law Institute's (ALI) Model Penal Code, permitted abortion if pregnancy would seriously and permanently injure the woman's health; if the fetus suffered from a grave, permanent, and irremediable mental or physical defect; or if the pregnancy resulted from rape. In a companion case to *Roe*, Doe v. Bolton, 410 U.S. 179 (1973), the Court invalidated Georgia's ALI-inspired statute, including its procedural requirements of hospitalization, accreditation, committee approval, two-doctor concurrence, and residency.

4. **Viability.** Many early abortion restrictions disallowed abortions only after quickening (the first perception of fetal movement, usually between 16 and 18 weeks of gestation). Although quickening had no biological significance, it became important, in the absence of pregnancy tests, as the first indication of pregnancy. Without such evidence, prosecutors could not establish the elements of criminal

---

[8]. Robin West, From Choice to Reproductive Justice: De-Constitutionalizing Abortion Rights, 118 Yale L.J. 1394, 1409 (2009) (positing as costs, inter alia, inadequate social welfare for those who have children).

[9]. David J. Garrow, Liberty and Sexuality: The Right to Privacy and the Making of Roe v. Wade 541-544 (updated ed. 1998).

abortion. See James C. Mohr, Abortion in America: The Origins and Evolution of National Policy, 1800-1900, at 4 (1978).

Roe emphasizes viability, not quickening. Why? In invoking the role of viability in prenatal torts, *Roe* used an analysis that was becoming out of date. Although early cases permitted recovery for prenatal injuries by children subsequently born alive only if the injuries occurred after viability, many cases abandoned the requirement before *Roe*. See, e.g., Hornbuckle v. Plantation Pipe Line Co., 93 S.E.2d 727 (Ga. 1956).

Does the Court satisfactorily explain why the state's interest in protecting "potential life" becomes compelling only after viability? See Linda Greenhouse, Becoming Justice Blackmun: Harry Blackmun's Supreme Court Journey 96-98 (2005) (recounting how viability became the compelling point in *Roe*). See also Mark Osler, *Roe*'s Ragged Remnant: Viability, 24 Stan. L. & Pol'y Rev. 215, 219 (2013) (defending "viability as a meaningful threshold").

5. Timing of viability. In 1973, *Roe* placed viability at approximately 28 weeks. Although a later medical consensus identified 24 weeks as the earliest point of potential viability, evidence from newer studies could justify a shift to 22 weeks. Compare Maria A. Morgan et al., Obstetrician-Gynecologists' Practices Regarding Preterm Birth at the Limit of Viability, 21 J. Maternal-Fetal & Neonatal Med. 115 (2008), with Matthew A. Rysavy et al., Between-Hospital Variation in Treatment and Outcomes in Extremely Pre-Term Infants, 372 N. Eng. J. Med. 1801 (2015). What explains such changes? What if technology can advance viability still further? Or make available "artificial wombs"? See City of Akron v. Akron Ctr. for Reprod. Health, 462 U.S. 416, 458 (1983) (O'Connor, J., dissenting) (suggesting this prospect puts *Roe* on a "collision course" with itself); Jennifer S. Hendricks, Not of Woman Born: A Scientific Fantasy, 62 Case W. Res. L. Rev. 399 (2011). Will the state have authority to prohibit abortions earlier in pregnancy? Alternatively, might artificial wombs or abortion methods compatible with fetal survival give pregnant women *more* freedom to terminate their pregnancies by allowing the state to protect potential life without continued physical imposition on women? What interest of the pregnant woman does *Roe* protect: The freedom to terminate the physical burdens of pregnancy? The freedom to escape reproduction?

6. Physician's role. According to *Roe*, to whom does the privacy right belong—the woman or the physician? *Roe*'s emphasis on the physician receives reinforcement from Doe v. Bolton's broad interpretation of "health," which allows the physician to consider "all factors—physical, emotional, psychological, familial, and the woman's age—relevant to the well-being of the patient." 410 U.S. at 192. See id. at 196-197. What role *should* a physician play in the decision to terminate a pregnancy?

7. Gender equality. What alternative approaches might the Supreme Court have used? Many feminist commentators prefer an equal protection, over a privacy-based, approach on the theory that abortion freedom is essential for gender equality. For example, Professor Sylvia Law has argued:

> Nothing the Supreme Court has ever done has been more concretely important for women [than Roe v. Wade]. Laws denying access to abortion have a sex-specific

impact. Although both men and women seek to control reproduction, only women become pregnant. Only women have abortions. Laws restricting access to abortion have a devastating sex-specific impact. Despite the decision's overwhelming importance to women, it was not grounded on the principle of sex equality. . . .

. . . An equality doctrine that ignores the unique quality of [women's reproductive] experiences implicitly says that women can claim equality only insofar as they are like men. Such a doctrine demands that women deny an important aspect of who they are. . . .[10]

What are the advantages and disadvantages of an equal protection rationale for the right to abortion? Proponents of this approach include Justice Ginsburg, who as a litigator persuaded the Supreme Court to apply the Equal Protection Clause to gender discrimination. See, e.g., Ruth Bader Ginsburg, Some Thoughts on Autonomy and Equality in Relation to Roe v. Wade, 63 N.C. L. Rev. 375, 386 (1985).

8. Potential life and sex discrimination. How far should the state go in protecting *potential* life? Professor Frances Olsen ponders this question:

. . . How would men react to a law that forbad them to ejaculate outside a fertile woman's vagina? While most heterosexual men would probably prefer to ejaculate into a vagina, the idea that they could not ejaculate anywhere else would probably come to seem oppressive and absurd to them. Yet such a law would seem to promote a state interest in *potential life*, as well as a state interest in the life of sperm. To avoid overbreadth, the law could provide that if a man does ejaculate where he is not allowed to, he could avoid criminal liability by collecting as many of the sperm as possible and rushing them to a sperm bank. . . .

Of course, the burden such a law would place upon men is nothing like the burden that antiabortion laws place upon women. Many men would not be affected at all; other men would simply have to make periodic trips to sperm banks. . . . They would disrupt no one's life, disturb no long-range plans. The trips would be even less disruptive than a woman's menstrual period, so really no one could properly complain. Perhaps some disgruntled men, whose real complaint might be that they were born male, might object. Their objection, however, should be lodged against mother nature, not against the law—a law reasonably drafted to maximize a man's freedom, consistent with the state's obligation to preserve life.

Many people would consider this example silly, but this putative silliness reflects the value that society places upon men's lives and their freedom. Only convenience prevents us from valuing sperm. . . .[11]

Olsen goes on to say that, in order to reduce abortion, the state could provide social support for pregnant women and children; improve access to contraceptives; and "outlaw" the act of impregnating women who do not wish to become pregnant, by both requiring a woman's informed consent and imposing a waiting period before a man could risk impregnating her.[12]

9. Abortion and motherhood. Sociologist Kristin Luker attributes the sharp differences concerning abortion to a war over two opposing visions of motherhood.

---

[10]. Sylvia A. Law, Rethinking Sex and the Constitution, 132 U. Pa. L. Rev. 955, 980-981, 1007 (1984).

[11]. Frances Olsen, Comment: Unraveling Compromise, 103 Harv. L. Rev. 105, 129-130 (1989).

[12]. Id. at 130.

Generally, the pro-choice position embraces feminist and progressive objectives, including equal opportunities for men and women in education and employment, freedom from gender-based assumptions and stereotypes, and the elimination of paternalism. By contrast, abortion opponents do not regard equality as a primary value because "they believe that men and women are intrinsically different [with] different roles in life" and that "motherhood—the raising of children and families—is the most fulfilling role that women can have."[13] See also Linda Gordon, The Moral Property of Women: A History of Birth Control Politics in America 304-305 (2002); Reva Siegel, Reasoning from the Body: A Historical Perspective on Abortion Regulation and Questions of Equal Protection, 44 Stan. L. Rev. 261, 308-314 (1992).

What insights does this analysis provide in evaluating *Roe*? In understanding the controversy that followed *Roe* and persists today? See Mary Ziegler, The Bonds That Tie: The Politics of Motherhood and the Future of Abortion Rights, 21 Tex. J. Women & L. 47 (2011). Can one argue that abortion freedom advances respect for motherhood? Priscilla J. Smith, Responsibility for Life: How Abortion Serves Women's Interests in Motherhood, 17 J.L. & Pol'y 97 (2009). Does the protection of childrearing in *Meyer* and *Pierce*, supra, support this argument?

10. Abortion and crime. Two economists cite empirical evidence to claim that legalizing abortion explains large decreases in crime.[14] The authors theorize that abortion prevented the birth of unwanted children who would have grown up to commit crimes. What relevance, if any, do such findings have for the legal and constitutional questions posed by *Roe*?

11. Comparative law. Today, wide variations in abortion policy exist throughout the world. At the more permissive end of the spectrum, most European Union nations recognize abortion as a "fundamental human right."[15] Liberalization of abortion law has occurred in over 30 countries since 1994, while El Salvador, Nicaragua, and Poland all tightened existing restrictions during this period.[16] Recent efforts to secure abortion freedom worldwide invoke the jurisprudence of international human rights.[17] To the extent that China's notorious policy of one child per family (which was replaced by a two-child policy, effective in 2016) resulted in forced abortions and involuntary birth control, as critics claim,[18] it illustrates the different forms that government interference with reproductive autonomy can take.

---

[13]. Kristin Luker, Abortion and the Politics of Motherhood 118, 159-160 (1984).

[14]. John J. Donahue III & Steven D. Levitt, The Impact of Legalized Abortion on Crime, 116 Q.J. Econ. 379 (2001).

[15]. Chad M. Gerson, Development, Toward an International Standard of Abortion Rights: Two Obstacles, 5 Chi. J. Int'l L. 753, 757 (2005).

[16]. Center for Reproductive Rights, Abortion Worldwide: 20 Years of Reform (August 2014) (briefing paper), http://www.reproductiverights.org/sites/crr.civicactions.net/files/documents/20Years_Reform_Report.pdf. On Nicaragua's complete ban, see Sarah Helena Lord, Comment, The Nicaraguan Abortion Ban: Killing in Defense of Life, 87 N.C. L. Rev. 537 (2009).

[17]. E.g., Martha F. Davis, Abortion Access in the Global Marketplace, 88 N.C. L. Rev. 1657 (2010); Barbara Stark, The Women's Convention, Reproductive Rights, and the Reproduction of Gender, 18 Duke J. Gender L. & Pol'y 261 (2011).

[18]. See Chris Buckley, China Approves Two-Child Policy to Improve Economy, N.Y. Times, Oct. 30, 2015, at A1. See also Associated Press, China Teacher Allowed to Give Birth and Ordered to Abort, N.Y. Times, May 19, 2015, http://www.nytimes.com/aponline/2015/05/19/world/asia/ap-as-china-one-child-policy.html (illustrating conflicting provincial laws).

b. Anti-Abortion Laws: Historical and Philosophical Perspectives

Kristin Luker, Abortion and the Politics of Motherhood

20-29 (1984)

In the second half of the nineteenth century, abortion began to emerge as a social problem: newspapers began to run accounts of women who had died from "criminal abortions," although whether this fact reflects more abortions, more lethal abortions, or simply more awareness is not clear. Most prominently, physicians became involved, arguing that abortion was both morally wrong and medically dangerous.

The membership of the American Medical Association (AMA), founded in 1847 to upgrade and protect the interests of the profession, was deeply divided on many issues. But by 1859 it was able to pass a resolution condemning induced abortion and urging state legislatures to pass laws forbidding it; in 1860, Henry Miller, the president-elect of the association, devoted much of his presidential address to attacking abortion. . . . Slowly, physicians responded to the AMA's call and began to lobby in state legislatures for laws forbidding abortion. . . .

Why should nineteenth-century physicians have become so involved with the question of abortion? . . . First, [the physicians themselves] argued, they were compelled to address the abortion question because American women were committing a moral crime based on ignorance about the proper value of embryonic life. According to these physicians, women sought abortions because the doctrine of quickening led them to believe that the embryo was not alive, and therefore aborting it was perfectly proper. Second, they argued, they were obliged to act in order to save women from their own ignorance because only physicians were in possession of new scientific evidence which demonstrated beyond a shadow of a doubt that the embryo was a child from conception onward. . . .

This stand had an important advantage for physicians. It meant that the American women who practiced abortion (and who were generally thought to be members of the "better classes") could be defined as *inadvertent* murderesses. . . . Thus, a physician could condemn the "sin" without the necessity of condemning the "sinner." . . .

[N]either part of the physicians' claim was, strictly speaking, true. Women (and the general public) knew that pregnancy was a *biologically* continuous process from beginning to end, and physicians were not in possession of remarkable new scientific discoveries to use to prove the case. . . . What the anti-abortion physicians achieved, therefore, was a subtle transformation of the grounds of the debate. . . .

[W]hy in the middle of the nineteenth century, did some physicians become anti-abortionists? James Mohr, in a pioneering work on this topic, argues that the proliferation of healers in the nineteenth century created a competition for status and clients. The "regular" physicians, who tended to be both wealthier and better educated than members of other medical sects, therefore sought to distinguish themselves both scientifically and socially from competing practitioners. . . . The abortion issue [gave the "regulars"] a way of demonstrating that they were both more scientifically knowledgeable and more morally rigorous than their competitors.

Mohr suggests that . . . outlawing abortion would remove a lucrative source of income from competitors [whom the "regulars"] called "quacks" and perhaps remove that temptation from the path of the "regulars" as well. In addition, the "regulars" were predominantly white, upper-income, and native-born; as such, they belonged to precisely the same group that was thought to harbor the primary users of abortion. As a result, they were likely to be concerned about the depopulation of their group in the face of mounting immigration (and the higher fertility of immigrants) and about "betrayal" by their own women (because abortion required less male control and approval than the other available forms of birth control). . . .

As we know, regular physicians succeeded in their campaign. . . . More than almost any other profession, medicine now rigorously exercises the right to control who shall enter the profession, how they shall practice, and how competitors will be treated; its nineteenth-century stand against abortion contributed substantially to this ultimate success. It is in the context of this drive of professionalization that the political activity of American physicians against abortion must be understood. When examined closely in this context, their actual behavior raises serious doubts about whether they had . . . an unparalleled commitment to the "sanctity of life" of the embryo. . . .

Judith Jarvis Thomson, A Defense of Abortion

1 Phil. & Pub. Aff. 47-63 (1971)

[Assuming we grant that the fetus is a person from the moment of conception, how,] precisely, are we supposed to get from there to the conclusion that abortion is morally impermissible? . . .

[L]et me ask you to imagine this. You wake up in the morning and find yourself back to back in bed with an unconscious violinist. A famous unconscious violinist. He has been found to have a fatal kidney ailment, and the Society of Music Lovers has canvassed all the available medical records and found that you alone have the right blood type to help. They have therefore kidnapped you, and last night the violinist's circulatory system was plugged into yours, so that your kidneys can be used to extract poisons from his blood as well as your own. The director of the hospital now tells you, "Look, we're sorry the Society of Music Lovers did this to you—we would never have permitted it if we had known. But still, they did it and the violinist now is plugged into you. To unplug you would be to kill him. But never mind, it's only for nine months. By then he will have recovered from his ailment, and can safely be unplugged from you." Is it morally incumbent on you to accede to this situation? No doubt it would be very nice of you if you did, a great kindness. But do you *have* to accede to it? . . .

In this case, of course, you were kidnapped; you didn't volunteer for the operation that plugged the violinist into your kidneys. Can those who oppose abortion on the ground I mentioned make an exception for a pregnancy due to rape? Certainly. . . .

[I]t cannot seriously be thought to be murder if the mother performs an abortion on herself to save her life. It cannot seriously be said that she *must* refrain, that she *must* sit passively by and wait for her death. . . . If anything in the world is true, it is that you do not commit murder, you do not do what is impermissible, if you reach around to your back and unplug yourself from that violinist to save your life. . . .

. . . Where the mother's life is not at stake, the argument [based on the fetus's right to life] seems to have a much stronger pull[:] "Everyone has a right to life, so the unborn person has a right to life." And isn't the child's right to life weightier than anything other than the mother's own right to life, which she might put forward as ground for an abortion?

This argument treats the right to life as if it were unproblematic. It is not, and this seems to me to be precisely the source of the mistake. [T]o return to the story I told earlier, the fact that for continued life that violinist needs the continued use of your kidneys does not establish that he has a right to be given the continued use of your kidneys. He certainly has no right against you that *you* should give him continued use of your kidneys. For nobody has any right to use your kidneys unless you give him such a right; and nobody has the right against you that you shall give him this right—if you do allow him to go on using your kidneys, this is a kindness on your part, and not something he can claim from you as his due. . . . Certainly he had no right against the Society of Music Lovers that they should plug him into you in the first place. And if you now start to unplug yourself, having learned that you will otherwise have to spend nine years in bed with him, there is nobody in the world who must try to prevent you, in order to see to it that he is given something he has a right to be given. . . .

But it might be argued that there are other ways one can have acquired a right to the use of another person's body than by having been invited to use it by that person. Suppose a woman voluntarily indulges in intercourse, knowing of the chance it will issue in pregnancy, and then she does become pregnant; is she not in part responsible for the presence, in fact the very existence, of the unborn person inside her?

[D]etails make a difference. If the room is stuffy, and I therefore open a window to air it, and a burglar climbs in, it would be absurd to say, "Ah, now he can stay, she's given him a right to the use of her house—for she is partially responsible for his presence there, having voluntarily done what enabled him to get in, in full knowledge that there are such things as burglars, and that burglars burgle." It would be still more absurd to say this if I had had bars installed outside my windows, precisely to prevent burglars from getting in, and a burglar got in only because of a defect in the bars. It remains equally absurd if we imagine it is not a burglar who climbs in, but an innocent person who blunders or falls in. Again, suppose it were like this: people-seeds drift about in the air like pollen, and if you open your windows, one may drift in and take root in your carpets or upholstery. You don't want children, so you fix up your windows with fine mesh screens, the very best you can buy. As can happen, however, and on very, very rare occasions does happen, one of the screens is defective. . . . Someone may argue that you are responsible for its rooting, that it does have a right to your house, because after all you *could* have lived out your life with bare floors and furniture, or with sealed windows and doors. But this won't do—for by the same token anyone can avoid a pregnancy due to rape by having a hysterectomy, or anyway by never leaving home without a (reliable!) army. . . .

[I]t is worth drawing attention to the fact that in no state in this country is any man compelled by law to be even a Minimally Decent Samaritan to any person. . . . By contrast, in most states in this country women are compelled by law to be not merely Minimally Decent Samaritans, but Good Samaritans to unborn persons inside them. This [at least shows] that there is a gross injustice in the existing state of the law.

Sidney Callahan, Abortion and the Sexual Agenda

113 Commonweal 232, 232-236 (1986)

. . . Pro-life feminists, like myself, argue on good feminist principles that women can never achieve the fulfillment of feminist goals in a society permissive toward abortion. . . . The moral right to control one's own body does apply to cases of organ transplants, mastectomies, contraception, and sterilization; but it is not a conceptualization adequate for abortion. The abortion dilemma is caused by the fact that 266 days following a conception in one body, another body will emerge. One's own body no longer exists as a single unit but is engendering another organism's life. . . . Strained philosophical analogies fail to apply: having a baby is not like rescuing a drowning person, being hooked up to a famous violinist's artificial life-support system, donating organs for transplant—or anything else. . . . It does not matter (*The Silent Scream* notwithstanding) whether the fetus being killed is fully conscious or feels pain. . . . Pro-life feminists who defend the fetus empathetically identify with an immature state of growth passed through by themselves, their children, and everyone now alive.

It also seems a travesty of just procedures that a pregnant woman now, in effect, acts as sole judge of her own case, under the most stressful conditions. Yes, one can acknowledge that the pregnant woman will be subject to the potential burdens arising from a pregnancy, but it has never been thought right to have an interested party, especially the more powerful party, decide his or her own case when there may be a conflict of interest. If one considers the matter as a case of a powerful versus a powerless, silenced claimant, the pro-choice feminist argument can rightly be inverted; since hers is the body, hers the risk, and hers the greater burden, then how in fairness can a woman be the sole judge of the fetal right to life? . . .

As the most recent immigrants from non-personhood, feminists have traditionally fought for justice. . . . A woman, involuntarily pregnant, has a moral obligation to the now-existing dependent fetus whether she explicitly consented to its existence or not. . . . The woman's moral obligation arises both from her status as a human being embedded in the interdependent human community and her unique lifegiving female reproductive power. . . .

. . . Pitting women against their own offspring is not only morally offensive, it is psychologically and politically destructive. Women will never climb to equality and social empowerment over mounds of dead fetuses. [Women] stand to gain from the same constellation of attitudes and institutions that will also protect the fetus in the woman's womb—and they stand to lose from the cultural assumptions that support permissive abortion. . . . By pro-choice reasoning, a man who does not want to have a child, or whose contraceptive fails, can be exempted from the responsibilities of fatherhood and child support. . . .

For that matter, why should the state provide a system of day-care or child support, or require workplaces to accommodate women's maternity and the needs of childrearing? Permissive abortion, granted in the name of women's privacy and reproductive freedom, ratifies the view that pregnancies and children are a woman's private individual responsibility. . . .

3. Burdens on Privacy

GONZALES v. CARHART

550 U.S. 124 (2007)

Justice Kennedy delivered the opinion of the Court.

These cases require us to consider the validity of the Partial Birth Abortion Ban Act of 2003 (Act), 18 U.S.C. §1531 (2000 ed., Supp. IV), a federal statute regulating abortion procedures. In recitations preceding its operative provisions the Act refers to the Court's opinion in Stenberg v. Carhart, 530 U.S. 914 (2000), which also addressed the subject of abortion procedures used in the later stages of pregnancy. . . . We conclude the Act should be sustained against the objections lodged by the broad, facial attack brought against it. . . .

The Act proscribes a particular manner of ending fetal life, so it is necessary here . . . to discuss abortion procedures in some detail. Three United States District Courts heard extensive evidence describing the procedures. [Each court held the statute unconstitutional, and the courts of appeals affirmed. Two of these cases are before the Supreme Court here.]

Abortion methods vary depending to some extent on the preferences of the physician and, of course, on the term of the pregnancy and the resulting stage of the unborn child's development. Between 85 and 90 percent of the approximately 1.3 million abortions performed each year in the United States take place in the first three months of pregnancy, which is to say in the first trimester. The most common first-trimester abortion method is vacuum aspiration (otherwise known as suction curettage) in which the physician vacuums out the embryonic tissue. Early in this trimester, an alternative is to use medication, such as mifepristone (commonly known as RU-486), to terminate the pregnancy. The Act does not regulate these procedures.

Of the remaining abortions that take place each year, most occur in the second trimester. The surgical procedure referred to as "dilation and evacuation" or "D&E" is the usual abortion method in this trimester. Although individual techniques for performing D&E differ, the general steps are the same.

[After dilation of her cervix, the] woman is placed under general anesthesia or conscious sedation. The doctor, often guided by ultrasound, inserts grasping forceps through the woman's cervix and into the uterus to grab the fetus. The doctor grips a fetal part with the forceps and pulls it back through the cervix and vagina, continuing to pull even after meeting resistance from the cervix. The friction causes the fetus to tear apart. For example, a leg might be ripped off the fetus as it is pulled through the cervix and out of the woman. . . . A doctor may make 10 to 15 passes with the forceps to evacuate the fetus in its entirety. . . . Some doctors, especially later in the second trimester, may kill the fetus [by injection] a day or two before performing the surgical evacuation. . . . Fetal demise may cause contractions and make greater dilation possible. Once dead, moreover, the fetus' body will soften, and its removal will be easier. Other doctors refrain from injecting chemical agents, believing it adds risk with little or no medical benefit.

The abortion procedure that was the impetus for the numerous bans on "partial-birth abortion," including the Act, is a variation of this standard D&E. The medical community has not reached unanimity on the appropriate name for this D&E variation [which we will refer to] as intact D&E. The main difference between the two procedures is that in intact D&E, a doctor extracts the fetus intact or largely intact with only a few passes. There are no comprehensive statistics indicating what percentage of all D&Es are performed in this manner. . . .

Intact D&E gained public notoriety when, in 1992, Dr. Martin Haskell gave a presentation describing his method of performing the operation. In the usual intact D&E, the fetus' head lodges in the cervix, and dilation is insufficient to allow it to pass. Haskell explained the next step as follows:

> At this point, the right-handed surgeon slides the fingers of the left [hand] along the back of the fetus and "hooks" the shoulders of the fetus with the index and ring fingers (palm down).
>
> While maintaining this tension, lifting the cervix and applying traction to the shoulders with the fingers of the left hand, the surgeon takes a pair of blunt curved Metzenbaum scissors in the right hand. He carefully advances the tip, curved down, along the spine and under his middle finger until he feels it contact the base of the skull under the tip of his middle finger.
>
> The surgeon then forces the scissors into the base of the skull or into the foramen magnum. Having safely entered the skull, he spreads the scissors to enlarge the opening.
>
> The surgeon removes the scissors and introduces a suction catheter into this hole and evacuates the skull contents. With the catheter still in place, he applies traction to the fetus, removing it completely from the patient.

This is an abortion doctor's clinical description. Here is another description from a nurse who witnessed the same method performed on a 26-week fetus and who testified before the Senate Judiciary Committee:

> Dr. Haskell went in with forceps and grabbed the baby's legs and pulled them down into the birth canal. Then he delivered the baby's body and the arms—everything but the head. The doctor kept the head right inside the uterus. . . .
>
> The baby's little fingers were clasping and unclasping, and his little feet were kicking. Then the doctor stuck the scissors in the back of his head, and the baby's arms jerked out, like a startle reaction, like a flinch, like a baby does when he thinks he is going to fall.
>
> The doctor opened up the scissors, stuck a high-powered suction tube into the opening, and sucked the baby's brains out. Now the baby went completely limp. . . .
>
> He cut the umbilical cord and delivered the placenta. He threw the baby in a pan, along with the placenta and the instruments he had just used.

Dr. Haskell's approach is not the only method of killing the fetus once its head lodges in the cervix, and "the process has evolved" since his presentation. [Other doctors use different techniques to crush the fetus's skull. Further,] D&E and intact D&E are not the only second-trimester abortion methods. [Other methods include medical induction and surgical procedures, hysterotomy and hysterectomy, which present risks of complications.]

After Dr. Haskell's procedure received public attention, with ensuing and increasing public concern, bans on "partial birth abortion" proliferated. By the time of [this Court's decision in Stenberg v. Carhart, 530 U.S. 914 (2000), in which a 5-4 majority invalidated a Nebraska statute], about 30 States had enacted bans designed to prohibit the procedure. [Congress approved bills banning partial-birth abortion in 1996 and 1997, but President Bill Clinton vetoed both. Congress passed this ban in 2003, which President George W. Bush signed into law.]

The Act responded to *Stenberg* in two ways. First, Congress made factual findings. . . . Congress found, among other things, that "[a] moral, medical, and ethical consensus exists that the practice of performing a partial-birth abortion . . . is a gruesome and inhumane procedure that is never medically necessary and should be prohibited." Second, and more relevant here, the Act's language differs from that of the Nebraska statute struck down in *Stenberg*. The operative provisions of the Act provide in relevant part: . . .

> (b) As used in this section—
>
> (1) the term "partial-birth abortion" means an abortion in which the person performing the abortion—
>
> (A) deliberately and intentionally vaginally delivers a living fetus until, in the case of a head-first presentation, the entire fetal head is outside the body of the mother, or, in the case of breech presentation, any part of the fetal trunk past the navel is outside the body of the mother, for the purpose of performing an overt act that the person knows will kill the partially delivered living fetus; and
>
> (B) performs the overt act, other than completion of delivery, that kills the partially delivered living fetus. . . .

[The Act includes an exception when the woman's life is endangered by physical disorder, illness, or injury. Physicians violating the Act face fines and imprisonment, but the woman may not be prosecuted. A provision authorizes civil actions. Below, the district courts and courts of appeals held the Act unconstitutional under *Stenberg*.]

II

The principles set forth in the joint opinion in Planned Parenthood of Southeastern Pa. v. Casey, 505 U.S. 833 (1992), [which upheld portions of Pennsylvania's abortion statute,] did not find support from all those who join the instant opinion [citing the opinions of Justices Scalia and Thomas]. Whatever one's views concerning the *Casey* joint opinion, it is evident a premise central to its conclusion—that the government has a legitimate and substantial interest in preserving and promoting fetal life—would be repudiated were the Court now to affirm the judgments of the Courts of Appeals.

Casey involved a challenge to Roe v. Wade, 410 U.S. 113 (1973). The opinion contains this summary:

> It must be stated at the outset and with clarity that *Roe*'s essential holding, the holding we reaffirm, has three parts. First is a recognition of the right of the woman to choose to have an abortion before viability and to obtain it without undue interference from the State. Before viability, the State's interests are not strong enough to support a prohibition of abortion or the imposition of a substantial obstacle to the woman's effective right to elect the procedure. Second is a confirmation of the State's power to restrict abortions after fetal viability, if the law contains exceptions for pregnancies which endanger the woman's life or health. And third is the principle that the State has legitimate interests from the outset of the pregnancy in protecting the health of the woman and the life of the fetus that may become a child. These principles do not contradict one another; and we adhere to each. 505 U.S., at 846 (opinion of the Court).

Though all three holdings are implicated in the instant cases, it is the third that requires the most extended discussion; for we must determine whether the Act furthers the legitimate interest of the Government in protecting the life of the fetus that may become a child. To implement its holding, *Casey* rejected both *Roe*'s rigid trimester framework and the interpretation of *Roe* that considered all previability regulations of abortion unwarranted. 505 U.S., at 875-876, 878 (plurality opinion). . . .

. . . We assume the following principles for the purposes of this opinion. Before viability, a State "may not prohibit any woman from making the ultimate decision to terminate her pregnancy." 505 U.S., at 879 (plurality opinion). It also may not impose upon this right an undue burden, which exists if a regulation's "purpose or effect is to place a substantial obstacle in the path of a woman seeking an abortion before the fetus attains viability." Id., at 878. On the other hand, "regulations which do no more than create a structural mechanism by which the State, or the parent or guardian of a minor, may express profound respect for the life of the unborn are permitted, if they are not a substantial obstacle to the woman's exercise of the right to choose." Id., at 877. *Casey*, in short, struck a balance. The balance was central to its holding. We now apply its standard to the cases at bar.

III . . .

The Act punishes "knowingly performing" a "partial-birth abortion." It defines the unlawful abortion in explicit terms [that specify several distinct requirements, including the delivery of a living fetus to a stage at which certain "anatomical landmarks" are met, an overt act that kills the partially delivered living fetus, and the intentional and deliberate performance of both of these physical elements].

[Invoking these elements, the Court rejects Respondents' contention that the Act is unconstitutionally vague on its face, distinguishing the Act from the statute invalidated in *Stenberg*. The Court also rejects the argument that the Act on its face imposes an undue burden because its restrictions on second-trimester abortions are too broad, covering standard D&E abortions, explaining as follows:] The Act excludes most D&Es in which the fetus is removed in pieces, not intact. If the doctor intends to remove the fetus in parts from the outset, the doctor will not have the requisite intent to incur criminal liability. A doctor performing a standard D&E procedure can often "take about 10-15 'passes' through the uterus to remove the entire fetus." Removing the fetus in this manner does not violate the Act because the doctor will not have delivered the living fetus to one of the anatomical landmarks or committed an additional overt act that kills the fetus after partial delivery. [I]nterpreting the Act so that it does not prohibit standard D&E is the most reasonable reading and understanding of its terms [and comports with the canon of constitutional avoidance].

IV

Under the principles accepted as controlling here, the Act [which applies pre- and postviability], as we have interpreted it, would be unconstitutional "if its purpose or effect is to place a substantial obstacle in the path of a woman seeking an abortion before the fetus attains viability." *Casey*, 505 U.S., at 878 (plurality opinion). . . .

. . . The Act's purposes are set forth in recitals preceding its operative provisions. . . . The Act proscribes a method of abortion in which a fetus is killed just inches before completion of the birth process. Congress stated as follows: "Implicitly approving such a brutal and inhumane procedure by choosing not to prohibit it will further coarsen society to the humanity of not only newborns, but all vulnerable and innocent human life, making it increasingly difficult to protect such life." The Act expresses respect for the dignity of human life. Congress was concerned, furthermore, with the effects on the medical community and on its reputation caused by the practice of partial-birth abortion [as its findings show].

Casey reaffirmed these governmental objectives. The government may use its voice and its regulatory authority to show its profound respect for the life within the woman. A central premise of the opinion was that the Court's precedents after *Roe* had "undervalued the State's interest in potential life." . . . Where it has a rational basis to act, and it does not impose an undue burden, the State may use its regulatory power to bar certain procedures and substitute others, all in furtherance of its legitimate interests in regulating the medical profession in order to promote respect for life, including life of the unborn. The Act's ban on abortions that involve partial delivery of a living fetus furthers the Government's objectives.

Respect for human life finds an ultimate expression in the bond of love the mother has for her child. The Act recognizes this reality as well. Whether to have an abortion requires a difficult and painful moral decision. While we find no reliable data to measure the phenomenon, it seems unexceptionable to conclude some women come to regret their choice to abort the infant life they once created and sustained. See Brief for Sandra Cano et al. as Amici Curiae in No. 05-380, pp. 22-24. Severe depression and loss of esteem can follow.

In a decision so fraught with emotional consequence some doctors may prefer not to disclose precise details of the means that will be used, confining themselves to the required statement of risks the procedure entails. From one standpoint this ought not to be surprising. Any number of patients facing imminent surgical procedures would prefer not to hear all details, lest the usual anxiety preceding invasive medical procedures become the more intense. This is likely the case with the abortion procedures here in issue.

It is, however, precisely this lack of information concerning the way in which the fetus will be killed that is of legitimate concern to the State. *Casey*, supra, at 873 (plurality opinion) ("States are free to enact laws to provide a reasonable framework for a woman to make a decision that has such profound and lasting meaning"). The State has an interest in ensuring so grave a choice is well informed. It is self-evident that a mother who comes to regret her choice to abort must struggle with grief more anguished and sorrow more profound when she learns, only after the event, what she once did not know: that she allowed a doctor to pierce the skull and vacuum the fast-developing brain of her unborn child, a child assuming the human form.

It is a reasonable inference that a necessary effect of the regulation and the knowledge it conveys will be to encourage some women to carry the infant to full term, thus reducing the absolute number of late-term abortions. The medical profession, furthermore, may find different and less shocking methods to abort the fetus in the second trimester, thereby accommodating legislative demand. The State's interest in respect for life is advanced by the dialogue that better informs the political and legal systems, the medical profession, expectant mothers, and society as a whole of the consequences that follow from a decision to elect a late-term abortion.

It is objected that the standard D&E is in some respects as brutal, if not more, than the intact D&E, so that the legislation accomplishes little. . . . Partial-birth abortion, as defined by the Act, differs from a standard D&E because the former occurs when the fetus is partially outside the mother to the point of one of the Act's anatomical landmarks. It was reasonable for Congress to think that partial-birth abortion, more than standard D&E, "undermines the public's perception of the appropriate role of a physician during the delivery process, and perverts a process during which life is brought into the world." . . .

[The Court next considers whether the Act imposes an undue burden because of the absence of an exception that would allow the procedure when necessary to preserve the woman's health, as required by the Court's precedents:] Respondents presented evidence that intact D&E may be the safest method of abortion. . . . Abortion doctors testified, for example, that intact D&E decreases the risk of cervical laceration or uterine perforation because it requires fewer passes into the uterus with surgical instruments and does not require the removal of bony fragments of the dismembered fetus, fragments that may be sharp. [Respondents presented additional evidence on safety advantages.] These contentions were contradicted by other doctors who testified in the District Courts and before Congress. They concluded that the alleged health advantages were based on speculation without scientific studies to support them. They considered D&E always to be a safe alternative.

There is documented medical disagreement whether the Act's prohibition would ever impose significant health risks on women. [Medical] uncertainty does not foreclose the exercise of legislative power in the abortion context any more than it does in other contexts. The medical uncertainty over whether the Act's prohibition creates significant health risks provides a sufficient basis to conclude in this facial attack that the Act does not impose an undue burden.

The conclusion that the Act does not impose an undue burden is supported by other considerations. Alternatives are available to the prohibited procedure. [T]he Act does not proscribe D&E [a commonly used and generally accepted method]. If the intact D&E procedure is truly necessary in some circumstances, it appears likely an injection that kills the fetus is an alternative under the Act that allows the doctor to perform the procedure. . . .

[Given disagreement within the medical community, a zero tolerance policy for uncertainty] is too exacting a standard to impose on the legislative power, exercised in this instance under the Commerce Clause [over physicians in or affecting interstate commerce], to regulate the medical profession. . . .

V

The considerations we have discussed support our further determination that these facial attacks should not have been entertained in the first instance. In these circumstances the proper means to consider exceptions is by as-applied challenge. . . . This is the proper manner to protect the health of the woman if it can be shown that in discrete and well-defined instances a particular condition has or is likely to occur in which the procedure prohibited by the Act must be used. In an as-applied challenge the nature of the medical risk can be better quantified and balanced than in a facial attack.

[We need not resolve here the debate about what plaintiffs must show to succeed in a facial challenge to an abortion statute.] [R]espondents have not [even] demonstrated that the Act would be unconstitutional in a large fraction of relevant cases. *Casey*, supra, at 895 (opinion of the Court). We note that the statute here applies to all instances in which the doctor proposes to use the prohibited procedure, not merely those in which the woman suffers from medical complications. It is neither our obligation nor within our traditional institutional role to resolve questions of constitutionality with respect to each potential situation that might develop. . . . The Act is open to a proper as-applied challenge in a discrete case. [Reversed.]

Justice GINSBURG, with whom Justice STEVENS, Justice SOUTER, and Justice BREYER join, dissenting. . . .

. . . Today's decision is alarming. It refuses to take *Casey* and *Stenberg* seriously. It tolerates, indeed applauds, federal intervention to ban nationwide a procedure found necessary and proper in certain cases by the American College of Obstetricians and Gynecologists (ACOG). It blurs the line, firmly drawn in *Casey*, between previability and postviability abortions. And, for the first time since *Roe*, the Court blesses a prohibition with no exception safeguarding a woman's health. . . .

. . . As *Casey* comprehended, at stake in cases challenging abortion restrictions is a woman's "control over her [own] destiny." 505 U.S., at 869 (plurality opinion).

"There was a time, not so long ago," when women were "regarded as the center of home and family life, with attendant special responsibilities that precluded full and independent legal status under the Constitution." Id., at 896-897. . . . Women, it is now acknowledged, have the talent, capacity, and right "to participate equally in the economic and social life of the Nation." Their ability to realize their full potential, the Court recognized, is intimately connected to "their ability to control their reproductive lives." Thus, legal challenges to undue restrictions on abortion procedures do not seek to vindicate some generalized notion of privacy; rather, they center on a woman's autonomy to determine her life's course, and thus to enjoy equal citizenship stature.

. . . The Court offers flimsy and transparent justifications for upholding a nationwide ban on intact D&E *sans* any exception to safeguard a women's health. [T]he Act scarcely furthers [the state's interest in preserving fetal life]: The law saves not a single fetus from destruction, for it targets only a *method* of performing abortion. . . . As another reason for upholding the ban, the Court emphasizes that the Act does not proscribe the nonintact D&E procedure. But why not, one might ask. Nonintact D&E could equally be characterized as "brutal," involving as it does "tearing [a fetus] apart" and "ripping off" its limbs. . . .

Ultimately, the Court admits that "moral concerns" are at work, concerns that could yield prohibitions on any abortion. . . . Revealing in this regard, the Court invokes an antiabortion shibboleth for which it concededly has no reliable evidence: Women who have abortions come to regret their choices, and consequently suffer from "severe depression and loss of esteem." Because of women's fragile emotional state and because of the "bond of love the mother has for her child," the Court worries, doctors may withhold information about the nature of the intact D&E procedure. The solution the Court approves, then, is *not* to require doctors to inform women, accurately and adequately, of the different procedures and their attendant risks. Instead, the Court deprives women of the right to make an autonomous choice, even at the expense of their safety.[8]

This way of thinking reflects ancient notions about women's place in the family and under the Constitution—ideas that have long since been discredited. Compare, e.g., Muller v. Oregon, 208 U.S. 412, 422-42 (1908) ("protective" legislation imposing hours-of-work limitations on women only held permissible in view of women's "physical structure and a proper discharge of her maternal function"); Bradwell v. State, 83 U.S. 130 (1873) (Bradley, J., concurring) ("Man is, or should be, woman's protector and defender. The natural and proper timidity and delicacy which belongs to the female sex evidently unfits it for many of the occupations of civil life. . . . The paramount destiny and mission of woman are to fulfill the noble and benign offices of wife and mother."), with United States v. Virginia, 518 U.S. 515, 533, 542, n.12 (1996) (State may not rely on "overbroad generalizations" about the "talents, capacities, or preferences" of women; "such judgments have . . . impeded . . . women's progress toward full citizenship stature throughout our

---

8. Eliminating or reducing women's reproductive choices is manifestly not a means of protecting them. When safe abortion procedures cease to be an option, many women seek other means to end unwanted or coerced pregnancies [citing links found between abortion restrictions and incidence of unsafe abortions].

Nation's history"); Califano v. Goldfarb, 430 U.S. 199, 207 (1977) (gender-based Social Security classification rejected because it rested on "archaic and overbroad generalizations" "such as assumptions as to [women's] dependency" (internal quotation marks omitted)). . . .

. . . The Court's hostility to the right *Roe* and *Casey* secured is not concealed. [T]he opinion refers to obstetrician-gynecologists and surgeons who perform abortions not by the titles of their medical specialties, but by the pejorative label "abortion doctor." A fetus is described as an "unborn child" and as a "baby"; second-trimester, previability abortions are referred to as "late-term"; and the reasoned medical judgments of highly trained doctors are dismissed as "preferences" motivated by "mere convenience." Instead of the heightened scrutiny we have previously applied, the Court determines that a "rational" ground is enough to uphold the Act. And, most troubling, *Casey*'s principles, confirming the continuing vitality of "the essential holding of *Roe*," are merely "assumed" for the moment, rather than "retained" or "reaffirmed." . . .

. . . Though today's opinion does not go so far as to discard *Roe* or *Casey*, the Court, differently composed than it was when we last considered a restrictive abortion regulation, is hardly faithful to our earlier invocations of "the rule of law" and the "principles of *stare decisis*." . . .

John Leland, Beyond the Slogans: Inside an Abortion Clinic

N.Y. Times, Sept. 18, 2005, §1, at 1

At Little Rock Family Planning Services, the women filed in without making eye contact. [W]omen from as far away as Oklahoma joined the more than one million American women who will probably have abortions this year. Their experiences, at one of only two clinics in the state, offer a ground-level view of abortion in 2005, a landscape altered by shifts in technology, law, demographics and the political climate. . . .

More than 25 million Americans have had abortions since [Roe v. Wade]. Often kept secret, even from close friends or family members, the experience cuts across all income levels, religions, races, lifestyles, political parties, and marital circumstances. Though abortion rates have been falling since 1990, to their lowest level since the mid-1970's, abortion remains one of the most common surgical procedures for women in America. More than one in five pregnancies end in abortion.

In the squat, nondescript brick building here, the lofty rhetoric that has billowed through public debate for the last 32 years gave way to the mundane realities of the armed security guard and the metal detector, the surgical table and the settling of the bill before the procedure—$525 to $1,800, cash or credit card only. . . .

The solitary protester outside, Jim Dawson, 74, stood a court-mandated distance from the clinic with a video camera, taping women as they entered, and promising them hellfire if they went through with it—as he has for a decade. . . .

At the clinic, patients . . . spoke only if they could use just their first names. "It's not something I would talk about," said "M," a high school teacher who agreed to be identified only by her middle initial. . . . She said she had never discussed abortion with relatives or colleagues. Only two friends knew she was here. "I'd lose my job," she said. "My family's reputation would be ruined. It makes me nervous even being in the waiting room. You don't want to know who's here, you don't want to be recognized. . . ." Even most staff members at the clinic insisted on using only their first names—"to protect my identity from the anti-choice people," said Lori, a nurse practitioner. . . .

While abortion rates have been falling generally since 1990, the decline has been steepest among teenagers, and rates are lowest among educated, financially secure women. Researchers attribute the drop in teenage abortion to reduced rates of pregnancy, as a result of better access to contraception—including the three-month Depo-Provera injections—and abstinence. Conversely, for poor and low-income women, rates increased during the 1990's, possibly in response to the 1996 welfare overhaul, which reduced support systems for women who carry their fetuses to term. At every income level . . . , African-American women were more likely to terminate their pregnancies than white women.

Leah, 26, said money was a factor in her decision to have an abortion. A former college track athlete, she works in a clothing boutique, a job that she said did not pay enough to support a child. Like many women at the clinic, Leah had conflicted feelings about what she was doing. "I always said I would never, ever have an abortion," she said. "I probably will regret it. I'm pro-choice for cases of incest or rape, but if it's your own fault, you should accept responsibility. And it's my own fault." . . . Karen, 29, who arrived at the clinic 20 weeks pregnant, expressed no qualms about ending her pregnancy. [She did not come in earlier in the pregnancy, she said, because she did not have the money.] Like nearly half of all women who have abortions, she had had one before, when she was 18. . . . She has a 9-year-old son, and she said she felt she could not start again with a newborn child. This, too, is common. More than half of all women having abortions have had children. . . .

For many women at the clinic, their desire to end their pregnancy clashed with their religious beliefs. Tammy, a Muslim, had her first abortion a year ago, after having three children. She is married and works in a coffee shop in Tennessee. She became pregnant this time after erratically taking her birth control pills. [Similarly, Regina, 28, blamed a faulty contraceptive Depo-Provera shot from an Army nurse in Iraq for her pregnancy. "Every woman has second thoughts, especially because I'm Catholic," she said. She went to confession and met with her priest, she added. "The priest didn't hound me. He said, 'People make mistakes.'" She arrived at the clinic with cuts and bruises sustained after disclosing her pregnancy to her boyfriend, who is now in jail.]

Since 1992, when the Supreme Court recognized states' authority to restrict abortion as long as they did not create an "undue burden," states have enacted 487 laws restricting patients or providers, in many cases calling for mandatory counseling, waiting periods and parental consent for minors. [T]he result is a patchwork of laws and regulations that vary from state to state. . . .

At the clinic in Little Rock, patients and staff members said the restrictions were more inconveniences than roadblocks. Patients nodded dutifully as the staff members asked [state-scripted] questions like, "Do you understand that the father of the child must provide financial assistance if you deliver the pregnancy?" . . . For the clinic, the regulations add paperwork and require extra staff members [and impose extra costs that are passed on to the patients]. New licensing laws . . . require providers to comply with state codes for equipment, record-keeping, building grounds and other areas, which small businesses can find onerous. [Clinics call these] TRAP laws, for targeted regulation of abortion providers. [One physician] likened the regulations to "death by a thousand scratches."

In part because of the legal, financial, and emotional pressures, the number of doctors in Arkansas who perform more than occasional abortions has fallen to three, down from six in the late 1990's. The youngest . . . is 59. . . . [Dr. Jerry] Edwards, 63, said he felt an obligation to stay in business. "If we retired, I'm not sure anybody else would come to Arkansas and practice," he said. . . .[19]

Notes and Questions

1. Continuity or change? To what extent does *Gonzales* reflect an abortion jurisprudence that follows *Roe*, supra? To what extent does it depart? Does abortion remain a "fundamental right"? Does it still rest on the right of privacy? What is the standard of review? To what extent has the Court retained *Roe*'s controversial point of viability? How does the majority treat the absence of a health exception in the statute? May *Gonzales* and the statute it upholds be regarded as incremental steps in a larger strategy designed to overturn *Roe*? See Steven G. Calabresi, How to Reverse Government Imposition of Immorality: A Strategy for Eroding Roe v. Wade, 31 Harv. J.L. & Pub. Pol'y 85, 89-90 (2008).

2. Standard of review. *Gonzales* recalls Planned Parenthood of Southeastern Pennsylvania v. Casey, 505 U.S. 833 (1992), a challenge to several Pennsylvania abortion restrictions. In *Casey*, the sharply divided Court could not agree on the governing standard of review. The "joint opinion" (presented by Justices O'Connor, Kennedy, and Souter) embraced *Roe*'s protection for abortion freedom but rejected *Roe*'s trimester framework, announcing the *undue burden standard* in place of *Roe*'s strict scrutiny. Under this approach, these Justices voted to uphold several provisions of the Pennsylvania law, including the requirement that at least 24 hours before the abortion the physician must provide the woman detailed information about the procedure, its risks, and its alternatives as well as the "probable gestational age of the unborn child" and the availability of printed materials on child support, adoption, and other services.

Four justices (Chief Justice Rehnquist and Justices White, Scalia, and Thomas), who would have overruled *Roe* altogether, voted with the joint opinion authors to uphold these statutory sections under the *rational basis standard*. Two others

[19]. From the New York Times, Sept. 18, 2005 © 2005 The New York Times. All rights reserved. Used by permission and protected by the Copyright Laws of the United States. The printing, copying, redistribution, or retransmission of the material without express written permission is prohibited.

(Justices Blackmun and Stevens), following *Roe*, would have applied *strict scrutiny*, which Justice Blackmun said would invalidate all the challenged provisions.

In Stenberg v. Carhart, 530 U.S. 914 (2000), which *Gonzales* examines, a majority of the Justices embraced the undue burden standard for the first time. What makes a restriction an undue burden, according to *Casey* and *Gonzales*?

After *Gonzales*, does the undue burden standard still supply the governing rule? Why does the *Gonzales* majority conclude that the federal statute does not impose an undue burden? To what extent does the majority distinguish the statute struck down in *Stenberg* to reach this result? Or, does the majority opinion of Justice Kennedy (who dissented in *Stenberg*) alter the applicable legal principles? How does Justice Ginsburg's dissent answer this question? How does each opinion address the absence of a health exception? In an omitted separate concurring opinion joined by Justice Scalia, Justice Thomas took the opportunity to "reiterate [his] view that the Court's abortion jurisprudence, including *Casey* and [*Roe*], has no basis in the Constitution." 550 U.S. at 169.

3. Abortion participants.

a. Physician's role. How has the Court's understanding of reproductive autonomy evolved since *Roe*? *Roe*'s emphasis on the physician's role gave way in later cases to more explicit recognition of the woman's freedom. What does *Gonzales* say about physicians who provide abortions? About the medical profession? See Linda Greenhouse, How the Supreme Court Talks About Abortion: The Implications of a Shifting Discourse, 42 Suffolk U. L. Rev. 41 (2008).

Did the health exception required in all cases from *Roe* to *Stenberg* give physicians too much authority? How did the majority respond to the asserted medical uncertainty about the need for the prohibited procedure in some cases? In *Stenberg*, Justice Kennedy criticized the majority for "view[ing] the procedures from the perspective of the abortionist." 530 U.S. at 914 (Kennedy, J., dissenting). Whose perspective does he use in *Gonzales*? Why does his opinion contain such graphic descriptions of the medical procedures? Are these descriptions necessary to the reasoning and result? Gratuitous? See Neil S. Siegel, The Virtue of Judicial Statesmanship, 86 Tex. L. Rev. 959, 1022-1024 (2008) (critiquing Justice Kennedy's language).

b. Women's role. Citing the brief of Sandra Cano (who under the pseudonym "Mary Doe" prevailed in *Roe*'s companion case, Doe v. Bolton, 410 U.S. 179 (1973)), the *Gonzales* majority justifies abortion restrictions in part as a means of protecting women from decisions they do not understand and might come to regret. Justice Ginsburg condemns this paternalistic approach to reproductive autonomy. *Gonzales*'s treatment of regret, moreover, contrasts with that found in cases about other reproductive decisions and outcomes, such as adoption surrender or child support after an unintended conception. See Susan Frelich Appleton, Reproduction and Regret, 23 Yale J.L. & Feminism 255 (2011). In contrast to the Court's assumptions, a longitudinal study shows that most women (99 percent) regard their abortions as "the right decision" afterward.[20]

---

[20]. Corinne H. Rocca et al., Decision Rightness and Emotional Responses to Abortion in the United States: A Longitudinal Study. PLoS ONE 10(7): e0128832 (2015), http://journals.plos.org/plosone/article?id=10.1371/journal.pone.0128832.

Gonzales's regret rationale reflects modern efforts to restrict abortion by invoking women's interests, rather than fetal interests. See Reva B. Siegel, The Right's Reasons: Constitutional Conflict and the Spread of the Woman-Protective Antiabortion Argument, 57 Duke L.J. 1641 (2008). Would this basis for restricting abortion violate the Equal Protection Clause? One theory roots the woman-protective approach in the trauma discourse propounded by feminists seeking to reform the law of rape and domestic violence.[21] The view of women as abortion victims is also reflected in their longstanding exemption from criminal liability, a pattern continued in the federal statute. See generally McCormack v. Hiedeman, 694 F.3d 1004 (9th Cir. 2012); Ashley Gorski, The Author of Her Trouble: Abortion in Nineteenth- and Early Twentieth-Century Judicial Discourses, 32 Harv. J.L. & Gender 431 (2009).

Does the majority's reasoning rank protecting women from abortion regret as a more important value than protecting them from other health risks, physical and emotional? How does such reasoning stigmatize abortion and with what effect? See Paula Abrams, Abortion Stigma: The Legacy of *Casey*, 35 Women's Rts. L. Rep. 299 (2014).

4. The road to *Casey* and *Gonzales*. After Roe v. Wade and Doe v. Bolton invalidated then-existing abortion laws, state legislatures sought to fill the gap. Several "second-generation challenges" tested the limits of the Court's holdings.

a. Abortion funding. In 1977 the Court decided three cases permitting states to refuse Medicaid coverage for nontherapeutic abortions: Beal v. Doe, 432 U.S. 438 (1977); Maher v. Roe, 432 U.S. 464 (1977); and Poelker v. Doe, 432 U.S. 519 (1977). Although the government subsidized medical services for continued pregnancy and childbirth but not abortion for the indigent, the majority in *Maher* found no "unduly burdensome interference" with the abortion decision, distinguishing the "obstacle" invalidated in *Roe*. The Court treated the refusal to fund abortion as state inaction calling for the rational basis test rather than the strict scrutiny applied in *Roe*. State encouragement of childbirth over abortion, a "value judgment," satisfied this less demanding standard of review.

The Court used a similar analysis to reject challenges to governmental refusals to fund abortions necessary to preserve the woman's health. In Harris v. McRae, 448 U.S. 297 (1980), the Court held that *Roe*'s protection of the right to abortion does not confer an entitlement to funds to realize that right. How meaningful is the right to choose abortion without the means to effectuate this choice? Does the holding in *McRae* conflict with the importance ascribed to maternal health, at least pre-*Gonzales*? For a poor woman, is the state's offer of subsidized medical care for childbirth accompanied by its refusal to pay for an abortion an undue burden? Issues of funding have arisen anew in the context of the ACA (discussed infra).

b. The undue burden standard. Justice O'Connor was an early critic of *Roe*'s trimester framework. In her dissent in City of Akron v. Akron Center for Reproductive Health, Inc., 462 U.S. 416, 452-475 (1983), she announced a preference for

[21]. Jeannie Suk, The Trajectory of Trauma: Bodies and Minds of Abortion Discourse, 110 Colum. L. Rev. 1193 (2010).

strict scrutiny review only for "unduly burdensome" abortion restrictions, such as bans or third-party consent, asserting that the state has compelling interests in both maternal health and potential life throughout pregnancy. Later, however, she simply labeled the trimester framework "problematic," Webster v. Reproductive Health Servs., 492 U.S. 490, 529 (1989) (O'Connor, J., concurring). Is the undue burden standard that *Stenberg* and *Gonzales* take from *Casey* the same test used in the abortion-funding cases? In Justice O'Connor's earlier opinions?

Under the undue burden standard, *Casey*'s joint opinion expressly permits some measures "designed to persuade [the woman] to choose childbirth over abortion." 505 U.S. at 878. What measures does this language allow states to enact? Can you name other protected rights whose exercise the states can try to discourage, with the Supreme Court's blessing?

c. Informed consent. Soon after *Roe,* the Court upheld state regulations mandating that the physician obtain the patient's prior written consent, regardless of the stage of pregnancy. Planned Parenthood v. Danforth, 428 U.S. 52 (1976). When states required a detailed list of abortion warnings, however, the Court invalidated these measures because of both their interference with the doctor-patient relationship and their underlying anti-abortion motivation. *Akron,* 462 U.S. at 442-449; Thornburgh v. American College of Obstetricians & Gynecologists, 476 U.S. 747, 759-765 (1986). Why did *Casey* change this result, allowing mandated pre-abortion information and waiting periods?

Today, 35 states require pre-abortion counseling, and 27 states have written materials on abortion (with 10 requiring distribution to the woman and 17 requiring that they be offered to her).[22] Some states have imposed 72-hour waiting periods, e.g., Mo. Rev. Stat. §188.039(2). Are detailed informed consent requirements that apply only to abortion paternalistic? Do they discriminate on the basis of sex? See generally Maya Manian, The Irrational Woman: Informed Consent and Abortion Decision-Making, 16 Duke J. Gender L. & Pol'y 223 (2009). Do states enacting such requirements treat abortion patients as "inadvertent murderesses"? Recall the excerpt from Luker, supra. Note how Justice Kennedy's opinion in *Gonzales* deploys the justifications used to uphold information requirements to support a *ban* on a specific abortion procedure.

Currently 12 states include in their information requirements statements about the "fetal pain" caused by abortion, and 24 cover pre-abortion ultrasounds (including mandated ultrasounds in 13 states).[23] What legal rationale and scientific basis support such laws? See Carol Sanger, Seeing and Believing: Mandatory Ultrasound and the Path to Protected Choice, 56 UCLA L. Rev. 351 (2008). Do such laws compel speech in violation of the physician's First Amendment rights? See Stuart v. Camnitz, 774 F.3d 238 (4th Cir. 2014) (invalidating requirement that physician in all cases describe fetus to abortion patient during ultrasound), *cert. denied sub nom.* Walker-McGill v. Stuart, 135 S. Ct. 2838 (2015); Sonia M. Suter, The First Amendment and Physician Speech in Reproductive Decision Making, 43 J. L. Med. & Ethics 22 (2015).

---

[22]. Guttmacher Inst., State Policies in Brief: Counseling and Waiting Periods (July 1, 2015), http://www.guttmacher.org/statecenter/spibs/spib_MWPA.pdf.

[23]. Id.; Guttmacher Inst., State Policies in Brief: Requirements for Ultrasound (July 1, 2015), http://www.guttmacher.org/statecenter/spibs/spib_RFU.pdf.

Issues of informed consent and abortion funding coalesced in Rust v. Sullivan, 500 U.S. 173 (1991), in which the Court upheld regulations disallowing physicians in federally funded clinics from discussing abortion, despite the patient's request for information, the physician's judgment that the patient should consider abortion, the health risks of pregnancy, or state malpractice laws requiring disclosure. Does a physician's state-compelled silence on abortion create an undue burden for the patient?

d. Politics and a changing Court. To what extent is the road from *Roe* to *Casey,* and then to *Gonzales,* best understood as a reflection of changes in the Supreme Court's composition, in an era when presidential candidates often make explicit campaign promises about how their judicial nominees will address abortion cases? See Mary Ziegler, After *Roe*: The Lost History of the Abortion Debate (2015) (revealing how political pressure reshaped interests of diverse activists responding to *Roe*); Linda Greenhouse & Reva B. Siegel, Before (and After) Roe v. Wade: New Questions About Backlash, 120 Yale L.J. 2028 (2011) (challenging conventional wisdom that *Roe* politicized abortion). Where should matters of "family values" and morality be decided: in the home, the legislature, or the courts?

5. Morality. Justice Kennedy reasons in *Gonzales* that the banned procedure differs, as a moral matter, from other abortion techniques. What is the appropriate role of morality in constitutional adjudication? Would Justice Kennedy's approach require overturning *Roe* altogether—on the ground that some legislatures will find all abortions immoral? Can a state ban "dismemberment abortion" (nonintact D&E) on moral grounds, as anticipated in Justice Ginsburg's dissent? See Erik Eckholm, Judge Delays Kansas Ban on 2nd-Trimester Abortion Procedure, N.Y. Times, June 26, 2015, at A12 (noting bans passed in Kansas and Oklahoma).

Does prevention of "fetal pain" provide a morality-based justification for banning abortion after 20 weeks? Several states have enacted such laws based on this rationale, despite the absence of medical evidence. See Isaacson v. Horne, 716 F.3d 1213 (9th Cir. 2013) (holding such laws unconstitutional). Other states have banned abortion as soon as a fetal heartbeat can be detected. See Edwards v. Beck, 786 F.3d 1113 (8th Cir. 2015) (holding that Arkansas heartbeat law violates a woman's right to terminate a pregnancy before viability).

6. Abortion access. What access problems can you identify from the data and experiences reported in the *New York Times* story, supra?[24] What has the change in constitutional standard from *Roe* to *Casey* meant in practice? How far can a state go in impeding access without creating an undue burden? Do "TRAP" laws that force clinic closures, compelling women to seek abortions out of state, impose an undue burden? Compare Whole Women's Health v. Cole, 790 F.3d 563, 597 (5th Cir.), *mandate stayed,* 135 S. Ct. 2923 (2015), with Jackson Women's Health Org. v. Currier, 760 F.3d 448, 457 (5th Cir. 2014). Should the Supreme Court hear

[24]. A surge of recent enactments have made abortions much more difficult to obtain and have compelled the closure of clinics. See Heather D. Boonstra & Elizabeth Nash, A Surge of State Abortion Restrictions Puts Providers—and the Women They Serve—in the Crosshairs, 17 Guttmacher Pol. Rev. 1 (2014), http://www.guttmacher.org/pubs/gpr/17/1/gpr170109.pdf.

Whole Women's Health to clarify the undue burden standard? See generally John A. Robertson, Science Disputes in Abortion Law, 93 Tex. L. Rev. 1849 (2015).

Despite access problems, African-American women and poor women are more likely to terminate pregnancies than their white counterparts.[25] The increased demand for abortion during times of economic crisis highlights the financial constraints that influence reproductive decisionmaking.[26] Thus, Professor Dorothy Roberts observes that "[t]he primary concerns of white, middle-class women are laws that restrict choices otherwise available to them [while the] main concern of poor women of color . . . are the material conditions of poverty and oppression that restrict their choices."[27] See also Mary Ziegler, *Roe*'s Race: The Supreme Court, Population Control, and Reproductive Justice, 25 Yale J.L. & Feminism 1 (2013) (providing history of abortion's racial politics to illuminate current access issues).

7. Clinic violence. Violence creates access problems by dissuading both patients and abortion providers.[28] A federal statute, the Freedom of Access to Clinic Entrances Act (FACE) (18 U.S.C. §248), bars force, threats of force, or physical obstruction aimed at injuring, intimidating, or interfering with any patient or provider of reproductive health services. Some states have imposed "buffer zones" designed to keep protestors and "sidewalk counselors" a specific distance from clinic entrances; the Supreme Court has held that such measures survive First Amendment challenge only when alternatives that burden substantially less speech would fail to achieve the government's interests in protecting safety. McCullen v. Coakley, 134 S. Ct. 2518, 2540 (2014).

Laws protecting clinics, staff, and patients have neither increased nor decreased the incidence of abortion-related crimes. See William Alex Pridemore & Joshua Freilich, The Impact of State Laws Protecting Abortion Clinics and Reproductive Rights on Crimes Against Abortion Providers: Deterrence, Backlash, or Neither?, 31 Law & Hum. Behav. 611 (2007). In one famous case, Dr. George Tiller, whom anti-abortion activists had demonized because he performed late-term procedures, was murdered while attending church in Wichita, Kansas—an event that echoes in ongoing harassment of providers. See David S. Cohen & Krysten Connon, Living in the Crosshairs: The Untold Stories of Anti-Abortion Terrorism 1-5 (2015).

---

[25]. Non-Hispanic Black women account for 30 percent of abortions and Hispanic women for 25 percent, while 42 percent of women obtaining abortions are below the federal poverty level. Moreover, three-quarters of women obtaining abortions say they cannot afford a child. Guttmacher Inst., Fact Sheet, Induced Abortion in the United States, July 2014, http://www.guttmacher.org/pubs/fb_induced_abortion.pdf.

[26]. See Kimi Yoshino, Women's Clinics See Rise in Calls: As the Economy Falters, Some Family Planning Agencies Are Reporting a Record Number of Abortions, L.A. Times, May 9, 2009, at A3. See also Sam Roberts, Birth Rate Is Said to Fall as a Result of Recession, N.Y. Times, Aug. 7, 2009, at A9.

[27]. Dorothy E. Roberts, Punishing Drug Addicts Who Have Babies: Women of Color, Equality, and the Right of Privacy, 104 Harv. L. Rev. 1419, 1461 (1991).

[28]. Supporters of reproductive choice attribute to anti-abortion violence 8 murders, 17 attempted murders, and 6,923 other incidents of violence (i.e., bombings, arsons, death threats, kidnappings, and assaults), as well as more than 194,000 reported acts of disruption (i.e., bomb threats and harassing phone calls), during 1977-2014. National Abortion Fed'n, NAF Violence and Disruption Statistics, Incidents of Violence & Disruption Against Abortion Providers, http://prochoice.org/wp-content/uploads/Stats_Table_2014.pdf. Meanwhile, abortions have been declining, with approximately 1.06 million performed in the United States in 2011, compared to 1.21 million in 2008. Guttmacher Inst., supra note [25].

8. Impact on birth control. To what extent does use of the undue burden test signal not just a retreat from *Roe,* but also a retreat from *Griswold,* supra? What consequences follow for the use of modern birth control methods? Suppose that the intrauterine device (IUD) and emergency contraception (ordinary birth control pills taken in appropriate doses within 72 hours of intercourse) prevent implantation of fertilized ova and they work just as ordinary birth control pills do. Such questions have emerged in an ongoing clash between women's access claims and asserted conscience objections by some pharmacists and other health care providers[29] as well as some employers covered by the ACA's contraception mandate. See Burwell v. Hobby Lobby Stores, Inc., 134 S. Ct. 2751 (2014) (noted supra).

9. Medical abortion. What does the undue burden test mean for RU-486, or mifepristone, the "abortion pill" developed by French scientists for termination of early pregnancies and approved in 2000 by the FDA as safe and effective? Under *Gonzales,* can the government ban medical abortions (abortions accomplished through medication) so long as surgical abortions remain available? Must there be a health exception? What must states show to justify applying to medical abortions their restrictions on surgical abortions (for example, clinic regulations, specified procedures for disposal of fetal remains, and reporting requirements)? May states impose greater restrictions than the FDA? Compare Planned Parenthood Southwest Ohio Region v. Dewine, 696 F.3d 490 (6th Cir. 2012), with Planned Parenthood Arizona, Inc. v. Humble, 753 F.3d 905 (9th Cir. 2014). See also Planned Parenthood of the Heartland, Inc. v. Iowa Bd. of Medicine, 865 N.W.2d 252 (Iowa 2015) (finding undue burden imposed by rule prohibiting telemedicine or videoconferencing for prescription and administration of abortion-inducing drugs). How might a pill make access to abortion more "private"? See McCormack v. Hiedeman, 694 F.3d 1004 (9th Cir 2012).

10. Transitory abortion. Crossing state lines to find a more hospitable legal regime has long been a common phenomenon in family law. For example, before *Roe,* abortion restrictions primarily affected poor women because women with means could travel to more permissive jurisdictions.[30] Today, waiting periods and other restrictions enacted under the undue burden standard prompt abortion travel. May a state's TRAP law that forces clinic closures survive constitutional scrutiny because local women may obtain abortions in neighboring states? Compare *Whole Women's Health,* supra (yes), with *Jackson Women's Health Org.,* supra (no).

Scholars question the commonly held belief that states cannot prosecute out-of-state conduct that is legal where performed. Hence, if the Justices overturn *Roe,* they might later need to confront whether constitutional protections for due process, full faith and credit, and the right to travel prevent prosecuting abortions obtained in permissive states by women domiciled in restrictive states. See Susan

---

[29]. For the range of different approaches across the states, see Guttmacher Inst., State Policies in Brief: Emergency Contraception (July 1, 2015), http://www.guttmacher.org/statecenter/spibs/spib_EC.pdf.

[30]. See Sherri Finkbine, "The Lesser of Two Evils," in The Case for Legalized Abortion Now 15 (Alan F. Guttmacher ed., 1967) (presenting account of a woman who went to Sweden to terminate a pregnancy following use of thalidomide).

Frelich Appleton, Gender, Abortion, and Travel After *Roe*'s End, 51 St. Louis U. L.J. 655 (2007); Richard H. Fallon, Jr., If *Roe* Were Overruled: Abortion and the Constitution in a Post-*Roe* World, 51 St. Louis U. L.J. 611 (2007).

11. Federal abortion law. What does *Gonzales* mean for federal (rather than state) abortion laws? Note that, depending on the prevailing political winds, Congress might legislate to protect reproductive autonomy or to prohibit abortion. See, e.g., H.R. 36, 114th Cong. (2015) (the "Pain-Capable Unborn Child Protection Act," which would ban abortion at 20 weeks or later). On what basis does Congress have the authority to ban particular abortion procedures—or to regulate abortion at all? Is abortion interstate commerce? (*Gonzales* did not address these issues.)

12. Fetal protection measures. Most states have fetal homicide laws. They vary regarding the stage of fetal development when criminal liability attaches. See Marka B. Fleming, Feticide Laws: Contemporary Legal Applications and Constitutional Inquiries, 29 Pace L. Rev. 43 (2008). When, if at all, may they apply against the woman herself? State ballot measures to establish fetal "personhood" have failed to win approval, following campaigns emphasizing how they might ban contraception and in vitro fertilization. E.g., Denise Grady, Medical Nuances Drove "No" Vote in Mississippi, N.Y. Times, Nov. 14, 2011, at D1. See also In re Initiative Petition No. 395, 286 P.3d 637 (Okla. 2012).

Federal law addresses the status of the fetus in two respects. First, the federal Unborn Victims of Violence Act, 18 U.S.C. §1841, enacted in 2004, creates a separate criminal offense for killing or injuring an unborn child (at any stage of gestation) during the commission of a federal crime against the pregnant woman. Second, revisions to the State Children's Health Insurance Program (SCHIP) include the unborn in the definition of "child." 42 C.F.R. §457.10. SCHIP provides health coverage for uninsured children in families at the poverty level. What impact, if any, does such legislation have on abortion rights?

13. Federalism in family law.

a. Background. The advent of federal abortion legislation raises questions of federalism. Traditionally, the subject of the domestic relations was said to belong exclusively to the states. *Griswold* changed the traditional approach, signaling that the Constitution limits the states' authority over family law.

In recent years, Congress repeatedly has invoked—not always with success—the Commerce Clause and the Fourteenth Amendment to legislate on many family law subjects. E.g., Violence Against Women Act of 1994, 42 U.S.C. §13981, *invalidated by* United States v. Morrison, 529 U.S. 598 (2000) (holding that §13981 exceeds Congress's power). Congress has also conditioned the states' use of federal funds on compliance with federal requirements for laws governing the family, as it did in welfare reform legislation, for example. E.g., 42 U.S.C. §666. Such federal measures, which shape family life especially among the poor, have prompted some observers to reject as a myth the "canonical story" that family law is local. See Jill Elaine Hasday, Family Law Reimagined 17-20 (2014).

b. Health care reform. The ACA, 42 U.S.C. §18001, and its regulatory scheme address several family law matters. Although these reforms purport to maintain the status quo on abortion funding (by providing no federal funds for abortion coverage or care) and allowing health plans to choose the extent to which they cover abortion, if at all, critics condemn the disproportionate impact on poor women and, more generally, the exclusion of abortion from health care. See Nicole Huberfeld, With Liberty and Access for Some: The ACA's Disconnect for Women's Health, 40 Fordham Urb. L.J. 1357 (2013). Per published rules, employer plans and insurance coverage must include prescription contraception without additional cost, a requirement that some for-profit corporations successfully challenged on religious grounds. See *Hobby Lobby* (noted supra). Such reforms sparked many efforts to limit services for women, through the elimination of funding for Planned Parenthood and the enactment of new abortion restrictions and expansive conscience clauses. See Janet L. Dolgin & Katherine R. Dieterich, The "Other" Within: Health Care Reform, Class, and the Politics of Reproduction, 35 Seattle U. L. Rev. 377, 410 (2012) (finding an "ideology of class" and resistance to universal health care).

The Supreme Court upheld most of the ACA, using analysis with significant family law implications. National Fed'n of Indep. Bus. v. Sebelius, 132 S. Ct. 2566 (2012). First, the Court limited the reach of congressional authority under the Commerce Clause. Second, it limited congressional use of conditional funding, reasoning that Congress may attempt to persuade states to expand their Medicaid coverage by offering additional support but may not eliminate existing federal Medicaid funds for those states that decline to participate in the expansion—a ruling with implications for many federally supported state family laws.

c. Policy. Should family law reflect national policy or should it vary from state to state? What explains the traditional allocation of authority over questions of family law? The increasing federalization? See generally Meredith Johnson Harbach, Is the Family a Federal Question?, 66 Wash. & Lee L. Rev. 131 (2009); Sylvia Law, Families and Federalism, 4 Wash. U. J.L. & Pol'y 175 (2000). What impact will the Supreme Court's limitations on federal power have on family law? Will these limitations also prevent Congress from imposing national standards on family law through its provision of federal funds? Should family law devote more attention to federal laws that affect poor families, including for example welfare laws, the food stamp program, Medicaid, and punishment to enforce child support obligations? See Hasday, supra, at 195-220 ("family law of the poor"); Clare Huntington, Failure to Flourish: How Family Law Undermines Family Relationships (2014) (adopting expansive understanding of family law, including direct and indirect regulation of families).

Problems

1. A South Dakota statute requires that physicians inform abortion patients in writing that "the abortion will terminate the life of a whole, separate, unique, living human being" and that abortion poses risks of "depression and related psychological distress [and] increased risk of suicide ideation and suicide." Is the law constitutional? Why? See Planned Parenthood Minn., N.D., S.D. v. Rounds, 530 F.3d

724 (8th Cir. 2008), *after remand*, 686 F.3d 889 (8th Cir. 2012); Jeremy Blumenthal, Emotional Paternalism, 35 Fla. St. U. L. Rev. 1 (2007); Alex Stuckey, Judge Hears Case Over Abortion Restrictions, Religious Beliefs, St. Louis Post-Dispatch, Sept. 29, 2015, at A3. In the absence of such legislation, suppose that a patient sues a provider for malpractice as well as negligent infliction of emotional distress for failing to inform her before an abortion that the procedure will kill "an existing living human being." May the jury award damages? See Acuna v. Turkish, 930 A.2d 416 (N.J. 2007).

2. In an effort to encourage work and "personal responsibility" and to discourage out-of-wedlock births and welfare dependency, New Jersey has adopted a "family cap." Previously, a welfare recipient received an increased allotment of public assistance on the birth of each child. On enactment of the family cap, a welfare recipient gets no such increase regardless of how large her family thereafter becomes. For those newly joining the welfare rolls even after the family cap, however, the allotment is calculated on the basis of actual family size. Hence, for example, the assistance for a family of three children varies, depending on when the children are born (before or after enactment of the family cap) and whether the parent is receiving welfare at the time of the births.

What constitutional challenges might be brought on behalf of those adversely affected by the family cap? Does the law encourage abortion? Given the state's justifications, what result and why? See C.K. v. New Jersey Dept. of Health & Human Servs., 92 F.3d 171 (3d Cir. 1996); Sojourner A. v. New Jersey Dept. of Human Servs., 828 A.2d 306 (N.J. 2003). See generally, e.g., Dorothy Roberts, Killing the Black Body: Race, Reproduction, and the Meaning of Liberty 202-245 (1999); Susan Frelich Appleton, When Welfare Reforms Promote Abortion: "Personal Responsibility," "Family Values," and the Right to Choose, 85 Geo. L.J. 155 (1996).

4. The Liberation of Privacy

LAWRENCE v. TEXAS

539 U.S. 558 (2003)

Justice KENNEDY delivered the opinion of the Court.

Liberty protects the person from unwarranted government intrusions into a dwelling or other private places. In our tradition the State is not omnipresent in the home. And there are other spheres of our lives and existence, outside the home, where the State should not be a dominant presence. Freedom extends beyond spatial bounds. Liberty presumes an autonomy of self that includes freedom of thought, belief, expression, and certain intimate conduct. The instant case involves liberty of the person both in its spatial and more transcendent dimensions.

I

The question before the Court is the validity of a Texas statute making it a crime for two persons of the same sex to engage in certain intimate sexual conduct. In

Houston, Texas, officers of the Harris County Police Department were dispatched to a private residence in response to a reported weapons disturbance. They entered an apartment where one of the petitioners, John Geddes Lawrence, resided. . . . The officers observed Lawrence and another man, Tyron Garner, engaging in a sexual act. The two petitioners were arrested, held in custody overnight, and charged and convicted before a Justice of the Peace. . . .

. . . The applicable state law is Tex. Penal Code Ann. §21.06(a) (2003). It provides: "A person commits an offense if he engages in deviate sexual intercourse with another individual of the same sex." The statute defines "deviate sexual intercourse" as follows:

> "(A) any contact between any part of the genitals of one person and the mouth or anus of another person; or
> "(B) the penetration of the genitals or the anus of another person with an object." §21.01(1). . . .

[In a trial *de novo*, petitioners raised an unsuccessful equal protection challenge to the law, which criminalizes sexual intimacy by same-sex couples but not identical behavior by different-sex couples. Then, petitioners entered pleas of *nolo contendere*, were each fined $200, and were assessed court costs. On appeal, the court rejected petitioners' equal protection and due process arguments.]

II

We conclude the case should be resolved by determining whether the petitioners were free as adults to engage in the private conduct in the exercise of their liberty under the Due Process Clause of the Fourteenth Amendment to the Constitution. For this inquiry we deem it necessary to reconsider the Court's holding in [Bowers v. Hardwick, 478 U.S. 186 (1986)].

There are broad statements of the substantive reach of liberty under the Due Process Clause in earlier cases [citing *Pierce* and *Meyer*]; but the most pertinent beginning point is our decision in Griswold v. Connecticut, 381 U.S. 479 (1965). [The Court then reviews *Griswold, Eisenstadt, Roe,* and Carey v. Population Services International, 431 U.S. 678 (1977) (invalidating restrictions on minors' contraceptive choices).] [These subsequent cases] confirmed that the reasoning of *Griswold* could not be confined to the protection of rights of married adults. . . .

The facts in *Bowers* had some similarities to the instant case [including police entry into Hardwick's bedroom while he was engaged in sexual conduct with another male]. One difference between the two cases is that the Georgia statute prohibited the conduct whether or not the participants were of the same sex, while the Texas statute, as we have seen, applies only to participants of the same sex. Hardwick was not prosecuted, but he brought an action in federal court to declare the state statute [unconstitutional].

The Court began its substantive discussion in *Bowers* as follows: "The issue presented is whether the Federal Constitution confers a fundamental right upon homosexuals to engage in sodomy and hence invalidates the laws of the many States that still make such conduct illegal and have done so for a very long time." [478 U.S. at 190.] That statement, we now conclude, discloses the Court's own failure to appreciate the extent of the liberty at stake. To say that the issue in *Bowers* was simply the right to engage in certain sexual conduct demeans the claim the individual put forward, just as it would demean a married couple were it to be said marriage is simply about the right to have sexual intercourse. The laws involved in *Bowers* and here are, to be sure, statutes that purport to do no more than prohibit a particular sexual act. Their penalties and purposes, though, have more far-reaching consequences, touching upon the most private human conduct, sexual behavior, and in the most private of places, the home. The statutes do seek to control a personal relationship that, whether or not entitled to formal recognition in the law, is within the liberty of persons to choose without being punished as criminals.

This, as a general rule, should counsel against attempts by the State, or a court, to define the meaning of the relationship or to set its boundaries absent injury to a person or abuse of an institution the law protects. It suffices for us to acknowledge that adults may choose to enter upon this relationship in the confines of their homes and their own private lives and still retain their dignity as free persons. When sexuality finds overt expression in intimate conduct with another person, the conduct can be but one element in a personal bond that is more enduring. The liberty protected by the Constitution allows homosexual persons the right to make this choice.

Having misapprehended the claim of liberty there presented to it, and thus stating the claim to be whether there is a fundamental right to engage in consensual sodomy, the *Bowers* Court said: "Proscriptions against that conduct have ancient roots." Id., at 192. In academic writings, and in many of the scholarly *amicus* briefs filed to assist the Court in this case, there are fundamental criticisms of the historical premises relied upon by the majority and concurring opinions in *Bowers*. . . . At the outset it should be noted that there is no longstanding history in this country of laws directed at homosexual conduct as a distinct matter. Beginning in colonial times there were prohibitions of sodomy derived from the English criminal laws passed in the first instance by the Reformation Parliament of 1533. The English prohibition was understood to include relations between men and women as well as relations between men and men. Nineteenth-century commentators similarly read American sodomy, buggery, and crime-against-nature statutes as criminalizing certain relations between men and women and between men and men. The absence of legal prohibitions focusing on homosexual conduct may be explained in part by noting that according to some scholars the concept of the homosexual as a distinct category of person did not emerge until the late 19th century. . . .

Laws prohibiting sodomy do not seem to have been enforced against consenting adults acting in private. A substantial number of sodomy prosecutions and convictions for which there are surviving records were for predatory acts against those who could not or did not consent, as in the case of a minor or the victim of an assault. . . .

It was not until the 1970's that any State singled out same-sex relations for criminal prosecution, and only nine States have done so. Post-*Bowers* even some of these States did not adhere to the policy of suppressing homosexual conduct. Over the course of the last decades, States with same-sex prohibitions have moved toward abolishing them. In summary, the historical grounds relied upon in *Bowers* are more complex than [Justice White's] majority opinion and the concurring opinion by Chief Justice Burger indicate. Their historical premises are not without doubt and, at the very least, are overstated.

It must be acknowledged, of course, that the Court in *Bowers* was making the broader point that for centuries there have been powerful voices to condemn homosexual conduct as immoral. The condemnation has been shaped by religious beliefs, conceptions of right and acceptable behavior, and respect for the traditional family. For many persons these are not trivial concerns, but profound and deep convictions accepted as ethical and moral principles to which they aspire and which thus determine the course of their lives. These considerations do not answer the question before us, however. The issue is whether the majority may use the power of the State to enforce these views on the whole society through operation of the criminal law. "Our obligation is to define the liberty of all, not to mandate our own moral code." Planned Parenthood of Southeastern Pa. v. Casey, 505 U.S. 833, 850 (1992).

[O]ur laws and traditions in the past half century are of most relevance here. These references show an emerging awareness that liberty gives substantial protection to adult persons in deciding how to conduct their private lives in matters pertaining to sex. . . . This emerging recognition should have been apparent when *Bowers* was decided. In 1955 the American Law Institute promulgated the Model Penal Code and made clear that it did not recommend or provide for "criminal penalties for consensual sexual relations conducted in private." ALI, Model Penal Code §213.2, Comment 2, p 372 (1980). It justified its decision on three grounds: (1) The prohibitions undermined respect for the law by penalizing conduct many people engaged in; (2) the statutes regulated private conduct not harmful to others; and (3) the laws were arbitrarily enforced and thus invited the danger of blackmail. ALI, Model Penal Code, Commentary 277-280 (Tent. Draft No. 4, 1955). [Illinois and other states changed their laws accordingly.]

The sweeping references by Chief Justice Burger [concurring in *Bowers*] to the history of Western civilization and to Judeo-Christian moral and ethical standards did not take account of other authorities pointing in an opposite direction. A committee advising the British Parliament recommended in 1957 repeal of laws punishing homosexual conduct. The Wolfenden Report: Report of the Committee on Homosexual Offenses and Prostitution (1963). Parliament enacted the substance of those recommendations 10 years later. Sexual Offences Act 1967, §1. Of even more importance, almost five years before *Bowers* was decided the European Court of Human Rights considered a case with parallels to *Bowers* and to today's case. . . . The court held that the laws proscribing the conduct were invalid under the European Convention on Human Rights. Dudgeon v. United Kingdom, 45 Eur. Ct. H.R. (1981) P 52. Authoritative in all countries that are members of the Council of Europe (21 nations then, 45 nations now), the decision is at odds with the premise in *Bowers* that the claim put forward was insubstantial in our Western civilization.

In our own constitutional system the deficiencies in *Bowers* became even more apparent in the years following its announcement. The 25 States with laws prohibiting the relevant conduct referenced in the *Bowers* decision are reduced now to 13, of which 4 enforce their laws only against homosexual conduct. In those States where sodomy is still proscribed, whether for same-sex or heterosexual conduct, there is a pattern of nonenforcement with respect to consenting adults acting in private. The State of Texas admitted in 1994 that as of that date it had not prosecuted anyone under those circumstances.

Two principal cases decided after *Bowers* cast its holding into even more doubt. In Planned Parenthood of Southeastern Pa. v. Casey, 505 U.S. 833 (1992), the

Court reaffirmed the substantive force of the liberty protected by the Due Process Clause. The *Casey* decision again confirmed that our laws and tradition afford constitutional protection to personal decisions relating to marriage, procreation, contraception, family relationships, child rearing, and education. Id., at 851. In explaining the respect the Constitution demands for the autonomy of the person in making these choices, we stated as follows:

> "These matters, involving the most intimate and personal choices a person may make in a lifetime, choices central to personal dignity and autonomy, are central to the liberty protected by the Fourteenth Amendment. At the heart of liberty is the right to define one's own concept of existence, of meaning, of the universe, and of the mystery of human life. Beliefs about these matters could not define the attributes of personhood were they formed under compulsion of the State."

[505 U.S. at 851.] Persons in a homosexual relationship may seek autonomy for these purposes, just as heterosexual persons do. The decision in *Bowers* would deny them this right.

The second post-*Bowers* case of principal relevance is Romer v. Evans, 517 U.S. 620 (1996). There the Court struck down class-based legislation directed at homosexuals as a violation of the Equal Protection Clause. *Romer* invalidated an amendment to Colorado's constitution which named as a solitary class persons who were homosexuals, lesbians, or bisexual either by "orientation, conduct, practices or relationships," id., at 624, and deprived them of protection under state antidiscrimination laws. We concluded that the provision was "born of animosity toward the class of persons affected" and further that it had no rational relation to a legitimate governmental purpose. Id., at 634.

[Although petitioners have a tenable equal protection argument under *Romer,* we must] address whether *Bowers* itself has continuing validity. Were we to hold the statute invalid under the Equal Protection Clause, some might question whether a prohibition would be valid if drawn differently, say, to prohibit the conduct both between same-sex and different-sex participants.

Equality of treatment and the due process right to demand respect for conduct protected by the substantive guarantee of liberty are linked in important respects, and a decision on the latter point advances both interests. . . . When homosexual conduct is made criminal by the law of the State, that declaration in and of itself is an invitation to subject homosexual persons to discrimination both in the public and in the private spheres. The central holding of *Bowers* has been brought in question by this case, and it should be addressed. Its continuance as precedent demeans the lives of homosexual persons [by imposing the stigma of a misdemeanor, with resulting sex-offender registration requirements and disclosure requirements for job applications].

The foundations of *Bowers* have sustained serious erosion from our recent decisions in *Casey* and *Romer.* When our precedent has been thus weakened, criticism from other sources is of greater significance [citing commentators, state constitutional decisions, and authorities from other countries that rejected *Bowers's* reasoning]. The doctrine of *stare decisis* is essential to the respect accorded to the judgments of the Court and to the stability of the law. It is not, however, an inexorable command. . . . *Bowers* was not correct when it was decided, and it is not correct today. It ought not to remain binding precedent. Bowers v. Hardwick should be and now is overruled.

The present case does not involve minors. It does not involve persons who might be injured or coerced or who are situated in relationships where consent might not easily be refused. It does not involve public conduct or prostitution. It does not involve whether the government must give formal recognition to any relationship that homosexual persons seek to enter. The case does involve two adults who, with full and mutual consent from each other, engaged in sexual practices common to a homosexual lifestyle. The petitioners are entitled to respect for their private lives. The State cannot demean their existence or control their destiny by making their private sexual conduct a crime. Their right to liberty under the Due Process Clause gives them the full right to engage in their conduct without intervention of the government. "It is a promise of the Constitution that there is a realm of personal liberty which the government may not enter." *Casey*, supra, at 847. The Texas statute furthers no legitimate state interest which can justify its intrusion into the personal and private life of the individual.

Had those who drew and ratified the Due Process Clauses of the Fifth Amendment or the Fourteenth Amendment known the components of liberty in its manifold possibilities, they might have been more specific. They did not presume to have this insight. They knew times can blind us to certain truths and later generations can see that laws once thought necessary and proper in fact serve only to oppress. As the Constitution endures, persons in every generation can invoke its principles in their own search for greater freedom. [Reversed.]

Justice O'CONNOR, concurring in the judgment. . . .

This case raises a different issue than *Bowers*: whether, under the Equal Protection Clause, moral disapproval is a legitimate state interest to justify by itself a statute that bans homosexual sodomy, but not heterosexual sodomy. It is not. Moral disapproval of this group [homosexuals], like a bare desire to harm the group, is an interest that is insufficient to satisfy rational basis review under the Equal Protection Clause. See, e.g., Department of Agriculture v. Moreno, [413 U.S. 528, 534 (1973)]; Romer v. Evans, 517 U.S., at 634-635. . . . The Texas sodomy law "raises the inevitable inference that the disadvantage imposed is born of animosity toward the class of persons affected." Id., at 634.

. . . While it is true that the law applies only to conduct, the conduct targeted by this law is conduct that is closely correlated with being homosexual. Under such circumstances, Texas' sodomy law is targeted at more than conduct. It is instead directed toward gay persons as a class. [T]he State cannot single out one identifiable class of citizens for punishment that does not apply to everyone else, with moral disapproval as the only asserted state interest for the law. . . .

. . . Texas cannot assert any legitimate state interest here, such as national security or preserving the traditional institution of marriage. Unlike moral disapproval of same-sex relations—the asserted state interest in this case—other reasons exist to promote the institution of marriage beyond mere moral disapproval of an excluded group. A law branding one class of persons as criminal solely based on the State's moral disapproval of that class and the conduct associated with that class runs contrary to the values of the Constitution and the Equal Protection Clause, under any standard of review. . . .

Justice SCALIA, with whom THE CHIEF JUSTICE and Justice THOMAS join, dissenting. . . .

I begin with the Court's surprising readiness to reconsider a decision rendered a mere 17 years ago in Bowers v. Hardwick. . . . Today's approach to *stare decisis* invites us to overrule an erroneously decided precedent (including an "intensely divisive" decision) *if*: (1) its foundations have been "eroded" by subsequent decisions; (2) it has been subject to "substantial and continuing" criticism; and (3) it has not induced "individual or societal reliance" that counsels against overturning. The problem is that [Roe v. Wade] itself—which today's majority surely has no disposition to overrule—satisfies these conditions to at least the same degree as *Bowers*. . . .

[To] distinguish the rock-solid, unamendable disposition of *Roe* from the readily overrulable *Bowers* [we need to examine] the third factor. . . . It seems to me that the "societal reliance" on the principles confirmed in *Bowers* and discarded today has been overwhelming. Countless judicial decisions and legislative enactments have relied on the ancient proposition that a governing majority's belief that certain sexual behavior is "immoral and unacceptable" constitutes a rational basis for regulation [citing cases relying on *Bowers*]. State laws against bigamy, same-sex marriage, adult incest, prostitution, masturbation, adultery, fornication, bestiality, and obscenity are likewise sustainable only in light of *Bowers*' validation of laws based on moral choices. Every single one of these laws is called into question by today's decision. . . .

What a massive disruption of the current social order, therefore, the overruling of *Bowers* entails. Not so the overruling of *Roe*, which would simply have restored the regime that existed for centuries before 1973, in which the permissibility of and restrictions upon abortion were determined legislatively State-by-State. . . .

[To establish that *Bowers* was wrongly decided, the majority relies on an] *emerging awareness* that liberty gives substantial protection to adult persons in deciding how to conduct their private lives *in matters pertaining to sex* (emphasis added). Apart from the fact that such an "emerging awareness" does not establish a "fundamental right," the statement is factually false. States continue to prosecute all sorts of crimes by adults "in matters pertaining to sex": prostitution, adult incest, adultery, obscenity, and child pornography. Sodomy laws, too, have been enforced "in the past half century," in which there have been 134 reported cases involving prosecutions for consensual, adult, homosexual sodomy. [W. Eskridge, Gaylaw: Challenging the Apartheid of the Closet 375 (1999).]

In any event, an "emerging awareness" is by definition not "deeply rooted in this Nation's history and traditions," as we have said "fundamental right" status requires. Constitutional entitlements do not spring into existence because some States choose to lessen or eliminate criminal sanctions on certain behavior. Much less do they spring into existence, as the Court seems to believe, because *foreign nations* decriminalize conduct. . . .

The Texas statute undeniably seeks to further the belief of its citizens that certain forms of sexual behavior are "immoral and unacceptable," *Bowers*, supra, at 196—the same interest furthered by criminal laws against fornication, bigamy, adultery, adult incest, bestiality, and obscenity. *Bowers* held that this *was* a legitimate state interest. The Court today reaches the opposite conclusion. . . . This effectively decrees the end of all morals legislation. If, as the Court asserts, the promotion of majoritarian sexual morality is not even a *legitimate* state interest, none of the above-mentioned laws can survive rational-basis review. . . .

Finally, I turn to petitioners' equal-protection challenge. . . . To be sure, §21.06 does distinguish between the sexes insofar as concerns the partner with whom the sexual acts are performed: men can violate the law only with other men, and women only with other women. But this cannot itself be a denial of equal protection, since it is precisely the same distinction regarding partner that is drawn in state laws prohibiting marriage with someone of the same sex while permitting marriage with someone of the opposite sex. . . .

[Justice O'Connor's] reasoning leaves on pretty shaky grounds state laws limiting marriage to opposite-sex couples. . . . [Her] "preserving the traditional institution of marriage" is just a kinder way of describing the State's *moral disapproval* of same-sex couples. . . .

Today's opinion is the product of a Court, which is the product of a law-profession culture, that has largely signed on to the so-called homosexual agenda, by which I mean the agenda promoted by some homosexual activists directed at eliminating the moral opprobrium that has traditionally attached to homosexual conduct. . . . It is clear from this that the Court has taken sides in the culture war, departing from its role of assuring, as neutral observer, that the democratic rules of engagement are observed. Many Americans do not want persons who openly engage in homosexual conduct as partners in their business, as scoutmasters for their children, as teachers in their children's schools, or as boarders in their home. They view this as protecting themselves and their families from a lifestyle that they believe to be immoral and destructive. . . . So imbued is the Court with the law profession's anti-anti-homosexual culture, that it is seemingly unaware that the attitudes of that culture are not obviously "mainstream"; that in most States what the Court calls "discrimination" against those who engage in homosexual acts is perfectly legal; that proposals to ban such "discrimination" under Title VII have repeatedly been rejected by Congress; and that in some cases such "discrimination" is a constitutional right, see Boy Scouts of America v. Dale, 530 U.S. 640 (2000).

Let me be clear that I have nothing against homosexuals, or any other group, promoting their agenda through normal democratic means. Social perceptions of sexual and other morality change over time, and every group has the right to persuade its fellow citizens that its view of such matters is the best. . . . But persuading one's fellow citizens is one thing, and imposing one's views in absence of democratic majority will is something else. I would no more *require* a State to criminalize homosexual acts—or, for that matter, display *any* moral disapprobation of them—than I would *forbid* it to do so. . . .

Patty Reinert, Pair Proud They Could Get Sodomy Law Thrown Out

Hous. Chron., Apr. 25, 2004, at A1

Almost six years after police stormed his apartment and arrested him for having sex with another man, this is what John Lawrence remembers: Harris County Sheriff's Department officers shoving him to the couch, shattering the

Tyron Garner (left) and John Lawrence celebrate the Supreme Court victory.

porcelain birds that were a gift from his mother. The humiliating ride to the station, wearing only handcuffs and underwear. The fingerprinting and mugshot, the bologna sandwich he ate in jail, the jeans another inmate gave him for the ride home, the cabbie who took him, though he had no wallet to pay. And the call to his elderly father to tell him what had happened. . . .

. . . In [their first interview] since the case began, Lawrence and Garner said they are proud to have helped defeat an unjust law, overwhelmed by the support they've received and so glad it's over. "I got a sense of justice for being wronged by the state of Texas," Lawrence said as he sat with Garner in lawyer Mitchell Katine's office. "I feel I've been vindicated." . . . "Would I have done the same thing again? Yes," he said. "When somebody is wronged and they don't stand up for themselves, they're going to get wronged again. I wasn't going to stand for it."

Garner, 36, who sells barbecue from a street stand, agreed. "It was worth it," he said. On Sept. 17, 1998, Garner and his boyfriend, Robert Royce Eubanks, were drinking margaritas and eating dinner at a Mexican restaurant with their friend, Lawrence. . . . Back at [Lawrence's] apartment after dinner, though, Eubanks and Garner argued. Eubanks left angry, saying he was going to buy a soda. Instead, he went to a pay telephone and called the police, reporting that there was a man with a gun in Lawrence's apartment. "I think he was jealous," Garner said.

When two Harris County deputies arrived, the door to the apartment was unlocked. They walked in with Eubanks following and discovered Lawrence and Garner having sex. Lawrence and Garner said they had no idea why they were being arrested. They spent the night in jail.

The charges stemmed from the 1973 Texas Homosexual Conduct Law. . . . At the time, Kansas, Oklahoma and Missouri had similar laws, and nine other states—Louisiana, Mississippi, Alabama, Florida, South Carolina, North Carolina, Virginia, Idaho and Utah—made sodomy a crime for heterosexuals as well as homosexuals. . . . Eubanks was convicted and sentenced to 30 days in jail for filing a false report to a peace officer. Garner forgave him and continued their relationship; Lawrence couldn't. . . .

[After their arrest], Lawrence and Garner returned to their lives. But Lawrence was stewing. When Katine, a partner at Houston's Williams, Birnberg & Andersen, and the New York-based Lambda Legal Defense and Education Fund offered their services for free, Lawrence decided to fight. Garner was reluctant, but he agreed. "I didn't think we'd win," Garner said. And though his friends and family knew he was gay, he said, "I didn't enjoy being outed with my mugshot on TV. It was degrading to me." . . .

Lawrence, who works nights, set his alarm for 9 a.m. the day the court was expected to rule. He flipped on CNN and heard the announcement. "I bolted out of bed and shouted, 'Thank you, God!'" he said. . . . "I called my brother, and we celebrated with a couple of bottles of champagne," Garner said.

By nightfall, hundreds had gathered for a rally at City Hall. Katine, who had spent years shielding his clients from the media, introduced them to the crowd. People stood in line to meet them.

Today, Lawrence and Garner remain friends and date other people. Neither were activists before their case, and they still aren't. . . . Both support the right of gay people to marry but aren't interested themselves. "I'm single and love it," Lawrence said.

Garner is touched by people who recognize him at the grocery store or on the street, and Lawrence loves to tell the story of two burly cops, working security outside a gay nightclub, approaching to give them a hug. Both laugh at the idea of cashing in with a book or a TV movie deal, and they shun comparisons some have made to Jane Roe of abortion rights fame or Rosa Parks, a civil rights icon. "I don't really want to be a hero," Garner said. "But I want to tell other gay people, 'Be who you are, and don't be afraid.'" . . .[31]

Tony Mauro, A "Cultural Milestone" at the High Court: Lawrence Gay Attorneys Turned Out in Force to Witness Lawrence Arguments

Tex. Law., Mar. 31, 2004, at 11

Paul Smith brought energy, agility and a full command of the case to the podium when he argued on behalf of the Lambda Legal Defense and Education Fund . . . in the landmark gay rights case Lawrence v. Texas. He also brought personal experience. Smith, managing partner in Jenner & Block's Washington, D.C., office, is gay, a fact that was not widely talked about. . . .

"I think it gave me a greater comfort level answering questions . . . ," says Smith, 48, a veteran of eight [previous] U.S. Supreme Court arguments . . . . "And I think there is a symbolic importance to the community that I was up there. . . ." The symbolism was palpable in the courtroom. Dozens of prominent gay lawyers filled the lawyers' section of the gallery. "The most remarkable thing about the argument was the audience," said Walter Dellinger of O'Melveny & Myers, who wrote an amicus curiae brief for several gay and civil rights groups. The presence of so many [gay] prominent lawyers . . . was a "cultural milestone," Dellinger said. . . .

Smith's advocacy also marked a milestone for Jenner & Block, which has become well-known as a firm that welcomes gay and lesbian lawyers. . . . He joined the firm 10 years ago "when I was not very 'out' in general, but it has been a very supportive place." . . .

Smith's sexual orientation is notable for another reason: He clerked for the late Justice Lewis Powell in 1981. Five years later, historians have noted that as

[31]. Both challengers died just a few years later. Adam Liptak, John Lawrence, 68, Plaintiff in Gay Rights Case, Dies, N.Y. Times, Dec. 24, 2011, at D8; Douglas Martin, Tyron Garner, 39, Plaintiff in Sodomy Case, N.Y. Times, Sept. 14, 2006, at D8.

Powell deliberated in Bowers v. Hardwick, he mused to a law clerk that "I don't believe I've ever met a homosexual." Powell was apparently unaware not only that the clerk he was speaking to was gay, but also that several of his previous clerks were gay.

. . . Smith holds no animosity toward Powell, who was the deciding vote in favor of upholding Georgia's anti-sodomy law. Smith notes that after Powell left the court in 1987, he said he regretted his vote in *Bowers*. "Obviously it was very troubling to him, and he came to believe he had made a mistake," Smith says, "Justice Powell was very much on my mind as I argued."

Notes and Questions

1. Constitutional basis. What is the constitutional right protected by *Lawrence*? The majority's opinion begins with the word "liberty" and ends with the word "freedom." Does the Court's opinion reflect a broad libertarian approach under which substantive due process presumptively protects all personal interests? See, e.g., Randy E. Barnett, Justice Kennedy's Libertarian Revolution: Lawrence v. Texas, 2002-2003 Cato Sup. Ct. Rev. 21. What does *Lawrence*'s liberty mean for the right to privacy? See Jamal Greene, The So-Called Right to Privacy, 43 U.C. Davis L. Rev. 715 (2010).

2. Equality. What role do equality principles play in the majority opinion? How does the majority respond to Justice O'Connor's reliance on the Equal Protection Clause? Why do you suppose the majority did not use the Equal Protection Clause to decide *Lawrence,* as it did Romer v. Evans, 517 U.S. 620 (1996), a precedent cited in *Lawrence*? What difference would it have made? What role does the type of "animosity" found in *Romer* play in *Lawrence*?

Despite the *Lawrence* majority's use of due process, not equal protection, commentators say the opinion synthesizes autonomy and equality principles by rejecting criminal statutes that subordinate a particular group of citizens. See, e.g., Pamela S. Karlan, Foreword: Loving *Lawrence*, 102 Mich. L. Rev. 1447, 1449 (2004) ("*Lawrence* is a case about liberty that has important implications for the jurisprudence of equality."); Kenji Yoshino, The New Equal Protection, 124 Harv. L. Rev. 747, 749 (2011) (naming "such hybrid equality/liberty claims as 'dignity' claims"). This synergy between liberty and equality as a foundation for gay rights culminated 12 years later in Obergefell v. Hodges, 135 S. Ct. 2584 (2015), guaranteeing for same-sex couples access to marriage and marriage recognition (reprinted in Chapter II).

3. Bowers. In Bowers v. Hardwick, 478 U.S. 186 (1986), the Supreme Court held that enforcement of a state sodomy statute did not violate the Constitution. Citing the "ancient roots" of sodomy proscriptions, the majority opinion in *Bowers* found no fundamental right to privacy at stake and saw no connection between "family, marriage, or procreation on the one hand and homosexual activity on the other." Id. at 191. Why did the Supreme Court overturn *Bowers*? How does *Lawrence* explain its overruling of *Bowers,* consistent with the doctrine of *stare decisis*?

4. Liberty's scope. *Bowers* had invoked history and tradition to determine whether an asserted interest merits constitutional protection. What methodology does *Lawrence* use to determine what's "in" and what's "out" of substantive due process? See David A. Strauss, The Modernizing Mission of Judicial Review, 76 U. Chi. L. Rev. 859 (2009) (discerning new approach that looks forward instead of back to history and tradition).

What is the scope of the liberty protected in *Lawrence*? Does the majority hew to *Griswold*'s focus on the spatial privacy of the bedroom and the home? What do the "more transcendent dimensions" of "liberty of the person" encompass?

Lawrence quotes language from Planned Parenthood of Southeastern Pennsylvania v. Casey, 505 U.S. 833, 851 (1992), that critics, including Justice Scalia (in an omitted portion of his dissent), call the "sweet-mystery-of-life passage." See 539 U.S. at 588 (Scalia, J., dissenting). Does this language help define the interest at stake? Cf. Washington v. Glucksberg, 521 U.S. 702, 720-721 (1997) (requiring interests protected by substantive due process to be deeply rooted in history and tradition and susceptible to "careful description").

5. Standard of review. *Bowers*, which saw no fundamental right at stake, used the rational basis test. What standard of review does *Lawrence* use? Why?

Professor Mary Anne Case identifies the following as the critical sentence, asserting that the Court's use of the nonrestrictive "which" instead of the restrictive "that" reveals the application of rationality review: "The Texas statute furthers no legitimate state interest which can justify its intrusions into the personal and private life of the individual."[32] But see Matthew Coles, Lawrence v. Texas and the Refinement of Substantive Due Process, 16 Stan. L. & Pol'y Rev. 23, 30-31, 37 (2005) (finding the Court used a balancing test); Laurence H. Tribe, Essay, Lawrence v. Texas: The "Fundamental Right" That Dare Not Speak Its Name, 117 Harv. L. Rev. 1893, 1917 (2004) (finding the Court used strict review).

6. Morality. In *Bowers*, the Supreme Court concluded that Georgia satisfied the rational basis test because its electorate regarded sodomy as immoral and unacceptable. In *Lawrence*, why do majoritarian moral values fail to justify the Texas statute? Evaluate Justice Scalia's prediction that the *Lawrence* majority's approach dooms "all morals legislation."

Consider philosopher John Stuart Mill's tenet that "the only purpose for which power can be rightfully exercised over any member of a civilised community, against his will, is to prevent harm to others." John Stuart Mill, On Liberty 13 (Gateway ed. 1955) (originally published in 1859). To what extent does Mill satisfactorily resolve the issue in *Lawrence*? Does Mill's "harm principle" preclude legislation based on morality alone? Even under Mill's harm test, don't moral judgments remain relevant? As Justice Scalia intimates, why can't a legislature regard its disapproval of gay sex as a means of protecting children from the "harm" of exposure "to a lifestyle [believed] to be immoral and destructive"? Cf. Chai R. Feldblum, Gay Is Good: The Moral Case for Marriage Equality and More, 17 Yale J.L. & Feminism 139, 139 (2005) (contending that *Lawrence* provides an

---

[32]. Mary Anne Case, Of "This" and "That" in Lawrence v. Texas, 2003 Sup. Ct. Rev. 75, 83-84.

opportunity "to make a moral case for supporting the range of . . . creative ways in which we currently construct our intimate relations outside of marriage").

Justice Scalia's use of the term "culture war" evokes a discourse about a number of contested family law (and family values) issues, including reproductive rights, gender equality, gay rights, end-of-life decisions, and the legislatures' and courts' roles in such matters. Why has family law, in particular, become the site of such controversy? What role should religion and religious beliefs play in official resolutions of such disputes?

7. Foreign law. What is the appropriate role for foreign legal authorities, such as those cited by the *Lawrence* majority, when battles in the culture wars reach American courts? Note that the Supreme Court has relied on foreign and international law to invalidate certain punishments, such as juvenile life sentences. See Graham v. Florida, 560 U.S. 48 (2010); Stephen C. McCaffrey, There's a Whole World Out There: Justice Kennedy's Use of International Sources, 44 McGeorge L. Rev. 201 (2013).

8. Legislative vs. judicial reform. Justice Scalia's dissent advocates leaving the issue of gay rights to the legislature. In an omitted portion, he asserts that "the people, unlike judges, need not carry things to their logical conclusion. The people may feel that their disapprobation of homosexual conduct is strong enough to disallow homosexual marriage, but not strong enough to criminalize private homosexual acts—and may legislate accordingly." 539 U.S. at 604. Must courts take matters to their logical conclusions? Do they? What does Justice Scalia's distinction mean in family law, with its religious and cultural roots? Note that this "Who decides?" issue also divided the majority and dissents in the marriage-equality case, *Obergefell*, supra.

9. The anti-subordination theme. In an omitted sentence, Justice O'Connor states that the Texas statute violates equal protection because it "threatens the creation of an underclass." The majority, rejecting Texas's argument that the statute simply punishes conduct, condemns the statute for targeting "gay persons as a class." Such language suggests an anti-subordination approach (which requires invalidation of laws and legal structures that perpetuate the subordination of disadvantaged groups, such as women or African-Americans). See generally Kenneth L. Karst, The Liberties of Equal Citizens: Groups and the Due Process Clause, 55 UCLA L. Rev. 99 (2007). What groups count for purposes of this anti-subordination analysis? Is Justice Scalia correct that the most salient classification in the Texas law is sex-based, the same classification that long restricted access to traditional marriage to one man and one woman? Should sexual orientation trigger suspect-class status (and hence strict scrutiny)?

10. Conduct and identity. The majority opinion refers to "homosexual conduct," "homosexual persons," and "a homosexual lifestyle." What connection does the majority see among these? Justice O'Connor discerns a close correlation between the prohibited conduct and "being homosexual." Is Justice Scalia correct that one might invoke the same analysis for any criminal law? In an omitted portion of his dissent, he analogizes: "A law against public nudity targets 'the conduct that is closely correlated with being a nudist,' and hence 'is targeted at more than conduct'; it is 'directed toward nudists as a class.'" 539 U.S. at 600. Is the analogy apt? Does "conduct" suggest choice and "identity" suggest immutability? What are the legal implications? Cf. Jessica A. Clarke, Against Immutability, 125 Yale L.J. 2 (2015).

11. A relationship test? The majority envisions sexual intimacy as one part of a more encompassing relationship, criticizing *Bowers* for its assumption that the case concerned "simply the right to engage in certain sexual conduct . . . , just as it would demean a married couple were it to be said marriage is simply about the right to have sexual intercourse." Lawrence and Garner had no ongoing relationship, as noted in the interview, supra. Does that matter? Does *Lawrence* assume that, for constitutional protection, sex must be part of an intimate relationship like marriage in *Griswold*, supra? See Laura A. Rosenbury & Jennifer E. Rothman, Sex In and Out of Intimacy, 59 Emory L.J. 809 (2010). For more details on the facts of the case, see Dale Carpenter, Flagrant Conduct: The Story of Lawrence v. Texas (2012).

Alternatively, do all consensual sexual encounters, however fleeting, evoke the protection that *Lawrence* requires? How "discreet" must one keep the relationship? What is the boundary that separates "private" from "public" sex? Privacy from "the closet"? See Carlos A. Ball, Privacy, Property, and Public Sex, 18 Colum. J. Gender & L. 1 (2008).

12. A right to sex? Is *Lawrence* simply a "sex positive" case, embracing a jurisprudence of sexual pleasure, regardless of the nature of the underlying relationships? What are the implications for family law? Soon after *Bowers*, Professor Sylvia Law linked Georgia's sodomy law with the statutes overturned in *Griswold*, *Eisenstadt*, and *Roe* by explaining how all these measures burden the capacity to enjoy sexual activity:

> People have a strong affirmative interest in sexual expression and relationships. Through sexual relationships, we experience deep connection with another, vulnerability, playfulness, surcease, connection with birth and with death, and *transcendence*. The power of sexual experience is such that, in every culture, the basic units of human community, nurturing, acculturation, economic sharing, companionship and daily life are built around relationships of sexual expression and taboo.[33]

Is this what *Lawrence* had in mind in protecting liberty in its "more transcendent dimensions"? What does this liberty include? See Melissa Murray, Marriage as Punishment, 112 Colum. L. Rev. 1, 54 (2012) ("*Lawrence* interposed a space between marriage and crime that, in the relative absence of legal regulation, offered the possibility of sexual liberty untethered to the disciplinary domains of the state."). But see Mary Ziegler, The (Non-)Right to Sex, 69 U. Miami L. Rev. 631 (2015).

---

[33]. Sylvia A. Law, Homosexuality and the Social Meaning of Gender, 1988 Wis. L. Rev. 187, 225 (emphasis added).

Does the Court, along with family law more generally, show solicitude for men's sexual pleasure, but not women's? See Susan Frelich Appleton, Toward a "Culturally Cliterate" Family Law?, 23 Berkeley J. Gender L. & Just. 267 (2008); Kim Shayo Buchanan, Lawrence v. Geduldig: Regulating Women's Sexuality, 56 Emory L.J. 1235 (2007). What does family law's focus on sex mean for self-identified asexuals? See Elizabeth F. Emens, Compulsory Sexuality, 66 Stanford L. Rev. 303 (2014).

13. *Lawrence* and other family laws. What implications does *Lawrence* have for other family law issues? Consider, for example, the Court's abortion jurisprudence. Evaluate Justice Scalia's assertion in his dissent in *Lawrence* that *Roe* stands out as a more compelling case for overruling than *Bowers*. Can you reconcile the treatment of morality and criminal law in Justice Kennedy's majority opinions in *Lawrence* and *Gonzales*, supra?

As Justice Scalia, predicted, *Lawrence* paved the way for constitutional protection of same-sex marriage. See Chapter II. What does *Lawrence* mean for nonmarital relationships and families? See Ariela R. Dubler, From McLaughlin v. Florida to Lawrence v. Texas: Sexual Freedom and the Road to Marriage, 106 Colum. L. Rev. 1165 (2006); Courtney G. Joslin, Marital Status Discrimination 2.0, 95 B.U. L. Rev. 805, 815 (2015); Murray, supra. Identify other aspects of family law that *Lawrence* might unsettle.

14. Race, class, and power. Given its emphasis on *consensual* sex, to what extent should the Court's analysis have paid more attention to race, class, and age—and power disparities? Consider the following facts, not all apparent from the case or the interview: Lawrence, age 59 and white, was a medical technician; Garner, some 20 years younger, an unemployed African-American, had a white roommate-boyfriend (Eubanks), who summoned police to Lawrence's residence with a false report of "a black male going crazy with a gun." Professor Carpenter explores such background facts, including conflicting reports of the arresting officers, whose own racial backgrounds might have shaped their understandings of what they saw at Lawrence's residence.[34] What should be the legal relevance of such details?

15. Critiques. Predictably, *Lawrence* has many critics. Some condemn the "judicial activism" exemplified by the majority opinion. E.g., Nelson Lund & John O. McGinnis, Lawrence v. Texas and Judicial Hubris, 102 Mich. L. Rev. 1555 (2004). Some supporters of gay rights also find fault with *Lawrence*. According to Professor Catharine MacKinnon, *Lawrence* reinforces the pervasive problem of gender inequality, "securing for homosexuals heterosexuality's substantive privileges, including its male gendered dominance, by extending rather than dismantling them."[35] Professor Marc Spindelman agrees, identifying as the source of the problem *Lawrence*'s "'like-straight' logic," which protects gays and lesbians on the theory that their lives and relationships mirror those of heterosexuals.[36]

---

[34]. Dale Carpenter, Flagrant Conduct: The Story of Lawrence v. Texas 96-104 (2012).

[35]. Catharine A. MacKinnon, The Road Not Taken: Sex Equality in Lawrence v. Texas, 65 Ohio St. L.J. 1081, 1094 (2004).

[36]. Marc Spindelman, Surviving Lawrence v. Texas, 102 Mich. L. Rev. 1615, 1619-1632 (2004).

This assimilationist approach also has a confining, rather than a liberating effect, according to Professor Katherine Franke, who writes:

> I fear that *Lawrence* and the gay rights organizing that has taken place in and around it have created a path dependency that privileges privatized and domesticated rights and legal liabilities, while rendering less viable projects that advance nonnormative notions of kinship, intimacy, and sexuality.[37]

Problem

On several occasions, R.L.C., age 14, had vaginal intercourse with his girlfriend, O.P.M., age 12. Despite their youth and a state statutory rape law that places the age of consent at 16, this conduct was not illegal because of a "Romeo and Juliet exception" applicable to minors no more than three years apart in age. The state's prohibition against the "crime against nature," which includes oral sex, does not contain a similar exception, however. After the couple engaged in oral sex, R.L.C. was convicted and adjudicated a felony delinquent, entailing punishment and required registration as a sex offender. R.L.C. now challenges this outcome as unconstitutional, based on *Lawrence*. What result and why? See In re R.L.C., 643 S.E.2d 920 (N.C. 2007); Michael Kent Curtis & Shannon Gilreath, Transforming Teenagers into Oral Sex Felons: The Persistence of the Crime Against Nature After Lawrence v. Texas, 43 Wake Forest L. Rev. 155 (2008); Daniel Allender, Applying *Lawrence*: Teenagers and the Crime Against Nature, 58 Duke L.J. 1825 (2009). See also State v. Limon, 122 P.3d 22 (Kan. 2005).

B. When Privacy Rights Conflict

1. Wives and Husbands

PLANNED PARENTHOOD OF SOUTHEASTERN PENNSYLVANIA v. CASEY

505 U.S. 833 (1992)

Justice O'Connor, Justice Kennedy, and Justice Souter announced the judgment of the Court and delivered the opinion of the Court [for Part V-C]:

Section 3209 of Pennsylvania's abortion law provides, except in cases of medical emergency, that no physician shall perform an abortion on a married woman without receiving a signed statement from the woman that she has notified her spouse that she is about to undergo an abortion. The woman has the option of

[37]. Katherine M. Franke, The Domesticated Liberty of Lawrence v. Texas, 104 Colum. L. Rev. 1399, 1414 (2004).

providing an alternative signed statement certifying that her husband is not the man who impregnated her; that her husband could not be located; that the pregnancy is the result of spousal sexual assault which she has reported; or that the woman believes that notifying her husband will cause him or someone else to inflict bodily injury upon her. A physician who performs an abortion on a married woman without receiving the appropriate signed statement will have his or her license revoked, and is liable to the husband for damages.

The District Court heard the testimony of numerous expert witnesses, and made detailed findings of fact regarding the effect of this statute. These included:

> "273. The vast majority of women consult their husbands prior to deciding to terminate their pregnancy. . . .
>
> "281. Studies reveal that family violence occurs in two million families in the United States. This figure, however, is a conservative one that substantially understates (because battering is usually not reported until it reaches life-threatening proportions) the actual number of families affected by domestic violence. In fact, researchers estimate that one of every two women will be battered at some time in their life. . . .
>
> "282. A wife may not elect to notify her husband of her intention to have an abortion for a variety of reasons, including the husband's illness, concern about her own health, the imminent failure of the marriage, or the husband's absolute opposition to the abortion. . . .
>
> "283. The required filing of the spousal consent form would require plaintiff-clinics to change their counseling procedures and force women to reveal their most intimate decision-making on pain of criminal sanctions. The confidentiality of these revelations could not be guaranteed, since the woman's records are not immune from subpoena. . . .
>
> "284. Women of all class levels, educational backgrounds, and racial, ethnic and religious groups are battered. . . .
>
> "285. Wife-battering or abuse can take on many physical and psychological forms. The nature and scope of the battering can cover a broad range of actions and be gruesome and torturous [including murder, rape, child abuse, psychological intimidation, and emotional harm].
>
> "289. Mere notification of pregnancy is frequently a flashpoint for battering and violence within the family. The number of battering incidents is high during the pregnancy and often the worst abuse can be associated with pregnancy. . . . The battering husband may deny parentage and use the pregnancy as an excuse for abuse. . . .
>
> "290. Secrecy typically shrouds abusive families. . . . Battering husbands often threaten [the wife] or her children with further abuse if she tells an outsider of the violence and tells her that nobody will believe her. A battered woman, therefore, is highly unlikely to disclose the violence against her for fear of retaliation by the abuser. . . ."

These findings are supported by studies of domestic violence. . . . In well-functioning marriages, spouses discuss important intimate decisions such as whether to bear a child. But there are millions of women in this country who are the victims of regular physical and psychological abuse at the hands of their husbands. . . . Many may fear devastating forms of psychological abuse from their husbands, including [abuse of their children,] verbal harassment, threats of future violence, the destruction of possessions, physical confinement to the home, the withdrawal of financial support, or the disclosure of the abortion to family and friends. These methods of psychological abuse may act as even more of a deterrent to notification than the possibility of physical violence, but women who are the victims of the abuse are not exempt from §3209's notification requirement. And many women who are pregnant as a result of sexual assaults by their husbands will be unable to avail themselves of the exception for spousal sexual assault, §3209(b)(3), because the exception requires that the woman have notified law enforcement authorities within 90 days of the assault, and her husband will be notified of her report once an investigation begins, §3128(c). If anything in this field is certain, it is that victims of spousal sexual assault are extremely reluctant to report the abuse to the government. . . . We must not blind ourselves to the fact that the significant number of women who fear for their safety and the safety of their children are likely to be deterred from procuring an abortion as surely as if the Commonwealth had outlawed abortion in all cases.

Respondents attempt to avoid the conclusion that §3209 is invalid by pointing out that it imposes almost no burden at all for the vast majority of women seeking abortions. . . . Legislation is measured for consistency with the Constitution by its impact on those whose conduct it affects. . . . The unfortunate yet persisting conditions we document above will mean that in a large fraction of the cases in which §3209 is relevant, it will operate as a substantial obstacle to a woman's choice to undergo an abortion. It is an undue burden, and therefore invalid. . . .

We recognize that a husband has a "deep and proper concern and interest . . . in his wife's pregnancy and in the growth and development of the fetus she is carrying." [Planned Parenthood of Central Mo. v. Danforth, 428 U.S. 52, 69 (1976).] With regard to the children he has fathered and raised, the Court has recognized his "cognizable and substantial" interest in their custody. Stanley v. Illinois, 405 U.S. 645, 651-652 (1972). . . .

Before birth, however, the issue takes on a very different cast. It is an inescapable biological fact that state regulation with respect to the child a woman is carrying will have a far greater impact on the mother's liberty than on the father's. The effect of state regulation on a woman's protected liberty is doubly deserving of scrutiny in such a case, as the State has touched not only upon the private sphere of the family but upon the very bodily integrity of the pregnant woman. The Court has held that "when the wife and the husband disagree on this decision, the view of only one of the two marriage partners can prevail. Inasmuch as it is the woman who physically bears the child and who is the more directly and immediately affected by the pregnancy, as between the two, the balance weighs in her favor." *Danforth*, supra, at 71. This conclusion rests upon the basic nature of marriage and the nature of our Constitution: "The marital couple is not an independent entity with a mind and heart of its own, but an association of two individuals each with a separate intellectual and emotional makeup. If the right of privacy means anything, it is the right of the *individual*, married or single, to be free from unwarranted governmental intrusion into matters so fundamentally affecting a person as the decision whether to bear or beget a child." Eisenstadt v. Baird, 405 U.S. at 453 (emphasis in original). . . .

There was a time, not so long ago, when a different understanding of the family and of the Constitution prevailed. In Bradwell v. State, 83 U.S. (16 Wall.) 130 (1872), three Members of this Court reaffirmed the common-law principle that "a woman had no legal existence separate from her husband, who was regarded as her head and representative in the social state; and, notwithstanding some recent modifications of this civil status, many of the special rules of law flowing from and dependent upon this cardinal principle still exist in full force in most States." Id., at 141 (Bradley, J., joined by Swayne and Field, JJ., concurring in judgment). Only one generation has passed since this Court observed that "woman is still regarded as the center of home and family life," with attendant "special responsibilities" that precluded full and independent legal status under the Constitution. Hoyt v. Florida, 368 U.S. 57, 62 (1961). These views, of course, are no longer consistent with our understanding of the family, the individual, or the Constitution.

[T]he Court held in *Danforth* that the Constitution does not permit a State to require a married woman to obtain her husband's consent before undergoing an abortion. . . . For the great many women who are victims of abuse inflicted by their husbands, or whose children are the victims of such abuse, a spousal notice requirement enables the husband to wield an effective veto over his wife's decision [contrary to *Danforth*].

The husband's interest in the life of the child his wife is carrying does not permit the State to empower him with this troubling degree of authority over his wife. . . . A husband has no enforceable right to require a wife to advise him before she exercises her personal choices. If a husband's interest in the potential life of the child outweighs a wife's liberty, the State could require a married woman to notify her husband before she uses a postfertilization contraceptive. Perhaps next in line would be a statute requiring pregnant married women to notify their husbands before engaging in conduct causing risks to the fetus. After all, if the husband's interest in the fetus' safety is a sufficient predicate for state regulation, the State could reasonably conclude that pregnant wives should notify their husbands before drinking alcohol or smoking. Perhaps married women should notify their husbands before using contraceptives or before undergoing any type of surgery that may have complications affecting the husband's interest in his wife's reproductive organs. And if a husband's interest justifies notice in any of these cases, one might reasonably argue that it justifies exactly what the *Danforth* Court held it did not justify—a requirement of the husband's consent as well. A State may not give to a man the kind of dominion over his wife that parents exercise over their children. . . .

Chief Justice Rehnquist, with whom Justice White, Justice Scalia, and Justice Thomas join, . . . dissenting in part. . . .

[T]he provision here involves a much less intrusive requirement of spousal notification, not consent. . . . *Danforth* thus does not control our analysis. . . .

The question before us is therefore whether the spousal notification requirement rationally furthers any legitimate state interests. We conclude that it does. First, a husband's interests in procreation within marriage and in the potential life of his unborn child are certainly substantial ones. The State itself has legitimate interests both in protecting these interests of the father and in protecting the potential life of the fetus, and the spousal notification requirement is reasonably related to advancing those state interests. By providing that a husband will usually know of his spouse's intent to have an abortion, the provision makes it more likely that the husband will participate in deciding the fate of his unborn child, a possibility that might otherwise have been denied him. This participation might in some cases result in a decision to proceed with the pregnancy. As Judge Alito observed in his dissent below, "the Pennsylvania legislature could have rationally believed that some married women are initially inclined to obtain an abortion without their husbands' knowledge because of perceived problems—such as economic constraints, future plans, or the husbands' previously expressed opposition—that may be obviated by discussion prior to the abortion." 947 F.2d at 726 (opinion concurring in part and dissenting in part).

The State also has a legitimate interest in promoting "the integrity of the marital relationship." 18 Pa. Cons. Stat. §3209(a) (1990). [T]he spousal notice requirement is a rational attempt by the State to improve truthful communication between spouses and encourage collaborative decisionmaking, and thereby fosters marital integrity. . . .

Notes and Questions

1. Rationale. Why did the Court strike down the spousal notification provision? How many rationales do you see in the opinion? How does a requirement of spousal notification differ from one of spousal consent, which the Court struck down in Planned Parenthood v. Danforth, 428 U.S. 52, 67-72 (1976)? Should one trigger a higher level of scrutiny? Which one? Does the answer depend on the meaning of "privacy"?

2. Undue burden. Why do Justices O'Connor, Kennedy, and Souter conclude that spousal notification constitutes an undue burden, but the 24-hour waiting period does not? See *Casey,* 505 U.S. at 881-887. Realistically, couldn't a woman more easily surmount the former simply by forging her husband's signature? Compare the Court's treatment of the two requirements, considering both the number of women apparently affected and the difficulty of the obstacle created.

3. Whose privacy? Does privacy emerge from *Casey* as protection for the individual? The family unit? One approach advocates a constitutional doctrine that favors the "objectively weaker" party in family conflicts. See Jane Rutherford, Beyond Individual Privacy: A New Theory of Family Rights, 39 U. Fla. L. Rev. 627, 652 (1987). Who is "objectively weaker" in reproductive decisionmaking—the woman or the man? What role does privacy doctrine play when the family unit is divided? See David D. Meyer, The Paradox of Family Privacy, 53 Vand. L. Rev. 527, 554-558 (2000) (in "splintered" families, privacy does not keep the state out but locates in the Constitution "a substantive rule for resolving a family's internal conflict").

4. Who decides? Who should make the determination when women's and men's rights conflict? Should the state provide preabortion hearings at which an impartial arbiter decides? Can you imagine circumstances in which the male should prevail? Suppose that the man seeks to avoid having a child, but the woman chooses to carry to term. Must he pay child support under all circumstances, or does he have a right to a "financial abortion"? See Dubay v. Wells, 506 F.3d 422

(6th Cir. 2007) (unsuccessful challenge in case dubbed "Roe v. Wade for men"). Compare Shari Motro, The Price of Pleasure, 104 Nw. U. L. Rev. 917 (2010) (urging additional financial obligations for men who conceive), with Lisa Lucile Owens, Coerced Parenthood as Family Policy: Feminism, the Moral Agency of Women, and Men's "Right to Choose," 5 Ala. C.R. & C.L. L. Rev. 1, 33 (2013) (urging a "new reproductive policy that gives men a meaningful opportunity to choose whether to become legal and social fathers" even after pregnancy).

5. Empirical data. To what extent did the Court rely on empirical data in invalidating the spousal notification requirement? Although most women report that the man knew about and supported the abortion decision, studies also show an association between intimate partner violence and pregnancy termination.[38] What do such data mean for the *Casey* dissent's view of the notification requirement as a valid means of furthering the state's interest in promoting marital integrity and spousal communication?

6. Vision of marriage. What vision of marriage does *Casey* reflect? Does the rejection of traditional gender-based roles provide a better explanation for the outcome than the empirical data? How persuasive is the majority's "parade of horribles" that might follow if the notification requirement were upheld? Do the joint opinion authors have a consistent view of women and their decisionmaking capacity, considering the approach to spousal notification, on the one hand, and the 24-hour waiting period (which they upheld), on the other?

Contrast the majority's reasoning with this assessment of the consequences: "women alone have been given all the power of choice to abort and so are often left with all the responsibility for their child when they do not[, thus offering] the man a rationale for neglecting to support a child to whose existence he failed to consent."[39] But see Susan Frelich Appleton, Illegitimacy and Sex, Old and New, 20 Am. U. J. Gender Soc. Pol'y & L. 347, 360-369 (2012) (noting emphasis on sexually conceiving fathers' "personal responsibility," including child support).

7. Gender stereotypes. *Casey*'s rejection of the traditional concept of marriage, with its subordination of women, complements a line of cases invalidating under the Equal Protection Clause (or other equality principles) laws resting on gender-based stereotypes of males and females. The resulting "gender neutralization" of family law stands out as one of the most transformative developments in the field. (See Chapter III.)

---

[38]. Most married and cohabiting women (88 and 87 percent, respectively) report that their spouses and partners knew of and supported their abortion decisions. Most women conceiving outside a relationship also report men's knowledge and support. However, 7 percent of abortion patients report exposure to intimate partner violence (IPV) by the man with whom the pregnancy was conceived; such exposure, in turn reduced the likelihood of reports that such men knew about or supported the abortion. Rachel K. Jones et al., Perceptions of Male Knowledge and Support Among U.S. Women Obtaining Abortions, 21 Women's Health Issues 117, 119-121 (2010). See also Megan Hall et al., Associations Between Intimate Partner Violence and Termination of Pregnancy: A Systematic Review and Meta-Analysis, 11 PLoS Med. e1001581 (2014), http://www.plosmedicine.org/article/fetchObject.action?uri=info:doi/10.1371/journal.pmed.1001581&representation=PDF.

[39]. Erika Bachiochi, Embodied Equality: Debunking Equal Protection Arguments for Abortion Rights, 34 Harv. J.L. & Pub. Pol'y 889, 944 (2011).

To what extent does this egalitarian understanding of family law presuppose a woman's reproductive autonomy, including abortion rights? See generally, e.g., Jennifer S. Hendricks, Body and Soul: Equality, Pregnancy, and the Unitary Right to Abortion, 45 Harv. C.R.-C.L. L. Rev. 329 (2010). See also Mary Ziegler, Abortion and the Constitutional Right (Not) to Procreate, 48 U. Rich. L. Rev. 1263 (2014) (showing how spousal "consent wars" invoked gender stereotypes in parenting). According to a biographer of Justice Blackmun, author of *Roe*'s majority opinion, he initially resisted the Court's gender equality rulings but came to understand the link between them and abortion rights, around the time of *Casey*.[40] What does the Court's reliance on the asserted government interest in protecting against postabortion regret in *Gonzales*, supra, portend for the jurisprudence of gender equality?

Problem

Wife becomes pregnant for the purpose of terminating the pregnancy and donating the fetal tissue to Husband, who suffers from Parkinson's disease, a condition that has been shown to respond favorably to fetal tissue transplantation. See generally, e.g., The President's Council on Bioethics, Monitoring Stem Cell Research (2004). All physicians refuse to participate in the plan, however, because of the following state criminal statute:

> 1. No physician shall perform an abortion on a woman if the physician knows that the woman conceived the unborn child for the purpose of providing fetal organs or tissue for medical transplantation to herself or another, and the physician knows that the woman intends to procure the abortion to utilize those organs or tissue for such use for herself or another.
>
> 2. No person shall utilize the fetal organs or tissue resulting from an abortion for medical transplantation, if the person knows that the abortion was procured for the purpose of utilizing those organs or tissue for such use.

Wife and Husband consult you, an attorney, about filing suit to challenge the constitutionality of the statute. How would you proceed? What additional information would you need? If you file suit, assess the chances of success. To what extent would your arguments change if the proposed procedure were sought to benefit the ten-year-old son of Wife and Husband, rather than Husband himself?

See Mo. Rev. Stat. §188.036. See also, e.g., S.D. Codified Laws §§34-14-16 to 34-14-20 (prohibiting research that destroys a human embryo when research is not intended to help preserve life and health of the particular embryo). See generally John A. Robertson, Embryo Stem Cell Research: Ten Years of Controversy, 38 J.L. Med. & Ethics 191 (2010).

---

[40]. Linda Greenhouse, Becoming Justice Blackmun: Harry Blackmun's Supreme Court Journey 207-227 (2005).

2. Children and Parents

CINCINNATI WOMEN'S SERVICES, INC. v. TAFT

468 F.3d 361 (6th Cir. 2006)

R. GUY COLE, JR., Circuit Judge. . . .

In this facial constitutional attack, [plaintiffs] appeal the district court's judgment upholding [an abortion regulation that] limits minors seeking a judicial bypass of the statutory parental-consent requirement to one petition per pregnancy ("Single-Petition Rule"). [We reverse.]

Until 1998, Ohio law did not impose any restrictions upon the number of times a minor woman could petition for a judicial bypass of the prior parental-notification rule. The 1998 amendments, however, included the Single-Petition Rule, which limits to once per pregnancy the number of times a minor may seek a judicial bypass in lieu of parental consent. Ohio law makes it a misdemeanor and a tort for any person to perform an abortion on an unemancipated minor unless the attending physician has "secured the written informed consent of the minor and one parent, guardian, or custodian." Ohio Rev. Code §2919.121(B)(1) (2005). The statutory amendment permits a minor woman to petition a juvenile court for a judicial bypass of parental consent if "the court finds that the minor is sufficiently mature and well enough informed to decide intelligently whether to have an abortion" or that "the abortion is in the best interests of the minor." Id. §2919.121(C)(3). The Single-Petition Rule further provides that "[n]o juvenile court shall have jurisdiction to rehear a petition concerning the same pregnancy once a juvenile court has granted or denied the petition." Id. §2919.121(C)(4).

In evaluating the probable impact of the Single-Petition Rule, the district court found that "[m]ost judicial bypasses occur in the first trimester of a minor's pregnancy." The district court also found that "there have been times when it was apparent that a bypass was denied because the minor failed by oversight to adequately discuss facts that the minor knew or could easily learn." One witness, a part-time magistrate in the Cuyahoga County Juvenile Court in Cleveland, testified that in such situations he has advised the minor's attorney to file another bypass petition during the same pregnancy. [The district court upheld the constitutionality of the Single-Petition Rule.]

If a state requires parental consent before an unemancipated minor woman receives an abortion, it must provide for a judicial or administrative procedure so that a minor woman who satisfies certain conditions may bypass the consent requirement. See Bellotti v. Baird, 443 U.S. 622, 647-51 (1979) (plurality opinion) ("*Bellotti II*"). If a minor woman establishes either "that she is mature enough and well enough informed to make the abortion decision independently" or "that the abortion would be in her best interests," the reviewing court or agency must issue the bypass. Lambert v. Wicklund, 520 U.S. 292, 295 (1997) (citation omitted). Otherwise, the attendant bypass procedure is constitutionally invalid. See *Bellotti II*, 443 U.S. at 643-44.

Ohio provides for a judicial-bypass procedure that apparently encompasses the procedural requirements set forth in *Lambert* and *Bellotti II*. Ohio, however, seeks to limit a minor woman to filing one petition for a bypass per pregnancy. The

Supreme Court has never determined whether an abortion restriction preventing a minor woman from filing multiple bypass petitions violates the Constitution. . . .

In [Planned Parenthood of Southeastern Pennsylvania v. Casey, 505 U.S. 833 (1992),] the Supreme Court analyzed a spousal-notification law that required a married woman who wished to abort her pregnancy to first notify her husband, unless she fit into a statutorily exempted category. The Supreme Court held that, in determining whether this restriction was an undue burden, the "proper focus of constitutional inquiry is the group for whom the law is a restriction, not the group for whom the law is irrelevant." . . . [*Casey*] requires courts to determine whether a large fraction of the women "for whom the law is a restriction" will be "deterred from procuring an abortion as surely as if the [government] has outlawed abortion in all cases." . . .

Applying *Casey* to the Single-Petition Rule before us, we find that the group of women for whom the restriction actually operates are women who are denied a bypass and who have changed circumstances such that if they were able to reapply for a bypass, it would be granted. The group of women who will be deterred from procuring an abortion because of the restriction are women with changed circumstances who would apply for another bypass if allowed. The record shows that second petitioners exist under Ohio's current bypass scheme, and that practically all second petitioners allege changed circumstances such that, if believed, a reviewing court must issue a bypass [including increased maturity, greater knowledge about abortion, and the discovery of fetal anomalies.] The record further shows that most women who are denied a bypass but who experience a change in their circumstances will subsequently seek another bypass procedure. Because Ohio's law preventing more than one petition per procedure acts as a substantial obstacle to a woman's right to an abortion in a large fraction of the cases in which the single petition is relevant, we find that the Single-Petition Rule is an undue burden and, therefore, is facially unconstitutional. . . .

ROGERS, Circuit Judge, concurring. . . .

. . . The *Bellotti II* Court explained that every minor must have the opportunity to establish that she should not have to seek parental consent based on her current level of maturity or her current best interests. . . . Accordingly, under *Bellotti II*, the single petition rule is facially invalid because, after a failed first petition, the rule does not permit a judge to evaluate the petitioner's current maturity or interest in abortion in light of new developments. . . .

Angela Bonavoglia, Kathy's Day in Court

Ms., Apr. 1988, at 46-49

On Wednesday, September 23, 1987, at 7:30 a.m., a pregnant 17-year-old we will call "Kathy"—her court-designated name—left her home in a working-class neighborhood of Birmingham, Alabama, and drove alone to the Jefferson County Family Courthouse. Kathy wanted an abortion. But in Alabama, as in [many] other states in the nation, a law exists that forbids a minor (anyone under the age of 18) to give her own consent for an abortion. Alabama's minors must ask one parent for permission, and if they can't do that, they must get a judge's approval before they can have an abortion.

Kathy is a friendly young woman with a big hearty laugh. Her face is round with residues of baby fat, and framed in a mane of blond hair. People tend to describe her as "sensible," which she is, but her sense of competence comes from having had to take care of herself much too early in life. Six years ago her mother remarried, to a man who is an alcoholic. For the last year and a half Kathy has lived mainly on her own, since she doesn't get along with her stepfather. . . .

Waiting for her at the courthouse that September day was the abortion provider Kathy had contacted when she realized she was pregnant [Diane Derzis, the director of Summit Medical Center]. Diane Derzis wanted to find a teenager willing to go to court and take her chances with the ambiguous law. If a judge turned this test case down, she would help the girl appeal, going as far as necessary in the court system to show how punitive the statute is. [Kathy had previously called the Medical Center to arrange an abortion. Her maturity led Derzis to ask her if she would wait five days until the consent law became effective and then go to court to test the new law. In exchange, Derzis would arrange for Kathy to have a free abortion.]

"The money was a little bit of why I did it," said Kathy, "but I could have paid." More to the point for Kathy was that "Diane told me it would be a big help to the people who came after me. Everyone thought I was the perfect person to try this out: seventeen, living on my own. And, I thought, with all I've been through, I'm still here, I *know* I can handle this."

Following the instructions set forth in the Alabama law, Derzis had submitted Kathy's request for a judicial hearing to the Jefferson County Family Court. By law, the court had to provide Kathy with free legal representation for her hearing. Her papers were brought by a court officer to a Legal Aid lawyer, J. Wynell (Wendy) Brooks Crew, on September 21. [Judge Charles Nice would be hearing the case two days later.]

But on the day after Crew believed herself to have been appointed as Kathy's attorney, Judge Nice's bailiff approached her and a private attorney, Marcus Jones. According to Crew, the bailiff told Jones *he* had been appointed to represent the minor, and she was to represent the fetus. Wendy Crew said no. She pointed out that she had already talked to Kathy. She also noted that appointing a lawyer for the fetus would be unconstitutional, since, under Roe v. Wade, the fetus cannot be considered a person and does not have a right to representation. . . .

Crew and Jones went into the judge's office. Nice, 68, a slightly built, benevolent-looking man, had in his office pamphlets for Lifeline, an adoption agency run by the virulently anti-choice Sav-A-Life Christian ministry. Hanging on his wall was a photo of some of Lifeline's adoptive parents at their last reunion. Crew told him she wanted to stay on the case. She asked to be appointed Kathy's guardian or to be co-counsel. Judge Nice refused both requests and dismissed Crew.

Now Marcus Jones went into the conference room to meet Kathy. "I was mad," said Kathy. "I felt like I could pull this through with Wendy. Then they bring some man in fifteen minutes before the trial. Men don't really know about this. How is some man gonna stand up there and fight for me when he doesn't even know what's going on? I thought to myself, 'I'm gonna lose.'"

At approximately 9:45 a.m., Kathy and Diane Derzis walked down the hall from the conference room to Judge Nice's courtroom. . . . "I was having heart failure," [Kathy] said. She wanted Derzis to stay, but only court personnel were allowed in the room. That left Kathy in a room with four men—Nice, Jones, the bailiff, and the court officer. . . .

Jones began his questioning. . . . Kathy testified that she would not be 18 until the end of the year, and was therefore still affected by the parental consent law. To establish her maturity, Jones asked her about school. She told him that since she had not graduated, she planned to take the high school equivalency test. She also testified that she had been working full-time and part-time for the last two years and contributed to her own support.

Marcus Jones asked about her family. Kathy testified that her alcoholic stepfather abused her mother and herself. According to Kathy, he beat her so badly one night, she left and moved in with friends. . . . Kathy said she was 10 weeks pregnant. She didn't want to tell her mother about the pregnancy because her mother told her stepfather everything and if he found out about this he might get mad and end by beating her mother.

Kathy testified that she had considered adoption as well as abortion and remembers being surprised when Judge Nice continued to question her about this. . . . After 45 minutes of testimony, Judge Nice left the courtroom to make his decision. . . . Judge Nice returned and read his decision: he would not grant Kathy's request for an abortion; she was not mature enough, it was not in her best interest. The judge told Kathy she should talk to her mother about this decision.

Kathy was stunned. "I was about in tears. How can he say this about me? He didn't feel I was mature enough to make this decision myself? I could feel my eyes start pooling up, and I was going, 'Don't cry, don't cry.'"

"Everyone here at the clinic thinks I'm such a hard bitch," said Diane Derzis, "but I came back the day of that hearing and cried to think of what Kathy went through. I called Wendy and said 'I can't believe we put her through that. Why didn't we just take her to Georgia?'"

But they persevered, filing an appeal of Judge Nice's decision. [Kathy] has never said that she regrets her decision to go to court, but admits that the waiting was terrible: "I kept wishing I had already gotten it over with."

Fourteen days after the hearing, the Alabama Court of Civil Appeals overturned the judge's opinion . . . : "The trial judge in this case abused his discretion by denying the minor's request. . . . More importantly, we can neither discern from the trial court's judgment nor from the record any ground upon which the trial court's conclusion could rest. We can safely say, having considered the record, that, should this minor not meet the criteria for 'maturity' under the statute, it is difficult to imagine one who would." . . .

Notes and Questions

1. Minors' abortion decisionmaking. Both opinions in *Taft* discuss Bellotti v. Baird, 443 U.S. 622 (1979), which triggered the creation of "judicial bypass" procedures in states with parental consent or notification requirements (discussed infra). The *Bellotti* plurality offers three reasons why the Constitution permits greater regulation of minors' abortions compared to adults'. Consider each in turn:

a. Vulnerability. What does "vulnerability" encompass? *Bellotti* elaborates with references to the Court's holdings protecting minors' constitutional rights. 443 U.S. at 634. Would a more apt focus consider the emotional effects of abortions on minors? Psychological data fail to show that adolescent abortion causes negative psychological or health consequences. See Anne R. Davis & Anitra D. Beasley, Abortion in Adolescents: Epidemiology, Confidentiality, and Methods, 21 Current Op. Obstet. & Gynecol. 390, 394 (2009).

b. Decisionmaking capacity. Are adolescents less able to make informed, mature decisions than adults? Compare J. Shoshanna Ehrlich, Who Decides? The Abortion Rights of Teens 61-62, 93-95 (2006) (asserting few differences in cognitive abilities of adults and adolescents, in terms of decisionmaking processes), with American College of Pediatricians, Parental Notification/Consent for Treatment of the Adolescent, 30 Issues L. & Med. 99 (2015) (emphasizing importance of parental guidance for adolescents making life-changing decisions). Scholars argue that minors' decisionmaking capacity varies by context, a position supported by social science evidence. See Richard J. Bonnie & Elizabeth S. Scott, The Teenage Brain: Adolescent Brain Research and the Law, 22 Current Directions in Psych. Science 158 (2013) (emphasizing developmental view of teen risk taking and criminal activity). See also Emily Buss, What the Law Should (and Should Not) Learn from Child Development Research, 38 Hofstra L. Rev. 13 (2009).

c. Promoting parental involvement. Do laws requiring parental consent or notice promote family unity? Parental control? Result in more informed decisions? Prompt actual consultation between parents and their daughters? See Davis & Beasley, supra, at 394. If the Constitution protects a parent's right to control the upbringing of children under *Meyer* and *Pierce*, supra, why don't parents have absolute authority to prevent a daughter's abortion if they see fit? See Richard F. Storrow & Sandra Martinez, "Special Weight" for Best-Interests Minors in the New Era of Parental Autonomy, 2003 Wis. L. Rev. 789. Or, to direct a teenage daughter to have an abortion despite her wishes to the contrary? See In the Matter of Mary P., 444 N.Y.S.2d 545 (Fam. Ct. 1981).

2. Parental involvement laws. Currently, a majority of states require parental involvement for a minor's abortion. Twenty-one states require parental consent; 12 states require parental notification; 5 states require both. Most states require consent or notification of only one parent (with only 3 states requiring both parents to consent and one requiring notification of both parents); and 7 states permit other adult relatives instead of parents to be involved. Should the same rules apply to minors' access to abortion and to contraception? Does *Eisenstadt*, supra, apply to minors?[41]

---

[41]. See Guttmacher Inst., State Policies in Brief: Parental Involvement in Minors' Abortions (Sept. 1, 2015), http://www.guttmacher.org/statecenter/spibs/spib_PIMA.pdf. All minors age 12 and older may consent to contraceptive services in 26 states and D.C.. Guttmacher Inst., State Policies in Brief: An Overview of Minors' Consent Law (Sept. 1, 2015), http://www.guttmacher.org/statecenter/spibs/spib_OMCL.pdf.

3. Federal proposals and laws. *Bellotti*, supra, emphasized the importance of the parental role in minors' decisionmaking. May Congress prohibit other adults from fulfilling this function? Data reveal that virtually all minors consult at least one adult (often relatives or health care professionals). Ehrlich, supra, at 102-103. Proposed federal legislation would subject to both criminal and civil liability anyone, other than a parent, who knowingly transports a minor to a less restrictive state to obtain an abortion; it also would prohibit a physician from performing an abortion on a minor from another state absent parental notification or compliance with a local notification requirement. H.R. 803, 114th Cong. (2015-2016).

Historically, Congress focused on teen pregnancy in welfare reform. Under such legislation, states can provide assistance only to minor parents who meet specific educational and residential requirements, states can get grants for abstinence education, and states should aggressively enforce statutory rape laws. 42 U.S.C. §§602(a)(1)(A)(v), 608(a)(4), 608(a)(5), 710, 14016. In 2010, Congress left abstinence-only grants in place but, as part of health care reform, also made funds available to the states for "personal responsibility education," which teaches about abstinence, contraception, and protection from sexually transmitted diseases. Id. §713.

4. Judicial bypass. All 38 states requiring parental involvement have a judicial bypass procedure, developed in response to the Court's rulings.[42] A judicial bypass has "saved" several different parental involvement laws. See, e.g., Hodgson v. Minnesota, 497 U.S. 417 (1990) (two-parent notification requirement with judicial bypass); Lambert v. Wicklund, 520 U.S. 292 (1997) (one-parent notification 48 hours pre-abortion with judicial bypass with waiver when notification is not in minor's best interest); Planned Parenthood of Southeastern Pa. v. Casey, 505 U.S. 833, 899-900 (1992) ("informed parental consent" with bypass). Does the judicial bypass make sense as a means of operationalizing the competing interests at stake? What does *Kathy's Day in Court* suggest?

a. Rationale? Why might the Constitution allow state age based lines for some constitutionally protected activities (for example, the right to marry) but require case-by-case assessments of maturity and best interests when the minor seeks an abortion? See Martin Guggenheim, What's Wrong with Children's Rights 237-244 (2005) (asserting that the Court pragmatically responded to social costs of teen pregnancy). Does the bypass regime conflict with criminal prohibitions on consensual sex with minors—that is, statutory rape and similar provisions that *always* make the minor's own consent legally irrelevant? See Jones v. State, 640 So. 2d 1084 (Fla. 1994).

b. Scope. Can a state with a parental notice requirement provide for a bypass procedure only for minors with documented experiences of child abuse or neglect? Compare Planned Parenthood v. Miller, 63 F.3d 1452 (8th Cir. 1995) (no), with Planned Parenthood of Blue Ridge v. Camblos, 155 F.3d 352 (4th Cir. 1998) (yes).

c. Judicial role. Do judges have the requisite expertise to assess maturity? To what extent is the judgment about maturity or best interests shaped by the judge's ideology and values? See, e.g., Ex parte Anonymous, 806 So. 2d 1269 (Ala. 2001).

---

[42]. Guttmacher Inst., State Policies in Brief: Parental Involvement in Minors' Abortions, supra note [41].

Will a judge think it mature or immature for a young woman to become pregnant? Not to want to involve her parents? To choose to assume responsibility herself? What other value judgments might prove influential? *Kathy's Day in Court* illustrates one possibility. Should judges with moral or religious objections to abortion recuse themselves? See Eric Parker Babbs, Note, Pro-Life Judges and Judicial Bypass Cases, 22 Notre Dame J.L. Ethics & Pub. Pol'y 473 (2008). Would widespread judicial recusals impose an undue burden? See Lauren Treadwell, Note, Informal Closing of the Bypass: Minors' Petitions to Bypass Parental Consent for Abortion in an Age of Increasing Judicial Recusals, 58 Hastings L.J. 869 (2007). Suppose a judge believes that forcing an unwilling minor to carry to term can never serve her best interests. See Nanette Dembitz, The Supreme Court and a Minor's Abortion Decision, 80 Colum. L. Rev. 1251, 1255-1256 (1980). See generally Helena Silverstein, Girls on the Stand: How Courts Fail Pregnant Minors (2007).

d. Determining maturity. The notion of a "mature minor" developed in tort law as a malpractice defense for physicians who failed to obtain parental consent before providing medical treatment to a minor. In borrowing this idea for abortion cases, the Supreme Court has not clarified the meaning of "maturity." How is a trial court to make such determinations? For example, how relevant is the minor's composure (or lack thereof) during her testimony? See Ex parte Anonymous, 812 So. 2d 1234 (Ala. 2001) (affirming finding of immaturity based on "rehearsed" testimony and lack of emotion). Her academic record? See In re Anonymous, 888 So. 2d 1265, 1271 (Ala. Civ. App. 2004) (rejecting academic standing as basis for finding lack of maturity, but upholding finding based on "demeanor"). Her failure to consult her mother? See In re Doe, 33 A.3d 615 (Pa. 2011). The suspicion that she deceived her parents? See In re Doe 13-A, 136 So. 3d 723, 723 (Fla. Dist. Ct. App. 2014) (Roberts, J., concurring). The absence of evidence of her knowledge of the risks (immediate or long-term) of having an abortion? In re Doe, 973 So. 2d 548, 552 (Fla. Dist. Ct. App. 2008). What role should the possibility of postabortion regret, invoked in *Gonzales*, supra, play in bypass proceedings? Do you agree with the concurring judge in *Taft* that the Supreme Court's emphasis on current maturity (and best interests) necessarily invalidates Ohio's single-petition rule?

e. Representation. Does the Constitution require court-appointed counsel for minors in bypass proceedings? In some proceedings, judges can appoint guardians ad litem for the fetus, as *Kathy's Day in Court* illustrates. Do such appointments constitute an undue burden on the minor's right to an abortion? See Helena Silverstein, In the Matter of Anonymous, A Minor: Fetal Representation in Hearings to Waive Parental Consent for Abortion, 11 Cornell J.L. & Pub. Pol'y 69 (2001).

5. Comparing burdens. Do parental consent requirements impose more onerous burdens than notification requirements? See Planned Parenthood of Cent. N.J. v. Farmer, 762 A.2d 620, 629 (N.J. 2000). How does going to court compare? Is this alternative itself "unduly burdensome"? See id. at 634-638. See Caitlin E. Borgmann, Abortion, the Undue Burden Standard, and the Evisceration of Women's Privacy, 16 Wm. & Mary J. Women & L. 291, 315-316 (2010). Cf. Alexandra Rex, Note, Protecting the One Percent: Relevant Women, Undue Burdens, and Unworkable Judicial Bypasses, 114 Colum. L. Rev. 85 (2014) (arguing that parental involvement laws, like spousal notice requirements, violate the Constitution).

6. Remedies under the undue burden standard. *Taft* applies the undue burden standard first announced and used in *Casey*, supra. Does *Gonzales* clarify this standard? Change it? After *Gonzales*, how would the Court determine whether spousal notification imposes an undue burden? Whether Ohio's single-petition rule for judicial bypass does so? How would such analysis treat the number of women affected by each requirement? Would the analysis still require determining whether the law has an impact on a "large fraction" of relevant cases?

Recall that *Gonzales* rejects a facial challenge to the federal statute, deeming as-applied challenges more appropriate. Must as-applied challenges be brought on an individual basis, for each woman who encounters problems or risks as a result of an abortion restriction? Or is it possible to bring wider challenges? In an omitted portion of Justice Ginsburg's *Gonzales* dissent, she provides this analysis of the statute's failure to include a health exception:

> Surely the Court cannot mean that no suit may be brought until a woman's health is immediately jeopardized by the ban on intact D&E. A woman "suffering from medical complications" needs access to the medical procedure at once and cannot wait for the judicial process to unfold. The Court appears, then, to contemplate another lawsuit by the initiators of the instant actions [who] could succeed upon demonstrating that "in discrete and well-defined instances a particular condition has or is likely to occur in which the procedure prohibited by the Act must be used."

550 U.S. at 189-190. See B. Jessie Hill, A Radically Immodest Judicial Modesty: The End of Facial Challenges to Abortion Regulations and the Future of the Health Exception in the Roberts Era, 59 Case W. Res. L. Rev. 997 (2009). Do you agree with Justice Ginsburg? How might the process play out in a post-*Gonzales* challenge to a spousal notification requirement? To Ohio's single-petition rule for judicial bypass? To a TRAP law that forces clinic closures and requires abortion patients to travel great distances or go out of state?

7. Role of physicians and other professionals. What role should the physician play in the minor's abortion decision? Should judges delegate the determination of maturity to the physicians who perform the abortions? Would such deference create a conflict of interest? Suppose that the physician cannot be associated with the physician who would perform the procedure? See W. Va. Code §16-2F-3.

Missouri, which requires parental consent, now has legislation subjecting to civil liability any person who "shall intentionally cause, aid, or assist a minor to obtain an abortion" without such consent. Mo. Rev. Stat. §188.250. The law seeks to stop Missouri minors from traveling to clinics in other states that do not require parental consent. Can parents sue a Missouri physician, counselor, clergy, or attorney who simply responds to a minor's questions about whether nearby states require parental consent? What constitutional issues does the law raise? See Planned Parenthood of Kan. & Mid-Mo. v. Nixon, 220 S.W.3d 732 (Mo. 2007).

Under child abuse reporting requirements, can law enforcement officials compel health care professionals to submit medical records of sexually active minors who had abortions as evidence of statutory rape or sexual abuse? See Aid for Women v. Foulston, 441 F.3d 1101 (10th Cir. 2006); Alpha Med. Clinic v. Anderson, 128 P.3d 364 (Kan. 2006); Roe v. Planned Parenthood Southwest Ohio Region, 912 N.E.2d 61 (Ohio 2009).

8. Medical exceptions. Must parental involvement requirements include exceptions for the minor's life and health? If the state seeks to involve a parent in a daughter's important medical decision (with a judicial bypass for appropriate cases), why can't the state assume that the parent (or the judge) will protect the minor's health? Do the legislatures assume that health care providers will be less likely to include parents in their daughters' abortions than in other medical decisions? Or, do the courts assume that parents will exhibit less concern for a daughter's health in the abortion context than they would in connection with any other medical treatment?

9. State constitutions. Some courts have struck down under state constitutions measures that have survived federal constitutional challenge. Compare, e.g., State v. Planned Parenthood of Alaska, 171 P.3d 577 (Alaska 2007) (parental consent or bypass requirement violates fundamental state constitutional rights to privacy and equal protection), with Hope Clinic for Women, Ltd. v. Flores, 991 N.E.2d 745 (Ill. 2013) (parental notice requirement does not violate state constitutional protection of due process, equal protection, privacy, or gender equality).

10. Vision of the family. What is the vision of the family reflected in parental consent and notification statutes? See generally Guggenheim, supra, at 231-244; Anne C. Dailey, Constitutional Privacy and the Just Family, 67 Tul. L. Rev. 955 (1993). Does this vision support (or require) parental involvement laws for minors who want to carry their pregnancies to term? See Emily Buss, The Parental Rights of Minors, 48 Buff. L. Rev. 785 (2000). How is this vision informed by evidence that pregnant teens' parents favor abortion by a four to one ratio? William Saletan, Bearing Right: How Conservatives Won the Abortion War 192 (2003) (citing study). See also Maya Manian, Functional Parenting and Dysfunctional Abortion Policy: Reforming Parental Involvement Legislation, 50 Fam. Ct. Rev. 241 (2012) (advocating expanded laws to include, as an alternative to parents, other designated adults to assist minors, based on family law's modern emphasis on function and pluralism).

11. Empirical data. Recall the Court's reliance on empirical data in invalidating the spousal notification requirement in *Casey*, supra. What role should the following data play in the constitutional analysis of restrictions on minors' abortions?

a. Teen sexual activity. By age 17, half of all teens have had sexual intercourse, with 16 percent experiencing sexual initiation by age 15.[43]

b. Teen pregnancies and births. The rates of teen pregnancy and birth in the United States are among the highest in the developed world, despite a recent decline because of improved access to contraception.[44] The data (and analyses) vary by race, with Black women having the highest teen pregnancy rate (100 per

[43]. Guttmacher Inst., Fact Sheet, American Teens' Sexual and Reproductive Health, May 2014, http://www.guttmacher.org/pubs/FB-ATSRH.pdf.

[44]. See id. "The birth rate for teenagers aged 15-19 declined 10% in 2013 from 2012, to 26.5 births per 1,000 teenagers . . . another historic low for the nation." Joyce A. Martin et al., Births: Final Data for 2013, 64 Nat'l Vital Statistics Rep., no. 1, at 2 (2015), http://www.cdc.gov/nchs/data/nvsr/nvsr64/nvsr64_01.pdf.

thousand), followed by Hispanics (84 per thousand) and non-Hispanic whites (38 per thousand).[45]

c. Teen abortions. Abortion rates for teens exceed those for women generally. In 2010, 26 percent of teen pregnancies ended in abortion.[46]

d. Reasons for nondisclosure. For what reasons would a teenager not wish to notify her parents of her pending abortion? Based on in-depth interviews with 26 minors who received judicial authorization for an abortion, Professor Shoshanna Ehrlich found that these teens feared that their parents would be extremely upset or would have a severe adverse reaction (ejecting them from the home or inflicting physical harm or other abuse), or they anticipated parental opposition, pressure to have the baby or get married, or problematic family dynamics.[47]

e. Reasons for choosing abortion. According to Ehrlich, minors also gave multiple reasons for choosing an abortion, such as not being ready for motherhood (feelings of insufficient maturity or responsibility); interference with future plans (such as the desire to complete education); present circumstances (such as already having a child, not having a place to live, or health problems); concerns about the child's well-being (inability to support the child); and anticipated adverse parental response.[48]

f. Consequences of parental involvement laws. What are the consequences of parental involvement laws for minors? See Davis & Beasley, supra (highlighting health-related effects). For families? For society? In *Hodgson*, supra, Minnesota bypass judges testified that the "court experience produced fear, tension, anxiety, and shame among minors, causing some who were mature, and some whose best interests would have been served by an abortion, to 'forego the bypass option and either notify their parents or carry to term.'" 497 U.S. at 441-442. *Hodgson* also indicates that in some states minors' petitions are routinely granted. Id. at 441 (of 3,573 bypass petitions considered between 1981 and 1986, courts granted all but 15). In terms of the impact of bypass laws on teen behavior and teen abortions, the data remain largely inconclusive.[49]

12. Epilogue. After *Taft*, Ohio revised its statute, limiting venue for bypass proceedings, requiring that the judge question the minor specifically about her awareness of the "possible physical and emotional complications of abortion,"

---

[45]. Guttmacher Inst., supra note [43], at 3. See Martin et al., supra note [44], at 6 (birth rates for women aged 10-19).

[46]. Guttmacher Inst., supra note [43], at 3.

[47]. J. Shoshanna Ehrlich, Who Decides? The Abortion Rights of Teens 117-125 (2006).

[48]. Id. at 86-93.

[49]. Compare Andrew Lehren & John Leland, Scant Drop Seen in Abortions If Parents Are Told, N.Y. Times, Mar. 6, 2006, at A1, with Associated Press, Study Links Abortion Drop in Texas to Notification, St. Louis Post-Dispatch, Mar. 9, 2006, at A3. One empirical study concludes that parental involvement requirements decrease risky sexual behavior among teens by raising the cost in terms of consequences. See Jonathan Klick & Thomas Stratmann, Abortion Access and Risky Sex Among Teens: Parental Involvement Laws and Sexually Transmitted Diseases, 24 J.L. Econ. & Org. 2 (2008) (using gonorrhea rates and finding differences by race). Other research reveals that parental involvement laws prompt minors to travel to more permissive states. Amanda Dennis et al., The Impact of Laws Requiring Parental Involvement for Abortion: A Literature Review (Guttmacher Inst. Mar. 2009), http://www.guttmacher.org/pubs/ParentalInvolvementLaws.pdf.

and imposing a clear and convincing evidence standard for the findings to be made. Ohio Rev. Code Ann. §2919.121. What explains this reform?

Problems

1. You are an attorney helping a colleague prepare for the court appearance of a 14-year-old petitioner seeking an abortion without parental involvement. In rehearsing for the hearing, your colleague elicits the following responses from the minor:

Q: At the time that the Complaint in this matter was signed, you were pregnant?
A: Yes.
Q: You had consulted with a counselor about that pregnancy?
A: Yeah.
Q: You had determined after talking to the counselor that you felt you should get an abortion?
A: Yes.
Q: You felt that you did not want to notify your parents—
A: Right.
Q: —of that decision? You did not feel for your own reasons that you could discuss it with them?
A: Right.
Q: After discussing the matter with a counselor, you still believed that you should not discuss it with your parents?
A: Right.
Q: And they shouldn't be notified?
A: Right.
Q: After talking the matter over with a counselor, the counselor concurred in your decision that your parents should not be notified?
A: Right.
Q: You were advised that an abortion couldn't be performed without notifying them?
A: Yes.
Q: You then came to me to see about filing a suit?
A: Right.
Q: You and I discussed it as to whether or not you had a right to do what you wanted to do?
A: Yes.
Q: You decided that, after our discussion, you should still proceed with the action to try to obtain an abortion without notifying your parents?
A: Right.
Q: Now, at the time that you signed the Complaint and spoke with the counselor and spoke with me, you were in the first trimester of pregnancy, within your first twelve weeks of pregnancy?
A: Yes.

Q: You feel that, from talking to the counselor and thinking the situation over and discussing it with me, that you could make the decision on your own that you wished to abort the pregnancy?
A: Yes.
Q: You are living at home?
A: Yes.
Q: You still felt, even though you were living at home with your parents, that you couldn't discuss the matter with them?
A: Right.

H.L. v. Matheson, 450 U.S. 398, 402-403 n.6 (1981) (quoting transcript). Would you advise your colleague that a judge is likely to grant the petition on this evidence? If not, what questions would you recommend to elicit the information necessary for a successful petition, assuming truthful answers from the minor? In particular, what questions could help show a judge that this minor is well informed? Mature? That an abortion would serve her best interests? See also In re Doe 13-A, 136 So. 3d 723, 723 (Fla. Dist. Ct. App. 2014) (Roberts, J., concurring).

2. Early studies from an experimental program in Colorado, funded by a private grant from the Susan Thompson Buffett Foundation, show that cost-free access to long-acting reversible contraceptives (LARCs) can dramatically reduce the teen pregnancy rate. Sabrina Tavernise, Colorado's Effort Against Teenage Pregnancies Is a Startling Success, N.Y. Times, July 7, 2015, at A1. Based on such data, what law reforms would you recommend? What difficulties or challenges would they present? See Isabel V. Sawhill, Generation Unbound: Drifting into Sex and Parenthood Without Marriage (2014).

3. Life and Death

CRUZAN v. DIRECTOR, MISSOURI DEPARTMENT OF HEALTH

497 U.S. 261 (1990)

Chief Justice Rehnquist delivered the opinion of the Court.

. . . On the night of January 11, 1983, Nancy Cruzan lost control of her car as she traveled down Elm Road in Jasper County, Missouri. The vehicle overturned, and Cruzan was discovered lying face down in a ditch without detectable respiratory or cardiac function. Paramedics were able to restore her breathing and heartbeat at the accident site, and she was transported to a hospital in an unconscious state. [P]ermanent brain damage usually results after 6 minutes in an anoxic state; it was estimated that Cruzan was deprived of oxygen from 12 to 14 minutes. She remained in a coma for approximately three weeks and then progressed to an unconscious state in which she was able to orally ingest some nutrition. In order to ease feeding and further the recovery, surgeons implanted a gastrostomy feeding and hydration tube in Cruzan with the consent of her then husband. Subsequent rehabilitative efforts proved unavailing. She now lies in a Missouri state hospital

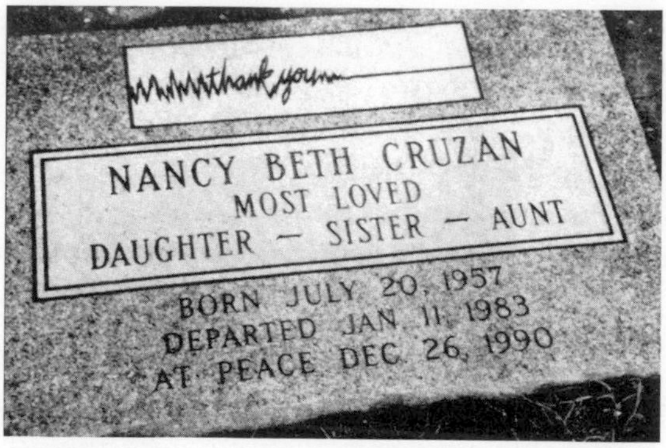

Nancy Cruzan's gravestone (with a "thank you," a flatline, and dates of birth, "departure," and "at peace")

in what is commonly referred to as a persistent vegetative state: generally, a condition in which a person exhibits motor reflexes but evinces no indications of significant cognitive function. The State of Missouri is bearing the cost of her care.

After it had become apparent that Nancy Cruzan had virtually no chance of regaining her mental faculties, her parents asked hospital employees to terminate the artificial nutrition and hydration procedures. All agree that such a removal would cause her death. The employees refused to honor the request without court approval. . . .

We granted certiorari to consider the question of whether Cruzan has a right under the United States Constitution which would require the hospital to withdraw life-sustaining treatment from her under these circumstances.

At common law, even the touching of one person by another without consent and without legal justification was a battery. . . . This notion of bodily integrity has been embodied in the requirement that informed consent is generally required for medical treatment. . . .

The logical corollary of the doctrine of informed consent is that the patient generally possesses the right not to consent, that is, to refuse treatment. Until about 15 years ago and the seminal decision in In re Quinlan, 355 A.2d 647 [(N.J.)], *cert. denied sub nom.* Garger v. New Jersey, 429 U.S. 922 (1976), the number of right-to-refuse-treatment decisions were relatively few. [W]ith the advance of medical technology capable of sustaining life well past the point where natural forces would have brought certain death in earlier times, cases involving the right to refuse life-sustaining treatment have burgeoned.

In the *Quinlan* case, young Karen Quinlan suffered severe brain damage as the result of anoxia, and entered a persistent vegetative state. Karen's father sought judicial approval to disconnect his daughter's respirator. The New Jersey Supreme Court granted the relief, holding that Karen had a right of privacy grounded in the Federal Constitution to terminate treatment. Recognizing that this right was not absolute, however, the court balanced it against asserted state interests. Noting that the State's interest "weakens and the individual's right to privacy grows as the degree of bodily invasion increases and the prognosis dims," the court concluded that the state interests had to give way in that case. The court also concluded that the "only practical way" to prevent the loss of Karen's privacy right due to her incompetence was to allow her guardian and family to decide "whether she would exercise it in these circumstances."

After *Quinlan*, however, most courts have based a right to refuse treatment either solely on the common law right to informed consent or on both the common law right and a constitutional privacy right. . . . This is the first case in which we have been squarely presented with the issue of whether the United States Constitution grants what is in common parlance referred to as a "right to die." . . .

. . . The principle that a competent person has a constitutionally protected liberty interest in refusing unwanted medical treatment may be inferred from our prior decisions. In Jacobson v. Massachusetts, 197 U.S. 11, 24-30 (1905), for instance, the Court balanced an individual's liberty interest in declining an unwanted smallpox vaccine against the State's interest in preventing disease . . . . But determining that a person has a "liberty interest" under the Due Process Clause does not end the inquiry;[7] "whether respondent's constitutional rights have been violated must be determined by balancing his liberty interests against the relevant state interests."

Petitioners insist that under the general holdings of our cases, the forced administration of life-sustaining medical treatment, and even of artificially-delivered food and water essential to life, would implicate a competent person's liberty interest. Although we think the logic of the cases discussed above would embrace such a liberty interest, the dramatic consequences involved in refusal of such treatment would inform the inquiry as to whether the deprivation of that interest is constitutionally permissible. But for purposes of this case, we assume that the United States Constitution would grant a competent person a constitutionally protected right to refuse lifesaving hydration and nutrition.

Petitioners go on to assert that an incompetent person should possess the same right in this respect as is possessed by a competent person. . . . The difficulty with petitioners' claim is that in a sense it begs the question: an incompetent person is not able to make an informed and voluntary choice to exercise a hypothetical right to refuse treatment or any other right. Such a "right" must be exercised for her, if at all, by some sort of surrogate. Here, Missouri has in effect recognized that under certain circumstances a surrogate may act for the patient in electing to have hydration and nutrition withdrawn in such a way as to cause death, but it has established a procedural safeguard to assure that the action of the surrogate conforms as best it may to the wishes expressed by the patient while competent. Missouri requires that evidence of the incompetent's wishes as to the withdrawal of treatment be proved by clear and convincing evidence. The question, then, is whether the United States Constitution forbids the establishment of this procedural requirement by the State. We hold that it does not.

[Missouri asserts] its interest in the protection and preservation of human life, and there can be no gainsaying this interest. [T]he majority of States in this country have laws imposing criminal penalties on one who assists another to commit suicide. We do not think a State is required to remain neutral in the face of an informed and voluntary decision by a physically-able adult to starve to death.

But in the context presented here, a State has more particular interests at stake. The choice between life and death is a deeply personal decision of obvious and overwhelming finality. We believe Missouri may legitimately seek to safeguard the personal element of this choice through the imposition of heightened evidentiary requirements [specifically, clear and convincing evidence]. It cannot be disputed that the Due Process Clause protects an interest in life as well as an interest in

7. Although many state courts have held that a right to refuse treatment is encompassed by a generalized constitutional right of privacy, we have never so held. We believe this issue is more properly analyzed in terms of a Fourteenth Amendment liberty interest. See Bowers v. Hardwick, 478 U.S. 186, 194-195 (1986).

refusing life-sustaining medical treatment. Not all incompetent patients will have loved ones available to serve as surrogate decisionmakers. And even where family members are present, "[t]here will, of course, be some unfortunate situations in which family members will not act to protect a patient." A State is entitled to guard against potential abuses in such situations. . . .

. . . We believe that Missouri may permissibly place an increased risk of an erroneous decision on those seeking to terminate an incompetent individual's life-sustaining treatment. An erroneous decision not to terminate results in a maintenance of the status quo; the possibility of subsequent developments such as advancements in medical science, the discovery of new evidence regarding the patient's intent, changes in the law, or simply the unexpected death of the patient despite the administration of life-sustaining treatment, at least create the potential that a wrong decision will eventually be corrected or its impact mitigated. An erroneous decision to withdraw life-sustaining treatment, however, is not susceptible of correction. . . .

The Supreme Court of Missouri held that in this case the testimony adduced at trial did not amount to clear and convincing proof of the patient's desire to have hydration and nutrition withdrawn. . . . The testimony adduced at trial consisted primarily of Nancy Cruzan's statements made to a housemate about a year before her accident that she would not want to live should she face life as a "vegetable," and other observations to the same effect. The observations did not deal in terms with withdrawal of medical treatment or of hydration and nutrition. We cannot say that the Supreme Court of Missouri committed constitutional error in reaching the conclusion that it did.

Petitioners alternatively contend that Missouri must accept the "substituted judgment" of close family members even in the absence of substantial proof that their views reflect the views of the patient. They rely primarily upon our decisions in Michael H. v. Gerald D., 491 U.S. 110 (1989), and Parham v. J.R., 442 U.S. 584 (1979). . . . In *Michael H.*, we *upheld* the constitutionality of California's favored treatment of traditional family relationships; such a holding may not be turned around into a constitutional requirement that a State *must* recognize the primacy of those relationships in a situation like this. And in *Parham*, where the patient was a minor, we also *upheld* the constitutionality of a state scheme in which parents made certain decisions for mentally ill minors. Here again petitioners would seek to turn a decision which allowed a State to rely on family decisionmaking into a constitutional requirement that the State recognize such decisionmaking. But constitutional law does not work that way.

No doubt is engendered by anything in this record but that Nancy Cruzan's mother and father are loving and caring parents. If the State were required by the United States Constitution to repose a right of "substituted judgment" with anyone, the Cruzans would surely qualify. But we do not think the Due Process Clause requires the State to repose judgment on these matters with anyone but the patient herself. Close family members may have a strong feeling—a feeling not at all ignoble or unworthy, but not entirely disinterested, either—that they do not wish to witness the continuation of the life of a loved one which they regard as hopeless, meaningless, and even degrading. But there is no automatic assurance that the view of close family members will necessarily be the same as the patient's would have been had she been confronted with the prospect of her situation while competent. All of the reasons previously discussed for allowing Missouri to require clear and convincing evidence of the patient's wishes lead us to conclude that the State may choose to defer only to those wishes, rather than confide the decision to close family members. . . .

Justice O'CONNOR, concurring. . . .

I . . . write separately to emphasize that the Court does not today decide the issue whether a State must also give effect to the decisions of a surrogate decisionmaker. . . . In my view, such a duty may well be constitutionally required to protect the patient's liberty interest in refusing medical treatment. Few individuals provide explicit oral or written instructions regarding their intent to refuse medical treatment should they become incompetent. States which decline to consider any evidence other than such instructions may frequently fail to honor a patient's intent. Such failures might be avoided if the State considered an equally probative source of evidence: the patient's appointment of a proxy to make health care decisions on her behalf. Delegating the authority to make medical decisions to a family member or friend is becoming a common method of planning for the future. Several States have recognized the practical wisdom of such a procedure [by living wills and durable power of attorney statutes for health care decisionmaking]. Moreover, as patients are likely to select a family member as a surrogate, giving effect to a proxy's decisions may also protect the "freedom of personal choice in matters of . . . family life." Cleveland Board of Education v. LaFleur, 414 U.S. 632, 639 (1974).

[N]o national consensus has yet emerged on the best solution for this difficult and sensitive problem. Today we decide only that one State's practice does not violate the Constitution; the more challenging task of crafting appropriate procedures for safeguarding incompetents' liberty interests is entrusted to the "laboratory" of the States. . . .

Justice SCALIA, concurring. . . .

. . . I would have preferred that we announce, clearly and promptly, that the federal courts have no business in this field; that American law has always accorded the State the power to prevent, by force if necessary, suicide—including suicide by refusing to take appropriate measures necessary to preserve one's life; that the point at which life becomes "worthless," and the point at which the means necessary to preserve it become "extraordinary" or "inappropriate," are neither set forth in the Constitution nor known to the nine Justices of this Court any better than they are known to nine people picked at random from the Kansas City telephone directory; and hence, that even when it is demonstrated by clear and convincing evidence that a patient no longer wishes certain measures to be taken to preserve her life, it is up to the citizens of Missouri to decide, through their elected representatives, whether that wish will be honored. . . .

The text of the Due Process Clause [protects individuals] against deprivations of liberty "without due process of law." [N]o "substantive due process" claim can be maintained unless the claimant demonstrates that the State has deprived him of a right historically and traditionally protected against state interference. That cannot possibly be established here. At common law in England, a suicide—defined as one who "deliberately puts an end to his own existence, or commits any unlawful malicious act, the consequence of which is his own death," 4 W. Blackstone,

Commentaries *189—was criminally liable. . . . Thus, "there is no significant support for the claim that a right to suicide is so rooted in our tradition that it may be deemed 'fundamental' or 'implicit in the concept of ordered liberty.'" . . .

. . . Are there, then, no reasonable and humane limits that ought not to be exceeded in requiring an individual to preserve his own life? There obviously are, but they are not set forth in the Due Process Clause. . . . Our salvation is the Equal Protection Clause, which requires the democratic majority to accept for themselves and their loved ones what they impose on you and me. This Court need not, and has no authority to, inject itself into every field of human activity where irrationality and oppression may theoretically occur, and if it tries to do so it will destroy itself.

Justice BRENNAN, with whom Justice MARSHALL and Justice BLACKMUN join, dissenting. . . .

[I]f a competent person has a liberty interest to be free of unwanted medical treatment, as both the majority and Justice O'Connor concede, it must be fundamental. Whatever other liberties protected by the Due Process Clause are fundamental, "those liberties that are 'deeply rooted in this Nation's history and tradition'" are among them. [T]he State has no legitimate general interest in someone's life, completely abstracted from the interest of the person living that life, that could outweigh the person's choice to avoid medical treatment. . . .

Moreover, there may be considerable danger that Missouri's rule of decision would impair rather than serve any interest the State does have in sustaining life. Current medical practice recommends use of heroic measures if there is a scintilla of a chance that the patient will recover, on the assumption that the measures will be discontinued should the patient improve.

[In addition, Missouri's rule does not enhance the accuracy of a determination of Nancy Cruzan's wishes, because it] imposes a markedly asymmetrical evidentiary burden. Only evidence of specific statements of treatment choice made by the patient when competent is admissible to support a finding that the patient, now in a persistent vegetative state, would wish to avoid further medical treatment. Moreover, this evidence must be clear and convincing. No proof is required to support a finding that the incompetent person would wish to continue treatment. [Yet,] from the point of view of the patient, an erroneous decision in either direction is irrevocable. . . . Even more than its heightened evidentiary standard, the Missouri court's categorical exclusion of relevant evidence dispenses with any semblance of accurate factfinding. . . . While it might be a wise social policy to encourage people to furnish [a living will,] no general conclusion about a patient's choice can be drawn from the absence of formalities. . . .

Finally, I cannot agree with the majority that where it is not possible to determine what choice an incompetent patient would make, a State's role as parens patriae permits the State automatically to make that choice itself. [Even if family members and the patient might have different views, is] there any reason to suppose that a State is *more* likely to make the choice that the patient would have made than someone who knew the patient intimately? To ask this is to answer it. . . . .

[Justice Stevens, dissenting, writes that the Constitution requires respect for Nancy Cruzan's "own best interests."]

Notes and Questions

1. **Epilogue.** At a subsequent hearing, a probate court determined that the Cruzans had presented sufficient additional evidence to halt artificial nutrition and hydration. Nancy died 12 days after removal of the feeding tube. The outcome deeply troubled the hospital staff who had cared for her for seven years; they felt "violated and betrayed," observing that "it would be easier for them to cope with the process if Miss Cruzan were allowed to die quickly by lethal injection."[50] The case took its toll on the Cruzans as well, and Nancy's father committed suicide in 1996.

2. **A constitutional right?** Does the majority recognize a right on the part of *competent* patients to refuse life-sustaining treatment? To the extent that the majority finds such right, what is its constitutional source? Is it "fundamental"? Would legislation giving physicians discretion whether or not to follow the patient's request violate this right? See Christina Q. Nguyen, Comment, Death as Liberty, 49 U.S.F. L. Rev. 387 (2015). Does the right extend to incompetent patients?

3. **Rationale.** How does the rationale of *Cruzan* compare to the privacy-based rationale of In re Quinlan, 355 A.2d 647 (N.J. 1976), cited by the majority? Which rationale is more persuasive? What are the implications of each approach?

4. **History and tradition.** If the Court must look to history and tradition to determine whether an interest merits constitutional protection, then how should the Court resolve evidence of conflicting traditions, for example, the traditional prohibition against suicide (per Justice Scalia) or the tradition of patient self-determination (per Justice Brennan)?

5. **Choice.** The right to die, like the abortion decision, entails making a personal choice. How can such choices be made by incompetent individuals such as Nancy Cruzan? Why wasn't Nancy Cruzan's past expression of her preferences adequate? How can *prior* directives ever express what the patient wants *now*? See Nancy K. Rhoden, Litigating Life and Death, 102 Harv. L. Rev. 375, 410-419 (1988). What is "substituted judgment," to which the majority alludes? Should a court simply impute to an incompetent patient, who had not made her wishes known, what most people would prefer?

6. **Vision of the family.** What vision of the family emerges from the *Cruzan* opinions? Is this vision consistent with the portrayal of the family in the minors' abortion cases? Suppose that the family is divided? Compare the "asymmetrical evidentiary burden" approved in *Cruzan* (as characterized by dissenting Justice Brennan) with the asymmetry of requiring bypass proceedings for minors seeking abortions without parental involvement (but not for those carrying a pregnancy to term).

---

[50]. Anger in Hospital at Death Order, N.Y. Times, Dec. 16, 1990, §1, at 29.

7. Competing interests. Should courts be involved routinely in right-to-die cases to ascertain and weigh the competing interests? In situations of doubt, who should have the burden of proof? Should there be a presumption of family decisionmaking? On the other hand, *why* would the Constitution disallow a state to "err on the side of life" in response to a given request to withdraw nutrition and hydration from an incompetent patient? What practical effects might follow from *Cruzan*?

8. Advance directives. Justice O'Connor urges the use of patient-executed documents to avoid the dilemma in *Cruzan*. If Nancy Cruzan had executed a "living will" directing termination of treatment, would that have changed the result? Missouri law imposes two limitations on such advance directives that would have posed problems in this case. The statute excludes nutrition and hydration from "death prolonging procedures" that one may refuse, and it makes such declarations operative only for patients in a "terminal condition." Mo. Rev. Stat. §§459.010-459.025. Missouri (like many states), however, authorizes nomination of a surrogate decisionmaker for health care with specific authority to withhold or withdraw artificially supplied nutrition and hydration (Mo. Rev. Stat. §404.820).

The Uniform Health-Care Decisions Act allows a competent individual to declare in advance the wish to withhold or withdraw life-sustaining treatment (§§2-4). The Act also allows certain third parties to consent to the withholding or withdrawal of such treatment for incompetent patients who have made no effective declaration—in order of priority: a spouse, an adult child, a parent, an adult sibling (§5).

Federal law requires Medicare and similarly funded providers (hospitals, skilled nursing facilities, home health agencies, and hospice programs) to inform adult recipients of the right under state law to refuse treatment. 42 U.S.C. §1395cc(f). When Congress debated health care reform, ultimately enacting the ACA, coverage of consultations regarding end-of-life care was deleted after provoking accusations about federal "death panels." Later, opposition softened, with such coverage offered by private insurers, Medicaid in some states, and ultimately Medicare.[51]

9. Gender. Justice Scalia recommends resorting to the Equal Protection Clause. How would this approach work? Will it guard against unreasonable impositions of forced medical treatment? Unreasonable abortion restrictions? Do men and women have equal opportunities to exercise the right to die? Consider the following evidence of gender bias:

> Appellate court rulings show four major differences in how courts speak of previously competent women's or men's moral preferences. The first difference is the courts' view that a man's opinions are rational and a woman's remarks are unreflective, emotional, or immature. Second, women's moral agency in relation to medical decisions is often not recognized. Third, courts apply evidentiary standards differently to evidence about men's and women's preferences. Fourth, life-support dependent men are seen as subjected to medical assault; women are seen as vulnerable to medical neglect. Not all of these differences are present in any one case. Each difference (e.g., language describing a woman's reasoning as immature)

---

[51]. Robert Pear, New Medicare Rule Authorizes End-of-Life Consultations, N.Y. Times, Oct. 31, 2015, at A14.

is present in at least three cases of the gender to which it is attributed and none of the cases of the opposite gender.[52]

10. State experimentation. Justice O'Connor stresses that these problems belong in the "'laboratory' of the States." What are the likely consequences of this approach? Can a state prevent its domiciliaries from crossing state lines to evade restrictive laws? See In re Christine Busalacchi, 1991 WL 10048 (Mo. Ct. App. 1991) (enjoining father, who desires to remove daughter's feeding tube, from moving her to a more permissive state); I. Glenn Cohen, Circumvention Tourism, 97 Cornell L. Rev. 1309 (2012).

11. A constitutional right to assisted suicide? Do *Cruzan* and the abortion cases together establish a foundation for a constitutionally protected right to assisted suicide? Advocates of an expanded right to die that includes physician-assisted suicide claimed to find support in *Casey*'s "sweet-mystery-of-life passage," subsequently invoked in *Lawrence*, supra. See also Ronald Dworkin, Life's Dominion: An Argument About Abortion, Euthanasia, and Individual Freedom (1993).

Unpersuaded, the Supreme Court has upheld prohibitions against substantive due process challenge, rejecting the argument that *Casey* warranted "the sweeping conclusion that any and all important, intimate, and personal decisions are so protected." Washington v. Glucksberg, 521 U.S. 702, 727 (1997). See also Vacco v. Quill, 521 U.S. 793 (1997) (rejecting equal protection challenge). Does *Lawrence* require a second look at physician-assisted suicide? What are the implications of *Gonzales*, supra, for the issue? See generally Symposium, *Glucksberg* and *Quill* at Ten. Death, Dying and the Constitution, 106 Mich. L. Rev. 1453-1667 (2008).

12. "Death with Dignity" in Oregon. In declining to recognize a constitutional right to assisted suicide, the Court expressly left the issue for democratic resolution. *Glucksberg*, 521 U.S. at 735. A few states now allow the practice, with Oregon leading the way. Its legislation allows a competent adult who resides in Oregon, suffers from a terminal disease according to physicians, and voluntarily expresses a wish to die to request and then obtain, after a waiting period, medication "for the purpose of ending his or her life in a humane and dignified manner." Or. Rev. Stat. §127.805. According to 2014 data, 859 patients have died under the terms of the law since its passage.[53] Physician-assisted suicide is also permitted per voter initiative in Vermont (Vt. Stat. tit. 18 §5281) and Washington State (Wash. Rev. Code §70.245.020) and in Montana per state supreme court ruling (Baxter v. State, 224 P.3d 1211 (Mont. 2009)). Momentum for such reforms increased following the well-publicized case of Brittany Maynard, a terminally ill 29-year-old woman who moved from California to Oregon to take advantage of its law.[54] California then changed its law, becoming the fifth state to allow physician-assisted suicide.[55]

---

[52]. Steven H. Miles & Allison August, Courts, Gender and "The Right to Die," 18 Law, Med. & Health Care 85, 87 (1990).

[53]. Oregon Pub. Health Div., Death with Dignity Act—2014, http://public.health.oregon.gov/ProviderPartnerResources/EvaluationResearch/DeathwithDignityAct/Documents/year17.pdf.

[54]. See Brittany Maynard, My Right to Death with Dignity at 29, CNN, Nov. 2, 2014, http://www.cnn.com/2014/10/07/opinion/maynard-assisted-suicide-cancer-dignity/.

[55]. See Ian Lovett & Richard Pérez-Peña, Brown Signs "Right to Die" Into Law in California, N.Y.Times, Oct. 6, 2015, at A10. For the status of reform efforts in other states, see Death with Dignity Around the U.S. (July 6, 2015), http://www.deathwithdignity.org/advocates/national.

Do such laws advance autonomy, expanding the "private realm of family life"? Do they present a danger of involuntary euthanasia? Although critics contend that permitting assisted suicide poses special risks to undervalued and self-sacrificing persons (including women, minorities, and the elderly), empirical data show members of vulnerable groups are less likely than others to select aid in dying. See Jackson Pickett, Can Legalization Improve End-of-Life Care? An Empirical Analysis of the Results of the Legalization of Euthanasia and Physician-Assisted Suicide in the Netherlands and Oregon, 16 Elder L.J. 333, 363-365 (2009). Other critics argue that the law's scope should be broadened to cover patients with dementia or severe physical impairments such as Lou Gehrig's disease.

Congress has prohibited the use of federal funds for assisted suicide. 42 U.S.C. §§14401-14408; 42 U.S.C. §238o; 25 U.S.C. §1621x; 38 U.S.C. §1707.

Problems

1. Terri Schiavo, age 26 and living in Florida, suffered severe brain damage from oxygen deprivation resulting from cardiac arrest of undetermined origin. After attempted treatments failed to improve her condition, which physicians diagnosed as a persistent vegetative state (PVS), her husband and guardian, Michael Schiavo, eventually sought to withdraw her artificial nutrition and hydration (feeding tube), based on her previously asserted wishes. Her parents, Robert and Mary Schindler, objected, disputing both Michael's claims about Terri's wishes and the PVS diagnosis, and sued to enjoin removal of the feeding tube. They also persuaded then–Florida governor Jeb Bush, the Florida legislature, and the U.S. Congress, as well as pro-life and disability rights activists, to intervene in their effort to continue use of the feeding tube. How should the law address such controversies involving divided families? In the wake of this highly publicized controversy, what law reform measures would you recommend? Why?

For analyses of the controversy, see, e.g., Lois Shepherd, If That Ever Happens to Me: Making Life and Death Decisions After Terri Schiavo (2009); Rebecca Dresser, Schiavo and Contemporary Myths About Dying, 61 U. Miami L. Rev. 821 (2007). For suggested approaches, see, e.g., Nancy N. Dubler & Carol B. Liebman, Bioethics Mediation: A Guide to Shaping Shared Solutions (2004); I. Glenn Cohen, Negotiating Death: ADR and End of Life Decision-making, 9 Harv. Negot. L. Rev. 253 (2004).

2. A.C. was first diagnosed with cancer at the age of 13. At age 27, while her illness was in remission, she married, and she and her husband decided to start a family. When she was 25 weeks pregnant, doctors found an apparently inoperable tumor. After admission to the hospital in the District of Columbia, when asked if she really wanted to have her baby, A.C. replied that she did. Over the next few days, A.C.'s condition worsened considerably. Accordingly, members of the medical staff treating A.C. assembled, along with her family, in A.C.'s room. The doctors then informed her that her illness was terminal, and A.C. agreed to palliative treatment designed to extend her life until at least her twenty-eighth week of pregnancy, which would improve the chances of a positive outcome for the fetus. A.C. knew that the palliative treatment she had chosen presented some increased risk to the fetus, but she opted for this course both to prolong her life

for at least another two weeks and to maintain her own comfort. When asked if she still wanted to have the baby, A.C. replied, "I don't know—I think so." As the day moved toward evening, A.C.'s condition grew still worse, and she consented to intubation to facilitate her breathing.

The hospital sought a declaratory judgment authorizing delivery by caesarean section. A trial judge convened a hearing at the hospital. The court appointed counsel for both A.C. and the fetus, and the District of Columbia was permitted to intervene for the fetus as parens patria. A neonatologist testified that the chances of survival for a 26-week fetus delivered at the hospital might be as high as 80 percent, but that this particular fetus, given the mother's medical history, had only a 50 to 60 percent chance of survival. This physician estimated that the risk of substantial impairment for the fetus, if delivered promptly, would be less than 20 percent. However, she noted that the fetus's condition was worsening appreciably at a rapid rate, and another doctor—an obstetrician who was one of A.C.'s treating physicians—stated that any delay in delivering the child by caesarean section would lessen its chances of survival. Another treating obstetrician testified that A.C. would probably die within 24 hours if absolutely nothing else were done. This doctor also stated that A.C. had limited ability to interact because of the heavy sedation applied to maintain her ventilatory function.

There was no evidence showing that A.C. discussed with her physician the option of a caesarean section before her twenty-eighth week of pregnancy. A.C.'s mother opposed surgical intervention, testifying that A.C. wanted "to live long enough to hold that baby" and that she expected to do so, "even though she knew she was terminal."

On these facts, should the trial court issue a declaratory judgment ordering a caesarean section to try to save the fetus? Has A.C. provided sufficient consent? Suppose she has not. On what basis should the court decide? What reasons support your conclusion? What additional information should the judge have? What role should A.C.'s husband play? Her parents? To what extent does your analysis of the case change if you know that, after a court-ordered caesarean, the baby lived only for a few hours and A.C. died two days later? What legal principles should guide courts faced with such situations? See In re A.C., 573 A.2d 1235 (D.C. 1990) (en banc).

Does the case represent a "maternal-fetal conflict" to which abortion jurisprudence might apply? Which doctrines from abortion cases should govern? Compare Helen Alvaré, Gonzales v. Carhart: Bringing Abortion Law Back into the Family Law Fold, 69 Mont. L. Rev. 409 (2008), with Donald H. Regan, Rewriting Roe v. Wade, 77 Mich. L. Rev. 1569 (1979).

Would a more helpful analysis present all such situations as "maternal-doctor conflicts," rather than maternal-fetal conflicts, given physicians' "central role in generating and escalating these conflicts"? See Michelle Oberman, Mothers and Doctors' Orders: Unmasking the Doctor's Fiduciary Role in Maternal-Fetal Conflicts, 94 Nw. U. L. Rev. 451, 454, 500 (2000). See also Rona Kaufman Kitchen, Holistic Pregnancy: Rejecting the Theory of the Adversarial Mother, 26 Hastings Women's L.J. 207 (2015). Should they be viewed as reflections of the subordination of women generally and "outsider women" in particular? See April L. Cherry, *Roe*'s Legacy: The Nonconsensual Medical Treatment of Pregnant Women and Implications for Female Citizenship, 6 U. Pa. J. Const. L. 723, 740-751 (2004); Linda C. Fentiman, Are Mothers Hazardous to Their Children's Health?: Law, Culture, and the Framing of Risk, 21 Va. J. Soc. Pol'y & L. 295 (2014).

II

Getting Married

A. Introduction: Public Versus Private Dimensions of Courtship and Marriage

The decision to marry is one of life's most important choices. This chapter explores the law that governs the individual's decision to marry, emphasizing both the private nature of the decision and the state's regulatory authority. What are the personal interests at stake? The state interests? What are the constitutional limits on state regulation?

The chapter opens with a focus on the premarital relationship, including courtship, engagement, and premarital agreements. Next, the chapter examines a broad range of restrictions on entry into marriage, including substantive and procedural regulations. Rapid changes in this regulatory regime in recent years challenge some of family law's basic foundations—the role of tradition, the importance of gender, and the understanding of marriage itself.

1. Courtship Patterns

The premarital relationship has become increasingly private. The excerpts below explore the public and private dimensions of courtship over time.

John Demos, A Little Commonwealth: Family Life in Plymouth Colony

152, 154-155, 157-162 (2000)

[W]hen a courtship had developed to a certain point of intensity, the parents became directly involved. [If a man proposed marriage without first securing parental consent, the law provided fines or corporal punishment but placed limits on the power of parents to refuse their consent. Following parental approval, a series of steps remained.]

[T]he "betrothal" or "contract" [was] a simple ceremony which bears comparison to our own custom of "engagement." [This] was a very serious undertaking [as] failure to fulfill such a contract would create the likelihood of legal action. [S]exual intimacies between the contracted parties fell into a category all their own. [Although they were not officially condoned, the usual penalty was relatively light.]

[A]nother formal step became necessary: the "publishing" of the banns [that is, posting notice of the parties' intent to marry for 14 days or making an announcement to this effect three times in a public meeting]. [Still another important matter] was a set of transactions designed to underwrite the economic welfare of the contracted couple. [A] young man would receive the bulk of his portion in the form of land and housing, a woman would be given a variety of domestic furnishings, cattle, and/or money. . . .

[F]ourteen days was the minimum interval allowable between the betrothal ceremony and the wedding itself—between "contract and covenant," in the language of the time. [M]ost couples waited considerably longer: two or three months seems to have been quite customary. [T]radition has it that this was an occasion for sober reflection, and if need be, for reconsideration—before the final step was taken. . . .

Beth L. Bailey, From Front Porch to Back Seat: Courtship in Twentieth-Century America

19-22 (1988)

Between 1890 and 1925, dating . . . had gradually, almost imperceptibly, become a universal custom in America. By the 1930s it had transcended its origins. [Dating had its origins in the urban lower classes, who lacked the family space (such as the parlor) in which to conduct courtship activities and who took advantage of the excitement and opportunities presented by the urban environment.] The rise of dating was usually explained, quite simply, by the invention of the automobile [but the automobile simply accelerated] a process already well under way. . . .

Dating not only transformed the outward modes and conventions of American courtship, it also changed the distribution of control and power in courtship. One change was generational: the dating system lessened parental control and gave young men and women more freedom. The dating system also shifted power from women to men. [The older courtship practice of "calling" on a woman] gave women a large portion of control. First of all, courtship took place within the girl's home—in women's "sphere," as it was called in the nineteenth century—or at entertainments largely devised and presided over by women. Dating moved courtship out of the home and into man's sphere—the world outside the home. . . .

Second, in the calling system, the woman took the initiative. . . . Contrast these strictures with advice on dating etiquette from the 1940s and 1950s: An advice book for men and women warns that "girls who [try] to usurp the right of boys to choose their own dates" will "ruin a good dating career. . . ." An invitation to go out on a date . . . was an invitation into man's world—not simply because dating took place in the public sphere (commonly defined as belonging to men) [but also] because dating moved courtship into the world of the economy. Money—men's money—was at the center of the dating system. [M]oney shift[ed] control and initiative to men by making them the "hosts," [and] led contemporaries to see dating as a system of exchange. . . .

Jennifer Egan, Love in the Time of No Time[1]

N.Y. Times, Nov. 23, 2004, §6 (Mag.), at 66

Online dating is a key source of potential partners.

. . . Online dating is the most lucrative form of legal paid online content. [S]ocietal reasons for this flurry of activity are so profound that it's almost surprising that online dating didn't take off sooner: Americans are marrying later and so are less likely to meet their spouses in high school or college. They spend much of their lives at work, but the rise in sexual harassment suits has made workplace relationships tricky at best. Among a more secular and mobile population, social institutions like churches and clubs have faded in importance. That often leaves little more than the "bar scene" as a source of potential mates. . . .

Improved technology—namely, the proliferation of broadband and the abrupt ubiquity of digital cameras—partly explains online dating's surge in popularity. More critical still is the fact that the first generation of kids to come

[1]. The full article is available at http://jenniferegan.com/non-fiction/love-in-the-time-of-no-time.

of age on the Internet are now young adults, still mostly single, and for them, using the Web to find what they need is as natural as using a lung to suck in air. They get jobs and apartments and plane tickets online—why not dates?

Still, a fair number of people continue to feel a stigma about dating online, ranging from the waning belief that it's a dangerous refuge for the desperate and unsavory to the milder but still unappealing notion that it's a public bazaar for the sort of people who thrive on selling themselves. The shopping metaphor is apt; online dating involves browsing and choosing among a seemingly infinite array of possible mates. But those who see a transactional approach to coupling as something new and unseemly would do well to pick up a novel by Jane Austen, where characters are introduced alongside their incomes. There is nothing new about the idea of marriage as a business transaction. . . .

How do [online personals change] the nature of courtship? [F]or the serious online dater, the personal profile—the page allotted to each client on dating Web sites—quickly assumes a pivotal importance. . . . Dating profiles are works in progress, continually edited and tweaked, fortified with newer, more flattering pictures. . . . The exact progression from first contact to in-the-flesh-meeting varies among daters and age groups. For younger people, who grew up with instant-messaging programs, e-mail will often lead to an instant-message exchange (or several), followed by a meeting; those over 30 tend to prefer the phone. . . .

. . . Relationships begun online have a tendency to end there too. This generally happens one of two ways: by e-mail or by no e-mail—i.e., someone disappears. . . . People in fledgling relationships begun online can vanish from one another's lives with the same breathtaking efficiency as a line of text deleted from a word processing document. . . . For some, an awareness of this exit strategy permeates the enterprise, allowing them to skimp on the niceties they would more or less have to extend toward a person they were likely to meet again. . . .

[E]ven the most jaundiced view of online personals must contend with the fact that people manage to find one another this way—again and again and again. . . .

The success rate of online dating is high. Almost one-fourth of online daters have entered into marriage or a long-term relationship with someone they met through a dating site or dating app.[2]

2. The Marriage Contract

A classic question asks: Is marriage a contract (a private agreement between two parties) or a status (a public institution regulated by the state)? Or does marriage retain features of both? In the following classic case affirming the state's right to regulate marriage and divorce, the Supreme Court addressed these questions.

[2]. PEW Research Center, Online Dating and Relationships, Oct. 21, 2013, http://www.pewinternet.org/2013/10/21/online-dating-relationships/.

MAYNARD v. HILL

125 U.S. 190 (1887)

Mr. Justice Field.

[While] marriage is often termed by text writers and in decisions of courts as a civil contract—generally to indicate that it must be founded upon the agreement of the parties, and does not require any religious ceremony for its solemnization—it is something more than a mere contract. The consent of the parties is of course essential to its existence, but when the contract to marry is executed by the marriage, a relation between the parties is created which they cannot change. Other contracts may be modified, restricted, or enlarged, or entirely released upon the consent of the parties. Not so with marriage. The relation once formed, the law steps in and holds the parties to various obligations and liabilities. It is an institution, in the maintenance of which in its purity the public is deeply interested, for it is the foundation of the family and of society, without which there would be neither civilization nor progress.

[The Supreme Court then cited approvingly a state supreme court's description of marriage as]

> a social relation like that of parent and child, the obligations of which arise not from the consent of concurrent minds, but are the creation of the law itself, a relation the most important, as affecting the happiness of individuals, the first step from barbarism to incipient civilization, the purest tie of social life, and the true basis of human progress. [Adams v. Palmer, 51 Me. 481, 484-485 (Me. 1863)] . . . .

Henry Maine, Ancient Law

163-165 (1963)

The movement of the progressive societies has been uniform in one respect. [I]t has been distinguished by the gradual dissolution of family dependency and the growth of individual obligation in its place. The Individual is steadily substituted for the Family, as the unit of which civil laws take account. The advance has been accomplished at varying rates of celerity, and there are societies not absolutely stationary in which the collapse of the ancient organization can only be perceived by careful study. . . . But, whatever its pace, the change has not been subject to reaction or recoil, and apparent retardations will be found to have been occasioned through the absorption of archaic ideas and customs from some entirely foreign source. Nor is it difficult to see what is the tie between man and man which replaces by degrees those forms of reciprocity in rights and duties which have their origin in the Family. It is Contract. Starting, as from one terminus of history, from a condition of society in which all the relations of Persons are summed up in the relations of Family, we seem to have steadily moved towards a phase of social order in which all these relations arise from the free agreement of individuals. In Western Europe the progress achieved in this direction has been considerable. Thus the status of the Slave has disappeared—it has been superseded by the contractual relation of the servant to his master. The status of the Female under Tutelage, if the tutelage be understood of persons other than her husband, has also ceased to exist; from her coming of age to her marriage all the relations she may form are relations of contract. [W]e may say that the movement of the progressive societies has hitherto been a movement *from Status to Contract.*

Susan Moller Okin, Justice, Gender, and the Family

122-123 (1989)

[M]arriage itself has long been regarded as a contract, though it is a very peculiar one: it is a contract that does not conform with the *principles* (let alone the counter principles) of liberal contract doctrine. It is a preformed status contract, which restricts the parties' freedom to choose their partners (for example, there must be only one partner, and [traditionally] of the opposite sex) and of which they are not free to choose the terms.

The courts' refusal to enforce explicit contracts between husband and wife has been by no means completely attributable to reluctance to intrude into a private community supposedly built upon trust. It has been due at least as much to the fact that the courts have regarded the terms of marriage as already established. When, for example, they have refused to enforce intramarital agreements in which wives have agreed to forgo support for other consideration, and in which husbands have agreed to pay their wives for work done in a family business, they have done so on the grounds that the wife's right to support, in the former case, and her obligation to provide services for her husband, in the latter, are fixed by the marriage contract itself. Likewise, when courts have showed a reluctance to enforce the terms of the preformed contracted itself—for example, refusing to establish a level of adequate support that a wife must receive—it has been on the grounds that, so long as husband and wife cohabit, it is up to him as the family head to determine such matters. Another respect in which marriage is an anomalous contract is that the parties to it are not required to be familiar with the terms of the relationship into which they are entering. . . .

B. Preparing to Marry: Premarital Controversies

1. Breach of Promise to Marry

RIVKIN v. POSTAL

2001 WL 1077952 (Tenn. Ct. App. 2001)

KOCH, J.

. . . David Rivkin and Lori Postal met in April 1994 at a music convention in Memphis. Mr. Rivkin was a successful, award-winning producer [who was married with three children]. Ms. Postal was a 28-year-old divorcée [who] sold bathing suits at wholesale and had also started a record label. Ms. Postal was attending the Memphis convention to obtain a record contract for a singer and a band that she represented. . . . Within a short period of time, they began living together.

In early 1995, Ms. Postal discovered she was pregnant. . . . Mr. Rivkin suggested an abortion, but Ms. Postal did not agree. Their child was born in September 1995. Shortly after their child was born, Mr. Rivkin sold the house in Memphis, [and they moved to the Nashville area where they believed that he would have greater success as a producer.] Mr. Rivkin was the parties' sole source of support, and he was able to provide an exceptionally affluent lifestyle for Ms. Postal and their child despite his continuing obligations to his wife and children. He purchased a $420,000 home in Williamson County and horses for Ms. Postal. He also hired a nanny for the child. Not surprisingly, Ms. Postal took to this lifestyle. She did not work outside the home but rather spent her time raising the parties' child, training her horses, and entertaining her personal friends and Mr. Rivkin's business associates.

But all was not well with the parties. They entered counseling in an effort to save their relationship. One of their problems stemmed from Ms. Postal's concern that her family knew that she was living with a married man and had given birth to his child. She insisted that Mr. Rivkin buy her an engagement ring to enable her to save face with her family. When Mr. Rivkin did not purchase a ring for her, Ms. Postal ordered a ring herself. [She] told her parents that she and Mr. Rivkin were planning to wed after he was divorced, and Mr. Rivkin did not contradict her. However, the parties themselves never discussed specific wedding plans. . . .

Mr. Rivkin was finally divorced from his wife in March 1997. [Three months later, he ended the relationship with Ms. Postal.] [N]either party followed Emily Post's sage advice "to take the high road—and move on." In September 1997, Mr. Rivkin filed suit [seeking] partition of the parties' jointly-owned property and the return of his personal property that was still in Ms. Postal's possession. Ms. Postal responded with a counterclaim seeking damages for breach of promise to marry. . . .

In England, before the founding of this country, questions touching on marriage and breach of a promise of marriage were chiefly the province of the ecclesiastical courts. . . . Eventually, as marriage began to be viewed as "largely a property transaction, entered into as much for material advantages as for reasons of sentiment," actions for breach of promise to marry found their way into the King's Courts [where the parties obtained damages].

The common-law action for breach of promise to marry made its way to the American colonies along with most of the common law of England. Here, it started out as "popular means of soothing the sufferings of rejected love." In time, however, it became subject to abuse. Borrowing ideas from tort law, the courts began permitting juries to award punitive damages. Most breach of promise to marry actions were brought by women against men, and men's fears of excessive verdicts and their distaste for the scandal surrounding such suits gave women the power to wield the cause of action almost as blackmail.

By the 1930s, newspapers were publishing accounts of "spectacular 'extortion and blackmail rackets'" based on these claims. The publicity of the "unfounded suits, perjury, and excessive verdicts at the hands of . . . seemingly ever gullible [juries] armed with unrestrained discretion" eventually prompted a movement to reform these claims. Beginning with Indiana in 1935, the states began enacting statutes aimed at ending the perceived abuses associated with breach of promise claims.

Many states abolished the cause of action altogether, prompting courts to jump on a bandwagon of sorts that some thought went too far. It became increasingly evident that the pendulum was swinging too far in the other direction. The barriers erected to correct one evil gave legal protection to another. The courts, perhaps overzealous in their interpretation of legislative intent, construed these statutes as prohibiting tort actions between formerly betrothed parties for fraud and deceit.

Tennessee chose a middle course. Rather than abolish the common-law cause of action for breach of promise to marry, this state chose to rein it in a bit. In 1949, the Tennessee General Assembly passed [Tenn. Code Ann. §§36-3-401 to -405] which, according to its caption, was designed "to prevent certain injustices in suits for damages for the breach of promise or contract of marriage." This act circumscribes breach of promise claims in four significant ways [by providing that these claims could not be joined with other damage claims; requiring that promises or contracts of marriage could only be established using either signed, written evidence of the promise or contract or the testimony of at least two disinterested witnesses; requiring juries to consider the parties' age and experience in calculating damages; and, prohibiting punitive damages in cases where the alleged breaching party was over 60 years old].

. . . To meet [Ms. Postal's] burden of proof in this case, Tenn. Code Ann. §36-3-401 requires her to present either "written evidence of such contract, signed by the party against whom the action is brought" or with the testimony of "at least two disinterested witnesses." . . . We turn first to the "written evidence." [O]ne month after he purchased the Williamson County house, Mr. Rivkin executed a quitclaim deed conveying the property to himself and Ms. Postal as joint tenants with right of survivorship. . . .

"It is obvious," as one treatise puts it, "that not only are most engagements to marry arrived at informally and without witnesses or written record, but in many instances there is no explicit exchange of promises at all." [1 Homer H. Clark, Law of Domestic Relations §1.2 (1968).] Accordingly, proof of an engagement would be impossible if the plaintiff were required to produce evidence that at some specific moment the parties formally exchanged promises and reduced these promises to writing. Tenn. Code Ann. §36-3-401 is not intended to go that far. Rather, it calls for signed, written evidence that the parties were, by mutual agreement, on the way to becoming husband and wife. Many kinds of writings would suffice.[10]

Mr. Rivkin testified that he gave Ms. Postal a joint tenant's interest in the Williamson County house as a way of making sure that their child would be provided for should something happen to him. [He] never explained to her why he quitclaimed an interest in the Williamson County property to her.

Thus, the only evidence we have regarding the significance of the deed is the deed itself. Nothing within the four corners of the deed alludes to any promise or contract of marriage or to the parties' betrothed status. Executing quitclaim

10. While not intended to be an exhaustive list, the following signed writings might fit the bill: an application for a marriage license, an attested petition to waive the age or waiting requirements for marriage, correspondence between the parties, writing dealing with wedding arrangements, or prenuptial agreements.

deeds is not only within the province of persons who have agreed or contracted to marry the grantee named in the deed. Quitclaim deeds are commonly used for business transactions between partners, conveyances between family members, cleaning up a title for title insurance purposes, or gifts. Thus, in light of the ubiquitous nature of quitclaim deeds, we decline to hold that an unexplained quitclaim deed between an unmarried man and an unmarried woman, without much, much more, suffices as signed, written evidence of a promise of marriage. . . .

Without a writing signed by Mr. Rivkin, Ms. Postal's only remaining avenue for proving that Mr. Rivkin promised to marry her consisted of presenting at least two disinterested witnesses who could substantiate Mr. Rivkin's promise. [T]he only witnesses she called regarding this issue were her parents. . . . While it is doubtful that a claimant's parent can ever be a disinterested witness in cases of this sort, Ms. Postal's parents are clearly not disinterested witnesses because at the time of trial they were also Ms. Postal's creditors. [W]e have concluded that Ms. Postal failed to carry the statutory burden of proof placed on persons seeking money damages for a breach of promise or contract of marriage. . . .

Notes and Questions

1. Majority view. Only a few jurisdictions still recognize the claim for breach of promise to marry. See, e.g., Dellinger v. Barnes, 218 N.C. App. 454 (N.C. Ct. App. 2012). Some of these states impose limitations. See, e.g., Md. Code Ann., Fam. Law §3-102 (permitting action only if plaintiff is pregnant); Tex. Civ. Prac. & Rem. Code Ann. §16.002 (setting a one-year statute of limitations). Do these limitations, as well as the limitation in *Rivkin,* appropriately "rein in" the cause of action?

2. Historical background. The modern action of breach of promise reflects Roman, Germanic, and canon law influences. In early Roman law, the consequences of a broken promise to marry were mild, reflecting a belief in contractual freedom.[3] In contrast, Germanic custom (adopting a moral stance) awarded damages to "punish" the breach.[4] In both traditions, the consequences were more severe if the woman broke the engagement. The Germanic view of marriage influenced English ecclesiastical courts.[5]

Criticisms of the action first emerged in the nineteenth century. In America, the controversy culminated in a movement in the 1930s when many states enacted statutes (termed "heartbalm" or "anti-heartbalm" legislation) to eliminate the action. Parliament abolished the action in 1970.[6]

---

[3]. Patrick MacChombaich de Coloquhoun, 1 A Summary of the Roman Civil Law 455 (1988). See also H.F. Jolowicz & Barry Nicholas, Historical Introduction to the Study of Roman Law 233 (3d ed. 1972).

[4]. Rudolf Huebner, A History of Germanic Private Law 601 (1918); Paul Weidenbaum, Breach of Promise in Private International Law, 14 N.Y.U. L.Q. Rev. 451, 452 (1937).

[5]. Jean Brissaud, A History of French Private Law 99 (1912); 3 William Blackstone, Commentaries *92-94.

[6]. Law Reform (Miscellaneous Provisions) Act, 1970, ch. 33, §1 (Eng.). On the abolition movement in the United States, see Joanna L. Grossman & Lawrence M. Friedman, Inside the Castle: Law and the Family in Twentieth-Century America 96-106 (2011).

3. Damages. Breach of promise to marry is a hybrid action, reflecting roots in both contract and tort law. Traditionally, a plaintiff could recover the monetary and social value of the marriage (expectation damages), as well as expenses incurred in preparation for the marriage (reliance damages). Damages for mental anguish and humiliation, not normally compensable in contract, could also be recovered. Punitive damages are sometimes permitted.

In light of contemporary social norms and values, should states abolish such actions? If not, what damages should they allow? Loss of anticipated social position? Expectation damages? Reliance damages? Damages for emotional distress, or only economic loss? How significant are reliance damages for a broken engagement? Consider the average cost of a wedding of $31,000.[7] As the wedding approaches, few costs are recoverable in the event of cancellation.

> Engagement rings can usually be returned for a full refund for 60 to 100 days after purchase. But some cities, including New York, allow caterers and hotels to charge for services and rooms that cannot be rebooked when canceled with less than six month[s'] notice. Wedding gown makers typically require an initial nonrefundable deposit of half the price of the dress, with the balance on delivery. The week before the wedding, the cake and flowers are delivered. When an engagement is broken the day of the wedding, almost none of the cost can be recovered.[8]

Should couples have premarital agreements that specify responsibility for expenses if the wedding is canceled? Should they purchase "wedding insurance"?

4. Defenses. Traditional defenses to breach-of-promise claims include physical and mental defects, plaintiff's lack of chastity or love for the defendant, and mutuality of the decision to end the engagement. Should a plaintiff's obsessive-compulsive disorder excuse a defendant's performance? See Wildey v. Springs, 840 F. Supp. 1259 (N.D. Ill. 1994), *rev'd*, 47 F.3d 1475 (7th Cir. 1995). Should public policy preclude enforcement if unmarried parties are living together at the time of the promise? See Kelley v. Cooper, 751 S.E.2d 889 (Ga. Ct. App. 2013).

5. Seduction. At common law, tort liability existed for seduction (i.e., consent to sexual intercourse by an unmarried, previously chaste, woman in reliance on a false promise to marry). The action was maintainable *not* by the woman, but by one entitled to her services (such as her father or someone in loco parentis). A few jurisdictions still recognize the tort for minors. See, e.g., Alaska Stat. §09.15.020; Md. Code Ann., Fam. Law §5-206. Some states impose criminal liability. See, e.g., Mich. Comp. Laws §750.532. Should legislatures abolish such actions, given that a woman's loss of virginity no longer adversely affects marital prospects? On criminalization of seduction, see Melissa Murray, Marriage as Punishment, 112 Colum. L. Rev. 1 (2012).

---

[7]. Quentin Fottrell, American Wedding Costs Soar 16% in Four Years, Market Watch, Mar. 14, 2015, http://www.marketwatch.com/story/american-wedding-costs-soar-16-in-four-years-2015-03-12.

[8]. Keith Bradsher, Ditching Your Betrothed May Cost You: Wedding Rings, Gowns, Cakes, and Deposits Add Up, S.F. Chron., Mar. 20, 1990, at B5.

6. Online dating fraud. Fraudulent representations regarding marital status, height, wealth, age, and weight are common in online dating.[9] Suppose the online dating service advertises that it serves only a specific population (e.g., a given religious faith, race, or ethnic group). Should such claims make the service responsible for misrepresentations? Should antidiscrimination laws apply? See Elizabeth F. Emens, Intimate Discrimination: The State's Role in the Accidents of Sex and Love, 122 Harv. L. Rev. 1307 (2009).

Only a few states regulate online services for purposes of consumer safety. Should state law require that online dating services conduct mandatory background checks? How effective is such screening? New Jersey became the first state in 2008 to require dating sites to *disclose* whether they perform criminal background checks (although without requiring actual screening). N.J. Stat. Ann. §56:8-171. Three other states (Illinois, New York, and Texas) also adopted regulations.[10] However, some of the latter states merely require inclusion of safety notifications (e.g., N.Y. Gen. Bus. Law § 394-cc). Subsequently several online services reached an agreement with the California Attorney General to screen for sexual predators against sex offender registries. The agreement stemmed from a lawsuit by a Match.com user who was attacked by a date who turned out to be a registered sex offender.[11]

Are such safety concerns unique to *online* dating? Should online service providers face liability for these risks of online dating? Or does such exposure "seriously and unnecessarily" threaten the websites' success? See Lindsey A. Datte, Chaperoning Love Online: Online Dating Liability and the Wavering Application of CDA §230, 20 Cardozo J.L. & Gender 769 (2014) (so arguing).

7. Class and gender. Historically, most breach-of-promise plaintiffs were women (often working-class women). The decline of such claims parallels the decline in the value of middle-class female chastity. Lawrence M. Friedman, Guarding Life's Dark Secrets: Legal and Social Controls over Reputation, Propriety, and Privacy 205-212 (2007).

8. Conflict of laws. May a plaintiff recover for breach of promise to marry if the "promise" occurs in a jurisdiction that recognizes the cause of action, but the "breach" occurs in a jurisdiction that does not? See Callahan v. Parker, 824 N.Y.S.2d 768 (Sup. Ct. 2006) (dismissing claim based on statute banning such suits whether arising "within or without the state").

---

[9]. Jonathan Sidener, Tall Tales: Fibs About Height, Wealth, Age, and Weight Not Uncommon at Online Dating Sites, San Diego Union-Trib., Feb. 9, 2004, at C1 (noting that 11 percent of clients are married).

[10]. Sharon Jayson, Online and Mobile Dating Face Privacy, Safety Concerns, USA Today, Mar. 27, 2014, http://www.usatoday.com/story/news/nation/2014/02/27/online-dating-privacy/6957331/.

[11]. David Lazarus, Dating Sites Finally Meeting Responsibility, L.A. Times, Mar. 23, 2012, at 1. See generally Phyllis Coleman, Online Dating: When "Mr. (or Ms.) Right" Turns out All Wrong, Sue the Service!, 36 Okla. City U. L. Rev. 139, 144 (2011).

Problem

Marilyn is dating Donald, a married man, when she discovers that she is pregnant. He promises her that if she has the abortion, he will pay her $75,000 plus medical and legal expenses. He also tells her that he will marry her when his divorce is final and that they can later have a baby together. Marilyn accepts payment and has the abortion. When they break up, she sues for intentional and negligent infliction of emotional distress, battery, fraud, and misrepresentation. She alleges that the settlement agreement is unconscionable, violates public policy, and was subject to duress. Donald moves for summary judgment on the ground that the jurisdiction bans claims for breach of promise to marry. What result? See M.N. v. D.S., 616 N.W.2d 284 (Minn. Ct. App. 2000).

2. Gifts in Contemplation of Marriage

CAMPBELL v. ROBINSON

726 S.E.2d 221 (S.C. Ct. App. 2012)

THOMAS, J.

These cross appeals arise out of a broken engagement between Matthew Campbell and Ashley Robinson. . . . Campbell proposed and presented a ring to Robinson in December 2005. In a spring 2006 phone conversation, they agreed to postpone the wedding. The engagement was later cancelled, and a dispute ensued over ownership of the ring.

. . . At trial, Robinson testified the engagement ended simply because Campbell cancelled it. She also testified that after the engagement was cancelled, she asked Campbell twice whether she should return the ring. She maintained that Campbell, in response to her inquiries, said she should keep the ring. Campbell testified that he gave Robinson the ring believing they would get married. He denied ending the engagement by himself and contended the cancellation was mutual. He also denied telling Robinson that she should keep the ring. He contended Robinson refused to give him the ring after he asked for its return. [He brought an action against Robinson to seek return of the engagement ring.]

An engagement ring by its very nature is a symbol of the donor's continuing devotion to the donee. Once an engagement is cancelled, the ring no longer holds that significance. Thus, if a party presents evidence a ring was given in contemplation of marriage, the ring is an engagement ring. As an engagement ring, the gift is impliedly conditioned upon the marriage taking place. Until the condition underlying the gift is fulfilled, the attempted gift is unenforceable and must be returned to the donor upon the donor's request.

The person challenging the assertions that the ring is an engagement ring and therefore impliedly conditioned upon marriage has the burden of presenting evidence to overcome those assertions. This burden may be satisfied by presenting evidence showing that the ring was not given in contemplation of marriage—it was not an engagement ring—or was not conditioned upon the marriage. If the parties do not dispute that the ring was originally an engagement ring conditioned upon the marriage, the burden may also be satisfied by presenting evidence establishing the ring subsequently became the challenger's property.

Jurisdictions differ on whether ownership of an engagement ring may be based upon fault in the breakup. Courts that do consider fault generally reason that it is unfair for a person to retain the fruit of a broken promise. In contrast, courts with a "no-fault" approach often base their decision upon the abolishment of heart balm actions, adoption of no-fault divorce, desire to limit courtroom dramatics, and reduction of the difficulty in determining the issue of what constitutes fault in the decline of a relationship.

We hold that the consideration of fault has no place in determining ownership of an engagement ring. . . . In other contexts, the culpability of one's conduct is determined by legal standards such as the reasonable person. In contrast, no legal standard exists by which a fact finder can adjudge culpability or fault in a prenuptial breakup. See, e.g., Aronow v. Silver, 538 A.2d 851, 853-854 (N.J. Super. Ct. Ch. Div. 1987) ("What fact justifies the breaking of an engagement? The absence of a sense of humor? Differing musical tastes? Differing political views? . . . They must be approached with intelligent care and should not happen without a decent assurance of success. When either party lacks that assurance, for whatever reason, the engagement should be broken. No justification is needed. Either party may act. Fault, impossible to fix, does not count."). . . .

[T]he adoption of the fault approach could cause ironic results. Two of the main purposes of an engagement are to prepare the couple for marriage and test the permanency of their compatibility. In some circumstances, the fault approach may penalize a party who innocently recognizes the couple's incompatibility. On the other hand, adoption of the no-fault approach would not diminish our state's intent to protect the marital relationship. . . .

Here, Campbell gave Robinson the ring during his proposal. Thus, he presented evidence that the ring was given in contemplation of marriage and therefore was an engagement ring conditioned upon the marriage occurring. Although Robinson kept the ring in a safe deposit box after the engagement was cancelled, without further evidence the ring would remain a conditional gift and Campbell would be entitled to recover it as a matter of law.

Robinson explicitly characterizes the ring as an engagement ring. However, she has presented evidence that the ring was converted into an absolute gift by testifying Campbell told her to keep the ring after the engagement was cancelled. Because Campbell disputes this contention, the evidence conflicts as to whether the ring was conditioned upon marriage. Accordingly, ownership of the ring was a jury issue, and a directed verdict on Campbell's claims for declaratory judgment and claim and delivery were not warranted. . . .

Here, the trial court provided an erroneous jury charge. . . . While the charge instructed the jury that the gift was conditional, it did not explain that the gift could become absolute. Moreover, the jury charge and verdict form hinged ownership of the ring upon fault in the breakup [which we hold has no place in determining ownership of an engagement ring]. [Campbell] is entitled to a new trial on those claims. . . .

Notes and Questions

1. Historical background. Legal disputes about the return of an engagement ring are far more common than actions for breach of promise to marry. The gift of a diamond engagement ring is a relatively recent custom. Before the Great Depression, etiquette did not require a diamond engagement ring. By 1945, however, the diamond engagement ring had evolved into an American tradition based on an extensive advertising campaign by the diamond industry, as well as the abolition of breach-of-promise suits. Some commentators speculate that the abolition of breach-of-promise claims resulted in the need to give some item as a form of pledge, perhaps as "virginity insurance"![12]

2. Theories of recovery. At common law, actions for recovery of gifts given in contemplation of marriage were distinct from breach-of-promise actions. As a result, anti-heartbalm laws do not bar the former action. Courts generally hold that recovery of such gifts rests on *conditional gift* theory: the gift is conditioned on performance of the marriage. If the condition fails, the donor may recover the gift. The central question, as *Campbell* reveals, is whether the gift is conditional or absolute. Courts consider the nature of the gift, circumstances, and cause of the broken engagement.

3. Fault. Traditionally, fault barred recovery or retention of the engagement ring. Thus, the man could recover the ring if the woman unjustifiably ended the engagement or if the couple mutually dissolved it, but not if he unjustifiably terminated the engagement. The modernization of divorce law revealed the shortcomings of a fault-based analysis of personal relationships and their dissolution. Hence, the modern trend, as *Campbell* indicates, makes fault irrelevant. But cf. Walton v. Snow, 2014 WL 820579 (Del. Com. Pl. 2014). Do you find *Campbell*'s reasons persuasive for adopting this approach?

4. Other gifts. Sometimes, plaintiffs seek recovery of *other* gifts given during an engagement. Should such gifts receive different treatment from engagement rings? See Northern Trust, NA v. Delley, 935 N.Y.S.2d 805 (App. Div. 2011) (real property). Suppose the man gives the woman other jewelry. How does one determine which gifts are "in contemplation of marriage"? Can gifts to a *third party* qualify? See Cooper v. Smith, 800 N.E.2d 372 (Ohio Ct. App. 2003) (gifts to mother-in-law).

5. Married donee. Should it matter if the donee is still married to someone else at the time of the engagement? See Lipschutz v. Kiderman, 905 N.Y.S.2d 247 (App. Div. 2010). Should the donee's marital status matter in states that follow the modern trend of making fault irrelevant? What is the status of the ring if the couple marries but subsequently divorces? See Randall v. Randall, 56 So. 3d 817 (Fla. Dist. Ct. App. 2011).

---

[12]. See Margaret F. Brinig, Rings and Promises, 6 J.L. Econ. & Org. 203, 204 (1990); Matthew O'Brien, The Strange (and Formerly Sexist) Economics of Engagement Rings, The Atlantic, Apr. 5, 2012, http://www.theatlantic.com/business/archive/2012/04/the-strange-and-formerly-sexist-economics-of-engagement-rings/255434/.

6. Gender-based nature of rule. Given that etiquette and custom dictate that the bride pays for the wedding and the groom pays for the ring, do women bear a disproportionate burden for a broken engagement? Should courts hold that an engagement ring is an irrevocable gift to avoid gender bias? See Albinger v. Harris, 48 P.3d 711, 720 (Mont. 2002) (so holding). How should the gender basis of the rule be addressed? See, e.g., Rebecca Tushnet, Rules of Engagement, 107 Yale L.J. 2583 (1998) (advocating joint liability for expenses). What do these gendered rules and customs mean for same-sex couples?

7. Policy. With the abolition movement for breach-of-promise suits, should the law also abolish actions for recovery of engagement rings and let the loss fall where it lies? Are remedies of the marketplace appropriate for courtship controversies? Should courts refuse to intrude on this private matter? Or should the law facilitate the breaking of engagements? If so, what rule best achieves this goal? See generally Viviana A. Zelizer, The Purchase of Intimacy (2007).

Problems

1. Virginia, a nurse practitioner, and Stephen, an attorney, plan a lavish wedding and reception. He buys her a Tiffany engagement ring and gives it to her on Valentine's Day. They agree that, as professionals, Virginia will pay for wedding costs and, in return, Stephen will convey to her a half interest in his condo (which he does). When the engagement ends by mutual agreement, Stephen seeks return of the ring and restoration of full ownership of his condo. Virginia argues that Stephen referred to the ring as "a Valentine's Day present." He counters that the ring remained covered by his homeowner's policy. She seeks $16,000 for wedding expenses and the value of five engagement gifts that Stephen retained after the broken engagement. New York has anti-heartbalm legislation but permits actions for the return of gifts in contemplation of marriage. What result? DeFina v. Scott, 755 N.Y.S.2d 587 (Sup. Ct. 2003).

Suppose, instead, that Stephen receives pressure from his family members, who are opposed to the marriage because they do not like Virginia. Whose fault is it when Stephen decides to break off the engagement because Virginia is not the "right person" for him? How might this turn of events change the result? Clippard v. Pfefferkorn, 168 S.W.3d 616 (Mo. Ct. App. 2005).

2. Three months after Jody and Layne start dating, Layne gives Jody a ring. They make plans to marry once their finances improve. Jody loves to travel and, during their engagement, asks Layne to pay for trips to Alaska and France. She also asks him to purchase a car for her son and to have a vasectomy. Layne pays for a seven-day Alaskan cruise, a three-week trip to France, $2,400 toward Jody's son's car, and $3,500 for the vasectomy. Jody then breaks off the engagement, without any excuse, and returns the ring. Layne sells the ring for only half its purchase price. He then brings suit under theories of conditional gift and unjust enrichment, seeking reimbursement of $25,000 for the cost of the trips, the money he paid for the son's car, the cost of the vasectomy and a reversal procedure, and the difference between the ring's purchase price and sale price. What result? Hess v. Johnston, 163 P.3d 747 (Utah Ct. App. 2007).

Suppose Layne also gives Jody an engagement present of a pedigree dog, which they register with the Kennel Club in their joint names. When they break up, Layne refuses to give Jody the dog as he allegedly promised to do. She files suit under theories of conditional gift and breach of an oral agreement, seeking specific performance. What result? Houseman v. Dare, 966 A.2d 24 (N.J. Super. Ct. App. Div. 2009).

C. Premarital Contracts

SIMEONE v. SIMEONE

581 A.2d 162 (Pa. 1990)

FLAHERTY, Justice.

At issue in this appeal is the validity of a prenuptial agreement executed between the appellant, Catherine E. Walsh Simeone, and the appellee, Frederick A. Simeone. At the time of their marriage, in 1975, appellant was a twenty-three-year-old nurse and appellee was a thirty-nine-year-old neurosurgeon. Appellee had an income of approximately $90,000 per year, and appellant was unemployed. Appellee also had assets worth approximately $300,000. On the eve of the parties' wedding, appellee's attorney presented appellant with a prenuptial agreement to be signed. Appellant, without the benefit of counsel, signed the agreement. Appellee's attorney had not advised appellant regarding any legal rights that the agreement surrendered. The parties are in disagreement as to whether appellant knew in advance of that date that such an agreement would be presented for signature. . . .

The agreement limited appellant to support payments of $200 per week in the event of separation or divorce, subject to a maximum total payment of $25,000. The parties separated in 1982, and, in 1984, divorce proceedings were commenced. Between 1982 and 1984 appellee made payments which satisfied the $25,000 limit. In 1985, appellant filed a claim for alimony pendente lite [i.e., temporary support pending a divorce or separation]. . . .

We granted this appeal because uncertainty was expressed by the Superior Court regarding the meaning of our plurality decision in Estate of Geyer, 533 A.2d 423 (1987) [upholding a premarital agreement if it either made reasonable provision for the spouse or was entered into after full and fair disclosure]. Inasmuch as the courts below held that the provision made for appellant was a reasonable one, appellant's efforts to overturn the agreement here focused on an assertion that there was an adequate disclosure of statutory rights. Appellant continues to assert, however, that the payments provided in the agreement were less than reasonable.

The statutory rights in question are those relating to alimony pendente lite. . . . The present agreement [expressly stated] that alimony pendente lite was being relinquished. It also recited that appellant "has been informed and understands" that, were it not for the agreement, appellant's obligation to pay alimony pendente lite "might, as a matter of law, exceed the amount provided." Hence, appellant's claim is not that the agreement failed to disclose the particular right affected, but rather that she was not adequately informed with respect to the nature of alimony pendente lite. . . .

There is no longer validity in the implicit presumption that supplied the basis for *Geyer* and similar earlier decisions. Such decisions rested upon a belief that spouses are of unequal status and that women are not knowledgeable enough to understand the nature of contracts that they enter. Society has advanced, however, to the point where women are no longer regarded as the "weaker" party in marriage, or in society generally. Indeed, the stereotype that women serve as homemakers while men work as breadwinners is no longer viable. Quite often today both spouses are income earners. Nor is there viability in the presumption that women are uninformed, uneducated, and readily subjected to unfair advantage in marital agreements. Indeed, women nowadays quite often have substantial education, financial awareness, income, and assets.

Accordingly, the law has advanced to recognize the equal status of men and women in our society. Paternalistic presumptions and protections that arose to shelter women from the inferiorities and incapacities which they were perceived as having in earlier times have, appropriately, been discarded. It would be inconsistent, therefore, to perpetuate the standards governing prenuptial agreements that were described in *Geyer* and similar decisions, as these reflected a paternalistic approach that is now insupportable.

Further, *Geyer* and its predecessors embodied substantial departures from traditional rules of contract law, to the extent that they allowed consideration of the knowledge of the contracting parties and reasonableness of their bargain as factors governing whether to uphold an agreement. Traditional principles of contract law provide perfectly adequate remedies where contracts are procured through fraud, misrepresentation, or duress. Consideration of other factors, such as the knowledge of the parties and the reasonableness of their bargain, is inappropriate. Prenuptial agreements are contracts, and, as such, should be evaluated under the same criteria as are applicable to other types of contracts. Absent fraud, misrepresentation, or duress, spouses should be bound by the terms of their agreements.

Contracting parties are normally bound by their agreements, without regard to whether the terms thereof were read and fully understood and irrespective of whether the agreements embodied reasonable or good bargains. Based upon these principles, the terms of the present prenuptial agreement must be regarded as binding, without regard to whether the terms were fully understood by appellant. *Ignorantia non excusat.*

Accordingly, we find no merit in a contention raised by appellant that the agreement should be declared void on the ground that she did not consult with independent legal counsel. To impose a per se requirement that parties entering a prenuptial agreement must obtain independent legal counsel would be contrary to traditional principles of contract law, and would constitute a paternalistic and unwarranted interference with the parties' freedom to enter contracts.

Further, the reasonableness of a prenuptial bargain is not a proper subject for judicial review. . . . By invoking inquiries into reasonableness, [the] functioning and reliability of prenuptial agreements is severely undermined. Parties would not have entered such agreements, and, indeed, might not have entered their marriages, if they did not expect their agreements to be strictly enforced. If parties viewed an agreement as reasonable at the time of its inception, as evidenced by their having signed the agreement, they should be foreclosed from later trying to evade its terms by asserting that it was not in fact reasonable. Pertinently, the present agreement contained a clause reciting that "each of the parties considers this agreement fair, just, and reasonable. . . ."

Further, everyone who enters a long-term agreement knows that circumstances can change during its term, so that what initially appeared desirable might prove to be an unfavorable bargain. Such are the risks that contracting parties routinely assume. Certainly, the possibilities of illness, birth of children, reliance upon a spouse, career change, financial gain or loss, and numerous other events that can occur in the course of a marriage cannot be regarded as unforeseeable. If parties choose not to address such matters in their prenuptial agreements, they must be regarded as having contracted to bear the risk of events that alter the value of their bargains.

We are reluctant to interfere with the power of persons contemplating marriage to agree upon, and to act in reliance upon, what they regard as an acceptable distribution scheme for their property. A court should not ignore the parties' expressed intent by proceeding to determine whether a prenuptial agreement was, in the court's view, reasonable at the time of its inception or the time of divorce. These are exactly the sorts of judicial determinations that such agreements are designed to avoid. Rare indeed is the agreement that is beyond possible challenge when reasonableness is placed at issue. Parties can routinely assert some lack of fairness relating to the inception of the agreement, thereby placing the validity of the agreement at risk. And if reasonableness at the time of divorce were to be taken into account an additional problem would arise. Virtually nonexistent is the marriage in which there has been absolutely no change in the circumstances of either spouse during the course of the marriage. Every change in circumstance, foreseeable or not, and substantial or not, might be asserted as a basis for finding that an agreement is no longer reasonable.

In discarding the approach of *Geyer* that permitted examination of the reasonableness of prenuptial agreements and allowed inquiries into whether parties had attained informed understandings of the rights they were surrendering, we do not depart from the longstanding principle that a full and fair disclosure of the financial positions of the parties is required. . . . Parties to these agreements do not quite deal at arm's length, but rather at the time the contract is entered into stand in a relation of mutual confidence and trust that calls for disclosure of their financial resources. It is well settled that this disclosure need not be exact, so long as it is "full and fair." In essence therefore, the duty of disclosure under these circumstances is consistent with traditional principles of contract law.

If an agreement provides that full disclosure has been made, a presumption of full disclosure arises. . . . The present agreement recited that full disclosure had been made, and included a list of appellee's assets totaling approximately $300,000. Appellant contends that this list understated by roughly $183,000, the value of a classic car collection which appellee had included at a value of $200,000. The master, reviewing the parties' conflicting testimony regarding the value of the car collection, found that appellant failed to prove by clear and convincing evidence that the value of the collection had been understated. . . .

Appellant's final contention is that the agreement was executed under conditions of duress in that it was presented to her at 5 p.m. on the eve of her wedding, a time when she could not seek counsel without the trauma, expense, and embarrassment of postponing the wedding. . . . Although appellant testified that she did not discover until the eve of her wedding that there was going to be a prenuptial agreement, testimony from a number of other witnesses was to the contrary. . . . [T]he courts below properly held that the present agreement is valid and enforceable. Appellant is barred, therefore, from receiving alimony pendente lite. . . .

McDermott, Justice, dissenting. . . .

I am not willing to believe that our society views marriage as a mere contract for hire. . . . Our courts must seek to protect, and not to undermine, those institutions and interests which are vital to our society. [W]hile I acknowledge the longstanding rule of law that prenuptial agreements are presumptively valid and binding upon the parties, I am unwilling to go as far as the majority to protect the right to contract at the expense of the institution of marriage. Were a contract of marriage, the most intimate relationship between two people, not the surrender of freedom, an offering of self in love, sacrifice, hope for better or for worse, the begetting of children and the offer of effort, labor, precious time and care for the safety and prosperity of their union, then the majority would find me among them. . . .

At the time of dissolution of the marriage, a spouse should be able to avoid the operation of a prenuptial agreement upon clear and convincing proof that, despite the existence of full and fair disclosure at the time of the execution of the agreement, the agreement is nevertheless so inequitable and unfair that it should not be enforced in a court of this state. . . .

[T]he passage of time, accompanied by the intervening events of a marriage, may render the terms of the agreement completely unfair and inequitable. While parties to a prenuptial agreement may indeed foresee, generally, the events which may come to pass during their marriage, one spouse should not be made to suffer for failing to foresee all of the surrounding circumstances which may attend the dissolution of the marriage. Although it should not be the role of the courts to void prenuptial agreements merely because one spouse may receive a better result in an action under the Divorce Code to recover alimony or equitable distribution, it should be the role of the courts to guard against the enforcement of prenuptial agreements where such enforcement will bring about only inequity and hardship. It borders on cruelty to accept that after years of living together, yielding their separate opportunities in life to each other, that two individuals emerge the same as the day they began their marriage. . . .

IN RE MARRIAGE OF SHANKS

758 N.W.2d 506 (Iowa 2008)

Hecht, Justice.

. . . Randall Shanks is an attorney with a successful personal injury and workers' compensation practice in Council Bluffs. Teresa Shanks holds an associate degree in court reporting and a Bachelor of Science degree in marketing management. She has been employed in various roles, including a position in the marketing department of a casino, and employment as a bookkeeper, secretary, and office manager in Randall's law office.

Attorney Randall J. Shanks

Randall and Teresa were married in Jamaica on April 23, 1998. This was a second marriage for both parties. Randall had two children and Teresa had three children from prior marriages. While contemplating marriage, Randall and Teresa discussed Randall's goal of preserving his current and future assets for his children in the event their marriage were to end by his death or a divorce. Randall suggested they enter a premarital agreement, and Teresa agreed. . . .

[Randall drafted a premarital agreement and presented it to Teresa ten days before their wedding. After receiving the draft, Teresa asked Randall several questions. He answered her questions, but insisted that she seek independent legal advice as to the meaning and effect of the agreement. She consulted a friend, who referred her to an out-of-state attorney, who in turn asked her associate to review the draft. The associate made several handwritten comments, including an exclamation that the proposed agreement would force Teresa to "waive all rights as spouse!" in Randall's pension assets. The associate also suggested that Teresa should have an Iowa attorney review the document, but Teresa chose not to do so. In response to the associate's suggestions, Randall made some revisions and again told Teresa to review it with her lawyer.]

Despite Randall's urging that she have her lawyer review the revised draft, Teresa did not seek further counsel. . . . Randall attached to the revised agreement separate schedules listing the assets of each party. The parties signed the agreement [and] departed for Jamaica the next day. [Six years later, when the marriage ended Randall sought, and Teresa opposed, enforcement of the premarital agreement]. . . .

[P]remarital agreements [are] subject to the requirements of the Iowa Uniform Premarital Agreement Act (IUPAA), Iowa Code §596.12 [invalidating agreements if]: (1) The person did not execute the agreement voluntarily; (2) The agreement was unconscionable when it was executed; (3) Before the execution of the agreement the person was not provided a fair and reasonable disclosure of the property or financial obligations of the other spouse; and the person did not have, or reasonably could not have had, an adequate knowledge of the property or financial obligations of the other spouse. . . .

A. VOLUNTARINESS

The district court found the premarital agreement in this case was not executed voluntarily because Randall, as an attorney, had substantially greater power under the circumstances and Teresa did not receive the advice of independent Iowa counsel. . . . Neither the IUPAA nor the UPAA defines the term "voluntarily."

[Prior case law explains that a voluntarily executed premarital agreement was one free from duress and undue influence.] There are two essential elements to a claim of duress in the execution of a contract: (1) one party issues a wrongful or unlawful threat and (2) the other party had no reasonable alternative to entering the contract. Here, Randall informed Teresa he would not get married again without a premarital agreement. We rejected [in prior case law] the argument that such an ultimatum was wrongful or unlawful. [Additionally] Teresa had the reasonable alternative of cancelling the wedding in the face of such a threat. These facts fall far short of a showing of duress sufficient to support a finding that Teresa involuntarily executed the agreement.

. . . Despite the potential for abuse inherent in the parties' complex relationship, we find the evidence presented was insufficient to establish undue influence. . . . Randall encouraged Teresa to seek the advice of counsel as to both drafts of the agreement. The facts presented here simply do not demonstrate the "improper or wrongful constraint, machination, or urgency of persuasion" required for a finding of undue influence. We are not persuaded that Randall's will was substituted for Teresa's own judgment in deciding to sign the agreement. . . . We next consider whether the agreement is unconscionable and therefore unenforceable.

B. UNCONSCIONABILITY

While the IUPAA largely adopts the provisions of the Uniform Premarital Agreement Act (UPAA) verbatim, section 596.8(1) of the IUPAA differs from the UPAA in two important particulars. First, the UPAA (§6(a)(2)) allows a party to modify or eliminate spousal support in a premarital agreement, as long as the modification or elimination does not cause the other party to be eligible for public assistance at the time of enforcement. The IUPAA, on the other hand, prohibits premarital agreements from adversely affecting spousal support. Iowa Code §596.5(2). Thus, the district court correctly concluded the purported alimony waiver in this premarital agreement is invalid and unenforceable.

Second, under UPAA section 6(a)(2), a court may not consider the alleged unconscionability of the agreement unless it first finds there was no fair and reasonable financial disclosure, voluntary waiver of such disclosure, and the challenging party did not have, or reasonably could not have had an adequate knowledge of the other party's property and financial obligations. . . . Neither the IUPAA nor the UPAA attempts to define "unconscionability" in the context of premarital agreements. The comment to UPAA section 6 indicates the concept is patterned after section 306 of the Uniform Marriage and Divorce Act (UMDA), which states:

> The standard of unconscionability is used in commercial law, where its meaning includes protection against one-sidedness, oppression, or unfair surprise, and in contract law. . . . In the context of negotiations between spouses as to the financial incidents of their marriage, the standard includes protection against overreaching, concealment of assets, and sharp dealing not consistent with the obligations of marital partners to deal fairly with each other. . . .

The concept of unconscionability includes both procedural and substantive elements. . . .

1. Substantive Unconscionability

At the outset, we acknowledge premarital agreements are typically financially one-sided in order to protect the assets of one prospective spouse. Courts must resist the temptation to view disparity between the parties' financial circumstances as requiring a finding of substantive unconscionability. [T]he focus of the substantive unconscionability analysis is upon whether "the provisions of the contract are mutual or the division of property is consistent with the financial condition of the parties at the time of execution."

The district court found the agreement executed by Randall and Teresa was not substantively unconscionable. We agree. Most, but not all, of the provisions of the agreement are mutual in scope. The agreement basically sought to maintain the parties' premarital assets as separate property and to perpetuate their premarital financial conditions throughout the marriage. The parties agreed to maintain separate property during the marriage, with the exceptions of a marital home and a joint checking account. Any property acquired by either party in their sole name during the marriage was to remain separate property. The parties' earnings during the marriage were to remain separate, except to the extent they were deposited in the joint checking account.

The agreement specifically provides for the allocation of any jointly-owned property in the event of a dissolution. The accord dictates such property will be allocated between the parties in different percentages depending on the nature of the property and the length of the marriage. . . . While these provisions clearly contemplated the allocation of a greater portion of the marital assets to Randall than Teresa, we believe they were at least consistent with the parties' financial conditions at the time of the marriage, and were not so oppressive to Teresa as to justify a finding of unconscionability.

Additionally, although Teresa unilaterally waived any marital interest in certain assets (such as Randall's retirement assets), she also derived some potential benefits under the agreement [20 percent of any net proceeds in the marital home upon divorce, being named as a beneficiary of Randall's life insurance, and a percentage of the value of his law practice upon his death]. Because the agreement contemplated leaving both parties substantially in the same financial condition as they were before the marriage, included primarily mutual covenants and obligations, and provided for some potential financial benefits to Teresa, we conclude the agreement was not unduly harsh or oppressive, and therefore was not substantively unconscionable.

2. Procedural Unconscionability

[T]he primary focus of the procedural unconscionability inquiry is the advantaged party's exploitation of the disadvantaged party's lack of understanding or unequal bargaining power. Courts have found the following factors, among others, are relevant to procedural unconscionability: the disadvantaged party's opportunity to seek independent counsel; the relative sophistication of the parties in legal and financial matters; the temporal proximity between the introduction of the premarital agreement and the wedding date; the use of highly technical or confusing language or fine print; and the use of fraudulent or deceptive practices to procure the disadvantaged party's assent to the agreement.

In holding the agreement procedurally unconscionable, the district court stressed the fact that Randall is an attorney and therefore was in a vastly superior bargaining position to Teresa. It appears the district court believed there are no circumstances under which an attorney could enter into an enforceable premarital agreement with a spouse who is not represented by independent legal counsel. Although any doubt as to the conscionability of the agreement at issue in this case could have likely been avoided if both parties had been represented by competent Iowa-licensed counsel, we conclude such legal representation is not a condition of enforceability. While Randall certainly had greater inherent bargaining power as both the party whose assets were primarily protected by the agreement and as an attorney, he twice insisted Teresa should seek the advice of counsel in connection with the agreement. [Her out-of-state attorney] also urged Teresa to do so. The anti-paternalistic notions underlying the IUPAA lead us to conclude Teresa's decision to forgo her opportunity to seek further legal advice [was a choice] that emasculates her unconscionability claim. Equitable principles will not permit a party to eschew an opportunity to consult counsel as to the legal effect of a proposed contract, execute the contract, and then challenge the enforceability of the agreement on the ground she did not have adequate legal advice.

Temporal considerations can in some instances support a finding of unconscionability. Although Randall presented the agreement only ten days before the wedding date, Teresa had sufficient time to consider the implications of the agreement and an opportunity to seek advice of counsel. . . . [Moreover, the trial court found Teresa was not an unsophisticated party because she was a college graduate, was previously divorced, and was a court reporter and paralegal.]

[In addition] Randall communicated to Teresa his desire for a premarital agreement to protect his assets for his children. Teresa responded that she was not marrying Randall for his money, and acted accordingly by acquiescing, without thorough investigation or objection, to a premarital agreement that facilitated her marriage. Teresa's words and actions demonstrate she placed higher value on marriage and Randall's companionship than the opportunity for greater financial security. "Buyer's remorse" will not excuse Teresa's voluntary relinquishment of her marital property rights. . . .

[Finally, when the parties executed the agreement], schedules listing the parties' respective assets and their approximate value were attached. Teresa nonetheless contends the agreement is unenforceable under Iowa Code section 596.8(3) because Randall failed to provide her with fair and reasonable disclosure of his property and financial obligations. The trial court rejected this assertion, finding Teresa [who was Randall's paralegal and secretary] was sufficiently knowledgeable about Randall's financial circumstances to satisfy the IUPAA. We agree. . . .

Notes and Questions on *Simeone* and *Shanks*

1. Epilogue. After the events in the principal case, Randall Shanks became president of the Iowa Academy of Trial Attorneys and was invited to join the prestigious American College of Trial Lawyers. Teresa Shanks later became a financial adviser. Personal communication, Randall Shanks, Shanks Law Firm, July 27, 2015.

On remand in *Shanks*, the trial court divided the property according to the premarital agreement and awarded spousal support to Teresa. The appellate court reversed the award of $4,000/month rehabilitative alimony as "excessive," based on the short duration of the marriage and Teresa's ability to support herself. 805 N.W.2d 175 (Iowa Ct. App. 2011).

2. Modern view. Premarital (also "antenuptial" or "prenuptial") agreements generally limit property rights in the event of dissolution and death. Enforcement of these agreements combines traditional contract principles respecting private ordering with family law principles of equitable distribution. Prior to the 1970s, courts held that these agreements violated public policy as an inducement to divorce.

3. Ordinary contracts distinguished. How do premarital agreements differ from ordinary contracts? First, the state has a greater interest in premarital agreements because it wishes to protect the welfare of the couple and their children, and also to preserve the privacy of the family, according to Professor Judith Younger. She continues:

> The second difference is the relationship of the parties to each other. It is a confidential relationship involving parties who are usually not evenly matched in bargaining power. The possibility, therefore, that one party may overreach the other is greater than in the case of ordinary contracts.
>
> The third difference is the fact that antenuptial agreements are to be performed in the future, in the context of a relationship which the parties have not yet begun and which may continue for many years after the agreement is executed and before it is enforced. The possibility that later events may make it unwise, unfair, or otherwise undesirable to enforce such agreements is also greater than in the case of ordinary contracts.[13]

4. Requirements. *Simeone* and *Shanks* reflect different approaches. *Simeone,* out of deference to private ordering, treats such agreements as ordinary contracts. *Shanks* underscores the need for special protection. Further, *Simeone* rejects an examination of substantive fairness (although still requiring voluntariness and adequate disclosure), whereas *Shanks* requires both substantive fairness and procedural fairness. Why does *Simeone* reject judicial review of reasonableness? Should a recitation of reasonableness in the agreement serve as a presumption of fairness? Or are premarital agreements "in the nature of contracts of adhesion" (as an omitted concurrence in *Simeone* states)? Why did the plaintiff in *Shanks* contend the prenuptial agreement was invalid? What was the court's response in the principal case?

A few states hold that a premarital agreement cannot waive spousal support, or else that such waiver must be made after consultation with independent counsel. See, e.g., Cal. Fam. Code §1612(7)(c). On the evolution in the policy disallowing waivers, see In re Marriage of Melissa, 151 Cal. Rptr. 3d 608 (Ct. App. 2013). What does Iowa law require for waivers of spousal support? What rationale explains these rules?

---

[13]. Judith T. Younger, Perspectives on Antenuptial Agreements: An Update, 8 J. Am. Acad. Matrimonial Law 1, 3 (1992).

a. UPAA: Unconscionability. The UPAA, although calling for review of both procedural and substantive fairness, sets a high standard for substantive unfairness, requiring "unconscionability." How does unconscionability differ from "fair and reasonable"? Is unconscionability (the standard for invalidating commercial contracts) an appropriate standard to apply to marital relationships?

UNIFORM PREMARITAL AGREEMENT ACT (UPAA)

§6(a) A premarital agreement is not enforceable if the party against whom enforcement is sought proves that:

(1) that party did not execute the agreement voluntarily; or

(2) the agreement was unconscionable when it was executed and, before execution of the agreement, that party:

(i) was not provided a fair and reasonable disclosure of the property or financial obligations of the other party;

(ii) did not voluntarily and expressly waive, in writing, any right to disclosure of the property or financial obligations of the other party beyond the disclosure provided; and

(iii) did not have, or reasonably could not have had, an adequate knowledge of the property or financial obligations of the other party.

Recent cases illustrate premarital agreements that courts have found to be unconscionable. See, e.g., Fetters v. Fetters, 26 N.E.3d 1016 (Ind. Ct. App. 2015) (wife was a pregnant teen, agreement was proposed to evade husband's prosecution, and significant benefits inured to husband but no comparable benefits to wife); Kelcourse v. Kelcourse, 23 N.E.3d 124 (Mass. App. Ct. 2015) (agreement left wife with negative equity and required her to pay for major structural home repairs).

b. ALI Principles. Under rules approved by the American Law Institute (ALI), premarital agreements must meet standards of procedural fairness (i.e., informed consent and disclosure) and substantive fairness. A rebuttable presumption arises that the agreement satisfies the informed consent requirement if (1) it was executed at least 30 days prior to the marriage; (2) both parties had, or were advised to obtain, counsel and had the opportunity to do so; and (3) if one of the parties did not have counsel, the agreement contained understandable information about the parties' rights and the adverse nature of their interests. ALI, Principles of the Law of Family Dissolution: Analysis and Recommendations §7.04(3)(a), (b), and (c) (2002).

Finally, the court must undertake a review of substantive fairness at the time of enforcement, specifically regarding whether enforcement would work a "substantial injustice" based on the passage of time, the presence of children, or changed circumstances that were unanticipated and would have a significant impact on the parties or their children. Id. §7.05. Which approach do you favor—the UPAA or the ALI Principles? Why?

c. UPMAA. The UPAA has been adopted by 26 states and the District of Columbia.[14] In 2012, the Uniform Law Commissioners approved the Uniform Premarital

[14]. Uniform Law Comm'n, Legislative Fact Sheet—Premarital Agreement Act, http://www.uniformlaws.org/LegislativeFactSheet.aspx?title=Premarital%20Agreement%20Act.

and Marital Agreements Act (UPMAA) in an effort to treat premarital and marital agreements alike.[15] The UPMAA requires both types of agreements to be in writing; provides a framework for determining validity; specifies that unconscionability and failure of disclosure are alternative grounds to deny enforcement; bars enforcement if an agreement is involuntary or results from duress; and affirms traditional principles of conflict of laws in determining an agreement's validity and meaning. Only two states (Colorado and North Dakota) have adopted the new act.

5. Time of determination. If substantive fairness is considered, should it be determined as of execution and/or enforcement? Compare the approaches in *Simeone* and *Shanks* with those of the UPAA and ALI Principles.

The dissent in *Simeone* suggests (in an omitted section) that the following circumstances at divorce might lead to invalidation of a premarital agreement: (1) a spouse's diminished employment prospects if that spouse remained home due to family responsibilities, such that the spouse would become a public charge or suffer a significantly reduced standard of living; (2) a dependent spouse in a long marriage who helped increase the value of the other's property; (3) an unanticipated serious illness rendering the spouse unable to provide self-support. Note that the UPAA provides that a premarital agreement will not be enforced at divorce if the enforcement of a provision that modifies or eliminates spousal support would cause one spouse to become a public charge (UPAA §6(b)).

6. Relative bargaining power. *Simeone* and *Shanks assume* that prospective spouses have equal bargaining power. On what basis might you question this assumption in either case? What relevance should a court attach to such factors as age, financial position, business acumen, obtaining (or rejecting) legal advice, the selection of counsel by the defendant, or a previous divorce?

One legal scholar comments on the gendered aspects of premarital contracts as follows:

> By enforcing them, the courts are enabling the dominant party to acquire financial advantages and to shift the risk of a failed relationship from him, even though he can afford to bear it, to her, the weaker party who cannot easily bear such a burden. These judicial decisions work not only to her detriment but to the public's detriment as well.[16]

She recommends: (1) independent counsel for each party, with the requirement that each party have ample time and money for consultation; (2) a reasonable provision for post-divorce support if a party gives up income to become a homemaker; and (3) prior judicial approval of such agreements. What do you think of these suggestions?

---

[15]. Uniform Law Comm'n, Uniform Premarital and Marital Agreements Act (2012), http://www.uniformlaws.org/shared/docs/premarital%20and%20marital%20agreements/2012_pmaa_final.pdf.

[16]. Judith T. Younger, Lovers' Contracts in the Courts: Forsaking the Minimum Decencies, 13 Wm. & Mary J. Women & L. 349, 427 (2007).

7. Timing of agreement. The plaintiffs in *Simeone* and *Shanks* claim duress based on the proximity of the execution of the agreement to the wedding. How do these courts resolve this issue? Should statutes require execution of premarital agreements a minimum amount of time before marriage? What do the ALI Principles require? Should a presumption apply that all premarital contracts executed within a short period of marriage are void?

8. Disclosure. What do *Simeone* and *Shanks* require in terms of disclosure? Is this synonymous with "detailed" disclosure? Is a general approximation of income, assets, and liabilities sufficient? Can a party's conduct constitute a waiver of the right to full disclosure? See In re Marriage of Hill & Dittmer, 136 Cal. Rptr. 3d 700 (Ct. App. 2011) (upholding premarital agreement because bride never took steps to obtain financial information). Should courts require an attached list of assets? See Cannon v. Cannon, 865 A.2d 563 (Md. 2005) (rejecting idea). Does a prospective spouse have a legal duty to inquire into the other's financial status before executing the agreement? See Oldani v. Oldani, 34 A.3d 407, 414 (Conn. Ct. App. 2011).

9. Confidential relationship. A majority of jurisdictions hold that prospective spouses have a confidential relationship. See Friezo v. Friezo, 914 A.2d 533, 549 (Conn. 2007) (survey). What does that term mean? How might that status affect the requirements for a valid premarital agreement?

10. Independent counsel. How does the court in *Shanks* respond to the plaintiff's claim that she did not have adequate legal advice in executing the premarital agreement? Many states emphasize the importance of providing an opportunity for the parties to consult independent counsel if they so choose. However, no state requires such consultation. What reforms, if any, would you recommend?

11. Same-sex couples. How should same-sex couples approach the possible termination of their relationships? What areas are of special importance to same-sex couples? Do these issues differ from those facing opposite-sex couples? See generally Jeffrey N. Greenblatt & Roberta Oluwaseun, Same-Sex but Not Same Old, Same Old: Special Considerations for Drafting Same-Sex Prenuptial Agreements, 41 Fam. L. Rptr. 1101 (2014).

12. Scope and limitations. UPAA supports a wide latitude regarding prospective spouses' contractual freedom. Among the permissible areas for premarital agreements, UPAA specifies "any other matter, including personal rights and obligations, not in violation of public policy or a statute imposing a criminal penalty." UPAA §3(a). The comment enumerates such examples as choice of abode, the freedom to pursue career opportunities, and the upbringing of children. Does this provision interfere with the doctrine of family privacy?

According to the general rule, premarital agreements may not restrict judicial discretion regarding either child custody or child support because of the state's concern with child welfare. See also id. §3(b) (setting forth limitation regarding child support).

Problems

1. Suppose you are about to marry (or begin a committed relationship). What roles, responsibilities, and other decisions might you want to allocate? Support? Property rights? Names? Employment and its consequences? Domicile? Responsibilities for birth control? Number of children? Parenting responsibilities? Draft an agreement to govern your relationship. Assuming you and your partner reach a satisfactory agreement, should the courts enforce it?

2. Which of the following provisions are enforceable under the UPMAA? Which provisions *should* the law enforce?

a. A parent shall not interfere, in the presence of the children, in punishments by the other parent (e.g., Ball v. Ball, 36 So. 2d 172, 174 (Fla. 1948)).
b. Sexual intercourse shall be limited to once per week (e.g., Favrot v. Barnes, 332 So. 2d 873, 875 (La. Ct. App.), *rev'd on other grounds*, 339 So. 2d 843 (La. 1976)).
c. One of the spouses shall reside in a certain locale (e.g., Isaacs v. Isaacs, 99 N.W. 268 (Neb. 1904)).
d. The husband's mother shall live with the parties (e.g., Koch v. Koch, 232 A.2d 157 (N.J. Super. Ct. App. Div. 1967)), but not the children of the wife's prior marriage (e.g., Mengal v. Mengal, 103 N.Y.S.2d 992 (Fam. Ct. 1951)).
e. Each spouse must undergo counseling before seeking a divorce and must not seek a divorce absent fault grounds or a two-year separation.
f. If the husband obtains a no-fault divorce, he must pay the wife $15,000/month for five years, but if he divorces her on fault grounds, she pays him $5,000/month for two years.
g. The wife will receive half of the husband's property upon divorce only if the parties remain married ten years or more; if the marriage ends sooner, she will receive only 25 percent.

3. Major League Baseball (MLB) player Barry Bonds meets Susann ("Sun") in Montreal after she emigrates from Sweden. Both are 23 years of age. Sun is working as a waitress and planning a career as a makeup artist for the rich and famous. The two take up residence in Phoenix, Arizona, and decide to marry. Barry is earning $106,000 at this time. The day before the wedding, the couple signs a premarital contract at Barry's lawyers' office by which each waives any interest in the earnings and acquisitions of the other during the marriage. Sun declines the lawyers' advice that she retain her own counsel. The attorneys read the agreement to her and explain that it waives her community property rights. After a six-year marriage, Barry petitions for dissolution in California. At the time, he is earning $8 million annually. Sun, who has custody of the couple's two children, is awarded child support of $20,000 per month and spousal support of $10,000 per month for a four-year period.

Sun argues that the premarital agreement was not executed voluntarily. She claims that she did not understand the terms because of her limited English skills. She also asserts that she believed the agreement pertained only to property that was owned prior to the marriage. Barry's attorneys later testify that she understood the agreement and did not appear pressured or confused but rather seemed confident and happy. What result? Is legal counsel essential to the enforceability of premarital contracts? How relevant is a party's waiver of legal counsel? See In re Marriage of Bonds, 5 P.3d 815 (Cal. 2000). Suppose Sun argues that the agreement is unconscionable because of drastically changed circumstances (i.e., Barry's increased wealth). What result? See Blue v. Blue, 60 S.W.3d 585 (Ky. Ct. App. 2001).

D. Getting Married: Substantive and Procedural Regulations

1. Constitutional Limits on State Regulation of Entry into Marriage

LOVING v. VIRGINIA

388 U.S. 1 (1967)

Mr. Chief Justice Warren delivered the opinion of the Court.

This case presents a constitutional question never addressed by this Court: whether a statutory scheme adopted by the State of Virginia to prevent marriages between persons solely on the basis of racial classifications violates the Equal Protection and Due Process Clauses of the Fourteenth Amendment. . . .

In June 1958, two residents of Virginia, Mildred Jeter, a Negro woman, and Richard Loving, a white man, were married in the District of Columbia pursuant to its laws. Shortly after their marriage, the Lovings returned to Virginia and established their marital abode in Caroline County. [A] grand jury issued an indictment charging the Lovings with violating Virginia's ban on interracial marriages. [T]he Lovings pleaded guilty to the charge and were sentenced to one year in jail; however, the trial judge suspended the sentence for a period of 25 years on the condition that the Lovings leave the State and not return to Virginia together for 25 years. He stated in an opinion that:

> Almighty God created the races white, black, yellow, malay and red, and he placed them on separate continents. And but for the interference with his arrangement there would be no cause for such marriages. The fact that he separated the races shows that he did not intend for the races to mix. . . .

Virginia is now one of 16 States which prohibit and punish marriages on the basis of racial classifications. Penalties for miscegenation arose as an incident to slavery and have been common in Virginia since the colonial period. The present statutory scheme dates from the adoption of the Racial Integrity Act of 1924, passed during the period of extreme nativism which followed the end of the First World War. The central features of this Act, and current Virginia law, are the absolute prohibition of a "white person" marrying other than another "white person," a prohibition against issuing marriage licenses until the issuing official is satisfied that the applicants' statements as to their race are correct, certificates of "racial composition" to be kept by both local and state registrars [and a penalty of one to five years imprisonment].

In upholding the constitutionality of these provisions in the decision below, the Supreme Court of Appeals of Virginia referred to its 1955 decision in Naim v. Naim, 197 Va. 80, 87 S.E.2d 749, as stating the reasons supporting the validity of these laws. In *Naim*, the state court concluded that the State's legitimate purposes were "to preserve the racial integrity of its citizens," and to prevent "the corruption of blood," "a mongrel breed of citizens," and "the obliteration of racial pride," obviously an endorsement of the doctrine of White Supremacy. The court also reasoned that marriage has traditionally been subject to state regulation without federal intervention, and, consequently, the regulation of marriage should be left to exclusive state control by the Tenth Amendment.

[T]he State contends that, because its miscegenation statutes punish equally both the white and the Negro participants in an interracial marriage, these statutes, despite their reliance on racial classifications do not constitute an invidious discrimination based upon race. The second argument . . . is that, if the Equal Protection Clause does not outlaw miscegenation statutes because of their reliance on racial classifications, the question of constitutionality would thus become whether there was any rational basis for a State to treat interracial marriages differently from other marriages. On this question, the State argues, the scientific evidence is substantially in doubt and, consequently, this Court should defer to the wisdom of the state legislature in adopting its policy of discouraging interracial marriages.

Because we reject the notion that the mere "equal application" of a statute containing racial classifications is enough to remove the classifications from the Fourteenth Amendment's proscription of all invidious racial discriminations, we do not accept the State's contention that these statutes should be upheld if there is any possible basis for concluding that they serve a rational purpose. . . . The clear and central purpose of the Fourteenth Amendment was to eliminate all official state sources of invidious racial discrimination in the States.

There can be no question but that Virginia's miscegenation statutes rest solely upon distinctions drawn according to race. The statutes proscribe generally accepted conduct if engaged in by members of different races. Over the years, this Court has consistently repudiated "(d)istinctions between citizens solely because of their ancestry" as being "odious to a free people whose institutions are founded upon the doctrine of equality." At the very least, the Equal Protection Clause demands that racial classifications, especially suspect in criminal statutes, be subjected to the "most rigid scrutiny," and, if they are ever to be upheld, they must be shown to be necessary to the accomplishment of some permissible state objective, independent of the racial discrimination which it was the object of the Fourteenth Amendment to eliminate. . . .

There is patently no legitimate overriding purpose independent of invidious racial discrimination which justifies the classification. The fact that Virginia prohibits only interracial marriages involving white persons demonstrates that the racial classifications must stand on their own justification, as measures designed to maintain White Supremacy. We have consistently denied the constitutionality of measures which restrict the rights of citizens on account of race. There can be no doubt that restricting the freedom to marry solely because of racial classifications violates the central meaning of the Equal Protection Clause.

These statutes also deprive the Lovings of liberty without due process of law in violation of the Due Process Clause of the Fourteenth Amendment. The freedom to marry has long been recognized as one of the vital personal rights essential to the orderly pursuit of happiness by free men.

Marriage is one of the "basic civil rights of man," fundamental to our very existence and survival. Skinner v. State of Oklahoma, 316 U.S. 535, 541 (1942). See also Maynard v. Hill, 125 U.S. 190 (1888). To deny this fundamental freedom on so unsupportable a basis as the racial classifications embodied in these statutes, classifications so directly subversive of the principle of equality at the heart of the Fourteenth Amendment, is surely to deprive all the State's citizens of liberty without due process of law. The Fourteenth Amendment requires that the freedom of choice to marry not be restricted by invidious racial discriminations. Under our Constitution, the freedom to marry or not marry, a person of another race resides with the individual and cannot be infringed by the State. These convictions must be reversed. . . .

Robert A. Pratt, Crossing the Color Line: A Historical Assessment and Personal Narrative of Loving v. Virginia

41 How. L.J. 229, 234-244 (1998)

Mildred and Richard Loving, the couple who challenged Virginia's ban on interracial marriage

. . . Richard Perry Loving and Mildred Delores Jeter had known each other practically all of their lives, as their families lived just up the road from each other in the rural community of Central Point, Virginia, located in Caroline County. . . . For twenty-three years, Richard's father had defied the racial mores of southern white society by working for Boyd Byrd, one of the wealthiest black farmers in the community. [T]he close-knit nature of their community [led] to an acceptance of personal relationships in a particular setting that would have been anathema elsewhere. So when white Richard Loving, age seventeen, began courting "colored" Mildred Jeter, age eleven, their budding romance drew little attention from either the white or the black communities.

Mildred (part-black and part-Cherokee) had a pretty light-brown complexion accentuated by her slim figure, which was why practically everyone who knew her called her "Stringbean" or "Bean" for short. Richard (part-English and part-Irish) was a bricklayer by trade, but spent much of his spare time drag racing a car that he co-owned with two black friends, Raymond Green (a mechanic) and Percy Fortune (a local merchant). Despite their natural shyness, both Richard and Mildred were well-liked in the community, and the fact that they attended different churches and different schools did not hinder their courtship. When he was twenty-four and she was eighteen, Richard and Mildred decided to legalize their relationship by getting married.

Mildred did not know that interracial marriage was illegal in Virginia, but Richard did. This explains why, on June 2, 1958, he drove them across the Virginia state line to Washington, D.C., to be married. . . . Mr. and Mrs. Loving returned to Central Point to live with Mildred's parents; however, their marital bliss was short-lived. [Five weeks later], their quiet life was shattered when they were awakened early in the morning as three law officers "acting on an anonymous tip" opened the unlocked door of their home, walked into their bedroom, and shined a flashlight in their faces. Caroline County Sheriff R. Garnett Brooks demanded to know what the two of them were doing in bed together. Mildred answered, "I'm his wife," while Richard pointed to the District of Columbia marriage certificate that hung on their bedroom wall. "That's no good here," Sheriff Brooks replied. He charged the couple with unlawful cohabitation, and then he and his two deputies hauled the Lovings off to a nearby jail in Bowling Green.

[After their conviction and suspended sentences, the Lovings moved to Washington, D.C.] The years in Washington were not happy ones for the couple. Richard struggled to maintain permanent employment while Mildred busied herself tending to the needs of their three children. "I missed being with my family and friends, especially Garnet [her sister]. I wanted my children to grow up in the country, where they could run and play, and where I wouldn't worry about them so much. I never liked much about the city."

Virginia law would not allow Richard and Mildred Loving [to be] in the state at the same time; however, that did not stop them from trying or from succeeding on various occasions. Mildred and the children made frequent visits to Battery, Virginia, the rural black community where her sister and brother-in-law lived. When Mildred would arrive in Battery, some of the neighbors would begin to look at their watches to see how long it would be before Richard's car came cruising through the neighborhood. During those early years, Richard's visits [occurred] almost exclusively after dark. . . .

The Lovings had not really been that interested in the civil rights movement, nor had they ever given much thought to challenging Virginia's law. But with a major civil rights bill being debated in Congress in 1963, Mildred decided to write to Robert Kennedy, the Attorney General of the United States. The Department of Justice referred the letter to the American Civil Liberties Union [ACLU]. Bernard S. Cohen, a young lawyer doing pro bono work for the ACLU in Alexandria, Virginia, agreed to take the case. He would later be joined by another young attorney, Philip J. Hirschkop. . . .

[T]he U.S. Supreme Court agreed to hear the case. . . . In concluding his oral argument on April 10, 1967, Cohen relayed a message to the Justices from Richard Loving: "Tell the Court I love my wife, and it is just unfair that I can't live with her in Virginia." . . .

Mildred Loving [remained] the same intensely shy woman she has always been. [She saw] herself as an ordinary black woman who fell in love with an ordinary white man. [She] puts it this way:

> We weren't bothering anyone. And if we hurt some people's feelings, that was just too bad. All we ever wanted was to get married, because we loved each other. Some people will never change, but that's their problem, not mine. I married the only man I had ever loved, and I'm happy for the time we had together. For me, that was enough.

ZABLOCKI v. REDHAIL

434 U.S. 374 (1978)

Justice MARSHALL delivered the opinion of the Court.

At issue in this case is the constitutionality of a Wisconsin statute, Wis. Stat. §245.10(1), (4), (5) (1973), which provides that members of a certain class of Wisconsin residents may not marry, within the State or elsewhere, without first obtaining a court order granting permission to marry. The class is defined by the statute to include any "Wisconsin resident having minor issue not in his custody and which he is under obligation to support by any court order or judgment." The statute specifies that court permission cannot be granted unless the marriage applicant submits proof of compliance with the support obligation and, in addition, demonstrates that the children covered by the support order "are not then and are not likely thereafter to become public charges." . . .

Appellee Redhail is a Wisconsin resident who, under the terms of §245.10, is unable to enter into a lawful marriage in Wisconsin or elsewhere so long as he maintains his Wisconsin residency. [W]hen appellee was a minor and a high school student, a paternity action was instituted against him in Milwaukee County Court, alleging that he was the father of a baby girl born out of wedlock on July 5, 1971. After he appeared and admitted that he was the child's father, the court [adjudged him] the father and ordered him to pay $109 per month as support for the child until she reached 18 years of age. From May 1972 until August 1974, appellee was unemployed and indigent, and consequently was unable to make any support payments.

On September 27, 1974, appellee filed an application for a marriage license with appellant Zablocki, the County Clerk of Milwaukee County, and a few days later the application was denied on the sole ground that appellee had not obtained a court order granting him permission to marry, as required by §245.10. [I]t is stipulated that he would not have been able to satisfy either of the statutory prerequisites for an order granting permission to marry. First, he had not satisfied his support obligations to his illegitimate child, and as of December 1974 there was an arrearage in excess of $3,700. Second, the child had been a public charge since her birth, receiving [welfare benefits]. [Appellee filed a class action, claiming violations of equal protection and due process. He prevailed in the District Court.] We agree with the District Court that the statute violates the Equal Protection Clause.

[The Court turns to the issue of the appropriate level of scrutiny.] Since our past decisions make clear that the right to marry is of fundamental importance, and since the classification at issue here significantly interferes with the exercise of that right, we believe that "critical examination" of the state interests advanced in support of the classification is required.

The leading case of this Court on the right to marry is Loving v. Virginia, 388 U.S. 1 (1967). [*Loving*] could have rested solely on the ground that the statutes discriminated on the basis of race in violation of the Equal Protection Clause. But the Court went on to hold that the laws arbitrarily deprived the couple of a fundamental liberty protected by the Due Process Clause, the freedom to marry. . . . Although *Loving* arose in the context of racial discrimination, prior and subsequent decisions of this Court confirm that the right to marry is of fundamental importance for all individuals. . . .

More recent decisions have established that the right to marry is part of the fundamental "right of privacy" implicit in the Fourteenth Amendment's Due Process Clause. . . . Cases subsequent to *Griswold* and *Loving* have routinely categorized the decision to marry as among the personal decisions protected by the right of privacy. . . . It is not surprising that the decision to marry has been placed on the same level of importance as decisions relating to procreation, childbirth, child rearing, and family relationships. [I]t would make little sense to recognize a right of privacy with respect to other matters of family life and not with respect to the decision to enter the relationship that is the foundation of the family in our society. . . .

By reaffirming the fundamental character of the right to marry, we do not mean to suggest that every state regulation which relates in any way to the incidents of or prerequisites for marriage must be subjected to rigorous scrutiny. To the contrary, reasonable regulations that do not significantly interfere with decisions to enter into the marital relationship may legitimately be imposed. See Califano v. Jobst, 434 U.S. 47 (1977). The statutory classification at issue here, however, clearly does interfere directly and substantially with the right to marry.

Under the challenged statute, no Wisconsin resident in the affected class may marry in Wisconsin or elsewhere without a court order, and marriages contracted in violation of the statute are both void and punishable as criminal offenses. Some of those in the affected class, like appellee, will never be able to obtain the necessary court order, because they either lack the financial means to meet their support obligations or cannot prove that their children will not become public charges. These persons are absolutely prevented from getting married. Many others, able in theory to satisfy the statute's requirements, will be sufficiently burdened by having to do so that they will in effect be coerced into forgoing their right to marry. And even those who can be persuaded to meet the statute's requirements suffer a serious intrusion into their freedom of choice in an area in which we have held such freedom to be fundamental.[12]

When a statutory classification significantly interferes with the exercise of a fundamental right, it cannot be upheld unless it is supported by sufficiently important state interests and is closely tailored to effectuate only those interests. Appellant asserts that two interests are served by the challenged statute: the permission-to-marry proceeding furnishes an opportunity to counsel the applicant as to the necessity of fulfilling his prior support obligations; and the welfare of the out-of-custody children is protected. We may accept for present purposes that these are legitimate and substantial interests, but, since the means selected by the State for achieving these interests unnecessarily impinge on the right to marry, the statute cannot be sustained.

State interest.

12. The directness and substantiality of the interference with the freedom to marry distinguish the instant case from Califano v. Jobst, 434 U.S. 47 [(1977) (upholding the Social Security Act provision for termination of a dependent child's benefits upon marriage to a person not entitled to benefits under the Act)]. The Social Security provisions placed no direct legal obstacle in the path of persons desiring to get married, and . . . there was no evidence that the laws significantly discouraged, let alone made "practically impossible," any marriages. Indeed, the provisions had not deterred the individual who challenged the statute from getting married, even though he and his wife were both disabled (because of availability of other federal benefits, total payments to the Jobsts after marriage were only $20 per month less than they would have been had Mr. Jobst's child benefits not been terminated).

There is evidence that the challenged statute, as originally introduced in the Wisconsin Legislature, was intended merely to establish a mechanism whereby persons with support obligations to children from prior marriages could be counseled before they entered into new marital relationships and incurred further support obligations. Court permission to marry was to be required, but apparently permission was automatically to be granted after counseling was completed. The statute actually enacted, however, does not expressly require or provide for any counseling whatsoever, nor for any automatic granting of permission to marry by the court, and thus it can hardly be justified as a means for ensuring counseling of the persons within its coverage. Even assuming that counseling does take place—a fact as to which there is no evidence in the record—this interest obviously cannot support the withholding of court permission to marry once counseling is completed.

With regard to safeguarding the welfare of the out-of-custody children, appellant's brief does not make clear the connection between the State's interest and the statute's requirements. At argument, appellant's counsel suggested that, since permission to marry cannot be granted unless the applicant shows that he has satisfied his court-determined support obligations to the prior children and that those children will not become public charges, the statute provides incentive for the applicant to make support payments to his children. This "collection device" rationale cannot justify the statute's broad infringement on the right to marry.

First, with respect to individuals who are unable to meet the statutory requirements, the statute merely prevents the applicant from getting married, without delivering any money at all into the hands of the applicant's prior children. More importantly, regardless of the applicant's ability or willingness to meet the statutory requirements, the State already has numerous other means for exacting compliance with support obligations, means that are at least as effective as the instant statute's and yet do not impinge upon the right to marry. . . .

There is also some suggestion that §245.10 protects the ability of marriage applicants to meet support obligations to prior children by preventing the applicants from incurring new support obligations. But the challenged provisions of §245.10 are grossly underinclusive with respect to this purpose, since they do not limit in any way new financial commitments by the applicant other than those arising out of the contemplated marriage. The statutory classification is substantially overinclusive as well: given the possibility that the new spouse will actually better the applicant's financial situation, by contributing income from a job or otherwise, the statute in many cases may prevent affected individuals from improving their ability to satisfy their prior support obligations. And, although it is true that the applicant will incur support obligations to any children born during the contemplated marriage, preventing the marriage may only result in the children being born out of wedlock, as in fact occurred in appellee's case. Since the support obligation is the same whether the child is born in or out of wedlock, the net result of preventing the marriage is simply more illegitimate children.

The statutory classification created by §245.10(1), (4), (5) thus cannot be justified by the interests advanced in support of it. The judgment of the District Court is, accordingly, [a]ffirmed.

Justice Stewart, concurring in the judgment.

I cannot join the opinion of the Court. To hold, as the Court does, that the Wisconsin statute violates the Equal Protection Clause seems to me to misconceive the meaning of that constitutional guarantee. The Equal Protection Clause deals not with substantive rights or freedoms but with invidiously discriminatory classifications. . . . The problem in this case is not one of discriminatory classifications, but of unwarranted encroachment upon a constitutionally protected freedom. I think that the Wisconsin statute is unconstitutional because it exceeds the bounds of permissible state regulation of marriage, and invades the sphere of liberty protected by the Due Process Clause of the Fourteenth Amendment. . . .

The Constitution does not specifically mention freedom to marry, but it is settled that the "liberty" protected by the Due Process Clause of the Fourteenth Amendment embraces more than those freedoms expressly enumerated in the Bill of Rights. And the decisions of this Court have made clear that freedom of personal choice in matters of marriage and family life is one of the liberties so protected. . . . It is evident that the Wisconsin law now before us directly abridges that freedom. The question is whether the state interests that support the abridgement can overcome the substantive protections of the Constitution. . . .

As directed against either the indigent or the delinquent parent, the law is substantially more rational if viewed as a means of assuring the financial viability of future marriages. In this context, it reflects a plausible judgment that those who have not fulfilled their financial obligations and have not kept their children off the welfare rolls in the past are likely to encounter similar difficulties in the future. But the State's legitimate concern with the financial soundness of prospective marriages must stop short of telling people they may not marry because they are too poor or because they might persist in their financial irresponsibility. . . . A legislative judgment so alien to our traditions and so offensive to our shared notions of fairness offends the Due Process Clause of the Fourteenth Amendment. . . .

Justice STEVENS, concurring in the judgment. . . .

Under this statute, a person's economic status may determine his eligibility to enter into a lawful marriage. A noncustodial parent whose children are "public charges" may not marry even if he has met his court-ordered obligations. Thus, within the class of parents who have fulfilled their court-ordered obligations, the rich may marry and the poor may not. This type of statutory discrimination is, I believe, totally unprecedented, as well as inconsistent with our tradition of administering justice equally to the rich and to the poor. . . .

The statute prevents impoverished parents from marrying even though their intended spouses are economically independent. Presumably, the Wisconsin Legislature assumed (a) that only fathers would be affected by the legislation, and (b) that they would never marry employed women. The first assumption ignores the fact that fathers are sometimes awarded custody, and the second ignores the composition of today's work force. To the extent that the statute denies a hard-pressed parent any opportunity to prove that an intended marriage will ease rather than aggravate his financial straits, it not only rests on unreliable premises, but also defeats its own objectives.

These questionable assumptions also explain why this statutory blunderbuss is wide of the target in another respect. The prohibition on marriage applies to the noncustodial parent but allows the parent who has custody to marry without the State's leave. Yet the danger that new children will further strain an inadequate budget is equally great for custodial and non-custodial parents. . . .

. . . Even assuming that the right to marry may sometimes be denied on economic grounds, this clumsy and deliberate legislative discrimination between the rich and the poor is irrational in so many ways that it cannot withstand scrutiny under the Equal Protection Clause of the Fourteenth Amendment.

[Justice Rehnquist, dissenting, would have upheld the statute under the rational basis test as a permissible exercise of the state's power to regulate family life and to assure child support.]

Notes and Questions on *Loving* and *Zablocki*

1. Epilogue. Mildred Loving died of pneumonia in 2008 at age 68. Her husband, Richard, predeceased her in 1975, as explained below:

> Less than a month after the Lovings' fourteenth anniversary and slightly more than eight years after they had earned the right to live as husband and wife in Virginia, Richard was killed. The couple and Mildred's sister Garnet were returning from a visit with friends when their car was broadsided by a drunk driver who had run a stop sign on route 721 in Caroline County, just thirteen miles from their home. Richard, forty-two, died instantly. Mildred lost her right eye, and Garnet suffered minor injuries.
>
> There was a tremendous outpouring of sympathy from the community for this woman who, not so long before, had been an exile from the state. . . . Richard is buried in a mostly black graveyard just outside the local Baptist church. Even in death, he refused to be bound by the laws of segregation. . . .[17]

2. Historical background. The antimiscegenation statute under which the Lovings were convicted reflected a widespread policy stemming from beliefs about racial superiority. At one time, 38 states prohibited relationships between Blacks and whites. Even before Virginia enacted its prohibition in 1662, state officials whipped and publicly humiliated persons who entered into Black-white sexual relationships.[18] Authorities claimed to be concerned, in large part, about the status of mulatto offspring in an economy based on slavery.

Anxieties over miscegenation increased after the Civil War, when the emancipation of slaves heightened racial tension. Bolstering this climate was the eugenics movement, which preached that most maladies were hereditary and that social engineering would improve the human race. This theory led to many state restrictions on marriage. From 1880 to 1920, 20 states and territories revised or added antimiscegenation laws.[19]

---

[17]. Phyl Newbeck, Virginia Hasn't Always Been for Lovers: Interracial Marriage Bans and the Case of Richard and Mildred Loving, 219-220 (2004). See also Peter Wallenstein, Race, Sex, and the Freedom to Marry: Loving v. Virginia (2015).

[18]. Rachel F. Moran, Interracial Intimacy: The Regulation of Race and Romance 17, 19 (2001).

[19]. Michael Grossberg, Governing the Hearth: Law and the Family in Nineteenth-Century America 136, 138-139 (1985).

3. Empirical data. *Loving* marked the beginning of a steady increase in multiracial marriages.[20] As intermarriage became more common, the public became more accepting.[21] Currently, 6.3 percent of marriages are between spouses of a different race, compared to less than 1 percent in 1970.[22]

4. Marrying in another state. Although Virginia's 1924 Racial Purity statute prohibited interracial marriage, the Lovings were convicted for violating a *different* statute (Va. Code §20-58, enacted in 1878) forbidding residents from leaving the state to marry, with intent to evade the state antimiscegenation law, and then returning to cohabit. This scenario raises questions of choice of law, full faith and credit, and marriage evasion acts.

a. Choice of law. One state will ordinarily recognize a marriage validly celebrated in another state under the common law rule of lex loci (the "place of celebration" rule), which provides that a marriage that is valid where performed is valid everywhere. Why didn't this choice of law rule apply in *Loving*? States considered some marriages (for example, interracial, polygamous, or incestuous unions) so offensive that they carved out exceptions to the rule based on public policy grounds, even without the existence of state bans on marriage evasion.

The Restatement (Second) of Conflict of Laws §283(1) (1971) addresses the issue as follows:

RESTATEMENT (SECOND) OF CONFLICT OF LAWS

§283. VALIDITY OF MARRIAGE

(1) The validity of a marriage will be determined by the local law of the state which, with respect to the particular issue, has the most significant relationship to the spouses and the marriage. . . .

(2) A marriage which satisfies the requirements of the state where the marriage was contracted will everywhere be recognized as valid unless it violates the strong public policy of another state which had the most significant relationship to the spouses and the marriage at the time of the marriage.

§284. INCIDENTS OF FOREIGN MARRIAGE

A state usually gives the same incidents to a foreign marriage, which is valid under the principles stated in §283, that it gives to a marriage contracted within its territory.

---

[20]. Steven A. Holmes, Study Finds Rising Number of Black-White Marriages, N.Y. Times, July 4, 1996 (noting that percentage of Blacks who were married to whites increased from 1.7 percent in 1960 to almost 6 percent in 1990), http://www.nytimes.com/1996/07/04/us/study-finds-rising-number-of-black-white-marriages.html.

[21]. Frank Newport, In U.S., 87% Approve of Black-White Marriage vs. 4% in 1958, July 25, 2013, http://www.gallup.com/poll/poll/163697/approve-marriage-blacks-whites.aspx.

[22]. Wendy Wang, Interracial Marriage: Who is "Marrying Out"? June 12, 2015, http://www.pewresearch.org/fact-tank/2015/06/12/interracial-marriage-who-is-marrying-out/. See also William Frey, Diversity Explosion: How New Racial Demographics Are Remaking America (2014) (pointing out that new minorities (i.e., Hispanics and Asians) are poised to exert a profound impact on society, economy, and politics).

b. Full Faith and Credit. The Full Faith and Credit Clause (art. IV, §1) of the Constitution and federal statutes implementing it require that one state give full faith and credit to "the public acts, records, and judicial proceedings" of sister states. Courts have interpreted the language to require the most rigorous respect for "judicial proceedings," foreclosing choice-of-law analysis in a second state once a court in the first state rendered a final judgment or decree. Marriage is not a judicial decree, so it does not evoke mandatory recognition and respect, even though a second state typically will choose to treat it as valid under lex loci or the Restatement. This approach leaves room for a state like Virginia to rely on its own public policy against interracial relationships to refuse to recognize the marriage that the Lovings validly celebrated in Washington, D.C.

c. Marriage evasion acts. The subject of marriage evasion was addressed by the Uniform Marriage Evasion Act (UMEA). Approved in 1912, UMEA did the following: (1) declared void all marriages of parties who married in another state for the purpose of evading home state restrictions; (2) allowed out-of-state residents to marry only if their marriage would be permissible in their home state; (3) required state officers to obtain proof that out-of-state applicants would be permitted to marry in their home state; and (4) provided misdemeanor liability for violations. The Uniform Marriage and Divorce Act (UMDA) superseded UMEA in 1970, with a requirement that states recognize marriages deemed valid either at the place of celebration or the parties' domicile (UMDA §210).[23]

5. *Loving* and precedent. *Loving* cites precedents concerning divorce (Maynard v. Hill), compulsory sterilization (Skinner v. Oklahoma), and, in an omitted section, parental rights (Meyer v. Nebraska). Are the cases apt? Curiously, *Loving* does not cite *Griswold*, decided two years earlier. What explains this omission? What contribution might *Griswold* and subsequent privacy cases make to the analysis in *Loving*?

6. *Loving*'s constitutional basis. Is *Loving* a case about race or about freedom of choice in marriage? What standard of review does the Court apply? What triggers such review? *Loving* establishes that the right to marry is constitutionally protected. Why should the Constitution protect the right to marry? Where in the Constitution is this right? Does it rest on substantive due process or equal protection? What difference does that make? On the basis of which approach did the Court decide *Zablocki*? Why?

7. Relevance of *Loving* to marriage for same-sex couples. Before the advent of marriage equality, advocates of same-sex marriage often equated the ban on same-sex marriage with antimiscegenation laws. This analogy is explored later in the chapter.

8. Degrees of scrutiny. *Zablocki* establishes different degrees of scrutiny for classifications infringing the right to marry; that is, rigorous scrutiny for a significant

---

[23]. On the history of the UMEA, see Joanna Grossman, Fear and Loathing in Massachusetts: Same-Sex Marriage and Some Lessons from the History of Marriage and Divorce, 14 B.U. Pub. Int. L.J. 87, 103, 113 (2004); Edward Stein, Past and Present Proposed Amendments to the United States Constitution Regarding Marriage, 82 Wash. U. L.Q. 611, 638 (2004) (pointing out that only Vermont, Massachusetts, Louisiana, Illinois, and Wisconsin adopted UMEA in whole or in part).

interference but minimal scrutiny for "reasonable regulations that do not significantly interfere with decisions to enter into the marital relationship." Justice Powell (in an omitted concurrence) suggests that the Court does not present any means to distinguish between the two types of regulations. Do you agree? What distinguishes the regulation in *Zablocki* from that in Califano v. Jobst (cited in *Zablocki*)?

According to *Zablocki*, a significant interference calling for rigorous scrutiny must be "direct" and "substantial." Are these distinct requirements? What guidelines does *Zablocki* give for identifying a "direct" interference?

9. **Post-*Zablocki* regulation of the procreation-support link.** The Wisconsin statute invalidated in *Zablocki* arose from legislative concern about the nonpayment of child support by "deadbeat dads." How does *Zablocki* inform our understanding of the normative link between marriage and procreation and/or support? See Melissa Murray, Marriage as Punishment, 112 Colum. L. Rev. 1, 43-47 (2012).

Problems

1. Which, if any, of the following statutes, regulations, or policies are unconstitutional infringements on the right to marry?

   a. Prohibition on married students' participation in athletic programs (Indiana High Sch. Athletic Ass'n v. Raike, 329 N.E.2d 66 (Ind. Ct. App. 1975));
   b. State agency's employment policy terminating a county clerk (an at-will employee) after she accepted a proposal of marriage from an attorney whose divorce from another county clerk (in an adjacent office) was not yet final (Beecham v. Henderson Cty., 422 F.3d 372 (6th Cir. 2005));
   c. State agency's denial to a governmental employee of extended state workers' compensation disability benefits based on the employee's spouse's income (Johnson v. Pomeroy, 294 Fed. Appx. 397 (10th Cir. 2008));
   d. Judicial imposition of a no-contact restriction between defendant and her husband as a condition of her suspended sentence for sexual crimes that she committed with her husband (sexual abuse of her stepdaughter) (State v. Guill, 248 P.3d 826 (Mont. 2011)).

2. As part of welfare reform, Congress enacted the Deficit Reduction Act of 2005 (DRA), 42 U.S.C. §603(a)(2), appropriating $150 million in grants annually for five years to implement the Healthy Marriage and Responsible Fatherhood Initiative. Congress reauthorized the program by the Claims Resolution Act of 2010 (Pub. L. No. 111-291). The objective of the legislation is to promote and strengthen marriages and relationships in low-income families as a national strategy for enhancing children's well-being. Activities include premarital education and marriage skills training emphasizing the value of healthy marriage and responsible parenting.

Do such programs, as applied to recipients of public assistance, directly and substantially interfere with the right to marry? What policy issues should the implementing states consider? See generally Vivian Hamilton, Will Marriage Promotion Work?, 11 J. Gender Race & Justice 1 (2007); R.A. Lenhardt, Marriage as Black Citizenship?, 66 Hastings L.J. 1317 (2015) (arguing that marriage regulation—historically and in contemporary times—has contributed to cumulative racial disadvantage for African Americans).

3. Kaniska Berashk is a citizen of Afghanistan. Based on his marriage to Fauzia Din, a naturalized U.S. citizen, he applies to a consular officer in the U.S. embassy in Islamabad, Pakistan, for a visa to enter the United States. The official denies Kaniska's visa application. The officer gives no specific reason but merely relies on the immigration statute's broad definition of "terrorist activities." Kaniska presumes that the denial is based on his possible connection to the Taliban – that is, his job as a payroll clerk for the Afghan Ministry of Social Welfare, which was part of the national government that was at one time controlled by the Taliban. His wife, Fauzia, seeks judicial review of her husband's visa denial and his forced separation from her. She alleges that the visa denial violates her constitutional right to marry. What result? See Kerry v. Din, 135 S. Ct. 2128 (2015).

TURNER v. SAFLEY

482 U.S. 78 (1987)

Justice O'CONNOR delivered the opinion of the Court.

This case requires us to determine the constitutionality of regulations promulgated by the Missouri Division of Corrections relating to inmate marriages [that permit] an inmate to marry only with the permission of the superintendent of the prison, and provide that such approval should be given only "when there are compelling reasons to do so." The term "compelling" is not defined, but prison officials testified at trial that generally only a pregnancy or the birth of an illegitimate child would be considered a compelling reason. [Plaintiff inmates, who desire to marry, bring a class action for injunctive relief and damages.]

In support of the marriage regulation, petitioners first suggest that the rule does not deprive prisoners of a constitutionally protected right. They concede that the decision to marry is a fundamental right [under *Zablocki* and *Loving*], but they imply that a different rule should obtain "in . . . a prison forum." Petitioners then argue that even if the regulation burdens inmates' constitutional rights, the restriction should be tested under a reasonableness standard. They urge that the restriction is reasonably related to legitimate security and rehabilitation concerns.

We disagree with petitioners that *Zablocki* does not apply to prison inmates. It is settled that a prison inmate "retains those [constitutional] rights that are not inconsistent with his status as a prisoner or with the legitimate penological objectives of the corrections system." The right to marry, like many other rights, is subject to substantial restrictions as a result of incarceration.

Many important attributes of marriage remain, however, after taking into account the limitations imposed by prison life. First, inmate marriages, like others, are expressions of emotional support and public commitment. These elements are an important and significant aspect of the marital relationship. In addition, many religions recognize marriage as having spiritual significance; for some inmates and their spouses, therefore, the commitment of marriage may be an exercise of religious faith as well as an expression of personal dedication. Third, most inmates eventually will be released by parole or commutation, and therefore most inmate marriages are formed in the expectation that they ultimately will be fully consummated. Finally, marital status often is a precondition to the receipt of government benefits (e.g., Social Security benefits), property rights (e.g., tenancy by the entirety, inheritance rights), and other, less tangible benefits (e.g., legitimation of children born out of wedlock). These incidents of marriage, like the religious and personal aspects of the marriage commitment, are unaffected by the fact of confinement or the pursuit of legitimate corrections goals.

Taken together, we conclude that these remaining elements are sufficient to form a constitutionally protected marital relationship in the prison context. Our decision in Butler v. Wilson, 415 U.S. 953 (1974), is not to the contrary. That case involved a prohibition on marriage only for inmates sentenced to life imprisonment; and, importantly, denial of the right was part of the punishment for crime.

The Missouri marriage regulation prohibits inmates from marrying unless the prison superintendent has approved the marriage after finding that there are compelling reasons for doing so. . . . In determining whether this regulation impermissibly burdens the right to marry, we note initially that the regulation prohibits marriages between inmates and civilians, as well as marriages between inmates. Although not urged by respondents, this implication of the interests of nonprisoners . . . may entail a "consequential restriction on the [constitutional] rights of those who are not prisoners." We need not reach this question, however, because even under the reasonable relationship test, the marriage regulation does not withstand scrutiny.

Petitioners have identified both security and rehabilitation concerns in support of the marriage prohibition. The security concern emphasized by petitioners is that "love triangles" might lead to violent confrontations between inmates. With respect to rehabilitation, prison officials testified that female prisoners often were subject to abuse at home or were overly dependent on male figures, and that this dependence or abuse was connected to the crimes they had committed. The [prison] superintendent, petitioner William Turner, testified that in his view, these women prisoners needed to concentrate on developing skills of self-reliance, and that the prohibition on marriage furthered this rehabilitative goal. Petitioners emphasize that the prohibition on marriage should be understood in light of Superintendent Turner's experience with several ill-advised marriage requests from female inmates.

We conclude that on this record, the Missouri prison regulation, as written, is not reasonably related to these penological interests. No doubt legitimate security concerns may require placing reasonable restrictions upon an inmate's right to marry, and may justify requiring approval of the superintendent. The Missouri regulation, however, represents an exaggerated response to such security objectives. . . . Moreover, with respect to the security concern emphasized in petitioners' brief—the creation of "love triangles"—petitioners have pointed to nothing in the record suggesting that the marriage regulation was viewed as preventing such entanglements. Common sense likewise suggests that there is no logical connection between the marriage restriction and the formation of love triangles: surely in prisons housing both male and female prisoners, inmate rivalries are as likely to develop without a formal marriage ceremony as with one. Finally, this is not an instance where the "ripple effect" on the security of fellow inmates and prison staff justifies a broad restriction on inmates' rights. . . .

Nor, on this record, is the marriage restriction reasonably related to the articulated rehabilitation goal. First, in requiring refusal of permission absent a finding of a compelling reason to allow the marriage, the rule sweeps much more broadly than can be explained by petitioners' penological objectives. Missouri prison officials testified that generally they had experienced no problem with the marriage of male inmates, and the District Court found that such marriages had routinely been allowed as a matter of practice at Missouri correctional institutions prior to adoption of the rule. The proffered justification thus does not explain the adoption of a rule banning marriages by these inmates. Nor does it account for the prohibition on inmate marriages to civilians. Missouri prison officials testified that generally they had no objection to inmate-civilian marriages, and Superintendent Turner testified that he usually did not object to the marriage of either male or female prisoners to civilians. The rehabilitation concern appears from the record to have been centered almost exclusively on female inmates marrying other inmates or ex-felons. . . .

Moreover, although not necessary to the disposition of this case, we note that on this record the rehabilitative objective asserted to support the regulation itself is suspect. Of the several female inmates whose marriage requests were discussed by prison officials at trial, only one was refused on the basis of fostering excessive dependency. The District Court found that the Missouri prison system operated on the basis of excessive paternalism in that the proposed marriages of *all* female inmates were scrutinized carefully even before adoption of the current regulation . . . whereas the marriages of male inmates during the same period were routinely approved. That kind of lopsided rehabilitation concern cannot provide a justification for the broad Missouri marriage rule.

[On this record] the almost complete ban on the decision to marry is not reasonably related to legitimate penological objectives. We conclude, therefore, that the Missouri marriage regulation is facially invalid.

Sheila Isenberg, Women Who Love Men Who Kill[24]

34-35, 223-236 (2000)

Unbelievable as it may seem, there is a population of women who are deeply drawn to men who have murdered. They meet the men while working in prison as nurses, teachers, social workers, or volunteers. Others become pen pals with murderers. Some, who are infatuated, write fan/love letters to celebrity killers [or] serial killers. . . . Women who love killers were often little girls lost, reared in dysfunctional families where they were victims of abuse at the hands of harsh, dictatorial fathers aided by passive mothers. A large percentage were raised as Catholics and were severely affected by oppressive church teachings, including sexism, subjugation of women, and repression of sexuality.

[24]. Sheila Isenberg, a journalist, developed a profile of women who love convicted murderers based on her interviews with mental health professionals, law enforcement, and the couples themselves. The topic of prison marriages with non-inmates is also explored in a recent National Geographic documentary, Taboo: Prison Love, http://www.watchdocumentary.tv/taboo-prison-love-documentary.

Fathers were missing: divorced, dead, always working, drunk, withdrawn. Occasionally, mothers took on fathers' role and behaved like demanding authoritarians. Women who love killers frequently found that their relationships with men mimicked the one they had with their fathers. . . .

As it was between medieval maidens and the courtly knights who protected them, sex and true intimacy between women and the killers they love is usually forbidden by prison systems. These women feel deeply, but what they feel is not mature love or adult sexual passion. It is *romantic* passion—a passion fueled by deprivation and suffering, enhanced by anguish. These women have found the key to never-ending romance: suffering and pain.

Because many women who love killers have real difficulties with intimacy because of the damage done to them in childhood, they have chosen to live a fantasy. The majority of these women don't love real men but an illusion that is based on denial. Each woman separates, or compartmentalizes, the murder from the man she loves. She denies his crime. For women who love serial killers, or other notorious murderers, there is the added thrill of fame. Each serial killer's status gives a woman with low self-esteem a sense of importance; her prestige rises in direct proportion with the heinousness of his crimes.

In our patriarchal culture, murderers are often viewed as more than male: the most macho, strong, violent, and brutal of all men. In a majority of movies and television shows, the violent mystique of the murderer—or the cop, spy, undercover agent, etc.—is the erotic centerpiece. . . . For some women, it *is* thrilling to dance with a master of death. If a woman is seeking excitement, passion, a meaning to life, loving a murderer can make her feel intensely alive. She becomes important, perhaps famous, because she loves a man who has killed. . . .

A murderer is often a con man who wins a woman by manipulation and lying. Some women, gullible, vulnerable, and needy, are ready to believe these charmers. Each woman hears a story that fits her needs: If she needs to believe that he's religious, he'll tell her that. If she wants sweet talk, he'll woo her. If she needs a brilliant existentialist hero, he'll sweep her off her feet with his verbiage. Some murderers are unbelievably charismatic. These men exude self-confidence. The narcissistic and antisocial personalities of these murderers cause them to act as though rules don't apply to them. They act tough and superior. They believe in themselves (or pretend they do) and easily convince susceptible women (literally little girls lost) to believe in them too. But, in truth, these are deeply disturbed men who, by murdering, have irrevocably broken one of our most basic laws. . . .

Notes and Questions

1. Precedents. Does *Turner*'s holding follow automatically from *Loving* and *Zablocki*?

2. Rationale. What rationale supports depriving life-sentence inmates of the right to marry, as the Court previously held (in Butler v. Wilson, cited in *Turner*)?

Does this rationale dictate the automatic *dissolution* of marriages entered into by these inmates prior to incarceration? Cf. Langone v. Coughlin, 712 F. Supp. 1061 (N.D.N.Y. 1989) (invalidating a ban on marriages by "lifers" that exempted marriages of those "lifers" who were already married, as not reasonably related to legitimate penological objectives).

3. Gender. Why did the Department of Corrections policy in *Turner* focus on female inmates? Why did prison officials conclude that marriage could thwart the rehabilitation of females but not males? Are the problems of abuse and dependency in marriage gender specific? What additional "gendered" insights does Isenberg's excerpt, supra, provide?

Problems

1. Alfie, an indigent prison inmate who is serving a life sentence, is denied a marriage license when he is unable to comply with state law by personally appearing at the county clerk's office. The prison offers two accommodations: transportation by the Sheriff's Office for a fee or application by video conferencing at the prison, subject to judicial approval. However, Alfie does not have the resources to pay transportation costs, and the court does not have equipment for video conferencing. Does *Turner* require prison officials to facilitate and pay for benefits to enable prisoners to comply with procedural requirements to marry? See In re Coats, 849 A.2d 254 (Pa. Super. Ct. 2004); Toms v. Taft, 338 F.3d 519 (6th Cir. 2003). Must the prison permit solemnization of marriages at the corrections facility? See Lambert v. Myers, 2004 WL 1452423 (N.D. Ill. 2004).

2. Suppose that Alfie prevails (in the above Problem) and the prison allows him to marry. Afterwards, he and his wife, who is 44 years old, wish to have a child. Alfie learns that the California Department of Corrections (CDC) prohibits conjugal visits for inmates serving life sentences. He requests that (1) a lab be permitted to mail him a semen collection container with a prepaid return mailer, (2) he be permitted to ejaculate into the container, and (3) the filled container be returned to the laboratory via overnight mail. Alternatively, he requests that his attorney be permitted to transport the specimen to the lab. He is willing to bear all costs. When the CDC refuses his requests, he brings an action alleging a violation of his constitutional right to procreate pursuant to 42 U.S.C. §1983 and the Due Process Clause. What result? If the court were to agree that Alfie has a constitutional right to procreate noncoitally in this manner, does a female inmate have a right to be artificially inseminated? See Gerber v. Hickman, 291 F.3d 617 (9th Cir. 2002); Goodwin v. Turner, 908 F.2d 1395 (8th Cir. 1990).

3. Suppose that Alfie's lawsuit (in Problem 2) is denied. Alfie then files a class action suit on behalf of all inmates at his prison challenging the denial of conjugal visitation. He argues that the policy violates: (1) prisoners' and spousal rights to marital privacy; (2) the right to procreate; (3) the constitutional prohibition on cruel and unusual punishment; and (4) the First Amendment right to religious freedom. What result? Does it follow from *Turner* that a prisoner must be permitted

conjugal visits? See Robertson v. Kansas, 2007 WL 4322781, at *2 (D. Kan. 2007). Does it matter if the inmate is married or not? Are there valid reasons for denial of conjugal visits? See Newson v. Noble, 2007 WL 471005 (E.D. Cal. 2007); Doe v. Coughlin, 518 N.E.2d 536 (N.Y. 1987). How meaningful is recognition of the right to marry without the provision of conjugal visits? See generally Megan Comfort, Doing Time Together: Love and Family in the Shadow of the Prison (2008).

The following excerpt explores the actual practice of conjugal visits.

Dana Goldstein, Conjugal Visits

Marshall Project (Feb. 11, 2015)[25]

Although conjugal, or "extended," visits play a huge role in prison lore, in reality, very few inmates have access to them. Twenty years ago, 17 states offered these programs. Today, just four do: California, Connecticut, New York, and Washington. No federal prison offers extended, private visitation.

Last April, New Mexico became the latest state to cancel conjugal visits for prisoners after a local television station revealed that a convicted killer, Michael Guzman, had fathered four children with several different wives while in prison. Mississippi had made a similar decision in January 2014.

In every state that offers extended visits, good prison behavior is a prerequisite, and inmates convicted of sex crimes or domestic violence, or who have life sentences, are typically excluded.

The visits range from one hour to three days, and happen as often as once per month. They take place in trailers, small apartments, or "family cottages" built just for this purpose, and are sometimes referred to as "boneyards." At the MacDougall-Walker Correctional Institution in Connecticut, units are set up to imitate homes. Each apartment has two bedrooms, a dining room, and a living room with a TV, DVD player, playing cards, a Jenga game, and dominoes. In Washington, any DVD a family watches must be G-rated. Kitchens are typically fully functional, and visitors can bring in fresh ingredients or cooked food from the outside.

In California, inmates and their visitors must line up for inspection every four hours throughout the weekend visit, even in the middle of the night. Many prisons provide condoms for free. In New Mexico, before the extended visitation program was canceled, the prisoner's spouse could be informed if the inmate had tested positive for a sexually transmitted infection. After the visit, both inmates and visitors are searched, and inmates typically have their urine tested to check for drugs or alcohol, which are strictly prohibited.

Conjugal visits are not just about sex. In fact, they are officially called "family visits," and kids often are allowed to stay overnight, too. . . .

---

[25]. The full article is available at https://www.themarshallproject.org/2015/02/11/conjugal-visits.

2. State Regulation of Entry into the Marital Relationship

a. Substantive Restrictions

(i) Capacity to Marry

(1) Same Sex

UNITED STATES v. WINDSOR

133 S. Ct. 2675 (2013)

Justice KENNEDY delivered the opinion of the Court.

. . . In 1996, as some States were beginning to consider the concept of same-sex marriage, and before any State had acted to permit it, Congress enacted the Defense of Marriage Act (DOMA). DOMA contains two operative sections: Section 2, which has not been challenged here, allows States to refuse to recognize same-sex marriages performed under the laws of other States. See 28 U.S.C. §1738C. Section 3 is at issue here. It amends the Dictionary Act in Title 1, §7, of the United States Code to provide a federal definition of "marriage" and "spouse." Section 3 of DOMA provides as follows:

> "In determining the meaning of any Act of Congress, or of any ruling, regulation, or interpretation of the various administrative bureaus and agencies of the United States, the word 'marriage' means only a legal union between one man and one woman as husband and wife, and the word 'spouse' refers only to a person of the opposite sex who is a husband or a wife." 1 U.S.C. §7.

The definitional provision does not by its terms forbid States from enacting laws permitting same-sex marriages or civil unions or providing state benefits to residents in that status. The enactment's comprehensive definition of marriage for purposes of all federal statutes and other regulations or directives covered by its terms, however, does control over 1,000 federal laws in which marital or spousal status is addressed as a matter of federal law.

Edith Windsor and Thea Spyer met in New York City in 1963 and began a long-term relationship. Windsor and Spyer registered as domestic partners when New York City gave that right to same-sex couples in 1993. Concerned about Spyer's health, the couple made the 2007 trip to Canada for their marriage, but they continued to reside in New York City. The State of New York deems their Ontario marriage to be a valid one.

Spyer died in February 2009, and left her entire estate to Windsor. Because DOMA denies federal recognition to same-sex spouses, Windsor did not qualify for the marital exemption from the federal estate tax, which excludes from taxation "any interest in property which passes or has passed from the decedent to his surviving spouse." 26 U.S.C. §2056(a). Windsor paid $363,053 in estate taxes and sought a refund. The Internal Revenue Service denied the refund, concluding that, under DOMA, Windsor was not a "surviving spouse." Windsor commenced this refund suit [contending] that DOMA violates the guarantee of equal protection, as applied to the Federal Government through the Fifth Amendment. . . .

When at first Windsor and Spyer longed to marry, neither New York nor any other State granted them that right. After waiting some years, in 2007 they traveled to Ontario to be married there. It seems fair to conclude that, until recent years, many citizens had not even considered the possibility that two persons of the same sex might aspire to occupy the same status and dignity as that of a man and woman in lawful marriage. For marriage between a man and a woman no doubt had been thought of by most people as essential to the very definition of that term and to its role and function throughout the history of civilization. That belief, for many who long have held it, became even more urgent, more cherished when challenged. For others, however, came the beginnings of a new perspective, a new insight. Accordingly some States concluded that same-sex marriage ought to be given recognition and validity in the law for those same-sex couples who wish to define themselves by their commitment to each other. The limitation of lawful marriage to heterosexual couples, which for centuries had been deemed both necessary and fundamental, came to be seen in New York and certain other States as an unjust exclusion.

Slowly at first and then in rapid course, the laws of New York came to acknowledge the urgency of this issue for same-sex couples who wanted to affirm their commitment to one another before their children, their family, their friends, and their community. And so New York recognized same-sex marriages performed elsewhere; and then it later amended its own marriage laws to permit same-sex marriage [as did several other states]. . . .

Against this background of lawful same-sex marriage in some States, the design, purpose, and effect of DOMA should be considered as the beginning point in deciding whether it is valid under the Constitution. By history and tradition the definition and regulation of marriage . . . has been treated as being within the authority and realm of the separate States. [Within the context] of limited federal laws that regulate the meaning of marriage in order to further federal policy, DOMA has a far greater reach; for it enacts a directive applicable to over 1,000 federal statutes and the whole realm of federal regulations. And its operation is directed to a class of persons that the laws of New York, and of 11 other States, have sought to protect.

In order to assess the validity of that intervention, it is necessary to discuss the extent of the state power and authority over marriage as a matter of history and tradition. State laws defining and regulating marriage, of course, must respect the constitutional rights of persons [citing *Loving*]; but, subject to those guarantees, "regulation of domestic relations" is "an area that has long been regarded as a virtually exclusive province of the States."

The recognition of civil marriages is central to state domestic relations law applicable to its residents and citizens. The definition of marriage is the foundation of the State's broader authority to regulate the subject of domestic relations with respect to the "[p]rotection of offspring, property interests, and the enforcement of marital responsibilities." "[T]he states, at the time of the adoption of the Constitution, possessed full power over the subject of marriage and divorce [and] the Constitution delegated no authority to the Government of the United States on the subject of marriage and divorce." . . .

Against this background, DOMA rejects the long-established precept that the incidents, benefits, and obligations of marriage are uniform for all married couples within each State. . . . Here [New York's] decision to give this class of persons the right to marry conferred upon them a dignity and status of immense import. When the State used its historic and essential authority to define the marital relation in this way, its role and its power in making the decision enhanced the recognition, dignity, and protection of the class in their own community. DOMA, because of its reach and extent, departs from this history and tradition of reliance on state law to define marriage. "'[D]iscriminations of an unusual character especially suggest careful consideration to determine whether they are obnoxious to the constitutional provision.'" . . .

The Federal Government uses this state-defined class for the opposite purpose—to impose restrictions and disabilities. That result requires this Court now to address whether the resulting injury and indignity is a deprivation of an essential part of the liberty protected by the Fifth Amendment. . . .

The States' interest in defining and regulating the marital relation, subject to constitutional guarantees, stems from the understanding that marriage is more than a routine classification for purposes of certain statutory benefits. Private, consensual sexual intimacy between two adult persons of the same sex may not be punished by the State, and it can form "but one element in a personal bond that is more enduring." Lawrence v. Texas, 539 U. S. 558, 567 (2003). By its recognition of the validity of same-sex marriages performed in other jurisdictions and then by authorizing same-sex unions and same-sex marriages, New York sought to give further protection and dignity to that bond. For same-sex couples who wished to be married, the State acted to give their lawful conduct a lawful status. This status is a far-reaching legal acknowledgment of the intimate relationship between two people, a relationship deemed by the State worthy of dignity in the community equal with all other marriages. It reflects both the community's considered perspective on the historical roots of the institution of marriage and its evolving understanding of the meaning of equality.

DOMA seeks to injure the very class New York seeks to protect. By doing so it violates basic due process and equal protection principles applicable to the Federal Government. The Constitution's guarantee of equality "must at the very least mean that a bare congressional desire to harm a politically unpopular group cannot" justify disparate treatment of that group. In determining whether a law is motived by an improper animus or purpose, "'[d]iscriminations of an unusual character'" especially require careful consideration [Romer v. Evans, 517 U.S. 620, 633 (1996)].

DOMA cannot survive under these principles. The responsibility of the States for the regulation of domestic relations is an important indicator of the substantial societal impact the State's classifications have in the daily lives and customs of its people. DOMA's unusual deviation from the usual tradition of recognizing and accepting state definitions of marriage here operates to deprive same-sex couples of the benefits and responsibilities that come with the federal recognition of their marriages. This is strong evidence of a law having the purpose and effect of disapproval of that class. The avowed purpose and practical effect of the law here in question are to impose a disadvantage, a separate status, and so a stigma upon all who enter into same-sex marriages made lawful by the unquestioned authority of the States.

The history of DOMA's enactment and its own text demonstrate that interference with the equal dignity of same-sex marriages, a dignity conferred by the States in the exercise of their sovereign power, was more than an incidental effect of the federal statute. It was its essence. The House Report announced its conclusion that "it is both appropriate and necessary for Congress to do what it can to defend the institution of traditional heterosexual marriage. . . . The effort to redefine 'marriage' to extend to homosexual couples is a truly radical proposal that would fundamentally alter the institution of marriage." The House concluded that DOMA expresses "both moral disapproval of homosexuality, and a moral conviction that heterosexuality better comports with traditional (especially Judeo-Christian) morality." The stated purpose of the law was to promote an "interest in protecting the traditional moral teachings reflected in heterosexual-only marriage laws." Were there any doubt of this far-reaching purpose, the title of the Act confirms it: The Defense of Marriage.

. . . The Act's demonstrated purpose is to ensure that if any State decides to recognize same-sex marriages, those unions will be treated as second-class marriages for purposes of federal law. This raises a most serious question under the Constitution's Fifth Amendment. DOMA's operation in practice confirms this purpose. When New York adopted a law to permit same-sex marriage, it sought to eliminate inequality; but DOMA frustrates that objective through a system-wide enactment with no identified connection to any particular area of federal law. DOMA writes inequality into the entire United States Code. The particular case at hand concerns the estate tax, but DOMA [also applies to federal statutes and regulations such as Social Security, housing, taxes, criminal sanctions, copyright, and veterans' benefits among others].

DOMA's principal effect is to identify a subset of state-sanctioned marriages and make them unequal. The principal purpose is to impose inequality, not for other reasons like governmental efficiency. Responsibilities, as well as rights, enhance the dignity and integrity of the person. And DOMA contrives to deprive some couples married under the laws of their State, but not other couples, of both rights and responsibilities. By creating two contradictory marriage regimes within the same State, DOMA forces same-sex couples to live as married for the purpose of state law but unmarried for the purpose of federal law, thus diminishing the stability and predictability of basic personal relations the State has found it proper to acknowledge and protect.

By this dynamic DOMA undermines both the public and private significance of state-sanctioned same-sex marriages; for it tells those couples, and all the world, that their otherwise valid marriages are unworthy of federal recognition. This places same-sex couples in an unstable position of being in a second-tier marriage. The differentiation demeans the couple, whose moral and sexual choices the Constitution protects [citing *Lawrence*], and whose relationship the State has sought to dignify. And it humiliates tens of thousands of children now being raised by same-sex couples. The law in question makes it even more difficult for the children to understand the integrity and closeness of their own family and its concord with other families in their community and in their daily lives.

Under DOMA, same-sex married couples have their lives burdened, by reason of government decree, in visible and public ways. By its great reach, DOMA touches many aspects of married and family life, from the mundane to the profound. It prevents same-sex married couples from obtaining government healthcare benefits they would otherwise receive. It deprives them of the Bankruptcy Code's special protections for domestic-support obligations. It forces them to follow a complicated procedure to file their state and federal taxes jointly. It prohibits them from being buried together in veterans' cemeteries. . . . DOMA also brings financial harm to children of same-sex couples. It raises the cost of health care for families by taxing health benefits provided by employers to their workers' same-sex spouses. And it denies or reduces [Social Security] benefits allowed to families upon the loss of a spouse and parent, benefits that are an integral part of family security.

DOMA divests married same-sex couples of the duties and responsibilities that are an essential part of married life and that they in most cases would be honored to accept were DOMA not in force. . . . What has been explained to this point should more than suffice to establish that the principal purpose and the necessary effect of this law are to demean those persons who are in a lawful same-sex marriage. This requires the Court to hold, as it now does, that DOMA [§3] is unconstitutional. . . . The federal statute is invalid, for no legitimate purpose overcomes the purpose and effect to disparage and to injure those whom the State, by its marriage laws, sought to protect in personhood and dignity. By seeking to displace this protection and treating those persons as living in marriages less respected than others, the federal statute is in violation of the Fifth Amendment. This opinion and its holding are confined to those lawful marriages. . . .

Chief Justice ROBERTS, dissenting.

Interests in uniformity and stability amply justified Congress's decision to retain the definition of marriage that, at that point, had been adopted by every State in our Nation, and every nation in the world.

The majority sees a more sinister motive, pointing out that the Federal Government has generally (though not uniformly) deferred to state definitions of marriage in the past. That is true, of course, but none of those prior state-by-state variations had involved differences over something—as the majority puts it—"thought of by most people as essential to the very definition of [marriage] and to its role and function throughout the history of civilization." That the Federal Government treated this fundamental question differently than it treated variations over consanguinity or minimum age is hardly surprising—and hardly enough to support a conclusion that the "principal purpose," of the 342 Representatives and 85 Senators who voted for it, and the President who signed it, was a bare desire to harm. Nor do the snippets of legislative history and the banal title of the Act to which the majority points suffice to make such a showing. At least without some more convincing evidence that the Act's principal purpose was to codify malice, and that it furthered no legitimate government interests, I would not tar the political branches with the brush of bigotry.

But while I disagree with the result to which the majority's analysis leads it in this case, I think it more important to point out that its analysis leads no further. . . . We may in the future have to resolve challenges to state marriage definitions affecting same-sex couples. That issue, however, is not before us in this case. . . .

Justice SCALIA, with whom Justice THOMAS joins, and with whom THE CHIEF JUSTICE joins as to Part I (affirming jurisdiction), dissenting.

This case is about power in several respects. It is about the power of our people to govern themselves, and the power of this Court to pronounce the law. Today's opinion aggrandizes the latter, with the predictable consequence of diminishing the former. We have no power to decide this case. And even if we did, we have no power under the Constitution to invalidate this democratically adopted legislation. . . .

There are many remarkable things about the majority's merits holding. The first is how rootless and shifting its justifications are . . . Equally perplexing are the opinion's references to "the Constitution's guarantee of equality." [I]f this is meant to be an equal-protection opinion, it is a confusing one. The opinion does not resolve and indeed does not even mention what had been the central question in this litigation: whether, under the Equal Protection Clause, laws restricting marriage to a man and a woman are reviewed for more than mere rationality. That is the issue that divided the parties and the court below. . . . I would review this classification only for its rationality. . . .

The majority opinion need not get into the strict-vs.-rational-basis scrutiny question, and need not justify its holding under either, because it says that DOMA is unconstitutional as "a deprivation of the liberty of the person protected by the Fifth Amendment of the Constitution," that it violates "basic due process" principles—and that it inflicts an "injury and indignity" of a kind that denies "an essential part of the liberty protected by the Fifth Amendment." The majority never utters the dread words "substantive due process," perhaps sensing the disrepute into which that doctrine has fallen, but that is what those statements mean. Yet the opinion does not argue that same-sex marriage is "deeply rooted in this Nation's history and tradition," a claim that would of course be quite absurd. . . . The sum of all the Court's nonspecific hand-waving is that this law is invalid (maybe on equal-protection grounds, maybe on substantive-due-process grounds, and perhaps with some amorphous federalism component playing a role) because it is motivated by a " 'bare . . . desire to harm' " couples in same-sex marriages . . .

As I have observed before, the Constitution does not forbid the government to enforce traditional moral and sexual norms. [T]he Constitution neither requires nor forbids our society to approve of same-sex marriage, much as it neither requires nor forbids us to approve of no-fault divorce, polygamy, or the consumption of alcohol. . . .

The majority concludes that the only motive for this Act was the "bare . . . desire to harm a politically unpopular group." [The Court] accuses the Congress that enacted this law and the President who signed it of [acting] with malice—with the "*purpose*" "to disparage and to injure" same-sex couples. It says that the motivation for DOMA was to "demean"; to "impose inequality"; to "impose . . . a stigma"; to deny people "equal dignity"; to brand gay people as "unworthy"; and to "*humiliat*[*e*]" their children (emphasis added). I am sure these accusations are quite untrue. To be sure (as the majority points out), the legislation is called the Defense of Marriage Act. But to defend traditional marriage is not to condemn, demean, or humiliate those who would prefer other arrangements. . . .

The penultimate sentence of the majority's opinion is a naked declaration that "[t]his opinion and its holding are confined" to those couples "joined in same-sex marriages made lawful by the State." . . . It takes real cheek for today's majority to assure us, as it is going out the door, that a constitutional requirement to give formal recognition to same-sex marriage is not at issue here—when what has preceded that assurance is a lecture on how superior the majority's moral judgment in favor of same-sex marriage is to the Congress's hateful moral judgment against it. . . .

Jill Hamburg Coplan, When a Woman Loves a Woman[26]

NYU Alumni Magazine (Fall 2011), at 38

Edie Windsor (right) and her spouse Thea Spyer (left, now deceased)

The year was 1963, the restaurant was Portofino [a fashionable Friday-night spot in Greenwich Village], and about the only place a white-collar lesbian could be out and at ease. Edith Schlain Windsor—Monroe-esque, cherubic cheeked, and her hair in a perfect flip—was an NYU-trained mathematician and fast-rising IBM programmer, just back from a fellowship at Harvard University. She was tired of being single and past ready to jettison the "therapy" to make her straight.

Friends brought Thea Clara Spyer to her table. A child of European refugees, Thea was charismatic and intellectual, a psychology PhD from Adelphi University who'd interned at St. Vincent's Hospital. The angular brunette mesmerized Edie. Thea was more experienced, having been expelled from Sarah Lawrence College for kissing an older woman. And she seemed a bit more comfortable in the Village's small lesbian underground of bars, run by the Mafia, where even huge bouncers at the doors couldn't prevent the occasional violent police raid.

They danced. "We immediately just fit." [Thea later recalled]. Their connection was passionate, and they became inseparable. In 1967, Thea proposed with a round diamond pin, because a ring would draw unwanted attention. "She was beautiful," Edie said in a recent interview. "It was joyful, and that didn't go away."

For more than four decades, they shared life and love in an apartment on Fifth Avenue near Washington Square, where Thea also saw patients. But while straight friends married and raised children, those doors were closed to the couple. IBM rejected Edie's insurance form naming Thea as beneficiary. Legally, they remained strangers—when Thea was diagnosed, at 45, with multiple sclerosis; when Edie took early retirement and evolved into her full-time caregiver; when they did financial planning. Until 2007. Thea's doctor said she had only one year left. Thea, by then paralyzed, proposed again.

This time, doors were open. With friends, they flew to Toronto (Canada had enacted marriage equality in 2005), hauling a duffel bag of tools to take apart and reassemble Thea's giant motorized wheelchair. Edie festooned an airport hotel conference room with palms and white fabric. She wore pastel silk, offset by a burst of fresh white flowers, while Thea chose all black with one red rose. Canada's first openly gay judge officiated: "You have found joy and meaning together and have chosen to live your lives together," he intoned. "To this

[26]. The full article is available at http://www.nyu.edu/alumni.magazine/issue17/17_FEA_DOMA.html.

moment you've brought the fullness of your hearts and the dreams that bind you together." When Thea welled up with tears, Edie dabbed them dry. They exchanged wedding bands.

Two years later, Thea was gone. Edie suffered a heart attack in her grief. And then the Defense of Marriage Act (DOMA), a 1996 federal statute, kicked in, transforming Edie's story from personal tragedy to public issue. . . . Married couples, according to the federal tax code, can transfer money or property from spouse to spouse upon death without triggering estate taxes (the "unlimited marital deduction"). But gay couples, after DOMA, have no such rights, even if the marriage is recognized by their state of residence, as Edie and Thea's was by New York.

So at 80, alone and living on a fixed income with a weakened heart, Edie paid a $363,053 widow's tax from her retirement savings. And with that payment, *Windsor v. United States* was born. . . .

OBERGEFELL v. HODGES

135 S. Ct. 2584 (2015)

Justice KENNEDY delivered the opinion of the Court.

The Constitution promises liberty to all within its reach, a liberty that includes certain specific rights that allow persons, within a lawful realm, to define and express their identity. The petitioners in these cases seek to find that liberty by marrying someone of the same sex and having their marriages deemed lawful on the same terms and conditions as marriages between persons of the opposite sex. . . . [The first question here] is whether the Fourteenth Amendment requires a State to license a marriage between two people of the same sex. The second is whether the Fourteenth Amendment requires a State to recognize a same-sex marriage licensed and performed in a State which does grant that right.

. . . [T]he annals of human history reveal the transcendent importance of marriage. The lifelong union of a man and a woman always has promised nobility and dignity to all persons, without regard to their station in life. Marriage is sacred to those who live by their religions and offers unique fulfillment to those who find meaning in the secular realm. . . . Rising from the most basic human needs, marriage is essential to our most profound hopes and aspirations. The centrality of marriage to the human condition makes it unsurprising that the institution has existed for millennia and across civilizations. . . . There are untold references to the beauty of marriage in religious and philosophical texts spanning time, cultures, and faiths, as well as in art and literature in all their forms. It is fair and necessary to say these references were based on the understanding that marriage is a union between two persons of the opposite sex.

That history is the beginning of these cases. [For respondents], it would demean a timeless institution if the concept and lawful status of marriage were extended to two persons of the same sex. Marriage, in their view, is by its nature a gender-differentiated union of man and woman. . . . The petitioners acknowledge this history but contend that these cases cannot end there. Were their intent to demean the revered idea and reality of marriage, the petitioners' claims would be of a different order. . . . To the contrary, it is the enduring importance of marriage that underlies the petitioners' contentions. . . . Far from seeking to devalue marriage, the petitioners seek it for themselves because of their respect—and need—for its privileges and responsibilities. . . .

[T]hese cases illustrate the urgency of the petitioners' cause from their perspective. [James Obergefell and John Arthur established a committed relationship two decades ago. After Arthur was diagnosed with amyotrophic lateral sclerosis (ALS), which is progressive and incurable, they resolved to marry before he died. They arranged a medical transport jet to travel from Ohio to Maryland, which allowed same-sex marriage. Arthur died three months later.] Ohio law does not permit Obergefell to be listed as the surviving spouse on Arthur's death certificate. By statute, they must remain strangers even in death, a state-imposed separation Obergefell deems "hurtful for the rest of time." He brought suit to be shown as the surviving spouse on Arthur's death certificate.

[Plaintiffs April DeBoer and Jayne Rowse, both nurses, celebrated a commitment ceremony in 2007. They adopted infants with special needs, one of whom requires round-the-clock care.] Michigan, however, permits only opposite-sex married couples or single individuals to adopt, so each child can have only one woman as his or her legal parent. [The couple fears the problems the children would face in case of an emergency or if the legal parent died.] . . . [Plaintiffs Army Reserve Sergeant First Class Ijpe DeKoe and Thomas Kostura married in New York just after DeKoe received orders to deploy to Afghanistan. They now reside in Tennessee, where DeKoe works full-time for the Army Reserve.] Their lawful marriage is stripped from them whenever they reside in Tennessee, returning and disappearing as they travel across state lines. DeKoe, who served this Nation to preserve the freedom the Constitution protects, must endure a substantial burden. . . .

The ancient origins of marriage confirm its centrality, but it has not stood in isolation from developments in law and society. The history of marriage is one of both continuity and change. That institution—even as confined to opposite-sex relations—has evolved over time. . . . This dynamic can be seen in the Nation's experiences with the rights of gays and lesbians. Until the mid-20th century, same-sex intimacy long had been condemned as immoral . . . a belief often embodied in the criminal law. For this reason, among others, many persons did not deem homosexuals to have dignity in their own distinct identity. A truthful declaration by same-sex couples of what was in their hearts had to remain unspoken. Even when a greater awareness of the humanity and integrity of homosexual persons came in the period after World War II, the argument that gays and lesbians had a just claim to dignity was in conflict with both law and widespread social conventions. Same-sex intimacy remained a crime in many States. Gays and lesbians were prohibited from most government employment, barred from military service, excluded under immigration laws, targeted by police, and burdened in their rights to associate.

For much of the 20th century, moreover, homosexuality was treated as an illness. When the American Psychiatric Association published the first Diagnostic and Statistical Manual of Mental Disorders in 1952, homosexuality was classified as a mental disorder, a position adhered to until 1973. Only in more recent years have psychiatrists and others recognized that sexual orientation is both a normal expression of human sexuality and immutable.

In the late 20th century, [same-sex couples] began to lead more open and public lives and to establish families. . . . After years of litigation, legislation, referenda, and the discussions that attended these public acts, the States are now divided on the issue of same-sex marriage.

. . . The fundamental liberties protected by [the Due Process Clause] extend to certain personal choices central to individual dignity and autonomy, including intimate choices that define personal identity and beliefs. The identification and protection of fundamental rights is an enduring part of the judicial duty to interpret the Constitution. . . . History and tradition guide and discipline this inquiry but do not set its outer boundaries. . . .

The nature of injustice is that we may not always see it in our own times. The generations that wrote and ratified the Bill of Rights and the Fourteenth Amendment did not presume to know the extent of freedom in all of its dimensions, and so they entrusted to future generations a charter protecting the right of all persons to enjoy liberty as we learn its meaning. When new insight reveals discord between the Constitution's central protections and a received legal stricture, a claim to liberty must be addressed.

[T]he Court has long held the right to marry is protected by the Constitution [citing *Loving*; *Zablocki*; and *Turner*]. Over time and in other contexts, the Court has reiterated that the right to marry is fundamental under the Due Process Clause. [F]our principles and traditions . . . demonstrate that the reasons marriage is fundamental under the Constitution apply with equal force to same-sex couples.

A first premise of the Court's relevant precedents is that the right to personal choice regarding marriage is inherent in the concept of individual autonomy. This abiding connection between marriage and liberty is why *Loving* invalidated interracial marriage bans under the Due Process Clause. Like choices concerning contraception, family relationships, procreation, and childrearing, all of which are protected by the Constitution, decisions concerning marriage are among the most intimate that an individual can make . . .

The nature of marriage is that, through its enduring bond, two persons together can find other freedoms, such as expression, intimacy, and spirituality. This is true for all persons, whatever their sexual orientation. There is dignity in the bond between two men or two women who seek to marry and in their autonomy to make such profound choices.

A second principle in this Court's jurisprudence is that the right to marry is fundamental because it supports a two-person union unlike any other in its importance to the committed individuals. . . . The right to marry thus dignifies couples who "wish to define themselves by their commitment to each other." Marriage responds to the universal fear that a lonely person might call out only to find no one there. It offers the hope of companionship and understanding and assurance that while both still live there will be someone to care for the other.

As this Court held in *Lawrence*, same-sex couples have the same right as opposite-sex couples to enjoy intimate association. [*Lawrence*] acknowledged that "[w]hen sexuality finds overt expression in intimate conduct with another person, the conduct can be but one element in a personal bond that is more enduring." But while *Lawrence* confirmed a dimension of freedom that allows individuals to engage in intimate association without criminal liability, it does not follow that freedom stops there. Outlaw to outcast may be a step forward, but it does not achieve the full promise of liberty.

A third basis for protecting the right to marry is that it safeguards children and families and thus draws meaning from related rights of childrearing, procreation, and education [citing *Meyer* and *Pierce*]."[T]he right to 'marry, establish a home and bring up children' is a central part of the liberty protected by the Due Process Clause." [M]arriage also confers more profound benefits. By giving recognition and legal structure to their parents' relationship, marriage allows children "to understand the integrity and closeness of their own family and its concord with other families in their community and in their daily lives." Marriage also affords the permanency and stability important to children's best interests.

[M]any same-sex couples provide loving and nurturing homes to their children, whether biological or adopted. . . . This provides powerful confirmation from the law itself that gays and lesbians can create loving, supportive families. . . . Without the recognition, stability, and predictability marriage offers, their children suffer the stigma of knowing their families are somehow lesser. They also suffer the significant material costs of being raised by unmarried parents, relegated through no fault of their own to a more difficult and uncertain family life. The marriage laws at issue here thus harm and humiliate the children of same-sex couples. . . .

Fourth and finally, this Court's cases and the Nation's traditions make clear that marriage is a keystone of our social order. . . . For that reason, just as a couple vows to support each other, so does society pledge to support the couple, offering symbolic recognition and material benefits to protect and nourish the union. Indeed, while the States are in general free to vary the benefits they confer on all married couples, they have throughout our history made marriage the basis for an expanding list of governmental rights, benefits, and responsibilities. . . .

There is no difference between same- and opposite-sex couples with respect to this principle. Yet by virtue of their exclusion from that institution, same-sex couples are denied the constellation of benefits that the States have linked to marriage. This harm results in more than just material burdens. Same-sex couples are consigned to an instability many opposite-sex couples would deem intolerable in their own lives. As the State itself makes marriage all the more precious by the significance it attaches to it, exclusion from that status has the effect of teaching that gays and lesbians are unequal in important respects. It demeans gays and lesbians for the State to lock them out of a central institution of the Nation's society. . . .

The limitation of marriage to opposite-sex couples may long have seemed natural and just, but its inconsistency with the central meaning of the fundamental right to marry is now manifest. With that knowledge must come the recognition that laws excluding same-sex couples from the marriage right impose stigma and injury of the kind prohibited by our basic charter.

[Respondents contend that petitioners seek a new "right to same-sex marriage." They argue that the Due Process Clause safeguards only those fundamental rights and forms of liberty that were specifically protected when the Constitution was ratified (citing Washington v. Glucksberg, 521 701 (1997) (refusing to recognize a right to physician-assisted suicide)]. Yet [that approach] is inconsistent with the approach this Court has used in discussing other fundamental rights, including marriage and intimacy. *Loving* did not ask about a "right to interracial marriage"; *Turner* did not ask about a "right of inmates to marry"; and *Zablocki* did not ask about a "right of fathers with unpaid child support duties to marry." Rather, each case inquired about the right to marry in its comprehensive sense, asking if there was a sufficient justification for excluding the relevant class from the right. . . . If rights were defined by who exercised them in the past, then received practices could serve as their own continued justification and new groups could not invoke rights once denied. This Court has rejected that approach, both with respect to the right to marry and the rights of gays and lesbians [citing *Loving* and *Lawrence*].

. . . Many who deem same-sex marriage to be wrong reach that conclusion based on decent and honorable religious or philosophical premises, and neither they nor their beliefs are disparaged here. But when that sincere, personal opposition becomes enacted law and public policy, the necessary consequence is to put the imprimatur of the State itself on an exclusion that soon demeans or stigmatizes those whose own liberty is then denied. Under the Constitution, same-sex couples seek in marriage the same legal treatment as opposite-sex couples, and it would disparage their choices and diminish their personhood to deny them this right.

The right of same-sex couples to marry that is part of the liberty promised by the Fourteenth Amendment is derived, too, from that Amendment's guarantee of the equal protection of the laws. The Due Process Clause and the Equal Protection Clause are connected in a profound way, though they set forth independent principles. Rights implicit in liberty and rights secured by equal protection may rest on different precepts and are not always co-extensive, yet in some instances each may be instructive as to the meaning and reach of the other. In any particular case, one Clause may be thought to capture the essence of the right in a more accurate and comprehensive way, even as the two Clauses may converge in the identification and definition of the right. This interrelation of the two principles furthers our understanding of what freedom is and must become.

The Court's cases touching upon the right to marry reflect this dynamic. In *Loving* the Court invalidated a prohibition on interracial marriage under both the Equal Protection Clause and the Due Process Clause. The Court first declared the prohibition invalid because of its unequal treatment of interracial couples. . . . With this link to equal protection, the Court proceeded to hold the prohibition offended central precepts of liberty. . . .

The synergy between the two protections is illustrated further in *Zablocki*. There the Court invoked the Equal Protection Clause as its basis for invalidating the challenged law, which, as already noted, barred fathers who were behind on child-support payments from marrying without judicial approval. The equal protection analysis depended in central part on the Court's holding that the law burdened a right "of fundamental importance." It was the essential nature of the marriage right, discussed at length in *Zablocki*, that made apparent the law's incompatibility with requirements of equality. Each concept—liberty and equal protection—leads to a stronger understanding of the other.

Indeed, in interpreting the Equal Protection Clause, the Court has recognized that new insights and societal understandings can reveal unjustified inequality within our most fundamental institutions that once passed unnoticed and unchallenged [citing the history of coverture as well as case law invalidating gender roles and stereotypes]. Like *Loving* and *Zablocki*, these precedents show the Equal Protection Clause can help to identify and correct inequalities in the institution of marriage, vindicating precepts of liberty and equality under the Constitution.

Other cases confirm this relation between liberty and equality. . . . In *Lawrence*, the Court acknowledged the interlocking nature of these constitutional safeguards in the context of the legal treatment of gays and lesbians. Although *Lawrence* elaborated its holding under the Due Process Clause, it acknowledged, and sought to remedy, the continuing inequality that resulted from laws making intimacy in the lives of gays and lesbians a crime against the State. *Lawrence* therefore drew upon principles of liberty and equality to define and protect the rights of gays and lesbians, holding the State "cannot demean their existence or control their destiny by making their private sexual conduct a crime."

This dynamic also applies to same-sex marriage. It is now clear that the challenged laws burden the liberty of same-sex couples, and it must be further acknowledged that they abridge central precepts of equality. Here the marriage laws enforced by the respondents are in essence unequal: same-sex couples are denied all the benefits afforded to opposite-sex couples and are barred from exercising a fundamental right. Especially against a long history of disapproval of their relationships, this denial to same-sex couples of the right to marry works a grave and continuing harm. The imposition of this disability on gays and lesbians serves to disrespect and subordinate them. And the Equal Protection Clause, like the Due Process Clause, prohibits this unjustified infringement of the fundamental right to marry.

These considerations lead to the conclusion that the right to marry is a fundamental right inherent in the liberty of the person, and under the Due Process and Equal Protection Clauses of the Fourteenth Amendment, couples of the same-sex may not be deprived of that right and that liberty. The Court now holds that same-sex couples may exercise the fundamental right to marry. . . . [S]tate laws challenged by Petitioners in these cases are now held invalid to the extent they exclude same-sex couples from civil marriage on the same terms and conditions as opposite-sex couples.

There may be an initial inclination in these cases to proceed with caution—to await further legislation, litigation, and debate [before] deciding an issue so basic as the definition of marriage. [The Court was asked to adopt a cautious approach in recognizing fundamental rights in Bowers v. Hardwick, 478 U.S. 186 (1986) (upholding a state sodomy law).] Although *Bowers* was eventually repudiated in *Lawrence*, men and women were harmed in the interim, and the substantial effects of these injuries no doubt lingered long after *Bowers* was overruled. Dignitary wounds cannot always be healed with the stroke of a pen.

[P]etitioners' stories make clear the urgency of the issue they present to the Court. James Obergefell now asks whether Ohio can erase his marriage to John Arthur for all time. April DeBoer and Jayne Rowse now ask whether Michigan may continue to deny them the certainty and stability all mothers desire to protect their children, and for them and their children the childhood years will pass all too soon. Ijpe DeKoe and Thomas Kostura now ask whether Tennessee can deny to one who has served this Nation the basic dignity of recognizing his New York marriage. [T]he Court has a duty to address these claims and answer these questions. . . .

The respondents also argue allowing same-sex couples to wed will harm marriage as an institution by leading to fewer opposite-sex marriages. This may occur, the respondents contend, because licensing same-sex marriage severs the connection between natural procreation and marriage. That argument, however, rests on a counterintuitive view of opposite-sex couple's decisionmaking processes regarding marriage and parenthood. Decisions about whether to marry and raise children are based on many personal, romantic, and practical considerations; and it is unrealistic to conclude that an opposite-sex couple would choose not to marry simply because same-sex couples may do so. The respondents have not shown a foundation for the conclusion that allowing same-sex marriage will cause the harmful outcomes they describe. . . .

Finally, it must be emphasized that religions, and those who adhere to religious doctrines, may continue to advocate with utmost, sincere conviction that, by divine precepts, same-sex marriage should not be condoned. The First Amendment ensures that religious organizations and persons are given proper protection as they seek to teach the principles that are so fulfilling and so central to their lives and faiths, and to their own deep aspirations to continue the family structure they have long revered. . . .

These cases also present the question whether the Constitution requires States to recognize same-sex marriages validly performed out of State. As made clear by the case of Obergefell and Arthur, . . . the recognition bans inflict substantial and continuing harm on same-sex couples. Being married in one State but having that valid marriage denied in another is one of "the most perplexing and distressing complication[s]" in the law of domestic relations [citing multistate divorce case law]. Leaving the current state of affairs in place would maintain and promote instability and uncertainty. For some couples, even an ordinary drive into a neighboring State to visit family or friends risks causing severe hardship in the event of a spouse's hospitalization while across state lines. . . .

[I]f States are required by the Constitution to issue marriage licenses to same-sex couples, the justifications for refusing to recognize those marriages performed elsewhere are undermined. The Court, in this decision, holds same-sex couples may exercise the fundamental right to marry in all States. It follows that the Court also must hold—and it now does hold—that there is no lawful basis for a State to refuse to recognize a lawful same-sex marriage performed in another State on the ground of its same-sex character.

No union is more profound than marriage, for it embodies the highest ideals of love, fidelity, devotion, sacrifice, and family. In forming a marital union, two people become something greater than once they were. As some of the petitioners in these cases demonstrate, marriage embodies a love that may endure even past death. It would misunderstand these men and women to say they disrespect the idea of marriage. Their plea is that they do respect it, respect it so deeply that they seek to find its fulfillment for themselves. Their hope is not to be condemned to live in loneliness, excluded from one of civilization's oldest institutions. They ask for equal dignity in the eyes of the law. The Constitution grants them that right. . . .

Chief Justice Roberts, with whom Justice Scalia and Justice Thomas join, dissenting.

Petitioners make strong arguments rooted in social policy and considerations of fairness. . . . But this Court is not a legislature. Whether same-sex marriage is a good idea should be of no concern to us. Under the Constitution, judges have power to say what the law is, not what it should be . . .

Although the policy arguments for extending marriage to same-sex couples may be compelling, the legal arguments for requiring such an extension are not. The fundamental right to marry does not include a right to make a State change its definition of marriage. And a State's decision to maintain the meaning of marriage that has persisted in every culture throughout human history can hardly be called irrational. In short, [t]he people of a State are free to expand marriage to include same-sex couples, or to retain the historic definition. . . .

. . . Supporters of same-sex marriage have achieved considerable success persuading their fellow citizens—through the democratic process—to adopt their view. That ends today. Five lawyers have closed the debate and enacted their own vision of marriage as a matter of constitutional law. Stealing this issue from the people will for many cast a cloud over same-sex marriage, making a dramatic social change that much more difficult to accept.

The majority's decision is an act of will, not legal judgment. The right it announces has no basis in the Constitution or this Court's precedent. The majority expressly disclaims judicial "caution" and omits even a pretense of humility, openly relying on its desire to remake society according to its own "new insight" into the "nature of injustice." As a result, the Court invalidates the marriage laws of more than half the States and orders the transformation of a social institution that has formed the basis of human society for millennia. . . . Just who do we think we are?

This Court's precedents have repeatedly described marriage in ways that are consistent only with its traditional meaning. . . . As the majority notes, some aspects of marriage have changed over time [i.e., arranged marriages, coverture, or racial restrictions]. The majority observes that these developments "were not mere superficial changes" in marriage, but rather "worked deep transformations in its structure." They did not, however, work any transformation in the core structure of marriage as the union between a man and a woman. . . .

[The majority resolves these cases] almost entirely on the Due Process Clause. The majority purports to identify four "principles and traditions" in this Court's due process precedents that support a fundamental right for same-sex couples to marry. In reality, however, the majority's approach has no basis in principle or tradition, except for the unprincipled tradition of [judicial activism reflected in *Lochner* v. *New York*, 198 U. S. 45 (1905), which relied on substantive due process to invalidate laws on minimum wages, child labor, and other economic and social regulations]. Stripped of its shiny rhetorical gloss, the majority's argument is that the Due Process Clause gives same-sex couples a fundamental right to marry because it will be good for them and for society. If I were a legislator, I would certainly consider that view as a matter of social policy. But as a judge, I find the majority's position indefensible as a matter of constitutional law . . .

. . . Neither *Lawrence* nor any other precedent in the privacy line of cases supports the right that petitioners assert here. Unlike criminal laws banning contraceptives and sodomy, the marriage laws at issue here involve no government intrusion. They create no crime and impose no punishment. [T]he laws in no way interfere with the "right to be let alone." [T]he privacy cases provide no support for the majority's position, because petitioners do not seek privacy. Quite the opposite, they seek public recognition of their relationships, along with corresponding government benefits. [A]though the right to privacy recognized by our precedents certainly plays a role in protecting the intimate conduct of same-sex couples, it provides no affirmative right to redefine marriage and no basis for striking down the laws at issue here. . . .

One immediate question invited by the majority's position is whether States may retain the definition of marriage as a union of two people. [The majority] offers no reason at all why the two-person element of the core definition of marriage may be preserved while the man-woman element may not. Indeed, from the standpoint of history and tradition, a leap from opposite-sex marriage to same-sex marriage is much greater than one from a two-person union to plural unions, which have deep roots in some cultures around the world. If the majority is willing to take the big leap, it is hard to see how it can say no to the shorter one.

It is striking how much of the majority's reasoning would apply with equal force to the claim of a fundamental right to plural marriage. If "[t]here is dignity in the bond between two men or two women who seek to marry and in their autonomy to make such profound choices," why would there be any less dignity in the bond between three people who, in exercising their autonomy, seek to make the profound choice to marry? If a same-sex couple has the constitutional right to marry because their children would otherwise "suffer the stigma of knowing their families are somehow lesser," why wouldn't the same reasoning apply to a family of three or more persons raising children? If not having the opportunity to marry "serves to disrespect and subordinate" gay and lesbian couples, why wouldn't the same "imposition of this disability," serve to disrespect and subordinate people who find fulfillment in polyamorous relationships? . . .

Near the end of its opinion, the majority offers perhaps the clearest insight into its decision. Expanding marriage to include same-sex couples, the majority insists, would "pose no risk of harm to themselves or third parties." [T]his assertion of the "harm principle" sounds more in philosophy than law. . . . [A] Justice's commission does not confer any special moral, philosophical, or social insight sufficient to justify imposing those perceptions on fellow citizens under the pretense of "due process." . . .

In addition to their due process argument, petitioners contend that the Equal Protection Clause requires their States to license and recognize same-sex marriages. . . . The central point seems to be that there is a "synergy between" the Equal Protection Clause and the Due Process Clause, and that some precedents relying on one Clause have also relied on the other. Absent from this portion of the opinion, however, is anything resembling our usual [means-end] framework for deciding equal protection cases. . . . [T]he marriage laws at issue here do not violate the Equal Protection Clause, because distinguishing between opposite-sex and same-sex couples is rationally related to the States' "legitimate state interest" in "preserving the traditional institution of marriage." . . .

[Today's decision] creates serious questions about religious liberty. Many good and decent people oppose same-sex marriage as a tenet of faith, and their freedom to exercise religion is—unlike the right imagined by the majority—actually spelled out in the Constitution. Respect for sincere religious conviction has led voters and legislators in every State that has adopted same-sex marriage democratically to include accommodations for religious practice. . . . The majority graciously suggests that religious believers may continue to "advocate" and "teach" their views of marriage. The First Amendment guarantees, however, the freedom to "*exercise*" religion. Ominously, that is not a word the majority uses. . . . Unfortunately, people of faith can take no comfort in the treatment they receive from the majority today.

If you are among the many Americans—of whatever sexual orientation—who favor expanding same-sex marriage, by all means celebrate today's decision. Celebrate the achievement of a desired goal. Celebrate the opportunity for a new expression of commitment to a partner. Celebrate the availability of new benefits. But do not celebrate the Constitution. It had nothing to do with it. . . .

Michael S. Rosenwald, How Jim Obergefell Became the Face of the Supreme Court Gay Marriage Case[27]

Wash. Post, Apr. 6, 2015

Plaintiff Jim Obergefell (left) and his spouse John Arthur (now decreased)

. . . It was not a long marriage, just three months and 11 days—the time it took his husband, John Arthur, to struggle to say, "I thee wed," and then die from [amyotrophic lateral sclerosis] [ALS]. Now their union, and the 20-year relationship that preceded it, is at the center of *Obergefell v. Hodges*. . . . For Jim Obergefell, the case is simply about that tricky-to-pronounce name [*Oh-ber-guh-fell*]: He wants it on Arthur's death certificate as the surviving spouse . . .

How Obergefell, a soft-spoken real estate broker with little previous interest in political activism, wound up in this spot is a story of judicial chance, but it's also about resolve, fate, and heartbreak. . . . Arthur was essentially on his deathbed when the couple decided to marry. He could no longer walk. Speaking was difficult. . . .

In their two decades together, the couple talked about marriage but never considered it seriously . . . . But in 2013, the Supreme Court struck down a key portion of the Defense of Marriage Act, giving same-sex married couples federal benefits in the states where such unions were legal. Obergefell saw the news online. He leaned over, kissed Arthur on the head, and said, "Let's get married." "Okay," Arthur said.

Their wedding was a production. Obviously, they needed to travel to a different state, choosing Maryland on a friend's suggestion. But how to get there? A car trip was out. A medical flight was their only option, but how could they arrange one, much less come up with the $13,000 to pay for it? Obergefell sought advice on Facebook. Their friends and family offered more than guidance—[they] funded the entire trip.

And so on the morning of July 11, 2013, an ambulance transported them to the airport, where they boarded a medical jet with a nurse and Arthur's aunt, Paulette Roberts, who became ordained online to perform weddings. They flew to Baltimore-Washington International Marshall Airport. Roberts began the

[27]. The full article is available at http://www.washingtonpost.com/local/how-jim-obergefell-became-the-face-of-the-supreme-court-gay-marriage-case/2015/04/06/3740433c-d958-11e4-b3f2-607bd612aeac_story.html.

ceremony on the tarmac, in the plane, shortly after landing. The couple held hands, Obergefell's thumb rubbing Arthur's. They stared into each other's eyes. "With this ring," said Obergefell, slipping a ring on Arthur's hand, "I thee wed." Then he gently helped Arthur guide a ring onto his own hand. "With this ring," said Arthur, his speech distorted by ALS, "I thee wed." . . .

Today, Obergefell lives alone in the couple's condo. . . . In the TV room, a large painting of the couple hangs above the couch. They are young and in love and smiling at a beautiful old cemetery where they used to take long walks. . . .

Jim Obergefell comments below on his role in history and the significance of his case for the family as an institution.

Jim Obergefell, The Legacy of Obergefell v. Hodges

Personal communication, July 28, 2015

I understand that this is a landmark decision that impacts our entire country, and also has an impact around the world. From an intellectual point of view, I know that my name and our case has become part of history. But I'm still coming to grips with that emotionally. I am hearing [that people are calling me] "hero" more and more [often]. While I understand why people say that, all I did was stand up for our marriage, and then fight to live up to the commitments I made to my husband.

This ruling means that all committed couples are able to make their relationship legal and public, and by doing so, enjoy the same rights and protections as any other couple. Because of this ruling, I—and other LGBT citizens—feel more like equal citizens. However, no matter how far we've come, there are still far too many individuals who are content to focus on how people differ instead of focusing on the fact that we're all humans who want the same basic things – the right to life, liberty, and the pursuit of happiness. Instead of embracing the ways we're the same and celebrating the beauty our differences bring to our country, too many people use those differences as reasons to hate. So the fight continues for all of us.

From the standpoint of the family, this ruling recognizes that families come in all shapes and sizes. Children need to be loved and brought up by two parents who nurture and support them as they journey from toddler to adolescence and beyond. Two dads, two moms, a mom and a dad—no matter the equation, the effect on the family overall is a positive one.

The following narrative provides background on Mary Bonauto, the pioneering attorney who argued *Obergefell* before the Supreme Court as well as other landmark marriage equality cases (i.e., cases involving civil unions in Vermont, the ban on same-sex marriage in Massachusetts, and several federal challenges to DOMA).

David J. Garrow, Toward a More Perfect Union

N.Y. Times, May 9, 2004, §6 (Mag.), at 52

Attorney Mary Bonauto who won several landmark cases on marriage equality

Mary Bonauto vividly remembers her first day as a lawyer at Gay and Lesbian Advocates and Defenders (GLAD), the small public-interest law office that represents gays and lesbians in the six New England states. "When I came here on March 19, 1990," she recalled not long ago, "one of the things waiting for me on my desk was a request from a lesbian couple in western Massachusetts who wanted to get married." At that time, though, she believed a lawsuit seeking a right to gay marriage had no chance of success in any American appellate court.

"It was absolutely the wrong time," she told me, "and I said no." A generation or two from now, March 19, 1990, may appear in history books the same way that another date appears in accounts of Brown v. Board of Education: Oct. 6, 1936, the day that Thurgood Marshall accepted a full-time job at the N.A.A.C.P. Legal Defense Fund. Marshall, too, said no—for more than a decade—to petitioners who asked him to challenge public-school segregation in the South. Only in 1950, as the legal landscape began to shift, did Marshall finally say yes. For Bonauto, the wait was shorter but the outcome no less momentous. . . .

Bonauto grew up with her three brothers in what she describes as a "highly Catholic" family. Her father worked as a pharmacist and her mother as a teacher. [She attended Hamilton College and Northeastern University Law School.] When she joined a small law firm in Portland, Me., in 1987, Bonauto was one of only three openly gay lawyers in private practice in the state. In Portland, she also met her life partner, Jennifer Wriggins, now a professor at the University of Maine School of Law.

The late 1980s were an auspicious time for a young lawyer in New England with a commitment to gay equality. In 1989, Massachusetts became the second state, after Wisconsin, to provide anti-discrimination protection to gays in employment, housing, and public accommodations. When GLAD advertised for a lawyer to help enforce the new law, Bonauto jumped at the opportunity and moved back to Boston. . . .

[In July 1997 Bonauto filed the successful challenge to the constitutionality of Vermont's exclusion of same-sex couples from the right to marry. But the Vermont legislature ultimately enacted civil union legislation granting all the benefits of marriage to gay and lesbian couples, but not the label.] The distinction evoked a phrase that Thurgood Marshall knew all too well: "separate but equal," the pre-*Brown* label for the fictional fairness of segregation.

Bonauto decided to try again. [When she argued the *Goodridge* case before the Massachusetts Supreme Judicial Court], she insisted that "civil unions" would not satisfy the requirements of the Massachusetts Constitution. "The Vermont approach is not the best approach for this Court to take," she emphasized, for "when it comes to marriage, there really is no such thing as separating the word 'marriage' from the protections it provides. The reason for that is that one of the most important protections of marriage is the word, because the word is what conveys the status that everyone understands as the ultimate expression of love and commitment." To follow Vermont, she continued, by "creating a separate system, just for gay people, simply perpetuates the stigma of exclusion that we now face because it would essentially be branding gay people and our relationships as unworthy of this civil institution of marriage." . . .

While Bonauto waited for a decision, the legal climate improved [with the Supreme Court's decision in Lawrence v. Texas, invalidating anti-sodomy laws]. Five months later, the Massachusetts Supreme Judicial Court handed down the ruling for which Bonauto had been waiting [the *Goodridge* case, legalizing same-sex marriage in Massachusetts]. . . .

The moral influence of the *Lawrence* decision on the Massachusetts court was made explicit at the very beginning of the *Goodridge* majority opinion, in which Massachusetts Chief Justice Margaret H. Marshall cited *Lawrence* three times in her first three paragraphs. As Matt Coles, head of the American Civil Liberties Union's Lesbian and Gay Rights Project, observes, *Goodridge* "answered that question that *Lawrence* begged." And while "*Goodridge* is the earthquake," Coles says, *Goodridge* is the earthquake because of *Lawrence*. . . .

When asked to talk about herself, Bonauto insists that "it's totally not about me." [A colleague] emphasizes Bonauto's "modesty and humility," but insiders who fully appreciate how a very small network of gay lawyers has brought America to the threshold of another civil rights milestone know whom to credit. . . .[28]

Notes and Questions on *Windsor* and *Obergefell*

1. Background and epilogue. *Windsor* was the first time that the U.S. Supreme Court addressed the constitutionality of DOMA. The significance of *Windsor* is explored below.

Obergefell invalidated same-sex marriage bans in 13 states. The Supreme Court announced *Obergefell* on the same day (June 26) that *Lawrence* was decided 12 years earlier and exactly two years after *Windsor*. Within hours after the decision in *Obergefell*, all but three states allowed gay marriages to take place. State officials in those states (Alabama, Louisiana, and Texas) refused to issue marriage licenses to same-sex couples until federal judges in their respective states ruled that they had to abide by *Obergefell*. Nationwide, the number of legally married same-sex couples more than doubled from the time of *Windsor* until *Obergefell*.[29]

---

[28]. Mary Bonauto and her spouse (law professor Jennifer Wriggens), who are Maine residents, faced a long uphill battle, first, to marry and, second, to have their marriage recognized in their home state. Bonauto successfully argued *Goodridge* in 2003, thereby bringing marriage equality to Massachusetts. But she was unable to marry there until 2008, when Massachusetts repealed its marriage evasion statute. However, because the couple lived in Maine at the time (where Wriggens teaches), their marriage was not recognized there until 2012, when Maine voters passed an initiative favoring marriage equality.

[29]. Williams Inst., 700,000 Americans Are Married to a Same-Sex Spouse, Married Same-Sex Couples More Likely to Raise Adopted, Foster Children and Are More Economically Secure, New Reports Show (Mar. 5, 2015), http://williamsinstitute.law.ucla.edu/press/press-releases/married-same-sex-couples-more-likely-to-raise-adopted-foster-children-and-have-more-economic-resources-new-reports-show/.

2. DOMA. Congress enacted the federal DOMA in 1996 in response to the first state judicial ruling favorable to same-sex marriage (Baehr v. Lewin, 852 P.2d 44 (Haw. 1993)), which was decided by the Hawaii Supreme Court in 1993. *Baehr* held that the denial of marriage licenses to same-sex couples constitutes gender discrimination under the state constitution. The ruling in *Baehr* mobilized opponents of same-sex marriage to influence Congress to enact DOMA, stemming from their fear that if Hawaii legalized same-sex marriage, then same-sex marriage would be valid everywhere based on the doctrine of lex loci.

The federal DOMA has two parts: Section 2 specifies that states are not required to give effect to same-sex marriages validly celebrated in another state (28 U.S.C. §1738C). What is the purpose of this section? DOMA's Section 3 (1 U.S.C. §7) provides a heterosexual and gendered definition for the terms "marriage" and "spouse" for purposes of federal benefits. In the wake of DOMA, a majority of the states enacted a version of the federal law or amended their state constitutions to prohibit same-sex marriage, or both.

Which section of DOMA did *Windsor* hold unconstitutional? What impact did *Windsor* have on the issue of the legalization of same-sex marriage in the states? What is the impact of *Obergefell* on the remaining section of DOMA? If *Obergefell* had preceded (rather than followed) *Windsor*, would *Windsor* have been necessary? The Court had the opportunity to decide the issues presented in *Obergefell* during the same term that it decided *Windsor*. Why do you think the Court postponed these issues?

3. Holding and rationale. On what constitutional provision(s) does *Obergefell* rest? On which does *Windsor* rest? Is marriage a "fundamental right" after *Windsor*? After *Obergefell*? How does the Court link the concepts of "liberty" and "equality"? Why does it? What were the two questions before the Court in *Obergefell*, and how did the Court answer them? Could the Court have answered one question affirmatively and the other negatively? Did the Court create a new right or simply extend an existing right to same-sex couples? Why does it matter? How does *Obergefell* respond to the argument that same-sex marriage cannot be a fundamental right because it is not deeply rooted in "history and tradition"?

a. Liberty. What is the *Obergefell* majority's understanding of liberty? How does it resemble the freedoms recognized in the reproductive privacy cases and *Lawrence*? How does it differ? How would you answer Chief Justice Roberts's assertion that marriage differs from the interests at stake in those precedents? See also *Obergefell*, 135 S.Ct. at 2631 ("Since well before 1787, liberty has been understood as freedom from government action, not entitlement to government benefits.") (Thomas, J., dissenting).

b. Equality. The Supreme Court has adopted different standards of review to evaluate the constitutionality of discriminatory classifications under the Equal Protection Clause. To survive constitutional attack, the classification must be (1) necessary to a compelling state interest (strict scrutiny), or (2) substantially related to an important governmental objective (intermediate scrutiny), or (3) rationally related to a legitimate government purpose (lowest level of scrutiny). The Court evaluates racial classifications under the first test; sex-based classifications are scrutinized under the middle-tier test (although a few states, such as California, apply higher scrutiny to gender-based classifications). What level of scrutiny does the Court apply in *Windsor*? In *Obergefell*? Why? What level of scrutiny *should* the Court adopt regarding challenges based on sexual orientation and why?

c. Views of marriage. In *Windsor*, Justice Alito (in a dissent omitted here) posits two contrasting views of marriage: the traditional or conjugal view and the more modern, consent-based view. 133 S. Ct. at 2718. He sees either as a legitimate legislative choice and condemns the majority for enshrining the latter view in the Constitution. What happens to the traditional or conjugal understanding of marriage after *Windsor* and *Obergefell*?

4. Historical background.

a. Stonewall sets the stage. The gay liberation movement was triggered by a police raid of the Stonewall Inn, a popular Greenwich Village gay bar in Manhattan, in the early-morning hours of June 28, 1969. This raid led to six days of spontaneous demonstrations by members of the LGBT community that served as the catalyst for the gay rights movement.[30]

b. Early challenges. Same-sex couples began challenging the ban on marriage in the 1970s. Courts in these early cases held that same-sex marriages were invalid based on either lack of capacity or the dictionary definition of marriage, thereby avoiding resolution of the constitutional issues.[31] The Supreme Court first considered a gay marriage case in Baker v. Nelson (409 U.S. 810 (1972) (dismissing an appeal from a Minnesota case upholding a state ban for "want of a substantial federal question"). *Obergefell* explicitly overruled *Baker*.

The 1990s brought a resurgence of state litigation. See, e.g., Baehr v. Lewin, supra (denial of marriage licenses to same-sex couples constitutes gender discrimination under state constitution); Brause v. Bureau of Vital Statistics, 1998 WL 88743 (Alaska Super. Ct. 1998) (invalidating ban based on state constitutional rights to privacy and equality). Subsequent state constitutional amendments (e.g., Haw. Const. art. 1, §23; Alaska Const. art 1, §25) nullified those decisions.

c. Goodridge. A landmark Massachusetts case set the stage for subsequent challenges to state bans of same-sex marriage. Goodridge v. Department of Public Health, 798 N.E.2d 941 (Mass. 2003), struck down the state ban, finding that under the state constitutional protections of liberty and equality, the ban did not even survive rational basis review. In May 2004, Massachusetts became the first state to permit same-sex marriage. *Goodridge* followed closely on the heels of *Lawrence*. Why?

d. California background. Soon after *Goodridge,* in a move that stunned the nation, San Francisco mayor Gavin Newsom ordered city officials to issue marriage licenses to same-sex couples. The first same-sex marriage in California took place on Valentine's Day in 2004. The California Supreme Court later ruled that the mayor had overstepped his authority, reasoning that his belief in the unconstitutionality of the law failed to justify his action. Lockyer v. City & County of San Francisco, 95 P.3d 459 (Cal. 2004). Gay rights advocates then challenged

---

[30]. On the history of the movement, see David Carter, Stonewall: The Riots That Sparked the Gay Revolution (2004); Linda Hirshman, Victory: The Triumphant Gay Revolution (2012).

[31]. On the early same-sex marriage cases, see Michael Boucai, Glorious Precedents: When Gay Marriage was Radical, 27 Yale J.L. & Hum. 1 (2015).

California's definition of marriage (Cal. Fam. Code §§300, 308.5). The California Supreme Court legalized same-sex marriage in In re Marriage Cases, 183 P.3d 384 (Cal. 2008) (based on the state's guarantee of equal protection and the fundamental privacy interest in family relationships, relying on strict scrutiny review). In response, voters passed a state constitutional ban (Proposition 8). Proponents of same-sex marriage subsequently filed a successful *federal* challenge to the ban (Hollingsworth v. Perry, 133 S. Ct. 2652 (2013)).[32]

5. Public opinion. Public opinion on same-sex marriage has changed dramatically. When *Obergefell* was decided, 60 percent of Americans supported same-sex marriage. A decade before, approximately the same number *opposed* marriage equality.[33]

6. Significance for family law. Is the significance of *Obergefell* limited to the legal status of marriage? Or, will the case have a broader impact on other family law issues? For example, what is the likely impact of *Obergefell* on parentage issues? Does *Obergefell* obviate the need for same-sex partners to adopt each other or to adopt a partner's children? What is the likely impact of the case on other nontraditional families? Does the emphasis on children in both *Windsor* and *Obergefell* require relaxing restrictions on assisted reproduction, such as the ban in some states on commercial surrogacy? See Compensated Surrogacy in the Age of *Windsor*, 89 Wash. L. Rev. 1069-1373 (2014) (symposium). Do you agree with Justice Roberts in his dissent that *Obergefell* will lead to recognition of plural marriage? Or are there differences between same-sex marriage and polygamy that compel a different analysis?

7. Role of the judiciary. How does the majority in *Windsor* and *Obergefell* see the role of the judiciary in influencing (or responding to) social change? How does it see the role of the Constitution as society evolves?

8. Government interests. What were the governmental interests advanced by defendants in *Windsor* and *Obergefell*? Consider the extent to which the challenged bans are related to each of the possible interests below. Compare the views of *Windsor* and *Obergefell* regarding these interests. Then contrast the majority and dissenting opinions in *Obergefell* regarding those same interests.

a. "Responsible procreation." In some cases, judges theorized that the possibility of accidental heterosexual procreation justifies excluding same-sex couples from marriage. As the appellate court in the case that became *Obergefell* reasoned: "[G]overnments got into the business of defining marriage, and remain in the business of defining marriage, not to regulate love but to regulate sex, most especially the intended and unintended effects of male-female intercourse." DeBoer v. Snyder, 772 F.3d 388, 404 (6th Cir. 2014). Under this theory, marriage provides a means to connect biological parents to their offspring for purposes of

---

[32]. On the history of this litigation, see Theodore B. Olson & David Boies, Redeeming the Dream: The Case for Marriage Equality (2014); Kenji Yoshino, Speak Now: Marriage Equality on Trial (2015).

[33]. Scott Clement & Robert Barnes, Poll: Gay Marriage Support at Record High, Wash. Post, Apr. 23, 2015, available at http://www.washingtonpost.com/politics/courts_law/poll-gay-marriage-support-at-record-high/2015/04/22/f6548332-e92a-11e4-aae1-d642717d8afa_story.html.

nurturing and support. By contrast, same-sex couples do not procreate by accident, and hence society has no need to offer them access to marriage or to reward them for making such commitments.

How does this argument fare in the principal cases? Is encouragement of "responsible procreation" a legitimate governmental interest? Is a ban on same-sex marriage rationally related to the government's interest in responsible procreation? Substantially related? Necessary? How does the availability of reproductive technology, such as donor insemination and surrogacy, affect this evaluation?

b. Religious liberty. Some opponents of same-sex marriage argue that a ban is necessary to protect clergy from having to marry same-sex couples in contravention of their religious beliefs. Does the First Amendment protect their beliefs? Can public officials, such as county clerks, refuse to issue marriage licenses on religious grounds? What redress does a same-sex couple have in such cases? Will a civil rights action lie for violation of 42 U.S.C. §1983? Can private businesses (such as bakeries or wedding planners) refuse services to same-sex partners who wish to marry?[34] Does *Hobby Lobby* (discussed supra Chapter I) protect those who seek religious exemptions from marrying or providing services to same-sex couples?

Should state legislators enact "marriage conscience protection" clauses that provide religious exemptions?[35] How do *Windsor and Obergefell* treat these concerns? How does Justice Roberts's dissent in *Obergefell* differ from the majority opinion on this point?

c. Promoting uniformity of laws. How important is the government interest in promoting a uniform definition of marriage? How does the Court in *Windsor* and *Obergefell* respond to this argument? What are the implications of a lack of uniformity?

d. Tradition. Marriage laws have long been justified as based on tradition. How do *Windsor* and *Obergefell* evaluate this argument? Could same-sex marriage lead to a society without civil marriage at all? See Summer L. Nastich, Questioning the Marriage Assumptions: The Justifications for "Opposite-Sex Only" Marriage as Support for the Abolition of Marriage, 21 Law & Ineq. 114 (2003). Given the majority's treatment of marriage in *Obergefell* as a protected liberty, could a state "get out of the marriage business" without violating the Constitution?

e. Moral disapproval. Moral disapproval of particular conduct underlies many regulatory laws. How do *Windsor* and *Obergefell* make clear that animosity toward a particular class of people is not a legitimate governmental interest that can support an otherwise discriminatory classification?

f. Harm. To what extent do *Windsor* and *Obergefell* address the harm caused by state bans on gay marriage? Does Justice Roberts in his dissent in *Obergefell* take harm into account? If so, how?

g. Children's interests. To what extent do *Windsor* and *Obergefell* address the effect of the state bans on children's interests?

---

[34]. See, e.g., Judge Rules Oregon Bakery Discriminated Against Gay Couple, Newsmax, Feb. 2, 2015, http://www.newsmax.com/US/judge-bakery-discriminated-gay/2015/02/02/id/622259/.

[35]. For a discussion of conscience-based claims in marriage equality litigation, see Douglas NeJaime & Reva Siegel, Conscience Wars: Complicity-Based Conscience Claims in Religion and Politics,124 Yale L.J. 2516 (2015); Douglas NeJaime, Marriage Inequality: Same-Sex Relationships, Religious Exemptions, and the Production of Sexual Orientation Discrimination, 100 Cal. L. Rev. 1169 (2012).

9. Loving **analogy.** Are antimiscegenation laws analogous to restrictions against same-sex marriage?[36] Evaluate Justice Scalia's rejection of the analogy in *Lawrence* on the basis that the law in *Loving* "was designed to maintain White Supremacy" but that no discriminatory purpose underlies the sex classifications in Texas's sodomy ban or traditional marriage restrictions. 539 U.S. at 600 (Scalia, J., dissenting).

10. Civil unions. How do civil unions and domestic partnerships differ from marriage? Vermont was the first state to enact civil unions (Vt. Stat. Ann. tit. 15, §§1201-1207) in response to the state supreme court's ruling that the same-sex marriage ban violated the state constitution's Common Benefits Clause. Baker v. State, 744 A.2d 864 (Vt. 1999).

To enter a civil union (or domestic partnership), parties must register with the state. To terminate such a union, a party must file a written declaration. Civil unions and domestic partnerships are available to same-sex partners, and sometimes to opposite-sex couples as well. Currently, approximately a dozen states recognize civil unions or domestic partnerships. Some statutory schemes offer the same rights as married couples; some states offer more limited rights.[37] What is the effect of *Windsor* and *Obergefell* on civil unions or domestic partnerships, respectively? What happens to these alternatives to marriage now that all same-sex couples who want to marry may do so? Following the passage of some same-sex marriage laws, several states provided that existing civil unions would cease and would be converted to marriages.

11. Criticisms. Some gay and lesbian activists initially refused unqualified support for same-sex marriage. Why might they have felt this way?[38]

12. International developments. Currently, almost two dozen countries have same-sex marriage. Countries include (in chronological order of legalization): the Netherlands (2001); Belgium (2003); Canada and Spain (both 2005); South Africa (2006); Norway and Sweden (both 2009); Portugal, Argentina, and Iceland (all 2010); Denmark (2012); Brazil, England, France, New Zealand, and Uruguay (all 2013); Luxembourg and Scotland (both 2014); Finland, Slovenia, Republic of Ireland, and Mexico (all 2015).[39]

---

[36]. See Andrew Koppelman, The Gay Rights Question in Contemporary American Law 63, 71 (2002); R.A. Lenhardt, Beyond Analogy: Perez v. Sharp, Antimiscegenation Law, and the Fight for Same-Sex Marriage, 96 Cal. L. Rev. 839 (2008).

[37]. As of April 2015, four states (Colorado, Hawaii, Illinois, and New Jersey) allow civil unions. Findlaw, Which States Have Civil Unions?, http://family.findlaw.com/domestic-partnerships/which-states-have-civil-unions.html (Apr. 2015). As of November 2014, five states (California, Maine, Nevada, Oregon, Washington, and Wisconsin) and the District of Columbia provided for domestic partnerships. Hawaii allows a similar relationship, known as "reciprocal beneficiaries." Nat'l Conf. of State Legislatures, Civil Unions, and Domestic Partnership Statutes (Nov. 18, 2014), http://www.ncsl.org/research/human-services/civil-unions-and-domestic-partnership-statutes.aspx. Colorado has a Designated Beneficiary Act, Colo. Rev. Stat. §§15-22-101-15.22-112, that is unusually broad, applying to any two unmarried persons (even friends and relatives).

[38]. For an early debate on the benefits and shortcomings of marriage equality for the gay rights movement, see Paula L. Ettelbrick, Wedlock Alert: A Comment on Lesbian and Gay Family Recognition, 5 J.L. & Pol'y 107 (1996); Nancy D. Polikoff, Symposium, We Will Get What We Ask For: Why Legalizing Gay and Lesbian Marriage Will Not "Dismantle the Legal Structure of Gender in Every Marriage," 79 Va. L. Rev. 1535 (1993). See also Nancy D. Polikoff, Beyond (Straight and Gay) Marriage: Valuing All Families Under the Law (2009).

[39]. Pew Research Center, Gay Marriage Around the World (June 2015), http://www.pewforum.org/2015/06/26/gay-marriage-around-the-world-2013/.

13. Same-sex marriage and immigration. Prior to *Windsor*, binational same-sex couples faced immigration issues. An openly gay or lesbian partner could enter the country under the Immigration Act of 1990, 8 U.S.C. §§1101-1525 (repealing the federal ban on entry of homosexuals (§1182(a)(1)-(9)). But same-sex couples confronted two primary problems if the foreign partner desired to remain for any significant length of time: deportation for overstaying a visa and ineligibility to work without a "green card" (proof of legal residency permanent status that permits a person to reside and work in the country). These problems were widespread because nearly 80,000 same-sex couples included a noncitizen-partner.[40]

For foreign nationals who were able to marry their U.S. citizen-partner, the situation was not much better. Foreign spouses of citizens receive preferential treatment in issuance of permanent resident status. But such preferential treatment did not apply to same-sex partners due to DOMA. Proposed legislation was unsuccessful in amending the Immigration and Nationality Act to allow a U.S. citizen to sponsor a same-sex "permanent partner" for legal residence. See Uniting American Families Act (UAFA), H.R. 1537, S. 821, 112th Cong. (2011). In 2011, the Obama administration suspended deportation of undocumented immigrants who posed no security risk, and the Department of Homeland Security extended eligibility to foreign same-sex partners of citizens. *Windsor* finally allowed same-sex partners to sponsor their foreign spouses for residency.

14. Transgender persons and marriage. Will *Windsor* or *Obergefell* have any effect on the marriage of a transgender (formerly "transsexual") person? Previously, some courts in states limiting marriage to opposite-sex couples determined marriage validity based on a person's genetic makeup and childbearing capacity (aspects not altered by gender-conforming surgery or other medical interventions). Compare In re Marriage of Simmons, 825 N.E.2d 303 (Ill. App. Ct. 2005), with M.T. v. J.T. 355 A.2d 204 (N.J. Super. Ct. App. Div. 1976). Should the validity of a marriage depend on whether the transgender person discloses his or her gender identity?[41] Do the rules on marriage fraud and annulment apply?

Problems

1. On May 18, 1970, Richard John Baker and James Michael McConnell sought a marriage license in Minnesota. The license was denied "on the sole ground that [Baker and McConnell] were of the same sex." They challenged this denial, thus initiating the first same-sex marriage case in the United States. In 1971, the Minnesota Supreme Court summarily rejected their constitutional arguments. The brief opinion invoked the dictionary definition of marriage (which assumes a male and a female) and held insufficient the two principal cases cited by the plaintiffs in support of their due process and equal protection arguments, Griswold v. Connecticut and Loving v. Virginia. The U.S. Supreme Court denied *certiorari* for

---

[40]. Craig J. Konnoth, Gary J. Gates, & Williams Inst., Report: Same-Sex Couples and Immigration in the United States (Nov. 2011).

[41]. See Sherry F. Colb, Is There a Moral Duty to Disclose That You're Transgender to a Potential Partner?, June 18, 2015, https://verdict.justia.com/2015/06/18/is-there-a-moral-duty-to-disclose-that-youre-transgender-to-a-potential-partner.

want of a substantial federal question. See Baker v. Nelson, 191 N.W.2d 185 (Minn. 1971), *cert. denied*, 409 U.S. 810 (1972).

Family law has changed enormously since 1971. What particular developments might help explain the contrast between the Minnesota Supreme Court's approach in Baker v. Nelson in 1971 and the analysis in the recent *Windsor* and *Obergefell* majority opinions? Consider the following changes in family law: (a) the recognition of reproductive rights, including rights to use and have access to contraceptives and to decide whether to terminate a pregnancy; (b) the invalidation of laws assuming or imposing gender-based roles; (c) the invalidation of laws discriminating against children born outside marriage; and (d) the advent of no-fault divorce throughout the United States. Explain the possible connection of each to same-sex marriage and the reasons why the particular development might be relevant to the increasing legitimacy of claims, like Baker's and McConnell's, that were flatly rejected in 1971.

2. In oral arguments before the U.S. Supreme Court in Obergefell v. Hodges, the Supreme Court justices questioned the principal lawyer representing the state of Michigan (John J. Bursch), who argued that states should not be required to license same-sex marriages. Justice Alito posed the following friendly question to Mr. Bursch: "If the reason . . . for marriage is to provide a lasting bond between people who love each other and make a commitment to take care of each other, . . . do you see a way in which that logic can be limited to two people who want to have sexual relations . . . ?" Mr. Bursch obligingly responded: ". . . It can't be."[42] To restate the hypothetical: Suppose two people, who are *not* romantically involved, wish to form a commitment together. Is there any reason to deny them a marriage license once the right to marry is extended to same-sex couples? To what extent does marriage require sexual affiliation? What problem might such a requirement pose? See Nancy Polikoff, Beyond Straight (and Gay) Marriage, supra; Laura A. Rosenbury, Friends with Benefits?, 106 Mich. L. Rev. 189 (2007). See also Colorado's Designated Beneficiary Act, Colo. Rev. Stat. 15-22-101-15.22-112.

(2) Incest

IN RE ADOPTION OF M.

722 A.2d 615 (N.J. Super. Ct. Ch. Div. 1998)

BATTEN, J.S.C.

. . . The undisputed facts are troubling beyond description. [On] January 5, 1991, adoptive parents sought to adopt child M (hereinafter "petitioner"), born November 24, 1975, and voluntarily surrendered by her natural parents to the Division of Youth and Family Services, in May 1989. The adoption was uncontested. Final judgment of adoption entered January 25, 1991 [when] [p]etitioner

---

[42]. The exchange formed the basis of a critique by Sherry F. Colb, Justice Alito Asks Whether Non-Romantic Couples Should Have the Right to Marry: Absurd Question?, Verdict: Legal Analysis and Commentary from Justicia, May 5, 2015, https://verdict.justia.com/2015/05/05/justice-alito-asks-whether-non-romantic-couples-should-have-the-right-to-marry-absurd-question.

was then fifteen years old. Two years and ten months later, on November 21, 1993, petitioner attained age eighteen.

At some point in time subsequent to the final judgment of adoption yet prior to September 8, 1997, the marital relationship between the adoptive parents failed. Adoptive mother, on this latter date, filed her complaint for divorce against adoptive father, alleging acts of extreme cruelty. [The adoptive parents actually separated several years prior to the time they filed for divorce.] On November 18, 1997, final judgment of divorce dissolved the marriage of the adoptive parents. On July 29, 1998, petitioner, then twenty-two years of age, gave birth to an infant son. The parties acknowledge that adoptive father is the natural father of the infant.

Poignant realities emerge. First, petitioner and the adoptive father conceived the infant child in or about October 1997, at which time petitioner was twenty-one years of age. Second, conception between petitioner and adoptive father therefore likely occurred *prior* to the November 18, 1997, dissolution of his marriage to adoptive mother. Third, *a fortiori*, adoptive father engaged in a carnal relationship with his adult adoptive daughter while he was yet married to her adoptive mother. Fourth, the foregoing circumstances suggest—and the record stipulated before the court specifically confirms—that the relationship between petitioner and adoptive father had transgressed the parameters of a parent-child relationship well prior to the act of conception. Now the natural parents of the minor child, they desire to marry. Their present legal relationship as adoptive father and adoptive daughter, however, clearly renders the former an "ancestor" of, and the latter a "descendant" to, the other, thereby precluding lawful marriage between them. N.J.S.A. 37:1-1 [invalidating marriage between persons and their siblings, nephews, nieces, ancestors, or descendants]. Hence, petitioner brings this application. [Although petitioner originally moved to vacate the adoption as to both her adoptive parents, she and her adoptive mother subsequently decided to leave their relationship undisturbed. Petitioner thus sought to vacate the adoption as to her adoptive father only.]

Final judgment of adoption marks a turning point in the status of the natural and adoptive parents. Entry of such a judgment terminates all relationships between the adopted child and his/her natural parents and all of the rights, duties, and obligations of any persons that are founded on such relationships. . . . Subsequent to judgment, the adoptive parents are, as a matter of law, the parents of that child as if the child had been born to the adoptive parents in lawful wedlock.

Under New Jersey law [a] final judgment of adoption "should not be set aside unless it is in the best interest of the child and adoptive parents," and upon the showing of "truly exceptional circumstances" as determined by the particular facts of each case. . . . Indeed, the Legislature has mandated that the Adoption Act of New Jersey "shall be liberally construed to the end that the *best interests of children* be promoted," and "*due regard shall be given to the rights of all persons affected by an adoption.*" N.J.S.A. 9:3-37. [Emphasis added.] . . .

Certainly, the interests of "all persons affected" by this adoption have changed measurably. First, the adoptive child, in whose best interests the adoption occurred, is now, seven years later, (A) twenty-two years of age, (B) a natural mother of a two-month-old infant son, and (C) intent upon marriage to her son's natural father. The absence of any facts of record which might support a finding of abuse, neglect, domestic violence, or other unlawful act suggests a petitioner's conscious decision that her legal relationship with her adoptive father had achieved its purpose and, parent-child status notwithstanding, the complexities and realities of human emotions and relationships warrant transposition of that status from father-daughter co-parents to husband and wife. Through marriage, petitioner legitimizes not only her relationship with her son's father but the status of her infant son as well. . . .

Clearly, the facts here . . . constitute "truly exceptional circumstances" for several reasons. First, all reported cases contemplate an application to vacate a final judgment of adoption at a time during the minority of the adoptive child; here, the petitioner, as adopted child, moves post-emancipation to vacate the judgment of adoption. In this sense, the "best interests" standard of N.J.S.A. 9:2-4 no longer pertains to the adoptive child. Second, the stated purpose of the petition to vacate is eradication of a legal impediment to petitioner's marriage to her adoptive father, a relationship to which petitioner and adoptive father would be entitled absent their present legal status as father-daughter. Third, vacation of the final judgment of adoption would also shed adoptive father of his simultaneous status as natural father and legal grandfather of the minor infant, leaving him the natural father only. Fourth, vacation of the adoption judgment, through its cure of the statutory impediment to marriage, would further legitimize the infant, thereby advancing long-standing policy of this state to protect the status of children. More "truly exceptional circumstances" are difficult to imagine. . . . Petitioner's application to vacate the final judgment of adoption as pertains to her adoptive father is—as it must be—granted. . . .

NOTE: VOID AND VOIDABLE DISTINCTION

Statutes and the common law classify invalid marriages as either void or voidable. A void marriage is one that is invalid from inception (void ab initio), that is, it never had legal existence. On the other hand, a voidable marriage is valid until subsequently declared invalid. The distinction becomes important in terms of who may assert the invalidity of a marriage and whether the validity of the marriage may be collaterally attacked.

If a marriage is void, then either party or a third party may challenge the validity of the marriage at any time and in any proceeding. On the other hand, the invalidity of a voidable marriage can be asserted only by one of the parties and only during the marriage (that is, not after death of one of the parties). Further, voidable marriages cannot be collaterally attacked (that is, in a related proceeding).

The consequences of a particular defect stem from history (ecclesiastical law) as well as public policy (the degree to which the defect offends public policy). Substantive defects (same-sex, bigamous, and incestuous unions) render the marriage void. Less serious substantive defects, such as age, may render the marriage voidable.

Notes and Questions

1. **Historical background.** Virtually all societies have some form of incest taboos. Classic formulations exist in the psychoanalytic, sociological, and

anthropological literature. After William the Conqueror ascended the throne, incest became an ecclesiastical offense (similar to adultery and bigamy). Until the seventeenth century, prohibitions on incestuous marriages were extensive, but mitigated by dispensations to the wealthy. Incest became a crime in 1650, punishable by death.[43] In 1908, the Punishment of Incest Act (8 Edw. 7, ch. 45) proscribed three to seven years' imprisonment.

2. Civil and criminal consequences. Every state specifies the degrees of consanguinity and affinity within which persons may marry. ("Consanguinity" refers to blood relations, while "affinity" refers to relations by marriage.) Marriage to one's parent, grandparent, brother, or sister is universally prohibited, as is marriage between an aunt and nephew, and between an uncle and niece. Occasionally, states extend the prohibition to marriages to relatives by adoption and to step-relationships. Many states exempt first-cousin marriages. Most jurisdictions regard incestuous marriages as void ab initio. Note that the degrees of relation for civil marriage restrictions and for the imposition of criminal liability may differ.

3. State interests. According to *Zablocki*, regulations that substantially and directly interfere with the freedom to marry must receive elevated scrutiny. Do incest laws qualify? What state interests are at stake? Several have been suggested, including the protection of the gene pool from harmful consequences of inbreeding; protection of persons from exploitation; protection of the family from the assumption of incompatible familial roles; and protection of societal concepts of decency. Are these state interests "sufficiently important" to justify the restrictions? Experts disagree about the consequences of inbreeding.[44] If these state interests are sufficiently important, are the proscriptions sufficiently closely tailored to achieve these goals?

If the goal is prevention of the harmful consequences of procreation, should the state exempt those too old to reproduce? Require genetic testing for a marriage license? Prohibit marriages when one partner carries harmful genetic traits? Is the protection of the gene pool a justifiable function of government? Does the right to privacy dictate that the decision to perpetuate harmful genetic traits should be left to prospective parents?

4. Consensual relationships. In *Adoption of M.*, the father and daughter's sexual relationship was consensual. Incest laws are applicable to both nonconsensual and consensual acts of sexual intercourse or marriage between qualifying individuals. What is the impact of *Lawrence* on incest laws?

5. Relatives by adoption. *Adoption of M.* addresses prohibitions on marriage of persons related by adoption. What state interest supports such restrictions? How can that interest be served by prohibiting marriage by adoptive siblings who have grown up in separate households? Compare Israel v. Allen, 577 P.2d 762 (Colo. 1978), with In re Marriage of MEW, 4 Pa. D. & C. 3d 51 (1977).

---

[43]. 4 William Blackstone, Commentaries *64.

[44]. Compare Sarah Kershaw, Shaking off the Shame, N.Y. Times, Nov. 26, 2009, at D1 (children of first cousins carry high risk of birth defects), with Denise Grady, Few Risks Seen to the Children of 1st Cousins, N.Y. Times, Apr. 4, 2002, at A1 (reporting studies that discount harmful genetic consequences).

6. Criminal liability for parties and officials. Many statutes not only classify certain marriages as presumptively void but also subject to criminal liability those officials who knowingly issue marriage licenses to such couples. The parties themselves are also subject to criminal penalties—sometimes draconian ones. See, e.g., Cal. Penal Code §285 (previous incest statute authorized up to 50 years' imprisonment). Are criminal sanctions appropriate to enforce civil limitations on marriage?

7. Choice of law. Suppose first cousins marry in a jurisdiction permitting such marriages, but they move to a state with a prohibition. Which law applies? See Ghassemi v. Ghassemi, 998 So. 2d 731 (La. Ct. App. 2008) (holding that, because Iranian citizens were married pursuant to Iranian law permitting first-cousin marriages, such a marriage is valid in Louisiana for purposes of issuance of a divorce). Does the result change if the parties chose the place of celebration for the purpose of evading their domicile's restrictions? See In re May's Estate, 114 N.E.2d 4 (N.Y. 1953).

Problem

Movie director Woody Allen, age 56, had an affair with Soon-Yi Previn, age 22, the adopted daughter of Allen's long-term lover, actress Mia Farrow. (Soon-Yi Previn's adoptive father is Andre Previn, Farrow's former husband.) Although Allen and Farrow had had a biological child together and are the adoptive parents of two other young children, Allen and Farrow never married; in fact, they maintained separate residences. Should a state legislature criminalize sexual relationships such as Allen and Soon-Yi Previn's? Bar the issuance of marriage licenses to such couples? Declare any ensuing marriages void?

How does the incest taboo apply in the modern family, with the rise of divorce, remarriage, and cohabitation? Commentators suggest that the most significant damage from incest is psychological; i.e., the disruption of the process of emotional separation from the family of origin.[45] How might this factor play a role in the Allen-Previn relationship? Does Lawrence v. Texas affect the analysis? See Lowe v. Swanson, 663 F.3d 258 (6th Cir. 2011); Muth v. Frank, 412 F.3d 808 (7th Cir. 2005).

(3) Bigamy

BROWN v. BUHMAN

947 F. Supp. 2d 1170 (D. Utah 2013)

WADDOUPS, J.

[Plaintiffs Kody Brown and his four "wives" brought an action in federal court against county attorney Jeffrey Buhman, challenging the constitutionality of Utah's bigamy statute. Only one marriage license was recorded, between Kody

[45]. See Anastasia Toufexis, What Is Incest?, Time, Aug. 31, 1992, at 57 (quoting views of a child psychologist).

Brown and his first wife, Meri Brown.]

"Sister Wives" Christine Brown, Janelle Brown, Robyn Brown, and Meri Brown (left to right) with Kody Brown (center)

This decision is fraught with both religious and historical significance for the State of Utah because it deals with the question of polygamy, an issue that played a central role in the State's development and that of its dominant religion. . . . The Brown Plaintiffs are not members of the [Church of Jesus Christ of Latter-day Saints or LDS], but do adhere to the beliefs of a fundamentalist church that shares its historical roots with Mormonism. . . .

It would be an easy enough matter for the court to [find against the Plaintiffs], defaulting simply to Reynolds v. United States, 98 U.S. 145 (1879), without seriously addressing the much developed constitutional jurisprudence that now protects individuals from the criminal consequences intended by legislatures to apply to certain personal choices. [T]his would not be the legally or morally responsible approach in this case. [The intervening years since *Reynolds* have witnessed] a practical and morally defensible identification of "penumbral" rights "of privacy and repose" emanating from key provisions of the Bill of Rights, as the Supreme Court has over decades assumed a general posture that is less inclined to allow majoritarian coercion of unpopular or disliked minority groups. . . .

[I]t is perhaps a bitter irony of the history at issue here that it is possible to view the LDS Church as playing the role of both victim and violator in the saga of religious polygamy in Utah (and America). When the federal government targeted Mormon polygamy for elimination . . . , the "good order and morals of society" served as an acceptable basis for a legislature, it was believed, to identify "fundamental values" through a religious or other perceived ethical or moral consensus, enact criminal laws to force compliance with these values, and enforce those laws against a targeted group. [T]his has remained true in various forms (depending on the particular right and constitutional provision at issue) until the Supreme Court's decision in Lawrence v. Texas, 539 U.S. 558 (2003). . . .

Plaintiffs challenge the constitutionality of the Statute on multiple grounds, arguing both that the Statute is facially unconstitutional and unconstitutional as applied to the Plaintiffs. The Statute provides that "[a] person is guilty of bigamy when, knowing he has a husband or wife or knowing the other person has a husband or wife, the person purports to marry another person or cohabits with another person." Utah Code Ann. §76–7–101(1) [enacted in 1973]. The court [is bound] by the Utah Supreme Court's interpretation of the Statute, most recently in State of Utah v. Holm, 137 P.3d 726 (Utah 2006). In *Holm,* the Utah Supreme Court affirmed the defendant's conviction for unlawful sexual conduct with a minor under section 76–5–401.2 of the Utah Code, as well as bigamy under the Statute, but did not find occasion to construe the phrase "or cohabits with another person" because it rested its holding as to the bigamy conviction on its interpretation of the term "marry" and the phrase "purports to marry." . . . .

[The court first addresses whether there is a fundamental right to engage in polygamy or to engage in "religious cohabitation."] [N]o "fundamental right" exists to have official State recognition or legitimation of individuals' "purported" polygamous marriages—relationships entered into knowing that one of the parties to such a plural marriage is already legally married in the eyes of the State. [Washington v. Glucksberg, 521 U.S. 702 (1997)] is instructive for the analysis of whether the asserted right to polygamy is "deeply rooted in this Nation's history and tradition, and implicit in the concept of ordered liberty." [T]o identify a fundamental right to assisted suicide, the Court "would have to reverse centuries of legal doctrine and practice, and strike down the considered policy choice of almost every State." . . . The prohibition against polygamy has similarly ancient roots in Anglo–American law. . . . .

The relationship at issue in this lawsuit, which the court has termed "religious cohabitation," has been aptly described by then-Chief Justice Durham of the Utah Supreme Court [as occurring] when "[t]hose who choose to live together without getting married enter into a personal relationship that resembles a marriage in its intimacy but claims no legal sanction." *Holm*, 137 P.3d at 773 (Durham, C.J., dissenting). . . . A defining characteristic of such cohabitation [is] that, in choosing "to enter into a relationship that [the persons know] would not be legally recognized as marriage, [they use] religious terminology to describe the relationship," and this terminology—"'marriage' and 'husband and wife'—happens to coincide with the terminology used by the state to describe the legal status of married persons." Stated succinctly, Plaintiffs "appropriate the terminology of marriage, a revered social and legal institution, for [their] own religious purposes," though not purporting "to have actually acquired the legal status of marriage." But this religious cohabitation also fails to qualify as a fundamental right or fundamental liberty interest triggering heightened scrutiny. . . .

[The court then turns to the plaintiffs' Free Exercise claim under the First Amendment.] *Reynolds* held that Congress's long history of specifically targeting Mormons based on the fear that their practice of polygamy posed a threat to American democracy, and the resulting federal legislation prohibiting polygamy did not violate the Mormons' right to the free exercise of their religion. *Reynolds*, therefore, still controls the analysis of straightforward polygamy or bigamy in which there is a claim to multiple simultaneous *legal* marriages. *Reynolds*, however, is not controlling for the cohabitation prong *under the 1973 Statute*. . . .

[The court sets forth the rule that facially neutral laws of general applicability do not violate the First Amendment. The court then concedes that specific language in the statute is facially neutral—i.e., the phrase "or cohabits with another person"—because that language does not refer to religion or facially imply a response to religiously motivated conduct. However, according to the court, the "problematic portion" of the statute is the "operational application" of the statute because "few if any cohabitations are prohibited other than religious cohabitations."]

Given the fact that all prosecutions under the Statute's cohabitation prong . . . have been of those cohabiting for religious reasons underscores that, in practice, the law is not operationally neutral. . . . The State's argument reveals that the object of the Statute "is to infringe upon or restrict practices because of their religious motivation." This it may not do unless it is a narrowly tailored means of advancing a compelling state interest. . . .

[The court next explores possible state interests to determine whether the statute is justified by a compelling state interest.] [First, we consider] the State's interest in regulating marriage, an interest which "has resulted in a network of laws, many of which are premised upon the concept of monogamy," and held that the Statute is rationally related to that interest. . . . The *Holm* Court, also applying rational basis review, re-emphasized this State interest in protecting monogamous marriage as a social institution. Applying strict scrutiny, however, the court agrees with Chief Justice Durham [dissenting in *Holm*] that "the state has an important interest in regulating marriage, but only insofar as marriage is understood as a legal status." The court therefore finds Chief Justice Durham's observation to be well-taken, that the Statute "protects marriage, as a legal union, by criminalizing the act of purporting to enter a *second legal union*. Such an act defrauds the state and perhaps an innocent spouse or purported partner. It also completely disregards the network of laws that regulate entry into, and the dissolution of, the *legal status of marriage,* and that limit to one the number of partners with which an individual may enjoy this status." (emphasis added).

[T]he incongruity between criminalizing religious cohabitation but not adulterous cohabitation, or rather selectively prosecuting the former while not prosecuting the latter at all, demonstrates that the cohabitation prong is not narrowly tailored to advance a compelling state interest. "That the state perceives no need to prosecute non-religiously motivated cohabitation, whether one of the parties to the cohabitation is married to someone else or not, demonstrates that, in the absence of any claim of legal marriage, neither participation in a religious ceremony nor cohabitation can plausibly be said to threaten marriage as a social or legal institution." Thus, "any interest the state has in maintaining this network of laws does not logically justify its imposition of criminal penalties on those who deviate from that domestic structure, particularly when they do so for religious reasons." Accordingly, "such criminal penalties are simply unnecessary to further the state's interest in protecting marriage" [citing Justice Durham, C.J., dissenting in *Holm*].

The court acknowledges [that] "some in society may feel that the institution of marriage is diminished when individuals consciously choose to avoid it," but agrees that "it is generally understood that the state is not entitled to criminally punish its citizens for making such a choice, even if they do so with multiple partners. . . ." [In addition, the defendant does not adequately explain] "how the institution of marriage is abused or state support for monogamy threatened simply by an individual's choice to participate in a religious ritual with more than one person outside the confines of legal marriage." [T]he court also feels compelled to identify an absurdity in the State's position against religious cohabitation in this context of trying to "protect" the institution of marriage by criminalizing religious cohabitation. . . . Encouraging adulterous cohabitation over religious cohabitation that resembles marriage in all but State recognition seems counterproductive to the goal of strengthening or protecting the institution of marriage . . . .

[Second,] the Statute addresses the State's "interest in preventing the perpetration of marriage fraud, as well as its interest in preventing the misuse of government benefits associated with marital status." The Statute's relationship to this interest makes even less sense to the court than the first interest discussed above, particularly when reviewed under strict scrutiny. "This interest focuses on preventing the harm caused to the state, to society, and to defrauded individuals when someone purports to have entered the legal status of marriage, but in fact is not eligible to validly enter that status because of a prior legal union. This interest is simply not implicated here, where no claim to the legal status of marriage has been made." *Holm*, 137 P.3d at 773–774 (Durham, C.J., dissenting in part). Moreover, it is "difficult to understand how those in polygamous relationships that are ineligible to receive legal sanction are committing welfare abuse when they seek benefits available to unmarried persons." [This court] accordingly finds the cohabitation prong of the Statute not even rationally related to this inapposite State interest.

Third, and of most concern, [we consider] "the State's interest in protecting vulnerable individuals from exploitation and abuse." [In the case of State v. Green, 99 P.3d 320 (Utah 2004), the court stated]: "The practice of polygamy, in particular, often coincides with crimes targeting women and children. Crimes not unusually attendant to the practice of polygamy include incest, sexual assault, statutory rape, and failure to pay child support." But, once again, the court agrees with Chief Justice Durham's assessment of *Green*'s rational basis review of this "State interest":

> Because the [*Green* Court applied rational basis review under the First Amendment challenge], the court was content to rely on assertions in a student law review piece that polygamy was frequently related to other criminal conduct, together with two local cases, including the case of Green himself. . . . Upon closer review, the student Note is unconvincing. The State has provided no evidence of a causal relationship or even a strong correlation between the practice of polygamy, whether religiously motivated or not, and the offenses of 'incest, sexual assault, statutory rape, and failure to pay child support' . . . Even if there were support for this claim in the record, *I would consider it inappropriate to let stand a criminal law simply because it enables the state to conduct a fishing expedition for evidence of other crimes*. . . . *Holm*, 137 P.3d at 775 (Durham, C.J., dissenting in part).

The court is aware of the many reports that circulate implying "the possibility that other criminal conduct may accompany the act of bigamy."

> It seems to the court that the Statute has unintentionally become a bottleneck to the straightforward prosecution of [incest, rape, unlawful sexual conduct with a minor, child abuse] precisely because of the State's general policy not to prosecute religiously motivated polygamy under the Statute in the absence of age concerns or evidence of "collateral" crimes. With the cohabitation prong stricken, the Statute can no longer function as this kind of barrier, and investigators and prosecutors can focus directly on the independent crimes that are being committed, if any. Accordingly, despite the gravity of this concern, the court finds that the cohabitation prong not only is not narrowly tailored to advance a compelling State interest but that it actually inhibits the advancement of this compelling State interest of "protecting vulnerable individuals from exploitation and abuse." *Green*, 99 P.3d at 830.

For all of these reasons, the cohabitation prong of the Statute cannot survive strict scrutiny and must be stricken as a facial violation of the free exercise of religion under the First Amendment. . . .

[The court next addresses whether the cohabitation prong violates substantive due process.] Consensual sexual privacy is the touchstone of the rational basis review analysis in this case, as in *Lawrence*. The court believes that Plaintiffs are correct in their argument [that] in the case of people who have not even claimed to be legally married, "[i]t is the state that is treating the relationship as a form of marriage and prosecuting on that basis." As such, this, in effect, criminalizes "the private consensual relations of adults." . . .

Adultery, including adulterous cohabitation, is not prosecuted. Religious cohabitation, however, is subject to prosecution at the limitless discretion of local and State prosecutors. . . . The court finds no rational basis to distinguish between the two, not least with regard to the State interest in protecting the institution of marriage. . . . [T]here can be no rational basis for this approach, particularly under *Lawrence* and its focus on the deeper liberty interests at issue in the home and personal relationships. [T]he cohabitation prong of the Statute does not survive rational basis review and must be stricken as a violation of substantive due process under *Lawrence*. . . .

[Plaintiffs next argue that the statute is void for vagueness in terms of its "arbitrary or discriminatory enforcement."] Here, the State seems to have various policies about whether to prosecute polygamists. Defendant himself has sent mixed signals about his intention to prosecute, currently claiming in an affidavit [that] he has established a policy that his office will not prosecute religiously motivated cohabitation (or cohabitation at all) absent the presence of some collateral crime. But Defendant disclaims adherence to this policy by any successors in his office.

These various policies create substantial uncertainty about whether one will be prosecuted under the Statute if engaging in religiously motivated cohabitation, or simple cohabitation with no religious motivation, or for one but not the other, or even about whether the Statute is moribund as a result of widespread prosecutorial inaction. The apparently limitless prosecutorial discretion in whether and whom to prosecute under the Statute "vests virtually complete discretion in the hands of [law enforcement and prosecutors] to determine whether" people cohabiting in the State of Utah for whatever reason, but particularly those involved in religiously motivated cohabitation, have violated the Statute's cohabitation prong. The cohabitation prong is therefore void for vagueness and will be stricken.

. . . With the cohabitation prong thus stricken, the Statute now reads as follows: "A person is guilty of bigamy when, knowing he has a husband or wife or knowing the other person has a husband or wife, the person purports to marry another person." Utah Code Ann. §76-7-101(1) (2013). [T]he phrase "purports to marry another person" raises the same constitutional concerns addressed in relation to the cohabitation prong above. [The court concludes that the phrase] should be interpreted "as referring to an individual's claim of entry into a legal union recognized by the state as marriage. The phrase does not encompass an individual's entry into a religious union where there has been no attempt to elicit the state's recognition of marital status or to procure the attendant benefits of this status under the law, and where neither party to the union believed it to have legal import." [This narrowing construction allows] the Statute to remain in force as prohibiting bigamy [only] in the literal sense—the fraudulent or otherwise impermissible possession of two purportedly valid marriage licenses for the purpose of entering into more than one purportedly legal marriage. . . .

Jack Anderson, Adventures Among the Polygamists[46]

1 Investigative Rep. Mag. (Jan. 1982), at 4-42

. . . Growing up in a devout Mormon home, I was duly drilled in the subjugation of the flesh and shielded from the lustier chapters of my heritage. But now and again, I picked up a mournful whisper among the adults about some fallen soul who had sunk back into the old ways. I was 18 and a fledgling reporter for The Salt Lake Tribune when whispers of [my second cousin's] relapse made the family rounds. [M]y curiosity was reinforced by the reporter's license to snoop into the hidden and illegal. In due course, I located [an elderly man with a saintly visage, Joseph Musser].

[Musser] outlined a "fundamentalist" faith which stressed the traditional doctrines and the old-fashioned virtues. [H]is main theme [was] a review of the moral shambles of modern life, [which he traced to monogamy] with its inevitable spawn of divorces and mistresses, unmarried mothers and bachelor fathers, cast-off wives and abandoned children. Did not the rise of abortion and contraception clearly foreshadow its ultimate ends: the destruction of the family? Opposed to this theme of abominations, he said, was the sacred institution of plural marriage, practiced by the Old Testament prophets and rooted in God's great commandment to the human race:

"Be fruitful and multiply and replenish the earth." [He said that we] must restore the patriarchal order [and] aspire to stand at the head of a family as numerous as the sands on the seashore. . . . God would provide women in abundance who were prepared to do their duty; we bearers of the seed must extend ourselves to the utmost. . . .

Mormonism [is] a product of the frontier. [Thousands of converts followed founder Joseph Smith to Missouri in the 1830s.] Most of the converts to Mormonism came out of New England. They were a puritanical people, reserved in conduct and strict about sex—attitudes further stiffened by their new faith. [When Smith revealed to the Church leaders the religious basis for polygamy, they quickly divided over the issue.] Even Smith's great disciple, Brigham Young, teetered for a time on the brink of rejection, later saying of his initial reaction: "It was the first time in my life that I desired the grave." But in time, Young not only accepted polygamy but warmed to it and acquired 27 wives.

[T]he Mormons had settled a thousand miles from their nearest neighbors in a land so inhospitable they thought no one else would ever want it, in order to pursue their faith without friction. At last, they felt safe, far from vigilantes, in a territory they controlled. But they underestimated the righteous enmity of the fellow who hears that someone else is savoring a fruit forbidden to him. . . . In 1869, the geographic isolation of the Mormons was broken by the completion of the transcontinental railroad, and they found themselves invaded by miners, railroaders and entrepreneurs, a rowdy bunch not previously noted for

---

[46]. Jack Anderson, a Pulitzer Prize–winning journalist, was one of the founders of investigative reporting. He contributed to the exposure of Senator Joseph McCarthy's Communist witch hunts and the Nixon-era Watergate hearings. This excerpt is from his first investigative story.

their sexual scruples, who set up a great lamentation over Mormon heresies and inequities. It was aimed more at Washington than at heaven, however, for the enterprising Mormons controlled not only the women of Utah, but the land, the commerce, and the public offices. [In response to congressional efforts from 1862-1887 to make bigamy a federal crime and to limit the power of the Mormon Church, the Mormons provided that anyone practicing polygamy would be excommunicated.] So thorough going was the Mormon effort to obliterate all traces of plural marriage that by the time I came along in the third generation, only whispers remained of it. . . .

[The polygamous families that the author met] were generally hardworking and frugal. Although the upwardly mobile polygamist aspired for a separate home for each of his wives and broods, thus to perambulate from one to the other, most had to house their multiple families under one roof. . . . To neighbors, the proliferation of brassieres on clotheslines, or new female faces at the windows or a platoon of strange tots romping in the yard, were explained away as visiting aunts and cousins. . . .

The polygamists also appeared to be a sober people of earnest disposition, who would have been enraged to hear themselves called immoral. . . . Among the men, there was no locker-room hee-hawing and lip-smacking about things sexual. Procreation was seen as the central duty of their lives. . . . Such gratifications, as attended this duty, were to be accepted as the unmentioned rewards of a job well done. [But] I struck up conversations with wives who, once their hair was down, acknowledged it was a problem being forever a regimented and scheduled shareholder in love and home. . . .

[T]he most critical operation in a polygamous society is the selection process by which spouses are distributed. . . . I came quickly to suspect that the prophet Musser was making very liberal interpretations of the Lord's messages. Either that or the Lord had an unerring partiality for old codgers. The choicest girls were going to the leaders themselves or to the wealthier laymen who were the biggest contributors to the cause. . . .

Unknown to me, I was not the only investigator on the beat. [Church elders] hired trusted private investigators to keep an eye on the polygamists. [During meetings of polygamists] the investigators would slip among the parked cars outside and copy the license numbers. [T]hus, it was that the license number of my father's old Plymouth, the only wheels available to me, kept appearing in the investigators' reports. In due course, my father was called in by his spiritual superiors for a confrontation that utterly confounded him. . . . [O]ne day I came home to find my father in a towering rage. The unspeakable had been spoken: He had been accused of an undercover flirtation with the polygamists. . . . I was a long time in the doghouse. [S]o ended my first adventures with the polygamists. . . .

Notes and Questions

1. Epilogue. Plaintiffs, who appear in the TLC reality TV series *Sister Wives,* are highly visible advocates of plural marriage. Threats of prosecution forced them to move from Utah to Nevada. Professor Jonathan Turley of George Washington University School of Law served as lead counsel in the principal case.

2. Historical background. Bigamy has a long history. In medieval England, bigamy was an ecclesiastical offense. Ecclesiastical law made bigamous marriages void. In 1603, Parliament made bigamy a felony. In the United States, polygamy has been associated primarily with the Mormon religion, even though the LDS Church formally repudiated the practice when Utah became a state.

Law enforcement efforts took the form of raids of polygamist communities. In a famous raid on Short Creek, an isolated community straddling the Arizona-Utah border (now Colorado City), law enforcement officials took mothers and children into custody and prosecuted the men. See In re State ex rel. Black, 283 P.2d 887 (Utah 1955). Law enforcement officials again raided a polygamist compound in 2008 in Eldorado, Texas, and took 400 children into custody following a report of sexual abuse by a 16-year-old girl that was later determined to be a hoax.[47]

3. Prevalence. Although mainstream members of the LDS Church reject polygamy, an estimated 38,000 persons identify as fundamentalist Mormons and practice polygamy, primarily in the southwestern United States.[48] Despite such estimates, prosecutions are rare. The prosecution of Mormon fundamentalist Tom Green by the state of Utah in 2000 was the first in nearly 50 years.[49]

4. Civil and criminal consequences. Bigamy, like incest, has criminal and civil consequences. Civil restrictions limit the ability to contract a second marriage (while a valid first marriage exists) by making such marriages void. Such a marriage needs no decree to establish its invalidity. States also impose criminal penalties when a prior valid marriage exists. Utah's statute was unique in extending its prohibition to "cohabitation in a marriage-like relationship" while one person is legally married to another person.

5. Constitutional challenges to polygamy laws.

a. First Amendment. Most challenges to polygamy laws are based on claims that such laws infringe on the free exercise of religion. How does *Brown* respond to such claims? Why doesn't *Reynolds* control? What level of scrutiny does the court apply to plaintiffs' free exercise claim and why? In an omitted portion of the case, the Court explains that hostility to polygamy reflected views of racial superiority, particularly the association of polygamy with nonwhite races (such as Asians, Africans, and Middle Easterners) in an era of xenophobia.[50]

b. Due process and precedent. Why does Lawrence v. Texas mandate reconsideration of polygamy laws? What level of scrutiny does *Brown* apply to plaintiffs' due process claim and why? What are the possible state interests that support the

---

[47]. David Fahrenthold, In Texas, an Unusual Prosecution of a Way of Life, Wash. Post, Apr. 26, 2008, at A3.

[48]. A.P., Governor: Utah Should Defend Anti-Polygamy Law, N.Y. Times, Aug. 28, 2014, http://www.nytimes.com/aponline/2014/08/28/us/ap-us-sister-wives-polygamy.html.

[49]. Pamela Manson, The Law Has Been Slow to Step In, Salt Lake Trib., Mar. 14, 2004, at G1.

[50]. *Brown*, 947 F. Supp. 2d at 1182. For background on the case, see Martha M. Ertman, The Story of Reynolds v. United States: Federal "Hell Hounds" Punishing Mormon Treasure, in Family Law Stories 51-75 (Carol Sanger ed., 2008).

imposition of criminal sanctions? How does the court evaluate those interests? Does the case hold that state bans on polygamy are unconstitutional? What might be the effect of *Brown* on polygamous families? On the LDS Church?

Do polygamy bans violate the right to marry based on *Zablocki*? To what extent are such prohibitions "direct" and "substantial" interferences with the right to marry? Or are such bans "reasonable regulations that do not significantly interfere with decisions to enter into the marital relationship"? What light does *Brown* shed on these questions?

Brown was decided before *Obergefell*. What implications does *Obergefell* have regarding the legal status of polygamy? How expansive or limited is *Obergefell's* rationale as applied to polygamy? See generally Symposium, Polygamous Unions? Charting the Contours of Marriage Law's Frontiers, 64 Emory L.J. 1669 (2015).

Do *Lawrence, Obergefell*, and *Brown* call into question all state "morals legislation" that implicate sexual privacy? What about adult incest? Adultery? Prostitution? Obscenity? See generally Gillian Calder & Lori Beaman eds., Polygamy's Rights and Wrongs: Perspectives on Harm, Family, and the Law (2015) (questioning assumptions about the harmful nature of polygamy).

c. Void for vagueness. Why does the *Brown* court hold that the bigamy law is void for vagueness? What is the harm of a vague law?

6. Other legal consequences. In addition to civil restrictions and criminal sanctions, polygamy may trigger other adverse legal consequences. See, e.g., Potter v. Murray City, 760 F.2d 1065 (10th Cir. 1985) (loss of employment); Shepp v. Shepp, 906 A.2d 1165 (Pa. 2006) (loss of child custody); Matter of Adoption of W.A.T., 808 P.2d 1083 (Utah 1991) (dismissal of adoption); Herman Miller Inc. Ret. Income Plan v. Magallon, 2010 WL 2940943, at *3 (E.D. Cal. 2010) (loss of retirement benefits). Should such consequences continue in light of *Lawrence, Obergefell*, and *Brown*? See also Hope Marie Deutsch, Marrying Polygamy into Title VII, 16 Rutgers J.L. & Religion 145 (2014).

7. Birth of a social movement. Pro-polygamy and polyamory activists seek the repeal of polygamy laws by minimizing the link between polygamy and abuse. They emphasize the consensual nature of the relationships and evoke the rhetoric of sexual liberation.

Anti-polygamists also seek law reform (increased enforcement of the law) by highlighting the occurrence of abuse, as illustrated in accounts of women who fled polygamous relationships. Compare Jeffrey Michael Hayes, Polygamy Comes out of the Closet: The New Strategy of Polygamy Activists, 3 Stan. J. C.R.-C.L. 99, 105 (2007), with Kristyn Decker, Fifty Years in Polygamy: Big Secrets and Little White Lies (2013); and Susan Schmidt, Favorite Wife: Escape from Polygamy (2014). As part of the anti-polygamy movement, a new reality TV series (*Escaping Polygamy*) recently debuted on the Lifetime Movie Network to portray the lives of people who flee from polygamous households.

8. Utah's child bigamy law. Among the state interests underlying polygamy prohibitions, as mentioned in *Brown*, is the interest in preventing sexual exploitation. Should criminal liability attach only in cases involving teenage wives, and not in cases involving adult women who freely consent to such relationships? See Maura I. Strassberg, The Crime of Polygamy, 12 Temp. Pol. & Civ. Rts. L. Rev. 353 (2003) (so arguing).

To address this problem, the Utah legislature enacted the Child Bigamy Amendment, which increases the penalties in cases involving teenage brides. Utah Code Annotated §76-7-101.5 provides that marriage or cohabitation with a person under age 18, while the actor is validly married to another, constitutes a second-degree felony punishable by up to 15 years in prison. (In contrast, adult bigamy is a third-degree felony, pursuant to Utah Code Ann. §76-7-101(2), punishable by up to five years in prison.) Is this provision constitutional after *Brown*? A different criminal provision provides that a parent who knowingly allows a minor to enter into a marriage that is prohibited is guilty of a third-degree felony. Utah Code Ann. §30-1-9.1. The legislature considered, but ultimately rejected, a provision that would have created the crime of inducing a minor to enter into a polygamous relationship and would have enabled prosecution of church leaders who arrange such marriages.

9. Harm. Why does Judge Waddoups believe that the state's interest in protecting vulnerable individuals from exploitation does not satisfy rational basis review? Note that Judge Waddoups concurs with Chief Justice Durham (the dissenting judge in *Holm*) that evidence of a correlation between polygamy and other crimes exploiting women and children (e.g., incest, sexual assault, statutory rape, etc.) is "unconvincing."

Consider that Warren Jeffs, the famous leader of a fundamentalist Mormon sect in Colorado City, was sentenced to two consecutive life terms in 2011 for sexually assaulting two underage girls (one was 12 years old) when he took them as "brides" in "spiritual marriages." Of Jeffs's 79 wives, 24 were under the age of 17.[51] What light does such evidence shed on the correlation between polygamy and crimes of sexual exploitation? See also Maura I. Strassbeg, Scrutinizing Polygamy: Utah's Brown v. Buhman and British Columbia's Reference re: Section 293, 64 Emory L.J. 1815 (2015) (comparing *Brown* with a recent Canadian case that explains the harm of polygamy).

10. Conflict of laws. Suppose a man marries multiple wives in a country where this practice is permitted. The couple then moves to a U.S. state that prohibits such marriages. Should the second jurisdiction recognize the marriages? Should it matter for what purpose the validity is at issue? Compare In re Dalip Singh Bir's Estate, 188 P.2d 499 (Cal. Ct. App. 1948) (inheritance law), with Al Sharabi v. Heinauer, 2011 WL 3955027 (N.D. Cal. 2011) (immigration).

---

[51]. Texas: Polygamist Leader Gets Life Sentence, N.Y. Times, Aug. 10, 2011, at A15; Cathy Scott, FLDS Girls Vindicated as Pedophile "Prophet" Awaits Sentencing, Forbes, Aug. 5, 2011, http://www.forbes.com/sites/shenegotiates/2011/08/05/flds-girls-vindicated-as-pedophile-prophet-awaits-sentencing.

Elizabeth Joseph, My Husband's Nine Wives

N.Y. Times, May 23, 1991, at A15

I married a married man. In fact, he had six wives when I married him 17 years ago. Today, he has nine. . . .

. . . At first blush, [polygamy] sounds like the ideal situation for the man and an oppressive one for the women. For me, the opposite is true. [C]ompelling social reasons make the life style attractive to the modern career woman.

Pick up any women's magazine and you will find article after article about the problems of successfully juggling career, motherhood, and marriage. It is a complex act that many women struggle to manage daily. . . .

When I leave for the 60-mile commute to court at 7 A.M., my 2-year-old daughter, London, is happily asleep in the bed of my husband's wife, Diane. London adores Diane. When London awakes, about the time I'm arriving at the courthouse, she is surrounded by family members who are as familiar to her as the toys in her nursery. . . .

I share a home with Delinda, another wife, who works in town government. [Alex Joseph shares another house with seven other wives and their children.] Most nights, we agree we'll just have a simple dinner with our three kids. . . . Mondays, however, are different. That's the night Alex eats with us. . . . The same system with some variation governs our private time with him. While spontaneity is by no means ruled out, we basically use an appointment system. . . .

Plural marriage is not for everyone. But it is the life style for me. It offers men the chance to escape from the traditional, confining roles that often isolate them from the surrounding world. More important, it enables women, who live in a society full of obstacles, to fully meet their career, mothering and marriage obligations. Polygamy provides a whole solution. I believe American women would have invented it if it didn't already exist.

(4) Age

KIRKPATRICK v. DISTRICT COURT

64 P.3d 1056 (Nev. 2003)

SHEARING, J. . . .

SierraDawn Kirkpatrick Crow is the daughter of Karen Karay and petitioner Bruce Kirkpatrick. . . . As part of the divorce decree, Karay and Kirkpatrick were awarded joint legal and physical custody of SierraDawn. In 1992, Karay and SierraDawn moved from California to New Mexico. In December 2000, when SierraDawn was fifteen years old, she informed her mother that she desired to marry her guitar teacher, 48-year-old Sauren Crow. SierraDawn's mother approved of the marriage.

However, under New Mexico law, SierraDawn was not permitted to marry. Therefore, SierraDawn, her mother, and Crow traveled to Las Vegas where

SierraDawn and Crow could marry, if granted permission by the court. [New Mexico law (N.M. Stat. Ann. §§40-1-5, 40-1-6(B)) provides that a minor under age 16 shall not marry unless the marriage legitimizes a nonmarital child or the minor is pregnant, whereas Nevada law (Nev. Rev. Stat. §122.025) permits a minor under age 16 to marry based on one parent's consent and judicial authorization.]

Karay filed a petition [for] judicial authorization for SierraDawn's marriage. [In addition] Karay filed an affidavit consenting to the marriage, in which she stated that she has "seen no other couple so right for each other," that they "have very real life plans at home, in the town in which we all reside," and that "[t]heir partnership and their talents will be most effectively utilized by this marriage." [The court found good cause under Nevada law for the marriage and ordered issuance of the license. The couple married in Las Vegas.]

When Kirkpatrick first learned of SierraDawn's marriage, he sought an ex parte temporary restraining order in the New Mexico district court. That court granted the temporary restraining order, and awarded Kirkpatrick immediate legal and physical custody of SierraDawn. Four days later, however, the court rescinded its order because it found that SierraDawn's marriage was valid under Nevada law, and that SierraDawn was emancipated as a result of the marriage.[3] . . . Thereafter, Kirkpatrick filed this petition seeking a writ of mandamus to compel the district court to vacate its order authorizing SierraDawn's marriage and to annul the marriage. . . .

It is well settled that states have the right and power to establish reasonable limitations on the right to marry. This power is justified as an exercise of the police power, which confers upon the states the ability to enact laws in order to protect the safety, health, morals, and general welfare of society. Pursuant to this power, the Nevada Legislature enacted Nev. Rev. Stat. §122.025 [requiring one parent consent and judicial authorization for underage marriages].

Kirkpatrick argues that this statute violates his constitutional interest in the care, custody, and management of his daughter since it neither requires his consent nor gives him an opportunity to be heard on the issue of his daughter's marriage. The United States Supreme Court has held that parents have a fundamental liberty interest in the care, custody, and management of their children. However, the United States Supreme Court has also held that, although these rights are fundamental, they are not absolute. The state also has an interest in the welfare of children and may limit parental authority. The Supreme Court has even held, where justified, that parents can be totally deprived of their children forever. If the state can completely eliminate all parental rights, it can certainly limit some parental rights when the competing rights of the child are implicated.

The United States Supreme Court has held that the right to marry is a fundamental right [citing *Loving* and *Zablocki*]. . . . The Supreme Court has made it clear that constitutional rights apply to children as well as adults. . . . Marriage is the cornerstone of the family and our civilization. As marriage comprises the most sacred of relationships, the decision of whom and when to marry is highly personal, often involving reasons that are complex and vary from individual to individual. The decision to marry should rest primarily in the hands of the individual,

3. At common law, marriage is generally sufficient to constitute emancipation. . . . It does not appear that judicial action is required for emancipation to occur. . . .

with little government interference. As a society, we recognize that reasonable constraints on the right to marry are appropriate, especially when the marriage involves a minor.

There is no one set of criteria that can be set forth as a litmus test to determine if a marriage will be successful [or] whether a person is mature enough to enter a marriage. Age alone is an arbitrary factor. The Nevada Legislature recognized that although most fifteen-year-olds would not be mature enough to enter into a marriage, there are exceptions. Nevada provided for the exceptional case by allowing a fifteen-year-old to marry if one parent consents and the court approves. The statute provides a safeguard against an erroneous marriage decision by the minor and the consenting parent, by giving the district court the discretion to withhold authorization if it finds that there are no extraordinary circumstances and/or the proposed marriage is not in the minor's best interest, regardless of parental consent. The statute strikes a balance between an arbitrary rule of age for marriage and accommodation of individual differences and circumstances.

Consent of both parents is by no means a constitutional requirement for even the most important of decisions regarding minors [citing Hodgson v. Minnesota, 497 U.S. 417 (1990) (declaring a *two-parent* notification requirement for an abortion unconstitutional in the absence of a judicial bypass)]. The *Hodgson* Court went on to hold that two-parent notification "is an oddity among state and federal consent provisions governing the health, welfare, and education of children," such as enlisting in the armed services, obtaining a passport, participating in medical research, or submitting to any surgical or medical procedure. When the state requires the consent of only one parent for significant events in a minor's life, the state implicitly recognizes the common reality of modern families. A significant percentage of children under the age of eighteen live in single-parent households. . . .

Kirkpatrick asserts that he has been deprived of his fundamental right to the parent-child relationship, like the parents whose parental rights have been terminated. Contrary to what is apparently Kirkpatrick's view, the parental relationship does not end with the emancipation of a child. The only right that he has lost by his daughter's emancipation is his right to exercise legal control over his daughter during her minority. He still has all the other legal and social attributes of parenthood. Kirkpatrick retains the legal rights of inheritance, as well as all the bonds of love, care, companionship, and influence that any parents have after emancipation of their children. How he chooses to foster those bonds is up to him.

The Supreme Court has held that the usual standard for analyzing a substantive due process challenge to the constitutionality of a state statute that impinges on a fundamental constitutional right is whether the statute is narrowly tailored so as to serve a compelling interest. In family privacy cases involving competing interests within the family, however, the Court has deviated from the usual test. Various child rearing and custody cases demonstrate the Court's application of a more flexible "reasonableness" test, which "implicitly calibrat[es] the level of scrutiny in each case to match the particular degree of intrusion upon the parents' interests."

In this case, we have the interest of the daughter in marriage and the interest of the mother in her daughter's welfare and happiness balanced against the father's interest in the legal control of his daughter for the remainder of her minority. Nev. Rev. Stat. §122.025 strikes an appropriate balance between the various interests. . . .

Notes and Questions

1. **Minimum age.** All states have a minimum age for marriage, generally age 18. Underage minors need parental and/or (in some jurisdictions) judicial consent. See, e.g., Ariz. Rev. Stat. §25-102 (persons under 18 require parental consent; those under 16 must also have judicial consent). Some states permit pregnant minors to marry at a younger age. See, e.g., N.C. Gen. Stat. Ann. §51-2.1 (age 14, with judicial consent).

Why did SierraDawn in *Kirkpatrick* decide to marry in Nevada rather than New Mexico? Are minors, such as SierraDawn, capable of informed consent on such "private" matters as marriage and abortion?

2. **Historical background.** The age of consent for marriage at early common law was 7. Such marriages, however, were voidable if either party was too young to consummate the marriage. Betrothals of children occurred in order to ensure the passage of estates, settle disputes, and prevent the sovereign from selecting a youth's spouse.[52] Ultimately, the Church proscribed such betrothals. Parliament raised the age of consent in 1653 to 16 for boys and 14 for girls. For the first time, parental consent was required for children under 21. Subsequent legislation declared a marriage void if either party was under 16.[53]

In the United States, the development of restrictions on youthful marriages reflects an ambivalence concerning respect for family privacy versus deference to state intervention. Historian Michael Grossberg writes:

> Early in the nineteenth century most states resolved [uncertainty about the state's treatment of underage marriage] in favor of a youthful freedom to wed free of public restraints. . . . A series of acts in the late nineteenth century and early twentieth [century] succeeded in raising the average national statutory age of marriage to sixteen for women and eighteen for men. By 1906 the legal trend had become so commonplace that only seventeen states and territories clung to the old common law standard of twelve and fourteen.
>
> These nuptial law revisions occurred amidst a broader reassessment of the social and economic place of youth in American life. Persuaded by educators, physicians, and reformers . . . , legislators began legally to segregate youths through compulsory school laws, to provide special courts for them with vast discretionary power over status offenses, as well as to limit nuptial freedom. These statutes used the law to protect a Victorian conception of youth development and marital conduct by prolonging childhood and by saving children from themselves and their misguided parents. . . .[54]

3. **Empirical data.** Both men and women are marrying later, although men marry later than women. In 2013, the median age at first marriage was almost 27 for women and 29 for men (compared to almost 24 for women and 26 for men in

---

[52]. Frederick Pollock & Frederic William Maitland, The History of English Law Before the Time of Edward I 390-391 (S.F.C. Milsom ed., 1968).

[53]. Id. at 389-390. See generally Vivian E. Hamilton, The Age of Marital Capacity: Reconsidering Civil Recognition of Adolescent Marriage, 92 B.U. L. Rev. 1817, 1823-1831 (2012).

[54]. Michael Grossberg, Guarding the Altar: Physiological Restrictions and the Rise of State Intervention in Matrimony, 26 Am. J. Legal Hist. 197, 206-209 (1982). See also Michael Grossberg, Governing the Hearth: Law and Family in Nineteenth-Century America 105-108, 142 (1985).

1990).[55] What factors contribute to this gender-based difference? To delayed marriage? What are the consequences for society of a later first-marriage age?

4. Instability. Early marriages are particularly unstable. Teenage marriages are two to three times more likely to end in divorce.[56] Should states require premarital counseling prior to teen marriages? See, e.g., Cal. Fam. Code §304; Mont. Code Ann §40-1-213(1). Should laws facilitate the marriage of pregnant teens to promote economic stability? What might the state do to enhance the stability of underage marriages?

5. Void-voidable distinction. State statutes reflect inconsistent treatment of the legal effect of nonage on marriage validity: Some classify such marriages as void, while others regard them as voidable. Historically, nonage was classified as a civil, rather than a canonical, disability. Civil disabilities rendered marriages void; canonical disabilities made them voidable.

How do these rules apply in practice? Suppose Tom marries Jenny when he is 17. The marriage is rocky from its inception. Tom, discovering that the statutory minimum age is 18, decides to leave Jenny. Later, he meets and marries Polly, but without securing an annulment of his prior marriage. Tom is prosecuted for bigamy. May he raise the invalidity of his prior marriage in the criminal proceeding? If a statute makes the marriage void, then he may. But if the statute classifies the marriage as voidable, the marriage remains valid until annulled, thereby precluding collateral attack.

6. Parental rights. Parental consent proves important if underage marriages are void and thus vulnerable to third-party attack. Requiring parental consent lessens the likelihood of subsequent parental efforts to invalidate a marriage, such as in *Kirkpatrick*. Why did the court in *Kirkpatrick* refuse to permit SierraDawn's father to annul her marriage? How should a court balance the interests of the child, parents, and state in minors' decision to marry? How should a court balance these interests when parents disagree, as in *Kirkpatrick*? Should the state ensure that parents exercise their consent wisely? If so, how? Did SierraDawn's mother exercise her responsibility wisely?

Suppose SierraDawn's father has sole (rather than joint) custody, and her mother has a history of mental illness and attempts to evade the father's role in decisionmaking. Should those factors change the result? See In re J.M.N., 2008 WL 2415490 (Tenn. Ct. App. 2008).

7. Minors' rights. Should the law require parental consent alone or require *both* parental consent and judicial authorization? Compare UMDA §§203-204 (minor may marry with either parent's consent or after a finding that the minor is capable of assuming the responsibilities of marriage and that the marriage would be in his or her best interests), with Cal. Fam. Code §302 (requiring both parental consent and judicial authorization).

---

[55]. U.S. Census Bureau, Median Age at First Marriage 1890–present (table), http://www.census.gov/hhes/familiesfilesms2.csv.

[56]. Sarah Kershaw, Now the Bad News on Teenage Marriage, N.Y. Times, Sept. 4, 2008, at G1, http://www.nytimes.com/2008/09/04/fashion/04marriage.html?_r=0.

Does an underage minor whose parents refuse consent have any recourse? Case law sometimes requires that the parents' refusal not be unreasonable. However, many statutes do not provide for override procedures. Should states institute judicial bypass proceedings to parental consent requirements that are similar to those in abortion decisionmaking?

8. Legislative reform. In the past few years, several state legislatures increased the minimum age for marriage in response to a Nebraska case involving the marriage of a 14-year-old girl (see Problem 1, below), and also a Colorado case that allowed a 15-year-old girl to enter a common law marriage with a felon (In re Marriage of J.M.H. & Rouse, 143 P.3d 1116 (Colo. Ct. App. 2006)). See, e.g., Colo. Rev. Stat. §14-2-109.5(1) and Kan. Stat. Ann. §2502 (both setting 18 as minimum age to enter common law marriage). What considerations should determine the minimum marital age?

9. International perspectives. Many countries allow child marriages. The reasons for this are primarily economic (i.e., to relieve parents of economic burdens) and the control of female sexuality. What, if anything, can be done to address this problem? The Violence Against Women Reauthorization Act of 2013 requires the Secretary of State to develop and implement a strategy to prevent child marriage. This strategy focuses on empowering girls and reflects an awareness of "the unique needs, vulnerabilities, and potential of girls younger than 18 years of age in developing countries." 122 U.S.C.A §7104(j). In 2014, 118 countries sponsored a United Nations (UN) resolution to end child and forced marriage. Although the resolution is not legally binding, it may increase political pressure on countries to pass and enforce child marriage laws.[57]

Problem

Crystal meets Matthew when he comes to play video games with her half-brother. When she is 12 and he is 20, they become a couple. A year later, Crystal's divorced mother petitions for a protective order restraining Matthew from seeing Crystal. Despite the court order, the two continue to see each other and eventually develop a sexual relationship. After Crystal becomes pregnant in 2005, her mother has a change of heart and, together with Matthew's parents, drives the couple to Kansas, where persons as young as 12 may marry with parental consent.

Nebraska, where the couple resides, prohibits marriages of persons under age 17, and also provides that sexual intercourse between a person who is 19 or older and another person who is younger than age 16 is statutory rape. Should the Kansas county clerk grant the marriage license? Should Matthew be charged

[57]. Miriam Donath, United Nations Members Resolve to End Child Marriages, Reuters, Nov. 24, 2014, http://www.reuters.com/article/2014/11/24/us-children-un-rights-idUSKCN0J81O320141124. See generally U.N. Population Fund Report, Marrying Too Young (2012), http://www.unfpa.org/end-child-marriage.

with statutory rape in Nebraska? How should the state of Nebraska reconcile these laws? Should Nebraska take any action against Crystal's mother?[58]

The Kosos later had another child. Does it affect your answers to the above questions to learn that the state child protective services temporarily removed the Koso children from their parents' custody due to neglect in 2010? Or that in 2012, a court-appointed attorney filed a petition to terminate parental rights?[59]

(ii) State of Mind Restrictions: Fraud and Duress

BLAIR v. BLAIR

147 S.W.3d 882 (Mo. Ct. App. 2004)

JOSEPH M. ELLIS, Judge.

William Jerry Blair (Husband) appeals from a judgment entered in the Circuit Court of Platte County denying his petition for annulment of his marriage to Nancy Blair. For the following reasons, we affirm.

In July 1976, Husband and Wife had sexual intercourse on one occasion after having worked together for a couple of years. At that time, Wife was married to Jim Farra and was also involved in a long-standing sexual relationship with Sam Kelly. Subsequently, Wife gave birth to a son, Devin, on April 26, 1977. Husband visited Wife in the hospital shortly after Devin's birth, but did not discuss the paternity of the child with her and had no further contact with Wife until 1979.

In January 1979, Wife contacted Husband, told him that he was Devin's father, and asked whether he had any history of disease in his family that might affect Devin later in life. Husband met with Wife and Devin, and he resumed a sexual relationship with Wife a few days later. In March 1979, Wife separated from Mr. Farra and filed a petition for dissolution of that marriage. Subsequently, Wife became pregnant with Husband's child, and on March 13, 1980, Wife gave birth to their daughter, Oralin.

Wife's marriage to Mr. Farra was dissolved in December 1980. Several days after her divorce from Mr. Farra became final, Husband and Wife were married on December 22, 1980. Husband later adopted both Devin and Oralin.

On November 20, 2001, Wife filed a petition for dissolution of her marriage to Husband. . . . Husband filed an amended answer and cross-petition requesting that the marriage be annulled. In support of his annulment claim, Husband averred that Wife had fraudulently represented to him before their marriage that he was Devin's father and had thereby induced him to marry her. Subsequent testing proved that Husband was indeed not Devin's father and that he [Devin] was the son of Sam Kelly. . . .

---

[58]. See Colleen Kenney, Koso Set to Come Home from Prison, Lincoln J. Star, May 5, 2007, at A1; Jodi Wilgoren, Rape Charge Follows Marriage to a 14-Year-Old, N.Y. Times, Aug. 30, 2005, at A1. See generally Melissa Murray, Strange Bedfellows: Criminal Law, Family Law, and the Legal Construction of Intimate Life, 94 Iowa L. Rev. 1253, 1273-1293 (2009) (discussing case).

[59]. See Joanne Young, Years After Controversial Marriage, Falls City Couple at Risk of Losing Children, Lincoln J. Star, July 22, 2012, http://journalstar.com/news/local/years-after-controversial-marriage-falls-city-couple-at-risk-of/article_16b4ea35-a638-5d92-923c-c9d43fcb2c31.html.

As grounds for granting an annulment, Husband asserted that Wife perpetrated a fraud upon him regarding Devin's paternity. In order to establish fraud, Husband was required to plead and prove the following elements: (1) a representation by Wife; (2) its falsity; (3) its materiality; (4) Wife's knowledge of its falsity or ignorance of its truth; (5) Wife's intent that the representation be acted upon by Husband; (6) Husband's ignorance of the falsity of the representation; (7) Husband's reliance on the truth of the representation; (8) Husband's right to rely on the representation; and (9) that Husband sustained consequent and proximate injury. . . .

Husband notes that he testified at trial that he would not have married Wife if he had known that he was not Devin's father. [T]he trial court was not required to accept Husband's own self-serving testimony that he would not have married Wife but for her representations related to Devin's paternity. Indeed, the overall gist of Husband's testimony appears to have been that he would never have seen Wife again after their one-night-stand if it had not been for her calling and telling him that he had a child and that the marriage was, therefore, the result of that representation. Such testimony does not establish that Husband relied upon the representations regarding Devin's paternity in deciding whether to marry Wife, only that it played a part in his decision to begin a relationship with her.

Sufficient evidence in the record supports the trial court's determination that Husband would have married Wife regardless of the representation as to Devin's paternity. Wife testified that Husband was crazy about her and that she was certain that he would have left his girlfriend and had a relationship with her regardless of Devin's paternity. Husband admitted on cross-examination that, during the two-year courtship the couple had between Wife's initial phone call and their marriage, he fell in love with Wife. In addition, nine months before their marriage, Oralin, who is undisputedly Husband's child, was born. The trial court could reasonably have inferred that Oralin's paternity would have been sufficient to cause Husband to marry Wife. Furthermore, testimony from both Husband and Wife reflects that Husband had questions about Devin's paternity prior to marriage, that he married her anyway, and that he subsequently adopted both children.

Based upon the foregoing testimony, the trial court could more than reasonably have found that Husband would have married Wife regardless of Wife's representations related to Devin's paternity. . . . Having determined that this ground for the trial court's denial of Husband's request for an annulment is not erroneous, we need not address Husband's remaining points. . . .

Notes and Questions

1. Consent requirement. A marriage may be set aside for lack of consent. Fraud (like duress) vitiates consent and serves as a ground for annulment. Because of the public policy in favor of marriage preservation, many courts apply a strict test for fraud, requiring that the misrepresentation go to the "essentials." "Essentials" generally includes the ability and willingness to engage in sexual relations and childbearing. Given the ease in obtaining a divorce, does this strict test make sense? Some states require only that the fraud be *material;* that is, the plaintiff would not have married defendant but for the fraud. Which test does the court use in *Blair*?

2. Annulment versus divorce. An annulment declares that no marriage occurred because some impediment existed at the time of the ceremony. In contrast, divorce terminates a valid marriage, enabling the parties to remarry. Annulments were important when divorce was difficult to obtain, particularly in England before the Matrimonial Causes Act of 1857. Discontented marital partners could secure an annulment for fraud, duress, or nonage. Following modern divorce reform, the importance of annulments decreased. On the historical treatment of fraud in annulments, see Angela Onwuachi-Willig, According to Our Hearts: Rhinelander v. Rhinelander and the Law of the Multiracial Family (2013).

3. Procedural differences and relation-back doctrine. Different procedural rules govern annulment and divorce. First, annulment jurisdiction exists at either party's domicile, the state where the marriage was celebrated, or any state with personal jurisdiction over the spouses. In contrast, divorce jurisdiction rests on domicile. Second, an invalid marriage generally precluded spousal and child support and property division. Today, many states, by equitable remedies or statute, equate the financial consequences of annulment to those of divorce. Third, the "relation back" doctrine applies only to annulments. Because an annulment decree establishes that a marriage never existed, benefits lost by virtue of the marriage may be reinstated. See Haacke v. Glenn, 814 P.2d 1157 (Utah Ct. App. 1991) (annulment eliminates wife's employment-related conflict of interest stemming from husband's concealment of his felon status).

Why might the plaintiff in *Blair* have sought an annulment rather than a divorce? Why did the court deny his request?

4. Consummation. When considering fraud to annul marriage, courts often distinguish between consummated and unconsummated marriages, sometimes requiring a higher standard for the former. Why? Given current sexual mores, should consummation continue to influence the law of annulment?

5. Privacy. Does judicial examination of marriage for purposes of fraud constitute an invasion of privacy?

6. Policy. How does marriage fraud harm the public? See generally Kerry Abrams, Marriage Fraud, 100 Cal. L. Rev. 1, 48-54 (2012).

7. Tort liability. Some jurisdictions recognize the tort of fraudulent inducement to marry. See, e.g., Desta v. Anyaoha, 371 S.W.3d 596 (Tex. App. 2012). However, the quantum of fraud for annulment purposes is considerably less than that required for tort liability. Should a plaintiff be able to secure an annulment as well as tort damages for the same legal wrong?

8. Limited-purpose marriages. Prior to the legalization of abortion, some couples who conceived a child would agree to marry "in name only" to legitimate the child, and then, after the birth, obtain a divorce. However, the parties agreed that no other marital rights and responsibilities would attach. Many American cases recognized such "limited-purpose" or "sham" marriages to avoid the stigma of illegitimacy. See, e.g., Schibi v. Schibi, 69 A.2d 831 (Conn. 1949). What purposes are served by failing to recognize such marriages? Are marriages to legitimate a child distinguishable from marriages that facilitate an alien's entry into the country (discussed later in this chapter)?

9. Duress. Agreements to marry that are procured by force, fear, or coercion are unenforceable. Although duress generally requires physical force or threat of force, lesser forms of duress may suffice if sufficient to overcome plaintiff's free will. English cases disagree about whether the test should be subjective or objective.[60] What difference does it make?

10. Forced marriage: Empirical data. A nationwide study found 3,000 cases of known or suspected forced marriage in the United States over a recent two-year period.[61] Few legal resources exist to prevent or punish parents from forcing daughters into marriage. In the United States, 10 states have laws on forced marriage. In 2013, Nevada, Maryland, and the District of Columbia amended their statutes by increasing the penalties for violations.[62]

11. Forced marriage: International perspective. Forced marriage is still practiced outside the United States, primarily in parts of the Middle East, Asia, and Africa. In addition, an estimated 30,000 forced brides live in Germany and Austria, where support groups help youth with annulments, housing, and new identities to avoid discovery.[63] Commentators point to the harm of forced child marriages: high maternal and infant mortality rates, as well as violence against women.[64]

Some countries have passed law reforms addressing the problem. In 2011, Germany enacted a new law imposing a five-year sentence on a person who forces a woman into marriage.[65] In the United Kingdom, the Forced Marriage Act 2007 authorizes restraining orders that *prevent* forced unions.[66] France raised the minimum age for marriage in an effort to discourage forced marriages.[67] In 2014, England and Wales criminalized forced marriage by punishing parents who force children into marriage with a prison sentence of 7 years, and criminalized the violation of protective orders with a 5-year prison sentence.[68] Evaluate the effectiveness of these approaches.

---

[60]. Homer H. Clark, Law of Domestic Relations 103-104 (2d ed. 1988).

[61]. See Tahirih Justice Center, Forced Marriage in Immigrant Communities in the United States (2011), 2011 National Survey Results, http://www.tahirih.org/pubs/forced-marriage-in-immigrant-communities-in-the-united-states/.

[62]. See Tahirih Justice Center, Criminal Laws Addressing Forced Marriage in the United States (2011), http://preventforcedmarriage.org/resources/criminal-laws-address-forced-marriage-in-the-united-states/.

[63]. Eric Geiger, Muslim Girls in Austria Fighting Forced Marriages, S.F. Chron., Dec. 4, 2005, at A15.

[64]. Rena Silverman, Millions of Young Girls Forced Into Marriage, Nat'l Geographic, Mar. 15, 2013, http://news.nationalgeographic.com/news/2013/13/130313-child-brides-marriage-women-sinclair-photography/.

[65]. Soeren Kern, Germans Stunned by Report on Forced Marriages, Gatestone Inst., Nov. 10, 2011, http://www.gatestoneinstitute.org/2575/german-forced-marriages.

[66]. Laws in the UK: Forced Marriage Act, http://www.bbc.co.uk/ethics/forcedmarriage/crime_1.shtml

[67]. France: Marriage Age for Women Raised to 18, N.Y. Times, Mar. 24, 2006, at A9.

[68]. Steven Erlanger, Law in Britain Makes Forcing Anyone to Wed a Criminal Act, N.Y. Times, June 17, 2014, at A8.

Problem

Mr. Patel, an Indian engineer who resides in New Jersey, travels to India to seek a wife of the same caste. A marriage broker arranges a match with Ms. Navitlal. They meet twice to discuss marriage and their respective backgrounds. Ms. Navitlal informs him that her parents are separated. She does not tell him that her mother is living with a person of a different caste. The couple is married in a civil ceremony, and the marriage is consummated. Mr. Patel returns to the United States but later returns to India, where he undergoes a religious ceremony with his wife. He later testifies that he underwent the Hindu ceremony only because of threats by his wife's brothers. Ms. Navitlal tires of waiting for her husband to send for her and travels to the United States. There, she discovers that her husband has no desire to live with her. He asserts that she married him for the sole purpose of gaining entry into the United States. He files for annulment. She counterclaims for divorce. What result? Patel v. Navitlal, 627 A.2d 683 (N.J. Super. Ct. Ch. Div. 1992).

NOTE: MARRIAGE FRAUD IN IMMIGRATION

Marriage to a U.S. citizen exempts an alien from the quota restrictions of the Immigration and Nationality Act (INA), 8 U.S.C. §1151(a), (b), thereby avoiding lengthy delays in entering the country. According to the Act, a U.S. citizen can petition on behalf of designated "immediate relatives" (defined as a legal spouse, child, or parent) in order to adjust the relatives' legal permanent residence status (entitling them to "green cards"). This rule contributes to a strong incentive for aliens to marry citizens.

Marriage fraud in immigration has been a longstanding problem for the U.S. Citizenship and Immigration Services (USCIS). To determine the validity of a marriage between a citizen and an alien, immigration officials conduct investigations that explore such factors as whether the couple are cohabiting, commingling resources, and holding property jointly. Do these investigations violate the right to privacy? Are they based on stereotypical views of marriage? See Olga Grosh, Note, Foreign Wives, Domestic Violence: U.S. Law Stigmatizes and Fails to Protect "Mail-Order Brides," 22 Hastings Women's L.J. 81, 92 (2011) (discussing procedures for detection of marriage fraud).

In the past several decades, an international marriage broker (IMB) industry has flourished. Congressional findings suggest that a substantial number of mail-order marriages are fraudulent. See Illegal Immigration Reform and Immigrant Responsibility Act (IIRIRA), (8 U.S.C. §1375a). The Internet contributed to the rapid growth of the mail-order industry. Until 1996, mail-order matchmaking was largely unregulated. In that year, Congress enacted §652 of the IIRIRA to obligate international marriage brokers to require American clients to submit to extensive background checks (about previous marriages and criminal histories) and then to disclose this information to mail-order brides. International marriage brokers must also disseminate information to foreign clients about the "battered spouse waiver" for conditional permanent residents, enacted as part of the Violence Against Women Act of 1994 (VAWA) (8 U.S.C. §1154(a)(1)(A)(iii)), which allows battered immigrant women to apply for permanent legal residence without their abusive citizen-spouse's participation. (Before VAWA, immigration law mandated the cooperation of the citizen spouse in order for the alien spouse to obtain lawful status.)

To remedy shortcomings in the legislation, Congress enacted the Battered Immigrant Women Protection Act of 2000 as part of the Victims of Trafficking and Violence Protection Act, Pub. L. No. 106-386, 114 Stat. 1464, §§1501-1513. This law facilitates self-petitioning by abused spouses, expands the categories of eligible spouses, and establishes a special visa for those victims of domestic violence who are not eligible for self-petition or cancellation of deportation. Congress enacted the International Marriage Broker Regulation Act (IMBRA), in 2005 as part of the reauthorization of VAWA, Pub. L. No. 109-162, 119 Stat. 2960, to prohibit IMBs from providing contact information about minors, require IMBs to advise foreign clients of the rights and resources for victims of domestic violence, require sharing of criminal background checks with the foreign fiancée or spouse, and prohibit simultaneous petitions for visas for multiple fiancées.

With its recent reauthorization of VAWA in 2013, Congress improved oversight of the mail-order bride industry by authorizing the Attorney General to designate a specific office to bring criminal or civil charges against IMBs that violate IMBRA (S. 47, 113th Cong. Title VIII, Sec. 808(a)(2)(A)); mandating recordkeeping by IMBs showing their compliance with background checks and age requirements for foreign brides (Sec. 808(3)(A)(ii)); and providing penalties for clients who lie or fail to disclose a violent or criminal history (Sec. 808(4)(B)). For a famous case imposing liability on an IMB, see Fox v. Encounters Int'l, 2006 WL 952317 (4th Cir. 2006) (finding that IMB failed to tell client about battered spouse waiver and was negligent in assuring her that her abusive husband had been carefully screened).

b. Procedural Restrictions

(i) Licensure and Solemnization

CARABETTA v. CARABETTA

438 A.2d 109 (Conn. 1980)

PETERS, Associate Justice. . . .

The plaintiff and the defendant exchanged marital vows before a priest in the rectory of Our Lady of Mt. Carmel Church of Meriden, on August 25, 1955, according to the rite of the Roman Catholic Church, although they had failed to obtain a marriage license. Thereafter they lived together as husband and wife, raising a family of four children, all of whose birth certificates listed the defendant as their father. [After a 20-year marriage, the wife petitioned for divorce. The husband sought dismissal of her claim, arguing that the court lacked jurisdiction because the marriage was void.] Until the present action, the defendant had no memory or recollection of ever having denied that the plaintiff and the defendant were married.

The issue before us is whether, under Connecticut law, despite solemnization according to an appropriate religious ceremony, a marriage is void where there has been noncompliance with the statutory requirement of a marriage. This is a question of first impression in this state. The trial court held that failure to obtain a marriage license was a flaw fatal to the creation of a legally valid marriage and that the court therefore lacked subject matter jurisdiction over an action for dissolution. We disagree with the court's premise and hence with its conclusion.

The determinants for a legally valid marriage are to be found in the provisions of our statutes. . . . The governing statutes at the time of the purported marriage between these parties contained two kinds of regulations concerning the requirements for a legally valid marriage. One kind of regulation concerned substantive requirements determining those eligible to be married. Thus General Statutes (Rev. 1949) §7301 declared the statutorily defined degrees of consanguinity within which a "marriage shall be void." . . . For present purposes, it is enough to observe that, on this appeal, no such substantive defect has been alleged or proven.

The other kind of regulation concerns the formalities prescribed by the state for the effectuation of a legally valid marriage. These required formalities, in turn, are of two sorts: a marriage license and a solemnization. In Hames v. Hames, [316 A.2d 379 (1972)], we interpreted our statutes not to make void a marriage consummated after the issuance of a license but deficient for want of due solemnization. Today we examine the statutes in the reverse case, a marriage duly solemnized but deficient for want of a marriage license.

As to licensing, the governing statute in 1955 was a section entitled "Marriage licenses." It provided, in subsection (a): "No persons shall be joined in marriage until both have joined in an application . . . for a license for such marriage." Its only provision for the consequence of noncompliance with the license requirement was contained in subsection (e): ". . . any person who shall join any persons in marriage without having received such (license) shall be fined not more than one hundred dollars." General Statutes (Rev. 1949) §7302, as amended by §1280b (1951 Supp.) and by §2250c (1953 Supp.). Neither this section, nor any other, described as void a marriage celebrated without license.

As to solemnization, the governing section, entitled "Who may join persons in marriage," [provides that] the celebration of a marriage by a person not authorized by this section to do so, renders a marriage void. We have enforced the plain mandate of this injunction. State ex rel. Felson v. Allen, 29 A.2d 306 (Conn. 1942).

In the absence of express language in the governing statute declaring a marriage void for failure to observe a statutory requirement, this court has held in an unbroken line of cases since Gould v. Gould, 61 A. 604 (Conn. 1905), that such a marriage, though imperfect, is dissoluble rather than void. . . . Then as now, the legislature had chosen to use the language of voidness selectively, applying it to some but not to all of the statutory requirements for the creation of a legal marriage. Now as then, the legislature has the competence to choose to sanction those who solemnize a marriage without a marriage license rather than those who marry without a marriage license. In sum, we conclude that the legislature's failure expressly to characterize as void a marriage properly celebrated without a license means that such a marriage is not invalid.

The plaintiff argues strenuously that our statutes, far from declaring void a marriage solemnized without a license, in fact validate such a marriage whenever it has been solemnized by a religious ceremony. The plaintiff calls our attention to the language of §7306, as amended, that "all marriages . . . solemnized according to the forms and usages of any religious denomination in this state shall be valid." To the extent that this language suggests greater validity for a marriage solemnized by a religious ceremony than for one solemnized by a civil ceremony, it is inconsistent with other provisions of the statutes with regard to solemnization and licensing. It has long been clear that, under our laws, all authority to join parties in matrimony is basically secular. . . . Whatever may be its antecedents, for present purposes it is sufficient to note that §7306 at the very least reenforces our conclusion that the marriage in the case before us is not void.

The conclusion that a ceremonial marriage contracted without a marriage license is not null and void finds support, furthermore, in the decisions in other jurisdictions. In the majority of states, unless the licensing statute plainly makes an unlicensed marriage invalid, "the cases find the policy favoring valid marriages sufficiently strong to justify upholding the unlicensed ceremony. This seems the correct result. Most such cases arise long after the parties have acted upon the assumption that they are married, and no useful purpose is served by avoiding the long-standing relationship." [Homer Clark, Law of Domestic Relations 41 (1968)].

Since the marriage that the trial court was asked to dissolve was not void, the trial court erred in granting the motion to dismiss. . . .

Wedding ceremonies vary significantly, as the excerpts below demonstrate.

Harriette Cole, Jumping the Broom: The African-American Wedding Planner

16-18 (1993)

When West Africans were brought forcibly to these shores some four hundred years ago, they were stripped of much of what was theirs. [A]fter the beginning of slavery, Africans were also denied the right to marry in the eyes of the law. Slaveholders apparently thought that their captives were not real people but were, instead, property to be bought and sold. As such, they had no rights. Further, if allowed formally to marry and live together, slaves might find strength in numbers that could lead to revolt. . . .

Yet the enslaved were spiritual people who had been taught rituals that began as early as childhood to prepare them for that big step into family life. . . . Out of their creativity came the tradition of jumping the broom. The broom itself held spiritual significance for many African peoples, representing the beginning of homemaking for a couple. For the Kgatla people of southern Africa, it was customary, for example, on the day after the wedding for the bride to help the other women in the family to sweep the courtyard clean, thereby symbolizing her willingness and obligation to assist in housework at her in-laws' residence until the couple moved to their own home. During slavery . . . a couple would literally jump over a broom into the seat of matrimony. Today, this tradition and many others are finding their way back into the wedding ceremony.

Ginia Bellafante, Even in Gay Circles, the Women Want the Ring

N.Y. Times, May 8, 2005, §6 (Mag.), at 91

[T]hree months after the Massachusetts Supreme Judicial Court ruled [in *Goodridge*] that it was unconstitutional to ban gay couples from marrying, a young woman named Bernadette Smith embarked on a [new career as] a wedding planner for gay couples, declaratively naming the new business she created "It's About Time." [O]ne consistent trend has emerged in her operation: most of her clients have been women. . . .

Sociologists and gay-marriage advocates explain the discrepancy largely in terms of the social and economic realities that shape conflicting attitudes about marriage. [T]he numbers may reflect a wish among women to override the economic vulnerability of living independently. "Women are situated differently in the occupational labor force; there's more value to their marrying," said Christopher Carrington, an anthropologist who has studied gay and lesbian couples. . . .

In many instances, though, there's another force at play: the cultural programming that prompts fantasies of tiered cakes and lilies in 6-year-old girls. For Abby McDonald and Tara Donner, who are to walk down the aisle of the Arlington Street Church in Boston on June 11 in white gowns, accompanied by their fathers, the desire to marry was driven almost entirely by intimate and conformist urges. Ms. Donner, a Wellesley graduate, read *Martha Stewart Weddings* in college. [T]hey purchased matching diamond engagement rings, proposed to each other on the Wellesley campus on June 11, and elected to spend a year planning a wedding. . . . The couple's reception for 120 guests will be held at the College Club of Boston, paid for in large part by their parents. . . .

In the view of Gary Gates, the senior research fellow at the Charles R. Williams Project on Sexual Orientation Law and Public Policy, at the University of California, Los Angeles, Law School, [the fact] that many gay couples, both female and male, seem inclined toward conventional weddings in Massachusetts reflects the changing demographics of gay life. "For a long time the gay rights movement was about the right to be different; now it's very much about the right to be the same," Dr. Gates said. . . .

Postscript. A study of marriage licenses granted to same-sex couples confirms that female couples are more likely to formalize their relationships. Female couples account for more than two-thirds of same-sex couples who marry.[69]

[69]. M.V. Lee Badgett & Christy Mallory, New Data from Marriage Licenses for Same-Sex Couples, Williams Inst. Report (Dec. 2014), http://williamsinstitute.law.ucla.edu/research/census-lgbt-demographics-studies/relationship-data-2014/.

Notes and Questions

1. Licensure requirements. Statutes in every jurisdiction provide for the issuance of marriage licenses. Yet, the policy favoring marriage validity gives rise to the rule announced in *Carabetta* that a violation of formality requirements, such as the failure to obtain a marriage license, will not invalidate a marriage. This rule operates unless the jurisdiction has a statute *expressly* making a marriage invalid without a license. See, e.g., Rivera v. Rivera, 243 P.3d 1148 (N.M. Ct. App. 2010) (upholding a marriage, performed without a license because the relevant statute was only directory).

Three justifications exist for licensure statutes: (1) they aid in enforcing marriage laws by requiring persons not qualified to marry for reasons of age, health, or existing marital status to disclose such information; (2) they serve as public health measures by preventing marriages that would be damaging to the health of one spouse or would produce unhealthy children; and (3) licensure serves as proof that the marriage has occurred.[70]

2. Solemnization. States mandate not only a marriage license but also solemnization by an authorized individual. Such persons include religious officials (for example, clergy) and some government officials. See, e.g., Ala. Code §30-1-9 (probate judges); Kan. Stat. Ann. §23-2505 (county clerks or judges). See also Universal Life Church v. Utah, 189 F. Supp. 2d 1302 (D. Utah 2002) (challenging statute prohibiting ordination of minister by mail and the Internet).

3. Formalities.

a. Where, how long, cost. Statutes in half the states require that licenses be procured in the county where one party resides or where the marriage is to be performed. The marriage license generally expires within a short time (typically 30 to 60 days).

Some states insist on the presence of both parties to apply for a license, while others allow one party to apply by affidavit. Parenthetically, the dual-presence requirement posed a problem for the named plaintiffs in *Obergefell* (supra this chapter) because one of the same-sex partners was too ill to cross state lines and he would have needed to do so twice (once to apply for the license, and the second time to get married). As a result, the couple chose to marry in the state of Maryland, where only one party was required to apply for a marriage license.

In some states, marriage license fees fund domestic violence shelters. See, e.g., Cal. Welf. & Inst. Code §18305; Fla. Stat. Ann. §741.01. Does such a fee unconstitutionally interfere with the right to marry? See Jacobsen v. King, 971 N.E.2d 620 (Ill. App. Ct. 2012).

b. Waiting periods. A majority of jurisdictions require a waiting period (one to five days) between issuance of the license and the ceremony. What explains this requirement? Waiting periods can be waived for exigent circumstances.

---

[70]. Clark, Law of Domestic Relations, supra note [60], at 34.

4. Premarital blood tests. Many states have abolished premarital physical exams. Some states still require proof of immunity or vaccination for certain diseases (i.e., venereal diseases, rubella, tuberculosis, and sickle-cell anemia). Although no state requires a mandatory premarital HIV/AIDS test, some states require that applicants for a marital license must be offered an HIV test and/or must be provided with information on AIDS and available tests.

The rationale for the enactment of premarital blood test requirements in the early twentieth century stemmed from concerns about eugenics, urbanization, rising rates of immigration, and the pervasive sexual double standard that reflected fears of the consequences for innocent young women of men's "sowing their wild oats." See generally Allan M. Brandt, No Magic Bullet: A Social History of Venereal Disease in the United States Since 1880 (1987).

5. Effectiveness of procedural requirements. Do licensure statutes accomplish their purposes? For example, do they aid in the detection of marriages in which one partner already has a spouse? Does the possibility of sanctions, such as a penalty for perjury on a license application, deter violations? How can we enforce licensure statutes if a marriage is held to be valid in the absence of a license? Alternatively, are waiting periods effective? Do they represent unnecessary state paternalism? Are they constitutional? Do they meet the *Zablocki* standard? Finally, what purpose underlies the solemnization requirement by authorized persons?

Problems

1. Anna and Dickie are involved in a sexual relationship. Dickie tells Anna that his family believes that he will go to hell if they do not marry. He proposes a "fake" ceremony, and she agrees. They have a ceremony, solemnized by a minister, but fail to file the marriage license with the county clerk within 60 days of issuance as required by statute. Instead, Anna burns the license with Dickie's knowledge and consent. They live together for almost two months. Later, Dickie files for divorce and requests a division of property. Anna responds by denying the existence of the marriage or, in the alternative, for an order annulling the marriage on the basis of fraudulent inducement. What result? See Fryar v. Roberts, 57 S.W.3d 727 (Ark. 2001).

2. Deborah and Richard decide to marry during an extraordinarily busy time in their lives when they are buying a new house and Richard is starting a new business. They set a wedding date, but neither of them obtains the necessary marriage license. When the rabbi arrives to perform the ceremony, he is surprised to learn of the absence of the license. Nonetheless, he and the couple decide to "deal with that problem later" because everyone is gathered for the wedding. Two weeks after the ceremony, the couple obtains the license and mails it to the rabbi who signs it, as of that date, and then submits it to the proper state authorities.

Ten years later, Richard wants to end the couple's relationship. He petitions for a declaration of marital status, contending that the parties were not lawfully married because they did not have a marriage license at the time of the ceremony. The applicable state law requires that, "[T]o contract a lawful marriage, the parties must obtain a license and afterward solemnize their union," along with a requirement that "a marriage occur within 60 days after obtaining a license," and a provision attaching a criminal penalty for the performance of a marriage ceremony without a license. What should the court rule? MacDougall v. Levick, 776 S.E. 2d 456.

3. Traditionally, states require couples' presence within their boundaries for a valid marriage ceremony. In light of modern technology, two law professors propose a reform in marriage procedure (dubbed "E-marriage"). They suggest that states liberalize the rules about marriage procedure by offering marriages to persons outside state boundaries via such means as videoconference, the Internet, and telephone. Evaluate the advantages and disadvantages of this proposal. Do territorial restrictions continue to make sense today? See Adam Candeub & Mae Kuykendall, Modernizing Marriage, 44 U. Mich. J.L. Reform 735 (2011); Mae Kuykendall & Adam Candeub, Symposium Overview: Perspectives on Innovative Marriage Procedure, 2011 Mich. St. L. Rev. 1 (2011).

(ii) Note: Procedural Variations

(1) Proxy Marriages

A proxy marriage is one in which at least one party is represented at the ceremony by an agent. Marriage by proxy, once the exclusive practice of royalty, was valid in England until the mid-nineteenth century when legislation required the presence of both parties at the ceremony.[71] Marriage by proxy has been most visible in the modern era in time of war, frequently to legitimize children.[72] Marriages by mail, telephone, cable, and radio have occurred. In 2003, as a result of Operation Iraqi Freedom, the California legislature provided statutory authority for proxy marriages for service members who were serving in an armed conflict or war (Cal. Fam. Code §420(b)).

Another use of proxy marriages is to circumvent immigration laws. Prior to 1924 when Congress prohibited the practice, proxy marriages were valid for immigration purposes so long as the marriage was valid in the country where performed.[73] Proxy marriage has also been used to assist political refugees. See, e.g., Apt v. Apt, 1 All. E.R. 620 (1947) (permitting Jewish refugee from Nazi Germany to marry by proxy in Argentina, where husband resided). Yet another group resorting to proxy marriages is prisoners. Courts are suspect about the use of proxies in deathbed ceremonies. See, e.g., In re Estate of Crockett, 728 N.E.2d 765 (Ill. App. Ct. 2000).

States that allow proxy marriages generally require the presence of *either* the bride or groom. Until recently, Montana was the only state that permitted a "double-proxy" wedding, in which both parties were represented by proxies. The dramatic increase in such marriages there, stemming from Internet publicity, led the state legislature to enact an amendment (Mont. Code Ann. §40-1-301) requiring

---

[71]. Comment, Persons—Marriage—Validity of Proxy Marriages, 25 S. Cal. L. Rev. 181, 182 (1952).

[72]. W.H. Howery, Marriage by Proxy and Other Informal Marriages, 13 UMKC L. Rev. 48, 54 (1944).

[73]. 8 U.S.C. §224(m) (1924) (superseded by 8 U.S.C. §1101(a)(35) (2006)) (the terms "spouse," "wife," or "husband" do not include a spouse, wife, or husband by reason of any marriage ceremony where the contracting parties thereto are not physically present in the presence of each other, unless the marriage shall have been consummated).

that at least one party be either a state resident or a member of the armed services on active duty.

Federal law reflects inconsistent treatment of proxy marriages by its recognition of such marriages for federal survivorship benefits but not for immigration purposes absent subsequent consummation. Thus, in a highly publicized case, a Marine died in combat in Iraq one month after he married his pregnant Japanese fiancée by proxy. Although his widow was able to collect survivors' benefits, she was denied permission to immigrate to the United States to raise their child with her husband's family in Tennessee because the marriage was unconsummated *after* the ceremony due to the husband's deployment. See generally Kathryn Rae Edwards, Note, Kicking the INA out of Bed: Abolishing the Consummation Requirement for Proxy Marriages, 22 Hastings Women's L.J. 55 (2011).

(2) *Confidential Marriages*

Some states permit "confidential" marriages, which enable a couple to dispense with some procedural requirements. See, e.g., Cal. Fam. Code §§500-536; Mich. Comp. Laws Ann. §§551.201. For example, the California statute permits unmarried cohabitants to marry without procuring a marriage license or filing a health certificate. However, they must participate in a ceremony by an authorized person and file a marriage certificate that is not open to public inspection except upon a showing of good cause. The purpose of the statute is to encourage cohabitants to legalize their relationship and legitimize children.

(3) *Other Variations*

Some states provide for other variations that dispense with licensure or solemnization requirements. A few states permit marriage by declaration (e.g., Mont. Code Ann. §40-1-311; Tex. Fam. Code Ann. §§2.401-2.402). Others permit marriage by contracts acknowledged before a judge (e.g., N.Y. Dom. Rel. Law §11(4)). Unlike a marriage by declaration, however, the parties to a marriage by contract first must obtain a license. Finally, tribal marriages, contracted according to Native American laws or customs, are also recognized in some jurisdictions. See, e.g., Nev. Rev. Stat. Ann. §122.170.

c. Informal Marriages

(i) Common Law Marriage

JENNINGS v. HURT

N.Y. L.J., Oct. 4, 1989, at 24 (Sup. Ct. N.Y. Cty), *aff'd*, 554 N.Y.S.2d 220 (App. Div. 1990), *appeal denied*, 568 N.Y.S.2d 347 (N.Y. 1991)

Justice SILBERMANN.

[Plaintiff, Sandra Jennings, alleged the existence of a common law marriage. Defendant, actor William Hurt, moved to dismiss.]

South Carolina is one of thirteen states (including the District of Columbia) that recognize common-law marriages. South Carolina became a common law state early in the eighteenth century when it adopted the law of common-law marriage which was recognized in the Ecclesiastic Courts in England. . . .

South Carolina law is aptly stated in the case of Fryer v. Fryer, S.C. Eq. 85 (S.C. App. 1832):

> Marriage, with us, so far as the law is concerned has ever been regarded as a mere civil contract. Our law prescribes no ceremony. It required nothing but the agreement of the parties, with an intention that the agreement shall, per se, constitute the marriage. They may express the agreement by parol, they may signify it by whatever ceremony their whim, or their taste, or their religious belief, may select: it is the agreement itself, and not the form in which it is couched, which constitutes the contract. The words used, or the ceremony performed, are mere evidence of a present intention and agreement of the parties. . . .

Although common-law marriages were abolished in New York as of April 29, 1933, New York does give effect to common-law marriages if they are recognized as valid under the law of the state in which it was supposedly contracted.

The sole question to be decided by this court is whether Sandra Jennings is the common-law wife of William Hurt. Since it is conceded that the parties never had a ceremonial marriage, the answer to that question rests upon certain events that allegedly transpired during the parties' stay in South Carolina and the law of South Carolina. . . .

Jennings and Hurt met in Saratoga, New York, in the summer of 1981 while each of them was working there. Shortly thereafter, upon their return to New York City, the parties began living together. [They ceased living together in 1984.] At the time their relationship began, Jennings knew Hurt was still married. The parties had many discussions in which Hurt explained to Jennings his disappointment at his own failure in marriage and his family's history in terms of failed marriages. Hurt frequently discussed his belief that marriage was a promise or a commitment to "God" and that he was experiencing "dismay about having broken that promise." Because of his feelings and pain relating to this subject, Hurt explained that marriage was "not in the cards" for him. This is corroborated by Hurt's conversation with Mary Beth Hurt when he asked for a divorce. Jennings herself stated "he wanted me to know that he did not necessarily mean a marital commitment. . . ."

In the Spring of 1982 Jennings became pregnant. Hurt's counsel began drafting an agreement governing the parties' financial arrangements of living together and for the support of the expected child. The earliest of these agreements is dated May 1982. The pregnancy prompted Hurt to commence divorce proceedings to terminate his marriage to Mary Beth Hurt. In September 1982, Hurt went to see his former wife to tell her he wanted to finalize the divorce since "Sandy is having a baby."

On October 31, 1982, Jennings joined Hurt in South Carolina where he was already engaged in the filming of the "Big Chill." During their stay in South Carolina from October 31, 1982, to January 10, 1983, the parties lived in the same house and shared a bed. Their social circle consisted of the cast and others connected with the film project. During this period as well as earlier and later times, their relationship was volatile and permeated by arguments.

On December 3, 1982, Hurt's divorce became final. He learned this sometime later from counsel. Jennings testified that she learned of his divorce on December

27, 1982 when he approached her with another version of the "prenuptial agreement" that had been the subject of negotiations between the parties and their counsel. That on that date he said they should sign the agreement, have blood tests and get married. Parenthetically, it is noted that South Carolina does not require blood tests in order to obtain a marriage license. She testified that they then went to a Notary Public to get the agreement signed and returned home. Hurt then spoke to his attorney and after that conversation a fight ensued in which he stated Jennings had tricked him, that the agreement was not valid because she did not have legal counsel. Jennings then allegedly went into the bedroom and started packing to go home to her mother, whereupon Hurt, according to Jennings, . . . "threw my suitcase on the ground and we had a huge fight and he ended up telling me that it didn't matter because as far as he was concerned we were married in the eyes of God and we had a spiritual marriage and this didn't matter. We were more married than married people."

Jennings' claim to be Hurt's common-law wife is based inter alia, on these events. . . .

Documents admitted in evidence indicate [that] on December 27, 1982, Hurt's signature was notarized on the document entitled "Paternity Acknowledgment"; that on December 28, 1982, Jennings' signature was notarized on a sublease for her New York apartment, and that on December 28, 1982, Jennings spoke with someone at her attorneys' telephone number for 17 minutes. [T]he undisputed fact that Hurt signed a paternity acknowledgment on [December 27, 1982] is inconsistent with any immediate intention to marry, but is consistent with Hurt's testimony that though his commitment to his child was unequivocal, he had deep reservations about his relationship with Jennings.

The only evidence introduced of a holding forth as husband and wife while the parties were in South Carolina was a conversation with [lessors] in connection with the parties' renting of accommodations for their stay in South Carolina in which Hurt allegedly referred to Jennings as his wife and a telephone call by Hurt to Jennings' obstetrician, Dr. Credle's office, in which he asked about his "wife." The conversation with the [lessors] occurred on October 31, 1982 and thus is irrelevant because it predates the removal of the impediment to marriage. The date of the conversation with Dr. Credle is unknown but in any event is of little significance.

It is clear . . . that the community with whom the parties socialized knew Jennings and Hurt were not married. Nor is there a preponderance of credible evidence that the parties held themselves out as husband and wife after December 27, 1982. There is no evidence that Jennings filed tax returns or other forms as married. Significantly, the one document on which Jennings is alleged to have her name "Sandra Cronsberg Hurt" is clearly an altered xerox copy of the original with "Hurt" added afterwards and the document re-xeroxed. Indeed, documents signed by Hurt prior to the commencement of a lawsuit, i.e., will, pension, jury form—all indicated he considered himself single. Hurt's accountant testified that but for one tax return, where by error, the box "married" was checked, all taxes have been filed by Hurt as "single."

The testimony of persons who worked for Jennings for several months, years ago, and who each remember one isolated incident of Hurt referring to Jennings as his "wife" is unbelievable and even if true is barely relevant to prove a holding forth as husband and wife. Scheible, Hurt's employee's testimony is rejected as totally unworthy of belief. She appears as a disgruntled former employee attempting to get even as well as protect her own interests in a lawsuit. . . .

The courts of South Carolina [are] reluctant to declare a common-law marriage unless the proof of such marriage is shown by strong and competent testimony. . . . Jennings's claim that a common-law marriage existed stems, to a large extent, from her present recollection of Hurt's alleged utterance after an argument on December 27, 1983, about seven years ago, that as far as he was concerned they were married in the eyes of God and had a spiritual marriage. To which utterance Jennings says she agreed. Even were this court to find this testimony credible, the event described by Jennings and the words allegedly spoken do not evince an "intent" to solemnize a marriage but rather the kind of words used by one desiring to continue the parties' present state of living together, i.e., in a relationship short of marriage. . . .

Moreover, where as in this case, the relationship began while one of them was already married, a subsequent divorce does not per se transform this illicit relationship into a common-law marriage. Instead the prior relationship is presumed to continue and the party claiming a common-law marriage must show by a preponderance of the evidence that the relationship underwent some fundamental change following the removal of the impediment. . . . Accordingly, it would be incumbent on Jennings to show an agreement to enter a common-law marriage after the impediment was removed. . . . The evidence shows a paucity of any "declaration or acknowledgement of the parties" of a marital state. Not one friend of either of the parties testified that the parties held themselves out as married.

Indeed, [a cast member] testified that at his wedding Jennings "wished us luck and that we have a good marriage and expressed the hope that she would be next." This statement belies any change in the relationship of the parties having taken place on December 27 or 28, 1982. It indicates that the prior illicit relationship continued although a hope, at least by one of the parties, to one day marry existed. . . .

. . . For all the foregoing reasons the court finds that Sandra Jennings is not the common-law wife of William Hurt.

Notes and Questions

1. Epilogue. Jennings sought equitable distribution of Hurt's assets of $5–7 million. Following their separation, Hurt began paying approximately $60,000 annually in child support despite Jennings's request for $192,000. In the course of the litigation, Hurt married bandleader Skitch Henderson's daughter, Heidi. Subsequently, an appellate court affirmed the judgment in Hurt's favor. 554 N.Y.S.2d 220, 221 (App. Div. 1990). In 2011, Jennings and Hurt's son, Alex, completed a graduate degree in acting from New York University and acted alongside his father in a Harold Pinter play in Oregon.[74]

---

[74]. Ben Waterhouse, William Hurt Returning to Artists Rep, Bringing Son Along, Willamette Wk. News, July 13, 2011, http://www.wweek.com/portland/blog-3464-william_hurt_returning_to_artists_rep.html.

2. Historical background. American jurisdictions, which adopted common law marriage, followed English ecclesiastical law. Following the Norman Conquest, when ecclesiastical authorities regulated marriage in England, the Church recognized two types of informal marriage: (1) the exchange of promises to be husband and wife from the present moment; and (2) the exchange of promises to be husband and wife in the future, followed by sexual intercourse. Under the second form, the marriage became valid on subsequent consummation. Such marriages were recognized until the enactment of Lord Hardwicke's Act, 26 Geo. II, c. 33, in 1753, which required formalities of church ceremony, publication of banns, and a license. Subsequently, informal marriages continued to be valid only beyond the statute's jurisdiction in Scotland (hence the importance of the first town across the border, Gretna Green) and Ireland.

Professor Lawrence Friedman explains that common law marriage in the United States stemmed from several social conditions:

> [T]here was a shortage of clergymen of every faith in some parts of the United States. Most of the population lived outside the cities; and parts of the country were thinly populated. [Couples] lived together after makeshift ceremonies, or no ceremony at all. . . . The doctrine of common-law marriage allowed the law to treat these "marriages" as holy and valid. . . .
>
> [T]he early settlers were inclined to make a virtue of necessity, or at least come to terms with it. Despite their "pure morals and stern habits," the settlers could not or would not go along with the strict English marriage laws or their American counterparts. . . . This was not just a matter of social stigma: It was a question of who got the farm, the house, the country acreage, the lot in town. . . .[75]

3. Requirements. Common law marriage has four elements: capacity to enter a marital contract, present agreement to be married, cohabitation, and holding out as husband and wife. Only eight states recognize common law marriage.[76] Some states limit application of the doctrine. See, e.g., Tex. Fam. Code Ann. §2.401 (requiring suit within two years after separation, or else the proponent must overcome a rebuttable presumption that no agreement to marry existed); N.H. Rev. Stat. Ann. §457:39 (recognizing common law marriage only for probate purposes).

Did Jennings and Hurt hold themselves out as married? What is the evidence for and against this position? The main reason for the requirement of a public reputation as man and wife is to prevent fraud. Although an agreement between the parties is necessary, the agreement may be inferred from cohabitation or other circumstantial evidence. How did Jennings attempt to prove their "agreement"? In terms of the standard of proof, South Carolina to the contrary, many states require clear and convincing evidence.

Jennings also discusses the problem of an impediment: A valid common law marriage cannot come into existence while a prior marriage exists for one spouse. Why? Many jurisdictions require that the parties must renew their "agreement"

---

[75]. Lawrence M. Friedman, A History of American Law, 141-142 (2005).

[76]. Nat'l Conf. of State Legislatures, Common-Law Marriage (2015), http://www.ncsl.org/default.aspx?tabid=4265 (listing Colorado, Iowa, Kansas, Montana, New Hampshire, South Carolina, Texas, and Utah).

and meet the other requirements following the removal of the impediment (in Hurt's case, following his divorce).

4. Dissolution or death. Many cases arise at dissolution of the relationship, as in *Jennings*, or at death when the survivor attempts to claim inheritance or health insurance benefits, workers' compensation, or Social Security benefits. One problem in establishing a common law marriage after the death of one party is the Dead Man's Act, which prohibits parties from testifying about communications or transactions with a deceased person. How is a surviving "spouse" to establish a common law marriage in the face of a statute that precludes such testimony? See Crenshaw v. Bussey, 100 P.3d 568 (Colo. Ct. App. 2004). Occasionally, claims of common law marriage arise in other contexts. See, e.g., Mesa v. United States, 875 A.2d 79 (D.C. 2005) (attempt to invoke marital privilege).

5. Choice of law. Can a couple who are domiciliaries in a non–common law jurisdiction obtain marital status by virtue of residing in another jurisdiction that does recognize common law marriage, and then returning to the non–common law state? Why did the New York court look to South Carolina law to determine whether the two New Yorkers had entered a common law marriage, given New York's abolition of common law marriage? See also Fritsche v. Vermilion Parish Hosp. Serv. Dist., 893 So. 2d 935 (La. Ct. App. 2005) (holding that a court is obliged to give effect to such marriages validly created in another state).

A common misconception is that the parties must cohabit for a specified period of time. How long a stay in the non-domiciliary state is sufficient to confer common law marital status? A few days? Compare In re Estate of Bivans, 652 P.2d 744 (N.M. Ct. App.), *cert. quashed*, 652 P.2d 1213 (N.M. 1982), and Kennedy v. Damron, 268 S.W.2d 22 (Ky. 1954) (mere visits are not enough), with Madewell v. United States, 84 F. Supp. 329 (E.D. Tenn. 1949) ("a number of days and nights" sufficient), and Metropolitan Life Ins. Co. v. Holding, 293 F. Supp. 854 (E.D. Va. 1968) (one year sufficient). The equities of the situation often influence courts.

6. Policy. Would you support a revival of common law marriage? Commentators suggest that failure to recognize the doctrine has adverse consequences for women and minorities, especially the poor. See Cynthia Grant Bowman, A Feminist Proposal to Bring Back Common Law Marriage, 75 Or. L. Rev. 709, 769-770 (1996); Sarah Primrose, The Decline of Common Law Marriage and the Unrecognized Cultural Effect, 34 Whittier L. Rev. 187 (2013).

In contrast, critics of the doctrine point to modern social conditions (urbanization) that have eliminated the need for it, the need to prevent fraud in the transmission of property, confusion of public records, the difficulty of surmounting problems of proof, the desire to enforce health-related marital requirements through the licensing process, and administrative and judicial efficiency (Bowman, supra). See also Goran Lind, Common Law Marriage: A Legal Institution 955-1072 (2008) (summarizing arguments). Which arguments are most convincing? In the face of this debate, UMDA includes alternative provisions of §211, leaving the question of whether to allow common law marriage to the states.

Problems

1. Sandra, a university student, begins dating baseball player Dave Winfield. The couple spends frequent time in California, New Jersey, and Texas. After Sandra becomes pregnant, they discuss marriage. Dave, concerned about his image as fathering a nonmarital child, tells Sandra he wants a private ceremony (just the two of them). He instructs Sandra to make a reservation at the Amfac Hotel under the name "Mr. and Mrs. David Winfield." After a three-day stay in the honeymoon suite, Sandra tells her mother she and Dave are married. She rents a condo in Houston for them; the name "Winfield" is on the mailbox. Dave pays for rent, food, furniture, medical, and travel expenses. Pursuant to Dave's instructions, Sandra continues to use her surname and signs the baby's birth certificate with her name.

A neighbor, who gave a party in their honor, is prepared to testify that she thought they were married. Further, when the couple vacations in the Bahamas, a local newspaper describes them as husband and wife, as does an announcer at a softball game. Dave does not contradict this or ask for retraction. Sandra files income tax returns and health insurance forms as single, per Dave's instructions. She does not wear a wedding ring. While living with Sandra, Dave is dating other women, one of whom he eventually marries. Sandra files for divorce, claiming she is his common law wife. Dave testifies that he never agreed to be married, bought the condo to provide for his child and, further, does not recall staying at the Amfac Hotel. Texas recognizes common law marriage, although California and New Jersey do not. What result? Winfield v. Renfro, 821 S.W.2d 640 (Tex. App. 1991).

2. Maurice and Anne meet at a restaurant where Anne works as a waitress. Soon thereafter, they move into a home purchased by Maurice and titled in his name. Maurice gives Anne an engagement ring and matching wedding band and asks her to marry him (although the wedding never takes place). Anne wears the engagement ring but not the wedding band because she does not believe that she has the right to do so without a formal ceremony. A sign outside their home reads "Hunsakers, Home of the Classics" (referring to the classic car business they operate together). The telephone answering message states "This is the Hunsaker residence." A grandfather clock, displayed in the living room, has the letters "A," "M," and "H" intertwined. Anne is listed as Maurice's spouse on his insurance policy. They own shares of stock and a time-share condominium as joint tenants. They keep separate bank accounts because Maurice has poor credit; they file income tax returns that list themselves as single. Maurice is listed as Anne's "significant other" on two hospital consent forms that Anne signed.

Shortly before his death, Maurice tells his attorney that he wants to bequeath his entire estate to Anne, whom he refers to as his "common law wife." He says that if he does not have a will, his family will "eat [Anne] alive." However, before the will can be drafted, Maurice dies. His surviving sister and brothers claim his estate. Anne claims she was his common law wife based on their ten years' cohabitation. The jurisdiction recognizes common law marriage. What result? In re Estate of Hunsaker, 968 P.2d 281 (Mont. 1998).

3. Sabrina Maurer and Kimberly Underwood, longstanding same-sex partners, celebrate a commitment ceremony in Pennsylvania in 2001. They live together

in the state for 12 years until Underwood's death in 2013 from heart disease. Although they wanted to marry, they were unable to do so because Underwood's death occurred six months before Pennsylvania legalized same-sex marriage.

Since her partner's death, Maurer has been unsuccessful in her efforts to be recognized as Underwood's spouse and to collect either spousal survivorship rights under Underwood's employer benefits plan or federal Social Security survivor benefits. In addition, Maurer was required to pay inheritance taxes on Underwood's estate that she would not have had to pay if the couple had been legally married.

Maurer files suit for a declaratory judgment, claiming that she and her deceased partner had a "common law marriage" dating from the date of their commitment ceremony in 2001. Pennsylvania law recognized common law marriages until 2004. In that year, the state legislature abolished common law marriage except for those marriages that "occurred prior to January 1, 2005."

Does Maurer have a right to retroactive application of the state common law marriage doctrine? Does *Obergefell* establish a constitutional right to common law marriage? After *Obergefell*, must states that allow common law marriage for opposite-sex couples also allow it for same-sex couples? What result? See Gina Passarella, Common Law Retroactively Applied to Same-Sex Couple, Legal Intelligencer, July 29, 2015.[77]

(ii) The Putative Spouse Doctrine and Other Curative Devices

Courts and legislatures often strain to recognize marriages that fail to comply with the formal requirements. In so doing, they have developed a variety of doctrines that cure or mitigate the harsh consequences of invalidity.

The most important of these devices is the putative spouse doctrine. This doctrine recognizes the marriage of an individual who participated in a marriage ceremony in good faith, in the belief that a valid marriage took place and in ignorance of an impediment making the marriage void or voidable (for example, a preexisting marriage or a disability such as nonage). In some states, putative spouses may obtain only limited benefits and privileges of a legal marriage.[78]

Must the belief be reasonable? See Xiong v. Xiong, 800 N.W.2d 187 (Minn. Ct. App. 2011) (holding that wife had good-faith reasonable belief that their Hmong cultural marriage ceremony satisfied state requirements). Is the standard subjective or objective? See, e.g., Ceja v. Rudolph & Sletten, Inc., 302 P.3d 211 (Cal. 2013) (holding that the proper standard is subjective good faith that does not require the belief to be objectively reasonable).

Section 209 of UMDA takes the following approach:

> Any person who has cohabited with another to whom he is not legally married in the good faith belief that he was married to that person is a putative spouse until knowledge of the fact that he is not legally married terminates his status and prevents acquisition of further rights. A putative spouse acquires the rights conferred upon a legal spouse, including the right to maintenance following termination of his status, whether or not the marriage is prohibited (Section 207) or declared invalid (Section 208). If there is a legal spouse or other putative spouses,

---

[77]. The full article is available at http://www.thelegalintelligencer.com/id=1202733414697/CommonLaw-Marriage-Retroactively-Applied-to-SameSex-Couple?slreturn=20150810111033.

[78]. For example, in California, putative spouses are not eligible for a family allowance during administration of the decedent spouse's estate. See Helen Chang, California Putative Spouses: The Innocent, the Guilty, and the Law, 44 Sw. L. Rev. 327, 328 (2014).

> rights acquired by a putative spouse do not supersede the rights of the legal spouse or those acquired by other putative spouses, but the court shall apportion property, maintenance, and support rights among the claimants as appropriate in the circumstances and in the interests of justice.

In addition, presumptions can sometimes function as curative devices. Rules of evidence in some states raise a presumption of a valid marriage based on a couple's "holding [themselves] out" as husband and wife, even if the jurisdiction has abolished common law marriage by statute. See, e.g., Thomson v. Thomson, 163 S.W.2d 792 (Mo. Ct. App. 1942). Similarly, some states attach a presumption of validity to the later of two (or the latest in a series of) marriages. Thus, for example, if A, who is already married to B, marries C, this second marriage, although bigamous and void, may be presumed valid. To rely on this presumption, one must introduce evidence that the later marriage occurred, and to rebut it, one must show "cogent and conclusive" evidence that the earlier marriage continues. This presumption rests on policies favoring validation of marriages and "the need to make good the parties' expectations."[79]

Other courts have developed additional equitable remedies. For example, some courts have created "marriage by estoppel." See, e.g., Farnham v. Farnham, 323 S.W.3d 129 (Tenn. Ct. App. 2009). Note that some courts apply equitable remedies to putative spouses' claims or common law marriages in order to permit determinations of spousal support, property, and child support. See, e.g., Combs v. Tibbitts, 148 P.3d 430 (Colo. Ct. App. 2006).

Problems

1. When Dr. Norman J. Lewiston, a renowned expert in cystic fibrosis at Stanford University, dies of a heart attack in 1991, three women claim to be his widow. Records reveal that he married Diana Lewiston in 1960 in Connecticut, naming her in a 1966 will as his sole heir. (He suffers his fatal heart attack in the home they share in Palo Alto, California.) They have three children, all now adults. Katy Mayer-Lewiston, who marries him in 1985, attends university events with him. His colleagues believe that she is his wife. The two own a house in a town ten miles away. Robin Phelps of San Diego marries Dr. Lewiston in 1989 during his sabbatical in that city. Believing that he plans to retire soon in San Diego, Robin remains there. See Katherine Bishop, Respected Doctor, Professor and Family Man—3 Families, in Fact, N.Y. Times, Oct. 23, 1991, at A7. Assume that California's community property law would give half of Dr. Lewiston's property acquired during marriage to the surviving spouse. If all three purported widows seek a share of his estate, to what extent do any of the curative and mitigative devices, discussed above, help resolve their claims? See also In re Estate of Vargas, 111 Cal. Rptr. 779 (Ct. App. 1974); In re Estate of Collier, 2011 WL 2420989 (Tex. App. 2011).

2. Several couples, noncitizens who reside in Alabama and desire to obtain a license to marry, challenge a policy that was recently implemented by a probate judge there, requiring non-U.S. citizens who are applicants for marriage licenses

[79]. Clark, Law of Domestic Relations, supra note [60], at 72-73.

to present certain forms of documentation. The policy states: "Non-citizens of the United States must provide proof of legal presence in the United States in the form of valid immigration documents or passport. Each applicant must provide one of the following: (1) an official picture ID; (2) an original certified copy of the state-issued birth certificate and original Social Security card; or (3) U.S. Government-issued Immigration Services Picture ID Card." Neither the Code of Alabama nor the Alabama Constitution requires applicants to provide proof of legal presence to secure a marriage license.

Plaintiffs, who are unable to provide the required documentation, seek declaratory and injunctive relief for violations of their Fourteenth Amendment rights to due process and equal protection. In response, the defendant-probate judge contends that plaintiffs have not sustained any injury and thus lack standing because (1) they have not yet applied for a marriage license; and (2) Alabama recognizes common-law marriage, and therefore the couples could simply enter into a common law marriage. What result? Does the availability of common law marriage solve the problem? See Loder v. McKinney, 896 F. Supp. 2d 1116 (M.D. Ala. 2012). See also Buck v. Stankovic, 485 F. Supp. 2d 576 (M.D. Pa. 2007); Ohio ex rel. Ten Residents of Franklin County v. Belskis, 755 N.E.2d 443 (Ohio Ct. App. 2001).

III

Being Married: Regulation of the Intact Marriage

A. Introduction: The Changing Nature of Marriage

Marriage and the family have evolved over time. Marriage has become more companionate.[1] The family has lost some of its functions and others have altered.[2] The legalization of same-sex marriage has fundamentally altered the traditional definition of marriage and the family. Significantly, these and other changes have contributed to an increase in family privacy[3]—but not always with positive consequences.

Despite the increase in family privacy, the state continues to exercise significant control over marriage. The cases and materials that follow focus on the changing nature of marital rights, roles, and responsibilities. They explore the duty of support during marriage; the regulation of naming, employment, and parenting; the application of tort law to spouses; and evidentiary privileges arising from the marital relationship.

This exploration raises important questions: As a matter of law, what are the consequences of being married? How does the law regulate the relationship between the spouses? Between spouses and third parties? To what extent does marriage as a legal institution diverge from marriage as practiced within families? In what ways has the

[1]. See Ernest Watson Burgess & Harvey James Locke, The Family: From Institution to Companionship (1953).

[2]. William Fielding Ogburn & Meyer Francis Nimkoff, Technology and the Changing Family (1955).

[3]. For classic historical studies of family privacy, see Philippe Aries, Centuries of Childhood: A Social History of Family Life (1962); David H. Flaherty, Privacy in Colonial New England (1972); Barbara Laslett, The Family as a Public and Private Institution: An HistoricalPerspective, 35 J. Marriage & Fam. 480 (1973).

increase in family privacy over time represented a positive versus negative development? Going forward, should state regulation in this realm grow or diminish?

John W. Blassingame, The Slave Community: Plantation Life in the Antebellum South

171-174, 177 (1979)

[In the antebellum South] many slaves had only one partner. Henry Box Brown, for instance, refused his master's order to take another mate after his wife was sold because he felt marriage "was a sacred institution binding upon me." Affection was apparently the most important factor which kept partners together. This emerges most clearly in the lamentations and resentments which pervade the autobiographies over the separation of family members. Frequently when their mates were sold, slaves ran away in an effort to find them. . . . Because they were denied all the protection which the law afforded, slaves had an almost mythological respect for legal marriage. . . .

[T]he slave faced almost insurmountable odds in his efforts to build a strong stable family. First, and most important of all, his authority was restricted by his master. . . . The master determined when both he and his wife would go to work, when or whether his wife cooked his meals, and was often the final arbiter in family disputes. . . . Some planters punished males by refusing to let them visit their mates when they lived on other plantations. . . . When the slave lived on the same plantation with his mate, he could rarely escape frequent demonstrations of his powerlessness. The master, and not the slave, furnished the cabin, clothes, and the minimal food for his wife and children. Under such a regime, slave fathers often had little or no authority.

The most serious impediment to the man's acquisition of status in his family was his inability to protect his wife from the sexual advances of whites and the physical abuse of his master. Instead, according to Austin Steward, slave husbands had to "submit without a murmur" when their wives were flogged. Sometimes, in spite of the odds, the men tried to protect their mates . . . Generally, however, the women had no choice but to submit to the sexual advances of white men. . . .

By all odds, the most brutal aspect of slavery was the separation of families. This was a haunting fear which made all of the slave's days miserable. [P]ractically all of the black autobiographers were touched by the tragedy. Death occurred too frequently in the master's house, creditors were too relentless in collecting their debts, the planter's reserves ran out too often, and the master longed too much for expensive items for the slave to escape the clutches of the slave trader. Nothing demonstrated his powerlessness as much as the slave's inability to prevent the forcible sale of his wife and children. . . .[4]

---

[4]. For other historical sources on the slave family, see Herbert G. Gutman, The Black Family in Slavery and Freedom, 1750-1925 (1977); Jacqueline Jones, Labor of Love, Labor of Sorrow: Black Women, Work, and the Family, from Slavery to the Present (2009); Dorothy Roberts, Killing the Black Body: Race, Reproduction, and the Meaning of Liberty 22-55 (1997).

Theodore Caplow et al., The Quality of Marriage in Middletown: 1924-1976

Middletown Families: Fifty Years of Change and Continuity 116-118, 120-121, 124-125, 126, 127, 135 (1982)

[Social scientists assessed the quality of marriages in Middletown (a fictional name for a midwestern city) in the 1920s, 1930s, and 1970s.]

Marriage in the 1920s

[T]he average marriage in the Middletown of the 1920s was a dreary one, especially for the working class. Marriage for many husbands meant weariness from trying to provide for their families, numerous children, and wives weary from doing other people's washing. For many wives, marriage meant poverty, cruelty, adultery, and abandonment. [M]ost families, although less than happy, were held together by community values discouraging divorce. . . . Married life was disappointing, but the prospect of a divorce was even more painful. . . .

Observations of husbands and wives revealed that most of them developed a relationship with limited companionship. In the social and recreational activities of the 1920s, the sexes were separated more often than not. At dinners, parties, and other social gatherings, men and women seemed to form separate groups so that the men could talk about business, sports and politics and the women could discuss children, dress styles, and local gossip. Men's leisure activities generally excluded women. Business-class husbands played golf or cards at their clubs without their wives. . . . The one recreational activity that husbands and wives shared was card playing with friends in their homes. . . . The limited communication between husbands and wives and the trivial nature of their conversation left many of them isolated in their separate worlds, his pertaining to work and friends and hers to the children and the home. In many marriages, they shared a house, each other's bodies, and little else.

. . . Lack of information about birth control and the prejudice against its use made babies the inevitable consequence of physical intimacy for most working-class couples. The uncertainty of employment often made another child an unwanted burden. The conflict between not wanting more children and needing the physical pleasures of marriage, and the resulting stress placed on the marriage, were evident. [C]omments provide considerable insight into Middletown's working-class marriages of the 1920s. The fact that a wife might not dare ask her husband what he thought about birth control, let alone what he felt about practicing it, shows how shallow some of the relationships were. . . .

Marriage in the 1930s

The Great Depression was thought by Middletown people to have mixed effects on marital happiness. On the one hand, they spoke of how married couples spent more time together and became more dependent on each other, and this enforced togetherness was perceived as strengthening the quality of Middletown's marriages. [T]he Depression did increase the amount of time husbands and wives spent together by making outside activities unaffordable.

[On the other hand,] [a]lthough couples spent more time together, they often reacted to economic pressures by mutual recrimination. The wives were quick to reproach their husbands for failing to provide for the family's needs, and the husbands were equally quick to defend their wounded egos by lashing out at wives and children. Despite these mounting tensions, the typical marital relationship during the Depression was similar to that of the 1920s. . . .

Marriage in the 1970s

[We] have witnessed a major change in the style of communication between husbands and wives. [Women have been encouraged to assert their needs and preferences.] Marriage-enrichment programs . . . have purported to teach thousands of American couples how to communicate with each other more effectively. The women's rights movement [has] fostered a more equal marriage relationship in which the needs and wishes of the wife are considered to be at least as important as those of the husband.

It is difficult to imagine many contemporary wives who would be afraid to discuss birth control with their husbands, particularly after the couple has had several children. The taboo on discussing financial matters observed in the 1920s [also] has almost disappeared, and today nearly all wives play an active role in the management of family finances, especially when they work and contribute to the family income. . . .

Not only are contemporary husbands and wives talking to each other, they are engaging in a great deal of leisure activity together. Shopping; eating out; going for drives and to movies, sporting events, fairs, and musical presentations; and taking part in physical fitness activities are frequently shared by husbands and wives. . . .

There is additional evidence suggesting that the quality of the average marital relationship has improved over the past 50 years—the number of wives who mentioned their husbands as a source of strength during difficult times. [W]hen a 1924 sample of Middletown housewives was asked the question "What are the thoughts and plans that give you courage to go on when thoroughly discouraged?," not a single wife mentioned her husband as a source of reassurance. . . . [H]usbands and wives share each other's burdens and provide emotional support to a greater degree now than then. . . .

All things considered, the quality of marriage seems to have improved substantially in Middletown during the past half a century. Such dismal marriages as [were] typical in the 1920s are now relatively rare. The overwhelming majority of contemporary husbands and wives say that their marriages are happy and fulfilling.

We do not mean to imply that all marriages in Middletown are happy. The data indicate that most are, but the divorce rate is a reminder that many unhappy marriages occur. Indeed, the high divorce rate is one important reason why contemporary marriages are so happy; most of the unhappy ones have been terminated. . . .

Postscript. When sociologists replicated the above study, they identified the following major differences between marriages in the 1920s and today: (1) married women with children did not work in the 1920s; (2) premarital sexual activity was taboo; (3) cohabitation was virtually nonexistent; (4) nonmarital births were heavily stigmatized; (5) housework took up a major fraction of the day; and (6) fathers spent little time with children.[5]

Social scientists have identified a phenomenon over the past fifty years that has been called the "retreat from marriage," that is, a major decline in the marriage rate. Fewer Americans are marrying today than ever before.[6] The dwindling numbers of married adults is attributable, in part, to the fact that young adults increasingly are delaying entrance into marriage and also because more adults are entering nontraditional family arrangements, such as single parenthood and cohabitation.

The "retreat from marriage" has serious consequences for society: it has enhanced socioeconomic inequality. That is, fewer adults are able to experience the economic gains that generally accompany marriage.[7] "The net result is that a marriage gap and a socioeconomic gap have been growing side by side for the past half century."[8]

The retreat from marriage also has serious consequences for the family and gender roles. The excerpt below explains some of these ramifications.[9]

W. Bradford Wilcox, Marriage in Decline: No Big Deal?[10]

Institute of Family Studies, Apr. 1, 2015

[M]arriage is declining and it's no big deal, right? Wrong. . . .

[O]ne of marriage's core social functions [is] attaching men to the children they help to bring into this world. [T]he rituals, customs, and norms associated with marriage have generally increased the odds that men will invest financially, practically, and emotionally in the lives of their children. . . . But because of the decline of marriage, fewer and fewer men have the opportunity to be this kind of father in America, and that matters for them, their kids, and the

[5]. Theodore Caplow et al., The First Measured Century: An Illustrated Guide to Trends in America, 1900-2000 (2000). This work is known as "Middletown IV" because it followed other replications of the original study.

[6]. For example, in 1960, 72 percent of American adults were married, compared to 52 percent in 2008 (the most recent year for which data are available). Pew Research Ctr., The Decline of Marriage and Rise of New Families (Nov. 18, 2010), http://www.pewsocialtrends.org/2010/11/18/the-decline-of-marriage-and-rise-of-new-families/.

[7]. Id. In 1960, the median household income of married adults differed from that of unmarried adults by 12 percent. However, in 2008, the difference was 41 percent.

[8]. Id. The decline in marriage and the socioeconomic gap cannot be explained by the fact that low-income adults are less eager to marry. The authors of the Pew Research Center Report explain that poor adults share the same desire to marry as wealthier adults. However, the poor are more likely to believe that economic security is a prerequisite for marriage. Because they have such difficulty obtaining economic security, they perceive marriage as an unobtainable goal. (Nonetheless, they do not delay parenting.) See also June Carbone & Naomi Cahn, Marriage Markets: How Inequality Is Remaking the American Family (2014); Kathryn Eden & Maria Kefalas, Promises I Can Keep: Why Poor Women Put Motherhood Before Marriage (2011). But cf. Charles Murray, Coming Apart: The State of White America, 1960-2010 (2012) (contending that the poor value marriage less than the middle class).

[9]. Other legal consequences for nonmarital families and children (for example, discrimination in housing, employment and familial benefits) are explored in Chapter V.

[10]. The full article is available at http://family-studies.org/marriage-in-decline-yglesias/.

families that they failed to form or sustain. . . . That's because families formed outside of marriage (or split by divorce) typically end with the kids living with mom, while dad's day-to-day involvement declines.

What's more: because the decline of marriage is concentrated in working-class and poor communities, [these] disconnected dads are most likely to be found in the very communities that can least afford to support lots of single-mother-headed households. . . . The decline of marriage thus ends up being a major contributor to economic inequality, gender inequality, and social inequality. How does that work?

When a man is not married to the mother of his children, both the mother and those children are much less likely to see his money, and to enjoy the economies of scale that come from two parents sharing a household. [This gives rise to] broader economic implications of the growing class divide in marriage and family instability: namely, rising levels of single parenthood in poor and working-class communities, coupled with high levels of marital stability among more educated and affluent communities, necessarily translate into greater economic inequality between these two groups.

[A]lmost one-third of the growth in family income inequality since the 1970s can be connected to this decline in marriage. . . . The decline of marriage is not the only story here, of course: declining real wages for men without college degrees are also a major part of our growing economic divide. . . .

The retreat from marriage also fuels two kinds of gender inequality. . . . First, working-class and poor mothers end up carrying a much bigger share of the load associated with raising children than do (absent) fathers: The parent who lives with the children, in most cases the mother, is predictably going to do most of the day-to-day household and child care chores.

Second, boys from working-class and poor communities struggle more than their female peers to navigate life without the steady involvement of their fathers. [L]acking a father seems to hurt boys' performance and behavior at school more than girls', and boys may also be less likely to imagine a future tied to work and family life because their own father is not in the picture. By contrast, girls being raised by a single mother anticipate having and supporting children as adults, with or without a man. . . .

[Finally], marital happiness has *declined* since the divorce revolution. In the 1970s, about 66 percent of husbands and wives were very happy, whereas in the 2000s only about 60 percent were, despite the fact that a lower share of Americans were getting and staying married. . . . Not only has marital quality declined, on average, but we're also seeing a growing class-based divide in marital quality as the soul-mate model of marriage gains ground. Well-educated Americans who have the financial means and the social skills to navigate today's "more optional and more brittle" soul-mate marriage model [continue] to enjoy high-quality marriages, but less-educated Americans are markedly less happy than they used to be. . . .

These are but a few of the reasons why the nation's retreat from marriage is a big deal. . . . But the bottom line is this: the decline of marriage is a problem because it is one of the primary reasons that the richer and poorer classes in our country are increasingly separate and unequal.[11]

---

[11]. For other studies of the social transformation wrought by the decline of marriage on low-income families, see Paul R. Amato et al., Families in an Era of Increasing Inequality: Diverging Destinies (2014); Carbone & Cahn, Marriage Markets, supra note [8]; Andrew J. Cherlin, Labor's Love Lost: The Rise and Fall of the Working-Class Family in America (2014).

The following excerpt explores a taken-for-granted assumption about marriage and its exclusionary implications.

Michael Warner, Beyond Gay Marriage

in Left Legalism/Left Critique 260
(Wendy Brown & Janet Halley eds., 2002)

Marriage sanctifies some couples at the expense of others. It is selective legitimacy. This is a necessary implication of the institution, and not just the result of bad motives. . . . To a couple that gets married, marriage just looks ennobling. . . . But stand outside it for a second and you see the implication: if you don't have it, you and your relations are less worthy. Without this corollary effect, marriage would not be able to endow anybody's life with significance. The ennobling and the demeaning go together. Marriage does one only by virtue of the other. Marriage, in short, discriminates.

That is one reason why same-sex marriage provokes such powerful outbursts of homophobic feeling in many straight people, when they could just as easily view marriage as the ultimate conformity of gay people to their own norms. They want marriage to remain a privilege, a mark that they are special. Often, they are willing to grant all or nearly all the benefits of marriage to gay people, as long as they don't have to give up the word *marriage*. They need some token, however magical, of superiority. But what about the gay people who want marriage? Would they not in turn derive their sense of pride from the invidious and shaming distinction between the married and the unmarried?

The final excerpt below explores the gender-based aspects of marriage.

Jessie Bernard, The Future of Marriage

16-18, 26-28, 40-41, 49-50 (1982)

There are few findings more consistent, less equivocal, more convincing than the sometimes spectacular and always impressive superiority on almost every index—demographic, psychological, or social—of married over never-married men. Despite all the jokes about marriage in which men indulge, all the complaints they lodge against it, it is one of the greatest boons of their sex. Employers, bankers, and insurance companies have long since known this. And whether they know it or not, men need marriage more than women do. . . .

The research evidence is overwhelmingly convincing. Although the physical health of married men is no better than that of never-married men until middle age, their mental health is far better, fewer show serious symptoms of psychological distress, and fewer of them suffer mental health impairments. [M]arriage is an asset in a man's career, including his earning power. The value of marriage for sheer male survival is itself remarkable. It does, indeed, pay men to be married. [Men] profit greatly from having a wife to help them to take care of their health. . . . In the United States, the suicide rate for single men is almost twice as high as for married men. . . .

The actions of men with respect to marriage speak far louder than words; they speak, in fact, with a deafening roar. Once men have known marriage, they can hardly live without it. Most divorced and widowed men remarry. . . . Half of all divorced white men who remarry do so within three years after divorce. . . .

[I]t is hard for us to see how different the wife's marriage really is from the husband's, and how much worse. But, in fact, it is. [M]ore wives than husbands report marital frustration and dissatisfaction; more report negative feelings; more wives than husbands report marital problems; more wives than husbands consider their marriages unhappy, have considered separation or divorce, have regretted their marriages; and fewer report positive companionship. [Yet it is not] the complaints of wives that demonstrate how bad the wife's marriage is, but rather the poor mental and emotional health of married women as compared not only to married men's but also to unmarried women's.

Although the physical health of married women, as measured by absence of chronic conditions or restricted activity, is as good as, and in the ages beyond sixty-five even better than, that of married men, they suffer far greater mental-health hazards and present a far worse clinical picture. [M]ore married women than married men have felt they were about to have a nervous breakdown; more experience psychological and physical anxiety; more have feelings of inadequacy in their marriages and blame themselves for their own lack of general adjustment. [M]ore married women than married men show phobic reactions, depression, and passivity; greater than expected frequency of symptoms of psychological distress; and mental-health impairment. . . .

The problem is not why do young women marry, but why, in the face of all the evidence, do more married than unmarried women report themselves as happy? [One way] to look at the seeming anomaly involved here . . . is that happiness is interpreted in terms of conformity. Wives may in effect be judging themselves happy by definition. They are conforming to expectations and are therefore less vulnerable to the strains accompanying nonconformity. The pressures to conform are so great that few young women can resist them. Better, as the radical women put it, dead than unwed. Those who do not marry are made to feel inferior, failures. . . . [S]ince marriage is set up as the *summum bonum* of life for women, they interpret their achievement of marriage as happiness, no matter how unhappy the marriage itself may be. They have been told that their happiness depends on marriage, so, even if they are miserable, they *are* married, aren't they? . . .

Postscript. Bernard's thesis (that marriage is good for men, but bad for women) has been validated by other scholars. Sociologist Linda Waite concurs that marriage affects men and women differently: husbands derive greater health benefits, but wives reap greater comparative financial advantages. Yet Waite also notes that both married men and women live longer, healthier, and wealthier lives than do the unmarried.[12]

---

[12]. Linda J. Waite & Maggie Gallagher, Is Her Marriage Really Worse Than His?, in The Case for Marriage: Why Married People Are Happier, Healthier, and Better Off Financially 162-163 (2001).

B. Roles and Responsibilities in Marriage

1. The Common Law View

1 William Blackstone, Commentaries

**442-445*

Husband beating his wife, from a 19th century illustration

By marriage, the husband and wife are one person in law: that is, the very being or legal existence of the woman is suspended during the marriage, or at least is incorporated and consolidated into that of the husband: under whose wing, protection, and *cover,* she performs everything; and is therefore called in our law-French a *ferne-covert;* is said to be *covert-baron,* or under the protection and influence of her husband, her baron, or lord; and her condition during her marriage is called her *coverture.* Upon this principle, of a union of person in husband and wife, depend almost all the legal rights, duties, and disabilities, that either of them acquire by the marriage. . . .

For this reason, a man cannot grant anything to his wife, or enter into covenant with her: for the grant would be to suppose her separate existence; and to covenant with her, would be only to covenant with himself: and therefore it is also generally true, that all compacts made between husband and wife, when single, are voided by the intermarriage. . . . The husband is bound to provide his wife with necessities by law, [and] if she contracts debts for them, he is obliged to pay them: but for anything besides necessaries, he is not chargeable. . . . If the wife be indebted before marriage, the husband is bound afterwards to pay the debt; for he has adopted her and her circumstances together. If the wife be injured in her person or her property, she can bring no action for redress without her husband's concurrence, and in his name, as well as her own: neither can she sue or be sued, without making the husband a defendant. . . . In criminal prosecutions, it is true, the wife may be indicted and punished separately; for the union is only a civil union. But, in trials of any sort, they are not allowed to be evidence for, or against, each other: partly because it is impossible their testimony should be indifferent; but principally because of the union of person.

But, though our law in general considers man and wife as one person, yet there are some instances in which she is separately considered; as inferior to

> him, and acting by his compulsion. And therefore all deeds executed, and acts done, by her, during her coverture, are void, or at least voidable; except it be a fine, or the like matter of record, in which case she must be solely and secretly examined, to learn if her act be voluntary. She cannot by will devise lands to her husband, [because] she is supposed to be under his coercion. And in some felonies, and other inferior crimes, committed by her, through constraint of her husband, the law excuses her: but this extends not to treason or murder.
>
> The husband also (by the old law) might give his wife moderate correction. For, as he is to answer for her misbehavior, the law thought it reasonable to entrust him with this power of restraining her, by domestic chastisement, in the same moderation that a man is allowed to correct his servants or children; for whom the master or parent is also liable in some cases to answer. But this power of correction was confined within reasonable bounds; and the husband was prohibited to use any violence to his wife [other than what is reasonably necessary to the discipline and correction of the wife]. . . .
>
> These are the chief legal effects of marriage during the coverture; upon which we may observe that even the disabilities, which the wife lies under, are for the most part intended for her protection and benefit. So great a favorite is the female sex of the laws of England.

2. Marital Property Regimes

a. Introduction

The state, through its treatment of property acquired during marriage, regulates certain rights of spouses upon marriage. According to historian Sir William Holdsworth:

> No legal system which deals merely with human rules of conduct desires to pry too closely into the relationship of husband and wife. Dealings between husband and wife are for the most part privileged. But some rules it must have to regulate the proprietary relationships of the parties. . . .[13]

Two marital property regimes exist in the United States: (1) the common law approach and (2) the community property approach. Each reflects a different philosophy. In the common law system, followed by most jurisdictions, the husband and wife own all property separately. During marriage, property belongs to the spouse who acquired it (traditionally, the wage-earning husband) unless he chooses another form of ownership.

On the other hand, in the community property system, the husband and wife own some property jointly. Equality of treatment of the spouses is the cardinal rule of the community property system. The community property system is characterized by the concept of a community of ownership under which the spouses

[13]. 3 W.S. Holdsworth, A History of English Law 404 (2d ed. 1909). See also 2 Frederick Pollock & Frederic William Maitland, The History of English Law Before the Time of Edward I 406 (S.F.C. Milsom, ed., 1968) (1898).

are partners. Each spouse has a present, undivided, one-half interest in all property acquired by the efforts of either spouse during marriage. Unlike the common law system, community property recognizes the contributions, for example, of the homemaker spouse. Moreover, the community property system respects each spouse's separate property, such as the property that each brought to the marriage. Separate property also includes property acquired by a spouse during the marriage by means of gift or inheritance.[14] The community property system is in effect in nine states (Arizona, California, Idaho, Louisiana, Nevada, New Mexico, Texas, Washington, and Wisconsin).

b. Common Law Disabilities

The common law and community property systems reflect fundamental differences concerning the position of married women. Until the mid-nineteenth century, Blackstone's famous quotation on coverture, quoted above, described the status of married women at common law. The common law imposed on a married woman many disabilities, summarized below:[15]

(1) *Wife's real property.* The husband acquired an estate in the wife's real property for the duration of the marriage. His interest, termed *jure uxoris,* entitled him to sole possession and control of any real property that the wife owned in fee—whether acquired by her before or after the marriage. If a child was born, the husband's rights became a life estate. Further, the husband could alienate the wife's real property without her consent.

(2) *Dower.* During marriage, the wife's primary protection from her husband's conveyances consisted of her right of dower—her life estate of one-third of any land of which the husband was seised in fee at any time during the marriage.[16] The husband could not bar her dower right without her consent. She came into enjoyment of her dower right if she survived her husband.

(3) *Wife's personal property.* The wife, similarly, had no right to possess personal property. Whatever personal property she owned before marriage, or might acquire after, became her husband's. She also lacked a right of testamentary disposition.[17]

(4) *Wife's lack of rights to husband's personal property.* During the marriage, the husband had the power of disposition (inter vivos or by will) over his personal property. Similarly, all his personal property (including what we might think of as the wife's property) was subject to his creditors. The only exception was the wife's necessary clothes. However, the husband could sell or give away his wife's jewels, trinkets, or ornaments (termed her "paraphernalia") during his lifetime.

(5) *Husband's liability.* The husband was liable for the wife's premarital debts, as well as for torts she committed before or during the marriage.

---

[14]. Note, however, that some states' equitable distribution schemes take separate property into account in awarding the marital property.

[15]. Pollock & Maitland, supra note [13], at 403-405.

[16]. *Dower,* not to be confused with *dowry,* is an inchoate property interest of a married woman that comes into beneficial enjoyment upon widowhood. *Dowry* refers to goods with which some women, historically, were endowed in anticipation of marriage.

[17]. As Holdsworth points out: "The logical consequence of the views of the common lawyers was the denial to married women of all testamentary capacity, for it is useless to say that a person may make a will if she has nothing to leave." Holdsworth, supra note [13], at 425-426.

(6) *Wife's contracts*. A wife could not execute contracts except as her husband's agent.

The legal status of married women changed little until many states enacted Married Women's Property Acts, which enabled women to own property that they brought to the marriage or acquired thereafter by gift or inheritance. The movement began in 1839 when Mississippi enacted a statute specifying that the wife could continue to possess slaves she owned prior to marriage or thereafter acquired (although the husband continued to manage them and reap the profits of their labor). New York legislation, the most progressive, enabled married women to sue and to retain their own earnings. By 1865, 29 states had Married Women's Property Acts.[18] The legislation significantly liberalized the rules to which married women had been subject for centuries.

c. Managerial Rules

The husband as master of the household was an entrenched common law principle. Paradoxically, the community property system also reflected this rule because statutes placed management of community property in husbands' hands. Limited exceptions to male management and control existed. For example, in many community property states, the wife retained management and control of her earnings. And the joinder requirement for the conveyance or encumbrance of community real property gave the wife some control. The Supreme Court marked the end of such gender-based rules in Kirchberg v. Feenstra, 450 U.S. 455 (1981), which invalidated, on equal protection grounds, a Louisiana statute designating the husband "head and master" of the community.

Three different, facially gender-neutral rules emerged in response to the unconstitutionality of male managerial rules: (1) extension of the separate property philosophy to link management to the source of earnings; (2) joint control (requiring consent of both spouses for community property transactions); and (3) equal control (either may manage community property regardless of the source of earnings or without the other's consent). Most community property jurisdictions follow the last approach.

Reforms narrowed the gap between the common law and community property systems. Although title theory determines ownership and management in common law states during an intact marriage, many common law states permit spouses to opt for a tenancy by the entireties in which spouses share the right of control (i.e., neither can alienate or encumber property without the other's consent). At divorce, common law states now follow an equitable distribution approach. Equitable distribution, which attempts to divide marital property in a fair or equitable manner based on a number of factors, purports to achieve more equal treatment of women.

Another significant development, the Uniform Marital Property Act (UMPA), imposes a sharing rule from the beginning of the marriage. Under UMPA §5, absent an agreement, a spouse acting alone can manage and control marital property held in that spouse's name alone, that not held in the name of either spouse, and that held in the name of both spouses in the alternative ("A or B" form). Spouses

---

[18]. Norma Basch, In the Eyes of the Law: Women, Marriage, and Property in Nineteenth-Century New York 27-28 (1982).

must act together with respect to marital property held in the name of both. The UMPA also allows spouses to enter into agreements with each other regarding the management and control of property. Id. §10(c)(2).

3. Duty of Support

McGUIRE v. McGUIRE

59 N.W.2d 336 (Neb. 1953)

MESSMORE, Justice.

The plaintiff, Lydia McGuire, brought this action . . . against Charles W. McGuire, her husband . . . to recover suitable maintenance and support money. [A] decree was rendered in favor of the plaintiff.

The record shows that the plaintiff and defendant were married in Wayne, Nebraska, on August 11, 1919. At the time of the marriage the defendant was a bachelor 46 or 47 years of age and had a reputation for more than ordinary frugality, of which the plaintiff was aware. She had visited in his home and had known him for about 3 years prior to the marriage. [P]laintiff had been previously married. Her first husband . . . died intestate, leaving 80 acres of land in Dixon County. The plaintiff and each of [their two] daughters inherited a one-third interest therein. At the time of the marriage of the plaintiff and defendant, the plaintiff's daughters were 9 and 11 years of age. By working and receiving financial assistance from the parties to this action, the daughters received a high school education in Pender. One daughter attended Wayne State Teachers College for 2 years and the other daughter attended a business college in Sioux City, Iowa, for 1 year. [Both] are married and have families of their own. [At trial] plaintiff was 66 years of age and the defendant nearly 80 years of age. No children were born to these parties. . . .

The plaintiff testified that she was a dutiful and obedient wife, worked and saved, and cohabited with the defendant until the last 2 or 3 years. She worked in the fields, did outside chores, cooked, and attended to her household duties such as cleaning the house and doing the washing. For a number of years she raised as high as 300 chickens, sold poultry and eggs, and used the money to buy clothing, things she wanted, and for groceries. She further testified that the defendant was the boss of the house and his word was law; that he would not tolerate any charge accounts and would not inform her as to his finances or business; and that he was a poor companion. . . . On several occasions the plaintiff asked the defendant for money. He would give her very small amounts, and for the last 3 or 4 years he had not given her any money nor provided her with clothing, except a coat about 4 years previous. . . . The defendant had not taken her to a motion picture show during the past 12 years. . . .

For the past 4 years or more, the defendant had not given the plaintiff money to purchase furniture or other household necessities. Three years ago he did purchase an electric, wood-and-cob combination stove which was installed in the kitchen, also linoleum floor covering for the kitchen. [T]he house is not equipped with a bathroom, bathing facilities, or inside toilet [or kitchen sink]. Hard and soft water is obtained from a well and cistern. She has a mechanical Servel refrigerator, and the house is equipped with electricity. . . . She had requested a new furnace but the defendant believed the one they had to be satisfactory. She related that the furniture was old and she would like to replenish it, [that] one of her daughters was good about furnishing her clothing, at least a dress a year, or sometimes two; that the defendant owns a 1929 Ford coupe equipped with a heater which is not efficient, and on the average of every 2 weeks he drives the plaintiff to Wayne to visit her mother; and that he also owns a 1927 Chevrolet pickup which is used for different purposes on the farm. The plaintiff was privileged to use all of the rent money she wanted to from the 80-acre farm, and when she goes to see her daughters, which is not frequent, she uses part of the rent money for that purpose, the defendant providing no funds for such use. . . . At the present time the plaintiff is not able to raise chickens and sell eggs. [P]laintiff has had three abdominal operations for which the defendant has paid. [P]laintiff further testified that [the] telephone was restricted [because] defendant did not desire that she make long distance calls. . . .

It appears that the defendant owns 398 acres of land with 2 acres deeded to a church, the land being of the value of $83,960; that he has bank deposits in the sum of $12,786.81 and government bonds in the amount of $104,500; and that his income, including interest on the bonds and rental for his real estate, is $8,000 or $9,000 a year. . . .

[Defendant appeals, alleging that the decree is not supported by sufficient evidence and is contrary to law.] While there is an allegation in the plaintiff's petition to the effect that the defendant was guilty of extreme cruelty towards the plaintiff, and also an allegation requesting a restraining order be entered against the defendant for fear he might molest plaintiff or take other action detrimental to her rights, the plaintiff made no attempt to prove these allegations and the fact that she continued to live with the defendant is quite incompatible with the same.

The plaintiff relies upon the following cases. [In] Earle v. Earle, 43 N.W. 118 (Neb. 1889), [t]he defendant sent his wife away from him, did not permit her to return, [and] later refused and ceased to provide for her support and the support of his child. The wife instituted a suit in equity against her husband for maintenance and support without a prayer for divorce or from bed and board. The question presented was whether or not the wife should be compelled to resort to a proceeding for a divorce, which she did not desire to do, or from bed and board. . . . [A]t the present time there is no statute governing this matter. The court stated that it was a well-established rule of law that it is the duty of the husband to provide his family with support and means of living—the style of support, requisite lodging, food, clothing, etc., to be such as fit his means, position, and station in life—and for this purpose the wife has generally the right to use his credit for the purchase of necessaries. The court held that if a wife is abandoned by her husband, without means of support, a bill in equity will lie to compel the husband to support the wife without asking for a decree of divorce. . . .

In the case of Brewer v. Brewer, 113 N.W. 161 (Neb. 1907), the plaintiff lived with her husband and his mother. The mother dominated the household. The plaintiff went to her mother. . . . The court held that a wife may bring a suit in equity to secure support and alimony without reference to whether the action is for divorce or not; that every wife is entitled to a home corresponding to the circumstances and condition of her husband over which she may be permitted to preside as mistress; and that she does not forfeit her right to maintenance by refusing to live under the control of the husband's mother. . . .

In the instant case the marital relation has continued for more than 33 years, and the wife has been supported in the same manner during this time without complaint on her part. The parties have not been separated or living apart from each other at any time. In the light of the cited cases it is clear, especially so in this jurisdiction, that to maintain an action such as the one at bar, the parties must be separated or living apart from each other.

The living standards of a family are a matter of concern to the household, and not for the courts to determine, even though the husband's attitude toward his wife, according to his wealth and circumstances, leaves little to be said in his behalf. As long as the home is maintained and the parties are living as husband and wife it may be said that the husband is legally supporting his wife and the purpose of the marriage relation is being carried out. Public policy requires such a holding. It appears that the plaintiff is not devoid of money in her own right. She has a fair sized bank account and is entitled to use the rent from the 80 acres of land left by her first husband, if she so chooses. [Reversed.]

One source of marital difficulty in *McGuire* was the husband's neglect of his role of "good provider." The excerpt below explores the development of this gender-based role and its consequences.

Jessie Bernard, The Good-Provider Role: Its Rise and Fall

36 Am. Psychol. 2 10 (1981)

. . . Webster's second edition defines the good provider as "one who provides, especially, colloq., one who provides food, clothing, etc. for his family; as, he is a good or an adequate provider." More simply, he could be defined as a man whose wife did not have to enter the labor force. . . .

The good provider as a specialized male role seems to have arisen in the transition from subsistence to market—especially money—economies that accelerated with the industrial revolution. The good-provider role for males emerged in this country roughly, say, from the 1830s, when de Tocqueville was observing it, to the late 1970s, when the 1980 census declared that a male was not automatically to be assumed to be head of household. This gives the role a life span of about a century and a half. Although relatively short-lived, while it lasted the role was a seemingly rock-like feature of the national landscape.

As a psychological and sociological phenomenon, the good-provider role had wide ramifications for all of our thinking about families. . . . It did not have good effects on women: The role deprived them of many chips by placing them in a peculiarly vulnerable position. Because she was not reimbursed for her contribution to the family in either products or services, a wife was stripped to a considerable extent of her access to cash-mediated markets. By discouraging labor force participation, it deprived many women, especially affluent ones, of opportunities to achieve strength and competence. It deterred young women from acquiring productive skills. They dedicated themselves instead to winning a good provider who would "take care" of them. . . .

. . . The good-provider role, as it came to be shaped [was] restricted in what it was called upon to provide. Emotional expressivity was not included in that role. One of the things a parent might say about a man to persuade a daughter to marry him, or a daughter might say to explain to her parents why she wanted to, was not that he was a gentle, loving, or tender man but that he was a good provider. He might have many other qualities, good or bad, but if a man was a good provider, everything else was either gravy or the price one had to pay for a good provider. . . . Loving attention and emotional involvement in the family were not part of a woman's implicit bargain with the good provider. . . .

. . . To be a man one had to be not only a provider but a *good* provider. Success in the good-provider role came in time to define masculinity itself. The good provider had to achieve, to win, to succeed, to dominate. He was a bread *winner*. . . . The good provider became a player in the male competitive macho game. What one man provided for his family in the way of luxury and display had to be equaled or topped by what another could provide. . . . The psychic costs could be high. . . .

[I]n an increasing number of cases the wife has begun to share this role. [T]he role-sharing wife now feels justified in making demands on [her husband]. [Two such demands are (1) greater intimacy, expressivity, and nurturance; and (2) more sharing of housework and childcare.] The good-provider role with all its prerogatives and perquisites has undergone profound changes. It will never be the same again. . . .

Postscript. Research confirms that fathers are adopting a more active role in family life. A new male ideal has emerged that subjects fathers to increasing social pressure to act as both engaged parents and equal partners in the division of labor. This new masculine ideal means that men now face the same competing demands in the workplace as women do.[19] Moreover, both women and men under age 40 appear to have similar aspirations of an egalitarian marriage, in which both partners share breadwinning, housekeeping, and child rearing.[20]

Surprisingly, more and more women are taking on the role of the primary breadwinner. Forty percent of households with children now include a mother who is either the sole or primary breadwinner.[21] More than one-third of these "breadwinner moms" are married mothers who earn higher incomes than their husbands; almost two-thirds of the "breadwinner moms" are single mothers.

---

[19]. Erin Rehel & Emily Baxter, Men, Fathers, and Work-Family Balance, Ctr. for Am. Progress, Feb. 4, 2015, https://www.americanprogress.org/issues/women/report/2015/02/04/105983/men-fathers-and-work-family-balance/

[20]. Kathleen Gerson, The Unfinished Revolution: Coming of Age in a New Era of Gender, Work, and Family (2010).

[21]. Wendy Wang et al., Pew Research Ctr., Social and Demographic Trends Project, Breadwinner Moms (2013), http://www.pewsocialtrends.org/2013/05/29/breadwinner-moms/.

Regrettably, however, the demise of the male good-provider role has taken a major toll on women because it has *not* resulted in an accompanying reallocation of the household division of labor. Married female primary breadwinners continue to take on a larger share of household work and childcare than their husbands.[22]

Notes and Questions

1. Doctrines of support and nonintervention. *McGuire* illustrates two doctrines. First, *McGuire* reflects the common law duty of support. At common law, a husband had a duty to provide support to his wife; the wife had a correlative duty to render domestic services. Second, the common law *doctrine of nonintervention* specifies that the state rarely will adjudicate spousal responsibilities in an ongoing marriage. Thus, marital support obligations are enforceable only *after* separation or divorce. This principle of family privacy stems from judicial reluctance to disrupt marital harmony or to interfere with the husband's authority.

Was there any marital harmony in the McGuires' marriage to disrupt? Should stereotypical rationale trump spousal welfare? Why do you think Mrs. McGuire did not seek a divorce instead of filing this lawsuit?

2. Necessaries doctrine. The common law *doctrine of necessaries* was the basis of the lower court opinion in Mrs. McGuire's favor. This doctrine imposed liability on a husband to a merchant who supplied necessary goods to a wife. "Necessaries" generally include food, clothing, shelter, and medical care. Case law sometimes extends the term's meaning. See, e.g., Shepard v. Moore, 83 Va. Cir. 377 (Va. Cir. 2011) (funeral expenses); In re Hofmann, 823 N.Y.S.2d 397 (App. Div. 2006) (legal fees).

Many American jurisdictions codified the common law duty of support of dependents via so-called family expense statutes, which render both spouses liable for the support of family members. Such statutes are broader than the common law doctrine (that is, applying to "family expenses" rather than merely "necessaries").

3. Third-party interests. Why should the state permit a creditor, but not a spouse, a remedy for support? Professor Marjorie Shultz argues that "the presence of third-party interests, even though minimal compared to the spouses' duties to one another, has been viewed as sufficient to allow disruption of the domestic harmony that could not be disturbed for the sake of resolving the spouses' own problems."[23] Further, Shultz points out, the necessaries doctrine encourages dealings with a creditor behind the back of the other spouse. Does this approach promote marital harmony?

4. Criticisms. Feminist commentators have been especially critical of the doctrine of nonintervention. Professors Nadine Taub and Elizabeth Schneider note:

---

[22]. Marianne Bertrand et al., Gender Identity and Relative Income Within Households, Nat'l Bureau of Econ. Res. (NBER) Working Paper No. 19023 (May 2013), http://www.nber.org/papers/w19023.

[23]. Marjorie Maguire Shultz, Contractual Ordering of Marriage: A New Model for State Policy, 70 Cal. L. Rev. 204, 238 (1982).

> The state's failure to regulate the domestic sphere is now often justified on the ground that the law should not interfere with emotional relationships involved in the family realm because it is too heavy-handed. Indeed, the recognition of a familial privacy right in the early twentieth century [Meyer v. Nebraska, 262 U.S. 390 (1923); Pierce v. Society of Sisters, 268 U.S. 510 (1925)] has given this rationale a constitutional dimension. . . .
>
> Isolating women in a sphere divorced from the legal order contributes directly to their inferior status by denying them the legal relief that they seek to improve their situations and by sanctioning conduct of the men who control their lives. . . . But beyond its direct, instrumental impact, the insulation of women's world from the legal order also conveys an important ideological message to the rest of society. Although this need not be the case in all societies, in our society the law's absence devalues women and their functions. . . .[24]

5. Equal protection problems. The gender-based common law necessaries doctrine poses equal protection problems. The issue has arisen when health care providers attempt to impose liability on a wife for services rendered prior to the husband's death. Most jurisdictions today, by statute or case law, impose a gender-neutral rule for interspousal liability for debts. See, e.g., Va. Code Ann. §55-37; St. Luke's Episcopal Presbyterian Hosp. v. Underwood, 957 S.W.2d 496 (Mo. Ct. App. 1997).

6. Civil and criminal remedies for nonsupport. What additional remedies might Mrs. McGuire have had? Civil remedies include suits for separate maintenance based either on statute or equity jurisdiction if the couple is living apart. Criminal remedies also exist in many states for nonsupport of a child and spouses. What purposes do criminal remedies serve? Would you advise Mrs. McGuire to pursue these?

Problem

During the course of their marriage, Wife pays for most household expenses, although Husband occasionally contributes to the utility and grocery bills. After 12 years of marriage, Wife informs Husband that she wants a divorce and asks him to leave. She informs him that she is removing him from her health insurance policy. Husband refuses to leave and makes no effort to secure his own coverage. Two years later, Wife files for divorce. They sign an agreement whereby each takes responsibility for his or her own debts. Two days later, Husband is admitted to the hospital with a terminal condition. He submits an outdated insurance card from Wife's policy. Finding it unnecessary to pursue the divorce, Wife instructs her attorney to dismiss the proceedings. Husband dies, leaving a hospital debt of $150,000. The hospital seeks to recover payment from Wife. The jurisdiction has a spousal liability statute providing that both spouses shall be liable "for all debts contracted for necessaries for themselves, one another, or their family during the marriage." What result? Queen's Medical Ctr. v. Kagawa, 967 P.2d 686 (Haw. Ct.

---

[24]. Nadine Taub & Elizabeth M. Schneider, Women's Subordination and the Role of Law, in The Politics of Law: A Progressive Critique 328, 333 (David Kairys ed., 1998).

App. 1998). See also Moses H. Cone Mem'l Hosp. Operating Corp. v. Hawley, 672 S.E.2d 742 (N.C. Ct. App. 2009).

NOTE: CONSTITUTIONAL LIMITS ON SEX-STEREOTYPED ROLE ASSIGNMENTS

Marriage has been described as "the vehicle through which the apparatus of the state can shape the gender order."[25] Constitutional law once reflected the common law's prescription of appropriate gender roles for husbands and wives. In the late nineteenth and early twentieth century, the Supreme Court upheld discrimination against women in employment based on the "separate spheres doctrine" (that is, women occupy the private sphere of home and family while men occupy the public arena of work and politics). Thus, for example, the Court upheld rules barring married women from the practice of law (Bradwell v. Illinois, 83 U.S. (16 Wall.) 130 (1873)) and laws giving working women special legislation to protect them in their childbearing capacity (Muller v. Oregon, 208 U.S. 412 (1908)).

The women's movement in the 1960s triggered major reform in constitutional doctrine. In 1971, the Supreme Court first held that sex discrimination violated the Fourteenth Amendment's Equal Protection Clause. In Reed v. Reed, 404 U.S. 71 (1971), the Court invalidated an Idaho law that gave preference to men over women as administrators of intestate estates. The Court reasoned that the statute, which was based on stereotypical gender roles, lacked a rational basis. *Reed* heralded the beginning of an era of equal protection challenges to sex-based legislation.

The Court announced the applicable level of constitutional scrutiny for gender-based distinctions in Craig v. Boren, 429 U.S. 190 (1976), a challenge to the constitutionality of an Oklahoma statute proscribing different ages for men and women to drink beer. The Court applied an intermediate standard of review, maintaining that the classification must serve *important* governmental objectives and must be *substantially* related to achievement of those objectives. This standard, although lower than the strict scrutiny applied to race discrimination ("necessary to a compelling state interest"), was higher than the rational basis test ("rationally related to a legitimate governmental objective") applied to most social legislation. The Supreme Court later elevated the standard of review slightly and now requires an "exceedingly persuasive justification" for gender classifications. United States v. Virginia, 518 U.S. 515 (1996). Note that some *states* go further, applying strict scrutiny to gender-based classifications (e.g., Sail'er Inn v. Kirby, 485 P.2d 529 (Cal. 1971)).

Over the years, the Court has wrestled with the meaning of "equal treatment" for men and women in many different contexts. Cases invalidated gender-based distinctions between widows and widowers in terms of government benefits and, thereby, rejected the gender-based assumption that the husband was the breadwinner and the wife the dependent. See, e.g., Califano v. Goldfarb, 430 U.S. 199 (1977); Weinberger v. Wiesenfeld, 420 U.S. 636 (1975); Frontiero v. Richardson, 411 U.S. 677 (1973). Outside the constitutional context, the Supreme Court has

---

[25]. Nancy F. Cott, Public Vows: A History of Marriage and the Nation 3 (2000).

embraced measures designed to dismantle traditional gender stereotypes. For example, reading the family care provisions of the Family and Medical Leave Act (FMLA)(discussed later in this chapter) as an antidiscrimination measure, the Court has approved this legislative effort to combat "[s]tereotypes about women's domestic roles [and] parallel stereotypes presuming a lack of domestic responsibilities for men." Nevada Dept. of Human Res. v. Hibbs, 538 U.S. 721, 736 (2003). The Court has had far more difficulty applying equal protection when confronted with classifications that it interpreted to reflect "real" differences, however. See Michael M. v. Superior Court, 450 U.S. 464, 469 (1981) (stating that the Court has upheld gender classifications that "realistically reflect[] the fact that the sexes are not similarly situated in certain circumstances").

Our abstract standard of equality, based on the Aristotelian notion, guarantees that likes (that is, "those similarly situated") will be treated alike. But how does one treat women like men in the face of biological differences? And should men provide the norm? Difficulties arose particularly in the Court's treatment of pregnancy. Further, the Court's preference for analyzing cases about reproduction under the Fourteenth Amendment's Due Process Clause ("privacy") left this strand of equal protection doctrine incomplete.[26] In other cases, the Court treated socially imposed differences (for example, the male as aggressor) as biological differences to justify differential treatment. Thus, despite disclaimers, the Court relied on gender-based stereotypes to exclude women from combat (Rostker v. Goldberg, 453 U.S. 57 (1981)) and certain employment (for example, prison guards) (Dothard v. Rawlinson, 433 U.S. 321 (1977)), and to uphold criminal laws applicable to only one sex (for example, statutory rape laws) (*Michael M.*, supra).

The same-sex marriage debate prompted renewed examination of the Supreme Court's jurisprudence on gender equality. In fact, some marriage equality advocates contend that the exclusion of same-sex couples from marriage reflected stereotypical understandings of the different marital roles of men and women that were previously condemned by the Supreme Court.[27]

4. Names in the Family

NEAL v. NEAL

941 S.W.2d 501 (Mo. 1997)

COVINGTON, Judge.

. . . Melissa J. Neal and Bruce L. Neal were married on September 10, 1994. They separated in February 1995. [Wife filed a petition for dissolution in March.] On July 16, 1995, Wife gave birth to the parties' child, a son. On the birth certificate she denominated her maiden name, Gintz, as the child's surname. She did not include the name of Husband on the birth certificate. The parties were

---

[26]. See Sylvia A. Law, Rethinking Sex and the Constitution, 132 U. Pa. L. Rev. 955, 1007 (1984).

[27]. See, e.g., Cary Franklin, The Anti-Stereotyping Principle in Constitutional Sex Discrimination Law, 85 N.Y.U. L. Rev. 83 (2010).

divorced by a decree of dissolution filed on September 14, 1995. [After making orders for custody, visitation, and support], [t]he court also ordered correction of the Certificate of Live Birth to reflect that Husband is the natural father of the minor child and ordered the surname of the minor child changed to Neal. Wife appealed. . . .

The first issue is Wife's claim of trial court error in refusing to restore her maiden name. Matter of Natale, 527 S.W.2d 402 (Mo. App. 1975), controls disposition of the issue. . . . In that case, Judith Natale, with her husband's consent, petitioned pursuant to section 527.270, RSMo 1969, and Rule 95.01 to have her maiden name restored. She desired to change her name for purposes of professional and personal identity and convenience to her husband and herself in carrying out their professional careers. The trial court denied the petition for change of name. The trial court's refusal was based upon the fact that the petitioner was lawfully married and residing with her legal spouse. Under such circumstances, the trial court reasoned, the granting of the petition could be detrimental to others in the future.

In reversing the judgment, the court of appeals provided historical background of the common law right to change of name, regardless of marital status. The court noted that the common law and statutory methods of changing names coexist for the reason that no constitutional or statutory mandate has invalidated the common law. The court of appeals found that, although it is within the trial court's discretion to find a change of name to be detrimental, the scope of discretion in the trial court to deny a petition for change of name is narrow, even within the marital relationship.

Following the teachings of *Natale,* the court of appeals in Miller v. Miller, 670 S.W.2d 591 (Mo. App. 1984), addressed precisely the issue presented here, a request pursuant to a dissolution proceeding that wife's maiden name be restored. Because there were two children born to Mr. and Mrs. Miller, the trial court refused to change Mrs. Miller's name. As the court of appeals stated in reversing the trial court, no law presumes that it is detrimental for a child to have a name that is different from the parent. A general concern of possible detriment is insufficient to deny a petition for change of name in light of the obvious legislative intent that such a procedure be available, and by reason of the teachings of *Natale.*

In the present case, the trial court provided no reason for its declination to order restoration of Wife's maiden name. There is no substantial evidence to support the trial court's decision. . . . Under the teachings of *Natale* and *Miller,* the trial court erred in refusing to restore Wife's maiden name. . . .

Wife next contends the trial court erred in granting Husband's request to change the child's name to Neal, Husband's surname. Wife attacks the trial court's decision on abuse of discretion grounds; however, there is a threshold issue that must be decided. . . .

To hold that the trial court in a dissolution proceeding has authority to change the name of a minor child does not, however, confer upon the trial court authority to change a child's name in the absence of proper procedure. Proper procedure first requires that notice be given by the party seeking to have the child's name changed. Notice is required because in changing a child's name, the trial court's discretion is guided by a determination of what is in the best interests of the child. . . .

In the present case, there was no notice to Wife of Husband's intent to change the name of the minor child. . . . Because the trial court erred in granting Husband's request to change the child's name to Neal for the reasons stated above, it is unnecessary to reach the question of whether there was sufficient evidence in the record to prove that the name change was in the best interest of the child. . . . .

Does state regulation of naming children treat men and women differently?

HENNE v. WRIGHT

904 F.2d 1208 (8th Cir. 1990)

BRIGHT, Senior Circuit Judge.

. . . Plaintiffs brought this action under 42 U.S.C. §1983 individually and as next friends to their daughters alleging that Neb. Rev. Stat. §71-640.01 (1986) unconstitutionally infringes their fundamental Fourteenth Amendment right to choose surnames for their daughters. . . .

On April 4, 1985, Debra Henne gave birth to Alicia Renee Henne at a hospital in Lincoln, Nebraska. Following Alicia's birth, Debra completed a birth certificate form at the request of a hospital employee. Debra listed Gary Brinton as the father and entered the name Alicia Renee Brinton in the space provided for the child's name. Brinton, also present at the hospital, completed and signed a paternity form.

At the time of the birth, Debra was still married to Robert Henne. Although Debra and Robert Henne had filed for a divorce prior to Alicia's birth, the decree dissolving the marriage did not become final until after the birth. As a result of her marital status, hospital personnel, acting on instructions from the Department of Health, informed Debra that she could not surname her daughter "Brinton." Debra then filled out a second birth certificate form, entering the child's name as Alicia Renee Henne and leaving blank the space provided for the father's name. Robert Henne has never claimed to be Alicia's father and, pursuant to the divorce decree, pays no child support for her.

[O]n February 4, 1988, Debra Henne went in person to the Bureau of Vital Statistics of the Nebraska Department of Health and requested that Alicia's surname be changed to Brinton and that Gary Brinton be listed on the birth certificate as the father. . . . She also presented a signed acknowledgement of paternity from Gary Brinton and a letter from him requesting that the birth certificate be changed. [Officials at the Bureau of Vital Statistics denied Debra's request.]

. . . On June 17, 1988, at St. Elizabeth's Hospital in Lincoln, Nebraska, Linda Spidell gave birth to a daughter, Quintessa Martha Spidell. Linda wished to give Quintessa the surname "McKenzie," the same surname as her other two children, who were born in California. Hospital personnel, acting upon instructions from the Department of Health, informed Linda that Quintessa could not be surnamed McKenzie and that if Linda did not complete the birth certificate form the hospital would enter Quintessa's last name as Spidell. Linda completed the form, entering "Spidell" as Quintessa's surname and leaving blank the space provided for the father's name.

Linda surnamed her other children McKenzie simply because she liked that name and not because of any familial connection. For that reason, and because she wishes all three children to share the same name, she wants Quintessa surnamed McKenzie. Linda was not married at the time of Quintessa's birth or at the time of this action and there has been no judicial determination of paternity. At trial, however, both Linda and Ray Duffer, who lives with Linda and her children, testified that Duffer is Quintessa's biological father. . . .

This case presents the issue whether a parent has a fundamental right to give a child a surname at birth with which the child has no legally established parental connection. We frame the issue this way because each plaintiff wishes to enter on her daughter's birth certificate a surname proscribed by section 71-640.01. . . .

We now turn to the question whether the right at issue is fundamental. A long line of Supreme Court cases have established that "liberty" under the Fourteenth Amendment encompasses a right of personal privacy to make certain decisions free from intrusive governmental regulation absent compelling justification [citing Zablocki v. Redhail; Moore v. City of East Cleveland; Roe v. Wade; and Loving v. Virginia]. Two of the earliest right to privacy cases, Meyer v. Nebraska, 262 U.S. 390 (1923), and Pierce v. Society of Sisters, 268 U.S. 510 (1925), established the existence of a fundamental right to make child rearing decisions free from unwarranted governmental intrusion. *Meyer* and *Pierce* do not, however, establish an absolute parental right to make decisions relating to children free from government regulation.

In determining whether a right not enumerated in the Constitution qualifies as fundamental, we ask whether the right is "deeply rooted in this Nation's history and tradition". . . . While *Meyer* and *Pierce* extended constitutional protection to parental decisions relating to child rearing, the parental rights recognized in those cases centered primarily around the training and education of children. . . . By contrast, the parental decision in this case relates to the choice of a child's surname. This subject possesses little, if any, inherent resemblance to the parental rights of training and education recognized by *Meyer* and *Pierce*. [Thus] constitutional protection for the right to choose a non-parental surname at birth must flow, if at all, from an extension of *Meyer* and *Pierce*. Furthermore, any logical extension of *Meyer* and *Pierce* has to be grounded in the tradition and history of this nation. Given this standard, we necessarily conclude that plaintiffs have presented no fundamental right.

The custom in this country has always been that a child born in lawful wedlock receives the surname of the father at birth, and that a child born out of wedlock receives the surname of the mother at birth. While some married parents now may wish to give their children the surname of the mother or a hyphenated surname consisting of both parents' surname, and some unmarried mothers may wish to give their children the surname of the father, we can find no American tradition to support the extension of the right of privacy to cover the right of a parent to give a child a surname with which that child has no legally recognized parental connection. Plaintiffs therefore have not asserted a right that is fundamental under the Fourteenth Amendment right of privacy, and Neb. Rev. Stat. §71-640.01 need only rationally further legitimate state interests to withstand constitutional scrutiny. . . .

[T]he law rationally furthers at least three legitimate state interests: the state's interest in promoting the welfare of children, the state's interest in insuring that the names of its citizens are not appropriated for improper purposes and the state's interest in inexpensive and efficient record keeping. Specifically, a reasonable legislature could believe that in most cases a child's welfare is served by bearing a surname possessing a connection with at least one legally verifiable parent. Furthermore, the legislature could reasonably perceive that in the absence of a law such as section 71-640.01, the name of a non-parent could be improperly appropriated to achieve a deliberately misleading purpose, such as the creation of a false implication of paternity. Finally, the legislature could reasonably conclude that it is easier and cheaper to verify and index the birth records of a person who has a surname in common with at least one legally verifiable parent. . . . Although the Nebraska legislature could perhaps tailor the statute to more closely serve these purposes, we cannot say that section 71-640.01 bears no rational relationship to the state's legitimate interests. . . .

ARNOLD, Circuit Judge, concurring in part and dissenting in part.

. . . I respectfully dissent. The fundamental right of privacy, in my view, includes the right of parents to name their own children, and the State has shown no interest on the facts of these cases sufficiently compelling to override that right. . . .

[F]amily matters, including decisions relating to child rearing and marriage, are on almost everyone's list of fundamental rights. The right to name one's child seems to me, if anything, more personal and intimate, less likely to affect people outside the family, than the right to send the child to a private school, or to have the child learn German. We know, moreover, from Roe v. Wade, 410 U.S. 113 (1973), that these women had a fundamental right to prevent their children from being born in the first place. It is a bizarre rule of law indeed that says they cannot name the children once they are born. If there was ever a case of the greater including the less, this ought to be it. . . .

Notes and Questions

1. Name retention. The feminist movement highlighted the impact of marital surname changes on a woman's identity. At common law, adoption of the husband's surname was a custom rather than a legal requirement. Early litigation focused on married women's right to have their birth name (formerly "maiden name") entered on voting records, automobile registration, and drivers' licenses. Currently, all states recognize a woman's right to retain her birth name upon marriage.

2. Empirical data. The number of women choosing to retain their birth names increased dramatically from the 1980s to 1990s (rising from 1 to 23 percent), but declined in the 2000s.[28] The practice is again on the upswing, although

[28]. Stephanie Pappas, Most Modern Wives Still Take Husband's Name (Nov. 1, 2011), http://www.livescience.com/16813-women-husband.html. On trends in marital name changes, see Suzanne A. Kim, Marital Naming/Naming Marriage: Language and Status in Family Law, 85 Indiana L.J. 893, 910-914 (2010).

the current reasons for women's surname retention are different.[29] What do you think explains the change? What factors influence the name change decision? What surname choices are available to spouses? What are the advantages and disadvantages of each choice?

3. Methods of name change. Two methods of name change exist: the common law method of consistent nonfraudulent use and a statutorily prescribed judicial procedure. Most women change their name upon marriage by the first method. Married women who elect to change their names must alter their driver's licenses, vehicle titles, voter registrations, passports, bank records, credit cards, medical records, insurance forms, wills, contracts, Social Security card, and Internal Revenue Service forms. Given the complications of name change, would a requirement of *name retention* be less confusing, less onerous, and pose less risk of fraud to creditors?

4. Postdivorce name resumption. Statutes often provide for a married woman to restore her birth name upon divorce. As *Neal* illustrates, early cases wrestled with whether the denial of the wife's request could rest on possible detriment to children from having a different last name. Should courts take this factor into account? Cf. Cal. Fam. Code §2081 (restoration of surname shall not be denied "(a) on the basis that the party has custody of a minor child who bears a different name or (b) for any other reason other than fraud"). In *Neal,* the wife failed to secure her husband's consent to restore her surname. Is a wife required to do so? Should judges have complete discretion to grant or deny a name change?

5. Men's surnames upon marriage. Men occasionally adopt wives' surnames or adopt hyphenated or blended surnames. Few statutes provide for men's right to change their names at marriage; fewer still provide for their postdivorce name resumption.

6. Name change: Contemporary contexts.

a. Same-sex couples. In the past, members of same-sex couples have faced difficulties changing partners' surnames. Often they were compelled to use the standard formal procedure requiring a judicial hearing and publication. Increasingly, however, jurisdictions are more receptive to name change requests by same-sex partners. See, e.g., Cal. Fam. Code §306.5.

b. Transgender persons. Transgender persons have encountered problems changing their name and gender on legal documents. States have refused such requests absent medical proof of gender conforming surgery. Currently, some states permit issuance of new birth certificates with name and gender changes merely upon proof of "clinically appropriate treatment" (i.e., adherence to transitioning guidelines) without requiring gender-conforming surgery. See, e.g., Cal. Health & Safety Code §103425. Gender can be changed on Social Security records

---

[29]. Claire Cain Miller & Derek Willis, Maiden Names on the Rise Again, N.Y. Times, June 28, 2015, at ST1. See also Upshot Staff, Readers' Turn: The Nuisances of a Marriage Name Decision, N.Y. Times, June 30, 2015, http://www.nytimes.com/2015/07/01/upshot/readers-turn-the-nuisances-of-a-marriage-name-decision.html?em_pos=small&emc=edit_up_20150630&nl=upshot&nlid=59943788&ref=headline&abt=0002&abg=0.

based on proof of government-issued documentation reflecting the gender change or a physician's confirmation that the person has undergone appropriate clinical treatment for gender transition.

c. Victims of domestic violence. Victims of domestic violence sometimes change their names in an effort to hide from abusers. Statutes that require the publication of name-change requests pose the risk of disclosure of the new identity. Some state laws address this problem by sealing records of a name change and providing that publication may be waived in cases of threats to safety. See, e.g., N.M. Stat. Ann. §40-8-2(B); Wash. Rev. Code §4.24.130(5).

7. Children's surnames.

a. Nonmarital children. What assumptions about naming do the rules in *Henne* reflect? Traditionally, children born in wedlock are given their father's surname. In response to the women's movement, however, statutes give parents the right to choose the father's surname, the mother's birth surname, or a hyphenated surname for a child. Nonmarital children, historically, took the mother's surname absent the father's consent or a judicial determination of paternity.

b. Standards to resolve disagreements. Currently, in name disputes between parents, courts resort to one of three standards: a custodial parent presumption, a presumption favoring the status quo, or a test to determine the best interests of the child. The best interests approach is followed by a majority of jurisdictions. See Emma v. Evans, 71 A.3d 862 (N.J. 2013).

How relevant are the following factors in the best interests determination: the child's preference, effect of the name change on parent-child relationships, length of time the child used the surname, identification of the child as part of a family unit, social difficulties the child might encounter, and the presence of parental misconduct or neglect (such as failure to maintain contact or provide support)? Is the mother's surname postdivorce relevant in the determination of the child's surname? See Foster v. Foster, 802 N.W.2d 755 (Minn. Ct. App. 2011).

What other factors might be relevant? How applicable are the above factors for an infant or toddler? Should the relevant standard apply regardless of the parents' marital status? Should third parties have standing to object to the child's proposed surname change? See In re Adoption of Jon L., 625 S.E.2d 251 (W. Va. 2005).

c. Same-sex parents and birth certificates. Same-sex couples have faced challenges in state recognition of both partners as parents on such documents as children's hospital records, birth certificates, and death certificates.[30] See, e.g., Gartner v. Iowa Dept. of Pub. Health, 830 N.W.2d 335 (Iowa 2013) (ordering issuance of birth certificate listing both lesbian mothers). See generally Nancy D. Polikoff, The New "Illegitimacy": Winning Backward in the Protection of the Children of Lesbian Couples, 20 Am. U. J. Gender Soc. Pol'y & L. 721 (2012).

---

[30]. A plaintiff-couple in *Obergefell* experienced a similar problem when a hospital nurse refused to allow the second mother to consent to her infant's treatment during an emergency without contacting the birth mother. Stories of Love, Life, Death in High Court Gay Marriage Case, N.Y. Times, Apr. 16, 2015, http://www.nytimes.com/aponline/2015/04/16/us/politics/ap-us-supreme-court-gay-marriage-the-plaintiffs.html?_r=0.

8. Paternal bias. To what extent do *Neal* and *Henne* show that the law of surnames reflects Blackstone's regime, with its connotation of men's property interests in their wives and children? Some cases continue to adhere to this view. See, e.g., Rice v. Merkich, 34 So. 3d 555 (Miss. 2010) (party must establish that child's best interests dictate that surname not be that of the father).

9. Constitutional issues. The *Henne* majority determines that the right to choose a child's surname is not "fundamental." Do you agree that this parental decision "possesses little, if any, inherent resemblance to the parental rights of training and education recognized by *Meyer* and *Pierce*"? See generally Carlton F.W. Larson, Naming Baby: The Constitutional Dimensions of Parental Naming Rights, 80 Geo. Wash. L. Rev. 159 (2011).

10. Policy. Should the state regulate name changes or defer to personal autonomy? Should the state encourage gender-neutral choices based on public policy concerns through the selection of a default rule? See generally Elizabeth F. Emens, Changing Name Changing: Framing Rules and the Future of Marital Names, 74 U. Chi. L. Rev. 761 (2007).

11. International perspectives. Some countries have quite different customs and regulations about names. For example, Latin American and Spanish customs use a two-part surname representing both parents' lineage. Some countries require governmental approval of a child's name. For example, Germany has an approved list of names and limits the number of first names and hyphenated surnames. The European Union (EU) also regulates surnames. How do other countries resolve children's surname disputes? For example, in China, authorities draw lots to decide between parents' choices.[31] What do you think of these various rules?

Problems

1. When Lisa and Robb Stratton divorced, the court awarded custody of their daughters (Lana, age 13, and Cara, age 16) to Lisa and visitation to Robb. Robb has not participated in the girls' lives for the past six years because he chooses to avoid family conflicts and to not jeopardize his tenuous bonds with his daughters. He pays child support and health insurance premiums. When Lisa remarried, she and the girls began using her new husband's surname, Kelley. To enable Cara to obtain a driver's license, Lisa filed a petition to change the children's surname from Stratton to Kelley. Robb objected, arguing that his surname is the girls' last link to his family and that it should not be severed merely on the grounds of convenience. What result? In re Stratton ex rel. Kelley, 90 P.3d 566 (Okla. Civ. App. 2003).

Suppose, instead, that when Lisa remarried, she wanted Lana and Cara to bear a hyphenated name that includes the surnames of both fathers. However, Robb

---

[31]. Nicholas Kulish, High Court in Germany Pops Names That Balloon, N.Y. Times, May 6, 2009, at A6; Surname Disputes to Be Settled by Lots, China Post, May 10, 2008, available at 2008 WLNR 8788276. For international perspectives on marital surname regulation, see Heather MacClintock, Sexism, Surnames, and Social Progress: The Conflict of Individual Autonomy and Government Preferences in Laws Regarding Name Changes at Marriage, 24 Temp. Int'l & Comp. L.J. 277 (2010).

wants the girls to retain his surname, contending that it is in their best interests for traditional reasons and to promote their self-identification. What result? In re Eberhardt, 920 N.Y.S.2d 216 (App. Div. 2011).

2. A married couple, Barbara and John Smith, who are each the fifth child in their respective families, decide to call their newborn son by the name of "5 + 5." They agree to call him "5" for short. When Barbara attempts to enter that name on the birth certificate, hospital personnel (on instructions from the Department of Health) inform Barbara that she cannot do so based on a state statute that limits the choice of a child's surname to that of the mother's birth name, father's surname, or a combination of the two. What arguments would you make on Barbara's and John's behalf? See In re Ritchie III, 206 Cal. Rptr. 239 (Ct. App. 1984) (name change request to "III"); In re Change of Name of Ravitch, 754 A.2d 1287 (Pa. Super. Ct. 2000) (name change request to "R").

Suppose, instead, that Barbara and John want to give their son the name "Adolf Hitler." Can (should) hospital personnel and/or state authorities reject the name? See Lisa W. Foderaro, Naming Children for Nazis Puts Spotlight on the Father, N.Y. Times, Jan. 19, 2009, at A28.

5. Employment

BRADWELL v. ILLINOIS

83 U.S. (16 Wall.) 130 (1873)

Myra Bradwell (1870), one of the first women lawyers

[Mrs. Myra Bradwell, a resident of Illinois, applied to the Illinois State Supreme Court for a license to practice law. Accompanying her petition was the requisite certificate attesting to her good character and qualifications. The Supreme Court of Illinois denied her application. The United States Supreme Court affirmed. Justice Bradley's concurring opinion below is a classic statement of separate spheres ideology.]

Mr. Justice BRADLEY [joined by Justices SWAYNE and FIELD], concurring: . . .

. . . The Supreme Court of Illinois denied the application on the ground that [the legislature] had simply provided that no person should be admitted to practice as attorney or counsellor without having previously obtained a license for that purpose from two justices of the Supreme Court, and that no person should receive a license without first obtaining a certificate from the court of some county of his good moral character. In other respects it was left to the discretion of the court to establish the rules by which admission to the profession should be determined. The court, however, regarded itself as bound by at least two limitations. One was that it should establish such terms of admission as would promote the proper administration of justice, and the other that it should not admit any persons, or class of persons, not intended by the legislature to be admitted, even though not expressly excluded by statute. In view of this latter limitation the court felt compelled to deny the application of females to be admitted as members of the bar. Being contrary to the rules of the common law and the usages of Westminster Hall from time immemorial, it could not be supposed that the legislature had intended to adopt any different rule.

The claim . . . under the Fourteenth Amendment of the Constitution, which declares that no State shall make or enforce any law which shall abridge the privileges and immunities of citizens of the United States . . . assumes that it is one of the privileges and immunities of women as citizens to engage in any and every profession, occupation, or employment in civil life.

It certainly cannot be affirmed, as an historical fact, that this has ever been established as one of the fundamental privileges and immunities of the sex. On the contrary, the civil law, as well as nature herself, has always recognized a wide difference in the respective spheres and destinies of man and woman. Man is, or should be, woman's protector and defender. The natural and proper timidity and delicacy which belongs to the female sex evidently unfits it for many of the occupations of civil life. The constitution of the family organization, which is founded in the divine ordinance, as well as in the nature of things, indicates the domestic sphere as that which properly belongs to the domain and functions of womanhood. The harmony, not to say identity, of interest and views which belong, or should belong, to the family institution is repugnant to the idea of a woman adopting a distinct and independent career from that of her husband. So firmly fixed was this sentiment in the founders of the common law that it became a maxim of that system of jurisprudence that a woman had no legal existence separate from her husband, who was regarded as her head and representative in the social state; and, notwithstanding some recent modifications of this civil status, many of the special rules of law flowing from and dependent upon this cardinal principle still exist in full force in most States. One of these is that a married woman is incapable, without her husband's consent, of making contracts which shall be binding on her or him. This very incapacity was one circumstance which the Supreme Court of Illinois deemed important in rendering a married woman incompetent fully to perform the duties and trusts that belong to the office of an attorney and counsellor.

It is true that many women are unmarried and not affected by any of the duties, complications, and incapacities arising out of the married state, but these are exceptions to the general rule. The paramount destiny and mission of woman are to fulfill the noble and benign offices of wife and mother. This is the law of the Creator. And the rules of civil society must be adapted to the general constitution of things, and cannot be based upon exceptional cases. . . .

Notes and Questions

1. **Holding.** The Illinois Supreme Court denied Mrs. Bradwell's application to the bar, in part, based on *married* women's inability to contract. Why, then, could *unmarried* women not practice law?

2. Equal protection. The Supreme Court determined that *admission* to the bar was a matter reserved to the states and not one of the privileges and immunities belonging to citizens. Thus, the Court found inapplicable the privilege and immunities guarantees of both Article IV and the Fourteenth Amendment. In so doing, the Court failed to consider the applicability of the Equal Protection Clause. When the Fourteenth Amendment was ratified in 1868, it engrafted the word "male" in the Constitution for the first time, causing considerable concern to nineteenth-century feminists. The Equal Protection Clause was not applied to invalidate gender-based discrimination until Reed v. Reed, 404 U.S. 71 (1971).

3. Separate spheres ideology. What authority does Justice Bradley cite in his concurrence to support his recognition of women's separate spheres? What is the danger of relying on history when considering the expansion of constitutional rights? See Aviam Soifer, Complacency and Constitutional Law, 42 Ohio St. L.J. 383, 409 (1981) ("To settle for the constitutionalization of the status quo is to bequeath a petrified forest.").

Early cases denying women admission to the bar rested on legal and social rationales that were directed at married women in particular, as the following article reveals.

D. Kelly Weisberg, Barred from the Bar: Women and Legal Education in the United States 1870-1890

28 J. Legal Educ. 485, 488-493 (1977)

One of the paramount concerns of any skilled profession is the regulation of access to the profession. As Chroust has pointed out, in colonial America any person desiring to be admitted to the legal profession had four major avenues of entry. He might, by his own efforts and through self-directed reading and study, acquire whatever scraps of legal information were available in books, statutes, or reports; he could work in the clerk's office of some court of record; he could serve as an apprentice or clerk in the law library of a reputable lawyer, preferably one with a law library; or he could enter one of the four Inns of Court in London and receive there the "call to the bar."

Chroust's use of the masculine pronoun above is not entirely without significance. "Any" person in colonial America did have four avenues of legal education open to him, provided that that person was male. The first hundred years of American legal education were characterized by a glaring absence of woman lawyers. . . .

The struggle for women to gain entrance to the legal profession began in the late 1860's with Ada Kepley the first woman to graduate from the Union College of Law (now Northwestern) in 1870 and Arabella Mansfield the first woman to be admitted to the bar of any state (Iowa, 1869). However, the battle was by no means over; in reality it had just begun.

Scarcely two months after Arabella Mansfield was admitted to the Iowa bar, Myra Bradwell passed an examination for the Chicago bar, but the Illinois

Supreme Court refused to grant her a license to practice law on the grounds of her sex. [In] the United States Supreme Court, she was once again unsuccessful. In other landmark cases, Lavinia Goodell was refused admission to the Wisconsin bar in 1875, Lelia Josephine Robinson was refused admission to the bar of Massachusetts in 1881, and Belva Lockwood [was] still refused admission to the Virginia bar in the 1890's because of her sex.

Even after the turn of the century, when women were admitted to the bar of almost every state, the battle continued for women's admission to law school. Columbia University first admitted women law students in 1929, Harvard University in 1950 (although women had first applied to Harvard in the 1870s), the University of Notre Dame in 1969, and the last male bastion Washington and Lee University in 1972. . . .

[A] common rationale utilized to bar women from the legal profession was the argument that the impediments growing out of women's legal status at the common law prevented them from gaining access to the profession. [T]he most serious common law disability which would interfere with women practicing law, or so women's opponents maintained, concerned married women's inability to contract.

This legal rationale was based on the fact that married women at this time were disqualified from entering into contracts with third persons without their husband's consent. In both the *Bradwell* and *Lockwood* decisions, it was held that because of this disability at common law, married women could not be permitted to gain admission to the bar. . . .

[Another] social rationale utilized to bar women from the legal profession centered on woman's traditional role in the family. The professional role of the lawyer was seen to be in direct conflict with the traditional roles of woman as wife and mother. In both the *Bradwell* and *Goodell* decisions, the judges delivered a lengthy discourse on woman's "sphere." The proper sphere for woman, they maintained, citing by way of authority the law of nature and the law of the Creator, was in the home. . . .

Woman's traditional role conflicted with the professional role of lawyer in terms of the divergent sets of priorities of the role sets. The socially approved role for woman as wife and mother had duties associated with it which were expected to be woman's first and primary obligation, superseding any other claim. For the lawyer, obviously, his occupation was intended to be his first priority. Or, as Justice Ryan had asserted in *Goodell*: "The profession enters largely into the wellbeing of society; and to be honorably filled and safely to society, exacts the devotion of life." . . . The requisite personality attributes of the lawyer, moreover, were seen as incompatible with those necessary for the role of wife and mother. The lawyer was supposed to be aggressive—a skilled combatant in the juridical conflicts of the courtroom. Woman was seen as nurturant, gentle, tender. In short, she possessed personality attributes required for the fulfillment of the role of wife and mother. . . .

. . . For the single woman who was not engaged in fulfilling the role of "her destiny," the law was still not to be considered as a possible occupation. The court in *Goodell* had this to say:

> The cruel chances of life sometimes baffle both sexes, and may leave women free from the peculiar duties of their sex. These may need employment. . . . But

it is public policy to provide for the sex, not for its superfluous members; and not to tempt women from the proper duties of their sex by opening to them duties peculiar to ours. There are many employments in life not unfit for female character. The profession of law is surely not one of these. [In re Goodell, 39 Wis. 232, 244-245 (Wis. 1875).]

The single woman, thus, was free to enter some other occupation to provide for herself. The legal profession, women's opponents stoutly maintained, should remain forever barred both to her and to her married sisters. . . .

NOTE: MARRIED WOMAN'S DOMICILE

Domicile is, essentially, a person's legal home. The law of the state of domicile is relevant to determination of marriage validity, the award of a divorce, custody, adoption, tax liability, probate and guardianship, as well as the right to vote, to hold and run for public office, to receive state benefits, or to qualify for tuition benefits at state colleges and universities.

Domicile requires two elements: presence plus intent to remain. A "domicile of choice" is acquired by persons who have legal capacity. A "domicile by operation of law" is assigned to those without legal capacity—traditionally, a category that included married women. At common law, the fiction of marital unity led to the assignment to a married woman of her husband's legal domicile. The Restatement of Conflict of Laws reflected this rule.[32]

The common law rule caused married women hardship and inconvenience. The rule began to change in the 1970s. "The harshness of the common law rule [first] became apparent in the field of divorce."[33] Constitutional challenges contributed to the rule's demise.[34] Finally, in 1988, the American Law Institute (ALI) revised the Restatement of Conflict of Laws to confer upon married women the ability to acquire a domicile of choice.[35] Case law now recognizes that neither spouse has a paramount right to select the marital domicile.[36] For a challenge to the entire concept of domicile, based on family life and family law today, see Susan Frelich Appleton, Leaving Home? Domicile, Family, and Gender, 47 UC Davis L. Rev. 1453 (2014).

---

[32]. Restatement of Conflict of Laws §§26, 27, 30, 40 (1934). Only a wife living apart from her husband but not guilty of desertion could have a separate domicile. Id. §38.

[33]. Restatement (Second) of Conflict of Laws §28 cmt. a (Tent. Draft No. 2, 1954).

[34]. See, e.g., Samuel v. University of Pittsburgh, 375 F. Supp. 1119 (W.D. Pa. 1974), *decision to decertify class vacated*, 538 F.2d 991 (3d Cir. 1976) (invalidating, on equal protection grounds, university residency rules that assign husband's domicile to the wife for determination of tuition).

[35]. Restatement (Second) of Conflict of Laws §21 ("rules for the acquisition of a domicile of choice are the same for both married and unmarried persons").

[36]. See Szumanski v. Szumanska, 611 N.Y.S.2d 737 (Sup. Ct. 1994) (wife's refusal to join husband does not constitute abandonment for divorce purposes because each spouse has the same right to choose a domicile).

VAUGHN v. LAWRENCEBURG POWER SYSTEM

269 F.3d 703 (6th Cir. 2001)

BOGGS, Circuit Judge.

Plaintiffs Keith Vaughn and Jennifer Vaughn, former employees of defendant Lawrenceburg Power System (LPS), filed an action in Tennessee state court alleging that their terminations [violated their rights] pursuant to 42 U.S.C. §1983, and under the Tennessee Human Rights Act (THRA), Tenn. Code Ann. §4-21-101 et seq. Specifically, the Vaughns objected to LPS's "anti-nepotism" policy, which requires the resignation of one spouse in the event two employees marry. . . .

Keith Vaughn began work for LPS in 1987, and has worked there in several capacities [including maintaining grounds and buildings] over a ten-year period. [Jennifer Vaughn] began working at LPS while in high school, and after her graduation in 1996, started a full-time job as a cashier. [I]n September 1997, they became engaged. Unfortunately for the Vaughns, their marriage was against power system policy. The "employment of relatives" or "anti-nepotism" portion of the LPS manual, which it is undisputed that both Vaughns received, reads as follows:

> It is the policy of the System to employ only one member of a family. No immediate relatives of employees, officers, members of the city governing body, by blood, marriage or adoption, shall be employed for permanent positions. . . . For purposes of this policy, said relatives are as follows: Spouse, parent, child, brother, sister, grandparent, grandchild, son-in-law, daughter-in-law, father-in-law, mother-in-law, brother-in-law, and sister-in-law. *When two employees working for the Lawrenceburg Power system are subsequently married, one must terminate employment.* (Emphasis added.)

The Vaughns ran afoul of the second part of this section forbidding marriages within the system, which may be termed LPS's rule of "exogamy."

It soon became common knowledge that the Vaughns were to be married. . . . Over the course of that autumn, [LPS Superintendent Ronald Cato] met with the Vaughns several times to inform them of the policy and to request that they decide which one of them was going to leave LPS. Cato told them he would need a decision before the marriage took place; he also told them that if they remained unmarried and merely lived together, there would be no problem with the exogamy rule. The Vaughns were reluctant to pursue this option, in large part because Jennifer had become pregnant that fall with Keith's son, who was born the following July.

The Vaughns disagreed with the policy's applicability to their situation. Mr. Vaughn knew of three other groups of relatives working at LPS, two brother-in-law/sister-in-law dyads, and a father-in-law/son-in-law pair. Keith Vaughn interpreted the overall anti-nepotism policy as being contravened by the presence of these related co-workers. He states that he so informed Michael Meek, the Administrative Services Manager, who Vaughn claims told him that the other employees were "grandfathered in." . . . Despite urging from Cato, neither of the Vaughns indicated they would resign. Instead, they took their case to a meeting of the Power Board in mid-December 1998, where Keith argued he should be "treated like everybody else." The Power Board was not convinced by the

Vaughns' interpretation, apparently distinguishing between the first part of the employment of relatives policy, which does not mandate termination, and the second part, the exogamy rule dealing specifically with employee intermarriage, which does. The Board also refused to change the rule or make an exception. . . .

Jennifer and Keith's wedding day was January 16, 1998. Keith had met with Cato the previous day and said "okay" in response to Cato's request for a decision. But Keith did not then tell Cato whether he or Jennifer would leave LPS. When the couple arrived back from their honeymoon, they found a letter suspending both of them for a minimum of two weeks, until February 9, 1998 (or until they reached a decision). . . . On February 6, 1998, Keith Vaughn met with Ron Cato and told him the couple planned to have Keith, who was paid more than Jennifer, continue working at LPS while Jennifer resigned. . . . The following Monday, February 9, Keith Vaughn, but not Jennifer Vaughn, arrived at LPS at 8 a.m. to begin work. Cato called Vaughn [into his office]. Fifteen to thirty minutes later, when Vaughn left Cato's office, he had been fired [presumably because the couple did not provide their employer with the requested letter of resignation from Jennifer]. . . .

[In response,] the Vaughns filed a lawsuit [alleging] violations of 42 U.S.C. §1983 based on "the fundamental right of marriage and freedom of association." . . .

We must first decide at what "level of scrutiny" to evaluate the challenged provision in the LPS manual. In order to trigger heightened constitutional scrutiny, the challenged portion of the anti-nepotism policy, the exogamy rule requiring termination of employment, must be shown to place "a 'direct and substantial' burden on the right of marriage." Our analysis of the case law . . . indicated that we would find direct and substantial burdens only where a large portion of those affected by the rule are absolutely or largely prevented from marrying, or where those affected by the rule are absolutely or largely prevented from marrying a large portion of the otherwise eligible population of spouses.

[T]he essential fact [is] that the policy did not bar Jennifer or Keith from getting married, nor did it prevent them marrying a large portion of population even in Lawrence County. It only made it economically burdensome to marry a small number of those eligible individuals, their fellow employees at LPS. Once Jennifer and Keith decided to marry one another, LPS's policy became onerous for them, but ex ante, it did not greatly restrict their freedom to marry or whom to marry. As a consequence, the exogamy rule in itself must be considered a non-oppressive burden on the right to marry, and so subject only to rational basis review. . . .

. . . LPS asserts that its rule exists to (1) prevent one employee from assuming the role of "spokesperson" for both, (2) to avoid involving or angering a second employee when an employee is reprimanded, (3) and to avoid marital strife or fraternization in the workplace. [A] government employer may have a legitimate concern about the inherent loyalty that one spouse will show to another, making discipline more difficult. Therefore, we conclude LPS has demonstrated its exogamy rule advances a legitimate governmental interest.

The Vaughns claim that the rule, even if advancing a legitimate interest, is an unreasonable means of doing so. They point out that the rule does not affect those willing merely to cohabitate (which in their case would have also involved the bearing of an out-of-wedlock child); the Vaughns note that cohabitating couples may well show a similar degree of loyalty and create the same problems the rule seeks to avoid. . . . There is, no doubt, wide variation in the nature and intensity of the relationships one finds among both married and unmarried couples. Yet there is good reason to believe that the level of commitment signified by marriage—and its attendant legal, moral, and financial obligations—marks those relationships in which, on average, there is likely to be intense loyalty. Whatever the situation may be, de facto, married and unmarried couples are not the same de jure; the law treats them differently, and LPS may do so as well.

The Vaughns raise a better argument by noting again that the consequences to them are inherently more severe than those affecting the couple in [Montgomery v. Carr, 101 F.3d 1117 (6th Cir. 1996) where the antinepotism policy required one spouse to transfer]. Here, both the Vaughns were terminated, and the policy mandated this for, at least, one of them. . . . In response, LPS points out that they simply do not have the option of having a transfer policy, because LPS is an operation of only 50 to 70 employees. . . .

Keith Vaughn claimed [also] to have been terminated in violation [of the Tennessee Human Rights Act]. An employee-at-will generally may not be discharged for attempting to exercise a statutory or constitutional right or for other reasons that violate a clear public policy evidenced by an unambiguous constitutional, statutory or regulatory provision. [T]he Tennessee Human Rights Act prevents "discrimination because of race, creed, color, religion, sex, age or national origin." Tenn. Code Ann. §4-21-101. The Act also "makes it a discriminatory practice to retaliate against a person because such person has opposed a practice declared discriminatory by" the Act. Tenn. Code Ann. §4-21-301. It is this latter "opposition" provision that has been asserted by the Vaughns. As the defendant points out, however, this provision is integrally connected to the types of discrimination the THRA has specifically forbidden. Tennessee has not included marital status in its list of forbidden employment classifications, and without an unambiguous provision, it is unlikely that a Tennessee court would abrogate its employment-at-will doctrine. . . . Keith Vaughn's claim under THRA was properly dismissed. . . .

Notes and Questions

1. **Historical background.** Derived from the Latin word for "nephew," the word *nepotism* was coined during the Middle Ages to describe Pope Calixtus III's appointment of his unqualified nephews as cardinals.[37]

2. **"No-spouse rules."** Some antinepotism policies limit employment specifically of "spouses." Other policies also apply to "close relatives." Policies generally prohibit hiring, employment in the same department, and/or supervision of work. Antinepotism rules create severe hardship in small communities and narrow specialties where the lack of alternatives may make one spouse unemployable. Do female employees disproportionately bear the burden of the no-spouse rule? If so, why?

[37]. Joan G. Wexler, Husbands and Wives: The Uneasy Case for Antinepotism Rules, 62 B.U. L. Rev. 75, 75 (1982). Some "nephews" may actually have been the pope's illegitimate sons. Id. at 75 n.3.

3. Business rationale. Antinepotism policies attempt to ensure that unqualified relatives are not hired. Yet, paradoxically, they ban qualified relatives from being hired as well. The following arguments support antinepotism policies: Spouses bring quarrels to work; they advance their own interests, leading to complaints of favoritism; and their employment promotes dual absenteeism because both partners want the same vacation or shifts.

Opposing arguments include: The best candidate should not be passed over (or fired) simply because of being married to an employee; the willingness to hire couples enables employers to hire a "star"; personnel benefits for employee-spouses are less costly; no-spouse restrictions violate public policy by encouraging cohabitation; and no-spouse policies discriminate against female employees. What do you think of these rationales—both in general and as applied to the plaintiffs in the principal case?

4. Causes of action. Federal and state grounds exist to challenge antinepotism rules.

a. Constitutional challenges—marriage is a fundamental right. This cause of action is available only to public employees because constitutional limitations do not apply to private employers. To date, challenges on this ground (such as *Vaughn*) have not been successful. When might a no-spouse rule "directly and substantially" interfere with the right to marry?

b. Title VII. Title VII of the Civil Rights Act of 1964, 42 U.S.C. §2000e-2(a)(1), has provided another avenue of attack on antinepotism policies. Title VII prohibits discrimination in the workplace based on race, color, religion, sex, or national origin (*but not marital status*). Claims may be based on either disparate treatment (that is, express classifications) or disparate impact. Most antinepotism litigation under Title VII is based on the latter, challenging policies that do not facially distinguish between employees but, in practice, adversely affect a particular class of employees. For example, note that in *Vaughn*, Jennifer planned to resign because Keith earned more money. Given that women on average earn less than men, no-spouse rules might result in the loss of a wife's job more often than her husband's. However, an employer in a disparate impact action may successfully defend by showing that the policy was justified (for example, by business necessity).

c. State civil rights statutes. In contrast to Title VII, some *state* civil rights statutes prohibit discrimination based on marital status. Why weren't the Vaughns successful under their state statute? Cases often turn on the interpretation of the term "marital status." Some jurisdictions apply the term broadly to include the identity of the spouse, while others limit it to only the status of being married, single, divorced, or widowed. Compare Minn. Stat. §363A.03 ("identity, situation, actions, or beliefs of a spouse or former spouse"), with Wowkun v. Closter Bd. of Educ., 2005 WL 1252398 (N.J. Super. Ch. Ct. 2005) (restrictive definition). This distinction also arises when an employee claims marital status discrimination if termination occurs because of an employer's hostility toward an employee's spouse. See, e.g., Donato v. AT&T, 767 So. 2d 1146 (Fla. 2000).

5. Empirical data. How common is romance in the workplace? Studies report that from 38 to 59 percent of employees admit they have dated a co-worker.[38] Moreover, attitudes toward office romance are becoming more liberal.[39] Few companies have formal prohibitions on dating co-workers. Should they?

6. Policy. Do no-dating policies in the workplace constitute employment discrimination? See McCavitt v. Swiss Reinsurance Am. Corp., 237 F.3d 166 (2d Cir. 2001). Should employers impose their code of morality outside the office? Are antinepotism policies out of sync with the modern workplace, or should workplace romances be regulated because they create a hostile work environment for *other* employees? See Miller v. Department of Corr., 30 Cal. Rptr. 3d 797, 802 (Cal. 2005).

7. Lawyer-spouses. Marriage between lawyers sometimes poses ethical problems. Does the possibility of breaches of confidentiality, conflicts of interest, and the appearance of impropriety require a per se rule barring lawyer-spouses from representing clients with adverse interests? If so, should the disqualification extend to other lawyers in their firms? Formerly, the ABA's Model Rules of Professional Conduct, Rule 1.8(I), provided for automatic disqualification of lawyer-spouses (as well as some relatives), absent consent and disclosure. In 2000, the ABA deleted the automatic disqualification policy and recharacterized such representation as a conflict of interest. However, because it constitutes a "*personal interest* conflict," according to the Model Rules, the conflict will not ordinarily be imputed to other members of a firm under Rule 1.10 ("Imputation of Conflicts"), provided that it does not present a "significant risk of materially limiting the representation of the client by the remaining lawyers in the firm" (Rule 1.10(a)).

Problems

1. Jim and Coleen are state troopers in the same squad in a small Illinois town. Their district is patrolled by three one-person squads (each person patrols in a separate car). The squads rotate every eight hours. Jim and Coleen decide to marry. When they notify their supervisor, he informs them of an unwritten policy that prohibits spouses from working on the same shift in the patrol area. Jim and Coleen could remain in the same patrol area on different shifts, or one could transfer to a different patrol area and work the same shift. Jim chooses the latter. After their marriage, they challenge the no-spouse policy under state law, which prohibits workplace discrimination based on marital status (defined as "the legal status of being married, single, separated, divorced, or widowed"). What result? See Boaden v. Department of Law Enforcement, 664 N.E.2d 61 (Ill. 1996).

---

[38]. Susan Adams, Behind the Numbers of Office Romance in 2012, Forbes, Feb. 14, 2012, http://today.msnbc.msn.com/id/46368364/ns/today-money/t/behind-numbers-office-romance/#.T_9yb5HlfK1.

[39]. Rieva Lesonsky, Office Romances on the Rise Among Millennial Employees: Survey Says, Huffington Post, Apr. 9, 2012 (reporting that 84 percent of workers from age 18-29 report their willingness to engage in a romantic relationship with a co-worker, compared to 36 percent of those age 30-46 and 29 percent of those age 47-66), http://www.huffingtonpost.com/2012/04/09/office-romances-on-the-rise-among-millennial-employees_n_1412190.html.

2. Some employers are addressing workplace romances by means of "love contracts"—a required document signed by employees in a dating relationship that declares the consensual nature of their relationship and their agreement to adhere to appropriate workplace behavior. As general counsel for a corporation, you have been asked to draft a "love contract" policy. Draft an opinion as to the scope of the policy, likely effectiveness, and advantages/disadvantages in comparison to an antinepotism policy.

6. Parenting

a. Pregnancy Leave

CLEVELAND BOARD OF EDUCATION v. LaFLEUR

414 U.S. 632 (1974)

Mr. Justice STEWART delivered the opinion of the Court. . . .

Jo Carol LaFleur and Ann Elizabeth Nelson . . . are junior high school teachers employed by the Board of Education of Cleveland, Ohio. Pursuant to a rule first adopted in 1952, the school board requires every pregnant school teacher to take maternity leave without pay, beginning five months before the expected birth of her child. . . . The teacher on maternity leave is not promised re-employment after the birth of the child; she is merely given priority in reassignment to a position for which she is qualified. Failure to comply with the mandatory maternity leave provisions is ground for dismissal.

Neither Mrs. LaFleur nor Mrs. Nelson wished to take an unpaid maternity leave; each wanted to continue teaching until the end of the school year.[2] Because of the mandatory maternity leave rule, however, each was required to leave her job in March 1971. The two women then filed separate suits. . . .

[Another petitioner,] Susan Cohen, was employed by the School Board of Chesterfield County, Virginia. That school board's maternity leave regulation requires that a pregnant teacher leave work at least four months prior to the expected birth of her child. [The teacher is] re-eligible for employment when she submits written notice from a physician that she is physically fit for re-employment, and when she can give assurance that care of the child will cause only minimal interference with her job responsibilities. The teacher is guaranteed re-employment no later than the first day of the school year following the date upon which she is declared re-eligible.

[Mrs. Cohen, who expected her baby around April 28, 1971] initially requested that she be permitted to continue teaching until April 1, 1971. The school board rejected the request, as it did Mrs. Cohen's subsequent suggestion that she be allowed to teach until January 21, 1971, the end of the first school

---

2. Mrs. LaFleur's child was born on July 28, 1971; Mrs. Nelson's child was born during August of that year.

semester. Instead, she was required to leave her teaching job on December 18, 1970. She subsequently filed this suit under 42 U.S.C. §1983. . . . We granted certiorari in both cases, in order to resolve the conflict between the Courts of Appeals regarding the constitutionality of such mandatory maternity leave rules for public school teachers.[8]

This Court has long recognized that freedom of personal choice in matters of marriage and family life is one of the liberties protected by the Due Process Clause of the Fourteenth Amendment. As we noted in Eisenstadt v. Baird, 405 U.S. 438, 453 [1972], there is a right "to be free from unwarranted governmental intrusion into matters so fundamentally affecting a person as the decision whether to bear or beget a child."

By acting to penalize the pregnant teacher for deciding to bear a child, overly restrictive maternity leave regulations can constitute a heavy burden on the exercise of these protected freedoms. Because public school maternity leave rules directly affect "one of the basic civil rights of man," the Due Process Clause of the Fourteenth Amendment requires that such rules must not needlessly, arbitrarily, or capriciously impinge upon this vital area of a teacher's constitutional liberty. The question before us in these cases is whether the interests advanced in support of the rules of the Cleveland and Chesterfield County School Boards can justify the particular procedures they have adopted.

The school boards in these cases have offered two essentially overlapping explanations for their mandatory maternity leave rules. First, they contend that the firm cutoff dates are necessary to maintain continuity of classroom instruction, since advance knowledge of when a pregnant teacher must leave facilitates the finding and hiring of a qualified substitute. Secondly, the school boards seek to justify their maternity rules by arguing that at least some teachers become physically incapable of adequately performing certain of their duties during the latter part of pregnancy. By keeping the pregnant teacher out of the classroom during these final months, the maternity leave rules are said to protect the health of the teacher and her unborn child, while at the same time assuring that students have a physically capable instructor in the classroom at all times.[9]

8. . . . The practical impact of our decision in the present cases may have been somewhat lessened by several recent developments. At the time that the teachers in these cases were placed on maternity leave, Title VII . . . did not apply to state agencies and educational institutions. On March 24, 1972, however, the Equal Employment Opportunity Act of 1972 amended Title VII to withdraw those exemptions. Shortly thereafter, the Equal Employment Opportunity Commission promulgated guidelines providing that a mandatory leave or termination policy for pregnant women presumptively violates Title VII. While the statutory amendments and the administrative regulations are, of course, inapplicable to the cases now before us, they will affect like suits in the future. . . .

9. The records in these cases suggest that the maternity leave regulations may have originally been inspired by other, less weighty, considerations. For example, Dr. Mark C. Schinnerer, who served as Superintendent of Schools in Cleveland at the time the leave rule was adopted, testified in the District Court that the rule had been adopted in part to save pregnant teachers from embarrassment at the hands of giggling schoolchildren; the cutoff date at the end of the fourth month was chosen because this was when the teacher "began to show." Similarly, at least several members of the Chesterfield County School Board thought a mandatory leave rule was justified in order to insulate schoolchildren from the sight of conspicuously pregnant women. . . . The school boards have not contended in this Court that these considerations can serve as a legitimate basis for a rule requiring pregnant women to leave work; we thus note the comments only to illustrate the possible role of outmoded taboos in the adoption of the rules.

It cannot be denied that continuity of instruction is a significant and legitimate educational goal. [W]hile the advance-notice provisions in the Cleveland and Chesterfield County rules are wholly rational and may well be necessary to serve the objective of continuity of instruction, the absolute requirements of termination at the end of the fourth or fifth month of pregnancy are not. Were continuity the only goal, cutoff dates much later during pregnancy would serve as well as or better than the challenged rules, providing that ample advance notice requirements were retained. Indeed, continuity would seem just as well attained if the teacher herself were allowed to choose the date upon which to commence her leave, at least so long as the decision were required to be made and notice given of it well in advance of the date selected.

In fact, since the fifth or sixth month of pregnancy will obviously begin at different times in the school year for different teachers, the present Cleveland and Chesterfield County rules may serve to hinder attainment of the very continuity objectives that they are purportedly designed to promote. For example, the beginning of the fifth month of pregnancy for both Mrs. LaFleur and Mrs. Nelson occurred during March of 1971. Both were thus required to leave work with only a few months left in the school year, even though both were fully willing to serve through the end of the term. Similarly, if continuity were the only goal, it seems ironic that the Chesterfield County rule forced Mrs. Cohen to leave work in mid-December 1970 rather than at the end of the semester in January, as she requested.

We thus conclude that the arbitrary cutoff dates embodied in the mandatory leave rules before us have no rational relationship to the valid state interest of preserving continuity of instruction. As long as the teachers are required to give substantial advance notice of their condition, the choice of firm dates later in pregnancy would serve the boards' objectives just as well, while imposing a far lesser burden on the women's exercise of constitutionally protected freedom.

The question remains as to whether the cutoff dates at the beginning of the fifth and sixth months can be justified on the other ground advanced by the school boards—the necessity of keeping physically unfit teachers out of the classroom. There can be no doubt that such an objective is perfectly legitimate, both on educational and safety grounds. . . .

The mandatory termination provisions of the Cleveland and Chesterfield County rules surely operate to insulate the classroom from the presence of potentially incapacitated pregnant teachers. But the question is whether the rules sweep too broadly. That question must be answered in the affirmative, for the provisions amount to a conclusive presumption that every pregnant teacher who reaches the fifth or sixth month of pregnancy is physically incapable of continuing. There is no individualized determination by the teacher's doctor—or the school board's—as to any particular teacher's ability to continue at her job. [T]he Due Process Clause requires a more individualized determination.

. . . While the medical experts in these cases differed on many points, they unanimously agreed on one—the ability of any particular pregnant woman to continue at work past any fixed time in her pregnancy is very much an individual matter. Even assuming, arguendo, that there are some women who would be physically unable to work past the particular cut-off dates embodied in the challenged rules, it is evident that there are large numbers of teachers who are fully capable of continuing work for longer than the Cleveland and Chesterfield County regulations will allow. Thus, the conclusive presumption embodied in these rules . . . is neither "necessarily (nor) universally true," and is violative of the Due Process Clause.

The school boards have argued that the mandatory termination dates serve the interest of administrative convenience, since there are many instances of teacher pregnancy, and the rules obviate the necessity for case-by-case determinations. Certainly, the boards have an interest in devising prompt and efficient procedures to achieve their legitimate objectives in this area. . . . While it might be easier for the school boards to conclusively presume that all pregnant women are unfit to teach past the fourth or fifth month or even the first month, of pregnancy, administrative convenience alone is insufficient to make valid what otherwise is a violation of due process of law.[13] The Fourteenth Amendment requires the school boards to employ alternative administrative means, which do not so broadly infringe upon basic constitutional liberty, in support of their legitimate goals. . . .

In addition to the mandatory termination provisions, both the Cleveland and Chesterfield County rules contain limitations upon a teacher's eligibility to return to work after giving birth. Again, the school boards offer two justifications for the return rules—continuity of instruction and the desire to be certain that the teacher is physically competent when she returns to work. As is the case with the leave provisions, the question is not whether the school board's goals are legitimate, but rather whether the particular means chosen to achieve those objectives unduly infringe upon the teacher's constitutional liberty. . . .

The respondents . . . do not seriously challenge either the medical requirements of the Cleveland rule or the policy of limiting eligibility to return to the next semester following birth. The provisions concerning a medical certificate or supplemental physical examination are narrowly drawn methods of protecting the school board's interest in teacher fitness; these requirements allow an individualized decision as to the teacher's condition, and thus avoid the pitfalls of the presumptions inherent in the leave rules. Similarly, the provision limiting eligibility to return to the semester following delivery is a precisely drawn means of serving the school board's interest in avoiding unnecessary changes in classroom personnel during any one school term.

The Cleveland rule, however, [requires] the mother to wait until her child reaches the age of three months before the return rules begin to operate. The school board has offered no reasonable justification for this supplemental limitation, and we can perceive none. To the extent that the three-month provision reflects the school board's thinking that no mother is fit to return until that point in time, it suffers from the same constitutional deficiencies that plague the

---

13. This is not to say that the only means for providing appropriate protection for the rights of pregnant teachers is an individualized determination in each case and in every circumstance. We are not dealing in these cases with maternity leave regulations requiring a termination of employment at some firm date during the last few weeks of pregnancy. We therefore have no occasion to decide whether such regulations might be justified by considerations not presented in these records—for example, widespread medical consensus about the "disabling" effect of pregnancy on a teacher's job performance during these latter days, or evidence showing that such firm cutoffs were the only reasonable method of avoiding the possibility of labor beginning while some teacher was in the classroom, or proof that adequate substitutes could not be procured without at least some minimal lead time and certainty as to the dates upon which their employment was to begin.

irrebuttable presumption in the termination rules. The presumption, moreover, is patently unnecessary, since the requirement of a physician's certificate or a medical examination fully protects the school's interests in this regard. And finally, the three-month provision simply has nothing to do with continuity of instruction, since the precise point at which the child will reach the relevant age will obviously occur at a different point throughout the school year for each teacher.

Thus, we conclude that the Cleveland return rule, insofar as it embodies the three-month age provision, is wholly arbitrary and irrational, and hence violates the Due Process Clause of the Fourteenth Amendment. The age limitation serves no legitimate state interest, and unnecessarily penalizes the female teacher for asserting her right to bear children. . . .

We perceive no such constitutional infirmities in the Chesterfield County rule. In that school system, the teacher becomes eligible for re-employment upon submission of a medical certificate from her physician; return to work is guaranteed no later than the beginning of the next school year following the eligibility determination. The medical certificate is both a reasonable and narrow method of protecting the school board's interest in teacher fitness, while the possible deferring of return until the next school year serves the goal of preserving continuity of instruction. . . .

Jo Carol LaFleur, "Go Home and Have Your Baby"

in The Courage of Their Convictions 320-328 (Peter Irons ed., 1988)

Jo Carol LaFleur (now Jo Carol Nesset-Sale), the former high school teacher who challenged maternity leave laws

I learned around January of 1971 that I was pregnant, with the child due to be born around the end of July. Teaching out the school year made perfect sense to me. . . . I thought I was actually contributing, partly by being a good role model [being] a married woman, having a baby, going to a doctor, getting good care. . . . Little did I know that you could not teach in the Cleveland schools past the fourth month of pregnancy.

[The principal, Mr. Wilkins, called Ms. LaFleur to his office about the first of March.] Mr. Wilkins said, "I understand you're having a baby in August. . . . You've got to go on maternity leave; you've got to fill out your papers." I said, "I don't have to do that, because I'm not leaving. I'm just going to teach until the end of the year." He said, "You can't do that; we have rules." I said, "My baby isn't scheduled to be born until the summer. I just want to teach school. This class that you just put me in has already lost one teacher. And I teach students who are pregnant." . . . He said, "You're a good teacher. I'm not going to fire you, but you've got to take this leave." Mr. Wilkins filled out the maternity leave papers for me, because I wouldn't fill them out. . . . I couldn't believe that anybody would yank from an inner-city school a person who was specially trained to teach there and who *wanted* to teach. . . .

[Ms. LaFleur then asked the teachers' union for help.] The union leader, who was a man, said, "Oh, Mrs. LaFleur, just go home and have your baby." . . . It was clear the union had no interest or sympathy whatever. [Later, she called the Women's Equity Action League, who referred her to a constitutional law professor, Jane Picker.]

Mr. Wilkins had given me a deadline to leave—near the end of March. . . . Jane tried to get an injunction in the federal court against the schools, to prevent them from barring me from my class. This district court judge, whose name was Connell—elderly, in his seventies—said at the injunction hearing, "Mrs. LaFleur will get exactly what she deserves, and she doesn't deserve an injunction." Since we knew he was the trial judge, Jane said, "This doesn't bode well. . . ."

. . . The school board put on a doctor, a male obstetrician, whose testimony I found really annoying. He was talking about all of the horrible complications that were possible with pregnancy, like placenta previa. There was absolutely *no* data that showed that the act of teaching made it more likely that you would have one of these conditions. . . . It was almost hilarious, in a very pathetic sense, listening to testimony about all of the possible complications of pregnancy. It's a wonder women *ever* have babies, if all of these horrible things happen. . . . The week before my son was born, I played nine holes of golf and I played a set of tennis. The only thing I didn't do was jump the net. . . .

[After losing, she appealed to the Sixth Circuit Court of Appeals and prevailed. The Supreme Court granted certiorari.] I remember Justice Blackmun asking the question of Jane Picker [at oral argument], whether she really saw any difference between a man losing his job because he refuses to shave his beard, and a woman losing her job because she's pregnant. And she stood up there, and she put her hands on both hips and she said, "Your Honor, that analogy is ludicrous. Simply *ludicrous.* What's the remedy for a man? You shave! For a woman it's abortion, to get rid of the problem. It's a little different, Your Honor." And I could see her husband at counsel table, with his head in his hands—"Jane, you shouldn't *say* such things." But Blackmun voted for us. . . .

. . . I remember the day the decision came down. I was teaching a social studies class [with a guest speaker], and we were discussing death and dying. . . . I got called out of the class for a telephone call from a radio station that wanted my opinion on the decision. . . . I called Jane's office. They said, "The only thing we know is that you won." . . .

I went running back to my class, doing these *jetés,* these giant leaps down the hall. I went into my class and I calmed down, and I said, "Mr. Smith, could I have just one moment? I need to tell the class something." They knew I had been waiting every day. "*We won!* Thank you, please resume." He doesn't know what's going on. The kids are screaming, "*All right!*" . . .

Looking back, I'm not quite sure why I started my case. . . . When I got pregnant, I knew I wasn't sick. I knew I wasn't ill. How could a male-dominated school system say to me, Even though you're not ill, and pregnancy is a perfectly normal condition, you are unfit to teach. The fundamental unfairness of it seemed morally wrong, not just stupid but wrong. . . .

Postscript. Jo Carol LaFleur (now Jo Carol Nesset-Sale) later attended the University of Utah Law School. For several years, she practiced criminal defense work, medical malpractice, and mediation. In 1994, she accepted a position at the University of Georgia Law School as assistant director of the Legal Aid Clinic. She later taught criminal law at a small Atlanta law school. Currently, she teaches on the faculty of Emory University School of Law in the Kessler-Eidson Trial Techniques Program.[40]

PREGNANCY DISCRIMINATION ACT OF 1978

The Pregnancy Discrimination Act of 1978 (PDA) amends, as follows, the definitional section of Title VII of the Civil Rights Act of 1964 that prohibits, inter alia, sex discrimination in employment:

> The terms "because of sex" or "on the basis of sex" include, but are not limited to, because of or on the basis of pregnancy, childbirth, or related medical conditions; and women affected by pregnancy, childbirth, or related medical conditions shall be treated the same for all employment-related purposes, including receipt of benefits under fringe benefit programs, as other persons not so affected but similar in their ability or inability to work. . . .

42 U.S.C. §2000e(k).

CALIFORNIA FEDERAL SAVINGS & LOAN ASSOCIATION v. GUERRA

479 U.S. 272 (1987)

Lillian Garland (the fired employee in California Federal Savings & Loan v. Guerra) and her daughter

Justice Marshall delivered the opinion of the Court.

The question presented is whether Title VII of the Civil Rights Act of 1964, as amended by the Pregnancy Discrimination Act of 1978, preempts a state statute that requires employers to provide leave and reinstatement to employees disabled by pregnancy.

California's Fair Employment and Housing Act (FEHA), Cal. Gov't Code Ann. §12900 et seq., is a comprehensive statute that prohibits discrimination in employment and housing. In September 1978, California amended the FEHA to proscribe certain forms of employment discrimination on the basis of pregnancy. Subdivision (b)(2)—the provision at issue here—is the only portion of the statute that applies to employers subject to Title VII. It requires these employers to provide

[40]. For an autobiographical account, see Jo Carol Nesset-Sale, From Sideline to Frontline: The Making of a Civil Rights Plaintiff—A Retrospective by the Plaintiff in Cleveland Board of Education v. LaFleur, A Landmark Pregnancy Discrimination Case, 7 Geo. J. Gender & L. 1 (2006).

female employees an unpaid pregnancy disability leave of up to four months. Respondent Fair Employment and Housing Commission, the state agency authorized to interpret the FEHA, has construed §12945(b)(2) to require California employers to reinstate an employee returning from such pregnancy leave to the job she previously held, unless it is no longer available due to business necessity. In the latter case, the employer must make a reasonable, good faith effort to place the employee in a substantially similar job. The statute does not compel employers to provide paid leave to pregnant employees. Accordingly, the only benefit pregnant workers actually derive from §12945(b)(2) is a qualified right to reinstatement.

Title VII of the Civil Rights Act of 1964, also prohibits various forms of employment discrimination, including discrimination on the basis of sex. However, in General Electric Co. v. Gilbert, 429 U.S. 125 (1976), this Court ruled that discrimination on the basis of pregnancy was not sex discrimination under Title VII. In response to the *Gilbert* decision, Congress passed the Pregnancy Discrimination Act of 1978 (PDA) [specifying] that sex discrimination includes discrimination on the basis of pregnancy.

Petitioner California Federal Savings and Loan Association (Cal. Fed.) is a federally chartered savings and loan association based in Los Angeles; it is an employer covered by both Title VII and §12945(b)(2). Cal. Fed. has a facially neutral leave policy that permits employees who have completed three months of service to take unpaid leaves of absence for a variety of reasons, including disability and pregnancy. Although it is Cal. Fed.'s policy to try to provide an employee taking unpaid leave with a similar position upon returning, Cal. Fed. expressly reserves the right to terminate an employee who has taken a leave of absence if a similar position is not available.

Lillian Garland was employed by Cal. Fed. as a receptionist for several years. In January 1982, she took a pregnancy disability leave. When she was able to return to work in April of that year, Garland notified Cal. Fed., but was informed that her job had been filled and that there were no receptionists or similar positions available. Garland filed a complaint with respondent Department of Fair Employment and Housing. . . . [Prior to the hearing before the Fair Housing and Employment Commission, Cal. Fed. brought this action seeking a declaration that §12945(b)(2) is inconsistent with, and preempted by, Title VII, and also an injunction against enforcement of the section.]

. . . In order to decide whether the California statute requires or permits employers to violate Title VII, as amended by the PDA, or is inconsistent with the purposes of the statute, we must determine whether the PDA prohibits the States from requiring employers to provide reinstatement to pregnant workers, regardless of their policy for disabled workers generally.

Petitioners argue that the language of the federal statute itself unambiguously rejects California's "special treatment" approach to pregnancy discrimination, thus rendering any resort to the legislative history unnecessary. They contend that the second clause of the PDA forbids an employer to treat pregnant employees any differently than other disabled employees. Because "[t]he purpose of Congress is the ultimate touchstone" of the preemption inquiry, however, we must examine the PDA's language against the background of its legislative history and historical context. . . .

By adding pregnancy to the definition of sex discrimination prohibited by Title VII, the first clause of the PDA reflects Congress' disapproval of the reasoning in *Gilbert* [holding that pregnancy discrimination was not sex discrimination]. Rather than imposing a limitation on the remedial purpose of the PDA, we believe that the second clause was intended to overrule the holding in *Gilbert* and to illustrate how discrimination against pregnancy is to be remedied. Accordingly, subject to certain limitations, we agree with the Court of Appeals' conclusion that Congress intended the PDA to be "a floor beneath which pregnancy disability benefits may not drop—not a ceiling above which they may not rise."

The context in which Congress considered the issue of pregnancy discrimination supports this view of the PDA. Congress had before it extensive evidence of discrimination against pregnancy, particularly in disability and health insurance like those challenged. . . . The reports, debates, and hearings make abundantly clear that Congress intended the PDA to provide relief for working women and to end discrimination against pregnant workers. In contrast to the thorough account of discrimination against pregnant workers, the legislative history is devoid of any discussion of preferential treatment of pregnancy, beyond acknowledgments of the existence of state statutes providing for such preferential treatment. Opposition to the PDA came from those concerned with the cost of including pregnancy in health and disability benefit plans and the application of the bill to abortion, not from those who favored special accommodation of pregnancy.

In support of their argument that the PDA prohibits employment practices that favor pregnant women, petitioners and several amici cite statements in the legislative history to the effect that the PDA does not *require* employers to extend any benefits to pregnant women that they do not already provide to other disabled employees. . . . On the contrary, if Congress had intended to *prohibit* preferential treatment, it would have been the height of understatement to say only that the legislation would not *require* such conduct. It is hardly conceivable that Congress would have extensively discussed only its intent not to require preferential treatment if in fact it had intended to prohibit such treatment.

We also find it significant that Congress was aware of state laws similar to California's but apparently did not consider them inconsistent with the PDA. . . . Title VII, as amended by the PDA, and California's pregnancy disability leave statute share a common goal. The purpose of Title VII is "to achieve equality of employment opportunities and remove barriers that have operated in the past to favor an identifiable group of . . . employees over other employees." Rather than limiting existing Title VII principles and objectives, the PDA extends them to cover pregnancy. As Senator Williams, a sponsor of the Act, stated: "The entire thrust . . . behind this legislation is to guarantee women the basic right to participate fully and equally in the workforce, without denying them the fundamental right to full participation in family life." 123 Cong. Rec. 29658 (1977).

Section 12945(b)(2) also promotes equal employment opportunity. By requiring employers to reinstate women after a reasonable pregnancy disability leave, §12945(b)(2) ensures that they will not lose their jobs on account of pregnancy disability. . . . California's pregnancy disability leave statute allows women, as well as men, to have families without losing their jobs. Thus, petitioners' facial challenge to §12945(b)(2) fails. The statute is not preempted by Title VII, as amended by the PDA, because it is not inconsistent with the purposes of the federal statute. . . .

Justice WHITE, with whom THE CHIEF JUSTICE and Justice POWELL join, dissenting. . . .

The second clause [of the PDA] could not be clearer: it mandates that pregnant employees "shall be treated the same for all employment-related purposes" as non-pregnant employees similarly situated with respect to their ability or inability to work. This language leaves no room for preferential treatment of pregnant workers. . . . In sum, preferential treatment of pregnant workers is prohibited by Title VII, as amended by the PDA. Section 12945(b)(2) of the California Gov't Code, which extends preferential benefits for pregnancy, is therefore preempted. . . .

Epilogue. After being fired and unemployed, Lillian Garland was evicted from her apartment. She then lost custody of her daughter to her ex-husband because she could afford neither rent nor legal representation. However, before *Cal. Fed.* settled, she returned to school and became a real estate agent and insurance broker. She purchased a franchise for a real estate agency that serves veterans. She later married her childhood sweetheart, a Black Hawk helicopter mechanic who had served four tours of duty in Vietnam. They currently live in Virginia, where she serves on the board of a nonprofit agency that offers home repairs to low-income seniors, the disabled, and veterans.

She is proud of the role that she played in combating pregnancy discrimination. Her fondest memory stems from a conversation at a ceremony where she was honored. She found herself seated next to Rosa Parks, the African-American seamstress who sparked the civil rights movement by refusing to give up her seat on a Montgomery, Alabama, bus to a white man in 1955. "Little sister," Rosa Parks told her, "I've had my eye on you. I've been following your career for years—and I am so proud of you!" "Imagine that," Ms. Garland remarks, with wonder. "Rosa Parks was proud of *me*!"[41]

Wendy W. Williams, Equality's Riddle: Pregnancy and the Equal Treatment/Special Treatment Debate

13 N.Y.U. Rev. L. & Soc. Change 325, 333-349 (1984-1985)

The treatment of pregnancy and maternity under the law developed in stages. . . .

A. STAGE ONE: 1870 TO 1970

[W]omen's "maternal functions" formed the basis of a dual system of law. The system treated women differently than men under the claim that it sought to accommodate to and provide for women's special needs. . . .

[41]. Phone conversation with Lillian Garland, December 31, 2012. See also Stephanie M. Wildman, Pregnant and Working: The Story of California Federal Savings & Loan Ass'n v. Guerra, in Women and the Law Stories 253 (Elizabeth M. Schneider & Stephanie M. Wildman eds., 2011).

[T]here were, beginning in the 1940's, a very few provisions dealing specifically with pregnancy. [T]he U.S. Department of Labor recommended that pregnant women not work for six weeks before and two months after delivery. Some states adopted laws prohibiting employers from employing women for a period of time before and after childbirth to protect the health of women and their offspring during that vulnerable time. Where leaves were not accompanied by a guarantee of job security or wage replacement, they "protected" pregnant women right out of their jobs. . . . At the same time, the unemployment insurance laws of many states rendered otherwise eligible women [pregnant workers] ineligible for unemployment insurance if they were pregnant or had recently given birth. Women unemployed because of state laws or employer policies or mandatory unpaid leave thus were precluded from the resources available to other unemployed workers. Four states, including California, created disability insurance programs to provide partial wage replacement to temporarily disabled workers, but those programs either excluded pregnancy-related disabilities altogether or provided restricted benefits. . . . The absence of legislation concerning pregnancy and employment meant that the issue was left to employers (and, where there were unions, to collective bargaining).

By 1960, the dawn of a new decade that would usher in Title VII, many employers simply fired women who became pregnant. Others provided unpaid maternity leaves of absence, frequently accompanied by loss of seniority and accrued benefits. Few provided job security, much less allowed paid sick leave and vacation time to be used for maternity leave. Payment of disability benefits for childbirth was, at best, restricted, and employer sponsored medical insurance provided, at most, limited coverage of pregnancy-related medical treatment and hospitalization. Pervasively, pregnancy was treated less favorably than other physical conditions that affected workplace performance. The pattern of rules telegraphed the underlying assumption: a woman's pregnancy signaled her disengagement from the workplace. [These rules reflected a normative judgment]: when wage-earning women became pregnant they did, and should, go home.

B. STAGE TWO: 1970-1976

By 1970, women were in the workforce in unprecedented numbers. Moreover, an increasing number of them were staying after the birth of children. . . . Suits were filed under Title VII and the Equal Protection Clause on the theory that treating pregnancy disabilities differently and less favorably than other disabilities discriminates on the basis of sex. . . .

In 1974, however, the United States Supreme Court eliminated the Equal Protection Clause as a vehicle for an "equal treatment" attack on legislation singling out pregnancy for special treatment. The state statute challenged in Geduldig v. Aiello [417 U.S. 484 (1974)] created a state disability fund, providing temporary, partial wage replacement to private sector workers who became physically unable to work. The statute was liberally interpreted to cover every conceivable work disability, including, according to the record in the case, disability arising from cosmetic surgery, hair transplants, skiing accidents and prostatectomies. It excluded only one type of work disability from coverage—those "arising out of or in connection with" pregnancy. . . .

Justice Stewart, on behalf of a majority of the court, [stated] that the case did not involve discrimination based on gender as such: "The California insurance program does not exclude anyone from benefit eligibility because of gender but merely removes one physical condition—pregnancy—from the list of compensable disabilities." Translated, this means that the statute bases the exclusion on pregnancy, not on sex itself. . . . .

The conclusion that discrimination on the basis of pregnancy was not sex discrimination freed the Court from the obligation to engage in the more activist review it reserves for sex discrimination cases. Indulging the strong presumption of constitutionality appropriate to rational basis review, it concluded that a legislature legitimately could exclude a costly disability. . . . The Court's explanation that exclusion was rational because the "additional" cost of covering pregnancy would upset the preestablished contribution rate or benefit level would apply to any frequent or prolonged disability that had been excluded from the program, however arbitrarily. . . .

Justice Brennan, joined in dissent by Justices Marshall and Douglas, adopted the plaintiffs' position in its entirety. Women disabled by pregnancy-related causes were comparable to other disabled workers for purposes of the California program. . . . Moreover, the exclusion of pregnancy-related disabilities constituted sex discrimination. . . .

[Yet], when the Court struck down the pregnancy policies in [Cleveland Board of Education v. LaFleur, 414 U.S. 632 (1974)], it invoked not the sex discrimination cases decided under the equal protection clause, but rather, the reproductive choice cases, such as [Eisenstadt v. Baird, 405 U.S. 438 (1972) and Roe v. Wade, 410 U.S. 113 (1973)]. . . . The doctrinal distinction between due process and equal protection analysis of pregnancy issues represented by *LaFleur* and *Geduldig* is in a sense a reiteration of the special treatment/equal treatment dichotomy. To oversimplify, the due process approach is not troubled by and, indeed, invokes a form of special treatment analysis. The liberty interest at stake, defined as the right to choose whether to bear or beget a child without undue state interference, is recognized as "fundamental" precisely because of the central and unique importance to the individual of reproductive choice. The characterization of pregnancy discrimination as sex discrimination, by contrast, requires the comparative analysis of the equal protection mode. Its emphasis is on what is not unique about the reproductive process of women. . . .

C. STAGE THREE: 1976-1978

In General Electric Company v. Gilbert, [429 U.S. 125 (1976)] the Supreme Court dropped the other shoe. Relying heavily on Geduldig v. Aiello, it interpreted Title VII as it had the equal protection clause: it held that discrimination on the basis of pregnancy was not sex discrimination. *Gilbert,* on its facts, was very similar to *Geduldig*. It involved a private employer's disability insurance plan almost identical to the California state plan both in its general scope and in its exclusion of pregnancy-related disabilities. . . .

Under Title VII, rules that are "neutral" but have a disproportionate sex-based effect may also violate the Act. However, the particular "neutral" General Electric pregnancy disability rule, said Justice Rehnquist [writing for the majority], could not even be viewed as having a discriminatory *effect* on women. Men and women, he said, are both covered by the disability program. Moreover, they are covered for the disabilities common to both sexes. Pregnancy disabilities are therefore an "*additional* risk, unique to women." Failure to compensate women for them does not upset the basic sex equality of the program. In a footnote, he drove home the point: Title VII does not require "that 'greater economic benefit[s]' . . . be paid to one sex or the other because of their differing roles in the 'scheme of human existence.'" This conclusion makes breathtakingly explicit the underlying philosophy of the majority of the justices in *Geduldig* and *Gilbert*. Pregnancy, for Rehnquist, is an "extra," an add-on to the basic male model for humanity. Equality does not contemplate handing out benefits for extras—indeed, to do so would be to grant special benefits to women, possibly discriminating against men. The fact that men were compensated under the program for disabilities unique to their sex troubled his analysis not at all.

Justice Brennan, in his dissent in *Geduldig,* almost grasped the essence of the problem when he observed that "the State has created a double standard for disability compensation; a limitation is imposed upon the disabilities for which women workers may recover, while men receive full compensation for all disabilities suffered, including those that affect only or primarily their sex. . . ." What eluded even Justice Brennan was that the statute did not create a "double" standard. Rather, it made man the standard (whatever disabilities men suffer will be compensated) and measured women against that standard (as long as she is compensated for anything he is compensated for, she is treated equally).

For Rehnquist, as long as women are treated in the same way as men in the areas where they are like men—in the disability program, this would mean coverage for things like heart attacks, broken bones, appendicitis—that's equality. To the extent the Court will consider the equities with respect to childbearing capacity, it will consider them only in the category where they belong—extra, separate, different. A family, marital, or reproductive right—yes, in appropriate circumstances. A public matter of equality and equal protection of women—no. . . .

[In response to the above Supreme Court decisions, Congress passed the PDA in 1978, thereby transforming employers' treatment of pregnancy and adopting the equal treatment model.]

Notes and Questions

1. Rationale. *LaFleur,* decided before the PDA, was based on due process. Why did the Supreme Court base its decision on due process rather than equal protection?

2. Antidiscrimination rule. The PDA does not mandate pregnancy leave. Rather, it is an antidiscrimination rule that requires employers to treat pregnancy the same as other physical conditions in terms of leave and other employment benefits. How does an employer treat pregnant women *the same as* "other persons not so affected but similar in their ability or inability to work"? And what should be the comparison group of disabled employees—employees with *occupational* injuries who are unable to work, employees who are injured off the job (such as in recreational activities), or both?

3. Pregnancy discrimination after the PDA. Despite the PDA, workers continue to report pregnancy discrimination. Complaints of pregnancy discrimination filed with the Equal Opportunity Employment Commission (EEOC)(the agency charged with administering the PDA) are made primarily by women in low-wage jobs. The largest number of cases in 2013 were found in the health care and social assistance fields, followed by the retail industry, accommodations and food services, administrative support, and manufacturing.[42]

4. Criticisms of PDA. Commentators have criticized the PDA for its failure to protect women who are fired not *during* pregnancy but *after* their return from leave, because of employers' fears that the women may become pregnant again, or because of gender-based stereotypes about pregnant women's lack of competence.[43] In addition, employers may offer nonpregnancy reasons (i.e., pretexts) for discharge or demotion. See, e.g., Groves v. Cost Planning & Mgmt. Int'l, Inc., 372 F.3d 1008 (8th Cir. 2004) (holding that economic downturn was justifiable reason for termination despite prima facie case of discrimination).

5. Pregnancy Accommodations. After passage of the PDA, many courts interpreted the federal law narrowly, allowing employers to refuse to accommodate pregnant employees with medical needs despite accommodating workers with other disabilities. The issue of pregnancy accommodations came before the Supreme Court recently in Young v. UPS, 135 S. Ct. 1338 (2015). In this case, a pregnant delivery driver was restricted by her physician from lifting more than 20 pounds. Because UPS policy required employees to lift parcels weighing up to 70 pounds, UPS placed Young on leave without pay. She filed suit, alleging pregnancy discrimination. Reversing the summary judgment in favor of UPS, the Supreme Court held that the employer cannot treat pregnant employees less favorably than others similar in their ability or inability to work simply because it would be "more expensive or less convenient." The Court also held that failure to accommodate pregnant workers violates the PDA when the employer's policies impose a "significant burden" on pregnant workers that outweighs any justification that the employer offers for those policies. The Court remanded for a determination whether the employer's policies and the burdens imposed show intentional discrimination.

a. ADAA Amendments. Amendments to the Americans with Disabilities Act (ADAA) in 2008 extended the law to require employers to provide necessary accommodations for pregnancy-related conditions that met the definition of "disability." Note, however, that courts do not consider normal pregnancy as a disability under the ADAA, 42 U.S.C. §§ 12101-12213, although a pregnancy-related impairment may qualify as a disability (42 USCA §12101).

b. Proposed reforms. To strengthen the treatment of pregnancy accommodations, Congress is presently considering the Pregnant Workers Fairness Act

[42]. Brigid Schulte, New Claims: Pregnancy Discrimination Hits Low-Wage Workers Hardest, Wash. Post., Aug. 5, 2014, http://www.washingtonpost.com/blogs/she-the-people/wp/2014/08/05/new-statistics-pregnancy-discrimination-claims-hit-low-wage-workers-hardest/.

[43]. Susan E. Huhta et al., Looking Forward and Back: Using the Pregnancy Discrimination Act and Discriminatory Gender/Pregnancy Stereotyping to Challenge Discrimination Against New Mothers, 7 Employee Rts. & Emp. Pol'y J. 303, 306 (2003).

(PWFA), S. 1512, H.R. 2654), 114th Cong. (2015-2016). The act aims to require employers to make the same accommodations for pregnant workers as for those employees with disabilities. Specifically, the PWFA would (1) require employers to make reasonable accommodations for employees who have limitations stemming from pregnancy, childbirth, or related medical conditions, unless the accommodation would impose an undue hardship on the employer; (2) prohibit employers from discriminating against employees if they need such reasonable accommodations; and (3) prohibit employers from forcing a pregnant employee to take paid or unpaid leave if a reasonable accommodation could be provided.

6. Equal treatment versus special treatment. To what extent does the "special treatment" approach of providing benefits for pregnant workers compromise women's employment opportunities? Might it revitalize early twentieth-century attitudes that women needed protective labor legislation (limiting the hours that women could work because of women's childbearing potential)? See Muller v. Oregon, 208 U.S. 412 (1908). On the other hand, without "special treatment," what will happen to the majority of female employees who are likely to require time off from work because of pregnancy?

7. Parental leave and the right to privacy. Do state parental leave statutes violate the right to privacy by compelling men and women to jeopardize job security in order to have children? If so, should these regulations be subject to higher scrutiny? What does *LaFleur*, supra, suggest?

8. PDA and infertility treatment. Does the PDA cover discrimination against women who miss work to undergo infertility treatments? See LaPorta v. Wal-Mart Stores, Inc., 163 F. Supp. 2d 758 (W.D. Mich. 2001). Is infertility "a pregnancy-related medical condition" covered by Title VII? Or, is infertility distinct from issues of pregnancy? Does an employer violate the PDA by firing an employee for her expressed *intent* to become pregnant? See Batchelor v. Merck & Co., 2008 WL 5191426 (N.D. Ind. 2008).

Note that under the Patient Protection and Affordable Care Act (known as the ACA), 42 U.S.C. §300gg, insurance plans must cover family-planning care without copayments or deductibles. However, coverage for infertility treatment is not mandated by the ACA except in those few states that selected this feature in their benchmark plans. Even in these states, the scope of coverage for infertility treatment varies considerably from state to state (for example, some of these state plans do not cover in vitro fertilization).

Problems

1. Hunter Tylo is a soap opera star on prime-time television. On "Melrose Place," she plays a happily married woman who suddenly begins an affair. Shortly after she accepts the job, Hunter becomes pregnant. She informs her employer, Spelling Entertainment Group. One month later, she is fired. Spelling informs her that they have a contractual right to terminate her if there was a "material change in [her] appearance." Further, Spelling argues that her pregnancy does not

conform to the character she portrays. Tylo alleges a violation of the PDA. What result? See Tylo v. Superior Court, 64 Cal. Rptr. 2d 731 (Ct. App. 1997). Recall that the Supreme Court recently decided Young v. UPS. How would *Young* influence the result?

2. When a public high school honors student becomes pregnant during her senior year, the principal informs her that she can no longer attend class "due to safety concerns," and that she is not permitted to attend commencement or to have her name printed in the graduation program. However, the school permits the baby's father to continue to participate in commencement exercises. The student comes to you for advice. Does she have a claim for pregnancy discrimination? Sex discrimination? See Sally Kalson, Graduation Pregnant with Inequity, Pittsburgh Post-Gazette, May 25, 2005, at A2.

b. Balancing Work and Family

CALDWELL v. HOLLAND OF TEXAS, INC.

208 F.3d 671 (8th Cir. 2000)

BRIGHT, Circuit Judge.

[Juanita Caldwell, mother of three-year-old Kejuan, had an excellent record working for three years for Holland, Inc., the owner of several Kentucky Fried Chicken restaurants in Texarkana, Arkansas, before she was fired based on the following events.]

On Saturday, June 7, 1997, Kejuan awoke with a high fever, pain in his ears, and congestion. Caldwell promptly notified Assistant Manager Loyce, prior to the start of her morning shift, that she would be absent because Kejuan required immediate medical attention. Loyce gave Caldwell permission to miss her shift. That morning, a doctor at an emergency clinic diagnosed Kejuan as having an acute ear infection. During this visit, the doctor prescribed a ten-day course of antibiotics and a two-day decongestant for Kejuan. At the same time, the treating physician informed Caldwell that her son's condition probably would require surgery if her son was to avoid permanent hearing loss, and he recommended that Caldwell schedule a follow-up examination with her son's regular pediatrician, Dr. Mark Wright.

Later that Saturday night, upon the request of an assistant manager, Caldwell worked an evening shift at one of Holland's other restaurant locations. While Caldwell was working, her elderly mother cared for her son and administered his medications. Caldwell did not have any shifts on Sunday. When Caldwell returned to her regular work on Monday morning, June 9, 1997, Mark Monholland, a manager at the Hickory Street restaurant, abruptly fired Caldwell without discussing her absence of June 7, 1997. [She filed suit, alleging that her termination violated the FMLA.]

The FMLA allows eligible employees to take up to a total of twelve workweeks of leave per year for, among other things, "serious health conditions" that afflict their immediate family members [such as a "spouse, son, daughter, or parent].

See 29 U.S.C. §2612(a)(1)(C). The employee must show that her family member suffered a serious health condition and that her absence was attributable to the family member's serious health condition.

A "serious health condition" occurs, under the regulations, when the family member suffers an "illness, injury, impairment, or physical or mental condition" that requires "inpatient care" or "continuing treatment" by a health care provider. See 29 C.F.R. §825.114(a). Here, the parties agree that Kejuan never received inpatient care. The pertinent issue is whether Kejuan received continuing treatment. A family member receives continuing treatment if the person experiences "[a] period of *incapacity* . . . of more than three consecutive calendar days" and then receives subsequent treatment, or experiences further incapacity relating to, the same condition. The subsequent treatment must include, either "[t]reatment two or more times by a health care provider . . . ," or "[t]reatment by a health care provider on at least one occasion which results in a regimen of continuing treatment under the supervision of the health care provider." . . .

The applicability of the FMLA, here, turns on whether Caldwell can prove a two-pronged inquiry: first, she must show that Kejuan suffered "a period of incapacity of more than three consecutive calendar days"; second, she must show that Kejuan subsequently received continued, supervised treatment relating to the same condition. . . .

In assessing the first prong of Caldwell's case, we note at the outset that the question of what constitutes incapacity of a three-year-old raises an issue not directly addressed by the regulations. The regulations state that incapacity may be determined based on an individual's "inability to work, attend school, or perform other regular daily activities due to the serious health condition, treatment therefor, or recovery therefrom." Because most three-year-old children do not work or attend school, the standard offered by the regulations is an insufficient guide. The fact finder must determine whether the child's illness demonstrably affected his normal activity. In making this determination, the fact finder may consider a variety of factors, including but not limited to: whether the child participated in his daily routines or was particularly difficult to care for during that period, and whether a day-care facility would have allowed a child with Kejuan's illness to attend its sessions.

Caldwell avers that Kejuan's ear infection, which was severe enough to warrant emergency treatment, required constant care for a period of more than three days. She states in her supplemental affidavit that Kejuan was incapacitated beginning Saturday, June 7, 1997, for more than three consecutive days. She further states:

> He [Kejuan] remained inside the house and was kept in bed as much as possible. He did not participate in any of his normal activities. He was under the constant care of me (his mother) and his grandmother, and both the prescribed medications and a fever reducer were administered to him during this entire time.

In addition to Caldwell's affidavit, the medical records show that Kejuan's ear infection was a continuing, persistent condition that could only be treated by surgery. Kejuan's period of incapacity, therefore, may be measured over the entire time during which he was suffering from this illness and being treated for it. We note that Kejuan was treated for his condition for ten days following his first visit to the emergency clinic. The medical records state that the condition did not improve, and as a result, Dr. Wright, his regular physician, prescribed another ten-day course of antibiotics. Despite the two medical treatments, Kejuan's condition continued to persist until Dr. Trone, a surgical specialist, performed surgery to remove his tonsils and adenoids on July 17, 1997. This entire period, from June 7-July 17, 1997, may constitute Kejuan's period of incapacity if his illness and these various treatments disrupted his basic daily routines, and if, as the record suggests, his ongoing treatment was not successfully alleviating his condition of disability. . . .

Alternatively, the ten-day period beginning on June 7, 1997 could constitute Kejuan's period of incapacity. As we have noted, his mother's supplemental affidavit refers to constant care and administration of prescribed medications during "this entire time." . . . Even if Kejuan did not sustain "incapacity" under the regulations *prior* to his surgery, the record clearly shows that the inflammation and infection in his ears resulted in a period of incapacity that lasted more than three days once he had the tonsillectomy and adenoidectomy. . . .

FMLA's purpose is to help working men and women balance the conflicting demands of work and personal life. The law requires courts to consider the seriousness of the afflicted individual's condition because the law was designed to prevent individuals like Juanita Caldwell from having to choose between their livelihood and treatment for their own or their family members' serious health conditions. Upon examining the seriousness of Kejuan's ear infection, which required surgery to prevent deafness, we hold that there is at least a question of fact as to whether Kejuan's condition was "serious" under the regulations. . . .

On the second prong of the threshold inquiry, we believe that Caldwell has generated a genuine issue of fact regarding whether Kejuan received "subsequent treatment." Here, after the first ten-day antibiotic treatment, Kejuan was treated by Dr. Wright and later by Dr. Trone in surgery. . . . Furthermore, the record shows at least two postoperative medical visits to monitor Kejuan's condition. [T]he district court erred in granting a summary judgment of dismissal. . . .

FAMILY AND MEDICAL LEAVE ACT

29 U.S.C. §§2601, 2611, 2612, 2614

§2601. FINDINGS AND PURPOSES

(a) *Findings*. The Congress finds that

(1) the number of single-parent households and two-parent households in which the single parent or both parents work is increasing significantly; . . .

(3) the lack of employment policies to accommodate working parents can force individuals to choose between job security and parenting; . . .

(5) due to the nature of the roles of men and women in our society, the primary responsibility for family caretaking often falls on women, and such responsibility affects their working lives more than it affects the working lives of men; and

(6) employment standards that apply to one gender only have serious potential for encouraging employers to discriminate against employees and applicants for employment who are of that gender.

(b) *Purposes.* It is the purpose of this Act

(1) to balance the demands of the workplace with the needs of families, to promote stability and economic security of families, and to promote national interests in preserving family integrity;

(2) to entitle employees to take reasonable leave for medical reasons, for the birth or adoption of a child, and for the care of a child, spouse, or parent who has a serious health condition;

(3) to accomplish such purposes . . . in a manner that accommodates the legitimate interests of employers;

(4) to accomplish [such] purposes . . . in a manner that, consistent with the Equal Protection Clause of the Fourteenth Amendment, minimizes the potential for employment discrimination on the basis of sex by ensuring generally that leave is available for eligible medical reasons (including maternity-related disability) and for compelling family reasons, on a gender-neutral basis; and

(5) to promote the goal of equal employment opportunity for women and men, pursuant to such clause.

§2611. DEFINITIONS . . .

(2)(A) "[E]ligible employee" means an employee who has been employed

(i) for at least 12 months by the employer with respect to whom leave is requested under section 2612; and

(ii) for at least 1,250 hours of service with such employer during the previous 12-month period. . . .

(4)(A) "[E]mployer"

(i) means any person engaged in commerce or in any industry or activity affecting commerce who employs 50 or more employees [for each workday, for 20 or more weeks in the current or proceeding year]. . . .

(5) "[E]mployment benefits" means all benefits provided or made available to employees by an employer, including group life insurance, health insurance, disability insurance, sick leave, annual leave, educational benefits, and pensions. . . .

(7) "[P]arent" means the biological parent of an employee or an individual who stood in loco parentis to an employee when the employee was a son or daughter. . . .

(11) "[S]erious health condition" means an illness, injury, impairment, or physical or mental condition that involves —

(A) inpatient care in a hospital, hospice, or residential medical care facility; or

(B) continuing treatment by a health care provider.

(12) "[S]on or daughter" means a biological, adopted, or foster child, a stepchild, a legal ward, or a child of a person standing in loco parentis, who is [under 18, or mentally or physically disabled].

(13) "[S]pouse" means a husband or wife, as the case may be.

§2612. LEAVE REQUIREMENT

(a) In General.

(1) Entitlement to leave. [A]n eligible employee shall be entitled to a total of 12 workweeks of leave during any 12-month period for one or more of the following:

(A) Because of the birth of a son or daughter of the employee and in order to care for such son or daughter.

(B) Because of the placement of a son or daughter with the employee for adoption or foster care.

(C) In order to care for the spouse, or a son, daughter, or parent, of the employee, if such spouse, son, daughter, or parent has a serious health condition.

(D) Because of a serious health condition that makes the employee unable to perform the functions of the position of such employee.

(E) Because of any qualifying exigency (as the Secretary shall, by regulation, determine) arising out of the fact that the spouse, or a son, daughter, or parent of the employee is on active duty (or has been notified of an impending call or order to active duty) in the Armed Forces. . . .

(b) [Leave generally shall not be taken intermittently unless the employer and employee agree otherwise.]

(c) Unpaid Leave Permitted. [L]eave granted under subsection (a) may consist of unpaid leave. [However, the employee may choose to substitute, or the employer may require, accrued paid leave or sick leave be substituted for the unpaid 12-week leave.]

. . .

(e) Foreseeable leave.

(1) Requirement of notice

[For a foreseeable leave based on a birth or child placement], the employee shall provide the employer with not less than 30 days' notice [except if] the date of the birth or placement requires leave to begin in less than 30 days, the employee shall provide such notice as is practicable. . . . [For a foreseeable leave based on planned medical treatment, the employee shall provide at least 30 days' notice or such notice as is practicable under the circumstances].

(f) Spouses Employed by the Same Employer. [If husband and wife] are employed by the same employer, the aggregate number of workweeks of leave to which both may be entitled may be limited to 12 workweeks during any 12-month period. . . .

§2614. EMPLOYMENT AND BENEFITS PROTECTION

(a) Restoration to Position.

(1) In general. Except as provided in subsection (b), any eligible employee who takes leave under section 2612 for the intended purpose of the leave shall be entitled, on return from such leave —

(A) to be restored by the employer to the position of employment held by the employee when the leave commenced; or

(B) to be restored to an equivalent position with equivalent employment benefits, pay, and other terms and conditions of employment.

[The taking of leave shall not result in the loss of any employment benefit accrued prior to the date on which the leave commenced, but the restored employee has no right to the accrual of any seniority benefits during any period of leave.]

(b) Exemption Concerning Certain Highly Compensated Employees.

(1) Denial of restoration. An employer may deny restoration under subsection (a) to any eligible employee [if] —

(A) such denial is necessary to prevent substantial and grievous economic injury to the operations of the employer; . . .

(2) Affected employees. An eligible employee described in paragraph (1) is a salaried eligible employee who is among the highest paid 10 percent of the employees employed by the employer within 75 miles of the facility at which the employee is employed.

(c) [Employer is required to maintain health benefits for the duration of the leave.]

Notes and Questions

1. Background. The public outcry for family leave dates from the 1970s. After the women's liberation movement expanded employment opportunities, the number of mothers who were working outside the home dramatically increased. The largest increase occurred for mothers with preschool children.[44] Currently, almost 70 percent of mothers in the workforce have children under age 18; slightly more than half of mothers in the workforce have children under one year old.[45]

The FMLA became law after a lengthy battle. Opponents originally charged that the legislation would have a negative impact on industry. First proposed in 1985, the act was twice passed by Congress but vetoed by President George H.W. Bush. Former President Bill Clinton signed the act in 1993. Currently, one-sixth of the FMLA-covered workforce (or 14 million employees) take leave annually for FMLA-covered reasons.[46]

2. Purposes. How does the FMLA redress the PDA's shortcomings? What is the purpose of the FMLA? To what extent does the FMLA accomplish the purposes enumerated in the statute?

3. Criticisms. The FMLA mandates *unpaid leave*. Are most employees able to take unpaid leave?[47] Does the FMLA address the needs of *single parents*? *Fathers*? Does it achieve its vision of caretaking leaves to men and women on equal terms? Professor Joanna Grossman responds:

> If only mothers take leave, then the FMLA only accommodates women's caretaking, protection that gives them a measure of job security but at the same time preserves employers' incentives to prefer male employees. It also does nothing to equalize the burdens of caretaking themselves.[48]

---

[44]. "Between 1959 and 1974, the employment rate for mothers with children under three more than doubled, from 15 to 31 percent." Marie Richmond-Abbott, Women Wage Earners, in Feminist Philosophies 135, 136 (Janet A. Kourany et al. eds., 1992).

[45]. Bureau of Labor Statistics, U.S. Dept. of Labor, Latest Annual Data: Women of Working Age (2013), http://www.dol.gov/wb/stats/recentfacts.htm.

[46]. Nat'l P'ship for Women & Families, U.S. Dept. of Labor, A Look at the U.S. Department of Labor's 2012 Family and Medical Leave Act Employee and Worksite Surveys (Feb. 2013), http://www.nationalpartnership.org/research-library/search.jsp?query=worksite+surveys&type=file.

[47]. Id. at 5 (78 percent of employees who need family leave do not take it because they cannot afford to miss a paycheck).

[48]. Joanna L. Grossman, Job Security Without Equality: The Family and Medical Leave Act of 1993, 15 Wash. U. J.L. & Pol'y 17, 18 (2004).

See also Knussman v. Maryland, 272 F.3d 625 (4th Cir. 2001) (state trooper told "only mothers can be primary caregivers").

Does the FMLA go far enough to meet the needs of working parents? For example, is 12 weeks' leave sufficient? Given that the period applies both to pregnancy and infant care, might a mother with pregnancy complications use all her leave before birth? Will it achieve the antidiscrimination goals of "degendering" responsibilities for care work? See Nevada Dept. of Human Res. v. Hibbs, 538 U.S. 721 (2003).

4. FMLA and nontraditional families. How well does the FMLA address the needs of gay and lesbian co-parents? In 2010, the U.S. Department of Labor issued regulations that expanded FLMA coverage to those same-sex partners who are in an "in loco parentis" relationship with a child, and explicitly affirmed that the standard *does* apply to same-sex partners.[49] Proposed FMLA amendments would permit an employee to take FMLA leave to care for a same-sex spouse or domestic partner or, alternatively, for the spouse's or domestic partner's child or parent. (Family and Medical Leave Inclusion Act, S. 846, H.R. 1751, 113th Cong. (2013-2014).) The bill died in committee and has not been reintroduced. Do *Windsor* and *Obergefell* render this issue moot?

Does the FMLA provide for such nontraditional caregivers as grandmothers? Proposed FMLA amendments, supra, would remedy this shortcoming. See generally Jessica Dixon Weaver, Grandma in the White House: Legal Support for Intergenerational Caregiving, 43 Seton Hall L. Rev. 1, 36-42 (2013).

5. Range of childcare tasks. Does the FMLA provide for the *full* range of a parent's childcare responsibilities, such as the need to attend school appointments or to provide childcare in the event of school closures? Proposed amendments would provide FMLA leave to cover some important, but non-medical, parenting responsibilities. See Family and Medical Leave Enhancement Act, H.R. 3999, 113th Cong. (2013-2014) (allowing FMLA leave of 24 hours at most per year to participate in a child's or grandchild's school activities). However, the bill died in committee and has not been reintroduced.

6. Paid leave. A few states offer paid leave. California was the first state to do so in 2003 via the disability insurance model, funded by employee contributions. See Cal. Unemp. Ins. Code §3301(a)(1) (providing six weeks' wage replacement of up to 55 percent of salary, up to a maximum of $738/week). See also N.J. Stat. Ann. §§43:21-4, 43:21-7; Wash. Rev. Code §§49.86.030 et seq. Congress has unsuccessfully considered paid federal family leave since 2000 (Federal Employees Paid Parental Leave Act of 2015, H.R. 532, 114th Cong. (2015-2016)).

7. Serious health condition. *Caldwell* is an important case that interprets the FMLA requirement of a "serious health condition." How does the FMLA define the term? Did the toddler's ear infection in *Caldwell* qualify? What is a "serious health condition" for an infant or toddler? Does the definition differ for an adult? What qualifies as "subsequent treatment"? FMLA revisions in 2013 impose a timetable within which visits to a health care provider must occur in order for a "serious

---

[49]. Wage & Hour Div., U.S. Dept. of Labor, Fact Sheet #28B (July 2010), http://www.dol.gov/whd/regs/compliance/whdfs28B.htm.

health condition" to qualify. The incapacity must last more than three consecutive days and also involve one or more treatments by a health care provider within 30 days of the first day of incapacity.29 C.F.R. §825.115. Chronic conditions are treated differently.

8. Notice requirements. What notice requirements does the FMLA impose? Should an employee's failure to comply with notice requirements constitute grounds for denial of leave? Who decides whether an employee is physically fit to return to work—the physician or the employer? See Budhun v. Reading Hosp. & Med. Ctr., 765 F.3d 245 (3d Cir. 2014).

9. Privacy. Does an employer's inquiry to health care providers (to ascertain whether an employee's leave qualifies under the FMLA) invade the employee's privacy? FMLA regulations permit contacting health care providers to verify a medical certification or clarify information. However, only designated company officials (such as human resources personnel) may make the contact. See 29 C.F.R. §825.307(a). Do these new regulations adequately address privacy concerns?

10. Domestic violence. Domestic violence affects victims in the workplace by limiting productivity and increasing absenteeism. Proposed legislation, the Domestic Violence Leave Act, H.R. 3151, 112th Cong., would expand the FMLA (§§2601-2653) to provide leave to employees (1) who are addressing domestic violence, sexual assault, or stalking and their effects, if the employee is unable to perform any of the functions of the job; and (2) to care for a family member who is addressing domestic violence, sexual assault, or stalking and their effects. Specifically, leave would be available for seeking medical attention to recover from injuries; legal assistance; obtaining psychological counseling; participating in safety planning (including relocation); and participating in any other activity necessitated by domestic violence which must be undertaken during hours of employment. Do the proposals go far enough?

In response to the lack of federal protection, many states have enacted laws requiring leave for victims of domestic violence. All of these states require leave for medical needs and psychological counseling, obtaining social services, relocating, legal assistance, and participating in legal proceedings. Some of these states prohibit discrimination or retaliation against an employee who requests or takes leave for domestic-violence-related reasons.

11. Innovative state reforms. Some states expand FMLA rights by covering newer employees and smaller employers; allowing paid sick leave to substitute for unpaid family leave; and providing unpaid leave for school meetings and activities. In 2015, some major companies voluntarily responded to President Barack Obama's plea in his State of the Union address to enact *paid* sick leave legislation. For example, Microsoft announced that it would require many of its contractors and vendors to provide their employees with either 10 paid vacation days and 5 paid sick days or 15 days of unrestricted paid time off.[50]

---

[50]. Claire Cain Miller, Microsoft Tells Its Partners to Provide Paid Sick Leave, N.Y. Times, Mar. 26, 2015, at A3.

12. International perspective. Most industrialized countries provide significant paid parental leave, ranging from three months to one year.[51] In addition, such paid leave policies apply to *all* parents, whereas the FMLA covers only about 60 percent of employees.[52] Further, more than two dozen countries now offer *paid paternity* leave (as the excerpted article below reveals). Why is U.S. government support for parental leave so limited compared with that of other industrialized nations?

Sweden has long been known for its generous parental leave policy. In 1974, Sweden transformed its maternity leave policy to *parental* leave. Currently, both parents share 16 months of paid parental leave. They can decide how to allocate the time between themselves and whether to take the leave concurrently or consecutively. They can use the leave at any time before the child's eighth birthday. To encourage paternal involvement, the law provides that if each parent takes at least two months' leave, the family receives two extra months. As of 2016, Sweden is planning to introduce a third month of paid parental leave, reserved for fathers, in an effort to further increase gender equality.[53] As a result of this liberal policy, 90 percent of Swedish fathers take parental leave.[54] What are some of the effects of generous governmental leave policies—for mothers, fathers, children, and society?

Problems

1. Martha, a lawyer for a large corporation, and Michael, a computer engineer, are expecting quadruplets. During the fifth month of Martha's pregnancy, her physician advises complete bed rest. Martha can use her medical leave for this purpose. However, she will need someone to take care of her (fix her meals, run errands, and so forth). Michael, as well as Martha's sister, Miriam (who works for a brokerage firm), consider taking leave under the FMLA to care for Martha for the remainder of her pregnancy. What advice would you give them about the likelihood that their requests will be granted? Suppose after the quadruplets' birth, Martha claims she should be entitled to family leave to care for them. What result? See Navarro v. Pfizer Corp., 261 F.3d 90 (1st Cir. 2001). See also Jill Hasday, Family Law Reimagined 163 (2014) (arguing that family law, and the FMLA specifically, should extend protections for caretaking broadly).

2. Catherine Marzano is hired by Computer Science Co. (CSC) as a "junior technical recruiter." She is promoted several times. Shortly after her assignment to Mr. Marzi's unit, she learns that she is pregnant. She is reluctant to tell her boss because seven employees previously were terminated after their maternity leaves. After she does tell him, she notices that Mr. Marzi speaks "as if she wasn't coming back." During her leave, her unit begins experiencing losses (despite the stellar

---

[51]. Gretchen Livingston, Pew Research Ctr., Among 38 Nations, U.S. is the Outlier When It Comes to Paid Parental Leave, Dec. 12, 2013, http://www.pewresearch.org/fact-tank/2013/12/12/among-38-nations-u-s-is-the-holdout-when-it-comes-to-offering-paid-parental-leave/.

[52]. Nat'l P'ship for Women & Families, Facts About the FMLA: What Does It Do, Who Used It, and How? 1 (20015), http://www.nationalpartnership.org/site/DocServer/FMLAWhatWhoHow.pdf?docID=965.

[53]. Swedish Fathers to Get Third Month of Paid Parental Leave, The Guardian, May 28, 2015, http://www.theguardian.com/world/2015/may/28/swedish-fathers-paid-paternity-parental-leave.

[54]. Why Swedish Men Take So Much Paternity Leave, The Economist, July 22, 2014, http://www.economist.com/blogs/economist-explains/2014/07/economist-explains-15.

financial performance of CSC). Mr. Marzi eliminates Catherine's position and nine others. He notifies Catherine by saying that she "would be better off if [she] stays home with the baby and collects unemployment." Catherine alleges pregnancy discrimination and unlawful interference with her rights under the FMLA. What result? Marzano v. Computer Sci. Corp., 91 F.3d 497 (3d Cir. 1996).

How do employers accommodate fathers' need for parental leave? The next excerpt addresses this issue.

National Partnership for Women & Families, Dads Expect Better

2-4 (2012)

[T]oo few workplaces and too few public policies help new fathers when a child arrives and needs care. The absence of public policies that enable men to take leave to care for their children increases the conflict between work and family for working fathers and fosters the continuation of inequities in household caregiving responsibilities. . . .

[Research reveals that when] fathers take leave after a child's birth, they are more likely to be involved in the direct care of their children long term. One longitudinal study of U.S. families shows that fathers who took two or more weeks off after the birth of their children were involved in the direct care of their children at higher rates nine months later than fathers who took no leave. . . .

Internationally, at least 66 countries ensure that fathers either receive or have a right to paid leave when a new child arrives; at least 31 of these countries offer 14 or more weeks of paid leave. . . .

Employers' voluntary policies fail the nation's fathers. According to a recent national employer study, just 14 percent of men have access to paternity leave with some pay through their employers. . . . Even many industry leaders—companies that are regarded as the most "family friendly" by offering paid leave and other benefits that help workers manage the dual demands of work and family—have room for improvement. [T]hese companies provided only three weeks of fully paid paternity leave—far less than parents need to care adequately for their new children. . . .

DIKE v. SCHOOL BOARD

650 F.2d 783 (5th Cir. 1981)

GODBOLD, Chief Judge:

[Janice] Dike is employed by the school board as a kindergarten teacher at an elementary school. After giving birth to her child she returned to her teaching post. Having chosen to breastfeed her child, Dike wished to feed the child in this manner at all feedings, including the one feeding necessary during the school day. She sought a means of doing so that would not disrupt the education of children attending the school or interfere with her discharge of work responsibilities.

Dike therefore arranged for her husband or her babysitter to bring the child to school during her lunch period, when she was free from any duties. Dike would then nurse the child in privacy in a locked room into which other persons could not see. On occasions when the school asked Dike to perform duties during her lunch period, she would hand the infant to her husband or babysitter. She was thus always available for work even during her duty-free hour. She alleges that this routine did not disrupt the educational process at the school or her work performance.

After three months of this routine without disruption or incident the school principal directed Dike to stop nursing her child on campus, citing a school board directive prohibiting teachers from bringing their children to work with them for any reason. The rule's stated rationale is to avoid possible disruptions by the children of teachers and to avoid the possibility of the children having an accident and subjecting the school board to litigation. The principal threatened disciplinary action should Dike continue to nurse the child at school.

Dike heeded these warnings and stopped nursing her child during the school day. But because the child developed an allergic reaction to formula milk, Dike had to artificially extract milk with a breast pump and leave it for the child's mid-day feeding. Dike asserts this new routine caused the child to develop observable psychological changes that also affected her own emotional well-being. She requested permission to resume her earlier procedure, alternatively requesting permission to nurse the child off campus during her non-duty time or to nurse the child in her camper van in the school parking lot. The school board denied these requests, apparently relying on another policy prohibiting teachers from leaving school premises during the school day.

A short time later the infant began refusing to nurse from a bottle. Dike thus had no choice but to breastfeed the child. Because the school board denied her permission to breastfeed on campus or off, Dike was compelled to take an unpaid leave of absence for the remainder of the school term.

Dike sued [the school board under 42 U.S.C. §1983], alleging that it had unduly interfered with a constitutionally protected right to nurture her child by breastfeeding. [The district court, deeming the action frivolous, dismissed her complaint and awarded attorneys' fees to the defendants.]

The Constitution protects from undue state interference citizens' freedom of personal choice in some areas of marriage and family life. These protected interests have been described as rights of personal privacy or as "fundamental" personal liberties. . . . Among these protected liberties are individual decisions respecting marriage [citing *Zablocki* and *Loving*], procreation [citing *LaFleur* and *Skinner*], contraception [citing *Griswold* and *Eisenstadt*], abortion [citing Roe v. Wade], and family relationships. The Supreme Court has long recognized that parents' interest in nurturing and rearing their children deserves special protection against state interference [citing Pierce v. Society of Sisters, and Meyer v. Nebraska].

Breastfeeding is the most elemental form of parental care. It is a communion between mother and child that, like marriage, is "intimate to the degree of being sacred," Griswold v. Connecticut, 381 U.S. at 486. Nourishment is necessary to maintain the child's life, and the parent may choose to believe that breastfeeding will enhance the child's psychological as well as physical health. In light of the spectrum of interests that the Supreme Court has held specially protected, we conclude that the Constitution protects from excessive state interference a woman's decision respecting breastfeeding her child.

Our conclusion that Dike's interest in breastfeeding is a protected liberty interest, however, is the beginning rather than the end of the constitutional inquiry. . . . The Constitution does not prohibit all restrictions of protected liberties, and the school board may establish by appropriate pleading and proof that its regulations prohibiting teachers from leaving campus or bringing children to school, as applied to teachers who wish to breastfeed their children during non-duty time, further sufficiently important state interests and are closely tailored to effectuate only those interests. . . . The school board's interests in avoiding disruption of the educational process, in ensuring that teachers perform their duties without distraction, and in avoiding potential liability for accidents are presumably legitimate. Whether these or other interests are strong enough to justify the school board's regulations, and whether the regulations are sufficiently narrowly drawn, must be determined at trial. . . .

Notes and Questions

1. **Background.** A significant number of mothers choose to breastfeed their babies. However, as *Dike* illustrates, some women find that they must choose between breastfeeding and keeping their jobs. The lack of workplace accommodations may also force some mothers to discontinue nursing.

2. **Federal protection for breastfeeding and pumping breast milk.** Until recently, federal protection for breastfeeding was quite limited. The PDA does not require accommodations for lactating employees. The Affordable Care Act (ACA) (29 U.S.C. §207(r)(1)-(4)) significantly improves federal protection by amending Section 7 of the Fair Labor Standards Act (FLSA) to require reasonable unpaid break time for an employee to express breast milk for one year after the child's birth. The employer must also provide a place, other than a bathroom, for that purpose. Smaller employers (those with fewer than 50 employees) are exempt if the requirements impose undue hardship. See generally Marcy Karin & Robin Runge, Breastfeeding and a New Type of Employment Law, 63 Cath. U. L. Rev. 329 (2014) (exploring breastfeeding protection before and after the ACA).

Does the PDA protect employees form being discharged for nursing their infants at work? See EEOC v. Houston Funding II, Ltd., 717 F. 3d 425 (5th Cir. 2013); EEOC v. Vamco Sheet Metals, Inc., 2014 WL. 2619812 (S.D.N.Y. 2014). How should *Dike* be decided under the PDA? Under the FMLA? Under Title VII? Under the ACA? Under the ADA, is breastfeeding a "disability"? For purposes of the PDA and Title VII, how does one equate breastfeeding women to a "similarly situated" class of men? Should pumping of breast milk be considered a product or a service, for the purposes of consumer protection laws? See generally Kara W. Swanson, Banking on the Body: The Market in Blood, Milk, and Sperm in Modern America (2014).

3. Criticisms of special treatment. Can an employer grant special treatment for breastfeeding mothers without providing parental leave to fathers or to non-breastfeeding women? Professor Sylvia Law, who staunchly supports gender equality and reproductive rights, believes that special treatment for nursing mothers serves to perpetuate inequality and reinforces the gender-based expectation that women's destiny is to be mothers. She elaborates as follows:

> [T]he state's interest in promoting the physical or psychic benefits of nursing is not sufficiently substantial to justify the burden upon men and women who would choose to take child care leave but who cannot nurse. Also, the oppressive effect upon women who would prefer not to nurse but are compelled to do so in order to qualify for the leave is not justified by the state's interest.[55]

Is her reasoning persuasive?

4. Limitation on *Dike*. *Dike*'s holding that breastfeeding is a constitutional right based on the right of privacy has been narrowed by subsequent case law. The district court dismissed Dike's claim on remand, finding that the school board's policy was narrowly tailored and based on compelling state interests. Shahar v. Bowers (discussed in Chapter V), overruled *Dike* insofar as it implicated strict scrutiny review of a government employee's freedom of intimate association claim and upheld, instead, the use of the balancing-test approach.

5. Different state approaches. Statutory protection for breastfeeding includes (a) exemptions of breastfeeding from public nudity and other criminal statutes, (b) protection of breastfeeding mothers in any public or private location, (c) protection of breastfeeding via civil rights remedies, (d) encouragement or mandating employer accommodation of breastfeeding, and (e) exemptions of breastfeeding women from jury duty.[56] Florida (site of *Dike*) became the first state to guarantee the right to breastfeed in public (Fla. Stat. Ann. §§800.02-04, 847.001) after the media publicized an incident of a security guard harassing a nursing mother at a shopping center.

6. Innovative practices. Several states have launched innovative practices to encourage mothers to breastfeed. In 2011, Rhode Island became the first state to end the widespread practice of giving away free formula to new mothers. Massachusetts soon followed suit. In New York City, Mayor Michael Bloomberg initiated a controversial program to require new mothers in participating hospitals to sign out formula (similar to the hospital practice for medications), and also to require nurses to give new mothers a talk on the advantages of breastfeeding.[57] Evaluate the likely success of these initiatives.

---

[55]. Law, supra note [26], at 1033-1034.

[56]. See Nat'l Conf. of State Legislatures, Breastfeeding State Laws (Mar. 31, 2015), http://www.ncsl.org/research/health/breastfeeding-state-laws.aspx (explaining that virtually all states allow breastfeeding in public or private, 29 states exempt breastfeeding from public indecency laws, 27 states have laws related to breastfeeding in the workplace, 17 states exempt breastfeeding mothers from jury duty, and five states have implemented breastfeeding awareness programs).

[57]. K.J. Dell'Antonia, Bloomberg's Breastfeeding Nudge—or Shove, N.Y. Times, July 31, 2012, http://parenting.blogs.nytimes.com/2012/07/31/bloombergs-breast-feeding-nudge-%E2%80%94-or-shove.

Arlie Hochschild & Ann Machung, The Second Shift: Working Families and the Revolution at Home

4, 7-10 (rev. ed., 2012)

[How well do couples work two full-time jobs and raise young children? The author interviewed 50 couples to answer this question by determining their allocation of household tasks.]

[I] discovered that women worked roughly fifteen hours longer [at home] each week than men. Over a year, they worked an *extra month of twenty-four-hour days a year*. . . . Just as there is a wage gap between men and women in the workplace, there is a "leisure gap" between them at home. Most women work one shift at the office or factory and a "second shift" at home. . . .

Men who share the load at home seemed just as pressed for time as their wives, and as torn between the demands of career and small children. . . . But the majority of men did not share the load at home. Some refused outright. Others refused more passively, often offering a loving shoulder to lean on, an understanding ear as their working wife faced the conflict they both saw as hers. . . . But I came to realize that those husbands who helped very little at home were often indirectly just as deeply affected as their wives by the need to do that work, through the resentment their wives feel toward them. . . .

[E]ven when husbands happily shared the hours of work, their wives felt more *responsible* for home and children. More women kept track of doctors' appointments and arranged for playmates to come over. More mothers than fathers worried about the tail on a child's Halloween costume or a birthday present for a school friend. They were more likely to think about their children while at work and to check in by phone with the baby-sitter. . . .

Partly because of this, more women felt torn between one sense of urgency and another, between the need to soothe a child's fear of being left at day care and the need to show the boss she's "serious" at work. More women than men questioned how good they were as parents. . . .

Twenty percent of the men in my study shared housework equally. Seventy percent of men did a substantial amount (less than half but more than a third), and 10 percent did less than a third. Even when couples share more equitably in the work at home, women do two-thirds of the *daily* jobs at home, like cooking and cleaning up—jobs that fix them into a rigid routine. Most women cook dinner and most men change the oil in the family car. But, as one mother pointed out, dinner needs to be prepared every evening around six o'clock, whereas the car oil needs to be changed every six months. . . . A child needs to be tended daily, while the repair of household appliances can often wait. . . .

Another reason women may feel more strained than men is that women more often do two things at once—for example, write checks and return phone calls, vacuum and keep an eye on a three-year-old, fold laundry and think out the shopping list. . . . Beyond doing more at home, women also devote *proportionately more* of their time at home to housework and proportionately less of it to child care. Of all the time men spend working at home, more of it goes to child care. . . . Since most parents prefer to tend to their children rather than clean house, men do more of what they'd rather do. . . . Men also do fewer of the "undesirable" household chores: fewer men than women wash toilets and scrub the bathroom. . . .

All, in all, if in this period of American history, the two-job family is suffering from a speed-up of work and family life, working mothers are its primary victims. It is ironic, then, that often it falls to women to be the "time and motion expert" of family life. Watching inside homes, I noticed it was often the mother who rushed children, saying "Hurry up! It's time to go." . . . Sadly enough, women are more often the lightning rod for family aggressions aroused by the speed-up of work and family life. They are the "villains" in a process by which they are the primary victims. More than the longer hours, the sleeplessness, and feeling torn, this is the saddest cost to women of the extra month a year.

Postscript. Recent research confirms the above findings regarding the gender-based division of household labor. In households where both spouses work full time, the wife performs significantly more housework and childcare. In 2013, almost half of women did housework (e.g., cleaning or doing laundry), compared to about one-fifth of men. In households with children under the age of six, women spent an average of 1 hour a day in childcare activities (e.g., bathing or feeding), while men spent 26 minutes doing those activities. The study also found that men spent more time on leisure activities (e.g., participating in sports, exercise, or recreation) than women. [58]

NOTE: WORK-FAMILY CONFLICT ISSUES

1. Mothers' dilemmas. Despite their gains in the workplace, women face more hurdles than men in the working world. The biggest career obstacle is the work-family conflict; i.e., the need to raise children at the same time as women are progressing in their careers. When women leave their careers to raise children, they find themselves at a huge career disadvantage. Children impact women professionally more than men. For example, women's time out of the workplace has a significant effect on their salaries (the "motherhood penalty"). Highly skilled mothers who work outside the home are hit the hardest. They earn one-third less over their careers than their childless counterparts. The income of lower-skilled mothers also drops, but by less than 15 percent.[59] Mothers suffer economic loss depending on the length of time they are absent from the workplace. For example, women who take one year off sacrifice 20 percent of their lifetime earnings, while women who take two or three years off sacrifice 30 percent.[60]

In response to these difficulties, some women are opting out of the workplace. The proportion of stay-at-home mothers has been rising steadily (from 23 percent

[58]. Bureau of Labor Statistics, American Time Use Survey Summary—2014 Results, http://www.bls.gov/news.release/atus.nr0.htm.

[59]. Stephen Gandel, Will Your Baby Cost You a Raise?, Time, Dec. 10, 2010 (citing research), http://business.time.com/2010/12/10/what-do-babies-cost/print/.

[60]. Joan C. Williams, Reshaping the Work-Family Debate: Why Men and Class Matter 25 (2010).

in 2000 to 29 percent in 2012).[61] These stay-at-home mothers occupy both ends of the socioeconomic scale: highly educated women who choose not to work, and low-income women, who calculate that, after paying for child care, their salaries do not justify the time spent away from their children. The lack of favorable parental leave policies means that women are far more likely to take extensive time off or stop pursuing their careers when they have children.

2. Restructuring the workplace. Professor Joan Williams, a prominent feminist legal scholar, argues that the modern workplace is structured around the "ideal worker," a norm that is based on the male model—that is, persons who have no childcare responsibilities, who are able to work 40 hours per week, and who can work overtime on short notice.[62] This view leads to significant difficulties for mothers in the workplace as they attempt to juggle work and family responsibilities. In response to this issue, Williams emphasizes the need to redesign the workplace. Other scholars similarly have argued that the state must take responsibility for structuring societal institutions to address the work-family conflict and support families' caretaking functions.[63]

3. Part-time employment and childcare. One solution to the work-family conflict is for employers to offer more *part-time employment.* Many parents prefer to work part time, especially when their children are young. Yet part-time employees face many work-related difficulties, such as arbitrary and irregular shift schedules. They do not receive proportionately equal compensation in terms of salary, benefits, and bonuses. They are generally ineligible for health benefits, pension plans, and retirement plans. Female part-time employees are less likely than their full-time counterparts to have access to parental leave with reemployment rights, and they are typically excluded from the benefits of the FMLA. Part-time workers are also taken less seriously by employers and often lack opportunities for advancement.[64]

4. Affordable childcare. Another solution is *affordable childcare.* Mothers are more than twice as likely to quit their jobs when the employer offers inadequate or no childcare.[65] One solution is increasing federal funding of childcare and early childhood education. In 1971, Congress passed the Comprehensive Child Development Act, a federally funded universal childcare measure; but President Richard Nixon vetoed the legislation.[66] Some solutions for governments and

---

[61]. The Return of the Stay-at-Home Mother, The Economist, Apr. 19, 2014 (chart #1), http://www.economist.com/news/united-states/21600998-after-falling-years-proportion-mums-who-stay-home-rising-return.

[62]. Joan Williams, Unbending Gender: Why Family and Work Conflict and What to Do About It 2-3 (2010).

[63]. See generally Maxine Eichner, The Supportive State (2010); Martha Albertson Fineman, The Autonomy Myth (2004); Clare Huntington, Failure to Flourish: How Law Undermines Family Relationships (2014).

[64]. On the inequities between part-time and full-time employment, see Arne L. Kalleberg, Part-Time Work and Workers in the United States: Correlates and Policy Issues, 52 Wash. & Lee L. Rev. 771 (1995); Nantiya Ruan & Nancy Reichman, Hours Equity Is the New Pay Equity, 59 Vill. L. Rev. 35 (2014).

[65]. Mildred Warner et al., Addressing the Affordability Gap: Framing Child Care as Economic Development, 12 J. Affordable Housing & Community Dev. L. 294, 295 (2003).

[66]. For a discussion of this legislation, see Deborah Dinner, The Costs of Reproduction: History and the Legal Construction of Sex Equality, 46 Harv. C.R.-C.L. L. Rev. 415, 457-464 (2011).

employers to make childcare more accessible and affordable include (1) government-provided child care, (2) government funding of private childcare, (3) loans and subsidies for childcare costs, and (4) mandates for employers and/or landlords to provide childcare.[67]

5. The "Mommy Track" and its effects on the family. Given the disproportionate impact of the work-family conflict on mothers, one reform might be separate employment tracks for different categories of women. In a classic article, Felice Schwartz (founder of the nonprofit consulting firm Catalyst) proposes that corporations distinguish between "career-primary" and "career-and-family" women by identifying the former early and giving them the same opportunities, while recognizing that they face sex stereotypes. On the other hand, she suggests that corporations recognize the need to retain career-and-family women by providing parental leave, support during relocation, flexible benefits, and quality affordable childcare. Her point of departure is that women in management are more costly for the corporation because such women often interrupt careers for family responsibilities.[68]

Professor Karen Czapanskiy worries about the impact of the "mommy track" (the name given by the media to Schwartz's proposal):

> An ideology of unequal labor allocation is not benign for fathers, either. By permitting employers to assume that every male worker has a female partner caring for the home and children, employers are freed to burden workers with schedules and demands that are inconsistent with family responsibilities or enjoyment. Men are denied social support for developing close relationships with their children. In the event of divorce, men may find themselves deprived of a realistic claim to custody because they have not provided daily care for their children nor learned to be fully competent and involved parents.
>
> Children may be victimized the most by gendered parenting and its second shift consequences. First, they experience and learn to replicate exploitative, antidemocratic family lives. [T]hey will learn that boys fulfill a role which includes very little nurturing behavior, and that girls fulfill one loaded with nurturing, but at a high cost when the nurturing is done by one who works for money. [Both boys and girls may] decide not to have children [or] that someone else, either a wife or a day care worker, will have to take care of any children they have. Because their gendered parents have modeled ways to allocate household labor through exploitation, rather than through mutual respect, negotiation, and power sharing, the relationship of the grownup child from the gendered household with a spouse or day care worker is also likely to be unequal and exploitative. . . .[69]

For additional commentary on the work-family conflict, see Jeanne M. Brett, Thirty-Five Years of Studying Work and Family, 35 Psychol. Women Q. 500 (2011); Anne-Marie Slaughter, Why Women Still Can't Have It All, Atlantic Mag., July/Aug. 2012, at 84.

---

[67]. Catherine Schur, Conspicuous by Their Absence: How Childcare Can Help Women Make It to the Top, 27 Geo. J. Legal Ethics 859 (2014).

[68]. Felice N. Schwartz, Management Women and the New Facts of Life, 67 Harv. Bus. Rev. 65 (Jan.-Feb. 1989).

[69]. Karen Czapanskiy, Volunteers and Draftees: The Struggle for Parental Equality, 38 UCLA L. Rev. 1415, 1455-1456 (1991).

6. Stereotypes and family responsibilities discrimination. Mothers in the workplace may face gender stereotypes about their lack of competence and commitment. Such stereotypes are illustrations, according to Joan Williams, of the "maternal wall"—barriers in the form of the perception that devotion to one's family renders one less capable of performing a job. The maternal wall may arise upon pregnancy, motherhood, or working part time.[70]

Williams also identifies another form of discrimination—"family responsibilities discrimination (FRD)"—stemming from the stereotyping of employees who take on caregiving responsibilities for children, elderly parents, spouses, or partners.[71] Common forms of this discrimination include (1) New Supervisor Syndrome (supervisors who change work arrangements); (2) Second Child Bias (treatment based on assumptions about employees' additional family responsibilities); and (3) the Elder Care Effect (treatment based on similar assumptions about commitment).[72] Men can also be victims of family responsibilities discrimination.

7. Class and the work-family conflict. The work-family conflict affects all women—the poor as well as professionals and the middle class. Joan Williams contends that strategies to address the work-family conflict require an examination of class-based as well as gender-based assumptions.[73] In a recent study, she identifies several ways that the work-family conflict affects low-income families. For example, their jobs often involve unpredictable schedules that make it difficult to schedule child care. Government policies to aid their families, such as low-cost child care, are often unavailable or underfunded. One-quarter of poor single mothers do not participate in the labor force, partly because the cost of child care would eliminate most or all of their earnings. Moreover, low-income mothers are more likely to be providing direct care for elders because they cannot afford to pay others to do so.[74]

Many low-wage workers are at the mercy of "just-in-time scheduling," in which employers give employees very little advance notice of their schedules, call upon workers at the last minute, during non-scheduled times, to meet unforeseen consumer demand, and send workers home before the scheduled end of their shifts if business slows. These problems exacerbate employees' difficulties in juggling the work-family balancing act.[75]

The fundamental problem is that today's workplace is still "perfectly designed for the workplace of 1960," when only 20 percent of mothers worked.[76] Today, 70 percent of American children live in households where all adults are working. Professor Williams urges the government to take a more active role in addressing these work-family issues. Specifically, she emphasizes a focus on four work-family

---

[70]. Joan C. Williams et al., eds., The Maternal Wall: Research and Policy Perspectives on Discrimination Against Mothers (2004).

[71]. See Joan C. Williams & Nancy Segal, Beyond the Maternal Wall: Relief for Family Caregivers Who Are Discriminated Against on the Job, 26 Harv. Women's L.J. 77 (2003).

[72]. Cynthia Thomas Calvert, Center for WorkLife Law, Family Responsibilities Discrimination: Litigation Update, 2010, at 2-3 (2010).

[73]. Joan C. Williams & Heather Boushey, The Three Faces of Work-Family Conflict: The Poor, Professionals, and the Missing Middle, Ctr. for Am. Progress & Work Life Law (Jan. 2010). See also Williams, Reshaping the Work-Family Debate, supra note [60].

[74]. Williams & Boushey, Three Faces of Work-Family Conflict, supra note [73].

[75]. Charlotte Alexander et al., Stabilizing Low-Wage Work, 50 Harv. C.R.-C.L. L. Rev. 1 (2015).

[76]. Williams & Boushey, Three Faces of Work-Family Conflict, supra note [73], at 3.

issues that cut across class-based lines: (1) workplace flexibility; (2) short-term and extended time off; (3) child care, adult care, and after-school care; and (4) the elimination of FRD. In short, the government must send the message that the "work-family conflict is not just a personal problem."[77]

Problem

Diane McCourtney's employer, Seagate Technology, dismisses the accounts clerk for excessive absenteeism. McCourtney's absences stem from her inability to find affordable day care for her infant, who suffers frequent respiratory ailments. Following her dismissal, she files a claim for unemployment benefits, which is contested by Seagate and denied by the state Jobs and Training Department. She appeals. Minnesota, similar to many states, requires claimants to show that they are "available" for work, although such availability may be restricted for "good cause." To what extent is McCourtney available for work? Do the restrictions on her availability reflect "good cause"? Should the result depend on the availability for childcare of McCourtney's husband? See McCourtney v. Imprimis Tech., 465 N.W.2d 721 (Minn. Ct. App. 1991). Cf. Phillips v. Martin Marietta Corp., 400 U.S. 542 (1971).

C. Tort Law

1. Tort Actions Against Third Parties: Alienation of Affections and Criminal Conversation

JONES v. SWANSON

341 F.3d 723 (8th Cir. 2003)

Bye, Circuit Judge.

. . . Donna Jones and Todd Swanson grew up in a small rural South Dakota community. They became romantically involved for a short time [after high school]. [T]he two did not see one another for twenty years until 1998.

In the interim, Todd became an orthopedic surgeon and moved to Las Vegas, Nevada. He married and raised a family. Donna met Richard Jones shortly after the relationship with Todd ended and was married to him in 1981. Donna and Richard have four children and settled in Sioux Falls, South Dakota. Richard worked as a hospital administrator at Sioux Valley Hospital where Donna also worked as a nurse. . . .

On September 23, 1998, Todd's father suffered a heart attack and was taken to Sioux Valley hospital. [Donna ran into Todd when he came to the hospital.] The

[77]. Id. at 60-62.

two struck up a conversation, and Donna mentioned she was having a birthday the next day. Todd asked if he could buy her lunch and Donna agreed. The next day Donna and Todd met at a restaurant. Todd presented her with a birthday card and informed the waiter it was Donna's birthday. Todd also made arrangements for a special birthday dessert. Todd testified Donna talked about her dissatisfaction with her job and marriage during lunch. In particular, she complained she was not getting as much sex from her husband as she wanted. Todd also testified Donna rubbed her leg against his during lunch.

After lunch, Donna and Todd took a walk in a nearby park. As they walked, Todd put his arm around Donna. When they sat down on a bench, Todd put his hand on her knee. Donna again voiced her dissatisfaction with her marriage, saying she "loved Richard as the father of her children but not as a woman loves a man." Donna invited Todd to kiss her and they kissed several times. Todd remarked he had made a "huge mistake" letting Donna go twenty years earlier, and Donna told Todd she had always loved him.

Todd returned to Las Vegas but about a week later the two spoke over the telephone. There was conflicting evidence at trial as to who placed the first call; both said the other called, but it is undisputed over the next several weeks Todd and Donna spoke hundreds of times.[3] . . . Todd told Donna he was planning to attend a meeting in San Francisco and asked if she could meet him. Donna agreed. . . .

Before leaving for San Francisco, Todd sent Donna a CD and told her to listen to a song entitled "I'll Go On Loving You." When she arrived at the airport, Todd was there to meet her and gave her a bouquet of flowers. . . . Over the course of the weekend, Todd bought Donna a number of gifts and also took her to some of the meetings he attended. . . .

After San Francisco, Donna and Todd went back to exchanging telephone calls, cards and gifts. During their calls they talked about leaving their respective spouses and making a life together, including where they would live and how their children would react. Among other things, Todd promised Donna a "Brady Bunch" family and future. In cards to Donna, Todd told her how much he cared for and loved her and how much he looked forward to being with her again. He also expressed concern and guilt over the affair. . . . In mid-November, [Donna] told Richard she was contemplating divorce. Donna denied any involvement with another man and told Richard she was not sure she loved him anymore.

Days later, Donna's sister-in-law and nephew were killed in a car accident. Todd, who was in Sioux Falls for Thanksgiving, attended the funeral. It was then Richard began to suspect something between Todd and Donna. . . . A few days later, Donna admitted to Richard she was having an affair with Todd. . . .

In December 1998, Donna and Todd went to Europe as planned. . . . After their European vacation Todd and Donna began joint and individual counseling sessions to prepare for what lay ahead. In January, Donna moved out of the family home. Todd had encouraged her to get her own place so he could call whenever he wanted. [S]he traveled to California to meet [Todd] at a medical convention where they spent two days and nights together. It was there, for the first time, Todd suggested ending the affair.

---

3. Telephone records show Donna placed approximately 386 calls and Todd placed 186 calls. Todd gave Donna access to a calling card [so] she would not have to pay for them.

Todd testified he began having doubts about the affair and suggested they reconcile with their spouses. Todd testified he told Donna that Richard was a good man and father, and she needed to work on her marriage because their relationship was not going to work out. Todd's, emotions, however, proved fickle. He later sent Donna a Valentine's Day card telling her how much he loved her. . . . In April 1999, Donna moved back home with Richard and they attempted counseling to save the marriage. On July 4, 1999, Richard gave Donna a diamond ring and begged her to stay and work things out. Later that month, when Todd returned to Sioux Falls for his sister's wedding, Donna contacted him and asked to meet. [They had a picnic lunch together and then had sex at Donna's house.]

After Todd's trip to Sioux Falls in July, the relationship continued to cool until November 1999, when Donna flew to Seattle, Washington [to meet Todd]. This was the last time Todd and Donna were intimate together. Afterwards, Todd told Donna to go home and reconcile with her husband because it was not going to work out. Instead of flying home, Donna flew to San Diego where she planned to reconnect with Todd who was attending another seminar. . . . When he arrived in San Diego, he left a message telling Donna he would not be able to meet her. Donna was not dissuaded. Instead she waited for Todd at the airport in San Diego because "she wanted [him] to see [her] one more time."

In May 2000, Richard filed suit against Todd for alienation of affection. Donna moved out of the family home permanently [and] Richard sued for divorce. . . . On appeal, Todd argues: 1) there was insufficient evidence to prove the tort of alienation of affection, 2) there was no causal connection between the affair and the breakup of the marriage, [and] 3) the compensatory and punitive damages awards were unwarranted by the evidence and excessive.[5]

. . . The elements of a claim for alienation of affection are 1) wrongful conduct of the defendant, 2) loss of affection or consortium, and 3) a causal connection between the wrongful conduct and the loss of affection or consortium. The essence of the action is malicious interference with the marriage relationship, and a loss of consortium is the actionable consequence of an action for alienation of affection. Consortium is a right growing out of the marital relationship, and includes the right of either spouse to the society, companionship, conjugal affection, and assistance of the other.

> A wife conceivably may transfer her affection from her husband to another because of the latter's kindliness, attractiveness, desirability, financial superiority, or some other reason. Such motivation for transfer of affection may be a substantial factor even though the defendant had nothing to do with it. *The gravamen of an action for alienation of affection [therefore] is enticement. It is based on an intentional tort, not negligence.* The acts which lead to the loss of affection must be wrongful and intentional, calculated to entice the affection of one spouse away from the other. . . . (Emphasis added.)

[Pankratz v. Miller, 401 N.W.2d 543, 548-549 (S.D. 1987).]

---

5. Todd also complains the tort of alienation of affection is an anachronism and points out its continued viability as a legitimate cause of action has been roundly criticized. The propriety of South Dakota's decision to recognize alienation of affection as a tort claim is not an issue for this court. Despite repeated invitations, the Supreme Court of South Dakota has refused to judicially abolish the cause of action. . . .

. . . Todd argues the evidence showed the marriage between Donna and Richard was over before he arrived on the scene and his actions did not cause the alienation of Donna's affection. In other words, Todd argues his actions were not the proximate cause of Donna's loss of affection for her husband.

There was considerable evidence tending to show the marriage was on precarious footing before Todd arrived on the scene. In the months leading up to the affair, Donna repeatedly expressed dissatisfaction with her marriage and frequently stayed out late drinking with friends. The encounter [at a party when she was drunk and ended up in bed with a man] further illustrates the uncertainty of the marriage's future, and seriously undermines Donna's testimony claiming she loved Richard. Finally, Donna's counselor testified he met with Donna in November 1998, just as the affair was beginning, and Donna was already on her way out of the marriage.

There was, however, also evidence suggesting the marriage may have survived or, at the very least, Donna still had affection for Richard. Donna testified the marriage had been near perfect and minimized the problems leading up to the affair. As the affair wound down, Donna moved back home with Richard and started marriage counseling in an attempt to save the relationship. Despite Donna's attempts to reconcile with Richard, Todd continued to pursue the relationship. Clearly Donna was dissatisfied with the marriage, but the evidence was sufficient for the jury to conclude she harbored affection for Richard which was alienated as a result of Todd's involvement.

Todd also argues he was not solely to blame for the affair. Rather, Donna was infatuated with him and pursued the relationship with even greater enthusiasm than he. Richard's cause of action is not dependent upon finding Donna was an unwilling participant in the affair. . . . [E]vidence of infatuation may be offered to prove the absence of wrongful conduct or to demonstrate a lack of causation, but it does not obviate a defendant's wrongful conduct. Here, the jury was free to conclude Donna was infatuated but left Richard because of Todd's active enticement.

Todd also argues he never intended to harm Richard. The intent to inflict harm, however, is not an element of the tort. . . .

[Finally, Todd argues the damages were excessive.] [E]vidence of Donna's pre-affair conduct and her dissatisfaction with the marriage undermines Richard's claim for damages. Accordingly, we conclude the evidence does not support the $450,000 award of compensatory damages and must be reduced [to $150,000] or a new trial ordered. [The court also finds that the punitive damages award of $500,000 was excessive and ordered a remitter in the amount of $250,000, based on the facts that Donna was a willing participant and the marriage was in jeopardy before Todd arrived; Todd repeatedly expressed remorse; and the award represented nearly half of Todd's income and 25 percent of his net worth.] We conditionally affirm the judgment entered on the verdict in favor of Richard, subject to his acceptance of a remittitur judgment. . . .

Notes and Questions

1. Epilogue. In a fascinating aftermath Donna later contacted Todd and told him that she had lied when she testified that (1) she still had feelings for Richard when the affair began and (2) the affair caused the marriage to fail. Todd recorded her admissions and sought to vacate the judgment. In the meantime, Richard, who had filed for bankruptcy and assigned his interest in the (still unpaid) judgment to his lawyers, became convinced that Donna had lied at trial and also sought a dismissal of the judgment. The district court denied Todd's motion, reasoning that deception by a non-party does not warrant extension of the limitations period. Jones v. Swanson, 512 F.3d 1045 (8th Cir. 2008).

2. Elements. At common law, interference with the marital relationship was remediable by tort actions for *alienation of affections* and *criminal conversation.* Alienation of affections requires: (1) a valid marriage; (2) wrongful conduct by the defendant with the plaintiff's spouse; (3) the loss of affection or consortium; and (4) a causal connection between the defendant's conduct and the deprivation of affection. Restatement (Second) of Torts §683 (1977).

Unlike alienation of affections, criminal conversation requires sexual intercourse. Restatement (Second) of Torts §685 (1977). Criminal conversation has been called a strict liability tort because the only defenses are the plaintiff's (that is, the injured spouse's) consent and the statute of limitations. The participating spouse's consent is not a defense.

3. Abolition movement. After its initial recognition by New York in 1866, the tort of alienation of affections was adopted by virtually every state. Currently, however, most jurisdictions have abolished alienation of affections and criminal conversation either by statute or by case law.[78]

4. Rationales. What are the rationales for retaining tort liability for alienation of affections and criminal conversation? Does abolition of these torts "send the message that we are devaluing the marriage relationship"? Gorman v. McMahon, 792 So. 2d 307 (Miss. Ct. App. 2001). Do the rationales support liability for *post-separation* sexual misconduct? Can a parent be liable for alienating the affection of a child? See In re Noland-Vance, 321 S.W.3d 398 (Mo. Ct. App. 2010); Sandi S. Varnado, Inappropriate Parental Influence: A New App for Tort Law and Upgraded Relief for Alienated Parents, 61 DePaul L. Rev. 113 (2011).

Should the torts of alienation of affections and criminal conversation be abolished? Should divorce provide the sole remedy for marriages beset by adultery? Some jurisdictions have abolished criminal conversation while retaining alienation of affections. See, e.g., Saunders v. Alford, 607 So. 2d 1214 (Miss. 1992); Norton v. Macfarlane, 818 P.2d 8 (Utah 1991). Does this approach make sense?

5. Damages. In *Jones,* the appellate court found excessive the jury award of $450,000 in compensatory damages and $500,000 in punitive damages. Is the harm caused by adultery alleviated by money damages? Some courts have awarded multimillion dollar verdicts for alienation of affections. Do such huge damage awards argue for or against retention of tort liability?

---

[78]. See Jean M. Cary & Sharon Scudder, Breaking up Is Hard to Do: North Carolina Refuses to End Its Relationship with Heart Balm Torts, 4 Elon L. Rev. 1, 14 (2012) (reporting that 45 states and the District of Columbia have "abolished or severely limited" the cause of action for alienation of affection, and 42 states and the District of Columbia have "repealed or restricted" criminal conversation). See also State ex rel. Golden v. Kaufman, 760 S.E.2d 883 (W. Va. 2014).

6. Liability for marriage counselors. The abolition of alienation of affections and criminal conversation in many jurisdictions left an unanswered question about the viability of claims against marriage counselors who engage in an affair with one of the spouses. Courts are split about such claims. Compare Bailey v. Faulkner, 940 So. 2d 247 (Ala. 2006), with Scamardo v. Dunaway, 650 So. 2d 417 (La. Ct. App. 1995). Should anti-heartbalm statutes preclude such suits? Alternatively, should recovery be based on alternative theories, such as intentional or negligent infliction of emotional distress? Are such theories distinguishable from alienation of affections? What are the arguments pro and con the imposition of liability? What other possible theories might lead to imposition of liability?

7. Choice of law. May a plaintiff recover for alienation of affections if the plaintiff is domiciled in a state that recognizes the tort but the adultery occurs in a state that does not? See Jones v. Skelley, 673 S.E.2d 385 (N.C. Ct. App. 2009) (ruling that choice of law is based on where the injury occurs and finding that phone calls from one state to another that led to clandestine meetings could suffice). But cf. Nordness v. Faucheaux, 170 So. 3d 454 (Miss. 2015).

8. Delayed discovery. Some extramarital affairs remain secret for a considerable time. If a spouse discovers the affair long after it ends, does the statute of limitations bar suit? Compare Hancock v. Watson, 962 So. 2d 627 (Miss. Ct. App. 2007) (relevant time is when wife's and not plaintiff's affections were alienated), with Misenheimer v. Burris, 637 S.E.2d 173 (N.C. 2006) (statute begins to run upon discovery of affair, not its commission). Will the innocent party be judicially estopped if his delayed discovery of the affair led him to pursue a divorce on grounds other than adultery? See Wood v. Cooley, 78 So. 3d 920 (Miss. Ct. App. 2011).

9. Loss of consortium. Early authorities recognized only the husband's right to loss of consortium caused by injury to the wife. A claim for loss of consortium encompasses not merely loss of the sexual relationship, but also loss of comfort, affection, and companionship. The historical reluctance to recognize the wife's cause of action stemmed from concerns that her injury was indirect, the damages were too speculative, a damage award would result in double recovery, and the liability might extend too far to other classes of plaintiffs. A majority of jurisdictions now recognize the wife's cause of action. See, e.g., Rodriguez v. Bethlehem Steel Corp., 525 P.2d 669 (Cal. 1974).

Problem

Nicole and Vinnie have been married for five years. They have two children, ages two and four. Nicole consults Dr. Charles Brent for neck pain. Thereafter, Nicole and Dr. Brent begin talking on the phone and exchanging text messages, and eventually, they engage in consensual sexual relations on two occasions. Nicole's husband, Vinnie, discovers the text messages on Nicole's phone and immediately files for divorce. He then sues Dr. Brent, individually and on behalf of his two children, alleging the torts of alienation of affections and negligent infliction of emotional distress. Dr. Brent moves for summary judgment on the children's claims. Do children have standing to sue a parent's paramour who caused their parents to divorce? See Brent v. Mathis, 154 So. 3d 842 (Miss. 2014).

2. Tort Actions Between Spouses

KOHL v. KOHL

149 So. 3d 127 (Fla. Dist. Ct. App. 2014)

Gross, J.

[I]n January 2009, the former wife [filed] a cause of action for negligent transmission of a sexually transmissible disease, specifically HPV [human papillomavirus]. This claim was based upon the former husband's failure to warn the former wife during their marriage that he had HPV. The disease manifested in June 2008, when the former wife learned from a routine Pap smear that she had contracted "high-risk" HPV, resulting in the development of "precancerous cell changes."

[T]here were no allegations that the former husband had been diagnosed with HPV or that he had experienced symptoms of the disease. [T]he former wife alleged that [the husband] "had a duty of reasonable care . . . either to warn her or take other precautions to prevent the spread of the [HPV]," [that he] breached this duty and, in turn, proximately caused the former wife to contract HPV, resulting in damages for "past and future pain and suffering, past and future medical expenses, past and future mental pain and suffering, and past and future loss of full function of mind and body." . . .

Nationwide, [common law] courts "have long imposed liability on individuals who have harmed others by transmitting communicable diseases," paving the way for recognition of "a cause of action for the negligent transmission of sexually transmitted diseases." While Florida courts have embraced this national consensus, Florida case law has suggested that such a suit must be predicated on a statutory violation. [This] limitation on a common law cause of action derives from the application of [our] criminal statute that makes it a first-degree misdemeanor to knowingly transmit certain sexually transmissible diseases. The statute provides in relevant part:

> It is unlawful for any person who has chancroid, gonorrhea, granuloma inguinale, lymphogranuloma venereum, genital herpes simplex, chlamydia, nongonococcal urethritis (NGU), pelvic inflammatory disease (PID)/acute salpingitis, or syphilis, when such person knows he or she is infected with one or more of these diseases and when such person has been informed that he or she may communicate this disease to another person through sexual intercourse, to have sexual intercourse with any other person, unless such other person has been informed of the presence of the sexually transmissible disease and has consented to the sexual intercourse. Fla. Stat. § 384.24.

[However] we disagree [that the above statute] exclusively controls the elements of the negligence cause of action to which it applies [because the statute fails to] "unequivocally state that it changes the common law, or is so repugnant to the common law that the two cannot coexist." [E]ven though HPV is not one of the diseases enumerated in the statute, its transmission could still form the basis of a common law negligence claim. . . .

Our next task is to determine whether the former wife's complaint stated a cause of action. The linchpin of liability for imposing a legal duty to avoid negligent transmission of a sexually transmissible disease is the defendant's knowledge that he or she harbors the disease. A duty will not lie where the defendant is unaware of the condition, since the risk created by his or her sexual activity is unforeseen. See Restatement (Second) of Torts § 289 cmt. b (1965). In other states, courts require the plaintiff to "show that the defendant had actual or *constructive* knowledge that he or she was infected with the transmitted STD." The availability of a constructive knowledge showing is critical, since "[a] plaintiff will rarely be able to show that a defendant had actual knowledge of his or her infection." . . . We see no reason to depart from the majority view. . . .

Applying an actual or constructive knowledge standard, our sister states have carved out two situations sufficient to impose a duty. . . . First, a defendant will have the requisite knowledge if he or she has been formally diagnosed with a sexually transmissible disease by a medical professional. Second, the existence of obvious symptoms—such as rashes, genital warts, or discharge—will suffice to impute constructive knowledge. [H]owever, a requirement of actual knowledge to establish a legal duty is applicable [here] where the disease at issue is HPV, which is uniquely prevalent and often not symptomatic.

In this case, the former wife's complaint raises two allegations to infer the former husband's knowledge of his HPV infection. . . . First, the complaint contended that the former husband engaged in "high-risk" sexual behavior, such as having sexual relations outside his marriage and sleeping with prostitutes. Second, it contends that the former husband "knew or should have known he was exposed to HPV as his ex-wife had undergone a hysterectomy." Both grounds seek to extend liability beyond constructive knowledge, from what the defendant "should have known," to what "may have happened"—a privacy invasion we believe "open[s] a door better left closed."

The complaint's "high-risk" allegation is similar to one [we previously rejected]. . . . "Policy considerations strongly suggest that merely engaging in 'high risk' activity does not satisfy the should-have-known standard and does not, nor should it, impose a duty upon individuals to disclose previous high-risk behavior." From a logistical standpoint, developing the contours of "high-risk" behavior would be an unwieldy, unpredictable task. . . . As the court explained in Doe v. Johnson, 817 F. Supp. 1382 (W.D. Mich.1993):

> [I]mposition of a duty to disclose one's "high-risk" status raises a number of questions. [E]ven if a workable definition of "high-risk" were discovered, would a duty be imposed on non-high-risk group members to disclose to every potential sex partner all prior sexual contacts with partners who were so-called "high-risk" group members? . . . What are the privacy implications of imposing such a standard on a class of people? Would the duty eventually extend to everyone who has had any sexual contact outside of a monogamous relationship? [Id. at 1394.]

[W]e decline to open Pandora's box by imposing a duty in negligence for engaging in "high-risk" sexual behavior.

Similar logic bars the imposition of a legal duty based on the former wife's allegation that the former husband knew of his HPV because his prior wife underwent a hysterectomy. [W]ithout evidence linking the hysterectomy to HPV, there is no justifiable reason to believe a reasonable person in the former husband's shoes should have *known* he had HPV from that fact alone. The former husband's "knowledge" in this case cannot be predicated on remote chance and guesswork. For these reasons, we hold that the former wife's complaint failed to state a claim for negligent transmission of a sexually transmissible disease. . . .

Notes and Questions

1. **Interspousal immunity.** At common law, the doctrine of interspousal immunity precluded interspousal tort suits. The doctrine was premised on the legal fiction of marital unity (i.e., because husband and wife shared a legal identity, interspousal tort suits were impossible), and later on concerns that litigation would undermine marital harmony and invade marital privacy. Abrogation occurred first for intentional acts and, subsequently, for negligent acts. Even after abrogation, however, some states continued to disallow spousal suits deemed to intrude on marital privacy. Almost all states have abrogated the doctrine either fully or partially. See Bozman v. Bozman, 830 A.2d 450, 487 (Md. Ct. App. 2003) (explaining history).

2. **Transmission of venereal disease: Background.** Since the late nineteenth century, courts have recognized tort liability for negligent transmission of venereal disease. Historical concern about the impact of venereal disease on the family stemmed from the influence of the eugenics movement (i.e., the belief that social ills are transmitted through the family by heredity); concerns about immigration (i.e., the myth that immigrants had high rates of infection); worries about industrialization (i.e., a preoccupation with the immorality engendered by city living); and concerns about the sexual double standard (i.e., fear that dissolute husbands transmitted venereal disease to chaste young women). See generally Allan M. Brandt, No Magic Bullet: A Social History of Venereal Disease in the United States Since 1880 (1987); Sex, Sin, and Suffering: Venereal Disease and European Society Since 1870 (Roger Davidson & Lesley A. Hall eds., 2001).

3. **Duty to disclose?** The Restatement of Torts postulates that a spouse has a duty to disclose physical conditions that make cohabitation dangerous. Restatement (Second) of Torts §554. How far does the obligation to disclose extend? Does it extend to sexually transmissible conditions? To intimate partners? See Deuschle v. Jobe, 30 S.W.3d 215 (Mo. Ct. App. 2000). To third parties, such as the spouse of one's *paramour*? See Carsanaro v. Colvin, 716 S.E.2d 40 (N.C. Ct. App. 2011).

4. **Standard.** Does an infected spouse's ignorance of the infection preclude liability? What does *Kohl* say about this matter? Does liability extend to constructive, and not merely actual, notice? If so, why? Should the defendant's misrepresentation that he or she is not infected toll the statute of limitations? See Beller v. Tilbrook, 571 S.E.2d 735 (Ga. 2002). See generally Deana Pollard Sacks,

Intentional Sex Torts, 77 Fordham L. Rev. 1051 (2008); Michele L. Mekel, Note: Kiss and Tell: Making the Case for the Tortious Transmission of Herpes and Human Papillomavirus, 66 Mo. L. Rev. 929 (2001).

5. Statutes of limitations. Spouses pursue interspousal tort litigation at separation or divorce. Common theories of liability include battery, fraud, intentional infliction of emotional distress, negligence, and negligence per se. What was the plaintiff's theory? Why did the state statute pose an obstacle? How did the court overcome that obstacle? Short statutes of limitations for intentional torts (especially compared to longer statutes of limitations for negligent torts) may bar plaintiffs' claims. See Jennifer B. Wriggins, Domestic Violence in the First-Year Torts Curriculum, 54 J. Legal Educ. 511, 513 (2004) (criticizing short limitations periods in interspousal context).

6. Scope of liability. Should interspousal liability, which first emerged in cases of negligent driving, extend to *household accidents* between husband and wife? See Brown v. Brown, 409 N.E.2d 717 (Mass. 1980) (wife injured as a result of husband's negligent snow removal). Are there aspects of marital life that should *not* give rise to liability? Consider the following (posed by the husband's attorney in *Brown*): (1) Wife puts too much salt in meals and Husband gets high blood pressure. (2) Wife does not want children but she becomes pregnant. (3) Husband normally takes out the garbage. When he forgets, Wife hurts her back lifting the heavy bag. 6 Fam. L. Rep. (BNA) 1162 (Aug. 26, 1980).

7. Privacy. What aspects of privacy does *Kohl* address? Is the court concerned with marital privacy, sexual privacy, or both? What role *should* the couple's marriage play in suits such as this one?

How does *Kohl* weigh the privacy versus public health and safety questions that arise in tort law? How *should* a court weigh the privacy costs against the traditional duty to warn in tort law in the context of sexual transmission cases? Should the balance change depending on the seriousness of the harm to plaintiff? Professor Eugene Volokh responds as follows:

> Under standard tort law principles, there would be a good case for a duty to warn about much of this high-risk behavior. The potential benefit in disease averted is great. The likelihood of transmission is substantial [and] the financial cost of disclosure is generally nil. Warning of risk is thus a cost-effective precaution, which can help avoid the injury that would otherwise have been caused by the potential defendant. And tort law routinely imposes a duty to warn even about relatively modest risks. . . .
>
> Of course, this cost-benefit analysis does not mean that such warnings should be mandated by the duty of reasonable care, especially as to some risk factors (such as a history of promiscuity or same-sex sexual behavior): The warnings carry a privacy cost as well as a financial cost, and the privacy cost may make it unreasonable to require such warnings. The point here, though, is that if the duty to warn of certain risk factors is rejected, it would likely be precisely because privacy costs are included as part of the risk-benefit analysis.[79]

---

[79]. Eugene Volokh, Tort Law Versus Privacy, 114 Colum. L. Rev. 879, 892-893 (2014).

Volokh makes no distinction between marital couples and other sexual partners. Should this factor affect the analysis?

8. Spousal spying. Spouses sometimes spy on each other to discover evidence of extramarital affairs. Does such spying violate the law? Federal law (known as the Wiretap Act or Title III) imposes liability for nonconsensual intentional interception of wire, oral, or electronic communications. The Wiretap Act, enacted in 1968, imposes civil and criminal liability and creates special evidentiary rules that exclude use of the contents. It provides for a minimum fine of $100 per day or $10,000, whichever is greater, plus punitive damages. 18 U.S.C. §2520(c)(2)(B). A number of states have similar statutes.

Before the Internet, spousal spying consisted of tapping telephones. The Wiretap Act applied only to wire and oral communications until 1986. In that year, Congress amended the Wiretap Act by adding the term "electronic communications." Electronic Communications Privacy Act (ECPA), Pub. L. No. 99–508, 100 Stat. 1848.

Should interspousal immunity apply to the Wiretap Act because of privacy concerns? According to the majority of federal courts, spouses are not shielded from liability. Glazner v. Glazner, 347 F.3d 1212 (11th Cir. 2003). Should liability extend to spousal *installation* of "spyware"? See LaRocca v. LaRocca, 86 F. Supp. 3d 540 (E.D. La. 2015)? To global positioning satellite (GPS) electronic tracking devices?

Problems

1. Jane Doe contracts HIV from her fiancé, Albert Dilling. Shortly after Albert dies of AIDS, Jane sues his estate and his parents, alleging that the parents misrepresented his condition to her as metal poisoning and Lyme disease. Doe is prepared to testify that when she fell ill with flulike symptoms and a high fever, she thought that she had the flu and did not see a doctor. Had Albert's parents told her the truth, she alleges, she would have been tested immediately for HIV and would have commenced treatment. What should be the extent of liability for a defendant's *family members* in an action for failure to disclose to a plaintiff that she was exposed to a sexually transmissible disease? Does the defendant's insurer owe a duty to defend the action? Compare Doe v. Dilling, 861 N.E.2d 1052 (Ill. App. Ct. 2006), with F.S. v. L.D., 827 A.2d 335 (N.J. Super. Ct. 2003).

2. Actor Alec Baldwin and his ex-wife, actress Kim Basinger, share joint custody of their 11-year-old daughter, Ireland. One day, Ireland fails to answer a prearranged phone call from her father. He then leaves the following message on her cell phone: "You have insulted me for the last time. I don't give a damn that you're 12 years old or 11 years old, or a child, or that your mother is a thoughtless pain in the ass who doesn't care about what you do." He calls her a "rude, thoughtless little pig." "You don't have the brains or the decency as a human being." He threatens: "I am going to get on a plane [and] straighten your ass out when I see you!" He screams, "This crap you pull on me . . . you would never dream of doing to your mother, and you do it to me constantly." The press prints the story. Baldwin

believes that Basinger released the message to the press. Does Baldwin have a cause of action against Basinger for violation of wiretapping laws? See Sean Hannity & Alan Colmes, Alec Baldwin Leaves Abusive Message for His Daughter, FDCH Ent. Transcripts, Apr. 23, 2007, 2007 WLNR 7651405.

D. Evidentiary Privileges Arising from the Marital Relationship

TRAMMEL v. UNITED STATES

445 U.S. 40 (1980)

Mr. Chief Justice BURGER delivered the opinion of the Court.

We granted certiorari to consider whether an accused may invoke the privilege against adverse spousal testimony so as to exclude the voluntary testimony of his wife. . . .

On March 10, 1976, petitioner Otis Trammel was indicted with two others . . . for importing heroin into the United States from Thailand and the Philippine Islands and for conspiracy to import heroin. . . . The indictment also named six unindicted co-conspirators, including petitioner's wife Elizabeth Ann Trammel.

[P]etitioner and his wife flew from the Philippines to California in August 1975, carrying with them a quantity of heroin. . . . Elizabeth Trammel then traveled to Thailand where she purchased another supply of the drug. On November 3, 1975, with four ounces of heroin on her person, she boarded a plane for the United States. During a routine customs search in Hawaii, she was searched, the heroin was discovered, and she was arrested. After discussions with Drug Enforcement Administration agents, she agreed to cooperate with the Government.

Prior to trial on this indictment, petitioner . . . advised the court that the Government intended to call his wife as an adverse witness and asserted his claim to a privilege to prevent her from testifying against him. At a hearing on the motion, Mrs. Trammel was called as a Government witness under a grant of use immunity. She testified that she and petitioner were married in May 1975 and that they remained married.[1] She explained that her cooperation with the Government was based on assurances that she would be given lenient treatment. She then described, in considerable detail, her role and that of her husband in the heroin distribution conspiracy.

After hearing this testimony, the District Court ruled that Mrs. Trammel could testify in support of the Government's case to any act she observed during the marriage and to any communication "made in the presence of a third person"; however, confidential communications between petitioner and his wife were held to be privileged and inadmissible. . . .

---

1. In response to the question whether divorce was contemplated, Mrs. Trammel testified that her husband had said that "I would go my way and he would go his."

At trial, Elizabeth Trammel testified within the limits of the court's pretrial ruling; her testimony, as the Government concedes, constituted virtually its entire case against petitioner. He was found guilty on both the substantive and conspiracy charges. [Petitioner appealed, claiming that the admission of his wife's adverse testimony, over his objection, constituted reversible error.]

The privilege claimed by petitioner has ancient roots. Writing in 1628, Lord Coke observed that "it hath beene resolved by the Justices that a wife cannot be produced either against or for her husband." 1 E. Coke, A Commentarie upon Littleton 6b (1628). This spousal disqualification sprang from two canons of medieval jurisprudence: first, the rule that an accused was not permitted to testify in his own behalf because of his interest in the proceeding; second, the concept that husband and wife were one, and that since the woman had no recognized separate legal existence, the husband was that one. From those two now long-abandoned doctrines, it followed that what was inadmissible from the lips of the defendant-husband was also inadmissible from his wife.

[T]his rule of spousal disqualification remained intact in most common-law jurisdictions well into the 19th century. . . . Indeed, it was not until 1933, in Funk v. United States, 290 U.S. 371, that this Court abolished the testimonial disqualification in the federal courts, so as to permit the spouse of a defendant to testify in the defendant's behalf. *Funk,* however, left undisturbed the rule that either spouse could prevent the other from giving adverse testimony. The rule thus evolved into one of privilege rather than one of absolute disqualification.

The modern justification for this privilege against adverse spousal testimony is its perceived role in fostering the harmony and sanctity of the marriage relationship. Notwithstanding this benign purpose, the rule was sharply criticized. Professor Wigmore termed it "the merest anachronism in legal theory and an indefensible obstruction to truth in practice." 8 Wigmore §2228, at 221. The Committee on Improvements in the Law of Evidence of the American Bar Association called for its abolition. 63 American Bar Association Reports 594-595 (1938). In its place, Wigmore and others suggested a privilege protecting only private marital communications, modeled on the privilege between priest and penitent, attorney and client, and physician and patient. See 8 Wigmore §2332 et seq.

These criticisms influenced the American Law Institute, which, in its 1942 Model Code of Evidence advocated a privilege for marital confidences, but expressly rejected a rule vesting in the defendant the right to exclude all adverse testimony of his spouse. In 1953 the Uniform Rules of Evidence [followed] a similar course. . . . Several state legislatures enacted similarly patterned provisions into law. In Hawkins v. United States, 358 U.S. 74 (1958), this Court considered the continued vitality of the privilege against adverse spousal testimony in the federal courts. [*Hawkins*] left the federal privilege for adverse spousal testimony where it found it, continuing "a rule which bars the testimony of one spouse against the other unless both consent." Id., at 78. . . .

[T]he long history of the privilege suggests that it ought not to be casually cast aside. That the privilege is one affecting marriage, home, and family relationships—already subject to much erosion in our day—also counsels caution. At the same time, we cannot escape the reality that the law on occasion adheres to doctrinal concepts long after the reasons which gave them birth have disappeared and after experience suggests the need for change. . . .

Since 1958, when *Hawkins* was decided, support for the privilege against adverse spousal testimony has been eroded further. Thirty-one jurisdictions, including Alaska and Hawaii, then allowed an accused a privilege to prevent adverse spousal testimony. The number has now declined to 24. . . .

[W]e must decide whether the privilege against adverse spousal testimony promotes sufficiently important interests to outweigh the need for probative evidence in the administration of criminal justice.

It is essential to remember that the *Hawkins* privilege is not needed to protect information privately disclosed between husband and wife in the confidence of the marital relationship. . . . Those confidences are privileged under the independent rule protecting confidential marital communications. The *Hawkins* privilege is invoked, not to exclude private marital communications, but rather to exclude evidence of criminal acts and of communications made in the presence of third persons.

No other testimonial privilege sweeps so broadly. The privileges between priest and penitent, attorney and client, and physician and patient limit protection to private communications. These privileges are rooted in the imperative need for confidence and trust. . . . The *Hawkins* rule stands in marked contrast to these three privileges. Its protection is not limited to confidential communications; rather it permits an accused to exclude all adverse spousal testimony. As Jeremy Bentham observed more than a century and a half ago, such a privilege goes far beyond making "every man's house his castle," and permits a person to convert his house into "a den of thieves." 5 Rationale of Judicial Evidence 340 (1827). It "secures, to every man, one safe and unquestionable and ever ready accomplice for every imaginable crime." Id., at 338.

The ancient foundations for so sweeping a privilege have long since disappeared. Nowhere in the common-law world—indeed in any modern society—is a woman regarded as chattel or demeaned by denial of a separate legal identity and the dignity associated with recognition as a whole human being. Chip by chip, over the years those archaic notions have been cast aside. . . .

The contemporary justification for affording an accused such a privilege is also unpersuasive. When one spouse is willing to testify against the other in a criminal proceeding—whatever the motivation—their relationship is almost certainly in disrepair; there is probably little in the way of marital harmony for the privilege to preserve. In these circumstances, a rule of evidence that permits an accused to prevent adverse spousal testimony seems far more likely to frustrate justice than to foster family peace. Indeed, there is reason to believe that vesting the privilege in the accused could actually undermine the marital relationship. For example, in a case such as this the Government is unlikely to offer a wife immunity and lenient treatment if it knows that her husband can prevent her from giving adverse testimony. If the Government is dissuaded from making such an offer, the privilege can have the untoward effect of permitting one spouse to escape justice at the expense of the other. It hardly seems conducive to the preservation of the marital relation to place a wife in jeopardy solely by virtue of her husband's control over her testimony.

Our consideration of the foundations for the privilege and its history satisfy us that "reason and experience" no longer justify so sweeping a rule as that found acceptable by the Court in *Hawkins*. Accordingly, we conclude that the existing rule should be modified so that the witness-spouse alone has a privilege to refuse to testify adversely; the witness may be neither compelled to testify nor foreclosed from testifying. This modification—vesting the privilege in the witness-spouse—furthers the important public interest in marital harmony without unduly burdening legitimate law enforcement needs.

Here, petitioner's spouse chose to testify against him. That she did so after a grant of immunity and assurances of lenient treatment does not render her testimony involuntary. [Affirmed.]

Notes and Questions

1. Spousal privileges. The common law recognized two different privileges. Under the confidential marital communications privilege, private communications between husband and wife are privileged absolutely; either spouse may invoke this privilege. This rule is independent of the privilege at issue in *Trammel*: the ability of a spouse to exclude evidence by the other spouse of criminal acts and of communications in the presence of third parties. *Trammel* left the former privilege untouched in the federal courts. Should courts and legislatures also vest the confidential marital communications privilege in the witness spouse alone? Abolish it? Should the adverse spousal testimonial privilege apply in federal civil trials, as well as criminal trials?

2. Impact of *Trammel*. *Trammel* had several consequences. First, different rules now apply in the federal (and many state) courts concerning the two different types of spousal communications. Second, *Trammel* influenced many states to limit significantly the adverse spousal testimonial privilege.

3. Exceptions.

a. Joint participation. Should the law recognize an exception for either or both privileges when the spouses have *jointly participated* in the crime? Compare United States v. Miller, 588 F.3d 897, 905 (5th Cir. 2009) (privilege is unavailable), with Appeal of Malfitano, 633 F.2d 276 (3d Cir. 1980) (contra).

b. Separated spouses. Some courts have held that permanent, separated status at the time of the communication makes the marital communications privilege inapplicable. See, e.g., United States v. Singleton, 260 F.3d 1295, 1299 (11th Cir. 2001). Why?

c. Familial offenses. An exception exists for offenses committed against a spouse or a child of a spouse. See, e.g., United States v. Chandler, 2011 WL 1871223 (D. Nev. 2011) (holding marital communications privilege inapplicable when spouse is victim); Sherman v. State, 690 S.E.2d 915 (Ga. Ct. App. 2010) (same for child victim). What is the rationale for this exception?

d. Other exceptions. Should there be a "fraudulent marriage exception" to the marital privilege? Compare Glover v. State, 836 N.E.2d 414 (Ind. 2005) (refusing to engraft such an exception to the confidential communications privilege to exclude testimony of a woman who married a male co-worker solely to prevent him from being deported), with Commonwealth v. Lewis, 39 A. 3d 341 (Pa.

Super. Ct. 2012) (stating that statute did not authorize an exception, even in the case of collusive marriages or premarriage events).

4. Voluntariness. In vesting the adverse spousal testimony privilege in the witness-spouse, *Trammel* emphasizes that Mrs. Trammel gave her testimony voluntarily. The Supreme Court reasons that because her testimony was voluntary, there was little marital harmony to preserve. Was her testimony really voluntary? Is one spouse's willingness to testify against the other an indication that the marriage is past saving?

5. Images of marriage and family. What images of marriage and the family does *Trammel* reflect? Further, how does vesting the privilege in the witness-spouse "further the important public interest in marital harmony"? Alternatively, how does vesting it in the defendant-spouse "actually undermine the marital relationship"? Doesn't the rule in *Trammel* put the government in the position of "forc[ing] or encourag[ing] testimony which might alienate husband and wife, or further inflame existing domestic differences," Hawkins v. United States, 358 U.S. at 79 (cited in *Trammel*)? Is this an appropriate governmental role? For arguments that *Trammel* encourages the government to turn spouses against each other, see Richard O. Lempert, A Right to Every Woman's Evidence, 66 Iowa L. Rev. 725 (1981).

6. Policy reform. As society grows more accepting of cohabitation, does the evidentiary privilege need to be expanded to intimate partners and members of nontraditional families? See, e.g., Lisa Yurwit Bergstrom & W. James Denvil, Availability of Spousal Privileges for Same-Sex Couples, 11 U. Md. L.J. Race, Religion, Gender, & Class 224 (2011). Or should the adverse spousal testimony privilege be abolished altogether?

Problems

1. Kenneth Taylor, a police officer, is charged with aggravated battery of his girlfriend, Glenda Richard. The battery consisted of a severe beating with his fists, police flashlight, and service revolver. After Glenda's hospitalization, she agrees to testify against Kenneth and provides a typed statement, an affidavit expressing her desire to prosecute, and a videotape affirming that desire. Ten days before the trial, Glenda marries Kenneth. At trial, when the prosecutor calls Glenda as a victim-witness of the assault, she refuses to testify, invoking the spousal privilege for adverse testimony. Louisiana has no spousal crime exception to the privilege. What arguments would you advance on behalf of Glenda? On behalf of the prosecution? See Louisiana v. Taylor, 642 So. 2d 160 (La. 1994).

2. Former President Bill Clinton is accused of having an extramarital affair with former White House intern Monica Lewinsky and of having committed perjury by denying it before a grand jury investigating his liaison with another woman, Paula Jones. To help build a case against Clinton, independent counsel Kenneth Starr calls Marcia Lewis, the mother of Lewinsky, to testify before a federal grand jury

regarding her discussions about Lewinsky's relationship with Clinton. The resultant controversy (regarding the wisdom of compelling a mother to testify against her daughter) evokes a demand for an adverse testimonial privilege for parents and children. Do the rationales employed by *Trammel* with respect to the adverse spousal testimonial privilege apply with equal force to parents and children? See Hillary B. Farber, Do You Swear to Tell the Truth, the Whole Truth, and Nothing but the Truth Against Your Child?, 43 Loy. L.A. L. Rev. 551 (2010).

IV

Intimate Partner Violence

A. Introduction

This chapter explores the legal response to the social problem of intimate partner violence (IPV).[1] The occurrence of IPV pits the need for state intervention against respect for family privacy, raising questions about the appropriate relationship of the state to the family and its members.

First, the chapter presents background about the nature and scope of IPV. Introductory materials focus on the dynamics of abuse and the role of influential factors in domestic violence (such as age, gender, sexual orientation, disability, mental illness, race, ethnicity, immigration status, and social class).

Second, the chapter turns to the civil law response in the form of civil protection orders. Third, materials follow that focus on the criminal justice response. Criminal topics include self-defense, mandatory arrest, no-drop policies, the duties of law enforcement, and high-lethality crimes (marital rape, threats to kill, and stalking). Next, the chapter explains the provisions of the landmark Violence Against Women Act (VAWA). The text concludes by examining the problem of children's exposure to IPV, highlighting the contrast between the criminal justice response and that of the child protection system in the context of IPV.

[1]. Formerly, domestic violence was called "wife beating." The name was changed to "intimate partner violence" to reflect the fact that not all victims are "wives," and also that victimization involves many forms of abuse (not merely "beating").

Richard J. Gelles & Murray A. Straus, Intimate Violence

84, 88-96 (1988)

. . . The range of homes where wife beating occurs seems to defy categorization. . . . The profile of those who engage in violence with their partners is quite similar to the profile of the parents who are abusive toward their children. The greater the stress, the lower the income, the more violence. Also, there is a direct relationship between violence in childhood and the likelihood of becoming a violent adult. . . .

One of the more interesting aspects of the relationship between childhood and adult violence is that *observing* your parents hit one another is a more powerful contributor to the probability of becoming a violent adult than being a victim of violence. The learning experience of seeing your mother and father strike one another is more significant than being hit yourself. Experiencing, and more importantly observing, violence as a child teaches three lessons:

1. Those who love you are also those who hit you, and those you love are people you can hit.
2. Seeing and experiencing violence in your home establishes the moral rightness of hitting those you love.
3. If other means of getting your way, dealing with stress, or expressing yourself do not work, violence is permissible. . . .

Lurking beneath the surface of all intimate violence are confrontations and controversies over power. [T]he risk of intimate violence is the greatest when all the decisionmaking in a home is concentrated in the hands of one of the partners. . . .

It goes without saying that intimate violence is most likely to occur in intimate settings. . . . [T]he bedroom is the most lethal room in the house. . . . The kitchen and dining room are the other frequent scenes of lethal violence between family members.

After 8:00 p.m., the risk for family violence increases. This is almost self-evident, since this is also the time when family members are most likely to be together in the home. . . . The temporal and spatial patterns of intimate violence support our notion that privacy is a key underlying factor. . . .

Centers for Disease Control & Prevention (CDC), National Intimate Partner and Sexual Violence Survey (NISVS): Executive Summary 2 (2011)

[The National Intimate Partner and Sexual Violence Survey (NISVS) surveyed 16,507 adults about their experiences of sexual assault and IPV, and found the following results.]

VIOLENCE BY AN INTIMATE PARTNER

- More than 1 in 3 women (35.6%) and more than 1 in 4 men (28.5%) in the United States have experienced rape, physical violence, and/or stalking by an intimate partner in their lifetime.
- Among victims of intimate partner violence, more than 1 in 3 women experienced multiple forms of rape, stalking, or physical violence; 92.1% of male victims experienced physical violence alone. . . .
- Nearly 1 in 10 women in the United States (9.4%) has been raped by an intimate partner in her lifetime, and an estimated 16.9% of women and 8.0% of men have experienced sexual violence other than rape by an intimate partner at some point in their lifetime.
- About 1 in 4 women (24.3%) and 1 in 7 men (13.8%) have experienced severe physical violence by an intimate partner (e.g., hit with a fist or something hard, beaten, slammed against something) at some point in their lifetime.
- An estimated 10.7% of women and 2.1% of men have been stalked by an intimate partner during their lifetime. . . . .

Shannan Catalano et al., Bureau of Criminal Statistics, Female Victims of Violence

2-3 (2009)

FATAL INTIMATE PARTNER VIOLENCE

- [I]ntimate partners committed 14% of all homicides in the U.S. . . . Females made up 70% of victims killed by an intimate partner. . . . Females were killed by intimate partners at twice the rate of males. . . .
- 24% of female homicide victims were killed by a spouse or ex-spouse; 21% were killed by a boyfriend or girlfriend; and 19% by another family member. . . .
- [B]lack female victims of intimate partner homicide were twice as likely as white female homicide victims to be killed by a spouse. . . . Black females were four times more likely than white females to be murdered by a boyfriend or girlfriend. . . .
- Among male homicide victims in 2007, 16% were murdered by a family member or intimate partner. Of male homicide victims, 2% were killed by a spouse or ex-spouse and 3% were killed by a girlfriend or boyfriend. . . .

Judith A. Wolfer, Top Ten Myths About Domestic Violence

42 Md. Bar J. 38, 38-41 (2009)

[This list of 10 myths refutes common assumptions about domestic violence.]

MYTH #1: *Domestic violence happens when a batterer loses control of himself.*

Many of us hold the view that individuals who batter their partners simply lose control of themselves and their emotions; that, in an excess of anger or passion, batterers lose their reason and lash out at their partners. These outbursts are seen as unpredictable and, therefore, almost impossible to prevent. [However] domestic violence researchers and advocates have roundly rejected this explanation for domestic violence. We now know that domestic violence arises from a batterer's desire to control and dominate his (usually) female partner because he feels entitled to do so, not because he is suddenly angry.

Batterers utilize a wide array of coercive tactics to cement their control of their partners, such as isolating them from sources of help; humiliating them privately and in public; controlling their access to money, food, community and transportation; and micro-regulating their personal lives and those of their children. Physical violence only punctuates these coercive tactics—not the other way around. . . .

MYTH #2: *Men and women beat one another in equal numbers.*

The rates of domestic violence for both men and women have been studied regularly over the past 20 years with remarkably consistent results. Domestic violence continues to be the number one health and safety issue affecting women, but not men, in the United States. . . . Not only are women beaten more by male partners, but they are injured more. . . .

Women die at the hands of their intimate partners more often than men do. Of all the women killed annually in the United States, 40 to 50 percent of them are killed by an intimate partner. Only 3 percent of all men who are killed die at the hands of female intimate partners. . . .

MYTH #3: *If a woman doesn't leave her abuser, she must not really be afraid of him.*

Research demonstrates that a woman is most at risk of serious injury or death when she leaves her abuser than if she stays with him, so a battered woman's fear that leaving might be worse for her safety is an objectively reasonable fear. . . . In a Department of Justice study, 75 percent of the domestic assaults reported to law enforcement agencies were perpetrated on victims who were either divorced or separated from their assailants. . . .

Despite this grim reality, studies have also found that battered women often make multiple attempts to leave their abusers before they are finally successful in leaving their abusers permanently. A battered woman is often forced to weigh a staggering number of conflicting needs and realities against her fear of being abused again: she may have no other place to live, she may depend upon her partner's financial support to make ends meet, she may still care for him or feel responsible for him, she may stay with him for the sake of minor children, she may be too embarrassed to ask for help or too afraid to go out on her own, she may be isolated from family and friends and have no other source of help, or she may be simply too tired to move. These reasons are all highly rational and do not negate her fear of her abuser.

MYTH #4: *Getting a protective order does no good—it's just a sheet of paper.*

In fact, a protective order is much more than a mere piece of paper. It is quite clear now from the research that protective orders make a significant positive difference in victims' long-term experiences of safety and security. In a large study, researchers discovered that victims who had obtained protective orders experienced an 80 percent reduction in police-reported physical violence 12 months following the first reported incident. . . . This same effect did not occur, however, for victims who only obtained temporary orders . . . .

MYTH #5: *When a man threatens to kill his spouse or girlfriend, he doesn't really mean it—he's just blowing off steam.*

Statistically, it is more likely that he does mean it. In a large study involving 12 different cities across the country, researchers found that battered women who had been threatened with being killed were 15 times more likely to be killed than battered women who had never been threatened by their partners. . . .

MYTH #6: *There is no way to predict if a particular man will kill or seriously injure his partner.*

Actually, there is. Over the last few years, a group of public health researchers have disseminated the results of carefully designed, rigorous studies that looked for factors that were predictive of death from domestic violence. . . . The most predictive factor was the use or threatened use of a weapon.

The second most predictive factor was the batterer's threat to kill his partner. Other factors include the batterer's abuse of alcohol or drugs, an increase in the frequency or severity of battering, a report of choking or strangulation, forced sex, the presence of a child in the home from a previous relationship, abuse while pregnant, his unemployment, previous separations by the victim, stalking behavior, the existence of a new intimate partner for the victim, and the victim's subjective belief that the batterer could kill her. . . .

MYTH #7: *Just because a father abuses the mother of his children doesn't mean that he's not a good parent.*

Many members of the legal profession try to draw this distinction between how an abusive partner treats his intimate partner and what kind of parent he is. This distinction may be a false one in a majority of families. One study analyzed 36 separate studies that all looked at the risk of abuse of children where the mother reported being abused by the father. These studies revealed that 30 to 60 percent of those children whose mothers had been abused were themselves likely to be abused.

Even if children are not themselves physically abused, it is well settled in the field that living in a domestically violent home creates four distinct types of physical and emotional harms: the risk of exposure to traumatic events, the risk of neglect, the risk of being directly abused, and the risk of losing one or both of their parents. . . .

MYTH #8: *Women apply for protective orders to get a leg up on a custody case.*

[V]ictims apply for protective orders simply to get the abuse to stop. But they need a custody order to insure that there is no child snatching back and forth between the victim and abuser, and that exchanges can be safe and regulated. . . .

MYTH #9: *[Most state laws do not address domestic violence.]*

[In fact, most states have a variety of civil and criminal laws that address domestic violence. Protective orders and state criminal laws are explored infra this chapter.]

MYTH #10: *Rape or sexual assault really doesn't happen in a marriage.*

No act communicates domination and control better than rape or sexual assault. Rape and sexual assault occur in approximately 40 to 45 percent of all battering relationships, whether the parties are married or not. . . . [Sexual assault in intimate partner relationships is also a high-lethality indicator.]

B. The Role of Age: Teen Dating Violence

Teen dating violence is society's first indication of the problem of IPV. Today's teenagers who experience dating violence often become tomorrow's adult victims. This section focuses on the role of *age* in the law's response to IPV. It explores the unique problems that teenagers face in seeking and obtaining legal relief.

EMILY K. v. LUIS J.

997 N.Y.S.2d 510 (N.Y. App. Div. 2014)

GARRY, J.

[P]etitioner commenced this [protection order] proceeding on behalf of her daughter. . . . Respondent and the daughter were each 13 years old when the petition was filed, and they had been in an on-and-off dating relationship for several years. Following a fact-finding hearing, Family Court granted the petition, finding that the daughter and respondent were in an intimate relationship within the meaning of Family Ct. Act §812(1)(e) and that respondent had committed the family offenses of forcible touching and sexual misconduct. After a dispositional hearing, the court issued a two-year order of protection in the daughter's favor. Respondent appeals from both orders.

Respondent contends that petitioner lacks standing to bring this family offense proceeding. [I]t is well established that a parent has standing to commence a family offense proceeding on behalf of his or her child. However, the substance of respondent's argument is not truly addressed to standing, but instead challenges Family Court's subject matter jurisdiction. . . .

Respondent contends that his relationship with the daughter did not fall within the parameters of Family Ct. Act §812(1). This provision [provides] that Family Court has jurisdiction over family offense proceedings arising from certain acts committed by a respondent against a "member [ ] of the same family or household." Before 2008, the statutory definition of this phrase embraced only persons who were related by consanguinity or affinity, who were or had been married to one another, or who shared a common child. In 2008, the Legislature expanded the scope of the statute's protection by amending the definition to include "persons who are not related by consanguinity or affinity and who are or have been in an intimate relationship regardless of whether such persons have lived together at any time" (Family Ct. Act §812[1][e]).

The amended statute does not define the phrase "intimate relationship," but instead provides a nonexhaustive list of factors for consideration in determining whether such a relationship exists, including "the nature or type of relationship, regardless of whether the relationship is sexual in nature; the frequency of interaction between the persons; and the duration of the relationship" . . .

The daughter testified that she and respondent had been classmates since kindergarten and began a "boyfriend-girlfriend" relationship in fifth grade that continued, on and off, through eighth grade. At first, the relationship consisted of holding hands, kissing, and exchanging texts and phone calls. By sixth grade, according to the daughter, respondent was texting or calling her 5 or 10 times daily and becoming jealous, "controlling," and "isolat[ing]." The daughter testified that she and respondent had some sexual contact in sixth grade, including an incident in which he allegedly caused her to touch his erect penis at school in the presence of other students, and another in which he put his hand down her shirt to touch her breasts without her permission.

According to the daughter, she and respondent did not date for most of seventh grade. However, late in that year they began talking again, and in eighth grade they met twice, each time at respondent's request. The daughter testified that during the first encounter, she reluctantly acceded to respondent's request for oral sex, believing that he would "leave [her] alone" if she did so. When they met the second time, they had sexual intercourse; the daughter testified that she asked respondent to stop and that he complied at first, but then continued. The daughter distanced herself from respondent after these events, and reported them to petitioner after she began having suicidal thoughts.

Respondent did not dispute the factual accuracy of this testimony. Contrary to his claim, the youth of the participants does not preclude a determination that their relationship was intimate within the meaning of the statute; Family Ct. Act §812(1) expressly extends its jurisdiction to include respondents who are too young to be held criminally responsible, and nothing in the statutory language excludes young victims as participants in intimate relationships. Further, as the legislation expressly directs that such a relationship may exist between persons who have never lived together, the fact that the participants lived in their parents' separate households does not exclude them from the ambit of the statute. The record supports Family Court's determination that the intermittent dating relationship between respondent and the daughter qualified as an intimate relationship within the expanded reach of the revised statute. Accordingly, the Family Court had subject matter jurisdiction to entertain the proceeding . . . .

Notes and Questions

1. Background. IPV affects teenagers as well as adults. Dating violence starts early—as young as age 11 or 12.[2] Violence in teen dating relationships may be guite severe and escalates into adult partner violence.[3] Teen dating violence has been called a "hidden epidemic." Why do you think that label applies?

2. Similarities and differences. Teen dating violence has many of the same signs as adult IPV: excessive jealousy; controlling behavior; rapid involvement in the relationship; unpredictable mood swings; explosive anger; threats of violence; verbal abuse; use of force during arguments; attempts at isolation from friends and family; hypersensitivity; belief in rigid sex roles; blame of others for problems or feelings; cruelty to animals; and mistreatment of other people.[4] Teen dating violence also consists of the same forms of violence as adult IPV: physical, sexual, and psychological abuse.[5] Electronic harassment is especially common among teen victims. However, differences also exist: female teen victims are not typically financially dependent on their partners; they lack experience in negotiating romantic relationships; and they are more subject to the influence of peers.

3. Order of protection. An order of protection is a legal document sought by victim ("petitioner") against an alleged perpetrator ("respondent") that is intended to prevent abuse. It can be temporary or permanent. A temporary ex parte order is issued without prior notice. After a hearing at which both parties have the opportunity to present evidence, the court can issue a permanent protection order. Protection orders are explored in more detail later in this chapter.

a. Grounds. What are the alleged acts of abuse triggering the order of protection in *Emily K.*? Did the boyfriend commit any criminal offenses? If so, which? Were criminal charges brought? If not, why not? How does a restraining order proceeding differ from a criminal proceeding? How does a restraining order differ from a harassment prevention order? Which of Emily's claims involved abuse and which involved harassment?

---

[2]. Michele C. Black et al., Ctrs. for Disease Control & Prevention, National Intimate Partner and Sexual Violence Survey (NISVS): 2010 Summary Report 49 (2011) [hereinafter NISVS] (more than one in five women first experience rape, physical violence, and/or stalking by a partner between ages 11 to 17); Danice K. Eaton et al., Ctrs. for Disease Control & Prevention, Youth Risk Behavior Surveillance—United States, 61 Morbidity & Mortality Wkly. Rep. 1, 66 (2011) (almost 10 percent of dating high school students report physical abuse by a dating partner); Robert Wood Johnson Fdn. & Blue Cross of Cal. Fdn., Prevention in Middle School Matters: A Summary of Findings of Teen Dating Violence Behaviors and Associated Risk Factors Among 7th-Grade Students: Executive Summary 2, 4 (2012) (more than one in three seventh graders report abuse).

[3]. Females aged 16-19 are victims in 22% of all intimate partner homicides; those aged 12 to 15 are victims in 10% of such homicides. Callie Marie Rennison, Bureau of Justice Statistics, Special Report, Intimate Partner Violence and Age of Victim, 1993-1998 (Table 3) (2001). Teens aged 12-18 who experience dating violence are two to three times more likely to be in violent relationships as adults. Deinera Exner-Cortens et al., Longitudinal Associations Between Teen Dating Violence Victimization and Adverse Health Outcomes, Pediatrics 131:1-8 (Aug. 10, 2012).

[4]. Nat'l Ctr. on Domestic and Sexual Violence, What Are the Early Warning Signs of Teen Dating Violence?, www.ncdsv.org/images/WarningSignsofTeenDatingViolence.pdf.

[5]. Ctrs. for Disease Control & Prevention, Injury Ctr.: Violence Prevention, Teen Dating Violence 1 (2012), http:// www.cdc.gov/ViolencePrevention/intimatepartnerviolence/teen_dating_violence.html.

b. Eligible parties. Did Emily petition on her own behalf? Could she have? What problems are posed by statutes that require parents to petition on a minor's behalf? Only nine states explicitly permit minors to petition on their own.[6] In other states, application of the law to minors remains unclear.

c. Conditions. What was the nature of the order of protection sought by Emily's mother? What restrictions on the respondent should the judge impose?

d. Barriers for teens. What barriers do teens face in terms of their access to protection orders? How are these obstacles similar to, and different from, those facing adult victims?[7]

4. Statutory application. How does the New York statute define the phrase "intimate relationship"? How did the statutory amendment change the definition? Would Emily have prevailed under prior law?

a. Age of victim. In some states, including New York, the law does not specify the age at which a juvenile is eligible to petition for an order. Should laws specify an age limit? If so, what age? See, e.g., Neilson ex rel. Crump v. Blanchette, 201 P.3d 1089 (Wash. Ct. App. 2009) (denying petition of 14-year-old girl who fell below eligible age of 16).

b. "Same household." Some statutes apply to victims who are members of the offender's "family or household." What explains this limitation? How did the New York legislature expand the statutory definition? Why?

c. Definition of a "dating" or "intimate" relationship. Many statutes refer to "dating" relationships rather than "intimate" relationships. For example, the Washington statute provides:

> "Dating relationship" means a social relationship of a romantic nature. Factors that the court may consider in making this determination include: (a) The length of time the relationship has existed; (b) the nature of the relationship; and (c) the frequency of interaction between the parties.

Wash. Rev. Code §26.50.010(3). What issues arise in applying the terms "dating relationship" to teen relationships?

"Dating relationships" are not covered in *all* state statutes or federal statutes. For example, pending federal legislation would expand the Lautenberg Amendment, 18 U.S.C. §922(g)(9), to prohibit firearm possession by persons who are convicted of misdemeanor crimes of domestic violence against partners in, specifically, dating relationships or former dating relationships. See S.B. 1834, 114th Cong. (2014-15). Formerly, these firearm restrictions applied only to offenders who are current or former spouses, parents or guardians, persons who share a child in common, or current or former cohabitants of the victim.

---

[6]. Break the Cycle: Empowering Youth to End Domestic Violence, 2010 State Law Report Cards: A Nat'l Survey of Teen Dating Violence Laws, at 7, http://www.breakthecycle.org/sites/default/files/pdf/2010-Dating-Violence-State-Law-Report-Card-Full-Report.pdf.

[7]. See Andrew Klein, NIJ, An Exploratory Study of Juvenile Orders of Protection as a Remedy for Dating Violence (Apr. 2013), https://www.ncjrs.gov/pdffiles1/nij/grants/242131.pdf (identifying widespread ignorance of the law, peer pressure, and intimidation posed by the court system, among others).

5. School-based responses. How do middle and high schools better address teen dating violence? Currently, about 20 states have legislation that confers a proactive role upon middle and high schools for TDV prevention education. What components should be included in such programs? See generally D. Kelly Weisberg, Lindsay's Legacy: The Tragedy That Triggered Law Reform to Prevent Teen Dating Violence, 24 Hastings Women's L.J. 27 (2013).

Congress authorized funds in the VAWA Reauthorization Act of 2013, Pub. L. No. 113-4, for grants to address TDV prevention in the schools by developing programs that change attitudes and behavior, provide teacher training, and formulate policies targeted to prevention. Saving Money and Reducing Tragedies Through Prevention (SMART Prevention) Act, 42 U.S.C. 14043d-2.

6. Campus sexual assault. College women are also victims of dating violence. In fact, 20 percent of college students report that they have experienced domestic violence—the same percent as those who report sexual assaults.[8] This prevalence rate is not surprising given that women age 18-24 experience the highest rates of partner violence. Most assaults on college campuses are committed by acquaintances.

The issue of acquaintance rape came before the U.S. Supreme Court in United States v. Morrison, 529 U.S. 598 (2000). A female college student at Virginia Polytechnic Institute was raped by two football players. When the school failed to punish the perpetrators, she filed an action alleging a violation of the Violence Against Women Act, 42 U.S.C. §13981, that provided a federal tort remedy for gender-motivated crimes. The U.S. Supreme Court held that Congress exceeded its power under the Commerce Clause in enacting the provision, reasoning that crime was an inherently local concern and that any aggregate effect of crime on the economy was insufficient to invoke federal regulation. Although a federal remedy no longer exists for gender-motivated violence, some states have similar laws.[9]

Federal law addresses dating abuse on campus. The Jeanne Clery Disclosure of Campus Security Policy and Campus Crime Statistics Act or Clery Act, 20 U.S.C. §1092(f)), requires all colleges and universities participating in federal financial aid programs to compile and disclose information about campus crimes. (The law is named after a 19-year-old student at Lehigh University who was raped and murdered in her campus residence hall in 1986.) In October 2014, the U.S. Department of Education published its final regulations (34 CFR §668.46) to implement Clery Act amendments that were enacted pursuant to the Violence Against Women Reauthorization Act (VAWA) of 2013.

The new rules require colleges and universities to compile statistics not only for sexual assault, but also for dating violence, domestic violence, and stalking. The rules strengthen victims' rights by (1) requiring notice of students' rights to seek protective orders as well as to seek assistance from law enforcement and campus authorities; (2) providing both victims and alleged perpetrators with the right

---

[8]. DV as Prevalent as Sexual Assault on College Campuses, 21 Nat'l Bull. Domestic Violence Prevention 1 (Feb. 2015); Heather M. Karjane, Nat'l Inst. of Justice, Sexual Assault on Campus: What College and Universities Are Doing About It 2 (Dec. 2005), http://www.ncjrs.gov/pdffiles1/nij/205521.pdf.

[9]. See Julie Goldscheid, The Civil Rights Remedy of the 1994 Violence Against Women Act: Struck Down But Not Ruled Out, 39 Fam. L.Q. 157, 168 (2005) (surveying states).

to have others present in campus disciplinary proceedings and also to receive written notification of the outcome; (3) establishing a preponderance-of-the-evidence standard of proof; and (4) requiring training for campus personnel, assurances of confidentiality for the parties, and the written specification of possible sanctions for perpetrators.

Problem

Karen Muscato and Mary Moore, who are both fourteen-year old eighth graders, live in the state of Blackacre. They are best friends who are also "going out together." Karen's mother, Mrs. Muscato, finds what she believes to be inappropriate and sexually explicit text messages between the two girls on her daughter's cell phone. The text messages allegedly contain information intimating that Mary is sexually active and that Mary's mother had purchased a sex toy (a vibrator) for her daughter. After that discovery, Mrs. Muscato tells her daughter that she does not want her spending time with Mary any longer. Mrs. Muscato repeats that message to Mary's mother and warns both Mary's mother and Mary from contacting her daughter again. Karen is unhappy about her mother's actions because she wants to continue her relationship with Mary, despite her mother's objections.

Mary's mother (Mrs. Moore) decides to ignore Mrs. Muscato's request. Mrs. Moore continues to text Karen and to encourage contact between the girls. In fact, Mrs. Moore sends Karen a text message urging her to hide all communications from her mother. The next Sunday, Mrs. Moore appears at Karen's church, when she knows that Karen will be volunteering in the religious school class, in an attempt to contact Karen and reunite the two friends. Karen sees Mrs. Moore coming into the church and unsuccessfully tries to evade her. The ensuing conversation with Mrs. Moore makes Karen so uncomfortable that she opts to spend the rest of her class in the ladies' room.

When Mrs. Muscato learns of these incidents, she files a police report and petitions for a protection order on behalf of her daughter, Karen. (In Blackacre, adult family or household members must file on behalf of teens under age 16.) Mrs. Muscato alleges that Mrs. Moore and her daughter Mary are guilty of stalking. The Blackacre Protection from Abuse Act contains the following definitions of stalking:

> **Section 61a**. "Stalking" consists of: the willful, malicious, and repeated following or harassment of a person by an adult, emancipated minor, or minor thirteen years of age or older, in a manner that would cause a reasonable person to feel frightened, intimidated, threatened, harassed, or molested and actually causes the person being followed or harassed to feel terrorized, frightened, intimidated, threatened, harassed or molested.
>
> **Section 61b.** "Stalking" also means a course of conduct composed of a series of two or more separate acts over a period of time, however short, evidencing a continuity of purpose or unconsented contact with a person that is initiated or continued without the consent of the individual or in disregard of the expressed desire of the individual that the contact be avoided or discontinued.

Should the court grant Mrs. Muscato's petition for a protection order against Mrs. Moore? Against Mary? Should the issue of consent be considered from the perspective of the minor (Karen) or the minor's parent (Mrs. Muscato)?

Should it matter if Mrs. Muscato's goal is to prevent the girls' sexual conduct rather than physical violence? Should it matter if the sexual conduct is a crime in Blackacre? Suppose that there is no hint of any sexual relationship between the two girls, but Mrs. Muscato merely objects to the girls' friendship on religious, racial, or ethnic grounds? Would you suggest any statutory reforms to prevent parental "meddling" and judicial entanglement in similar private family disputes? The Problem is a modified version of Muscato ex rel Butler v. Moore, 338 P.3d 643 (2014).[10]

NOTE: THE ROLE OF OTHER INFLUENTIAL FACTORS

Various factors play an important role in the law's response to IPV, such as: age, gender, sexual orientation, disability, mental illness, race and ethnicity, immigration status, and social class. Consider how each of these factors plays a role in a victim's experience of IPV as well as the law's response.

1. Elder abuse. Domestic violence occurs at both ends of the life cycle. All states have laws addressing elder abuse. Spouses perpetrate one-fifth of such cases.[11] Most elder abuse consists of physical abuse, abandonment, psychological abuse, financial abuse, and neglect. Financial abuse takes subtle forms, such as persuasion to transfer title of an asset or to create a testamentary instrument. Signs of abuse may be missed by professionals due to a lack of training in detection. Victims are often reluctant to report their abuse because of fear of retaliation, abandonment, or lack of ability to report. Federal law consists of the Elder Justice Act, enacted in 2010 as Section 6703 of the Affordable Care Act (commonly known as the ACA), Pub. Law No. 111-148, Title VI, §6703(d)(1), to "prevent, detect, treat, understand, intervene in and, where appropriate, prosecute elder abuse, neglect and exploitation."

2. Gender. Women are significantly more likely than men to be victims of IPV – regardless of the type of abuse (physical, sexual, psychological, or stalking).[12] Women are also more likely than men to suffer severe injuries[13] and to be killed by an intimate partner.[14] Nonetheless, a controversy exists regarding whether female intimate partners are as violent (or more violent) than male partners. Supporters of the "gender symmetry" argument claim that women and men commit IPV at equal rates. Opponents refute that assertion by claiming that proponents of the gender-symmetry claim simply count up the number of incidents

---

[10]. See also Eugene Volokh, The Volokh Conspiracy, (Possibly Lesbian) Teenagers, Interceding Mothers, and Restraining Orders, Wash. Post (Jan. 2, 2014) (raising many of these questions), https://www.washingtonpost.com/news/volokh-conspiracy/wp/2015/01/02/teenagers-interceding-mothers-and-restraining-orders/.

[11]. U.S. Dept. of Health & Human Servs., Nat'l Ctr. on Elder Abuse, National Elder Abuse Incidence Study (NEAIS), Executive Summary 4-28 (1998).

[12]. NISVS, supra note [2], at 1-2.

[13]. Id. at iv.

[14]. Rennison, supra note [3], at 1 (2003) (three times as many female victims).

(without regard to their seriousness), omit measures of context (such as self-defense), and rely on narrow definitions of violence (without accounting for multiple forms of victimization and former, as well as present, intimate partners).

3. Sexual orientation. IPV among same-sex couples occurs with the same frequency as opposite-sex partner violence.[15] Although same-sex partner violence bears many similarities to that of opposite-sex couples, important differences exist. For example, same-sex partners have an additional weapon of abuse (the threat to "out" their partners).[16] In addition, lesbian, gay, bisexual, and transgender (LGBT) victims are often reluctant to seek help because they fear legal consequences, such as loss of custody or housing due to homophobic attitudes.[17]

Congress expanded federal protection for LGBT victims in the VAWA Reauthorization Act of 2013 (discussed infra this chapter) based on the recognition that LGBT victims face obstacles in accessing services (such as shelter services) by providers who lacked "cultural competency" (an understanding of diversity). As a result, VAWA 2013 lists both "sexual orientation" and "gender identity" in the revised definition of "underserved populations" in order to expand eligibility of LGBT victims for various grant programs. (42 U.S.C.A. §13925(a)(39)). VAWA 2013 also prohibits discrimination on the basis of sexual orientation or gender identity in all VAWA-funded programs. 42 U.S.C.A. §13925(b)(13)(A). The provisions of VAWA and its reauthorizations are discussed later in this chapter.

4. Disability. Disabled women face a higher risk of IPV than nondisabled victims.[18] They also suffer abuse by multiple partners, more severe abuse, more types of abuse, and abuse for longer durations.[19] The original VAWA omitted to provide services for disabled victims. However, VAWA 2000 remedied this omission by providing funding for education and technical assistance to improve services. 42 U.S.C. §§3796gg, 3796hh. VAWA 2005 provided additional funding for education, training, and direct services for disabled victims of sexual assault, domestic violence, dating violence, and stalking. 42 U.S.C. §3796gg. Note that the Americans with Disabilities Act of 1990 (ADA) (codified in relevant part at 42 U.S.C. §12182(a)) does not address domestic violence.

5. Mental illness. Male perpetrators of IPV manifest high rates of personality disorders, especially antisocial, borderline, dependent, depressed, and narcissistic personality traits. A multistate study of male batterers in treatment programs

---

[15]. Patricia Tjaden & Nancy Thoennes, Nat'l Inst. of Justice, Extent, Nature, and Consequences of Intimate Partner Violence, at iv, v (2000).

[16]. Janice Ristock & Norma Timbang, Moving Beyond a Gender-Based Framework: Relationship Violence in Lesbian/Gay/Bisexual/Transgender/Queer Communities (2005), http://www.mincava.umn.edu/documents/lgbtqviolence/lgbtqviolence.html.

[17]. Jennifer L. Hardesty et al., Lesbian/Bisexual Mothers and Intimate Partner Violence: Help Seeking in the Context of Social and Legal Vulnerability, 17 Violence Against Women 28, 39-40 (2011).

[18]. Douglas A. Brownridge, Violence Against Women: Vulnerable Populations 236 (2009); Nat'l Coalition Against Domestic Violence (NCADV), Fact Sheet, Domestic Violence and Disabilities, http://www.hope-eci.org/_documents/disabilities.pdf.

[19]. Dena Hassouneh-Phillips & Elizabeth McNeff, "I Thought I was Less Worthy": Low Sexual and Body Esteem and Increased Vulnerability to Intimate Partner Abuse in Women with Physical Disabilities, 23 Sexuality & Disability, 227, 229 (2005).

found that almost one-fourth displayed symptoms associated with severe mental disorders, more than one-third displayed symptoms associated with an anxiety disorder, one-fourth manifested narcissistic traits, and another fourth manifested passive-aggressive behavior.[20]

Victims, similarly, suffer high rates of mental illness.[21] Abuse by an intimate partner elevates a victim's risk of depression, posttraumatic stress disorder (PTSD), substance abuse, suicidality, and many chronic health conditions.[22] Causation runs in two directions: mental illness can result from experiencing domestic violence, and abuse can worsen a preexisting mental health condition.

6. Race and ethnicity. Domestic violence affects members of all race and ethnic groups. However, Native American women and African-American women are at particularly high risk.[23] In fact, Native American women experience higher rates of physical assaults that are domestic in nature than any other demographic group in the United States.[24] African-American women face unique problems in obtaining legal relief. They often hesitate to report the abuse because of their fear of discrimination by law enforcement. They worry that they will be labeled or blamed for the violence. They feel protective of their abuser (i.e., reluctant to subject him to a possibly racist or violent response from the police). They also refrain from reporting in order to combat stereotypes of the African-American family.[25]

7. Immigration status. Immigrant women also suffer high rates of domestic violence. They face difficulties, in part, because their home cultures are more tolerant of domestic violence, so they believe that the abuse is acceptable. In addition, they face language barriers, social isolation, and the lack of financial resources. Moreover, abusers frequently use their partners' immigration status as a tool to force victims to remain in the relationship.[26]

Congressional hearings prior to the original VAWA shed light on the problem of domestic violence in marriages between foreign women and U.S. citizens. In

---

[20]. Edward W. Gondolf, Characteristics of Court-Mandated Batterers in Four Cities: Diversities and Dichotomies, 11 Violence Against Women 1277, 1285-1286 (1999) (study of 840 batterers).

[21]. Between 60-90 percent of battered women suffer from "significant" mental health issues. Denice Wolf Markham, Mental Illness and Domestic Violence: Implications for Family Law Litigation, J. Poverty Law & Policy, 23, 23 (May-June 2003).

[22]. Victims are three times as likely to develop PTSD, twice as likely to develop symptoms of depression, and three times as likely to develop major depressive disorder compared to women who have not experienced such abuse. Nat'l Ctr. on Domestic Violence, Trauma, & Mental Health, Current Evidence: Intimate Partner Violence, Trauma-Related Mental Health Conditions & Chronic Illness, Fact Sheet 2014, at 1, 2.

[23]. Nat'l Ctr. for Injury Prevention and Control Division of Violence Prevention, Nat'l Intimate Partner and Sexual Violence Survey 2010 Summary Report, at 39 (reporting that approximately 40% of 10 Black women and 40% of American Indian women have been victims of rape, physical violence, and/or stalking by an intimate partner in their lifetime).

[24]. Jacqueline P. Hand & David C. Koelsch, Shared Experiences, Divergent Outcomes: American Indian and Immigrant Victims of Domestic Violence, 25 Wis. J.L. Gender & Soc'y 185, 188 (2010).

[25]. Lisa M. Martinson, Comment, An Analysis of Racism and Resources for African-American Female Victims of Domestic Violence in Wisconsin, 16 Wis. Women's L.J. 259, 264-273 (2001).

[26]. Futures Without Violence, Fact Sheet, The Facts on Immigrant Women and Domestic Violence, https://www.futureswithoutviolence.org/userfiles/file/Children_and_Families/Immigrant.pdf.

response, VAWA created a "self-petitioning" option to allow an abused foreign wife to submit a special petition to immigration authorities for legalization of her residency status. A battered foreign wife no longer must remain married and living with her abusive husband for two years prior to requesting an adjustment to lawful permanent residency status. VAWA also provides for "suspension of deportation" or "cancellation of removal" for victims without the need for the assistance of their citizen-spouses. 8 U.S.C. §1229b(b)(2). Requirements for self-petitioning include proof that the foreign spouse entered into the marriage in good faith and that she, or her children, has been battered or subjected to extreme cruelty. 8 U.S.C. 1154(a)(1)(A)(iii)(I)(aa), (bb).

VAWA 2000, 8 U.S.C. §1101 created a nonimmigrant U-visa to enable a victim of crime, who cooperates with law enforcement, to petition for a temporary visa (even if her presence in the United States is unlawful). Victims must have suffered "substantial physical or mental abuse" as the result of a designated crime (e.g., rape, trafficking, domestic violence, sexual assault, or felonious assault).

A victim of domestic violence also may apply for asylum. To obtain asylum, a person must prove that she is a "refugee," defined as a person who cannot return to her country of origin based on a well-founded fear of persecution by a government or group that the government is unable or unwilling to control on account of race, religion, nationality, membership in a "particular social group," or political opinion. 8 U.S.C. §1101(a)(42); 8 U.S.C. §1158. Until recently, domestic violence victims faced difficulties in obtaining asylum. However, in August 2014, the U.S. Board of Immigration Appeals acknowledged that women fleeing domestic violence could meet the definition of "refugee" and qualify for asylum. See Matter of A-R-C-G- et al., 26 I&N Dec. 388 (BIA 2014) (concerning a Guatemalan victim of spousal abuse who encountered extreme indifference from Guatemalan police).

8. Social class. The "universal risk theory" suggests that all women are equally victimized by IPV. However, the relationship between income and domestic violence is complex and influenced by multiple marginalization factors. Women in low-income households experience a higher rate of nonlethal violence. Women whose partners are unemployed also have high rates of partner violence.[27] At least half of women receiving public benefits have experienced physical abuse by an intimate partner, compared to 22 percent of the general population.[28] However, socioeconomic factors complicate victimization rates because certain factors that are associated with poverty (i.e., higher rates of unemployment and substance abuse) also contribute to domestic violence.[29]

Congress addressed the domestic-violence-related difficulties faced by low-income victims in regard to their need to meet work requirements of Temporary

---

[27]. Lawrence A. Greenfeld et al., U.S. Dept. of Justice, Violence by Intimates: Analysis of Data on Crimes by Current or Former Spouses, Boyfriends, and Girlfriends 14 (1998).

[28]. Sharmila Lawrence, Research Forum on Children, Families, and the New Federalism, Nat'l Ctr. for Children in Poverty, Domestic Violence and Welfare Policy: Research Findings That Can Inform Policies on Marriage and Child Well-Being, Issue Brief (2002); Richard Tolman & Jody Raphael, A Review of the Research on Welfare and Domestic Violence, 56 J. Soc. Issues 655 (2000).

[29]. See Hillary Potter, Battle Cries: Black Women and Intimate Partner Abuse 8 (2008) (citing "multiple marginalization factors").

Assistance to Needy Families (TANF) (Pub. L. No. 104-193) (a program for single parents that requires them to cooperate with child support agencies in establishing paternity, locating the absent parent, and obtaining child support orders). Recognizing that such requirements put survivors at risk of violence from their partners, Congress included a Family Violence Option (FVO) in the Personal Responsibility and Work Opportunity Reconciliation Act (PRWORA) that was designed to provide exemptions from TANF requirements to victims of domestic violence (42 U.S.C.A. §602(a)(7)(A)(iii)).

C. Civil Protection Orders: Nature and Scope

All states currently provide civil protection orders for victims of domestic violence. Historically, courts issued injunctions against interspousal violence only in conjunction with divorce proceedings. However, in 1976, Pennsylvania became the first state to authorize restraining orders regardless of whether the victim was seeking a divorce. Within two decades, all states had similar laws. This section explores the nature of these orders.

What are they?

A protection order is a civil order that is issued by a court to a petitioner (the victim) against a respondent (the offender). The goal is immediate protection rather than punishment. A protection order directs a person to do or refrain from doing certain acts. States use different terms for this order, such as a "restraining order," "protection order", "domestic violence protection order," "personal protection order," "civil protection order," and "protection from abuse" order. Victims often seek protection orders in order to stop the abuse rather than to punish the abuser. However, petitioning for a protection order does not preclude imposition of criminal charges.

Who can obtain an order of protection?

State statutes specify who may petition. Eligible parties include spouses and former spouses, "family and household members," cohabitants and former cohabitants, boyfriends/girlfriends and former boyfriends/girlfriends, co-parents, and, in some states, dating partners and former dating partners.

What acts do protection orders cover?

The specific restrictions in a protection order depend on the circumstances of each case and state law. A protection order can prohibit a person from threatening or harming the petitioner; entering the petitioner's home ("kick-out order"); coming within a certain distance of the petitioner and/or her children or coming to the petitioner's home, work, school, or the children's home or school ("stay-away" order); contacting the petitioner directly or indirectly, in person, by phone, email, texting, mail, or through a third party; purchasing or owning firearms; and prohibiting the transfer or disposal of property. The order can also grant temporary child custody and award temporary child or spousal support; prevent the removal of children from a jurisdiction; require payment of rent, mortgage costs, medical costs or property damage; order police to help the victim remove possessions from the home; and protect a family pet.

What acts are beyond the scope of protection orders?

A protection order *cannot* make a final child custody determination or determine title to property.

What are the types of protection orders?

An order of protection may be temporary or permanent. States have different forms of temporary orders: (1) an *emergency protection order* (EPO) issued upon exigent circumstances when a responding police officer requests the order from a judge (by phone, at any hour of day or night); (2) a *temporary restraining order* (TRO) issued by a family court upon the victim's petition and affidavit that demonstrate reasonable proof of past acts of domestic violence pursuant to statute, and (3) a *permanent protection order* issued after an adversarial hearing on the merits, at which time both parties have the opportunity to present evidence.

Proceedings for restraining orders are subject to a preponderance-of-the-evidence standard. Both emergency and temporary protective orders are issued ex parte. In each case, the order must be served on the restrained party to be effective.

How long does a protection order last?

The court specifies the duration of the order. The maximum period is designated by statute. Orders of protection may be renewed at the petitioner's request if the abuser has threatened the petitioner, caused her to fear for her safety, or has violated the order. Note that "permanent" protection orders are rarely permanent.

What is the consequence of the violation of a protection order?

Traditionally, civil protection orders were enforced by contempt proceedings. Today, most states make the violation of a protection order a crime. Although violations of protection orders generally are misdemeanors, some states treat repeat violations or those involving a weapon as felonies.

How do civil and criminal protective orders differ?

Civil protection orders can be supplemented by criminal protection orders. Criminal protective orders can be issued during arraignment, bail, pretrial release, and also as a postconviction condition of probation. Criminal protection orders provide less relief than civil protection orders for several reasons. Criminal orders do not address issues of visitation or child support. Nor do they mandate treatment or enable eviction of the abuser. Moreover, criminal no-contact orders last only so long as criminal charges are pending.

D. Criminal Justice Response

1. Self-Defense

HAWTHORNE v. STATE

408 So. 2d 801 (Fla. Dist. Ct. App. 1982)

Per Curiam. . . .

[Defendant's husband was shot to death in the home in the early morning hours of January 28, 1977, by bullets fired from a number of weapons belonging to the deceased. This was appellant's second trial for the murder of her husband after her first conviction for first-degree murder was reversed.]

The [first] argument by appellant that warrants discussion is that the trial court erred in disallowing the testimony of Dr. Lenore Walker, a clinical psychologist who would have testified as an expert with regard to the battered-woman syndrome. The purpose of such testimony would have been to give the jury a basis for considering whether appellant suffered from the battered-woman syndrome, not in order to establish a novel defense, but as it related to her claim of self-defense. We are aware of the conflicting decisions of various jurisdictions as to the admissibility of this type of expert testimony. The courts that have considered the admissibility of this type of expert testimony have generally analyzed it to see whether it meets three basic criteria: (1) the expert is qualified to give an opinion on the subject matter; (2) the state of the art or scientific knowledge permits a reasonable opinion to be given by the expert; and (3) the subject matter of the expert opinion is so related to some science, profession, business, or occupation as to be beyond the understanding of the average layman. . . .

The few case authorities which have considered the admissibility of this type of expert testimony disagree primarily with regard to (1) whether the study of the battered-woman syndrome is an area sufficiently developed to permit an expert to assert a reasonable opinion, and (2) whether the battered-woman syndrome is beyond the knowledge and experience of most laymen.

In [Ibn-Tamas v. United States, 407 A.2d 626 (D.C. 1979)] and [Smith v. State, 277 S.E.2d 678 (Ga. 1981),] the courts concluded that the expert testimony should have been allowed, inasmuch as the subject matter was "beyond the ken of the average layman." "[T]he expert's testimony explaining why a person suffering from battered woman's syndrome would not leave her mate, would not inform police or friends, and would fear increased aggression against herself, would be such conclusions that jurors could not ordinarily draw for themselves." . . . The *Ibn-Tamas* court determined, however, that the trial court had not ruled on whether the expert, Dr. Lenore Walker, was sufficient qualified to give an opinion on whether "the state of the pertinent art or scientific knowledge" would permit an expert opinion. The court said that this third criterion depended on "whether Dr. Walker's methodology for identifying and studying battered women" was generally accepted. The question whether the [criteria] were satisfied was remanded to the trial court. . . .

[Similarly, in the instant case,] there has been no determination below as to the adequacy of Dr. Walker's qualifications or the extent to which her methodology is generally accepted, indicating that the subject matter can support a reasonable expert opinion. Our determination that this expert testimony would provide the jury with an interpretation of the facts not ordinarily available to them is subject to the trial court determining that Dr. Walker is qualified and that the subject is sufficiently developed and can support an expert opinion.

Appellee argues that to admit this type of expert testimony would violate the rule [that] "testimony regarding the mental state of a defendant in a criminal case is inadmissible in the absence of a plea of not guilty by reason of insanity." In this case, a defective mental state on the part of the accused is not offered as a defense [to show that she was not responsible for her actions]. Rather, the specific defense is self-defense which requires a showing that the accused reasonably believed it was necessary to use deadly force to prevent imminent death or great bodily harm to herself or her children. The expert testimony would have been offered in order to aid the jury in interpreting the surrounding circumstances as they affected the reasonableness of her belief. . . . It is precisely because a jury would not understand why appellant would remain in the environment that the expert testimony would have aided them in evaluating the case. [Reversed and remanded.]

Dr. Lenore Walker, Terrifying Love: Why Battered Women Kill and How Society Responds

23-41 (1989)

I first met Joyce Hawthorne three years after [her husband] Aubrey's death. An ordinary-looking woman of forty, about 5'3" tall, weighing about 150 lbs., she didn't attract much attention. Her smile was rare but sweet; her eyes sparkled when she laughed. She looked just like the church-going mother of five that she was. Judging by her appearance alone, no one would have known that she'd killed a man much larger than herself, firing five guns in the process, even if sometimes her facial expression, at rest, revealed her fear and unhappiness. . . . Joyce never denied that she'd fired the fatal shots; rather, although she had no memory of it, she claimed that she had been justified in firing them because she had wanted to protect herself and her family from assault, rape, and death. . . . Although she did not remember shooting her husband, she had initially confessed to doing it in order to get the police to release her five children, who were being held for questioning at the time.

In reversing the judge's previous decision, an appellate court had ruled that evidence about the extensive family abuse in this case could be introduced in the upcoming trial; but nothing had been specifically stated about the permissibility of allowing an expert witness to explain what Joyce's behavior had meant. . . .

Battered Woman Syndrome had not previously been used in the state of Florida to support a self-defense argument (although several other states had, by that time, permitted such testimony in courts of law). Before, it would have been much more common for a woman like Joyce to plead insanity, arguing that her husband's terrible abuse had rendered her temporarily insane. . . . Shortly after Aubrey's death, Joyce Hawthorne had been examined by a psychiatrist, who had found that she knew right from wrong, the legal standard for Florida's insanity plea. I, too, would find that Joyce Hawthorne was legally sane—but terrified that she and her family would be slaughtered, just as Aubrey had threatened. In my opinion, her belief that she and her children were in danger that night had been reasonable, and reasonable perception of imminent physical danger is the legal standard for acting in self-defense.

. . . I agreed with [defense attorney] Leo Thomas that . . . without understanding the long history of marital abuse Joyce had endured, the average person sitting on a jury could not be expected to comprehend why she had believed her husband would kill her when she refused his sexual advances. . . . But Battered Woman Syndrome would provide the appropriate explanation; it would delineate the perception of imminence, and show how that perception was affected by the woman's state of mind. It would make her state of mind comprehensible, because battered women are always afraid of being hurt; any crisis situation may be perceived as a matter of life or death. . . .

Leo Thomas realized that he would have to [help the jury] understand why Joyce hadn't divorced Aubrey despite the daily horror of their marriage; he would have to corroborate Joyce's reports of domestic violence, even if no one else had seen Aubrey beat her; he would have to introduce convincing evidence to demonstrate that Joyce's fear had been reasonable on the night she finally killed him. All this would mean persuading the jury that Aubrey Hawthorne's repeated abuse of his wife had so affected her state of mind that she'd believed she needed to shoot him, to stop him from hurting her—as she perceived him coming toward her, even before he'd actually touched her—on that night in January 1977. Leo would have to help Joyce persuade the jury that her acute state of terror had induced her to use no less than five guns that night, firing at least nine bullets into her husband's body; that, in fact, her behavior had been a demonstration not of anger but of fear. . . .

. . . Most women are at a serious disadvantage when facing an attack from a man who is not only physically stronger but more ready and willing to fight. And battered women who kill are really like battered women who don't kill—they endure the same harassment, the same psychological torture; they experience the same terror—except that they have partners who are ready, able, and willing to kill them. When a battered woman kills her abuser, she has reached the end of the line. She is absolutely desperate, in real despair. She believes, with good reason, that if she does not kill, she will be killed. . . .

Notes and Questions

1. Background and epilogue. *Hawthorne* was one of the first cases in which defense attorneys sought to introduce evidence about the dynamics of domestic violence for the purpose of helping a decisionmaker decide whether a defendant acted reasonably in exercising self-defense. All states now admit such evidence.

Joyce Hawthorne's initial conviction was reversed because of her illegally obtained confession and the exclusion of testimony about her husband's violent acts. 377 So. 2d 780 (Fla. Dist. Ct. App. 1979). Her second conviction was reversed when the appellate court remanded for a determination of the admissibility of "battered woman syndrome" (BWS) evidence (the principal case here). Upon rehearing, the trial court rejected the evidence, reasoning that its scientific basis was not sufficiently accepted. The appellate court affirmed. 470 So. 2d 770 (Fla. Dist. Ct. App. 1985). At Hawthorne's next trial, her attorney successfully argued that a retrial would constitute cruel and unusual punishment. All charges against her were dismissed.

2. Common law. English common law recognized the right of husbands to discipline their wives by use of physical force (the "privilege of chastisement"). Recall Blackstone (supra pp. 229-230). Divorce, rather than criminal sanctions, was considered the appropriate remedy. Further, interspousal immunity precluded tort recovery. During the late nineteenth century, most courts declared wife beating illegal. Currently, all jurisdictions offer a range of remedies such as civil protection orders, tort suits, and criminal sanctions.

On the history of domestic violence legislation, see Linda Gordon, Heroes of Their Own Lives: The Politics and History of Family Violence, Boston, 1880-1960 (2002); Elizabeth Haflin Pleck, Domestic Tyranny: The Making of Social Policy Against Family Violence from Colonial Times to the Present (1989); Elizabeth Schneider, Battered Women and Feminist Lawmaking (2002).

3. Battered woman syndrome (BWS). Battered women who kill their partners often rely on evidence of BWS as part of their self-defense claim. BWS is a theory of behavior that derives from the research of psychologist Lenore Walker in the 1970s with 400 battered women. BWS has two components: a three-stage cycle of violence and "learned helplessness."

The cycle of violence consists of (a) a tension-building phase—a gradual escalation of tension during which the batterer displays hostility and the woman attempts to placate him; (b) an acute battering incident, in which the batterer explodes into uncontrollable disproportionate rage; and (c) the contrition phase, in which the batterer shows remorse and promises to end the abuse. "Learned helplessness" purports to explain why women stay in a battering relationship. Relying on the research of psychologist Martin Seligman involving shocks to laboratory animals, Walker posits that a battered woman becomes so depressed from repeated battering that she loses the motivation to respond.[30] According to Walker, BWS is not a mental disorder, but rather the psychological reaction of a normal person when exposed to traumatic events. Walker has since recharacterized BWS as a component of PTSD.

4. Criticisms. BWS has prompted many criticisms: (1) it stereotypes victims as helpless, (2) it portrays them as mentally ill and hysterical, (3) it fails to explain that victims respond in different ways, (4) it disadvantages minorities, (5) it

---

[30]. Lenore Walker, The Battered Woman Syndrome 71 (3d ed. 2009).

provides special treatment in violation of equal protection, and (6) it is subject to sexist applications by judges and juries.[31]

5. Defenses. Traditionally, the battered woman who kills her intimate partner faces difficulties in using self-defense because of the traditional elements: (1) a person must use only proportional force against unlawful armed force; (2) the defendant must reasonably fear that she is in imminent danger of bodily harm (and definitions of "reasonableness" and "imminence" were developed for paradigms such as "the barroom brawl," not intimate violence); (3) the defendant cannot have been the aggressor; and (4) in some jurisdictions, she must seek to retreat before use of deadly force (referred to as "the castle doctrine").[32]

Several facts suggest the need for BWS testimony in such cases. First, the woman may use lethal force against a man who attacked with his hands. Second, the victim may not pose an immediate threat because he may be incapacitated (for example, asleep or drunk). Third, the woman appears to be the aggressor. Finally, her abuser is a lawful occupant of the dwelling. BWS evidence overcomes these problems by addressing misconceptions that jurors hold about battered women as well as their views about the reasonableness of the women's perception of the imminence and seriousness of the danger.

Applying Walker's theory, the woman experiences the growing tension of phase one and the acute incident in phase two. In response, she develops a constant fear of serious bodily harm that she perceives as imminent partially because of the unpredictability of her spouse's rage. The cycle theory of violence also addresses the element of the reasonableness of the amount of force necessary to repel the attack by suggesting that the woman perceives herself trapped in a cycle of potentially deadly violence and feels compelled to use deadly force to preempt the attack of the more powerful (even though perhaps unarmed) aggressor. Does this theory explain why Joyce Hawthorne used *five* weapons to kill her husband?

6. Admissibility of evidence: *Frye* and *Daubert*. All states and the District of Columbia now admit BWS evidence, at least to some degree, either by statute or case law. BWS has achieved such acceptance that cases hold that an attorney's failure to present expert testimony on Battered Woman Syndrome constitutes ineffective assistance of counsel. See, e.g., Smith v. State, 144 P.3d 159 (Okla. Crim. App. 2006).

To determine the admissibility of novel scientific evidence, federal courts traditionally relied on the standard in Frye v. United States, 293 F. 1013 (D.C. Cir. 1923): Evidence is admissible if it has become generally accepted by scientists in the particular field of study. This classic formulation was superseded by Daubert v. Merrell Dow Pharmaceuticals, Inc., 509 U.S. 579 (1993), which adopted Federal Rule of Evidence 702, and provided that evidence may be admitted if it is helpful to the trier of fact and also if the methodology is scientifically valid. Many state courts also adhere to these standards. Which test did *Hawthorne* follow? In

---

[31]. For a discussion of these criticisms, see Sharan K. Suri, Note, A Matter of Principle and Consistency: Understanding the Battered Woman and Cultural Defenses, 7 Mich. J. Gender & L. 107, 126-127 (2000).

[32]. Some states have abrogated the duty to retreat. For a discussion of the "new" castle doctrine, see Jeannie Suk, At Home in the Law: How the Domestic Violence Revolution is Transforming Privacy 73-80 (2009).

addition, some courts admit BWS testimony for other purposes, such as to bolster the woman's credibility if she recants her testimony. See, e.g., Minnesota v. Vance, 685 N.W.2d 713 (Minn. Ct. App. 2004).

7. Exit from abusive relationships.

a. Why didn't she leave? One of the most difficult issues for jurors to understand, as *Hawthorne* explains, is why the battered woman killed rather than left her abuser. Professor Martha Mahoney sheds light on this issue:

> The "shopworn question" [Why didn't she leave?] reveals several assumptions about separation: that the right solution is separation, that it is the woman's responsibility to achieve separation, and that she could have separated. . . . When we ask the woman, "Exactly what did you do in your search for help?" the answer often turns out to be that she left—at least temporarily. In [one] study, more than seventy percent of the women had left home at some time in response to violence. . . .
>
> [T]he assumption that the woman's first separation should be permanent ignores the real dangers that the man will seek actively—and sometimes violently—to end the separation. [W]e need to reckon with the dangers she faces. . . . The story of the violent pursuit of the separating woman must become part of the way we understand domestic violence to help eliminate the question "Why didn't she leave?" from our common vocabulary.[33]

b. Separation assault. Professor Mahoney explains the primary reason that abused women are reluctant to leave: They fear their abusers will kill them if they do. Mahoney points out that, contrary to common belief, separation does not end the violence. In fact, victims' attempts to leave actually increase the violence because the abuser retaliates against them to force them to stay. Mahoney coined the term "separation assault" to signify the violence that erupts when a victim attempts to leave. She was influential in debunking the idea (derived from learned helplessness theory) that battered women are passive victims of circumstances. She refutes the question "why didn't the woman leave?" by contending that women *repeatedly try* to leave, but abusers sabotage their efforts. What are the implications of "separation assault" for legal policy?

c. Stages of change. The Transtheoretical Model of behavioral change (or "stages-of-change" model) brings a new understanding to IPV by explaining that the exit from abusive relationships is a *process* with five stages: Precontemplation, Contemplation, Preparation, Action, and Maintenance. Progression through the stages is not linear. That is, the individual may revisit earlier stages before she reaches the final stage when she successfully exits the relationship. Interventions in the early stages, when the individual has not yet decided to leave the relationship, are unlikely to have a positive impact.[34]

---

[33]. Martha Mahoney, Legal Images of Battered Women: Redefining the Issue of Separation, 90 Mich. L. Rev. 1, 61-62 (1991).

[34]. For a discussion and application of the stages-of-change model to IPV, see Jane K. Stoever, Freedom from Violence: Using the Stages of Change Model to Realize the Promise of Civil Protection Orders, 72 Ohio St. L.J. 303 (2011). See also Edward W. Gondolf & Ellen R. Fisher, Battered Women as Survivors: An Alternative to Treating Learned Helplessness 11-18, 20-24 (1988).

Problem

Ann and her husband, Jeff, are at a bar. When Jeff goes to the bathroom, Greg begins talking to Ann. Jeff returns and becomes jealous. He retrieves two handguns and shoots Greg when he exits. However, the grand jury indicts both Ann and Jeff after Ann lies to police that she fired the fatal shot accidentally during a struggle between the men. Ann and Jeff are convicted of first-degree murder and sentenced to life imprisonment. Ann files an application for postconviction relief, alleging that, as a victim of BWS, her husband forced her to relate the false account. She claims that he beat her over an 18-month period whenever she failed to relate the story to his satisfaction. What result? McMaugh v. State, 612 A.2d 725 (R.I. 1992). See also Dixon v. United States, 548 U.S. 1 (2006). For a debate on the duress doctrine and domestic violence, see Joshua Dressler, Battered Women and Sleeping Abusers: Some Reflections, 3 Ohio St. J. Crim. L. 457 (2006); Joan H. Krause, Distorted Reflections of Battered Women Who Kill: A Response to Professor Dressler, 4 Ohio St. J. Crim. L. 555 (2007).

2. Law Reform: Mandatory Arrest and No-Drop Policies

Police traditionally responded to domestic violence with indifference. Throughout the 1970s and early 1980s, police officers ignored domestic violence calls; intentionally delayed responding; attempted to mediate cases of violence with the parties; dealt with the violence by telling the abuser to take a "time out" by walking around the block; and admonished the victim to be a better wife.[35] Police rationalized their refusal to intervene on the ground that domestic violence was a private matter.

The battered women's movement in the 1970s sought to improve the police response. The first step required changing the *common law warrant rule*. This rule prohibited arrests of misdemeanants without a warrant. The common law had different rules for arrest of felons and misdemeanants. A police officer could make a warrantless arrest for a misdemeanor *only* in cases in which the suspect committed the criminal act in the officer's presence. In contrast, when a police officer believed a person has committed a felony, the officer does not actually have to witness the act. Rather, the officer can arrest the suspect without a warrant based on probable cause that the suspect had committed the felony.

Of course, abusers do not commit acts of domestic violence in a police officer's presence. Because the warrant requirement came from the common law, battered women's advocates pressured state legislatures to change that rule. By the 1980s, reformers had convinced many state legislatures to enact warrantless arrest statutes permitting police to arrest an alleged misdemeanant, provided that the officer has probable cause to believe that domestic violence has occurred and that the suspect was the perpetrator. All 50 states now provide for warrantless misdemeanor arrests in domestic violence cases.

---

[35]. Joan Zorza, The Criminal Law of Misdemeanor Domestic Violence, 1970-1990, 83 J. Crim. L. & Criminology 46, 47-48 (1992).

The enactment of warrantless arrest laws, however, failed to alter the policy of nonintervention. As a result, reformers called for an even stronger policy to limit police discretion. They advocated "mandatory arrest" laws that would *require* police to arrest an offender whenever police have probable cause to believe the offender has committed the crime.

Considerable support for mandatory arrest laws stemmed from: (1) a landmark study of police responses to misdemeanor domestic assaults that concluded that arrest was the most effective approach;[36] (2) class-action lawsuits against the police for failure to respond (discussed infra this chapter); and (3) the Violence Against Women Act, 42 U.S.C. §3796hh(c)(1)(a), requiring state and local governments to follow either a mandatory or preferred arrest policy if they wished to receive federal funding (discussed infra this chapter).

Many states subsequently enacted mandatory arrest statutes (although some states enacted pro-arrest statutes). However, the benefits and detriments of mandatory arrest remain contested. Advocates argue that the policy (1) communicates to offenders that society will not tolerate their behavior; (2) protects victims more effectively; (3) empowers victims; (4) equalizes the position of women; (5) clarifies the role of police by providing guidelines; (6) decreases police injuries during domestic disturbances; and (7) ensures that all perpetrators are treated similarly. On the other hand, opponents contend that mandatory arrest contributes to the escalation of violence, increases arrests of women who fight back and minority victims, deters women from contacting police, and reinforces the idea that a woman cannot make her own life decisions.[37]

The role of the *prosecutor* also has evolved since the early days of the battered women's movement. In the 1970s and 1980s, prosecutors often failed to initiate charges, citing victim noncooperation and recantation as reasons. Domestic violence advocates pushed for reforms. Many prosecutors now follow "no-drop" policies that limit prosecutorial discretion. Some states follow "hard" no-drop policies, in which cases proceed regardless of the victim's wishes, whereas other states follow "soft" no-drop policies, in which prosecutors merely encourage victims to proceed and provide support services.[38]

The traditional reluctance of law enforcement personnel to interfere in domestic disputes also precipitated another response in the form of civil lawsuits, such as the following:

---

[36]. See Lawrence W. Sherman & Richard A. Berk, The Specific Deterrent Effects of Arrest for Domestic Assault, 49 Am. Soc. Rev. 261 (1984).

[37]. For a summary of the debate, see Cheryl Hanna, No Right to Choose: Mandated Victim Participation in Domestic Violence Prosecutions, 109 Harv. L. Rev. 1849, 1860 n.37 (1996).

[38]. Id. at 1863.

3. Duties of Law Enforcement

TOWN OF CASTLE ROCK v. GONZALES

545 U.S. 748 (2005)

Justice SCALIA delivered the opinion of the Court.

. . . The horrible facts of this case are contained in the complaint that respondent Jessica Gonzales filed in Federal District Court. [At] about 5 or 5:30 P.M. on Tuesday, June 22, 1999, respondent's [ex-]husband took [their] three daughters [ages 10, 9, and 7] while they were playing outside the family home. No advance arrangements had been made for him to see the daughters that evening. When respondent noticed the children were missing, she suspected her husband had taken them. At about 7:30 P.M., she called the Castle Rock Police Department, which dispatched two officers. The complaint continues: "When [the officers] arrived . . . , she showed them a copy of the TRO [that had been issued to her in conjunction with her divorce proceedings that ordered her ex-husband not to "molest or disturb the peace of [respondent] or of any child," and to remain at least 100 yards from the family home at all times.] [She] requested that it be enforced and the three children be returned to her immediately. [The officers] stated that there was nothing they could do about the TRO and suggested that [respondent] call the Police Department again if the three children did not return home by 10:00 P.M.

At approximately 8:30 P.M., respondent talked to her husband on his cellular telephone. He told her "he had the three children [at an] amusement park in Denver." She called the police again and asked them to "have someone check for" her husband or his vehicle at the amusement park and "put out an [all-points bulletin]" for her husband, but the officer with whom she spoke "refused to do so," again telling her to "wait until 10:00 P.M., and see if" her husband returned the girls.

At approximately 10:10 P.M., respondent called the police and said her children were still missing, but she was now told to wait until midnight. She called at midnight and told the dispatcher her children were still missing. She went to her husband's apartment and, finding nobody there, called the police at 12:10 A.M., she was told to wait for an officer to arrive. When none came, she went to the police station at 12:50 A.M. and submitted an incident report. The officer who took the report "made no reasonable effort to enforce the TRO or locate the three children. Instead, he went to dinner."

At approximately 3:20 A.M., respondent's husband arrived at the police station and opened fire with a semiautomatic handgun he had purchased earlier that evening. Police shot back, killing him. Inside the cab of his pickup truck, they found the bodies of all three daughters, whom he had already murdered.

[Gonzales brought a civil rights action against the municipality and police officers under 42 U.S.C. §1983, claiming that she had a property interest in enforcement of the restraining order; and that the town deprived her of this property interest without due process by having a policy that tolerated nonenforcement of restraining orders.]

[W]e left a similar question [whether a statute conferred an entitlement to due process protection] unanswered in DeShaney v. Winnebago County Dept. of Social Servs., 489 U.S. 189 (1989), another case with "undeniably tragic" facts: Local child-protection officials had failed to protect a young boy from beatings by his father that left him severely brain damaged. We held that the so-called "substantive" component of the Due Process Clause does not "requir[e] the State to protect the life, liberty, and property of its citizens against invasion by private actors." We noted, however, that the petitioner had not properly preserved the argument that—and we thus "decline[d] to consider" whether—state "child protection statutes gave [him] an 'entitlement' to receive protective services in accordance with the terms of the statute, an entitlement which would enjoy due process protection."

The procedural component of the Due Process Clause does not protect everything that might be described as a "benefit." . . . Our cases recognize that a benefit is not a protected entitlement if government officials may grant or deny it in their discretion. . . .

. . . The Court of Appeals in this case determined that Colorado law created an entitlement to enforcement of the restraining order because the "court-issued restraining order . . . specifically dictated that its terms must be enforced" and a "state statute command[ed]" enforcement of the order when certain objective conditions were met (probable cause to believe that the order had been violated and that the object of the order had received notice of its existence). . . .

[The Tenth Circuit based its reasoning primarily on] language from the restraining order, the statutory text, and a state-legislative-hearing transcript. . . . The critical language in the restraining order [came from] the preprinted notice to law-enforcement personnel that appeared on the back of the order. [describing] "peace officers' duties" related to the crime of violation of a restraining order [*A peace officer shall use every reasonable means to enforce a restraining order. . . . A peace officer shall arrest, or, if an arrest would be impractical under the circumstances, seek a warrant for the arrest of a restrained person. . . . A peace officer shall enforce a valid restraining order whether or not there is a record of the restraining order in the registry.* Colo. Rev. Stat. §18-6-803.5(3) (emphasis added).]

The Court of Appeals concluded that this statutory provision [about police officers' duties regarding enforcement of TROs]—especially taken in conjunction with a statement from its legislative history, and with another statute restricting criminal and civil liability for officers making arrests—established the Colorado Legislature's clear intent "to alter the fact that the police were not enforcing domestic abuse retraining orders," and thus its intent "that the recipient of a domestic abuse restraining order have an entitlement to its enforcement." Any other result, it said, "would render domestic abuse restraining orders utterly valueless."

This last statement is sheer hyperbole. Whether or not respondent had a right to enforce the restraining order, it rendered certain otherwise lawful conduct by her husband both criminal and in contempt of court. The creation of grounds on which he could be arrested, criminally prosecuted, and held in contempt was hardly "valueless"—even if the prospect of those sanctions ultimately failed to prevent him from committing three murders and a suicide.

We do not believe that these provisions of Colorado law truly made enforcement of restraining orders *mandatory*. A well-established tradition of police discretion has long coexisted with apparently mandatory arrest statutes [in the criminal law generally]. [A] true mandate of police action would require some stronger indication from the Colorado Legislature than "shall use every reasonable means to enforce a restraining order" (or even "shall arrest . . . or . . . seek a warrant"), §§18-6-803.5(3)(a), (b). That language is not perceptibly more mandatory than the Colorado statute which has long told municipal chiefs of police that they "shall pursue and arrest any person fleeing from justice in any part of the state" and that they "shall apprehend any person in the act of committing any offense . . . and, forthwith and without any warrant, bring such person before a . . . competent authority for examination and trial." Colo. Rev. Stat. §31-4-112.

It is hard to imagine that a Colorado peace officer would not have some discretion to determine that—despite probable cause to believe a restraining order has been violated—the circumstances of the violation or the competing duties of that officer or his agency counsel decisively against enforcement in a particular instance. The practical necessity for discretion is particularly apparent in a case such as this one, where the suspected violator is not actually present and his whereabouts are unknown.

The dissent correctly points out that, in the specific context of domestic violence, mandatory-arrest statutes have been found in some States to be more mandatory than traditional mandatory-arrest statutes. . . . Even in the domestic-violence context, however, it is unclear how the mandatory-arrest paradigm applies to cases in which the offender is not present to be arrested. As the dissent explains, much of the impetus for mandatory-arrest statutes and policies derived from the idea that it is better for police officers to arrest the aggressor in a domestic-violence incident than to attempt to mediate the dispute or merely to ask the offender to leave the scene. Those other options are only available, of course, when the offender is present at the scene. . . .

Respondent does not specify the precise means of enforcement that the Colorado restraining-order statute assertedly mandated—whether her interest lay in having police arrest her husband, having them seek a warrant for his arrest, or having them "use every reasonable means, up to and including arrest, to enforce the order's terms," Brief for Respondent 29-30. Such indeterminacy is not the hallmark of a duty that is mandatory. . . . The dissent, after suggesting various formulations of the entitlement in question, ultimately contends that the obligations under the statute were quite precise: either make an arrest or (if that is impractical) seek an arrest warrant. The problem with this is that the seeking of an arrest warrant would be an entitlement to nothing but procedure—which we have held inadequate even to support standing; much less can it be the basis for a property interest. . . .

Even if the statute could be said to have made enforcement of restraining orders "mandatory" because of the domestic-violence context of the underlying statute, that would not necessarily mean that state law gave *respondent* an entitlement to *enforcement* of the mandate. . . . Respondent's alleged interest stems only from a State's *statutory* scheme. . . . She does not assert that she has any common-law or contractual entitlement to enforcement. If she was given a statutory entitlement, we would expect to see some indication of that in the statute itself. . . .

Even if we were to think otherwise concerning the creation of an entitlement by Colorado, it is by no means clear that an individual entitlement to enforcement of a restraining order could constitute a "property" interest for purposes of the Due Process Clause. Such a right would not, of course, resemble any traditional conception of property. Although that alone does not disqualify it from due process protection . . . , the right to have a restraining order enforced does not "have some ascertainable monetary value." . . . Perhaps most radically, the alleged property interest here arises *incidentally,* not out of some new species of government benefit or service, but out of a function that government actors have always performed—to wit, arresting people who they have probable cause to believe have committed a criminal offense. . . . We conclude, therefore, that respondent did not, for purposes of the Due Process Clause, have a property interest in police enforcement of the restraining order against her husband. . . .

Jessica Gonzales subsequently filed a petition with the Inter-American Commission on Human Rights (IACHR), alleging that the actions of the police violated her human rights. Below is her testimony before the commission.

Testimony of Jessica Gonzales Before the Inter-American Commission on Human Rights

Washington, D.C. (March 2, 2007)

Jessica Gonzales Lenahan, holding a picture of her three daughters who were murdered by their father

. . . I met my previous husband, Simon Gonzales, while still in high school. I married Simon in 1990 and we moved to Castle Rock, Colorado, in 1998. We lived together with our three children—Rebecca, Katheryn, and Leslie—and my son Jessie, from a previous relationship.

Throughout our relationship, Simon was erratic and abusive toward me and our children. By 1994, he was [becoming] more and more controlling, unpredictable, and violent. He would break the children's toys and other belongings, harshly discipline the children, threaten to kidnap them, drive recklessly, exhibit suicidal behavior, and verbally, physically, and sexually abuse me. He was heavily involved with drugs. Simon's frightening and destructive behavior got worse and worse as the years went by. One time I walked into the garage, and he was hanging there with a noose around his neck, with the children watching. I had to hold the rope away from his neck while my daughter Leslie called the police. Simon and I separated in 1999 when my daughters were 9, 8, and 6. But he continued scaring us. He would stalk me inside and outside my house, at my job, and on the phone at all hours of the day and night.

On May 21, 1999, a Colorado court granted me a temporary restraining order that required Simon to stay at least 100 yards away from me, my home, and the children. The judge told me to keep the order with me at all times, and that the order and Colorado law required the police to arrest Simon if he violated the order. Having this court order relieved some of my anxiety. But Simon continued to terrorize me and the children even after I got the restraining order. He broke into my house, stole my jewelry, changed the locks on my doors, and loosened my house's water valves, flooding the entire street. I called the Castle Rock Police Department to report these and other violations of the restraining order. The police ignored most of my calls. . . .

On June 4, Simon and I appeared in court, and the judge made the restraining order permanent. The new order granted me full custody of Rebecca, Katheryn, and Leslie, and said that Simon could only be with our daughters on alternate weekends and one prearranged dinner visit during the week. Less than 3 weeks later, Simon violated the restraining order by kidnapping my three daughters from our yard on a day that he wasn't supposed to see the girls. When I discovered they were missing, I immediately called the police, told them that the girls were missing and that I thought Simon had abducted them in violation of a restraining order, and asked them to find my daughters. . . .

[T]wo officers came to my house. I showed them the restraining order and explained that it was not Simon's night to see the girls, but that I suspected he had taken them. The officers said, "Well, he's their father; it's okay for them to be with him." And I said, "No, it's not okay. There was no prearranged visit for him to have the children tonight." The officers said there was nothing they could do, and told me to call back at 10 P.M. if the children were still not home. . . .

Soon afterwards, Simon's girlfriend called me and told me that Simon called her and was threatening to drive off a cliff. She asked me if he had a gun and whether or not he would hurt the children. I began to panic. I finally reached Simon on his cell phone around 8:30 P.M. He told me he was with the girls at an amusement park in Denver, 40 minutes from Castle Rock. I immediately communicated this information to the police. I was shocked when they responded that there was nothing they could do, because Denver was outside of their jurisdiction. . . . The officer told me I needed to take this matter to divorce court, and told me to call back if the children were not home in a few hours. The officer said to me, "At least you know that the children are with their father." . . .

I called the police again and again that night. When I called at 10 P.M., the dispatcher said to me that I was being "a little ridiculous making us freak out and thinking the kids are gone." Even at that late hour, the police were still scolding me and not acknowledging that three children were missing. [After midnight] I drove to the police station and told yet another officer about the restraining order and that the girls had been gone for seven hours. After I left, that officer went to a two-hour dinner and never contacted me again. I asked the police for help nine separate times that night—two times in person and seven times on the phone. . . .

I later learned that Simon had driven up to the Castle Rock Police station at 3:20 A.M. and opened fire with a semiautomatic handgun he had purchased earlier that evening, after he had abducted the children. The police returned fire, spraying the truck with bullets. After Simon was killed, they searched his truck and found the bodies of my three little girls inside. I was told that Simon had killed them earlier that evening. . . .

I never received an explanation for why Simon was approved in the FBI's background check system when he went to purchase the gun that night. Under federal law, gun dealers can't sell guns to people subject to domestic violence restraining orders. . . . So why did the police ignore my calls for help? Was it because I was a woman? A victim of domestic violence? A Latina? Because the police were just plain lazy? . . .

. . . I brought [a] petition to the Inter-American Commission on Human Rights because I have been denied justice in the United States. It's too late for Rebecca, Katheryn, and Leslie, but it's not too late to create good law and policies for others. Police have to be required to enforce restraining orders or else these orders are meaningless. . . .

Epilogue. In a landmark decision, the IACHR ruled that the American Declaration of the Rights and Duties of Man (the source of legal obligation for the commission's member-states) imposes an affirmative duty to protect citizens from private acts of domestic violence.[39] The commission recommended a full investigation into the "systemic failures" in the enforcement of Gonzales/Lenahan's restraining order. It also recommended the enactment of legislation to strengthen protection orders, protect children in cases of domestic violence, eliminate "sociocultural patterns" that impede victims' protection, and the development of protocols for investigating reports of missing children in the context of restraining order violations.

Notes and Questions

1. No-duty rule. *Castle Rock* is one of several cases instituted by battered women beginning in the 1970s, to force local police departments to treat their complaints seriously. Many suits, like *Castle Rock,* were brought pursuant to the Civil Rights Act of 1964, 42 U.S.C. §1983, which requires a plaintiff to show a deprivation under color of law of a constitutional right. Generally, no right to police protection exists for private acts of violence.

2. Exceptions. Two possible exceptions exist to the no-duty rule: (1) the special relationship doctrine; and (2) the state-created danger doctrine.

a. Special relationship doctrine. The special relationship doctrine was first applied to battered spouses in Balistreri v. Pacifica Police Department, 855 F.2d 1421 (9th Cir. 1988), upholding application of the doctrine to impose a duty of protection by law enforcement based on their repeated notice of the husband's assaults and the wife's restraining order. However, after the Supreme Court severely limited the doctrine in DeShaney v. Winnebago County Department of Social

---

[39]. Jessica Lenahan (Gonzales) v. United States of America, Inter-American Commission on Human Rights Report No. 80/11, Para. 170, http://internationalhumanrightslaw.net/wp . . . /01/Lenahan-et-al.-excerpt1.doc.

Services, 489 U.S. 189 (1989), the Ninth Circuit reheard *Balistreri* and found no substantive due process violation for the police's failure to protect. 901 F.2d 696 (9th Cir. 1990).

DeShaney had significant implications for battered women despite its child abuse context. In *DeShaney*, the Court found that, absent a special relationship, state social workers did not violate a child's *substantive* due process rights by their failure to protect him from his father's abuse.

Post-*DeShaney*, plaintiffs were restricted to other theories, such as claiming (1) an exception to *DeShaney* (i.e., such as invocation of the "custodial relationship doctrine" conferring on police an affirmative duty to protect a victim who is in state custody); (2) a violation of procedural, rather than substantive, due process (i.e., the claim of an entitlement to procedural safeguards); (3) a violation of equal protection; and (4) liability under state tort theories.[40] Because *DeShaney* failed to raise the *procedural* due process claim in a timely manner (the issue raised in *Castle Rock*), the Supreme Court had refused to consider it.

b. State-created danger doctrine. The state-created danger doctrine (another exception to *DeShaney*) allows victims to seek redress from state actors who increase the harm. In a landmark case, the Second Circuit Court of Appeals made it easier for victims to prove their §1983 claims in the domestic violence context by liberalizing the requirement that police must explicitly enhance the danger. The Second Circuit permitted an affirmative act to qualify if it merely communicated an implicit sanction of the violence and also allowed repeated inaction to suffice to condone the violence. Okin v. Village of Cornwall-on-Hudson Police Dept., 577 F.3d 415 (2d Cir. 2009). Would *Okin* have helped Jessica Gonzales?

3. *Castle Rock*: Dissent. In a sharp dissent in *Castle Rock*, Justice Stevens (joined by Justice Ginsburg) charged that the majority failed to take seriously (1) the purpose and nature of restraining orders, and (2) other state laws recognizing that mandatory arrest statutes and restraining orders create a private right to police action. The dissent criticized the majority's lack of regard for legislative intent in the passage of state mandatory arrest statutes as part of the law reform movement to redress police reluctance to enforce restraining orders. According to the dissent, mandatory arrest statutes "undeniably create an entitlement to police enforcement of restraining orders" because, under the state statute, the police were *required* to provide enforcement; they *lacked the discretion to do nothing*. 545 U.S. at 784-785 (emphasis in the original). Finally, the dissent added that cases have found "property interests" in other state benefits and services (such as welfare benefits, disability benefits) and, therefore, reasoned that police enforcement of a restraining order is a government service that is "no less concrete." Id. at 791 (Stevens, J., dissenting).

4. Police nonintervention. What factors explain the refusal of the police to intervene in *Castle Rock*? Gonzales herself speculates about various possibilities in her testimony above. What other reasons might exist?

---

[40]. Developments in the Law: Legal Responses to Domestic Violence, Making State Institutions More Responsive, 106 Harv. L. Rev. 1551, 1560 (1993).

5. Victim cooperation. Police are sometimes reluctant to intervene because of the difficulty of securing the victim's cooperation to testify. Prosecutors have known for years that victims frequently recant or refuse to testify. Perhaps as many as 80 percent of domestic violence cases that reach the court system involve victim recantation or refusal to testify.[41] Why does a victim refuse to cooperate or recant her testimony? What role should her decision play in prosecution of the abuser? Are there sound policy reasons to compel her to testify? Or should the criminal justice system honor her wishes? What other strategies might the prosecutor adopt to encourage the victim to testify?

6. Restraining orders: Effectiveness. How effective are restraining orders—before and after *Castle Rock*? Are they "valueless" or is that "sheer hyperbole"? A significant percentage of battered women seek and obtain restraining orders. Victims resort to restraining orders not as a form of early intervention, but rather as a last resort.[42] Further, temporary restraining orders are violated frequently.[43] Problems of enforcement abound: Many state courts fail to issue restraining orders regularly; many restraining orders are never served; and lax enforcement exists regarding restrictions on firearm possession.[44] What legal reforms might make restraining orders more effective?

7. Mandatory arrest. As we have seen, many states provide mandatory arrest for misdemeanor domestic violence offenses. Do mandatory arrest laws give rise to a private cause of action for failure to protect victims, according to *Castle Rock*? Why or why not?

8. Other remedies.

a. Contempt. Justice Scalia claims that the restraining order was not "valueless" because Jessica Gonzales had an alternative—an action for contempt. Is his reasoning persuasive?

b. State tort theories. Courts have been reluctant to recognize claims that police were negligent in the performance of their duties. Law enforcement agencies have protection from suit by virtue of state tort immunity laws. Such laws require plaintiffs to file a written "notice of claim," subject them to shorter statutes of limitations than those applicable to nongovernmental defendants, and provide immunity from certain types of lawsuits and from claims for punitive damages.

c. Human rights violation. An innovative remedy is to treat domestic violence as a violation of human rights (recall Jessica Gonzales's victory before the IACHR). Following *Castle Rock*, several municipalities passed domestic violence-related

---

[41]. Ami E. Bonomi et al., New Insights on the Process of Victim Recantation, 18 Domestic Violence Rep. 49 (April/May 2013).

[42]. Nat'l Inst. of Justice, Practical Implications of Current Domestic Violence Research: For Law Enforcement, Prosecutors and Judges, Section 9, June 2009 (victims petition for protection orders after failing to stop the abuse through other means), http://www.nij.gov/nij/topics/crime/intimate-partner-violence/practical-implications-research/ch7/civil-protection-orders-when.htm.

[43]. Id. (almost 50 percent of protective orders are violated within two years).

[44]. Office of Attorney General, Attorney General Lockyer Report on Domestic Violence Finds Criminal Justice System Is Failing to Protect Victims, Families AG's Task Force Makes 44 Recommendations to Reduce Domestic Violence, July 26, 2005, http://www.ag.ca.gov/newsalerts/release.php?id=1197.

human rights resolutions recognizing freedom from domestic violence as a fundamental human right.[45] In 2014, President Barack Obama issued two proclamations concerning violence against women, affirming the "basic human right to be free from violence and abuse."[46] Also in 2014, the Colorado Senate acknowledged Jessica Gonzales's efforts on behalf of survivors of domestic violence, affirming that "freedom from domestic violence is a basic human right that government must ensure for all."[47] Evaluate the effectiveness of this human rights remedy.

9. Reform after *Castle Rock*. One suggested reform is to make mandatory arrest statutes "more" mandatory. How could this be accomplished? Professor Kristian Miccio responds with cynicism:

> After *Castle Rock*, advocates believed that if we did what Scalia told us to do, specifically go back to the legislative drawing board and make our laws "more mandatory," the promise of the Fourteenth Amendment Due Process Clause would be attainable in our lifetime. Remember, Scalia told us that "shall," meant "maybe or maybe not," dismissing out of hand the legislative history of thirty-two states and the plain statutory meaning of the word. I guess to the good Justice, the Ten Commandments are merely the ten suggestions. From a policy standpoint, I cannot envision how one makes "a peace officer shall arrest, or . . . seek a warrant," more mandatory.[48]

Should mandatory arrest laws be amended to include unambiguous mandatory language that "police will arrest without discretion" if a protective order is violated? Should reformers pressure legislators to craft exceptions to governmental immunity for police failure to protect victims? What is the likelihood of success of these approaches?

Problem

Shala wants to leave her abusive husband, Dwayne. One Sunday, she tells Dwayne that she wants to attend church. He threatens to kill her two children if she fails to return. Instead of attending church, Shala informs police that Dwayne has violated an order of protection. She explains that she fears him because he has beaten her and threatened to kill her, and that he possesses a handgun. She begs them to help her remove her personal belongings and remove her children. Two officers accompany her home. When they see Dwayne, they do not separate him or search him. While Shala is retrieving her personal belongings, Dwayne draws a revolver from a pocket, kills Shala, and then kills himself. The personal representative of Shala's estate brings a §1983 claim, claiming that the city violated her due process rights. What result? See Simmons v. City of Inkster, 323 F. Supp. 2d 812 (E.D. Mich. 2004); Zelig v. County of Los Angeles, 45 P.3d 1171 (Cal. 2002). Cf. Freeman v. Ferguson, 911 F.2d 52 (8th Cir. 1990). See generally Laura Oren,

---

[45]. Charlotte Cassel et al., Innovative Perspectives on Domestic Violence: Using a Human Rights Framework, 20 Domestic Violence Rep. 33, 35 (2015).

[46]. Id. at 45.

[47]. Id. at 46.

[48]. G. Kristian Miccio, The Death of the Fourteenth Amendment: *Castle Rock* and Its Progeny, 17 Wm. & Mary J. Women & L. 277, 293 (2011).

Some Thoughts on the State-Created Danger Doctrine: *DeShaney* is Still Wrong and *Castle Rock* Is More of the Same, 16 Temp. Pol. & Civ. Rts. L. Rev. 47 (2006).

E. High-Lethality Crimes: Marital Rape, Threats to Kill, and Stalking

1. Lethality Assessment

Lethality assessment is the evaluation of various risk factors to predict cases in which IPV is likely to be fatal. Below, criminologist Neil Websdale explains the markers that identify the risk of death based on his work with fatality review teams.

Neil Websdale, Assessing Risk in Domestic Violence Cases

in Encyclopedia of Domestic Violence 38, 38-40 (Nicky Ali Jackson ed., 2007)

Risk assessment procedures seek to identify the most dangerous perpetrators. [I]dentifying cases that will escalate to the occurrence of the abuse victim's death is an inexact science at best. Nevertheless, risk assessment and management are integral and important aspects of the delivery of all kinds of services to victims. . . .

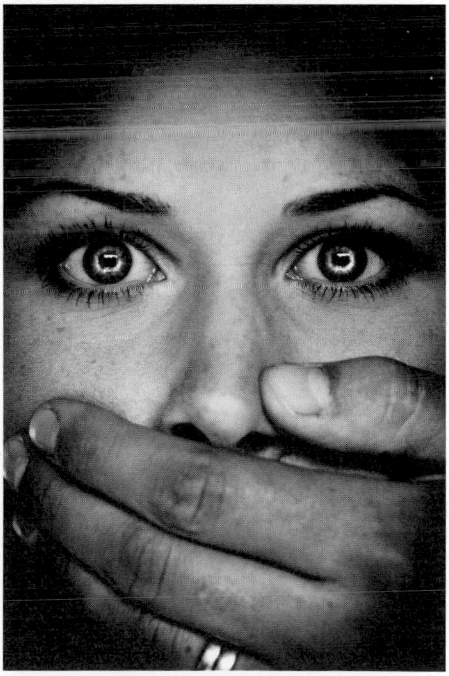

Red flags, such as threats to kill, forced sex, and non-fatal strangulation, loom large as predictive factors in the murder of intimate partners.

RED FLAGS OR RISK MARKERS

. . . Certain red flags loom large in both the research literature and in risk assessment instruments. These red flags are outlined below.

A PRIOR HISTORY OF INTIMATE PARTNER VIOLENCE

The first and most important red flag is a prior history of intimate partner violence. Under this broad umbrella of "prior history," some researchers note the predictive significance of particular forms of violence such as "choking" and "forced sex." Using data from the Danger Assessment Instrument, Campbell et al., found that compared with the control group of abused women, murdered women were forced to have sex 7.6 more times and were 9.9 times more likely to be choked.

"Stalking" appears as a prominent correlate in a number of works. According to the research of McFarlane et al., "Stalking is revealed to be a correlate of lethal and near lethal violence against women and, coupled with physical assault, is significantly associated with murder and attempted murder."

A prior history of intimate partner violence may include the use of a weapon. According to Campbell et al.'s Danger Assessment study, abused women who were threatened or assaulted with a gun or other weapon were 20 times more likely than other women to be murdered. "The mere presence of a gun in the home meant that an abused woman "was six times more likely than other abused women to be killed." . . .

PENDING OR ACTUAL SEPARATION OR ESTRANGEMENT

The extant research literature contends that women experience an increased risk of lethal violence when they leave intimate relationships with men. More recent research from Campbell et al.'s eleven-city case control study found, "Women who separated from their abusive partners after cohabitation experienced increased risk of femicide, particularly when the abuser was highly controlling."

OBSESSIVE POSSESSIVENESS OR MORBID JEALOUSY

The research literature consistently identifies obsessive or morbid jealousy as central to intimate partner homicides. For example, [some researchers point to the role of male sexual proprietariness in homicides cross-culturally, particularly obsessive or pathological jealousy in terms of the perpetrator seeing his partner as part of his own identity]. Consequently, any threat of the female's leaving threatens the man's identity. The emphasis with this red flag is firmly on "extreme" or "morbid" forms of jealousy.

MAKING THREATS TO KILL

Threats to kill constitute one of the most consistent correlates of intimate partner homicide when compared with abused women in general. "Women whose partners threatened them with murder were 15 times more likely than other women to be killed." Batterers' threats to take their own lives, perhaps as a means of gaining some control in the relationship, also appear as risk indicators for homicide. [B]atterers' suicidal threats, ideation, and plans [are] very significant risk markers. . . .

An important tool for measuring a victim's risk of homicide or severe physical violence is the Danger Assessment Instrument. The tool was developed by

Professor Jacquelyn Campbell of Johns Hopkins University School of Nursing after consultation with victims and professionals. Her assessment device measures the severity and frequency of IPV by means of the use of a calendar to increase a victim's recall, raise the consciousness of the victim, and reduce the victim's denial or minimization of the abuse. A fascinating finding of Campbell's research is the inaccuracy of women's own perceptions of their risk. That is, fewer than half of the women who are eventually killed by their partners accurately perceived their risk of death.[49]

The Danger Assessment Instrument is one of the few evidence-based measures of lethality. Its predictive value rests on the fact that it has been scientifically validated in multicity studies. The tool has become so widely accepted that many states now require or encourage its use by police, prosecutors, court personnel, and service providers. In fact, the VAWA Reauthorization Act of 2013 emphasizes the need to integrate lethality assessments in VAWA-funded programs.

Caption: Red flags, such as threats to kill and non-fatal strangulation, loom large as predictive factors in the murder of intimate partners.

2. Marital Rape

PEOPLE v. HARRIS

2012 WL 1651015 (Cal. Ct. App. 2012)

O'Rourke, J.

A jury convicted Shawn Michael Harris of forcible oral copulation [pursuant to California Penal Code §288a, subd. (c)(2)]. It deadlocked on charges of sodomy by force and forcible spousal rape, and the court dismissed those charges. . . . Harris contends the court erred in admitting an "excessive" number of prior acts evidence under Evidence Code sections 1108 [permitting the admission of evidence of a prior sexual assault by defendant] and 1109 [permitting evidence of defendant's other acts of domestic violence] . . .

Harris's wife, C.H., testified that the day before Easter in 2008, which was one week before the forcible oral copulation incident, Harris was driving a car with her and their son in it through their church parking lot, when someone drove towards them. Harris made a rude gesture to the other driver, and C.H. criticized him for it. Harris responded by striking a snow cone out of C.H.'s hand, pressed her neck hard, and said, "Don't push my buttons." . . .

The relationship between C.H. and Harris reached a critical point on March 28, 2008, when the oral copulation incident occurred. As soon as C.H. got home from work that afternoon, Harris, a stay-at-home father, asked her, "Do you want to leave or do you want me to because I can't stand to be around you." C.H. went to the master bedroom to nap. Shortly afterwards, Harris asked her if she wanted to have sex. She said no, because they needed to discuss events of the past week.

---

[49]. See Jacquelyn C. Campbell et al., The Danger Assessment: Validation of a Lethality Risk Assessment Instrument for Intimate Partner Femicide, 24 J. Interpersonal Violence 653, 669 (2009).

Harris asked C.H. if she had called a woman friend of his, whom he had met at a "mommy and me class." Based on her answer, he accused her of lying to him and said she needed to be punished. C.H. excused herself to the bathroom, and used a tape recorder to secretly record the entire ensuing interaction with Harris. A copy of the recording was played for the jury.

On the audiotape, Harris gave C.H. this ultimatum: "You suck or get butt fucked." She interpreted that as a demand to perform oral sex on him or he would force her to have anal sex. While he was choking her, she protested that he was hurting her neck, and said, "Okay, okay, okay! I'll suck it!" She testified that she relented out of fear, and to avoid the hurt from forced anal sex. [During the oral copulation incident,] C.H. protested, "I can't breathe. I can't breathe. I'm sorry, I'm sorry, I can't breathe. I'm sorry, I can't . . ." [She repeatedly] tried to talk her way out of orally copulating him. She pleaded, "I don't want to be raped. Nobody deserves to be raped." Harris responded, "I'll go get a knife downstairs if I fucking have to." He added that she was not dumb or confused, and he would "be sure to carve that on [her] fuckin' head when [he dumped her] body." . . . [At one point] Harris asked C.H. if she was going to call the police. . . . She retorted, "If I could survive the phone call, I would have called." C.H. testified that her retort referred to her fear of calling the police because Harris had threatened that if she did call, he would kill her before the police arrived. She was certain he would carry out the threat. . . .

Before trial, the People moved *in limine* to admit testimony regarding Harris's prior acts under Evidence Code sections 1108 and 1109. [O]ver Harris's objections, the court admitted C.H.'s testimony regarding [several] prior incidents of sexual or domestic abuse during their marriage [as follows]. . . .

C.H. testified that in 1998, approximately two years after they were married, she and Harris got into an argument, he called her a "bitch," and hit her as they were driving to work. She got a restraining order against him, and he was convicted of misdemeanor battery. In November 2003, Harris and C.H. got into an argument and he threatened to throw a four-foot tall play structure for cats at her. Police were called, but she filed no charges against Harris. In April 2004, Harris poured water on their bed, and C.H. went to sleep on a couch. He followed her, pushed her head into the ground. . . . She called police, initially sought a restraining order, but withdrew the request because she hoped Harris would change.

In an August 2007 incident, C.H. sought to discuss their outstanding problems, but Harris did not want to; therefore, C.H. hid his keys to stop him from leaving the house. He pressed her head to the floor as hard as he could, and kicked her. She said she would divorce him, and he threatened to kill her, telling her no one would protect her, not even the police. She called 911, and the recording of the call was played for the jury. In November or December 2007, while they were discussing their marriage, Harris pretended to fall asleep; therefore, C.H. lied about having an affair, in order to get a reaction out of him. Harris immediately straddled her and started choking her. She did not report the incident to police because she was afraid of Harris's death threats. . . .

[At trial] Harris testified that both before and throughout their marriage, he and C.H. had engaged in sexual role playing, and the March 28, 2008 incident was a scenario they had acted out several times before. While acknowledging C.H. had orally copulated him, Harris denied it was forcible and dismissed the notion he was choking her. He insisted, "It's all verbal. It's just acting. I'm not punching her, holding her, tying her down, none of that." . . . He testified C.H. enjoyed the role play. . . . He denied threatening to kill C.H. that night, saying, "I have no desire to kill my ex-wife. It's [*sic*] the mother of my children. I've got no interest in that." . . .

On Harris's cross-examination, this exchange took place:

> "[Prosecutor:] On the recording that we heard here in court during your—your role play with [C.H.] on March 28th, 2008, do you know approximately how many times she expresses to you 'No' or 'Stop' or 'I don't want to do this'?
>
> "[Harris:] No. But I'm sure you're going to tell me.
>
> "[Prosecutor:] She tells you that approximately 50 times. Does that sound about right?
>
> "[Harris:] Whatever is in the scene is in the scene."

Harris generally denied C.H.'s testimony regarding each prior act, and denied ever threatening to kill C.H., choking her, or forbidding her from calling the police. . . . Harris contends the court erred in admitting evidence of his prior acts under Evidence Code sections 1108 and 1109 because "the sheer number of the other incidents resulted in a clear portrayal of [himself] in an extremely negative light, one that would necessarily influence the jury. . . ."

Under Evidence Code section 352, the trial court has discretion to exclude evidence "if its probative value is substantially outweighed by the probability that its admission will . . . create substantial danger of undue prejudice, of confusing the issues, or of misleading the jury." . . . In other words, in cases involving the proffer of evidence of prior acts of domestic violence under Evidence Code section 1109, the question is whether there is a likelihood the evidence will inflame the jury members so that they will base their verdict not on the evidence presented as to the charged offenses, but rather on an emotional response to the defendant's commission of other acts or crimes. . . . We review for abuse of discretion a court's ruling on relevance and admission or exclusion of evidence. . . .

As a preliminary matter, the approximately eight prior acts that were admitted into evidence were not excessive. Also, they were not cumulative, in that they showed different ways Harris exerted control over C.H. at different times during their marriage. Next, we conclude it was not reasonably likely the prior acts evidence so inflamed the jury that it based its verdict on those incidents. It was not likely the jury was confused regarding the specific charged offense of a forcible oral copulation incident, which was more egregious than the prior act incidents because of its sustained duration, and the sexual aggression it entailed. Further, that incident was unique in that the audiotape documented it from start to finish. . . .

Harris's belief that he was prejudiced amounts to speculation. The jury was specifically instructed [that] it may consider [prior acts of domestic violence] in assessing guilt. "Jurors are presumed able to understand and correlate instructions and are further presumed to have followed the court's instructions." Moreover, the jury acquitted Harris of two charges, showing the jurors limited their consideration of the Evidence Code section 1109 evidence as instructed.

Finally, we note that Harris denied C.H.'s versions of each of the prior incidents. Therefore, the jury was afforded an opportunity to evaluate the conflicting versions and make credibility determinations. Based on the above, we conclude that the trial court did not err in admitting evidence of Harris's prior domestic violence and sexual assault. . . .

Notes and Questions

1. **Epilogue.** Harris was sentenced to six years in prison. In a remarkable outcome, the judge in the parallel divorce proceedings awarded spousal support to Harris, a stay-at-home father (upon his release from prison), in the amount of $1,000 per month, as well as $47,000 in legal fees. In response, the state legislature enacted California Family Code §4324.5, precluding spousal support in cases in which a spouse convicted of a sexual felony against the other spouse would otherwise be entitled to spousal support.

2. **Lethality assessment.** Lethality assessment, as the above excerpt by Neil Websdale reveals, seeks to identify the most dangerous cases of abuse that might escalate to the victim's death. Forced sex is one of the lethality indicators. What lethality indicators do you discern in *Harris*?

3. **Frequency.** Sexual assaults are a common feature of IPV. About 10 percent of women are sexually assaulted by an intimate partner.[50] Physical abuse often accompanies sexual assault.[51] Did C.H. in the principal case experience both types of violence?

4. **Abusers' motivation.** Sexual assaults in intimate relationships can be an alternative form of physical abuse, a form of punishment, or a reconciliation tactic.[52] Such assaults reflect the abuser's sense of entitlement to the partner's sexual and reproductive services.[53] What evidence suggests any of these motivations for the defendant in *Harris*?

5. **Victims' voluntary "consent."** Many victims "consent" to sexual activity with an abusive partner because they fear retaliation or hope to deescalate a conflict. Given these motivations, how can a fact finder determine whether the sexual activity was truly consensual? What factors militated against a jury finding in *Harris* that the sexual activity was consensual? Why do you think the jury deadlocked on the charges of sodomy by force and forcible spousal rape?

Should a victim's engaging in consensual sex *following* an incident of physical assault preclude her eligibility for a protection order? See Durham v. Metzger, 2012 WL 1556490 (Ky. App. Ct. 2012). See generally Robin West, Sex, Law, and Consent, in The Ethics of Consent: Theory and Practice 221 (Franklin G. Miller & Alan Wertheimer eds., 2010); Robin West, The Harms of Consensual Sex, in The Philosophy of Sex: Contemporary Readings 317 (Alan Soble & Nicholas Power eds., 5th ed. 2008).

---

[50]. NISVS, supra note [2], at 39.

[51]. Jennifer A. Bennice & Patricia A. Resick, Marital Rape: History, Research, & Practice, 4 Trauma, Violence, & Abuse 228, 234, 238 (2003) (reporting that from one-third to one-half of battered women are also sexually assaulted).

[52]. T.K. Logan et al., A Mixed-Methods Examination of Sexual Coercion and Degradation Among Women in Violent Relationships Who Do and Do Not Report Forced Sex, 22 Violence & Victims 71, 87, 89 (2007); Bennice & Resick, supra note [51], at 237.

[53]. Margo Wilson & Martin Daly, 'Til Death Do Us Part, in Femicide: The Politics of Woman Killing 83, 85 (Jill Radford & Diana E.H. Russell eds., 1992).

6. Use of evidence. What is the inference that follows from admission of prior acts evidence ("propensity evidence")? Why did the court in *Harris* overrule the defendant's objection to the prosecutor's motion to admit the evidence? Suppose the defendant wanted to admit "propensity evidence" on the part of the victim? See Deborah Tuerkheimer, Judging Sex, 97 Cornell L. Rev. 1461 (2012). Did the defendant's claim that the couple was "role-playing" a sexual fantasy carry any weight with the jury? Should it have? What other problems do victims face in convincing fact finders of the occurrence of marital rape?

7. Spectrum of assaults. Sexual assault of an intimate partner spans a spectrum, including coercion to engage in sex or particular sexual acts; degrading and/or humiliating tactics before, during, or after sex; forced sex on a partner who is sleeping, physically ill, or who recently gave birth; being hit, kicked, or burned during sex; coerced substance abuse during sex; use of sex as punishment; nonconsensual insertion of objects; holding a partner captive during sex; forcing the partner to have sex in public (e.g., in a parked car); and coercing the partner to involve others in sexual acts.[54]

8. Contraceptive sabotage. Some victims of IPV experience contraceptive sabotage, also known as reproductive coercion, in which a partner makes threats or commits acts of violence against a partner's reproductive health or reproductive decisionmaking. What are the motivations for this form of abuse? Not surprisingly, sabotage of birth control leads to a large number of unintended pregnancies and abortions. See generally Jay G. Silverman et al., Male Perpetration of Intimate Partner Violence and Involvement in Abortions and Abortion-Related Conflict, 100 Am. J. Pub. Health 1415 (2010). What, if anything, can the legal system do to address birth control sabotage? Men are not the only intimate partners who sabotage birth control. "Contraceptive fraud" consists of cases in which a woman stops using birth control because she wants to get pregnant, but she fails to inform her partner of her decision. See Wallis v. Smith (infra Chapter V).

9. Severity. A commonly held belief is that intimate partner rape is less serious than stranger rape. What is the basis for this belief? In fact, research reveals that relationships accompanied by physical violence and rape are marked by *more* severe violence and *repeated* sexual victimizations.[55]

10. Marital rape exemption. At common law, a husband was exempt from prosecution for raping his wife. American law reflected the "marital rape exemption" based on British jurist Sir Matthew Hale's assertion that marriage signified a wife's presumed and irrevocable consent to her husband's sexual demands.[56]

---

[54]. Bennice & Resick, supra note [51], at 237; Logan et al., supra note [52], at 75, 81-86, 89.

[55]. Bennice & Resick, supra note [51], at 238-239; Logan et al., supra note [52], at 71.

[56]. For a discussion of the marital rape exemption, see Jill Elaine Hasday, Contest and Consent: A Legal History of Marital Rape, 88 Cal. L. Rev. 1373, 1396-1398 (2000).

The marital rape exemption existed until People v. Liberta, 474 N.E.2d 567 (N.Y. 1984), in which the court held that the marital exemption, as well as the female exemption, to the rape and sodomy statutes violated equal protection. The court reasoned that the underlying rationales (wives' irrevocable consent to sex and wives-as-property) were archaic notions that did not withstand rational basis review. The court also rejected the justification of marital privacy, reasoning that the marital rape exemption fails to accomplish that objective because the privacy right protects only consensual acts. Should the right to marital privacy ever supersede the individual right to privacy?

Following *Liberta*, courts and legislatures gradually abrogated the marital rape exception. Despite widespread reform, however, many states still treat marital rape differently from stranger rape. Some states impose special procedural requirements (e.g., mandating reports to designated professionals or within certain time periods), subject marital rape to less severe sanctions, or criminalize a narrower range of offenses.[57]

11. Strangulation. C.H. was choked by the defendant in the course of the assault. Nonfatal strangulation (commonly referred to as "choking") is a frequent occurrence in IPV. Such incidents are also highly predictive of homicide. The occurrence of prior strangulation attempts has been identified in 25 percent of women killed by an intimate partner.[58]

Strangulation is difficult to discover because it often leaves no visible marks. As a result, police need to be trained to look for subtle signs, such as visual changes, dizziness, changes in the victim's voice, petechiae (small red spots created by increased venous pressure), loss of consciousness, or the victim's urination or defecation during an assault (indicators of lack of oxygen). If bruises do occur, they may not appear until several days after the incident. In fact, some victims, without visible symptoms, may die 36 or more hours after the incident due to internal swelling and undetected internal injuries. Repeated nonfatal strangulation assaults often result in long-term neurological consequences.[59]

A common belief is that abusers choke their victims with the intent to kill them. However, research reveals that abusers choke their victims to show that they *can* kill them any time they wish.[60] What message was Harris attempting to convey to his ex-wife by choking her? Should Harris have been criminally charged for strangling C.H.?

12. State and federal law reform. Awareness of the lethality of nonfatal strangulation assaults prompted many states to enact laws designating felony liability for such conduct. Currently, 37 states have strangulation laws.[61] Previously,

---

[57]. Samantha Allen, Marital Rape is Semi-Legal in 8 States, Daily Beast, June 9, 2015, http://www.thedailybeast.com/articles/2015/06/09/marital-rape-is-semi-legal-in-8-states.html (pointing out that Ohio and Oklahoma still distinguish between marital and nonmarital rape by requiring a greater degree of force for marital rape).

[58]. Gael B. Strack et al., Investigation and Prosecution of Strangulation Cases, 19 Domestic Violence Rep. 83 (Aug./Sept. 2014) (explaining that 30-60% of domestic violence victims are victims of nonfatal strangulation by their partners).

[59]. Mary Carr, Increasing Awareness about Possible Neurological Alterations in Brain Status Secondary to Intimate Violence, 4 Brain Injury Source 30 (Summer 2000).

[60]. Casey Gwinn et al., Law Reform Targets the Crime of Strangulation, 19 Domestic Violence Rep. 81, 81 (Aug./Sept. 2014).

[61]. Id.

strangulation attempts were not charged, were prosecuted as misdemeanors, were reduced to lesser charges, or simply dismissed altogether. In addition, the 2013 reauthorization of VAWA amends the federal assault statute (18 USCA §113(8)) to recognize the seriousness of nonfatal strangulation by punishing "assault of a spouse, intimate partner, or dating partner by strangling, suffocating, or attempting to strangle or suffocate, by a fine under this title, imprisonment for not more than 10 years, or both."

Problems

1. Henry met Donna in their church choir when both were almost 70 years old and had suffered the death of their respective spouses. Henry was a member of the Iowa House of Representatives. Two years later, they married. By all accounts, they were quite affectionate with each other and held hands wherever they went. Four years into the marriage, Donna was diagnosed with early-onset Alzheimer's. She suffered frequent bouts of forgetfulness, drove on the wrong side of the road, and once put a single sock into the dryer instead of a full load of laundry. When her daughter once took her out for lunch, Donna wore a coat over pajamas that left her breasts exposed and she tried to wash her hands in the restaurant toilet. Soon thereafter, Donna's two adult daughters by a prior marriage, moved Donna into a nursing home—a move that Henry resisted. Her daughters drew up a care plan for her with the nursing home staff that concluded that Donna was no longer able to make decisions about her well-being, including consent to sex. They informed Henry of that fact.

But one week later, a surveillance video showed Henry spending a half hour in his wife's room. When he left, he was holding Donna's underwear, which he dropped into a laundry bag in the hallway. Donna's roommate told nursing home staff that Henry had entered the room and closed the privacy curtain around his wife's bed. The roommate then heard noises indicating that the couple was having sex. A rape test kit and analysis of her underwear and bedding confirmed that account. Shortly thereafter, a state investigator interviewed Henry about the incident. Henry admitted having "sexual contact" with his wife on the relevant date. However, he argued that it was consensual and that Donna still enjoyed his expressions of affection. Henry was arrested and charged with marital rape. What result?[62]

How would the following additional information (introduced as expert testimony) affect your answer? Some experts in geriatric health care have begun to emphasize the value of touch, intimacy, and sex among older adults, especially those in care facilities. For example, the Hebrew Home in Riverdale, N.Y., has pioneered a "sexual rights policy" for its residents. As one expert explains: "Touch is one of the last pleasures we lose . . . . So much of aging and so much of being in a long-term care facility is about loss, loss of independence, loss of friends, loss of ability to use your body. Why would we want to diminish that?" Others have analogized sexual relations to eating and drinking—a basic instinct that should be satisfied

[62]. For a discussion of the case, see Sarah Kaplan, In an Iowa Courtroom, an Astonishing Case of Sex and Alzheimer's, Wash. Post, Apr. 7, 2015, http://www.washingtonpost.com/news/morning-mix/wp/2015/04/07/in-an-iowa-courtroom-an-astonishing-case-of-sex-and-alzheimers/.

even among the elderly with impaired cognitive functioning. See Pam Belluck, Sex, Dementia, and a Husband on Trial at Age 78, N.Y. Times, Apr. 14, 2015, at A1.

2. Craig Hutchinson has been involved in an intimate relationship with Jane Smith for the past six months. Jane insists that he wear condoms whenever they have sex because, as she repeatedly explains, she does not want to become pregnant. After Jane expresses some doubt about continuing with their relationship, Craig decides to sabotage the condoms. Over a period of several weeks, he pokes holes in the condoms in an effort to impregnate Jane and thus encourage her to stay with him. After Jane becomes pregnant, she questions Craig about his use of birth control. He admits his deceit in a series of text messages to her.

Jane promptly obtains an abortion and then reports Craig's conduct to the police. Craig is charged with aggravated sexual assault. A defense to the jurisdiction's Criminal Code governing sexual assault is the "voluntary agreement of the complainant to engage in the sexual activity in question." At trial, Craig contends that he cannot be convicted of sexual assault because Jane consented to sex, and his deceit about the condition of the condoms did not invalidate her consent to have sex. What result? Does Jane have any civil remedies against Craig? Should rape law be revised to take this form of intimate partner abuse into account? See R. v. Hutchinson, [2014] 1 SCR 346.

3. Threats to Kill and Stalking

ELONIS v. UNITED STATES

135 S. Ct. 2001 (2015)

Chief Justice Roberts delivered the opinion of the Court.

Federal law makes it a crime to transmit in interstate commerce "any communication containing any threat . . . to injure the person of another." 18 U.S.C. §875(c). Petitioner was convicted of violating this provision under instructions that required the jury to find that he communicated what a reasonable person would regard as a threat. The question is whether the statute also requires that the defendant be aware of the threatening nature of the communication, and—if not—whether the First Amendment requires such a showing.

Anthony Douglas Elonis was an active user of the social networking Web site Facebook. Users of that Web site may post items on their Facebook page that are accessible to other users, including Facebook "friends" who are notified when new content is posted. In May 2010, Elonis's wife of nearly seven years left him, taking with her their two young children. Elonis began "listening to more violent music" and posting self-styled "rap" lyrics inspired by the music. Eventually, Elonis changed the user name on his Facebook page from his actual name to a rap-style nom de plume, "Tone Dougie," to distinguish himself from his "on-line persona." The lyrics Elonis posted as "Tone Dougie" included graphically violent language and imagery. This material was often interspersed with disclaimers that the lyrics were "fictitious," with no intentional "resemblance to real persons." Elonis posted an explanation to another Facebook user that "I'm doing this for me. My writing is therapeutic."

Elonis's co-workers and friends viewed the posts in a different light. Around Halloween of 2010, Elonis posted a photograph of himself and a co-worker at a "Halloween Haunt" event at the amusement park where they worked. In the photograph, Elonis was holding a toy knife against his co-worker's neck, and in the caption Elonis wrote, "I wish." . . . [T]he chief of park security was a Facebook "friend" of Elonis, saw the photograph, and fired him. In response, Elonis posted a new entry on his Facebook page [that included his claim that he still had the keys to the park, and also included his threat to break into the park at night during the Halloween Haunt.] This post became the basis for Count One of Elonis' subsequent indictment, threatening park patrons and employees.

Elonis's posts frequently included crude, degrading, and violent material about his soon-to-be ex-wife. [In one example, he wrote: "I'm not going to rest until your body is a mess, soaked in blood and dying from all the little cuts."] Shortly after he was fired, Elonis posted an adaptation of a satirical sketch that he and his wife had watched together. In the actual sketch, called "It's Illegal to Say . . . ," a comedian explains that it is illegal for a person to say he wishes to kill the President, but not illegal to explain that it is illegal for him to say that. When Elonis posted the script of the sketch, however, he substituted his wife for the President. The posting was part of the basis for Count Two of the indictment, threatening his wife:

> "Hi, I'm Tone Elonis.
>
> Did you know that it's illegal for me to say I want to kill my wife? . . .
>
> It's one of the only sentences that I'm not allowed to say . . . .
>
> Now it was okay for me to say it right then because I was just telling you that it's illegal for me to say I want to kill my wife . . . .
>
> Um, but what's interesting is that it's very illegal to say I really, really think someone out there should kill my wife . . . .
>
> But not illegal to say with a mortar launcher.
>
> Because that's its own sentence . . . .
>
> I also found out that it's incredibly illegal, extremely illegal to go on Facebook and say something like the best place to fire a mortar launcher at her house would be from the cornfield behind it because of easy access to a getaway road and you'd have a clear line of sight through the sun room . . . .
>
> Yet even more illegal to show an illustrated diagram [revealing a diagram of his ex-wife's house]."

At the bottom of the post, Elonis included a link to the video of the original skit, and wrote, "Art is about pushing limits. I'm willing to go to jail for my Constitutional rights. Are you?"

After viewing some of Elonis's posts, his wife felt "extremely afraid for [her] life." A state court granted her a three-year protection-from-abuse order. . . . [Elonis questioned whether the protection order was "thick enough to stop a bullet," and maintained that he had "enough explosives to take care of the State Police and the Sheriff's Department."] At the bottom of this post was a link to the Wikipedia article on "Freedom of speech." Elonis's reference to the police was the basis for Count Three of his indictment, threatening law enforcement officers.

Anthony Elonis, who asserted a First Amendment defense after he posted threats to kill his wife on Facebook

. . . Elonis [later] posted an entry that gave rise to Count Four of his indictment [by threatening to "make a name for himself" and "initiat[ing] the most heinous school shooting ever imagined" and "hell hath no fury like a crazy man in a Kindergarten class"]. [After this post, FBI Agent Denise Stevens and her partner visited Elonis at his house.] Following their visit, during which Elonis was polite but uncooperative, Elonis posted another entry on his Facebook page, called "Little Agent Lady," which led to Count Five. [He threatened that it took all his strength, when she knocked, not to "Pull my knife, flick my wrist, and slit her throat/ Leave her bleedin' from her jugular in the arms of her partner" . . . and suggested that he was a "crazy sociopath" who was "strapped with a bomb" and warned that if law enforcement returned to his home, they better bring a SWAT team].

A jury convicted Elonis on four of the five counts against him [threatening his estranged wife, police officers, a kindergarten class, and an FBI agent], acquitting only on the charge of threatening park patrons and employees. Elonis was sentenced to three years, eight months' imprisonment and three years' supervised release. Elonis renewed his challenge to the jury instructions [contending] that the jury should have been required to find that he intended his posts to be threats.

. . . This statute requires that a communication be transmitted and that the communication contain a threat. It does not specify that the defendant must have any mental state with respect to these elements. In particular, it does not indicate whether the defendant must intend that his communication contain a threat. . . .

[Elonis' conviction] was premised solely on how his posts would be understood by a reasonable person. Such a "reasonable person" standard is a familiar feature of civil liability in tort law, but is inconsistent with "the conventional requirement for criminal conduct—*awareness* of some wrongdoing." Having liability turn on whether a "reasonable person" regards the communication as a threat—regardless of what the defendant thinks—"reduces culpability on the all-important element of the crime to negligence," and we "have long been reluctant to infer that a negligence standard was intended in criminal statutes" . . . .

In light of the foregoing, Elonis's conviction cannot stand. The jury was instructed that the Government need prove only that a reasonable person would regard Elonis's communications as threats, and that was error. Federal criminal liability generally does not turn solely on the results of an act without considering the defendant's mental state. . . .

There is no dispute that the mental state requirement in Section 875(c) is satisfied if the defendant transmits a communication for the purpose of issuing a threat, or with knowledge that the communication will be viewed as a threat. In response to a question at oral argument, Elonis stated that a finding of recklessness would not be sufficient. Neither Elonis nor the Government has briefed or argued that point, and we accordingly decline to address it. Given our disposition, it is not necessary to consider any First Amendment issues.

Both Justice Alito and Justice Thomas complain about our not deciding whether recklessness suffices for liability under Section 875(c). . . . We may be "capable of deciding the recklessness issue," but following our usual practice of awaiting a decision below and hearing from the parties would help ensure that we decide it correctly. . . . [T]he case is remanded for further proceedings consistent with this opinion.

Justice ALITO, concurring in part and dissenting in part.

. . . It is settled that the Constitution does not protect true threats. And there are good reasons for that rule: True threats inflict great harm and have little if any social value. A threat may cause serious emotional stress for the person threatened and those who care about that person, and a threat may lead to a violent confrontation. It is true that a communication containing a threat may include other statements that have value and are entitled to protection. But that does not justify constitutional protection for the threat itself.

Elonis argues that the First Amendment protects a threat if the person making the statement does not actually intend to cause harm. In his view, if a threat is made for a "'therapeutic' purpose," to 'deal with the pain' . . . of a wrenching event," or for "cathartic" reasons, the threat is protected. But whether or not the person making a threat intends to cause harm, the damage is the same. And the fact that making a threat may have a therapeutic or cathartic effect for the speaker is not sufficient to justify constitutional protection. Some people may experience a therapeutic or cathartic benefit only if they know that their words will cause harm or only if they actually plan to carry out the threat, but surely the First Amendment does not protect them.

Elonis also claims his threats were constitutionally protected works of art. Words like his, he contends, are shielded by the First Amendment because they are similar to words uttered by rappers and singers in public performances and recordings. To make this point, his brief includes a lengthy excerpt from the lyrics of a rap song in which a very well compensated rapper imagines killing his ex-wife and dumping her body in a lake. If this celebrity can utter such words, Elonis pleads, amateurs like him should be able to post similar things on social media. But context matters. "Taken in context," lyrics in songs that are performed for an audience or sold in recorded form are unlikely to be interpreted as a real threat to a real person. Statements on social media that are pointedly directed at their victims, by contrast, are much more likely to be taken seriously. To hold otherwise would grant a license to anyone who is clever enough to dress up a real threat in the guise of rap lyrics, a parody, or something similar. . . .

There was evidence that Elonis made sure his wife saw his posts. And she testified that they made her feel "'extremely afraid'" and "'like [she] was being stalked.'" Considering the context, who could blame her? Threats of violence and intimidation are among the most favored weapons of domestic abusers, and the rise of social media has only made those tactics more commonplace. A fig leaf of artistic expression cannot convert such hurtful, valueless threats into protected speech.

It can be argued that §875(c), if not limited to threats made with the intent to harm, will chill statements that do not qualify as true threats, e.g., statements that may be literally threatening but are plainly not meant to be taken seriously. We have sometimes cautioned that it is necessary to "exten[d] a measure of strategic protection" to otherwise unprotected false statements of fact in order to ensure enough "'breathing space'" for protected speech. A similar argument might be made with respect to threats. But we have also held that the law provides adequate breathing space when it requires proof that false statements were made with reckless disregard of their falsity. . . . I would vacate the judgment below and remand for the Court of Appeals to decide in the first instance whether Elonis's conviction could be upheld under a recklessness standard. . . .

Notes and Questions

1. Epilogue. At the time of his postconviction appeal before the U.S. Supreme Court, Elonis had served over three years in prison. In April 2015, Elonis was arrested for a domestic violence-related assault for allegedly hitting his new girlfriend's mother in the head with a metal pot during an argument. He is currently serving time for this incident as a violation of the conditions of his supervised release from federal prison.[63]

2. Holding. In the principal case, Elonis is charged with violating the Interstate Communications Act, 18 U.S.C. §875(c), which makes it a federal crime to transmit in interstate commerce "any communication containing any threat . . . to injure the person of another." Congress enacted the statute in 1939 to regulate threatening speech as one of a series of laws directed at extortion in kidnapping cases, stemming from the Lindbergh baby kidnapping incident in 1932. Under the federal statute, what elements does the prosecutor have to prove? What mental state is required?

3. Standard. The Supreme Court regulates the content of speech very reluctantly, although exceptions exist. One such exception is the "true threats" doctrine that prohibits statements that communicate a serious expression of an intent to commit an act of violence to a particular individual or group. *Elonis* raised the issue of the *standard* for determining whether speech constitutes a "true threat." The trial court adopted a negligence standard. What standard did the defendant advocate? What standard did the appellate court adopt? What standard did the Supreme Court adopt? On remand, what standard *should* the court adopt? How should a court apply that standard on remand in Elonis's case?

4. First Amendment. What was the defendant's argument about whether the federal law violated his First Amendment rights? The amicus brief of the American Civil Liberties Union (ACLU) expressed concern that "criminalizing threats that may be considered merely offensive or crude statements" might impinge upon "core political, artistic, and ideological speech."[64] On the other hand, the amicus brief of the Domestic Violence Legal Empowerment and Appeals Project (DVLEAP)

---

[63]. Jessica Mason Pieklo, More Domestic Violence Charges for Man in Supreme Court Facebook Threats Case, RH Reality Check, May 8, 2015, http://rhrealitycheck.org/article/2015/05/08/domestic-violence-charges-man-scotus-facebook-threats-case.

[64]. Brief for American Civil Liberties Union et al. as Amici Curiae Supporting Petitioner, Elonis v. United States of America, 2014 WL 4215752 (Aug. 22, 2014) (No. 13-983), at 5.

emphasized that "threats are the essence of domestic violence and most protection order cases."[65] How should this conflict between free speech and victim protection be resolved? What was the Supreme Court's response to the First Amendment issue?

5. Stalking: Elements. Stalking is a pattern of repeated and unwanted attention, harassment, contact, or other course of conduct that is directed at a specific person that would cause a reasonable person to feel fear. Stalking, an indicator of high lethality in the domestic violence context, may take the form of contact via phone calls, letters, e-mails, and sometimes even presents or flowers. Victims are followed, spied upon, and subject to rumors. Stalking frequently leads to murder.[66]

Could the defendant have been charged with stalking under the state law below? Pennsylvania law provides that a person commits stalking when he or she either:

> (1) engages in a course of conduct or repeatedly commits acts toward another person, including following the person without proper authority, under circumstances which demonstrate either an intent to place such other person in reasonable fear of bodily injury or to cause substantial emotional distress to such other person; or
> (2) engages in a course of conduct or repeatedly communicates to another person under circumstances which demonstrate or communicate either an intent to place such other person in reasonable fear of bodily injury or to cause substantial emotional distress to such other person. (18 Pa. C.S.A. §2709.1).

What elements does the statute require? Some states enhance the penalties for stalking if the stalker is subject to a restraining order. See, e.g., Fla. Stat. §784.048(4). Assess the lethality of the risk that defendant posed to his ex-wife.

6. Stalking: Characteristics. Most stalking victims tend to be *former* intimate partners. Separated partners have an especially high rate of victimization. Stalkers often intend to coerce the victim to remain in the relationship. What do you think was Elonis's motivation for his conduct?

Studies suggest that "threats of violence by former partners who are stalking are an even better predictor of future violence than the prior violence used by these ex-partners."[67] Another study found that of women murdered by their abusers, approximately half had previously been threatened with death.[68] Does the Supreme Court's decision take into account this reality?

7. Policy. What would be the implications of a ruling that specific intent to harm was required in order for communication of a "true threat"? The amicus brief of DVLEAP was concerned about the implications for protection orders if Elonis's conviction had been overturned on this basis. What would be the implications of such a holding for stalking laws?

---

[65]. Brief for Domestic Violence Legal Empowerment and Appeals Project (DVLEAP) & Prof. Margaret Drew as Amici Curiae Supporting Respondent, Elonis v. United States of America, 2014 WL 5035111 (Oct. 6, 2014) (No. 13-983), at 23.

[66]. Katrina Baum et al., Bureau of Justice Statistics, Department of Justice, Stalking Victimization in the United States (2009).

[67]. DVLEAP Amicus Brief, supra note [65], at 25.

[68]. Id.

8. State and federal stalking laws. Both state and federal laws address stalking.

a. State laws. Prior to the enactment of stalking laws, victims had limited recourse absent physical injury or conduct involving specific offenses (i.e., annoying or obscene phone calls). California was the first state to enact a stalking law in 1990 after an obsessed fan stalked and killed television actress Rebecca Schaeffer, following his acquisition of her address from the Department of Motor Vehicles.[69] Schaeffer's murder also led to enactment of the Driver's Privacy Protection Act, 18 U.S.C. §§2721-2725.

In most states, stalking is a misdemeanor. States enhance the penalty if the defendant is a repeat offender; violates a protection order or conditions of probation, pretrial release, or bond; commits stalking with a deadly weapon; or physically harms the victim. Stalking statutes underwent several stages of revision, including expansion of categories of victims; increases in penalties; expansion of types of threats; revision of the intent and fear requirements (from narrow definitions of "death or great bodily" harm to threats intended to place the victim in reasonable fear for his/her safety or that "of a family member"); notification of victims prior to stalkers' release; provisions enabling prosecution of stalkers who threaten victims from prison; and requirements that stalkers register as sex offenders.

b. Federal law. Federal law also covers stalking. VAWA enacted the federal crime of interstate stalking, 18 U.S.C §2261A, defined as interstate travel with the intent to "kill, injure, harass, or place under surveillance with intent to kill, injure, harass, or intimidate" a person. The statute requires that the victim experience "reasonable fear" of death or serious bodily injury. The federal crime of interstate stalking also covers use of the "mail, any interactive computer service, or any facility of interstate or foreign commerce" with the above intent in order to place a victim in reasonable fear of death or serious bodily injury. Did Elonis commit the crime of interstate stalking? The federal criminal provisions of VAWA are discussed later in this chapter.

9. Cyberstalking. Modern forms of communication, such as cell phones and the Internet, facilitate stalking. Formerly, abusers who wanted to track a partner were limited to the use of car odometers for measuring a partner's mileage. Now, stalkers can install monitoring software and/or hardware in computers to locate and harass victims. Some abusers use surveillance techniques, such as GPS devices—often with little legal oversight.

a. State cyberstalking law. State legislatures have expanded stalking statutes to address the newest forms of electronic surveillance devices. Forty-nine states have laws that address cyber harassment, cyber stalking, or both. See generally Steven D. Hazelwood & Sarah Koon-Magnin, Cyber Stalking and Cyber Harassment Legislation in the United States: A Qualitative Analysis, 7 Int'l J. of Cyber Criminology, 155 (2013).

b. Federal cyberstalking laws. Several federal laws address cyberstalking. In addition to the Interstate Communications Act at issue in *Elonis*, the Telephone Harassment Act, as amended by VAWA 2000, 47 U.S.C. §223 & 223(a)(1)(C), makes

---

[69]. Naomi Harlin Goodno, Cyberstalking, A New Crime: Evaluating the Effectiveness of Current State and Federal Laws, 72 Mo. L. Rev. 125, 127 (2007).

it a crime to use a telephone or an interactive computer service to transmit in interstate or foreign commerce any message "to annoy, abuse, harass, or threaten a person."

In March 2014, Senator Al Franken (D-MN) introduced the Location Privacy Protection Act of 2014 (S. 2171, 113th Cong. (2013-2014)) to ban apps that track the location of another person's smartphone, citing concerns about the misuse of such apps to enable domestic violence. As an illustration of how such apps can be misused, Franken recounts the story of a woman who, while at the courthouse petitioning for a restraining order, received a text from her husband asking why she was at the courthouse.[70] What concerns jeopardize its passage?

F. Violence Against Women Act (VAWA)

In 1994, Congress enacted the Violence Against Women Act (VAWA), Pub. L. No. 103-322, 108 Stat. 1796, as part of major anti-crime legislation. VAWA's primary goals are to improve law enforcement as well as community-based responses to domestic violence. To accomplish these ends, VAWA provided grants for investigation and prosecution, created a federal tort remedy for gender-motivated violence (later ruled unconstitutional), authorized interstate enforcement of protection orders, established new federal crimes, and created firearm restrictions.

VAWA has been reauthorized three times. The first reauthorization, in 2000, 22 U.S.C. §§7101 et seq., increased funding for law enforcement and shelters; expanded services to the elderly, disabled, and Native Americans; incorporated the crimes of dating violence and stalking; improved legal services for victims; expanded transitional housing; promoted supervised visitation; and strengthened protections for immigrant victims by creating U- and T-visas. VAWA's second reauthorization in 2005 (codified in scattered sections of 42 U.S.C.), added protections against housing discrimination, provided funding for rape centers; developed culturally and linguistically specific services; and enhanced services for disabled victims and children.

The most recent reauthorization, the VAWA Reauthorization Act of 2013, provides funds for programs for LGBT victims and prohibits discrimination in services based on sexual orientation or gender identity; integrates lethality assessments in VAWA-funded programs; expands tribal court jurisdiction over non-Indian perpetrators; expands housing protections (against denial or eviction from public and Section 8 housing) to additional federal housing programs; provides funding for services for schools and other agencies for victims of teen dating violence; and requires that victims of domestic violence, dating violence, sexual assault, and stalking on college campuses be informed of their rights, available resources, and the prevalence of such crimes on campus.

The primary provisions of VAWA are explored below.

1. Grants. VAWA's grant programs address domestic violence, dating violence, sexual assault, and stalking by strengthening victim services. The most important

[70]. Julie Bort, Why Senator Al Franken Wants to Make "Stalking" Apps Illegal, Bus. Insider, Jun. 4, 2014, http://www.businessinsider.com/al-franken-tries-to-ban-stalking-apps-2014-6.

grant program, the STOP Violence Against Women Formula Grant Program provides funding for law enforcement and prosecution.

2. VAWA's civil rights remedy. VAWA also created a federal civil rights remedy (Title III) for victims of gender-motivated violent crimes. The Supreme Court invalidated this remedy in United States v. Morrison, 529 U.S. 598 (2000) (discussed supra this chapter).

3. Interstate enforcement of restraining orders. The effectiveness of restraining orders is problematic if the victim relocates from the issuing state to a different state. To address this problem, VAWA specifies that protection orders are entitled to full faith and credit, so long as the issuing state had personal and subject matter jurisdiction and also that the defendant had reasonable notice and an opportunity to be heard. 18 U.S.C. §2265(a). Subsequently, in 2000, the Uniform Law Commission promulgated the Uniform Interstate Enforcement of Domestic-Violence Protection Orders Act (UIEDVPOA) to improve interstate enforcement of protection orders. Specifically, the Act establishes uniform procedures that enable courts to enforce valid domestic protection orders issued in other jurisdictions. It supplements VAWA's full faith and credit provisions for protection orders.

4. VAWA's federal criminal provisions. The original VAWA created several federal criminal provisions: (1) interstate crimes of domestic violence, and (2) firearm restrictions. Prior to VAWA, crimes of domestic violence were traditionally subject to state jurisdiction. Jurisdictional gaps led to interstate offenses going unpunished because of the difficulty of determining the state in which a given offense began and/or ended—a prerequisite for establishing jurisdiction over offenders who committed crimes in two or more states. VAWA also enables federal prosecutors to devote superior resources to prosecution of interstate offenses and provided for harsher sentences.

a. Interstate crimes of domestic violence. VAWA created three new federal crimes: interstate travel to commit domestic violence, interstate stalking, and interstate travel to violate an order of protection. These crimes are explained below.

1. Interstate Travel to Commit Domestic Violence, 18 U.S.C. §2261

It is a federal crime to travel across state lines to commit domestic violence or to cause a victim to cross state lines in the commission of an act of domestic violence. Specifically, this law provides:

> A person who travels in interstate or foreign commerce . . . with the intent to kill, injure, harass, or intimidate a spouse, intimate partner, or dating partner, and who, in the course of or as a result of such travel, commits or attempts to commit a crime of violence against that spouse, intimate partner, or dating partner, shall be punished. . . .

The law also prohibits causing an intimate partner (by "force, coercion, duress, or fraud") to travel in interstate commerce and, in the course of such travel, committing or attempting to commit a crime of violence against that intimate partner.

2. Interstate Stalking, 18 U.S.C §2261A

This law criminalizes interstate travel for the purpose of stalking. Specifically, it prohibits:

> (1) travel in interstate or foreign commerce . . . with the intent to kill, injure, harass, intimidate, or place under surveillance with intent to kill, injure, harass, or intimidate another person, and in the course of, or as a result of, such travel or presence engages in conduct that—
>
> (A) places that person in reasonable fear of the death of, or serious bodily injury. . . . or
>
> (B) causes, attempts to cause, or would be reasonably expected to cause substantial emotional distress to a person described [above]; or
>
> (2) with the intent to kill, injure, harass, intimidate, or place under surveillance with intent to kill, injure, harass, or intimidate another person, uses the mail, any interactive computer service or electronic communication service or electronic communication system of interstate commerce, or any other facility of interstate or foreign commerce to engage in a course of conduct that [causes the above response in the victim]. . . .

3. Interstate Travel to Violate an Order of Protection, 18 U.S.C. §2262(a)

This offense prohibits interstate travel with the intent to violate an order of protection. Specifically, the law provides:

> A person who travels in interstate or foreign commerce . . . with the intent to engage in conduct that violates the portion of a protection order that prohibits or provides protection against violence, threats, or harassment against, contact or communication with, or physical proximity to, another person, or that would violate such a portion of a protection order in the jurisdiction in which the order was issued, and subsequently engages in such conduct, shall be punished. . . .

b. VAWA's firearm offenses. Firearms pose special threats to victims of IPV because they are the abuser's weapon of choice to threaten, harm, or kill.[71] In 1994, as part of the original VAWA, Congress amended the Gun Control Act (GCA) of 1968 (18 U.S.C. §921 et seq.) to prevent individuals who are subject to orders of protection from owning firearms (18 U.S.C. §922(d)(8), (g)(8)). In 1996, Congress amended the GCA with the Lautenberg Amendment to criminalize firearm possession for those who commit "misdemeanor crimes of domestic violence" (MCDV) under state law (18 U.S.C. §921(a)(33)(A); §922(d)(8)-(9); §922(g)(8)-(9)).

Pending legislation would extend restrictions on gun ownership to those persons subject to *temporary* restraining orders. See Lori Jackson Domestic Violence Survivor Protection Act, S. 1834, 114th Cong. (2014-2015).

Sometimes, law enforcement officers are abusers (called "batterers in blue"). These officers may be able to take advantage of an "official use exemption" to the federal firearm restrictions. Although law enforcement personnel who are subject to restraining orders may resort to an "official use exemption" that enables them

[71]. Lindsay Nichols, State Laws to Prevent Domestic Abusers from Access to Guns, 20 Domestic Violence Rep. 1,3 (Oct./Nov. 2014).

to continue to use their service weapon to perform their official duties, there is no similar exemption for persons who have been convicted of MCDVs.

A serious criticism is that federal firearm law fails to ensure that prohibited abusers actually surrender their firearms. The federal law is not self-executing but rather depends on state law to require firearm relinquishment. Only a few states have strong relinquishment laws.[72]

In addition to the above firearm regulations, Congress enacted the Brady Handgun Violence Prevention Act, Pub. L. No. 103–159, 107 Stat. 1536, in 1993 to require federally-licensed firearm dealers to conduct a background check of "prohibited persons" who are listed in the federal Gun Control Act and who desire to purchase firearms and ammunition. Private sales of firearms and online sales are not subject to this law. Many states have similar laws.

Problem

Alex is in a three-year intimate relationship with Tim in the state of Blackacre. One night, in the middle of a drunken brawl concerning overdue rent, Tim beats Alex with a baseball bat, breaks his arm, chokes him, and threatens to kill him. Alex moves out and files for a restraining order. A judge grants Alex a three-year protection order that requires Tim to refrain from "abusing, harassing, or molesting" Alex and also prohibits Tim from having any contact with Alex, including requiring him to "stay away" from Alex, his home, place of employment, business or school. Shortly thereafter, Tim's employer transfers Tim to the state of Greenacre. Alex is relieved that Tim has left Blackacre. He is looking forward to moving on with his life. Tim, however, is still angry that Alex left him. One weekend, Tim drives from Greenacre to Blackacre with the intent to kill Alex. A drunken Tim appears, without warning, at Alex's apartment. Tim bangs on the door, yells and screams at Alex, and threatens to kill him. Alex immediately calls the police. Is Tim subject to any federal charges under the criminal provisions of VAWA?[73] Does the parties' sexual orientation matter? Would Tim be subject to any federal charges if he had made the same threat via the Internet?

G. Children's Exposure to IPV

The past few decades have witnessed increasing awareness of the overlap between domestic violence and child maltreatment. Approximately 1 in 15 children experienced exposure to IPV between a parent and the parent's partner in the past year.[74]

---

[72]. Id. (identifying California, Connecticut, Hawaii, New York, and Pennsylvania as states with strong relinquishment laws). A few more state laws apply specifically to offenders convicted of MCDVs (Colorado, Illinois, Iowa, Minnesota, and Tennessee). Id. at 3-4.

[73]. This problem is a revised version of a hypothetical problem in YWCA, Criminal Provisions of the Violence Against Women Act – Who's Covered?, www.ywcahbg.org/sites/default/files/legal%20news%20winter.pdf.

[74]. David Finkelhor et al., Children's Exposure to Violence, Crime, and Abuse: An Update, OJJDP Juvenile Justice Bulletin 1, 8 (Sept. 2015) (finding 6.1 percent of children were exposed to IPV in a national sample), http://www.ojjdp.gov/publications/index.html.

Such children are referred to as "witnessing" or "being exposed to" domestic violence. State law increasingly recognizes that these children also suffer harm by the occurrence of violence in the home. How does the law respond to the problem?

NICHOLSON v. SCOPPETTA

820 N.E.2d 840 (N.Y. 2004)

KAYE, Chief Judge.

. . . Sharwline Nicholson, on behalf of herself and her two children [and similarly situated mothers and children], brought an action pursuant to 42 U.S.C. §1983 against the New York City Administration for Children's Services (ACS). . . . Plaintiffs alleged that ACS, as a matter of policy, removed children from mothers who were victims of domestic violence [solely on the ground that the mothers had failed to prevent their children from witnessing acts of domestic violence against the mothers] without probable cause and without due process of law. That policy, and its implementation—according to plaintiff mothers—constituted, among other wrongs, an unlawful interference with their liberty interest in the care and custody of their children in violation of the United States Constitution. . . .

[The District Court granted a preliminary injunction. In re Nicholson, 181 F. Supp. 2d 182 (E.D.N.Y. 2002). The Second Circuit Court of Appeals affirms the finding that ACS's practice of removing children from the home based on parents' failure to prevent their children from witnessing domestic violence amounted to a policy or custom of ACS and that, in some circumstances, the removals raised serious questions of federal constitutional law. However, the court certified questions regarding the scope of the state statutes under which the city had acted, in particular the question of whether New York law authorized such a policy and whether the definition of child neglect included a parent's exposure of the child to domestic violence.]

Certified Question: Neglect

"Does the definition of a 'neglected child' under N.Y. Family Ct. Act §1012(f), (h)I include instances in which the sole allegation of neglect is that the parent or other person legally responsible for the child's care allows the child to witness domestic abuse against the caretaker?" . . .

Family Court Act §1012(f) is explicit in identifying the elements that must be shown to support a finding of neglect. . . . [A] party seeking to establish neglect must show, by a preponderance of the evidence, first, that a child's physical, mental or emotional condition has been impaired or is in imminent danger of becoming impaired and second, that the actual or threatened harm to the child is a consequence of the failure of the parent or caretaker to exercise a minimum degree of care in providing the child with proper supervision or guardianship. The drafters of article 10 were "deeply concerned" that an imprecise definition of child neglect might result in "unwarranted state intervention into private family life."

The first statutory element requires proof of actual (or imminent danger of) physical, emotional or mental impairment to the child. This prerequisite to a finding of neglect ensures that the Family Court, in deciding whether to authorize state intervention, will focus on serious harm or potential harm to the child, not just on what might be deemed undesirable parental behavior. "Imminent danger" reflects the Legislature's judgment that a finding of neglect may be appropriate even when a child has not actually been harmed; "imminent danger of impairment to a child is an independent and separate ground on which a neglect finding may be based." Imminent danger, however, must be near or impending, not merely possible.

In each case, additionally, there must be a link or causal connection between the basis for the neglect petition and the circumstances that allegedly produce the child's impairment or imminent danger of impairment. [In Matter of Nassau County Dept. of Social Servs. (*Dante M.*) v. Denise J., 637 N.Y.S.2d 666 (N.Y. 1995)], for example, we held that the Family Court erred in concluding that a newborn's positive toxicology for a controlled substance alone was sufficient to support a finding of neglect because the report, in and of itself, did not prove that the child was impaired or in imminent danger of becoming impaired. We reasoned, "[r]elying solely on a positive toxicology result for a neglect determination fails to make the necessary causative connection to all the surrounding circumstances that may or may not produce impairment or imminent risk of impairment in the newborn child"[id. at 669]. . . .

The cases at bar concern, in particular, alleged threats to the child's emotional, or mental, health. The statute specifically defines "[i]mpairment of emotional health" and "impairment of mental or emotional condition" to include

> a state of substantially diminished psychological or intellectual functioning in relation to, but not limited to, such factors as failure to thrive, control of aggressive or self-destructive impulses, ability to think and reason, or acting out or misbehavior, including incorrigibility, ungovernability or habitual truancy.

Family Ct. Act §1012[h]. Under New York law, "such impairment must be clearly attributable to the unwillingness or inability of the respondent to exercise a minimum degree of care toward the child." Here, the Legislature recognized that the source of emotional or mental impairment—unlike physical injury—may be murky, and that it is unjust to fault a parent too readily. The Legislature therefore specified that such impairment be "clearly attributable" to the parent's failure to exercise the requisite degree of care.

Assuming that actual or imminent danger to the child has been shown, "neglect" also requires proof of the parent's failure to exercise a minimum degree of care. As the Second Circuit observed, "a fundamental interpretive question is what conduct satisfies the broad, tort-like phrase, 'a minimum degree of care.' [*Nicholson*, 344 F.3d at 169]. The Court of Appeals has not yet addressed that question, which would be critical to defining appropriate parental behavior."

"[M]inimum degree of care" is a "baseline of proper care for children that all parents, regardless of lifestyle or social or economic position, must meet." Notably, the statutory test is "minimum degree of care"—not maximum, not best, not ideal—and the failure must be actual, not threatened.

Courts must evaluate parental behavior objectively: would a reasonable and prudent parent have so acted, or failed to act, under the circumstances then and there existing? The standard takes into account the special vulnerabilities of the child, even where general physical health is not implicated. Thus, when the inquiry is whether a mother—and domestic violence victim—failed to exercise a minimum degree of care, the focus must be on whether she has met the standard of the reasonable and prudent person in similar circumstances.

[F]or a battered mother—and ultimately for a court—what course of action constitutes a parent's exercise of a "minimum degree of care" may include such considerations as: risks attendant to leaving, if the batterer has threatened to kill her if she does; risks attendant to staying and suffering continued abuse; risks attendant to seeking assistance through government channels, potentially increasing the danger to herself and her children; risks attendant to criminal prosecution against the abuser; and risks attendant to relocation. Whether a particular mother in these circumstances has actually failed to exercise a minimum degree of care is necessarily dependent on facts such as the severity and frequency of the violence, and the resources and options available to her.

Only when a petitioner demonstrates, by a preponderance of evidence, that both elements of section 1012(f) are satisfied may a child be deemed neglected under the statute. When "the sole allegation" is that the mother has been abused and the child has witnessed the abuse, such a showing has not been made. This does not mean, however, that a child can never be "neglected" when living in a household plagued by domestic violence. Conceivably, neglect might be found where a record establishes that, for example, the mother acknowledged that the children knew of repeated domestic violence by her paramour and had reason to be afraid of him, yet nonetheless allowed him several times to return to her home, and lacked awareness of any impact of the violence on the children; or where the children were exposed to regular and continuous extremely violent conduct between their parents, several times requiring official intervention, and where caseworkers testified to the fear and distress the children were experiencing as a result of their long exposure to the violence.

In such circumstances, the battered mother is charged with neglect not because she is a victim of domestic violence or because her children witnessed the abuse, but rather because a preponderance of the evidence establishes that the children were actually or imminently harmed by reason of her failure to exercise even minimal care in providing them with proper oversight. . . .

Jill M. Zuccardy, Nicholson v. Williams: The Case

82 Denv. U. L. Rev. 655, 657-660, 663-665, 667, 669 (2005)

[The author was co-counsel in Nicholson v. Williams, 203 F. Supp. 2d 153 (E.D.N.Y. 2002).]

[I]n 1999, I met Sharwline Nicholson. Sharwline had been separated from her child's father for some time. He lived in South Carolina. Although he had not been a model partner during the relationship, he was never physically abusive toward her or threatened physical abuse during the relationship.

From time to time [however] after Sharwline and her child's father separated, he came to New York to visit his infant daughter. During one visit, he got into an argument with Sharwline and became enraged. He beat her very badly. She managed to call 911, and he took off. Her son was at school and her infant daughter was asleep in the other room.

Sharwline was very seriously injured. She had a broken arm; she had a concussion; she was bleeding from numerous wounds. Yet, even before the police arrived, her first thought was of her children. She called her neighbor, who was her regular child care provider, and had the neighbor come over, get the baby, and pick up the son from school. Sharwline was removed by ambulance, thinking that her children were safely with the babysitter. . . .

While Sharwline was in the hospital, the police—and to this day we don't know why—went to the neighbor's home with their guns drawn and took custody of the children. This all sounds incredible, but it's true. They called Sharwline at the hospital and said, "We have your children here at the precinct. We can't allow them to be in the custody of a stranger," which is not an accurate statement of New York law by any means. A fit parent has the right to make child care arrangements for his or her child. In any event, they said, "You have to call a relative to take care of the children."

So, Sharwline called her cousin in New Jersey. By now, it was ten or eleven o'clock at night. Sharwline's cousin went to the hospital, told Sharwline that she would go to the precinct and get the children and everything would be okay. However, when Sharwline's cousin went to the precinct, the police refused to release the children, saying the children could not be taken out of state to New Jersey. Again, this was not a proper statement of the law.

Sharwline received a telephone call early the next morning—and the person on the other end of the line said, "This is ACS. We have your children. If you want to see them, you'll need to go to court. We'll call you back and tell you the date.". . . . When Sharwline finally had an opportunity to appear in court, she learned that she had been charged with child neglect for "engaging in domestic violence." Make no mistake. Sharwline was not accused of perpetrating any violence. She was accused of being a victim and she was accused of being a neglectful mother because she was a victim. . . .

When I got Sharwline's case, I was blown away. . . . I thought the case was some sort of aberration, some sort of a mistake. . . . In the class action which ultimately came to pass . . . the theory in all of [the] cases was that the children were suffering, or in danger of suffering, emotional harm from exposure to domestic violence against their mothers and, therefore, should be removed from their mothers. These were not cases in which the City alleged that the children were in danger of physical harm, or that the mother had failed to protect the child from physical harm. Rather, they all focused on the presumption that exposure to domestic violence, per se, constituted impairment rising to the level of imminent harm and neglect under our child welfare statutes. . . .

[T]he city put forth one defense only, "We don't do this. We don't remove children solely or primarily because of domestic violence, period." The city said, "We employ best practices. Look at our written policies." And, in fact, except for [their] mission statement . . . , the ACS domestic violence policies and guiding principles looked really good on paper. Thus, it made the case simpler for us that ACS actually agreed with us as to what constituted best practices in child welfare cases involving domestic violence. They claimed they already employed them; we claimed that they didn't. . . .

The city [] waved its written policies like a banner throughout the case. And, as I mentioned, their written policies were actually pretty good. The problem was the disconnection between the written policies and the actual policies and practices. We illustrated this disconnection. . . . The child protective managers' description of the agency's practices with regard to domestic violence supported our contentions. . . .

I think *Nicholson* was a unique case for systemic reform: we believed that due to the nature of the lawsuit, because the safety of children was involved, the case could not just be about proving that the city's practices were unconstitutional or that they violated the civil rights of battered mothers and their children. We firmly believed that in order to prevail, we must educate, and challenge head-on some of society's most deeply held biases and judgments regarding domestic violence and child welfare. And we had to show that what the city was doing was hurting children. . . .

We also felt that we had to challenge the notion that removing children from their parents is erring on the side of safety. You hear that a lot. There is a notion that foster care provides safety for children. This is simply not true. . . . Many of our clients' children suffered in foster care, ranging from the physical abuse of Sharwline's son, to various incidents of medical neglect and emotional harm. The mothers' testimony about their children's experience in foster care was very powerful. But we did not only use the mothers, the literature and the experts to help us establish the trauma and danger of foster care.

We called the older children as witnesses. Listening to one fourteen-year-old describe her experience, Judge Weinstein and everyone in the courtroom, including the city's attorneys, became teary-eyed and Judge Weinstein had to call a ten-minute recess. Listening to her describe her trauma of being taken from her mother and being placed in foster care was one of the most wrenching moments in the trial. . . .

The *Nicholson* decision had a domino effect locally and nationwide. ACS stopped removing children from battered mothers, and the case spurred them to make vast improvements in their child welfare practice . . .

NOTE: THE GREEN BOOK INITIATIVE

Traditionally, domestic violence advocates and child welfare professionals manifested a troubled relationship. Child welfare agencies often removed children from homes because of mothers' "failure to protect" their children from exposure to domestic violence. Domestic violence advocates criticized this approach for placing responsibility for the violence on the abused mother, rather than holding the batterer accountable. In addition, child welfare professionals, who tend to view domestic violence as a symptom of dysfunctional families, traditionally strive to reestablish the family unit. Conversely, domestic violence advocates view separation from the perpetrator as the best option to provide safety for the victim and her children.

Amidst this atmosphere, a collaboration of family court judges and experts in the fields of domestic violence and child welfare produced an influential report in 1999 that contained recommendations for the improvement of child welfare proceedings involving families that experience domestic violence.[75] The recommendations advocated culturally competent practice, batterer accountability,

[75]. See Nat'l Council of Juv. & Fam. Ct. Judges, Effective Intervention in Domestic Violence and Child Maltreatment Cases: Guidelines for Policy and Practice (1999), (popularly known as the "Green Book" because of the color of its cover).

improved services for battered immigrant women, and the use of supervised visitation. The project criticized the removal of a child from a nonabusive parent, and also prioritized the protection of the victim and child by all relevant agencies. The group recognized the need to improve collaboration between service providers to achieve these goals. The recommendations suggested the creation of multiple points of entry into the system for families needing services; the provision of services without the need to routinely open a child protection case; and continuous screening and assessment of the family by courts and welfare agencies. The report also advocated improved training for service providers and courts about the dynamics of domestic violence. In addition, it encouraged juvenile courts to remain in close contact with criminal courts to ensure batterer accountability.

The Green Book had a significant influence on legal policy when the trial court in In re Nicholson, 181 F. Supp. 2d 182 (E.D.N.Y. 2000), relied heavily on its findings. Together, the Green Book and the *Nicholson* decision fundamentally changed the approach of child protective services to cases involving domestic violence. They influenced child welfare agencies to revise their practice of removing children from abused mothers and also improved coordination between child welfare agencies and domestic violence advocates.

Notes and Questions

1. **Juvenile court jurisdiction for abuse and neglect.** Every state has a jurisdictional statute that authorizes courts to assume jurisdiction over children who are endangered because of parental abuse or neglect. Most states refer to the juvenile court's jurisdiction over child abuse and neglect as "dependency jurisdiction" because the child victims become "dependents" of the state. The source of such jurisdiction is the doctrine of "parens patriae" ("parent of the country"), that is, the state's power to intervene in cases of abuse or neglect and to act as the parent of any child who is in need of protection. Typically, these statutory standards are broad and vague.

2. **Constitutional right to family integrity.** The right to family integrity is protected by substantive due process. The U.S. Supreme Court cases of Meyer v. Nebraska, 262 U.S. 390 (1923), and Pierce v. Society of Sisters, 268 U.S. 510 (1925), established broad liberal principles of family autonomy in the face of government intervention. These foundational cases affirm that parents have a constitutional right to the care, custody, and control of their children. However, this parental right is not absolute. In Prince v. Massachusetts, 321 U.S. 158 (1944), the Supreme Court established that the state has the right to intervene to remove children from the home in cases of child endangerment based on the state's parens patriae power. What role does constitutional protection of the parent-child relationship play in the analysis in *Nicholson*? How did the New York child welfare procedures violate the mothers' constitutional rights?

3. **Stages of intervention.** State intervention in cases of child abuse and neglect takes two forms: summary seizure or the assertion of temporary custody. If the court determines that an emergency exists, the court may order (in an ex parte

hearing) that the child be immediately removed from the home. On the other hand, the adversarial proceeding regarding temporary custody (termed a "jurisdictional hearing") determines whether the child falls within the statutory definition of an abused or neglected child. The next stage of juvenile court intervention occurs after the jurisdictional determination—when the court conducts a "dispositional hearing." At that time, the court chooses among various dispositions (for example, imposition of conditions on custody, foster care, termination of parental rights). What were the various forms of state intervention in Sharwline Nicholson's case?

4. *Nicholson*: Holding. *Nicholson* involved a challenge to the New York child welfare system. Was *Nicholson* a challenge to the constitutionality of New York's child welfare law or practice? What does the New York statute require for a finding of child neglect? How were the children in *Nicholson* allegedly neglected by their mothers? What actions did the state social service workers take in response to their beliefs that the children were neglected? How did the state agencies' written policies differ from their actual practices? How did these practices violate plaintiffs' rights?

5. Exposure to domestic violence. Children's exposure to domestic violence can take several forms: hearing a violent event; being involved in an event (as an eyewitness, intervenor, or a shield); experiencing the aftermath of a violent event); being forced to watch or participate in the abuse of the parent; comforting a parent who is a victim of assault; being used as a spy to interrogate the parent; or being used as a pawn to coerce the victim into returning to the violent relationship. Children also suffer accidental harm, such as when the abused parent is holding the child or when children intervene in violent episodes. How were Sharwline Nicholson's children exposed to domestic violence?

6. Exposure to domestic violence as neglect. *Nicholson* dealt with an interpretation of state law that social service workers were applying to children who were exposed to domestic violence. The law takes three approaches to children's exposure to domestic violence: (1) imposition of tort liability for intentional infliction of emotional distress; (2) criminal liability; and (3) defining exposure to domestic violence as a form of maltreatment.

Some states, like New York in *Nicholson*, treat exposure of children to domestic violence as a form of child abuse and neglect.[76] Various policy rationales support this approach, including that the statutes: (1) bring children who are exposed to domestic violence to the attention of authorities, (2) make available the resources of the child protective system, (3) promote consistency in interagency handling of domestic violence among children, and (4) send a message to domestic violence perpetrators and the community that domestic violence is harmful. How well do the statutes accomplish these purposes?

---

[76]. For a discussion of state responses and policy rationales, see Lois A. Weithorn, Protecting Children from Exposure to Domestic Violence: The Use and Abuse of Child Maltreatment Statutes, 53 Hastings L.J. 1 (2001). See also David Finkelhor et al., OJJDP, Children's Exposure to Violence: A Comprehensive National Study (Oct. 2009), https://www.ncjrs.gov/pdffiles1/ojjdp/227744.pdf.

7. Blanket presumptions. In *Nicholson*, the New York Court of Appeals ruled that exposure to domestic violence does not presumptively establish neglect and that removal requires additional particularized evidence. Other blanket presumptions exist in the context of domestic violence. For example, one presumption prohibits court-ordered visitation to a parent who murdered the other parent (absent the child's consent). Does this last presumption have the same constitutional infirmities as the presumption in *Nicholson*?

8. Harm from exposure versus harm from removal. Children who are exposed to domestic violence face behavioral, social, and emotional problems (aggression, anger, hostility, fear, anxiety, withdrawal, depression, poor social relationships, low self-esteem); cognitive and attitudinal problems (lower cognitive functioning, poor academic performance, acceptance of violent behaviors and attitudes, belief in rigid gender stereotypes); and long-term consequences (depression, trauma symptoms, and tolerance for and use of violence in adult relationships).[77] Yet, as noted in *Nicholson*, sometimes the harm of removing a child from the home outweighs the harm experienced in the home where domestic violence occurs. *Nicholson*, 820 N.E.2d at 849. What explains this seeming paradox?[78]

In 2010, Attorney General Eric Holder launched Defending Childhood, a Department of Justice initiative that addressed the topic of children's exposure to violence. As part of the initiative, a 13-member National Task Force examined the extent and nature of the problem and then identified promising practices to address it. In 2012, the task force issued its recommendations emphasizing the importance of identifying children who are victims or witnesses of violence and providing services for them. The initiative also developed specific programs across the country to help children exposed to IPV. Finally, the task force called for earlier identification of children exposed to IPV by screening all children who enter the juvenile justice system. For the task force report, see Report of the Attorney General's National Task Force on Children Exposed to Violence (Dec. 12, 2012), available at www.justice.gov.

---

[77]. Jeffrey L. Edleson, Emerging Responses to Children Exposed to Domestic Violence (Oct. 2006), http://pdfbookeacre.org/k-59193495.html.

[78]. See Sharwline Nicholson, Balancing the Harms (Trailer), Jan. 15, 2007, http://www.youtube.com/watch?v=P5ne2rapK9M&feature=player_embedded#at=45.

V

The Nonmarital Family

The American family is experiencing dramatic changes. The traditional nuclear family (a husband and wife with their resident children) has been on the decline for some time. Currently, only one in five families fits this type.[1]

The transformation in family structure reflects three different trends. First, fewer Americans are getting married. Over the past four decades, the annual number of marriages has declined by more than 50 percent.[2] Instead of marrying, people are turning to *cohabitation*. The number of unmarried couples has increased almost 17 times since 1960.[3] Cohabitation serves as a step toward marriage for some people and an alternative to marriage for others.

A second development is the prevalence of *same-sex couples*. The number of same-sex couples increased by more than 20 percent in a recent five-year period.[4] Most of these same-sex partners are unmarried.[5] With marriage equality no longer the most pressing legal concern, the focus of attention for the LGBT community has shifted to discrimination in employment, housing, and familial benefits.[6]

---

[1]. Jonathan Vespra et al., U.S. Census Bureau, Current Population Reports, America's Families and Living Arrangements (2013).

[2]. Nat'l Marriage Project, Social Indicators of Marital Health & Well-Being: Trends of the Past Five Decades in The State of Our Unions: Marriage in America 62 (2012), http://www.stateofourunions.org/2012/SOOU2012.php [hereafter State of Our Unions).

[3]. Id. at 76.

[4]. Ramon Johnson, How Many Same-Sex Couples Are in the U.S.?, Gay Life (based on Williams Institute study), http://gaylife.about.com/od/comingout/a/numberofgaycouples.htm. Today, almost 727,000 same-sex households reside in the United States (based on 2013 data). However, the number probably reflects underreporting because some LGBT couples may prefer anonymity.

[5]. U.S. Census, Characteristics of Same-Sex Couple Households, Table 3: Same-Sex Couple Households: 2013 American Community Survey (revealing that only 34.6 percent of same-sex households contain same-sex spouses), http://www.census.gov/hhes/samesex/.

[6]. Only about half of the states explicitly prohibit marital status discrimination in housing, employment, or both. But in many of these states, the protections do not extend to unmarried couples (same-sex or opposite-sex). See Courtney G. Joslin, Marital Status Discrimination 2.0, 95 B.U. L. Rev. 805 (2015).

Third, and finally, the number of *children born to unwed parents* has increased significantly. The percentage of infants born to unmarried mothers has risen more than eight times since 1960.[7] Nonmarital births are such a common feature of the American family that nearly 40 percent of births today occur to unmarried mothers.[8] The rise in nonmarital births has profound social and economic consequences for children who live in single-parent families.[9]

This chapter explores the law's response to these changes in family structure with an emphasis on cohabitation and unwed parenthood. Two themes pervade the chapter. First, the introductory materials focus on the changing legal meaning of "family." To what extent is a "family" limited to ceremonially initiated or biologically-based relationships? Does this definition apply for some purposes but not others? Second, the chapter explores the extent to which the legal treatment of these families differs from that of the traditional family. How does and how should the law treat families that do not conform to traditional marital norms? Should the state impose a legal meaning of "family" on all persons without exception? Or should the state honor private choices, so long as a given unit performs familial functions?[10]

A. Constitutional Limits on Definitions of "Family"

1. Functional Definition of Family

U.S. DEPARTMENT OF AGRICULTURE v. MORENO

413 U.S. 528 (1973)

Mr. Justice Brennan delivered the opinion of the Court.

This case requires us to consider the constitutionality of §3(e) of the Food Stamp Act of 1964, 7 U.S.C. §2012(e) [established] in 1964 in an effort to alleviate hunger and malnutrition among the more needy segments of our society. Eligibility for participation in the program is determined on a household rather than an individual basis. An eligible household purchases sufficient food stamps to provide that household with a nutritionally adequate diet. The household pays for the stamps at a reduced rate based upon its size and cumulative income. The food stamps are then used to purchase food at retail stores, and the Government

---

[7]. State of Our Unions, supra note [2], at 95.

[8]. Stephanie Ventura, CDC, Changing Patterns of Nonmarital Childbearing in the United States, NCHS Data Brief, 2 (May 2009).

[9]. Forty percent of all children will spend some time growing up in a household with cohabiting adults. The percentage of children living in single-parent families has tripled compared to the same rate in 1960. State of Our Unions, supra note [2], 62, 95.

[10]. This chapter examines forms of unequal treatment of same-sex couples that are not explored in other chapters, such as discrimination in the areas of employment, housing, and familial benefits. The topics of discrimination in marriage, divorce, custody, child support, adoption, and assisted reproduction appear elsewhere in the book.

redeems the stamps at face value, thereby paying the difference between the actual cost of the food and the amount paid by the household for the stamps.

As initially enacted, §3(e) defined a "household" as "a group of related or non-related individuals, who are not residents of an institution or boarding house, but are living as one economic unit sharing common cooking facilities and for whom food is customarily purchased in common." In January 1971, however Congress redefined the term "household" so as to include only groups of related individuals. Pursuant to this amendment, the Secretary of Agriculture promulgated regulations rendering ineligible for participation in the program any "household" whose members are not "all related to each other."

Appellees in this case consist of several groups of individuals who allege that, although they satisfy the income eligibility requirements for federal food assistance, they have nevertheless been excluded from the program solely because the persons in each group are not "all related to each other." Appellee Jacinta Moreno, for example is a 56-year-old diabetic who lives with Ermina Sanchez and the latter's three children. They share common living expenses, and Mrs. Sanchez helps to care for appellee. Appellee's monthly income, derived from public assistance, is \$75; Mrs. Sanchez receives \$133 per month from public assistance. The household pays \$135 per month for rent, gas and electricity, of which appellee pays \$50. Appellee spends \$10 per month for transportation to a hospital for regular visits, and \$5 per month for laundry. That leaves her \$10 per month for food and other necessities. Despite her poverty, appellee has been denied federal food assistance solely because she is unrelated to the other members of her household. Moreover, although Mrs. Sanchez and her three children were permitted to purchase \$108 worth of food stamps per month for \$18, their participation in the program will be terminated if appellee Moreno continues to live with them.

Appellee Sheilah Hejny is married and has three children. Although the Hejnys are indigent, they took in a 20-year-old girl, who is unrelated to them because "we felt she had emotional problems." The Hejnys receive \$144 worth of food stamps each month for \$14. If they allow the 20-year-old girl to continue to live with them, they will be denied food stamps by reason of §3(e).

Appellee Victoria Keppler has a daughter with an acute hearing deficiency. The daughter requires special instruction in a school for the deaf. The school is located in an area in which appellee could not ordinarily afford to live. Thus, in order to make the most of her limited resources, appellee agreed to share an apartment near the school with a woman who, like appellee, is on public assistance. Since appellee is not related to the woman, appellee's food stamps have been, and will continue to be, cut off if they continue to live together.

These and two other groups of appellees instituted a class action . . . seeking declaratory and injunctive relief against the enforcement of the 1971 amendment of §3(e) and its implementing regulations. In essence, appellees contend, and the District Court held, that the "unrelated person" provision of §3(e) creates an irrational classification in violation of the equal protection component of the Due Process Clause of the Fifth Amendment. We agree. . . .

The challenged statutory classification (households of related persons versus households containing one or more unrelated persons) is clearly irrelevant to the stated purposes of the Act. As the District Court recognized, "(t)he relationships among persons constituting one economic unit and sharing cooking facilities have nothing to do with their abilities to stimulate the agricultural economy by purchasing farm surpluses, or with their personal nutritional requirements." 345 F. Supp., at 313.

Thus, if it is to be sustained, the challenged classification must rationally further some legitimate governmental interest. . . . Regrettably, there is little legislative history to illuminate the purposes of the 1971 amendment of §3(e). The legislative history that does exist, however, indicates that that amendment was intended to prevent so-called "hippies" and "hippie communes" from participating in the food stamp program. See H.R. Conf. Rep. No. 91-1793, p. 8; 116 Cong. Rec. 44439 (1970) (Sen. Holland). The challenged classification clearly cannot be sustained by reference to this congressional purpose. For if the constitutional conception of "equal protection of the laws" means anything, it must at the very least mean that a bare congressional desire to harm a politically unpopular group cannot constitute a legitimate governmental interest. . . .

Although apparently conceding this point, the Government maintains that the challenged classification should nevertheless be upheld as rationally related to the clearly legitimate governmental interest in minimizing fraud in the administration of the food stamp program.[7] In essence, the Government contends that, in adopting the 1971 amendment, Congress might rationally have thought (1) that households with one or more unrelated members are more likely than "fully related" households to contain individuals who abuse the program by fraudulently failing to report sources of income or by voluntarily remaining poor; and (2) that such households are "relatively unstable," thereby increasing the difficulty of detecting such abuses. But even if we were to accept as rational the Government's wholly unsubstantiated assumptions concerning the differences between "related" and "unrelated" households we still could not agree with the Government's conclusion that the denial of essential federal food assistance to all otherwise eligible households containing unrelated members constitutes a rational effort to deal with these concerns.

At the outset, it is important to note that the Food Stamp Act itself contains provisions, wholly independent of §3(e), aimed specifically at the problems of fraud. . . . The existence of these provisions necessarily casts considerable doubt upon the proposition that the 1971 amendment could rationally have been intended to prevent those very same abuses.

[I]n practical operation, the 1971 amendment excludes from participation in the food stamp program, not those persons who are "likely to abuse the program," but, rather, only those persons who are so desperately in need of aid that they cannot even afford to alter their living arrangements so as to retain their eligibility. Traditional equal protection analysis does not require that every classification be drawn with precise "mathematical nicety." But the classification here in issue is

---

7. The Government initially argued to the District Court that the challenged classification might be justified as a means to foster "morality." In rejecting that contention, the District Court noted that "interpreting the amendment as an attempt to regulate morality would raise serious constitutional questions." 345 F. Supp. 310, 314. Indeed, citing this Court's decisions [in Griswold v. Connecticut, Stanley v. Georgia, and Eisenstadt v. Baird], the District Court observed that it was doubtful at best, whether Congress, "in the name of morality," could 'infringe the rights to privacy and freedom of "association *in the home*." 345 F. Supp., at 314. (Emphasis in original.) Moreover, the court also pointed out that the classification established in §3(e) was not rationally related "to prevailing notions of morality, since it in terms disqualifies all households of unrelated individuals, without reference to whether a particular group contains both sexes." 345 F. Supp., at 315. The Government itself has now abandoned the "morality" argument.

not only "imprecise," it is wholly without any rational basis. The judgment of the District Court holding the "unrelated person" provision invalid under the Due Process Clause of the Fifth Amendment is therefore affirmed. . . .

Mr. Justice DOUGLAS, concurring. . . .

. . . As the facts of this case show, the poor are congregating in households where they can better meet the adversities of poverty. This banding together is an expression of the right of freedom of association that is very deep in our traditions.

Other like rights have been recognized that are only peripheral First Amendment rights—the right to send one's child to a religious school, the right to study the German language in a private school, the protection of the entire spectrum of learning, teaching, and communicating ideas, the marital right of privacy. As the examples indicate, these peripheral constitutional rights are exercised not necessarily in assemblies that congregate in halls or auditoriums but in discrete individual actions such as parents placing a child in the school of their choice. Taking a person into one's home because he is poor or needs help or brings happiness to the household is of the same dignity.

Congress might choose to deal only with members of a family of one or two or three generations, treating it all as a unit. Congress, however, has not done that here. Concededly an individual living alone is not disqualified from the receipt of food stamp aid, even though there are other members of the family with whom he might theoretically live. Nor are common-law couples disqualified: they, like individuals living alone, may qualify under the Act if they are poor—whether they have abandoned their wives and children and however antifamily their attitudes may be. In other words, the "unrelated" person provision was not aimed at the maintenance of normal family ties. It penalizes persons or families who have brought under their roof an "unrelated" needy person. It penalizes the poorest of the poor for doubling up against the adversities of poverty.

But for the constitutional aspects of the problem, the "unrelated" person provision of the Act might well be sustained as a means to prevent fraud. . . . I could not say that this "unrelated" person provision has no "rational" relation to control of fraud. We deal here, however, with the right of association, protected by the First Amendment. People who are desperately poor but unrelated come together and join hands with the aim better to combat the crises of poverty. The need of those living together better to meet those crises is denied, while the need of households made up of relatives that is no more acute is serviced. Problems of the fisc . . . are legitimate concerns of government. But government "may not accomplish such a purpose by invidious distinctions between classes of its citizens." . . . The right of association, the right to invite the stranger into one's home is too basic in our constitutional regime to deal with roughshod. If there are abuses inherent in that pattern of living against which the food stamp program should be protected, the Act must be "narrowly drawn," to meet the precise end. The method adopted and applied to these cases makes §3(e) of the Act unconstitutional by reason of the invidious discrimination between the two classes of needy persons. . . .

Mr. Justice REHNQUIST, with whom THE CHIEF JUSTICE concurs, dissenting.

[O]ur role is limited to the determination of whether there is any rational basis on which Congress could decide that public funds made available under the food stamp program should not go to a household containing an individual who is unrelated to any other member of the household. . . . I do not think it is unreasonable for Congress to conclude that the basic unit which it was willing to support with federal funding through food stamps is some variation on the family as we know it—a household consisting of related individuals. This unit provides a guarantee which is not provided by households containing unrelated individuals that the household exists for some purpose other than to collect federal food stamps. . . .

Notes and Questions

1. Definition of family. *Moreno* highlights the different definitions of "family." The formal definition characterizes a "family" according to blood ties (consanguinity) or legal ceremony (such as marriage or adoption). In contrast, the functional approach defines family by virtue of its functions (support, affection, caregiving, etc.). What are the advantages of the respective approaches to the definition of a family? Disadvantages? See generally Jessica A. Clarke, Identity and Form, 103 Calif. L. Rev. 747, 782-791 (2015).

2. "Family" or "household"? In *Moreno*, the Supreme Court was willing to include unrelated persons in a definition of "household" for food stamp purposes. Would the Court have reached the same result if the food stamp legislation determined eligibility on a "family" basis, instead of a "household" basis? How do the terms differ? If "family" were defined in terms of "a single housekeeping unit," how would that change the analysis?

In contrast to *Moreno*, consider Village of Belle Terre v. Boraas, 416 U.S. 1 (1974), in which the U.S. Supreme Court upheld a zoning ordinance that restricted land use to "one-family dwellings" and defined a "family" as follows:

> (o)ne or more persons related by blood, adoption, or marriage, living and cooking together as a single housekeeping unit, exclusive of household servants. A number of persons but not exceeding (2) living and cooking together as a single housekeeping unit though not related by blood, adoption, or marriage shall be deemed to constitute a family.

In this challenge to a zoning ordinance by a landlord who rented a house to six college students, Justice Douglas found no violation of the freedom of association (because a "family" may entertain whomever it pleases) or any other fundamental right. In upholding the ordinance, the Court analogized the group of students to other "urban problems" such as "boarding houses, fraternity houses, and the like . . ." in which "[m]ore people occupy a given space; more cars rather continuously pass by; more cars are parked; noise travels with crowds." Id. at 9. Applying the rational-basis test to the ordinance, the Court saw nothing impermissible in the Village's goal of "lay[ing] out zones where family values, youth values, and the blessings of quiet seclusion and clean air make the area a sanctuary for people." Id. A majority of states have upheld similar restrictions on the number of unrelated persons who live together.

3. Views of family. How do the Court's views of the "families" in *Moreno* and *Belle Terre* differ? For example, *Belle Terre* reveals concerns about transiency, overcrowding, and congestion. Yet *Moreno* is skeptical about the government's "unsubstantiated assumptions" about the instability of households of unrelated persons. What factors explain the different results? Why might the Court have shown greater deference to the government's interest in *Belle Terre* than in *Moreno*? Why does Justice Douglas concur in *Moreno*, given his majority opinion in *Belle Terre*? Was the outcome different, perhaps, because the *Moreno* plaintiffs conformed more to our concept of the traditional family?

4. **Family values.** What family values do the groups in *Moreno* and *Belle Terre* reflect? Did the group sharing a home in *Belle Terre* pose a greater risk to the "family value" of permanency than the groups excluded by the food stamp restriction that was invalidated in *Moreno*? Cf. Laurence H. Tribe, American Constitutional Law 1403 (2d ed. 1988).

5. **Federal constitutional rights.** Commentators have long criticized *Moreno* for its unwillingness to address the degree to which the Constitution protects the right to choose with whom to share a home. J. Harvie Wilkinson III & G. Edward White, Constitutional Protection for Personal Lifestyles, 62 Cornell L. Rev. 563, 584 (1977). For a criticism of *Belle Terre*'s assertion that the zoning ordinance implicates no fundamental right, such as association or privacy, see Kenneth L. Karst, The Freedom of Intimate Association, 89 Yale L.J. 624 (1980).

6. **Other group living arrangements.**

a. Student groups. In a post-*Belle Terre* case, ten college students challenged an ordinance of a New Jersey town that limited occupancy by defining a "family" as

> one or more persons occupying a dwelling unit as a single non-profit housekeeping unit, who are living together as a stable and permanent living unit, being a traditional family unit or the functional equivalency thereof.

Borough of Glassboro v. Vallorosi, 568 A.2d 888, 889 (N.J. 1990). The *Vallorosi* ordinance, similar to that in *Belle Terre,* aimed to preserve stable, permanent housing. Influenced by state precedents equating "single family" with "single housekeeping unit," the New Jersey Supreme Court adopted a functional standard and held that the group complied because they planned to live together for three years, ate together, and shared household tasks and expenses. Is *Vallorosi*'s functional standard superior to *Belle Terre*'s focus on associational ties?

***b. Impact of* Lawrence *and* Obergefell.** In *Belle Terre,* plaintiffs argued that the ordinance "reeks with an animosity to unmarried couples," 416 U.S. at 8, and asked why more than two unmarried persons could not constitute a family. How would the Supreme Court respond to an ordinance that excluded unmarried couples after Lawrence v. Texas? How does Obergefell v. Hodges affect the answer?

c. Group homes. *Belle Terre* (and *Vallorosi,* supra) illustrate the elasticity of the definition of "family" in the use of zoning as an agent of social control. The Supreme Court again examined the issue in City of Cleburne v. Cleburne Living Center, 473 U.S. 432 (1985), in which the city denied an exemption from the local ordinance to a home for the mentally retarded. In response to the group's claim that the ordinance violated equal protection, the Court held the ordinance invalid as applied, reasoning that the denial rested on irrational prejudice. Did the Belle Terre ordinance, as applied, rest on "irrational prejudice" against students? Is resort to the police power appropriate to exclude "undesirables" from the community?

Two of the three named family groups in *Moreno* consist of households of single mothers who are caring for dependent adults. The number of single-mother families has risen dramatically over the past four decades. African-American single mothers constitute a significant proportion of these families. The article below criticizes American family policy that prioritizes the marital family over other family forms, such as the single-parent family.

Vivian Hamilton, Mistaking Marriage for Social Policy

11 Va. J. Soc. Pol'y & L. 307, 355-360, 368-370 (2004)

In Sickness and in Health: The Caretaking Function of Marriage

Society currently designates the nuclear, preferably marital, family as the social structure that supports child caretaking. . . . The rhetorical importance placed on child caretaking in the U.S. stands in stark contrast to family support policies that are the stingiest in the industrial world. [O]ther countries consistently do more to assist caretakers. France and the Scandinavian countries are among those that have implemented family support policies that directly support caretaking. These policies include subsidized day care, paid parental leave, universal health care, and income supplements to low-earning caretakers. . . .

Married couples [in the United States] receive more protections and benefits than do nonmarital couples—Social Security, pension, and health insurance benefits are among the measures that assist marital families. . . . [U]nmarried men and women who live together are almost as likely to be raising children as are married couples. But because they have chosen not to formalize their relationships, they must manage caretaking without many of the benefits accorded marital families. Also, social support for single-parent families, the vast majority of which are headed by women, can vary dramatically. . . . Divorced and never-married mothers [are dependent] on the vicissitudes of the uncertain child support and welfare systems. Not only are these families affected materially, but they also suffer from a social stigma that is reinforced by the existing legal structure.

Some commentators retort that two-parent marital families are best for children, so it is therefore appropriate for the state to subsidize or privilege this family form over others. There are several problems with this argument. [S]ociologist Sara McLanahan has found that data does not support the conclusion that what harms children is the absence of one parent. Instead, McLanahan says, single parenting currently leads to certain types of instability that can harm children. Much of the link between single parenting and negative child outcomes can thus be attributed to low income, less-stable adult presence, and residential mobility after divorce. . . .

Rather than emphasizing the importance of marriage, government should instead enact more carefully targeted policies to support caretaking and the economic well-being of its citizenry. . . . What would this look like in practice? First, the state would deemphasize family form. It would eliminate government-sanctioned privileges that currently accompany heterosexual monogamous marriage and that devalue and stigmatize other family structures. It would also introduce programs that directly bolster dependent caretaking and the economic supports that make such caretaking possible. . . . Possible programs could include subsidized or public day care, longer school days and school years, more affordable health care, and workplace protections (including paid family leave policies and flexible schedules). To further ensure the economic security of dependents, the state should also make modifications to the welfare, social security, and tax systems. . . .

Some might suggest that it is incongruous to demand privacy from government intervention in certain aspects of family life but seek its intervention in other aspects. But incongruity appears only if the marital family is viewed as an indivisible unit. Dissecting that unit into its functional parts brings into sharp relief and permits examination of its different components. Once family life has been dissected, the question becomes not how one can justify treating certain aspects of the family differently, but instead how one can justify treating such radically different aspects of the family the same. Why should government privilege . . . one form of companionate relationship over others that may serve the same societal functions?

2. The Extended Family

MOORE v. CITY OF EAST CLEVELAND

431 U.S. 494 (1977)

Mr. Justice POWELL announced the judgment of the Court, and delivered an opinion in which Mr. Justice BRENNAN, Mr. Justice MARSHALL, and Mr. Justice BLACKMUN joined.

East Cleveland's housing ordinance, like many throughout the country, limits occupancy of a dwelling unit to members of a single family. But the ordinance contains an unusual and complicated definitional section that recognizes as a "family" only a few categories of related individuals, §1341.08.[2] Because her family, living together in her home, fits none of those categories, appellant stands convicted of a criminal offense. The question in this case is whether the ordinance violates the Due Process Clause of the Fourteenth Amendment.

---

2. Section 1341.08 (1966) provides:

"Family" means a number of individuals related to the nominal head of the household or to the spouse of the nominal head of the household living as a single housekeeping unit in a single dwelling unit, [including spouse, parent, or unmarried children, provided the unmarried children have no co-resident children, but] a family may include not more than one dependent married or unmarried child of the nominal head of the household or of the spouse of the nominal head of the household and the spouse and dependent children of such dependent child. . . .

Appellant, Mrs. Inez Moore, lives in her East Cleveland home together with her son, Dale Moore Sr., and her two grandsons, Dale, Jr., and John Moore, Jr. The two boys are first cousins rather than brothers; we are told that John came to live with his grandmother and with the elder and younger Dale Moores (sic) after his mother's death.

In early 1973, Mrs. Moore received a notice of violation from the city, stating that John was an "illegal occupant" and directing her to comply with the ordinance. When she failed to remove him from her home, the city filed a criminal charge. [She claimed that the ordinance was facially unconstitutional. She was convicted and sentenced to 5 days in jail and a $25 fine.]

The city argues that our decision in Village of Belle Terre v. Boraas, 416 U.S. 1 (1974), requires us to sustain the ordinance attacked here. . . . But one overriding factor sets this case apart from *Belle Terre*. The ordinance there affected only *unrelated* individuals. It expressly allowed all who were related by "blood, adoption, or marriage" to live together, and in sustaining the ordinance we were careful to note that it promoted "family needs" and "family values." East Cleveland, in contrast, has chosen to regulate the occupancy of its housing by slicing deeply into the family itself. This is no mere incidental result of the ordinance. On its face it selects certain categories of relatives who may live together and declares that others may not. In particular, it makes a crime of a grandmother's choice to live with her grandson in circumstances like those presented here.

When a city undertakes such intrusive regulation of the family, neither *Belle Terre* nor *Euclid* governs; the usual judicial deference to the legislature is inappropriate. "This Court has long recognized that freedom of personal choice in matters of marriage and family life is one of the liberties protected by the Due Process Clause of the Fourteenth Amendment." A host of cases, tracing their lineage to Meyer v. Nebraska, 262 U.S. 390, 399-401 (1923), and Pierce v. Society of Sisters, 268 U.S. 510, 534-535 (1925), have consistently acknowledged a "private realm of family life which the state cannot enter." Of course, the family is not beyond regulation. But when the government intrudes on choices concerning family living arrangements, this Court must examine carefully the importance of the governmental interests advanced and the extent to which they are served by the challenged regulation.

When thus examined, this ordinance cannot survive. The city seeks to justify it as a means of preventing overcrowding, minimizing traffic and parking congestion, and avoiding an undue financial burden on East Cleveland's school system. Although these are legitimate goals, the ordinance before us serves them marginally, at best. For example, the ordinance permits any family consisting only of husband, wife, and unmarried children to live together, even if the family contains a half dozen licensed drivers, each with his or her own car. At the same time it forbids an adult brother and sister to share a household, even if both faithfully use public transportation. The ordinance would permit a grandmother to live with a single dependent son and children, even if his school-age children number a dozen, yet it forces Mrs. Moore to find another dwelling for her grandson John, simply because of the presence of his uncle and cousin in the same household. . . .

The city would distinguish the cases based on *Meyer* and *Pierce*. It points out that none of them "gives grandmothers any fundamental rights with respect to grandsons," . . . and suggests that any constitutional right to live together as a family extends only to the nuclear family, essentially a couple and their dependent children.

To be sure, these cases did not expressly consider the family relationship presented here. They were immediately concerned with freedom of choice with respect to childbearing, or with the rights of parents to the custody and companionship of their own children, or with traditional parental authority in matters of child rearing and education. But unless we close our eyes to the basic reasons why certain rights associated with the family have been accorded shelter under the Fourteenth Amendment's Due Process Clause, we cannot avoid applying the force and rationale of these precedents to the family choice involved in this case. . . .

Substantive due process has at times been a treacherous field for this Court. There *are* risks when the judicial branch gives enhanced protection to certain substantive liberties without the guidance of the more specific provisions of the Bill of Rights. As the history of the *Lochner*-era demonstrates, there is reason for concern lest the only limits to such judicial intervention become the predilections of those who happen at the time to be Members of this Court. That history counsels caution and restraint. But it does not counsel abandonment, nor does it require what the city urges: cutting off any protection of family rights at the first convenient, if arbitrary boundary—the boundary of the nuclear family.

Appropriate limits on substantive due process come not from drawing arbitrary lines but rather from careful "respect for the teachings of history (and), solid recognition of the basic values that underlie our society." Griswold v. Connecticut, 381 U.S., at 501. Our decisions establish that the Constitution protects the sanctity of the family precisely because the institution of the family is deeply rooted in this Nation's history and tradition. It is through the family that we inculcate and pass down many of our most cherished values, moral and cultural.

Ours is by no means a tradition limited to respect for the bonds uniting the members of the nuclear family. The tradition of uncles, aunts, cousins, and especially grandparents sharing a household along with parents and children has roots equally venerable and equally deserving of constitutional recognition. Over the years millions of our citizens have grown up in just such an environment, and most, surely, have profited from it. Even if conditions of modern society have brought about a decline in extended family households, they have not erased the accumulated wisdom of civilization, gained over the centuries and honored throughout our history, that supports a larger conception of the family. Out of choice, necessity, or a sense of family responsibility, it has been common for close relatives to draw together and participate in the duties and the satisfactions of a common home. Decisions concerning child rearing, which *Yoder, Meyer, Pierce* and other cases have recognized as entitled to constitutional protection, long have been shared with grandparents or other relatives who occupy the same household, indeed who may take on major responsibility for the rearing of the children. Especially in times of adversity, such as the death of a spouse or economic need, the broader family has tended to come together for mutual sustenance and to maintain or rebuild a secure home life. This is apparently what happened here [when John Moore, Jr., came to live with his grandmother, as an infant, after his mother's death].

Whether or not such a household is established because of personal tragedy, the choice of relatives in this degree of kinship to live together may not lightly be denied by the State. [T]he Constitution prevents East Cleveland from standardizing its children and its adults by forcing all to live in certain narrowly defined family patterns. . . .

Mr. Justice BRENNAN, with whom Mr. Justice MARSHALL joins, concurring.

I join the plurality's opinion. . . . I write only to underscore the cultural myopia of the arbitrary boundary drawn by the East Cleveland ordinance in the light of the tradition of the American home that has been a feature of our society since our beginning as a Nation. . . .

. . . The "extended family" that provided generations of early Americans with social services and economic and emotional support in times of hardship, and was the beachhead for successive waves of immigrants who populated our cities, remains not merely still a pervasive living pattern, but under the goad of brutal economic necessity, a prominent pattern virtually a means of survival for large numbers of the poor and deprived minorities of our society. For them compelled pooling of scant resources requires compelled sharing of a household.

The "extended" form is especially familiar among black families. We may suppose that this reflects the truism that black citizens, like generations of white immigrants before them, have been victims of economic and other disadvantages that would worsen if they were compelled to abandon extended, for nuclear, living patterns. . . . In black households whose head is an elderly woman, as in this case, . . . 48% of such black households, compared with 10% of counterpart white households, include related minor children not offspring of the head of the household.[9]

I do not wish to be understood as implying that East Cleveland's enforcement of its ordinance is motivated by a racially discriminatory purpose: The record of this case would not support that implication. But the prominence of other than nuclear families among ethnic and racial minority groups, including our black citizens, surely demonstrates that the "extended family" pattern remains a vital tenet of our society. It suffices that in prohibiting this pattern of family living as a means of achieving its objectives, appellee city has chosen a device that deeply intrudes into family associational rights that historically have been central, and today remain central, to a large proportion of our population. . . .

[The concurring opinion of Justice Stevens, emphasizing Mrs. Moore's right to use her property as she sees fit, has been omitted.]

Mr. Justice STEWART, with whom Mr. Justice REHNQUIST joins, dissenting. . . .

The *Belle Terre* decision . . . disposes of the appellant's contentions to the extent they focus not on her blood relationships with her sons and grandsons but on more general notions about the "privacy of the home." Her suggestion that every person has a constitutional right permanently to share his residence with whomever he pleases, and that such choices are "beyond the province of legitimate governmental intrusion," amounts to the same argument that was made and found unpersuasive in *Belle Terre*. . . .

The appellant is considerably closer to the constitutional mark in asserting that the East Cleveland ordinance intrudes upon "the private realm of family life which the state cannot enter." Several decisions of the Court have identified specific aspects of what might broadly be termed "private family life" that are constitutionally protected against state interference.

Although the appellant's desire to share a single-dwelling unit also involves "private family life" in a sense, that desire can hardly be equated with any of the interests [which we have previously protected]. The ordinance about which the

9. [R. Hill, The Strengths of Black Families 5-6 (1972).]

appellant complains did not impede her choice to have or not to have children, and it did not dictate to her how her own children were to be nurtured and reared. The ordinance clearly does not prevent parents from living together or living with their unemancipated offspring.

But even though the Court's previous cases are not directly in point, the appellant contends that the importance of the "extended family" in American society requires us to hold that her decision to share her residence with her grandsons may not be interfered with by the State. This decision, like the decisions involved in bearing and raising children, is said to be an aspect of "family life" also entitled to substantive protection under the Constitution. Without pausing to inquire how far under this argument an "extended family" might extend, I cannot agree. . . . To equate [Moore's] interest with the fundamental decisions to marry and to bear and raise children is to extend the limited substantive contours of the Due Process Clause beyond recognition.

The appellant also challenges the single-family occupancy ordinance on equal protection grounds [an issue which the majority did not reach]. Her claim is that the city has drawn an arbitrary and irrational distinction between groups of people who may live together as a "family" and those who may not. . . . I do not think East Cleveland's definition of "family" offends the Constitution. The city has undisputed power to ordain single-family residential occupancy. And that power plainly carries with it the power to say what a "family" is. Here the city has defined "family" to include not only father, mother, and dependent children, but several other close relatives as well. The definition is rationally designed to carry out the legitimate governmental purposes identified in the *Belle Terre* opinion. . . .

Obviously, East Cleveland might have as easily and perhaps as effectively hit upon a different definition of "family." But a line could hardly be drawn that would not sooner or later become the target of a challenge like the appellant's. If "family" included all of the householder's grandchildren there would doubtless be the hard case of an orphaned niece or nephew. If, as the appellant suggests, a "family" must include all blood relatives, what of longtime friends? . . .

Peggy Cooper Davis, Moore v. East Cleveland: Constructing the Suburban Family

Family Law Stories 77, 88-89 (Carol Sanger ed., 2008)

The trouble seems to have begun for Inez Moore and her family in 1973 when John Jr. started school. It was then that Raiford Williams, an East Cleveland Deputy Housing Inspector, began to visit the Moore house on Garfield Road and to record violations. The structural violations—leaking sinks and tubs, a defective light, walls that needed replastering—Mrs. Moore began to repair. But there was one violation she would not address: "*John Moore, 7, is an illegal occupant. . . . Correct within 15 days.*" . . .

East Cleveland officials were proud of their zoning regulations. [T]he city had balanced its enforcement policies with a program of enlightened and socially responsible development. . . . The zoning regulations had been carefully considered and repeatedly refined: They were a key part of the city's strategy for attracting and maintaining a middle-class base and realizing the vision of East Cleveland as a "City of Achievement." Working from a vision of the prototypical middle-class suburban family, and undoubtedly having in mind both the problems of overcrowding and the pathologies thought to be associated with female-headed extended families, the regulations provided that a single-family dwelling could house spouses and their parents and children, but could house only one set of grandchildren. . . .

"On the surface, it looks like somebody's trying to be mean," said the city's Law Director, "but studies show a correlation between population density and trouble: more cars, crowded schools, more family fights that can lead to violence." . . . To Ms. Moore, the zoning regulations were not just mean, but also irrational. Speaking to a CBS News reporter, she said, "I could go out and bring in a foster child, and it would be legal. I could bring in a stepson or something, and it would probably be legal. But these are my grandchildren and it's not legal. I don't know why." The Law Director's statement to the same reporter was candid; he said that the zoning regulation "was written to avoid slums. It was written to avoid violence. It was written to avoid all the problems that the inner cities are experiencing throughout the country." But was it constitutionally permissible? . . .

Notes and Questions

1. **Formal versus functional definition.** Does the *Moore* family conform to the formal and/or functional definition(s) of the family? Given the presence of Mrs. Moore's blood ties with her grandsons, why doesn't the Moore household qualify as a "family" under the East Cleveland zoning ordinance?

2. **The tradition of the extended family.** Justice Powell's plurality opinion invalidates the East Cleveland ordinance based on the historical importance of the extended family. In fact, this view is a myth. The Cambridge Group for the History of Population and Social Structure documented, based on computer analysis, that the nuclear (rather than the extended) family predominated before industrialization. See Household and Family in Past Time (Peter Laslett ed., 1972); Peter Laslett, The World We Have Lost Further Explored 97-99 (3d ed. 1984). See also William J. Goode, World Revolution and Family Patterns 6 (1970) (referring to the extended family as the "family form of Western nostalgia"). Would such knowledge have changed the outcome in *Moore*?

3. **Role of race.** East Cleveland, a suburb of Cleveland, is a predominantly Black community. Mrs. Moore is African-American. Did the Court adequately take the role of race into account? Does Justice Powell's plurality opinion rest on a mythical model of *white* families? How does Justice Brennan respond in his concurrence? Although demographic data support the *mythical* status of the extended family among whites, empirical research supports the prevalence of this family form among African-Americans. Ronald L. Taylor, Diversity within African American Families, in Family in Transition: Families in Society 421, 430 (Arlene S. Skolnick & Jerome H. Skolnick, eds., 2011).

4. Return of the extended family. The extended family fell out of favor after World War II. In 1940, about 25 percent of the population lived in such households compared to 12 percent in 1980. Recently, the percentage of extended families has risen. About 16 percent of the population now lives in multigenerational households, such as the Moore family. The resurgence of the extended family stems from the economy (foreclosures, job loss) and the delayed first-marriage age causing young adults to live at home longer.[11] An increasing number of African-American grandmothers (like Mrs. Moore) are raising grandchildren. In addition to zoning problems, what other legal issues do these grandmothers face? See generally Jessica Dixon Weaver, Grandma in the White House: Legal Support for Intergenerational Caregiving, 43 Seton Hall L. Rev. 1 (2013) (pointing to loss of tax and employment benefits, as well as limitations on "granny" dwelling units).

5. *Belle Terre* distinguished. In applying a stricter standard of review than it used in *Belle Terre*, the Court treats *Moore* as involving not zoning, but rather family privacy. Why does the Belle Terre ordinance serve "family needs" and "family values" but the East Cleveland ordinance "slic[es] deeply into the family itself"? Is the latter ordinance directed at the same ends (eliminating traffic congestion and overcrowding) or at other family values? Professor Robert Burt responds:

> The plurality did not consider that the purpose of the ordinance was quite straightforward: to exclude from a middle-class, predominantly black community, that saw itself as socially and economically upwardly mobile, other black families most characteristic of lower-class ghetto life.
>
> Perhaps the Court did not see this purpose or, if it did, considered this an "illegitimate goal," though in other cases the Court had been exceedingly solicitous of white middle-class communities' attempts to preserve a common social identity—"zones," as the Court had put the matter [in *Belle Terre*]—"where family values, youth values, and the blessings of the quiet seclusion and clean air make the area a sanctuary for people." . . . I find in [Justice Brennan's] characterization of the East Cleveland ordinance, as "senseless" and "eccentric," precisely what he alleges in it: "a depressing insensitivity toward the economic and emotional needs" of the current majority of residents in East Cleveland.[12]

In an omitted dissent, Justice White disputes the idea that Mrs. Moore's interest in living with her grandchildren is protected by the Due Process Clause. He reasons that the ordinance prevents her from living only in East Cleveland but that she is free to move elsewhere in Cleveland. What do you think of his suggestion? Does it respond to Professor Burt's criticism above?

6. Criteria for family. Are blood and legal ties conclusive evidence of a family? Suppose John Moore, Jr. is an adult grandchild who is employed, financially independent, pays rent to his grandmother but seldom interacts with her. Or suppose that Inez Moore takes into her home a neighbor's child when the friend becomes terminally ill. Does a blood relationship merit protection of John Jr.'s residential right but not the child's? What factors, other than consanguinity and marriage, are suggestive of the existence of a family? A parent-child relationship? What problems

---

[11]. Pew Research Ctr., Return of the Multi-Generational Family Household, Mar. 18, 2010, http://www.pewsocialtrends.org/2010/03/18/the-return-of-the-multi-generational-family-household.

[12]. Robert A. Burt, The Constitution of the Family, 1979 Sup. Ct. Rev. 329, 389.

does this approach perpetuate? See generally Melissa Murray, The Networked Family: Reframing the Legal Understanding of Caregiving and Caregivers, 94 Va. L. Rev. 385 (2008); Laura A. Rosenbury, Friends with Benefits?, 106 Mich. L. Rev. 189 (2007) (both advocating legal support for broader notions of caregiving).

Problems

1. After their respective divorces, two friends, Alicia Wrob and Sheri Clark, rent a unit in a duplex in Eureka, Missouri. Wrob's two school-age children stay there every other week, and Clark's 21-year-old daughter has a room in the basement of the three-bedroom, two-bathroom dwelling. The city has cited them for illegal occupancy in an area zoned for "single families." Wrob and Clark claim they do constitute a family, sharing living expenses, dividing household labor, and relying on one another for emotional support. Eureka's zoning ordinance defines "family" as "[one] or more persons, related or unrelated, living together as a single integrated household unit." If the case goes to court, what arguments should Wrob and Clark make and what result should they obtain? See Sarah Wilson, Eureka Lawsuit Questions Living Situation, Definition of Family, Newsmagazine Network, Aug. 28, 2015, http://www.newsmagazinenetwork.com/nn/2013012330275/eureka-lawsuit-questions-living-situation-definition-of-family/.

2. John Smith wants to purchase property from the city of Blackacre to operate a commercial group home for foster children. John plans to delegate care of the children to licensed staff members who will work in alternating shifts around the clock. The children will live, sleep, and eat at the facility when they are not attending school. When Blackacre denies John's application to purchase the property on the basis that the property is zoned for "single family residences," John contends that the denial violates the Fair Housing Act (FHA), 42 U.S.C. §§3601 et seq., which requires that all persons be provided equal access to housing regardless of their "familial status."

"Familial status," according to *current* FHA rules, includes (1) one or more minors (2) domiciled with (3) a parent or other person having legal custody of the minor or the designee of such parent or custodian. 42 U.S.C. §3602(k). *Proposed* legislation would amend the definition of "familial status" to include minors residing with: (1) a foster parent or another person having lawful physical custody of such individuals; or (2) anyone standing in loco parentis of such individuals (currently, the designee of such parent or other person having such custody, with the parent's or other person's written permission). Housing Opportunities Made Equal Act, H.R. 2479, 113th Cong. (2013). What result under the existing and proposed FHA regulations? See Estvanko v. City of Perry, 2011 WL 1750232 (M.D. Ga. 2011).

B. Cohabitation: Unmarried Couples

The first three excerpts in the next section present background on the history of cohabitation in the United States as well as its demographic characteristics. The final excerpt offers a comparative view from an international perspective.

1. Introduction

Marsha Garrison, Nonmarital Cohabitation: Social Revolution and Legal Regulation

42 Fam. L.Q. 309, 311-314 (2008)

[Before the 1960s] cohabitation outside of marriage was widely viewed as shameful. . . . What almost no one foresaw [was] the rapidity with which the stigma traditionally attached to nonmarital cohabitation would vanish. . . .

Among the remarkable cultural shifts of the 1960s was a new attitude toward premarital sex. To be more precise, the 1960s witnessed a profound shift in attitudes toward *female* premarital sex. Before the 1960s, a young man could "sow a few wild oats" without fear of serious social censure. Of course, he risked venereal disease if he patronized a prostitute. And he risked a shotgun wedding if he impregnated a girl from a respectable family. But if the young man got away with it. . . . he typically suffered no reputational harm.

For young women, on the other hand, premarital sex posed extraordinary risks. The first and largest of these risks was pregnancy. The best outcome that pregnancy could produce was a shotgun wedding. A furtive stay at a home for unwed mothers or an illegal, and perhaps dangerous, abortion represented the only alternatives to that wedding. Even if pregnancy was averted, the young woman who engaged in premarital sex risked serious reputational loss. "Nice" girls did not; "fast" girls who did faced gossip, snickers, and damaged marriage prospects.

During the 1960s, technology and social change combined to change these traditional norms. The new birth control pill offered young women, for the first time, near certain protection from pregnancy. . . . The women's movement offered [these young women] the chance to imagine gaining what had always been male prerogatives, including the possibility of premarital sex without reputational loss. And the social upheaval that accompanied the civil rights movement and Vietnam War produced a new world in which the vision of sex without reputational harm became a reality. . . .

With premarital sex came open premarital cohabitation. What began as a countercultural innovation associated with hippies and antiwar activists became, with remarkable rapidity, an accepted part of youth culture. . . . Between 1970 and 2000, the number of U.S. unmarried-cohabitant households rose almost ten-fold, from 523,000 to 4,880,0000. . . . In recent years, the ranks of cohabitants have been further swelled by older couples who have already been married. Some of these older cohabitants have already been divorced and thus feel hesitant about a new marital commitment; some, making use of cohabitation's new respectability, have chosen cohabitation over marriage for more pragmatic reasons.

The net result is that cohabitation is now a multifaceted and multigenerational phenomenon. It includes young men and women who are sharing living space with a dating partner in order to save money, more committed couples who are testing the strength of their relationship, engaged couples who are planning to marry, committed couples who view their relationship as marital but have chosen to avoid marriage for practical reasons such as the potential loss of alimony or a surviving-spouse entitlement, and many couples whose motives are mixed or who disagree about the nature of their relationship. . . .[13]

The excerpt below explores the question of what persons are most likely to live together, considering such factors as age, education, and income level. It also explores the controversial issue of whether cohabitation leads to more stable subsequent marriages.

Nat'l Marriage Project, Social Indicators of Marital Health & Well-Being: Trends of the Past Five Decades: Unmarried Cohabitation in The State of Our Unions: Marriage in America 76-77 (2012)[14]

Between 1960 and 2009 . . . , the number of cohabiting couples in the United States increased more than fifteenfold. About a quarter of unmarried women age 25 to 39 are currently living with a partner, and an additional quarter has lived with a partner at some time in the past. More than 60 percent of first marriages are now preceded by living together, compared to virtually none 50 years ago. . . .

Cohabitation is more common among those of lower educational and income levels. Among women in the 25 to 44 age range, 75 percent of those who never completed high school have cohabited, compared to 50 percent of college graduates. Cohabitation is also more common among those who are less religious than their peers, those who have been divorced, and those who have experienced parental divorce, fatherlessness, or high levels of marital discord during childhood. A growing percentage of cohabiting-couple households, now over 40 percent, contain children.

The belief that living together before marriage is a useful way "to find out whether you really get along," and thus avoid a bad marriage and an eventual divorce, is now widespread among young people. But the available data on the effects of cohabitation fail to confirm this belief. In fact, a substantial body of evidence indicates that those who live together before marriage are more likely to break up after marriage.

This evidence is controversial, however, because it is difficult to distinguish the *selection effect* from the *experience of cohabitation effect*. The selection effect

---

[13]. A variation of unmarried partners' relationships is the phenomenon of "living apart together" (or LATs)—those couples who have committed relationships, often longstanding in duration, whose partners maintain separate residences. See generally Eric Klinenberg, Going Solo: The Extraordinary Rise and Surprising Appeal of Living Alone (2011); Lise Stryker Stoessel, Living Happily Ever After—Separately (2013); Constance Rosenblum, Living Apart Together, N.Y. Times, Sept. 13, 2013, at RE1.

[14]. The full report can be found at http://www.stateofourunions.org/2010/si-cohabitation .php.

refers to the fact that people who cohabit before marriage have different characteristics from those who do not, and it may be these characteristics, and not the experience of cohabitation, that leads to marital instability. . . . What can be said for certain is that no research from the United States has yet been found that those who cohabit before marriage have stronger marriages than those who do not.

The following excerpt focuses on the characteristics of *first* premarital cohabitation—its duration, demographic features, probability of pregnancies, and the probability that it will lead to marriage.

Casey E. Copen et al., CDC, First Premarital Cohabitation in the United States in Nat'l Health Statistics Reports 6-7 (Apr. 4, 2013)[15]

[Research shows] an increase in premarital cohabitation in the United States. The length, or median duration, of first premarital cohabitations among women in 2006–2010 increased over the past decade to 22 months, up from 13 months in 1995. Estimates [show] that 40% of women's first premarital cohabitations transitioned to marriage, which is larger than the percentages of cohabiting unions that remained intact (32%) or dissolved (27%) within the first 3 years following union formation. . . .

First premarital cohabitations were longest for foreign-born Hispanic women (33 months) and shortest for white women (19 months). A higher percentage of first premarital cohabitations among white women (44%) and foreign-born Hispanic women (42%) transitioned to marriage by 3 years, compared with cohabitations for both U.S.-born Hispanic women and black women (31% each).

[The rate and duration of cohabitation also differ by educational level.] [T]he increase between 1995 and 2006–2010 in the percentage of women who cohabited before marriage was larger for women with less than a high school diploma. . . . [These women also had longer cohabitations, and their cohabitation less frequently led to marriage.]

[We also studied] the probability of pregnancies within first premarital cohabiting unions. Nearly one out of five women experienced a pregnancy in the first year of a first premarital cohabitation. Probabilities of a pregnancy were higher among women who were under age 20 when they began cohabiting, among foreign-born Hispanic women, and among women with less than a high school diploma. Alongside the increase in fertility within cohabiting unions over the past decade was a decrease in the probability of marriage among women who became pregnant in a cohabiting union. . . . .

[15]. The full report is available at www.cdc.gov.

The final excerpt examines the comparative perspective. What countries have high cohabitation rates? What factors influence these rates?

Social Trends Institute, Global Family Structure (2011)[16]

[N]ot surprisingly, cohabitation is more common in countries with comparatively low marriage rates, and uncommon where marriage is stronger. There are several countries where less than 2 percent of adults are living together but unmarried: China, Taiwan, South Korea, Japan, Indonesia, Malaysia, Egypt, Saudi Arabia, and Nigeria. This list primarily consists of the high marriage-rate countries of Asia and the Middle East. . . .

There is considerable variation in cohabitation levels across Africa. For example, [the decline in cohabitation in Nigeria from 7 percent in 1990 to 1 percent in 2008] may be linked to religious changes in the country, as Islamic and evangelical Protestant groups have tried to assert more control over young adult sexuality in recent years. . . . In contrast, cohabitation is 4 percent in Kenya and 11 percent in South Africa.

Among European countries, Poland, Spain, and Italy have relatively low cohabitation rates, while France and Sweden have some of the highest rates. Cohabitation is obviously common in the Americas, but Colombia is still an outlier at 31 percent, 13 percentage points higher than even Sweden, the leader in cohabitation in Europe at 18 percent. However, it is important to note that consensual unions have a long history in Latin America, where they often function much like legal marriages and are typically more stable than cohabiting unions in North America.

When these statistics are taken together, adults in Asian countries are more likely to marry and less likely to cohabit than their counterparts in other regions, but the stability of their marriages has declined over time. Middle Eastern countries have not witnessed this same rise in divorce, and for them cohabitation is essentially nonexistent; consequently, these countries appear to maintain a traditional attitude toward marriage. Countries in Latin America exhibited low divorce rates in the 1970s (divorce was illegal in some of our target countries in 1970), but since that time, rising rates of divorce and high rates of cohabitation in many South and Central American countries demonstrate that marriage is not as normative a part of the adult life course in this region as it is in Asia and the Middle East. African adults are also spending fewer of their adult years married than they did in the past. . . .

Canada more closely resembles a European country than its neighbor, the United States. Similarly, Australia and New Zealand have marriage, divorce, and cohabitation rates that look more like Europe than like their Southeast Asian neighbors. Overall, then, marriage continues to play a strong role in guiding the adult life course in Asia and the Middle East, while its hold is somewhat weaker on nations in Africa, the Americas, Europe, and Oceania.

---

[16]. The full article is available at http://sustaindemographicdividend.org/articles/international-family-indicators/global-family-structure.

Postscript. Some countries offer cohabiting couples the option of entering a civil union that enables them to legalize their relationship without marriage but is subject to a registration requirement. Eleven countries authorize this legal status (Belgium, Denmark, Finland, France, Germany, Iceland, Luxembourg, the Netherlands, Norway, Sweden, and the United Kingdom).[17]

In some countries, cohabiting partners who have lived together for a specified period of time without registering are considered to have the same legal rights as couples who have formalized their relationship. For example, in both Australia and New Zealand, couples who have lived together for 6 months and 3 years, respectively, occupy a partnership status that is equivalent to marriage.[18]

France has the most famous civil union (*pacte civil de solidarité,* or PACS), created by the French Parliament in 1999. Originally, the status was heralded as a form of legal protection for gays and lesbians. Today, however, the overwhelming majority of PACS consist of opposite-sex couples. PACS are remarkably popular—two civil unions exist for every three marriages. French civil unions confer the right to file joint tax returns, exempt partners from inheritance taxes, permit partners to share insurance policies, ease access to residency permits for foreigners, and make partners responsible for each other's debts. To enter a civil union, the parties must appear before a judicial official. To end the status, they must send a registered letter to designated governmental officials.[19]

2. Traditional Response: Criminal Sanctions

Traditionally, nonmarital cohabitation and fornication were subject to criminal sanctions. Criminalization was aimed at prohibiting the affront to public morals and also encouraging marriage. Criminal sanctions also attempted to prevent the birth of nonmarital offspring that were regarded as imposing a financial burden on the state.[20]

Efforts to revise or repeal criminal statutes against cohabitation and fornication began in the 1950s. The Model Penal Code (MPC) proposed criminalizing cohabitation only if it was "open and notorious."[21] Subsequently, the ALI Council voted to delete the MPC section because the law was seldom enforced, inconsistent with the widespread policy of nonenforcement of moral standards, without deterrent value, and prone to discriminatory enforcement.[22] Many states followed suit by liberalizing the law.

Sexual activity between gays and lesbians, similarly, evoked punitive legal responses. Criminal prohibitions on sodomy (consensual oral or anal sex) existed in all 50 states before 1961. However, after the MPC recommended the decriminalization of cohabitation and fornication, states gradually began abrogating their

[17]. OECD Family Database, SF3.3: Cohabitation Rate and Prevalence of Other Forms of Partnership (Jan. 31, 2013), www.oecd.org/social/family/database.

[18]. Id.

[19]. Scott Sayare & Maïa de la Baume, In France, Civil Unions Gain Favor over Marriage, N.Y. Times, Dec. 16, 2010, at A1.

[20]. Joanne Sweeny, Undead Statutes: The Rise, Fall, and Continuing Uses of Adultery and Fornication Criminal Laws, 46 Loy. U. Chi. L.J. 127 (2014).

[21]. MPC §207.1 (Tent. Draft No. 4, 1955).

[22]. Id. at cmt.

sodomy laws.[23] In 2003, Lawrence v. Texas led to the repeal of sodomy laws in the remaining 13 states.[24]

3. Unmarried Couples' Rights Inter Se

MARVIN v. MARVIN

557 P.2d 106 (Cal. 1976)

TOBRINER, Justice.

During the past 15 years, there has been a substantial increase in the number of couples living together without marrying. Such nonmarital relationships lead to legal controversy when one partner dies or the couple separates. Courts of Appeal, faced with the task of determining property rights in such cases, have arrived at conflicting positions. . . . We take this opportunity to resolve that controversy and to declare the principles which should govern distribution of property acquired in a nonmarital relationship. . . .

. . . In the instant case plaintiff and defendant lived together for seven years without marrying; all property acquired during this period was taken in defendant's name. When plaintiff sued to enforce a contract under which she was entitled to half the property and to support payments, the trial court granted judgment on the pleadings for defendant, thus leaving him with all property accumulated by the couple. . . . [Plaintiff appeals.]

Plaintiff avers that in October of 1964 she and defendant "entered into an oral agreement" that while "the parties lived together they would combine their efforts and earnings and would share equally any and all property accumulated as a result of their efforts whether individual or combined." Furthermore, they agreed to "hold themselves out to the general public as husband and wife" and that "plaintiff would further render her services as a companion, homemaker, housekeeper and cook to . . . defendant."

Shortly thereafter plaintiff agreed to "give up her lucrative career as an entertainer [and] singer" in order to "devote her full time to defendant . . . as a companion, homemaker, housekeeper and cook"; in return defendant agreed to "provide for all of plaintiff's financial support and needs for the rest of her life."

Plaintiff alleges that she lived with defendant from October of 1964 through May of 1970 and fulfilled her obligations under the agreement. During this period the parties as a result of their efforts and earnings acquired in defendant's name substantial real and personal property, including motion picture rights worth over $1 million. In May of 1970, however, defendant compelled plaintiff to leave his household. He continued to support plaintiff until November of 1971, but thereafter refused to provide further support. . . .

[D]efendant offers some four theories to sustain the ruling. . . . Defendant first and principally relies on the contention that the alleged contract is so

[23]. MPC §207.5 (Tent. Draft No. 4, 1955); MPC §213.2 (Prop. Off. Draft 1962).
[24]. Lawrence v. Texas, 539 U.S. 558, 573 (2003) (explaining history).

Lee Marvin (left) and Michelle Marvin (a.k.a. Michelle Triola), the parties in Marvin v. Marvin

closely related to the supposed "immoral" character of the relationship between plaintiff and himself that the enforcement of the contract would violate public policy.[4] He points to cases asserting that a contract between nonmarital partners is unenforceable if it is "involved in" an illicit relationship. A review of the numerous California decisions concerning contracts between nonmarital partners, however, reveals that the courts have not employed such broad and uncertain standards to strike down contracts. The decisions instead disclose a narrower and more precise standard: a contract between nonmarital partners is unenforceable only *to the extent* that it *explicitly* rests upon the immoral and illicit consideration of meretricious sexual services. . . .

Although the past decisions hover over the issue in the somewhat wispy form of the figures of a Chagall painting, we can abstract from those decisions a clear and simple rule. The fact that a man and woman live together without marriage, and engage in a sexual relationship, does not in itself invalidate agreements between them relating to their earnings, property, or expenses. Neither is such an agreement invalid merely because the parties may have contemplated the creation or continuation of a nonmarital relationship when they entered into it. Agreements between nonmarital partners fail only to the extent that they rest upon a consideration of meretricious sexual services. Thus the rule asserted by defendant, that a contract fails if it is "involved in" or made "in contemplation" of a nonmarital relationship, cannot be reconciled with the decisions. . . .

The principle that a contract between nonmarital partners will be enforced unless expressly and inseparably based upon an illicit consideration of sexual services not only represents the distillation of the decisional law, but also offers a far more precise and workable standard than that advocated by defendant. [A] standard which inquires whether an agreement is "involved" in or "contemplates" a nonmarital relationship is vague and unworkable. Virtually all agreements between nonmarital partners can be said to be "involved" in some sense in the fact of their mutual sexual relationship, or to "contemplate" the existence of that relationship. Thus defendant's proposed standards, if taken literally, might invalidate all agreements between nonmarital partners, a result no one favors. Moreover, those standards offer no basis to distinguish between valid and invalid agreements. By looking not to such uncertain tests, but only to the consideration underlying the agreement, we provide the parties and the courts with a practical

4. Defendant also contends that the contract was illegal because it contemplated a violation of former Penal Code section 269a, which prohibited living "in a state of cohabitation and adultery." (§269a was repealed by Stats. 1975, ch. 71, eff. Jan. 1, 1976.) Defendant's standing to raise the issue is questionable because he alone was married and thus guilty of violating section 269a. . . . The numerous cases discussing the contractual rights of unmarried couples have drawn no distinction between illegal relationships and lawful nonmarital relationships. Moreover, even if we were to draw such a distinction, [plaintiff] sought to amend her complaint to assert that the parties reaffirmed their contract after [his] divorce.

guide to determine when an agreement between nonmarital partners should be enforced.

Defendant secondly relies upon the ground suggested by the trial court: that the 1964 contract violated public policy because it impaired the community property rights of Betty Marvin, defendant's lawful wife. . . . In the present case Betty Marvin, the aggrieved spouse, had the opportunity to assert her community property rights in the divorce action. The interlocutory and final decrees in that action fix and limit her interest. Enforcement of the contract between plaintiff and defendant against property awarded to defendant by the divorce decree will not impair any right of Betty's, and thus is not on that account violative of public policy.

Defendant's third contention is [that] that enforcement of the oral agreement between plaintiff and himself is barred by Civil Code section 5134, which provides that "All contracts for marriage settlements must be in writing. . . ." A marriage settlement, however, is an agreement in contemplation of marriage. . . . The contract at issue here does not conceivably fall within that definition. [The court also rejected "as a rather strained contention," defendant's fourth argument that plaintiff was asserting a claim for breach of promise to marry, barred by statute.]

In summary, we base our opinion on the principle that adults who voluntarily live together and engage in sexual relations are nonetheless as competent as any other persons to contract respecting their earnings and property rights. Of course, they cannot lawfully contract to pay for the performance of sexual services, for such a contract is, in essence, an agreement for prostitution and unlawful for that reason. . . . So long as the agreement does not rest upon illicit meretricious consideration, the parties may order their economic affairs as they choose, and no policy precludes the courts from enforcing such agreements.

In the present instance, plaintiff alleges that the parties agreed to pool their earnings, that they contracted to share equally in all property acquired, and that defendant agreed to support plaintiff. The terms of the contract as alleged do not rest upon any unlawful consideration. We therefore conclude that the complaint furnishes a suitable basis upon which the trial court can render declaratory relief. The trial court consequently erred in granting defendant's motion for judgment on the pleadings. . . .

As we have noted, both causes of action in plaintiff's complaint allege an express contract; neither assert any basis for relief independent from the contract. In In re Marriage of Cary, [109 Cal. Rptr. 862 (1973),] however, the Court of Appeal held that, in view of the policy of the Family Law Act, property accumulated by nonmarital partners in an actual family relationship should be divided equally. . . . Although our conclusion that plaintiff's complaint states a cause of action based on an express contract alone compels us to reverse the judgment for defendant, resolution of the *Cary* issue will serve both to guide the parties upon retrial and to resolve a conflict presently manifest in published Court of Appeal decisions.

Both plaintiff and defendant stand in broad agreement that the law should be fashioned to carry out the reasonable expectations of the parties. Plaintiff, however, presents the following contentions: that the decisions prior to *Cary* rest upon implicit and erroneous notions of punishing a party for his or her guilt in entering into a nonmarital relationship, that such decisions result in an inequitable distribution of property accumulated during the relationship, and that *Cary* correctly held that the enactment of the Family Law Act in 1970 overturned those prior decisions. Defendant in response maintains that the prior decisions merely applied common law principles of contract and property to persons who have deliberately elected to remain outside the bounds of the community property system. *Cary*, defendant contends, erred in holding that the Family Law Act vitiated the force of the prior precedents.

[T]he truth lies somewhere between the positions of plaintiff and defendant. . . . The cases prior to *Cary* exhibited a schizophrenic inconsistency. By enforcing an express contract between nonmarital partners unless it rested upon an unlawful consideration, the courts applied a common law principle as to contracts. Yet the courts disregarded the common law principle that holds that implied contracts can arise from the conduct of the parties. Refusing to enforce such contracts, the courts spoke of leaving the parties "in the position in which they had placed themselves," just as if they were guilty parties "in pari delicto."

Still another inconsistency in the prior cases arises from their treatment of property accumulated through joint effort. To the extent that a partner had contributed *funds* or *property*, the cases held that the partner obtains a proportionate share in the acquisition, despite the lack of legal standing of the relationship. Yet courts have refused to recognize just such an interest based upon the contribution of *services*. As Justice Curtis points out, "Unless it can be argued that a woman's services as cook, housekeeper, and homemaker are valueless, it would seem logical that if, when she contributes money to the purchase of property, her interest will be protected, then when she contributes her services in the home, her interest in property accumulated should be protected" [Vallera v. Vallera, 134 P.2d at 761, 764 (dissenting opinion)].

Thus as of 1973, the time of the filing of In re Marriage of Cary, the cases apparently held that a nonmarital partner who rendered services in the absence of express contract could assert no right to property acquired during the relationship. The facts of *Cary* demonstrated the unfairness of that rule.

Janet and Paul Cary had lived together, unmarried, for more than eight years. They held themselves out to friends and family as husband and wife, reared four children, purchased a home and other property, obtained credit, filed joint income tax returns, and otherwise conducted themselves as though they were married. Paul worked outside the home, and Janet generally cared for the house and children.

In 1971 Paul petitioned for "nullity of the marriage." Following a hearing on that petition, the trial court awarded Janet half the property acquired during the relationship, although all such property was traceable to Paul's earnings. The Court of Appeal affirmed the award [reasoning that prior cases that denied relief were based] upon a policy of punishing persons guilty of cohabitation without marriage. The Family Law Act, the court observed, aimed to eliminate fault or guilt as a basis for dividing marital property. But once fault or guilt is excluded, the court reasoned, nothing distinguishes the property rights of a nonmarital "spouse" from those of a putative spouse. Since the latter is entitled to half the "quasi marital property" (Civ. Code §4452), the Court of Appeal concluded that, giving effect to the policy of the Family Law Act, a nonmarital cohabitator should also be entitled to half the property accumulated during an "actual family relationship."

Cary met with a mixed reception in other appellate districts. [W]e agree [with the view] that *Cary* distends the act. No language in the Family Law Act addresses the property rights of nonmarital partners, and nothing in the legislative history of the act suggests that the Legislature considered that subject. [A]lthough we reject the reasoning of *Cary* . . . , we share the perception . . . that the application of former precedent in the factual setting of those cases would work an unfair distribution of the property accumulated by the couple. . . .

The principal reason why the pre-*Cary* decisions result in an unfair distribution of property inheres in the court's refusal to permit a nonmarital partner to assert rights based upon accepted principles of implied contract or equity. We have examined the reasons advanced to justify this denial of relief, and find that none have merit.

First, we note that the cases denying relief do not rest their refusal upon any theory of "punishing" a "guilty" partner. Indeed, to the extent that denial of relief "punishes" one partner, it necessarily rewards the other by permitting him to retain a disproportionate amount of the property. Concepts of "guilt" thus cannot justify an unequal division of property between two equally "guilty" persons.

Other reasons advanced in the decisions fare no better. The principal argument seems to be that "[e]quitable considerations arising from the reasonable expectation of . . . benefits attending the status of marriage . . . are not present (in a nonmarital relationship)" [Vallera v. Vallera, 134 P.2d 761, 763 (Cal. 1943)]. But, although parties to a nonmarital relationship obviously cannot have based any expectations upon the belief that they were married, other expectations and equitable considerations remain. The parties may well expect that property will be divided in accord with the parties' own tacit understanding and that in the absence of such understanding the courts will fairly apportion property accumulated through mutual effort. We need not treat nonmarital partners as putatively married persons in order to apply principles of implied contract, or extend equitable remedies; we need to treat them only as we do any other unmarried persons.

The remaining arguments advanced from time to time to deny remedies to the nonmarital partners are of less moment. There is no more reason to presume that services are contributed as a gift than to presume that funds are contributed as a gift; in any event the better approach is to presume . . . "that the parties intend to deal fairly with each other."

The argument that granting remedies to the nonmarital partners would discourage marriage [also] must fail. . . . Although we recognize the well-established public policy to foster and promote the institution of marriage, perpetuation of judicial rules which result in an inequitable distribution of property accumulated during a nonmarital relationship is neither a just nor an effective way of carrying out that policy.

[W]e believe that the prevalence of nonmarital relationships in modern society and the social acceptance of them, marks this as a time when our courts should by no means apply the doctrine of the unlawfulness of the so-called meretricious relationship to the instant case. As we have explained, the nonenforceability of agreements expressly providing for meretricious conduct rested upon the fact that such conduct, as the word suggests, pertained to and encompassed prostitution. To equate the nonmarital relationship of today to such a subject matter is to do violence to an accepted and wholly different practice.

We are aware that many young couples live together without the solemnization of marriage, in order to make sure that they can successfully later undertake marriage. This trial period, preliminary to marriage, serves as some assurance that the marriage will not subsequently end in dissolution to the harm of both parties. We are aware, as we have stated, of the pervasiveness of nonmarital relationships in other situations.

The mores of the society have indeed changed so radically in regard to cohabitation that we cannot impose a standard based on alleged moral considerations that have apparently been so widely abandoned by so many. Lest we be misunderstood, however, we take this occasion to point out that the structure of society itself largely depends upon the institution of marriage, and nothing we have said in this opinion should be taken to derogate from that institution. The joining of the man and woman in marriage is at once the most socially productive and individually fulfilling relationship that one can enjoy in the course of a lifetime.

We conclude that the judicial barriers that may stand in the way of a policy based upon the fulfillment of the reasonable expectations of the parties to a nonmarital relationship should be removed. As we have explained, the courts now hold that express agreements will be enforced unless they rest on an unlawful meretricious consideration. We add that in the absence of an express agreement, the courts may look to a variety of other remedies in order to protect the parties' lawful expectations.[24]

The courts may inquire into the conduct of the parties to determine whether that conduct demonstrates an implied contract or implied agreement of partnership or joint venture, or some other tacit understanding between the parties. The courts may, when appropriate, employ principles of constructive trust. Finally, a nonmarital partner may recover in quantum meruit for the reasonable value of household services rendered less the reasonable value of support received if he can show that he rendered services with the expectation of monetary reward.[25]

Since we have determined that plaintiff's complaint states a cause of action for breach of an express contract, and, as we have explained, can be amended to state a cause of action independent of allegations of express contract,[26] we must conclude that the trial court erred. . . . [Reversed and remanded.]

GONZALEZ v. GREEN

831 N.Y.S.2d 856 (Sup. Ct. 2006))

Gangel-Jacob, J.:

Plaintiff and defendant had been same-sex domestic partners since in or about 2001 when defendant, a person of considerable assets and income, invited plaintiff to move in with him. Plaintiff was a student with little or no income at the

24. We do not seek to resurrect the doctrine of common law marriage, which was abolished in California by statute in 1895. Thus we do not hold that plaintiff and defendant were "married," nor do we extend to plaintiff the rights which the Family Law Act grants valid or putative spouses; we hold only that she has the same rights to enforce contracts and to assert her equitable interest in property acquired through her effort as does any other unmarried person.

25. Our opinion does not preclude the evolution of additional equitable remedies to protect the expectations of the parties to a nonmarital relationship in cases in which existing remedies prove inadequate; the suitability of such remedies may be determined in later cases in light of the factual setting in which they arise.

26. We do not pass upon the question whether, in the absence of an express or implied contractual obligation, a party to a nonmarital relationship is entitled to support payments from the other party after the relationship terminates.

time. During the course of their relationship the defendant gave plaintiff expensive gifts, including two automobiles and a ski house in plaintiff's name. In 2005 the couple, whose primary residence was in Westchester, New York, decided to take advantage of recent Massachusetts legislation that permits people of the same sex to marry. They arranged for and took part in a marriage ceremony to each other in Massachusetts on February 14, 2005. [However, at that time, Massachusetts had the following marriage evasion law]:

§11. NONRESIDENTS, MARRIAGES CONTRARY TO LAWS OF DOMICILED STATE

> No marriage shall be contracted in this commonwealth by a party residing and intending to continue to reside in another jurisdiction if such marriage would be void if contracted in such other jurisdiction, and every marriage contracted in this commonwealth in violation hereof shall be null and void. [Mass. Gen. Laws ch. 207 §11]

As was their intention from the beginning, the parties left Massachusetts and returned to New York to continue to primarily reside in their Westchester domicile. They also frequently resided in a pied-à-terre shared by them in New York City. Over the next several months, the parties' relationship deteriorated and they separated. In September of 2005 defendant's attorney drafted a "separation agreement" (the "Agreement") which both parties executed . . . .

The Agreement recites in relevant part that

> "the parties desire to confirm their separation and make arrangements in connection therewith, including the settlement of their property rights, and other rights and obligations growing out of the marriage relation . . . . Now, therefore, in consideration of the premises and of the mutual promises hereinafter contained, the parties agree as follows . . . ."

Among other things, the Agreement provides for division of the real and personal property accumulated by the parties during their time together; it also provides for a one-time payment by defendant to plaintiff of the sum of $780,000, described as "the only support, maintenance, or other form of payment by either party hereto to the other" . . . .

On January 20, 2006, plaintiff commenced an "Action for a Divorce" . . . on the ground of cruel and inhuman treatment (DRL §170[1]). [D]efendant moved by Order to Show Cause for summary judgment dismissing plaintiff's action for failure to state a cause of action. Defendant's motion also seeks a declaration that as a matter of law, since the parties were never married, the Agreement was void ab initio and all property transferred by defendant to plaintiff thereunder must be returned to defendant . . . .

I find the parties' marriage to be void under the laws of either the state of New York, where both parties reside, or the state of Massachusetts, where the purported marriage ceremony took place [citing Hernandez v. Robles, 855 N.E.2d 1 (N.Y. 2006) (upholding state ban on same-sex marriage); Mass. Gen. L. Ann. Ch. 207, §11 (marriage evasion statute)]. Accordingly, defendant's motion is granted to the extent that it seeks dismissal of plaintiff's "Action for a Divorce" for failure to state a cause of action; in all other respects, defendant's motion is denied.

Plaintiff's cross-motion to dismiss defendant's counterclaims for rescission of the Agreement is granted. "New York courts have long accepted the concept that an express agreement between unmarried persons living together . . . is as enforceable as though they were not living together . . . provided only that illicit sexual relations were not part of the consideration of the contract . . . . The theory [is] that while cohabitation without marriage does not give rise to the property and financial rights which normally attend the marital relation, neither does cohabitation disable the parties from making an agreement within the normal rules of contract law . . . ."

Furthermore, "[New York's refusal to permit same-sex marriage in Hernandez v. Robles] does not negate the existence of same sex relationships, nor the reality that some same sex relationships dissolve, and the courts are called upon to resolve disputes regarding the distribution of assets of such relationships." In this regard there is "no impediment to enforcement in a contract action of the provisions of the parties' Agreement insofar as it concerns their personal property and . . . monetary obligations," and defendant's counterclaim that the Agreement is void ab initio as against public policy because the parties are a same sex couple who were not actually married when they entered into the Agreement is dismissed.

Defendant's claim of lack of consideration similarly fails. "The valid consideration which will support a contract need not be equal on both sides, and if a minimal yielding of a position by one side promotes an agreement, then it will be deemed enforceable. There is no need to measure the relative weight of the consideration provided by each party." [Here] the Agreement provides at the outset that it is made "in consideration of the premises and of the mutual promises hereinafter contained . . . ."

The Agreement, which was drafted with deliberation by defendant's own attorney, purports the settlement of all claims between the parties, indeed, it contains a mutual release of all claims, causes of action or demands that might arise in law or in equity which either party has, ever had or will have against the other which further supports this court's finding of valid consideration in support of enforcement of the Agreement.

Apparently, however, the defendant, who on each counterclaim seeks the return of the $780,000 he paid to plaintiff upon his execution, and thus his ratification, of the Agreement, mistakenly believes such things as promises to act or to forbear from acting that constitute detriment to the promisor are not sufficient consideration to support the Agreement in light of the tangible sums he paid to plaintiff upon its execution (which he selectively characterizes as support or maintenance, but which is also defined in the deliberately drafted Agreement as an "other form of payment by either party hereto to the other").

[T]he law is otherwise and defendant's assertions in this regard are intrinsically mistaken. Nevertheless, to further alleviate defendant's curious logic in this regard, I find that the plaintiff delivered tangible property of more than sufficient value to defendant in consideration of his entering into the Agreement. [A]s part of the division of property between the parties that is referred to in the Agreement was the transfer by plaintiff of title to his ski house to defendant. This valuable consideration is more than sufficient to support the enforceability of the Agreement . . . .

. . . Nor do I find that the Agreement is voidable under the doctrine of mutual mistake. Defendant claims that since both sides mistakenly thought they were married at the time they entered into the Agreement, with all of the rights and obligations that attend such status, the fact that they were not actually married when they believed they were should vitiate the Agreement. However, defendant defeats his own argument by his own statement in his moving papers in support of his motion; he asserts: "[t]he Court should note that the Plaintiff and I never filed Joint-tax Returns and always filed such returns as single and we never purchased property as married people and only had the marriage, because it seemed like a nice thing to have, since couples in the gay community are seeking such status."

It could not be more obvious that defendant never took the idea that he was married to plaintiff seriously. . . . Whether or not the parties considered themselves married in nature, defendant, a sophisticated businessman, must have considered the strong possibility of illegality while the law was in such a developing state. Accordingly, defendant's position that there was a mutual mistake of fact which impairs the validity of the Agreement is disingenuous . . . . Defendant's attorney drafted the Agreement. Its contents express the transaction as defendant desired it to be. [Although] the law of New York [at that time did not] recognize the validity of the cohabiting parties' marriage, it does recognize the validity of the cohabiting parties' right to settle their affairs by agreement . . . .

Notes and Questions

1. Epilogue.

a. ***Sequel to*** **Marvin.** On remand, the trial court found neither an express contract nor an implied contract based on the parties' conduct. Nonetheless, the trial judge awarded Michelle Marvin $104,000 in "rehabilitative alimony" based on several factors: the state supreme court's contemplation of broad equitable remedies (in footnote 25), the plaintiff's resort to unemployment benefits for support, and the defendant's net worth at separation exceeding $1 million. The trial judge arrived at the amount by calculating (for a two-year period) plaintiff's highest salary as a singer prior to the cohabitation. The appellate court reversed, reasoning that the trial court had merely established plaintiff's need and defendant's ability to pay. The court elaborated:

> . . . A court of equity admittedly has broad powers, but it may not create totally new substantive rights under the guise of doing equity. [I]n view of the already-mentioned findings of no damage (but benefit instead), no unjust enrichment and no wrongful act on the part of defendant with respect to either the relationship or its termination, it is clear that no basis whatsoever, either in equity or in law, exists for the challenged rehabilitative award.[25]

Lee later married his childhood sweetheart and remained married to her until his death in 1987. Michelle lived with actor Dick Van Dyke for 30 years until her death in 2009.[26]

---

[25]. 5 Fam. L. Rep. (BNA) 3079, 3085 (Apr. 24, 1979).

[26]. Dick Van Dyke, 86, Marries 40-Year-Old, Miami Herald, Mar. 13, 2012, available at 2012 WLNR 5392324.

b. *Sequel to* Gonzalez. When Steven Green met David Gonzalez, Green was a wealthy 41-year-old real estate developer, producer of independent films, owner of a small charter airline, philanthropist, and activist for gay causes. Gonzalez was an impoverished 29-year-old student. Subsequent to the case, Green pleaded guilty to income tax evasion and fraudulent use of a false Social Security number on a $9 million loan to purchase an apartment building. Gonzalez became a lawyer.[27]

2. State approaches. Jurisdictions adopt different approaches to the issue of cohabitants' postdissolution support claims. The majority follows *Marvin* in recognizing express and implied agreements as well as equitable remedies. However, some jurisdictions recognize only express agreements. See, e.g., Northrup v. Brigham, 826 N.E.2d 239, 244 (Mass. App. Ct. 2005); Basso v. LO Electric/Oliver, 46 Misc.3d 1227(A) (N.Y. Sup. Ct. 2014). Finally, until recently, a few jurisdictions refused to recognize cohabitants' claims based on public policy grounds. See, e.g., Hewitt v. Hewitt, 394 N.E.2d 1204 (Ill. 1979), *superseded by statute as stated in* Blumenthal v. Brewer, 24 N.E.3d 168 (Ill App. Ct. 2014) (*petition for leave to appeal granted by Illinois Supreme Court,* 31 N.E.3d 767 (2015)); Cates v. Swain, 116 So. 3d 1073 (Miss. Ct. App. 2012), *rev'd* 2013 WL 1831783 (Miss. 2013)

3. Extending *Marvin* to same-sex couples. How were the contracts in *Marvin* and *Gonzalez* similar? How were they different? Although each case arose at the termination of a relationship, how were the legal issues similar, and how were they different? What were the parties' various arguments? How does each court respond? Must Gonzalez return the gifts that Green gave him?

Before the advent of marriage equality, same-sex partners executed contracts (like that between Gonzalez and Green) because they had no other means of securing their legal rights. Only a few states (like New York in *Gonzalez*) recognized cohabitation contracts between same-sex partners before legalization of same-sex marriage. See, e.g., Doe v. Burkland, 808 A.2d 1090 (R.I. 2002); Gormley v. Robertson, 83 P.3d 1042 (Wash. Ct. App. 2004). But, the tide appears to be turning. See Blumenthal v. Brewer, supra (holding that former lesbian partner can bring claims against partner for unjust enrichment and quantum meruit regarding real property they owned); Cates v. Swain, supra (holding that lesbian partner can recover the amounts she contributed to her former partner on a theory of unjust enrichment). See also M. v. H., [1999] 2 S.C.R. 3 (landmark Canadian case recognizing property rights of same-sex partners at dissolution.)

4. Planning documents. Same-sex couples are more likely than opposite-sex couples to have estate planning documents and medical decisionmaking documents, such as wills and health care proxies. What explains this fact? See generally Ellen D.B. Riggle et al., The Execution of Legal Documents by Sexual Minority Individuals, 11 Psychol. Pub. Pol'y & L. 138 (2005). Do you think this will still be true after the advent of marriage equality?

5. Legal significance of *Marvin*. *Marvin* permits recovery based on express agreements, and in the absence thereof, implied-in-fact and implied-in-law agreements. Note that *Marvin*'s statements regarding implied agreements are dictum because the plaintiff pleaded an express agreement. Because most agreements between cohabitants are not express, *Marvin*'s importance rests on this dictum and on the suggestion

[27]. Anemona Hartocollis, Married or Not, Gay Couple's Separation Agreement Is Held Valid, N.Y. Times, Jan. 9, 2007, at B4; Dareh Gregorian, $hock in Gay Split – 'Alimony' Upheld, N.Y. Post, Jan. 9, 2007, at 23; Jeff Testerman, Philanthropist . . . and a Fraud, Tampa Bay Times, Feb. 20, 2007.

(in footnote 25) of "additional equitable remedies." Implied-in-fact remedies are applicable when a court infers contractual intent from the parties' conduct. Implied-in-law remedies are impressed judicially to prevent unjust enrichment, regardless of the parties' intent. Thus, the latter, of course, are not really contracts.

What guidelines does *Marvin* give for determining the existence of implied agreements or the application of additional equitable remedies? Does the court assume that the parties have identical expectations? In reality, don't parties' expectations frequently vary? In addition, the court advocates adherence to a presumption that the parties intend to deal fairly with each other. What facts should raise that presumption? Does this presumption interfere with freedom of contract and constitute impermissible state intervention?

6. Public policy rationale. In *Marvin,* the defendant argued that recognition of a contract would violate public policy by impairing the rights of his ex-wife (to whom he was married during part of the cohabitation). Should a cohabitant be disqualified by, preferred to, or share property equally with, a lawful spouse? See In re Long & Fregeau, 244 P.3d 26 (Wash. Ct. App. 2010).

7. Homemaking services. In *Marvin,* the plaintiff asserts that she provided homemaking services, among other services, in return for the defendant's promise of support. Under traditional contract doctrine, the provision of domestic services by an intimate partner does not constitute consideration because of the rationales that (1) the woman acted from affection rather than expectation of gain, (2) she intended her actions as a gift, or (3) her services are offset by the man's companionship and services. Should such services constitute consideration? If so, how do we value them? Apportion them?

Does the provision of homemaking services without compensation trigger the doctrine of "unjust enrichment" under restitutionary theory? Specifically, has the plaintiff conferred a benefit on the defendant at her expense? Was the enrichment "unjust"? See Robert C. Casad, Unmarried Couples and Unjust Enrichment: From Status to Contract and Back Again, 77 Mich. L. Rev. 47, 55 (1978). See also Blumenthal v. Brewer, supra; Cates v. Swain, supra.

8. Sexual services. *Marvin* stands for the rule that express contracts are enforceable except to the extent that they are premised on sexual services, assuming that cohabitants' agreements can be separated from the sexual relationship. How does a plaintiff show that the claim is independent from the sexual relationship? Aren't sexual services always an implicit part of cohabitants' agreements? Or is that confusing contractual terms with motive for entering the contract? See generally Jill Elaine Hasday, Family Law Reimagined 67-94 (2014). By refusing to recognize sexual services as consideration, is a court simply saying that it refuses to confer value on these services for policy reasons? Does recognition of sexual services implicate an invasion of privacy? Professor Fran Olsen counters:

> To make "whisperings across the pillows," sacred, private, and unrepeatable is to support the sexual status quo. . . . Sex is private in part because the state makes it private and because keeping sex private seems to serve the interests of those with power. . . .[28]

---

[28]. Frances E. Olsen, The Myth of State Intervention in the Family, 18 U. Mich. J.L. Reform 835, 857 n.57 (1985).

9. Undermining marriage. Does legal recognition of cohabitants' rights undermine marriage? Signify a return to common law marriage? How do the legal consequences of cohabitation and common law marriage differ? Would resurrection of common law marriage help cohabitants? Support or weaken marriage? See Cynthia Grant Bowman, Unmarried Couples, Law, and Public Policy (2010). Is the court or legislature the more appropriate body to reform the law about this issue? What impact does marriage equality have for these questions?

10. Gender equality. Does recognition of cohabitants' rights alleviate gender inequality? Is *Marvin* an advance or a setback for women?

11. Marriage as the standard. What public policy considerations support equating cohabitation with marriage for purposes of recognition of the partners' rights? Should all economic consequences of cohabitation imitate the rights and duties of marriage? For example, on remand in *Marvin*, the trial court awarded "rehabilitative alimony," using the traditional factors for spousal support of need versus ability to pay. Should cohabitants be entitled to postdissolution "spousal support" regardless of contractual intent?

12. Contract or status principles. *Marvin* disapproved the status approach of In re Marriage of Cary, 109 Cal. Rptr. 862 (Ct. App. 1973), which treated cohabitants like married persons by granting them half of the accumulated property, based on an extension of no-fault divorce and community property principles. Washington State pioneered this approach in Connell v. Francisco, 898 P.2d 831 (Wash. 1995), by developing an equitable doctrine that treats partners' jointly acquired property at dissolution as community property *if* the parties manifest a "meretricious relationship" (defined as a "stable, marital-like relationship where both parties cohabit with knowledge that a lawful marriage between them does not exist").

This equitable doctrine was later renamed the "committed intimate relationship (CIR)" doctrine. To determine the existence of a CIR, courts examine the following elements: (1) continuous cohabitation, (2) duration of the relationship, (3) purpose of the relationship, (4) pooling of resources and services for joint projects, and (5) the intent of the parties. See In re Kelly & Moesslang, 287 P.3d 12 (Wash. Ct. App. 2012).

Commentators have proposed variations of the status-based approach to operate independently of the parties' intentions. For example, Professor Grace Blumberg recommends, for purposes of support and property division, treating cohabitants similarly to married persons if they have remained together for two years. She rejects durational requirements if a child is born to the parties or, for inheritance purposes, if the relationship remains intact until the death of one partner.[29] The American Law Institute follows this approach (discussed below).

On the other hand, Professor Marsha Garrison favors the contract approach, arguing that cohabitation and marriage are not equivalent behavior because of the shorter duration of cohabitation and the lack of cohabitants' sharing expectations. She contends that the status-based approach presents "daunting fact-finding

---

[29]. Grace Ganz Blumberg, Cohabitation Without Marriage: A Different Perspective, 28 UCLA L. Rev. 1125, 1167-1168 (1981).

challenges" and worries that the benefits (financial, emotional) of marriage might be lost if people spent more time in cohabiting relationships.[30] Which approach do you favor and why?

13. Law reform. The ALI's Principles of the Law of Family Dissolution, favoring a status-based approach, apply the same rules to the property and support claims of domestic partners as to those of spouses. ALI, Principles of the Law of Family Dissolution: Analysis and Recommendations (2002) (Chapter 6: Domestic Partners). According to the ALI, a presumption of domestic partnership arises if the persons have maintained a household with their common child for a requisite period or if they have simply maintained a common household for the requisite period. If neither presumption applies, a person may still establish a domestic partnership by proof of various factors (i.e., statements made to each other or jointly to a third party, intermingling finances, economic dependence, emotional or physical intimacy, community reputation as a couple, participation in a commitment ceremony, naming each other as beneficiaries of life insurance or a will, or joint assumption of parenthood). Id. §6.03(7)(a) to (m).

The Restatement (Third) of Restitution permits cohabitants who have made "substantial uncompensated contributions in the form of property or services" to bring a claim of restitution at the end of the relationship. Restatement (Third) of Restitution and Unjust Enrichment §28 (2011). The Restatement rejects a moralistic stance that denies recovery, reasoning that such a bar merely leads to unjust enrichment. How would these approaches apply in *Marvin* and *Gonzalez*?

Problems

1. Patricia files suit against her long-term paramour, noted criminal defense attorney Johnnie L. Cochran, Jr. (who successfully defended O.J. Simpson at his murder trial). The couple's 17-year relationship began in 1966, when Johnnie was still married to his first wife (whom he divorced in 1978). In 1973, Patricia and Johnnie have a son, and the next year, they purchase a house together. Many people believe that the couple is married, especially after Patricia changes her surname to Cochran. Johnnie manages Patricia's finances and, at various times, directs her to quit her jobs and forgo her career in order to take care of him and their child. During his first marriage and until 1985, when Johnnie informs Patricia that he is remarrying another woman, he lives with Patricia from two to four nights per week. After his remarriage, they never again spend the night, although frequently visits Patricia and takes meals there.

Patricia contends that, in 1983, Johnnie orally promised to support her for the rest of her life, and that he did so until 1995, when he became angry after she discussed their relationship on television. Johnnie, citing *Marvin*, argues that the support agreement is unenforceable because the couple was not living together full time when the promise was made, and he also contends that it violates public policy because he was married. He characterizes the relationship as little more

[30]. Marsha Garrison, Nonmarital Cohabitation: Social Revolution and Legal Regulation, 42 Fam. L.Q. 309, 325-327 (2008).

than "dating." What result? See Cochran v. Cochran, 106 Cal. Rptr. 2d 899 (Ct. App. 2001).

2. Helen, age 23, works as a medical receptionist for an ophthalmologist, Frank, who is 51 years old and has been married for 20 years. They begin a romantic relationship. Frank continues living with his wife while providing Helen with expenses, a car, a home, and funds for her undergraduate and graduate education. They spend vacations together and dine together three or four times weekly, but rarely spend the night together. Helen contends that Frank told her repeatedly that he would divorce his wife and marry her. After a 20-year relationship, Frank ends the affair. After he discovers that Helen has started another relationship, Frank sues to eject her from the condo that he purchased for her. She counters with a complaint for palimony. Should a long-term intimate partner who has maintained a separate residence be entitled to enforce a support agreement? See Devaney v. L'Esperance, 949 A.2d 743 (N.J. 2008). Is this case distinguishable from *Cochran*, supra? Cf. Bergen v. Wood, 18 Cal. Rptr. 2d 75 (Ct. App. 1993).

4. Unmarried Couples, Third Parties, and the State

a. Tort Recovery

GRAVES v. ESTABROOK

818 A.2d 1255 (N.H. 2003)

DUGGAN, J.

[Catrina] Graves was engaged to Brett A. Ennis and had lived with him for approximately seven years. On September 23, 2000, Ennis was riding his motorcycle while Graves followed immediately behind him in a car. At an intersection, Estabrook's vehicle failed to yield at a stop sign and collided with Ennis. As Graves looked on, Ennis flipped over the hood of Estabrook's car and landed on the pavement. Graves immediately stopped her car and ran to the aid of her fiancé. She saw blood coming from his mouth and significant trauma to his head. She followed the ambulance that transported her fiancé to the hospital, stayed by his side while he was being treated, and attempted to comfort his parents and son. Ennis died the next day. Graves alleges that as a result of witnessing the collision and death of her fiancé, she suffered shock, severe mental pain and emotional distress.

The issue before us is whether a plaintiff who lived with and was engaged to marry the decedent may recover for negligent infliction of emotional distress. . . .

Many of the first states to recognize bystander liability for negligent infliction of emotional distress limited its scope by applying the "physical impact test," without considering foreseeability. Under the physical impact test, the plaintiff must have sustained a physical impact, no matter how slight, in order to recover. New Hampshire never adopted the physical impact test but instead followed the zone of danger rule [permitting] recovery only when the bystander was within a physical zone of danger created by the defendant's negligence. [However, the court later rejected the zone of danger rule in favor of the traditional negligence analysis of foreseeability.] We adopted the test first enunciated in Dillon v. Legg, 441 P.2d 912, 920 (Cal. 1968), in which the California Supreme Court set forth three factors for determining whether a defendant should reasonably foresee injury to a bystander: (1) Whether plaintiff was located near the scene of the accident as contrasted with one who was a distance away from it. (2) Whether the shock resulted from a direct emotional impact upon plaintiff from the sensory and contemporaneous observance of the accident, as contrasted with learning of the accident from others after its occurrence. (3) Whether plaintiff and the victim were closely related, as contrasted with an absence of any relationship or the presence of only a distant relationship. . . .

This case requires us to examine the scope of *Dillon*'s third factor. The defendant argues that we should continue to follow the California Supreme Court and adopt its subsequent holding in Elden v. Sheldon, 758 P.2d 582 (Cal. 1988). There, the court held that unmarried cohabitants are not "closely related" and cannot recover for negligent infliction of emotional distress. Other courts have adopted the same rule [citing cases in Florida, New Mexico, and Texas].

As noted by the New Jersey Supreme Court in Dunphy v. Gregor, 642 A.2d 372, 375 (N.J. 1994), the [California Supreme Court] in *Elden* was reacting to the experience of the California courts with bystander liability under the *Dillon* standard. After *Dillon*, California courts had significantly expanded the scope of bystander liability [e.g., to eliminate the requirement of visual perception of the injury and to expand the "closely related" factor to include foster parent-child relationships]. Thus, one reason for the holding in *Elden* was a need to rein in the expansion of bystander liability in California. [U]nlike the California Supreme Court, we are not faced with a need to curb bystander liability.

Notwithstanding this difference, the defendant urges us to construe the third factor [literally]. He argues that we should limit the meaning of "closely related" to a dictionary definition: people "connected by consanguinity," Webster's Third New International Dictionary 1916 (unabridged ed.1961), or "persons connected by kinship, common origin or marriage." American Heritage Dictionary 1473 (4th ed. 2000). . . . The defendant's argument, limiting the analysis to a dictionary definition, amounts to a "dry classification [that] puts the emphasis at the wrong place[]." . . . The appropriate analysis is not to resort to a dictionary definition but rather to use our traditional analysis of foreseeability.

In *Elden*, the California Supreme Court rejected a traditional analysis of foreseeability for three policy reasons. . . . First is the State's strong interest in marriage. . . . *Elden* found no convincing reason to permit recovery to couples who bear no legal obligations to each other to the same extent as those who undertake such obligations.

The court in *Elden* apparently relied upon the dubious assumption that the possibility of recovery in tort litigation is an incentive to marry. Rejecting this assumption, the New Jersey Supreme Court observed that "a person who would not otherwise choose to marry would not be persuaded to do so in order to assure his or her legal standing in a future personal injury action should that person have the misfortune of witnessing the serious injury of his or her spouse." *Dunphy*, 642 A.2d at 379. . . . We agree.

The second reason relied upon in *Elden* was the "difficult burden on the courts." *Elden* reasoned that "[a] determination whether a partner in an unmarried cohabitation relationship may recover damages for emotional distress based on such matters as the sexual fidelity of the parties and their emotional and economic ties would require a court to undertake a massive intrusion into the private life of the partners." Again, we agree with the New Jersey Supreme Court, which noted that "[o]ur courts have shown that the sound assessment of the quality of interpersonal relationships is not beyond a jury's ken and that courts are capable of dealing with the realities, not simply the legalities, of relationships to assure that resulting emotional injury is genuine and deserving of compensation." . . . Third, the court in *Elden* relied upon [the need to limit the class of plaintiffs by means of a bright line rule]. The court stated that the absence of a bright line rule "would result in the unreasonable extension of the scope of liability of a negligent actor." . . .

Rejecting the bright line rule in *Elden*, however, does not place an intolerable burden upon society or unfair burden upon a negligent defendant. Rather, it allows recovery for an eminently foreseeable class of plaintiffs. . . . *Elden* argued that "[t]he need to draw a bright line in this area of the law is essential" because there is no "principled distinction between an unmarried cohabitant who claims to have a de facto marriage relationship with his partner and de facto siblings, parents, grandparents or children." While this observation is accurate, it fails to consider that there is also no logical distinction between denying recovery to a fiancée who has lived with her betrothed for seven years and allowing recovery to a wife who met and married her husband a week before the accident. A bright line rule that includes only individuals related by blood or marriage is

> overinclusive because it permits recovery when the suffering accompanies a legal or biological link between bystander and victim, regardless of whether the relationship between the two is estranged, alienated, or in some other way removed. Conversely, the [rule] is underinclusive because it arbitrarily denies court access to persons with valid claims that they could prove if permitted to do so.

[Note, It's All Relative: A Graphical Reasoning Model for Liberalizing Recovery for Negligent Infliction of Emotional Distress Beyond the Immediate Family, 30 Val. U. L. Rev. 913, 917 (1996).]

More fundamentally, we decline to adopt a bright line rule when a "flexible approach, designed to account for factual nuances" is available. . . . We conclude that "to foreclose [an unmarried cohabitant] from making a claim based upon emotional harm because her relationship with the injured person does not carry a particular label is to work a potential injustice . . . where the emotional injury is genuine and substantial and is based upon a relationship of significant duration that . . . is deep, lasting and genuinely intimate." [*Dunphy*, 642 A.2d at 378.] A number of courts have reached a similar conclusion [citing cases in Hawaii, Nebraska, Ohio, Pennsylvania, Tennessee, West Virginia]. We thus recognize that unmarried cohabitants may have a close relationship, i.e., a "relationship that is stable, enduring, substantial, and mutually supportive . . . cemented by strong emotional bonds and provid[ing] a deep and pervasive emotional security." [Id. at 380.] In determining whether a relationship meets this standard, a court should

> take into account the duration of the relationship, the degree of mutual dependence, the extent of common contributions to a life together, the extent and quality of shared experience, and . . . whether the plaintiff and the injured person

> were members of the same household, their emotional reliance on each other, the particulars of their day to day relationship, and the manner in which they related to each other in attending to life's mundane requirements.

Id. at 378 (quotation omitted).

In this case, the plaintiff alleged in her complaint that she was engaged to the decedent and that they had lived together for seven years immediately preceding the accident. Construing all reasonable inferences in the light most favorable to the plaintiff, we conclude that it is reasonable to infer that in the course of their lengthy cohabitation the plaintiff and her fiancé enjoyed mutual dependence, common contributions to a life together, emotional reliance on each other and attended to life's mundane requirements together. . . .

The attorney who represented Catrina Graves provides the following background.

Roy A. Duddy, The Background Story of Graves v. Estabrook[31]

One late Saturday afternoon, 32-year-old Brett Ennis was riding his motorcycle on Route 102 in Londonderry, New Hampshire, after spending the day at a friend's home cleaning and polishing their motorcycles in preparation for a fund-raiser. Following immediately behind Brett in her vehicle was his long-term fiancée, Catrina Graves. They had just eaten lunch at a local restaurant and were on their way to a video store to rent a movie to watch that evening. Route 102 is a two-lane roadway that handles a large volume of traffic at a relatively high speed limit of 50 mph. As Brett approached an uncontrolled intersection (controlled via a STOP sign that required any driver on a secondary road to stop prior to entering Route 102), a vehicle owned by Franklin Estabrook accelerated into the intersection immediately in front of Brent's motorcycle. Brett, who was operating at 45-50 mph, swerved to avoid the Estabrook vehicle, but Estabrook's vehicle struck Brett. Brett was thrown into the air, striking the vehicle on the hood. He cartwheeled through the air, landing on his back in the middle of the traffic lane.

Catrina screamed when she saw what was happening. She saw Brett fly through the air and saw his feet hit the pavement, then his head. She swerved to avoid the crash. She immediately stopped her car, jumped out, and ran to Brett's side where she observed blood coming from his mouth. She attempted to clear his mouth and to loosen his jacket and sweatshirt. Brett's eyes were open, and he wasn't moving. Catrina held his hand and attempted to comfort him, all the while she was crying.

---

[31]. Roy A. Duddy, of Duddy Law Offices, Hampton, New Hampshire, was the attorney for Catrina Graves.

Catrina followed the ambulance to the medical center where she stayed at Brett's side for almost 30 hours until he was removed from life support. Brett was kept on life support in order to harvest certain organs and in order to allow Brett's son from a former marriage to arrive from Arkansas in order to "say his good-byes." Catrina sought counseling almost immediately after the accident to deal with the tragedy and remained in counseling for a considerable period of time.

Approximately one month after the accident, Catrina and Brett's father came to see me. It was very clear to me that Catrina and Brett, along with Brett's family, had a real and genuine love for one another. Catrina saw Brett's parents and sisters on a weekly basis. Brett's parents treated Catrina as though she were their own daughter. She called them "Mom" and "Dad." Catrina also had a good relationship with Brett's son. In fact, Catrina expressed concern that Brett's son should receive any insurance that Brett's estate might obtain. She was more concerned about making certain that Brett's son was taken care of than she was about her own future.

In my mind, this young woman had suffered more egregiously than almost anyone I had met in more than 20 years of practice. She was so selfless in her dealings with Brett's son and his family that I felt if ever there was a case to present the issue as to whether a bystander, not related by blood or marriage to the decedent—yet having the deep, intimate familial ties to the decedent—can recover on a claim for negligent infliction of emotional distress (NIED), this was the case.

I researched the law of New Hampshire and that of other jurisdictions. I also had two other lawyers who worked with me gather information in support of the social and demographic aspects of the cause of action. As expected, the superior court granted defense counsel's motion to dismiss on the ground that New Hampshire does not recognize the right of an unmarried cohabitant to maintain a cause of action for NIED. I filed a motion to reconsider—which was denied. I then appealed to the New Hampshire Supreme Court which accepted the case.

I approached the New Hampshire Trial Lawyers to ask them to submit an Amicus brief. The Amicus committee voted not to recommend to the Board of Governors that the case be accepted and an Amicus brief be filed. The majority of the Amicus committee felt that there was no likelihood of success and that the reputation of the Trial Lawyers would be tarnished by presenting a brief in support of my Appeal. I was very disheartened by its position. Nonetheless, at the next Board of Governors' meeting of the state Trial Lawyers' association, I presented my case to the whole Board in opposition to the Amicus committee's recommendation. After discussion, a vote was taken to support filing the brief. Attorney James Townsend, a member of the Board of Governors, volunteered to write the Association's Amicus brief.

Three months after oral argument, a divided New Hampshire Supreme Court (3 to 2) issued an opinion which held that Catrina Graves "may recover damages for emotional distress as the result of witnessing the collision." The case was remanded for trial. Subsequently, the parties reached a confidential settlement.

Notes and Questions

1. Tort recovery generally. Unmarried cohabitants sometimes try to recover for relationship injuries (such as those resulting from personal injury or death of a partner) through tort actions based on negligent infliction of emotional distress (NIED), loss of consortium, and wrongful death. Unlike claims for NIED and loss of consortium, actions for wrongful death are purely statutory. Wrongful death statutes restrict recovery only to legal spouses (although a few state laws permit recovery by a person who is named as a beneficiary in a decedent's will).

2. Negligent infliction claims. As *Graves* explains, under the traditional rule, recovery for NIED from witnessing the negligent injury to another was limited to persons who either suffered a physical impact or were in the zone of danger. Most jurisdictions follow Dillon v. Legg, 441 P.2d 912 (Cal. 1968), limiting recovery based on the foreseeability of the trauma to bystanders. Restatement (Third) of Torts: Physical and Emotional Harm §47 (2009). The third prong of *Dillon* focuses on whether the plaintiff had a *sufficiently close relationship* with the victim. As *Graves* explains, courts are split regarding such claims for unmarried cohabitants.

3. Rationale. According to *Graves*, what are the arguments pro and con recognizing cohabitants' claims for NIED? Justice Garibaldi, in a dissent in *Dunphy*, supra, protests that exclusion of cohabitants conforms to societal expectations regarding differential treatment of spouses and is less likely to lead to confusion because spouses are treated differently in many legal contexts (e.g., intestacy, alimony, etc.). 642 A.2d at 381, 382-383. She adds that exclusion is consistent with nonrecognition of common law marriage. How persuasive are these arguments? Does the extension of liability advance the objectives of the tort system?

4. Quality or status? According to *Graves*, how does a plaintiff prove the quality of the relationship? What evidence would minimize the quality of the relationship? How workable is the *Dunphy* standard (adopted by *Graves*) that focuses on the duration of the relationship, the degree of mutual dependence, the extent of common contributions to a life together, the extent and quality of shared experience, and co-residence?

How easy is the *Graves-Dunphy* standard to apply in the following situations: (a) Mary and Joe are engaged when defendant's negligence causes Mary's death. However, the couple are not living together because of opposition from Mary's parents (although the couple spend several nights per week together). They share all assets and expenses. (b) Carol and Paul are living together with their infant for six months before defendant's negligence causes Carol's death. The couple had no plans to marry and kept all accounts separate. Should recovery be allowed in either or both case(s)? Suppose that a relationship is not monogamous. Should that preclude recovery? How is "emotional reliance" determined?

5. Engaged couples. In *Graves*, the plaintiff and the victim were cohabitants who were engaged to marry. Does this latter factor strengthen plaintiff's claim? In whose favor does a long engagement cut? How does a plaintiff prove an engagement? A date to marry? Rings? If the accident occurs the day before the wedding? See, e.g., Smith v. Toney, 862 N.E.2d 656 (Ind. 2007).

In what ways are cohabitants' claims similar to, and different from, those of engaged persons? Professor Grace Blumberg advocates recovery by distinguishing cohabitants' claims as follows:

> The cohabitant was enjoying consortium at the time of the injury. More importantly, [it] is socially prudent to encourage fiancés and cohabitants to remain with the injured victims of tortfeasors. Denying them loss of consortium recovery on the ground that they were not legally bound to the injured person would seem to sanction and to encourage abandonment of the injured. . . . In this sense, fiancés and cohabitants are similarly situated: neither is bound to be virtuous.[32]

6. Loss of consortium. Most states deny recovery for loss of consortium to unmarried cohabitants. How should states treat *postmarital* loss of consortium involving these partners? That is, suppose, instead, that Brett Ennis in *Graves* was injured rather than killed, and that the couple marries after the accident. Should Graves be able to recover for the loss of consortium (i.e., the loss of companionship, affection, sex, economic contribution, and services) that she *subsequently* experienced stemming from the premarital injury? Compare Leonard v. John Crane, Inc., 142 Cal. Rptr. 3d 700 (Ct. App. 2012) (permitting postmarital recovery), with Bransteter v. Moore, 579 F. Supp. 2d 982 (N.D. Ohio 2008) (contra).

7. *Marvin* distinguished. Has California adopted a paradoxical position toward unmarried couples? Does it make sense to allow recovery by unmarried cohabitants in contract law (*Marvin*) but not tort law (*Elden*)?

8. Impact of *Lawrence*. *Graves* was decided before Lawrence v. Texas. What might be the impact of *Lawrence* on the rights of unmarried cohabitants to recover in tort for the injury or death of a partner?

b. Employment

SHAHAR v. BOWERS

114 F.3d 1097 (11th Cir. 1997)

Edmondson, Circuit Judge:

[Plaintiff Robin Shahar, a law student, worked as a law clerk with Georgia Attorney General Michael J. Bowers. In September 1990, the Attorney General offered Shahar the position of Staff Attorney when she graduated from law school. Shahar accepted the offer and was scheduled to begin work in September 1991.]

In the summer of 1990, Shahar began making plans for her "wedding." . . . [She] and her partner invited approximately 250 people, including two Department employees, to the "wedding." The written invitations characterized the ceremony as a "Jewish, lesbian-feminist, outdoor wedding." The ceremony took place in a public park in South Carolina in June 1991.

---

[32]. Blumberg, supra note [29], at 1138-1139 n.80.

In November 1990, Shahar filled out the required application for a Staff Attorney position. In response to the question on "marital status," Shahar indicated that she was "engaged." She altered "spouse's name" to read "future spouse's name" and filled in her partner's name: "Francine M. Greenfield." In response to the question "Do any of your relatives work for the State of Georgia?" she filled in the name of her partner as follows: "Francine Greenfield, future spouse."

Sometime in the spring of 1991, Shahar and her partner were working on their "wedding" invitations at an Atlanta restaurant. [While there, they met a paralegal and staff attorney, Susan Rutherford, from the Attorney General's office and mentioned to them the wedding preparations.] In June 1991, Shahar told Deputy Attorney General Robert Coleman that she was getting married at the end of July, changing her last name, taking a trip to Greece and, accordingly, would not be starting work with the Department until mid-to-late September. At this point, Shahar did not say that she was "marrying" another woman. [Eventually word got out that] Shahar was planning on "marrying" another woman. This revelation caused a stir.

Senior aides to the Attorney General became concerned about what they viewed as potential problems in the office resulting from the Department's employment of a Staff Attorney who purported to be part of a same-sex "marriage." Upon the Attorney General's return to the office, he was informed of the situation [and withdrew Shahar's offer by stating that it has]:

> become necessary in light of information which has only recently come to my attention relating to a purported marriage between you and another woman. As chief legal officer of this state, inaction on my part would constitute tacit approval of this purported marriage and jeopardize the proper functioning of this office.

[Shahar instituted suit seeking damages, injunctive relief, and "reinstatement." She argued that revocation of the employment offer based on her purported "marriage" to another woman violated the rights to free exercise and association, equal protection, and substantive due process. The district court granted the Attorney General's motion for summary judgment.]

Even when we assume, for argument's sake, that either the right to intimate association or the right to expressive association or both are present, we know they are not absolute. Georgia and its elected Attorney General also have rights and duties which must be taken into account. . . . In reviewing Shahar's claim, we stress that this case is about the government acting as employer.

Shahar argues that we must review the withdrawal of her job offer under strict scrutiny. The only precedent to which Shahar refers us for the proposition that strict scrutiny is to be applied to the government as employer is Dike v. School Board, 650 F.2d 783 (5th Cir. 1981). In *Dike*, the Fifth Circuit—our predecessor—implied that a school district's refusal to allow a teacher to breast-feed her child on her lunch hour must withstand strict scrutiny. To the extent that *Dike* might be interpreted as requiring strict scrutiny review of a government employee's freedom of intimate association claim, it misstates the appropriate standard; and we overrule it now. . . . We conclude that the appropriate test for evaluating the constitutional implications of the State of Georgia's decision [is] the same test as the test for evaluating the constitutional implications of a government employer's decision based on an employee's exercise of her right to free speech, that is, the *Pickering* [Pickering v. Board of Educ., 391 U.S. 563 (1968)] balancing test. . . .

. . . To decide this case, we are willing to accord Shahar's claimed associational rights (which we have assumed to exist) substantial weight. But, we know that the weight due intimate associational rights, such as, those involved in even a state-authorized marriage, can be overcome by a government employer's interest in maintaining the effective functioning of his office.

In weighing her interest in her associational rights, Shahar asks us also to consider the "nonemployment related context" of her "wedding" and "marriage" and that "[s]he took no action to transform her intimate association into a public or political statement." In addition, Shahar says that we should take into account that she has affirmatively disavowed a right to benefits from the Department based on her "marriage."

To the extent that Shahar disclaims benefits bestowed by the State based on marriage, she is merely acknowledging what is undisputed, that Georgia law does not and has not recognized homosexual marriage. We fail to see how that technical acknowledgment counts for much in the balance.

If Shahar is arguing that she does not hold herself out as "married," the undisputed facts are to the contrary. Department employees, among many others, were invited to a "Jewish, lesbian-feminist, out-door wedding" which included exchanging wedding rings: the wearing of a wedding ring is an outward sign of having entered into marriage. Shahar listed her "marital status" on her employment application as "engaged" and indicated that her future spouse was a woman. She and her partner have both legally changed their family name to Shahar by filing a name change petition with the Fulton County Superior Court. They sought and received the married rate on their insurance. And, they, together, own the house in which they cohabit. These things were not done secretly, but openly. . . .

[T]he Attorney General's worry about his office being involved in litigation in which Shahar's special personal interest might appear to be in conflict with the State's position [is] not unreasonable. In addition, the Department, when the job offer was withdrawn, had already engaged in and won a recent battle [Bowers v. Hardwick, 478 U.S. 186 (1986)] about homosexual sodomy—highly visible litigation in which its lawyers worked to uphold the lawful prohibition of homosexual sodomy. This history makes it particularly reasonable for the Attorney General to worry about the internal consequences for his professional staff (for example, loss of morale, loss of cohesiveness and so forth) of allowing a lawyer, who openly—for instance, on her employment application and in statements to coworkers—represents herself to be "married" to a person of the same sex, to become part of his staff. . . .

Shahar also argues that, at the Department, she would have handled mostly death penalty appeals and that the *Pickering* test requires evidence of potential interference with these particular duties. Even assuming Shahar is correct about her likely assignment within the Department, a particularized showing of interference with the provision of public services is not required. . . . [I]t is not for this court to tie the Department's hands by telling it which Staff Attorneys may be assigned to which cases or duties or to force upon the Attorney General a Staff Attorney of limited utility.

. . . Shahar argues that [the Attorney General] may not justify his decision by reference to perceived public hostility to her "marriage." We have held otherwise about the significance of public perception when law enforcement is involved. . . . [A]ssessing what the public perceives about the Attorney General and the Law Department is a judgment for the Attorney General to make in the day-to-day course of filling his proper role as the elected head of the Department, not for the federal judiciary to make with hindsight or from a safe distance away from the distress and disturbance that might result if the decision was mistaken. . . .

Shahar says that by taking into account these concerns about public reaction, the Attorney General impermissibly discriminated against homosexuals; and she refers us to the Supreme Court's recent decision in Romer v. Evans, [517 U.S. 620 (1996)]. In *Romer*, the Supreme Court struck down an amendment to a state constitution as irrational because the amendment's sole purpose was to disadvantage a particular class of people (to "den[y] them protection across the board"), and because the government engaged in "classification of persons undertaken for its own sake, something the Equal Protection Clause does not permit."

Romer is about people's condition; this case is about a person's conduct. And, *Romer* is no employment case. Considering (in deciding to revoke a job offer) public reaction to a future Staff Attorney's conduct in taking part in a same-sex "wedding" and subsequent "marriage" is not the same kind of decision as an across-the-board denial of legal protection to a group because of their condition, that is, sexual orientation or preference.

This case is about the powers of government as an employer, powers which are far broader than government's powers as sovereign. In addition, the employment in this case is of a special kind: employment involving access to the employer's confidences, acting as the employer's spokesperson, and helping to make policy. This kind of employment is one in which the employer's interest has been given especially great weight in the past. Furthermore, the employment in this case is employment with responsibilities directly impacting on the enforcement of a state's laws: a kind of employment in which appearances and public perceptions and public confidence count a lot.

Particularly considering this Attorney General's many years of experience and Georgia's recent legal history, we cannot say that he was unreasonable to think that Shahar's acts were likely to cause the public to be confused and to question the Law Department's credibility; to interfere with the Law Department's ability to handle certain controversial matters, including enforcing the law against homosexual sodomy; and to endanger working relationships inside the Department. We also cannot say that the Attorney General was unreasonable to lose confidence in Shahar's ability to make good judgments as a lawyer for the Law Department.

[W]e hold that the Attorney General's interest—that is, the State of Georgia's interest—as an employer in promoting the efficiency of the Law Department's important public service does outweigh Shahar's personal associational interests. . . . Georgia's Attorney General has made a personnel decision which none of the asserted federal constitutional provisions prohibited him from making. . . .

Postscript by Robin Shahar

Personal communication, July 8, 2015

Robin Shahar (the plaintiff in Shahar v. Bowers)

I hold two positions with the City of Atlanta. I am a Chief Counsel in the City of Atlanta Department of Law, and I also serve as Atlanta Mayor Kasim Reed's Advisor on LGBT Issues. My work as LGBT Advisor has been tremendously challenging and gratifying. Although Atlanta has municipal laws protecting LGBT individuals from discrimination, I am repeatedly reminded that equal protection is not synonymous with equal treatment. As the Mayor's Advisor, I am able to address both forms of inequality.

The year 2015 has been remarkable for me as a former plaintiff in a gay/lesbian rights case. The reasoning of the *Shahar vs. Bowers en banc* decision was profoundly hurtful and disturbing. As a lawyer, I struggled with my feelings of disillusionment about our country's judicial system—a system that is integral to my work. To make sense of the *en banc* ruling, I viewed the case within a historical context, as an early step in a long march for equal rights.

The Supreme Court's marriage equality ruling (*Obergefell*) affirmed my long-term perspective. It is an affirmation that I did not anticipate receiving during my lifetime. The current year has also been remarkable because Michael Bowers publicly and emphatically opined that firing people because of their sexual orientation is "dumb, plain dumb." As a vocal opponent of Georgia's pending RFRA (the "Religious Freedom" Restoration Act) bills, Mr. Bowers opined that the bills are unlawful, and are aimed at discriminating against disfavored groups including same-sex couples who want to marry. When asked about his decision to fire me in 1991, Mr. Bowers stated: "I wish it had never happened."[33]

Despite our incredible progress, the LGBT community is far from achieving our goal of full equality. An example that is particularly poignant for me is employment discrimination. Ironically, though United States courts have upheld the constitutional right to marriage equality, they have not yet upheld the constitutional right to LGBT workplace equality. Adverse employment decisions, such as mine, will continue to happen until Congress and more states enact laws (such as the Employment NonDiscrimination Act) that provide critical protection against workplace discrimination on the basis of sexual orientation and gender identity.

---

[33]. Both direct quotes are cited in Robin McDonald & Kathleen Baydala Joyner, ExAG Bowers: Religious Freedom Bills are 'Ill-Conceived' and 'Mean-Spirited,' Fulton Cty. Daily Rep., Feb. 24, 2015, http://www.dailyreportonline.com/id=1202718840481/ExAG-Bowers-Religious-Freedom-Bills-Are-IllConceived-and-MeanSpirited?slreturn=20150608114424.

Notes and Questions

1. Epilogue. Following plaintiff's appeal of the summary judgment in favor of the attorney general, the court of appeals initially upheld plaintiff's intimate association claim under the First Amendment, and ruled that strict scrutiny applied. 70 F.3d 1218 (11th Cir. 1995). However, after granting a rehearing en banc (78 F.3d 499 (11th Cir. 1996)), the court of appeals applied the *Pickering* balancing test to reach the conclusion in the principal case.

One week after the ruling in *Shahar*, former state attorney general Michael Bowers confessed his 15-year adulterous affair with a former employee. Shahar filed a motion for rehearing, arguing that Bowers' prohibited conduct under Georgia law undermined the court's reasoning. The Eleventh Circuit denied her petition, saying that she was terminated not because of her sexual conduct, but because of her marriage. Bowers resigned as state attorney general to run an unsuccessful gubernatorial campaign and then returned to private practice.[34] As the above excerpt reveals, he has changed his view on employment discrimination based on sexual orientation.

2. State interests. Plaintiff claims a violation of her constitutional rights because she lost her offer of employment at the hands of a state actor. The appellate court relies on the *Pickering* balancing test because of the state-employer's special interests. Do you believe that plaintiff's marriage would have interfered with the performance of her daily duties? What role should public perception play in employment decisions involving state actors?

3. Post-*Lawrence*. The *Shahar* court reached its decision six years before the Supreme Court decided Lawrence v. Texas (overturning Bowers v. Hardwick). What effect, if any, might *Lawrence* have had on the result in *Shahar*?

4. Public versus private. Does *Shahar* imply that plaintiff lost her employment only because she made "public" her relationship? The judicial attitude that penalizes some employees for certain behavior prompted one commentator to point out:

> [W]hat is seen as extravagant flaunting on the part of gay men and lesbians is routine, even expected behavior for heterosexuals in this society. Heterosexuals are free to reveal their status and preferences through public displays of affection as diverse as holding hands and sending out wedding announcements. Conversations among heterosexuals about "the process of forming couples" and one's life with one's partner are "expected and appropriate . . . in social and work settings."[35]

---

[34]. Lyle V. Harris, Out of the Wrestling Ring, into the Courtroom, Atlanta J. & Const., Mar. 3, 2000, at G1; Wendy Kaminer, Gay Rights, American Prospect, Feb. 28, 2000, at 67.

[35]. Mary Anne Case, Couples and Coupling in the Public Sphere: A Comment on the Legal History of Litigating for Lesbian and Gay Rights, 79 Va. L. Rev. 1643, 1672 (1993) (quoting Marc A. Fajer, Can Two Real Men Eat Quiche Together? Storytelling, Gender-Role Stereotypes, and Legal Protection for Lesbians and Gay Men, 46 U. Miami L. Rev. 511, 604 (1992)).

5. Employment discrimination: sexual orientation and gender identity. Federal efforts to ban employment discrimination based on sexual orientation date from 1974. A version of the Employment Nondiscrimination Act (ENDA) (H.R. 3685, 110th Cong.) finally passed the House of Representatives in 2007. However, that bill left transgender persons without employment protection, causing a rift in the LGBT community. The bill died in the Senate.

In July 2015, Congress introduced landmark legislation, the Equality Act (S.B. 1858, 114th Cong. (2015-2016)), that would expand the Civil Rights Act of 1964 and other nondiscrimination statutes by banning discrimination on the basis of sexual orientation or gender identity in employment, housing, credit, education, public accommodations (such as hotels, stores, and similar public places), and jury service. The bill also protects LGBT people against discrimination by any entity that receives federal funding. The bill faces an uphill battle in the current Republican-controlled Congress.

On the state level, 21 states have laws prohibiting employment discrimination based on sexual orientation, and 18 states also prohibit discrimination based on gender identity (but not Georgia, the setting of the principal case).[36]

6. Military discharge: Sexual orientation and gender identity. Traditionally, gay and lesbian service members faced discharge if they revealed their sexual orientation. The military policy of "Don't Ask, Don't Tell," (DADT), 10 U.S.C. §654, prohibited any person who was not heterosexual from disclosing his or her sexual orientation, or from speaking about any same-sex intimate relationships, while serving in the armed forces. Following adoption of the DADT policy in 1993, 12,500 gays and lesbians were discharged.[37]

Congress repealed DADT in 2012. Don't Ask, Don't Tell Repeal Act of 2010 (H.R. 2965, S. 4023, 111th Cong.). Soon after the Supreme Court decided *Obergefell* in 2015, the Pentagon announced that it will allow transgender members of the military to serve openly, thereby ending the DADT policy regarding these personnel. An estimated 150,000 transgender people have served in the military (despite the compulsion to conceal their identity). In addition, approximately 15,500 transgender people are currently on active duty in the armed forces or serving in the Guard or Reserve forces.[38]

7. Employment discrimination: Opposite-sex couples. Unmarried opposite-sex couples may also face adverse employment actions based on their sexual conduct, especially if one or both partners work in the public sector. Does Lawrence v. Texas preclude such actions? See, e.g., Sylvester v. Fogley, 383 F. Supp. 2d 1135 (W.D. Ark. 2005) (holding that investigation of police officer's off-duty sexual relationship with a female complainant did not violate his constitutional privacy right based on the public interest of achieving effective law enforcement).

---

[36]. Human Rights Campaign, Employment Non-Discrimination Act (2015), http://www.hrc.org/resources/entry/employment-non-discrimination-act.

[37]. Carolyn Lochhead, "Don't Ask" Repeal Losing Momentum, S.F. Chron., May 8, 2009, at A16.

[38]. Gary J. Gates & Jody J. Herman, Transgender Military Service in the United States, Williams Inst. (May 2014), http://williamsinstitute.law.ucla.edu/research/military-related/us-transgender-military-service/; AP, Pentagon to Repeal Ban on Transgender Service Members, S.F. Chron., July 14, 2015, at A12.

Problem

In 2011, Peter, a camera crewman at Onstage Productions, has been living with his partner, Austin, for 14 years. They jointly own real and personal property and name each other as beneficiaries of their respective life insurance policies and last will and testament documents. They have also designated each other as health care proxies (conferring medical decisionmaking power in the event of disability). They are open about their relationship.

Carolyn, another Onstage employee, has lived with her two children and her partner, Gordon, for two years. She and Gordon are beneficiaries of each other's life insurance policy and last will and testament. Peter asks his benefits manager to consider a welfare and pension benefits policy for employees with same-sex partners. The human resources committee considers two approaches: the "Lotus Alternative," named after a Cambridge, Massachusetts, software firm that was the first private corporation to grant benefits to same-sex partners, but not to opposite-sex cohabitants; and the "Ben and Jerry" model, named after the Vermont ice cream maker that offers health coverage to all unmarried partners.

What approach should the committee adopt, considering issues of cost, the potential for abuse, and the effects on morale and productivity? If a governmental employer (for example, a state university) were exploring similar options, what problems should it consider? With the advent of marriage equality nationwide in *Obergefell* in 2015, should those same-sex couples who choose not to marry be precluded from seeking partner benefits?

Suppose that new owners acquire Onstage in 2015, and they refuse to provide partner benefits to unmarried employees or to provide spousal benefits to employees married to a same-sex partner. The owners rely on a state law guaranteeing "conscience protection" for employers with religious or moral objections to employees' "lifestyle choices." What arguments can any affected employees make to challenge Onstage's new restrictive policy on partner and spousal benefits? Will such arguments succeed? Note that several states have enacted conscience clause legislation (i.e., versions of the federal Religious Freedom Restoration Act) that permits health care providers (and others providers of goods and services) to deny services for reasons of religion or conscience. What would be the impact on the challenge of the Supreme Court's decision in *Hobby Lobby* (discussed in Chapter I)? What approach does the Court suggest in *Obergefell* (discussed in Chapter II)? How would the enactment of the proposed federal Equality Act, supra p. 417, affect the issue?[39]

---

[39]. This is a modified version of the problem in Alice Rickel, Extending Employee Benefits to Domestic Partners: Avoiding Legal Hurdles While Staying in Tune with the Changing Definition of the Family, 16 Whittier L. Rev. 737, 739-742 (1995). On religious conscience legislation, see generally Douglas NeJaime & Reva B. Siegel, Conscience Wars: Complicity-Based Conscience Claims in Religion and Politics, 124 Yale L.J. 2516 (2015); Henry Bruinius, Indiana Religious Freedom Act: Does It Protect Faithful or Legalize Prejudice?, Christian Sci. Monitor, Mar. 24, 2015, http://www.csmonitor.com/USA/Society/2015/0324/Indiana-religious-freedom-act-Does-it-protect-faithful-or-legalize-prejudice-video.

c. Health

IN RE GUARDIANSHIP OF KOWALSKI (*KOWALSKI III*)

478 N.W.2d 790 (Minn. Ct. App. 1991)

DAVIES, Judge. . . .

Sharon Kowalski is 35 years old. On November 13, 1983, she suffered severe brain injuries in an automobile accident which left her in a wheelchair, impaired her ability to speak, and caused severe loss of short-term memory. At the time of the accident, Sharon was sharing a home in St. Cloud with her lesbian partner, appellant Karen Thompson. They had exchanged rings, named each other as insurance beneficiaries, and had been living together as a couple for four years. Sharon's parents were not aware of the lesbian relationship. . . .

In March of 1984, both Thompson and Sharon's father, Donald Kowalski, cross-petitioned for guardianship. Thompson, expecting that she would have certain visitation rights and input into medical decisions, agreed to the appointment of Mr. Kowalski as Sharon's guardian. The guardianship order, however, gave complete control of visitation to Kowalski, who subsequently received court approval to terminate Thompson's visitation rights on July 25, 1985. Kowalski immediately relocated Sharon from a nursing home in Duluth to one in Hibbing.

In May of 1988, Judge Robert Campbell ordered specialists at Miller-Dwan Medical Center to examine Sharon to determine her level of functioning and whether Sharon could express her wishes on visitation. The doctors concluded that Sharon wished to see Thompson, and the court permitted Thompson to reestablish visitation in January of 1989. The doctors also recommended in 1989 that Sharon be relocated to Trevilla at Robbinsdale, where she currently resides. After Sharon's move, Thompson was permitted to bring Sharon to her St. Cloud home for semi-monthly weekend visits.

In late 1988, Kowalski notified the court that, due to his own medical problems, he wished to be removed as Sharon's guardian. The court granted his request [and then Thompson filed a petition for appointment as successor guardian]. [At the hearing] Thompson called approximately 16 medical witnesses, [who] had first-hand knowledge of her condition and care. The court also heard testimony from three witnesses in opposition to Thompson's petition [including Karen Tomberlin, a Kowalski family friend]. These witnesses had no medical training, each had visited Sharon infrequently in recent years, and none had accompanied Sharon on any outings from the institution. Sharon's parents chose not to attend the hearing.

[The trial court denied Thompson's petition for guardianship, appointing Tomberlin instead. Thompson appealed. The Minnesota statute provides that the standard for appointment of a guardian is the best interests of the ward and enumerates the relevant criteria, discussed below.]

1. THE WARD'S EXPRESSED PREFERENCE

The court heard testimony from its appointed evaluation team at Miller-Dwan about Sharon's ability to express a reliable preference as to where and with whom she wanted to be. [T]he doctor overseeing the evaluation submitted the following recommendation to the court:

> We believe Sharon Kowalski has shown areas of potential and ability to make rational choices in many areas of her life and she has consistently indicated a desire to return home. And by that, she means to St. Cloud to live with Karen Thompson again. Whether that is possible is still uncertain as her care will be difficult and burdensome. We think she deserves the opportunity to try.

All the professional witnesses concurred. . . .

The three lay witnesses who opposed Thompson's petition were skeptical that Sharon could reliably express her wishes, saying that Sharon changed her mind too often to believe what she said, given her impaired short-term memory.

Despite the uncontradicted medical testimony about Sharon's capability to make choices in her life, the trial court concluded that Sharon could not express a reliable preference for guardianship. This court finds that, in the absence of contradictory evidence about Sharon's decision-making capacity from a professional or anyone in daily contact with her, the trial court's conclusion was clearly erroneous. . . .

2. PETITIONER'S QUALIFICATIONS

The medical professionals were all asked about Thompson's qualifications with respect to the statutory criteria. The testimony was consistent that Thompson: (1) achieves outstanding interaction with Sharon; (2) has extreme interest and commitment in promoting Sharon's welfare; (3) has an exceptional current understanding of Sharon's physical and mental status and needs, including appropriate rehabilitation; and (4) is strongly equipped to attend to Sharon's social and emotional needs.

Sharon's caretakers described how Thompson has been with Sharon three or more days per week, actively working with her in therapy and daily care. They described Thompson's detailed knowledge of Sharon's condition, changes, and needs.

The doctors unanimously testified that their long-term goal for Sharon's recovery is to assist her in returning to life outside an institution. It is undisputed that Thompson is the only person willing or able to care for Sharon outside an institution. In fact, Thompson has built a fully handicap-accessible home near St. Cloud in the hope that Sharon will be able to live there. On the other hand, Sharon's sister testified that none of her relatives is able to care for Sharon at home, and that her parents can no longer take Sharon for overnight visits. Tomberlin testified that she is not willing or able to care for Sharon at home and is in a position only to supervise Sharon's needs in an institution. . . .

The medical witnesses also testified about Thompson's effectiveness with Sharon's rehabilitation. They all agreed that Sharon can be stubborn and will often refuse to cooperate in therapy. They testified, however, that Thompson is best able to get Sharon motivated to work through the sometimes painful therapy. . . .

[The appellate court concludes that the trial court findings that Sharon's long-term care should take place in a neutral setting, such as a nursing home, and that

Karen Thompson was incapable of providing necessary health care at her home was] directly contradicted by the testimony of Sharon's doctors and other care providers.]

3. THE COURT'S CHOICE OF A "NEUTRAL" GUARDIAN

The trial court recognized Thompson and Sharon as a "family of affinity" and acknowledged that Thompson's continued presence in Sharon's life was important. In its guardianship decision, however, the court responded to the Kowalski family's steadfast opposition to Thompson being named guardian. Debra Kowalski [Sharon's sister] testified that her parents would refuse ever to visit Sharon if Thompson is named guardian. The trial court likened the situation to a "family torn asunder into opposing camps," and concluded that a neutral third party was needed as guardian.

The record does not support the trial court's conclusion that choosing a "neutral" third party is now necessary. Thompson testified that she is committed to reaching an accommodation with the Kowalskis whereby they could visit with Sharon in a neutral setting or in their own home. . . . Thompson's appointment as guardian would not, of itself, result in the family ceasing to visit Sharon. The Kowalskis are free to visit their daughter if they wish. It is not the court's role to accommodate one side's threatened intransigence, where to do so would deprive the ward of an otherwise suitable and preferred guardian.

The court seized upon Tomberlin as a neutral party in this case. This decision, however, is not supported by sufficient evidence in the record as to either Tomberlin's suitability for guardianship or her neutrality. [G]iven that Tomberlin rarely visited Sharon, it is unlikely that [the] witnesses would have been able to comment knowledgeably on Tomberlin's qualifications. . . . There was equally little evidence establishing Tomberlin's neutrality in this case. . . . Tomberlin lives near the Kowalskis and helped facilitate the appearance at the hearing of [the witnesses] in opposition to Thompson. Both in her deposition and at the hearing, Tomberlin testified that her first and primary goal as guardian was to relocate Sharon to the Iron Range, close to her family. This testimony undermines the one "qualification" relied on by the trial court in appointing Tomberlin—her role as an impartial mediator.

4. COURT-IDENTIFIED DEFICIENCIES IN APPELLANT'S PETITION

. . . The court found fault with Thompson on several issues the court viewed as contrary to Sharon's best interest. [T]he court suggested that Thompson's statement to the family and to the media that she and Sharon are lesbians was an invasion of privacy, perhaps rising to the level of an actionable tort. The court also took issue with Thompson taking Sharon to public events, including some gay and lesbian-oriented gatherings and other community events where Thompson and Sharon were featured guests. Finally, the court concluded that Thompson's solicitation of legal defense funds and her testimony that she had been involved in other relationships since Sharon's accident raised questions of conflicts of interest with Sharon's welfare.

The record does not support the trial court's concern on any of these issues. [First,] Sharon's doctor testified that it was in Sharon's best interest for Thompson to reveal the nature of their relationship promptly after the accident because it is crucial for doctors to understand who their patient was prior to the accident, including that patient's sexuality.

Second, there was no evidence offered at the hearing to suggest that Sharon is harmed or exploited by her attendance at public events. In fact, the court authorized Sharon to travel with Thompson to receive an award at the National Organization for Women's annual convention. A staff person who accompanied Sharon to one of these events testified that Sharon "had a great time" and interacted well with other people. . . .

Finally, there is no evidence in the record about a conflict of interest over Thompson's collection of defense funds or her other personal relationships. The evidence showed the money was raised in Thompson's own name to help defray the cost of years of litigation and that none of it was used for her personal expenses. Thompson testified that whatever extra money raised was used to purchase special equipment for Sharon, such as her voice machine, motorized wheelchair, hospital bed, and a special lift for transfers. . . .

Appellant also challenges the process by which Tomberlin was named guardian [specifically, that she] never submitted a formal petition and that the court never held a hearing on her qualifications. [T]his court is troubled by the trial court's failure to give notice and its naming of Tomberlin in this manner. . . . [I]t appears the trial court clearly abused its discretion in denying Thompson's petition and naming Tomberlin guardian instead. . . . We reverse the trial court and grant Thompson's petition. . . .

In the following excerpt, Karen Thompson describes her painful interactions with hospital personnel when she arrived at the hospital immediately after the car accident.

Casey Charles, The Sharon Kowalski Case: Lesbian and Gay Rights on Trial 16 (2003)

"Who will I say I am?" [Karen Thompson] asked herself, reading the instructions posed under the intercom [outside the intensive care unit]. Under the push-button intercom system to the left of the entrance, a set of regulations, posted by the hospital for the protection of its severely ill or injured patients, stated that only "family members" were allowed to visit patients. . . .

Trying to ignore the import of the regulations she had just finished reading, Thompson finally mustered enough courage to push the speaker button to ask

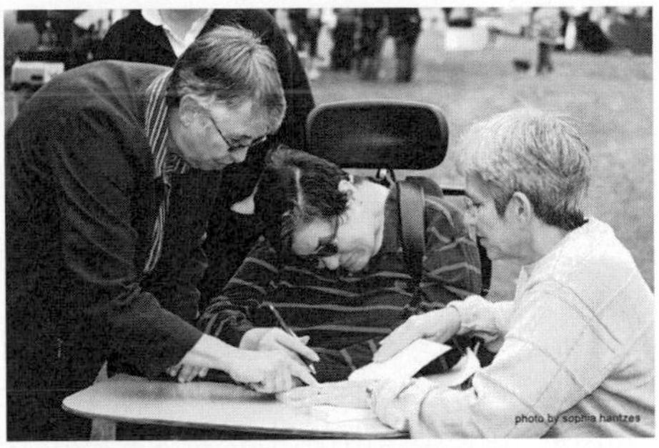

Sharon Kowalski (seated center), with her family: Karen Thompson (left) and Karen's current partner Patti Bresser (right) (photo by Sophia Hantzes)

if Sharon Kowalski was there and what her condition was. "What is your relationship?" a disembodied voice demanded over the intercom. Karen replied that she was a close friend who lived with Sharon. "I'm sorry," the speaker replied. "We can't give out information to anyone except immediate family members." Karen tried to explain, stating that she had come in place of Sharon's parents [who lived farther away], but the voice was adamant. Unsuccessful, Thompson walked in frustration from the intercom to the waiting room. The woman she loved for almost four years was probably less than a hundred feet away from her, but because she was not a family member, she was prevented from knowing whether Sharon was living or dying. . . .

Notes and Questions

1. Epilogue. After the accident, hostility developed between Karen and Sharon's parents because of Karen's frequent visits. On a psychologist's advice, Karen disclosed the women's relationship. The Kowalskis refused to believe Karen and responded by limiting her visitation privileges. Animosity continued as Karen questioned their choice of a nursing home rather than a brain injury treatment center. Sharon's parents ultimately moved their daughter to a distant nursing home where she was denied an electric wheelchair, typewriter (she could type short sentences), and visitation by friends, and was confined to bed. Contrary to guardianship requirements, her father refused competency testing for three years.

During the eight-year separation from Sharon, Karen fell in love with, and began living with, a nurse (Patti Bresser). Nonetheless, Karen remained devoted to her former partner. After the principal case, Sharon came to live with both women who still care for her in their home.

Kowalski was a landmark case in both the gay rights movement and the disability rights movement. It paved the way for the first successful marriage equality cases. See D. Kelly Weisberg, Karen Thompson's Role in the Movement for Marriage Equality, 25 Hastings Women's L.J. 3 (2014).

2. Functional versus formal definitions. The principal case, the third dispute between Karen and the Kowalskis, rests on a clash between a functional versus formal definition of "family." In *Kowalski I*, 382 N.W.2d 861 (Minn. Ct. App. 1986), Karen petitioned for appointment as guardian, contending that she was best suited based on her intimate relationship with Sharon as well as Sharon's preference. Sharon's father countered that his biological relationship and "unconditional parental love" supported his appointment. The trial court, influenced by a formal definition of "family," confirmed Sharon's father and gave him power to determine her visitors. In *Kowalski II*, 392 N.W.2d 310 (Minn. Ct. App. 1986), Karen unsuccessfully petitioned to find Mr. Kowalski in contempt for terminating her visitation and to remove him as guardian.

Both *Kowalski I* and *II* strongly affirm the role of biological relatives as guardians with broad powers over persons with disabilities. Moreover, both cases are laden with assumptions and stereotypes about the disabled (for example, reducing Sharon to a child, discounting her preferences, denying her sexuality) and about sexual orientation (for example, questioning Sharon's sexual preference and characterizing Karen as sexually abusive). How does *Kowalski III*, the principal case, address these issues?

3. Relevant factors. In a guardianship conflict between the family and a same-sex partner, what relevance, if any, should attach to:

a. The potential guardian's views of sexual orientation? Mr. Kowalski reportedly said, "On the farm and in the Army we called them queers and fruits" and also stated that Karen would never be granted guardianship because "there ain't a law in the United States that allows a lesbian relationship."[40] Are such views relevant in the selection of a guardian?

b. The manner in which the couple held themselves out? Sharon never told her family of her intimate relationship. Should that be relevant in the selection of her guardian?

c. The emotions experienced by the ward following the partner's visits? *Kowalski II* relied in part on Sharon's despondency following visits with Karen. Are these emotions relevant in the selection of her guardian? Would the battle over guardianship have differed had Sharon's partner been male? See generally Nancy J. Knauer, LGBT Issues and Adult Guardianship: A Comparative Perspective, in Comparative Perspectives on Guardianship (Kim Dayton ed., 2013) (explaining the manner in which seemingly neutral guardianship laws place LGBT families at risk).

4. Hospital visitation. As the above excerpt reveals, Karen Thompson was unable to visit her partner in the hospital because hospital policy permitted visitation by only designated "family members." In 2011, federal rules on hospital visitation went into effect, requiring hospitals that receive Medicare and Medicaid funding to inform patients (or attending friends or family members) of patients' rights to receive visitors of their choice. Further, the policy prohibits discrimination against visitors based on race, ethnicity, religion, sex, gender identity, sexual orientation, or disability. 75 Fed. Reg. 70,381-70,833.

The rules were prompted by the case of Janice Langbehn, who was barred from the hospital bedside of her partner of 18 years, Lisa Pond, after the latter suffered an aneurysm and died. See Langbehn v. Public Health Trust of Miami-Dade County, 661 F. Supp. 2d 1326 (S.D. Fla. 2009) (upholding denial of visitation by same-sex partner despite presentation of a valid designation of health care proxy). The new policy on hospital visitation does not provide a private cause of action or

---

[40]. Nancy Livingston, A Bitter Love Triangle: The Fight between Family and Lover to Control a Woman's Future, S.F. Chron., Sept. 11, 1988 (This World), at 10.

sanctions. What is the impact of *Obergefell* on the right to hospital visitation for same-sex partners?

5. Medical decisionmaking. Another difficulty faced by Karen Thompson after her partner's accident was her inability to acquire information about Sharon's medical condition and to make medical decisions for her (as the above excerpt reveals). What might cohabitants do, prior to incapacity, to ensure that they play a role in medical decisionmaking for each other? Will the advent of marriage equality obviate the need for same-sex couples—married and/or unmarried—to execute documents to guarantee their role in medical decisionmaking for each other? Why might Karen Thompson have commented about medical decisionmaking for same-sex partners, "While marriage for same-sex couples can help legitimize our relationships, it is not enough"?[41]

Many states now broaden common law preferences for family members to permit an incompetent to designate a proxy decisionmaker by means of a durable power of attorney for health care decisionmaking. Such a designation is especially important for unmarried couples.

In 2011, the federal Centers for Medicare and Medicaid Services issued a memorandum clarifying the rights of patients in hospitals receiving federal funding to delegate medical decisionmaking to persons of their choice.

6. Disposition of the body. Another health care-related problem arises after death regarding disposition of a partner's remains. Statutes give decisionmaking preference to a deceased's spouse (and afterwards to children, parents, and siblings). As a result, conflicts may arise between a surviving partner and relatives if the deceased partner was not married.

d. Familial Benefits: Housing and Inheritance

BRASCHI v. STAHL ASSOCIATES CO.

543 N.E.2d 49 (N.Y. 1989)

TITONE, Judge. . . .

Appellant Miguel Braschi was living with Leslie Blanchard in a rent-controlled apartment located at 405 East 54th Street from the summer of 1975 until Blanchard's death in September of 1986. [R]espondent, Stahl Associates Company, the owner of the apartment building, served a notice to cure on appellant contending that he was a mere licensee with no right to occupy the apartment since only Blanchard was the tenant of record [and threatened eviction proceedings]. The present dispute arises because the term "family" is not defined in the rent-control code and the legislative history is devoid of any specific reference to the noneviction provision. All that is known is the legislative purpose underlying the enactment of the rent-control laws as a whole.

---

[41]. 100 Women We Love, Go Magazine, June 15, 2012, http://www.gomag.com/article/100_women_we_love3/68.

Rent control was enacted to address a "serious public emergency" created by "an acute shortage in dwellings," which resulted in "speculative, unwarranted, and abnormal increases in rents" (L. 1946 ch. 274, codified, as amended, at McKinney's Uncons. Laws of N.Y. §8581 et seq.). These measures were designed to regulate and control the housing market so as to "prevent exactions of unjust, unreasonable, and oppressive rents and rental agreements and to forestall profiteering, speculation and other disruptive practices tending to produce threats to the public health [and] to prevent uncertainty, hardship and dislocation" (id.). [The legislation was] initially designed as an emergency measure to alleviate the housing shortage attributable to the end of World War II. . . .

To accomplish its goals, the Legislature recognized that not only would rents have to be controlled, but that evictions would have to be regulated and controlled as well. Hence, [New York City Rent and Eviction Regulations provide for] noneviction protection to those occupants who are either the "surviving spouse of the deceased tenant or *some other member of the deceased tenant's family* who has been living with the tenant [of record]" (emphasis supplied).

[R]espondent argues that the term "family member" as used in 9 NYCRR 2204.6(d) should be construed, consistent with this State's intestacy laws, to mean relationships of blood, consanguinity and adoption in order to effectuate the over-all goal of orderly succession to real property. Under this interpretation, only those entitled to inherit under the laws of intestacy would be afforded noneviction protection. [R]espondent relies on our decision in Matter of Robert Paul P., 471 N.E.2d 424 [(N.Y.1984)], arguing that since the relationship between appellant and Blanchard has not been accorded legal status by the Legislature, it is not entitled to the protections of section 2204.6(d). . . . Finally, respondent contends that our construction of the term "family member" should be guided by the recently enacted noneviction provision of the Rent Stabilization Code (9 NYCRR 2523.5[a], [b][1], [2]) [which includes a precise definition of family members based on the existence of marital or blood ties].

However, as we have continually noted, the rent-stabilization system is different from the rent-control system in that the former is a less onerous burden on the property owner, and thus the provisions of one cannot simply be imported into the other. Respondent's reliance on Matter of Robert Paul P. is also misplaced, since [that case] was based solely on the purposes of the adoption laws and has no bearing on the proper interpretation of a provision in the rent-control laws.

We also reject respondent's argument that the purpose of the noneviction provision of the rent-control laws is to control the orderly succession to real property in a manner similar to that which occurs under our State's intestacy laws. The noneviction provision does not concern succession to real property but rather is a means of protecting a certain class of occupants from the sudden loss of their homes. . . . Moreover, such a construction would be inconsistent with the purposes of the rent-control system as a whole, since it would afford protection to distant blood relatives who actually had but a superficial relationship with the deceased tenant while denying that protection to unmarried lifetime partners. . . .

Contrary to all of these arguments, we conclude that the term family, as used in 9 NYCRR 2204.6(d), should not be rigidly restricted to those people who have formalized their relationship by obtaining, for instance, a marriage certificate or an adoption order. The intended protection against sudden eviction should not rest on fictitious legal distinctions or genetic history, but instead should find its foundation in the reality of family life. In the context of eviction, a more realistic, and certainly equally valid, view of a family includes two adult lifetime partners whose relationship is long term and characterized by an emotional and financial commitment and interdependence.

This view comports both with our society's traditional concept of "family" and with the expectations of individuals who live in such nuclear units. In fact, Webster's Dictionary defines "family" first as "a group of people united by certain convictions or common affiliation" (Webster's Ninth New Collegiate Dictionary 448 [1984]). Hence, it is reasonable to conclude that, in using the term "family," the Legislature intended to extend protection to those who reside in households having all of the normal familial characteristics. Appellant Braschi should therefore be afforded the opportunity to prove that he and Blanchard had such a household. . . .

The determination as to whether an individual is entitled to noneviction protection should be based upon an objective examination of the relationship of the parties. In making this assessment, the lower courts of this State have looked to a number of factors, including the exclusivity and longevity of the relationship, the level of emotional and financial commitment, the manner in which the parties have conducted their everyday lives and held themselves out to society, and the reliance placed upon one another for daily family services. These factors are most helpful, although it should be emphasized that the presence or absence of one or more of them is not dispositive since it is the totality of the relationship as evidenced by the dedication, caring and self-sacrifice of the parties which should, in the final analysis, control. Appellant's situation provides an example of how the rule should be applied.

Appellant and Blanchard lived together as permanent life partners for more than 10 years. They regarded one another, and were regarded by friends and family, as spouses. The two men's families were aware of the nature of the relationship, and they regularly visited each other's families and attended family functions together, as a couple. Even today, appellant continues to maintain a relationship with Blanchard's niece, who considers him an uncle.

In addition to their interwoven social lives, appellant clearly considered the apartment his home. He lists the apartment as his address on his driver's license and passport, and receives all his mail at the apartment address. Moreover, appellant's tenancy was known to the building's superintendent and doormen, who viewed the two men as a couple.

Financially, the two men shared all obligations, including a household budget. The two were authorized signatories of three safe-deposit boxes, they maintained joint checking and savings accounts, and joint credit cards. In fact, rent was often paid with a check from their joint checking account. Additionally, Blanchard executed a power of attorney in appellant's favor so that appellant could make necessary decisions—financial, medical and personal—for him during his illness. Finally, appellant was the named beneficiary of Blanchard's life insurance policy, as well as the primary legatee and coexecutor of Blanchard's estate. Hence, a court examining these facts could reasonably conclude that these men were much more than mere roommates. [The court concludes that appellant has demonstrated a likelihood of success on the merits and remands the case.]

NORTH DAKOTA FAIR HOUSING COUNCIL v. PETERSON

625 N.W.2d 551 (N.D. 2001)

SANDSTROM, Justice.

In 1999, an unmarried couple tried to rent from David and Mary Peterson. The Petersons refused because the unmarried couple were seeking to cohabit. The North Dakota Fair Housing Council and Robert and Patricia Kippen—the unmarried couple, who had since married—sued, claiming housing discrimination in violation of the North Dakota Human Rights Act. . . . We are asked to decide whether refusing to rent to an unmarried couple because they are seeking to cohabit violates the discriminatory housing practices provision of the North Dakota Human Rights Act, N.D.C.C. §14-02.4-12 [as follows].

> It is a discriminatory practice for an owner of rights to housing or real property [to]:
>
> Refuse to transfer an interest in real property or housing accommodation to a person because of race, color, religion, sex, national origin, age, physical or mental disability, or status with respect to marriage or public assistance. . . .

We have not previously addressed the relationship between N.D.C.C. §§12.1-20-10 [the prohibition of cohabitation] and 14-02.4-12 [above]. The issue, however, has been addressed in a formal attorney general's opinion and in two federal district court opinions. We begin with a review of the history of the legislation.

North Dakota has prohibited unlawful cohabitation since statehood. The provision, as codified in 1895, remained essentially unchanged until the 1970s. . . . The 1971 legislative assembly provided for an interim committee to draft a new criminal code. The interim committee considered whether to recommend repeal of the prohibition on unlawful cohabitation. . . . Because sexual offenses were a controversial portion of the proposed new criminal code, alternative provisions were submitted to the 1973 legislature in three separate bills. All three bills contain the same language on unlawful cohabitation [with somewhat different penalties]. The new criminal code [retaining the prohibition] was approved by the 1973 legislature. . . .

The 1983 legislature adopted the North Dakota Human Rights Act. The legislative history reflects no discussion of the cohabitation statute.

The issue of a claimed conflict between the cohabitation statute and the Human Rights Act was presented to the attorney general in 1990. In a formal opinion, the attorney general wrote: . . .

> The North Dakota Supreme Court has not ruled on the apparent conflict between N.D.C.C. §§14-02.4-12's protection of a person's right to housing notwithstanding

> the person's marital status, and N.D.C.C. §12.1-20-10's prohibition against allowing unmarried couples to live as a married couple. However, there has been similar litigation in other states whose laws prohibit both cohabitation and discriminatory housing practices based on marital statutes. In McFadden v. Elma Country Club, 613 P.2d 146 (Wash. Ct. App. 1980), the court held that, notwithstanding a statute prohibiting discrimination based upon marital status, a country club could refuse to admit to membership an unmarried woman cohabiting with a man. The court's holding was based upon the fact the statute prohibiting cohabitation was not repealed when the discrimination statute was enacted. This fact the court said "would vitiate any argument that the legislature intended 'marital status' discrimination to include discrimination on the basis of a couple's unwed cohabitation." Id. at 150.
>
> As in the *McFadden* case, N.D.C.C. §12.1-20-10 was not repealed when N.D.C.C. §14-02.4-12 was enacted. Thus, the continuing existence of the unlawful cohabitation statute after the enactment of N.D.C.C. §14-02.4-12 vitiates "any argument that the legislature intended 'marital status' discrimination to include discrimination on the basis of a couple's unwed cohabitation." *McFadden, supra, at 150.* . . .

Attorney General's Opinion 90-12 (1990).

In 1991, House Bill 1403, a measure to repeal the cohabitation statute, was introduced, with the legislator who had requested the 1990 attorney general's opinion as the primary sponsor. . . . The House of Representatives defeated the bill by a vote of 27 yeas and 78 nays.

In 1999, the United States District Court for North Dakota decided a case involving the alleged conflict between the cohabitation statute and the Human Rights Act and concluded it was not unlawful to refuse to rent to an unmarried couple seeking to cohabit. . . . North Dakota Fair Housing Council, Inc. v. Halder, No. A1-98-077 (D.N.D. 1999). In 2000, the United States District Court for North Dakota decided a suit similar to this one brought by the Housing Council. North Dakota Fair Housing Council v. Woeste, No. A1-99-116 (D.N.D. 2000). The federal court, analyzing North Dakota law and distinguishing federal cases relied on by the Housing Council, concluded the Housing Council lacked standing to sue under the North Dakota Human Rights Act. . . .

With this historical background, we turn to the framework for analyzing statutes and claimed conflicts between statutes. . . . We now consider the meaning of the cohabitation statute and the meaning of the Human Rights Act discriminatory housing practices provision. . . . North Dakota's cohabitation statute, N.D.C.C. §12.1-20-10, states:

> A person is guilty of a class B misdemeanor if he or she lives openly and notoriously with a person of the opposite sex as a married couple without being married to the other person.

The 1973 amendment of the statute removed the language "cohabits as husband or wife" and added "lives openly and notoriously with a person of the opposite sex as a married couple."

Varying definitions of cohabitation exist. The 1996 edition of Merriam Webster's Dictionary of Law defines cohabit as "to live together as a married couple or in the manner of a married couple." The 1999 edition of Black's Law Dictionary, at page 254, defines cohabitation as "[t]he fact or state of living together, esp. as partners in life, usu. with the suggestion of sexual relations." Notorious cohabitation is the "act of a man and a woman openly living together under circumstances that make the arrangement illegal under statutes that are now rarely enforced."[4] Id. The Minnesota Supreme Court has defined "cohabit" as living "together in a sexual relationship when not legally married." State by Cooper v. French, 460 N.W.2d 2, 4 n.1 (Minn. 1990) (citing The American Heritage Dictionary of the English Language 259 (1980)). . . .

The Housing Council asserts that North Dakota has decriminalized all sexual relations among consenting adults. The assertion is contradicted by the cohabitation statute as well as the criminal penalties for adultery, bigamy, prostitution, or incest, notwithstanding the consent of the parties. . . .

At issue is the term "status with respect to marriage," which is undefined under the Human Rights Act. Analyzing other definitions under North Dakota law, the district court concluded the "Legislature intended the phrase to mean being married, single, separated or divorced." The Housing Council and the Kippens argue "status with respect to marriage" is simple: a person is either married or not married. Although it is unlawful to deny housing based solely on whether a person is or is not married, the relevant inquiry is whether a person is divorced, widowed, or separated, rather than simply married or unmarried.

The Petersons argue that although it is true that under the discriminatory housing provision a person cannot be discriminated against because of marital status, the Kippens were denied housing not because they were single, but because they were unmarried and were seeking to live together as if they were married. . . .

Numerous courts have addressed language similar to "status with respect to marriage," the language at issue here. Those courts disagree regarding the appropriate weight to give to words with an import similar to "status with respect to marriage." In McCready v. Hoffius, 564 N.W.2d 493, 495-96 (Mich. Ct. App. 1997), the court differentiated marital status from conduct by concluding the term "marital status" was legislatively intended to prohibit discrimination "based on *whether* a person is married" (quoting Miller v. C.A. Muer Corp., 362 N.W.2d 650 (Mich. 1984)).

The Wisconsin Supreme Court has also concluded [that] refusal to rent to unmarried tenants who choose to live together is based on conduct rather than status. See County of Dane v. Norman, 497 N.W.2d 714 (Wis. 1993). On the other hand, Alaska, Massachusetts, and California have concluded [that] refusal to rent to unmarried cohabitants is based upon status rather than conduct [Smith v. Fair Employment & Housing Comm'n, 913 P.2d 909 (Cal. 1996); Swanner v. Anchorage Equal Rights Comm'n, 874 P.2d 274 (Alaska 1994); Attorney General v. Desilets, 636 N.E.2d 233 (Mass. 1994)]. . . .

When the legislature enacted the Human Rights Act, it is presumed to have known of the existing criminal cohabitation statute. [B]y suggesting the Human Rights Act requires that housing be provided regardless of compliance with the criminal code, the Housing Council and the Kippens are asking us to repeal or to

4. Although it is argued cohabitation statutes are rarely enforced, this Court has held the lack of enforcement to be of no significance.

give new meaning to the cohabitation statute. We are then confronted with the well-established rule precluding amendment or repeal of legislation by implication. . . . The cohabitation statute and the discriminatory housing provision are harmonized by recognizing that the cohabitation statute regulates conduct, not status. The opposite interpretation would render the prohibition against cohabitation meaningless.

Like Michigan, Wisconsin, and Minnesota, we conclude these two provisions may be harmonized while still giving each of them full effect. It is unlawful to openly and notoriously live together as husband and wife without being married. It is unlawful to deny housing based on a person's status with respect to marriage (i.e., married, single, divorced, widowed, or separated). It is not unlawful to deny housing to an unmarried couple seeking to openly and notoriously live together as husband and wife. . . . Under the words of the statute, the rules of statutory construction, and the legislative, administrative, and judicial history, we conclude it is not an unlawful discriminatory practice under N.D.C.C. §14-02.4-12 to refuse to rent to unmarried persons seeking to cohabit. . . .

Notes and Questions

1. Functional definition. *Braschi*, like *Graves* (and *Dunphy* before it), adopts a functional definition of "family." The significance of this definition for the recognition of the gay and lesbian rights was monumental. See Paris R. Baldacci, Protecting Gay and Lesbian Families from Eviction from Their Homes: The Quest for Equality for Gay and Lesbian Families in Braschi v. Stahl Associates, 13 Tex Wesleyan L. Rev. 619 (2007).

2. Familial characteristics. *Braschi* reasons that the legislature intended to protect those who reside in households "having all of the normal familial characteristics." Which "normal familial characteristics" did the Braschi household exhibit? Which did it not? Should the state define and impose a legal meaning of "family" on all persons without exception, or should the law honor private choices, so long as a given unit acts like a family and performs familial functions? See generally Martha L. Minow, Redefining Families: Who's In and Who's Out?, 62 U. Colo. L. Rev. 269 (1991); Note, Looking for a Family Resemblance: The Limits of the Functional Approach to the Legal Definition of Family, 104 Harv. L. Rev. 1640 (1991).

3. Criticisms of factors. *Braschi* suggests factors to determine individual qualifications as a "family member" for noneviction protection. Do you agree with the dissent that these factors "produce[] an unworkable test that is subject to abuse" and lead to extended litigation "focusing on such intangibles as the strength and duration of the relationship and the extent of the emotional and financial interdependency"? Does the need for proof of financial interdependence cause difficulty for partners who keep their finances separate, or for low-income cohabitants?

Does *Braschi* sanction legal distinctions between those same-sex couples who do and those who do not fit the traditional family model? For example, Professor Mary Anne Case charges that several factors required of gay couples (such as sexual fidelity, sharing a domicile, and commingling finances) are not evidence of commitment that is similarly required for married couples.[42] See also Picon v. O.D.C. Assocs., No. 86-22894 (Sup. Ct. N.Y. County Jan. 28, 1991) (minimizing relevance of sexual affair for surviving tenant's occupancy claim because "peccadillos of this nature seem not to be uncommon, even in the marital life of normally married couples"). Do you agree with these criticisms?

4. Family definition. Why does the marital couple serve as the model for expanded definitions of "family"? Should the law also recognize nonconjugal relationships when providing familial benefits? If so, what nonconjugal relationships should be covered? For which benefits?

How does the public understand the term "family"? A study of attitudes about marriage and the family reveals that the public has an expansive view. The majority of the public believes that all of the following constitute a family: a single parent and child, an unmarried couple living together with a child, and a gay or lesbian couple raising a child.

However, if a cohabiting couple is childless, a majority believes that they are *not* a family—although if the childless couple is married, the majority do consider them to be a family.[43] Why might the presence of a child or the existence of marriage convey the image that the parties constitute a "family"?

5. Landlord-tenant law. Social forces historically play a role in the development of landlord-tenant law. For example, the civil rights movement and the Vietnam War influenced the "revolution" in tenant rights in the late 1960s and 1970s. The AIDS epidemic influenced the result in *Braschi*. See generally Edward H. Rabin, The Revolution in Residential Landlord-Tenant Law: Causes and Consequences, 69 Cornell L. Rev. 517, 546, 550 (1984).

6. Third parties. *Braschi*, like *Graves*, presents a dispute not of cohabitants inter se (as in *Marvin* and *Gonzalez*), but rather a dispute involving third parties. Does the presence of third parties dictate different treatment of cohabitants in the housing and tort contexts? Further, how relevant was the fact that *Braschi* did *not* present the court with two openly gay litigants in a dispute between themselves?[44]

7. Housing discrimination: Marital status. Unmarried couples face housing discrimination by landlords, real estate agents, and property owners who reject their applications or charge higher rent. They also confront discrimination by banks that sometimes require partners to have a higher income to qualify for a loan or that impose higher interest rates.[45] Only about half the states ban housing discrimination based on marital status. Even in some of these states, it is not clear

[42]. Case, supra note [35], at 1665.

[43]. Pew Research Ctr., Social and Demographic Trends Report, The Decline of Marriage and Rise of New Families, Executive Summary (Nov. 18, 2010), http://www.pewsocialtrends.org/2010/11/18/the-decline-of-marriage-and-rise-of-new-families/.

[44]. For a discussion of the stereotypes in *Braschi* about sexual orientation, see William Rubenstein, We Are Family: A Reflection on the Search for Legal Recognition of Lesbian and Gay Relationships, 8 J.L. & Pol'y 89 (1991). Rubenstein, a law professor at UCLA, was Braschi's attorney. For an in-depth account of the case, see Carlos A. Ball, From the Closet to the Courtroom, Five LGBT Rights Lawsuits That Have Changed Our Nation (2010).

[45]. Nat'l Fair Housing Alliance, Modernizing the Fair Housing Act for the 21st Century 14 (Apr. 11, 2013), www.nationalfairhousing.org/.../33/2013_fair_housing_trends_report.pdf.

that the statutory protection applies to *unmarried* couples rather than simply to those who are single, married, or divorced. Courts in only a few states (i.e., Alaska, California, Massachusetts, Michigan, and New Jersey) have ruled explicitly that the term "marital status" in state housing discrimination laws applies to unmarried couples.[46]

In states without protection against housing discrimination, landlords can legally refuse to rent to unmarried couples. Some states have express provisions that permit landlords to discriminate in this manner. See, e.g., Conn. Gen. Stat. Ann. § 46a-64c(b)(2) (provisions about housing discrimination "on the basis of marital status shall not be construed to prohibit the denial of a dwelling to a man or a woman who are both unrelated by blood and not married to each other"). See also Hawkins v. Community Bank of Raymore, 761 F.3d 937 (8th Cir. 2014) (questioning whether spousal guaranty requirements for residential loans constitute marital status discrimination pursuant to Equal Credit Opportunity Act), *cert granted,* 135 S. Ct. 1492 (2015).

8. Housing discrimination: Sexual orientation. Until recently, the federal Fair Housing Act (42 U.S.C. §§3601–3619) prohibited the refusal to rent or sell a dwelling *only* on the grounds of race, color, religion, sex, familial status (which pertains to the presence of children under age 18), or national origin. In 2012, the Department of Housing and Urban Development (HUD) issued regulations that (1) changed the definition of "family" to include families regardless of "marital status, sexual orientation, or gender identity"; (2) prohibit owners receiving HUD assistance from inquiring as to sexual orientation; and (3) prohibit consideration of sexual orientation when determining awards of mortgage loans insured by the Federal Housing Administration (FHA).[47] On the state level, of the 22 states that prohibit housing discrimination on the basis of sexual orientation, 17 also ban housing discrimination based on gender identity.[48]

9. Freedom of religion defense. *Peterson* addresses whether landlords' refusal to rent to an unmarried couple violates state law. The court wrestled with (1) whether the statutory protection regarding "status with respect to marriage" included nonmarital cohabitation, and (2) how to resolve the conflict between the state prohibition on cohabitation between unmarried persons and the state anti-housing discrimination provision. How did the court resolve each issue?

In 2005, the North Dakota House of Representatives upheld its prohibition against cohabitation based on the need to "send a message" to young people and to counter attacks on the "concept of traditional marriage."[49] However, in 2007, the legislature repealed the statute. S.L. 2007, ch. 131, § 4, eff. Aug. 1, 2007.

---

[46]. Ralph Warner et al., A Legal Guide for Unmarried Couples 119 (2013).

[47]. Equal Access to Housing in HUD Programs Regardless of Sexual Orientation or Gender Identity, 77 Fed. Reg. 5662 (Feb. 3, 2012) (to be codified at 24 C.F.R. pts. 5, 200, 203, 236, 400, 570, 574, 882, 891, and 982). HUD recently announced a settlement in a case involving a lesbian couple who were denied a mortgage in violation of HUD's new Equal Access rule (77 Fed. Reg. 5661). Jenna Greene, BofA Settles Claim of Bias Against Same-Sex Mortgage-Seekers, Legal Intelligencer, Jan. 7, 2013.

[48]. U.S. Dept. of Housing & Urban Dev., Ending Housing Discrimination against Lesbian, Gay, Bisexual and Transgender Individuals and their Families, http://portal.hud.gov/hudportal/HUD?src=/program_offices/fair_housing_equal_opp/LGBT_Housing_Discrimination.

[49]. Brenden Timpe, Cigarettes OK; Shacking up, No Way: Legislature Deals with Rules for Young Adults, Grand Forks Herald, Jan. 20, 2005, at A2.

Peterson does not elaborate on the landlords' reason for refusing to rent to the particular unmarried couple. Presumably, the landlords had moral objections. Suppose, however, that a landlord's refusal to rent to unmarried couples is based on religious grounds. Is the First Amendment a defense to violation of state housing discrimination law? See, e.g., Smith v. Fair Emp't & Hous. Comm'n, 913 P.2d 909 (Cal. 1996) (holding that state prohibition against discrimination based on "marital status" prohibits refusal to rent to unmarried couples on religious grounds); Swanner v. Anchorage Equal Rights Comm'n, 874 P.2d 274 (Alaska 1994) (accord). What might explain the different results in *Peterson* and *Smith*? Does the Supreme Court's decision in *Hobby Lobby* (discussed in Chapter I) have an impact on the issue?

Problem

Jill and Michael move together into a rent-stabilized apartment in New York. They live together in an exclusive relationship for 16 years. They represent to others that they are married. They pool their earnings. However, because Jill's earnings as a masseuse are small, Michael (who works in a family-owned business) pays almost all their expenses. They frequently travel together. Jill defines herself as "a stereotypical housewife"—doing all the cleaning and laundry, washing dishes, making the beds, and shopping. Jill does not file tax returns because she does not earn enough income. She does not register to vote. The address on her driver's license is her brother's address in Texas, which she never got around to changing. After the relationship ends, Michael still stays at the apartment occasionally when he is in town. Four years later, he fully vacates the apartment. The landlord then seeks to evict Jill. She claims that she is entitled to succeed to Michael's tenancy in the apartment because of the familial relationship.

For eviction protection, the state code requires that the claimant maintain a family-type relationship (including emotional and financial interdependence) with the tenant-of-record for the two-year period immediately preceding the tenant's permanent vacatur of the dwelling. Should *Braschi* apply if the partners' relationship ends by dissolution and not death? What guideposts should a court use to identify the "end" of a relationship for determination of eligibility for such housing benefits? See 72A Realty Assocs. v. Kutno, 838 N.Y.S.2d 334 (Sup. Ct. 2007).

BECKWITH v. DAHL

141 Cal. Rptr. 3d 142 (Ct. App. 2012)

O'Leary, P.J.

. . . [Brent] Beckwith and his partner, Marc Christian MacGinnis, were in a long-term, committed relationship for almost 10 years. They leased an apartment together and were occasional business partners. MacGinnis had no children and his parents were deceased. His sister, Susan Dahl, with whom he had an estranged relationship, was his only other living family member. At some point during their relationship, MacGinnis showed Beckwith a will he had saved on his computer. The will stated that upon MacGinnis's death, his estate was to be divided equally between Beckwith and Dahl. MacGinnis never printed or signed the will.

In May 2009, MacGinnis's health began to decline. On May 25, 2009, MacGinnis was in the hospital awaiting surgery to repair holes in his lungs. He asked Beckwith to locate and print the will so he could sign it. Beckwith went to their home and looked for the will, but he could not find it. When Beckwith told MacGinnis that he could not locate the will, MacGinnis asked Beckwith to create a new will so he could sign it the next day. That night, Beckwith created a new will for MacGinnis using forms downloaded from the Internet [stating that the estate was to be equally divided between Beckwith and Dahl].

Before Beckwith presented the will to MacGinnis, he called Dahl to tell her about the will and e-mailed her a copy. Later that night, Dahl responded to Beckwith's e-mail stating: "'I really think we should look into a Trust for [MacGinnis]. There are far less regulations and it does not go through probate. The house and all property would be in *our names* and if something should happen to [MacGinnis] *we* could make decisions without it going to probate and the taxes are less on a trust rather than the normal inheritance tax. I have [two] very good friends [who] are attorneys and I will call them tonight.' [Emphasis added.]" After receiving the e-mail, Beckwith called Dahl to discuss the details of the living trust. Dahl told Beckwith not to present the will to MacGinnis for signature because one of her friends would prepare the trust documents for MacGinnis to sign "in the next couple [of] days." Beckwith did not present the will to MacGinnis.

Two days later, on May 27, MacGinnis had surgery on his lungs. Although the doctors informed Dahl there was a chance MacGinnis would not survive the surgery, the doctors could not discuss the matter with Beckwith since he was not a family member under the law. . . . After the surgery, MacGinnis was placed on a ventilator and his prognosis worsened. Six days later, Dahl, following the doctors' recommendations, removed MacGinnis from the ventilator. On June 2, 2009, MacGinnis died intestate. He left an estate worth over $1 million.

. . . Two weeks [later], Dahl opened probate in Los Angeles Superior Court. . . . Beckwith e-mailed Dahl [several times], asking about the probate proceedings. [Eventually] Dahl responded by e-mail, stating: "'Because [MacGinnis] died without a will, and the estate went into probate. I was made executor of his estate. The court then declared that his assets would go to his only surviving family member which is me.'" [At the hearing on the petition for final distribution of the estate], the probate judge found that Beckwith had no standing because he was "not a creditor of the estate" and he had "no intestate rights". . . .

[T]he threshold question before this court is whether California should recognize a tort remedy for [Intentional Interference with Expected Inheritance (IIEI)]. [Although California has not yet recognized the tort, 25 of the 42 states that considered it have validated it.] In addition, IIEI is outlined in section 774B of the Restatement Second of Torts. . . . In general, most states recognizing the tort adopt it with the following elements: (1) an expectation of receiving an inheritance; (2) intentional interference with that expectancy by a third party; (3) the interference was independently wrongful or tortious; (4) there was a reasonable certainty that, but for the interference, the plaintiff would have received the inheritance; and (5) damages. . . .

In order to decide whether a new tort cause of action should be recognized, we must consider the relevant policy considerations and balance the benefits of such recognition against any potential burdens and costs that recognition of the tort would bring. . . . [One concern is] that an expectancy in an inheritance is too speculative to warrant a tort remedy because the testator may have changed his mind notwithstanding any interference from a third party. However, where there is a strong probability that an expected inheritance would have been received absent the alleged interference, whether or not the decedent changed his mind is a question of fact necessary to prove an element of the tort and is not a reason to refuse to recognize the existence of the tort altogether. . . .

[W]e conclude that a court should recognize the tort of IIEI if it is necessary to afford an injured plaintiff a remedy. The integrity of the probate system and the interest in avoiding tort liability for inherently speculative claims are very important considerations. However, a court should not take the "drastic consequence of an absolute rule which bars recovery in all . . . cases[]" when a new tort cause of action can be defined in such a way so as to minimize the costs and burdens associated with it. . . . California case law in analogous contexts shields defendants from tort liability when the expectancy is too speculative. In addition, case law from other jurisdictions bars IIEI claims when an adequate probate remedy exists. By recognizing similar restrictions in IIEI actions, we strike the appropriate balance between respecting the integrity of the probate system, guarding against tort liability for inherently speculative claims, and protecting society's interests in providing a remedy for injured parties. . . .

[Next,] we turn to whether Beckwith sufficiently stated the cause of action [for IIEI] in his complaint. . . . Here, Beckwith alleged he had an expectancy in MacGinnis's estate that would have been realized but for Dahl's intentional interference. However, Beckwith did not allege Dahl directed any independently tortious conduct at MacGinnis. The only wrongful conduct alleged in Beckwith's complaint was Dahl's false promise to him. Accordingly, Beckwith's complaint failed to sufficiently allege the IIEI tort.

We must still decide "whether there is a reasonable possibility that the defect can be cured by amendment. . . ." Under the circumstances here, Beckwith did not have a fair opportunity to correct the deficiencies with regard to his IIEI cause of action. The trial court found Beckwith's IIEI cause of action insufficient on its face, based on its conclusion the tort was not legally recognized in California. Accordingly, the court did not inquire into the sufficiency of the factual allegations supporting the IIEI claim. In light of the subsequent guidance provided by this opinion, we think it is appropriate Beckwith be given an opportunity to amend his complaint to address, if possible, the defects we have pointed out. . . .

[The court next turns to Beckwith's claim of promissory fraud.] [W]e conclude Beckwith's complaint sufficiently alleged each of the elements of fraud with the requisite specificity and particularity. [I]n a promissory fraud action, to sufficiently allege defendant made a misrepresentation, the complaint must allege (1) the defendant made a representation of intent to perform some future action, i.e., the defendant made a promise, and (2) the defendant did not really have that intent at the time that the promise was made, i.e., the promise was false. . . .

Beckwith's complaint alleged that on May 25, 2009, Dahl promised him, via e-mail and a telephone call, she would "promptly prepare and deliver trust documents to [MacGinnis] for him to sign, equally dividing [MacGinnis's] estate between [Dahl] and [Beckwith] in accordance with [MacGinnis's] wishes." The complaint also alleged, "[Dahl] did not intend to perform this promise when it was made." Thus, the complaint clearly and specifically alleged (1) who made the promise, (2) to whom the promise was made, (3) where and when the promise was made, (4) by what means the promise was made, and (5) that the promise was made with no intention of performance. Accordingly, Beckwith's complaint sufficiently alleged the first element of promissory fraud, a false promise. . . .

[The court then analyzes the requisite elements of intent, reliance, and damages.] Beckwith clearly alleged Dahl made specific promises to prepare and deliver trust documents to MacGinnis, but she did not intend to prepare them at all when she made that promise. . . . Further, Beckwith alleged that because of his "trust in [Dahl] to help effectuate [MacGinnis's] wishes, [Beckwith] reasonably relied on [Dahl's] representation that she would have trust documents prepared and that no will was necessary." Thus, Beckwith alleged he believed Dahl's promises to be true and in reliance on that belief, he did not present MacGinnis with the will. He sufficiently pled actual reliance. . . .

In addition to pleading actual reliance, the plaintiff must set "forth facts to show that his or her actual reliance on the representations was justifiable, so that the cause of the damage was the defendant's wrong and not the plaintiff's fault." . . . Here, the complaint alleged that "[g]iven the circumstances, [MacGinnis's] condition, [Beckwith's] emotionally vulnerable state, and [Beckwith's] trust in [Dahl] to help effectuate [MacGinnis's] wishes, [Beckwith] reasonably relied on [Dahl's] representations that she would have trust documents prepared and that no will was necessary." . . . . . . Beckwith has sufficiently alleged all of the elements of promissory fraud with the required specificity to state a claim. Accordingly, we conclude the trial court erred in sustaining Dahl's demurrer. . . .

Elaine Woo, Marc Christian MacGinnis Dies at 56; Rock Hudson's Ex-Lover

L.A. Times, Dec. 5, 2009, at 32

Marc Christian MacGinnis, who won a multimillion-dollar settlement in 1991 from the estate of his ex-lover, actor Rock Hudson, after convincing a jury Hudson had knowingly exposed him to AIDS, has died. He was 56.

Marc Christian MacGinnis, former partner of actor Rock Hudson

Known as Marc Christian, he died of pulmonary problems June 2 at Providence Saint Joseph Medical Center in Burbank. The details were confirmed Friday by his sister, Susan Dahl, who said she did not publicly announce his death earlier because of her brother's wish for privacy.

Christian, who went by his mother's maiden name, made headlines in 1985 when he sued Hudson's estate and his secretary, Mark Miller, for $10 million, alleging that he had suffered severe emotional distress after hearing on a news broadcast that the former matinee idol and television star had AIDS, which was claiming lives throughout the gay community.

Rock Hudson, actor and former partner of Marc Christian MacGinnis

Hudson was diagnosed in 1984 but did not publicly acknowledge his illness until July 1985; he died three months later at age 59. Christian tested negative for acquired immune deficiency syndrome several times after learning of Hudson's diagnosis but contended that the star put him at risk of contracting the disease by concealing his illness and continuing to have sexual relations with him. . . .

In 1989, a Los Angeles County Superior Court jury said Hudson had displayed "outrageous conduct" and awarded Christian $21.75 million in damages, later reduced to $5.5 million. The $5.5-million award was upheld by a state Court of Appeal, which called it just compensation for the "ultimate in personal horror, the fear of slow, agonizing death." After the California Supreme Court, citing requests from both sides in the dispute, decided not to hear the case, a private settlement was reached for an amount Christian later said was less than $6 million.

He was portrayed by Hudson estate lawyers as a gold-digging hustler and criticized in the gay community, which at the time had little understanding of the need for sexual responsibility.

"It was obviously a groundbreaking case," said Tammy Bruce, a former president of the National Organization for Women's Los Angeles chapter and an openly gay conservative talk-show host. "It was the first public acknowledgment that gay relationships are complicated, important, and that responsibility is attached to them. . . . A lot of people owe a great deal to that man and the way he handled it with particular grace, not only at the trial but in the years afterward."

Several years after the sensational case ended, Christian told *People* magazine that his purpose was "not to sleaze Rock. It was to say that if you have AIDS, you ought to tell your partner, whether you're a movie star or a postman." . . .

Christian met Hudson in late 1982 at a fundraiser for then-senatorial candidate Gore Vidal. . . . He and Hudson became lovers about five months later. By late 1983, they were living together in Hudson's Beverly Hills mansion.

When Hudson began losing weight and looking ill, he told Christian, who was about 27 years his junior, that he was merely dieting; later, associates said he was anorexic. Christian said he learned the true cause of his partner's increasing gauntness the way the rest of the world did—from a 1985 television broadcast from Paris, where Hudson had flown to seek treatment for AIDS. "I thought I was a dead man," Christian recalled thinking at the time.

He tested negative for the disease after several tests. Told by medical experts that the best treatment would cost $100,000 a year with a life expectancy of three years, he approached Hudson's managers after the actor's death and asked them to place $300,000 in a trust fund to cover his care if he developed AIDS, with the funds returning to the estate if he remained AIDS-free.

When the managers turned him down, "That's when he went to Marvin Mitchelson," the famous palimony attorney who filed the lawsuit against Hudson's estate, said Brent Beckwith, who was Christian's lover and best friend for nine years. . . .

Notes and Questions

1. **Inheritance law.** According to the general rule, unmarried cohabitants cannot inherit from their partners by intestate succession (i.e., when a person dies without a will). Nor do unmarried cohabitants have such "spousal" rights as the right to a family support allowance during estate administration, protection against disinheritance, priority in administration of the estate, and the right to control the disposition of the remains. Domestic partnership legislation in some states changes these results.

2. **Policy.** What policy arguments exist for and against allowing intestate succession by unmarried cohabitants? Should jurisdictions adopt a status-based approach or an intent-based approach? What difference would each approach have made in *Beckwith*?

3. **Holding.** What were Beckwith's legal theories? What elements did he have to prove? What legal obstacles did he face? What was he hoping to gain? Would it have made a difference in the outcome if Beckwith and MacGinnis had been registered partners? If they were an opposite-sex unmarried couple? Spouses? Why did the court recognize the tort?

What is the larger significance of the recognition of the tort of IIEI for family law generally and alternative families in particular? That is, to what extent is the case likely to benefit the LGBT community? See generally John C.P. Goldberg & Robert H. Sitkoff, Torts and Estates: Remedying Wrongful Interference with Inheritance, 65 Stanford L. Rev. 335 (2013).

4. **Meretricious relationships in Washington State.** Washington State was in the forefront of the movement to extend property rights to unmarried cohabitants *upon dissolution*. See Connell v. Francisco, 898 P.2d 831 (Wash. 1995) (adopting an equitable doctrine that confers property rights at dissolution for partners who have a "meretricious relationship" (a "stable, marital-like relationship where both parties cohabit with knowledge that a lawful marriage between them does not exist")). What are the policy arguments in favor of, and against, *restricting* the doctrine to dissolution? See also Olver v. Fowler, 168 P.3d 348 (Wash. 2007); Witt v. Young, 275 P.3d 1218 (Wash. Ct. App. 2012). The doctrine was later renamed the "committed intimate relationship" doctrine (discussed supra p. 403).

What information would you need to determine if MacGinnis and Beckwith shared the requisite "stable, marital-like relationship" under Washington State law? See Susan N. Gary, Adapting Intestacy Laws to Changing Families, 18 Law & Ineq. 1 (2000); E. Gary Spitko, An Accrual/Multi-Factor Approach to Intestate Inheritance Rights for Unmarried Committed Partners, 81 Or. L. Rev. 255 (2002) (both suggesting relevant factors).

5. **Adult adoption.** Adult adoption is another vehicle by which same-sex partners create a legally recognized relationship for inheritance purposes. Adult adoption generally requires only the parties' consent (unlike a child's adoption, which is predicated on the best interests standard). Almost all states permit adult adoption, but some traditionally imposed limitations (i.e., co-residence, consanguinity,

or age restrictions) that precluded gays or lesbians from adopting their partners. Would adoption have solved Beckwith's problem? Is adult adoption for same-sex partners still necessary after *Obergefell*?

In a much-publicized case, Olive Watson, a granddaughter of the founder of IBM, adopted her same-sex partner of 14 years, Patricia Spado, in Maine, where Watson's family owned a vacation home. When the couple broke up, Watson promised not to revoke the adoption. Watson family lawyers later attempted to abrogate the adoption, contending that it violated state residency requirements because Spado was not a Maine resident. However, the Maine Supreme Court upheld the adoption, construing the residency requirement liberally. Adoption of Spado, 912 A.2d 578 (Me. 2007). However, at a subsequent trial construing the terms of the Watson trust, a Connecticut probate court ruled that Spado was not a grandchild under the trust, based on the IBM founder's testamentary intent and his ignorance of the adoption. See Thomas B. Scheffey, IBM Heiress Case Pushes Legal Boundaries, Conn. L. Trib., Aug. 17, 2009, at 1.

6. Death benefits. Death benefits for surviving same-sex spouses of state employees traditionally were not available in states that did not recognize same-sex marriage. The same-sex partner of a deceased highway patrolman challenged this policy in Glossip v. Missouri Department of Transportation and Highway Patrol Employees' Retirement System (MPERS), 411 S.W.3d 796 (Mo. 2013), after his long-term partner died in the line of duty. Rejecting his claim, the Missouri Supreme Court concluded that the spousal limitation bore a reasonable relation to the legitimate state interests of administrative efficiency and the policy goal of ensuring support to dependent spouses who were economically dependent on the deceased, whereas no such duty of financial support exists for unmarried couples. What impact might *Obergefell* have on this case?

7. Estate planning for gay and lesbian clients. Over 25 years ago, Roberta Achtenberg (politician, gay rights activist, and civil rights attorney) gave the following advice about estate planning to same-sex couples. How much of her advice is still sound today?

> Early in the estate planning process, the lawyer should inquire as to the client's concerns about a will contest and should discuss the grounds for such contests and their applicability, if any, to the client's situation. This discussion should serve both to identify potential contestants (if there are any) and, in most cases, to reduce the client's fears. In this regard, it is important to the lawyer to have an accurate picture of the kind of emotional relationship the testator has with her or his biological family. Does the family know the testator is homosexual, or that the testator has a lover or friend whom she or he intends to benefit through the will? Does the testator hold property of such value that a contest by the biological family would be predictable? Is there anything the testator can do during her or his lifetime to minimize the shock which members of the biological family might experience if they were to discover that the bulk of the testator's estate was being left to an "unrelated" person?
>
> [T]he lawyer should not presume that just because a client is a lesbian or gay, she or he does not have a legal spouse from whom she or he was never divorced. . . . Special caution must be exercised where the client is terminally ill or otherwise in a weakened mental or physical state. Any documents executed under

such circumstances will probably be more susceptible to attack than documents executed when the client is healthy and clearly competent. . . .[50]

What documents should unmarried couples execute to plan for the disability or death of a partner? What are the lessons of *Beckwith* for unmarried couples? Do the lessons differ if the unmarried couple consists of opposite-sex or same-sex partners? See generally Joan M. Burda, ABA, Estate Planning for Same-Sex Couples (3d ed. 2015).

C. Parents' and Children's Rights in the Nonmarital Family

This section explores some of the issues that are faced by nontraditional families with children, such as the support rights of nonmarital children and limitations on the rights of unwed parents. In recent decades, society has witnessed a steady increase in the number of single-parent families and cohabiting couples. The rising rate of nonmarital children growing up in these families has consequences for children's well-being, as the excerpt below reveals.

Nat'l Marriage Project, Social Indicators of Marital Health & Well-Being: Trends of the Past Five Decades: Marriage[51]

in The State of Our Unions: Marriage in America 89 (2012)

FRAGILE FAMILIES WITH CHILDREN

. . . The trend toward single-parent families is probably the most important of the recent family trends that have affected children and adolescents. This is because the children in such families have negative life outcomes at two to three times the rate of children in married, two-parent families. While in 1960 only 9 percent of all children lived in single-parent families, a figure that had changed little over the course of the twentieth century, by 2011 the percentage had risen to 26.

An indirect indicator of fragile families is the percentage of children under age 18 living with two married parents. Since 1960 this percentage has declined substantially, by 23 percentage points. Unfortunately, this measure makes no distinction between natural and stepfamilies; it is estimated that some 88 percent of two-parent families consist of both biological parents, while 9 percent are stepfamilies. The problem is that children in stepfamilies, according to a substantial and growing body of social science evidence, fare no better in life

[50]. Sexual Orientation and the Law §4.04 (Roberta Achtenberg ed., 1991).
[51]. The full report can be found at http://www.stateofourunions.org/2010/si-cohabitation.php.

than children in single-parent families. Data on stepfamilies, therefore, probably are more reasonably combined with single-parent than with biological two-parent families. An important indicator that helps resolve this issue is the percentage of children who live apart from their biological fathers. That percentage has doubled since 1960, from 17 percent to 34 percent.

The dramatic shift in family structure indicated by these measures has been generated mainly by three burgeoning trends: divorce, unmarried births, and unmarried cohabitation. The incidence of divorce began to increase rapidly during the 1960s. The number of children under age 18 newly affected by parental divorce each year, most of whom have lost a resident father, grew from under 500,000 in 1960 to well over a million in 1975. After peaking around 1980, that number leveled off and remains close to a million new children each year. . . .

The second reason for the shift in family structure is an increase in the percentage of babies born to unwed mothers, which suddenly and unexpectedly began to increase rapidly in the 1970s. Since 1960, the percentage of babies born to unwed mothers has increased more than sevenfold. More than four in ten births and more than two-thirds of black births in 2011, the latest year for which we have complete data, were out-of-wedlock.

A third and still more recent family trend that has affected family structure is the rapid growth of unmarried cohabitation. In fact, more cohabiting couples are having children, or bringing children into their relationship. Consequently, there has been about a fifteen-fold increase in the number of cohabiting couples who live with children since 1960. Slightly more than 40 percent of all children are expected to spend some time in a cohabiting household during their childhood years.

In 2000, about 40 percent of unmarried-couple households included one or more children under age 18. For unmarried couples in the 25 to 34 age group, the percentage with children is higher still, approaching half of all such households. Seventy percent of the children in unmarried-couple households are the children of only one partner. Indeed, if one includes cohabitation in the definition of stepfamily, almost one half of stepfamilies today would consist of a biological parent and unrelated cohabiting partner.

Children who grow up with cohabiting couples tend to have worse life outcomes compared to those growing up with married couples. The primary reasons are that cohabiting couples have a much higher breakup rate than married couples, a lower level of household income, and higher levels of child abuse and domestic violence. The proportion of cohabiting mothers who eventually marry the fathers of their children is declining, a decline sadly predictive of increased problems for children.

For other recent studies that contend that single parenthood is a principal factor in the growth of inequality in the United States and also in the decline in children's well-being, see June Carbone & Naomi Cahn, Marriage Markets: How Inequality Is Remaking the American Family (2014); Isabel Sawhill, Generation Unbound: Drifting into Sex and Parenthood Without Marriage (2014).

1. Support Rights of Nonmarital Children

CLARK v. JETER

486 U.S. 456 (1988)

Justice O'CONNOR delivered the opinion of the Court.

Under Pennsylvania law, an illegitimate child must prove paternity before seeking support from his or her father, and a suit to establish paternity ordinarily must be brought within six years of an illegitimate child's birth. By contrast, a legitimate child may seek support from his or her parents at any time. . . .

On September 22, 1983, petitioner Cherlyn Clark filed a support complaint in the Allegheny County Court of Common Pleas on behalf of her minor daughter, Tiffany, who was born out of wedlock on June 11, 1973. Clark named respondent Gene Jeter as Tiffany's father. The court ordered blood tests, which showed a 99.3% probability that Jeter is Tiffany's father.

Jeter moved to dismiss the complaint on the ground that it was barred by the 6-year statute of limitations for paternity actions. In her response, Clark contended that this statute is unconstitutional under the Equal Protection and Due Process Clauses. . . .

[The trial court upheld the statute of limitations and Clark appealed. Before the court decided her case, however, the legislature enacted an 18-year statute of limitations for actions to establish paternity to comply with the federal Child Support Enforcement Amendments of 1984 requiring all states participating in the federal child support program to have procedures to establish the paternity of any child who is less than 18 years old. 42 U.S.C. §666(a)(5) (1982 ed., Supp. IV). The Superior Court concluded that Pennsylvania's new 18-year statute of limitations did not apply retroactively, and it affirmed the trial court's conclusion that the 6-year statute of limitations was constitutional. The Court granted Clark's petition for certiorari.]

In considering whether state legislation violates the Equal Protection Clause of the Fourteenth Amendment, we apply different levels of scrutiny to different types of classifications. . . . Between [the] extremes of rational basis review and strict scrutiny lies a level of intermediate scrutiny, which generally has been applied to discriminatory classifications based on sex or illegitimacy.

To withstand intermediate scrutiny, a statutory classification must be substantially related to an important governmental objective. Consequently we have invalidated classifications that burden illegitimate children for the sake of punishing the illicit relations of their parents, because "visiting this condemnation on the head of an infant is illogical and unjust." Weber v. Aetna Casualty & Surety Co., 406 U.S. 164, 175 (1972). Yet, in the seminal case concerning the child's right to support, this Court acknowledged that it might be appropriate to treat illegitimate children differently in the support context because of "lurking problems with respect to proof of paternity." Gomez v. Perez, 409 U.S. 535, 538 (1973).

This Court has developed a particular framework for evaluating equal protection challenges to statutes of limitations that apply to suits to establish paternity, and thereby limit the ability of illegitimate children to obtain support.

> First, the period for obtaining support . . . must be sufficiently long in duration to present a reasonable opportunity for those with an interest in such children to assert claims on their behalf. Second, any time limitation placed on that opportunity must be substantially related to the State's interest in avoiding the litigation of stale or fraudulent claims.

Mills v. Habluetzel, 456 U.S., at 99-100.

In *Mills*, we held that Texas' 1-year statute of limitations failed both steps of the analysis. We explained that paternity suits typically will be brought by the child's mother, who might not act swiftly amidst the emotional and financial complications of the child's first year. And, it is unlikely that the lapse of a mere 12 months will result in the loss of evidence or appreciably increase the likelihood of fraudulent claims. A concurring opinion in *Mills* explained why statutes of limitations longer than one year also may be unconstitutional. Id., at 102-106 (O'Connor, J., joined by Burger, C.J., and Brennan and Blackmun, JJ., and joined as to Part I by Powell, J., concurring). First, the State has a countervailing interest in ensuring that genuine claims for child support are satisfied. Second, the fact that Texas tolled most other causes of action during a child's minority suggested that proof problems do not become overwhelming during this period. Finally, the practical obstacles to filing a claim for support are likely to continue after the first year of the child's life.

In Pickett v. Brown, 462 U.S. 1 (1983), the Court unanimously struck down Tennessee's 2-year statute of limitations for paternity and child support actions brought on behalf of certain illegitimate children. Adhering to the analysis developed in *Mills*, the Court first considered whether two years afforded a reasonable opportunity to bring such suits. The Tennessee statute was relatively more generous than the Texas statute considered in *Mills* because it did not limit actions against a father who had acknowledged his paternity in writing or by furnishing support; nor did it apply if the child was likely to become a public charge. Nevertheless, the Court concluded that the 2-year period was too short in light of the persisting financial and emotional problems that are likely to afflict the child's mother.

Proceeding to the second step of the analysis, the Court decided that the 2-year statute of limitations was not substantially related to Tennessee's asserted interest in preventing stale and fraudulent claims. The period during which suit could be brought was only a year longer than the period considered in *Mills*, and this incremental difference would not create substantially greater proof and fraud problems. . . . Finally, scientific advances in blood testing had alleviated some problems of proof in paternity actions. For these reasons, the Tennessee statute failed to survive heightened scrutiny under the Equal Protection Clause.

In light of this authority, we conclude that Pennsylvania's 6-year statute of limitations violates the Equal Protection Clause. Even six years does not necessarily provide a reasonable opportunity to assert a claim on behalf of an illegitimate child. "The unwillingness of the mother to file a paternity action on behalf of her child, which could stem from her relationship with the natural father or . . . from the emotional strain of having an illegitimate child, or even from the desire to avoid community and family disapproval, may continue years after the child is born. The problem may be exacerbated if, as often happens, the mother herself is a minor." Not all of these difficulties are likely to abate in six years. A mother might realize only belatedly "a loss of income attributable to the need to care for the child." Furthermore, financial difficulties are likely to increase as the child matures and incurs expenses for clothing, school, and medical care. Thus, it is questionable whether a State acts reasonably when it requires most paternity and support actions to be brought within six years of an illegitimate child's birth.

We do not rest our decision on this ground, however, for it is not entirely evident that six years would necessarily be an unreasonable limitations period for child support actions involving illegitimate children. We are, however, confident that the 6-year statute of limitations is not substantially related to Pennsylvania's interest in avoiding the litigation of stale or fraudulent claims. In a number of circumstances, Pennsylvania permits the issue of paternity to be litigated more than six years after the birth of an illegitimate child [for example, for intestate succession purposes, in paternity actions initiated by the father, and tolls the limitation during minority in other civil actions as well]. In *Pickett* and *Mills,* similar tolling statutes cast doubt on the State's purposed interest in avoiding the litigation of fraudulent claims.

A more recent indication that Pennsylvania does not consider proof problems insurmountable is the enactment by the Pennsylvania Legislature in 1985 of an 18-year statute of limitations for paternity and support actions. 23 Pa. Cons. Stat. §4343(b) (1985). To be sure, the legislature did not act spontaneously, but rather under the threat of losing some federal funds. Nevertheless, the new statute is a tacit concession that proof problems are not overwhelming. The legislative history of the federal Child Support Enforcement Amendments explains why Congress thought such statutes of limitations are reasonable. Congress adverted to the problem of stale and fraudulent claims, but recognized that increasingly sophisticated tests for genetic markers permit the exclusion of over 99% of those who might be accused of paternity, regardless of the age of the child. This scientific evidence . . . is an additional reason to doubt that Pennsylvania had a substantial reason for limiting the time within which paternity and support actions could be brought.

We conclude that the Pennsylvania statute does not withstand heightened scrutiny under the Equal Protection Clause. We therefore find it unnecessary to reach Clark's due process claim. . . .

Notes and Questions

1. Common law rule. *Clark* reflects the trend of increasing constitutional protection for the rights of a nonmarital child. Traditionally, the law regarded such a child as *filius nullius* and a bastard ("illegitimate"). That status affected the child's right to support and inheritance. Only the mother had a common law duty of support for a nonmarital child. However, in Gomez v. Perez, 409 U.S. 535 (1973), the United States Supreme Court held that a state cannot grant marital children a statutory right to paternal support while denying this right to nonmarital children. Today, statutes require both parents to support the child regardless of the parents' marital status. Nonetheless, distinctions persisted for a long time in terms of inheritance law (as explained below).

2. Statutes of limitations. At the time of *Clark*, many states had statutes of limitations that restricted the time within which paternity suits could be brought. States justified these short periods in order to prevent the filing of stale claims and discourage fraud. After several Supreme Court cases prior to *Clark* invalidated various short statutes of limitations, many states lengthened their statutory periods. Congress also lengthened statutes of limitations in paternity establishment by means of the Child Support Enforcement Amendments of 1984, requiring states (as a condition for receipt of federal funds) to permit paternity establishment for 18 years after birth. 42 U.S.C. §666(a)(5)(A)(i). This requirement was incorporated subsequently into federal welfare reform legislation in 1996. See Personal Responsibility and Work Opportunity Act (PRWORA), 42 U.S.C. §666(a)(5)(A).

3. Inheritance rights of nonmarital children. Although the Supreme Court used intermediate scrutiny under the equal protection doctrine to strike down many laws disadvantaging nonmarital children, the Court declined to invalidate *all* such discrimination, most notably laws about inheritance rights.

Traditionally, most state laws provided that a nonmarital child occupied the same position as a child born within marriage with regard to inheritance rights vis-à-vis the child's *mother*. However, whereas a father could name a nonmarital child as a beneficiary in the father's will, the child would receive nothing if the father died intestate (without a will), a result stemming largely from a concern about proof of paternity.

Beginning in 1968, the Supreme Court decided a number of cases concerning the rights of nonmarital children. These early cases established that nonmarital children could be treated differently from their marital counterparts in some circumstances. Compare Levy v. Louisiana, 391 U.S. 68 (1969) (holding that nonmarital children could recover damages for the wrongful death of their mother); with Labine v. Vincent, 401, U.S. 532 (1971) (upholding a statutory distinction between nonmarital children and marital children regarding inheritance to a father's intestate estate).

The Court continued to affirm distinctions between nonmarital and marital children in terms of inheritance law throughout the next decade. See, e.g., Lalli v. Lalli, 439 U.S. 259 (1978) (holding that the state could require a higher level of proof, in the form of a judicial declaration of paternity, for a nonmarital child to inherit via intestate succession from their fathers); Trimble v. Gordon, 430 U.S. 762 (1977) (holding that, although the state could require a higher level of proof for nonmarital children to inherit via intestacy from their father, the state could not require that the child's parents marry after the child's birth). The opaque nature of the Supreme Court's jurisprudence on the rights of nonmarital children highlighted the need for law reform.

4. Statutory reform. Today, all states have expanded the inheritance rights of nonmarital children. Many states have done so by adopting the original Uniform Parentage Act (UPA).

a. Original UPA. The original UPA was promulgated in 1973 to address the prevailing unequal treatment of nonmarital children and also to respond to the need to provide guidance to the states in response to U.S. Supreme Court decisions on the rights of nonmarital children. The UPA was heavily influenced by the work of Professor Harry Krause, who was an early advocate of equal treatment for nonmarital and marital children.[52] Before the adoption of the UPA in 1973, most states failed to identify two legal parents for nonmarital children. In addition, considerable stigma attached to these "illegitimate" children, who were denied the financial and legal benefits that flowed from having two legal parents. The UPA transformed this policy.

In a classic law review article, Krause addressed the inequality of treatment by refuting the justifications for the discrimination: the uncertainty surrounding the paternity of nonmarital children, the desire to discourage promiscuity, the need to protect the family unit, the belief that nonmarital children lack a close relationship with their fathers, and the need to respect the father's choice whether to recognize the child. How would you refute these justifications?

In response to the above critique, the UPA provided for equal treatment for all children without regard to the marital status of their parents, so long as the father could be identified. To identify the father of a nonmarital child, the UPA replaced the traditional presumption of legitimacy with the following network of presumptions:

UNIFORM PARENTAGE ACT [ORIGINAL]

§4. [PRESUMPTIONS OF PATERNITY]

(a) A man is presumed to be the natural father of a child if:

(1) he and the child's natural mother are or have been married to each other and the child is born during the marriage, or within 300 days after the marriage is terminated by death, annulment, declaration of invalidity, or divorce, or after a decree of separation is entered by the court;

(2) before the child's birth, he and the child's natural mother have attempted to marry each other by a marriage solemnized in apparent compliance with the law, although the attempted marriage is or could be declared invalid, and

(i) if the attempted marriage could be declared invalid only by a court, the child is born during the attempted marriage, or within 300 days after its termination by death, annulment, declaration of invalidity, or divorce; or

(ii) if the attempted marriage is invalid without a court order, the child is born within 300 days after the termination of cohabitation;

(3) after the child's birth, he and the child's natural mother have married, or attempted to marry, each other by a marriage solemnized in apparent compliance with law, although the attempted marriage is or could be declared invalid, and

(i) he has acknowledged his paternity of the child in writing filed with the [appropriate court or Vital Statistics Bureau];

(ii) with his consent, he is named as the child's father on the child's birth certificate; or

(iii) he is obligated to support the child under a written voluntary promise or by court order;

---

[52]. For his classic law review article, see Harry D. Krause, Bringing the Bastard into the Great Society — A Proposed Uniform Act on Legitimacy, 44 Tex. L. Rev. 829 (1966). Discriminatory policies against "illegitimates" in the 1960s also stemmed from stereotypical beliefs about the convergence of race, class, and out-of-wedlock childbearing. See Martha F. Davis, Male Coverture: Law and the Illegitimate Family, 56 Rutgers L. Rev. 73, 107-09 (2003).

(4) while the child is under the age of majority, he receives the child into his home and openly holds out the child as his natural child; or

(5) he acknowledges his paternity of the child in a writing filed with the [appropriate court or Vital Statistics Bureau], which shall promptly inform the mother of the filing of the acknowledgment, and she does not dispute the acknowledgment within a reasonable time after being informed thereof, in a writing filed with the [appropriate court or Vital Statistics Bureau]. If another man is presumed under this section to be the child's father, acknowledgment may be effected only with the written consent of the presumed father or after the presumption has been rebutted.

(b) A presumption under this section may be rebutted in an appropriate action only by clear and convincing evidence. If two or more presumptions arise which conflict with each other, the presumption which on the facts is founded on the weightier considerations of policy and logic controls. The presumption is rebutted by a court decree establishing paternity of the child by another man.

Eighteen states adopted the original UPA. 9B U.L.A. at 377.

b. Revised UPA. In 2000, the Uniform Law Commission (ULC) promulgated a new UPA, which was revised in 2002. 9B U.L.A. 295. The new version was necessary because of technological advances (including assisted reproductive techniques and increasingly accurate genetic testing). The new UPA reaffirms the original policy of equal treatment of children regardless of the parents' marital status. UPA §202. For additional discussion of the new UPA, see infra.

c. Uniform Probate Code. The original UPA influenced the evolution of Uniform Probate Code (UPC) rules on the inheritance rights of nonmarital children. The UPC is model legislation governing inheritance of decedents' estates in the United States; streamlining the probate process; and modernizing state laws on wills, trusts, and intestate succession.

The UPC (promulgated in 1969) allowed a nonmarital child to inherit only from the mother in the event that she died without a will. However, in order for the child to inherit from the father via intestacy, the child had to establish any of the following: (1) the parents participated in a marriage ceremony after the birth; (2) paternity was judicially established prior to the father's death; or (3) paternity was judicially established after the father's death by clear and convincing proof. Following promulgation of the UPA in 1973, the ULC amended the UPC in 1975 to provide that if a state had enacted the UPA, then the UPA's alternative approach of paternity establishment would apply.

Significant revisions to the UPC in 1990, however, provided for broader equality of treatment of nonmarital and marital children for purposes of inheritance law. Adopting UPA language, the UPC provided: "an individual is the child of his natural parents, regardless of their marital status." UPC §2-114. In 2008, the ULC amended Article II of the UPC, and confirmed that a parent-child relationship exists regardless of the parents' marital status. Unif. Probate Code §2-117.[53]

---

[53]. On the evolution of the UPC's approach to the rights of nonmarital children, see Paula A. Monopoli, Toward Equality: Nonmarital Children and the Uniform Probate Code, 45 Univ. Mich. J.L. Ref. 995 (2012). On the evolution of the law's treatment generally of nonmarital children, see Solangel Maldonado, Illegitimate Harm: Law, Stigma, and Discrimination Against Nonmarital Children, 63 Fla. L. Rev. 345 (2011).

NOTE: PATERNITY ESTABLISHMENT

The traditional way to identify the father of a nonmarital child and impose a support obligation was a paternity suit. Paternity actions, rooted in the English bastardy proceedings, historically were quasi-criminal proceedings characterized by short statutes of limitations, proof beyond a reasonable doubt, and trial by jury. Increasing public awareness about the problem of child support enforcement on the federal level prompted law reform, including a reformulation of these elements. Paternity proceedings, now commonly viewed as civil proceedings, raise a number of issues.

a. Jurisdiction. To establish paternity of an out-of-state putative father, a court must obtain personal jurisdiction over him. Traditionally, courts use different theories to extend long-arm bases of jurisdiction: failure to support constitutes the "commission of a tortious act," the breach of a contractual obligation within the state, or "doing business" in the state. For the modern approach, see Uniform Interstate Family Support Act (UIFSA) (amended 2001), 9 U.L.A. (pt. IB) 484 (providing in §201(6) that a person who has sexual intercourse within the state thereby submits to jurisdiction regarding any ensuing child); UPA §604(b) (incorporating in the new UPA the UIFSA long-arm provision for establishing personal jurisdiction, now followed by every state).

b. Admissible evidence. Concerns about fraudulent paternity claims contributed to enactment of short statutes of limitations, as well as rules about the admissibility of evidence. Such concerns were eliminated by advances in scientific proof of paternity. Paternity testing was first performed in the middle half of the twentieth century and required blood tests. In the 1970s, a more effective blood test was developed (the Human Leukocyte Antigens (HLA) test) that was sufficiently accurate to exclude about 95 percent of falsely accused fathers. Far more accurate testing can now be obtained by DNA testing that involves swiping a cotton swab along the inner cheek. DNA testing can be performed even after death, such as by taking a blood or tissue sample from the alleged father's body or by testing close relatives of the deceased. Scientific advances in DNA testing now yield a 99.9 percent probability that a given man *is* in fact the child's father.

c. Plaintiffs. Traditionally, paternity actions were brought by the *mother* for support purposes. Gradually, states permitted such actions by the child, the child's representative, and the father. For many decades, *public welfare authorities* brought paternity suits, seeking reimbursement for public funds spent to support the child. This practice stemmed from federal interest in the identification of the father to enforce child support obligations. Welfare reform legislation (PRWORA), 42 U.S.C. §603, required states to adopt new paternity provisions in order to receive federal funds for child support enforcement programs and welfare programs. Under PRWORA, paternity can be established when *either parent* brings a paternity suit at any time until the child attains age 18 and also when both parents voluntarily acknowledge paternity.

d. Submission to genetic testing. According to PRWORA, upon either parent's request (if supported by a sworn statement "establishing a reasonable possibility of the requisite sexual contact between the parties"), the court must order genetic tests. 42 U.S.C. §666(a)(5)(B)(i)(I). However, under the revised UPA (§608), courts may deny requests for genetic testing based on estoppel principles "in the interests of preserving a child's ties to the presumed or acknowledged father who openly held himself out as the child's father regardless of whether he is in fact the genetic father." Once paternity is established, the court enters an order that often includes an award of child support. Paternity establishment procedures may create either a rebuttable or conclusive presumption of paternity—at the state's option. Id. §666(a)(5)(G).

e. Indigent defendants. Indigent defendants sometimes lack financial resources to pay for testing that might disprove paternity. In Little v. Streater, 452 U.S. 1 (1981), the U.S. Supreme Court held that the Due Process Clause guarantees the cost of blood testing to indigent defendants in paternity actions. However, courts are split regarding whether due process mandates indigent's right to counsel in such actions. See generally Laura K. Abel & Max Rettig, State Statutes Providing for a Right to Counsel in Civil Cases, 40 Clearinghouse Rev. 245 (2006).

f. Jury. Most states now provide that the parties in a paternity case are not entitled to a jury.

g. Standard of proof. The Supreme Court has held that due process requires only the "preponderance of the evidence" standard of proof in paternity proceedings. Rivera v. Minnich, 483 U.S. 574 (1987).

h. Voluntary paternity establishment. The shift from judicial hearings to voluntary affidavits has transformed paternity establishment. Beginning in 1992, a few states adopted voluntary programs that targeted mothers at birth facilities, providing that in-hospital affidavits established a rebuttable presumption of paternity. These programs were so successful that Congress included a requirement in the Omnibus Budget Reconciliation Act of 1993, 42 U.S.C. §666(a)(5)(C)(ii), for all states to adopt voluntary paternity establishment programs. PRWORA expanded these programs by providing that a valid, nonrescinded, and unchallenged acknowledgment of paternity is equivalent to a judicial determination of paternity (rather than a mere presumption) and is entitled to full faith and credit. 42 U.S.C. §666(a)(5). The revised UPA also complies with the federal mandate by providing for voluntary establishment of paternity and specifying that voluntary affidavits serve as judgments for enforcement purposes. UPA, art. 3 (prefatory cmt.) (amended 2002).

For recent scholarship on fatherhood, see Kathryn Edin & Timothy J. Nelson, Doing the Best I Can: Fatherhood in the Inner City (2013) (exploring obstacles faced by low-income fathers in forging relationships with their nonmarital children, based on 110 interviews with Black and white fathers); Laura King, Family Men: Fatherhood and Masculinity in Britain, 1914-1960 (2015) (exploring the emergence of fatherhood as an identity).

WALLIS v. SMITH

22 P.3d 682 (N.M. Ct. App. 2001)

Bosson, Judge.

[Peter] Wallis and [Kellie Rae] Smith began an intimate, sexual relationship. . . . They discussed contraceptive techniques and agreed that Smith would use birth control pills. Wallis and Smith further agreed that their sexual intimacy would last only as long as Smith continued to take birth control pills because Wallis made it clear that he did not want to father a child. Wallis participated in contraception only passively; he relied on Smith to use birth control and took no precautions himself.

As time went by, Smith changed her mind. She chose to stop taking birth control pills, but never informed Wallis of her decision. Wallis continued their intimate relationship, and Smith became pregnant. Smith carried the fetus to term and gave birth to a normal, healthy girl. [Thereupon, Wallis sued Smith for money damages, asserting four causes of action—fraud, breach of contract, conversion, and prima facie tort. The district court dismissed for failure to state a claim. Wallis appealed.]

Wallis alleges that he has suffered, and will continue to suffer, substantial economic injury as a proximate result of his unintended fatherhood because New Mexico law requires him to pay child support for the next eighteen years. Due to his statutory obligations, Wallis asserts that he has been injured by Smith's conduct, and requests compensatory and punitive damages from her. The district court determined that public policy prohibited the relief sought by Wallis, and dismissed the case with prejudice.

. . . At the onset of our discussion, it is important to distinguish the factual allegations of this case from other kinds of related lawsuits, and thus underscore the limited reach of this opinion. Wallis's complaint is not about sexually-transmitted disease, nor does it concern the damages arising from an unwanted pregnancy that led to an abortion, or an undesired pregnancy resulting in medical complications. This case is not even brought to recover the expense of giving birth. Wallis's complaint is limited to compensatory damages for the "economic injury" of supporting a normal, healthy child.

Although Wallis insists that he is not attempting to circumvent his child support obligations, we cannot agree. It is self-evident that he seeks to recover for the very financial loss caused him by the statutory obligation to pay child support. At oral argument when pressed by the Court to clarify what damages Wallis was seeking, his counsel stated that Wallis was seeking not punitive, but compensatory damages measured by his "out of pocket loss." Therefore, this case boils down to whether sound public policy would permit our courts to require Smith to indemnify Wallis for child support under the circumstances of this case.

Our legislature has spoken to the public policy that governs the economic consequences of sexual relationships that produce children, and that policy is reflected in New Mexico child support laws. In 1986, our legislature adopted, with minor revisions, the Uniform Parentage Act (UPA), which outlines the legal procedure to establish a parent-child relationship and the corresponding obligation of child support. See 1986 N.M. Laws, ch. 47, §§1-23; Unif. Parentage Act §§1-30, 9B U.L.A. 287 (West 1987). The UPA imposes a form of strict liability for child support, without regard to which parent bears the greater responsibility for the child's being.

Making each parent financially responsible for the conception and birth of children also illuminates a strong public policy that makes paramount the interests of the child. Our jurisprudence has abandoned the notion that the father of an "illegitimate" child could decline to accept the financial responsibility of raising that child. . . . Placing a duty of support on each parent has the added benefit of insulating the state from the possibility of bearing the financial burden for a child. In our view, it is difficult to harmonize the legislative concern for the child, reflected in the immutable duty of parental support, with Wallis's effort in this lawsuit to shift financial responsibility for his child solely to the mother.

New Mexico is not alone in its view of parental responsibility and the conflict created by lawsuits such as this. To our knowledge, no jurisdiction recognizes contraceptive fraud or breach of promise to practice birth control as a ground for adjusting a natural parent's obligation to pay child support. . . .

Some courts have dismissed contraceptive fraud cases on the ground that the claims reach too far into the realm of an individual's privacy interests. [Stephen K. v. Roni L., 164 Cal. Rptr. 618 (Cal. Ct. App. 1980)]. We agree that individuals are entitled a sphere of privacy into which courts should not tread. A person's choice whether or not to use contraceptives understandably fits into this sphere. We also believe that the "privacy interests involved . . . require a cautious approach," and therefore we elect to rely primarily on the prevailing public policy of child support, while at the same time recognizing the serious privacy concerns implicated and threatened by the underlying lawsuit.

Wallis's attempt to apply traditional contract and tort principles to his contraceptive agreement is unconvincing and, in the end, futile. The contract analogy fails because children, the persons for whose benefit child support guidelines are enacted, have the same needs regardless of whether their conception violated a promise between the parents. Further, a parent being sued for causing the conception and birth of a child is no ordinary tortfeasor; a defendant under these circumstances is legally entitled to collect financial support on behalf of the child.

We will not re-enter the jurisprudence of illegitimacy by allowing a parent to opt out of the financial consequences of his or her sexual relationships just because they were unintended. Nor will we recognize a cause of action that trivializes one's personal responsibility in sexual relationships. Indeed, permitting "such actions while simultaneously encouraging paternity actions for support flies in the face of all reason." We also observe that if Wallis did not desire children, he was free and able to practice contraceptive techniques on his own.

Wallis tries to make the basis for liability not so much the birth of the child, but the fact that Smith lied, and perpetrated a fraud on him. But not all misrepresentations are actionable. . . . Finally, Wallis argues that our courts have recognized tort claims which measure damages by the economic injury of supporting an unwanted child. See Lovelace Med. Ctr. v. Mendez, 805 P.2d 603, 612 (N.M. 1991) [(holding that a couple who sought to protect their financial resources by limiting the size of their family through sterilization could sue a negligent physician for economic damages measured by the cost of raising an additional child to the age of majority]. Because *Lovelace* does not speak to the issue of inter-parental liability, which is the crux of Wallis's appeal, it has no bearing on our decision. Accordingly, we hold that the actions asserted here cannot be used to recoup the financial obligations of raising a child. . . .

Notes and Questions

1. Basis for child support? Paternity establishment generally gives rise to a legal obligation to pay child support. Should the child support obligation be based on an adult's biological or social relationship to the child? Should either relationship alone be enough? For example, should a biological father who had sexual relations with the child's mother only once, and never had any relationship with the child, have a legal obligation to support the child? Should the child support obligation be based on the relationship of the parents, marital or otherwise? Is it more important to identify *a* father than to identify the "right" father?

2. Preconception agreements for support. Suppose that Wallis knew that Smith wanted to conceive a child, but the two had entered into a written preconception agreement relieving him of support. If a mother chooses not to enforce the support obligation against the father (or her same-sex partner, as the case may be), does that relieve the father (or the same-sex partner) of financial responsibility? Should it matter whether the mother would otherwise require public assistance to support the child? See Kristine M. v. David P., 37 Cal. Rptr. 3d 748 (Ct. App. 2006).

3. Contraceptive fraud. Should a father's child support obligation be affected by the mother's deception about birth control? *Wallis* illustrates the general rule that the mother's contraceptive fraud does not serve as a defense to a father's support obligation. Courts traditionally refuse to grant tort recovery for misrepresentations of contraceptive use unless serious physical injury results. What explains the court's reluctance? See generally Michelle Oberman, Sex, Lies, and the Duty to Disclose, 47 Ariz. L. Rev. 871 (2005).

4. Other wrongful conduct of mother. Should the mother's wrongful conduct *ever* relieve the father's liability for support? That is, should the general rule apply when the woman obtains unauthorized use of "purloined sperm" from: (a) an unconscious man [see, e.g., S.F. v. State ex rel. T.M., 695 So. 2d 1186 (Ala. Civ. App. 1996))]; (b) a teenage male victim of statutory rape (see, e.g., In re Paternity of K.B., 104 P.3d 1132 (Okla. Ct. App. 2004)); (c) a fertility clinic from deposited sperm long after the couple's intimate relationship terminates (see, e.g., In re Parentage of J.M.K., P.119 P.3d 840 (Wash. 2005)). See generally Michael J. Higdon, Fatherhood by Conscription: Nonconsensual Insemination and the Duty of Child Support, 46 Ga. L. Rev. 407 (2012); Donald C. Hubin, Daddy Dilemmas: Untangling the Puzzles of Paternity, 13 Cornell J.L. & Pub. Pol'y 29 (2003) (coining the term "purloined sperm").

5. Damages. Should a parent's support obligation in case of contraceptive fraud, if not dismissed, at least be reduced? To what extent does (or should) the mother have a duty to mitigate damages? Would the result change if the father had offered to pay for an abortion? If the defendant used birth control that failed? Does any man who engages in sexual relations with a woman "assume the risk" with all attendant duties? If so, why should actual paternity matter—why not impose shared liability on all men who might have fathered a particular child? See, e.g., State ex rel. Dept. of Soc. Servs. v. Howard, 898 So. 2d 443 (La. Ct. App. 2004) (holding that biological father cannot escape support obligation merely because a legal father could share the responsibility).

6. Tort claims. Should a father in Wallis's position be permitted to maintain a tort action for fraud or infliction of emotional distress instead? How much is the emotional harm of unwanted fatherhood worth? In dismissing Wallis's suit, the court did not address his claim of conversion (i.e., unauthorized use of his "property"). Did Smith "convert" sperm? See Phillips v. Irons, 2005 WL 4694579 (Ill. App. Ct. 2005).

7. **Constitutional claims.** Does Wallis have any constitutional claims? For example, would the right to privacy support or prohibit recognition of tort claims? Does a man have a constitutional right to avoid fatherhood? Is the Fourteenth Amendment violated if the woman has the right to reject parenthood after conception via abortion or adoption but the man has no corresponding right? See Dubay v. Wells, 506 F.3d 422 (6th Cir. 2007).

2. Limitations on Unmarried Parents' Rights

STANLEY v. ILLINOIS

405 U.S. 645 (1972)

Mr. Justice White delivered the opinion of the Court.

Joan Stanley lived with Peter Stanley intermittently for 18 years during which time they had three children. When Joan Stanley died, Peter Stanley lost not only her but also his children. Under Illinois law the children of unwed fathers become wards of the State upon the death of the mother. Accordingly, upon Joan Stanley's death, in a dependency proceeding instituted by the State of Illinois, Stanley's children were declared wards of the State and placed with court-appointed guardians. Stanley appealed, claiming that he had never been shown to be an unfit parent and that since married fathers and unwed mothers could not be deprived of their children without such a showing, he had been deprived of the equal protection of the laws guaranteed him by the Fourteenth Amendment. . . .

Stanley presses his equal protection claim here. The State continues to respond that unwed fathers are presumed unfit to raise their children. . . . We granted certiorari to determine whether this method of procedure by presumption could be allowed to stand in light of the fact that Illinois allows married fathers—whether divorced, widowed, or separated—and mothers—even if unwed—the benefit of the presumption that they are fit to raise their children.

We must [examine the following question]: Is a presumption that distinguishes and burdens all unwed fathers constitutionally repugnant? We conclude that, as a matter of due process of law, Stanley was entitled to a hearing on his fitness as a parent before his children were taken from him and that by denying him a hearing and extending it to all other parents whose custody of their children is challenged, the State denied Stanley the equal protection of the laws guaranteed by the Fourteenth Amendment.

Illinois has two principal methods of removing nondelinquent children from the homes of their parents. In a dependency proceeding, it may demonstrate that the children are wards of the State because they have no surviving parent or guardian. In a neglect proceeding, it may show that children should be wards of the State because the present parent(s) or guardian does not provide suitable care.

The State's right—indeed duty—to protect minor children through a judicial determination of their interests in a neglect proceeding is not challenged here. Rather, we are faced with a dependency statute that empowers state officials to circumvent neglect proceedings on the theory that an unwed father is not a "parent" whose existing relationship with his children must be considered. "Parents," says the State, "means the father and mother of a legitimate child, or the survivor of them, or the natural mother of an illegitimate child, and includes any adoptive parent" (Ill. Rev. Stat., c. 37, §701-14), but the term does not include unwed fathers.

Under Illinois law, therefore, while the children of all parents can be taken from them in neglect proceedings, that is only after notice, hearing, and proof of such unfitness as a parent as amounts to neglect, an unwed father is uniquely subject to the more simplistic dependency proceeding. By use of this proceeding, the State, on showing that the father was not married to the mother, need not prove unfitness in fact, because it is presumed at law. . . .

In considering this procedure under the Due Process Clause, we recognize, as we have in other cases, that due process of law does not require a hearing "in every conceivable case of government impairment of private interest." [The rule is] firmly established that "what procedures due process may require under any given set of circumstances must begin with a determination of the precise nature of the government function involved as well as of the private interest that has been affected by governmental action." . . . The private interest here, that of a man in the children he has sired and raised, undeniably warrants deference and, absent a powerful countervailing interest, protection. . . . The Court has frequently emphasized the importance of the family. The rights to conceive and to raise one's children have been deemed "essential," [citing Meyer v. Nebraska, among other cases]. . . .

Nor has the law refused to recognize those family relationships unlegitimized by a marriage ceremony. The Court has declared unconstitutional a state statute denying natural, but illegitimate, children a wrongful-death action for the death of their mother, emphasizing that such children cannot be denied the right of other children because familial bonds in such cases were often as warm, enduring, and important as those arising within a more formally organized family unit. Levy v. Louisiana, 391 U.S. 68, 71-72 (1968). "To say that the test of equal protection should be the 'legal' rather than the biological relationship is to avoid the issue. For the Equal Protection Clause necessarily limits the authority of a State to draw such 'legal' lines as it chooses." Glona v. American Guarantee Co., 391 U.S. 73, 75-76 (1968). These authorities make it clear that, at the least, Stanley's interest in retaining custody of his children is cognizable and substantial.

For its part, the State has made its interest quite plain: Illinois has declared that the aim of the Juvenile Court Act is to protect "the moral, emotional, mental, and physical welfare of the minor and the best interests of the community" and to "strengthen the minor's family ties whenever possible, removing him from the custody of his parents only when his welfare or safety or the protection of the public cannot be adequately safeguarded without removal. . . ." Ill. Rev. Stat., c. 37, §701-2. These are legitimate interests well within the power of the State to implement. We do not question the assertion that neglectful parents may be separated from their children.

But we are here not asked to evaluate the legitimacy of the state ends, rather, to determine whether the means used to achieve these ends are constitutionally defensible. What is the state interest in separating children from fathers without a hearing designed to determine whether the father is unfit in a particular disputed case? We observe that the State registers no gain towards its declared goals when it separates children from the custody of fit parents. Indeed, if Stanley is a fit father, the State spites its own articulated goals when it needlessly separates him from his family. . . .

It may be, as the State insists, that most unmarried fathers are unsuitable and neglectful parents. It may also be that Stanley is such a parent and that his children should be placed in other hands. But all unmarried fathers are not in this category; some are wholly suited to have custody of their children. This much the State readily concedes, and nothing in this record indicates that Stanley is or has been a neglectful father who has not cared for his children. Given the opportunity to make his case, Stanley may have been seen to be deserving of custody of his offspring. Had this been so, the State's statutory policy would have been furthered by leaving custody in him. . . .

It may be argued that unmarried fathers are so seldom fit that Illinois need not undergo the administrative inconvenience of inquiry in any case, including Stanley's. The establishment of prompt efficacious procedures to achieve legitimate state ends is a proper state interest worthy of cognizance in constitutional adjudication. But the Constitution recognizes higher values than speed and efficiency. . . . Procedure by presumption is always cheaper and easier than individualized determination. But when, as here, the procedure forecloses the determinative issues of competence and care, when it explicitly disdains present realities in deference to past formalities, it needlessly risks running roughshod over the important interests of both parent and child. It therefore cannot stand.

. . . The State's interest in caring for Stanley's children is de minimis if Stanley is shown to be a fit father. It insists on presuming rather than proving Stanley's unfitness solely because it is more convenient to presume than to prove. Under the Due Process Clause that advantage is insufficient to justify refusing a father a hearing when the issue at stake is the dismemberment of his family.

The State of Illinois assumes custody of the children of married parents, divorced parents, and unmarried mothers only after a hearing and proof of neglect. The children of unmarried fathers, however, are declared dependent children without a hearing on parental fitness and without proof of neglect. Stanley's claim in the state courts and here is that failure to afford him a hearing on his parental qualifications while extending it to other parents denied him equal protection of the laws. We have concluded that all Illinois parents are constitutionally entitled to a hearing on their fitness before their children are removed from their custody. It follows that denying such a hearing to Stanley and those like him while granting it to other Illinois parents is inescapably contrary to the Equal Protection Clause. . . .

MICHAEL H. v. GERALD D.

491 U.S. 110 (1989)

Justice SCALIA announced the judgment of the Court and delivered an opinion, in which THE CHIEF JUSTICE joins, and in all but note 6 of which Justice O'CONNOR and Justice KENNEDY join.

Under California law, a child born to a married woman living with her husband is presumed to be a child of the marriage. Cal. Evid. Code Ann. §621 (West Supp. 1989). The presumption of legitimacy may be rebutted only by the husband or wife, and then only in limited circumstances. The instant appeal presents the claim that this presumption infringes upon the due process rights of a man who wishes to establish his paternity of a child born to the wife of another man, and the claim that it infringes upon the constitutional right of the child to maintain a relationship with her natural father.

The facts of this case are, we must hope, extraordinary. On May 9, 1976, in Las Vegas, Nevada, Carole D., an international model, and Gerald D., a top executive in a French oil company, were married. The couple established a home in Playa del Rey, California, in which they resided as husband and wife when one or the other was not out of the country on business. In the summer of 1978, Carole became involved in an adulterous affair with a neighbor, Michael H. In September 1980, she conceived a child, Victoria D., who was born on May 11, 1981. Gerald was listed as father on the birth certificate and has always held Victoria out to the world as his daughter. Soon after delivery of the child, however, Carole informed Michael that she believed he might be the father.

In the first three years of her life, Victoria remained always with Carole, but found herself within a variety of quasi-family units. In October 1981, Gerald moved to New York City to pursue his business interests, but Carole chose to remain in California. At the end of that month, Carole and Michael had blood tests of themselves and Victoria, which showed a 98.07% probability that Michael was Victoria's father. In January 1982, Carole visited Michael in St. Thomas, where his primary business interests were based. There, Michael held Victoria out as his child. In March, however, Carole left Michael and returned to California, where she took up residence with yet another man, Scott K. Later that spring, and again in the summer, Carole and Victoria spent time with Gerald in New York City, as well as on vacation in Europe. In the fall, they returned to Scott in California.

In November 1982, rebuffed in his attempts to visit Victoria, Michael filed a filiation action in California Superior Court to establish his paternity and right to visitation. In March 1983, the court appointed an attorney and guardian ad litem to represent Victoria's interests. Victoria then filed a cross-complaint asserting that if she had more than one psychological or de facto father, she was entitled to maintain her filial relationship, with all of the attendant rights, duties, and obligations, with both. In May 1983, Carole filed a motion for summary judgment. During this period, from March through July 1983, Carole was again living with Gerald in New York. In August, however, she returned to California, became involved once again with Michael, and instructed her attorneys to remove the summary judgment motion from the calendar.

For the ensuing eight months, when Michael was not in St. Thomas, he lived with Carole and Victoria in Carole's apartment in Los Angeles and held Victoria out as his daughter. In April 1984, Carole and Michael signed a stipulation that Michael was Victoria's natural father. Carole left Michael the next month, however, and instructed her attorneys not to file the stipulation. In June 1984, Carole reconciled with Gerald and joined him in New York, where they now live with Victoria and two other children since born into the marriage.

In May 1984, Michael and Victoria, through her guardian ad litem, sought visitation rights for Michael *pendente lite*. To assist in determining whether visitation would be in Victoria's best interests, the Superior Court appointed a psychologist to evaluate Victoria, Gerald, Michael, and Carole. The psychologist recommended that Carole retain sole custody, but that Michael be allowed continued contact with Victoria pursuant to a restricted visitation schedule. The court concurred and ordered that Michael be provided with limited visitation privileges *pendente lite*.

On October 19, 1984, Gerald, who had intervened in the action, moved for summary judgment on the ground that under Cal. Evid. Code §621 there were no triable issues of fact as to Victoria's paternity. This law provides that "the issue of a wife cohabiting with her husband, who is not impotent or sterile, is conclusively presumed to be a child of the marriage." The presumption may be rebutted by blood tests, but only if a motion for such tests is made, within two years from the date of the child's birth, either by the husband or, if the natural father has filed an affidavit acknowledging paternity, by the wife. [The trial court granted Gerald's motion for summary judgment. Michael and Victoria appeal.]

. . . We address first the [due process] claims of Michael. At the outset, it is necessary to clarify what he sought and what he was denied. California law, like nature itself, makes no provision for dual fatherhood. Michael was seeking to be declared the father of Victoria. The immediate benefit he evidently sought to obtain from that status was visitation rights. But if Michael were successful in being declared the father, other rights would follow—most importantly, the right to be considered as the parent who should have custody. . . . All parental rights, including visitation, were automatically denied by denying Michael status as the father. . . .

Michael contends as a matter of substantive due process that, because he has established a parental relationship with Victoria, protection of Gerald's and Carole's marital union is an insufficient state interest to support termination of that relationship. This argument is, of course, predicated on the assertion that Michael has a constitutionally protected liberty interest in his relationship with Victoria. . . .

In an attempt to limit and guide interpretation of the [Due Process] Clause, we have insisted not merely that the interest denominated as a "liberty" be "fundamental" (a concept that, in isolation, is hard to objectify), but also that it be an interest traditionally protected by our society. . . . This insistence that the asserted liberty interest be rooted in history and tradition is evident, as elsewhere, in our cases according constitutional protection to certain parental rights. Michael reads the landmark case of Stanley v. Illinois, 405 U.S. 645 (1972), and the subsequent cases of Quilloin v. Walcott, 434 U.S. 246 (1978), Caban v. Mohammed, 441 U.S. 380 (1979), and Lehr v. Robertson, 463 U.S. 248 (1983), as establishing that a liberty interest is created by biological fatherhood plus an established parental relationship—factors that exist in the present case as well. We think that distorts the rationale of those cases. As we view them, they rest not upon such isolated factors but upon the historic respect—indeed, sanctity would not be too strong a term—traditionally accorded to the relationships that develop within the unitary family.[3] . . .

Thus, the legal issue in the present case reduces to whether the relationship between persons in the situation of Michael and Victoria has been treated as a protected family unit under the historic practices of our society, or whether on any other basis it has been accorded special protection. We think it impossible to find that it has. In fact, quite to the contrary, our traditions have protected the marital family (Gerald, Carole, and the child they acknowledge to be theirs) against the sort of claim Michael asserts.[4]

The presumption of legitimacy was a fundamental principle of the common law. Traditionally, that presumption could be rebutted only by proof that a husband was incapable of procreation or had had no access to his wife during the relevant period. As explained by Blackstone, nonaccess could only be proved "if the husband be out of the kingdom of England (or, as the law somewhat loosely phrases it, *extra quatuor maria* [beyond the four seas]) for above nine months. . . ." 1 Blackstone's Commentaries 456 (J. Chitty ed., 1826). And, under the common law both in England and here [neither parent could testify to bastardize the child]. The primary policy rationale underlying the common law's severe restrictions on rebuttal of the presumption appears to have been an aversion to declaring children illegitimate, thereby depriving them of rights of inheritance and succession, and likely making them wards of the state. A secondary policy concern was the interest in promoting the "peace and tranquillity of States and families," a goal that is obviously impaired by facilitating suits against husband and wife asserting that their children are illegitimate. . . .

We have found nothing in the older sources, nor in the older cases, addressing specifically the power of the natural father to assert parental rights over a child born into a woman's existing marriage with another man. Since it is Michael's burden to establish that such a power (at least where the natural father has established a relationship with the child) is so deeply embedded within our traditions as to be a fundamental right, the lack of evidence alone might defeat his case. But the evidence shows that even in modern times—when, as we have noted, the rigid protection of the marital family has in other respects been relaxed—the

3. Justice Brennan asserts that only "a pinched conception of 'the family'" would exclude Michael, Carole, and Victoria from protection. We disagree. The family unit accorded traditional respect in our society, which we have referred to as the "unitary family," is typified, of course, by the marital family, but also includes the household of unmarried parents and their children. Perhaps the concept can be expanded even beyond this, but it will bear no resemblance to traditionally respected relationships—and will thus cease to have any constitutional significance—if it is stretched so far as to include the relationship established between a married woman, her lover, and their child, during a 3-month sojourn in St. Thomas, or during a subsequent 8-month period when, if he happened to be in Los Angeles, he stayed with her and the child.

4. Justice Brennan insists that in determining whether a liberty interest exists we must look at Michael's relationship with Victoria in isolation, without reference to the circumstance that Victoria's mother was married to someone else when the child was conceived, and that that woman and her husband wish to raise the child as their own. We cannot imagine what compels this strange procedure of looking at the act which is assertedly the subject of a liberty interest in isolation from its effect upon other people—rather like inquiring whether there is a liberty interest in firing a gun where the case at hand happens to involve its discharge into another person's body. The logic of Justice Brennan's position leads to the conclusion that if Michael had begotten Victoria by rape, that fact would in no way affect his possession of a liberty interest in his relationship with her.

ability of a person in Michael's position to claim paternity has not been generally acknowledged. . . .

Moreover, even if it were clear that one in Michael's position generally possesses, and has generally always possessed, standing to challenge the marital child's legitimacy, that would still not establish Michael's case. As noted earlier, what is at issue here is not entitlement to a state pronouncement that Victoria was begotten by Michael. It is no conceivable denial of constitutional right for a State to decline to declare facts unless some legal consequence hinges upon the requested declaration. What Michael asserts here is a right to have himself declared the natural father and *thereby to obtain parental prerogatives*. What he must establish, therefore, is not that our society has traditionally allowed a natural father in his circumstances to establish paternity, but that it has traditionally accorded such a father parental rights, or at least has not traditionally denied them. . . . What counts is whether the States in fact award substantive parental rights to the natural father of a child conceived within, and born into, an extant marital union that wishes to embrace the child. We are not aware of a single case, old or new, that has done so. This is not the stuff of which fundamental rights qualifying as liberty interests are made.[6] . . .

We have never had occasion to decide whether a child has a liberty interest, symmetrical with that of her parent, in maintaining her filial relationship. We need not do so here because, even assuming that such a right exists, Victoria's claim must fail. Victoria's due process challenge is, if anything, weaker than Michael's. Her basic claim is not that California has erred in preventing her from establishing that Michael, not Gerald, should stand as her legal father. Rather, she claims a due process right to maintain filial relationships with both Michael and Gerald. This assertion merits little discussion, for, whatever the merits of the guardian ad litem's belief that such an arrangement can be of great psychological benefit to a child, the claim that a State must recognize multiple fatherhood has no support in the history or traditions of this country. . . .

Victoria claims in addition that her equal protection rights have been violated because, unlike her mother and presumed father, she had no opportunity to rebut the presumption of her legitimacy. We find this argument wholly without merit. We reject, at the outset, Victoria's suggestion that her equal protection challenge must be assessed under a standard of strict scrutiny because, in denying her the right to maintain a filial relationship with Michael, the State is discriminating against her on the basis of her illegitimacy. See Gomez v. Perez, 409 U.S. 535, 538

---

6. Justice Brennan criticizes our methodology in using historical traditions specifically relating to the rights of an adulterous natural father, rather than inquiring more generally "whether parenthood is an interest that historically has received our attention and protection." . . .

We do not understand why, having rejected our focus upon the societal tradition regarding the natural father's rights vis-à-vis a child whose mother is married to another man, Justice Brennan would choose to focus instead upon "parenthood." Why should the relevant category not be even more general—perhaps "family relationships"; or "personal relationships"; or even "emotional attachments in general"? Though the dissent has no basis for the level of generality it would select, we do: We refer to the most specific level at which a relevant tradition protecting, or denying protection to, the asserted right can be identified. If, for example, there were no societal tradition, either way, regarding the rights of the natural father of a child adulterously conceived, we would have to consult, and (if possible) reason from, the traditions regarding natural fathers in general. But there is such a more specific tradition, and it unqualifiedly denies protection to such a parent. . . .

(1973). Illegitimacy is a legal construct, not a natural trait. Under California law, Victoria is not illegitimate, and she is treated in the same manner as all other legitimate children: she is entitled to maintain a filial relationship with her legal parents. . . . Since it pursues a legitimate end [protecting the integrity of the marital family] by rational means, California's decision to treat Victoria differently from her parents is not a denial of equal protection. . . .

Justice BRENNAN, with whom Justice MARSHALL and Justice BLACKMUN join, dissenting. . . .

Today's plurality . . . does not ask whether parenthood is an interest that historically has received our attention and protection; the answer to that question is too clear for dispute. Instead, the plurality asks whether the specific variety of parenthood under consideration—a natural father's relationship with a child whose mother is married to another man—has enjoyed such protection. . . .

If we had looked to tradition with such specificity in past cases, many a decision would have reached a different result. Surely the use of contraceptives by unmarried couples, or even by married couples; the freedom from corporal punishment in schools; . . . and even the right to raise one's natural but illegitimate children, were not "interest[s] traditionally protected by our society" at the time of their consideration by this Court. . . .

In construing the Fourteenth Amendment to offer shelter only to those interests specifically protected by historical practice, moreover, the plurality ignores the kind of society in which our Constitution exists. We are not an assimilative, homogeneous society, but a facilitative, pluralistic one, in which we must be willing to abide someone else's unfamiliar or even repellant practice because the same tolerant impulse protects our own idiosyncracies. Even if we can agree, therefore, that "family" and "parenthood" are part of the good life, it is absurd to assume that we can agree on the content of those terms and destructive to pretend that we do. In a community such as ours, "liberty" must include the freedom not to conform. The plurality today squashes this freedom by requiring specific approval from history before protecting anything in the name of liberty. . . .

. . . This is not a case in which we face a "new" kind of interest, one that requires us to consider for the first time whether the Constitution protects it. On the contrary, we confront an interest—that of a parent and child in their relationship with each other—that was among the first that this Court acknowledged in its cases defining the "liberty" protected by the Constitution [citing Meyer v. Nebraska, Skinner v. Oklahoma, Prince v. Massachusetts].

The evidence is undisputed that Michael, Victoria, and Carole did live together as a family; that is, they shared the same household, Victoria called Michael "Daddy," Michael contributed to Victoria's support, and he is eager to continue his relationship with her. Yet they are not, in the plurality's view, a "unitary family," whereas Gerald, Carole, and Victoria do compose such a family. The only difference between these two sets of relationships, however, is the fact of marriage. . . . However, the very premise of *Stanley* and the cases following it is that marriage is not decisive in answering the question whether the Constitution protects the parental relationship under consideration. . . .

The plurality's exclusive rather than inclusive definition of the "unitary family" is out of step with other decisions as well. This pinched conception of "the family," crucial as it is in rejecting Michael's and Victoria's claims of a liberty interest, is jarring in light of our many cases preventing the States from denying important interests or statuses to those whose situations do not fit the government's narrow view of the family. From Loving v. Virginia, 388 U.S. 1 (1967), to Levy v. Louisiana, 391 U.S. 68 (1968), and Glona v. American Guarantee & Liability Ins. Co., 391 U.S. 73 (1968), and from Gomez v. Perez, 409 U.S. 535 (1973), to Moore v. East Cleveland, 431 U.S. 494 (1977), we have declined to respect a State's notion, as manifested in its allocation of privileges and burdens, of what the family should be. Today's rhapsody on the "unitary family" is out of tune with such decisions. . . .

Notes and Questions on *Stanley* and *Michael H.*

1. Father's rights. To what extent does *Stanley* recognize substantive rights for unwed fathers? Whose rights does the Court vindicate? To what extent does *Stanley* accord equal status to unwed fathers and mothers? Is *Stanley* a procedural due process case, dealing with the hearing rights of parents? A substantive due process case, limiting the circumstances when the state may remove children from parents? Or both?

2. Background. The Court addressed the constitutional claims of unmarried fathers in three cases decided after *Stanley* but before *Michael H.*:

In Quilloin v. Walcott, 434 U.S. 246 (1978), the Court upheld a Georgia adoption statute requiring only the consent of the mother unless the father had legitimated the child by marriage and acknowledgment or by court order. The mother, shortly after her child's birth, married a man who was not the child's father. The new husband petitioned for adoption after the child had lived with him for nine years. The biological father, who had been given notice of the adoption proceeding, requested that the court deny the adoption, declare him the legitimate father, and grant him visitation. Although he had never lived with or legitimated the child, he had made some support payments and had visited the child occasionally. The child expressed a desire to be adopted. The Supreme Court affirmed the stepparent adoption as consistent with the child's best interests. Rejecting the father's due process argument, the Court distinguished the case from *Stanley* because of this biological father's failure to have or seek child custody. The Court rejected his equal protection claim on the ground that his interests were distinguishable from those of a married father because the latter had borne legal responsibility for childrearing.

In Caban v. Mohammed, 441 U.S. 380 (1979), an unmarried father brought a successful equal protection challenge to a New York law that permitted the adoption of his children, without his consent, by the husband of the children's mother. Caban had lived with Mohammed for five years and had fathered their two children. When the couple separated, the mother married another man. Caban continued to see his children frequently, contributed to their support, and at one point had custody. After the mother and her new husband petitioned for adoption, Caban and his new wife cross-petitioned.

The Supreme Court found the statute, which required the consent of only the mother of a nonmarital child, an overbroad gender-based generalization. The Court pointed out both the mother and father had participated in the children's care and support, and also that the state's interest in promoting adoption was not advanced in cases such as this. The Court elaborated:

> In those cases where the father never has come forward to participate in the rearing of his child, nothing in the Equal Protection Clause precludes the State from withholding from him the privilege of vetoing the adoption of that child. . . . But in cases such as this, where the father has established a substantial relationship with the child and has admitted his paternity, a State should have no difficulty in identifying the father even of children born out of wedlock. Thus, no showing has been made that the different treatment afforded unmarried fathers and unmarried mothers under [the statute] bears a substantial relationship to the proclaimed interest of the State in promoting the adoption of illegitimate children.

Id. at 392-393

Finally, in Lehr v. Robertson, 463 U.S. 248 (1983), the Court upheld another New York adoption statute dispensing with notice of adoption proceedings for some fathers of nonmarital children. In *Lehr*, Lorraine married Richard Robertson eight months after the birth of her nonmarital child. The biological father, Jonathan Lehr, had never contributed to the child's support and had seen her only infrequently. When the child was two, the Robertsons filed an adoption petition. Lehr claimed that the Due Process and Equal Protection Clauses, as interpreted in *Stanley*, gave him a right to notice and an opportunity to be heard. New York law required notice for fathers who had registered with a "putative father registry," as well as those who were adjudicated to be the father, identified on the birth certificate, lived openly with the child and the child's mother, or were married to the mother before the child was six months old. Lehr fit none of these categories. Unanswered by *Quilloin* and *Caban* was the extent of constitutional protection required for a father, such as Lehr, who manifests only a biological relationship with his child. That is, was he entitled to notice and an opportunity to be heard before the child could be adopted?

The Supreme Court concluded that due process does not require notice to a biological father if he has not assumed any responsibility for the care of his child:

> The significance of the biological connection is that it offers the natural father an opportunity that no other male possesses to develop a relationship with his offspring. If he grasps that opportunity and accepts some measure of responsibility for the child's future, he may enjoy the blessings of the parent-child relationship and make uniquely valuable contributions to the child's development. If he fails to do so, the Federal Constitution will not automatically compel a state to listen to his opinion of where the child's best interests lie.

Id. at 262. Further, the Court reasoned that the statute did not constitute a denial of equal protection because "If one parent has an established custodial relationship with the child and the other parent has either abandoned or never established a relationship, the Equal Protection Clause does not prevent a state from according the two parents different legal rights." Id. at 267-268. The Court distinguished the developed parent-child relationship that was implicated in *Stanley* and *Caban*.

A troublesome issue, raised by the dissent in *Lehr,* concerns the degree of constitutional protection to be afforded if the mother *prevents* the father from establishing a relationship with the child. Lehr's efforts to establish a parent-child relationship were thwarted by the mother who concealed her whereabouts after the birth. What is the extent of an unwed biological father's obligation to discover a mother's deception about her whereabouts or her pregnancy? See In re Adoption of Baby Girl P., 242 P.3d 1168, 1175 (Kan. 2010).

The *Quilloin-Caban-Lehr* trilogy stands for the principle that an unwed father is entitled to constitutional protection so long as he is willing to accept the responsibilities of parenthood (the "biology plus test"). The extent of this constitutional protection varies according to the degree to which he manifests a custodial, personal, or financial relationship with the child ("the indicia of parenthood"). To what extent is *Michael H.* consistent with these precedents? For an excellent analysis of the *Quilloin-Caban-Lehr* trilogy, see Melissa Murray, What's So New About the New Illegitimacy? 20 Am. U. J. Gender Soc. Pol'y & L. 387 (2012).

3. Defining "family." Professor Janet L. Dolgin sees familial relationships as the determinative variables in these cases:

> [T]he unwed father cases, from *Stanley* through *Michael H.*, delineate three factors that make an unwed man a father. These are the man's biological relation to the child, his social relation to the child, and his relation to the child's mother. . . . In this regard, *Michael H.* clarifies the earlier cases. A biological father does protect his paternity by developing a social relationship with his child, but this step demands the creation of a family, a step itself depending upon an appropriate relationship between the man and his child's mother.[54]

See also Allison Anna Tait, A Tale of Three Families: Historical Households, Earned Belonging, and Natural Connections, 63 Hastings L.J. 1345 (2012) (pointing out that unwed fathers earn rights only if they subscribe to the idea of the nuclear family).

4. Defining "father." Both *Stanley* and *Michael H.* test the government's power to write its own definition of certain terms: "parent" in *Stanley* and "father" in *Michael H.* Can you reconcile *Michael H.* with *Stanley*? Is footnote 3 in the plurality opinion persuasive?

5. Marital presumption. Professor Michael Grossberg has traced the history of the presumption of legitimacy (also known as the *marital presumption*) to the strong reluctance to stigmatize illegitimate children in the post-Revolutionary period. He elaborates:

> In the agonizing conflict between a man's right to limit his paternity only to his actual offspring and the right of a child born to a married woman to claim family

---

[54]. Janet L. Dolgin, Just a Gene: Judicial Assumptions About Parenthood, 40 UCLA L. Rev. 637, 671 (1993).

membership, the common law, first in England and then in America, generally made paternal rights defer to the larger goal of preserving family integrity.[55]

What is the purpose of the presumption of legitimacy and the other paternity presumptions? *Michael H.* suggests that the presumption was designed to preserve marital harmony and establish the marital family as the norm. What other purposes does a paternity presumption serve? See generally Jeffrey A. Parnass & Zachary Townsend, Legal Paternity (and Other Parenthood) After *Lehr* and *Michael H.*, 43 U. Tol. L. Rev. 225 (2012). How strong is the continuing case for the marital presumption in light of the decreased stigma of illegitimacy and the increasing accuracy of paternity determinations?

6. Other parentage presumptions: UPA.

a. The original UPA. The presumption of legitimacy, which *Michael H.* analyzes, presumptively identifies the legal father only of children born to married women. To extend coverage to children born to *unmarried* women, the original UPA provided for several alternative presumptions, including one based on the *conduct* of a man who "while the child is under the age of majority, . . . receives the child into his home and openly holds out the child as his natural child." UPA §4(a)(4) (1973). When two presumptions conflict, the original UPA directs that "the presumption which on the facts is founded on the weightier considerations of policy and logic controls." Id. §4(b). See supra (quoting §4 in its entirety). Does *Michael H.* present a case of conflicting presumptions under this section of the original UPA? If so, which one should control?

b. The revised UPA. The advent of genetic testing and the rise of assisted reproductive technologies prompted the development of a new UPA in 2000 and some revisions in 2002. This statutory scheme contains the following relevant provisions:

UNIFORM PARENTAGE ACT [REVISED]

§201. ESTABLISHMENT OF PARENT-CHILD RELATIONSHIP

(a) The mother-child relationship is established between a woman and a child by:

(1) the woman's having given birth to the child[, except as otherwise provided in [Article] 8] [on "gestational agreements" or surrogacy arrangements];

(2) an adjudication of the woman's maternity; [or]

(3) adoption of the child by the woman[; or

(4) an adjudication confirming the woman as a parent of a child born to a gestational mother if the agreement was validated under [Article] 8 or is enforceable under other law].

(b) The father-child relationship is established between a man and a child by:

[55]. Michael Grossberg, Governing the Hearth: Law and the Family in Nineteenth-Century America 201-202 (1985).

(1) an unrebutted presumption of the man's paternity of the child under Section 204;

(2) an effective acknowledgment of paternity by the man under [Article] 3, unless the acknowledgment has been rescinded or successfully challenged;

(3) an adjudication of the man's paternity;

(4) adoption of the child by the man; [or]

(5) the man's having consented to assisted reproduction by a woman under [Article] 7 which resulted in the birth of the child[; or

(6) an adjudication confirming the man as a parent of a child born to a gestational mother if the agreement was validated under [Article] 8 or is enforceable under other law].

§204. PRESUMPTION OF PATERNITY

(a) A man is presumed to be the father of a child if:

(1) he and the mother of the child are married to each other and the child is born during the marriage;

(2) he and the mother of the child were married to each other and the child is born within 300 days after the marriage is terminated by death, annulment, declaration of invalidity, or divorce[, or after a decree of separation];

(3) before the birth of the child, he and the mother of the child married each other in apparent compliance with law, even if the attempted marriage is or could be declared invalid, and the child is born during the invalid marriage or within 300 days after its termination by death, annulment, declaration of invalidity, or divorce[, or after a decree of separation];

(4) after the birth of the child, he and the mother of the child married each other in apparent compliance with law, whether or not the marriage is or could be declared invalid, and he voluntarily asserted his paternity of the child, and:

(A) the assertion is in a record filed with [state agency maintaining birth records];

(B) he agreed to be and is named as the child's father on the child's birth certificate; or

(C) he promised in a record to support the child as his own; or

(5) for the first two years of the child's life, he resided in the same household with the child and openly held out the child as his own.

(b) A presumption of paternity established under this section may be rebutted only by an adjudication under [Article] 6 [on paternity proceedings].

Article 6 of the new UPA authorizes paternity proceedings, including genetic testing. For children with no presumed father, a paternity proceeding can be brought at any time. UPA §606. The following limitations apply to a child with a presumed father:

§607. LIMITATION: CHILD HAVING PRESUMED FATHER

(a) Except as otherwise provided in subsection (b), a proceeding brought by a presumed father, the mother, or another individual to adjudicate the parentage of a child having a presumed father must be commenced not later than two years after the birth of the child.

(b) A proceeding seeking to disprove the father-child relationship between a child and the child's presumed father may be maintained at any time if the court determines that:

(1) the presumed father and the mother of the child neither cohabited nor engaged in sexual intercourse with each other during the probable time of conception; and

(2) the presumed father never openly held out the child as his own.

How would a court following the new UPA decide the controversy in the *Michael H.* case? What is the reason for the two-year requirement in §204(a)(5) and the two-year limitation period in §607(a)?

7. Weight of genetic evidence. At one time, the presumption of legitimacy was conclusive if the spouses were cohabiting at conception and the husband was neither sterile nor impotent. Today, federal child support legislation gives states the option of making the presumption rebuttable or conclusive depending on genetic test results. 42 U.S.C. §666(5)(G). Most states now have a rebuttable presumption of legitimacy.

Given that parenthood currently can be scientifically determined, what role should genetic evidence play? Should such evidence always trump presumptions resting on social factors, such as marriage or "holding out" the child as one's own? Should legal paternity rest exclusively on biological paternity? To what extent would a regime of fatherhood resting exclusively on genetics best achieve equal treatment of all children, regardless of the marital status or living arrangement of mothers? Alternatively, when genetic evidence conflicts with the presumption of legitimacy or one of the other paternity presumptions, should courts consider a child's best interests in resolving the conflict?

8. Paternity disestablishment. Some jurisdictions permit, by case law or statute, the *disestablishment* of paternity, particularly in cases of paternity fraud. Typically, a former husband or unwed father will attempt to invalidate a support obligation after genetic evidence shows that a child is not biologically related to him. Some states require that the man act within a prescribed time. A few jurisdictions impose criminal penalties on mothers who intentionally establish paternity for a man who is not the biological father.

Does disestablishment constitute sound policy? Should a man be permitted to disestablish paternity once he has assumed the role of the child's father? Courts sometimes deny disestablishment based on equitable estoppel. See, e.g., Boone v. Ballinger, 228 S.W.3d 1 (Ky. Ct. App. 2007). Other courts bar disestablishment based on res judicata, treating as a final judgment the divorce decree or child support order establishing paternity. See, e.g., Department of Revenue ex rel. Donaldson v. Blocker, 988 So. 2d 1292 (Fla. Dist. Ct. App. 2009). If a would-be father is permitted to disestablish paternity, who becomes responsible for child support? Can the putative father who disestablishes paternity seek reimbursement from the biological father? See R.A.C. v. P.J.S., 927 A.2d 97 (N.J. 2007).

9. How many fathers? *Michael H.* is based on the assumption that a child may have only one father. Recall Justice Scalia's comment in *Michael H.* that "California law, like nature itself, makes no provision for dual fatherhood." What is the basis for this belief? Given modern sexual mores, the high divorce rate, and remarriage rate, does this assumption make sense?

Should states adopt the Louisiana model of "dual paternity" (La. Civ. Code art. 198), which confers rights on both the legally presumed father and biological father, provided that the latter demonstrates that his participation in the child's life meets the best interests of the child? Is the concept of dual paternity a workable solution to *Michael H.*? For other advocates of dual-paternity models, see Nancy E. Dowd, Multiple Parents/Multiple Fathers, 9 J.L. & Fam. Stud. 231 (2007); Melanie B. Jacobs, Overcoming the Marital Presumption, 50 Fam. Ct. Rev. 289 (2012).

10. Extant marriage. How relevant is the fact that when Victoria was born, Carole and Gerald were *physically* residing together? Because *Michael H.* was based in large part on reluctance to disrupt an intact marriage, should the traditional presumption of legitimacy be applicable if the married couple has separated or divorced when the putative father makes his claim? See, e.g., Brian C. v. Ginger K., 92 Cal. Rptr. 2d 294 (Ct. App. 2000).

11. Response to *Michael H.* Discomfort with the Court's holding in *Michael H.* led to its rejection by a majority of states and the advent of the revised UPA. California (the site of *Michael H.*) amended its conclusive presumption of legitimacy to allow a putative father to move for blood tests within two years of birth in some cases (i.e., if the putative father received the child into his home and openly held out the child as his child). Cal. Fam. Code §7541(b) (amending former Cal. Evid. Code §621). The new UPA incorporates California's two-year limitation on the putative father's ability to request blood tests subject to estoppel principles (regarding the conduct of the parties, the equities of disproving the father-child relationship, or the best interests of the child). UPA §608.

Problems

1. When Stephanie marries Jeffrey, she is not motivated by love, but by a desire to obtain military benefits and to share rent. Thereafter, Stephanie begins an intimate relationship with Paul and bears his child. Before the birth, they move in together. During the two years in which they live together, Paul holds the child out as his son. Subsequently, Stephanie and Paul break up. At that time, Stephanie lies to Paul, telling him that he might not be the father. Paul files suit to establish paternity in California after the legislature has amended the statute (discussed in Note 11) in response to *Michael H.* Stephanie defends, alleging that Jeffrey is the child's father based on the statutory presumption of legitimacy. What result? Comino v. Kelley, 30 Cal. Rptr. 2d 728 (Ct. App. 1994).

2. DeAndre, born out of wedlock, is killed in an auto accident at age 20. Although a judicial proceeding established his biological father's paternity years before, his father never openly acknowledged his son. After DeAndre's death, the young man's mother sues to sever any inheritance rights that his father might claim. State law precludes the father of a nonmarital child from inheriting

from the child if the father either failed or refused to provide support or openly acknowledged the child as his own. The father challenges the statute as an unconstitutional gender-based classification because unmarried mothers need not meet any requirements before inheriting from their children. DeAndre's mother and the state argue that the statute differentiates not on the basis of gender but rather distinguishes fathers who openly acknowledge their nonmarital children and those who do not. They also argue that the statute advances the state interest in encouraging fathers to take responsibility for their nonmarital children by precluding an uninvolved father from profiting from the child's death. What result? See Rainey v. Chever, 510 S.E.2d 823 (Ga. 1999); Eleanor Mixon, Note, Deadbeat Dads: Undeserving of the Right to Inherit from Their Illegitimate Children and Undeserving of Equal Protection, 34 Ga. L. Rev. 1773, 1775-1776 (2000).

3. Extending Paternity Laws to Same-Sex Couples

The preceding materials focus on statutory and constitutional frameworks to identify the fathers of nonmarital children. Paternity establishment has long been necessary to confer rights and obligations on nonmarital children and their parents. Traditionally, the law was not concerned with "maternity establishment" and its ensuing rights and obligations because the woman who gives birth to a child is easily identifiable. However, with the development of reproductive technology and the advent of marriage equality, this issue arises with greater frequency.

The following materials focus on these questions: Should paternity laws apply in a gender-neutral manner to mothers as well as fathers? Put another way, what role should paternity laws play in the establishment of the rights of children of lesbian couples and their corresponding parental obligations? How should such laws apply to gay male couples and their children?

CHATTERJEE v. KING

280 P.3d 283 (N.M. 2012)

CHÁVEZ, Justice.

Bani Chatterjee and Taya King are two women who were in a committed, long-term domestic relationship when they agreed to bring a child into their relationship. [W]ith Chatterjee's active participation, King adopted a child from Russia. Chatterjee supported King and Child financially, lived in the family home, and co-parented Child for a number of years before their commitment to each other foundered and they dissolved their relationship. Chatterjee never adopted Child. After they ended their relationship, King moved to Colorado and sought to prevent Chatterjee from having any contact with Child.

Chatterjee filed a petition to establish parentage and determine custody and timesharing. Chatterjee alleged that she was a presumed natural parent under the former codification of the New Mexico Uniform Parentage Act. [W]e must now determine whether Chatterjee, as a woman, can establish a presumed natural parent and child relationship under [N.M. Stat. Ann. §40-11-5(A)(4)].

Chatterjee argues that the Court of Appeals erred in holding that none of the UPA provisions relating to the father and child relationship may be applied to women. . . . We find support for Chatterjee's argument not only in the plain language of the statute itself, but also in the purpose of the UPA, the application of paternity provisions to women in jurisdictions with similar UPA provisions, and in public policy that encourages the love and support of children from able and willing parents. . . .

We begin our analysis with Section 40-11-2 of the UPA, which states that a "'parent and child relationship' means the legal relationship existing between a child and his natural or adoptive parents incident to which the law confers or imposes rights, privileges, duties, and obligations. It includes the mother and child relationship and the father and child relationship." For a mother, Section 40-11-4(A) provides that "the natural mother may be established by proof of her having given birth to the child, or *as provided by Section* [40-11-21 NMSA 1978]." ([E]mphasis added.) Section 40-11-21 states that "[a]ny interested party may bring an action to determine the existence or nonexistence of a mother and child relationship. Insofar as practicable, the provisions of the Uniform Parentage Act applicable to the father and child relationship apply."

[The court first held that Chatterjee had standing as an "interested party" because the term applied to any person who is able to establish presumed natural parenthood under Section 40-11-5(A)(4). The court then addressed the Court of Appeals' arguments that reading Section 40-11-21 to allow Chatterjee to establish parentage through Section 40-11-5(A)(4) was "impracticable" and that the legislature, in enacting Section 40-11-4(A), created separate sections for how a woman, as opposed to a man, can prove natural parenthood, implying that it intended each sex to have different means available for proving parenthood.] The Court therefore concluded that applying the means for proving paternity to proving maternity would contravene the legislature's intent. We disagree.

It is practicable to apply Section 40-11-5 to determine maternity in certain circumstances [because] Section 40-11-5(A)(4), which establishes a parental presumption is reasonably capable of being accomplished by either a man or a woman. [That section] provides, in relevant part, that "[a] man is presumed to be the natural father of a child if . . . while the child is under the age of majority, he openly holds out the child as his natural child and has established a personal, financial or custodial relationship with the child." Because the presumption is based on a person's conduct, not a biological connection, a woman is capable of holding out a child as her natural child and establishing a personal, financial, or custodial relationship with that child. This is particularly true when, as is alleged in this case, the relationship between the child and both the presumptive and the adoptive parent occurred simultaneously.

In addition, by limiting proof of natural motherhood to biology under Section 40-11-4(A), the Court of Appeals renders meaningless the clear instruction in Section 40-11-4(A) that a "natural mother may [also] be established . . . . as provided by Section 21 [40-11-21 NMSA 1978]." A straightforward reading of Section 40-11-4(A) is that motherhood may be established by giving birth, by adoption, and in any other way in which a father and child relationship may be established when it is practicable to do so. Because it is practicable for a woman to hold a child out as her own, the plain language instructs us to recognize that Section 40-11-5(A)(4) relating to the father and child relationship also applies to the mother and child relationship. . . .

Moreover, we seek to avoid an interpretation of a statute that would raise constitutional concerns. In this case, the Court of Appeals' reading would yield different results for a man than for a woman in precisely the same situation. If this Court interpreted Section 40-11-5(A)(4) as applying only to males, then a man in a same-sex relationship claiming to be a natural parent because he held out a child as his own would have standing simply by virtue of his gender, while a woman in the same position would not. . . . We avoid this disparate treatment, giving effect to the Legislature's intent, with a plain and simple application of Section 40-11-5(A)(4) to both men and women under Section 40-11-21.

The authors of the Uniform Parentage Act of 1973 (the original UPA), anticipating situations such as this case, provided in a comment that masculine terminology was used for the sake of simplicity and not to limit application of its provisions to males. . . . There is no indication that our Legislature intended a different reading of this statute in New Mexico when it adopted the original UPA. . . .

[The court next points out that other jurisdictions with virtually identical statutes have applied provisions relating to the father-child relationship to the mother-child relationship. [Further, the court explains, public policy supports applying the state version of the UPA to women.] [T]he state has a strong interest in ensuring that a child will be cared for, financially and otherwise, by two parents. If that care is lacking, the state will ultimately assume the responsibility of caring for the child. This is one of the primary reasons that the original UPA was created, and it makes little sense to read the statute without keeping this overarching legislative goal in mind. The original UPA was also written to address the interest that children have in their own support. The rationale underlying the original UPA is that every child should be treated equally, regardless of the marital status of the child's parents. In deciding illegitimacy cases, the United States Supreme Court recognized that it is "illogical and unjust" for a state to deny a child's essential right to be supported by two parents simply because the child's parents are not married. Gomez v. Perez, 409 U.S. 535, 538 (1973). . . . With this in mind, we see no reason for children to be penalized because of the decisions that their parents make, legal or otherwise.

Consistent with the underlying policy-based rationale of the New Mexico UPA that equality in child welfare requires laws that achieve equality in parentage, Child's need for love and support is no less critical simply because her second parent also happens to be a woman. Experts in child psychology recognize that sometimes the law is too limiting when it comes to actually addressing what is in the child's best interests. The attachment bonds that form between a child and a parent are formed regardless of a biological or legal connection. See Joseph Goldstein et al., Beyond the Best Interests of the Child 27 (rev. ed. 1979). These bonds are formed as a result of "provision of physical and emotional care, continuity or consistency in the child's life, and emotional investment in the child." The law needs to address traditional expectations in light of current realities to keep up with the changing demographic of American families and to protect the children born into them. . . .

It is inappropriate to deny Chatterjee the opportunity to establish parentage, when denying Chatterjee this opportunity would only serve to harm both Child and the state. In our view, it is against public policy to deny parental rights and responsibilities based solely on the sex of either or both of the parents. The better view is to recognize that the child's best interests are served when intending parents physically, emotionally, and financially support the child from the time the child comes into their lives. This is especially true when both parents are able and willing to care for the child. Therefore, we hold that the Legislature intended that Section 40-11-5(A)(4) be applied to a woman who is seeking to establish a natural parent and child relationship with a child whom she has held out as her natural child from the moment the child came into the lives of both the adoptive mother and the presumptive mother. . . .

The fact that Chatterjee did not adopt Child does not impact our decision. Section 40-11-5 of the New Mexico UPA delineates the ways in which parentage can be presumed. Thus, our Legislature has recognized that there will be many situations in which someone is caring for a child but has not taken any steps to legalize that relationship. While taking legal action is the best way to ensure that both the alleged parent and the child have rights arising from that relationship, both our Legislature and this Court have indicated a willingness to confer rights to relationships that have not been legally established. This is so because parental rights are not automatically conferred when there is a biological relationship, but rather when an alleged parent has taken the responsibility of caring for a child. Considering the specific facts of this case, we hold that Chatterjee has alleged sufficient facts to attempt to establish that she is an interested party, and therefore she has standing to establish parentage under Section 40-11-21 of the New Mexico UPA. . . .

[Finally, the court concludes by examining the argument that Chatterjee must establish King's unfitness as a parent based on the parental preference doctrine.] [T]he Court of Appeals held that, since Chatterjee could not establish a natural mother and child relationship under the New Mexico UPA, she therefore could not seek custody under the Dissolution of Marriage Act absent a showing of King's unfitness. . . . However, the parental preference doctrine does not apply between two parents in a custody dispute. [O]ur holding gives Chatterjee the opportunity to seek joint custody as a natural parent. . . .

Notes and Questions

1. **Holding and rationale.** What was the nature of the dispute in *Chatterjee*? What are the different views of the appellate and state supreme courts? Why did Chatterjee's former partner (Taya King) argue that Chatterjee had to make a showing of King's unfitness? What did the courts respond? Compare In re Wells, 373 S.W.3d 174 (Tex. App. 2012) (requiring proof of unfitness in dispute between former same-sex partners).

Suppose the women could have married. What would be the relevance of their choice not to do so? What is the relevance of the fact that Chatterjee never adopted the child? On the other hand, suppose that Chatterjee had adopted the child. Could the court nonetheless have denied her standing in the custody dispute? Compare L.M. v. M.G., 145 Cal. Rptr. 3d 97 (Ct. App. 2012), with Bates v. Bates, 730 S.E 2d 482 (Ga. Ct. App. 2012). Suppose that Chatterjee merely wanted to intervene in an adoption proceeding involving her former partner's next partner or spouse? Would she have standing? See In re Guardianship of Madelyn, 98

A.3d 494 (N.H. 2014) (reversing determination that second parent was not a "parent," thereby allowing her to intervene).

2. Benefit. Who benefits from the court's ruling in *Chatterjee*? Lesbian partners who are parents? Gay male partners who are parents? Birth mothers? The children? The state?

3. UPA. Which provision(s) of the UPA does the court apply? What is the basis of the court's reasoning that the UPA's paternity provisions should apply to women? Is the court's reasoning persuasive? As *Chatterjee* explains, the trend is to apply the UPA's presumed-parent provisions in a gender-neutral manner to same-sex partners. How might this trend evolve after the legalization of same-sex marriage?

4. Child support. What is the relationship between parental status and the support obligation? In Elisa B. v. Superior Court, 117 P.3d 660 (Cal. 2005), the California Supreme Court held that the presumed father provisions of the California UPA applied in order to impose child support obligations on a former lesbian partner. To what extent is judicial recognition of a former partner as a parent a prerequisite of the duty of child support? In other words, could a court obligate a same-sex partner to support a child without recognizing the partner as a parent? This last question assumed considerable importance in states that formerly did not recognize same-sex marriage, as well as those states that did not recognize second-parent adoption. The issue still has relevance because not all same-sex couples choose to marry or adopt. What room remains for equitable remedies and functional and formal approaches now that there is marriage equality?

5. Alternative theories. Chatterjee claimed alternatively that she was entitled to relief as the equitable or de facto parent of the child, although the court did not reach either issue. Should courts recognize parentage for former same-sex partners based on these common law theories that would estop a legal parent from denying the claimant's parental status? Compare D.M.T. v. T.M.H., 129 So. 3d 320 (Fla. 2013) (applying unmarried-father cases to recognize as a parent an egg donor who helped rear the child), with In re Custody of A.F.J., 260 P.3d 889 (Wash. Ct. App. 2011) (contra). See also L.S.K. v. H.A.N., 813 A.2d 872 (Pa. Super. Ct. 2002) (recognizing parents by estoppel). These theories are discussed later in this book, in Chapter VIII. Should courts recognize parentage by contract? See Frazier v. Goudschaal, 295 P.3d 542 (Kan. 2013).

6. Rebuttal. If genetic evidence is increasingly permitted to rebut parentage presumptions, what will this development signify for second parents? If genetic evidence controls, what good are parentage presumptions for same-sex couples, who must use donated genetic material? See generally Janet L. Dolgin, Biological Evaluations: Blood, Genes, and Family, 41 Akron L. Rev. 347 (2008) (pointing out that some courts are well aware of the limitations posed by increasing reliance on genetic testing). Will the advent of marriage equality cause weakening or dilution of parentage presumptions?

7. Gender neutrality. Does the court's holding make Chatterjee the child's father? Their second mother? Their parent? Does it matter? Professor Susan Dalton criticizes existing law for its asymmetrical treatment of parentage for males and females and the underlying incapacity for "imagining a gender-free subject" in this context.[56] She contends that, while the law has accorded a man parental status based on social factors, such as marriage to the child's mother or holding out a child as his own, biological ties remained essential for a woman to achieve such status. To what extent has the New Mexico Supreme Court addressed Dalton's critique?

How does *Chatterjee* address the application of the relevant doctrines and statutes to gay male couples? What would Dalton's call for gender neutrality mean here?

8. Marital presumption. Now that same-sex marriage is legal in all states, is there any reason that the marital presumption should *not* apply to same-sex married couples? Some issues may still need to be addressed by legal reforms. For example, how should the law address the traditional application of the marital presumption to the parentage rights of the spouse of the "birth mother" in order to take into account the rights of gay fathers? In addition, the marital presumption may be rebutted by proof of nonpaternity in some states. How should the rule be revised to apply to second parents who have no biological connection to the child?

9. Conflict of laws. How should the law resolve conflicting state approaches to parentage? See, e.g., Ex Parte N.B., 66 So. 3d 249 (Ala. 2010); Miller-Jenkins v. Miller-Jenkins, 12 A.3d 768 (Vt. 2010). See generally Steve Sanders, Interstate Recognition of Parent-Child Relationships: The Limits of the State Interests Paradigm and the Role of Due Process, 2011 U. Chi. Legal F. 233.

Problems

1. Melissa, who is bisexual, is currently involved in a rocky relationship with her female partner, Irene, in the state of Blackacre. After the women break up, Melissa starts an intimate relationship with Jesus. In the course of Melissa and Jesus's brief relationship, Melissa becomes pregnant. Toward the end of the pregnancy, however, Melissa and Irene reconcile and decide to marry. When Melissa gives birth to Emily, Melissa places both women's names on her birth certificate.

One day, in the midst of a verbal altercation, Melissa becomes infuriated, grabs a kitchen knife, and stabs Irene. Melissa is jailed on a charge of attempted murder. Irene lives but is hospitalized. Because neither mother can care for Emily, the state social services department takes her into custody. When Irene recovers, she seeks Emily's return. The Department of Social Services refuses on the grounds that Irene is unemployed and homeless. At this point, Jesus (Emily's biological father) asks the court to award custody to him on the grounds that he is Emily's "parent." Does Jesus have standing to claim parentage based on the UPA? How should the court rule? See In re M.C., 123 Cal. Rptr. 3d 856 (Ct. App. 2011).

---

[56]. Susan E. Dalton, From Presumed Fathers to Lesbian Mothers: Sex Discrimination and Legal Construction of Parenthood, 9 Mich. J. Gender & L. 261, 266 (2003).

Motivated by the above case, the Blackacre legislature is considering a bill that would amend Blackacre's version of the UPA to allow children to be granted more than two legal parents, and that would apply equally to opposite- and same-sex relationships. You are a legislative aide to the state senator who introduced the bill. Your boss asks you to evaluate the merits and shortcomings of the bill. Should custody be granted to more than two parents? If so, what rights and responsibilities would be affected, and how should they be allocated? Should the bill place a ceiling on the maximum number of parents? See S.B. 274, 2013-2014 Leg. Sess. (Cal. 2013) (authorizing a court to find that more than 2 persons with a claim to parentage, as specified, are parents if the court finds that recognizing only 2 parents would be detrimental to the child).

2. Elizabeth and Sabrina begin living together in an intimate relationship. They want to have a child together, and they agree that Sabrina will undergo artificial insemination. After one failed insemination attempt, and without telling Elizabeth, Sabrina asks a male friend, Mark, if he will agree to inseminate her through sexual intercourse. He does and she conceives a child (A.R.L.). Elizabeth is present at the birth. Both women agree to give the child Elizabeth's surname. The birth certificate lists Sabrina as the child's mother but does not identify a father. They all live together as a family for a year with both women sharing parenting. Elizabeth petitions for a second-parent adoption, but the court dismisses her petition. After the women separate, Elizabeth files a petition to establish her parentage under the state version of the UPA. Sabrina moves to dismiss Sabrina's petition and joins Mark as a party, but he later files a petition to relinquish his parental rights. Discuss Elizabeth's arguments and Sabrina's counterarguments. Should it matter whether they are an unmarried couple living together or a married couple? See In re Parental Responsibilities of A.L.R., 318 P.3d 581 (Colo. Ct. App. 2013).

VI

Divorce

A. Introduction

For centuries, marriage was regarded as a lifelong commitment. Today, developments in family law make it considerably easier for the spouses to dissolve their relationship. This chapter explores state regulation of the dissolution process. In particular, it contrasts the traditional fault-based system with the system of no-fault divorce that replaced it. It also addresses issues of access to divorce, the role of counsel, and divorce jurisdiction.

The evolution of divorce law and procedure raises important questions about individual autonomy and the interest of the state. How does divorce law change the parties' roles and responsibilities toward each other and the state? How have developments in divorce law altered the legal meaning of marriage? What additional divorce reforms would you recommend?

1. Divorce as a Historical Phenomenon

Lawrence M. Friedman, A History of American Law

142-144, 378-381 (3d ed. 2005)

England had been a "divorceless society," and remained that way until 1857. Henry VIII had gotten a divorce; but ordinary Englishmen had no such privilege.

The very wealthy might squeeze a rare private bill out of Parliament. Between 1800 and 1836 there were, on the average, three of these a year. For the rest, unhappy husbands and wives had to be satisfied with annulment (no easy matter), or divorce from bed and board (*a mensa et thoro*), a form of legal separation, which did not entitle either spouse to marry again. . . . No court before 1857 had authority to grant a divorce. The most common solutions, of course, when a marriage broke down, were adultery and desertion.

In the colonial period, the South was generally faithful to English tradition. . . . In New England, however, courts and legislatures occasionally granted divorce. In Pennsylvania, Penn's laws of 1682 gave spouses the right to a "Bill of Divorcement" if their marriage partner was convicted of adultery. Later, the governor or lieutenant governor was empowered to dissolve marriages, on grounds of incest, adultery, bigamy, or homosexuality. There is no evidence that the governor ever used this power. Still later, the general assembly took divorce into its own hands. The English privy council disapproved of this practice, and in the 1770's disallowed legislative divorces in Pennsylvania, New Jersey, and New Hampshire. The Revolution put an end to the privy council's power.

After Independence, the law and practice of divorce began to change, but regional differences remained quite strong. [In the South, legislatures passed private divorce laws.] North of the Mason-Dixon line, courtroom divorce became the normal mode rather than legislative divorce. Pennsylvania passed a general divorce law in 1785, Massachusetts one year later. Every New England state had a divorce law before 1800, along with New York, New Jersey, and Tennessee. Grounds for divorce varied somewhat from state to state. New York's law of 1787 permitted absolute divorce only for adultery. Vermont, on the other hand, in 1798 allowed divorce for impotence, adultery, intolerable severity, three years' willful desertion, and long absence with presumption of death. . . .

The outbreak of [these] divorce laws surely represented a real increase in the demand for legal divorce. More marriages seemed to be cracking under the strains of nineteenth-century life. . . . To many devout and respectable people, [the rising divorce rate] was an alarming fire bell in the night, a symptom of moral dry rot and a cause in itself of further moral decay. [T]he family was changing. There was a slow but real revolution in the way men and women related to each other. William O'Neill put it this way: "when families are large and loose, arouse few expectations, and make few demands, there is no need for divorce." That need arises when "families become the center of social organization." At this point, "their intimacy can become suffocating, their demands unbearable, and their expectations too high to be easily realizable. Divorce then becomes the safety valve that makes the system workable." Moreover, a divorceless state is not a state without adultery, prostitution, fornication. It is certainly not a place where there are no drunken, abusive husbands. What it may be—or rather, what it became later in the century—was a place where the official law and the world of real life were sharply different.

[By 1880, legislative divorce was abolished. From 1850 to 1870, many states adopted highly liberal divorce laws. Divorce was easiest to obtain in western states especially, those least stratified by class.] After 1870, the tide began to turn. Influential moral leaders had never stopped attacking loose divorce laws. Horace Greeley thought that "easy divorce" had made the Roman Empire rot.

America could suffer a similar fate. [In 1881, a New England Divorce Reform League was formed which later became the National Divorce Reform League. By 1882, the Connecticut law had been repealed.] Maine's law fell in 1883. A more rigorous divorce law replaced it, with tougher grounds, a six-month wait before divorce decrees became "absolute," and a two-year ban on remarriage of the plaintiff without court permission; the guilty defendant could *never* remarry without leave of the court.

Militant feminists, on the other hand, took up the cudgels for permissive divorce. A furious debate raged in New York. Robert Dale Owen, son of the Utopian reformer, went into battle against Horace Greeley. [Owen] felt that strict divorce laws, not lax ones, led to adultery. . . .

[A dramatic increase occurred in the divorce rate between 1867 and 1881 despite the stricter divorce laws.] What accounts for the rising demand for divorce? [A] large number of people simply wanted *formal* acceptance of the fact that their marriages were dead. Just as more of the middle class wanted, and need, their deeds recorded, their wills made out, [and] their marriages solemnized, so they wanted the honesty and convenience of divorce, the right to remarry in bourgeois style, to have legitimate children with their second wife (or husband), and the right to decent, honest disposition of their worldly goods. . . .

"Divorce rings" operated practically in the open. Manufactured adultery was a New York specialty. Henry Zeimer and W. Waldo Mason, arrested in 1900, had lured young secretaries and other enterprising girls for this business. The girls would admit on the witness stand that they knew the plaintiff's husband, then blush, shed a few tears, and leave the rest to the judge. . . .

The migratory divorce, for people with money and the urge to travel, was another detour around strict enforcement of divorce law. To attract the "tourist trade," a state needed easy laws and a short residence period. [I]n the twentieth century, Nevada become *the* place. . . .

The last part of the nineteenth century was an era of national panic over morality, eugenics, the purity of the bloodline, and the future of old-fashioned white America. Whores and divorce had to be constrained. An irresistible force (the demand) met an immovable object (the resistance to divorce). The result was a stalemate. [M]oralists had their symbolic victory, a stringent law strutting proudly on the books. But nobody enforced these laws, least of all the judges. A cynical traffic in runaway and underground divorce flourished in the shadows. . . .

World War II brought higher divorce rates stemming from the effects of wartime separation (i.e., adultery) and difficult postwar adjustments to married life. Divorce rates stabilized in the 1950s for about ten years.[1] Rates began rising sharply in the 1960s and 1970s with the advent of no-fault divorce, and reached a

[1]. Roderick Phillips, Putting Asunder: A History of Divorce Law in Western Society 557-564 (1988).

peak in 1981.[2] Since then, the divorce rate has declined.[3] Approximately half of all marriages today will end in divorce compared to 10 percent at the beginning of the twentieth century.[4] Currently, one in five adults has been divorced.[5] First marriages that end in divorce last about eight years; remarriages reflect the same dissolution rate and same average duration.[6]

2. Divorce as a Social Phenomenon

Paul Bohannon, The Six Stations of Divorce

in Divorce and After 29-32 (Paul Bohannon ed., 1970)

The complexity of divorce arises because at least six things are happening at once. They may come in a different order and with varying intensities, but [they include]: (1) the emotional divorce, which centers around the problem of the deteriorating marriage; (2) the legal divorce, based on grounds [and now, on no-fault]; (3) the economic divorce, which deals with money and property; (4) the coparental divorce, which deals with custody, single-parent homes, and visitation; (5) the community divorce, surrounding the changes of friends and community that every divorcee experiences; and (6) the psychic divorce, with the problem of regaining individual autonomy.

The first visible stage of a deteriorating marriage is likely to be what psychiatrists call emotional divorce. This occurs when the spouses withhold emotion from their relationship because they dislike the intensity or ambivalence of their feelings. They may continue to work together as a social team, but their attraction and trust for one another have disappeared. [They become] mutually antagonistic and imprisoned, hating the vestiges of their dependence. Two people in emotional divorce grate on each other because each is disappointed. . . .

The economic divorce must occur because in Western countries husband and wife are an economic unit. [T]hey certainly have many of the characteristics of a legal corporation. [A]n economic settlement must be made, separating the assets of the "corporation" into two sets of assets, each belonging to one person. This is the property settlement. . . .

The coparental divorce is necessary if there are children. When the household breaks up, the children have to live somewhere. Taking care of the children requires complex arrangements for carrying out the obligations of parents.

---

[2]. Andrew J. Cherlin, American Marriage in the Early Twenty-First Century, in 15 The Future of Children 33, 36 (2005); U.S. Dept. of Health & Human Servs., Nat'l Ctr. for Health Statistics, Monthly Vital Statistics Report, Divorces and Annulments and Rates, 1940-1990, at 1 (1995) (table 1).

[3]. Nat'l Marriage Project, The State of Our Unions: Marriage in America 2012, Divorce 69, http://nationalmarriageproject.org/reports. Scholars attribute the decline in divorce rates to delayed first marriage age, and the fact that marriage is increasingly sought by the well-educated—factors contributing to greater marital stability.

[4]. Cherlin, supra note [2], at 36.

[5]. U.S. Census Bureau, Number, Timing, and Duration of Marriages and Divorces: 2009, at 12 (May 2011), http://www.census.gov/prod/2011pubs/p70-125.pdf.

[6]. Id. at 15.

All divorced persons suffer more or less because their community is altered. Friends necessarily take a different view of a person during and after divorce—he ceases to be a part of a couple. . . .

Finally comes the psychic divorce. It is almost always last, and always the most difficult. Indeed, I have not found a word strong or precise enough to describe the difficulty of the process. Each partner to the ex-marriage, either before or after the legal divorce—usually after, and sometimes years after—must turn himself or herself again into an autonomous social individual. People who have been long married tend to have become socially part of a couple or a family; they lose the habit of seeing themselves as individuals. . . .

Divorce is an institution that nobody enters without great trepidation. In the emotional divorce, people are likely to feel hurt and angry. In the legal divorce, people often feel bewildered—they have lost control, and events sweep them along. In the economic divorce, the reassignment of property and the division of money (there is *never* enough) may make them feel cheated. In the parental divorce, they worry about what is going to happen to the children; they feel guilty for what they have done. With the community divorce, they may get angry with their friends and perhaps suffer despair because there seems to be no fidelity in friendship. In the psychic divorce, in which they have become autonomous again, they are probably afraid and are certainly lonely.

However, the resolution of any or all of these various six divorces may provide an elation of victory that comes from having accomplished something that had to be done and having done it well. . . . I know a divorced man who took great comfort in the fact that one of his business associates asked him, when he learned of his divorce, "Do I feel sorry for you or do I congratulate you?" He thought for a moment and said—out of bravado as much as conviction—"Congratulate me." It was, for him, the beginning of the road back.

3. Divorce as a Gender-Based Phenomenon

Men and women experience marriage differently (as we saw in Chapter III). Below, men and women report different experiences of divorce.

Catherine K. Riessman, Divorce Talk: Women and Men Make Sense of Personal Relationships

65-72 (1990)

. . . For women, marriage flounders because husbands fail to be emotionally intimate in the ways wives expect them to be. This element of the companionate marriage is the centerpiece in women's accounts, working class and middle class alike. For men, the explanatory schema is very different: particularly for more economically advantaged men, the marriage failed because other relationships—with children, kin, and friends—were not subordinated to it; the marital relationship was not self-contained or was not primary enough to the wife. For both husbands and wives there was a failure in companionship; yet the particular activities women and men wanted to "do together" are strikingly different, especially in working-class marriages. And both women and men lament acts of sexual infidelity and incompatibility, though the interpretations they place on these events are not the same. For women, infidelity is an act of betrayal, living proof the marriage is over. Men have complex and differentiated views of infidelity, even as sex is central to their definition of what a good marriage should provide.

Some might argue that these different constructions arise out of the very different personality structures of women and men. Feminist psychological theory suggests that masculinity becomes defined through separation, whereas femininity becomes defined through relationships. Women and men, in bringing these different orientations into marriage, put severe strains on it. Women define the institution of marriage interpersonally. The relationship with the spouse is one of a series of interpersonal ties that coexist for them—not without conflict, of course. Yet at the same time women want marriage to be emotionally intimate through talking about feelings, problems, and daily experiences, and through understandings that go beyond words. Further, they expect talk to be reciprocal: their husbands will disclose to them at the same time as they share with their husbands. Divorced women's accounts describe men who could not or did not express love in these ways, or whose needs for separation, some might argue, precluded this kind of emotional intimacy.

Men want something very different from marriage. Especially prominent is their desire for the undivided attention of their wives. [Men] want the marital relationship to be exclusive and primary; women in contrast, add it to their other relational investments. Men value the autonomy of the marital pair rather than its interconnectedness. They expect to achieve emotional closeness with their wives through sex and a particular kind of companionship. It is these "doing" aspects of marriage that they emphasize. [T]he masculine style of love emphasizes practical help, shared physical activities, spending time together, and sex—manifestations of love that achieve connection through action rather than talk, just as providing for a family does. This style of love fits well with cultural expectations for men more generally, for achievement, responsibility, instrumentality. . . .

Neither the women nor the men interviewed, whether working class or middle class, questioned the ideology of the companionate marriage. It was the failure of their particular partners to live up to the ideal that was defined as the problem, not the dream itself. . . .

Below, psychologist E. Mavis Hetherington explains the theory that women's experiences of divorce vary according to *marriage type.*

E. Mavis Hetherington, Marriage and Divorce American Style

The American Prospect Online, Mar. 25, 2002

GOOD MARRIAGES, BAD MARRIAGES

[In the authors' long-term study of 1,400 divorced families, they identified different types of marriages (described below), ranging from "pursuer-distancer" marriages, which are most likely to end in divorce, to traditional marriages, which reflect the most stability.]

Pursuer-distancer marriages are those mismatches in which one spouse, usually the wife, wants to confront and discuss problems and feelings and the other, usually the husband, wants to avoid confrontations and either denies problems or withdraws. In disengaged marriages, couples share few interests, activities, or friends. Conflict is low, but so is affection and sexual satisfaction. Operatic marriages involve couples who like to function at a level of extreme emotional arousal. They are intensely attracted, attached, and volatile, given both to frequent fighting and to passionate lovemaking. Cohesive-individuated marriages are the yuppie and feminist ideal, characterized by equity, respect, warmth, and mutual support, but also by both partners retaining the autonomy to pursue their own goals and to have their own friends. Traditional marriages are those in which the husband is the main income producer and the wife's role is one of nurturance, support, and home and child care. These marriages work well as long as both partners continue to share a traditional view of gender roles.

We found that not just the risk of divorce, but also the extent of women's psychological and health troubles, varies according to marriage type—with wives in pursuer-distancer and disengaged marriages experiencing the most problems, those in operatic marriages significantly fewer, and those in cohesive-individuated and traditional marriages the fewest. Like so many other studies, we found that men's responses are less nuanced; the only differentiation among them was that men in pursuer-distancer marriages have more problems than those in the other four types.

The issue is not simply the amount of disagreement in the marriage; disagreements, after all, are endemic in close personal relations. It is how people disagree and solve problems—how they interact—that turns out to be closely associated with both the duration of their marriages and the well-being of wives and, to a lesser extent, husbands. Contempt, hostile criticism, belligerence, denial, and withdrawal erode a marriage. Affection, respect, trust, support, and making the partner feel valued and worthwhile strengthen the relationship.

GOOD DIVORCES, BAD DIVORCES

Divorce experiences also are varied. Initially, especially in marriages involving children, divorce is miserable for most couples. In the early years, ex-spouses typically must cope with lingering attachments; with resentment and anger, self-doubts, guilt, depression, and loneliness; with the stress of separation from children or of raising them alone; and with the loss of social networks and, for women, of economic security. Nonetheless, we found that a gradual recovery usually begins by the end of the second year. And by six years after divorce, 80 percent of both men and women have moved on to build reasonably or exceptionally fulfilling lives.

Indeed, about 20 percent of the women we observed eventually emerged from divorce enhanced and exhibiting competencies they never would have developed in an unhappy or constraining marriage. They had gone back to school or work to ensure the economic stability of their families, they had built new social networks, and they had become involved and effective parents and socially responsible citizens. Often they had happy second marriages. Divorce had offered them an opportunity to build new and more satisfying relationships and the freedom they needed for personal growth. This was especially true for women moving from a pursuer-distancer or disengaged marriage, or from one in which a contemptuous or belligerent husband undermined their self-esteem and child-rearing practices. Divorced men, we found, are less likely to undergo such remarkable personal growth; still, the vast majority of the men in our study did construct reasonably happy new lives for themselves. . . .

Postscript. Hetherington elaborates that women are more likely than men to initiate divorce. The reasons to stay in an unhappy marriage also differ by gender. Women's motivations for remaining stem from concerns about finances and raising a male child alone. Men are hesitant to leave because they worry about the loss of their children, particularly their sons, which leads to the finding that marriages with sons are less likely to break up.[7]

B. Fault-Based Grounds for Divorce

1. Adultery

BROWN v. BROWN

665 S.E.2d 174 (S.C. Ct. App. 2008)

PER CURIAM.

. . . Husband and Wife (collectively the Browns) married in Ohio on November 27, 1982. They had five children together during their [20-year] marriage. . . . In 1995, Husband and Wife built a new home on the property in Traveler's Rest where they resided throughout the remainder of the marriage.

[7]. E. Mavis Hetherington & John Kelly, For Better or for Worse: Divorce Reconsidered 40-41 (2002).

Chris Craft sold and installed the windows in the Browns' new home. A few months later, Craft and his wife began socializing with the Browns. Around Christmas of 1996, Husband took the children to church while Wife remained at home with their baby. Husband returned home and unexpectedly discovered Craft there. In explaining Craft's presence, Wife told Husband Craft had stopped by to look at their Christmas lights.

Wife and Craft became close and began having lunch without either of their spouse's knowledge. On several occasions, Craft and Wife met in a remote part of a restaurant's parking lot and fondled each other in Wife's car. In 1998, Husband discovered Craft and Wife were having lunch together. After confronting Wife, she temporarily ceased contact with Craft but admitted to subsequently resuming their relationship. Additionally, Craft and Wife frequently talked on the phone. In late 2000, Husband discovered Wife had a cell phone for which she had the bill sent to her mother's address, and Husband testified Wife had called Craft several dozen times from Wife's cell phone. [Husband filed for divorce, alleging adultery. He contends that the family court erred in failing to find that Wife committed adultery.]

Proof of adultery as a ground for divorce must be "clear and positive and the infidelity must be established by a clear preponderance of the evidence." . . . Because of the "clandestine nature" of adultery, obtaining evidence of the commission of the act by the testimony of eyewitnesses is rarely possible, so direct evidence is not necessary to establish the charge. Accordingly, adultery may be proven by circumstantial evidence that establishes both a disposition to commit the offense and the opportunity to do so. Generally, "proof must be sufficiently definite to identify the time and place of the offense and the circumstances under which it was committed." Evidence placing a spouse and a third party together on several occasions, without more, does not warrant the conclusion the spouse committed adultery.

Our courts have not specifically stated what sexual acts constitute adultery. . . . South Carolina has rejected the argument equating adultery with intercourse. In [Nemeth v. Nemeth, 481 S.E.2d 181 (S.C. Ct. App. 1997),] the wife took a cruise and stayed in a cabin with a man other than her husband. The wife denied she committed adultery and introduced evidence she had chronic pain that made intercourse difficult for her. This Court found adultery, stating sexual intercourse is not required to establish adultery; sexual intimacy is enough. . . .

This Court [has asserted] that circumstantial evidence indicating opportunity and inclination is sufficient to sustain a finding of adultery. In [McLaurin v. McLaurin, 363 S.E.2d 110 (S.C. Ct. App. 1987),] we affirmed the family court's finding that the husband committed adultery when the only evidence of adultery was the wife's testimony that her husband admitted committing adultery and a process server's statement that the divorce pleadings were served on the husband at the alleged paramour's residence where the paramour answered the door "comfortably clothed". . . .

[Here] Husband has the burden of proving Wife committed adultery. While Husband is not required to show direct evidence of the actual act, he must demonstrate Wife's inclination and opportunity to commit adultery. The family court determined Wife and Craft may have had the opportunity to commit adultery at two locations: (1) in the Browns' home around Christmas when Husband was at church and (2) in the car in a parking lot at lunchtime. . . .

We agree that Craft and Wife's presence in the Browns' home, without more, is not sufficient to establish adultery. However, we disagree with the family court's finding that Wife and Craft's continued and secretive meetings in various parking lots did not provide sufficient evidence to establish an opportunity to commit adultery. The family court found Craft and Wife met approximately twenty-four times over a four-to-five-year period. While the admitted meetings were during the daytime in a car parked in public parking lots, Wife's and Craft's admissions to the conduct that occurred while in the car are circumstantial evidence that adultery was committed.

Furthermore, Wife's and Craft's own admissions establish they were inclined to commit adultery. Craft testified the activities he and Wife engaged in were sexual in nature. Wife and Craft admitted that when they would meet for lunch, they would often kiss in Wife's car. Craft also touched Wife's breast and removed her bra. Both Wife and Craft touched one another below the waist, outside of their clothing. Wife also admitted Craft touched Wife "under her panties" once or twice. Additionally, Wife stated she was in love with Craft and that she discussed marriage with him. Further, she admitted their relationship was sexual to a degree, and she desired to have sexual intercourse with Craft. . . .

The evidence here of opportunity and inclination is too compelling to be brushed aside on the basis of Wife's "strict moral upbringing" and her claims that the romantic rendezvous always stopped short of sexual intercourse. Therefore, based on the evidence Husband presented, we hold Husband met his burden in proving Wife committed adultery. . . .

Notes and Questions

1. Background. Historically, adultery was one of the most common fault-based grounds. Until the 1970s, adultery was a ground for divorce in all states. In New York, adultery was the only ground until 1967.

2. Elements. What are the requisite elements to establish adultery as a ground for divorce in South Carolina (the setting in *Brown*)? How did Mr. Brown establish those elements? What type of evidence is required, according to *Brown*? Why? What might have motivated Mr. Brown to file for divorce on a fault-based ground rather than a no-fault ground?

At common law, the crime of adultery could be committed only with a married woman. For divorce purposes, however, many states defined adultery as the voluntary sexual intercourse of a married person with someone other than his or her spouse. How does South Carolina law define adultery?

3. Double standard. A double standard once governed adultery. For purposes of divorce, a wife had to prove that a husband's adultery constituted a "course of conduct," although a husband merely had to prove that his wife committed a single act. Two possible reasons explain the gender bias: (1) a married woman was considered her husband's property (that is, adultery was regarded as a form of theft), and (2) adultery of a married woman threatened the lineage.[8]

---

[8]. Annette Lawson, Adultery: An Analysis of Love and Betrayal 42 (1988).

4. Influence of Lawrence v. Texas. At the time of *Lawrence* in 2003, adultery was a ground for divorce in 29 states, as well as a crime in 23 states and the District of Columbia.[9] Adultery is currently a crime in 21 states.[10] Does *Lawrence* raise constitutional questions about these laws?[11]

5. "Open" relationships. Contemporary adherents of polyamory engage in sexual relationships with multiple partners (often during marriage to one person). How does adultery law apply to persons who engage in such relationships? How does it apply to same-sex couples, given research findings that many same-sex partners have open relationships?[12]

6. Adultery in the military. Although state prosecutors rarely bring charges for adultery, the military still subjects service personnel who commit adultery to disciplinary action. See, e.g., Penland v. Mabus, 643 F. Supp. 2d 14 (D.D.C. 2009). The military prohibition on adultery is found in the Uniform Code of Military Justice, 10 U.S.C. §§933 ("conduct unbecoming an officer and a gentleman"), 934 ("disorders and neglects [leading] to the prejudice of good order and discipline in the armed forces"), and the Manual for Courts-Martial, MCM pt. IV ¶62 (setting forth requirements to establish adultery). What explains the military's concern with adultery? See generally Krista Bordatto, The Crime Behind the Bedroom Door: Unequal Governmental Regulation of Civilian and Military Spouses, 26 Hastings Women's L.J. 95 (2015).

In a well-publicized scandal, retired four-star general David Petraeus resigned abruptly as Director of the Central Intelligence Agency (CIA) after disclosure of his extramarital affair with his biographer, West Point graduate Paula Broadwell. Petraeus claimed that the affair began after he retired from the military when he started work at the CIA—hence, military law would not be applicable. He later pleaded guilty—not for adultery, but rather for providing his lover with classified information, subjecting him to two years' probation and a $40,000 fine.[13]

7. Policy. If adultery prohibitions are rarely enforced, why do they remain? With the evolution of sexual mores and the de-emphasis on marital fault, should adultery be decriminalized?

---

[9]. Nat'l Survey of State Laws 396-411 (Richard A. Leiter ed., 2003) (extrapolation from survey data); Melanie C. Falco, Comment, The Road Not Taken: Using the Eighth Amendment to Strike Down Criminal Punishment for Engaging in Consensual Sexual Acts, 82 N.C. L. Rev. 723, 744 (2004).

[10]. Jessica Feinberg, Exposing the Traditional Marriage Agenda, 7 Nw. J. L. & Soc. Pol'y 301, 329 (2012).

[11]. For a discussion of adultery bans after *Lawrence*, see Andrew D. Cohen, Note, How the Establishment Clause Can Influence Substantive Due Process: Adultery Bans After *Lawrence*, 79 Fordham L. Rev. 605 (2010); Joanne Sweeny, Undead Statutes: The Rise, Fall, and Continuing Uses of Adultery and Fornication Criminal Laws, 46 Loy. U. Chi. L.J. 127 (2014).

[12]. Scott James, Many Successful Gay Marriages Share an Open Secret, N.Y. Times, Jan. 29, 2010, at A17A (reporting infidelity rate of 50 percent among 556 gay male couples). See generally Peter Nicolas, The Lavender Letter: Applying the Law of Adultery to Same-Sex Couples and Same-Sex Conduct, 63 Fla. L. Rev. 97 (2011). On polyamorous relationships, see Elizabeth F. Emens, Monogamy's Law: Compulsory Monogamy and Polyamorous Existence, 29 N.Y.U. Rev. L. & Soc. Change 277 (2004).

[13]. See generally Scott Shane & Charlie Savage, Timeline Shows F.B.I. Discovered Affair in Summer, N.Y. Times, Nov. 12, 2012, at A1. Caitlin Dickson, The Petraeus Scandal: Where Are They Now?, Mar. 3, 2015, http://news.yahoo.com/the-petraeus-scandal--where-are-they-now-010846840.html.

8. Comparative perspective. All European nations have decriminalized adultery. However, two Asian countries (Taiwan and the Philippines) still maintain criminal sanctions. Countries governed by Islamic law all strictly prohibit sexual relations outside of marriage. Human rights advocates point to gender discrimination in the application of adultery law: Adultery laws in some Muslim countries are used against women who have been raped.[14]

9. Empirical data: Role of gender. Women are closing the adultery gender gap. In the 1940s and 1950s, half of married men compared to 26 percent of married women reported extramarital affairs.[15] The percentage of wives who engage in affairs has risen significantly over the past two decades; reasons include working wives have less to lose economically from divorce and also social media facilitate engaging in affairs.[16]

The following study explores the role of adultery in the decision to divorce.

Julie H. Hall & Frank D. Fincham, Relationship Dissolution Following Infidelity

in Handbook of Divorce and Relationship Dissolution 153, 154, 156, 157-158, 159-160 (Mark A. Fine & John H. Harvey eds., 2006)

Infidelity is the leading cause of divorce. . . . The impact of infidelity on a couple's decision to separate depends in large part on the nature of the infidelity and how it was discovered. . . . Catching one's partner red-handed [leads] to high rates of relationship dissolution (83.3 percent), whereas 68 percent of those who heard of their partner's infidelity from a third party then ended the relationship. Unsolicited disclosure by the unfaithful party was least likely to lead to relationship dissolution. This may be because individuals who voluntarily confess their infidelity to a partner are more committed to repairing the relationship and are willing to make amends. However, it may also be that these individuals provide more mitigating accounts of their infidelity. . . .

[Gender also has been shown to play a role in the relationship between infidelity and relationship dissolution.] [O]verall, women are more likely to report that their divorce was caused by infidelity, specifically their partners' infidelity, than are men. [I]t is evident that men and women react differently to infidelity. [W]omen tend to show a more negative overall emotional reaction to infidelity than do men. Women are more likely than men to feel nauseated or repulsed, depressed, undesirable or insecure, helpless or abandoned, or anxious in reaction to a partner's infidelity. . . .

---

[14]. Adultery Laws: Where Is Cheating Still Illegal?, The Week Magazine, Feb. 27, 2015, http://www.theweek.co.uk/62723/adultery-laws-where-is-cheating-still-illegal.

[15]. Alfred C. Kinsey et al., Sexual Behavior in the Human Male 585 (1948); Alfred C. Kinsey et al., Sexual Behavior in the Human Female 416 (1953).

[16]. Frank Bass, Cheating Wives Narrowed Infidelity Gap Over Two Decades, Bloomberg Business, July 1, 2013 (reporting survey findings that the percentage of wives who report affairs rose 40 percent in the past two decades), http://www.bloomberg.com/news/articles/2013-07-02/cheating-wives-narrowed-infidelity-gap-over-two-decades.

The association between infidelity and relationship dissolution may also vary depending on the nature or quality of the relationship. [T]he risk of divorce following infidelity appears to decrease with the length of the marriage. Couples who experience infidelity in the early years of marriage are more likely to divorce than those who experience infidelity later in marriage.

The likelihood of relationship termination following infidelity may also depend on the level of satisfaction within the primary relationship. Married or cohabiting partners who break up following infidelity recall lower relationship satisfaction than partners who stay together. . . . The discovery of a husband's infidelity or divorce following such infidelity is associated with increased risk of a major depressive episode. . . . [I]nfidelity-related divorces may be even greater stressors than other divorces, because the heavy emotional and psychological toll associated with adultery is compounded with the distress of divorce. Indeed, individuals who divorce following infidelity are more distressed after the dissolution than those who divorce without infidelity. They are also less well adjusted to the divorce and more attached to the former spouse than are those whose divorce was not related to infidelity. . . .

2. Cruelty

ANDERSON v. ANDERSON

54 So. 3d 850 (Miss. Ct. App. 2010)

Griffis, J., for the Court:

. . . Donald and Merlene were married on October 2, 1994. Donald had two children from a previous marriage [Samuel and Joshua]. . . . Donald was the pastor of Little Zion Missionary Baptist Church in Corinth, Mississippi, for seventeen years. . . . Merlene worked for the United States Army Reserve in Tupelo, Mississippi, for thirteen years. On January 31, 2006, Donald filed for divorce [based on habitual cruel and inhuman treatment and, alternatively, irreconcilable differences]. The issue is whether Donald proved he was entitled to a divorce on the ground of habitual cruel and inhuman treatment. . . .

Mississippi Code Annotated section 93-5-1 (Rev. 2004) provides that a divorce may be granted to the injured party based on the ground of habitual cruel and inhuman treatment [if evidence is established that the conduct of the spouse either]:

> (1) endangers life, limb, or health, or creates a reasonable apprehension of such danger, rendering the relationship unsafe for the party seeking relief or
> (2) is so unnatural and infamous as to make the marriage revolting to the non-offending spouse and render it impossible for that spouse to discharge the duties of marriage, thus destroying the basis for its continuance.

The supreme court has held [citations omitted] that more is required "than mere unkindness, rudeness, or incompatibility to support the granting of a divorce on the ground of 'cruel and in-human treatment.'" "There must be corroboration of the complaining party's testimony" for a divorce based upon habitual cruel and inhuman treatment.

Donald's evidence was that Merlene abused him, physically and emotionally abused his children, verbally threatened him, attempted to ruin his reputation at his church, falsely accused him of having affairs, and exhibited "dominant behavior." . . . [He] claimed that she yelled at him for no reason. He testified that she threatened him by reminding him multiple times about a minister's wife in Selmer, Tennessee, who had killed her husband. She also told him that God was upset with him for wanting to divorce her. In July 2006, a snake was in their home, and Merlene told Donald that the snake represented the devil and that it was God's way of telling Donald that He did not agree with Donald's filing for divorce. . . .

Samuel and Joshua also testified that Merlene was physically and mentally abusive to both of them several years prior to Donald's filing for divorce. . . . Both claimed that she hit them and that she favored Joshua over Samuel. Merlene admitted that she was hard on Samuel during his teenage years. Joshua testified that during a fight between Merlene and Donald, Donald left the house in his car, and Merlene followed after him in her car. While she was backing up in her car, she almost hit Joshua. The chancellor appointed a guardian ad litem [who did not find sufficient evidence of child abuse]. Without such a finding, this evidence cannot be used by Donald to prove his ground for divorce.

Donald accused Merlene of attempting to "bring his church down." According to Donald, Merlene discussed with members and with the head of the National Baptist Convention details of their marriage and Donald's alleged adultery. Merlene stood up during one church meeting and said the only person that really loved her was Joshua. Merlene's behavior embarrassed Donald.

Out of three fellow church members who testified, not one member corroborated Donald's allegation of Merlene "ranting and raving" at conventions and church meetings about their marital problems and Donald's alleged extra-marital affairs. Based on the testimony, it was not Merlene who "ranted and raved" about their marriage at a convention. Instead, it was a third person who had told the convention that Donald was treating Merlene badly. . . .

Donald claimed that Merlene attempted to "dominate" him and that "no real man [is] going to be dominated by his wife." His example of Merlene being dominant was that she refused to allow the boys to have a dog. She testified that she did not like animals and that was her reason for not wanting a dog.

Donald testified that Merlene publicly had accused him of having affairs and that she had harassed the ladies that he counseled at church because she believed that he was having affairs with them. He claimed that one lady had to change her phone number because Merlene called and harassed her.

The chancellor's decision was primarily based on the finding that Merlene's accusations of infidelity were unfounded, Merlene's ongoing abusive behavior toward the children, and Merlene's "ongoing activities which were oppressive to Donald, and made the relationship unbearable."

"[F]alse accusations of infidelity, made habitually over a long period of time without reasonable cause also constitute cruel and inhuman treatment." Richard v. Richard, 711 So. 2d 884, 889 (Miss. 1998). However, "honestly made claims, even when later found to have been erroneous, do not constitute habitual cruel and inhuman treatment." This brings us to consider the evidence of Donald's alleged infidelities.

Donald traveled to conferences throughout the year. Merlene found out that in August 2006, Donald traveled to New Orleans, Louisiana, for a meeting and booked a hotel room for two. At trial, Donald testified that his friend was supposed to go with him to New Orleans but backed out. He denied that a woman stayed with him in the hotel room. Donald testified that he regularly booked a room for two in case someone at the conference or meeting needed a place to stay, and he did so despite the price increase when a room is booked for two people versus one person.

Merlene also found an e-mail that Donald had sent to a female assistant. The e-mail was very short and explicit; it said, "good pu**y." Donald admitted that he had sent the e-mail to his assistant, but he claimed that it was taken out of context because it was the punch line of a joke that they had both heard while at a meeting. He sent the e-mail in an effort to cheer her up. The full context or the joke was not in the record. . . .

The chancellor's finding that Merlene's accusations of infidelity were unfounded is simply not supported by the record. Indeed, there was more than sufficient evidence to give Merlene reason to believe that Donald was in an adulterous relationship.

. . . Merlene's behavior may have been odd at times and embarrassing to Donald, but her conduct did not meet the standard set forth to prove the ground of cruel and inhuman treatment. The yelling, the accusations of infidelity, and the "dominant behavior" exhibited by Merlene are more akin to mere unkindness, rudeness, or incompatibility.

More importantly, Donald failed to show that Merlene's conduct had a negative impact on him. Our analysis must include the effect that Merlene's conduct had on Donald. The "impact of the conduct on the plaintiff is crucial[;] thus[,] we employ a subjective standard." . . . [T]here is no testimony or other evidence to indicate that Donald's health was even slightly impaired. Donald has no physical or mental health problems due to Merlene's conduct. There was no proof that Merlene's accusations, taunting, yelling, and alleged mistreatment of the children rendered cohabitation impossible, except at the risk of life, limb, or health on the part of Donald. . . .

While we agree that the parties' marriage is, indeed, troubled and possibly irreparable, we find that Donald presented insufficient evidence to prove the ground of habitual cruel and inhuman treatment. Accordingly, the chancellor's judgment is reversed and rendered.

Notes and Questions

1. **Elements.** Cruelty (termed "indignities" or "cruel and inhuman treatment") has provided a ground for divorce in most states. Courts generally require a *course of conduct* of cruel behavior that creates an *adverse health effect.* What is a "course of conduct"? "Adverse health effect"? What did the Mississippi statute

require in *Anderson*? How did the husband in *Anderson* attempt to establish the requisite elements? Why did the court find that such evidence was insufficient? What is the relationship between accusations of infidelity and habitual cruel and inhuman treatment?

How "adverse" does the effect on health have to be? See In re Guy, 969 A.2d 373 (N.H. 2009) (holding that wife's becoming "angry, upset, and distraught" upon discovery of husband's emails to other women was not sufficient). Further, several courts maintain that one incident will not satisfy the "course of conduct" requirement. However, a single incident may suffice if the act is particularly brutal. See, e.g., Rogers v. Rogers, 2002 WL 1335654 (Ark. Ct. App. 2002) (nonfatal strangulation). What option does a spouse have if the court denies the divorce?

2. Battered spouses. In the nineteenth century, divorce on grounds of cruelty was often the only remedy that was available to battered spouses. How effective was this remedy? See generally Elizabeth Pleck, Domestic Tyranny: The Making of Social Policy Against Family Violence from Colonial Times to the Present (1987).

3. Mental cruelty. English ecclesiastical courts required actual or threatened bodily harm. Courts gradually expanded the definition to include mental cruelty. Many states require that the cruelty be extreme and/or sufficiently severe as to threaten safety or health or make continued cohabitation "unreasonable" or "insupportable." See, e.g., N.J. Stat. Ann. §2A:34-2.

What acts establish mental cruelty? Engaging in an affair? Unreasonable demands regarding sex or birth control? See Jizmejian v. Jizmejian, 492 P.2d 1208 (Ariz. Ct. App. 1972); Goldstein v. Goldstein, 235 A.2d 498 (N.J. Super. Ct. Ch. Div. 1967). Would this requirement present constitutional problems? Excessive gambling? See Rocconi v. Rocconi, 196 S.W.3d 499 (Ark. Ct. App. 2004). Permitting relatives to live with the couple? See Ferro v. Ferro, 871 So. 2d 753 (Miss. Ct. App. 2004) (adult son from previous marriage). Sexual abuse of a child? See In re Henry, 37 A.3d 320 (N.H. 2012).

4. New York law. Until recently, New York had particularly strict requirements regarding proof of cruelty for divorce purposes, requiring a "course of conduct" and an adverse effect to physical or mental well-being. These requirements reflected a historical concern with preventing easy divorce. In addition, New York required a higher degree of proof of cruelty for divorce involving a long-term marriage. See S.C. v. A.C., 798 N.Y.S.2d 348 (Sup. Ct. 2004). What purpose does this last rule serve? Is it sound? New York's recent adoption of no-fault divorce is discussed later in this chapter, p. [495].

5. Corroboration. In the fault-based era, corroboration was widely required to prove acts of marital misconduct for purposes of divorce. The corroboration requirement necessitated eyewitness testimony and contributed to the adversarial nature of divorce proceedings. What was the corroborating evidence in *Anderson*? What is the rationale for the corroboration requirement? Does adherence to the requirement make sense today?

3. Desertion

REID v. REID

375 S.E.2d 533 (Va. Ct. App. 1989)

KOONTZ, Chief Judge.

[Judith N. Reid sought a divorce on the ground of constructive desertion. Dr. Robert Reid responded seeking a divorce on the ground of desertion. When the commissioner recommended denial of the divorce on fault grounds but the entry of a no-fault divorce decree, both parties filed exceptions and a motion requesting preservation of the issue of fault for appeal. This appeal by Dr. Reid followed.]

The parties were married on June 26, 1965, in Denver, Colorado. Mrs. Reid had obtained a degree in medical technology and was employed at a local hospital. Dr. Reid was in medical school. In 1966, the first of their four children was born. In 1967 the parties moved to New York City where Dr. Reid completed his internship and residency. [Following Dr. Reid's stint in the Navy,] the parties moved to Charlottesville, Virginia, where Dr. Reid obtained a position at the University. He ultimately became tenured, head of his division, and director of the nurse practitioner program. [He subsequently left the university position to establish a medical corporation.]

During the first years of the marriage in which the parties' remaining children were born, Mrs. Reid was a homemaker. In 1980 she began part-time employment with [her husband's corporation] and ultimately became its controller. In 1985 Mrs. Reid and two other individuals, with the concurrence of Dr. Reid, formed King Travel, Inc., a travel agency, [and became president].

In his report, the commissioner reflected: "The testimony of Dr. Reid and Mrs. Reid rarely conflicts. They were talking about two different aspects [perceptions] of what were actually separate lives." The record amply supports the appropriateness of this statement. Mrs. Reid testified in detail as to the gradual breakdown in the marital relationship during this nineteen year marriage. The commissioner concluded that in each specific instance Mrs. Reid identified a marital problem, Dr. Reid did not perceive a problem. In fact, almost to the very end of the marriage, as if they lived separate lives, Dr. Reid considered himself happily married, while Mrs. Reid considered her emotional health endangered.

[Mrs. Reid] does not challenge the chancellor's finding that Dr. Reid did not constructively desert her. [Rather, she asserts she was justified in leaving her husband when she moved out in 1984 because her emotional health was endangered by virtue of the following marital problems]: (1) sexual inactivity, (2) Dr. Reid's excessive work habits, (3) Dr. Reid's failure to assist in the disciplining and rearing of their children, and (4) a lack of "intimacy within the marriage." . . .

It is apparent from the record and particularly Mrs. Reid's testimony that, following the birth of their first child in 1966, the sexual pattern which developed between the couple can best be described as infrequent. While three additional children were conceived and born over the ensuing years, many months passed between acts of sexual intercourse. These periods of abstinence gradually increased until no intercourse occurred for approximately two to three years prior to the final separation. It is also apparent that Dr. Reid suffered periods of sexual impotency, and that the infrequency of intercourse was more a concern to Mrs. Reid than to Dr. Reid.

Compounding this difficult situation, Mrs. Reid described the work pattern of Dr. Reid which she considered excessive. From the beginning of the marriage, Dr. Reid held more than one job. During the Navy years, he worked at night conducting insurance physicals. After accepting the position at the University of Virginia, he worked at night at the emergency room of a nearby hospital, opened a nearby clinic with two other doctors, and ultimately formed Commonwealth Clinical. There is no dispute that these activities severely limited the time available for Dr. Reid to spend at home with his wife and children. . . . Mrs. Reid felt that Dr. Reid was not appropriately supportive of her efforts to discipline [one child in particular] and, rather, conveyed to her the sense that this problem was solely her responsibility.

Mrs. Reid's description of the lack of "intimacy within the marriage," while conceptually understandable, is nebulous at best. On brief, she partially summarizes it as Dr. Reid's refusal "to talk to her about their lives with its joys and its sorrows, about the family and where it was and where it was going, or any other matter not directly related to one of the family financial concerns." . . . It is fair to say that while Dr. Reid was financially supportive, Mrs. Reid bore the major responsibility for raising the children and maintaining the home. In the process she became unhappy and felt unfulfilled. We accept the commissioner's conclusion that this condition was due in major part to Dr. Reid's denial or lack of recognition of the needs and feelings of Mrs. Reid.

While not specifically asserted by Mrs. Reid as a justification for her leaving, it is clear from the evidence that the marital problems of this couple were compounded by the additional responsibilities assumed by Mrs. Reid when she undertook her duties at Commonwealth Systems and eventually King Travel. These activities were encouraged by Dr. Reid, but they did not produce the personal satisfaction or the lessening of Mrs. Reid's frustration as they both apparently had hoped. Finally, the purchase of a large sailing boat and Mrs. Reid's enthusiastic involvement in sailing without Dr. Reid, in turn, merely added more stress to the marriage.

. . . The issue remains, however, whether as a matter of law these circumstances provide a justification for leaving the marriage. In that regard, the additional facts surrounding her leaving become critical.

In April, 1983, in what she describes as an effort to get Dr. Reid's attention, Mrs. Reid informed Dr. Reid that she could no longer endure the stress created by the problems in their marriage. As a result, the parties underwent counseling, which was unsuccessful. Mrs. Reid asserts that at that point she was totally committed to saving the marriage, but that Dr. Reid did not perceive the extent of their problems. The record supports this assertion. Subsequently, in October of that year, Mrs. Reid went on a month-long sailing cruise to the Virgin Islands. Upon returning she advised Dr. Reid that she wanted a separation. The separation was delayed because Mrs. Reid underwent a gallbladder operation and she did not want to upset the children at Christmas. . . . Mrs. Reid testified that she eventually made a deposit on an apartment and on a Friday night again discussed the marriage with Dr. Reid. There was no agreement for a mutual separation. She described this conversation as "not being intimate" but rather, "a superficial sort of thing."

On the following Monday, without Dr. Reid's knowledge, Mrs. Reid moved to this apartment. She testified that her intent in leaving the marital home was to make Dr. Reid realize that they had a problem, and that she "couldn't go on with it without doing something about it." This separation occurred on April 16, 1984. Mrs. Reid filed her suit for divorce on June 13, 1984. The chancellor sustained the commissioner's finding that as a matter of law Mrs. Reid did not intend to desert the marriage. We disagree. . . . "Proof of an actual breaking off of matrimonial cohabitation combined with the intent to desert . . . constitutes desertion as grounds for divorce. However, reasons for leaving the marriage other than an intent to desert may justify discontinuance of the relationship without giving rise to grounds for divorce." Under the law existing at the time of the present suit, fault, such as desertion, was a bar to spousal support. . . .

Mrs. Reid's description of her feelings and emotional condition are understandable in terms of human experience. The *cause* of her feelings and emotional condition, however, cannot be attributed factually or legally solely to the conduct of Dr. Reid. Rather, the evidence established that the pattern of conduct, indeed the entire marital relationship, established by both parties in this marriage resulted in her frustration and guided her decision to terminate the marriage. Mrs. Reid's complaints that Dr. Reid absented himself from the home and his proper share of the child discipline while working to provide financially for her and the family cannot serve as the justification for leaving him. Mrs. Reid would have us draw a fine line between where perhaps he excelled in one duty to the family at a sacrifice of another duty. This we cannot do. Her complaint of a "lack of intimacy in the marriage" is, in the final analysis, no more than a reflection of the different personalities of these marital partners and their method of relating to each other. It can be considered no more than a general complaint of unhappiness on the part of one spouse, which is the regrettable risk in all marriages. Finally, her complaint of the infrequency of sexual intercourse was a pattern developed uniquely between them almost from the beginning of the marriage. Moreover, Dr. Reid's periodic impotency was a mutual problem; the solution to which, obviously, was not within his sole control.

Under these circumstances, the most that can be concluded is that there was a gradual breakdown in the marriage relationship. As a result, Mrs. Reid understandably became unhappy and believed her emotional health was endangered. Her response to this problem was to terminate matrimonial cohabitation. The fact that she filed for divorce within two months thereafter belies an intent for a temporary separation. In so doing, she legally deserted the marriage and forfeited her right to spousal support. For these reasons, the commissioner erred in his conclusions of law. . . .

Notes and Questions

1. **Background.** Virginia permits divorce on the no-fault ground of a year's separation as well as on fault-based grounds (adultery, conviction of a felony, cruelty, desertion or abandonment, or causing reasonable apprehension of bodily harm). Va. Code Ann. §20-91. If both fault-based and no-fault grounds exist, the judge may use discretion to select the most appropriate ground. When *Reid* was filed, proof of fault barred spousal support. Subsequently, the Virginia legislature

eliminated fault as a bar to spousal support in all cases except adultery. Va. Code Ann. §20-107.1.

2. Epilogue. Following the principal case, Dr. Reid petitioned for restitution of his spousal support previously paid to Mrs. Reid. A panel of the court of appeals affirmed the trial court's denial of the husband's motion. At a subsequent rehearing en banc, the court concluded that restitution could be ordered and remanded for a determination of the amount. However, the Virginia Supreme Court held that the trial court lacked the authority to order restitution of support. Reid v. Reid, 429 S.E.2d 208 (Va. 1993).

3. Elements. Desertion constitutes a ground for divorce in many jurisdictions. A spouse's mere departure is not sufficient to prove desertion. Desertion requires a cessation of cohabitation, without cause or consent, but with intent to abandon, continuing for a statutory period. Although intent (to desert, abandon, or terminate the relationship) is essential, the separation and intent need not occur contemporaneously. Separation without the requisite intent will not constitute desertion; subsequent intent formed after a separation will suffice, however. The desertion, then, dates from the time the intention is formed. Did Mrs. Reid satisfy the requisite elements? Desertion must also occur without justification. Why did the court deem Mrs. Reid's reason(s) unjustified?

Some statutes require that desertion be voluntary. Does desertion caused by imprisonment suffice? Can a spouse who was ordered out of the marital home claim desertion? Cf. Knepp v. Niece, 2003 WL 175192 (Va. Ct. App. 2003) (husband deserted by breaking off marital cohabitation when he ordered wife to leave), with Royer v. Royer, 2004 WL 2093443 (Va. Cir. Ct. 2004) (finding that wife's departure after being told to leave was not desertion). Must abandonment be total? See Jeffries v. Jeffries, 138 N.W.2d 882, 884 (Iowa 1965) (financial support by husband barred wife's claim).

Does refusal to engage in sexual relations constitute desertion? See, e.g., B.M. v. M.M., 880 N.Y.S.2d 850 (Sup. Ct. 2009) (granting divorce on ground of constructive abandonment). Suppose the refusal to engage in sex stems from health reasons? Religious beliefs? Objections to the other spouse's sexual practices?

4. Constructive desertion. Recall that Mrs. Reid filed for divorce on the ground of constructive desertion. Dr. Reid cross-complained for desertion. Constructive desertion constitutes intolerable conduct by one spouse toward an innocent spouse that causes the innocent spouse to leave the marital abode. Thus, if Dr. Reid's conduct gives the plaintiff justification for leaving the home, then Mrs. Reid is not guilty of desertion. Under this ground, a spouse (in this case, Dr. Reid) need not specifically intend that the plaintiff leave. Did Dr. Reid provide just cause for Mrs. Reid to leave?

5. Gender differences. To what extent does *Reid* exemplify the thesis of Catherine Riessman and E. Mavis Hetherington (in the above excerpts) about gender-based differences in divorce experiences? How does the judge in *Reid* interpret the facts? For example, compare the court's description of Dr. Reid's work, requiring absence from the home, as "excel[ling] in one duty," with its assessment of

Mrs. Reid's work, which the court found "[compounded] the marital problems of this couple."

6. Statutory period. Most states require that the desertion continue for at least one year. See, e.g., N.D. Stat. Ann. §14-05-09. Why require a statutory period of desertion for divorce? Should parties be able to file once the intent to desert is expressed? Does a statutory period assist courts in determining a party's intent?

7. Other fault-based grounds. Additional statutory fault-based grounds include willful nonsupport of wife by husband (e.g., R.I. Gen. Laws §15-5-2(7)); criminal conviction or imprisonment (e.g., Ala. Code §30-2-1(a)(4)); drunkenness and drug addiction (e.g., Tenn. Code Ann. §36-4-101(10)); impotence (Miss. Code §93-5-1); and insanity (e.g., Utah Code Ann. §30-3-1(3)(i)).

C. Fault-Based Defenses

1. Recrimination

JENKINS v. JENKINS

55 So. 3d 1094 (Miss. Ct. App. 2010)

MAXWELL, J., for the Court.

The Chancery Court of Copiah County granted Rose Jenkins a divorce from Edmond Jenkins on the ground of habitual cruel and inhuman treatment. Edmond appeals claiming the chancellor erred in rejecting his recrimination defense. . . .

Edmond and Rose were married for approximately twelve years before separating in June 2006. They had two children from their marriage.

At trial, Rose testified that Edmond exhibited a pattern of cruel behavior. One incident in May 2006 involved Edmond locking Rose and the children out of the house. He also disconnected the spark plugs in her car, forcing Rose to contact a friend to pick up her and the children. Another incident occurred in June 2006, soon after the two had separated, when Rose and the children visited Edmond at the marital home. After hugging his children and telling them goodbye, Edmond walked to the front porch, placed a noose around his neck, and tried to hang himself to death. His unsuccessful suicide attempt took place in front of the children. In another postseparation incident, Edmond argued with Rose while riding in a car with her and the children. According to Rose, Edmond became so enraged that he opened the door and threatened to jump from the vehicle. Rose managed to pull the car to the side of the road without Edmond injuring himself. When Rose attempted to discuss divorce with Edmond, he told her the only way they would separate would be by death.

Rose filed for divorce in June 2006, soon after the hanging incident. She asserted the fault-based grounds of adultery and habitual cruel and inhuman treatment. Edmond counterclaimed alleging these same grounds. In Rose's amended response to Edmond's counterclaim, she admitted committing adultery since November 2007. Edmond later withdrew his counterclaim.

The chancellor granted Rose a divorce based on Edmond's habitual cruel and inhuman treatment. [Edmond's sole argument] focuses on Rose's adultery, which he claims bars her from obtaining a divorce.

Under the common-law doctrine of recrimination, if each party to a marriage proved a fault-based ground for divorce, then neither party was entitled to a divorce. The doctrine is "founded on the basis that the equal guilt of a complainant bars his/her right to divorce[.]" Parker v. Parker, 519 So. 2d 1232, 1235 (Miss.1988). And under the common-law principle, "the complainant must come into court with clean hands." For the doctrine to apply, "[t]he offenses committed by each spouse need not be the same," but both spouses' offenses must be sufficient to constitute grounds for divorce.

But recrimination is no longer an absolute bar to divorce. In 1964, the Mississippi Legislature modified the common-law recrimination defense by enacting Mississippi Code Annotated section 93-5-3. Section 93-5-3 provides: "If a complainant or cross-complainant in a divorce action shall prove grounds entitling him to a divorce, it shall not be mandatory on any chancellor to deny such party a divorce, even though the evidence might establish recrimination on the part of such complainant or cross-complainant." As a result, chancellors are no longer bound by the strictures of the common-law doctrine. Therefore, under Section 93-5-3, "one party's adultery, even if established at trial, does not prevent the chancellor from granting a divorce to that party."

This Court has further held: "There can be but one divorce granted. . . . 'In a situation where both parties are at fault, if a divorce is to be granted, the chancellor must determine which party's conduct was the proximate cause of the deterioration of the marital relationship and the divorce itself.'" Garriga v. Garriga, 770 So. 2d 978, 983-84 (¶¶ 23-24) (Miss. Ct. App. 2000). . . .

Here, the chancellor rejected Edmond's recrimination defense and found:

> [Edmond] put on evidence that [Rose] had more than one adulterous affair as early as the year 2006. Obviously the evidence was put on to either condone [Edmond's] behavior toward his wife or to challenge the cause of the failed marriage. However, [Edmond] admits that he did not learn of [Rose's] affairs until November or December of 2007, and [Rose] denies any such behavior prior to [then]. From the evidence, the court can't find that it was [Rose's] behavior which caused the . . . separation. . . .
>
> [T]he Court is satisfied from the evidence that [Edmond] is guilty of habitual cruel and inhuman treatment toward[ ] his wife, and that his conduct is the proximate cause of the . . . separation.

Though Edmond resolutely asserts Rose engaged in adultery before the parties separated, he fails to point out specific evidence to support his claim. . . . Equally lacking is proof that her adulterous conduct proximately caused the parties' separation. Under these facts, we find the chancellor did not manifestly err in rejecting Edmond's recrimination defense and, therefore, affirm.

Notes and Questions

1. Policy. Recrimination "prevents the dissolution of those very marriages most appropriate for dissolution."[17] Should divorce be granted only to "innocent" parties? *Jenkins* discusses the policy underlying the recrimination defense:

> At least four policy-oriented justifications of the doctrine may be found in judicial opinions: (a) By rendering divorces more difficult to procure, recrimination promotes marital stability. (b) The rule tends to deter immorality, since a spouse is less likely to commit adultery (or any other marital offense) if he knows that his misdeed may bar him from obtaining a divorce at some future time. (c) The doctrine serves to protect the wife's economic status. (d) Recrimination prevents persons who are obviously poor marriage risks from being freed to contract—and probably ruin—another marriage.

519 So. 2d 1232, 1235-1236 (Miss. 1988). Do any of these policies justify the application of the recrimination doctrine in *Jenkins*? How determinative was Edmond's cruelty?

2. Financial issues. One commentator points out that the defense of recrimination tends to be raised "only when one party was dissatisfied with the property arrangements."[18] What considerations may have influenced Edmond's resort to the defense? If recrimination were abolished as a fault-based defense to divorce, should fault be retained, nonetheless, to determine alimony? That is, should fault trump financial need? Should fault be retained to determine child custody or support?

3. Modern applications. The recrimination defense still surfaces occasionally. See Morgan v. Morgan, 2014 WL 3387915 (Ala. Civ. App. 2014); Carambat v. Carambat, 72 So. 3d 505 (Miss. 2011).

2. Condonation

HAYMES v. HAYMES

646 N.Y.S.2d 315 (App. Div. 1996)

MAZZARELLI, Justice. . . .

Gail and Stephen Haymes were married in 1965 and lived together, without interruption, until 1987. They are the parents of two adult children, born in 1967 and 1975. According to plaintiff's allegations, beginning in December

---

[17]. Homer H. Clark, Jr., The Law of Domestic Relations in the United States 527 (2d ed. 1988). On the history of the doctrine, see J.G. Beamer, The Doctrine of Recrimination in Divorce Proceedings, 10 UMKC L. Rev. 213 (1942); J. Herbie DiFonzo, Alternatives to Marital Fault: Legislative and Judicial Experiments in Cultural Change, 34 Idaho L. Rev. 1, 18-19 (1997).

[18]. DiFonzo, supra note [17], at 19.

1984, defendant refused to have sexual relations with her, rejecting her repeated overtures. In September 1987, defendant moved out of the couple's home, an act which plaintiff maintains was without her consent and without justification. The plaintiff claimed that defendant engaged in several adulterous relationships with women identified in the complaint. Defendant retained legal counsel, who wrote to plaintiff, suggesting that she retain her own matrimonial lawyer. This action for divorce and related relief was commenced [by wife] in September of 1988. . . .

The couple attempted a reconciliation between November 18, 1988 and January 4, 1989, during which time they resumed residing unhappily together. According to Ms. Haymes, her husband expressed neither remorse for his adultery nor any affection for her during this six-week period. Unable to resolve their problems, Gail and Stephen Haymes returned to living apart and pursuing their respective marital claims. Indeed, in January 1989, defendant asserted his own counterclaim for divorce.

On January 23, 1995, on the eve of the trial herein, defendant moved in open court for dismissal [of wife's causes of action for abandonment and constructive abandonment]. He urged that these claims were precluded because of the wife's admission, during a wholly separate conversion action, that she and the husband resumed living together briefly between November 18, 1988 and January 4, 1989. The wife also conceded that during this time period, while on a family vacation in Vail, Colorado, she and her husband had engaged in sexual relations at least once. According to defendant, upon returning from the family vacation, plaintiff informed him that the attempted reconciliation was a failure and that he was not to come back to the marital home. [T]he parties had later visited Acapulco, Mexico, together in 1990. Plaintiff, in response, argued that a single unsuccessful effort at reconciliation after the matrimonial action had already been commenced is hardly sufficient to defeat, as a matter of law, her claims founded in abandonment. . . .

[T]here is a dearth of current appellate authority in this state directly addressing the legal question presented by this dispute, whether a relatively brief attempt at a reconciliation . . . should require plaintiff to forfeit these otherwise facially valid causes of action for divorce. . . . In our view, common sense teaches that it is consistent with the public policy of this state that couples enduring marital disharmony should be encouraged to attempt reconciliation, particularly when, as here, the marriage is one of long duration. That the courts should, when practicable, encourage the preservation of families, in all their permutations, is so painfully obvious, that the lack of appellate authority so declaring can only be explained by the failure heretofore of anyone to contest such a basic proposition.

The extant case law does not point to a contrary result. . . . Although not exactly on all fours with this case, we find that the authorities relied on by plaintiff, in that they discuss the effect of reconciliation attempts on causes of action other than abandonment, are at least supportive of her position. Moreover, we agree with plaintiff that there is more than an implication in several of the cases that an effort to reconcile is meaningless without a showing that it was made in good faith.

. . . In the case at bar, by granting the motion for summary judgment just prior to opening statements, the trial court prevented plaintiff from endeavoring to prove that defendant did not make a good faith effort to reconcile. The court held plaintiff's abandonment claims were forfeited as a matter of law by the fact she engaged in sexual relations with her husband during the failed reconciliation attempt. However, we view the extant record as ambiguous as to the frequency of those relations and whether they were entered into in good faith by the defendant husband. The prevailing legal authority, even if sparse, seems to hold that cohabitation by itself is insufficient to invalidate a separation agreement or an accrued claim for divorce. . . . Furthermore, in the context of a cruel and inhuman treatment cause of action, it has been held that a short period of cohabitation does not amount to condonation of the cruel and inhuman treatment asserted as the basis of a divorce. [Lowe v. Lowe, 324 N.Y.S.2d 229 (Sup. Ct. 1970), *aff'd*, 322 N.Y.S.2d 975 (App. Div. 1971).]

As long ago as 1928, this court declared, and the Court of Appeals agreed, in the context of a cause of action for cruel and inhuman treatment, that "[w]e are not in accord with defendant's argument that cohabitation after acts of cruelty may be considered as condonation, in the sense in which it would be after an act of adultery. We rule that endurance of unkind treatment in an effort to overcome its practice and continuance of cohabitation does not condone a course of inhuman conduct" [Fisher v. Fisher, 227 N.Y.S. 345 (Sup. Ct. 1928), *aff'd*, 165 N.E. 460 (N.Y. 1929)].

Today, we hold that an estranged couple's attempt at a reconciliation, even where it involves the brief and isolated resumption of cohabitation and/or sexual relations, after a matrimonial action has already been commenced, does not, as a matter of law, preclude an entry of judgment in favor of the spouse who originally had an otherwise valid claim for abandonment. Rather, the trial court should examine the totality of the circumstances surrounding the purported reconciliation, before determining its effect, if any, upon the pending marital proceeding. Among the many factors for the trial court to consider are whether the reconciliation and any cohabitation were entered into in good faith, whether it was at all successful, who initiated it and with what motivation. Although concededly more difficult to apply than a rule which automatically results in the forfeiture of abandonment claims upon the parties making even the most hollow attempt at reconciliation, we conclude that the approach we adopt is not only consonant with human experience and common sense, but with the public policy and law of our State as well. . . .

Notes and Questions

1. Definition. A spouse who has once condoned marital misconduct is barred from using that misconduct as grounds for divorce, according to the traditional rule. Grounds that may be condoned include adultery, cruelty, habitual drunkenness, and desertion (termed here "abandonment"). However, some courts limit the condonation defense to divorces based on adultery. See, e.g., P.K. v. R.K., 820 N.Y.S.2d 844 (Sup. Ct. 2006). What approach does *Haymes* adopt?

2. Requirements. Does condonation require *both* forgiveness of marital misconduct and resumption of sexual relations? See In re Marriage of Hightower, 830 N.E.2d 862, 867 (Ill. App. Ct. 2005) (condonation is "a question of intent [involving] a combination of factors" and finding that wife condoned husband's infidelity by her ensuing cohabitation).

Does condonation require *both* cohabitation and resumption of sexual relations? Is resumption of cohabitation alone sufficient to establish condonation? See Vinson v. Vinson, 880 So. 2d 469 (Ala. Civ. App. 2003) (holding that sexual intercourse may be presumed from cohabitation); Nemeth v. Nemeth, 481 S.E.2d 181 (S.C. Ct. App. 1997) (finding no condonation because spouses spent two nights together without sexual relations after wife confessed adultery).

Is it appropriate to assume that the resumption of sexual relations constitutes forgiveness by one party? See Hoffman v. Hoffman, 762 A.2d 766 (Pa. Super. Ct. 2000) (holding that husband's resumption of sexual relations was evidence of condonation despite his refusal to withdraw the custody action). Does the recurrence of defendant's wrongful conduct (after plaintiff's initial condonation) revive the previous offenses? See Lindsey v. Lindsey, 818 So. 2d 1191 (Miss. 2002).

3. Policy. Does the condonation doctrine raise constitutional issues of family privacy? Should condonation serve as grounds for denying divorce, or merely as a bar to alimony?

4. Attorneys' role. Because of the possible application of the condonation defense, should divorce attorneys regularly counsel their clients at their first interview and at every opportunity, "Do Not. Under Any Circumstances. Have Sex. With Your Spouse. Again."?[19]

5. Abolition. With the advent of no-fault divorce (discussed in the next section), many jurisdictions abolished fault-based defenses. Nonetheless, as *Haymes* reveals, some jurisdictions continue to recognize some or all of these defenses. See Ga. Code Ann. §19-5-4 (recognizing collusion, connivance, recrimination, and condonation); Edmisten v. Edmisten, 2003 WL 21077990 (Tenn. Ct. App. 2003). And, a few jurisdictions that have abolished recrimination as a defense still preserve the defense of condonation. See, e.g., Tex. Fam. Code Ann. §6.008. Does this last approach make sense?

6. Criticisms. The traditional condonation doctrine was harsh in its application to the forgiving spouse. One commentator notes:

> The practical effect of the rule of condonation is to impose a "do-or-die" decision upon the innocent spouse in the hour of crisis. Confronted suddenly with the knowledge of his partner's infidelity, he must decide promptly whether to pack his suitcase and leave what may have been and could be a very happy home, or to continue marital relations thereby forfeiting the right to dissolve the marriage if it should subsequently cease to be viable. The penalizing effect of the rule is to trap in a cancerous marriage those parties who have made laudable, although unsuccessful, attempts to reconcile.[20]

Is the approach adopted by *Haymes* an improvement?

---

[19]. See Res Ipsa Loquitur; Condonation, Aug. 12, 2004, http://www.res-ipsa.the-blinding-white-light.com/archives/002330.html (so suggesting in the context of a discussion of an unreported New York case, Ozkan v. Ozkan, for the reason that some "try to take advantage of that theory by conning the innocent spouse into bed, then using that to leverage a more 'favorable' settlement").

[20]. Arthur L. Fox II, Condonation: An Obstruction to Reconciliation, 2 Fam. L.Q. 259, 259-260 (1969).

NOTE: OTHER FAULT-BASED DEFENSES

In the fault-based era, other common defenses to divorce were connivance and collusion. Connivance constitutes express or implied consent by the plaintiff to the misconduct alleged. Three justifications exist for the connivance defense: First, according to the Latin maxim *volenti non fit injuria*, "He who consents cannot receive an injury." Second, a petitioner with unclean hands is not entitled to equitable relief. Third, some states limited divorce to the innocent party, and a conniving spouse was not an innocent party.[21]

Collusion is an agreement between husband and wife to (1) commit a marital offense in order to obtain a divorce, (2) introduce false evidence of a transgression not actually committed, or (3) suppress a valid defense. Before no-fault divorce, "[t]he collusive divorce, so far from being a rare phenomenon, appears to be the norm."[22] Courts sometimes have difficulty distinguishing collusion from connivance. See, e.g., Furst v. Furst, 78 N.Y.S.2d 608 (Sup. Ct. 1948), *modified*, 91 N.Y.S.2d 202 (App. Div. 1949). Professor Moore explains the distinctions:

> Although related in concept and function, collusion and connivance differ in two significant respects: First, connivance requires only the corrupt consent of the plaintiff, while collusion requires that of both spouses; and secondly, connivance cannot occur without the actual commission of a marital offense, while collusion can take place without either party's ever actually giving the other cause for divorce.[23]

Insanity traditionally provided a ground for divorce as well as a defense. See Rutherford v. Rutherford, 414 S.E.2d 157 (S.C. 1992). Because divorce required the presence of a "guilty" party, mental illness relieved the defendant from liability for marital misconduct.

Problems

1. Richard, an accountant, and Sandra, a schoolteacher, have been married for eight years. They have no children. Richard believes that a husband should be in charge of the family's finances. He puts Sandra on a strict allowance, insists that she account for every cent, forbids her from writing checks or using credit cards, and requires her to surrender all receipts of her purchases to him. He is highly critical of Sandra's spending habits, castigating her for the amount that she spends on groceries and gasoline, and at the beauty salon. In addition, he limits her to two showers per week to save money on hot water. He habitually belittles her, insults her in front of other people, refuses to allow her friends to visit, and makes baseless charges that she is unfaithful.

Sandra complains that she and Richard have little in common. She chides him that his only interests are football and other women. She yells at him for refusing

---

[21]. Marvin M. Moore, An Analysis of Collusion and Connivance, Bars to Divorce, 36 UMKC L. Rev. 193, 196-197 (1968).

[22]. Id. at 226.

[23]. Id. at 195.

to help around the house and leaving his dirty clothes everywhere for her to pick up. She subjects him to constant verbal abuse over their inability to conceive. Sandra is so upset by Richard's incessant harping at her about money that she suffers from insomnia and depression. She begins spending an increasing amount of time online. Sandra discovers an online game called "Second Life," which provides players with their own avatars and the opportunity to purchase services and goods. She soon begins playing "Second Life" six to eight hours daily. Richard, who declines to join Sandra in the virtual world, learns that Sandra has a "virtual husband," Oscar. Although Sandra never meets Oscar in real life, she begins skipping meals and outings to spend more time online with him. Richard feels angry and betrayed by Sandra's emotional withdrawal.

Richard, who has a drinking problem, attends Alcoholics Anonymous (AA) weekly. After a meeting, he invites an AA member, Lorraine, to have coffee with him. Richard starts coming home late from the meetings. Although Sandra has no evidence of Richard's infidelity, she gets so furious at his late hours that she confronts him with a handgun when he returns home one evening. Richard denies having an affair. The couple separates, reconciles briefly, but Richard eventually moves out. During the separation, Sandra observes his Mercedes parked in front of Lorraine's apartment at night.

Sandra and Richard decide to end the marriage. Their jurisdiction permits divorce based on either no-fault or fault-based grounds. Both Sandra and Richard consult attorneys to explore possible fault-based grounds and defenses. What should their respective attorneys advise them? See generally Sandi S. Varnado, Avatars, Scarlet "A"s, and Adultery in the Technological Age, 55 Ariz. L. Rev. 371 (2013).

2. Lois Hollis seeks a divorce from her husband, Rex, on the ground of adultery. During the divorce proceedings, Rex contends that Lois urged him to date other women during the marriage. He introduces into evidence her handwritten note to him, stating her hope that he would fall in love with another woman so that Lois could leave the marriage. After he began an affair, Lois again wrote to him that she hoped that he and his new love would live together for some time (prior to marriage). Further, Rex testifies that when he and his new woman friend first had sexual relations at a hotel, they received flowers and a card from Lois saying, "My very best wishes to you both today, to your new beginning." What result? See Hollis v. Hollis, 427 S.E.2d 233 (Va. Ct. App. 1993).

D. No-Fault Divorce

1. Divorce Reform

All states have some form of no-fault divorce. Considerable variation exists, however, as to that form. Two common models, the California Family Law Act and the Uniform Marriage and Divorce Act (UMDA), are discussed below.

Allen M. Parkman, Good Intentions Gone Awry: No-Fault Divorce and the American Family

72-75, 79-81 (2000)

California Governor Edmund ("Pat") Brown, who launched the first law reform commission that recommended no fault divorce

The nation's unequivocal no-fault law became effective in California in 1970. . . . It is impossible to identify exactly when the reform movement began, but the California legislature took its first steps in that direction in 1963. In that year, a House Resolution was passed that initiated a study of the laws on divorce, and an interim committee began the study. . . . Four major themes emerged from the 1964 hearings in the California Assembly which set the agenda for the legislative proposals that followed. There were widespread concerns about:

1. the high divorce rate,
2. the adversary process creating hostility, acrimony, and trauma,
3. a need to recognize the inevitability of divorce for some couples and attempt to make the legal process less destructive for them and their children, and
4. charges made by divorced men that the divorce law and its practitioners worked with divorced women to acquire an unfair advantage over former husbands.

The hearings reached no conclusions, nor was any legislation proposed. . . . In 1966, Governor Edmund G. Brown, who was enthusiastic about divorce law reform, established a twenty-two member Commission on the Family [consisting of] one minister, four legislators, six lawyers, four judges, three psychiatrists, two law professors, one medical doctor, and one member of the State Social Welfare Board. . . .

The commission reviewed the condition of the family and made recommendations in two areas: First, it suggested revisions in the substantive law of divorce. Second, it examined the feasibility of establishing a system of family courts. The commission proposed legislation in the form of a model Family Court Act that would have created a family court, eliminated fault as a ground for divorce, and revised the community property distribution rules. The family court proposal included both the creation of a family court system and the establishment of procedures to encourage the parties to use the court's conciliation and counseling services. The commission also recommended that dissolution should be granted whenever the court found that the legitimate objectives of the marriage had been destroyed and that there was no reasonable likelihood that the marriage could be saved.

[The major objection was the potentially high cost of the counseling.] James A. Hayes, a member of the Assembly Judiciary Committee, independently put together another proposal that eliminated the major cost-incurring features—a separate family court system and mandatory counseling structure—but kept the marriage-breakdown theory of divorce. [A subsequent bill, drafted by a conference committee of which he was a member, was enacted as the Family Law Act of 1969.]

The new Family Law Act established two grounds for marital dissolution, "irreconcilable differences which have caused the irremediable breakdown of the marriage" and incurable insanity. [The new act had no provision for a family court system or counseling.] Other changes emphasized a new orientation in divorce proceedings. The term *divorce* was replaced by *dissolution of marriage*. A neutral petition form, *In re the Marriage of Mrs. Smith and Mr. Smith*, replaced the adversarial form *Smith v. Smith*. The parties were called "petitioner" and "respondent" rather than "plaintiff" and "defendant." . . .

Under the prior law, the property division was unequal when the grounds for divorce were adultery, extreme cruelty, or incurable insanity, with the innocent party allocated a disproportionately large share of the community property. Under the new act, community property usually was to be divided equally, with no regard for fault, unless the division would impair the value of the property, such as a business, or when community funds had been deliberately squandered or misused by one spouse to the extent that an equal division of the remaining assets would no longer be equitable. Alimony was redefined as "support" and was determined by fairness rather than fault. . . .

. . . Often ignored in the histories of no-fault divorce in California was the special interest that Hayes brought to his advocacy of no-fault. James A. Hayes was involved in a bitter divorce action during the evolution of no-fault in the California legislature. [Hayes divorced his homemaker wife in 1969, after 25 years of marriage and four children. The final decree was generous to his wife. However, in 1973, Hayes successfully petitioned to reduce significantly his financial obligations to his wife because he had remarried and assumed new financial obligations.]

. . . Hayes was obviously not a casual observer. He was instrumental in enacting no-fault divorce in California; after its passage, in the report that rationalized its passage, he emphasized the equality between men and women. He then used the law and the report to attempt to reduce the financial arrangements to which he had agreed as a condition for his divorce. . . .

In most histories of the passage of the law, James Hayes's role is given only passing notice. If anything, he is pictured as a very active public servant. But the passage of no-fault in California bears witness to the process of legislative self-interest. . . . This is a law that was passed by a legislature dominated by men . . . reinforced by the lobbying efforts of men's interest groups and maneuvered through the California legislature by a man who personally had a great deal to gain from a reduction in the negotiating power of married women. . . .

Lynne Carol Halem, Divorce Reform: Changing Legal and Social Perspectives

269-277 (1980)

[The Uniform Marriage and Divorce Act: Background]

The idea of a national marriage and divorce statute, either in the form of an amendment to the Constitution or a singular law to be adopted by each state, was first proposed in 1884 and continued to spark debates for many years. [T]he Uniform Marriage and Divorce Act [was] ratified by the National Conference of Commissioners on Uniform State Laws in 1970. [The original intent was to remove the concept of fault by substituting the term "irretrievable breakdown" for fault-based grounds and to reject the no-fault ground of separation because it might be construed as a form of punishment.]

The critical blow came from the members of the Family Law Section of the American Bar Association. Whereas in the past, the ABA had been most supportive of the commissioners' bills, this statute proved to be the exception. Without discrediting the concept of no-fault, the Bar attacked the statute on three grounds: the ease and speed with which a divorce could be granted; the absence of conciliation provisions or other brakes on hasty divorce; and the lack of specificity in the regulations governing property division. . . . Using standard conservative arguments, the ABA charged that passage of the act would legalize "easy" or "quickie" divorces. It may be that this position reflected the fear of an insidious plot to minimize the role of legal counsel. . . .

[The commissioners drafted three versions of the statute before they received American Bar Association (ABA) endorsement in 1974. The 1973 version of the act reintroduced notions of fault.] If the commissioners' capitulation was not total, it was, nonetheless, significant. The new statute introduced a clause for the no-fault ground of separation even if the waiting period was abbreviated to 180 days; the term "marital discord" was implicitly linked to the ground of "cruel and inhuman treatment" even if "marital misconduct" was not mentioned; references to reconciliation were more obtrusive even if they were not clearly defined; and the ABA's denouncement of demand divorce received credence through the addition of new safeguards even if they were weak and inoperable.

In other ways, however, the Uniform Marriage and Divorce Act was more progressive than California's law. Issues of marital misconduct were considered irrelevant to custody. [Evidence of fault was relevant to custody in early versions of the California statute but not after 1993.] The effort to discourage spousal maintenance by basing awards on the needs and resources of the parties might eventually prove a more realistic and less acrimonious approach to the problem of postdivorce economics.

Further, incurable insanity and irreconcilable differences did not appear as grounds for dissolution. Whereas the former was largely superfluous in the California act, the latter troubled some purists who objected to the multiplicity of possible translations. Quite obviously the uniform bill had other vagaries. The term "irretrievably broken" was not defined, nor were precise directives furnished to curtail the discretionary powers of the judiciary. Hence many of the indeterminacies in the California model were duplicated in this statute. But in California the reformers could predict fairly accurately the court's interpretation would be liberal. This was not the case with the Uniform Act. . . .

Many states follow the California or UMDA model. Other jurisdictions have taken different approaches (illustrated below).

CALIFORNIA FAMILY CODE

§2310. GROUNDS FOR DISSOLUTION OR LEGAL SEPARATION

Dissolution of the marriage or legal separation of the parties may be based on either of the following grounds, which shall be pleaded generally [formerly, incurable insanity].:

(a) Irreconcilable differences, which have caused the irremediable breakdown of the marriage.

(b) Permanent legal incapacity to make decisions.

§2311. IRRECONCILABLE DIFFERENCES DEFINED

Irreconcilable differences are those grounds which are determined by the court to be substantial reasons for not continuing the marriage and which make it appear that the marriage should be dissolved.

§2335. MISCONDUCT; ADMISSIBILITY OF SPECIFIC ACTS OF MISCONDUCT

Except as otherwise provided by statute, in a pleading or proceeding for dissolution of marriage or legal separation of the parties, including depositions and discovery proceedings, evidence of specific acts of misconduct is improper and inadmissible.

UNIFORM MARRIAGE AND DIVORCE ACT

§302. DISSOLUTION OF MARRIAGE; LEGAL SEPARATION

(a) The [________] court shall enter a decree of dissolution of marriage if . . .

(2) the court finds that the marriage is irretrievably broken, if the finding is supported by evidence that (i) the parties have lived separate and apart for a period of more than 180 days next preceding the commencement of the proceeding, or (ii) there is serious marital discord adversely affecting the attitude of one or both of the parties toward the marriage. . . .

§305. IRRETRIEVABLE BREAKDOWN

(a) If both of the parties by petition or otherwise have stated under oath or affirmation that the marriage is irretrievably broken, or one of the parties has so stated and the other has not denied it, the court, after hearing, shall make a finding whether the marriage is irretrievably broken.

(b) If one of the parties has denied under oath or affirmation that the marriage is irretrievably broken, the court shall consider all relevant factors, including the circumstances that gave rise to filing the petition and the prospect of reconciliation, and shall:

(1) make a finding whether the marriage is irretrievably broken; or

(2) continue the matter for further hearing not fewer than 30 nor more than 60 days later, or as soon thereafter as the matter may be reached on the court's calendar, and may suggest to the parties that they seek counseling. The court, at the request of either party shall, or on its own motion may, order a conciliation conference. At the adjourned hearing the court shall make a finding whether the marriage is irretrievably broken.

(c) A finding of irretrievable breakdown is a determination that there is no reasonable prospect of reconciliation.

NEW YORK DOMESTIC RELATIONS LAW[24]

§170. ACTION FOR DIVORCE

An action for divorce may be maintained by a husband or wife to procure a judgment divorcing the parties and dissolving the marriage on any of the following grounds:

(1) The cruel and inhuman treatment of the plaintiff by the defendant such that the conduct of the defendant so endangers the physical or mental well being of the plaintiff as renders it unsafe or improper for the plaintiff to cohabit with the defendant.

(2) The abandonment of the plaintiff by the defendant for a period of one or more years.

(3) The confinement of the defendant in prison for a period of three or more consecutive years after the marriage of plaintiff and defendant.

(4) The commission of an act of adultery. . . .

(5) The husband and wife have lived apart pursuant to a decree or judgment of separation for a period of one or more years after the granting of such decree or judgment, and satisfactory proof has been submitted by the plaintiff that he or she has substantially performed all the terms and conditions of such decree or judgment.

(6) The husband and wife have lived separate and apart pursuant to a written agreement of separation, subscribed by the parties thereto and acknowledged or proved in the form required to entitle a deed to be recorded, for a period of one or more years after the execution of such agreement and satisfactory proof has been submitted by the plaintiff that he or she has substantially performed all the terms and conditions of such agreement. . . .

(7) The relationship between husband and wife has broken down irretrievably for a period of at least six months, provided that one party has so stated under oath. . . .

---

[24]. Until 2010, New York had the strictest divorce law in the country. New York permitted divorce only on fault-based grounds or subject to both parties' agreement (for example, if the spouses lived apart for at least one year pursuant to a written agreement or both sought a judicial separation). In 2010, the state legislature added a unilateral no-fault provision (N.Y. Dom. Rel. Law §170(7)).

2. Legal Problems Raised by No-Fault Divorce

a. Early Problems of No-Fault

The advent of no-fault divorce brought its share of legal problems. One of these focused on the method of proof to secure a no-fault divorce, stemming from reluctance from making divorce too easy to obtain. Early case law sometimes required that divorce petitioners make a personal appearance and attest to the existence of irreconcilable differences (rather than merely submitting an affidavit). See In re Marriage of McKim, 493 P.2d 868 (Cal. 1972). Many states now dispense with the need for a personal appearance. See, e.g., Fisher v. Fisher, 944 So. 2d 134 (Miss. Ct. App. 2006). Summary dissolution procedures also authorize divorce by affidavit in some circumstances (e.g., childless spouses, short marriages, lack of real property, few debts or assets, and a willingness to waive spousal support (e.g., Cal. Fam. Code §2400)).

Another problem concerned discomfort with unilateral divorce (i.e., a divorce desired by only one spouse). Some courts resisted no-fault divorce over the objection of one party. For example, in Shearer v. Shearer, 356 F.2d 391 (3d Cir. 1965), the court reversed a divorce granted to the husband. Despite the facts of the couple's constant bickering, their six-year separation initiated by the husband (and his overcoming alcoholism only after the separation), the court concluded that the finding of "incompatibility" was clearly erroneous in light of the wife's interest in continuing the marriage and the couple's ten years of cohabitation. Some states found other ways to make divorce more difficult when only one spouse wanted the divorce. See, e.g., Mo. Rev. Stat. §452.320 (requiring proof of fault or two-year separation in such cases).

Finally, opponents of no-fault divorce unsuccessfully challenged early legislation on constitutional grounds of vagueness, impairment of contract, equal protection, and freedom of religion. See, e.g., In re Walton's Marriage, 104 Cal. Rptr. 472 (Ct. App. 1972); In re Marriage of Franks, 542 P.2d 845 (Colo. 1975).

Problems

1. Blackacre just approved the adoption of domestic partnerships, available to same-sex and opposite-sex couples whose members do not wish to marry. A Blackacre legislator is proposing the following grounds for termination: adultery; willful and continued desertion for at least one year; physical or mental cruelty that endangers the plaintiff's safety or health or makes continued cohabitation unreasonable; separation for at least 18 months with no reasonable prospect of reconciliation; addiction to any narcotic drug; institutionalization for mental illness for two or more years; or imprisonment of the defendant for 18 or more months after establishment of the domestic partnership. In such proceedings, the court is not required to effectuate an equitable distribution of property. As the legislator's intern, you are asked for your advice on the proposed legislation.

2. Whiteacre recently simplified its divorce procedure. A newly enacted statute authorizes divorce-by-mail decrees. Such decrees allow petitioners to divorce

without making a personal appearance if (1) the couple has no minor children and the wife is not pregnant, (2) neither party has real property, (3) neither party desires spousal support, (4) the couple's debts do not exceed $10,000, and (5) the marital property totals less than $15,000. Mary Jones, a Whiteacre legislator, is concerned that cutbacks in legal services have resulted in vast numbers of persons whose needs for divorce are not being met. She would like to propose that the above simplified procedure be extended further. You are her legislative intern. What do you advise?

3. A bill pending in the Greenacre legislature would require that, in marriages with children, both parties to a no-fault divorce must consent to terminate the marriage. The state's current law requires that, in the absence of adultery or cruelty, either spouse can petition to end the marriage without the other's consent. You are a legislative aide who has been asked to comment on the proposed reform. What do you advise? See Lynne Marie Kohm, On Mutual Consent to Divorce: A Debate with Two Sides to the Story, 8 Appalachian J.L. 35 (2008).

b. Living Separate and Apart

BENNINGTON v. BENNINGTON

381 N.E.2d 1355 (Ohio Ct. App. 1978)

McCormac, Judge.

Mary Bennington commenced an action for alimony only, claiming gross neglect of duty and abandonment without just cause as grounds therefor. Larry Bennington answered, denying grounds for alimony, and counterclaimed for divorce, alleging gross neglect of duty and extreme cruelty. His counterclaim was later amended, asserting the grounds for divorce of living separate and apart for at least two years without cohabitation. . . .

Plaintiff and defendant were married in 1946. No children have been born to the marriage. In 1963, plaintiff suffered a stroke rendering her permanently and totally disabled and causing her left side to become paralyzed. There have been no sexual relations between the parties since that time.

In 1974, Larry Bennington moved out of the house and into a travel van located adjacent to the house on the same premises. His primary reason for moving into the van was that his wife kept the heat in the house at about 85 to 90 degrees Fahrenheit. He was also irritated about the fact that his wife locked and bolted the door to the house and, when he arrived home from work, it frequently took her fifteen to twenty minutes to come to the door to let him into the house. Her reason for locking the door was apparently for security purposes.

There were also other areas of conflict between the parties. However, there was no intention on the part of Larry Bennington to abandon his marital responsibilities when he moved from the house to the van in 1974. On the contrary, he continued to help his disabled wife with household chores, pretty much the same as before moving into the travel van. There was a conflict as to whether he ever slept inside the house again after moving to the van, or whether he used the house otherwise for his comfort and enjoyment. It is clear, however, that he did enter the house regularly to assist his disabled wife.

On November 26, 1976, Larry Bennington finally became thoroughly disenchanted with the entire arrangement and decided to leave home. He went to Arizona for about one month. He then returned, regaining his job. After his return, he lived off of the premises in the van for about three months and then obtained an apartment elsewhere.

R.C. §3105.01(K) provides grounds for divorce ". . . [w]hen husband and wife have, without interruption for two years, lived separate and apart without cohabitation. . . ."

The trial court found that when the husband moved from the house to the van located on the same premises that he was living separate and apart without cohabitation. . . .

The trial court erroneously included the time that the husband lived in the van adjacent to the house as part of the two-year period, as the parties were not living "separate and apart" during that time. During that time there was no cessation of marital duties and relations between the wife and husband. Approximately the same duties were performed by the husband to the wife and by the wife to the husband as prior to the time that the husband moved outside of the house to the van. . . . While the parties were living apart in a limited sense, they were not living separately in a marital sense. . . . Judgment reversed.

Notes and Questions

1. Mixed grounds. With the movement toward no fault, many states merely added no-fault grounds (for example, living separate and apart) to their traditional fault-based grounds. Thus, a large number of states reflect a "mixed" fault/no-fault regime. This approach contrasts with "pure" no-fault laws in some jurisdictions, such as California. If both fault and no-fault grounds exist, trial judges can use their discretion to select the ground upon which to grant the divorce.

2. Statutory variations. Statutes reflect different types of "living separate and apart" provisions. Currently, 28 states provide that "living separate and apart" is a ground for divorce.[25] Some states require that the parties live apart under a judicial decree or separation agreement for a prescribed period. Some states require that the spouses "mutually and voluntarily" live separate and apart, and sometimes specify a shorter duration for consensual compared to judicial separations. UMDA merely requires proof that the parties live apart for a statutorily designated period. UMDA §302(a)(2). Which does the statute in *Bennington* require?

3. Historical background. Many states had living-apart statutes prior to California's adoption of no fault.[26] However, such statutes were aimed at

---

[25]. Compiled from ABA, Grounds for Divorce and Residency Requirements (Chart 4), 45 Fam. L.Q. 500 (2012).

[26]. DiFonzo, supra note [17], at 39 (citing 23 states).

forestalling, rather than facilitating, divorce. In addition, the requisite statutory periods were so long (generally five to ten years) that the statutes were seldom utilized.

4. Duration. Durational periods for "living separate and apart" range from six months (e.g., UMDA §302(a)(2)) to five years (e.g., Idaho Code Ann. §32-610). In jurisdictions that require lengthy separations before filing for a no-fault divorce, an unhappy spouse must thereby resort to traditional fault-based grounds. What purposes do lengthy separation requirements serve? Do they undermine the purpose of no fault?

5. Elements. Why does *Bennington* conclude the parties were not "living separate and apart"? Suppose that the van were not adjacent to the house? Down the street? Across town? Is the geographic location determinative? Suppose Mr. Bennington moved out and obtained an apartment, yet still returned daily to assist his wife. Is he living separate and apart? May parties who separate to reside in different bedrooms ever establish that they are "living separate and apart"? Compare In re Marriage of Davis, 189 Cal. Rptr. 3d 835 (Cal. 2015), with In re Marriage of Tomlins, 983 N.E.2d 118 (Ill. App. Ct. 2013).

6. Outcome. Did Mrs. Bennington's acts constitute sufficient cruelty for divorce? How did her disability affect the outcome? Were Mr. Bennington's chores in the household, after moving to the van, "marital duties and relations" or caretaking of a disabled person? Should Mr. Bennington's altruistic behavior preclude his divorce?

7. Comparison. How is living separate and apart similar to, and different from, fault-based grounds generally? Similar to, and different from, desertion? Why is a statutory period required? What difference does it make when the period commences? What should toll the statutory period? Suppose the Benningtons were intimate once during the statutory period. Recall the condonation defense. Should fault-based defenses be available?

8. Economic Impact. Should a party wishing to separate be forced to vacate the marital home, even if not financially able? See Carol Bruch, The Legal Import of Informal Marital Separations: A Survey of California Law and a Call for Change, 65 Cal. L. Rev. 1015 (1977) (noting that the requirement causes financial hardship).

9. Privacy. One commentator suggests that living-apart statutes spared parties "the intrusion into their privacy which fault divorce proceedings mandated."[27] Is this an apt characterization of the proceedings in *Bennington*?

10. Legal separation distinguished. Legal separations, constituting an alternative to divorce, were quite common during the fault-based era, when divorce was difficult to obtain. Such separations were once called "divorce from bed and board" (from the Latin *divorce a mensa et thoro*) to be distinguished from absolute divorce (or *divorce a vinculo matrimonii* from the bonds of marriage). Decrees of

---

[27]. Id.

legal separation do not free the parties to remarry but do relieve them from cohabitation. Today, judicial decrees of separation are still necessary in some states to satisfy statutory requirements for "living separate and apart."

NOTE: ABOLITION OF FAULT-BASED DEFENSES

One important legal issue after the adoption of no fault was the status of fault-based defenses. Many states abolished them legislatively. See, e.g., Colo. Rev. Stat. Ann. §14-10-107(5); Fla. Stat. Ann. §61.044; Minn. Stat. Ann. §518.06. Some states abolished them judicially. See Flora v. Flora, 337 N.E.2d 846, 852 (Ind. Ct. App. 1975). On the other hand, some states that added no-fault divorce to their fault grounds still maintain the defenses. See, e.g., Me. Rev. Stat. Ann. tit. 19-A, §§902(3) (recrimination), 902(4) (condonation); N.Y. Dom. Rel. Law §171 (retaining connivance, condonation, recrimination, and statute of limitations defenses to adultery).

Fault-based defenses become important in states with lengthy separation requirements (which force parties who want a speedier divorce to resort to traditional fault-based grounds) and/or in jurisdictions in which fault still plays a role in spousal support or property division.

c. What Role for Fault?

FELTMEIER v. FELTMEIER

798 N.E.2d 75 (Ill. 2003)

Justice Rarick delivered the opinion of the court:

Plaintiff, Lynn Feltmeier, and defendant, Robert Feltmeier, were married on October 11, 1986, and divorced on December 16, 1997. [O]n August 25, 1999, Lynn sued Robert for the intentional infliction of emotional distress. . . . The first matter before us for review is whether Lynn's complaint states a cause of action for intentional infliction of emotional distress. . . . According to the allegations contained in Lynn's complaint, since the parties' marriage in October 1986, and continuing for over a year after the December 1997 dissolution of their marriage: "[Robert] entered into a continuous and outrageous course of conduct with either the intent to cause emotional distress to [Lynn] or with reckless disregard as to whether such conduct would cause emotional distress to [Lynn] . . . including, but not limited to, the following:

> A. On repeated occasions, [Robert] has battered [Lynn] by striking, kicking, shoving, pulling hair, and bending and twisting her limbs and toes. . . .
>
> B. On repeated occasions, [Robert] has prevented [Lynn] from leaving the house to escape the abuse. . . .
>
> C. On repeated occasions, [Robert] has yelled insulting and demeaning epithets at [Lynn]. Further, [Robert] has engaged in verbal abuse which included threats and constant criticism of [Lynn] in such a way as to demean, humiliate, and degrade [Lynn]. . . .

D. On repeated occasions, [Robert] threw items at [Lynn] with the intent to cause her harm. . . .

E. On repeated occasions, [Robert] attempted to isolate [Lynn] from her family and friends and would get very upset if [Lynn] would show the marks and bruises resulting from [Robert's] abuse to others.

F. On repeated occasions since the divorce, [Robert] has engaged in stalking behavior. . . .

G. On at least one occasion, [Robert] has attempted to interfere with [Lynn's] employment by confiscating her computer. Additionally, [Robert] broke into [Lynn's] locked drug cabinet for work on or about March 23, 1997.

[The court then sets forth the elements for intentional infliction of emotional distress (IIED): extreme and outrageous conduct; the actor must either intend that his conduct inflict severe emotional distress, or know that there is at least a high probability that his conduct will cause severe emotional distress; and the conduct must in fact cause severe emotional distress.]

In the case at bar, Robert first contends that the allegations of Lynn's complaint do not sufficiently set forth conduct which was extreme and outrageous when considered "[i]n the context of the subjective and fluctuating nature of the marital relationship." In support of this contention, Robert cites several cases from other jurisdictions that have addressed the policy ramifications of allowing a spouse to maintain an action for intentional infliction of emotional distress based upon acts occurring during the marriage. . . . [W]hile we agree that special caution is required in dealing with actions for intentional infliction of emotional distress arising from conduct occurring within the marital setting, our examination of both the law of this state and the most commonly raised policy concerns leads us to conclude that no valid reason exists to restrict such actions or to require a heightened threshold for outrageousness in this context.

One policy concern that has been advanced is the need to recognize the "mutual concessions implicit in marriage," and the desire to preserve marital harmony. See Henriksen v. Cameron, 622 A.2d 1135, 1138-39 (Me. 1993). However, in this case, brought after the parties were divorced, "there is clearly no marital harmony remaining to be preserved." Moreover, we agree with the Supreme Judicial Court of Maine that "behavior that is 'utterly intolerable in a civilized society' and is intended to cause severe emotional distress is not behavior that should be protected in order to promote marital harmony and peace." Indeed, the Illinois legislature, in creating the Illinois Domestic Violence Act of 1986 (Act) (750 ILCS 60/101 *et seq.* (West 2002)), has recognized that domestic violence is "a serious crime against the individual and society." . . . Thus, it would seem that the public policy of this state would be furthered by recognition of the action at issue.

A second policy concern is the threat of excessive and frivolous litigation if the tort is extended to acts occurring in the marital setting. Admittedly, the likelihood of vindictive litigation is of particular concern following a dissolution of marriage, because "the events leading to most divorces involve some level of emotional distress." *Henriksen*, 622 A.2d at 1139. However, we believe that the showing required of a plaintiff in order to recover damages for intentional infliction of emotional distress provides a built-in safeguard against excessive and frivolous litigation. . . .

Another policy consideration which has been raised is that a tort action for compensation would be redundant. [However,] the laws of this state provide no compensatory relief for injuries sustained [here]. An action for dissolution of marriage also provides no compensatory relief for domestic abuse. In Illinois, as in most other states, courts are not allowed to consider marital misconduct in the distribution of property when dissolving a marriage. See 750 ILCS 5/503(d) (West 2002). After examining case law from courts around the country, we find the majority have recognized that public policy considerations should not bar actions for intentional infliction of emotional distress between spouses or former spouses based on conduct occurring during the marriage.

[W]e now examine the allegations set forth in Lynn's complaint to determine whether Robert's conduct satisfies the "outrageousness" requirement. . . . The issue of whether domestic abuse can be sufficiently outrageous to sustain a cause of action for intentional infliction of emotional distress is apparently one of first impression in Illinois. Other jurisdictions, however, have found similar allegations of recurring cycles of physical and verbal abuse, wherein the conduct went far beyond the "trials of everyday life between two cohabiting people," to be sufficiently outrageous to fall within the parameters of section 46 of the Restatement (Second) of Torts. In the instant case, we must agree with the appellate court that, when the above-summarized allegations of the complaint are viewed in their entirety, they show a type of domestic abuse that is extreme enough to be actionable. . . .

[The court then rejected Robert's contention that Lynn did not suffer sufficiently severe emotional distress, pointing to her claims of loss of self-esteem, difficulty in forming other relationships, Post-traumatic Stress Disorder (PTSD), depression, fear of men, and curtailed enjoyment of life. Finally, the court considered Robert's argument that Lynn's claim was barred by the applicable statute of limitations.] The ultimate question, however, is when the statute of limitations began to run in the instant case. Generally, a limitations period begins to run when facts exist that authorize one party to maintain an action against another. However, under the "continuing tort" or "continuing violation" rule, "where a tort involves a continuing or repeated injury, the limitations period does not begin to run until the date of the last injury or the date the tortious acts cease." A continuing tort, therefore, does not involve tolling the statute of limitations because of delayed or continuing injuries, but instead involves viewing the defendant's conduct as a continuous whole for prescriptive purposes. . . .

In the instant case, Robert . . . maintains that "each of the alleged acts of abuse inflicted by Robert upon Lynn over a 12-year period are separate and distinct incidents which give rise to separate and distinct causes of action [and therefore, if occurring prior to August 25, 1997, would be time barred], rather than one single, continuous, unbroken, violation or wrong which continued over the entire period of 12 years." We must disagree. While it is true that the conduct set forth in Lynn's complaint could be considered separate acts constituting separate offenses of, *inter alia,* assault, defamation and battery, Lynn has alleged, and we have found, that Robert's conduct *as a whole* states a cause of action for intentional infliction of emotional distress. . . .

We believe the appellate court herein properly applied this reasoning to the facts of this case where:

> "The alleged domestic violence and abuse endured by Lynn . . . spanned the entire 11-year marriage. No one disputes that the allegations set forth the existence of

ongoing abusive behavior. Lynn's psychologist, Dr. Michael E. Althoff, found that Lynn suffered from the "battered wife syndrome." He described the psychological process as one that unfolds over time. The process by which a spouse exerts coercive control is based upon 'a systematic, repetitive infliction of psychological trauma' designed to 'instill terror and helplessness.' Dr. Althoff indicated that the posttraumatic stress disorder from which Lynn suffered was the result of the entire series of abusive acts, not just the result of one specific incident."

The purpose behind a statute of limitations is to prevent stale claims, not to preclude claims before they are ripe for adjudication, and certainly not to shield a wrongdoer. As the Superior Court of New Jersey stated, in finding that a wife diagnosed with battered woman's syndrome could sue her spouse in tort for physical and emotional injuries sustained by continuous acts of battering during the course of the marriage:

> "It would be contrary to the public policy of this State, not to mention cruel, to limit recovery to only those individual incidents of assault and battery for which the applicable statute of limitations has not yet run. The mate who is responsible for creating the condition suffered by the battered victim must be made to account for his actions—*all* of his actions. Failure to allow affirmative recovery under these circumstances would be tantamount to the courts condoning the continued abusive treatment of women in the domestic sphere." (Emphasis in original.) Cusseaux v. Pickett, 279 N.J. Super. 335, 345, 652 A.2d 789, 794 (1994).

Therefore, based upon the foregoing reasons, we agree [with] the growing number of jurisdictions that have found that the continuing tort rule should be extended to apply in cases of intentional infliction of emotional distress. . . . Applying the continuing tort rule to the instant case, Lynn's complaint, filed August 25, 1999, was clearly timely and her claims based on conduct prior to August 25, 1997, are not barred by the applicable statute of limitations. . . .

Notes and Questions

1. **Background.** Several factors contribute to the application of tort law to the divorce context, including the abolition of interspousal immunity, recognition and extension of tort liability for emotional injury, awareness of domestic violence, and the demise of fault-based divorce. *Feltmeier* reveals the split among jurisdictions over the recognition of interspousal suits for emotional distress in the divorce context. On what basis does *Feltmeier* decide to recognize such suits?

2. **High threshold?** Should courts adopt a high threshold for extreme and outrageous behavior in the marital context? See McCulloh v. Drake, 24 P.3d 1162, 1169-1170 (Wyo. 2001) (setting high standard for recovery "so that the social good which comes from recognizing the tort in a marital setting will not be undermined by an invasive flood of merit-less litigation" [and] "to protect defendants from the possibility of long and intrusive trials on frivolous claims").

Some commentators contend that determinations of "outrageousness" should be limited to cases in which a spouse's conduct is criminal.[28] What role does a high threshold play in the context of domestic violence?[29]

3. Policy. *Feltmeier* first explores whether courts should permit interspousal actions for IIED in divorce actions. Do you agree with *Feltmeier*'s resolution of this issue? Does recognition of emotional distress claims in the context of divorce undermine no-fault divorce law? Resurrect the fault-based ground of cruelty? Further or disserve the goals of tort law? Lead to recovery for domestic disputes that are trivial and/or widespread? Lead to double recovery in cases in which fault plays a role in property distribution? Do problems of causation militate against recovery (i.e., the difficulty of proving that the emotional distress was caused by the spouse's conduct and not by the marital difficulties)?

On the policy arguments, compare Ira Mark Ellman, The Place of Fault in a Modern Divorce Law, 28 Ariz. St. L.J. 773 (1996); Harry D. Krause, On the Danger of Allowing Marital Fault to Re-Emerge in the Guise of Torts, 73 Notre Dame L. Rev. 1355, 1363-1366 (1998), with Pamela Laufer-Ukeles, Reconstructing Fault: The Case for Spousal Torts, 79 U. Cin. L. Rev. 207 (2010). See also Brenda Cossman, The Story of Twyman v. Twyman: Politics, Tort Reform, and Emotional Distress in a Texas Divorce, in Family Law Stories 243, 259-265 (Carol Sanger, ed., 2008); Janet Halley, Split Decisions: How and Why to Take a Break from Feminism 348-364 (2006) (discussing Twyman v. Twyman).

4. Special rules? If tort claims are permitted in the divorce context, should courts limit them to interspousal torts involving injury or physical violence? How does *Feltmeier* resolve the issue whether statutes of limitations should be tolled for victims of spousal abuse who endure years of abuse before filing for divorce? Why do battered spouses often wait to file tort suits, thereby incurring problems with the statute of limitations? Should courts and legislatures recognize a tort of "domestic violence"? See Cal. Civ. Code §1708.6 (creating this tort). See also Pugliese v. Superior Court, 53 Cal. Rptr. 3d 681 (Ct. App. 2007) (adopting continuing tort theory to extend statute of limitations).

5. Privacy. Should notions of privacy militate against the recognition of IIED claims in the marital context?[30]

6. Joinder. Tort liability in the context of divorce also presents the issue of whether courts should *require* joinder of tort claims and divorce claims.

a. Different views. Courts that permit interspousal actions for IIED adopt different positions regarding joinder: some prohibit joinder, some mandate joinder,

---

[28]. See Ira Mark Ellman & Stephen D. Sugarman, Spousal Emotional Abuse as a Tort?, 55 Md. L. Rev. 1268, 1335 (1996).

[29]. For critical commentary, see Sarah M. Buel, Access to Meaningful Remedy: Overcoming Doctrinal Obstacles in Tort Litigation Against Domestic Violence Offenders, 83 Or. L. Rev. 945 (2004); Margaret E. Johnson, Redefining Harm, Reimagining Remedies, and Reclaiming Domestic Violence Law, 42 U.C. Davis L. Rev. 1107 (2009).

[30]. According to one critic, "It is ethically questionable for the state to be the sole arbiter of what should remain private and thus within the discretion of the spouses, and what may be considered by the court as within its purview." Buel, supra note [29], at 976.

and some adopt a permissive policy of joinder. Which approach do you favor? If a court does not permit joinder, is a plaintiff without remedy? May she pursue a separate action? Must she? Since *Feltmeier* was decided, a majority of jurisdictions have adopted a permissive approach—permitting, but not mandating joinder. See Chen v. Fischer, 843 N.E.2d 723, 726 (N.Y. 2005) (surveying jurisdictions).

b. Claim preclusion. If a spouse chooses to pursue a separate tort action postdivorce, can the tortfeasor spouse raise the affirmative defense of res judicata to bar her claim? Professor Sarah Buel charges:

> At first glance it would appear that most states are permissive regarding joinder of tort and divorce actions. However, closer scrutiny reveals that many divorce statutes include specific language that, although joinder is not strictly mandatory, if the subject of the subsequent tort action was at all part of the dissolution, the tort action will be disallowed on grounds of res judicata.[31]

Compare Brinkman v. Brinkman, 966 S.W.2d 780 (Tex. App. 1998) (holding that wife's subsequent tort claims were precluded by res judicata), with Boblitt v. Boblitt, 118 Cal. Rptr. 3d 788 (Ct. App. 2010) (contra).

c. Benefits of joinder. What benefits follow from joinder? Professor Andrew Schepard responds:

> Divorce litigation comprises a major portion of the caseload of many large state court systems. The policy interest in conserving scarce judicial resources by concentrating all claims between the divorcing couple into a single proceeding is thus great. . . . There is also a related social interest in reducing the private transaction costs (the most significant component of which is legal fees) of settling marital differences. Divorce is generally a zero sum economic transaction: there is not enough money in the marital settlement pot for both spouses to live postdivorce at the same standard of living as before the divorce. Increasing the transaction costs of the divorce settlement by reopening proceedings reduces further the total resources available for the postdivorce family to live on. . . .
>
> Also weighing in favor of [joinder] is the policy of repose that underlies [res judicata]. Divorce is a wrenching, all-consuming emotional experience. [The husband's and wife's] well-being, and their continued productive functioning as members of society, require that their emotional stability be reestablished quickly and firmly by a final settlement of marital differences.[32]

Do you find his reasoning persuasive?

d. Distinctions: Tort and divorce law. Do the different purposes of (or underlying legal theories) tort actions and divorce militate in favor of—or against—joinder? Do the different procedural characteristics? For example, if joinder is required, how should a court resolve access to jury trials (normally permitted in tort actions)? If a jury trial is ordered, where shall the claim be litigated—in family court or civil court? How should a court resolve the problem of attorneys' fees (because

[31]. Id. at 1000-1001.

[32]. Andrew Schepard, Divorce, Interspousal Torts, and Res Judicata, 24 Fam. L.Q. 127, 131-132 (1990). See also Tiffany Oliver, Intentional Infliction of Emotional Distress Between Spouses: New Mexico's Excessively High Threshold for Outrageous Conduct, 33 N.M. L. Rev. 381, 392 (2003) (arguing that the benefits outweigh concerns).

contingent fees are not permitted in divorce actions)? See *Chen*, 843 N.E.2d at 725-726 (addressing distinctions that militate against mandatory joinder).

7. Economic tort claims. Not all dissolution-related tort actions involve domestic violence. For example, in Schlueter v. Schlueter, 975 S.W.2d 584 (Tex. 1998), the Texas Supreme Court held that no independent action existed in a divorce proceeding for a spouse's fraudulent depletion of community assets. In so ruling, the court permitted joinder for personal injury claims but not economic torts. Does this rule make sense?

Problem

Jane and John Doe have been married for seven years and have a son and twin girls. Unbeknownst to John, his wife had a sexual affair during the marriage with her art professor. John discovers a letter that reveals to him that the children may have been fathered by the professor. DNA testing confirms that John is father of the son, but not the twins. The next day, John petitions for divorce, alleging adultery, and sues to recover damages for fraud and IIED. Should he be permitted to bring the tort claims in the divorce proceeding? Should his tort claims be barred by the interspousal immunity doctrine? Does the wife's conduct satisfy the requirements for IIED? See Doe v. Doe, 747 A.2d 617 (Md. 2000). See generally Linda L. Berger, Lies Between Mommy and Daddy: The Case for Recognizing Spousal Emotional Distress Claims Based on Domestic Deceit That Interferes with Parent-Child Relationships, 33 Loy. L.A. L. Rev. 449 (2000).

3. Assessment of the No-Fault "Revolution"

a. Divorce Reform in the United States

Deborah L. Rhode & Martha Minow, Reforming the Questions, Questioning the Reforms: Feminist Perspectives on Divorce Law

in Divorce Reform at the Crossroads 191-199, 209-210 (Stephen D. Sugarman & Herma Hill Kay eds., 1990)

Our central premise is that the legal issues surrounding divorce have been conceived too narrowly. Reform initiatives have too often treated divorce as a largely private dispute and have not adequately addressed its public dimensions. . . .

The leading proponents of initial no-fault reform were lawyers, judges, and law professors. Their primary focus was on the legal grounds for divorce; their primary purposes were to reduce expense, acrimony, and fraud in resolving matters envisioned as essentially private concerns. What is, perhaps, most revealing about these original efforts are the issues that were not on the agenda. Early reform strategies neglected gender equality and public responsibilities.

Although no-fault initiatives coincided with the resurgence of a women's rights movement, proponents of these reforms generally were not seeking to remedy women's disadvantages under traditional family policies. Indeed, to the extent that gender equity appeared at all in discussions among decision makers, the focus involved equity for men. The dominant concern was beleaguered ex-husbands, crippled by excessive alimony burdens, and threats of blackmail. Although this problem was grossly exaggerated, the absence of systematic data allowed policymakers to rely on anecdotal experiences to formulate the problem they sought to reform.

In part, the absence of women's concerns from the debate reflected the absence of women. Those with greatest influence in policy-making—practicing attorneys, politicians, and family law experts—were overwhelmingly male. The newly emerging women's rights movement was not significantly involved with early divorce reforms, in part because it was understaffed and overextended during this period, but more important, because the implications of such reforms were not yet apparent. Only as the divorce rate escalated and scholars concerned with women's issues began to chronicle its impact did the focus of debate begin to change.

Even when reformers identified gender equality as an objective, they relied almost exclusively on gender-neutral formulations. For example, they succeeded in eliminating explicitly sex-linked provisions (such as those granting alimony only to wives) and in reformulating rules for marital property distribution to require "equal" or "equitable" division of assets. Yet . . . such provisions have secured equality in form, but not equality in fact.

The assumptions underlying early reforms also marginalized the public implications of divorce doctrine. No-fault initiatives began from the premise that decisions involving the termination of marriage should rest with private parties; the public's responsibility was simply to provide efficient legal rules for processing their agreement and resolving any disputes. Within this framework, a couple's allocation of financial and child-rearing obligations appeared to be primarily matters for private ordering. If parties failed to reach agreement, their differences would be resolved under broad discretionary standards mandating equality or equity between the spouses in financial matters and the best interest of the child in custody contests. Public norms about the kinds of resolutions society should endorse receded to the background. As a result, the state was given little responsibility for guiding, enforcing, or supplementing judicial awards.

Paradoxically, this move toward private ordering failed adequately to acknowledge the diversity of private family circumstances. Those who framed and interpreted legal doctrine often overlooked the fact that marriages of different durations, formed during different decades with different expectations, could leave divorcing parties in sharply divergent situations. One single, discretionary standard was thought adequate to deal with circumstances ranging from a couple married for one year while the parties finished college to a couple married for twenty-five years while the woman worked in the home and the husband held paid employment.

Early no-fault reforms gave no special attention to the concerns of particularly vulnerable groups such as displaced homemakers with limited savings, insurance, and employment options; families with inadequate income to support two households (a problem disproportionately experienced by racial minorities); or couples with no children, no significant property, and no need for a formal adjudicative procedure. Nor was child support central to the reform agenda; it appeared only as a side issue, buried within custody and other financial topics.

It bears emphasis what such a limited conception of public responsibility left out. The early reform agenda did not specify clear public norms concerning financial and child-care responsibilities to guide parties' decisionmaking or judicial review. Nor did it mandate effective, affordable enforcement procedures for spousal and child support awards, or state subsidies where private resources were inadequate. Reformers also neglected the impact of postdivorce property divisions—such as the forced sale of the family home—on dependent children. And what was most critical, no-fault initiatives omitted criteria for assessing the outcomes of divorce, outcomes affecting not only the parties and their children but subsequent marriages, stepfamilies, and public welfare responsibilities.

In noting what was absent from the no-fault agenda, we do not mean to devalue its central objective. Reducing the acrimony, expense, and fraud associated with fault-based procedures was a goal worth pursuing on its own right. Given the opposition to liberalizing grounds for divorce, reformers may have been justifiably wary about raising other related issues. But we also believe that the limitations of the original reform movement reflect not only what was politically expedient at that historical moment but also more fundamental conceptual inadequacies. By remaining wedded to traditional public/private distinctions, early divorce reform tended to amplify rather than redress gender inequalities. . . .

. . . Norms governing termination of a marriage should be consistent with the ideal to which marriage aspires—that of equal partnerships between spouses who share resources, responsibilities, and risks. . . . Gender equality and child welfare should become priorities in practice, not just theory, under contemporary divorce law. . . .

b. Divorce Reform: The Comparative-Law Perspective

Carlos H. Conde, Philippines Stands All But Alone in Banning Divorce

N.Y. Times, June 17, 2011

When citizens of the small Mediterranean nation of Malta voted in a referendum last month to legalize divorce, they reignited debate in the Philippines, one of the last countries, along with Vatican City, where divorce is still banned.

Days later, the issue surfaced at a hearing in the Philippine House of Representatives on a long-dormant bill.

The Vatican City State, the only other sovereign state that bans divorce besides the Philippines

"The global reality is that divorce has been recognized as a legitimate option for couples, particularly for women, who are trapped in unhappy, even violent, unions," said Luz Ilagan, a congresswoman representing the Gabriela Women's Party and co-author of the bill. "If they can do it in Malta, we can do it here. Let us not remain in the Dark Ages."

But the re-emergence of the divorce proposal has inflamed opponents in this overwhelmingly Roman Catholic country and riled the church authorities, who have called it part of an "orchestrated war against the Filipino family."

Divorce is not an alien concept in the Philippines; it was legal during the U.S. and Japanese occupations in the early part of the 20th century. However, it was prohibited with the enactment of the 1949 Civil Code. . . .

The Family Code currently provides three options for spouses who want to get out of their marriage: legal separation, annulment or a declaration of nullity of marriage. Lawmakers who advocate the legalization of divorce say those are inadequate.

In a legal separation, they note, spouses cannot remarry because the marriage is not dissolved. An annulment, which requires the testimony of psychiatrists that one party is psychologically too incapacitated to sustain the marriage, is typically too complicated and costly for most people to pursue. A declaration of nullity requires a court to find that the marriage was never valid to begin with because of factors like fraud.

According to government records, thousands of Filipinos have filed for separation, mostly for infidelity, physical abuse and abandonment. And the numbers are growing. According to the Office of the Solicitor General, 7,753 petitions for legal separations, annulments, and declarations of nullity of marriage were filed in 2007, compared with 4,520 in 2001. . . .

[Congresswoman Ilagan] calls her bill "divorce, Filipino-style" because of its stringent requirements for applicants, among them that petitioner and spouse have been legally separated for at least five years. "There won't be any Britney Spears marriages under our divorce law," said Ms. Ilagan, referring to the singer's marriage to her high school sweetheart in 2004, which lasted less than three days.

Divorce is still not permitted in the Philippines. In other international developments, divorce was legalized in Chile in 2004, despite longstanding opposition from the Catholic Church and conservative groups. Ireland was the last European country in 1995 to legalize divorce (for spouses who have been separated for four of the last five years).

c. Divorce Reform: The Return of Fault Movement

A movement began in the late 1990s to reintroduce fault in the dissolution process. Many states have considered "covenant marriage" laws, which are designed to preserve the lifelong character of marriage. Such laws are characterized by (1) mandatory premarital counseling that emphasizes the seriousness of marriage; (2) execution of the parties' statement (the covenant) that contains their respective promises to take reasonable steps to preserve the marriage if marital problems arise; and (3) limitation on the grounds for divorce (i.e., fault on the part of one spouse or, in the absence of fault, a designated period of living separate and apart). See Ariz. Rev. Stat. Ann. §§25-901 & 25-903; Ark. Code Ann. §§9-11-801 to 9-11-811; La. Rev. Stat. Ann. §9:307.

Supporters of covenant marriage claim that, by making divorce more difficult to obtain, covenant marriage promotes children's well-being. Religious groups contend that covenant marriage reaffirms the meaning of marriage.[33] Critics charge, however, that these reforms raise constitutional concerns (placing an undue burden on the right to make decisions regarding family life); conflict-of-laws and choice-of-law questions (possibly forcing noncovenant marriage states to recognize covenant marriages and denying no-fault divorces to spouses who seek them outside their home state); unauthorized practice of law problems (requiring clergy marriage counselors to counsel couples regarding the "nature and purpose" of marriage); and policy debates (the effect of covenant marriages on preserving the family, protecting women and children, and lowering juvenile crime rates).[34]

Furthermore, some worry that covenant marriages may make it more difficult for victims of domestic violence to exit abusive marriages.[35] Covenant marriages have not been as popular as supporters initially hoped. For example, less than 2 percent of newly contracted marriages in Louisiana are covenant marriages.[36]

E. Access to Divorce

BODDIE v. CONNECTICUT

401 U.S. 371 (1971)

Mr. Justice Harlan delivered the opinion of the Court.

Appellants, welfare recipients residing in the State of Connecticut, brought this action in the Federal District Court for the District of Connecticut on behalf of

[33]. Cynthia DeSimone, Comment, Covenant Marriage Legislation: How the Absence of Interfaith Religious Discourse Has Stifled the Effort to Strengthen Marriage, 52 Cath. U. L. Rev. 391, 393-394 (2003).

[34]. Jay Macke, Note, Of Covenants and Conflicts—When "I Do" Means More Than It Used To, But Less Than You Thought, 59 Ohio St. L.J. 1377 (1998).

[35]. Robert M. Gordon, The Limits of Limits on Divorce, 107 Yale L.J. 1435, 1447-1449 (1998).

[36]. Steven L. Nock et al., Covenant Marriage Turns Five Years Old, 10 Mich. J. Gender & L. 169, 170 (2003). Similarly, only 57 licenses for covenant marriages were issued in Arkansas during the first year. Andrew Demillo, Covenant Couples Mean to Stay Wed, Ark. Post-Gazette, Aug. 25, 2002, at A7.

themselves and others similarly situated, challenging, as applied to them, certain state procedures for the commencement of litigation, including requirements for payment of court fees and costs for service of process, that restrict their access to the courts in their effort to bring an action for divorce.

It appears from the briefs and oral argument that the average cost to a litigant for bringing an action for divorce is $60. Section 52-259 of the Connecticut General Statutes provides: "There shall be paid to the clerks of the supreme court or the superior court, for entering each civil cause, forty-five dollars. . . . " An additional $15 is usually required for the service of process by the sheriff, although as much as $40 or $50 may be necessary where notice must be accomplished by publication.

There is no dispute as to the inability of the named appellants in the present case to pay either the court fees required by statute or the cost incurred for the service of process. The affidavits in the record establish that appellants' welfare income in each instance barely suffices to meet the costs of the daily essentials of life and includes no allotment that could be budgeted for the expense to gain access to the courts in order to obtain a divorce. . . .

[Appellants challenged the constitutionality of the statute and sought an injunction to permit them to proceed without payment of fees and costs. A three-judge court found the statute constitutional.] We now reverse. Our conclusion is that, given the basic position of the marriage relationship in this society's hierarchy of values and the concomitant state monopolization of the means for legally dissolving this relationship, due process does prohibit a State from denying, solely because of inability to pay, access to its courts to individuals who seek judicial dissolution of their marriages. . . .

. . . Without [the] guarantee [of the Fifth and Fourteenth Amendments] that one may not be deprived of his rights, neither liberty nor property, without due process of law, the State's monopoly over techniques for binding conflict resolution could hardly be said to be acceptable under our scheme of things. . . .

Such [due process] litigation has, however, typically involved rights of defendants—not, as here, persons seeking access to the judicial process in the first instance. This is because our society has been so structured that resort to the courts is not usually the only available, legitimate means of resolving private disputes. . . .

. . . As this Court on more than one occasion has recognized, marriage involves interests of basic importance in our society [citing *Loving*, *Skinner*, and Meyer v. Nebraska]. It is not surprising, then, that the States have seen fit to oversee many aspects of that institution. Without a prior judicial imprimatur, individuals may freely enter into and rescind commercial contracts, for example, but we are unaware of any jurisdiction where private citizens may covenant for or dissolve marriages without state approval. Even where all substantive requirements are concededly met, we know of no instance where two consenting adults may divorce and mutually liberate themselves from the constraints of legal obligations that go with marriage, and more fundamentally the prohibition against remarriage, without invoking the State's judicial machinery.

Thus, although they assert here due process rights as would-be plaintiffs, we think appellants' plight, because resort to the state courts is the only avenue to dissolution of their marriages, is akin to that of defendants faced with exclusion from the only forum effectively empowered to settle their disputes. Resort to the judicial process by these plaintiffs is no more voluntary in a realistic sense than that of the defendant called upon to defend his interests in court. For both groups this process is not only the paramount dispute-settlement technique, but, in fact, the only available one. In this posture we think that this appeal is properly to be resolved in light of the principles enunciated in our due process decisions that delimit rights of defendants compelled to litigate their differences in the judicial forum.

[P]recedent has firmly embedded in our due process jurisprudence two important principles upon whose application we rest our decision in the case before us. [First,] due process requires, at a minimum, that absent a countervailing state interest of overriding significance, persons forced to settle their claims of right and duty through the judicial process must be given a meaningful opportunity to be heard. . . . Our cases further establish that a statute or a rule may be held constitutionally invalid as applied when it operates to deprive an individual of a protected right although its general validity as a measure enacted in the legitimate exercise of state power is beyond question. . . .

No less than these rights, the right to a meaningful opportunity to be heard within the limits of practicality, must be protected against denial by particular laws that operate to jeopardize it for particular individuals. . . . Just as a generally valid notice procedure may fail to satisfy due process because of the circumstances of the defendant, so too a cost requirement, valid on its face, may offend due process because it operates to foreclose a particular party's opportunity to be heard. The State's obligations under the Fourteenth Amendment are not simply generalized ones; rather, the State owes to each individual that process which, in light of the values of a free society, can be characterized as due.

Drawing upon the [these] principles . . . we conclude that the State's refusal to admit these appellants to its courts, the sole means in Connecticut for obtaining a divorce, must be regarded as the equivalent of denying them an opportunity to be heard upon their claimed right to a dissolution of their marriages, and, in the absence of a sufficient countervailing justification for the State's action, a denial of due process.

The arguments for this kind of fee and cost requirement are that the State's interest in the prevention of frivolous litigation is substantial, its use of court fees and process costs to allocate scarce resources is rational, and its balance between the defendant's right to notice and the plaintiff's right to access is reasonable.

In our opinion, none of these considerations is sufficient to override the interest of these plaintiff-appellants in having access to the only avenue open for dissolving their allegedly untenable marriages. Not only is there no necessary connection between a litigant's assets and the seriousness of his motives in bringing suit, but it is here beyond present dispute that appellants bring these actions in good faith. Moreover, other alternatives exist to fees and cost requirements as a means for conserving the time of courts and protecting parties from frivolous litigation, such as penalties for false pleadings or affidavits, and actions for malicious prosecution or abuse of process, to mention only a few. In the same vein we think that reliable alternatives exist to service of process by a state-paid sheriff if the State is unwilling to assume the cost of official service. This is perforce true of service by publication which is the method of notice least calculated to bring to a potential defendant's attention the pendency of judicial proceedings. We think in this case service at defendant's last known address by mail and posted notice is equally effective as publication in a newspaper. . . .

In concluding that the Due Process Clause of the Fourteenth Amendment requires that these appellants be afforded an opportunity to go into court to obtain a divorce, we wish to re-emphasize that we go no further than necessary to dispose of the case before us, a case where the bona fides of both appellants' indigency and desire for divorce are here beyond dispute. We do not decide that access for all individuals to the courts is a right that is, in all circumstances, guaranteed by the Due Process Clause of the Fourteenth Amendment so that its exercise may not be placed beyond the reach of any individual, for, as we have already noted, in the case before us this right is the exclusive precondition to the adjustment of a fundamental human relationship. The requirement that these appellants resort to the judicial process is entirely a state-created matter. Thus we hold only that a State may not, consistent with the obligations imposed on it by the Due Process Clause of the Fourteenth Amendment, preempt the right to dissolve this legal relationship without affording all citizens access to the means it has prescribed for doing so. . . .

Mr. Justice DOUGLAS, concurring in the result. . . .

. . . The Court today puts "flesh" upon the Due Process Clause by concluding that marriage and its dissolution are so important that an unhappy couple who are indigent should have access to the divorce courts free of charge. Fishing may be equally important to some communities. May an indigent be excused if he does not obtain a license which requires payment of money that he does not have? How about a requirement of an onerous bond to prevent summary eviction from rented property? The affluent can put up the bond, though the indigent may not be able to do so. Is housing less important to the mucilage holding society together than marriage? The examples could be multiplied. I do not see the length of the road we must follow if we accept my Brother Harlan's invitation. . . .

An invidious discrimination based on poverty is adequate for this case. While Connecticut has provided a procedure for severing the bonds of marriage, a person can meet every requirement save court fees or the cost of service of process and be denied a divorce. Connecticut says in its brief that this is justified because "the State does not favor divorces; and only permits a divorce to be granted when those conditions are found to exist in respect to one or the other of the named parties, which seem to the legislature to make it probable that the interests of society will be better served and that parties will be happier, and so the better citizens, separate, than if compelled to remain together."

Thus, under Connecticut law, divorces may be denied or granted solely on the basis of wealth. . . . Affluence does not pass muster under the Equal Protection Clause for determining who must remain married and who shall be allowed to separate.

Notes and Questions

1. Background. On remand, the court ordered state officials to waive filing fees. Boddie v. Connecticut, 329 F. Supp. 844 (D. Conn. 1971). As *Boddie* reveals, states impose filing fees and costs for divorce petitions. Many jurisdictions permit indigents to avoid such fees by proceeding in forma pauperis. When *Boddie* was decided, approximately 32 states (excluding Connecticut) had such statutes.[37]

2. Limitations. In *Boddie*, Justice Harlan notes, "There is no dispute as to the inability of the named appellants [to pay]" and, later, "it is here beyond present dispute that appellants bring these actions in good faith." Thus, the holding is limited to plaintiffs who make a showing of indigency and who seek divorce in good faith. How does an indigent demonstrate these requirements?

3. Premises. The majority rests its opinion on "the basic position of the marriage relationship in this society's hierarchy of values and the concomitant state monopolization of the means for legally dissolving this relationship." Are both aspects necessary to the result, or are they independent grounds? How does the language about the importance of marriage in *Obergefell* (discussed in Chapter II) reinforce the reasoning in *Boddie*?

4. Extension to other divorce-related costs? If *Boddie* rests on both premises (societal values and monopoly), does an indigency exemption for other divorce expenses (for example, attorneys' fees) follow? Should it matter if the fees are paid to the court or to third parties? How meaningful is a right of access without an attorney? See In re Smiley, 330 N.E.2d 53 (N.Y. 1975).

5. Indigents' rights generally. How far does *Boddie* protect indigents' rights? If it rests on a monopoly rationale, then *Boddie* might guarantee access in civil cases generally. But cf. United States v. Kras, 409 U.S. 434 (1973) (no right to free bankruptcy discharge); Ortwein v. Schwab, 410 U.S. 656 (1973) (no right to waive filing fees for welfare appeals). How is divorce distinguishable from bankruptcy and welfare? Does *Boddie* mandate waiver of fees in other family law matters (for example, annulment, paternity, custody, or adoption)? Marriage license fees? Does *Boddie* mandate a right to publicly funded counsel in a dissolution action involving child custody? See King v. King, 174 P.3d 659 (Wash. 2007). In a civil contempt proceeding for failure to pay child support? See Turner v. Rogers, 131 S. Ct. 2507 (2011) (discussed in Chapter VII).

6. State grounds. At least one court has decided, based on state law rather than constitutional grounds, that an indigent has the right to appointed counsel in a divorce proceeding. Sholes v. Sholes, 760 N.E.2d 156 (Ind. 2001) (holding that state statute required appointment of counsel for life inmate in state prison who petitioned for relief from default judgment of divorce). The state legislature later amended the statute to limit the right to publicly appointed counsel to cases in which a party has a likelihood of success on the merits. Ind. Code Ann. §34-10-1-2.

7. Alternative rationale. How sound is *Boddie*'s approach? For example, what criteria does the Court suggest for determining which interests are fundamental for due process purposes? Is equal protection a superior approach, as Justice Douglas suggests (as does Justice Brennan in an omitted concurrence)? See Jeffreys

---

[37]. Charles Brooks, Note, Boddie v. Connecticut: The Rights of Indigents in a Divorce Action, 11 J. Fam. L. 121, 122 n.5 (1971).

v. Jeffreys, 296 N.Y.S.2d 74 (Sup. Ct. 1968) (state court costs for divorce violate indigents' state and federal rights to equal protection), *rev'd on other grounds*, 330 N.Y.S.2d 550 (App. Div. 1972) (requiring a state, but not a city, to pay such costs in absence of statutory authorization).

Problems

1. Blackacre has an explicit provision in its state constitution protecting the right to privacy. The Blackacre legislature has just repealed its no-fault laws and reintroduced fault. The Blackacre Family Code permits divorce only for adultery, cruelty, and desertion. John and Jane Doe, a married couple, challenge the statute, alleging that it violates their constitutional right of privacy by disallowing divorce by mutual consent. What result? Does *Boddie* guarantee a constitutional right to divorce, similar to the constitutional right to marry? See Ferrer v. Commonwealth, 4 Fam. L. Rep. (BNA) 2744 (Sept. 26, 1978) (deciding a somewhat similar issue based on Puerto Rican law). See generally Kenneth L. Karst, The Freedom of Intimate Association, 89 Yale L.J. 624, 671-672 (1980).

2. Public interest groups in Arkansas, Arizona, and Louisiana argue that "covenant marriage" laws are unconstitutional in light of *Boddie*. What arguments would they make? See generally David M. Wagner, The Constitution and Covenant Marriage Legislation: Rumors of a Constitutional Right to Divorce Have Been Greatly Exaggerated, 12 Regent U. L. Rev. 53 (1999).

NOTE: PRO SE DIVORCE

In the fault-based system, lawyers were essential to prove the existence of marital fault. The adoption of no-fault divorce eroded the role of lawyers and spurred the growth of pro se divorce. Divorce self-help kits and services proliferated in many states. Less than a decade after the advent of no fault, researchers conducted studies of the effectiveness of pro se divorce. One study by Yale law students found that most clients themselves resolved property, support, and custody issues. The authors expressed doubts about the need for counsel in terms of judicial efficiency or public welfare.[38]

Psychologists who conducted a subsequent empirical study funded by the ABA came to a different conclusion. After comparing self-represented versus attorney-represented litigants, these researchers identified various shortcomings of pro se divorce, including that (1) pro se litigants become progressively less satisfied with the terms of their divorces as their cases become more complex, (2) they are less likely to receive tax advice or information about alternative dispute resolution, and (3) many petitioners and respondents encounter difficulties that are never resolved.[39]

---

[38]. Ralph C. Cavanaugh & Deborah L. Rhode, Project, The Unauthorized Practice of Law and Pro Se Divorce: An Empirical Analysis, 86 Yale L.J. 104, 128-129 (1976).

[39]. Bruce D. Sales et al., Is Self-Representation a Reasonable Alternative to Attorney Representation in Divorce Cases?, 37 St. Louis U. L.J. 553 (1993).

Despite the shortcomings of pro se divorce, the number of litigants who choose to represent themselves in family law cases is remarkably high. In fact, the majority of divorce cases today have at least one pro se party. In some states, about 90 percent of divorce cases involve at least one self-represented litigant.[40] In California, approximately 75 percent of divorces are brought by pro se litigants, compared to 47 percent two decades ago.[41] To put these numbers in perspective, there are about 5 percent of self-represented litigants in civil litigation generally.[42] Moreover, the economic downturn has contributed to the increase in pro se litigants in family law cases, as more marriages fall apart because of financial difficulties and as more spouses decide to represent themselves to save money.[43]

The rise in the number of pro se litigants creates considerable difficulty for court personnel—for judges who must determine how to assure a fair trial to pro se litigants without appearing to compromise their own neutrality, and also for court officials who must distinguish between the provision of information versus legal advice.[44] In response to these problems, courts and legal service programs are simplifying legal forms and instructions, creating self-help centers, developing Internet-based forms of assistance, conducting clinics for litigants, and relying on commercial paralegals and document preparation services to assist litigants.[45]

Some states are responding to the growth in pro se divorce by permitting limited representation services. Thus, a lawyer might represent a parent in a child support matter, but not a related custody dispute. See, e.g., Kan. Rules Prof'l Conduct R. 1.2 (approving modification in rules of professional conduct to permit limited representation, provided that the limitation is reasonable and the client consents). Some commentators worry, however, that limited-scope representation will jeopardize clients' interests.[46]

NOTE: RELIGIOUS, SOCIAL, AND CULTURAL OBSTACLES SURROUNDING DIVORCE

Religious issues also present obstacles to divorce. Under traditional Jewish law, a religious divorce (known as a *get*) is necessary to end an Orthodox Jewish marriage. However, traditional Jewish divorce law reflects considerable gender bias. For example, only a husband may grant a wife a *get*. Some husbands use the threat of denying a *get* to extract concessions during the divorce. A wife whose husband refuses to give her a *get* remains a "bound" woman (*agunah*), and thus

---

[40]. Margaret Davis, A Legal Team of One: Pro Se Divorce in Cook County, 18 Pub. Int. L. Rep. 132, 132-133 (2013).

[41]. Frances L. Harrison et al., Courts Responding to Communities: California's Family Law Facilitator Program: A New Paradigm for the Courts, 2 J. Center Child. & Cts. 61, 61 (2000).

[42]. Bonnie Hough, Self-Represented Litigants in Family Law: The Response of California's Courts, 1 Cal. L. Rev. Circuit 15 (2010).

[43]. Steve Campbell, Do-It-Yourself Divorce Experiences Upswing: Deep Recession, Steep Legal Fees Spur Growth of Courthouse Trend, Times (Trenton, N.J), Apr. 28, 2009, at B8.

[44]. Carolyn D. Schwarz, Note, Pro Se Divorce Litigants, 42 Fam. Ct. Rev. 655, 657-659 (2004).

[45]. Steven K. Berenson, A Family Law Residency Program? A Model Proposal in Response to the Burdens Created by Self-Represented Litigants in Family Court, 33 Rutgers L.J. 105, 122-131 (2001); Jessica Pearson, Court Services: Meeting the Needs of Twenty-First-Century Families, 33 Fam. L.Q. 617, 627 (1999).

[46]. See, e.g., Suzanne Valdez, Addressing the Pro Se Litigant Challenge in Kansas State Courts, 78 J. Kan. B. Ass'n 25, 26-28 (2009).

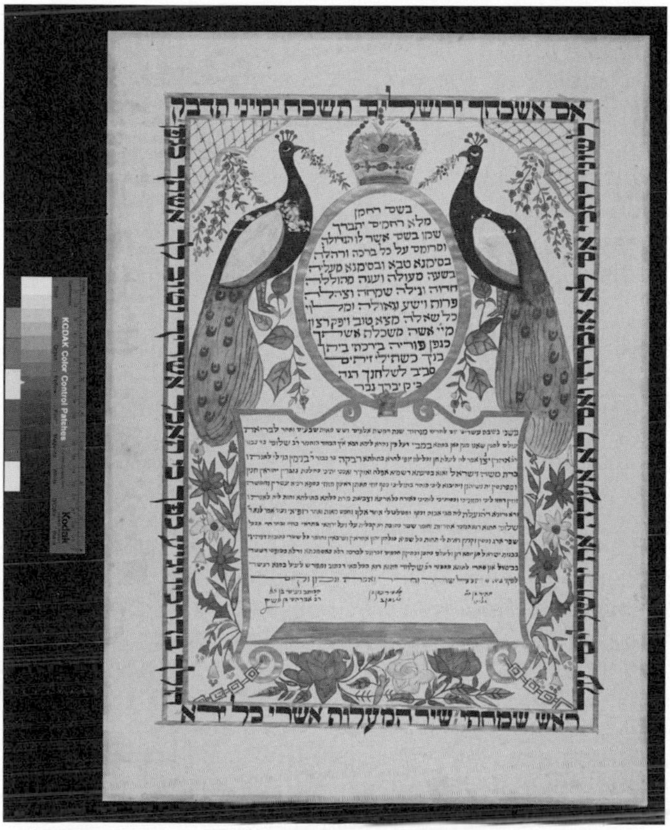

A traditional Jewish *Ketubah*, from Bombay, India, 1911

she is unable to remarry in the faith. If she does remarry without the *get,* she is considered an adulteress, and any of her subsequent children are considered illegitimate.

Dilemmas arise when American secular courts are asked to enforce either (1) the religious prenuptial agreement (called a *Ketubah*) that obligates the husband to provide the *get,* or (2) the decision of the religious tribunal (the *Beth Din*) that arranges religious divorces and orders husbands to grant the religious divorce. Constitutional issues involve the Free Exercise and Establishment Clauses of the First Amendment. Some courts avoid these constitutional issues by relying on contract principles to enforce the Jewish prenuptial agreement. See, e.g., Avitzur v. Avitzur, 446 N.E.2d 136 (N.Y. 1983).

In response to the problem of recalcitrant husbands, the New York legislature passed a *get* statute providing that no final judgment of divorce may be ordered unless the party who commences the proceeding alleges that he or she has taken or will take (prior to entry of judgment) "all steps" within his or her power to "remove any barrier" to the defendant's remarriage. N.Y. Dom. Rel. Law §253. Despite widespread doubts as to the statute's constitutionality, the legislature subsequently extended the statute by amending the equitable distribution law to permit a judge to consider the effect of any "barrier to remarriage" in postdivorce decisionmaking regarding property distribution and spousal support. N.Y. Dom. Rel. Law §236B(5)(h).[47]

Informal pressures, such as the threat of community ostracism, sometimes make husbands comply with the religious prenuptial agreement requiring the *get.* Occasionally, more direct pressure is applied.[48] Recently, the *Beth Din,* along with the Orthodox Caucus and the Rabbinical Council of America, approved a new prenuptial agreement form requiring a husband who refuses to appear before the *Beth Din* for divorce proceedings to pay his wife $150 for every day he fails to

---

[47]. On the legal strategies to surmount constitutional issues, see Lorelei Laird, Lawyers Look for Secular Solutions to the Orthodox Jewish Divorce Problem, ABAJ, Aug. 1, 2014, http://www.abajournal.com/magazine/article/lawyers_look_for_secular_solutions_to_the_jewish_divorce_problem.

[48]. In one well-publicized case, a rabbi kidnapped and tortured recalcitrant husbands in order to convince the men to grant a divorce. See, e.g., Sean Carlin, Rabbi Accused of Running Divorce Kidnap Team Heads to Trial, Wash. Times, Feb. 16, 2015, http://www.washingtontimes.com/news/2015/feb/16/rabbi-accused-of-running-divorce-kidnap-team-heads/.

appear.[49] The Israeli parliament has adopted a more strict approach: enactment of a law authorizing denials of employment, passports, driver's licenses, and banking privileges to recalcitrant husbands.[50] In the United States, constitutional issues preclude imposition of similar sanctions.

Religious issues also arise regarding Islamic marriage contracts. Such contracts make provision for a *mahr,* or a sum of money payable by the husband to the wife—part received upon marriage and the other part upon divorce or the husband's death. Some commentators suggest that judicial enforcement of these agreements may violate the Establishment Clause by giving rise to impermissible governmental entanglement in religion.[51]

Social and cultural obstacles also influence access to divorce. For example, vestiges of stigma still affect divorce. As one commentator explains the traditional beliefs underlying this stigma:

> Divorce is a neurotic procedure of neurotic people. In the great majority of cases, divorce is not a chance occurrence but unconsciously self-provoked, even if only by the choice of a neurotic partner. . . . Augmenting these clinical diagnoses were the data generated by empirical studies on the relationships between mental illness and divorce. [Some researchers] reported that divorced and separated parents had more emotional disturbances than the non-divorced. Although such studies were not conclusive or unchallenged, the affiliation between psychopathology and divorce was not to be broken. . . .
>
> In many respects it was this prognosis that brought divorce therapy into the arena of marriage counseling. Ostensibly the purpose behind clinical treatment was not chiefly to effect reconciliation but rather to help the divorced or the would-be divorced "to understand the causes of failure, to grow and to mature . . . , and to become potentially better candidates for some marriage in the future."[52]

Stigma about divorce sometimes plays a role in employment decisions. For example, in one case, an untenured elementary schoolteacher was not rehired by her school district despite excellent teaching evaluations, allegedly because she was in the midst of a divorce. She filed suit under 42 U.S.C. §1983, seeking reinstatement, back pay, and damages. She argued that her termination was based on her marital status (that is, her impending divorce) in violation of her constitutional rights of privacy and liberty. The Sixth Circuit held that the school board's action violated her right to privacy, reasoning that "[Roe v. Wade] clearly established the existence of a constitutionally protected right to privacy which includes matters relating to procreation and marriage." Littlejohn v. Rose, 768 F.2d 765, 769 (6th Cir. 1985).

The stigma surrounding divorce may affect men as well as women. In one case, a male English professor at an evangelical Christian liberal arts college resigned, rather than face being fired, because his pending divorce constituted a ground for firing. The college allowed faculty to continue employment if their divorces were based only on adultery or abandonment.[53]

---

[49]. Mark Oppenheimer, Where Divorce Can Be Denied, Orthodox Jews Look to Prenuptial Contracts, N.Y. Times, Mar. 17, 2012, at A19.

[50]. Pascale Fournier et al., Secular Rights and Religious Wrongs? Family Law, Religion, and Women in Israel, 18 Wm. & Mary J. Women & L. 333, 350-351 (2012).

[51]. See Nathan B. Oman, Bargaining in the Shadow of God's Law: Islamic Mahr Contracts and the Perils of Legal Specialization, 45 Wake Forest L. Rev. 579 (2010); Elaine Sciolino, Britain Grapples with Role for Islamic Justice, N.Y. Times, Nov. 19, 2008, at A1.

[52]. Cited in Lynn Halem, Divorce Reform: Changing Legal and Social Perspectives 181-183 (1980).

[53]. Catrin Einhorn, At College, a High Standard on Divorce, N.Y. Times, May 4, 2008, at 27.

F. The Role of Counsel

1. Emotional Aspects of Divorce

Kenneth Kressel et al., Professional Intervention in Divorce: The Views of Lawyers, Psychotherapists, and Clergy

in Divorce and Separation 246, 250-255
(George Levinger & Oliver C. Moles eds., 1979)

Much more frequently than either therapists or clergy, [the divorce lawyers in our sample] mentioned sources of stress inherent in the nature of their work. . . . Let us set forth the major sources of role strain reflected in the lawyer interviews.

The adversary nature of the legal proceedings. Despite many changes in recent years, divorce remains largely an adversary process in the eyes of the law. [T]he law's formal bias, the availability of legal threats and counter-threats, as well as the emotional agitation of clients, may push even the most cooperative of lawyers toward serious escalation of conflict. (No-fault divorce has not removed the problem; couples still file bitter suits and countersuits over who shall have custody, how much child support shall be paid, etc.)

The one-sidedness of the lawyer's view. The lawyer's objective appraisal of the marital situation is greatly limited by the professional injunction that lawyers deal with only one of the spouses. Our respondents referred frequently to the difficulty of ascertaining the true state of affairs from the perspective provided by their own clients. Hearing only one side, the lawyer is more easily led to over-identify with the client's point of view—and the client may have strong motives, conscious or unconscious, for wishing to use the adversary system as a vehicle for retribution.

The shortage of material resources. Since two households cannot be supported as cheaply as one, it is highly unlikely that both parties to a divorce will be happy with the terms of the economic settlement. The attorney, therefore, is often in the position of being the bearer of bad news. . . .

The economics of the law office. "There are some lawyers who want to litigate, litigate. They get better fees that way—the taxicab with the meter running." How widespread this phenomenon is nobody knows. It represents nonetheless a serious potential conflict of interest between lawyer and client.

Another potential source of conflict stems from the fact that it is generally the husband who pays the wife's legal costs. The lawyer who represents the wife, therefore, is in the anomalous position of having his fee paid by the opposing side. Unconscious pressures may thus be created for a less than totally effective representation of the wife's interests. The wife herself may have doubts about the degree of allegiance which she can expect from the arrangement.

The non-legal nature of many of the issues. In major areas of their activity, lawyers are operating largely outside the domain of law or legal training. Relatively few of the issues that arise are strictly "issues of law." Moreover, even many legal and financial issues engage psychological judgment and expertise, or personal values (e.g., custody or visitation arrangements that would best meet the emotional needs of both children and parents). Unfortunately, the training of lawyers poorly equips them to understand or handle the psychological and interpersonal issues in divorce, even though such issues may be crucial for creating equitable and workable agreements.

The difficulties in the lawyer-lawyer relationship. Almost universally the lawyers noted that a crucial determinant of divorce outcomes is the relationship between the two opposing attorneys. Indeed, for some respondents a constructive divorce was defined as one in which the two attorneys "come to operate within each other's framework." . . .

[The authors identify six roles that lawyers adopt in response to the problems of divorce practice:]

1. The Undertaker. This metaphor (supplied, incidentally, by one of our respondents) rests on two assumptions: that the job is essentially thankless and messy; and that the clients are in a state of emotional "derangement." This stance is also characterized by a general cynicism about human nature and the doubt that good or constructive divorces are ever possible. . . .

2. The Mechanic. This is a pragmatic, technically oriented stance. It assumes that clients are basically capable of knowing what they want. The lawyer's task primarily involves ascertaining the legal feasibility of doing what the client wants. . . . A good outcome lies in producing "results" for the client, "results" usually understood in financial terms. . . .

3. The Mediator. This stance is oriented toward negotiated compromise and rational problem solving, with an emphasis on cooperation with the other side and, in particular, the other attorney. . . . Unlike the Undertaker and Mechanic, but like the following three stances, the Mediator tends to downplay the adversary aspect of his role. [A] good outcome is a "fair" negotiated settlement that both parties can "live with" (a frequently used phrase). . . .

4. The Social Worker. This stance centers around a concern for the client's postdivorce adjustment and overall social welfare. Regarding women clients in particular, there may be an emphasis on the client's "marketability."

The main thing is to fully explore [the client's] ability to contribute to her own support. I have had agreements where I have been able to get money for college or a business course. . . .

Even though the attorney represents only one of the parties, there may also be a tendency to consider the interests of the entire family [such as the children]. This stance is also frequently associated with the view that, contrary to many clients' expectations, divorce is not usually an easy solution to marital unhappiness. The involvement of therapists or clergy is welcome. [A] "good" outcome is perceived to be one in which the client achieves social reintegration.

5. The Therapist. This stance involves active acceptance of the fact that the client is in a state of emotional turmoil. There is a concomitant assumption that the legal aspects of a divorce situation can be adequately dealt with only if the emotional aspects are engaged by the lawyer. Correspondingly, there is an orientation toward trying to understand the client's motivations. . . . A "good" outcome is conceptualized more or less as it would be in a therapeutically oriented crisis-intervention situation: personal reintegration of the client after a trying, stressful period. Predictably enough, this is also a stance that welcomes involvement of psychotherapists and in which clients may be encouraged to seek such assistance.

6. The Moral Agent. In this final stance there is a more or less explicit rejection of neutrality; it is assumed that the lawyer should not hesitate to use his or her sense of "right" and "wrong." This stance appears to be particularly salient when the divorcing couple has children, with the lawyer attempting to serve as a kind of guardian and protector of the children's interests. . . . A constructive outcome is one in which the lawyer's sense of "what is right" is satisfied, not only in relation to the client, but to the other spouse and the children.

We have sought to explain this typology of lawyer stances largely as a product of the role strains characteristic of matrimonial practice. . . .

MOSES v. MOSES

1 Fam. L. Rep. (BNA) 2604 (July 22, 1975), *aff'd*, 344 A.2d 912 (Pa. Super. Ct. 1975)

CERCONE, J.

This appeal has been taken by the husband, Dr. Lawrence Moses, from the lower court's award of attorney's fees and expenses to his wife's counsel. . . .

From December 16, 1968 until February 4, 1969, Mrs. Moses consumed many of the hours for which Mr. Fox billed Dr. Moses in personal and telephonic conversations of staggering numbers. Although the content of those conversations is privileged, there are indications in the record that large parts of the discussions are based upon Mr. Fox's friendship with both Dr. and Mrs. Moses, as well as his professional relationship with Mrs. Moses. Her phone calls to Mr. Fox at all hours of the day and night eventually grew so burdensome that they were apparently the principal case of Mr. Fox's withdrawal from the case in favor of Mr. Robinson.

After his withdrawal, Mr. Fox tendered a bill for $4,842 in counsel fees (121 hours and 5 minutes at $40 per hour) and expenses of $112.10. Only fifty-six days elapsed from the time that Mr. Fox began consulting with Mrs. Moses until he withdrew on February 10, 1969, so that he averaged two hours every day, including weekends and holidays, working on Mrs. Moses' problems. The only tangible result of this labor was the support award for Mrs. Fox and the children of $275 weekly. Indeed, to this day the parties are not divorced. . . .

The difficulty in the instant case is that there can be little doubt that Mr. Moses is able to pay, and Mrs. Moses is unable to pay, the fees charged by Mr. Fox. We also do not dispute the finding by the lower court that Mr. Fox actually spent

121 hours on the case, and that $40 per hour is a fair hourly charge for those services. We do challenge, however, the propriety of Mr. Fox investing so much time in this case. We feel that there is an obligation upon counsel, if he expects his fee to be paid by the other spouse, to control excessive demands upon his time, energy and intellect by the dependent spouse. We find that Mr. Fox failed to exercise such control in the instant case. [C]ase law in other jurisdictions . . . supports our view herein. . . .

Finally, our decision is supported by the American Bar Association's Code of Professional Responsibility, Disciplinary Rule 2-106 (1970), which sets forth the factors that counsel should consider in determining the reasonableness of his fee: "(1) The time and labor required, the novelty and difficulty of the questions involved, and the skill requisite to perform the legal service properly. (2) The likelihood, if apparent to the client, that the acceptance of the particular employment will preclude other employment by the lawyer. (3) The fee customarily charged in the locality for similar legal services. (4) The amount involved and the results obtained. (5) The time limitations imposed by the client or by the circumstances. (6) The nature and length of the professional relationship with the client. (7) The experience, reputation, and ability of the lawyer or lawyers performing the services. (8) Whether the fee is fixed or contingent."

We find that the time and labor required, the results obtained, and the nature and length of Mr. Fox's professional relationship with Mrs. Moses, all militate against the allowance of fees and expenses of roughly $5,000 in the instant case. [T]he allowance for attorney's fees and expenses is reduced to $3,000. . . .

Notes and Questions

1. Overlapping roles. *Moses* reveals the overlap between the divorce attorney's role as advocate and psychological counselor. Given the court's advice, how would you recommend that an attorney "control [such] excessive demands upon his time, energy, and intellect"?

2. Marital counseling. If the divorce attorney believes that a client should consult a therapist, should the attorney so suggest? How can the attorney do so in a nonthreatening manner? How might such a suggestion backfire? If the client refuses to heed the advice, should the attorney withdraw from the case? Some law firms address this problem by hiring full-time mental health professionals (and sometimes financial advisors) to assist clients with emotional and financial issues that arise during the divorce process.[54]

3. Empirical data. Many divorce lawyers provide far less emotional support than the attorney in *Moses*. An empirical study of 40 divorce cases in two states characterizes representation as a conversational tug-of-war: Clients seek to include a "broader picture of their lives, experiences, and needs" (especially regarding the

---

[54]. Elizabeth Millard, Continuum of Care: North Carolina Firm Adds Financial and Counseling Professionals to Its Staff, 4 ABAJ E-Rep. 6 (Apr. 15, 2005).

failure of their marriage), whereas lawyers resist these efforts. Lawyers tend to be interested "only in those portions of the client's life that have tactical significance for the prospective terms of the divorce settlement or the conduct of the case." Thus, lawyers do not usually provide psychological or emotional support, but rather emphasize communicating their legal knowledge in order "to move clients toward positions that [the lawyers] deem to be reasonable and appropriate."[55]

These findings confirm those of a small-scale empirical study (60 women) by sociologist Terry Arendell who reports that almost all the clients had complaints about their lawyers:

> Most of the women said their attorneys had showed little interest in their present or future problems and had not tried to keep them informed about divorce legalities and the overall legal process. Although they had been sought out as counselors in a personal life crisis, these lawyers soon appeared to be bureaucratic technicians, more concerned with forms, figures, and procedures than with a client's history, fears, or future well-being. . . . Oversights by attorneys provoked a great deal of anger and frustration. Failure to return phone calls, the most frequent complaint, eroded the attorney-client relationship and increased the woman's sense of stress. . . .[56]

What advice for the family lawyer do you derive from the above studies?

4. Risks for divorce attorneys. The emotionally charged divorce context can present dangers when some clients express their frustrations by resorting to violence against legal professionals. Causes of the violence have been attributed to (1) no-fault divorce, which makes litigants more angry and anxious to lash out at the legal system; and (2) pro se divorce, which eliminates the possibility that a lawyer can help the client understand the process and calm the client.[57] Do these incidents highlight the need for greater use of alternative dispute resolution? Or is some other strategy preferable?

2. Conflicts of Interest

FLORIDA BAR v. DUNAGAN

731 So. 2d 1237 (Fla. 1999)

PER CURIAM.

. . . After a formal hearing in this matter, the referee found the following facts. In July 1992, [attorney Walter Dunagan] prepared a bill of sale purporting to

[55]. Austin Sarat & William L.F. Felstiner, Divorce Lawyers and Their Clients: Power and Meaning in the Legal Process 144-145 (1995).

[56]. Terry Arendell, Mothers and Divorce: Legal, Economic, and Social Dilemmas 10-11 (1986). Of the seven women in Arendell's study who had no complaints about their lawyers, three prepared and filed their own divorce papers, three negotiated a spousal agreement before retaining an attorney, and the remaining woman was a law student!

[57]. Lisa Siegel & Keith Griffin, Middletown Shooting an Extreme Example of Risks Routinely Faced by Attorneys for Warring Spouses, Conn. L. Trib., June 21, 2005, at 1.

transfer certain assets of a restaurant business, "Biscuits 'N' Gravy 'N' More" ("B & G"), to the joint ownership of William and Paula Leucht. Dunagan also prepared the fictitious name filing for this business but, according to a letter sent by him to the Leuchts, inadvertently omitted Paula Leucht's name on the registration form.

Subsequently, a commercial lease dispute arose between B & G and Bay-Walsh Properties (Florida) Inc., d/b/a/ Nova Village Market Partnership ("Bay-Walsh"). The suit filed by Bay-Walsh named B & G, William Leucht, and Paula Leucht as defendants. Dunagan represented B & G and the Leuchts in this action and specifically moved to dismiss Paula Leucht as an improper party to the suit.

Later in 1994, Dunagan was involved in negotiations between the Leuchts and a third party to open another B & G restaurant in Daytona Beach and, in 1994 and 1995, also represented B & G and the Leuchts in an eminent domain suit against the Florida Department of Transportation.

On or about February 23, 1996, Dunagan sent a letter to the Port Orange Police Department and city attorney in which he stated that he represented William Leucht, that William Leucht was the sole owner of B & G, and that although there was a bill of sale which was "considered to put the business in the name of William and Paula Leucht," this "instrument and the legal consequences thereof were duly considered, and it was determined with deliberation that William Leucht would remain the sole owner." The letters further advised that Mr. Leucht intended to fire two employees, after which they would no longer be welcome on the premises of the restaurant, and that if they entered the premises, they would be ejected. The letters purported to notify the police "in order to prevent a breach of the peace from occurring."

Several days after sending these letters, Dunagan filed a petition for dissolution of marriage on behalf of William Leucht against Paula Leucht. A few days later, Paula Leucht called B & G Restaurant and was told by an employee that William Leucht was the sole owner and she could not come to the restaurant. Ms. Leucht went to the restaurant anyway and was arrested for disorderly conduct and forcibly removed from the premises. Prior to, during, and after her arrest, Ms. Leucht informed the police that she co-owned the restaurant.

Finally, on May 2, 1996, the judge in the divorce proceeding ordered that William and Paula Leucht were to share equally in the net proceeds from both B & G restaurants, and on October 31, 1996, Dunagan filed a motion to withdraw from representation of William Leucht in the divorce proceeding after Paula Leucht hired an attorney to file a malpractice lawsuit against him. [Dunagan seeks review of the referee's findings and recommendation.]

Dunagan first argues that the referee erred in finding that his representation of William Leucht in the divorce proceeding after having jointly represented William and Paula Leucht in matters relating to their business presented a conflict of interest. Dunagan argues that the business matters in which he represented the Leuchts were completely unrelated to the dissolution of marriage and that ownership of the business was not a central issue in the divorce; therefore, he reasons, there was no conflict of interest. This argument is without merit.

Rule 4-1.9(a) of the Rules Regulating the Florida Bar prohibits a lawyer who has formerly represented a client from representing another person "in the same or a substantially related matter" where that person's interests are materially adverse to the former client's interests. Whether two legal matters are substantially related depends upon the specific facts of each particular situation or transaction. Further, the comment to rule 4-1.9 states that "[w]hen a lawyer has been directly involved in a specific transaction, subsequent representation of other clients with materially adverse interests clearly is prohibited." . . .

[H]ere, Dunagan represented William and Paula Leucht in the formation of their business and, specifically, prepared a bill of sale transferring assets of the business to their joint ownership. Because the business was begun during the marriage, it was a marital asset and as such was inherently an issue in the divorce. Additionally, the petition for dissolution of marriage filed by Dunagan on William Leucht's behalf specifically raised the issue of the ownership of the business and impliedly disputed the validity of the bill of sale prepared by Dunagan in that it alleged that William Leucht "is the sole owner of the restaurant known as 'Biscuits 'N' Gravy 'N' More'." While ownership of the business may not have been a hotly contested issue, it was still an issue involved in the divorce; therefore, at least one prior matter in which Dunagan jointly represented the Leuchts was substantially related to the divorce. . . .

Dunagan next argues that the referee erred in finding that Paula Leucht did not consent to Dunagan's representation of William Leucht in the dissolution of marriage action. Under certain circumstances, a lawyer may be permitted to represent a client despite a conflict of interest, but only if he or she obtains the consent of the appropriate party or parties after consultation. See R. Regulating Fla. Bar 4-1.7(a)-(b); 4-1.9(a). Here, the referee found that "no disclosure of the conflict or waiver of same took place, given the uncontested fact that no testimony was provided that the respondent ever consulted with Paula Leucht as to the circumstances which led him to represent William Leucht in the divorce, and to what her position was vis-a-vis his representing William Leucht." This finding is supported by the evidence.

Without consulting with or obtaining Paula Leucht's consent, Dunagan filed a petition for dissolution of marriage against her and on behalf of William Leucht. Shortly thereafter, Paula Leucht arrived home from a trip and discovered that the dissolution petition had been filed. Only then, after first calling Mr. Dunagan's office, did Paula Leucht seek and retain another attorney to represent her in the divorce. Only after she had retained an attorney of her own did Dunagan claim he sought her consent through her attorney.

Dunagan testified that he contacted Ms. Leucht's original and subsequent attorneys who gave their consent as attorneys for her. Ms. Leucht's original attorney, Mr. Beck, submitted an affidavit stating that "pursuant to a conference with my client, Paula K. Leucht, it was agreed that there would be no objection raised to the Respondent, Walter B. Dunagan, Esq., representing William Leucht." Paula Leucht acknowledged that she discussed Dunagan's representation of William Leucht with Beck and he advised her that there were better attorneys to be up against; so, she testified, "we never did say anything about him representing me." However, Ms. Leucht also testified that Beck never clearly advised her of her rights or the possible prejudice Dunagan's representation of her ex-husband presented. Accordingly, Ms. Leucht's and her attorney's failure to affirmatively object cannot be construed as "consent after consultation" as required by the rules.

Dunagan makes much of the fact that he could not personally consult with and obtain Ms. Leucht's consent because she was represented by counsel. However, there was no reason that Dunagan could not have consulted with and attempted to obtain Paula Leucht's consent prior to filing the dissolution petition on behalf of William Leucht and, therefore, prior to the time Paula Leucht retained other counsel to represent her in the divorce. This, in fact, would have been the most appropriate course of action. . . . The rules state that an attorney *shall not represent* conflicting interests unless the client consents. Especially where the conflict exists prior to the beginning of the representation, this can only mean that the necessary consent should be obtained before the attorney agrees to represent the conflicting interest. This was clearly not done in this case. . . .

Dunagan also argues that the referee erred in concluding that his letters to the Port Orange police and city attorney violated rule 4-1.9(b). . . . Rule 4-1.9(b) prohibits a lawyer from using information relating to the representation of a former client to the former client's disadvantage except as permitted by rule 4-1.6 or when the information has become generally known. Dunagan essentially argues that the information in the letter was not used to Paula Leucht's disadvantage because it only addressed who had the right to sole possession of the premises, and Paula Leucht was arrested for disorderly conduct, not trespassing. Therefore, he argues, the letters did not cause her to be arrested.

However, the evidence supports the referee's finding that the letters contributed, at least to some degree, to Ms. Leucht's being arrested and forcibly removed from the premises of the business. Although she was charged with disorderly conduct, the arrest report filled out by the police officer clearly shows that the police officers relied on the letter from Dunagan. [B]ecause Dunagan clearly used information relating to his representation of Paula Leucht to her disadvantage and such disclosures were not permitted under rule 4-1.6, we approve the referee's conclusion that the letters at issue violated rule 4-1.9(b).

Finally, Dunagan argues that the recommended discipline, a ninety-one-day suspension, is too harsh. . . . We find that the recommended suspension is appropriate. [T]he Court has imposed similar suspensions for similar conduct. . . .

Notes and Questions

1. Epilogue. After Dunagan's 91-day suspension, he filed a petition for reinstatement. The referee recommended that he not be reinstated for the following reasons: he had remained the attorney of record in several cases during his suspension; he failed to notify an employer (a company for which he lectured) of his suspension; he disagreed with the finding that his representation constituted a conflict of interest; he failed to correct deficiencies in his trust accounting procedures; and he presented no evidence of postsuspension community service. Nonetheless, the Florida Supreme Court found the referee's factual findings insufficient to justify denying Dunagan's petition. Florida Bar ex rel. Dunagan, 775 So. 2d 959 (Fla. 2000).

2. Rationale. The divorce lawyer may face several ethical problems, including conflicts of interest. In *Dunagan,* what was the nature of the conflict of interest? Why does the court reject Dunagan's arguments that no conflict of interest existed? For example, how were the couple's business matters and divorce related? How were Mr. Leucht's interests materially adverse to his ex-wife's interests?

3. Scope. Courts wrestle with the issue how broadly to interpret the term "conflict of interest" for disciplinary or disqualification purposes. Courts also continue to address whether conflicts of interest arise from two legal matters being sufficiently "substantially related" to result in the disqualification of, or sanctions on, an attorney. See, e.g., Hurley v. Hurley, 923 A.2d 908 (Me. 2007) (holding that an attorney who previously represented a wife in a personal injury action was properly disqualified from later representing her husband in their divorce action given the fact that the attorney had obtained confidential information from wife previously about her health, employment history, and response to contested litigation); In re Conduct of Balocca, 151 P.3d 154 (Or. 2007) (finding a bankruptcy case and paternity action brought by the bankrupt to be "substantially related").

4. Joint representation. Is joint representation permissible? If so, when? According to current ethical rules (i.e., Model Code of Professional Responsibility and Model Rules of Professional Conduct), joint representation is permitted if the attorney reasonably believes he or she can adequately represent both clients' interests and if both clients consent after full disclosure of the risks of such representation. The Restatement (Third) of the Law Governing Lawyers §128 reaffirms this rule.

On the other hand, some states condemn the practice of joint representation by their disciplinary rules, case law, or state bar opinions. The American Academy of Matrimonial Lawyers (a voluntary association of lawyers and judges that establishes ethical standards for family law practitioners that exceed those of the ABA and most state ethics codes) also admonishes against joint representation, even if clients consent. Which point of view do you find more persuasive? See generally Avi Braz, Note, Out of Joint: Replacing Joint Representation with Lawyer-Mediation in Friendly Divorces, 78 S. Cal. L. Rev. 323 (2004); Mary E. Chesser, Comment, Joint Representation in a Friendly Divorce: Inherently Unethical?, 27 J. Legal Prof. 155 (2002-2003).

5. Client consent. Did Mrs. Leucht consent to Mr. Dunagan's representation of her ex-husband in the dissolution? Why did the Florida Supreme Court hold that her "failure to affirmatively object" could not be construed as consent pursuant to the state bar rules?

6. Judges and conflicts of interest. Judges also may be subject to sanctions for conflicts of interest in their representation of clients after leaving the bench. See, e.g., James v. Mississippi Bar, 962 So. 2d 528 (Miss. 2007) (reprimand of a former judge who presided over a child abuse proceeding and then represented one parent in a custody proceeding).

Problems

1. Wife files a petition for a restraining order for protection against domestic violence from her husband. The court grants her petition, but before the hearing to determine whether the order should be made permanent, Wife files a motion seeking disqualification of her husband's attorney, Charles Esposito. She alleges that she previously consulted Esposito's partner (Davis Upchurch) to ask him to represent her in divorce proceedings; in the course of that one consultation, she

claims that she divulged confidential information to Upchurch. Upchurch did not charge her for the consultation; he claims that he was not retained to represent Wife and does not remember anything she told him that might have been confidential. Should Wife's motion be granted?

Consider the following: (1) Can an attorney-client relationship be established based on one visit? (2) To fulfill the requirements for disqualification, must the client prove that confidential communications were actually disclosed? (3) Does the existence of the attorney-client privilege depend on whether the client actually hires the attorney? (4) Were the two proceedings (the restraining order and the dissolution) substantially related, i.e., did the law firm subsequently represent an interest adverse to the former client in a matter that was the same or substantially related to the matter in which it represented the former client? See Metcalf v. Metcalf, 785 So. 2d 747 (Fla. Dist. Ct. App. 2001).

2. After Marie and Theodore have been married for more than 25 years, Marie files for divorce. She seeks division of the couple's property, permanent spousal support, and attorney fees and costs. Theodore decides to retain their adult son, Mark, as his attorney. Marie then files a motion to disqualify Mark. Does representation by an adult child of one of the parents in a divorce action constitute a disqualifying conflict of interest? What additional facts might you want to know to make this determination? See Liapis v. District Court, 282 P.3d 733 (Nev. 2012). What should be the appropriate standard for disqualification in this case: avoidance of the appearance of impropriety or actual prejudice? See State v. Eighth Jud. Dist. Ct. (Zogheib), 321 P.3d 882 (Nev. 2014)

Ethics Committee, Mississippi State Bar Opinion 80

Law. Manual on Prof'l Conduct (ABA/BNA) 801:5104 (Mar. 25, 1983)

An attorney may not represent both parties in a no-fault divorce. The interests of the parties are conflicting, inconsistent, diverse, and otherwise discordant, no matter what the parties themselves believe. Serving one client's interest may result in not adequately representing the other client's interest. The lawyer's loyalty will be divided. DRs 5-105(A)[, 5-105](C); ECs 5-14, 5-15.

Ethics Committee, State Bar of Montana, Opinion 10

Law. Manual on Prof'l Conduct (ABA/BNA) 801:5401 (Dec. 1980)

A lawyer may represent both spouses in a joint petition for dissolution as a nonadversary procedure. A lawyer may represent both spouses if it is obvious that he can adequately represent the interest of each after each consents to the representation after full disclosure of the possible effect of such representation on the exercise of his independent professional judgment on behalf of each. DRs 5-104; Canon 5.

Robert G. Spector, The Do's and Don'ts When One Lawyer Represents Both Parties

Fam. Advoc. (Spring 1991), at 16-18

Representing both parties in an uncontested divorce has traditionally been viewed as an inherent conflict of interest and has been prohibited. However, the past decade has witnessed considerable disagreement over whether it is permissible for a lawyer to perform the role of the intermediary in a "friendly divorce." Many states still view divorce as a real conflict, despite any appearance of harmony [and prohibit joint representation]. Other states have ethics opinions that allow an attorney to represent both husband and wife, albeit under restrictive circumstances. . . .

The perils into which you advance in this situation are quite clear. If something goes wrong with the agreement that has been drafted, it may be set aside. In such a case, you may be sued for malpractice, particularly if the client believes that you truly represented only one of the parties. If that occurs, the existence of the attorney-client relationship may well be a jury question. Or you might be subject to discipline.

Despite all the potential trouble, however, lawyers do take on joint representation and must know how to proceed. In jurisdictions that have adopted the Model Rules of Professional Conduct and that do not otherwise prohibit joint representation, compliance with the strictures of the rule can present problems.

Model Rule 2.2, Intermediary, provides:

a) A lawyer may act as intermediary between clients if:

1) the lawyer consults with each client concerning the implications of the common representation, including the advantages and risks involved, and the effects on the attorney-client privilege, and obtains each client's consent to the common representation;

2) the lawyer reasonably believes that the matter can be resolved on terms compatible with the clients' best interests, that each client will be able to make adequately informed decisions in the matter, and that there is little risk of material prejudice to the interests of the clients if the contemplated resolution is unsuccessful; and

3) the lawyer reasonably believes that the common representation can be undertaken impartially and without improper effect on other responsibilities the lawyer has to any of the clients.

b) While acting as intermediary, the lawyer shall consult with each client concerning the decisions to be made and the considerations relevant in making them, so that each client can make adequately informed decisions.

c) A lawyer shall withdraw as intermediary if any of the clients so requests, or if any of the conditions stated in paragraph (a) is no longer satisfied. Upon withdrawal, the lawyer shall not continue to represent any of the clients in the matter that was the subject of intermediation.

The comment to Rule 2.2 specifically notes that this rule does not apply when you are acting as a mediator or arbitrator—roles the clients may not understand precisely. At the initial interview, you should explain the differences between a mediator, an arbitrator, an intermediary, and an advocate. If one of the clients mistakenly believes that he or she is engaging an advocate, the inevitable result will be an unhappy client and risk for you. . . .

If, in spite of all the warnings, you decide to act as an intermediary, . . . Model Rule 2.2(a)(2), (3) requires that you make three objective determinations: that the matter can be resolved on terms compatible with the clients' best interests with little risk of material prejudice, that the clients are able to make informed decisions, and that the common representation can be undertaken impartially. Once you have made these determinations and have made full disclosure to the clients, you must still obtain each client's consent. Rule 2.2(a)(1). In essence, Rule 2.2(a)(3) requires that you consider whether advocacy will be needed by one of the parties and whether an independent counsel will be required for each party. To determine if that is the case, consider the following factors:

1) *The parties' social and economic relationship*—When one party dominates another, it is unlikely that the dominated spouse will be able to make an informed decision in his or her best interest. The dominated party needs an independent advocate, not an intermediary.

2) *Each party's emotional condition*—Most parties to a divorce are under great stress. If either spouse is emotionally disturbed, it will impair his or her ability to make informed decisions. If you believe that this is the case, you should decline intermediary representation.

3) *Each party's understanding of divorce law*—The parties cannot arrive at an informal decision that is in their best interests unless they know the law that governs their relationship. . . .

4) *The extent of disclosure of assets and liabilities*—If there has not been full disclosure, an informed decision is impossible. If the parties balk at disclosure, obviously advocacy and independent counsel are needed.

5) *The agreement that has been reached*—If the parties have reached a general agreement on the various issues of their divorce, you can help them work out the detailed legal problems. However, be sure that the parties have discussed all the issues. If they have not discussed and agreed on most of the issues (you should have a list), contentious negotiations are likely. If this occurs, the spouses need advocates, not an intermediary.

6) *The existence of minor children and substantial assets or debts, and the need for alimony or maintenance*—The presence of these factors indicates that the divorce is likely to involve complexities. The more complex the divorce, the less likely it is that the parties have adequately discussed the issues. In some states, in fact, the existence of any of the above factors will prohibit your acting as an intermediary.

7) *Your relationship with either party*—Rule 2.2(a)(3) requires your independent judgment that you can impartially undertake joint representation without its affecting any other responsibilities to the clients. In practice, this means that if you have a close relationship with one of the parties, either personal or professional, you should decline joint representation. A lawyer who has previously represented one of the spouses may have to be disqualified anyway, on the basis of Rule 1.9, Former Client. Even if disqualification under Rule 1.9 would not be required, a lawyer can hardly be thought of as neutral when he or she has benefitted from one of the parties as a client or may do so in the future.

Client Consent

Rule 2.2(a)(1) requires that you consult with each client about the implications of common representation and that you get each client's consent to the representation. To obtain consent, follow these guidelines:

1) *Get separate consent for each client*—Rule 2.2 explicitly requires separate [written] consent from each client. . . .

2) *Explain attorney-client privilege in joint representation*—Tell clients that the normal attorney-client confidentiality provisions of Rule 1.6 do not apply to jointly represented parties. If you are later forced to withdraw from the case, either party will be able to call you to testify to communications made to you. The comment to Rule 2.2 notes that during common representation, you are still required to keep clients adequately informed and to maintain confidentiality of information. This balance is impossible to maintain. When acting as intermediator, you must maintain full communication with both clients. Rule 2.2(b) requires you to consult with each client concerning the decisions to be made. To ensure that the clients fully understand this point, clearly explain that you will communicate with them only together, never separately.

3) *Point out problems of advice*—Acknowledge to the clients that an attorney who is not acting as an advocate for either party will not be able to present the best position for either party. This is a point that many clients do not understand. Many of the suits that follow joint representation—either against the lawyer for malpractice or to set aside the agreement—allege that the attorney did not advise the client of the best position to take on certain issues.

4) *Explain withdrawal and its problems*—Tell the clients that if serious disagreement develops regarding any issue, you will have to withdraw from joint representation. If that occurs, you will not be able to represent either party, and each will have to hire new counsel. It's best to illustrate this with an example—to say, perhaps, that if you discover that one party has not made and does not intend to make full disclosure of assets, you will have to withdraw. . . .

5) *Communicate problems of fees*—The clients should know that even if you have to withdraw from the case, you will expect to be paid for the time expended. You should also tell them that if you have to withdraw and the clients hire separate counsel, the total fees for the divorce will be higher than if the clients had hired separate counsel at the outset.

6) *Explain the benefits of obtaining separate counsel*—The difficulties of joint representation are such that some courts have required that you suggest [the possibility and desirability of seeking independent legal advice].

7) *Discuss the finality of any agreement*—The parties should be informed that any agreement they conclude will likely be as binding as an agreement concluded with independent counsel. Even if a court later decides that the intermediary representation was unwise, the agreement may still be sustained. . . .

3. Sexual Ethics

IOWA SUPREME COURT ATTORNEY DISCIPLINARY BOARD v. MORRISON

727 N.W.2d 115 (Iowa 2007)

STREIT, J.

. . . William Morrison was admitted to the Iowa bar in 1989. . . . In June 2005, Morrison reported to the Iowa Supreme Court Attorney Disciplinary Board ("Board") he "engaged in a sexual relationship with a female client while representing her in a dissolution proceeding." Morrison represented this client from October 2004 through February 2005. They had sex on several occasions from November 2004 through March 2005. Morrison did not have a personal relationship with this client prior to November 2004.

The Board filed a complaint against Morrison alleging he violated the Iowa Code of Professional Responsibility for Lawyers by engaging in a sexual relationship with a client. In lieu of an evidentiary hearing before the Grievance Commission, the Board and Morrison agreed to submit the matter upon stipulation. The parties stipulated to the facts above. Morrison acknowledged his conduct was unethical. The Board noted Morrison cooperated with its investigation. The parties also included with the stipulation a private admonition Morrison received from the Board in March 2004. Morrison was admonished for "solicitation of a dissolution client for a social relationship by reason of that dissolution client's 'attractiveness.'" The parties jointly recommend Morrison's conduct warrants suspension of his Iowa law license for sixty days. The Grievance Commission recommends Morrison's license to practice law be suspended for six months and that he enter and complete a counseling program to address his "boundary issues." Morrison reports he has already completed such a counseling program with a psychologist in addition to marriage counseling. . . .

. . . Morrison admits he had a sexual relationship with a client. This is a patent violation of Iowa Code of Professional Responsibility for Lawyers DR 5-101(B) (lawyer shall not engage in sexual relations with a client) and DR 1-102(A)(1) and (6) (lawyer shall not violate a disciplinary rule or engage in any other conduct that adversely reflects on the fitness to practice law). "Professional responsibility involves many gray areas, but sexual relationships between attorney and client is not one of these. Such conduct is clearly improper." Iowa Supreme Ct. Bd. of Prof'l Ethics & Conduct v. Furlong, 625 N.W.2d 711, 714 (Iowa 2001). Before determining the appropriate sanction, we review the sound reasons for prohibiting attorney-client sexual relationships.

First, "[t]he unequal balance of power in the attorney-client relationship, rooted in the attorney's special skill and knowledge on the one hand and the client's potential vulnerability on the other, may enable the lawyer to dominate and take unfair advantage." Iowa Code of Prof'l Responsibility EC 5-25. This is why the client's consent is irrelevant. We have previously stated, "the professional relationship renders it impossible for the vulnerable layperson to be considered 'consenting.'" Iowa Supreme Ct. Bd. of Prof'l Ethics & Conduct v. Hill, 540 N.W.2d 43, 44 (Iowa 1995) (*Hill II*).

Second, a sexual relationship between attorney and client may be harmful to the client's interest. This is true in any legal representation but "presents an even greater danger to the client seeking advice in times of personal crises such as divorce, death of a loved one, or when facing criminal charges." Iowa Code of Prof'l Responsibility EC 5-25.

Third, an attorney-client sexual relationship may prevent the attorney from competently representing the client. An attorney must be able to objectively evaluate the client's case. The American Bar Association stated, "[t]he roles of lover and lawyer are potentially conflicting ones as the emotional involvement that is fostered by a sexual relationship has the potential to undercut the objective detachment that is often demanded for adequate representation." ABA Comm. on Ethics and Prof'l Responsibility, Formal Op. 92-364 (1992).

Finally, an attorney initiating a sexual relationship with a client or attempting to do so may undercut the client's trust and faith in the lawyer. "Clients may rightfully expect that confidences vouchsafed to the lawyer will be solely used to advance the client's interest, and will not be used to advance the lawyer's interest, sexual or otherwise." Iowa Code of Prof'l Responsibility EC 5-25.

We now turn to the appropriate sanction. We consider:

> the nature and extent of the respondent's ethical infractions, his fitness to continue practicing law, our obligation to protect the public from further harm by the respondent, the need to deter other attorneys from engaging in similar misconduct, our desire to maintain the reputation of the bar as a whole, and any aggravating or mitigating circumstances.

Iowa Supreme Ct. Bd. of Prof'l Ethics & Conduct v. Kallsen, 670 N.W.2d 161, 164 (Iowa 2003). . . .

. . . This court does not tolerate attorney-client sexual relationships. In the present case, the Grievance Commission recommends Morrison's license to practice law be suspended for six months and that he be required to complete a counseling program to address his "boundary issues." The Board on the other hand recommends a sixty-day suspension because "this case does not involve aggravating factors such as forced sexual advances or commercial exploitation."

Our review is hindered by a limited record. Based on the parties' stipulation, Morrison's conduct does not appear to be particularly egregious in comparison to our previous cases involving attorney-client sexual relationships. But even a purely consensual sexual relationship between attorney and client is clearly prohibited by DR 5-101(B) for the reasons we have already stated.

Like this case, *Hill I* involved an attorney representing a client in a dissolution action. There, we said:

> A lawyer undertaking a divorce action must recognize reconciliation is possible and may be in the best interest of his client. An attorney must be aware that the actions of the client and attorney may affect negotiations in the dissolution case, including determination of custody and visitation of minor children. Sexual intercourse between the lawyer and a client seeking a dissolution of marriage carries a great potential of prejudice both to the client and to the minor children of the marriage. *Hill I*, 436 N.W.2d at 59.

Morrison's client and her husband had at least one minor child. We do not know from the record if the relationship between Morrison and his client prejudiced her in the dissolution action. Nevertheless, at least the potential for harm existed and exists in any attorney-client representation. See Iowa Supreme Ct. Bd. of Prof'l Ethics & Conduct v. Steffes, 588 N.W.2d 121, 123 (Iowa 1999) (sexual harassment by attorney made client uncomfortable going to attorney's office so client did not seek attorney's advice regarding pending criminal charges).

Moreover, Morrison has previously been admonished for making a sexual advance toward another client. He became sexually involved with the client in this particular case just eight months after the admonishment. Clearly, Morrison has not learned his lesson. A suspension of Morrison's license to practice law is necessary and appropriate. We hereby suspend Morrison's license to practice law in Iowa for a minimum of three months. . . .

Notes and Questions

1. **Trend.** *Morrison* represents the current trend (influenced by the ABA) of prohibiting sexual relationships between attorneys and clients. In 2002, the ABA amended its Model Rules of Professional Conduct to provide that "a lawyer shall not have sexual relations with a client unless a consensual sexual relationship existed between them when the client-lawyer relationship commenced." Model Rules of Prof'l Conduct R. 1.8(j). Prior to this time, an ABA ethics opinion merely *recommended* a ban on sexual relationships between attorneys and clients. See ABA Comm. on Ethics and Prof'l Responsibility, Formal Op. 92-364 (1992). Although the Model Rules are not binding, many states have similar ethics rules.

2. **Background.** California was the first state whose bar association approved a rule proscribing attorney-client sexual relationships. California Rules of Prof'l Conduct R. 3-120(B) (effective 1992) prohibits an attorney from (1) requiring or demanding sexual relations as a condition of representation; (2) employing coercion, intimidation, or undue influence in entering into sexual relations; or (3) continuing to represent a client after having sexual relations with that client if the sexual relationship causes the attorney to perform legal services incompetently. The Rule exempts preexisting sexual relationships and spousal relationships. Id. R. 3-120(C). The California state bar rejected an absolute ban based on concerns that a per se rule was not the least restrictive alternative and also would infringe on freedom of association of the attorney and client.[58]

3. **Consensual nature of sexual relationship.** Does the consensual nature of the relationship militate against the imposition of sanctions? Are even apparently consensual attorney-client sexual relationships "dangerous and exploitative" such

[58]. For background on the California law, see Anthony E. Davis & Judith Grimaldi, Sexual Confusion: Attorney-Client Sex and the Need for a Clear Ethical Rule, 7 Notre Dame J.L. Ethics & Pub. Pol'y 57, 91 (1993); California Sex-with-Clients Rule, 7 Law. Manual on Prof'l Conduct (ABA/BNA) 279, 280 (Sept. 11, 1991).

that regulation is necessary to protect clients and establish public trust in the legal profession?[59]

Should it matter if the client, rather than the attorney, initiates the sexual relationship? See Committee on Prof'l Ethics & Conduct v. Hill, 436 N.W.2d 57 (Iowa 1989) (suspending attorney even though client initiated the sexual relationship, reasoning that attorney should have recognized the potential negative effects on her case). Some commentators argue that attorney-client sex can never be voluntary because of the power imbalance and the client's emotional and financial status.[60] Do you agree?

Do you think that the sanction (a three-month suspension) was appropriate in *Morrison*? Compare State ex rel. Okla. Bar Ass'n v. Downes, 121 P.3d 1058 (Okla. 2005) (one-year suspension); In re Hoffmeyer, 656 S.E.2d 376 (S.C. 2008) (nine-month suspension). Courts take a particularly dim view of attorneys' misconduct when the sexual relationship is coerced. See, e.g., Iowa Supreme Court Attorney Disciplinary Bd. v. McGrath, 713 N.W.2d 682 (Iowa 2006) (three-year suspension for soliciting sexual favors in exchange for legal services).

4. Harm. In cases in which no prejudice results to the client's case, what is the harm of attorney-client sexual conduct? To the profession? To the client? See In re Tsoutsouris, 748 N.E.2d 856 (Ind. 2001). How does *Morrison* respond to this issue?

5. Exceptions. Should rules regulating sexual conduct between lawyers and clients have exceptions? For example, should the rules exempt sexual relationships that predate the professional relationship? See the ABA Model Rule, supra. Does such an exemption adequately address the issue? See Phillip R. Bower & Tanya E. Stern, Current Development 2002-2003, Conflict of Interest? The Absolute Ban on Lawyer-Client Sexual Relationships Is Not Absolutely Necessary, 16 Geo. J. Legal Ethics 535, 545 (2003) (arguing that preexisting sexual relationships may be just as dangerous).

6. Empirical data. Although no empirical studies investigate the effects of lawyers' sexual misconduct with clients, the effects of sexual relations between therapists and clients are well known. For example, 90 percent of patients in one study suffered negative effects, including loss of motivation, impaired social adjustment, suicidal feelings or behavior, and increased substance abuse.[61] How is the attorney-client relationship similar to, and different from, the psychotherapist-client relationship? Are similar effects to attorneys' clients likely?

7. Therapist-client rules. Regulations currently prohibit sexual conduct between psychotherapists and clients. See, e.g., Cal. Bus. & Prof. Code §726. Although some statutes limit prohibitions to sexual conduct within two years of termination of therapy (e.g., Cal. Civil Code §43.93), most statutes contain *absolute* prohibitions (e.g., Fla. Stat. Ann. §491.0112). Which do you think is a better

---

[59]. Malinda L. Seymore, Attorney-Client Sex: A Feminist Critique of the Absence of Regulation, 15 Yale J.L. & Feminism 175 (2003) (so arguing).

[60]. Jennifer Tuggle Crabtree, Does Consent Matter? Relationships Between Divorce Attorneys and Clients, 23 J. Legal Prof. 221, 229-232 (1998).

[61]. Jacqueline Bouhoutsos et al., Sexual Intimacy Between Psychotherapists and Patients, 14 Prof. Psychol.: Res. & Prac. 185, 191 (1983) (sample of 559 patients).

approach? What might explain the difference in treatment between the lawyer-client relationship versus the psychotherapist-client relationship?

8. Different approaches. The ABA's enactment of Rule 1.8(j) prompted states to review their policies about attorney-client sexual relations. Approximately 27 states have proposed or adopted Rule 1.8(j) or a more stringent provision; 14 states have no rule covering sexual relationships.[62] Many states have only cautionary warnings. New York limits the ban to domestic relations attorneys. N.Y. Rules Prof'l Conduct R. 1.8. Does this last limitation make sense?

9. Other sanctions. Different types of sanctions also apply to sexual misconduct, such as those for violations of state business and professions codes. Suspensions and disbarment are possible. Tort remedies, such as IIED or malpractice, might apply (e.g., McDaniel v. Gile, 281 Cal. Rptr. 242 (Ct. App. 1991)). See also Doe v. Roe, 681 N.E.2d 640 (Ill. App. Ct. 1997) (breach of fiduciary duty). Criminal statutes also might be relevant. What approach do you favor?

10. Privacy. Does an outright ban on attorney-client sexual relations constitute an unconstitutional intrusion on the attorney's and client's respective rights to privacy? In Committee on Professional Ethics & Conduct v. Hill, 436 N.W.2d 57 (Iowa 1989), an attorney was disciplined for engaging in sexual intercourse, purportedly in exchange for money, with a divorce client involved in child custody litigation. The attorney argued that the court's consideration of his conduct violated his right to privacy, protecting private acts between two consenting adults. How should the court rule? What is the impact of Lawrence v. Texas?

11. Conduct that falls short of a sexual relationship. Does the act of engaging in flirtation violate a state's ban on attorney-client sexual relationships? See In re Poff, 714 S.E.2d 313 (S.C. 2011) (no violation without evidence that lawyer's feelings affected representation); Lawyer Disciplinary Bd. v. Chittum, 689 S.E.2d 811 (W. Va. Ct. App. 2010) (no violation where there was no evidence of physical sexual contact).

12. Same-sex issues. Not all sexual misconduct involves a male attorney and female client. After public attention focused on the California state bar rule (discussed above), the assemblywoman who proposed the legislation began receiving calls from heterosexual men complaining about advances by female attorneys and also from gay men complaining about advances from their male attorneys.[63]

Problems

1. You receive a telephone call from a former law school friend. He asks for your advice, explaining that he is very attracted to a woman whom he is representing in a contentious divorce case. Although he is eager to become romantically

---

[62]. Craig D. Feiser, Strange Bedfellows: The Effectiveness of Per Se Bans on Attorney-Client Sexual Relations, 33 J. Legal Prof. 53, 60 (2008).

[63]. Michele Fuetsch, Bar OK's Limits on Lawyer-Client Sex, L.A. Times, Apr. 21, 1991, at A-3.

involved, he would like to know more about potential ethical issues. He confesses that he is so smitten that he has lost his objectivity. Nonetheless, he believes he can continue to represent her effectively, even if they begin to see each other romantically.[64] What would you advise?

2. Cheryl retains Sam Drucker to represent her in her divorce. During an initial consultation, she discusses her marriage and treatment for an anxiety disorder. On her second visit, she alleges that Drucker held her hand, embraced her, and told her about his marriage. When he apologized and offered to refer her to another lawyer, she declined. Drucker called her at home to tell her that he was attracted to her. Cheryl alleges that they engaged in sexual activity three times. She pinpoints two of the encounters based on surrounding events (that is, Drucker's daughter was ill; another client was in the office). After Drucker ends the relationship, Cheryl's husband discovers her diary. He confronts her in the presence of their son, who is the subject of a custody dispute. Drucker denies the sexual relationship. The Committee on Professional Conduct seeks to suspend Drucker from practice. What result? Drucker's Case, 577 A.2d 1198 (N.H. 1990).

G. Divorce Jurisdiction

1. Over the Plaintiff and Defendant

IN RE MARRIAGE OF KIMURA

471 N.W.2d 869 (Iowa 1991)

LAVORATO, Justice. . . .

Ken and Fumi Kimura were married in Japan in 1965. Both are Japanese citizens. They have a daughter and a son. The daughter, Izumi, was twenty-three at the time of the dissolution hearing. The son, Naoki, was twenty-one. Ken and Fumi have lived apart since September 1973.

Ken graduated from Kobe University Medical School in Japan. Currently, he is a pediatric surgeon at the University of Iowa Hospitals and Clinics in Iowa City.

In July 1986 Ken was invited to come to the United States where he took a position at the Long Island Jewish Medical Center in New Hyde Park, New York. When he came to the States, Ken had an H-1 visa. Such a visa is a temporary one, issued to persons with special talents or abilities that may be useful to the United States. [The center filed an application on Ken's behalf for permanent residency status, which he received in October 1987. Subsequently, he was hired at the University of Iowa as an associate professor of medicine.]

In March 1988, Ken filed a divorce mediation proceeding with the family court in Japan. In July, he withdrew from the proceeding. Apparently he could not attend that court's reconciliation proceeding between himself and Fumi because of his work.

[64]. This problem is posed in Ethics: Affairs of the Heart, A.B.A. J., June 1990, at 82.

In December, Ken filed a petition for dissolution of marriage in Johnson County District Court. He alleged that he had resided in Iowa for more than one year. He further alleged that his residency was not just for the purpose of obtaining a dissolution. Finally, he alleged a breakdown of the marital relationship.

Because personal service was not possible on Fumi in Iowa, a copy of the petition was mailed to her in Japan. In addition, notice of the petition was published in the *Iowa City Press Citizen* on December 14, December 21, and December 28.

In February 1989 Fumi filed a preanswer motion in which she contested the district court's subject matter and personal jurisdiction. [Her affidavit pointed out that Ken could not obtain a divorce under Japanese law because his conduct caused the marital problems. At the final hearing, Fumi did not personally appear, but her attorney did. After testimony about Ken's employment, residence status, and the breakdown of the marriage, the court concluded that Ken satisfied the residency requirements and dissolved the marriage. Fumi appealed.]

II. THE DUE PROCESS CHALLENGE

Fumi poses the issue this way: "Iowa's assertion of jurisdiction over respondent (who has no contacts with Iowa) or her marriage based solely on petitioner's alleged residence in Iowa violates the due process clauses of the United States and Iowa Constitutions." . . .

Early on, due process required the personal presence of the defendant in the forum state as a condition for rendering a binding personal or in personam judgment against the defendant. Pennoyer v. Neff, 95 U.S. 714, 733 (1878). The rule was expanded in International Shoe Co. v. Washington, 326 U.S. 310 (1945). Now due process does not require such personal presence. Due process only requires that the defendant have certain minimum contacts with the forum state. However, those contacts must be such "that the maintenance of the suit does not offend traditional notions of fair play and substantial justice." *International Shoe*, 326 U.S. at 316. Simply put, there must be a connection among the forum, the litigation, and the defendant.

Fumi relies on [Shaffer v. Heitner, 433 U.S. 186 (1977)] in support of her contention that jurisdiction to grant the dissolution must be tested by the minimum contacts standard of *International Shoe*. A footnote in *Shaffer* suggests her reliance is misplaced. See *Shaffer*, 433 U.S. at 208 n.30. One commentator seems to agree:

> Although the *Shaffer* Court concluded that all assertions of state-court jurisdiction must conform to the standards of *International Shoe* and, thus, be based upon a nexus among the forum, the litigation, and the defendant, the nexus requirement is unlikely to apply to cases in which status provides the basis of the asserted jurisdiction. The power to dissolve the marriage status in an ex parte proceeding normally is thought to stem, at least in part, from the perception of the marriage status as a res, and thus, as a "thing" to which the court's jurisdiction can attach. Despite the obvious analogy between in rem and quasi in rem jurisdiction based on the presence of property and ex parte-divorce jurisdiction based on the presence of a res (marriage status), the Court specifically noted in a footnote [n.30] that it was not suggesting "that jurisdictional doctrines other than those discussed in text, such as the particularized rules governing adjudications of status, are inconsistent with the standard of fairness." The all-inclusive language of the *Shaffer*

> conclusion, therefore, may not include cases in which status is the basis of the asserted jurisdiction. As far as the *Shaffer* holding is concerned, the forum-litigation-plaintiff nexus recognized as sufficient by the Court in Williams v. North Carolina seems to remain a valid basis of jurisdiction for ex parte divorces.

State-Court Jurisdiction, 63 Iowa L. Rev. at 1005-06 (citations omitted).

In Williams v. North Carolina, 317 U.S. 287 (1942) [hereinafter *Williams I*], the question was whether full faith and credit had to be given to a foreign divorce decree where only one spouse was domiciled in the foreign state and the other spouse had never been there. *Williams I*, 317 U.S. at 298-99. The Supreme Court held that the foreign state's high interest in the marital status of its domiciliaries required that full faith and credit be given such a decree. The Court did require, however, that substituted service on the absent spouse meet due process standards, that is, reasonably calculated to give the absent spouse actual notice and an opportunity to be heard.

In *Williams I,* the Court had difficulty classifying dissolution proceedings. Though it did not view such proceedings as in rem actions, neither did it view them as mere in personam actions. According to the Court, domicile of one spouse within the forum state gave that state the power to dissolve the marriage regardless of where the marriage occurred. This court too has deemed domicile as essential to dissolution of marriage jurisdiction.

The cases generally adopt the following explanation of the components for a dissolution of marriage proceeding:

> It is commonly held that an essential element of the judicial power to grant a divorce, or jurisdiction, is domicile. A court must have jurisdiction of the res, or the marriage status, in order that it may grant a divorce. The res or status follows the domiciles of the spouses; and therefore, in order that the res may be found within the state so that the courts of the state may have jurisdiction of it, one of the spouses must have a domicile within the state.

24 Am. Jur. 2d Divorce & Separation §238, at 336 (1983).

Williams v. North Carolina reached the Supreme Court a second time. The Court held that while the finding of domicile by the state that granted the decree is entitled to prima facie weight, it is not conclusive in a sister state but might be relitigated there. Williams v. North Carolina, 325 U.S. 226, 238-39 (1945) [*Williams II*].

The divisible divorce doctrine emerged in Estin v. Estin, 334 U.S. 541, 549 (1948). In *Estin* the Court held that Nevada in an ex parte divorce proceeding could change the marital status of those domiciled within its boundaries. The power to do so stems from Nevada's "considerable interest in preventing bigamous marriages and in protecting the offspring of marriages from being [illegitimate]." *Estin*, 334 U.S. at 546. But Nevada could not wipe out the absent spouse's claim for alimony under a New York judgment in a prior separation proceeding because Nevada had no personal jurisdiction over the absent spouse. So New York did not have to give full faith and credit to that part of the Nevada decree which purported to eliminate the support obligation of its domiciliary. [The Supreme Court reaffirmed *Estin* in Vanderbilt v. Vanderbilt, 354 U.S. 416, 417-418 (1957).

Vanderbilt differed in the fact that the absent spouse's right to alimony had not been determined before the ex parte divorce in Nevada.]

The divisible divorce doctrine simply recognizes the court's limited power where the court has no personal jurisdiction over the absent spouse. In these circumstances, the court has jurisdiction to grant a divorce to one domiciled in the state but no jurisdiction to adjudicate the incidents of the marriage, for example, alimony and property division. In short, the divisible divorce doctrine recognizes both the in rem and in personam nature of claims usually raised in dissolution of marriage proceedings.

We conclude that the all-inclusive language of the *Shaffer* conclusion does not include dissolution of marriage proceedings. In other words, jurisdiction to grant such a dissolution is not to be tested by the minimum contacts standard of *International Shoe*.

We further conclude that domicile continues to be the basis for a court's jurisdiction to grant a dissolution of marriage decree. So the courts of this state have the power to grant dissolution of marriage decrees provided the petitioner is domiciled in this state. Such power exists even though the petitioner's spouse is absent from this state, has never been here, and was constructively rather than personally served. [W]e are left with the question whether Ken established his domicile or residency in this state. . . .

III. CHALLENGE TO DOMICILE OR RESIDENCY

The district court adjudicated only the marital status. And that was done based on Ken being domiciled in this state. None of the incidents of the marriage—for example, alimony and property division—were adjudicated because the court did not have personal jurisdiction over Fumi. . . .

Fumi contends that even if minimum contacts were not the standard, Ken still had to establish that he met the residency requirements of this state before the court could dissolve the marriage. She argues that Ken failed to establish those requirements and so the district court should not have dissolved the marriage. For reasons we discuss, we disagree. . . .

According to [Iowa Code §598.6] Ken had to establish the following: (1) he resided in Iowa for at least one year before the petition was filed; and (2) his residence here was in good faith and not just for the purpose of obtaining a marriage dissolution.

Residence for the purpose of section 598.6 has the same meaning as domicile. To have a residence or domicile within the meaning of this section, "one must have a fixed habitation with no intention of" leaving it.

Once a domicile is established, it continues until a new one is established. A new domicile is established if all of the following things happen: (1) the former domicile is abandoned; (2) there is an actual removal to, and physical presence in the new domicile; and (3) there is a bona fide intention to change and to remain in the new domicile permanently or indefinitely. This intention must be a present and fixed intention and not dependent on some future or contingent event. . . .

We think Ken amply proved that he met the residency requirements of section 598.6. . . . In the affidavit he swore to a number of facts showing that he had abandoned his domicile in Japan in favor of the one here. For example, he swore that he had no other permanent residence other than his residence in Johnson County. In addition, he swore that since moving to Iowa, he had obtained an Iowa driver's license and had opened bank accounts at local banks. Finally, he swore that he intends to remain here for an indefinite period so long as his employment at the university is satisfactory to him and the university. . . .

We see nothing in the evidence to support Fumi's contention that Ken's residence here was in bad faith and only for the purpose of obtaining a dissolution of marriage. It may be that one reason Ken came here was—as Fumi suggests—because of our liberal dissolution marriage law as compared to Japan's. But that fact is not sufficient to preclude Ken from establishing a domicile or residence in Iowa, especially in light of his intention to remain here indefinitely.

Nor does Ken's continued Japanese citizenship preclude such a domicile or residence. A foreign citizenship does not—standing alone—bar one from establishing a domicile or residence for dissolution of marriage purposes. . . .

IV. CHALLENGE TO COURT'S RULING REFUSING TO DECLINE JURISDICTION BASED ON FORUM NON CONVENIENS DOCTRINE

[Fumi contends the district court should have declined jurisdiction based on forum non conveniens, arguing] that Japan is the more convenient forum and is the nation with the most significant contacts to the marital status of the parties. . . . Forum non conveniens is a facet of venue. This doctrine presupposes at least two forums in which jurisdiction and venue are proper. Under the doctrine a court may decline to proceed with an action though venue and jurisdiction are proper. The doctrine is a self-imposed limit on jurisdictional power that can be used to avoid unfair, vexatious, oppressive actions in a forum away from the defendant's domicile. . . .

What the moving party must show is that the relative inconveniences are so unbalanced that jurisdiction should be declined on an equitable basis. Factors that bear on this determination include the following: the relative ease of access to sources of proof; the availability of compulsory process for attendance of unwilling, and the cost of obtaining attendance of willing, witnesses; the possibility of view of the premises, if view would be appropriate to the action; the enforceability of the judgment if one is obtained; and all other practical problems that make trial of a case easy, expeditious, and inexpensive. All of these factors pertain to the private interest of the litigant.

Factors of public interest are also considered. They include the administrative difficulties for courts, trial in the forum that is the home of the state law which governs the case, and the burden of jury duty imposed on citizens of a forum with no relation to the litigation. Residency of the plaintiff is also considered but only as one of the many factors in the balancing process.

Whether to apply the doctrine of forum non conveniens lies in the sound discretion of the district court. . . . In deciding whether the district court abused its discretion in this case, we think it would be helpful to look at the divorce process in Japan. Japan has a variety of ways to dissolve a marriage [in contested cases] . . . : divorce through mediation in the family court, divorce by judicial decree in the family court, and divorce by judicial decree in the district court. A person seeking a divorce by judicial decree in the district court must prove fault. . . .

The family court may grant a divorce without proof of such grounds. But a divorce by judicial decree in the family court is rare because if either party objects, the divorce becomes invalid. So a decree of divorce by judicial decision usually issues from the district court.

Before the parties may proceed to the district court they must attempt mediation in the family court. Divorce can be effected without resort to litigation if the parties can agree on terms. If the parties fail to reach agreement, a divorce petition may then be submitted to and processed by the district court. Mediators in family court have no power to arbitrate disputes and are likely to oppose the idea of divorce. As a practical matter, a failure to agree to terms in mediation may mean no divorce in district court.

A divorce in Japan means the severance of all ties between the parties—they virtually become strangers. Usually a lump sum property settlement occurs. Because of enforcement problems, a settlement involving installment payments is rare. Alimony and other postdivorce maintenance payments are not available under Japanese law. Indeed, there is no legal requirement that property be divided or that support be paid. . . .

It has been suggested that divorce in Japan is quick and easy if a party can bribe, coerce, threaten, or persuade the other party to a divorce by mutual consent. A nonconsensual divorce is difficult, if not impossible, to obtain. . . .

For several reasons, the district court here could have determined that Japan is the more convenient forum for the parties. First, Japan has complete jurisdiction over the marital status of the parties and over all the incidents of the marriage. Second, a Japanese court has a societal interest in the marital status of its citizens. Third, given the nature of the divorce proceedings in Japan, Fumi's bargaining power in a family court mediation may be reduced by permitting a dissolution of marriage here. Fourth, Fumi may be at a cultural disadvantage with regard to customs and language in an Iowa proceeding. Last, Iowa is an inconvenient forum in relation to her residence.

On the other hand we think the district court was well within its discretion to deny Fumi's request to decline jurisdiction. Iowa too has an interest in the marital status of its residents. Right or wrong, our legislature has opted for no-fault divorce. One reason, we suspect, was to eliminate the extortion leverage an "innocent" spouse had over a "guilty" spouse. Had the district court honored Fumi's request, Ken—an Iowa resident—would have been denied the protection of Iowa's dissolution law. In short, a ruling in Fumi's favor may have resulted in no dissolution at all for one of this State's residents.

In addition we are impressed with the vigorous representation Fumi enjoyed in the district court and here. We doubt there would be any less representation in a postdissolution action for alimony and property division. . . . Our liberal discovery rules should allow Fumi to discover all of Ken's assets and his income in such an action. This is in contrast to Japan where it is difficult to discover a party's assets in divorce proceedings. Given our liberal rules on alimony and property division, we suspect Fumi might even fare better here than in Japan. . . . The district court did not violate Fumi's rights under either the federal or state constitutions. . . .

Notes and Questions

1. Special rules. *Kimura* reveals that special jurisdictional rules, unlike those in other civil actions, apply to divorce. To terminate a marriage, the plaintiff must be domiciled in the forum state. Personal jurisdiction over the defendant is not required. (Although personal jurisdiction is not required merely to terminate the marriage, it is required to resolve the financial incidents of the marriage.) However, *notice* to the defendant that complies with due process is required to inform the defendant of the pendency of the action. A divorce without proper notice may be challenged for lack of jurisdiction.

2. Ex parte divorces. As *Kimura* indicates, some divorce decrees issued in one state may be collaterally attacked in another state for want of jurisdiction. Williams v. North Carolina, 317 U.S. 287 (1942), established that the domiciliary state of one spouse may grant an "ex parte" divorce entitled to full faith and credit in all other states. (The term *ex parte* here means that the forum lacks jurisdiction over the respondent-spouse.) Because divorce courts routinely apply local substantive law, *Williams I* reinforced the practice of migratory divorce during the fault era, when an unhappy spouse often traveled to a new "domicile" to seek a divorce under the latter state's more permissive grounds.

However, the Supreme Court limited that holding in Williams v. North Carolina, 325 U.S. 226 (1945). *Williams II* held that, although the full faith and credit obligation assumes that the forum has valid jurisdiction as the domicile of the petitioner, a subsequent showing of *lack of domicile* will allow sister states to *refuse* to recognize the divorce. The holding thus allowed North Carolina to prosecute for bigamy two North Carolina residents who purported to establish a domicile in Nevada where each got a divorce, married each other, and then immediately returned home.

What rationale underlies the judicial willingness to recognize ex parte divorces? Is the ex parte divorce fair to the "stay-at-home spouse"? To the state whose laws the migratory petitioning-spouse seeks to evade?

3. Bilateral divorce. In another line of cases, the Supreme Court indicated that, when the forum has personal jurisdiction over *both* spouses in a migratory divorce, the principles of full faith and credit forbid collateral attack. See, e.g., Johnson v. Muelberger, 340 U.S. 581 (1951); Sherrer v. Sherrer, 334 U.S. 343 (1948). If the petitioning spouse has not genuinely established a domicile in the divorce forum (a jurisdictional prerequisite for all divorces, ex parte and bilateral alike), why should personal jurisdiction over the respondent spouse prevent collateral attack, say, by way of a bigamy prosecution? What good is a state's restrictive divorce law if a resident spouse can simply cross state lines, purport to establish a new domicile, and—after the personal appearance of the other spouse—obtain a divorce immune from collateral attack?

4. Transitory presence. The Supreme Court elaborated on the standards for in personam jurisdiction over a defendant in Burnham v. Superior Court, 495 U.S. 604 (1990), which held that transitory presence can satisfy due process even when the defendant lacks a substantial connection to the forum. The Court upheld

California's assertion of jurisdiction over a New Jersey resident who was personally served during a brief business trip and visit to his children in California (his wife's home). The plurality determined that due process was satisfied because (1) the minimum-contacts/fairness approach (initiated by *International Shoe*) addresses only absent (not present) defendants, and (2) the longstanding rule conferring jurisdiction on defendants personally served in the forum accords with "traditional notions of fair play and substantial justice."

Note that, as a result of the Court's holding in *Burnham*, the divorce action in *Burnham* becomes a bilateral, rather than an ex parte, proceeding, allowing the forum to resolve the financial incidents of the dissolution.

5. Foreign-country divorces. In the fault era, disputes arose about foreign divorces obtained by U.S. residents seeking to evade restrictive laws. American courts do not owe full faith and credit to decrees from foreign countries, although they may recognize such divorces under principles of "comity." E.g., Rosenstiel v. Rosenstiel, 209 N.E.2d 709 (N.Y. 1965). Because comity is discretionary, some states refuse to apply the doctrine to recognize foreign divorces. See, e.g., Aleem v. Aleem, 947 A.2d 489 (Md. 2008) (refusing to recognize Pakistani divorce because the procedure denied due process to the wife by its limitation of her right to seek divorce only with her husband's permission); Jewell v. Jewell, 751 A.2d 735, 739 (R.I. 2000) (holding that a "fly-by-day divorce" obtained in the Dominican Republic where neither party was a resident or maintained any other connection to the forum was repugnant to state law).

6. Same-sex divorces. Prior to the legalization of same-sex marriage in *Obergefell*, many same-sex couples faced problems of access to divorce stemming from the jurisdictional requirement of domicile. To illustrate, suppose that a couple domiciled in a state with a same-sex marriage ban traveled to a state permitting such unions and wed there. Where can they obtain a divorce?

Sometimes the home state claimed an inability to dissolve a marriage that it did not recognize. Other times, however, the state issuing the marriage license offered the option to return there for a divorce, but without adherence to the domiciliary connection usually required for full faith and credit. Compare Christiansen v. Christiansen, 253 P.3d 153 (Wyo. 2011) (affirming divorce of same-sex couple married in Canada despite state Defense of Marriage Act), with O'Darling v. O'Darling, 188 P.3d 137 (Okla. 2008) (vacating an order dissolving the Canadian marriage of a lesbian couple). See generally Elisabeth Oppenheimer, No Exit: The Problem of Same-Sex Divorce, 90 N.C. L. Rev. 73 (2011). This reason helps explain why the Supreme Court in *Obergefell* (discussed in Chapter II) did not find the marriage-recognition issue moot, even though the Court had decided that all states must now offer same-sex couples marriage licenses on the same terms as opposite-sex couples.

7. Attorney's role. Has an attorney in a restrictive state violated ethical principles by facilitating a client's out-of-state or foreign-country divorce? See, e.g., In re Donnelly, 470 N.W.2d 305 (Wis. 1991) (suspending lawyer's license for two years for his national advertisements of his arrangement of Dominican Republic divorces, without cautioning clients about the questionable validity of such decrees).

Problem

According to Islamic law, a husband can end his marriage by telling his wife, "I divorce you" three times. A Muslim man sends his wife, who is residing in the American state of Greenacre, an e-mail message via the Internet, informing her that he is divorcing her. The husband relies on Internet notice because he is studying in a foreign country. Based on that notice, the wife subsequently remarries. After her first husband completes his studies, he returns to Greenacre. When he sees his ex-wife again, he changes his mind about the divorce. He threatens to sue the wife if she will not leave her new husband and return to him. The wife requests the court to rule on the sufficiency of the husband's e-mail notice. What result? If the court rules that the husband's notice is insufficient, can the wife be convicted of bigamy? Would the husband's notice comply with the requirements of due process? [65]

2. Durational Residency Requirements

SOSNA v. IOWA

419 U.S. 393 (1975)

Mr. Justice REHNQUIST delivered the opinion of the Court.

Appellant Carol Sosna married Michael Sosna on September 5, 1964, in Michigan. They lived together in New York between October 1967 and August 1971, after which date they separated but continued to live in New York. In August 1972, appellant moved to Iowa with her three children, and the following month she petitioned the District Court of Jackson County, Iowa, for a dissolution of her marriage. Michael Sosna, who had been personally served with notice of the action when he came to Iowa to visit his children, made a special appearance to contest the jurisdiction of the Iowa court. The Iowa court dismissed the petition for lack of jurisdiction, finding that Michael Sosna was not a resident of Iowa and appellant had not been a resident of the State of Iowa for one year preceding the filing of her petition. In so doing the Iowa court applied the provisions of Iowa Code §598.6 (1973) requiring that the petitioner in such an action be "for the last year a resident of the state." . . .

The durational residency requirement under attack in this case is a part of Iowa's comprehensive statutory regulation of domestic relations, an area that has long been regarded as a virtually exclusive province of the States. Cases decided by this Court over a period of more than a century bear witness to this historical fact. . . . In Pennoyer v. Neff, 95 U.S. 714, 734-735 (1878), the Court said: "The State . . . has absolute right to prescribe the conditions upon which the marriage

---

[65]. See Egypt Dismisses Net Divorce Case (AP), June 2000, http://www.beliefnet.com/Entertainment/2000/06/Egypt-Dismisses-Net-Divorce-Case.aspx. See also Andy Soltis, Islamic Ruling Is Bad News for Divorcée, N.Y. Post, June 2, 2000, 2000 WLNR 8156388.

relation between its own citizens shall be created, and the causes for which it may be dissolved." . . .

The imposition of a durational residency requirement for divorce is scarcely unique to Iowa, since 48 States impose such a requirement as a condition for maintaining an action for divorce. As might be expected, the periods vary among the States and range from six weeks to two years. The one-year period selected by Iowa is the most common length of time prescribed.

Appellant contends that the Iowa requirement of one year's residence is unconstitutional for two separate reasons: *first,* because it establishes two classes of persons and discriminates against those who have recently exercised their right to travel to Iowa, thereby contravening the Court's holdings in Shapiro v. Thompson, 394 U.S. 618 (1969); Dunn v. Blumstein, 405 U.S. 330 (1972); and Memorial Hospital v. Maricopa County, 415 U.S. 250 (1974); and, *second,* because it denies a litigant the opportunity to make an individualized showing of bona fide residence and therefore denies such residents access to the only method of legally dissolving their marriage.

State statutes imposing durational residency requirements were, of course, invalidated when imposed by States as a qualification for welfare payments, *Shapiro,* supra; for voting, *Dunn,* supra; and for medical care, *Maricopa County,* supra. But none of those cases intimated that the States might never impose durational residency requirements. . . . What those cases had in common was that the durational residency requirements they struck down were justified on the basis of budgetary or recordkeeping considerations which were held insufficient to outweigh the constitutional claims of the individuals. But Iowa's divorce residency requirement is of a different stripe. Appellant was not irretrievably foreclosed from obtaining some part of what she sought, as was the case with the welfare recipients in *Shapiro,* the voters in *Dunn,* or the indigent patient in *Maricopa County.* She would eventually qualify for the same sort of adjudication which she demanded virtually upon her arrival in the State. Iowa's requirement delayed her access to the courts, but, by fulfilling it, she could ultimately have obtained the same opportunity for adjudication which she asserts ought to have been hers at an earlier point in time.

Iowa's residency requirement may reasonably be justified on grounds other than purely budgetary considerations or administrative convenience. A decree of divorce is not a matter in which the only interested parties are the State as a sort of "grantor," and a divorce petitioner such as appellant in the role of "grantee." Both spouses are obviously interested in the proceedings, since it will affect their marital status and very likely their property rights. Where a married couple has minor children, a decree of divorce would usually include provisions for their custody and support. With consequences of such moment riding on a divorce decree issued by its courts, Iowa may insist that one seeking to initiate such a proceeding have the modicum of attachment to the State required here.

Such a requirement additionally furthers the State's parallel interests both in avoiding officious intermeddling in matters in which another State has a paramount interest, and in minimizing the susceptibility of its own divorce decrees to collateral attack. [See Williams v. North Carolina, 325 U.S. 226 (1945).] A State such as Iowa may quite reasonably decide that it does not wish to become a divorce mill for unhappy spouses who have lived there as short a time as appellant had when she commenced her action in the state court after having long resided elsewhere. . . .

Nor are we of the view that the failure to provide an individualized determination of residency violates the Due Process Clause. . . . An individualized determination of physical presence plus the intent to remain, which appellant apparently seeks, would not entitle her to a divorce even if she could have made such a showing. For Iowa requires not merely "domicile" in that sense, but residence in the State for a year in order for its courts to exercise their divorce jurisdiction.

In Boddie v. Connecticut, [401 U.S. 371 (1971),] this Court held that Connecticut might not deny access to divorce courts to those persons who could not afford to pay the required fee. Because of the exclusive role played by the State in the termination of marriages, it was held that indigents could not be denied an opportunity to be heard "absent a countervailing state interest of overriding significance." 401 U.S., at 377. But the gravamen of appellant Sosna's claim is not total deprivation, as in *Boddie*, but only delay. . . . Affirmed.

Mr. Justice Marshall, with whom Mr. Justice Brennan joins, dissenting. . . .

The Court omits altogether what should be the first inquiry: whether the right to obtain a divorce is of sufficient importance that its denial to recent immigrants constitutes a penalty on interstate travel. In my view, it clearly meets that standard. The previous decisions of this Court make it plain that the right of marital association is one of the most basic rights conferred on the individual by the State. The interests associated with marriage and divorce have repeatedly been accorded particular deference [citing *Loving* and *Boddie*]. . . .

Having determined that the interest in obtaining a divorce is of substantial social importance, I would scrutinize Iowa's durational residency requirement to determine whether it constitutes a reasonable means of furthering important interests asserted by the State. . . .

. . . Iowa's residency requirement, the Court says, merely forestalls access to the courts; applicants seeking welfare payments, medical aid, and the right to vote, on the other hand, suffer unrecoverable losses throughout the waiting period. This analysis, however, ignores the severity of the deprivation suffered by the divorce petitioner who is forced to wait a year for relief. The injury accompanying that delay is not directly measurable in money terms like the loss of welfare benefits, but it cannot reasonably be argued that when the year has elapsed, the petitioner is made whole. The year's wait prevents remarriage and locks both partners into what may be an intolerable, destructive relationship. . . . The Court cannot mean that Mrs. Sosna has not suffered any injury by being foreclosed from seeking a divorce in Iowa for a year. It must instead mean that it does not regard that deprivation as being very severe.

I find the majority's second argument no more persuasive. The Court forgoes reliance on the usual justifications for durational residency requirements—budgetary considerations and administrative convenience. . . . In their place, the majority invokes a more amorphous justification—the magnitude of the interests affected and resolved by a divorce proceeding. Certainly the stakes in a divorce are weighty both for the individuals directly involved in the adjudication and for others immediately affected by it. The critical importance of the divorce process, however, weakens the argument for a long residency requirement rather than strengthens it. . . .

The Court's third justification seems to me the only one that warrants close consideration. Iowa has a legitimate interest in protecting itself against invasion by those seeking quick divorces in a forum with relatively lax divorce laws, and it may have some interest in avoiding collateral attacks on its decrees in other States. These interests, however, would adequately be protected by a simple requirement of domicile—physical presence plus intent to remain—which would remove the rigid one-year barrier while permitting the State to restrict the availability of its divorce process to citizens who are genuinely its own. . . .

Notes and Questions

1. Residency requirements. As *Sosna* explains, many states require a divorce petitioner to reside in the forum state for a specified period of time. In some states, residence alone suffices for divorce jurisdiction. Other jurisdictions mandate both durational residence and domicile requirements.[66] Most states' durational residence requirements specify a six-month period.[67] Some states have special provisions for military service personnel to obtain divorce decrees.

2. Rationale. Justice Rehnquist distinguishes a one-year delay for permitting the dissolution of marriage from a delay for the purpose of allowing voting, welfare benefits, and medical aid. Is the distinction persuasive? See Shauhin A. Talesh, Note, Welfare Migration to Capture Higher Benefits: Fact or Fiction?, 32 Conn. L. Rev. 675, 683 (2000) (discussing application of residency requirements for different benefits).

3. Significance of delay. In *Sosna,* Justices Rehnquist and Marshall disagree about the significance of delay in petitions for dissolution and the consequences of such delay. Whose argument is more persuasive? Further, Justice Rehnquist distinguishes *Boddie* by claiming the filing fee foreclosed access while the residency requirement in *Sosna* imposes "only delay." Do you agree that indigent plaintiffs have a stronger claim than recent immigrants do? Does the decision in *Sosna* neglect the interests of recent immigrants and present hardships for victims of domestic violence? Does the decision reflect discrimination against women who tend to predominate among custodial parents (i.e., moving for jobs, proximity to parents, or a new relationship)?

4. Divorce mills. Justice Marshall, dissenting, intimates that the state's real goal is to avoid becoming known as a "divorce mill." During the fault era, because residency requirements for divorce varied from state to state, some states with shorter durational requirements and more lenient grounds for divorce (such as Arkansas, Idaho, Florida, and Nevada) developed a reputation of being divorce mills.[68] Why does such a reputation pose problems? How important are problems of migratory divorce and divorce mills in the no-fault era?

---

[66]. However, *Williams,* discussed in *Sosna,* makes clear that domicile is necessary for full faith and credit, regardless of the statutory language. In some instances, durational residency requirements may provide evidence of domicile.

[67]. Chart, Grounds for Divorce and Residency Requirements, supra note [25].

[68]. Max Rheinstein, Marriage Stability, Divorce, and the Law 76 (1972).

5. *Zablocki's* impact. One student commentator points out that *Sosna* was decided a decade before *Zablocki*. "The case is therefore not indicative either of how the Court would decide the right to divorce issue today nor how it should decide it." She elaborates: "[P]etitioners did not raise any challenges on substantive due process grounds or right to privacy grounds."[69] How would *Sosna* be decided today? Note Justice Marshall's view that the right to divorce is equivalent to the right to marry.

6. Policy. In our increasingly mobile society, does it make sense to limit divorce jurisdiction to the state of the parties' domicile?[70]

7. States' rights. How much deference do the majority and dissent give to the state's exclusive control over family law matters? The parameters of federal versus state authority are reflected in the case below.

8. Intent. Must a party intend to remain in the state after meeting the durational residency requirement to obtain a divorce? See Kar v. Nanda, 805 N.W.2d 609 (Mich. Ct. App. 2011); Rogers v. Rogers, 18 A.3d 491 (R.I. 2011). What intent does *Sosna* require?

Problem

Jeffrey, who has been living with his wife, Andrea, and their two children in Ohio for ten years, accepts a new job in California with Andrea's acquiescence. Together, they visit California to look for a house, visit churches, and familiarize themselves with the community. Four months later, they sell their Ohio home and move to California. A month later, Jeffrey tells Andrea that he has been having an affair. Andrea returns to Ohio with the children and files for divorce. Jeffrey moves for dismissal of her action for lack of subject matter jurisdiction, alleging that she has not satisfied the statutory six-month residency requirement. Andrea counters that Jeffrey fraudulently induced her to abandon her Ohio residency in order that he might take advantage of California's more liberal divorce laws. Should the court grant Jeffrey's motion to dismiss on jurisdictional grounds? Should there be a fraud exception to the residency requirements for divorce? That is, should a court consider the motives of either spouse with regard to his or her establishment of residency? Barth v. Barth, 862 N.E.2d 496 (Ohio 2007).

---

[69]. Laura Bradford, Note, The Counterrevolution: A Critique of Recent Proposals to Reform No-Fault Divorce Laws, 49 Stan. L. Rev. 607, 636 n.112 (1997).

[70]. For commentary advocating the abrogation of the domicile rule for divorce purposes, see Courtney Joslin, Modernizing Divorce Jurisdiction: Same-Sex Couples and Minimum Contacts, 91 B.U. L. Rev. 1669 (2011) (advocating the abrogation of domicile rule); Rhonda Wasserman, Divorce and Domicile: Time to Sever the Knot, 39 Wm. & Mary L. Rev. 1 (1997) (arguing that the domicile rule fails to preserve state sovereignty or assure the parties' convenience, and that federal legislation would better ensure interstate recognition of divorce decrees).

3. Domestic Relations Exception to Diversity Jurisdiction

ANKENBRANDT v. RICHARDS

504 U.S. 689 (1992)

Justice White delivered the opinion of the Court. . . .

Petitioner Carol Ankenbrandt, a citizen of Missouri, brought this lawsuit . . . on behalf of her daughters L.R. and S.R. against respondents Jon A. Richards and Debra Kesler, citizens of Louisiana, in the United States District Court for the Eastern District of Louisiana. Alleging federal jurisdiction based on the diversity-of-citizenship provision of §1332, Ankenbrandt's complaint sought monetary damages for alleged sexual and physical abuse of the children committed by Richards and Kesler. Richards is the divorced father of the children and Kesler his female companion. [T]he District Court granted respondents' motion to dismiss this lawsuit [concluding] that this case fell within what has become known as the "domestic relations" exception to diversity jurisdiction, and that it lacked jurisdiction over the case. . . .

We granted certiorari limited to the following questions: "(1) Is there a domestic relations exception to federal jurisdiction? (2) If so, does it permit a district court to abstain from exercising diversity jurisdiction over a tort action for damages?" . . . We address each of these issues in turn.

The domestic relations exception upon which the courts below relied to decline jurisdiction has been invoked often by the lower federal courts. The seeming authority for doing so originally stemmed from the announcement in Barber v. Barber, 21 How. 582 (1859), that the federal courts have no jurisdiction over suits for divorce or the allowance of alimony. In that case, the Court heard a suit in equity brought by a wife (by her next friend) in Federal District Court pursuant to diversity jurisdiction against her former husband. She sought to enforce a decree from a New York state court, which had granted a divorce and awarded her alimony. The former husband thereupon moved to Wisconsin to place himself beyond the New York courts' jurisdiction so that the divorce decree there could not be enforced against him; he then sued for divorce in a Wisconsin court, representing to that court that his wife had abandoned him and failing to disclose the existence of the New York decree. In a suit brought by the former wife in Wisconsin Federal District Court, the former husband alleged that the court lacked jurisdiction. The court accepted jurisdiction and gave judgment for the divorced wife.

On appeal [in *Barber*], it was argued that the District Court lacked jurisdiction on two grounds: first, that there was no diversity of citizenship because although divorced, the wife's citizenship necessarily remained that of her former husband; and second, that the whole subject of divorce and alimony, including a suit to enforce an alimony decree, was exclusively ecclesiastical at the time of the adoption of the Constitution and that the Constitution therefore placed the whole subject of divorce and alimony beyond the jurisdiction of the United States courts. Over the dissent of three Justices, the Court rejected both arguments. After an exhaustive survey of the authorities, the Court concluded that a divorced wife could acquire a citizenship separate from that of her former husband and that a suit to enforce an alimony decree rested within the federal courts' equity jurisdiction. The Court reached these conclusions after summarily dismissing the former husband's contention that the case involved a subject matter outside the federal courts' jurisdiction. In so stating, however, the Court also announced the following limitation on federal jurisdiction:

> Our first remark is—and we wish it to be remembered—that this is not a suit asking the court for the allowance of alimony. That has been done by a court of competent jurisdiction. The court in Wisconsin was asked to interfere to prevent that decree from being defeated by fraud.
>
> We disclaim altogether any jurisdiction in the courts of the United States upon the subject of divorce, or for the allowance of alimony, either as an original proceeding in chancery or as an incident to divorce *a vinculo*, or to one from bed and board.

Barber, supra, at 584. . . .

The statements disclaiming jurisdiction over divorce and alimony decree suits, though technically dicta, formed the basis for excluding "domestic relations" cases from the jurisdiction of the lower federal courts, a jurisdictional limitation those courts have recognized ever since. . . . Because we are unwilling to cast aside an understood rule that has been recognized for nearly a century and a half, we feel compelled to explain why we will continue to recognize this limitation on federal jurisdiction.

Counsel argued in *Barber* that the Constitution prohibited federal courts from exercising jurisdiction over domestic relations cases. An examination of Article III, *Barber* itself, and our cases since *Barber* makes clear that the Constitution does not exclude domestic relations cases from the jurisdiction otherwise granted by statute to the federal courts.

Article III, §2, of the Constitution . . . delineates the absolute limits on the federal courts' jurisdiction. But in articulating three different terms to define jurisdiction—"Cases, in Law and Equity," "Cases," and "Controversies"—this provision contains no limitation on subjects of a domestic relations nature. Nor did *Barber* purport to ground the domestic relations exception in these constitutional limits on federal jurisdiction. The Court's discussion of federal judicial power to hear suits of a domestic relations nature contains no mention of the Constitution, and it is logical to presume that the Court based its statement limiting such power on narrower statutory, rather than broader constitutional, grounds. Subsequent decisions confirm that *Barber* was not relying on constitutional limits in justifying the exception. . . .

. . . The dissenters in *Barber* [suggested] that the federal courts had no power over certain domestic relations actions because the court of chancery lacked authority to issue divorce and alimony decrees. . . . We have no occasion here to join the historical debate over whether the English court of chancery had jurisdiction to handle certain domestic relations matters. . . . We thus are content to rest our conclusion that a domestic relations exception exists as a matter of statutory construction not on the accuracy of the historical justifications on which it was seemingly based, but rather on Congress' apparent acceptance of this construction of the diversity jurisdiction provisions in the years prior to 1948, when [Congress last amended the rules applicable to federal diversity jurisdiction]. Considerations of *stare decisis* have particular strength in this context, where "the legislative power is implicated, and Congress remains free to alter what we have done." . . .

In the more than 100 years since this Court laid the seeds for the development of the domestic relations exception, the lower federal courts have applied it in a variety of circumstances. Many of these applications go well beyond the circumscribed situations posed by *Barber* and its progeny. *Barber* itself disclaimed federal jurisdiction over a narrow range of domestic relations issues involving the granting of a divorce and a decree of alimony, and stated the limits on federal-court power to intervene prior to the rendering of such orders:

> It is, that when a court of competent jurisdiction over the subject-matter and the parties decrees a divorce, and alimony to the wife as its incident, and is unable of itself to enforce the decree summarily upon the husband, that courts of equity will interfere to prevent the decree from being defeated by fraud. The interference, however, is limited to cases in which alimony has been decreed; then only to the extent of what is due, and always to cases in which no appeal is pending from the decree for the divorce or for alimony.

[*Barber*, supra, at 591.]

The *Barber* Court thus did not intend to strip the federal courts of authority to hear cases arising from the domestic relations of persons unless they seek the granting or modification of a divorce or alimony decree. The holding of the case itself sanctioned the exercise of federal jurisdiction over the enforcement of an alimony decree that had been properly obtained in a state court of competent jurisdiction. . . .

Subsequently, this Court expanded the domestic relations exception to include decrees in child custody cases. In a child custody case brought pursuant to a writ of habeas corpus, for instance, the Court held void a writ issued by a Federal District Court to restore a child to the custody of the father. "As to the right to the control and possession of this child, as it is contested by its father and its grandfather, it is one in regard to which neither the Congress of the United States nor any authority of the United States has any special jurisdiction." In re Burrus, [136 U.S. 586, 594 (1890)].

Although In re Burrus technically did not involve a construction of the diversity statute, as we understand *Barber* to have done, its statement that "[t]he whole subject of the domestic relations of husband and wife, parent and child, belongs to the laws of the States and not to the laws of the United States," id., at 593-594, has been interpreted by the federal courts to apply with equal vigor in suits brought pursuant to diversity jurisdiction. This application is consistent with *Barber*'s directive to limit federal courts' exercise of diversity jurisdiction over suits for divorce and alimony decrees. We conclude, therefore, that the domestic relations exception, as articulated by this Court since *Barber*, divests the federal courts of power to issue divorce, alimony, and child custody decrees. Given the long passage of time without any expression of congressional dissatisfaction, we have no trouble today reaffirming the validity of the exception as it pertains to divorce and alimony decrees and child custody orders.

Not only is our conclusion rooted in respect for this long-held understanding, it is also supported by sound policy considerations. Issuance of decrees of this type not infrequently involves retention of jurisdiction by the court and deployment of social workers to monitor compliance. As a matter of judicial economy, state courts are more eminently suited to work of this type than are federal courts, which lack the close association with state and local government organizations dedicated to handling issues that arise out of conflicts over divorce, alimony, and child custody decrees. Moreover, as a matter of judicial expertise, it makes far more sense to retain the rule that federal courts lack power to issue these types of decrees because of the special proficiency developed by state tribunals over the past century and a half in handling issues that arise in the granting of such decrees.

By concluding, as we do, that the domestic relations exception encompasses only cases involving the issuance of a divorce, alimony, or child custody decree, we necessarily find that the Court of Appeals erred by affirming the District Court's invocation of this exception. This lawsuit in no way seeks such a decree; rather, it alleges that respondents Richards and Kesler committed torts against L.R. and S.R., Ankenbrandt's children by Richards. Federal subject-matter jurisdiction pursuant to §1332 thus is proper in this case. . . .

Notes and Questions

1. Rule and rationale. Under the "domestic relations exception to federal jurisdiction," federal courts traditionally declined to exercise jurisdiction over matters of domestic relations even in cases in which plaintiffs could establish the requisite diversity of citizenship and amount in controversy. The rationale was that domestic relations cases involve matters peculiarly of state, rather than federal, law. *Ankenbrandt* narrowed this exception, limiting the types of cases that federal courts could refuse to adjudicate. After *Ankenbrandt*, federal courts could decline jurisdiction only over those cases involving the issuance of divorce decrees and the issuance or modification of child custody or alimony, including any enforcement of court orders. See, e.g., Ferlita v. Ferlita, 2011 WL 6288408 (S.D.N.Y. 2011) (declining jurisdiction where the action involved enforcement of a divorce settlement despite the existence of other tort claims).

2. Abstention doctrine. *Ankenbrandt* left open an alternative means by which federal courts can still "slam shut" the federal courthouse door to some domestic relations matters that do not involve divorce, alimony, or custody. In an omitted portion of the opinion, the Court holds that neither the domestic relations exception nor the "abstention doctrine" bars *Ankenbrandt*'s tort claim. The abstention doctrine, delineated in Younger v. Harris, 401 U.S. 37 (1971), is founded on principles of federalism. It provides that federal courts may refuse to adjudicate civil proceedings that involve important state interests or substantial policy concerns. *Ankenbrandt* concluded, by way of dicta, that abstention might be proper

> when a case presents "difficult questions of state law bearing on policy problems of substantial public importance whose importance transcends the result in the case then at bar" (citation omitted). Such might well be the case if a federal suit were filed prior to effectuation of a divorce, alimony, or child custody decree, and the suit depended on a determination of the status of the parties.

504 U.S. 689, 705 (1992).

3. Advantages? Why did Carol Ankenbrandt prefer to litigate her tort claim alleging sexual abuse in a federal, rather than state, court? What are the benefits, as well as detriments, that will ensue from *Ankenbrandt* for litigants? For families? For society?

4. Federalism. Various considerations have led federal courts to decline jurisdiction over domestic relations issues, including recognition of special state expertise, federal docket congestion, and the ability of state courts to provide local support assuring compliance with decrees. However, critics point out that federal courts are less susceptible to influence and have better evidentiary and discovery processes; state courts have often been criticized for their handling of family law cases (state judges rotate out of family law courts after only one year); the confining authority of local control over family law often restricts the rights of traditionally subordinated groups; distinctions between marital property and marital status are blurry; and federal courts have been willing to intervene in family law cases when constitutional rights were at issue. For example, Professor Anne Dailey, writing in defense of state sovereignty, notes:

> [N]ational authority over family law raises a serious threat of governmental tyranny over the moral identities of developing citizens. To begin with, a politics of the good family life entails a degree of civic engagement and a sense of shared community identity unattainable at the national level. Although family law does not require the moral homogeneity characteristic of strong communitarian cultures, it does demand a political discourse built upon the normative commitments of a specific historical community. States . . . are far better situated than the national government to develop and sustain a normative political discourse on family. Moreover, regulatory diversity among the fifty states preserves some measure of individual and family choice in matters touching upon the formative conditions of human identity.[71]

Professor Naomi Cahn counters:

> Throughout the country, family law has traditionally reflected community norms, [and] the federal courts have attempted to protect the local character of domestic relations law. . . . The belief in local control over family law, however, beyond suggesting an inevitability to this means of family regulation, also overlooks the negative aspects of the community. While community can be a powerfully positive force, it can also be an extremely confining form of authority. The courts' examination of whether certain customs are based in community traditions, for instance, may enshrine majoritarian conventions such as a ban on gay marriage or certain consensual sex. Within certain communities, expectations are that women will be confined within traditional roles, thus hindering women's efforts to achieve equality. The many and various state regulations held unconstitutional by

---

[71]. Anne C. Dailey, Federalism and Families, 143 U. Pa. L. Rev. 1787, 1791-1792 (1995). See also Brian H. Bix, State of the Union: The States' Interest in the Marital Status of Their Citizens, 55 U. Miami L. Rev. 1, 18-19 (2000) (suggesting that local control of family law matters may also be favored because it allows states to be treated as laboratories, developing a variety of responses to questions of law instead of having a uniform federal response); Jill Elaine Hasday, Family Law Reimagined 17 (2014) (challenging, as a myth, the story that family law is local, not federal).

the Supreme Court provide yet further examples of the danger of trusting family law to community mores.[72]

Which view do you find more persuasive?

Problems

1. Jeanne sues in state court, charging that Joseph (the man with whom she has been cohabiting) breached his agreement to provide financial support for the rest of her life. Joseph removes the case to federal court on the basis of diversity. The court raises, on its own motion, the issue whether this "palimony" case falls within the domestic relations exception to federal jurisdiction, requiring remand to state court. See Anastasi v. Anastasi, 544 F. Supp. 866 (D.N.J. 1982). How would this case be decided after *Ankenbrandt*? See also Carino v. O'Malley, 2007 WL 951953 (D.N.J. 2007).

2. Ariane Cometa and Gerard Dunn marry in 1989. In September 1994, while Ariane is pursuing a medical residency, Gerard suffers a catastrophic brain injury that leaves him severely disabled. In June 1997, Gerard's father is appointed his conservator and takes him to Georgia to live. Ariane subsequently enters into a liaison with another man; her petition for divorce is granted in December 1998. She is ordered to pay Gerard alimony for five years based on her ability to pay, employment potential, and Gerard's disability. One year later, Gerard's father, acting on behalf of himself and Gerard, brings an action against Ariane in federal district court in Maine, alleging her mismanagement of Gerard's care, private health insurance, and property; intentional and negligent infliction of emotional distress by keeping him in care facilities rather than at home so that she could conduct an affair; breaching a contract with Gerard's father as to payment for construction work on a Georgia house for Gerard; and unjust enrichment for the care provided to Gerard by his father. Ariane moves to dismiss the claims as within the domestic relations exception to federal court jurisdiction. What result? See Dunn v. Cometa, 238 F.3d 38 (1st Cir. 2001).

---

[72]. Naomi Cahn, Family Law, Federalism, and the Federal Courts, 79 Iowa L. Rev. 1073, 1123 (1994). See also Meredith Johnson Harbach, Is the Family a Federal Question?, 66 Wash. & Lee L. Rev. 131 (2009) (emphasizing the important role of federal courts in supporting and protecting the family).

VII

Financial Consequences of Dissolution

Approximately one in five adults in the United States has divorced.[1] Such dissolutions often require a division of property and an award of spousal support. In marriages with children, a divorce decree also provides for their support.

This financial framework raises foundational questions—such as the place of fault, the value of domestic labor, and policies about remarriage and new relationships. Additional complications arise from spousal investments in pensions and careers, college students' postmajority dependency, and rising bankruptcy and poverty rates.

This chapter emphasizes theory and practice, guided by the following inquiries: What are the distinct theoretical bases traditionally undergirding property division, spousal support, and child support? How have our understandings of each evolved in the era of no-fault divorce? What happens to these theoretical distinctions when, in practice, different financial issues typically get resolved together? Finally, what roles do the state and the parties themselves play in making and enforcing these financial decisions?

A. Introduction: The Demise of Fault?

Although every state now has some form of no-fault divorce, sharp differences persist in the role of fault in dividing property and determining spousal support

[1]. In 2009, 20.5 percent of the men and 22.4 percent of the women had divorced at least once. U.S. Census Bureau, Number, Timing, and Duration of Marriages and Divorces: 2009 (May 2011) (table 6), http://www.census.gov/prod/2011pubs/p70-125.pdf.

(once called "alimony" and now often referred to as "maintenance").[2] California's early adoption of "pure no-fault"[3] laws prompted a famous study by sociologist Lenore J. Weitzman.[4]

According to Weitzman, fault previously played a dual role in determining the economic consequences of divorce. First, marital misconduct provided a rationale for judicial awards and settlements, requiring a "guilty" husband to "pay for his transgressions with alimony" or with an additional portion of marital property.[5] Second, fault offered valuable leverage to an "innocent" spouse, who could obtain financial concessions in exchange for cooperation in settling the case.

Weitzman found that California's transition to a no-fault regime had unexpectedly impoverished women and children: Family homes, formerly awarded to "innocent wives," were now being sold (and children displaced) so the proceeds could be divided equally between the spouses. Likewise, support awards were shrinking for women, primarily mothers and homemakers, who were now expected to be self-sufficient. And even a "guilty" spouse could now divorce unilaterally, eliminating the bargaining power of the resisting spouse, often the wife.

Weitzman's empirical study concluded that, just one year after divorce, men were experiencing a 42 percent improvement in their standard of living and women a 73 percent decline.[6] These dramatic figures proved enormously influential, prompting not only a feminist critique of no-fault divorce,[7] but also the passage of 14 new laws in California.[8] Subsequent empirical studies substantiated Weitzman's general finding that men's standard of living rises after divorce, while that of women and children declines,[9] but cast doubt on her oft-quoted 42/73 percent statistic.[10] Recent data show a narrowed gender gap in postdissolution income.[11]

---

[2]. Charts (A Review of the Year in Family Law), 48 Fam. L.Q. 654-655 (2015) (listing 29 jurisdictions that consider marital fault as an alimony factor); id. at 666-668 (listing 35 jurisdictions that consider *economic* misconduct in dividing property).

[3]. The term describes states that, by statute, disregard *marital* misconduct in deciding both property division and support. See American Law Inst., Principles of the Law of Family Dissolution: Analysis and Recommendations 44-47 (2002).

[4]. Lenore J. Weitzman, The Divorce Revolution: The Unexpected Social and Economic Consequences for Women and Children in America (1985) (empirical study based on 2,500 court dockets over a ten-year period and interviews with 169 family law attorneys, 44 family law judges, and 228 divorced men and women approximately one year after their divorces).

[5]. Id. at 12-13.

[6]. Id. at 339.

[7]. See Herma Hill Kay, From the Second Sex to the Joint Venture: An Overview of Women's Rights and Family Law in the United States During the Twentieth Century, 88 Cal. L. Rev. 2017, 2066-2068 (2000).

[8]. Lenore J. Weitzman, The Economic Consequences of Divorce Are Still Unequal: Comment on Peterson, 61 Am. Soc. Rev. 537, 538 (1996).

[9]. See, e.g., Liana C. Sayer, Economic Aspects of Divorce and Relationship Dissolution, in Handbook of Divorce and Relationship Dissolution 385 (Mark A. Fine & John H. Harvey eds., 2006) (summarizing research). Data show that divorce economically harms African-American women even more than white women. Id. at 394.

[10]. E.g., Richard R. Peterson, A Re-Evaluation of the Economic Consequences of Divorce, 61 Am. Soc. Rev. 528 (1996) (finding data flawed, which Weitzman later conceded).

[11]. Pew Charitable Trusts, Ups and Downs: Americans' Prospects for Recovery After an Income Loss 2 (Jan. 2012) (Economic Mobility Project Fact Sheet), http://www.pewtrusts.org/~/media/legacy/uploadedfiles/pcs_assets/2012/EMPUpsandDownsFactSheetpdf.pdf.

Since California initiated no-fault divorce, three questions about the economic consequences have emerged: First, what role should fault play? Second, what theories for dividing property and awarding alimony might take the place of fault? Third, how should law ensure that one group (men, women, or children) does not bear an unfair economic burden? The next two sections explore these questions, examining several modern rationales for property division and spousal support awards, respectively, while subsequent sections on child support and enforcement consider dissolution's economic impact on children.

B. Property Distribution: From Title Theory to Contribution

What property can a court allocate between the spouses at dissolution? What theory determines how much to award to each?

FERGUSON v. FERGUSON

639 So. 2d 921 (Miss. 1994) (en banc)

PRATHER, Presiding Justice. . . .

[Linda Ferguson, age 44, and Billy Cleveland Ferguson, Sr., age 48, were married in 1967 and separated in 1991. They had two children. During their 24 years of marriage, Linda worked both as a homemaker and as a cosmetologist/beautician. Billy, employed by South Central Bell as a cable repair technician, installed and maintained local telephone service. Linda filed for divorce, which the chancellor awarded to her on the ground of Billy's adultery. The chancellor also awarded her custody of the 14-year-old son and $300 a month child support, as well as the marital home and its contents, four acres of land comprising the homestead, with title to the marital home to be divested from Billy and vested in Linda, debt free; one-half interest in Billy's pension plan, stock ownership plan, and savings and security plan; and periodic alimony in the amount of $400 per month and lump sum alimony in the sum of $30,000 to be paid at the rate of $10,000 annually beginning on January 1, 1992. Billy appeals.]

States have devised various methods to divide marital assets at divorce, and approaches have usually followed one of three systems [separate property, equitable distribution, and community property]. Mississippi [and some other states] previously followed the separate property system, which was a system that merely determined title to the assets and returned that property to the title-holding spouse.

Our separate property system at times resulted in unjust distributions, especially involving cases of a traditional family where most property was titled in the husband, leaving a traditional housewife and mother with nothing but a claim for alimony, which often proved unenforceable. In a family where both spouses worked, but the husband's resources were devoted to investments while the wife's earnings were devoted to paying the family expenses or vice versa, the same unfair results ensued. The flaw of the separate property system, however, is not merely that it will occasionally ignore the financial contributions of the non-titleholding spouse. The system . . . is also unable to take account of a spouse's non-financial contribution. In the case of many traditional housewives such non-financial contributions are often considerable.[2] Thus, to allow a system of property division to ignore non-financial contributions is to create a likelihood of unjust division of property.

The non-monetary contributions of a traditional housewife have been acknowledged by this Court, and to some extent, case law has helped lessen the unfairness to a traditional housewife in the division of marital property. [T]his Court has allowed lump sum alimony as an adjustment to property division to prevent unfair division. The lump sum award has been described as a method of dividing property under the guise of alimony. . . .

Courts have acknowledged that the power and authority of the chancery court to award alimony and child support have been historically derived from the legal duty of the husband to support the family. As to division of marital assets, it is the broad inherent equity powers of the chancery court that give it the authority to act. General equity principles of fairness undergird this authority. That duty was codified in Miss. Code. Ann. §93-5-23 (Supp. 1993). . . . This Court, therefore, holds that the chancery court is within its authority and power to equitably divide marital assets at divorce. . . .

[T]his Court recognizes the need for guidelines to aid chancellors in their adjudication of marital property division. Therefore, this Court directs the chancery courts to evaluate the division of marital assets by the following guidelines [including, inter alia, substantial contribution to the accumulation of the property, the market and emotional value of the assets, tax and other economic consequences of the distribution, the parties' needs, and any other factor relevant to an equitable outcome.]

[F]airness is the prevailing guideline in marital division. . . . All property division, lump sum or periodic alimony payment, and mutual obligations for child support should be considered together. "Alimony and equitable distribution are distinct concepts, but together they command the entire field of financial settlement of divorce. Therefore, where one expands, the other must recede." [LaRue v. LaRue, 304 S.E.2d 312, 334 (W. Va. 1983) (Neely, J., concurring).] Thus, the chancellor may divide marital assets, real and personal, as well as award periodic and/or lump sum alimony, as equity demands. [F]indings of fact by the chancellor, together with the legal conclusions drawn from those findings, are required. . . .

. . . Billy contends that he owned all the interest in the pension plan, stock, and savings [obtained through his employer, Bell South], and that it was his separate property. On appeal [of the chancellor's allocation of one-half these assets to Linda], Billy claims Linda in no way contributed to the acquisition of this property, and nothing was ever issued in her name. . . .

When a couple has been married for twenty-four years, yet the only retirement benefits accumulated throughout the marriage are titled in the name of only one spouse, is it equitable to find only one spouse entitled to financial security upon retirement when both have benefitted from the employer funded plan along the way? When one spouse has contributed directly to the fund, by virtue of his/

2. The persistent attempts made to put a monetary value on a homemaker's contribution are likely to undervalue the magnitude of such contributions. . . .

her labor, while the other has contributed indirectly, by virtue of domestic services and/or earned income which both parties have enjoyed rather than invested, the spouse without retirement funds in his/her own name could instead have been working outside the home and/or investing his/her wages in preparation for his/her own retirement. . . .

[In addition,] Billy contends the chancellor lacked the authority to order him to convey, free of all encumbrances, his one-half interest in the jointly owned four acres on which the marital home was situated. . . . "A spouse who has made a material contribution toward the acquisition of property which is titled in the name of the other may claim an equitable interest in such jointly accumulated property incident to a divorce proceeding." Jones v. Jones, 532 So. 2d 574, 580 (Miss. 1988). [W]e said that "[i]f 'contribution' toward the acquisition of assets is proven by a divorcing party, then the court has the authority to divide these 'jointly' accumulated assets." *Jones*, 532 So. 2d at 580. . . .

[There were two mortgages on the marital home.] This Court holds that under existing case law the chancellor was within his authority to order Billy to effect a transfer of title to Linda to the marital home and the surrounding four acres [free and clear of any liens] to accomplish an equitable division. . . . Nonetheless, this issue is remanded for consideration together with the other assets [for equitable] division to be guided by the factors promulgated today. . . .

The chancellor stated on the record that he tended to believe the testimony of [Billy's paramour that he] had withdrawn $30,000.00 from his Bell South Savings and Security Plan and put it where nobody could get to it or find it. He awarded this amount to Linda as lump sum alimony to be paid in three installments. . . . Linda worked and contributed to Billy's financial status, but had no assets of her own; her separate estate pales in comparison to Billy's. This award of lump sum alimony may have been made by the chancellor to give Linda financial security. An explanation of the basis of this award will help this Court determine whether the distribution represents an abuse of discretion or a division supported by the record. Therefore, a remand is warranted on this issue. . . .

UNIFORM MARRIAGE AND DIVORCE ACT

§307. [DISPOSITION OF PROPERTY][12]

(a) [The court in a dissolution or legal separation proceeding] shall assign each spouse's property to him. It also shall divide the marital property without regard to marital misconduct in just proportions considering all relevant factors including:

(1) contribution of each spouse to acquisition of the marital property, including contribution of a spouse as homemaker;

(2) value of the property set apart to each spouse;

(3) duration of the marriage; and

---

[12]. This provision appears in the original 1970 version of the Uniform Marriage and Divorce Act (UMDA). The drafters later replaced this provision with two alternatives, A for states following the common law approach and B for community property states.

(4) economic circumstances of each spouse when the division of property is to become effective, including the desirability of awarding the family home or the right to live therein for reasonable periods to the spouse having custody of any children.

(b) For purposes of this Act, "marital property" means all property acquired by either spouse subsequent to the marriage except:

(1) property acquired by gift, bequest, devise, or descent;

(2) property acquired in exchange for property acquired before the marriage or in exchange for property acquired by gift, bequest, devise, or descent;

(3) property acquired by a spouse after a decree of legal separation;

(4) property excluded by valid agreement of the parties; and

(5) the increase in value of property acquired before the marriage.

(c) All property acquired by either spouse after the marriage and before a decree of legal separation is presumed to be marital property, regardless of whether title is held individually or by the spouses in some form of co-ownership such as joint tenancy, tenancy in common, tenancy by the entirety, and community property. The presumption of marital property is overcome by a showing that the property was acquired by a method listed in subsection (b).

Stephen D. Sugarman, Dividing Financial Interests on Divorce

in Divorce Reform at the Crossroads 130, 136-141 (Stephen D. Sugarman & Herma Hill Kay eds., 1990)

[The author attempts to identify a theoretical framework or legal analogy for understanding the financial incidents of divorce. He rejects fault as a suitable principle, given the high social cost imposed. He also rejects the notion of "marriage as contract," in part because modern no-fault, unilateral divorce leaves no room for "the concept of breach and resultant damages." He then considers partnership law.]

Perhaps a better legal analogy to no-fault divorce can be found in partnership law. The idea is that through marriage the man and woman have joined together (50-50?) in an economic partnership, which, like partnerships generally, can be dissolved by either party. On the ending of the marriage partnership, like other partnerships, there is to be a winding up of the partnership's activities and a distribution of the partnership assets. . . .

Under the partnership analogy all earnings generated by the couple during the marriage would seem to belong to the partnership, as would any things bought with those earnings and any earnings left unspent and saved or invested. . . . In the marriage setting [unlike in traditional financial partnerships], it is as though, as a general rule, all the extra income and asset appreciation of the partnership is simply retained and reinvested in the partnership. . . .

[J]ust as financial partners contribute only some of their property to the typical partnership, certain items of property belonging to the husband and wife could be seen as outside the marital partnership and not subject to division on the marriage's termination. They might include assets the parties bring to the marriage and do not commingle with other marital property, and those gifts and inheritances separately received by either party during the marriage and maintained separately.

If marriage under no-fault is to be seen as a conventional partnership, no formal distinctions would be made between long- and short-duration marriages; to be sure, in long-duration marriages, there might be more assets to distribute. So, too, the family home would not be treated differently from any other asset. The implication of minor children would be ambiguous since there is no obvious counterpart in ordinary partnerships. Does gaining custody mean that you have obtained a partnership asset, or merely that you have assumed a partnership liability for which you should be compensated?

Most important, under the partnership analogy, there would be no spousal support. That is, in the traditional partnership, even though the partners agree to make their earning capacity available to the partnership during its lifetime, they ordinarily just walk away from the dissolved partnership with all their own human capital. This applies both to the human capital they brought to the partnership and to any enhanced human capital they gained during the operation of the partnership. . . .

Traditional financial partners, of course, may anticipate certain problems of partnership breakup and, if they wish, enter into alternative arrangements at the outset. . . . They [even] might agree to be other than 50-50 partners originally. Perhaps married couples could also be encouraged to make specific agreements in advance. . . .

Notes and Questions on the Theory of Property Division

1. Development of equitable distribution. Most U.S. states follow the common law approach to spousal ownership of property during marriage. Eight use a community property approach derived from their French or Spanish heritage; Wisconsin's system is modeled on the Uniform Marital Property Act (UMPA).

The common law scheme reflects "title theory." Title to property (as evidenced in a deed, for example) determines ownership between the spouses. Property acquired or earned during marriage belongs to the acquiring or earning spouse unless that spouse acts affirmatively to create joint ownership (for example, buying a house titled jointly in the names of both spouses). Upon divorce, the court assigns property to the owner. In the 1980s, after adopting no-fault grounds and witnessing a rising divorce rate, many states abandoned the title system in favor of a system of "equitable distribution" applicable at the end of marriage. In *Ferguson*, Mississippi became the last state to abandon the title system in divorce cases.

Before the development of equitable distribution laws, statutes permitting a court to divide property upon divorce were limited. A few states used equitable remedies to recognize a wife's contribution or to prevent the husband's unjust enrichment. One influential model was the original 1970 version of the Uniform Marriage and Divorce Act (UMDA). Using definitions typical of community property systems, UMDA distinguished separate property from marital property and listed factors that courts should consider in making a "just" division of the latter.

Laws following this model bring common law states much closer to community property states in the treatment of property at divorce. That is, equitable distribution laws in common law states create a deferred community property system, with the concept of marital property becoming effective upon divorce.

Although most states adopted equitable distribution by statute (often modeled on UMDA), Mississippi did so by judicial decision in *Ferguson*. What is the source of *Ferguson*'s authority to adopt a new property distribution system? Does the ruling deprive Billy Ferguson of his property without due process? Are the court's "guidelines" really "judicial legislation" in disguise? See *Ferguson*, 639 So. 2d at 940 (Lee, P.J., concurring and dissenting).

2. Homemaker services. Title theory, as *Ferguson* reveals, evokes criticism because of its treatment of the traditional homemaker. See generally Katharine Silbaugh, Turning Labor into Love: Housework and the Law, 91 Nw. U. L. Rev. 1 (1996). The longstanding devaluation of homemakers' activities followed from the common law doctrine of coverture, including the wife's duty to perform household services and the husband's rights to her property and earnings. During the era of divorce reform, feminist activists helped secure equitable distribution laws, designed to take into account at divorce unpaid homemaking contributions. See generally Mary Ziegler, An Incomplete Revolution: Feminists and the Legacy of Marital-Property Reform, 19 Mich. J. Gender & L. 259 (2013). UMDA served as an influential catalyst for such reform. How does UMDA treat homemaker services?

3. Partnership. Does *Ferguson*'s contribution theory treat marriage as a partnership, the approach examined by Professor Sugarman? What is the difference? Does the partnership analogy, first developed in community property states, provide fair outcomes for homemakers? See Alicia Brokars Kelly, Navigating Gender in Modern Intimate Partnership Law, 14 J.L. & Fam. Stud. 1 (2012).

4. What to divide and distribute?

a. Marital property versus "hotchpot." Note how UMDA identifies the property that is subject to division. Statutes in states following this model define "marital property" as that acquired by either spouse during the marriage, except when acquired by gift, inheritance, or in exchange for nonmarital or "separate property"; such statutes often presume that all property acquired during the marriage is marital. E.g., Ky. Rev. Stat. Ann. §403.190. What theory explains the distinct treatment of marital and separate property?

In a later version of UMDA §307, Alternative A (the model proposed for common law states) gives the court authority to divide equitably the great "hotchpot" of assets owned by either spouse, whenever and however acquired.[13] Can partnership or contribution theories explain judicial authority to divide property acquired before marriage or received by one spouse as a gift?

Under yet another approach, a "hybrid system," the court distributes nonmarital property only after the distribution of marital property, if equity requires. Which approach is more fair—marital property, hotchpot, or hybrid? Which approach does *Ferguson* follow? See generally Marsha Garrison, What's Fair in

[13]. See Charts, supra note [2], at 666-668 (listing 16 jurisdictions that do not limit property division to marital assets only).

Divorce Property Distribution: Cross-National Perspectives from Survey Evidence, 72 La. L. Rev. 57, 58 (2011) (noting lack of consensus about pool of divisible assets).

b. The ALI's model: Recharacterizing separate property. The American Law Institute's Principles of the Law of Family Dissolution ("ALI Principles"), published in 2002, seek to guide states in addressing divorce-related questions. As a general matter, the ALI Principles reconceptualize dissolution's financial consequences to enhance consistency among outcomes and to clarify rationales. The ALI Principles propose the use of presumptive mathematical formulas ("rules of statewide application") that will allow prediction of judicial outcomes, in turn facilitating settlement at dissolution or encouraging premarital contracts. These presumptive formulas serve as default rules applicable in the absence of agreement by the parties. Courts can depart from a formula's outcome only on written findings that substantial injustice would result.

ALI Principles of the Law of Family Dissolution

The ALI Principles would "recharacterize" as marital property some of each spouse's separate property, based on the length of the marriage. Specifically, according to §4.12, states should develop presumptive formulas under which, at dissolution, a portion of each spouse's separate property would be treated as marital property. Such formulas should specify how long a marriage must have lasted before such recharacterization begins, as well as how the portion to be recharacterized increases over time. Why should duration of marriage itself transform separate property into marital property (which the ALI Principles subject to presumptively equal division)? This approach claims to reflect the reasonable expectations of spouses, as the comments explain:

> After many years of marriage, spouses typically do not think of their separate-property assets as separate, even if they would be so classified under the technical property rules. Both spouses are likely to believe, for example, that such assets will be available to provide for their joint retirement, for a medical crisis of either spouse, or for other personal emergencies. The longer the marriage the more likely it is that the spouses will have made decisions about their employment or the use of their marital assets that are premised in part on such expectations about the separate property of both spouses.

American Law Institute Principles of the Law of Family Dissolution: Analysis and Recommendations §4.12 cmt. a (2002).

This explanation cites no empirical investigation of spousal attitudes about property ownership in long marriages, however. Would the same attitudes prevail among domestic partners, to whom these rules for family dissolution apply as well?

c. Debts. Equitable distribution includes debts as well as assets. For example, *Ferguson* addresses responsibility for mortgages. Typically, the same considerations that apply to assets govern the distinction between separate and marital debts and the distribution of the latter. Debts at divorce become increasingly prominent during a weak economy. E.g., Warren v. Warren, 773 S.E.2d 135 (N.C. Ct. App. 2015) (dividing wife's student loan debt); Margaret M. Mahoney, The Equitable Distribution of Marital Debts, 79 UMKC L. Rev. 445 (2010).

d. Dissipated assets. *Ferguson* acknowledges evidence that Billy withdrew and hid $30,000. Although the court below awarded this sum to Linda as lump-sum alimony, typically courts will include the value of such dissipated marital assets in determining the marital property available for division and then count that amount as part of the share of the dissipating spouse. What types of expenditures constitute dissipation? Frivolous household expenditures? Expenditures for treatment for alcohol abuse? See Stein v. Stein, 11 So. 3d 1288 (Miss. Ct. App. 2009). Loans and cash advances to a paramour? Compare In re Marriage of Sather, 2013 WL 6670299 (Ill. App. Ct. 2013), with Felis v. Felis, 72 A.3d 874 (Vt. 2013). Suppose that the wasted property is separate, not marital. See Owens v. Owens, 967 N.Y.S.2d 465 (App. Div. 2013). Can a court following a strict no-fault approach consider dissipated assets?

What time period is relevant? See, e.g., Finan v. Finan, 949 A.2d 468 (Conn. 2008) (only actions in contemplation of divorce or during marriage breakdown); Kittredge v. Kittredge, 803 N.E.2d 306, 317 (Mass. 2004) (counting only 10 percent of husband's gambling losses as dissipation of assets because "it was not something that started in response to the breakdown of the marriage or in anticipation of divorce").

5. "Equitable" distribution. Once a court determines the property subject to division and its value, how does the court determine the amount each party should get? UMDA §307 directs an "equitable" apportionment according to a wide-ranging list of factors of unidentified weight. Other statutes direct the court to divide such property "in just proportions." E.g., 750 Ill. Comp. Stat. §5/503(d). Are these standards helpful?

6. Fault. Should marital misconduct play a role in the equitable or just division of property? Does Billy's adultery in *Ferguson* explain the court's departure from title theory? Was the court punishing him for his "fault"? Does consideration of fault in dividing property mitigate harsh effects of no-fault divorce? Even if dissolution should be available without regard to fault, does it follow that law should not impose economic rewards and punishments for behavior during marriage? See generally Robin Fretwell Wilson, Beyond the Bounds of Decency: Why Fault Continues to Matter to (Some) Wronged Spouses, 66 Wash. & Lee L. Rev. 503 (2009). What position does UMDA take on the role of fault in property division? Today, fault considerations (other than financial misconduct) have receded in property division even more than in support awards (discussed infra).

7. Equal division. Community property principles, explicitly recognizing marriage as a partnership, give each spouse an undivided one-half interest in property acquired by spousal labor during the marriage. Most, but not all, community property states apply a rule or presumption of equal division at dissolution, in contrast to "equitable distribution" or "just division." Equal division contemplates equality in value, not dividing an asset in half.

The ALI Principles also dictate a presumption of equal division of marital property (§4.09). Although the Principles disregard fault in the distribution of property, they include an exception for financial misconduct with marital assets (§4.10). Why? (UMDA has a similar exception.)

For an equitable distribution, should a court use an equal division as a starting point? Do partnership and contribution rationales presume equal participation by both spouses? See Dawkins v. Dawkins, 687 S.E.2d 52, 53-54 (S.C. 2010) ("The purpose behind case law's imprimatur of a 50%-50% division was [not to impose a mandatory requirement, but] to foster amicable resolutions in family court matters and provide guidance on what would in effect be a safe harbor in most cases in the division of marital property in a long-term marriage."), *abrogated on other grounds*, Lewis v. Lewis, 709 S.E.2d 650 (S.C. 2011).

Does the absence of a presumption of equal division constitute sex discrimination? Will courts disproportionately favor breadwinners over homemakers if given unfettered discretion to achieve an equitable division of property? See Wendt v. Wendt, 757 A.2d 1225, 1241-1245 (Conn. App. Ct. 2000) (rejecting wife's challenge under state constitution's equal rights amendment).

8. Need. Does *Ferguson*'s reliance on a contribution rationale leave room to divide property based on need? On what basis did Linda "need" the marital home and the other property that was titled to her husband but awarded to her? Can need provide a theory for property division at dissolution? How would a need-based approach affect the share awarded to the homemaking spouse?

How would you reconcile need as a factor in property distribution with the egalitarian assumptions of the contribution and partnership rationales? See Martha Albertson Fineman, The Illusion of Equality: The Rhetoric and Reality of Divorce Reform 41-52 (1991). Does consideration of need in property distribution help expose family law's persistent gender inequalities? Cf. Jill Elaine Hasday, Family Law Reimagined 103-104 (2014). Alternatively, does need make more sense as a basis for alimony than for property division? Consider the materials in the next section.

Problem

Rolando and Julieta separated two years after marrying. During the separation, Rolando sent money to their children (all born before the marriage) and paid for Julieta's surgery. Eight years after separating, they reconciled for four years. In subsequent divorce proceedings, Rolando challenges the court's classification of assets he acquired during the separation as marital, rather than separate, property. Assuming UMDA governs (the original version, supra), what result and why? See Rodriguez v. Rodriguez, 908 P.2d 1007 (Alaska 1995); In re Marriage of Perez, 7 N.E.3d 1009 (Ind. Ct. App. 2014); In re Marriage of English, 194 P.3d 887 (Or. Ct. App. 2009). If only property acquired while spouses are "living separate and apart" is deemed separate, not marital or community, does this criterion require that they occupy separate residences? See In re Marriage of Davis, 352 P.3d 401 (Cal. 2015). See also Kosobud v. Kosobud, 817 N.W.2d 384 (N.D. 2012). Alternatively, suppose that the assets in question had been acquired by Rolando premaritally, while he and Julieta were cohabiting as a prelude to their marriage. See Collins v. Wassell, 323 P.3d 1216 (Haw. 2014).

C. Spousal Support: Theories of Need, Self-Sufficiency, and Beyond

The concept of divorce as the dissolution of a partnership leaves unexplained the duty to provide future support for a former spouse. What is the rationale for spousal support? How should the amount be determined? How long should the duty continue?

MANI v. MANI

869 A.2d 904 (N.J. 2005)

Justice LONG delivered the opinion of the Court. . . .

. . . Plaintiff, Brenda Mani and defendant, James Mani met in 1970 when she went to work for him in his seasonal amusement business on the Seaside Heights boardwalk. James, a college graduate, was at the time, a half-owner of the boardwalk business and a partner in a travel agency in Florida that later failed; Brenda was a college student. Brenda graduated in 1971 and taught preschool for two years while working with James at his business during the summer.

[The couple had no children. During summers, they worked together at the boardwalk business for a combined total of 100 hours per week. During winters, they vacationed in Florida and Mexico. Brenda received valuable gifts from her father, including $10,000 annually during the early years of the marriage; tax-free bonds; and stock in a family business, Ultimate Corporation, that later traded publicly, split several times, and appreciated considerably. In 1986, using proceeds from Brenda's stock and the first home, the parties built a lavish new home, titled in Brenda's name.]

In 1993, when they were in their 40's, the parties retired from the boardwalk business and lived, in the words of the trial judge, an "extravagant" lifestyle almost exclusively out of Brenda's investment income. Their monthly budgetary expenses ranged from $7,360 [Brenda's estimate] to $13,143 [James's estimate]. Following the conclusion of the boardwalk operation, James, who had obtained a real estate license in Florida, worked briefly for real estate brokers. Although he provided a few referrals, he never showed a property for the firms and earned only about $20,000 in income in all. The couple spent seven years together in retirement before Brenda discovered that her husband was having an affair with a woman with whom the parties socialized. Brenda filed a complaint for divorce alleging adultery and extreme cruelty. . . .

[At trial,] James claimed entitlement to a permanent alimony award of $68,320 per year and Brenda sought to deny alimony altogether. [After allocating the property,] the judge awarded James [alimony of] $610 per week based "in substantial part on the defendant's economic dependency." In reaching that conclusion, the judge attributed to James the ability to earn a minimum of $25,000 annually and denominated the alimony award as necessary to maintain the marital standard of living. [Both parties appealed.]

[In affirming, the Appellate Division] observed that "the Manis' standard of living was not the result of the parties' joint efforts, but rather solely due to gifts from plaintiff's father." [Also,] James' adultery was significant and his marital indiscretions warrant consideration in the amount of that award." . . .

James asks us to establish, as a rule of law, that in modern matrimonial practice, fault should play no part in an alimony determination or in an award of counsel fees. . . . Brenda counters that N.J.S.A. 2A:34-23(b) gives courts discretion to "consider any other factors which the court may deem relevant" in arriving at an alimony decision, including marital fault. . . . Amicus Curiae [the New Jersey State Bar Association] urges us to rule that fault should not be a factor in the determination of alimony except in the most egregious circumstances and that the focus of alimony should remain, as is the present practice, on the parties' financial circumstances. . . .

The history of alimony is instructive. In early England, two forms of marital dissolution existed. The most common was an ecclesiastical divorce from bed and board (a mensa et thoro) [or legal separation]. The other form—a civil divorce (a vinculo matrimonii)—which literally means severing the chains of matrimony, although technically available, was extremely rare because it required an act of Parliament. Alimony was granted only in the former class of cases on the theory that husband was obliged to continue to support his wife as long as they remained married. Somehow, with the passage of time, the distinction between true divorce and mere separation was obliterated and alimony began to be awarded in all cases. No rationale was advanced to explain why parties, who were no longer married, remained economically bound to one another.

Divorce based on the English practice was available in the American colonies from the earliest times. The concept of alimony also carried over. Again, as had been the case in England, the reason for alimony, outside the legal separation scenario, remained an enigma. . . . Indeed, many distinct explanations have been advanced for alimony. They include its characterization as damages for breach of the marriage contract; as a share of the benefits of the marriage partnership; as damages for economic dislocation (based on past contributions); as damages for personal dislocation (foregoing the chance to marry another); as compensation for certain specific losses at the time of the dissolution; as deterrence or punishment for marital indiscretion; and as avoidance of a drain on the public fisc. Obviously, some of those purposes favor consideration of fault and some disfavor it. . . .

New Jersey cases have long expressed the view that alimony is neither a punishment for the payor nor a reward for the payee. . . . N.J.S.A. 2A:34-23(b) provides that in all divorce actions "the court may award one or more of the following types of alimony: permanent alimony; rehabilitative alimony; limited duration alimony or reimbursement alimony to either party." When ordering alimony, a "court shall consider" a non-exclusive list of [13] enumerated factors [including the actual need and ability of the parties to pay; the duration of the marriage; the age, physical and emotional health of the parties; the standard of living established in the marriage and the likelihood that each party can maintain a reasonably comparable standard of living; the parties' earning capacities; the equitable distribution of property ordered; and any other factors which the court may deem relevant].

As is obvious, the words "marital fault" and "responsibility for the breakdown in the marriage" do not appear in the statute, although the so-called "catch all category" arguably permits a court to consider "any other factor" it may "deem relevant." [In addition, N.J.S.A. 2A:34-23(g) provides that, except in divorces based on the ground of separation, the court also *may consider the proofs made* in establishing such ground in determining an amount of alimony or maintenance that is fit, reasonable, and just.]

[In 1971, based on the recommendations of its Divorce Law Study Commission, New Jersey reformed its divorce law by adding to the existing fault-based grounds the no-fault ground of separation. The alimony statutes quoted above came word-for-word from language proposed by the Commission, which explicitly left room for judicial discretion to consider fault in alimony awards. The Commission] concluded that "perhaps the penalty should fit the 'crime,' i.e., the flagrant offender, whether plaintiff or defendant (husband or wife) may be subject to equitable principles when alimony, custody and property rights are determined." The Commission did not, however, further define flagrancy.

[A]lthough our case law has consistently recognized that, under our statutory scheme, fault may be considered in calculating alimony, for over a quarter of a century, courts have declined to place their imprimatur on a wide-ranging use of fault in that context. . . . The thirteen alimony factors listed in N.J.S.A. 2A:34-23(b) clearly center on the economic status of the parties. That is the primary alimony focus. . . .

[O]ur task in this case is to search for a principled approach to the relationship between fault and alimony consistent with legislative intent. [We have scoured the laws of the different states and the commentators' views. They] reflect the full spectrum of approaches. For example, one commentator argues that even in the era of no-fault divorce, there should be consideration of fault in determining alimony to morally coerce better marital conduct. Adrian M. Morse, Jr., Fault: A Viable Means of Re-Injecting Responsibility in Marital Relations, 30 U. Rich. L. Rev. 605, 651 (1996). Another contends that legal recognition of fault may "provide protection and compensation for victims of abuse [of] spousal trust." Barbara Bennett Woodhouse, Sex, Lies and Dissipation: The Discourse of Fault in a No-Fault Era, 82 Geo L.J. 2525, 2529-30 (1994). Other scholars counter that "the potentially valid functions of a fault principle are better served by the tort and criminal law, and attempting to serve them through a fault rule risks serious distortions in the resolution of the dissolution action." [Ira] Mark Ellman, The Place of Fault in a Modern Divorce Law, 28 Ariz. St. L.J. 773, 808-09 (1996). That view aligns with the most recent report of the American Law Institute on Principles of the Law of Family Dissolution: Analysis and Recommendations. That report concluded that economic fault is a valid alimony factor, but that consideration of non-economic fault should be avoided because of its deleterious effect on the dissolution action. More particularly, the ALI report notes that, in a scheme such as ours, in which alimony has economic roots, it will be the unusual case in which the fairness of the result will be improved by a judicial inquiry into the relative virtue of the parties' intimate conduct. . . .

We agree [with this last view] and hold that in cases in which marital fault has negatively affected the economic status of the parties it may be considered in the calculation of alimony. By way of example, if a spouse gambles away all savings and retirement funds, and the assets are inadequate to allow the other spouse to recoup her share, an appropriate savings and retirement component may be included in the alimony award.

[Although economic misconduct is relevant to alimony, the] same relevance notion does not apply to the ordinary fault grounds for divorce that lurk in the margins of nearly every case. . . . Moreover, without concomitant benefit, considering non-economic fault can only result in ramping up the emotional content of matrimonial litigation and encouraging the parties to continually replay the details of their failed relationship. Not only is non-economic fault nearly impossible to factor into an alimony computation, but any attempt to do so would have the effect of generating complex legal issues regarding the apportionment of mutual fault, which is present in nearly all cases. That, in turn, would result in the protraction of litigation and the undermining of the goals of no-fault divorce, again without a corresponding benefit.

Thus we hold that to the extent that marital misconduct affects the economic status quo of the parties, it may be taken into consideration in the calculation of alimony. Where marital fault has no residual economic consequences, it may not be considered in an alimony award.

The only exception to that rule is the narrow band of cases involving [egregious fault]. [E]gregious fault is a term of art that requires not simply more, or even more public acts of marital indiscretion, but acts that by their very nature, are different in kind. By way of example but not limitation, California has legislatively barred alimony payments to a dependent spouse who has attempted to murder the supporting spouse. Cal. Fam. Code §4324. Deliberately infecting a spouse with a loathsome disease also comes to mind. Underlying those examples is the concept that some conduct, by its very nature is so outrageous that it can be said to violate the social contract, such that society would not abide continuing the economic bonds between the parties. In the extremely narrow class of cases in which such conduct occurs, it may be considered by the court, not in calculating an alimony award, but in the initial determination of whether alimony should be allowed at all.

In this case, there was no allegation that James's marital fault had any economic consequences or that it was, in any way, egregious. . . . [W]e do not know whether the court would have reached the same conclusion in the absence of the fault consideration. We therefore reverse and remand the case to the Appellate Division for reconsideration of alimony without regard to fault. . . .

One final note on the alimony-fault intersection. This is nothing more than a case involving statutory interpretation. . . . This case codifies what has been the nearly universal practice in our courts. . . . By delimiting the kinds of fault that may be taken into account in an alimony calculus, we have not only created a template for uniformity and predictability in decision-making but have relieved matrimonial litigants and their counsel from the need to act upon the nearly universal and practically irresistible urge for retribution that follows on the heels of a broken marriage. . . .

Justice Rivera-Soto, concurring in part and dissenting in part. . . .

[T]he paradigm we adopt today undoubtedly will generate its own flood of litigation because it defies definition. As a result, it takes little imagination to foresee the unending number of claims the standard adopted today—that a party's fault "affected the parties' economic life"—will bring. . . . Similarly, determining what constitutes "fault [that] so violates societal norms that continuing the economic bonds between the parties would confound notions of simple justice" is too subjective a standard, converting the analysis into a simple question of whose personal value system will prevail. It is not a stretch to conclude that having your spouse engage in sexual relations with your friend and yet still demand that you support his lifestyle after divorce at the rate of over $150,000 per year "confounds notions of simple justice." If that is not what this standard means, then it is meaningless. If, on the other hand, that is precisely what this new standard means, then we have created a new and unproven process to achieve a result already reached by tried-and-true methods. . . .

UNIFORM MARRIAGE AND DIVORCE ACT

§308. [MAINTENANCE]

(a) [The court in a dissolution or legal separation proceeding] may grant a maintenance order for either spouse only if it finds that the spouse seeking maintenance:

(1) lacks sufficient property to provide for his reasonable needs; and

(2) is unable to support himself through appropriate employment or is the custodian of a child whose condition or circumstances make it appropriate that the custodian not be required to seek employment outside the home.

(b) The maintenance order shall be in amounts and for periods of time the court deems just, without regard to marital misconduct, and after considering all relevant factors including:

(1) the financial resources of the party seeking maintenance, including marital property apportioned to him, his ability to meet his needs independently, and the extent to which a provision for support of a child living with the party includes a sum for that party as custodian;

(2) the time necessary to acquire sufficient education or training to enable the party seeking maintenance to find appropriate employment;

(3) the standard of living established during the marriage;

(4) the duration of the marriage;

(5) the age and the physical and emotional condition of the spouse seeking maintenance; and

(6) the ability of the spouse from whom maintenance is sought to meet his needs while meeting those of the spouse seeking maintenance.

MASSACHUSETTS ALIMONY REFORM ACT

Mass Gen. Laws, Ch. 208

§49. TERMINATION, SUSPENSION, OR MODIFICATION OF GENERAL TERM ALIMONY . . .

(b) Except upon a written finding by the court that deviation beyond the time limits of this section are required in the interests of justice, if the length of the marriage is 20 years or less, general term alimony shall terminate no later than a date certain under the following durational limits:

(1) If the length of the marriage is 5 years or less, general term alimony shall continue for not longer than one-half the number of months of the marriage.

(2) If the length of the marriage is 10 years or less, but more than 5 years, general term alimony shall continue for not longer than 60 per cent of the number of months of the marriage.

(3) If the length of the marriage is 15 years or less, but more than 10 years, general term alimony shall continue for not longer than 70 per cent of the number of months of the marriage.

(4) If the length of the marriage is 20 years or less, but more than 15 years, general term alimony shall continue for not longer than 80 per cent of the number of months of the marriage.

(c) The court may order alimony for an indefinite length of time for marriages for which the length of the marriage was longer than 20 years. . . .

§53. DETERMINATION OF FORM, AMOUNT, AND DURATION OF ALIMONY, MAXIMUM AMOUNT; INCOME CALCULATION; DEVIATIONS; CONCURRENT CHILD SUPPORT ORDERS

(a) In determining the appropriate form of alimony and in setting the amount and duration of support, a court shall consider: the length of the marriage; age of the parties; health of the parties; income, employment and employability of both parties, including employability through reasonable diligence and additional training, if necessary; economic and non-economic contribution of both parties to the marriage; marital lifestyle; ability of each party to maintain the marital lifestyle; lost economic opportunity as a result of the marriage; and such other factors as the court considers relevant and material.

(b) Except for reimbursement alimony or circumstances warranting deviation for other forms of alimony, the amount of alimony should generally not exceed the recipient's need or 30 to 35 per cent of the difference between the parties' gross incomes established at the time of the order being issued. Subject to subsection (c), income shall be defined as set forth in the Massachusetts child support guidelines . . .

(e) In setting an initial alimony order, or in modifying an existing order, the court may deviate from duration and amount limits for general term alimony and rehabilitative alimony upon written findings that deviation is necessary. Grounds for deviation may include:

(1) advanced age; chronic illness; or unusual health circumstances of either party;

(2) tax considerations applicable to the parties;

(3) whether the payor spouse is providing health insurance and the cost of health insurance for the recipient spouse;

(4) whether the payor spouse has been ordered to secure life insurance for the benefit of the recipient spouse and the cost of such insurance;

(5) sources and amounts of unearned income, including capital gains, interest and dividends, annuity and investment income from assets that were not allocated in the [parties'] divorce;

(6) significant premarital cohabitation that included economic partnership or marital separation of significant duration, each of which the court may consider in determining the length of the marriage;

(7) a party's inability to provide for that party's own support by reason of physical or mental abuse by the payor;

(8) a party's inability to provide for that party's own support by reason of that party's deficiency of property, maintenance or employment opportunity; and

(9) upon written findings, any other factor that the court deems relevant and material.

(f) In determining the incomes of parties with respect to the issue of alimony, the court may attribute income to a party who is unemployed or underemployed.

(g) If a court orders alimony concurrent with or subsequent to a child support order, the combined duration of alimony and child support shall not exceed the longer of: (i) the alimony or child support duration available at the time of divorce; or (ii) rehabilitative alimony beginning upon the termination of child support.

Notes and Questions on the Rationales for Postdissolution Support

1. A continuing duty? *Mani* poses the unresolved question "why parties, who [are] no longer married, remain[] economically bound together." Which of the explanations for alimony listed in *Mani* is most persuasive? Even if an economically dependent spouse *needs* support after dissolution, why does a former spouse (rather than parents, children, or the state) bear this responsibility? See Anne Alstott, Private Tragedies: Family Law as Social Insurance, 4 Harv. L. & Pol'y Rev. 3 (2010).

2. Need and gender. Alimony has its roots in the necessaries doctrine, which imposed on husbands a duty to support their wives during marriage. (See McGuire v. McGuire, Chapter III.) The Supreme Court invalidated gender-specific alimony rules in Orr v. Orr, 440 U.S. 268 (1979). Applying intermediate scrutiny to an Alabama statute that allowed courts to require husbands, but not wives, to pay alimony upon divorce, the Court rejected as a legitimate purpose the state's preference for traditional sex-based roles in marriage. It also rejected gender as a proxy for financial need, whether based on a goal of helping needy spouses or compensating women for past discrimination. The Court reasoned that Alabama's individualized judicial hearings to set the amount of an alimony award make reliance on a proxy unnecessary and that a gender-neutral law would achieve the state's ends, while avoiding "the inherent risk of reinforcing stereotypes about the 'proper place' of women and their need for special protection." Id. at 283.

Orr thus suggests that "need" furnishes the underlying rationale for alimony but rejects reliance on gender to determine need. Despite *Orr*, however, Professor Ira Ellman invokes gendered roles to identify alimony's theoretical basis. He writes:

> [Marriage] is a relationship in which the wife makes many initial investments of value only to her husband, investments a self-interested bargainer would make only in return for a long-term commitment. [T]he traditional wife makes her marital investment early in the expectation of a deferred return: sharing in the fruits of her husband's eventual market success. The traditional husband realizes his gains from the marriage in its early years, in the form of increased earning capacity and the production of children; his contribution is deferred until the marriage's later years when he shares the fruits of his enhanced earning capacity with his wife.

> In any relationship in which the flow of payments and benefits to the parties is not symmetrical over time, [t]he party who has already received a benefit has an incentive to terminate the relationship before the balance of payments shifts. . . .
>
> The function of alimony [is thus] to reallocate the postdivorce financial consequences of marriage in order to prevent distorting incentives. [B]y eliminating any financial incentives or penalties that might otherwise flow from different marital lifestyles, this theory maximizes the parties' freedom to shape their marriage in accordance with their nonfinancial preferences. They can allocate domestic duties according to these preferences without putting one spouse at risk of a much greater financial loss than the other if the marriage fails. . . .[14]

Does this analysis successfully explain why the duty of spousal support continues after divorce?

3. Contract? Does the marriage contract explain why the duty of spousal support continues after divorce? According to one classic treatment, although "alimony and marriage cannot be separated, [alimony] would seem to be most readily justified on the ground that it places the obligation to support a spouse who is in need upon the party who has undertaken to share the responsibilities and pleasures of such spouse by entering into the solemn compact of marriage, rather than upon the state."[15] Does this explanation suggest that part of the marriage contract remains binding after divorce? Or that alimony serves as a remedy for breach of this contract? See Elizabeth S. Scott & Robert E. Scott, Marriage as Relational Contract, 84 Va. L. Rev. 1225, 1309-1310 (1998) (theorizing alimony as legally enforceable insurance payments, under analysis of marriage as long-term relational contract). Does Ellman's theory, supra, also reflect a contractual rationale?

4. "A residual role for fault?"[16] If alimony provides a remedy in contract, how does a court determine who breached? Does the contractual rationale require consideration of fault? If fault should enter the analysis, what role should it play? Should the court consider the recipient's misconduct (to preclude alimony, as argued by the wife in *Mani*), the obligor's misconduct (to increase the award), or both? See, e.g., Mick-Skaggs v. Skaggs, 766 S.E.2d 870 (S.C. Ct. App. 2014) (evidence of wife's adultery justifies denial of alimony even if an insufficient ground for fault-based divorce); Riley v. Riley, 138 P.3d 84, 88-89 (Utah Ct. App. 2006) (justifying an award to wife that exceeded her need, in part because of husband's fault).

Why does *Mani* limit consideration of fault in determining alimony? What explains *Mani*'s two exceptions to its no-fault approach, economic misconduct and egregious fault? Why should courts consider these exceptions "not in calculating an alimony award, but in the initial determination of whether alimony should be allowed at all"? Why would the New Jersey Bar Association urge a no-fault approach, with an exception for egregious circumstances?

Evaluate the *Mani* dissent's critique of the two exceptions. Does a subjective standard, such as egregious fault, create risks of gender or other bias? How would

---

[14]. Ira Mark Ellman, The Theory of Alimony, 77 Cal. L. Rev. 1, 42-43, 50-51 (1989).

[15]. 2 Chester G. Vernier, American Family Laws 259, 262 (1932).

[16]. Professor Sugarman poses this question. Stephen D. Sugarman, Dividing Financial Interests on Divorce, in Divorce Reform at the Crossroads 130, 136 (Stephen D. Sugarman & Herma Hill Kay, eds., 1990).

the *Mani* judges treat domestic violence for purposes of alimony awards? Cf. Cal. Fam. Code §§4320, 4325. Child sexual abuse in the family? Cf. Eileen G. v. Frank G., 934 N.Y.S.2d 785 (App. Div. 2011). Embezzlement from the family business? See Clark v. Clark, 2014 WL 1577760 (N.J. Super. Ct. App. Div. 2014).

An omitted footnote in *Mani* states that, in appropriate cases, tort damages can compensate for harm caused by noneconomic fault. Does a tort suit provide a better way to address marital misconduct? See, e.g., Pamela Laufer-Ukeles, Reconstructing Fault: The Case for Spousal Torts, 79 U. Cin. L. Rev. 207 (2010); Lance McMillian, Adultery as Tort, 90 N.C. L. Rev. 1987 (2012). (See Feltmeier v. Feltmeier, Chapter VI.)

5. Standard of living. What does "need" mean for the purposes of computing a support award? Does it refer only to necessities of life? The standard of living during the marriage? How does UMDA measure "reasonable needs"? Should the marital standard of living determine the level of support even after a brief marriage?[17]

6. Rehabilitation for self-sufficiency.

a. UMDA's influence. UMDA provided an early model for the revision of alimony statutes once based on fault and gender. Which approach is more "progressive," UMDA's or *Mani*'s? How does UMDA frame the parameters of "need"? Note that UMDA makes maintenance a remedy of last resort, to be awarded only when a spouse's "reasonable needs" remain unmet because of the absence of sufficient property or income from appropriate employment. Why did UMDA's drafters make maintenance a disfavored remedy, to be awarded only when equitable distribution of property fails to achieve economic justice? Once this need threshold is satisfied, however, the court has discretion to order support in an amount and duration that is "just," based on all relevant factors.

Jurisdictions following UMDA view self-sufficiency as an important objective, making support a temporary, transitional measure that often contemplates post-divorce paid employment even for homemaker spouses. E.g., Zaleski v. Zaleski, 13 N.E.3d 967 (Mass. 2014).

b. Duration. How long should rehabilitation take? Can it exceed the length of the marriage? See Solem v. Solem, 757 N.W.2d 748 (N.D. 2008). Must the recipient have a plan that will lead to greater self-sufficiency? See Weintraub v. Weintraub, 864 So. 2d 22 (Fla. Dist. Ct. App. 2003) (rejecting rehabilitative alimony claim of former trained geneticist for help starting a gourmet dessert business). Must the rehabilitation achieve a particular standard of living? What is "appropriate employment" under UMDA? How costly can the rehabilitation training be?

c. Critiques. Weitzman criticizes UMDA's approach as "unrealistic" in many cases and partly responsible for the economic harm women and children suffered from no-fault divorce. See Lenore J. Weitzman, Women and Children Last: The Social and Economic Consequences of Divorce Law Reforms, in Feminism, Children, and the New Families 212, 224-229 (Sanford M. Dornbusch & Myra H. Strober, eds., 1988).

---

[17]. A total of 48 jurisdictions consider the marital standard of living in setting alimony. Charts, supra note [2], at 654-655.

Does the rehabilitation principle address the traditional gender stereotypes underlying alimony, rejected in *Orr*, supra? What are the purposes of rehabilitative alimony? To spur women to financial independence? To relieve former husbands of long-term support obligations? To foster equality between spouses? As *Mani* illustrates, courts today award alimony to husbands as well as wives.

7. Types of alimony. States permit several types of alimony, based on different objectives and rationales. The types include permanent, rehabilitative, and limited duration or reimbursement alimony (as noted by *Mani*), with the terminology varying among jurisdictions. See, e.g., Holmes v. Holmes, 6 N.E.3d 1062, 1065 (Mass. 2014) (Massachusetts statute provides for general term, rehabilitative, reimbursement, and transitional alimony). What criteria justify permanent alimony? Should a disparity in the former spouses' incomes suffice? See, e.g., Wold v. Wold, 744 N.W.2d 541, 547-548 (N.D. 2008). Should the length of the marriage alone be determinative? See Gnall v. Gnall, 119 A.3d 891 (N.J. 2015) (no).

8. Alimony reform.

a. ALI's loss compensation theory and formulaic approach. The ALI Principles (for which Professor Ellman served as chief reporter) rely on a theory of alimony based on "loss compensation." Treating income disparity as a reflection of the economically dependent spouse's loss upon divorce, the ALI Principles invoke Ellman's rationale, supra, as the basis for "compensatory spousal payments." ALI Principles §5.04. This term covers "residual" financial awards (financial awards other than for child support or property division). See id. §5.01 cmt. a. The notion of loss compensation also helps explain the gradual recharacterization of separate property as marital property because this process protects a long-term spouse from the unexpected loss of assets (discussed supra). Both mechanisms require that the spouses share the economic losses that divorce would otherwise impose on the dependent spouse alone. Such sharing is accomplished by means of transfer payments from the economically stronger spouse to the economically weaker spouse. The ALI Principles invite states to develop presumptive rules (i.e., mathematical formulas for statewide application) that calculate such payments based on the differences in spousal incomes at the time of dissolution and the length of the marriage, with longer marriages requiring gradually increased "loss sharing."

Is "loss compensation" just another way of saying that marriage is a contract with liquidated damages as the remedy for breach?

b. The Massachusetts Alimony Reform Act of 2011. In contrast to UMDA's goal of just awards and durations, based on an open-ended list of factors, the Massachusetts statute provides durational guidelines and a presumption that the amount of alimony should generally not exceed the recipient's need or 30 to 35 percent of the difference between the spouses' gross incomes at the time of the alimony order. What theory of alimony do these legislative choices reflect? Who benefits from these provisions? Who might suffer disadvantages? How would you evaluate the Act's formulaic approach compared to UMDA? The particular formulas suggested, compared to the ALI Principles? See generally Cynthia Lee Starnes, The Marriage Buyout: The Troubled Trajectory of U.S. Alimony Law 84-88 (2015); Charles P. Kindregan, Jr., Reforming Alimony: Massachusetts Reconsiders Postdivorce Spousal Support, 46 Suffolk U. L. Rev. 13 (2013).

***c. Epilogue to* Mani.** The New Jersey legislature amended the alimony statute after *Mani.* A 2009 change preserves the section allowing the court to consider all relevant factors, but expressly identifies some criminal behaviors that disqualify a former spouse from receiving alimony, such as murder, manslaughter, criminal homicide, or aggravated assault of a family member. Does this amendment codify the egregious fault exception recognized in *Mani*? Might other types of conduct still trigger this exception?

Amendments in 2014 follow several features of the Massachusetts Alimony Reform Act, while renaming "permanent alimony" as "open durational alimony"; stating that neither party has a greater entitlement than the other to maintain the marital standard of living; and providing that, for marriages less than 20 years' duration, "the total duration of alimony shall not, except in exceptional circumstances, exceed the length of the marriage." How do these reforms change the theory underlying New Jersey's alimony law?

d. Extending the partnership model. The human capital acquired by a spouse during marriage and the earnings to be generated therefrom after divorce constitute partnership resources, observes Professor Cynthia Starnes. She would reconceive alimony using a "buyout" approach under which the spouse with such collective marital resources must buy out the other spouse's interest. According to Starnes, although conventional alimony encourages dependence, an "exit price" would appropriately "protect the party who has not broken the marriage promise," while also reflecting the partnership analogy and normative visions of egalitarian marriage.[18] See also Jane Rutherford, Duty in Divorce: Shared Income as a Path to Equality, 58 Fordham L. Rev. 539, 578 (1990) (proposing "income sharing," under which the postmarital incomes of the former spouses would be added together and the total divided equally).

Under such proposals, does alimony become a "lifetime pension" at the level of the marital standard of living? What are the advantages of these partnership-based models over UMDA's approach? Over the Massachusetts statute? The disadvantages? Does Starnes's proposal, although gender neutral, operate like other feminist arguments for alimony, "moraliz[ing] women's work in the family" and further entrenching gendered divisions of family labor? See Philomila Tsoukala, Gary Becker, Legal Feminism, and the Costs of Moralizing Care, 16 Colum. J. Gender & L. 357, 362 (2007) (showing insights that feminists can gain from applying economic analysis to the family).

9. Alimony, class, and race. Despite the statutory standards, attempts to maintain the marital standard of living in two postdivorce households usually prove unrealistic. Studies find that income should increase by at least 30 percent for individuals to maintain the same standard of living after dissolution compared with that enjoyed during marriage. E.g., Liana C. Sayer, Economic Aspects of Divorce and Relationship Dissolution, in Handbook of Divorce and Relationship Dissolution 385, 389 (Mark A. Fine & John H. Harvey, eds., 2006).

Critics have long contended that the quest for a modern theory of alimony not only reveals class-based divisions but also rests on stereotypes (that is, an

---

[18]. Cynthia Lee Starnes, The Marriage Buyout: The Troubled Trajectory of U.S. Alimony Law 27, 135, 157-161 (2014).

economically powerful husband and a wife who has chosen to give priority to her family over her career) that exclude many African-American marriages. See Twila L. Perry, Alimony: Race, Privilege, and Dependency in the Search for Theory, 82 Geo. L.J. 2481, 2493 (1994). For example, Professor Regina Austin points to both evidence that in "some segments of the heterosexual black population, saving and asset accumulation are gender roles assigned to women" and anecdotes that "men [are] the chief cause of black women's asset poverty."[19]

Problem

Brian, a 48-year-old commercial pilot, and Ruth, a 47-year-old schoolteacher, divorce after 27 years of marriage. They have no children. Brian's annual salary is $75,000; Ruth's is $43,000. The trial court divides the marital property equally and awards Ruth half the difference in their incomes for two years to enable her to obtain additional university credits. All alimony will cease at the end of the two-year period. Ruth appeals, asking for a higher monthly award and alimony for at least 12 years. She claims that even a doctorate degree would not significantly increase her income as a teacher, and Brian will continue to have much greater income than she can ever expect. Brian also appeals, arguing that Ruth does not need support and she never expressed interest in additional education before divorce. What result under UMDA and why? Under the Massachusetts statute? Under a "buyout" or "income-sharing" approach? See Gardner v. Gardner, 881 P.2d 645 (Nev. 1994).

D. "Winding up" a Marriage: Applying Theories of Property and Support

1. A Case Study

Despite different theoretical bases, courts typically confront property and support questions together, along with related questions such as attorneys' fees, tax liability, and pension rights. The following case presents one specific factual context in which to analyze the application of the theories explored above while illustrating the interconnections among all of dissolution's financial incidents. What result would be fair? Which approach of those canvassed above would most likely achieve it?

[19]. Regina Austin, Nest Eggs and Stormy Weather: Law, Culture, and Black Women's Lack of Wealth, in Feminism Confronts Homo Economicus 131, 139 (Martha Albertson Fineman & Terence Dougherty eds., 2005).

WOLFE v. WOLFE

273 P.3d 915 (Or. Ct. App. 2012)

HASELTON, P.J. . . .

[H]usband [age 63] and wife [age 60] met in 1974 while husband was completing his [ophthalmology] internship and wife, who was a nurse practitioner, was working at the same hospital. After the parties married in 1975, husband completed his residency and fellowships, one of which took them to London for a little over a year. [T]hey moved to Corvallis, where they lived until they separated in 2006.

[H]usband worked for a clinic in Corvallis, and wife worked as a nurse practitioner for the county health department. In 1980, the parties purchased a farm, and, in 1982, about the time that their daughter was born, they moved into the home that they had recently built there. Although wife planned to continue working in her profession, by the time that the parties' son was born in 1983, she chose to be a homemaker rather than to continue working as a nurse practitioner. [I]n addition to her homemaking responsibilities, wife also managed the parties' farm, which was set up as a business so that they could contribute to an individual retirement account for wife.

Wife [took steps to reenter] the workforce in 1991. However, when husband decided to leave the clinic and open his own medical practice, wife became directly involved in its operation [handling the bookkeeping, training and supervising employees, interacting with the community, and serving as a substitute when an employee missed work. Wife also upholstered furniture, volunteered in the children's school, carpooled, did volunteer work to network and attract patients to husband's medical practice, and oversaw the livestock and other aspects of the 78-acre farm].

Despite wife's significant contributions to the ophthalmology practice, for many years, she did not draw a salary in order to, as husband noted, "better [their] tax situation." Specifically, husband explained that, on the advice of the parties' accountant, wife did not draw a salary so that the parties would not have to pay Social Security and Medicare taxes related to her work in the practice. That arrangement, in turn, maximized the amount of husband's earnings that were ultimately deposited into joint accounts and used for family purposes. In other words, husband's earnings effectively included wife's compensation for her contributions to the ophthalmology practice. [After the parties separated, husband could not do all the work performed by wife, so he sold the practice to another physician, for whom he continued working part time,] earning approximately $11,000 per month, and wife was employed part time as a bookkeeper, earning approximately $2,300 per month. However, wife planned to retire in the near future, and husband planned to retire within a couple of years.

[T]he parties had a very comfortable, but not overly extravagant, standard of living during the marriage. Husband noted that he and wife "really never talked about money." As wife explained, "[m]oney wasn't a problem" and she could make "[a]ny purchases that [she] want[ed]." In fact, through their efforts, the parties acquired assets—including real property and retirement and investment accounts—worth approximately $5 million at the time of trial.

[In addition to the income generated by the medical practice and the parties' joint investments,] husband had other assets [called here the "disputed property"] that he would periodically use to supplement that income. . . . In particular, [husband's grandfather died when husband was a child, leaving] certain stocks, bonds, and real property to husband's father to hold in trust for the use and benefit of husband and his two siblings. Husband's father managed the property held in the testamentary trust, and, at some point, placed husband's earnings in an investment account [at Smith Barney and UBS] in husband's name. . . . At the time of the parties' marriage in 1975, husband "knew that there was some family money there" (i.e., in the testamentary trust) but he did not know the extent of that money. Moreover, before the marriage, husband and wife had not discussed their individual financial interests, generally, or the value of husband's interest in the testamentary trust, specifically. . . .

The disputed property—that is, the . . . trust and the Smith Barney and UBS accounts—was essentially managed by third parties [including husband's father and financial advisors]. Earnings from the disputed property were reinvested. Significantly, none of the parties' earned income was ever invested in the disputed property. To the extent that the disputed property appreciated in value during the marriage, that appreciation was passive and did not result through the efforts—either direct or otherwise—of husband or wife.

During the marriage, husband periodically used funds from what he referred to as his "separate money"—which included the Smith Barney account—to supplement the parties' earned income. Most substantially, husband used that money to (1) help finance the acquisition of the parties' farm and the construction of their home; (2) annually make maximum contributions to both parties' individual retirement accounts; and (3) pay for some incidental vacation expenses. Husband's use of those funds within his control occurred in an overarching context in which the parties generally made financial decisions together based on what was in the best interests of their family

. . . For example, a few years after the parties married, husband decided that he no longer needed life insurance because, if he had died, his wife and children would have received the benefit of all of his assets—including the disputed property. [Thanks to the disputed property, husband always could make maximal contributions to his retirement fund.]

It was against that historic and financial backdrop that the parties framed their respective positions concerning the division of property and spousal support to the trial court. . . . [W]ife contended that (1) husband's interest in the disputed property was a marital asset; (2) husband had not rebutted the presumption of equal contribution with regard to that property in light of wife's contributions to the ophthalmology practice and as a homemaker; and (3) in all events, a just and equitable division "dictates that the parties in this case leave the marriage on equal footing." Wife also requested spousal support—the amount of which would "depend on the court's determination of how the assets are to be divided."

Conversely, husband contended that the disputed property was a premarital asset because it originated from the devise from his grandfather in the 1950s. Alternatively, husband contended that, to the extent that a portion of the disputed property was a marital asset, he had rebutted the presumption of equal contribution by demonstrating that the disputed property was managed by third parties and that any appreciation was essentially passive. In all events, husband contended that it was just and equitable to award him the $10.3 million in disputed assets [and that a spousal support] award was unnecessary because the property division, without reference to the disputed property, would generate sufficient income to enable wife to be economically self-sufficient and to enjoy a standard of living not overly disproportionate to the one that the parties enjoyed during the marriage.

[T]he trial court awarded wife approximately $2.6 million in assets, and awarded husband approximately $2.4 million in assets [as a just and equitable division]. Further, the trial court awarded husband the disputed property valued at $10.3 million as his separate property. . . . With regard to spousal support, the trial court determined that wife was entitled to support until she reached full retirement age. For that reason, the court awarded wife maintenance support of $2,000 per month for two years, followed by $1,000 per month for three years thereafter. Finally, over wife's objection, the trial court determined that each party was responsible for his or her respective attorney fees and costs and disbursements. . . .

On appeal, wife [contends]: (1) The trial court erred in awarding the $10.3 million in disputed assets to husband. (2) The trial court erred in the amount and duration of its award of maintenance spousal support, which, wife contends, should be increased to $10,000 per month indefinitely. And (3) the trial court erred in denying her request for attorney fees before reviewing it.

. . . Our resolution of [the first] matter is guided and circumscribed by ORS 107.105(1)(f) (2007) [which] provided, in part: . . .

> "(f) For the division or other disposition between the parties of the real or personal property, or both, of either or both of the parties as may be just and proper in all the circumstances. . . . The court shall consider the contribution of a spouse as a homemaker as a contribution to the acquisition of marital assets. There is a rebuttable presumption that both spouses have contributed equally to the acquisition of property during the marriage, whether such property is jointly or separately held."

Under the statute, our initial inquiry is to determine when a disputed asset was acquired. [According to our precedents,]

> "[i]f the asset was acquired during the marriage, we apply the statutory presumption. . . . If the presumption of equal contribution is effectively rebutted, [then the court] considers only what is 'just and proper in all the circumstances,' including the proven contributions of the parties to the asset."

Accordingly, we begin by determining whether and to what extent husband's interest in the disputed property was acquired during the marriage—that is, whether and to what extent the disputed property is a "marital asset" to which the presumption of equal contribution applies. Although that inquiry is straightforward in many cases, it is not here. On this record—candidly—it is impossible to make that determination with any degree of precision. [W]e cannot ascertain the specific configuration or "mix" of devised property in which husband had an interest at any time after its original acquisition—including at the time of the parties' marriage in 1975—nor can we know the value of that property. Moreover, after the parties married, the configuration of property was continually evolving. . . .

Nevertheless, at least, it is patent that wife did not contribute to the initial devise of property to husband from his grandfather decades before the parties' marriage. Moreover, and in all events, to the extent that some portion of the disputed property is, doubtless, a marital asset, husband rebutted the presumption of equal contribution [on two bases.]

First, the earnings from the disputed property were reinvested, and none of the parties' earned income was deposited into the Smith Barney or UBS accounts. Under those circumstances, husband's entire interest in the disputed property at the time of trial is traceable to his premarital interest in the property. . . .

Second, to the extent that a portion of the disputed property is a marital asset—through either the acquisition of new property or appreciation—neither husband nor wife contributed to the acquisition of that property during the marriage. Instead, the disputed property was essentially managed by third parties, who reinvested the earnings. Under those circumstances, the acquisition of new property and the appreciation during the marriage occurred passively and independent of any contribution of either husband or wife.[14] . . .

Accordingly, husband has rebutted the presumption of equal contribution as to any portion of the disputed property that is a marital asset. [In apportioning it,] two equitable considerations—neither of which appears to have been considered by the trial court—guide our review of the just and proper distribution of the disputed property. First, we consider the "social and financial objectives of the dissolution." Second, we consider the extent to which husband has integrated his interest in the disputed property "into the common financial affairs of the marital partnership through commingling."

With respect to the first consideration, we have previously explained that, "in a long-term marriage, . . . 'the parties should separate on as equal a basis as possible.'" In re Marriage of Boyd, 203 P.3d 312 [(Or. Ct. App. 2009)]:

> "[w]hen couples enter marriage, they ordinarily commit themselves to an indefinite shared future of which shared finances are a part. Acquisitions are made, forgone, or replaced for the good of the family unit rather than for the financial interests of either spouse. Property is bought, sold, enhanced, diminished, intermixed and used without regard to ease of division upon termination of the marriage."

In fact, this long-term marriage was marked by the dynamic contemplated in *Boyd*.

With respect to the second consideration, as previously indicated, the parties generally made financial decisions together based on what was in the best interest of their family as a whole. For example [wife did not draw a salary and husband did not buy life insurance]. On balance, . . . it is just and proper for wife to receive a portion of those assets. In reaching a contrary determination, the trial court appears to have focused only on the fact that wife would achieve economic self-sufficiency without sharing in the disputed property. However, in a case such as this, in which the parties have more than ample assets, economic self-sufficiency is not the dispositive factor in the equitable calculus. . . .

---

14. Wife emphasizes that, during the marriage, she was the primary caretaker of the parties' two children, contributed to the family's earned income, and gave uncompensated time to managing husband's ophthalmology practice. However, she does not explain how or why those contributions—either directly or indirectly—somehow contributed to the portion of the disputed property that is a marital asset, particularly where the property was essentially managed by third parties.

[I]t is just and proper for wife to receive an additional $2 million in property. In the end, wife will leave the marriage with approximately $4.6 million in assets, and husband will leave the marriage with $10.7 million in assets. In order to effectuate that award, we will not disturb any portion of the trial court's property division other than to award wife an equalizing judgment in the amount of $2 million.

. . . On appeal, wife contends that, if she is not awarded half of the disputed property, she is entitled to $10,000 per month in indefinite maintenance support in light of the substantial income that husband's investment property will generate. We disagree.

"The loadstar of a court's charge is to make a spousal support award that is 'just and equitable,' ORS 107.105(1)(d), and the ultimate decision concerning the amount and duration of a maintenance spousal support award is a discretionary one." ORS 107.105(1)(d)(C) (2007) identified a nonexclusive list of factors that a court should consider in awarding maintenance support [including marriage duration; the parties' ages; their health; the marital standard of living; their relative income and earning capacity; their training, employments skills, and financial needs and resources; and other factors deemed just and equitable].

"[T]he primary goal of spousal support in a long-term marriage such as this is to provide a standard of living roughly comparable to the one enjoyed during the marriage." [*Boyd,* supra.] [W]ife will receive assets that will generate income sufficient to allow her to enjoy a standard of living that is not overly disproportionate to the one that the parties enjoyed during the marriage. Accordingly, we reject wife's contentions but otherwise affirm the trial court's spousal support award.

. . . Because we have significantly modified the trial court's property division, we vacate the trial court's decision concerning attorney fees and remand for reconsideration on that issue. . . .

Notes and Questions

1. Interwoven analysis. Questions of property division and spousal support typically arise together in divorce litigation, as *Wolfe* illustrates. See, e.g., Gershman v. Gershman, 943 A.2d 1091, 1097 (Conn. 2008) (financial orders resemble a "mosaic" with "carefully interwoven" components). See also Russell v. Russell, 430 S.W.3d 15, 20 (Ark. 2013) (describing property award and alimony as "complementary devices").

The analysis generally addresses property first, considering the following questions: "1. Is it in fact 'property' (the identification question)? 2. Is it marital or nonmarital (the characterization question)? 3. How much is it worth (the valuation question)? 4. How much of it does each spouse get (the distribution question)?"[20]

2. Classifying property. On the "characterization question," *Wolfe* presents the common situation of separate property brought into the marriage by one

[20]. Robert J. Levy, An Introduction to Divorce-Property Issues, 23 Fam. L.Q. 147, 147 (1989).

spouse that increases in value during the marriage. Why does the *Wolfe* court find "ascertain[ing] the specific configuration" of the "disputed property" so difficult? In the face of this difficulty, how does the court classify the disputed property—as marital asset, separate property, or some of each? On what rationale? In particular, how does the court treat the portion of the disputed property that represents appreciation of the original assets? Consider the extent to which *Wolfe* implemented any of the following approaches—tracing, marital efforts, and recharacterization.

a. Tracing. Most community property jurisdictions classify as separate property appreciation and income from separate property. This approach, the "American rule," traces existing assets to their source: Assets traceable to separate property are treated as separate property, while those traceable to marital funds are treated as marital. (The minority approach, the "Spanish rule," treats as community property any income generated during marriage, even income from separate property.)

b. Marital efforts. Equitable distribution states often treat income or appreciation from separate property as marital based on "marital efforts" or the active role of either spouse. E.g., Hedges v. Pitcher, 942 A.2d 1217 (Me. 2008); Baker v. Baker, 753 N.W.2d 644 (Minn. 2008). The classification of income or appreciation from separate property proves particularly important when a breadwinner spouse works in a family or other closely held business and can decide what portion of the business earnings to take as salary (marital property) and what portion to retain or reinvest in the company. See, e.g., Joynt v. Joynt, 874 N.E.2d 916 (Ill. App. Ct. 2007).

c. Recharacterization. Recall the gradual recharacterization of separate property in the ALI Principles. To what extent does the couple's own treatment of the "disputed property" in *Wolfe* mirror the ALI's rationale for recharacterization (discussed supra)? How far does the court go in embracing this rationale? What role should the parties' intent play? See Beals v. Beals, 303 P.3d 453, 460 (Alaska 2013) (emphasizing parties' intent).

3. Equitable distribution. After valuing the assets, which often requires expert testimony, the court must distribute the property to be divided. Should each spouse's contribution determine the allocation? Oregon has a presumption of equal contribution to marital assets. In *Wolfe,* how did husband rebut this presumption? How did the court decide that awarding wife an additional $2 million would be "just and proper"? What standards guide judicial discretion under standards like Oregon's or UMDA §307, supra? What role did wife's homemaking contributions play? Her own earnings? The "two equitable considerations" emphasized by the court? See generally Katharine B. Silbaugh, Money as Emotion in the Distribution of Wealth at Divorce, in Reconceiving the Family: Critique on the American Law Institute's Principles of the Law of Family Dissolution 234 (Robin Fretwell Wilson, ed., 2006).

On what rationale might the wife in *Wolfe* have merited *more* than roughly half the marital property? See, e.g., Cartee v. Cartee, 239 P.3d 707 (Alaska 2010) (affirming award of 60 percent to a wife who shouldered childrearing and forwent career opportunities).

What role should the reason for the marriage breakdown (or "fault") play in equitable property distribution? How much, in terms of property, should either spouse's adultery be worth? Substance abuse? Suppose that such factors were present in *Wolfe*. How might they change the analysis and outcome?

4. Support.

a. Amount. Why does the support award in *Wolfe* depend on the allocation of property? How does the court arrive at a support award that is "just and equitable"? Which of the following purposes does the support award serve? "Spousal maintenance has multiple purposes, including 'to correct the . . . inequality of income resulting from the divorce,' 'to equalize the standard of living of the parties for an appropriate period of time,' 'to assist the recipient-spouse in becoming self-supporting,' and 'to compensate a homemaker for contributions to family well-being not otherwise recognized in the property distribution.'" Gravel v. Gravel, 980 A.2d 242, 250 (Vt. 2009).

b. Duration. On what basis does the court affirm the trial court's decision to end maintenance after five years? When should courts award indefinite support, as the wife in *Wolfe* requested? Today, compared to the recent past, scholars discern "a greater willingness to award indefinite term alimony when parties are divorcing after a marriage of long duration, the parties' incomes are quite different, and the recipients cannot realistically be retrained."[21] How would this aspect of *Wolfe* be decided under the Massachusetts statute, supra?

5. Law and economics. In economic analysis, legal rules operate as incentives that influence choices. Thus, the legal rules of divorce might affect future behavior by shaping the expectations and behaviors of those entering marriage. Do you agree with Professor Herma Hill Kay that "[a] nonpunitive, nonsexist, and nonpaternalistic framework for marriage dissolution, then, should begin with recommendations that encourage sharing behavior during marriage without penalizing such behavior at divorce"?[22] What does that mean in practice? Does the outcome in *Wolfe* achieve such objectives?

Do approaches that acknowledge and compensate women's loss upon divorce encourage women to specialize in domestic matters, "ratify[ing] existing gender inequalities" and "increasing women's economic dependence on their husbands"?[23] But see Deborah A. Widiss, Changing the Marriage Equation, 89 Wash. U. L. Rev. 721, 757 (2012) (noting "compelling reasons" for better protection of dependent spouse, given how marriage continues to encourage specialization in gendered breadwinning versus caretaking roles).

6. Attorneys' fees and costs. Courts often require one spouse to pay the other's attorneys' fees and litigation costs, the issue remanded in *Wolfe*.

---

[21]. J. Thomas Oldham, Changes in the Economic Consequences of Divorces, 1958-2008, 42 Fam. L.Q. 419, 432 (2008).

[22]. Herma Hill Kay, Beyond No-Fault: New Directions in Divorce Reform, in Divorce Reform at the Crossroads, supra note [16], at 6, 31.

[23]. June R. Carbone, Economics, Feminism, and the Reinvention of Alimony: A Reply to Ira Ellman, 43 Vand. L. Rev. 1463, 1464-1465 (1990).

Historically, a gender-based rule premised on the duty to provide necessaries prevailed. Today, many jurisdictions impose the responsibility for fees on the spouse in the superior financial position, treating the award as an additional distribution of property or a species of spousal support and reflecting a balance of the equities. When the spouses occupy similar financial positions, they pay their own fees and costs. Cf. Tedder v. Gardner Aldrich, 421 S.W.3d 651, 655-656 (Tex. 2013) (imposing liability only when one spouse incurs the debt as the other's agent or the debt is for necessaries and rejecting "necessaries" classification for legal fees).

The appropriate *amount* of fees often generates dispute, given the emotional climate of divorce proceedings. Most jurisdictions disallow contingent fees in divorce litigation because (a) lawyers should not have financial incentives to discourage reconciliation and (b) such arrangements are not typically necessary for securing counsel in divorce cases. See Restatement (Third) of the Law Governing Lawyers §35 cmt. g (2000) (rejecting the prohibition when such policies are inapplicable).

Problem

Deborah and Dennis divorce after 15 years of marriage and no children. During the marriage, the couple relocated to different parts of the country several times because of Deborah's employment with a large corporation, which frequently promoted her. For five years of the marriage, Dennis, who had a master's degree in journalism, found work in the various cities in which they lived. Thereafter, pursuant to the couple's agreement, he stayed home to write fiction and perform the domestic tasks. None of his writing was accepted for publication, however, and evidence shows that Dennis's domestic habits were "lax." Under a statute identical to UMDA §307 and §308 (both reprinted supra), the trial court awards Deborah 75 percent of the marital property and Dennis 25 percent; further, it denies the maintenance that Dennis requested to pursue additional training so that he can succeed as a journalist. Dennis appeals both the property division and support denial, seeking more property and rehabilitative maintenance. What result and why? See Michael v. Michael, 791 S.W.2d 772 (Mo. Ct. App. 1990). Would your analysis change if the couple had a child? Suppose that, in this scenario, Deborah argues that Dennis's care for their child did not impede his career because Dennis chose to stay home while the parties could have afforded childcare. See Cartee v. Cartee, 239 P.3d 707 (Alaska 2010).

2. Special Problems in Achieving a Fair Dissolution

With courts attempting to divide property "equitably" and to award "just" support, general considerations of fairness often overshadow theoretical distinctions between the two remedies. Given the practice of blurring these lines, what difference does it make whether a particular payment represents property or support? Will the purpose of the payment as property distribution or support always be clear? The following scenarios highlight such difficulties.

a. Changing Circumstances

PAUL v. PAUL

60 A.3d 1080 (Del. 2012)

BERGER, Justice. . . .

In this appeal, we consider the meaning of the term "regularly residing" as used in Delaware's alimony statute. . . . Joseph and Shannon Paul (Husband and Wife) were divorced in 2006. The parties entered into a divorce agreement, which provided that alimony shall terminate upon "cohabitation of Wife as that term is defined in [the alimony statute]." At some time prior to 2010, Wife became romantically involved with Fletcher Vance. As a result, Husband hired an investigator to conduct surveillance for the purpose of determining whether Wife was cohabiting with Vance. Based on the investigator's report, which spanned 9 months, Husband filed a petition to terminate alimony.

At the hearing, [the] private investigator testified that over a period of about five months, he saw Vance's car at Wife's house 25 of the 37 days that he observed. The car was there late at night and early the next morning. In addition, [the investigator] observed Vance "[retrieving] the paper, taking the trash out, feeding the cat, opening the garage door (which he knew the code to), and watering plants, all on multiple occasions." He also saw Vance doing yard work and escorting a painter into the house.

Wife testified that she and Vance have an exclusive relationship and that he stays at her house about two to four nights a week. They go out for dinner and dancing, and take vacations together, but they share expenses. Wife testified that she could not live with Vance because he is neat and she is messy. She said that he keeps no clothing or personal effects at her house. Vance explained that he needs to feel independent and that maintaining his own home serves that purpose. In addition, he is emotionally attached to his home because it preserves memories of his late wife.

The Family Court held that Husband failed to establish that Wife permanently or continuously resides with Vance. The court . . . stated that the "term reside . . . excludes a couple who maintains separate and independent dwelling places." . . . The alimony statute provides, in relevant part:

> [T]he obligation to pay future alimony is terminated upon the death of either party or the remarriage or cohabitation of the party receiving alimony. As used in this section, "cohabitation" means regularly residing with an adult . . . if the parties hold themselves out as a couple, and regardless of whether the relationship confers a financial benefit on the party receiving alimony. Proof of sexual relations is admissible but not required to prove cohabitation. . . . [13 Del. C. §1512(g).]

Wife concedes that she and Vance have an exclusive relationship and hold themselves out as a couple. The remaining question is whether they are "regularly residing" together.

[The trial court] attempted to identify factors or "themes" that tend to prove or disprove the "regularly residing" requirement of cohabitation. It found that the most significant factor is the amount of non-working time the couple spends together. Another related factor is the extent to which the two people maintain independent lives, which includes both their daily activities and whether they keep separate residences.

. . . The trial court used the dictionary definition of "reside," which means "to dwell permanently or continuously. . . ." But the alimony statute includes the modifier, "regularly," which means "usually or ordinarily." Thus, the term "regularly residing" does not mean "residing." It means usually residing or, stated another way, "living together with some degree of continuity."

Perhaps because the Family Court used the wrong definition of "regularly residing," it also placed undue emphasis on factors that are not very significant. The court noted that Wife and Vance have unlimited free time because they are retired, but they pursue different hobbies during the day. The implicit premise is that married retired couples spend most of their time together. There is no evidence, however, to support that premise. Thus, their daytime activities have little relevance to the issue of whether they live together with some degree of continuity.

The . . . Family Court stated that, "[e]very . . . definition of the term reside . . . excludes a couple who maintains separate and independent dwelling places." That is incorrect. It is settled law that a person may have more than one residence at the same time. The fact that a couple maintains two residences is less important than the extent to which they are involved in the normal activities associated with home ownership. The Family Court found that Vance behaves like someone who lives at Wife's home. He has a key to Wife's house, takes out the garbage, does yard work, and showed a painter around the house.

In sum, we conclude that the Family Court evaluated the evidence against the wrong standard. Under the correct definition of "regularly residing," several of the factors that the trial court found important have little or no relevance. This matter must be remanded for the Family Court to address the petition to terminate alimony in accordance with this opinion. . . .

Notes and Questions

1. **Final versus modifiable?** Distributions of property upon divorce are final, even if the parties' circumstances change significantly after dissolution. By contrast, support awards typically allow modification. For example, UMDA provides that support is modifiable on "a showing of changed circumstances so substantial and continuing as to make the terms unconscionable" and that the obligation to pay future maintenance terminates upon the recipient's remarriage or the death of either party, absent agreement. UMDA §316. See also UMDA §307, supra. Which theories of property division and support awards best explain the finality of the former and the modifiability of the latter? Awards of "property in lieu of alimony" and lump-sum alimony challenge these bright-line distinctions. See McAllister v. McAllister, 21 A.3d 1010 (Me. 2011); Averitte v. Averitte, 2013 WL 357602 (Tenn. Ct. App. 2013).

2. **Automatic termination.** Some states have statutes like UMDA, automatically terminating maintenance upon the recipient's remarriage, absent a contrary agreement. E.g., Minn. Stat. Ann. §518A.39 subd. 3. What rationale supports this

rule? Is it *always* "unreasonable for a dependent spouse to receive financial support from a former spouse and a present spouse at the same time"? See Amundson v. Amundson, 645 N.W.2d 837, 839 (S.D. 2002). Why? Does the rule reflect outmoded understandings of marriage? See, e.g., Cynthia Lee Starnes, The Marriage Buyout: The Troubled Trajectory of U.S. Alimony Law 113-126 (2014). Or should remarriage be viewed as a path to "self-sufficiency" under the conceptualization of alimony as a transitional remedy? See Mavis Maclean, Surviving Divorce 69, 75-77 (1991) (so arguing).

3. Discretionary termination. In some states, remarriage will terminate maintenance only when it produces a substantial change in economic circumstances. E.g., In re Marriage of Tilson, 317 P.3d 391 (Or. Ct. App. 2013) (also noting that continued award must be just and equitable). Should the test be whether the new marriage allows continuation of the standard of living enjoyed during the earlier marriage? How does the type of maintenance or alimony award (e.g., reimbursement alimony) affect the analysis? See Starnes, supra, at 115-116.

4. Cohabitation. Should cohabitation and remarriage be equated for modification purposes? Compare Charette v. Charette, 60 A.3d 1264 (Me. 2013), with Hirtzinger v. Hirtzinger, 2014 WL 4267484 (Ohio Ct. App. 2014). What constitutes cohabitation? Is a sexual relationship necessary? See In re Raybeck, 44 A.3d 551 (N.H. 2012). Sufficient? See Murphy v. Murphy, 2013 WL 5927542 (Fla. Dist. Ct. App. 2013) (noting required "supportive relationship"). What other factors are relevant? See Coggins v. Coggins, 132 So. 3d 636, 644 (Miss. Ct. App. 2014) (absence of evidence that obligee is "avoiding marriage to continue alimony"); Reese v. Weis, 66 A.3d 157 (N.J. Super. Ct. App. Div. 2013) (lifestyle enhancements). What evidence of such relationships is admissible? See In re Marriage of Miller, 2015 WL 3444341 (Ill. App. Ct. 2015) (admitting obligee's Facebook posts). To what extent does scrutiny of such relationships violate the obligee's privacy?

On what basis does *Paul* find "cohabitation"? How does it interpret "regularly residing"? To what extent is *Paul* recognizing the emerging phenomenon of LATs—that is, couples who "live apart together"?[24]

5. Other changed circumstances. When should changes in the *obligor's* circumstances warrant reduction or termination of spousal support? For example, what should be the impact of an injury that prevents a professional golfer from continuing to earn income from competitions? See Delsing v. Delsing, 409 S.W.3d 574 (Mo. Ct. App. 2013). When should an *increase* in the obligor's income justify an upward modification? Why? See Dan v. Dan, 105 A.3d 118 (Conn. 2014). What sort of changes in the *obligee's* circumstances might justify an *upward* modification?

6. Burdens and default rules. Note that the type of alimony might well determine which party has the burden of showing changed circumstances. After an award of short-term rehabilitative maintenance, an obligee who does not achieve self-sufficiency must show changed circumstances in order to extend postdissolution support. By contrast, an award of permanent alimony will continue until the

---

[24]. See Charles Q. Strohm et al., "Living Apart Together" Relationships in the United States, 21 Demographic Res. 177 (2009).

obligor carries the burden of showing changed circumstances. Even when no alimony is warranted, some courts award a nominal amount, to preserve a basis for later modification.

Problem

One catalyst for the Massachusetts Alimony Reform Act of 2011, supra, was controversial case law refusing to recognize a presumption that alimony should terminate when the obligor reaches full retirement age. E.g., Pierce v. Pierce, 916 N.E.2d 330 (Mass. 2009). The statute now states as follows:

> (f) Once issued, general term alimony orders shall terminate upon the payor attaining the full retirement age. The payor's ability to work beyond the full retirement age shall not be a reason to extend alimony, provided that:
>
> (1) When the court enters an initial alimony judgment, the court may set a different alimony termination date for good cause shown; provided, however, that in granting deviation, the court shall enter written findings of the reasons for deviation.
>
> (2) The court may grant a recipient an extension of an existing alimony order for good cause shown; provided, however, that in granting an extension, the court shall enter written findings of:
>
> (i) a material change of circumstance that occurred after entry of the alimony judgment; and
>
> (ii) reasons for the extension that are supported by clear and convincing evidence.

Mass. Gen. Laws chap. 208, §49(f). You serve as an aide to a law reform commission established in another state, which has a law like UMDA §316, supra, allowing termination or modification upon a showing of changed circumstances. Would you support a statutory amendment to address the obligor's retirement specifically? Why? If so, would you support the language in the Massachusetts provision? What other approaches should the commission consider? See In re Marriage of Gust, 858 N.W.2d 402 (Iowa 2015).

b. Bankruptcy

HOWARD v. HOWARD

336 S.W.3d 433 (Ky. 2011)

MINTON, C.J. . . .

[In dissolving the marriage of Roy Shane Howard and Sondra Howard, the trial court divided the parties' marital property and marital debts, assigning to Shane liability for a National City loan on the parties' Dodge Durango, which was repossessed by the time of the divorce decree; Shane was also ordered to pay child support. Shortly thereafter, in a separate proceeding, Shane successfully filed in federal court a bankruptcy petition for a Chapter 7 discharge of his debts; Sondra, who received notice of the bankruptcy proceeding, did nothing.

[Shane then returned to state court, seeking to reduce his child support obligation, claiming health problems, inability to find correctional work (based on his prior job as a prison guard), and the bankruptcy discharge he received after entry of the divorce decree. In this modification proceeding, Sondra successfully moved to have Shane held in contempt of court for failure to pay the debt on the repossessed Durango, for which she had been subjected to collection efforts by the creditor. Shane appealed, citing his bankruptcy discharge. The state Court of Appeals affirmed the contempt finding, reasoning that Shane had an obligation to pay the Durango debt under the divorce decree based on the Bankruptcy Abuse Prevention and Consumer Protection Act (BAPCPA).] The Court of Appeals noted that this statute had been amended, effective in 2005, to provide that discharge under Chapter 7 does not discharge the debtor from any debt "to a spouse, former spouse, or child" for something other than a "domestic support obligation" (*i.e.*, child support or maintenance) that "is incurred by the debtor in the course of a divorce or separation or in connection with a separation agreement, divorce decree, or other order of a court of record, or a determination made in accordance with State or territorial law by a governmental unit." [Shane appeals to this court.]

As the Court of Appeals states, obviously Shane had an obligation to pay the Durango debt under the divorce decree. But the tricky question is whether this was a debt to his former spouse that would not be subject to discharge under the post-BAPCPA version of 11 U.S.C. §523(a)(15). Obviously, Shane was not required to make a direct payment to Sondra under the relevant divorce decree provision, which simply stated that he was responsible for making payments to the creditor. [The court summarizes earlier versions of the federal statute before the BAPCPA amendments, including procedural requirements.]

Following the BAPCPA amendments, 11 U.S.C. §523(a)(5) recognized an exception to discharge for debts "for a domestic support obligation" without explicitly requiring that such debts be to a spouse, former spouse, or child.[25] On the other hand, 11 U.S.C. §523(a)(15) was amended to add language requiring that other divorce-related debts be "to a spouse, former spouse, or child of the debtor" to be excepted from discharge.[26] 11 U.S.C. §523(a)(15) was also amended to delete the former language that allowed for discharge if the debtor was not reasonably able to pay the debt and the benefits to the debtor outweighed the detriment to the other person(s) affected.

[Under BAPCPA, if] the obligation to make payments on the bank loan on the repossessed Durango meets the requirements of 11 U.S.C. §523(a)(15) as a debt to Sondra under the divorce decree, then Sondra is correct that she was not required to file anything in bankruptcy court in order later to obtain enforcement of Shane's obligation to her under the divorce decree in state court. We conclude that the obligation does meet the requirements of 11 U.S.C. §523(a)(15) and that

25. 11 U.S.C. §523(a)(5) (2007) states that a Chapter 7 discharge does not discharge the debtor for a debt "for a domestic support obligation." 11 U.S.C. §101(14A)(B) (2007) defines a *domestic support obligation* as one "in the nature of alimony, maintenance or support. . . ."

26. 11 U.S.C. § 523(a)(15) (2007) (stating that a Chapter 7 discharge does not discharge the debtor for a debt "to a spouse, former spouse, or child of the debtor and not of the kind described in paragraph 5 that is incurred by the debtor in the course of a divorce or separation or in connection with a separation agreement, divorce decree or other of a court of record, or a determination made in accordance with State or territorial law by a governmental unit.").

Sondra was not required to file anything in bankruptcy court regarding Shane's Chapter 7 filing in order to preserve her right to enforcement in state court of Shane's obligation to her under the divorce decree. . . .

Actually, in the divorce decree provision incorporating the parties' agreement that Shane would make the payments on the bank loan on the repossessed Durango, "two distinct obligations" are at issue. Naturally, there is an underlying marital debt on the bank loan on the repossessed Durango. But the divorce decree also establishes a separate obligation to Sondra that Shane make payments on this loan as part of the division of marital property and debts even though there is no hold harmless provision. . . .

While the debtor's obligation on an underlying debt to a third-party creditor may be discharged because that underlying debt was not *to a spouse or former spouse or child*, the weight of authority holds that a separate, otherwise enforceable, obligation to one's present or former spouse under a separation agreement or a divorce decree to make payments on third-party debt is not dischargeable in Chapter 7 bankruptcy following the BAPCPA amendments. Our holding today is premised on the broad definition of debt encompassed within the bankruptcy statutes. This holding is especially clear in cases where the debtor-spouse has not only been ordered to, or agreed to, pay the debt, but has also been ordered to, or agreed to, hold the other spouse harmless or indemnify the other spouse.

When one spouse's obligation to make payments on third-party debt under a separation agreement or divorce decree is not accompanied by a hold harmless or indemnification clause [as here], the law is perhaps somewhat less settled. But some courts have still recognized that even in the absence of an indemnification or hold harmless provision, the debtor spouse's divorce-related obligation to make payments on third party debt is not dischargeable. . . .

In view of the broad definition of debt under federal bankruptcy law and a Kentucky trial court's authority to use its contempt powers to enforce obligations under divorce decrees, we conclude that Shane's obligation to Sondra under the divorce decree for him to make payments on the bank loan debt on the repossessed Durango was not discharged in Chapter 7 bankruptcy. . . .

Notes and Questions

1. Background. Under the Bankruptcy Code, when an individual petitions for bankruptcy, the debtor's property becomes part of the bankrupt's "estate," 11 U.S.C. §541, distributed among creditors. To further bankruptcy's protective policy, the debtor may claim exemption for certain property (for example, a home or car). The Code also allows a debtor spouse to be discharged from certain obligations. The longstanding nondischargeability of spousal support obligations derives from judicial origin, but the rule was subsequently codified and extended to child support in 1903 amendments to the Bankruptcy Act of 1898.[25] By contrast, the debtor could discharge obligations based on property division. What reasons explain the different treatment?

[25]. Jana B. Singer, Divorce Obligations and Bankruptcy Discharge: Rethinking the Support/Property Distinction, 30 Harv. J. Legis. 43, 47, 53 (1993).

2. Bankruptcy reform. As *Howard* explains, the Bankruptcy Abuse Prevention and Consumer Protection Act of 2005 (BAPCPA), which now applies to Chapter 7 bankruptcies, makes nondischargeable a "domestic support obligation," such as maintenance and child support obligations. 11 U.S.C. §523(a)(5). In addition, the new statute makes nondischargeable other divorce- or separation-related obligations to a spouse, former spouse, or child—that is, those that are not "domestic support obligations" (see id. §523(a)(15))—thus eliminating the different treatment of support and property that had bedeviled judges. See, e.g., In re Taylor, 737 F.3d 670 (10th Cir. 2013) (statutory history and analysis).

On the other hand, the support/property classification continues to control dischargeability in Chapter 13 bankruptcies. Id. §1328(a)(2) (excepting from discharge §523(a)(5) obligations but not §523(a)(15) obligations). Chapter 13 bankruptcies provide for debt restructuring by wage earners, while Chapter 7 bankruptcies entail liquidation of "non-exempt equity for the benefit of nonsecured creditors."[26]

3. Policy. State and federal courts have concurrent jurisdiction to construe a discharge and determine whether it includes a particular debt. What is the proper balance between bankruptcy law's objective of a "fresh start" for debtors and the fair resolution of the financial incidents of divorce? Why does BAPCPA continue to allow discharge of property division obligations in Chapter 13 bankruptcies? When categorizing obligations, how does a bankruptcy judge discern whether a particular state divorce-court award constitutes spousal support or an allocation of property? Cases under both the new and old statutes reveal judicial efforts to enlarge the definition of "support" and "alimony" to thwart the debtor's attempted discharge. See, e.g., Quinn v. Quinn, 528 B.R. 203 (Bankr. D. Mass. 2015) (construing indemnification payments on second mortgage as nondischargeable "support," although parties waived alimony); Deichert v. Deichert, 587 A.2d 319 (Pa. Super. Ct. 1991) (classifying divorce award to wife of family residence and car as nondischargeable support in the form of shelter and transportation). To what extent does *Howard* illustrate this expansive approach? Does the court correctly interpret the statute? Should the same result follow if the divorce court had ordered one spouse, who later declared bankruptcy, to pay to the I.R.S. part of the federal income taxes owed by the other spouse? See In re Mason, 58 A.3d 1153 (N.H. 2012).

4. Other consequences of classification. Bankruptcy law makes distinguishing support and property distribution obligations important for several reasons. The automatic stay of proceedings triggered by a bankruptcy petition does not apply to the collection of domestic support obligations from property not in the bankrupt's estate; similarly, the stay does not apply to the commencement or continuation of proceedings for the establishment or modification of domestic support orders or marriage dissolution, except to the extent that the latter proceeding "seeks to determine the division of property that is property of the [bankrupt's] estate." 11

---

[26]. Shayna M. Steinfeld & Bruce R. Steinfeld, A Brief Overview of Bankruptcy and Alimony/Support Issues, 38 Fam. L.Q. 127, 128 (2004). Those using Chapter 7 must meet means-testing requirements. See, e.g., Charles J. Tabb & Jillian K. McClelland, Living with the Means Test, 31 S. Ill. U. L.J. 463 (2007). Indeed, these requirements for Chapter 7's "unconditional discharges" push more debtors to Chapter 13, which permits only "conditional discharges." See 11 U.S.C. §707. See generally Robert D. Berger, Bankruptcy & Divorce: A Marriage of Inconvenience, 83-FEB J. Kan. B.A. 30 (2014).

U.S.C. §362(b)(2)(A) & (B). Otherwise exempt property of the debtor is liable for domestic support obligations. Id. §522(c)(1). In addition, unsecured claims for domestic support obligations have first priority. Id. §507(a)(1)(A).

5. Bankruptcy and modification. To the extent the support/property classification remains significant, as in Chapter 13 bankruptcies, should discharge of the debtor spouse's property obligation permit the divorce court to increase a support award by the same amount? Or would such modification, in effect, change the division of property, a final award? See, e.g., Murphy v. Murphy, 759 N.W.2d 710, 718-719 (Neb. Ct. App. 2008).

6. Debtor's bad faith. Under earlier versions of the bankruptcy law, obligors sometimes "were able to craftily draft settlement agreements to be in property rather than alimony terms and then discharge their marital obligations in bankruptcy." In re Butler, 186 B.R. 371, 372-373 (Bankr. D. Vt. 1995). How far does BAPCPA go in addressing this problem? Does the debtor's bad-faith aim of frustrating the divorce decree justify dismissing the bankruptcy petition altogether? See In re Muth, 514 B.R. 719 (B.A.P. 10th Cir. 2014). If one spouse files for bankruptcy before the divorce decree and obtains a discharge from credit card debts, may the divorce court still allocate to this spouse a share of the debts incurred by the other spouse during the marriage? See Horvath v. Horvath, 2010 WL 338209 (Ohio Ct. App. 2010) (so holding).

7. Bankruptcy data. Bankruptcy and divorce often coincide, especially during a weak economy. The three most prevalent reasons for bankruptcies are job loss, family dissolution, and health problems.[27] During the first year under BAPCPA, 7 percent of those filing for bankruptcy protection were noncustodial parents with child support orders, according to the U.S. Government Accountability Office. These debtors represented about one-half of 1 percent of the 9.9 million noncustodial parents subject to child support orders.[28] Critics contend that BAPCPA continues the gendered pattern evident under its predecessors. See, e.g., Linda Coco, Visible Women: Locating Women in Financial Failure, Bankruptcy Law, and Bankruptcy Reform, 8 Charleston L. Rev. 191 (2013-2014).

NOTE: THE FAMILY HOME

Frequently, the family home is the most significant marital asset and becomes the focus of the court's effort to effect an equitable distribution of property. Yet this property often serves a support function for the dependent spouse and children.

When one spouse owns the home premaritally as separate property, the other spouse's contributions (financial or homemaking) to its preservation and appreciation can make the increased equity achieved during marriage a divisible asset. E.g., Beals v. Beals, 303 P.3d 453 (Alaska 2013). Rules requiring or favoring equal division of marital property often result in the sale of the family home. If the couple

---

[27]. Elizabeth Warren & Amelia Warren Tyagi, The Two-Income Trap: Why Middle-Class Mothers and Fathers Are Going Broke 81 (2003).

[28]. See GAO Highlights, Bankruptcy and Child Support Enforcement (Jan. 2008), http://www.gao.gov/highlights/d08100high.pdf.

has no asset of comparable value to allocate to the spouse not to be awarded the home, the home must be sold so the proceeds can be shared, to the disadvantage of children.[29] To remedy this problem, some states allow courts to award the family home, at least temporarily, to the custodial parent, treating use of the residence as a form of child support and reflecting reluctance to uproot the children. See, e.g., Cal. Fam. Code §3802; ALI Principles §§3.11, 4.09(3).

When the family home represents a liability (because of a large mortgage), the court can allocate responsibility for the debts in the distribution of property. Alternatively, monthly maintenance obligations can include mortgage payments on behalf of a former spouse. With the recent economic downturn and spike in home foreclosures (which peaked in 2010), however, neither spouse might be able to occupy the family home postdivorce. See, e.g., Lorna Fox, Repossessing "Home": A Re-Analysis of Gender, Homeownership and Debtor Default for Feminist Legal Theory, 14 Wm. & Mary J. Women & L. 423, 472 (2008).

c. Pensions and Employee Benefits

BENDER v. BENDER

785 A.2d 197 (Conn. 2001)

BORDEN, J.

The principal issue in this certified appeal is whether, in a dissolution action, unvested pension benefits are property subject to equitable distribution. . . . The plaintiff and the defendant, who were married in 1976, have four children, two of whom were minors at the time of trial. . . . The principal cause for the breakdown of the marriage was the fact that nearly all of the defendant's free time was spent in pursuits that did not include the plaintiff or their children, [his] at least one adulterous relationship [and] some violence on the part of the defendant. Despite the defendant's fairly good income, . . . the parties had acquired virtually no assets and no savings. Furthermore, nearly all of the parties' discretionary income had been expended on the defendant's personal pursuits.

. . . At the time of trial, the defendant had been employed as a firefighter by the city of Meriden for approximately nineteen years. The defendant is entitled to a pension as a firefighter in the event that he reaches twenty-five years of service. His pension, therefore, is unvested, except for purposes of disability. If the defendant were to leave the fire department before twenty-five years of service, other than for a disability, he would receive only his contributions made to the pension, which, at the time of trial, were valued at approximately $27,741.

[The trial court dissolved the marriage, awarded the plaintiff joint custody of the minor children, ordered the defendant to pay child support, issued certain orders of property distribution, and ordered the defendant to pay the plaintiff alimony of $200 per week.] Pursuant to [a] domestic relations order, the trial court ordered "that until such time, if any, as [the] defendant's right to receive retirement benefits from the city of Meriden vests, [the] plaintiff shall be the beneficiary of, and be entitled to receive, the refundable contributions, with accrued interest

[29]. Weitzman, supra note [4], at 384-387.

or yield thereon, if any, made by or on behalf of [the] defendant if such contributions, etc., shall ever become payable by the city of Meriden. And there is hereby entered a [domestic relations order] assigning to [the] plaintiff one-half of the disability and/or retirement benefits earned by [the defendant] from his employment by the city of Meriden for his labors for said city through the date of this decree. (The court is aware that [the] defendant's right to receive retirement benefits has not yet vested.) [The court made the alimony award modifiable downward in the event plaintiff actually began receiving payments pursuant to the domestic relations order. The defendant appealed.]

I

[Defendant claims] that his unvested pension benefits are not property subject to equitable distribution under §46b-81. The plaintiff claims, to the contrary, that the defendant's interest in his unvested pension benefits is not a mere expectancy, but rather, a presently existing property interest, and, therefore, his unvested pension benefits constitute property subject to equitable distribution. We agree with the plaintiff.

The threshold question of whether unvested pension benefits constitute "property" pursuant to §46b-81 presents a question of statutory interpretation. . . ." Neither §46b-81 nor any other closely related statute defines property or identifies the types of property interests that are subject to equitable distribution in dissolution proceedings. . . . Black's Law Dictionary (6th Ed. 1990) defines property as the term commonly used to denote everything which is the subject of ownership, corporeal or incorporeal, tangible or intangible, visible or invisible, real or personal; everything that has an exchangeable value or which goes to make up wealth or estate. It extends to every species of valuable right and interest, and includes real and personal property, easements, franchises, and incorporeal hereditaments. . . ."

[Although this is a case of first impression, in past cases, we] repeatedly have stated, and several recent decisions from this court reflect, that trial courts are empowered "to deal broadly with property and its equitable division incident to dissolution proceedings." . . . In Thompson v. Thompson, 438 A.2d 839 [(Conn. 1981), we considered evidence of the pension benefits but did not treat them as property to be divided.] We reasoned that "[p]ension benefits represent a form of deferred compensation for services rendered. In re Marriage of Brown, 544 P.2d 561 [(Cal. 1976)]. As such they are conceptually similar to wages. . . ."

In Krafick v. Krafick, [663 A.2d 365 (Conn. 1995),] we concluded that *vested* pension benefits constitute property for the purposes of equitable distribution pursuant to §46b-81. In doing so, we emphasized that a broad construction of the term "property" is consistent with the purpose of §46b-81, namely, "to recognize that marriage is, among other things, a shared enterprise or joint undertaking in the nature of a partnership to which both spouses contribute—directly and indirectly, financially and nonfinancially—*the fruits of which* are distributable at divorce." We also recognized, however, that . . . "§46b-81 applies only to presently existing property interests, not mere expectancies." We thereafter engaged in an analysis whereby we determined that the contingencies to which the vested pension benefits were subject did not render them a mere expectancy because the holder of the benefits had a presently existing interest by way of an enforceable contract right. [Our] cases reflect a common theme, namely, that in determining whether a certain interest is property subject to equitable distribution under §46b-81, we look to whether a party's expectation of a benefit attached to that interest was too speculative to constitute divisible marital property. . . .

In the present case, it is, of course, theoretically possible that the defendant's pension will not vest, whether because of the defendant's resignation, misconduct on his part that results in his dismissal, the defendant's death, or a decision on the part of the municipality to discontinue the pension plan. We conclude, however, that the defendant's expectation in his pension plan, as a practical matter, is sufficiently concrete, reasonable and justifiable as to constitute a presently existing property interest for equitable distribution purposes. Therefore, his unvested pension benefits are not too speculative to be considered property subject to equitable distribution under §46b-81. We believe that any uncertainty regarding vesting is more appropriately handled in the valuation and distribution stages, rather than in the classification stage.

Our conclusion that the defendant's unvested pension benefits are not a mere expectancy is consistent with the nature of retirement benefits, and the fact that employers and employees treat retirement benefits as property in the workplace. We previously have stated [in *Krafick*, supra] that "pension benefits represent a form of deferred compensation for services rendered" because an employee earning pension benefits presumably would receive higher current wages if he or she did not participate in the pension plan. . . .

Furthermore, the theme running through this area of our jurisprudence . . . pays mindful consideration to the equitable purpose of our statutory distribution scheme, rather than to mechanically applied rules of property law. . . . In view of that equitable purpose, the fact remains that nineteen of the twenty-five years necessary for the vesting of the defendant's pension benefits were years in which the parties were partners in marriage. We recognize that retirement benefits, whether vested or unvested, are significant marital assets, and may be, as in the present case, the only significant marital asset. To consider the pension benefits a nondivisible marital asset would be to blink our eyes at reality.

The defendant argues that the portion of his pension benefits that "would result from [his] future labors" is not subject to equitable distribution, and that the only portion subject to equitable distribution is the amount of the contributions in the fund at the time of dissolution. We disagree. The fact that a portion of the pension benefits, once vested, will represent the defendant's service to the fire department after the dissolution does not preclude us from classifying the entire unvested pension as marital property. . . .

II

Having concluded that unvested pension benefits are property for equitable distribution under §46b-81, we next address the methods available to value and distribute such benefits. . . . First, the present value or immediate offset approach "'requires the court to determine the present value of the pension benefits, decide the portion to which the nonemployee spouse is entitled, and award other property to the nonemployee spouse as an offset to the pension benefits to which he or she is otherwise entitled.' . . ." The present value approach has the advantage of effecting a severance of the parties' economic ties. The present value approach also avoids extended supervision and enforcement by the courts, thereby saving the parties and the courts the time and expense of future litigation.

The major weakness of this approach is that it requires the court to base its division of the unvested pension benefits upon actuarial probabilities rather than actual events. . . . Stated another way, if the present value approach is applied and the pension never vests, the nonowning spouse will have received, at the time of dissolution, other property in return for a share in a pension that never yields an actual benefit. "Further, this method is not feasible when there are insufficient other assets by which to offset the value of the pension. If there are sufficient other assets, however, several courts have favored this approach. . . ." . . .

"The second and third recognized methods for valuing and distributing pensions involve delaying distribution until the pension matures. Under the 'present division' method, the trial court determines at the time of trial, the percentage share of the pension benefits to which the nonemployee spouse is entitled. . . . In other words, the court will declare that, upon maturity, a fixed percentage of the pension be distributed to each spouse. [U]nder the 'reserved jurisdiction' method, . . . the trial court reserves jurisdiction to distribute the pension until benefits have matured. *Once matured*, the trial court will determine the proper share to which each party is entitled and divide the benefits accordingly."

A significant advantage to the deferred distribution approaches is that, because they delay distribution until the pension benefits have vested and matured, they impose equally on the parties the risk of forfeiture. . . . One disadvantage of delaying distribution of the pension benefits is "the cost of prolonging the parties' entanglement with each other. . . ." . . . Although the advantages of the reserved jurisdiction approach are the same as those of the deferred distribution method, there are serious costs and uncertainties that result therefrom: (1) the court must hold a second hearing in order to determine the percentage to which the nonemployee spouse is entitled; and (2) witnesses must testify to events that occurred long ago. [The court concludes that trial judges have discretion on a case-by-case basis to choose the present value method, the present division method of deferred distribution, or any other method that facilitates equitable division, but not the reserved jurisdiction method because the statute bars retained jurisdiction over orders for lump sum alimony or property division.]

Zarella, J., dissenting. . . .

The majority correctly recognizes the three part analysis that a trial court must employ when effecting the distribution of property upon dissolution [determining (1) whether the interest is property subject to equitable distribution; (2) whether the interest reasonably could be valued; and, (3) if so, what is the most appropriate method of valuation. The majority, however,] collapses the classification stage of the analysis into the valuation stage, concluding that, if an expectation can be valued, then it is not speculative but, rather, is transformed into property subject to equitable distribution. [Yet this analysis would apply to an expected inheritance and thus conflicts with our earlier decision in Rubin v. Rubin, 527 A.2d 1184 (Conn. 1987).]

[A]lthough unvested pension benefits should not be classified as property subject to equitable distribution, §46b-81(c) requires the trial court to *consider* them in fashioning property distribution orders at the time of dissolution. When a pension benefit becomes vested and is in payment status, the trial court may treat this situation as a changed circumstance warranting a modification of an award of periodic alimony under §46b-86. This approach remains faithful to the case law, the language of the relevant statutes and the legislative intent to expand the resources available for equitable distribution. . . .

Notes and Questions

1. **Pensions at divorce.** In addition to the marital home, pension benefits constitute the most significant marital asset for many couples. They also serve as an important source of funds for meeting support obligations.

2. **Majority rule and rationale.** Virtually all jurisdictions follow the approach in *Bender*: Nonvested, as well as vested, pensions are marital property subject to division upon dissolution.

What arguments support recognition of vested pensions as marital assets? Nonvested pensions? Do pension benefits constitute mere expectancies (like an anticipated inheritance), rather than property interests? How does the *Bender* majority answer this question? The dissent? Should a court consider such contingent interests in determining support rather than property distribution (say, on the theory of compensable loss under the ALI Principles §5.04, supra p. 591)?

The landmark case In re Marriage of Brown, 544 P.2d 561 (Cal. 1976), established the majority rule. Rejecting precedents treating nonvested pension rights as a "mere expectancy," Justice Tobriner described pension benefits as a form of "deferred compensation" based on the employment contract, a form of property, subject to division. Id. at 565. *Brown* also noted the unfairness of classifying unvested pensions as separate property. Alimony cannot rectify this unfairness because the spouse "should not be dependent on the discretion of the court . . . to provide her with the equivalent of what should be hers as a matter of absolute right." Id. at 567.

Courts now use identical analysis to treat other employment benefits as divisible property when earned during marriage, regardless of vesting. See, e.g., Engstrom v. Engstrom, 350 P.3d 766 (Alaska 2015) (retirement health insurance benefits); Beecher v. Beecher, 417 S.W.3d 868 (Mo. Ct. App. 2014) (stock options).

3. **Integrating federal and state law.** The important role of pension plans in dissolution requires analysis under both federal and state law.

a. Federal regulation of private pension plans: ERISA and REA. The Employee Retirement Income Security Act (ERISA), enacted in 1974 and amended over the years, protects employee retirement benefits through comprehensive federal regulation of private pension plans. 29 U.S.C. §§1001 et seq. ERISA explicitly preempts state law. As originally enacted, ERISA accorded a nonemployee spouse (for example, the wife of a covered employee) limited rights to share in the employee's pension upon dissolution, the result of an "anti-alienation rule" barring assignment or alienation of pension plan benefits (although not welfare plan benefits). See ERISA §206(d)(1), 29 U.S.C. §1056(d)(1). This protective policy ensures that the participant cannot consume retirement savings before retirement. ERISA made no exceptions for domestic relations claims against an employee's pension plan. In the wake of ERISA, federal and state courts split on whether the anti-alienation rule barred distribution of pension benefits to a nonemployee spouse upon divorce.

The Retirement Equity Act of 1984 (REA) sought to remedy this and other problems experienced particularly by women. REA mandates that ERISA's anti-alienation rule must yield to certain state domestic relations decrees and permits a court to divide pension benefits in the same manner as other marital assets. That is, REA amends ERISA to provide for the enforcement of "qualified domestic relations orders" (QDROs) and removes such orders from ERISA's preemption scheme. See ERISA §§206(d)(3), 514(b)(7), 29 U.S.C. §§1056(d)(3), 1144(b)(7).

ERISA also limits the possibility of the scenario in *Bender* by specifying a relatively short term of service (e.g., five years) that triggers full vesting. ERISA §203(a), 29 U.S.C. §1053(a). Such minimum vesting requirements apply to almost all pension plans except for government plans (as in *Bender*) and church plans. Cf. Reese v. Reese, 155 S.W.3d 862 (Mo. Ct. App. 2005) (noting exemption of state-employee teachers' pensions from classification as marital property).

b. QDROs. Under the Act, a QDRO means a domestic relations order "which creates or recognizes the existence of an alternate payee's right to, or assigns to an alternate payee the right to, receive all or a portion of the benefits payable with respect to a participant under a plan"; for purposes of this provision, a domestic relations order is a judgment, decree, or order "which relates to the provision of child support, alimony payments, or marital property rights to a spouse, former spouse, child, or other dependent of a participant," made "pursuant to a State domestic relations law (including a community property law)." ERISA §206(d)(3)(B), 29 U.S.C. §1056(d)(3)(B). See also ERISA §206(d)(3)(K), 29 U.S.C. §1056(d)(3)(K) (defining "alternate payee").

To qualify as a plan beneficiary under a QDRO, the nonemployee spouse must obtain a state court or administrative agency decree (not merely a separation agreement), which specifies the extent to which the plan participant's liability shall be paid from pension assets. Note that pension assets can be distributed under a QDRO not only for property division, but also for spousal and child support obligations.

Although QDROs facilitate collection of divorce awards by directing retirement plan administrators to make payments directly to the "alternate payee," QDROs have several limitations. The extent of the nonemployee spouse's benefits is governed by those of the employee spouse—that is, the nonemployee former spouse may not obtain a lump sum distribution, for example, if this option is not available to the employee. Similarly, if the nonemployee spouse is divorced from an employee whose pension benefits are already subject to a QDRO from a prior divorce, the first ex-spouse prevails.

c. Federal pension benefits. Federal retirement benefit plans cover certain government employees. In response to U.S. Supreme Court rulings that federal law preempts the field, Congress enacted corrective legislation. See 45 U.S.C. §231a(c)(4) (amendments to the Railroad Retirement Act extending benefits to divorced spouses married to a railroad employee for at least ten years, among other conditions); 10 U.S.C. §1408 (Uniformed Services Former Spouses Protection Act, permitting state courts to apply their laws to military retirement benefits upon divorce, with enforcement mechanism available under certain conditions).

As a matter of policy, should military retirement benefits receive different treatment from any other retirement benefits? How does military service differ from other employment? What implications does that difference have for the contributions of the nonmilitary spouse? Suppose after the judgment dividing the military pension, the military spouse converts the retirement pay to disability pay, which state courts have no authority to divide. See Youngbluth v. Youngbluth, 6 A.3d 677 (Vt. 2010). Cf. Megee v. Carmine, 802 N.W.2d 669 (Mich. Ct. App. 2010) (requiring compensation). See generally John E. Kirchner, Division of Military Retired Pay, 43 Fam. L.Q. 367 (2009).

Should Congress reconsider the statute that disallows assignment of Social Security benefits? See 42 U.S.C. §407 (2006).[30] See, e.g., In re Marriage of Mueller, 34 N.E.3d 538, 545 (Ill. 2015) (holding that "Congress intended to keep Social Security benefits out of divorce cases," so courts should not consider such benefits at all). But see, e.g., In re Marriage of Herald & Steadman, 322 P.3d 546 (Or. 2014) (allowing consideration in effectuating equitable division).

4. Pension valuation and distribution. Equitable division of pension rights, under a traditional defined benefit pension plan, entails considering the speculative and nonmarketable nature of pension rights, with valuation and distribution often requiring the assistance of actuarial experts. *Bender* canvasses the available approaches. See also, e.g., Daniel v. Daniel, 11 N.E.3d 1119 (Ohio 2014). Which approach best achieves the objectives of equitable division? Why? (Today, defined benefit pension plans have become less common, with the growing use of defined contribution pension plans, which do not present such valuation challenges.)

Problems

1. Karen and Robert divorced after 26 years of marriage. Karen, a part-time secretary for a church, was earning $645 per month; Robert, an employee of Miller Brewing Co., was earning $2,900 per month. In the division of marital property, Robert got his pension, valued at $11,355, and Karen got other property of roughly the same value (but no interest in Robert's pension). The court ordered Robert to pay Karen $600 per month for maintenance. After taking voluntary retirement at age 55, Robert now seeks to terminate maintenance payments, arguing he has no income available. Karen seeks to continue maintenance, arguing that the $2,700 per month Robert gets from his pension is income available for maintenance. What result and why? Is it unfair "double counting" to consider Robert's pension plan both as an asset in the property division and as income for maintenance payments? See In re Marriage of Olski, 540 N.W.2d 412 (Wis. 1995). See also, e.g., N.J. Stat. Ann. § 2A:34-23(b); Kazakis v. Kazakis, 2013 WL 5476330 (Ohio Ct. App. 2013); Donald J. DeGrazia & Stacy Preston Collins, The Double-Dipping Arguments, 31 Fam. Advoc. 16 (Spring 2009).

2. Debbie and David, each previously married, signed a premarital agreement waiving any interest in any pension or retirement plan in which the other might participate. After the couple married in 1995, David joined a law firm and began participating in the firm's retirement plan. Debbie left David in 2005, and David committed suicide three days later, before either had filed for separation or

[30]. If the divorce occurs after at least ten years of marriage, however, an ex-spouse is entitled to Social Security benefits based upon the earnings record of his or her former spouse. 42 U.S.C. §§402, 416.

divorce. The law firm's retirement plan documents designate a surviving spouse as the default beneficiary of the retirement plan if the employee has not designated a different beneficiary and the surviving spouse has not consented in writing to the change. No such designation or consent had been recorded with the firm's retirement committee, as required. In a dispute over the retirement funds between David's children from his first marriage and Debbie, who should prevail? Why? See Greenebaum, Doll, & McDonald PLLC v. Sandler, 256 Fed. Appx. 765 (6th Cir. 2007). For the Supreme Court's analyses of related questions, see Hillman v. Maretta, 133 S. Ct. 1943 (2013); Kennedy v. Plan Adm'r for DuPont Sav. & Inv. Plan, 555 U.S. 285 (2009).

NOTE: MEDICAL COVERAGE FOLLOWING DISSOLUTION

Historically, an important issue for many spouses upon dissolution, especially homemakers, has been securing the continuation of medical benefits. Concern about the high cost of medical insurance and its unavailability for dependent ex-spouses resulted in the 1985 enactment of the Consolidated Omnibus Budget Reconciliation Act (COBRA), adding §§601-608 to ERISA. See 29 U.S.C. §§1161-1168.

COBRA requires, inter alia, employers maintaining certain group health plans to offer continued medical coverage at group rates to "qualified beneficiaries" who would otherwise lose benefits upon the occurrence of a "qualifying event." Qualified beneficiaries (a class including employees and their dependents who were plan beneficiaries on the day before the qualifying event) may make "elections" for continuation of the same coverage. Qualifying events include divorce and legal separation. A nonemployee spouse is entitled to continued coverage for 36 months following the date of divorce or legal separation. Coverage may not be conditioned on evidence of insurability. The qualified beneficiary must pay the required premiums after he or she makes the COBRA election. Several states supplement COBRA by providing for continuation coverage. E.g., Cal. Ins. Code §10116.5; N.Y. Ins. Law §4305(e).

Although federal health care reform does not directly alter COBRA, the ACA should diminish this costly option's importance at divorce. The ACA's relevant features include extended coverage of adult children dependents, the ability to acquire new coverage without regard to pre-existing conditions, increased marketplace options, and establishment of special enrollment periods. See, e.g., Robert Calandra, Insurance May No Longer Hinder Divorce, Phil. Inquirer, Mar. 2, 2014, at G01.

d. Investments in a Spouse's Future Success: Degrees, Earning Capacity, and Goodwill

---

IN RE MARRIAGE OF ROBERTS

670 N.E.2d 72 (Ind. Ct. App. 1996)

GARRARD, Judge. . . .

[Matthew and Leigh Anne Roberts] were married on June 24, 1989. In the fall of 1990, Matthew began attending the Valparaiso University Law School as a full-time student. Before law school, Matthew had been employed at Society Bank in

South Bend, Indiana and had been earning a salary of $30,000.00 per year at the time he left employment. Matthew and Leigh Anne agreed that Matthew should quit working and attend school full-time while Leigh Anne continued to work to support them. Leigh Anne also assumed primary responsibility for running the household so that Matthew could devote all of his time to his studies.

Two months before Matthew's graduation, Leigh Anne learned that she was pregnant, and thereafter the couple separated. Matthew finished third in his graduating class and also served as editor-in-chief of the Valparaiso Law Review. After graduation, he took an associate position with a large law firm in Chicago, Illinois. He filed his petition for dissolution of marriage on August 4, 1993.

The major asset of the parties was the marital home, valued at $70,000.00 with a mortgage of $63,245.00. The parties also owned certain personal property and each had 401(k) accounts and IRA accounts. The court determined that Matthew's law degree could not be considered a marital asset subject to distribution. However, the court did include Matthew's student loans, totaling $22,500.00, in valuing the marital estate, and the court found repayment to be the sole responsibility of Matthew. The court determined that, based upon the student loans, the disproportionate earnings history and the earning potential of the parties, the presumption of equal distribution had been rebutted. The court [allocated to Matthew $22,084.96 total assets and $24,500 total debts, resulting in a net debt of $2,415.04; it allocated to Leigh Anne $90,779.98 total assets and $65,245.00 total debts, amounting to net assets of $25,534.98].

Leigh Anne first argues that the trial court should have included Matthew's law degree as a marital asset subject to distribution. . . .

The specific issue of whether a degree obtained during a marriage by one party may be considered marital property upon divorce was addressed in Prenatt v. Stevens, 598 N.E.2d 616 (Ind. Ct. App. 1992). In *Prenatt*, the trial court found that the wife's doctoral degree in English, which was obtained during the marriage, was a marital asset. This determination was reversed on appeal, with the court relying upon Wilcox v. Wilcox [365 N.E.2d 792 (Ind. Ct. App. 1977)] and In re Marriage of McManama [399 N.E.2d 371 (Ind. 1980)]. In *Wilcox*, the court first noted that any award over and above the assets of the marriage must represent some form of support or maintenance. The court then held that the husband's future earnings could not be considered a marital asset as there was no vested present interest in such income. In *McManama*, the trial court had awarded the wife a lump sum in the amount she had contributed to help her husband obtain his advanced degree on the theory that there had been a dissipation of marital property. Our supreme court reversed, finding that the award was in actuality an award to be paid from the husband's future income. Such an award of future income could only be proper as either support or maintenance, and there was no evidence of any incapacity to support such an award.

Based upon this precedent, *Prenatt* concluded that, despite the legislature's intent for "property" to be interpreted as broadly inclusive, a degree simply does not possess the common characteristics of property:

> A degree is an intangible which is personal to the holder. It is a piece of paper and has no real value except for what the holder chooses to pursue with it. Potential worth is dependent upon choice and availability of work, whether the holder is good at what she does, or a myriad of other potentialities.

> Valuation of a degree is fraught with uncertainty because of the personal factors described above. Even if valuation could be made certain, such valuation, whether based on future earning capacity or upon cost of acquisition, would ultimately result in an award beyond the actual physical assets of the marriage. As noted in *Wilcox* and *McManama*, such award is improper.

Prenatt, 598 N.E.2d at 620.

The only statutory exception is I.C. §31-1-11.5-11(d), which states:

> When the court finds there is little or no marital property, it may award either spouse a money judgment not limited to the property existing at the time of final separation. However, this award may be made only for the financial contribution of one (1) spouse toward tuition, books, and laboratory fees for the higher education of the other spouse.

Thus, a spouse may be reimbursed, even above the assets of the marital estate, but reimbursement is strictly limited.

We agree with the finding in *Prenatt* that a degree does not constitute marital property. [W]hile Indiana does not permit a degree to be included as marital property, and further will not allow an award of future earnings unless the spouse qualifies for maintenance, nevertheless the earning ability of the degree-earning spouse may be considered in determining the distribution of the marital estate. . . .

Leigh Anne also argues that the trial court should have made an award to compensate her for the dissipation of the marital estate by Matthew as a result of the income which the family was deprived of while Matthew attended law school and the contributions Leigh Anne made toward Matthew's education and the household living expenses. [I]n employing the term "dissipation," our legislature intended that it carry its common meaning denoting "foolishly" or "aimlessly." Thus, under the circumstances of this case it cannot be said that the money expended in order to secure Matthew's law degree was dissipated, even though Leigh Anne did not receive the benefits she expected therefrom. . . .

We affirm the judgment. . . .

Joan Williams, Is Coverture Dead? Beyond a New Theory of Alimony

82 Geo. L.J. 2227, 2267-2272, 2274-2275 (1994)

Despite some early support for using the language of property to address the issue of postdivorce impoverishment, it is an article of faith among many family law courts and scholars today that property language is out of place and inherently unconvincing in this context. This dismissal is ironic because . . . conclusions about ownership are inevitable; the only question is whether the family wage will continue to be awarded one-sidedly to the husband. The disagreement is not over whether the family wage will be owned, but over who shall own it.

[T]he courts' and commentators' rejection of property language in this context reflects its linkage with arguments of human capital theorists. Such arguments generally have failed to persuade courts, leading many family law scholars to conclude that property rhetoric has failed them. In fact, property rhetoric is not the problem; human capital theory is. . . .

The typical degree case involves a wife who supported her husband through professional school and who claims "property in his degree" when he divorces her shortly after graduation. Courts, with few exceptions, have rejected wives' claims that the degrees are marital property, often using broad language to the effect that human capital does not have the attributes traditionally associated with property. To justify this rejection, courts rely on the traditional Blackstonian image of property rights as the absolute dominion of people over things. This imagery, however, was never an accurate description of property law, and was formally abandoned in the First Restatement of Property in 1936. The 1936 Restatement adopted instead Wesley Hohfeld's view that property rights defined the relationships among people with respect to some valuable interest. The image is not of "absolute" ownership but of an evolving set of claims, in which courts attach the name "property" as a signal they have accepted someone's claim. . . .

[In most degree cases, the] court starts out with a predefined notion of what "property" entails. It then inquires whether a degree "fits" that image. Upon deciding that it does not, it concludes that no property right exists in the wife. . . . In contrast to the Hohfeldian view's message that "property" is a word courts use to signal their legal conclusion that someone has an entitlement, the [court's] language sends the message that judges play no active role in determining entitlements. But they do. Conclusions about property are legal conclusions, made in a context where the court has to allocate the asset to someone. . . .

Many modern property rights . . . clash with a model of absolute, alienable, inheritable, and exchangeable entitlements. Examples are pensions and goodwill which are widely recognized as property despite their lack of heritability and their status as income streams provided by "many years of . . . hard work." . . . Courts' refusal to recognize "new property" rights in the context of the family stems not from the logic of property, but from unstated assumptions about who is entitled to what. . . .

If the courts' projected image of property rights is so inaccurate and their property theory half a century out of date, why have the degree cases proved so convincing? . . . Family court judges, almost by definition, are successful lawyers. Most are men who have conformed to an ideal worker pattern in a profession notorious for long hours. This workaholic culture tends to marginalize the ideal workers' wives, as they assume more and more family responsibilities to allow for their husbands' "success." It is also the (upper-middle) class context in which the ideology of gender equality is strongest. In short, the judges in degree cases are heavily invested in the polite fiction—observed in most intact marriages—that the husband's career success and the wife's marginalization both result not from a system that privileges ideal workers who can command a flow of domestic services from women, but from the idiosyncracies of two individuals residing in the republic of choice.[231]

The degree cases also reflect judges' sense that they worked long and hard for their degrees. Their reaction is colored by their struggles in law school and their sense that they have earned everything they have achieved through their own hard work. That degree holders worked long and hard is not the issue. So did their wives, both in the home and (often) at boring, dead-end jobs, passing up opportunities for better positions. The issue is not who worked hard, but whose hard work gives rise to entitlements. . . .

Notes and Questions

1. Majority rule. *Roberts* follows the majority of courts in refusing to treat advanced degrees and professional licenses, as well as the enhanced earning capacity therefrom, as property. Hence, the supporting spouse's contribution does not make them divisible assets upon divorce. Is Professor Williams's explanation for this rule persuasive?

2. Limited remedies. While applying the majority rule, *Roberts* states that Matthew's enhanced earning capacity is a factor in the distribution of property; the court, in turn, approves a disproportionate division favoring Leigh Anne and assigns debts for Matthew's student loans exclusively to him. Is this approach fair? Suppose that the couple had spent everything on the husband's degree, without accumulating any assets. Does the statute quoted in *Roberts* (now Ind. Code Ann. §31-15-7-6) solve the problem?

Alternatively, does this limited remedy result in unjust enrichment for Matthew? Would an analysis based on unjust enrichment require consideration of fault? (For example, would it matter whether Leigh Anne's pregnancy, about which she learned just before the couple separated, was conceived with Matthew or another man?) More generally, does the supporting spouse deserve compensation not just for financial contributions but also for the loss of a return on the investment in the supported spouse's career?

3. Maintenance as a remedy? If the couple has no assets to divide, should a court recognize the supporting spouse's contribution by awarding maintenance? Does Leigh Anne *need* support? See also Hodge v. Hodge, 520 A.2d 15, 18 (Pa. 1986) (purpose of alimony is "rehabilitation, not reimbursement"). In contrast to *Roberts*, other authorities look to maintenance to provide a remedy. E.g., Tenn. Code § 36-5-121(i)(10); In re Marriage of Harris, 244 P.3d 801 (Or. 2010). See

---

231. [See Joan Williams, Gender Wars: Selfless Women in the Republic of Choice, 66 N.Y.U. L. Rev. 1559, 1562-1608 (1991).] The relatively few female judges may be high-human-capital women who may not be sympathetic to the claims of mothers marginalized by motherhood. Id. at 1597-98, 1605-06.

also Cynthia Lee Starnes, The Marriage Buyout: The Troubled Trajectory of U.S. Alimony Law 160 (2014) (proposing alimony as a "buyout obligation" when one "spouse walks away at divorce with a larger share of wage-earning human capital that has become part of the marital pool").

4. A fair result by any means. Some courts have used a frankly flexible approach, stating that achieving a fair result is more important than whether a traditional "property" or "alimony" label fits. For example, in Washburn v. Washburn, 677 P.2d 152 (Wash. 1984) (en banc), the court declined to identify the husband's veterinary degree as property but went on to say:

> . . . A professional degree confers high earning potential upon the holder. The student spouse should not walk away with this valuable advantage without compensating the person who helped him or her obtain it.
>
> [T]he supporting spouse may be compensated through a division of property and liabilities. In many cases, however, the wealth of the marriage will have been spent toward the cost of the professional degree, leaving few or no assets to divide. Where the assets of the parties are insufficient to permit compensation to be effected entirely through property division, a supplemental award of maintenance is appropriate.
>
> [W]e recognize that the spouse who is capable of supporting someone through school will in most cases also be capable of supporting him or herself after the marriage is dissolved. However, under the extremely flexible provisions of [the statute], a demonstrated capacity of self-support does not automatically preclude an award of maintenance. . . .
>
> Under our opinion today, Mrs. Washburn may be entitled to an award as compensation for her contribution to her husband's education. Such compensation may be effected through property division, maintenance or a combination of both. . . .

Id. at 158, 161. Despite the Washington Supreme Court's lack of concern about the label for Mrs. Washburn's award, what difference will the label make? Under the more flexible approach approved in *Washburn*, how does a judge compute a fair result? See also Ashby v. Ashby, 227 P.3d 246 (Utah 2010) (allowing breach of contract remedy when spouses had entered a student support agreement).

5. New York's property treatment. In contrast to the majority approach, New York treats degrees and professional licenses as property subject to equitable division, based on the legislative definition of marital property. In O'Brien v. O'Brien, 489 N.E.2d 712, 715-716 (N.Y. 1985), the court invoked the language of the equitable distribution statute, which expressly mentions contributions to a spouse's career, career potential, or profession, concluding that an interest in a profession or professional career potential constitutes marital property subject to division, based on "direct or indirect contributions of the non-title-holding spouse, including financial contributions and nonfinancial contributions made by caring for the home and family."

Under this approach, the supporting spouse should get an "equitable portion" of this property, based on the present value of "the enhanced earning capacity it affords the holder." Id. at 718. Few other courts define property so expansively. New York has adhered to this approach even when the marriage endures well past the degree date so that both spouses have already enjoyed the enhanced earning capacity it created. See Holterman v. Holterman, 814 N.E.2d 765, 779-780, 783 (N.Y. 2004) (Smith, J., dissenting). Should courts extend the New York approach further to encompass enhanced earning capacity acquired with the help of a spouse but not based on a degree or license? See Sebastian Weiss, Note, Preventing Inequities in Divorce and Education: The Equitable Distribution of a Career Absent an Advanced Degree or License, 9 Cardozo Women's L.J. 133 (2002).

What are the implications of New York's approach for bankruptcy discharges? For modifiability? What happens when a professional former spouse, who is ordered to pay under New York law a particular sum as an equitable share of his enhanced earning capacity, suddenly becomes unable to work, say, because of illness?

6. ALI approach. Consistent with majority rule, the ALI Principles reject the treatment of earning capacity as divisible property. Instead, they provide for "compensatory spousal payments" to reimburse the supporting spouse for the financial contributions made to the other spouse's education or training. ALI Principles §§4.07, 5.12. For compensation under §5.12, the education must have been completed in less than a specified number of years (set out in a rule of statewide application) before the filing of the dissolution petition. See also Cal. Fam. Code §2641 (statute that provided the model for the ALI approach).

7. Comparing pensions and goodwill. The advanced degree cases test the limits of the "new property." See, e.g., Lenore J. Weitzman, The Divorce Revolution: The Unexpected Social and Economic Consequences for Women and Children in America 110-142 (1985). Weitzman's definition of the term includes "tangible and intangible assets that are acquired as part of either spouse's career or career potential" (id. at 110), and encompasses pensions and other retirement benefits, the goodwill value of a business or profession, insurance benefits, as well as professional degrees and licenses (id. at 110-142). Given that courts routinely treat pensions and retirement funds as marital property, what explains their reluctance to afford similar treatment to professional degrees and licenses? For example, on what basis would the Connecticut Supreme Court treat unvested pension benefits as divisible property (*Bender*, supra), but not advanced degrees (Simmons v. Simmons, 708 A.2d 949 (Conn. 1998))?

With respect to goodwill, the majority approach distinguishes personal goodwill (not divisible property) and professional or corporate goodwill (divisible property). E.g., Brave v. Brave, 433 S.W.3d 227 (Ark. 2014). How are the latter assets valued? The ALI Principles (§4.07) follow the majority approach on goodwill while excluding human capital from the definition of property.

8. Awards for lost future earnings. There is considerable authority for treating as divisible property some personal injury awards designed to compensate for lost future earnings. On what theory? Should the accrual date control? See Focht v. Focht, 32 A.3d 668 (Pa. 2011). Some authorities use a "replacement analysis," treating as marital property awards meant to compensate for wages that would have been earned during marriage, but treating as separate property damages meant to replace postdissolution earnings. See Grace v. Peterson, 269 P3d 663 (Alaska 2012). This analysis can also be applied to life insurance, disability pay, and workers' compensation awards. Why isn't a worker's disabled body considered separate property? See Gorman v. Gorman, 15 A.3d 217 (Del. 2011). Alternatively, why shouldn't the determinative question be whether the benefits in question were acquired through a spouse's labor during marriage? See, e.g., Grose v. Grose, 671 S.E.2d 727 (W. Va. 2008). Cf. Mickey v. Mickey, 974 A.2d 641 (Conn. 2009) (concerning postdissolution disability benefits).

Can a court divide a spouse's accrued vacation time or sick leave upon dissolution? Compare In re Marriage of Cardona and Castro, 316 P.3d 626 (Colo. 2014) (yes), with In re Marriage of Abrell, 923 N.E.2d 791 (Ill. 2010) (not when former spouse continues to work for same employer). An early retirement incentive package accepted by the employee spouse after divorce? See Olivo v. Olivo, 624 N.E.2d 151 (N.Y. 1993). An attorney's contingent fees for cases started during marriage? See Larsen-Ball v. Ball, 301 S.W.3d 228 (Tenn. 2010). Contractual rights for royalty payments on a novel authored by one spouse during the marriage? See Canisius v. Morgenstern, 35 N.E.3d 385 (Mass. Ct. App. 2015).

Problems

1. Upon dissolution of the 17-year marriage of New York opera singer Frederica von Stade Elkus, her husband argues that her career and celebrity status constitute marital property subject to equitable distribution. At the time of their marriage in 1973, von Stade had just begun her career and was performing minor roles with the Metropolitan Opera Company. During the marriage, she became a highly successful concert and television performer and international recording artist. Although in the first year of the marriage she earned $2,250, by 1989 she earned $621,878.

During the marriage, von Stade's husband served as her voice coach and photographer, traveling with her, critiquing her performance, and photographing her for albums and magazine articles. He claims he sacrificed his own career as an opera teacher and singer to devote himself to her career and to their two children. As a result of his efforts, Elkus contends that he is entitled to equitable distribution of the appreciation of the value of her career and her celebrity status as marital property.

According to New York Domestic Relations Law (see *O'Brien*, supra), marital property is defined as property acquired during the marriage "regardless of the form in which title is held." In enacting the Equitable Distribution Law, the legislature broadly defined the term "marital property" to give effect to the "economic partnership" concept of marriage.

What result and why? See Elkus v. Elkus, 572 N.Y.S.2d 901 (App. Div. 1991). Is celebrity status distinguishable from reputation, which courts in professional goodwill cases have held is not divisible? See also Golub v. Golub, 527 N.Y.S.2d 946 (Sup. Ct. 1988). How should a court in a state without New York's expansive definition of property rule? See In re Marriage of McTiernan, 35 Cal. Rptr. 3d 287 (Ct. App. 2005) (film director's celebrity goodwill); Ketterle v. Ketterle, 814 N.E.2d 385, 387 (Mass. App. Ct. 2004) (Nobel Prize-winning husband's status as

Divisible celebrity status? Mezzo soprano Frederica von Stade at the Metropolitan Opera

Divisible celebrity goodwill? Comedian Joe Piscopo performing

"superstar in the scientific and academic universe"); Piscopo v. Piscopo, 557 A.2d 1040 (N.J. Super. Ct. App. Div. 1989) (comedian's celebrity goodwill).

2. John and Margaret divorced when he was manager of municipal markets at Merrill Lynch and she was a housewife. The court equally divided their substantial assets and ordered John to pay half his monthly salary as alimony. After John became ill and lost his job, he successfully sought to reduce his alimony obligation based on the changed circumstances.

Margaret now appeals this modification, contending that the court underestimated John's ability to pay by ignoring his "experience as a savvy investor." She claims that John's "sophisticated investment skills are to him what Luciano Pavarotti's voice is to him: the 'asset' that is capable of earning a significant amount of money." She asks the court to measure John's ability to pay on the basis of the higher yield investments available to him, not his actual income. What result and why? See Miller v. Miller, 734 A.2d 752 (N.J. 1999). But cf. Clark v. Clark, 779 A.2d 42, 47 & n.3 (Vt. 2001).

e. Taxation

The Internal Revenue Code spells out different tax consequences for alimony, property division, and child support. What objectives do these variations in tax treatment achieve? How much room should federal law leave for the parties and/or the divorce court to decide such tax issues? Whom do the rules benefit—and disadvantage? Consider the following materials.

RYKIEL v. RYKIEL

838 So. 2d 508 (Fla. 2003)

SHAW, Senior Justice. . . .

Stephen Rykiel ("husband") appealed the final judgment in a divorce proceeding. The Fifth District Court of Appeal (the "Fifth District") reversed, holding as follows:

> Further, an obvious error was made with regard to the alimony award. First, the court ordered that the award of permanent periodic alimony be nontaxable to the receiving party, the former wife. This award cannot stand because there is no legal authority which would permit such a practice. Permanent periodic alimony (i.e., support money) is taxable to the recipient under federal income tax law. 26 U.S.C.A. §71. Its taxability cannot be changed by a state court order. State law creates legal interests, but federal law determines how those interests shall be taxed.

[795 So. 2d at 92.] [On rehearing, the Fifth District added that, under its reading of §71 and temporary Treasury Regulation 26 C.F.R. §1.71-1T, only the parties may agree to make alimony payments nondeductible by the payor and excludable from the payee's gross income and the parties must do so in a written document or on the record before the trial judge, which would be reduced to judgment. 795 So. 2d at 93 n.1.] Karen Rykiel ("wife") sought review [before this court of this pure question of law, which is] subject to de novo review. . . .

This case is governed by the provisions of the Internal Revenue Code and the Code of Federal Regulations governing the Internal Revenue Service, Department of the Treasury. Section 63, Internal Revenue Code (2001), provides as follows in relevant part:

> **§63. Taxable income defined**
>
> (a) In general
>
> Except as provided in subsection (b), for purposes of this subtitle, the term *"taxable income" means gross income. . . .*

I.R.C. §63 (2000) (emphasis added).

Section 71, Internal Revenue Code (2001), provides as follows in relevant part:

> **§71. Alimony and separate maintenance payments**
>
> (a) General rule
>
> *Gross income includes amounts received as alimony* or separate maintenance payments.
>
> (b) Alimony or separate maintenance payments defined
>
> For purposes of this section—
>
> (1) In general
>
> *The term "alimony* or separate maintenance payment" *means any payment in cash if—*
>
> (A) such payment is received by (or on behalf of) a spouse under a divorce or separation instrument,
>
> (B) *the divorce or separation instrument does not designate such payment as a payment which is not includible in gross income under this section and not allowable as a deduction . . .*

(C) in the case of an individual legally separated from his spouse under a decree of divorce or of separate maintenance, the payee spouse and the payor spouse are not members of the same household at the time such payment is made, and

(D) there is no liability to make any such payment for any period after the death of the payee spouse and there is no liability to make any payment (in cash or property) as a substitute for such payments after the death of the payee spouse.

(2) Divorce or separation instrument

The term "divorce or separation instrument" means—

(A) *a decree of divorce* or separate maintenance or a written instrument incident to such a decree,

(B) a written separation agreement, or

(C) a decree (not described in subparagraph (A)) requiring a spouse to make payments for the support or maintenance of the other spouse.

(c) Payments to support children

(1) In general

Subsection (a) shall not apply to that part of any payment which the terms of the divorce or separation instrument fix (in terms of an amount of money or a part of the payment) as a sum which is payable for the support of children of the payor spouse.

I.R.C. §71 (2000) (emphasis added).

The "question and answer" section in Temporary Treasury Regulation §1.71-1T(b) Q8 & A8 (2001), addresses this matter further:

> *Q.* How may spouses designate that payments otherwise qualifying as alimony or separate maintenance payments shall be excludible from the gross income of the payee and non-deductible by the payor?
>
> *A:* The spouses may designate that payments otherwise qualifying as alimony or separate maintenance payments shall be nondeductible by the payor and excludible from gross income by the payee by so providing in a divorce or separation instrument. . . .

Temp. Treas. Reg. §1.71-1T, Q8 & A8 (2001). . . .

[The Fifth District below] construed the above Code provisions and Treasury regulation to mean that a divorce court does not have the authority to order that "alimony shall be nontaxable to the receiving party." This construction, however, is inconsistent with the above Code provisions and Treasury regulation. Sections 63 and 71 of the Code may be paraphrased as follows:

— Gross income is taxable.
— Gross income includes alimony.
— Alimony includes monetary payments made to a spouse pursuant to a divorce instrument unless that instrument says that the payments are not includible in gross income and not allowable as a deduction.
— If the divorce instrument says that the payments are not includible in gross income and not allowable as a deduction, then the payments are not "alimony," are not included in gross income, and are not taxable.
— A divorce instrument includes a divorce decree.

Under the above provisions, a divorce decree may provide that alimony payments are to be excluded from the gross income of the payee and not deducted by the payor. In such a case, the payments do not constitute "alimony" for tax purposes, are not included in the gross income of the recipient, and are nontaxable to the recipient. Treasury regulation 1.71-1T, which the Fifth District relied on for the proposition that only the parties can agree to such an arrangement, simply states that the parties can agree to such an arrangement; it does not state that a court cannot order such an arrangement. . . . Contrary to the holding of the Fifth District, nothing in the above provisions prevents a court from ordering that alimony payments are to be excluded from the gross income of the payee and not deducted by the payor. . . .

Notes and Questions

1. Tax consequences. In reaching a fair and equitable result, courts often take into account the tax consequences of particular distributions of property or awards of support. See, e.g., In re Marriage of Johnston, 2014 WL 6977201, at *4 (Iowa Ct. App. 2014); L.J.S. v. J.E.S., 982 N.E.2d 1160 (Mass. 2013).

2. Spousal support. As *Rykiel* indicates, the Internal Revenue Code provides that "alimony" is deductible by the payor (or obligor)[31] and included in the gross income of the recipient (or obligee).[32] Hence, the obligee must pay income tax on such payments, just as on salary. Despite states' varying definitions of maintenance or spousal support, to qualify as "alimony" for federal income tax purposes, the payments must meet the statutory criteria listed in I.R.C. §71(b) (quoted in *Rykiel*). See generally Christopher C. Melcher, Simple Answers to Complex Alimony Questions, 27 J. Am. Acad. Matrim. Law 61 (2014-2015).

Rykiel also indicates, however, that tax law does not require divorcing couples to treat spousal support as alimony under §71. Couples may elect to treat the payments as nondeductible by the obligor and nontaxable to the obligee. Doing so might prove financially advantageous if, given the parties' respective incomes and tax rates, the deduction does not save the obligor as much money as inclusion in gross income costs the obligee in taxes. (Use of §71 has no direct tax effect if the parties are in the same bracket.) See Melvin B. Frumkes, Alimony Can Be Made Nontaxable, 17 Am. J. Fam. L. 187 (2004). So, for example, in *Rykiel,* if Karen's taxable income places her in the 28 percent tax bracket and Stephen's places him in the 25 percent bracket, they would minimize their total income tax liability by making Stephen's spousal support payments to Karen nondeductible by him and nontaxable to her.[33] The Rykiels must indicate this tax treatment in the divorce

---

[31]. I.R.C. §§62, 215. By specifically listing alimony as a deduction used to arrive at "adjusted gross income," §62 allows a dollar-for-dollar deduction from the gross income of the obligor, who can take, in addition, a standard deduction, if beneficial. As a result, the obligor can avoid paying the greater tax rate applicable to the portion of his or her income that would otherwise fall into a higher tax bracket. See I.R.C. §1.

[32]. I.R.C. §§71(a), 61(a)(8) (listing "alimony and separate maintenance payments" as one of 15 nonexclusive examples of income).

[33]. As an individual's taxable income for the year increases, the percentage of income owed for taxes increases, according to designated "tax brackets" specified in I.R.C. §1.

or separation agreement, and Karen must attach a copy of the instrument to her tax return.

Why did Congress choose the Code's approach to alimony? Should the divorce court as well as the parties be able to choose the tax treatment of spousal support payments? Why?

3. Other transfers and payments. For most transfers of property between spouses or former spouses, if "incident to the divorce," no gain or loss will be recognized.[34] I.R.C. §1041(b) treats the property transferred as a gift to the recipient. As a result, the value of the property is excluded from the recipient's income, under I.R.C. §102(a). Further, the recipient takes the transferor's basis in the property. Why did Congress decide to treat property transfers incident to divorce differently from support payments, with respect to taxation?

Unlike alimony, child support payments are nontaxable and nondeductible under I.R.C. §71(c) (quoted in *Rykiel*). What policy considerations does this rule reflect? What impact does it have? See Michael Waggoner, IRC §71 May Impoverish Children, Endanger Ex-Wives, and Disrupt Federalism, 46 Fam. Ct. Rev. 574 (2008).

4. Navigating the system. The different tax consequences of alimony, property transfers, and child support often determine the most financially advantageous way to "wind up" a marriage. The Code limits the parties' freedom to get the desired tax consequences, however. Consider the following examples:

a. "Excess alimony payments." Suppose that Karen's and Stephen's financial circumstances make it advantageous to have cash property distribution payments treated as alimony for tax purposes. If, for example, the parties were attempting to negotiate a settlement and Stephen wanted to treat cash property distribution payments as deductible alimony by making periodic payments that drop substantially within the first three postseparation years, I.R.C. §71(f) provides for recomputation to "recapture" the excess deductions over the amount permitted by the statute. Significantly, it is Stephen's *front-loading* of alimony payments that triggers the recapture of the excess, not his effort to characterize a cash property settlement as alimony. Thus, if Karen were willing to spread out evenly her receipt of the property distribution over the first three postseparation years, Stephen could avoid the recapture by paying Karen her alimony plus one-third of his property obligation during each of these years.

b. Disguising child support as alimony. Suppose, now, that Stephen and Karen have three children, ages 10, 15, and 20, and that Stephen wants to deduct as much of his postdivorce payments as possible. If the monthly "alimony" sums that Stephen pays drop each time one of the children reaches age 21, for example, the Internal Revenue Service (I.R.S.) will treat some of these payments as child support, based on §71(c), which classifies as child support payments sums specifically designated as child support by the divorce instrument, as well as payments otherwise classified as alimony to the extent that the amount paid is to be reduced by

---

[34]. I.R.C. §1041(a). See also id. §1041(e) (rule does not apply to transfers in trusts for the benefit of a spouse when liabilities exceed the basis). Property transfers cannot be "alimony" because they are not cash transfers; a cash transfer will constitute a "property settlement" if it does not meet the other requirements for "alimony" outlined in I.R.C. §71(b) (quoted in *Rykiel*).

the happening of a contingency related to the obligor's children or at a time that is clearly associated with such a contingency. In this illustration, only the portion of these obligations to remain unchanged after the youngest child turns 21 will be treated as alimony. Further, if Stephen pays less each year than the total amount of support specified in the divorce instrument for both Karen and the children, the money received will be regarded as child support first, with only the excess treated as deductible alimony. Careful planning, however, can help the parties structure payments to achieve the desired objective of treating as alimony for tax purposes payments intended as child support.[35]

c. Critique. What do these two illustrations reveal? Professor Deborah Geier would discard existing labels and

> explicitly [empower the parties] to determine whether cash transfers—whether denominated alimony, child support, a property settlement, an "equitable distribution" for state law purposes, or otherwise—are includable by the recipient and deductible by the payor, or excludable by the recipient and not deductible by the payor, with simple and clear default rules for taxpayers who fail to make their wishes known in their divorce, separation, or support instrument.[36]

Other critiques of tax law focus on the marriage-centric and gendered assumptions animating the Code. E.g., Anne L. Alstott, Updating the Welfare State: Marriage, the Income Tax, and Social Security in the Age of Individualism, 66 Tax L. Rev. 695 (2013); Martha T. McCluskey, Taxing the Family Work: Aid for Affluent Husband Care, 21 Colum. J. Gender & L. 109 (2011).

5. Other tax considerations. Divorce entails additional tax consequences because it changes the taxpayer's marital status. The couple can no longer file joint returns, so they must decide to file as either head of household or unmarried.[37] Between the two options, head of household is more advantageous, but it requires that the taxpayer must be unmarried on the last day of the taxable year and maintain as his or her home a household constituting the principal residence for an unmarried descendant or other dependent for more than half of the year. Thus, assuming that Karen receives custody of the children, she can file as head of household so long as the children live with her for more than half the year.[38] Because Karen and Stephen hypothetically have more than one child, Stephen would benefit if the court awarded him custody of at least one child, so he could also enjoy the preferential status of head of household.

The taxpayer's filing status determines the amount of the standard deduction available under I.R.C. §63(c). The standard deduction is a flat amount provided to all taxpayers of similar status. Deducted from the adjusted gross income, it operates with the personal exemptions (discussed next) to determine taxable income. If Stephen satisfies the requirements, he can take the head of household standard

---

[35]. I.R.C. §71(c)(3). See Temp. Treas. Reg. §1.71-1T(c) (1984); Schilling v. Commissioner, 104 T.C.M. (CCH) 272 (U.S. Tax Ct. 2012).

[36]. Deborah A. Geier, Simplifying and Rationalizing the Federal Income Tax Law Applicable to Transfers in Divorce, 55 Tax Law. 363, 364 (2002).

[37]. They can file a joint return if they have only a written separation agreement, rather than a decree of divorce or separate maintenance, I.R.C. §6013(d), but then §71(e) makes the favorable treatment of alimony unavailable.

[38]. I.R.C. §2(b).

deduction, a figure adjusted annually for cost of living according to §63(c)(4). Conversely, if Karen maintains the household for all three children, Stephen must file as unmarried. This status offers a lower standard deduction, again a figure adjusted annually for cost-of-living changes.[39] Thus, the standard deduction illustrates how filing status can directly affect tax liability.

Besides the standard deduction, Karen and Stephen will also be permitted personal exemptions to lower their taxable income. I.R.C. §151 allows an exemption for the taxpayer as well as for any eligible dependents. A parent may claim an exemption for a child (including an adopted child, a stepchild, and certain foster children) who has the same principal place of abode as the parent for more than one-half of the year, so long as the child does not provide more than one-half of her own support and has not attained the age of 19 by the close of the year, or is a student who has not attained age 24 by the end of the year. If no one can claim the child as a dependent under those rules—for example, because the age requirement is not satisfied—a parent may still claim the exemption if (1) the child's gross income for the calendar year is less than the exemption amount ($4,000 in 2015), and (2) the parent provides more than one-half of the child's support during the year.[40] For purposes of these support tests, §152(e) specifically refers to children of divorced parents and treats the custodial parent as providing over one-half of the child's support (regardless of actual contribution). Assuming that Karen retains custody of all three children, Stephen cannot take any additional personal exemptions. Nevertheless, Karen could sign a written declaration releasing her claim to one or more of her dependency deductions, enabling Stephen to take advantage of the available exemptions.[41]

After tax liability has been determined, additional tax preferences, known as *credits*, are available to qualifying taxpayers to reduce final tax liability on a dollar-for-dollar basis. Section 24 allows some taxpayers up to $1,000 credit for each child under 17 for whom the taxpayer is entitled to a dependency deduction.[42] In addition, I.R.C. §21 provides for some childcare credits incurred in order for a custodial parent to remain employed.[43]

---

[39]. I.R.C. §63(c)(2), (4).

[40]. I.R.C. §§151(c), 152(a). For the statutory definitions of "dependent," see I.R.C. §152(c) (qualifying child) & (d) (qualifying relative).

[41]. Id. §152(e)(2). State courts have split on the question whether they have the power to award the federal exemption to a noncustodial parent. Compare S. v. S., 2012 WL 1560401 (Del. Fam. Ct. 2012) (recognizing the court's authority to allocate exemption in appropriate cases), with Anderson v. Anderson, 861 N.W.2d 113 (Neb. 2015) (stating that courts lack power to allocate exemption directly but can order a custodial parent to execute a waiver in appropriate cases).

[42]. I.R.C. §24.

[43]. I.R.C. §21(a)(2). Another credit, the earned income credit, although targeted to low-income individuals, gives a larger credit to those with a qualifying child under the age of 19, or 24 if a student. I.R.C. §32(c)(3). The statute provides phaseout percentages based on income, increased in stages. Id. §32(b).

E. Child Support

1. From Discretion to Guidelines

A child support award typically requires the periodic transfer of funds from the noncustodial parent to the custodial parent for the benefit of their child. Once, courts determined child support in the same way that they set alimony—using open-ended standards to reach unpredictable results. Now, however, the regime of judicial discretion in the states has given way to a new approach prompted by federal legislation, the use of mathematical formulas called "guidelines." In the following materials, consider what objectives a child support award should seek to achieve and whether the current approach serves these goals.

TURNER v. TURNER

684 S.E.2d 596 (Ga. 2009)

THOMPSON, Justice.

Raymond and Jessica Turner were married in 1999 and had two children. Raymond filed for divorce in January 2008. The parties reached a partial settlement agreement which provided, inter alia, that husband and wife would share joint legal and physical custody of their two minor children, the custody arrangement being structured so husband is to have physical custody of the children from Friday a.m. until Tuesday a.m., and wife is to have physical custody from Tuesday a.m. through Friday a.m., with exceptions for holidays and other special occasions. [S]ubmitted to the trial court for determination were issues of child support and the division of extracurricular expenses. [The court] entered a final judgment and divorce decree which incorporated the partial settlement agreement, ordered husband to pay $552.09 in monthly child support, and apportioned the expenses for the children's extracurricular activities two-thirds to husband and one-third to wife. [Husband appeals.]

. . . The trial court's order includes a finding that husband earned gross monthly income of $5,483.56, approximately 65 percent of the parties' combined income. After determining a basic child support obligation of $1,582 for the parties' two minor children, the court calculated husband's pro rata share of the basic child support obligation to be $986.75. As evidenced in Schedule E attached to the court's order, however, the court applied a parenting time deviation of $434.66, reducing husband's monthly child support obligation to $552.09. See OCGA [Official Code of Georgia Annotated] §19-6-15(i)(2)(K). Husband does not on appeal challenge the court's decision to deviate from the presumptive child support obligation. Instead, he contends the trial court erred by failing to explain how the court calculated the deviation and failing to include express findings that the deviation was in the best interests of the children and would not seriously impair his ability to provide for the children. We agree. . . .

> [The applicable] guidelines permit the factfinder to deviate
>
> from the presumptive amount of child support when special circumstances make the presumptive amount of child support excessive or inadequate due to extended parenting time as set forth in the order of visitation or when the child resides with both parents equally.

OCGA §19-6-15(i)(2)(K)(i). Where a deviation is determined to apply and the factfinder deviates from the presumptive amount of child support, the order must explain the reasons for the deviation, provide the amount of child support that would have been required if no deviation had been applied, and state how application of the presumptive amount of child support would be unjust or inappropriate and how the best interest of the children for whom support is being determined will be served by the deviation. OCGA §§19-6-15(c)(2)(E) and (i)(1)(B). In addition, the order must include a finding that states how the court's or jury's application of the child support guidelines would be unjust or inappropriate considering the relative ability of each parent to provide support. OCGA §19-6-15(c)(2)(E)(iii). Because the court in this case applied a discretionary parenting time deviation from the presumptive amount of child support but failed to make all of the findings required under [the statute], we reverse the trial court's final judgment and remand this case to the trial court for further proceedings consistent with this opinion.

[We also] address husband's challenge to the trial court's apportionment of the expenses of the children's extracurricular activities because that issue is likely to recur on remand. The trial court's order requires husband to pay two-thirds of the children's extracurricular activities. Husband contends he is paying twice for the cost of extracurricular activities because such costs are included in the presumptive amount of child support. See OCGA §19-6-15(i)(2)(J)(ii).

The language of OCGA §19-6-15(i)(2)(J)(ii) makes clear that a portion of the basic child support obligation is intended to cover average amounts of special expenses for raising children, including the cost of extracurricular activities. If a factfinder determines that the full amount of special expenses described in that division exceeds seven percent of the basic child support obligation, the "additional amount of special expenses shall be considered as a deviation to cover the full amount of the special expenses." Id. Such a deviation must then be included in Schedule E of the Child Support Worksheet and, as with other deviations from the presumptive amount of child support, the factfinder must make the required written findings. See OCGA §19-6-15(i)(1)(B).

The trial court here made no provision in its Schedule E for a deviation for special expenses. Instead, the court included a provision in the final judgment apportioning among the parties the entire cost of the children's extracurricular expenses using essentially the same ratio as applied to the basic child support obligation. . . . Under the [applicable] guidelines, a court may only deviate from the presumptive child support amount based on special expenses incurred for child-rearing, including extracurricular expenses, by complying with OCGA §19-6-15(i)(2)(J)(ii) (defining "special expenses" as certain child-rearing expenses exceeding seven percent of basic child support obligation) and OCGA §19-6-15(i)(1)(B) (requiring written findings for all deviations). Thus, [the court] was without authority to make a separate child support award, one outside the parameters of the Child Support Worksheet, based on the cost of such activities. [Reversed and remanded.]

Notes and Questions

1. Historical background. William Blackstone described the duty of parents to provide for the support of their children as "a principle of natural law."[44] Traditionally, American divorce laws provided only vague guidance on postdissolution child support, using terms such as "just," "reasonable," or "necessary" to direct courts how to set an award.[45] Later, statutes listed factors to be considered, among others, in the exercise of judicial discretion to determine child support obligations,[46] much like the approach many states use for property distribution and spousal support.

Vague standards and judicial discretion resulted in inadequate (or sometimes nonexistent) awards, inconsistency from case to case, disrespect for support orders, and unpredictability, in turn discouraging settlement. Illinois and Maine responded by enacting optional guidelines.[47]

The fiscal burdens of providing subsidies for needy children also prompted federal concern. In 1984 Congress mandated that states use child support guidelines as rebuttable presumptions in "Title IV-D cases" (in which the state seeks to recover from an absent parent payments made to support a needy child). In 1988, Congress extended the guidelines requirement to all cases, 42 U.S.C. §667(a)-(b). Congress imposed these requirements on the states by making compliance a condition for receiving federal welfare funds, subsequently refining these measures and adding new enforcement tools. See Laura W. Morgan, Child Support Fifty Years Later, 42 Fam. L.Q. 365, 365-370 (2008).

2. Objectives. The unpredictability of a system entrusted entirely to judicial discretion was exacerbated by the absence of any clear theory or objective for child support awards. What purposes should an award seek to achieve? Fairness to the noncustodial parent? Prevention of child poverty? Support to the full extent possible? Continuation of the marital standard of living? Equalization of the standard of living in the custodial and noncustodial households? Then how should child support relate to alimony? In other words, does ensuring a standard of living for the child guarantee the same for the custodial parent? How should in-kind contributions of the custodial parent be evaluated? On the difficulty identifying the goals of various approaches to child support, see generally Marsha Garrison, Autonomy or Community? An Evaluation of Two Models of Parental Obligation, 86 Cal. L. Rev. 41 (1999).

What objectives for child support does *Turner* suggest? The federal Advisory Panel on Child Support Guidelines recommended that states should adhere to the following principles in developing guidelines: Both parents should share responsibility for child support; parental subsistence needs should be considered (but

---

[44]. 1 William Blackstone, Commentaries *447-448.

[45]. Vernier, supra note [15], at 193.

[46]. For example, §309 of UMDA directs courts to set an amount "reasonable or necessary," considering "all relevant factors including: (1) the financial resources of the child; (2) the financial resources of the custodial parent; (3) the standard of living the child would have enjoyed had the marriage not been dissolved; (4) the physical and emotional condition of the child and his educational needs; and (5) the financial resources and needs of the noncustodial parent."

[47]. Andrea H. Beller & John W. Graham, Small Change: The Economics of Child Support 165 (1993).

child support should virtually never be set at zero); child support should cover a child's basic needs while allowing enjoyment of a parent's higher standard of living; each child has an equal right to share in a parent's income, subject to factors such as age, income, and other dependents; child support determinations should not depend on the gender or the marital status of the parents; guidelines should not create economic disincentives for remarriage or work; and guidelines should encourage the involvement of both parents in the child's life.[48]

The ALI Principles list nine general objectives, including the child's ability to enjoy both a "minimum decent standard of living" when possible to achieve without impoverishing either parent and a "standard of living not grossly inferior to that of the child's higher income parent," protection of the child from "loss of important life opportunities," fairness to both parents, avoidance of disincentives that discourage parents from working or training for work, as well as fostering cooperation and minimizing parental conflict. ALI Principles §3.04.

3. State responses. Jurisdictions have complied with the federal mandate for guidelines in different ways.[49] All the models are designed to achieve uniformity and predictability, as *Turner* illustrates, by identifying a precise amount that the court presumptively orders.

The income-shares model is the most popular approach, used by 40 states.[50] As the statute cited in *Turner* shows, these states rely on a chart that lists the share of combined parental income allocated for child support at different levels; parents divide the obligation in proportion to their incomes. Twelve jurisdictions use, with some variations, the percentage-of-income model, which allocates a fraction of the noncustodial parent's income for child support.[51] Both rest on a "continuity of expenditures" approach that seeks to project what would have been spent on the child in an intact family. See Jane C. Venohr, Child Support Guidelines and Guidelines Reviews: State Differences and Common Issues, 47 Fam. L.Q. 327, 329 (2013).[52]

4. Different models. What are the advantages and disadvantages of the various approaches?

> The primary advantage of [the percentage-of-income model] is its simplicity. But its simplicity also forms the basis for criticism because the obligor will pay the same dollar amount whether the custodial parent earns no income or an amount equal to that of the obligor. Advocates have countered that the model contains the implicit assumption that the custodial parent contributes his or her share of financial support directly. . . .

[48]. See Laura W. Morgan, Child Support Guidelines: Interpretation and Application §1.04 (2d ed. 2012 & Supp. 2014).

[49]. Twenty-five jurisdictions adopted guidelines by statute, eight by administrative regulations, and 18 by court rule or decision. Id. §1.03 (table 1-2).

[50]. Charts, supra note [2], at 660-661.

[51]. Id.

[52]. Three jurisdictions use the "Melson formula." Morgan, supra note [48], §1.08. For the ALI's recommended formula, see Grace Ganz Blumberg, Balancing the Interests: The American Law Institute's Treatment of Child Support, 33 Fam. L.Q. 39 (1999).

> In addition to designating that both parents make a monetary contribution, the [income-shares] model is flexible in allowing for the apportionment between the parents of additional basic expenses such as work-related child care, extraordinary medical expenses, and a variety of custody arrangements. A disadvantage . . . is that it may reduce the incentive for the custodial parent to increase her work effort because the increased income may lower child support payments. Moreover, it can bring about what may seem like perverse changes in the noncustodial parent's contribution. An increase in the noncustodial parent's income could result in a decrease in the amount of child support owed, and a decrease in income could result in an increase in the amount owed. Any version of this model may be criticized for not acknowledging the nonmonetary contribution of the custodial parent in directly caring for the children. . . .[53]

5. Applying the guidelines. Determining child support awards under the guidelines requires several decisions, including the following: What counts as parental income? See, e.g., Matter of Maves, 101 A.3d 1 (N.H. 2014); Morrow v. Becker, 3 N.E.3d 144 (Ohio 2013). Who must pay whom? See Turk v. Turk, 12 N.E.3d 40 (Ill. 2014). Given that child support guidelines create a rebuttable presumption of the appropriate award, what findings justify deviating from the presumptive amount? See, e.g., In re Marriage of Hein, 253 P.3d 636 (Colo. Ct. App. 2010); Hults v. Hults, 11 So. 3d 1273 (Miss. Ct. App. 2009). How does the statute applicable in *Turner* answer this last question? Cf. McCarthy v. Ashment-McCarthy, 758 S.E.2d 306 (Ga. 2014) (ruling that issue in *Turner* is waived if not properly raised).

6. High- and low-income parents. Courts have struggled with how to apply the guidelines in cases of high-income parents whose numbers exceed those on the charts. Some jurisdictions reject extrapolations from the guidelines (i.e., determining the presumptive amount based on what the chart would have shown). E.g., Dudgeon v. Dudgeon, 318 S.W.3d 106, 110 (Ky. Ct. App. 2010). Without the guidelines, what criteria govern? "Appropriate needs"? See Nuveen v. Nuveen, 825 N.W.2d 863 (N.D. 2012). Continuation of the pre-divorce lifestyle? See Nash v. Nash, 307 P.3d 40 (Ariz. Ct. App. 2013). A "three pony rule" to the effect that, regardless of parental wealth, no child needs more than three ponies? See Schieffer v. Schieffer, 826 N.W.2d 627, 646 n.15 (S.D. 2013) (Konekamp, J., concurring in part and dissenting in part). The notion that the percentage of parental income spent on children decreases as the income itself rises? See Dowling v. Szymczak, 72 A.3d 1 (Conn. 2013). See generally Margaret Ryznar, The Obligations of High-Income Parents, 43 Hofstra L. Rev. 481 (2014).

Although most jurisdictions rely on economic data that reflect average child-rearing expenditures, almost all provide low-income adjustments for poor non-residential parents. The details for these adjustments, however, vary greatly from state to state. See Venohr, supra, at 340-341.

7. Marital status. Because of Supreme Court rulings giving nonmarital children a constitutional right to parental support equal to that of marital children, the guidelines apply to any child whose parents are not part of an intact family.

---

[53]. Beller & Graham, supra note [47], at 200-201. See also Douglas W. Allen & Margaret F. Brinig, Child Support Guidelines and Divorce Incentives, 32 Int'l Rev. L. & Econ. 309 (2012) (finding greater divorce incentives under percentage-of-income model than income-shares model).

See, e.g., Walsh v. Jodoin, 925 A.2d 1086 (Conn. 2007). Do both types of cases permit similar analyses? If one goal of child support is minimizing the effect of parental separation on the child, how does this consideration apply in cases in which the parents of a nonmarital child never cohabited and hence never shared a standard of living? See generally Katharine K. Baker, Homogeneous Rules for Heterogeneous Families: The Standardization of Family Law When There Is No Standard Family, 2012 U. Ill. L. Rev. 319.

8. Shared custody. Can mathematical formulas adequately address the variations and complexities of modern allocations of parental responsibility? Increasingly, courts must consider how to apply guidelines to joint custody and other shared parenting arrangements, such as that in *Turner*. Do such arrangements justify a deviation from the guidelines? Should each joint custodian be treated as a support obligor for the time the child spends with the other parent? See Charts (A Review of the Year in Family Law), 45 Fam. L.Q. 660-661 (2015) (showing how virtually every state addresses shared parenting as a deviation factor or as an offset). Does joint custody warrant a special formula? See, e.g., Rivero v. Rivero, 216 P.3d 213 (Nev. 2009) (using a special formula that is applicable when each parent has physical custody at least 40 percent of the time).

Should travel expenses for visitation be included in the guidelines amount or ordered as an "add-on" to such award? Or should such expenses be subtracted from the parental income available for child support? Compare Steinebach v. Steinebach, 957 So. 2d 291, 302-304 (La. Ct. App. 2007), with Inman v. Williams, 205 P.3d 185, 193-194 (Wyo. 2009). Should employment-related childcare expenses be treated the same way?

9. Family home. The ALI Principles, in §3.05(8), treat the use of the family home by the residential (custodial) parent as a form of additional child support beyond that resulting from the formula, apportioning the costs according to relative parental income and other equities. Under §3.11, an order deferring the sale of the family residence is justified only to avoid "significant detriment to the child"—an assessment based on all relevant factors including, for example, the time the child has lived there, the child's grade in school, and facilitation of the parent's employment. Does the additional benefit that the custodial parent will enjoy by living in the family home undercut the ALI Principles' strict formulaic approach?

10. Health care coverage. Federal law requires state child support guidelines to allocate health care costs (see 42 U.S.C. §652(f); 45 C.F.R. §302.56). Congress also mandates health care coverage for children otherwise ineligible under an employer-sponsored benefit plan (see 42 U.S.C. §1396g-1). State responses vary, with some guidelines "ordering one parent to pay, and then subtracting the cost from the income of that parent," and others either adding the cost to the child support award and prorating it between the parents or, alternatively, making this expense a factor for deviating from the guidelines.[54] Under the Affordable Care

---

[54]. Morgan, supra note [48], §7.01[A]. In terms of process, ERISA provides for Qualified Medical Child Support Orders (QMCSOs), similar to QDROs (discussed supra). ERISA §§609, 514(b)(7), 29 U.S.C. §§1169, 1144(b)(7).

Act, insurance plans providing dependent coverage must make such coverage available until a child turns 26 (42 U.S.C. §300gg-14).

11. Empirical research. Tentative findings from the period when guidelines were first adopted reveal they raise awards as intended—but only for divorced and separated non-Black mothers, not for the never-married and African-American mothers. Economists Andrea Beller and John Graham speculated that the older guidelines may have had loopholes that resulted in fewer awards for the latter populations.[55]

More recent data yield even more guarded conclusions. The poverty rate for families with a noncustodial parent remains higher than that for other families, and custodial mothers continue to be more likely to be poor than custodial fathers.[56] Despite use of guidelines, awards fail to meet the estimated childrearing expenditures.[57] Some contend the solution lies in new formulas. See, e.g., Sanford L. Braver et al., Public Intuitions About Fair Child Support Allocations: Converging Evidence for a "Fair Shares" Rule, 20 Psychol. Pub. Pol'y & L. 146 (2014) (based on lay judgments about fairness). The weak economy and current unemployment rates, however, suggest that the necessary resources often are not available.[58]

12. Beyond today's guidelines. Given the federal goals for child support guidelines, why has Congress not adopted a *national* guideline? Does the formulaic approach to child support work sufficiently well that it should be implemented for allocations of marital property and determinations of spousal support, as suggested by the ALI Principles, which used child support guidelines as a model, and as represented by the Massachusetts Alimony Reform Act (both discussed supra)? Who benefits from the trend toward greater consistency and predictability reflected in the adoption of numerical formulas? Cf. Jane C. Murphy, Eroding the Myth of Discretionary Justice in Family Law: The Child Support Experiment, 70 N.C. L. Rev. 209, 218 (1991) (attributing greater tolerance of discretion in family law than in commercial law to gender of parties seeking relief).

---

[55]. Beller & Graham, supra note [47], at 192, 194.

[56]. Poverty rates for custodial-parent families have remained higher than the poverty rates of other families, with the poverty rate for custodial mothers' families in 2011 (31.8 percent) significantly higher than that for custodial fathers' families (16.2 percent). Timothy S. Grall, U.S. Census Bureau, Custodial Mothers and Fathers and Their Child Support: 2011, at 4 (Oct. 2013), http://www.census.gov/prod/2013pubs/p60-246.pdf. See also Irwin Garfinkel et al., A Brief History of Child Support Policies in the United States, in Fathers Under Fire: The Revolution in Child Support Enforcement 22, 24 (Irwin Garfinkel et al. eds., 1998) (describing actual effect of guidelines as modest, despite large potential effects).

[57]. For the estimated costs of rearing a child for various income categories, see Mark Lino, Expenditures on Children by Families, 2013 (U.S. Dept. of Agric. 2014), http://www.cnpp.usda.gov/sites/default/files/expenditures_on_children_by_families/crc2013.pdf. See also Jane C. Venohr, Child Support Guidelines and Guidelines Reviews: State Differences and Common Issues, 47 Fam. L.Q. 327, 337-339 (2013).

[58]. Even with vigorous efforts to establish and enforce child support obligations, in 2010, 22 percent of children lived in families below the poverty line. Child Trends Data Bank, Children in Poverty: Indicators on Children and Youth 2 (Sept. 2014), http://www.childtrends.org/wp-content/uploads/2014/01/04_Poverty.pdf.

Problem

Denise appeals the trial court's order requiring her former husband, Kevin, to pay $816 monthly child support (instead of the presumptive amount of $1,121 required by the guidelines, based on Kevin's net disposable income). At the time of the order, Kevin was spending only one hour per week with the couple's two young daughters, subject to an order of supervised visitation, stemming from allegations of sexual abuse. In deviating from the guideline, the trial judge explained:

> Presumably the Legislature did not intend to create certain shortfalls in a payor's standard of living solely for the purpose of providing absolute windfalls to the payee parent's and children's standard of living. A child support order of $816 per month will allow Kevin to meet his monthly needs while yet providing Denise and the children with a surplus of $833 over her and the children's stated needs. Such a child support order is in the children's best interest, because to order a guidelines amount providing them with an even larger surplus while leaving Kevin unable to meet his own monthly cost of living would teach them disrespect for the fairness of the legislative and judicial branches of government.

What result when Denise appeals, seeking an award of $1,211 monthly? Was the deviation from the guideline justified? To what extent is the parents' division of time with the children (1 percent for Kevin and 99 percent for Denise) relevant? See In re Marriage of Denise & Kevin C., 67 Cal. Rptr. 2d 508 (Ct. App. 1997). Cf. Perkinson v. Perkinson, 989 N.E.2d 758 (Ind. 2013); In re Marriage of Krieger & Walker, 199 P.3d 450, 457 (Wash. Ct. App. 2008).

2. Postmajority Support

McLEOD v. STARNES

723 S.E.2d 198 (S.C. 2012)

Justice Hearn:

Less than two years ago, this Court decided Webb v. Sowell, 692 S.E.2d 543 [(S.C. 2010)], which held that ordering a non-custodial parent to pay college expenses violates equal protection, thus overruling thirty years of precedent flowing from Risinger v. Risinger, 253 S.E.2d 652 [(S.C. 1979), which had allowed a court to order a noncustodial parent, as an incident of child support, to pay for postsecondary education under appropriate and limited circumstances]. Today, we hold that *Webb* was wrongly decided and remand this matter for reconsideration in light of the law as it existed prior to *Webb*. . . .

Kristi McLeod (Mother) and Robert Starnes (Father) divorced in 1993 following five years of marriage. Mother received custody of their two minor children, and Father was required to pay child support in the amount of $212 per week, which was later reduced to $175 per week by agreement, in addition to thirty-five percent of his annual bonus. At the time, Father earned approximately $29,000 per year plus a $2,500 bonus. However, his salary steadily increased to over $120,000 per year and his bonus to nearly $30,000 by 2007. In 2008, his salary was almost $250,000. During the same time period, Mother's income increased and fluctuated from less than $12,000 per year to a peak of approximately $40,000 per year. Despite the rather sizable increases in Father's income, Mother never sought modification of his child support obligation because, as Father admitted, she had no way of knowing about them.

In August 2006, the parties' older child, Collin, reached the age of majority and enrolled as a student at Newberry College.[1] To help take advantage of this opportunity, he sought all scholarships, loans, and grants that he could. Father wholly supported Collin's decision to attend Newberry [and agreed to pay]. However, Father did not uphold his end of the bargain, nor did he regularly pay the percentage of his bonus as required. [Mother sought an award of college expenses but the court dismissed her claim on equal protection grounds. Mother appeals.]

In *Webb*, we were asked to determine whether requiring a non-custodial parent to pay college expenses was a violation of equal protection. [T]he majority viewed the classification created by *Risinger* for equal protection purposes as those parents subject to a child support order at the time the child is emancipated [rather than the classification raised by the parties: divorced and non-divorced parents]. Without any elaboration, the majority concluded that there is no rational basis for treating parents subject to such an order different than those not subject to one with respect to the payment of college expenses. Upon further reflection, we now believe that we abandoned our long-held rational basis rule that the party challenging a classification must prove there is no conceivable basis upon which it can rest and inverted the burden of proof. By not investigating whether there is any basis to support the alleged classification or refuting the bases argued, we effectively presumed *Risinger*'s reading of what is now section 63-3-530(A)(17) [on child support orders] unconstitutional. Our treatment of this issue thus essentially reviewed *Risinger* under the lens of strict scrutiny as opposed to rational basis. Our decision in *Webb* therefore rests on unsound constitutional principles, and stare decisis does not preclude our reconsideration of the issue addressed in that case.

As with any equal protection challenge, we begin by addressing the class *Risinger* created under section 63-3-530(A)(17). [We use] the same lens used by the family court: whether [*Risinger*] improperly treats divorced parents differently than non-divorced parents.

This State has a strong interest in the outcome of disputes where the welfare of our young citizens is at stake. As can hardly be contested, the State also has a strong interest in ensuring that our youth are educated such that they can become more productive members of our society. It is entirely possible "that most parents who remain married to each other support their children through college years. On the other hand, even well-intentioned parents, when deprived of the custody of their children, sometimes react by refusing to support them as they would if the family unit had been preserved." In re Marriage of Vrban, 293 N.W.2d 198, 202 (Iowa 1980). Therefore, it may very well be that *Risinger* sought to alleviate this harm by "minimiz[ing] any economic and educational disadvantages to children

1. Their younger son, Jamie, has autism; although he attained the age of majority in 2008, he is not expected to graduate from high school until he is twenty-one.

of divorced parents." Kujawinski v. Kujawinski, 376 N.E.2d 1382, 1390 (Ill. 1978); see also LeClair v. LeClair, 624 A.2d 1350, 1357 (N.H. 1993), *superseded by statute on other grounds* ("The legitimate State interest served by these statutes is to ensure that children of divorced families are not deprived of educational opportunities solely because their families are no longer intact."). There is no absolute right to a college education, and section 63-3-530(A)(17), as interpreted by *Risinger* and its progeny, does not impose a moral obligation on all divorced parents with children. Instead, the factors identified by *Risinger* and expounded upon in later cases seek to identify those children whose parents would *otherwise* have paid for their college education, but for the divorce, and provide them with that benefit.

We accordingly hold that requiring a parent to pay, as an incident of child support, for postsecondary education under the appropriate and limited circumstances outlined by *Risinger* is rationally related to the State's interest. . . . Indeed, Father's refusal to contribute towards Collin's college expenses under the facts of this case proves the very ill which *Risinger* attempted to alleviate, for Father articulated no defensible reason for his refusal other than the shield erected by *Webb*. What other reason could there be for a father with more than adequate means and a son who truly desires to attend college to skirt the obligation the father almost certainly would have assumed had he not divorced the child's mother? . . . Thus, this case amply demonstrates what we failed to recognize in *Webb*: sometimes the acrimony of marital litigation impacts a parent's normal sense of obligation towards his or her children. While this is a harsh and unfortunate reality, it is a reality nonetheless that *Risinger* sought to address. . . . We now hold *Risinger* does not violate the Equal Protection Clause because there is a rational basis to support any disparate treatment *Risinger* and its progeny created. . . .[8] . . .

Notes and Questions

1. Historical background. The problem of parental responsibility for postmajority education arose because of the national trend to lower the age of majority in the wake of the Vietnam War. The trend resulted from widespread public sentiment that youth who could enter combat should be able to drink, vote, and exercise other rights. In response, most statutes lowered the age of majority from 21 to 18. See Kathleen Conrey Horan, Postminority Support for College Education—A Legally Enforceable Obligation in Divorce Proceedings?, 20 Fam. L.Q. 589 (1987). This change, however, jeopardized the ability of many children of divorce to pursue a higher education.

As states responded to the ensuing problem of postmajority educational support, some legislatures explicitly addressed the question while some courts took

8. The family court also dismissed Mother's claim because Collin chose to attend a private college. While we agree that the cost of a child's education is a relevant consideration in light of the factors identified in *Risinger* and subsequent cases, attendance at a private school does not foreclose an award of expenses. Instead, the tuition amount is to be factored in with the child's attainment of scholarships, grants, and loans as well as the parents' ability to pay when determining whether to make such an award and in what amount.

the lead by construing existing statutory terms such as "children" and "education" broadly to fashion doctrines of extended dependency and deferred emancipation. Other states enacted special measures designed to supplement child support with postsecondary education subsidies. See In re Marriage of Mullen-Funderburk, 696 N.W.2d 607 (Iowa 2005). Some states later backed away from their expansive approach. E.g., Ex parte Christopher, 145 So. 3d 60 (Ala. 2013) (overturning previous broad judicial interpretation of "children"). Yet, today, most states do not authorize postmajority educational support. Charts (A Review of the Year in Family Law), 48 Fam. L.Q. 660-661 (2015) (chart listing 12 states that provide for college support). Under §3.12 of the ALI Principles, courts may require parents to provide for a child's "life opportunities." See generally Sally F. Goldfarb, Who Pays for the "Boomerang Generation"? A Legal Perspective on Financial Support for Young Adults, 37 Harv. J. L. & Gender 45 (2014).

2. Constitutional problems. Webb v. Sowell, which the principal case overrules, determined that parents under child support orders would suffer unconstitutional discrimination if a court could continue their obligations past the child's majority, given that parents not subject to orders have no legal obligation to provide such support. Thus, the court focused on "the rights of parents." 692 S.E.2d 543, 545 (S.C. 2010). By contrast, the court that struck down Pennsylvania's postmajority support statute as a violation of equal protection focused on the rights of children, given the disadvantage suffered by children in intact families (who have no right to postmajority support), compared to children of divorce. Curtis v. Kline, 666 A.2d 265 (Pa. 1995). What classification does *McLeod* scrutinize? An omitted dissent in *McLeod* describes the classes as "separated, divorced, or unmarried parents and their children versus the parents and children of intact families." To what extent does such framing dictate the result? If any such classifications raise constitutional problems, would this analysis jeopardize laws allowing courts to order divorced parents to pay a specific amount of child support to minors—a protection not provided to minors in intact families? See Stillman v. State, 87 P.3d 200 (Colo. Ct. App. 2003). Must laws providing postmajority educational support for children of divorce also apply to children of never-married parents? Compare Johnson v. Louis, 654 N.W.2d 886 (Iowa 2002), with Walsh v. Jodoin, 925 A.2d 1086 (Conn. 2007). How does the majority's analysis in *McLeod* address the equal protection concerns? What evidence does the court cite? See generally Emily A. Evans, A Jurisprudence Clarified or "McLeod-ed"?: The Real Constitutional Implications of Court-Mandated Postsecondary Educational Support, 64 S.C. L. Rev. 995 (2013).

Do support obligations for higher education interfere with the constitutionally protected autonomy of obligor parents to direct their children's upbringing? (See Meyer v. Nebraska and Pierce v. Society of Sisters, Chapter I.) Suppose a parent believes, as a matter of childrearing philosophy, that the student should be responsible for such expenses.

3. Reciprocal duties. At common law, the child had a right to support, and the parent had a right to the child's services and earnings. See 1 William Blackstone, Commentaries on the Laws of England *453. Although divorce may prevent fulfillment of this reciprocal relationship, the principle that child support is an individual parental responsibility still controls. Professor Harry Krause, however, suggests that family disruption's impact on this reciprocity has far-reaching consequences:

> . . . When Blackstone formulated the support obligation for the common law world, he was looking at a world that was centered on the ongoing family. Divorce did not exist. . . . Choosing to rest most of his case on natural law and what we now call sociobiology, Blackstone did not say that the support obligation was founded on the reciprocal relationship of parent and child in the ongoing family, but I think it was. This reciprocity had an economic and a social component.
>
> Economically, the support-obligated parent was entitled to the child's earnings until the child reached majority. More important, economic reciprocity extended to the parent's old age. Support received by the young child morally and legally obligated the adult child to support the aged parent. Thus, before we had Social Security, child support was an "investment" the parent made, to be recovered if needed. . . . Socially, parent and child reciprocity involved an ongoing family life. . . .
>
> The point is that the absent parent may fairly claim that he is not getting his money's worth for the support he is obligated to pay, not on the economic or social level. Today's enlarged child support obligation does not resemble what Blackstone was talking about. . . .[59]

Does increased reliance on public support follow from Krause's analysis? Do unmet needs for children?

4. **Applications.** In the states allowing courts to order postmajority support for higher education, reasonable expenses (not the guidelines) determine the amount. Such expenses may encompass such education-related costs as tuition, books, room, and board, as well as food, clothing, phone service, and transportation. E.g., Jacoby v. Jacoby, 47 A.3d 40 (N.J. Super. Ct. App. Div. 2012). Often, the student must achieve a particular level of academic success and provide the obligor with documentation. See, e.g., Cossitt v. Cossitt, 975 So. 2d 274 (Miss. Ct. App. 2008) (2.0 average); Waddington v. Cox, 247 S.W.3d 567 (Mo. Ct. App. 2008) (transcript). Do such requirements, imposed by statute or court order, unfairly burden the students to whom they apply? Violate their educational privacy rights? See 20 U.S.C. §1232g(d) (requiring consent of students over 18 under federal family and educational privacy rights legislation).

5. **Children with disabilities.** What postmajority obligations do parents have for children with disabilities, like Jamie in *McLeod* (see footnote 1 of the opinion)? Some states impose statutory duties for parents to support such children, regardless of age. E.g., Cal. Fam. Code §3910; V.L.-S. v. M.S., 266 P.3d 1267 (Mont. 2011). But see Hays v. Alexander, 114 So. 3d 704 (Miss. 2013) (no statutory or common law duty). In other states, courts lack jurisdiction over children with disabilities who reach adulthood before the parents divorce. E.g., Geygan v. Geygan, 973 N.E.2d 276 (Ohio Ct. App. 2012). If child support is ordered during the child's minority, however, it may continue indefinitely. See Weston v. Weston, 40 A.3d 934 (Me.

---

[59]. Harry D. Krause, Child Support Reassessed: Limits of Private Responsibility and the Public Interest, in Divorce Reform at the Crossroads, supra note [16], at 166, 178-180.

2011). See generally Anna Stępień-Sporek & Margaret Ryznar, Child Support for Adult Children, 30 Quinnipiac L. Rev. 359 (2012).

Problem

Patrick, the son of Cherry and John, was 12 at the time of their divorce. When Patrick turns 18, Cherry (who has custody) files a petition to increase John's child support payments to include $30,000 in combined tuition and expenses at Trinity College, a private college where Patrick has gained admission. Cherry shows that John's net worth exceeds $1 million. Assuming that the court has the authority to order postmajority support for education, what result on Cherry's petition and why? What additional evidence, if any, might be relevant in order for the court to decide?

Should the court consider the quality of the relationship between the noncustodial parent and child? See Mazurek v. Russell, 96 A.3d 372 (Pa. Super. Ct. 2014). The selection of the school without the parent's approval? See Dyke v. Scopetti, 121 A.3d 684 (Vt. 2015). What should be the extent of the noncustodial parent's obligation? Public higher education? Private? Graduate school? What facts must support the determination? Parents' educational background? Academic talent? A wealthy noncustodial parent? See, e.g., Ex parte Bayliss, 550 So. 2d 986 (Ala. 1989), *appeal after remand*, 575 So. 2d 1117 (Ala. Civ. App. 1990), *overruled*, Ex parte Christopher, supra. Cf. In re Marriage of Vaughan, 812 N.W.2d 688 (Iowa 2012).

3. Modification of Child Support

a. New Families

POHLMANN v. POHLMANN

703 So. 2d 1121 (Fla. Dist. Ct. App. 1997)

PETERSON, J. . . .

[The former husband unsuccessfully petitioned to reduce his child support obligation, alleging that this modification was justified by changed circumstances, including a permanent decrease in his income, his remarriage and his three children from this marriage, and his former wife's remarriage. He appeals.]

We first address the former husband's argument that subsection 61.30(12) is unconstitutional. The subsection provides:

> **61.30 Child Support Guidelines.**—. . .
>
> (12) A parent with a support obligation may have other children living with him or her who were born or adopted after the support obligation arose. The existence of such subsequent children should not as a general rule be considered by the court as a basis for disregarding the amount provided in the guidelines. The parent with a support obligation for subsequent children

may raise the existence of such subsequent children as a justification for deviation from the guidelines. However, if the existence of such subsequent children is raised, the income of the other parent of the subsequent children shall be considered by the court in determining whether or not there is a basis for deviation from the guideline amount. *The issue of subsequent children may only be raised in a proceeding for an upward modification of an existing award and may not be applied to justify a decrease in an existing award.*

(Emphasis added.) [W]e apply the rational basis standard of review because neither a suspect classification nor a fundamental right is involved. See Feltman v. Feltman, 434 N.W.2d 590 (S.D. 1989). . . . [W]e find that subsection 61.30(12) furthers a legitimate state interest and affirm the trial court's finding of constitutionality. The statute assures that noncustodial parents will continue to contribute to the support of their children from their first marriage notwithstanding their obligation to support children born during a subsequent marriage. Granting priority of child support to children of an earlier first marriage, the *Feltman* court determined that the South Dakota statute provided a fair and logical prioritization of claims against a noncustodial parent's income. "Without prioritization, the children from the first family might find their standard of living substantially decreased by the voluntary acts of a noncustodial parent. A noncustodial parent who elects to become responsible for supporting the children of a second marriage does so with the knowledge of a continuing responsibility to the children of the first marriage." [434 N.W.2d at 592.]

We also affirm the trial court's finding that the former husband failed to show a substantial change of circumstances. . . . In an attempt to manufacture a substantial change in circumstances, the former husband and his current wife produced the latter's petition for separate maintenance [and child support] which tellingly was filed only two weeks before trial. The current wife testified that while she filed such petition in order to assure that her three children would be provided for, nothing in their marital relationship has changed. The trial court did not abuse its discretion in finding that the former husband failed to meet his burden of proving a permanent, involuntary, and substantial change in circumstances. . . .

HARRIS, J., dissenting.

The issue in this case, quite simply, is whether it is a "legitimate government interest" for the State, through its legislative process, to prefer certain children over others. . . . It is not appropriate for the state to punish the children of a second marriage because their parent was involved in a previous divorce.

Although the state should not involve itself with the divorced parent's decision regarding remarriage, our statute is designed to discourage a parent from having a second family unless he or she is willing to support the second family at a lesser standard. . . . At least the parent has assumed the risk of state discrimination. But the children of the later marriage were not aware of the statutory provision nor did they consent to be born into state-mandated poverty. . . .

. . . The state's current approach is Cinderellian—it makes noncustodial parents appear as wicked stepparents to their own children by requiring them to provide new ball gowns for their first born while supplying hand-me-downs to their later children. . . . The children of the first marriage simply have no more veto power over the noncustodial parent's future reproductive decisions than a child of an intact marriage has over his parents' decision to have additional children. . . .

Because the state has no business discriminating between children based solely on the fact of a divorce, there is no legitimate state purpose in requiring a parent to allocate his or her income more to one child than another. . . .

Notes and Questions

1. Successive families. Several factors occurring after dissolution might implicate a parent's support obligations. The increasing incidence of multiple and "blended" families raises questions about the role subsequent family obligations should play in applying support guidelines to children of a prior marriage or other relationship. What are the rationale and implications of *Pohlmann*'s approach, sometimes called the "first family first" approach? See, e.g., Adrienne Jennings Lockie, Multiple Families, Multiple Goals, Multiple Failures: The Need for "Limited Equalization" as a Theory of Child Support, 32 Harv. J.L. & Gender 109, 110-111 (2009); Elizabeth S. Scott & Robert E. Scott, Parents as Fiduciaries, 81 Va. L. Rev. 2401, 2466-2468 (1995).

In applying the rule in *Pohlmann*, should "subsequent" refer to a child's age or the date of a support order? See Coleman v. McCullough, 290 P.3d 413 (Alaska 2012); Thompson v. Dehne, 220 P.3d 1132 (N.M. Ct. App. 2009). Why did the current wife in *Pohlmann* attempt to get a child support order? How should the court calculate the former husband's support obligation to his children with this wife, if faced with that issue?

2. Factual variations. Case law reveals many variations on the theme suggested by *Pohlmann*'s facts. Can the guidelines ignore a father's older children, born during his extant marriage, in determining the support that he must now pay for the child he conceived in an extramarital affair? See Gallaher v. Elam, 104 S.W.3d 455 (Tenn. 2003). What methodology should courts use to calculate support awards for children in multiple households? See Harte v. Hand, 105 A.3d 1171 (N.J. Super. Ct. Chan. Div. 2014). Suppose that the father in *Pohlmann* had taken a second job so that he could support his new family. See Fla. Stat. Ann. §61.30(12)(a).

3. Different approaches. When Congress directed states to adopt child support guidelines in 1988, it left to the states the weight to be given to a parent's obligations to successive families. In contrast to *Pohlmann*, some courts follow a "second family first" doctrine, deducting the support needed for the second family to determine the parent's available income before applying the guidelines to calculate the first family's support. Is this a better approach? Suppose that states following this approach allow the obligor to invoke support of the subsequent family defensively (to show why the court should not increase his present obligation to his prior family), but not offensively (to reduce support to the prior family). E.g., Schwarz v. Schwarz, 857 N.W.2d 802, 806 (Neb. 2015).

Alternatively, should courts take into account the obligor's subsequent family by recognizing it as a reason to deviate from the guideline amount in computing support owed to the earlier children? See State ex rel. J.V.G. v. Van Guilder, 154 P.3d 243 (Wash. Ct. App. 2007). Should child support received by a parent who is obligated to pay support for a different child count as part of that parent's income for computing the guideline amount? Compare Hammond v. Hammond, 651 S.E.2d 95 (Ga. 2007), with New Hanover Child Support Enforcement v. Rains, 666 S.E.2d 800 (N.C. Ct. App. 2008). See generally Martha Minow, How Should We Think About Child Support Obligations?, in Fathers Under Fire: The Revolution in Child Support Enforcement 302, 313-318 (Irwin Garfinkel et al., eds., 1998) (examining conflicting intuitions on support priorities in successive families).

4. Constitutionality. What constitutional problems does the dissent in *Pohlmann* identify? Is this analysis persuasive? Does the "second family first" approach have similar flaws because it treats unfairly the earlier children? Should states be required to consider all of an obligor's children, wherever they may be living, and then divide among them the money available for support? See Lockie, supra.

Can the state restrict the choice to have a second family to protect the first family's financial position? Does Zablocki v. Redhail (Chapter II) apply? As *Pohlmann* illustrates, constitutional challenges to state child support schedules have failed. See also, e.g., *Gallaher*, supra.

5. Obligations of stepparents. What financial responsibilities does law impose upon stepparents? At common law stepparents had no duty to support their stepchildren either during a marriage or following its dissolution, but courts and legislatures are changing these rules. See generally Margaret M. Mahoney, Stepparents as Third Parties in Relation to Their Stepchildren, 40 Fam. L.Q. 81 (2006).

Several states have statutes imposing financial responsibility on a stepparent who receives a child into the family, so long as the child remains in the home. E.g., Mo. Rev. Stat. §453.400. Others simply codify the doctrine of in loco parentis, presuming a stepparent who accepts and supports a child does so as a parent but allowing unilateral termination of that status at any time (e.g., Okla. Stat. Ann. tit. 43, §112.4), or look to stepparents only when a child would otherwise become destitute (e.g., Vt. Stat. Ann. tit. 15, §296). The obligation does not continue, however, upon dissolution of that marriage unless the stepparent has actively interfered with the child's support from the biological parent. See generally Cynthia Grant Bowman, The New Illegitimacy: Children of Cohabiting Couples and Stepchildren, 20 Am. U. J. Gender Soc. Pol'y & L. 437 (2012).

Under the ALI Principles, one who agrees or undertakes to assume a parental support obligation to a child might later be estopped from denying a parental support obligation. ALI Principles §3.03(1)(a). Accordingly, a court could impose a child support obligation on the stepparent after the dissolution of the relationship with the child's parent. See id. cmt. b. An adult obligated to pay child support is a parent by estoppel for purposes of determining custodial and decisionmaking responsibility. Id. §2.03. See also Mary Ann Mason & Nicole Zayac, Rethinking Stepparent Rights: Has the ALI Found a Better Definition?, 36 Fam. L.Q. 227 (2002).

6. New mate's income. Should a court, in computing a parent's child support obligation, take into account the resources of this parent's new spouse or partner? Why? See, e.g., Lockie, supra. How does the statute quoted in *Pohlmann* address this issue?

7. Policy. What stepparent obligations would make sound policy? Professor David Chambers has observed that residential stepparents often "replace" the absent biological parent, who recedes from the child's life emotionally and becomes less willing to pay child support. Yet, he would not adjust child support obligations whenever remarriage occurs, to avoid the risk of encouraging remarriage decisionmaking based on economic consequences or spite. Regarding stepparent responsibility for continued child support after the breakup of the subsequent relationship, Chambers suggests that relevant factors in this determination include the length of time the stepparent lived with the child, the extent of support the stepparent actually provided, and the extent of support the biological parents provided during the marriage.[60] Would a durational test provide a better means of determining economic interdependence? See Bowman, supra, at 465 (suggesting two-year co-residence, regardless of marriage).

8. Modification. The issue posed by *Pohlmann* often arises in litigation seeking to modify an existing child support award, because courts can modify child support awards based upon a showing of changed circumstances. The standards for modifying maintenance and child support are the same under UMDA §316 (discussed supra). Should the obligor's acquisition of a second family have the same impact in both contexts? Today, some states have replaced the changed circumstances test with an examination whether the award is inconsistent with an application of the guidelines. See Morales v. Morales, 984 N.E.2d 748 (Mass. 2013).

9. Retroactive modification. Most jurisdictions have long disallowed retroactive modification of child support obligations (that is, alterations of payments past due). E.g., Wiseman v. Wiseman, 863 N.W.2d 243 (S.D. 2015). Note that the rule against retroactive modification places the burden on the obligor to seek modification as soon as circumstances change.

Now, federal legislation requires all states to recognize child support obligations as judgments once due, entitled to full faith and credit, and to disallow retroactive modification. 42 U.S.C. §666(a)(9). Does this requirement mean that states lose the discretion to forgive arrearages even when equity dictates relief for the obligor or the facts show the obligor's inability to pay during the period in question? See James-Dickens v. Petit-Compere, 683 S.E.2d 83 (Ga. Ct. App. 2009). See also Harry D. Krause, Child Support Reassessed: Limits of Private Responsibility and the Public Interest, in Divorce Reform at the Crossroads at 166, 175 (Stephen D. Sugarman & Herma Hill Kay eds., 1990) (recommending forgiveness of arrears owed to government when obligor has no hope of repayment).

---

[60]. David L. Chambers, Stepparents, Biologic Parents, and the Law's Perceptions of "Family" After Divorce, in Divorce Reform at the Crossroads, supra note [16], 102, 117, 127-128.

b. Employment Changes

OLMSTEAD v. ZIEGLER

42 P.3d 1102 (Alaska 2002)

FABE, Chief Justice. . . .

William Olmstead and Elizabeth Ziegler married in August 1989. Their only child, Lauren, was born in January 1990. They divorced in December 1994. [Their settlement agreement, which was incorporated into the divorce decree,] provided for joint legal and physical custody of their daughter and specified that neither party would pay child support to the other. However, Olmstead did agree to pay for their daughter's daycare and education expenses. Their daughter no longer requires constant daycare, and she now attends public schools. Olmstead estimates that he spends approximately $80 per month on child care.

At the time of the divorce, the parties [both attorneys] submitted a child support affidavit, as required by Alaska Civil Rule 90.3(3). Olmstead's estimated 1994 annual gross income was $53,000 and Ziegler's was $25,000. Ziegler's estimate proved to be high, as she actually earned $16,753 in 1994. Ziegler was subsequently hired as an attorney with the firm of Baxter, Bruce & Brand in Juneau, where her annual income increased significantly. In 1998, she earned $53,761.

In August 1996 Olmstead's law partner of several years, Patrick Conheady, left the partnership. Conheady claimed that Olmstead was unproductive and frequently played card games on his computer instead of working on his cases. Olmstead became a solo practitioner. While he sought other positions and applied for several state jobs, he was apparently unsuccessful in obtaining other employment. Olmstead's income decreased significantly during this period. In 1996 his income dropped to $10,157. In 1998 he earned $13,075.

In March 1999 Olmstead informed his friends and colleagues in Juneau that he would be leaving the practice of law, as he had decided to go back to school to become a teacher. In order to make ends meet in the meantime, he offered his legal research and writing services to other attorneys. Olmstead has since remarried. Ziegler remains single.

On June 3, 1999, Olmstead filed a motion for an order modifying child support. . . . The trial court found that, although their financial situations may have changed, the parties still possessed equal earning capacities. The trial court also reasoned that, although Olmstead was free to change careers, he was not entitled to a modification of child support: "[Olmstead] has elected to learn new things for a while, and perhaps take on a new career. He is free to do so, but under our case law [Ziegler] and the child are not expected to finance these choices." Olmstead appeals. . . .

Olmstead claims that the court erred in finding that he was voluntarily underemployed and contends that the court improperly relied upon his decision to change careers in making that finding. Olmstead points out that he did not ask for a modification of child support based upon his income as a student or teacher. Rather, he requested a modification based entirely upon his earnings while he was a practicing attorney. He thus claims that it was improper for the trial court to rely on his career change when he did not make it a basis for his motion. Olmstead adds that he made a mistake by choosing law as a profession, and that he lacks the personality traits necessary for success in the field. . . . Ziegler counters that Olmstead's lack of success in law and subsequent move to teaching are the results of his voluntary actions. . . .

Voluntarily reducing one's income may not justify a modification of child support. Determining whether or not a parent is voluntarily and unreasonably underemployed is essentially a question of fact. . . . A trial court may find that underemployment is voluntary even if the obligor acted in good faith.

We conclude that the trial court did not err in finding that Olmstead was voluntarily and unreasonably underemployed. The evidence before the trial court established that Olmstead took many steps, including closing his office and failing to keep regular business hours, that demonstrated his intent to downsize his practice. He also significantly reduced his workload hoping to obtain a job with the Department of Transportation. In addition, the record contains an affidavit from Olmstead's former partner, Conheady, recounting his difficulties with Olmstead's lack of productivity: Conheady states that he left the partnership because Olmstead was not producing enough billable hours. While Olmstead has repeatedly stated that he was simply a failure at law and was not capable of earning the average lawyer's salary, he has provided scant support for his assertions. In addition, Olmstead's claims that he was unable to make a living practicing law are undermined by the fact that at one time he made over $53,000 a year.

[I]t was permissible for the trial court to consider Olmstead's career change in determining the issue of voluntary and unreasonable underemployment. . . . Moreover, . . . Civil Rule 90.3 recognizes that "[w]hen a parent makes a career change, this consideration should include the extent to which the children will ultimately benefit from the change." . . . Since Olmstead has failed to prove any benefit to the child from his decision to downsize his practice and change careers, the trial court did not err in finding that a modification is not warranted. . . .

[T]he record supports the trial court's view that Olmstead was not working at his full capacity. . . . The trial court based its view of Olmstead's earning capacity on his actual past earnings as well as on other factors discussed above. The trial court had before it ample evidence of Olmstead's work history, qualifications, and job opportunities. . . . The record also contains evidence that Olmstead at one time made over $50,000 per year while practicing law. Implicit in the trial court's evaluation of Olmstead's earning capacity is its rejection of his claims that he is simply not a successful solo practitioner. Also included in the record are Alaska Department of Labor statistics stating that the average income for male attorneys in Alaska is $65,811. In sum, the trial court's determination that Olmstead had the capacity to earn as much as Ziegler is not clearly erroneous. [Affirmed.]

Notes and Questions

1. Decreased income: Applicable test. Parental income provides the starting point for computing child support under the guidelines. How should courts respond when a parent who decides to switch careers or pursue additional education cites decreased income in seeking a reduction in child support? What test does *Olmstead* apply? Is the voluntary nature of the change controlling, or must the court deem the change unreasonable too? How should courts assess voluntariness? What criteria determine unreasonableness? Is the obligor's imprisonment a voluntary or involuntary change of circumstances? Compare Metz v. Metz, 711 S.E.2d 737 (N.C. Ct. App. 2011), with In re State and Lounder, 96 A.3d 970 (N.H. 2014). What about a decision to go to medical school if, before marriage, the parties agreed that the father could pursue such training after the mother completed her education? See Harvey v. Robinson, 665 A.2d 215 (Me. 1995). Suppose that the obligor must take a lower-paying job because he was fired from his prior job for misconduct. See In re Marriage of Applegate, 801 N.W.2d 627 (Iowa Ct. App. 2011).

An alternative approach articulates a motive-based test, disallowing modification only when the change in employment reflects bad faith. Compare Garcia v. Garcia, 288 P.3d 931 (Okla. 2012), with Iliff v. Iliff, 339 S.W.3d 74 (Tex. 2011). Other approaches include a "best interests" standard and a "balancing test." See Engle v. Landman, 212 P.3d 842 (Ariz. Ct. App. 2009). Are any of these standards preferable to the test used in *Olmstead*? See generally Lewis Becker, Spousal and Child Support and the "Voluntary Reduction of Income" Doctrine, 29 Conn. L. Rev. 647 (1997).

2. Imputation. By refusing to reduce Olmstead's child support obligation, the court is imputing his former income to him—that is, calculating his obligation as if he were earning at his capacity. Other courts perform a more searching inquiry before imputing income, looking beyond earning capacity and requiring proof of the availability of employment opportunities at the higher level. See In re Marriage of Berger, 88 Cal. Rptr. 3d 766 (Ct. App. 2008). See also Melinda H. v. William R., 742 S.E.2d 419 (W.Va. 2013) (using a three-part test). To what extent do dissolution and its financial obligations limit parental freedom to change careers and jobs?

Parents might also be "underemployed" to care for their children at home. Should income be imputed in such cases, for purposes of calculating the child support obligation, or should the law recognize a "nurturing parent" exception? See *Melinda H.*, supra. Should the answer turn on whether the parent in question has always stayed home (or had only part-time employment) or whether she left a full-time position in order to care for new children in a subsequent marriage? Compare, e.g., In re Marriage of Mosley, 82 Cal. Rptr. 3d 497, 506-509 (Ct. App. 2008), with Kraisinger v. Kraisinger, 928 A.2d 333, 342-343 (Pa. Super. Ct. 2007). See also Hollinsworth v. Hollinsworth, 757 N.W.2d 422 (N.D. 2008); Mark Strasser, Paying to Stay Home: On Competing Notions of Fairness and the Imputation of Income, in Reconceiving the Family: Critique on the American Law Institute's Principles of the Law of Family Dissolution 142 (Robin Fretwell Wilson ed., 2006).

3. Increased income. How should courts treat changes that *increase* the obligor's ability to pay? In Smith v. Freeman, 814 A.2d 65 (Md. Ct. Spec. App. 2002), a case about a professional football player whose salary increased significantly under a new contract, the court emphasized that either a change in the child's needs or a change in parental resources can justify an upward modification. What explains this approach? Would a child likely benefit from increased parental income in an intact family? Wouldn't all members in an intact family also experience decreases in income? Why should a child get the benefits but not the burdens of changes in the obligor's fortune? See also Steven K. Berenson, Economic Windfalls and Child Support: How Should Gifts, Inheritances, and Prizes Be Treated?, 47 Suffolk U. L. Rev. 701 (2014).

4. Automatic adjustment. Frequently, a child support award becomes inadequate over time. The applicable rule treats increases and decreases the same, requiring the party seeking modification to show sufficiently changed circumstances. This rule, which discourages modification to protect courts from the burden of such proceedings, has "impoverishing effects":

> The prevailing American rule for child support modification in many instances requires the custodial parent, usually the mother, to absorb the effects of inflation, the additional cost of raising older children, and changes in the child's needs, regardless of changes in the obligor's income. To remedy these imbalances, she must bear the cost of pursuing a new action and, in most states, prove that a party's circumstances have substantially changed since the date of the original order. Further, she must make this decision with little guidance as to the likelihood of success: she is generally ignorant of the obligor's true financial situation, and the judge's broad discretion to find that circumstances have or have not substantially changed creates even more uncertainty.[61]

Federal welfare reform law gives states three options for reviewing and adjusting awards: (1) required state review of guidelines every four years with administrative review of all awards in Title IV-D cases every three years and in all other cases when either parent so requests, (2) a cost-of-living adjustment (using a consumer price index to update the amount periodically), or (3) automated adjustment (based on tax or other records). 42 U.S.C. §666(a)(10)(A). The custodial parent still has the burden of requesting review, however. What problems might this burden cause? To remove the burden from the custodial parent, a few states make the passage of time sufficient for modification, by including in awards automatic "escalator clauses" tied to the cost of living or adopting procedures requiring review every three years. See Laura W. Morgan, Child Support Guidelines: Interpretation and Application §9.05 (2d ed. 2012 & Supp. 2014). Should Congress mandate such rules for all states?

Problem

At the time of divorce, the court ordered Samih, a chemist earning $46,000 annually in Indiana, to pay $174 per week in child support. When his employer required Samih to relocate to Minnesota, he refused because he wanted to remain close to his children in Indiana. Samih thereupon lost his job and started his own company, Vintage Chemicals. He earned $16,200 the first year and expected to earn $20,000 the following year. He seeks a decrease in his child support obligation

---

[61]. J. Thomas Oldham, Abating the Feminization of Poverty: Changing the Rules Governing Post-Decree Modification of Child Support Obligations, 1994 BYU L. Rev. 841, 843-844.

based on his reduced income. What result and why? Is Samih's reason for refusing to relocate relevant? See Abouhalkah v. Sharps, 795 N.E.2d 488 (Ind. Ct. App. 2003). See also Olson v. Mohammadu, 81 A.3d 215 (Conn. 2013); Payne v. Payne, 206 S.W.3d 379 (Mo. Ct. App. 2006).

F. Enforcement

Traditionally, enforcement of the financial consequences of family dissolution was largely a matter of private responsibility. Over the years, however, states and the federal government have assumed a significant role. Although child support enforcement in particular has become a national priority, problems in enforcing property divisions and alimony awards persist as well.

This section examines enforcement mechanisms, including traditional state-created private remedies and modern measures triggered by the "federalization" of this part of family law, with an emphasis on the collection of child support awards. Consider first how law should allocate enforcement responsibilities among individual obligees, the states, and the federal government. Further, consider how enforcement efforts might harm those whom the law seeks to help. Finally, consider whether the need for effective enforcement should trump even fundamental privacy rights and liberty interests, an issue posed by the following case.

1. Criminal Nonsupport

STATE v. OAKLEY

629 N.W.2d 200 (Wis.), *reconsideration denied & opinion clarified,* 635 N.W.2d 760 (Wis. 2001), *cert. denied,* 537 U.S. 813 (2002)

Jon P. Wilcox, J. . . .

David Oakley (Oakley), the petitioner, was initially charged with intentionally refusing to pay child support for his nine children he has fathered with four different women. The State subsequently charged Oakley with seven counts of intentionally refusing to provide child support as a repeat offender. [D]uring the relevant time period, Oakley had paid no child support and . . . there were arrears in excess of $25,000. [T]he State argued that Oakley should be sentenced to six years in prison. . . .

After taking into account Oakley's ability to work and his consistent disregard of the law and his obligations to his children, Judge Hazlewood observed that . . . "if Mr. Oakley goes to prison, he's not going to be in a position to pay any meaningful support for these children." [The judge imposed a term of probation and] then imposed the condition at issue here: while on probation, Oakley cannot have any more children unless he demonstrates that he had the ability to support them and that he is supporting the children he already had. After sentencing, Oakley filed for postconviction relief contesting this condition. . . .

Refusal to pay child support by so-called "deadbeat parents" has fostered a crisis with devastating implications for our children. [Census data show that, of] those single parent households with established child support awards or orders, approximately one-third did not receive any payment while another one-third received only partial payment. For example, in 1997, out of $26,400,000,000 awarded by a court order to custodial mothers, only $15,800,000,000 was actually paid, amounting to a deficit of $10,600,000,000. These figures represent only a portion of the child support obligations that could be collected if every custodial parent had a support order established. Single mothers disproportionately bear the burden of nonpayment as the custodial parent. On top of the stress of being a single parent, the nonpayment of child support frequently presses single mothers below the poverty line. In fact, 32.1% of custodial mothers were below the poverty line in 1997, in comparison to only 10.7% of custodial fathers. Indeed, the payment of child support is widely regarded as an indispensable step in assisting single mothers to scale out of poverty, especially when their welfare benefits have been terminated due to new time limits.

. . . In addition to engendering long-term consequences such as poor health, behavioral problems, delinquency and low educational attainment, inadequate child support is a direct contributor to childhood poverty. . . . Child support—when paid—on average amounts to over one-quarter of a poor child's family income. There is little doubt that the payment of child support benefits poverty-stricken children the most. Enforcing child support orders thus has surfaced as a major policy directive in our society.

In view of the suffering children must endure when their noncustodial parent intentionally refuses to pay child support, it is not surprising that the legislature has attached severe sanctions to this crime. Wis. Stat. §948.22(2). This statute makes it a Class E felony for any person "who intentionally fails for 120 or more consecutive days to provide spousal, grandchild or child support which the person knows or reasonably should know the person is legally obligated to provide. . . ."[19] A Class E felony is punishable with "a fine not to exceed $10,000 or imprisonment not to exceed 2 years, or both." The legislature has amended this statute so that intentionally refusing to pay child support is now punishable by up to five years in prison.

But Wisconsin law is not so rigid as to mandate the severe sanction of incarceration as the only means of addressing a violation of §948.22(2). In sentencing, a Wisconsin judge can take into account a broad array of factors, including the gravity of the offense and need for protection of the public and potential victims. . . . After considering all these factors, a judge may decide to forgo the severe punitive sanction of incarceration and address the violation with the less restrictive alternative of probation coupled with specific conditions. . . . As we have previously observed, "the theory of the probation statute is to rehabilitate the defendant and protect society without placing the defendant in prison." . . .

---

19. In Wisconsin, a circuit court typically orders support payments as a percentage of a parent's income, not as an invariable dollar amount. This means that it is within any parent's ability—regardless of his or her actual income or number of children he or she has—to comply with a child support order.

But Oakley argues that the condition imposed by Judge Hazlewood violates his constitutional right to procreate. This court, in accord with the United States Supreme Court, has previously recognized the fundamental liberty interest of a citizen to choose whether or not to procreate. [Citations omitted.] Accordingly, Oakley argues that the condition here warrants strict scrutiny. That is, it must be narrowly tailored to serve a compelling state interest. Although Oakley concedes, as he must, that the State's interest in requiring parents to support their children is compelling, he argues that the means employed here is not narrowly tailored to serve that compelling interest because Oakley's "right to procreate is not restricted but in fact eliminated." According to Oakley, his right to procreate is eliminated because he "probably never will have the ability to support" his children. Therefore, if he exercises his fundamental right to procreate while on probation, his probation will be revoked and he will face the stayed term of eight years in prison.

. . . We emphatically reject the novel idea that Oakley, who was convicted of intentionally failing to pay child support, has an absolute right to refuse to support his current nine children and any future children that he procreates, thereby adding more child victims to the list. In an analogous case, Oregon upheld a similar probation condition to protect child victims from their father's abusive behavior in State v. Kline, 963 P.2d 697, 699 (Or. Ct. App. 1998). Furthermore, Oakley fails to note that incarceration, by its very nature, deprives a convicted individual of the fundamental right to be free from physical restraint, which in turn encompasses and restricts other fundamental rights, such as the right to procreate. . . .

[The condition of probation is not overly broad. Oakley can satisfy it] by making efforts to support his children as required by law. Judge Hazlewood placed no limit on the number of children Oakley could have. Instead, the requirement is that Oakley acknowledge the requirements of the law and support his present and any future children. If Oakley decides to continue his present course of conduct—intentionally refusing to pay child support—he will face eight years in prison regardless of how many children he has. Furthermore, this condition will expire at the end of his term of probation. He may then decide to have more children, but of course, if he continues to intentionally refuse to support his children, the State could charge him again. . . .

[T]he condition essentially bans Oakley from violating the law again. . . . Accordingly, this condition is reasonably related to his rehabilitation because it will assist Oakley in conforming his conduct to the law. . . .

Ann Walsh Bradley, J. [joined by Shirley S. Abrahamson, C.J., and Diane S. Sykes, J.] (dissenting). . . .

. . . Today's decision makes this court the only court in the country to declare constitutional a condition that limits a probationer's right to procreate based on his financial ability to support his children. . . . While on its face the order leaves room for the slight possibility that Oakley may establish the financial means to support his children, the order is essentially a prohibition on the right to have children. Oakley readily admits that unless he wins the lottery, he will likely never be able to establish that ability. . . . In a similar context, the United States Supreme Court has explained that a statutory prohibition on the right to marry, a right closely aligned with the [fundamental] right at issue, was not a justifiable means of advancing the state's interest in providing support for children. Zablocki v.

Redhail, 434 U.S. 374, 388-90 (1978). . . . The narrowly drawn means described by the Supreme Court in *Zablocki* still exist today and are appropriate means of advancing the state's interest in a manner that does not impair the fundamental right to procreate. See, e.g., Wis. Stat. §767.265 (garnishment/wage assignment); §767.30 (lien on personal property); §785.03 (civil contempt). These means, as well as other conditions of probation or criminal penalties, are available in the present case. . . .

[U]pholding a term of probation that prohibits a probationer from fathering a child without first establishing the financial wherewithal to support his children [also] carries unacceptable collateral consequences and practical problems. First, prohibiting a person from having children as a condition of probation has been described as "coercive of abortion." . . . Because the condition is triggered only upon the birth of a child [not upon intercourse], the risk of imprisonment creates a strong incentive for a man in Oakley's position to demand from the woman the termination of her pregnancy. It places the woman in an untenable position: have an abortion or be responsible for Oakley going to prison for eight years. . . .

Second, by allowing the right to procreate to be subjected to financial qualifications, the majority imbues a fundamental liberty interest with a sliding scale of wealth. . . . Third, the condition of probation is unworkable. . . . The condition of probation will not be violated until the woman with whom he has sexual relations carries her pregnancy to term. Then, Oakley will be imprisoned, and another child will go unsupported. . . .

I, too, am troubled by the societal problem caused by "deadbeat" parents. . . . Let there be no question that I agree with the majority that David Oakley's conduct cannot be condoned. It is irresponsible and criminal. However, we must keep in mind what is really at stake in this case. The fundamental right to have children, shared by us all, is damaged by today's decision. . . .

David Ray Papke, State v. Oakley, Deadbeat Dads, and American Poverty

26 W. New Eng. L. Rev. 9, 10-15 (2004)

[David Oakley] was born in 1966 in the Taycheedah Correctional Institution, a women's prison in Fond du Lac, Wisconsin. Sharon Oakley, his mother, remained incarcerated until 1974, but authorities, of course, removed Oakley from the prison. After a period in state care, he was raised primarily by his maternal grandparents. Run-ins with law enforcement officials marked his youth, and while in his teens Oakley was sent to Lincoln Hills School, a home for delinquent boys located near Wausau, Wisconsin. . . .

After completing his sentences in juvenile facilities, Oakley lived largely in an area on the western shore of Lake Michigan in central Wisconsin [in rust-belt towns with] significant unemployment [and poverty]. In keeping with national patterns showing that poverty is "particularly rampant among children living in mother-only households," poverty in Manitowoc County is especially pronounced among families with a female family-head and no husband present.

With a limited formal education and virtually no skills, Oakley was unable to find or hold meaningful jobs. . . . As with many of the poor, Oakley's ability to find and get to work was limited by his lack of a motor vehicle. [W]ithout genuine and meaningful work opportunities, [he might well have ceased] to assume work is a regular and regulating factor in [his daily life]. Oakley's lengthy criminal record [for disorderly conduct, receipt of stolen property, illegal firearm possession, and witness intimidation] also without doubt made him less than an ideal hire in the minds of some employers.

The [four] mothers of Oakley's [nine] children, themselves among Manitowoc County's poor, do not unanimously condemn Oakley. . . . Cheri Pasdo, who gave birth to one of Oakley's sons but never married Oakley, considers him dangerously bewitching. "He could talk an Eskimo into buying an ice cube," she said. Jill Cochrane, mother of four of Oakley's children, thinks he never understood the seriousness of parenthood. "He likes having the kids but once they're there to him that's a punishment. He doesn't like them once he's got them," Cochrane said. On the other side, Lucretia Thompson-Smith and Rachel Ward remain sympathetic to Oakley. Thompson-Smith, mother of Oakley's fourteen year-old daughter, does not see much difference between Oakley and the two other fathers of her children when it comes to paying child support faithfully. Even if Oakley had a minimum-wage job, his child support would eat it up. "How could he live?" she asked. . . . The four women and their children survived on an unpredictable combination of welfare payments, earnings from various jobs, and occasional support from Oakley. . . . For what it's worth, Oakley claimed that he paid over seventy percent of his child support to the mothers of his children, and courtroom records confirm that he did at least pay some child support. . . .

Although the specifics of David Oakley's life and the Constitutional issues considered in [*Oakley*] are unique, the ultimate decision in the case and attitudes which buoyed that decision are part of a larger trend. Since at least the mid-1980's, men like Oakley have been demonized [as] "deadbeat dads." . . . The policing and punishing of David Oakley sanctioned by the Wisconsin [courts] had much the same animus as the national legislative and popular campaigns against "deadbeat dads."

"Enough is enough," the judges and legislators [and the community] want to shout. But has anything really been accomplished for Oakley, his children, and the mothers of those children? Does the national campaign have the capacity to affect significantly the conduct of transient, uneducated, and impoverished men or to reduce the poverty of their children and their children's mothers?

Notes and Questions

1. Reconciling *Zablocki*. What does *Oakley* hold? Does the majority successfully distinguish this case from *Zablocki* (Chapter II), and other constitutional authorities? Does the immediate availability of a prison sentence distinguish these facts from *Zablocki*'s? How should a court apply *Zablocki*'s "narrow tailoring" requirement to a particular obligor after less onerous means of support enforcement have failed?

2. Probation conditions and collateral consequences. The majority emphasizes that the defendant could have been incarcerated for the crime of intentional failure to support his children; hence, probation with conditions, however demanding, constitutes a less intrusive alternative. But see State v. Talty, 814 N.E.2d 1201 (Ohio 2004). Is Judge Hazlewood's approach a welcome innovation designed to address a difficult social problem? Or does it exemplify the excessive discretion that judges have to fashion probation conditions? Contemporary critiques take aim at the wide array of collateral consequences that impose conditions, restrictions, and burdens beyond the term of incarceration. See Christopher Uggen & Robert Stewart, Piling On: Collateral Consequences and Community Supervision, 99 Minn. L. Rev. 1871 (2015).

3. Impact on women. To what extent does the "practical problem" of abortion coercion, which troubles the dissent, undermine the majority's analysis and conclusion? Suppose the defendant had been a "deadbeat mom" or female substance abuser. See, e.g., Joanna Naim, Is There a Right to Have Children? Substantive Due Process and Probation Conditions That Restrict Reproductive Rights, 6 Stan. J. C.R.-C.L. 1 (2010) (advocating invalidation of such conditions).

As commentators have noted, all of the male members of the Wisconsin Supreme Court joined the majority opinion, and all of the female members dissented. How might you explain this division, particularly given the data about the disproportionate impact on single mothers of unpaid support obligations? To avoid the impact on women, should the court have offered Oakley a vasectomy as a probation condition? Could it have done so? See Naim, supra.

4. Reasons for nonsupport. *Oakley* cites data demonstrating the enormity of the problem of unmet support obligations. Commentators advance several possible explanations why noncustodial parents—generally fathers—fail to pay support:

> [Fathers often] begin their postdivorce lives with a strong commitment to support their children. Over time, their resolution weakens as relations with their children become emotionally less rewarding or they acquire a new set of family commitments. In effect, these men trade in old obligations for new ones. From their point of view, they are not callously disregarding their family responsibilities but rather redefining them as they move from one marriage to the next. . . .[62]

More recent studies find a similar pattern, albeit with marriage and remarriage playing less prominent roles:

> When fathers can't satisfy their desire to be a fully engaged father to one child their motivation to *avoid* fathering another child with a new partner may be diminished. [F]athers who enter into new partnerships and have more children are subsequently less likely to marshal their time and money in service of older children. . . . [F]or men with limited means, adequate role performance in one

---

[62]. Frank F. Furstenberg, Jr., & Andrew J. Cherlin, Divided Families: What Happens to Children When Parents Part 59-60 (1991).

father-child relationship seems to virtually require placing all of one's eggs in a single basket.[63]

Professor David Chambers points to the anger, confusion, and depression fathers feel upon divorce; their resentment toward relinquishing part of their earnings; their association of money with marital failure; and their weak attachment to their children.[64]

5. David Oakley in context. What insights does Oakley's own history provide? To what extent do enforcement efforts aid those whom the law purports to help? See generally Stacy Brustin, Child Support: Shifting the Financial Burden in Low-Income Families, 20 Geo. J. on Poverty L. & Pol'y 1 (2012); Daniel L. Hatcher, Forgotten Fathers, 93 B.U. L. Rev. 897 (2013).

6. Criminal nonsupport in context. All 50 states have criminal nonsupport statutes, with punishments ranging from small fines to lengthy prison sentences.[65] What should be the impact of a weak job market, racial disproportionality in the child welfare and criminal justice systems, and mass incarceration? See Young Disadvantaged Men: Fathers, Families, Poverty, and Policy, 635 Annals Am. Acad. Pol. & Soc. Sci. 6-261 (May 2011) (symposium issue); Ann Cammett, Deadbeats, Deadbrokes, and Prisoners, 18 Geo. J. on Poverty L. & Pol'y 127 (2011). Such issues captured national attention after a police officer in South Carolina fatally shot fleeing Walter Scott in the back; Scott's previous incarceration for failure to pay child support, resulting in the loss of employment, reportedly prompted his decision to run from a traffic stop. See Frances Robles & Shaila Dewan, Skip Child Support. Go to Jail. Lose Job. Repeat., N.Y. Times, Apr. 20, 2105, at A1.

7. Reform proposals. Given Oakley's story, evaluate the following proposals for rethinking child support obligations and their enforcement: (a) Statutorily authorize courts to issue temporary no-procreation orders to those unfit to parent. See Carter Dillard, Child Welfare and Future Persons, 43 Ga. L. Rev. 367 (2009). (b) At the time of birth, recognize as a parent only someone who meets a minimum threshold of fitness. See James G. Dwyer, The Relationship Rights of Children (2006). (c) Increase the involvement of poor fathers in their children's lives after divorce by redefining child support to include nonfinancial and informal contributions. See Solangel Maldonado, Deadbeat or Deadbroke: Redefining Child Support for Poor Fathers, 39 U.C. Davis L. Rev. 991 (2006). (d) Revise the law to link child support and visitation orders, allowing the former only after evaluating the propriety of the latter. See Clare Huntington, Postmarital Family Law: A Legal Structure for Nonmarital Families, 67 Stan. L. Rev. 167, 231 (2015). (e) Strengthen efforts to keep fragile families together, including increasing voluntary

---

[63]. Kathryn Edin & Timothy J. Nelson, Doing the Best I Can: Fatherhood in the Inner City 192 (2013).

[64]. David L. Chambers, Making Fathers Pay: The Enforcement of Child Support 71-75 (1979). On paternal disengagement after divorce, see Judith S. Wallerstein & Julia M. Lewis, Divorced Fathers and Their Adult Offspring: Report from a Twenty-Five-Year Longitudinal Study, 42 Fam. L.Q. 695 (2009).

[65]. For a state-by-state listing, see National Conference of State Legislatures, Criminal Nonsupport and Child Support (June 2015), http://www.ncsl.org/research/human-services/criminal-nonsupport-and-child-support.aspx.

acknowledgments of paternity. See Leslie Joan Harris, Questioning Child Support Enforcement Policy for Poor Families, 45 Fam. L.Q. 157 (2011). (f) Establish a special court to address "fathering" problems. See Milton C. Lee, Fatherhood in the Child Support System: An Innovative Problem-Solving Approach to an Old Problem, 50 Fam. Ct. Rev. 59 (2012). (g) Prioritize children's economic support by requiring states to give families on welfare all child support collected through the assignment process. See Tonya L. Brito, Fathers Behind Bars: Rethinking Child Support Policy Toward Low-Income Noncustodial Fathers and Their Families, 15 J. Gender Race & Just. 617, 660 (2012). (h) Pursue support enforcement less aggressively to avoid discouraging men who are not biological fathers from assuming the role of father. See Jane C. Murphy, Legal Images of Fatherhood: Welfare Reform, Child Support Enforcement, and Fatherless Children, 81 Notre Dame L. Rev. 325 (2005). (i) Allow prisoners to pause child support obligations. See Eli Hager, For Prisoners, Child-Support Debt Can Be Crushing, Wash. Post, 2015 WLNR 30996851 (Oct. 19, 2015) (citing new federal regulations).

2. Civil Contempt and the Transformation of Enforcement

TURNER v. ROGERS

131 S. Ct. 2507 (2011)

Justice Breyer delivered the opinion of the Court. . . .

In June 2003 a South Carolina family court entered an order [that] required petitioner, Michael Turner, to pay $51.73 per week to respondent, Rebecca Rogers, to help support their child. . . . Over the next three years, Turner repeatedly failed to pay the amount due and was held in contempt on five occasions [sometimes paying and sometimes serving time in custody. He remained in arrears. After the clerk issued a new "show cause" order, a civil contempt hearing took place]. Turner and Rogers were present, each without representation by counsel.

The hearing was brief. The court clerk said that Turner was $5,728.76 behind in his payments. The judge asked Turner if there was "anything you want to say." Turner [apologized, cited his substance abuse, and said]: "I mean, I know I done wrong, and I should have been paying and helping her, and I'm sorry. I mean, dope had a hold to me."

[The court found Turner in willful contempt and imposed a 12-month sentence, while allowing him to purge himself of the contempt and avoid the sentence by achieving a zero balance on or before release. The court placed a lien on his Social Security and other benefits. The court made no inquiry or finding about Turner's ability to pay. While serving his sentence, Turner appealed through his pro bono attorney, claiming a federal constitutional right to counsel.]

We must decide whether the Due Process Clause grants an indigent defendant, such as Turner, a right to state-appointed counsel at a civil contempt proceeding, which may lead to his incarceration. [The Sixth Amendment's right to counsel in criminal cases, including criminal contempt,] does not govern civil cases. Civil contempt differs from criminal contempt in that it seeks only to "coerc[e] the defendant to do" what a court had previously ordered him to do. A court may not impose punishment "in a civil contempt proceeding when it is clearly established that the alleged contemnor is unable to comply with the terms of the order." Hicks v. Feiock, 485 U.S. 624, 638, n.9 (1988). And once a civil contemnor complies with the underlying order, he is purged of the contempt and is free. [Id. at 633] (he "carr[ies] the keys of [his] prison in [his] own pockets").

Consequently, the Court has made clear (in a case not involving the right to counsel) that, where civil contempt is at issue, the Fourteenth Amendment's Due Process Clause allows a State to provide fewer procedural protections than in a criminal case. This Court has decided only a handful of cases that more directly concern a right to counsel in civil matters. And the application of those decisions to the present case is not clear. On the one hand, the Court has held that the Fourteenth Amendment requires the State to pay for representation by counsel in a *civil* "juvenile delinquency" proceeding (which could lead to incarceration). In re Gault, 387 U.S. 1, 35-42 (1967). . . . [I]n Lassiter v. Department of Social Servs. of Durham Cty., 452 U.S. 18 (1981), a case that focused upon civil proceedings leading to loss of parental rights, the Court [generalized that the right to counsel exists only when the litigant may lose his physical liberty]. We believe those statements are best read as pointing out that the Court previously had found a right to counsel "*only*" in cases involving incarceration, not that a right to counsel exists in *all* such cases. . . .

Civil contempt proceedings in child support cases constitute one part of a highly complex system designed to assure a noncustodial parent's regular payment of funds typically necessary for the support of his children. Often the family receives welfare support from a state-administered federal program, and the State then seeks reimbursement from the noncustodial parent. See 42 U.S.C. §§ 608(a)(3) (2006 ed., Supp. III), 656(a)(1) (2006 ed.); S. C. Code Ann. §§ 43-5-65(a)(1), (2) (2010 Cum. Supp.). Other times the custodial parent (often the mother, but sometimes the father, a grandparent, or another person with custody) does not receive government benefits and is entitled to receive the support payments herself.

The Federal Government has created an elaborate procedural mechanism designed to help both the government and custodial parents to secure the payments to which they are entitled. See generally Blessing v. Freestone, 520 U.S. 329, 333 (1997) (describing the "interlocking set of cooperative federal-state welfare programs" as they relate to child support enforcement); 45 CFR pt. 303 (2010) (prescribing standards for state child support agencies). These systems often rely upon wage withholding, expedited procedures for modifying and enforcing child support orders, and automated data processing. But sometimes States will use contempt orders to ensure that the custodial parent receives support payments or the government receives reimbursement. Although some experts have criticized this last-mentioned procedure, and the Federal Government believes that "the routine use of contempt for non-payment of child support is likely to be an ineffective strategy," the Government also tells us that "coercive enforcement remedies, such as contempt, have a role to play." South Carolina, which relies heavily on contempt proceedings, agrees that they are an important tool.

We . . . determine the "specific dictates of due process" by examining the "distinct factors" that this Court has previously found useful in deciding what specific safeguards the Constitution's Due Process Clause requires in order to make a civil proceeding fundamentally fair. [T]hose factors include (1) the nature of "the private interest that will be affected," (2) the comparative "risk" of an "erroneous deprivation" of that interest with and without "additional or substitute procedural safeguards," and (3) the nature and magnitude of any countervailing interest in not providing "additional or substitute procedural requirement[s]." [Mathews v. Eldridge, 424 U.S. 319, 335 (1976).]

The "private interest that will be affected" . . . consists of an indigent defendant's loss of personal liberty through imprisonment. . . . Given the importance of the interest at stake, it is obviously important to assure accurate decisionmaking in respect to the key "ability to pay" question. Moreover, the fact that ability to comply marks a dividing line between civil and criminal contempt, *Hicks*, 485 U.S., at 635, n.7, reinforces the need for accuracy. . . . And since 70% of child support arrears nationwide are owed by parents with either no reported income or income of $10,000 per year or less, the issue of ability to pay may arise fairly often.

On the other hand, the Due Process Clause does not always require the provision of counsel in civil proceedings where incarceration is threatened. And in determining whether the Clause requires a right to counsel here, we must take account of opposing interests, as well as consider the probable value of "additional or substitute procedural safeguards." Doing so, we find three related considerations that, when taken together, argue strongly against the Due Process Clause requiring the State to provide indigents with counsel in every proceeding of the kind before us.

First, the critical question likely at issue in these cases concerns, as we have said, the defendant's ability to pay. That question is often closely related to the question of the defendant's indigence. But when the right procedures are in place, indigence can be a question that in many—but not all—cases is sufficiently straightforward to warrant determination *prior* to providing a defendant with counsel, even in a criminal case. Federal law, for example, requires a criminal defendant to provide information showing that he is indigent, and therefore entitled to state-funded counsel, *before* he can receive that assistance. See 18 U.S.C. §3006A(b).

Second, sometimes, as here, the person opposing the defendant at the hearing is not the government represented by counsel but the custodial parent *un*represented by counsel. The custodial parent, perhaps a woman with custody of one or more children, may be relatively poor, unemployed, and unable to afford counsel. Yet she may have encouraged the court to enforce its order through contempt. And the proceeding is ultimately for her benefit.

A requirement that the State provide counsel to the noncustodial parent in these cases . . . could mean a degree of formality or delay that would unduly slow payment to those immediately in need. And, perhaps more important for present purposes, [the asymmetry] could make the proceedings *less* fair overall, increasing the risk of a decision that would erroneously deprive a family of the support it is entitled to receive. . . .

Third, as the Solicitor General points out, there is available a set of "substitute procedural safeguards," which, if employed together, can significantly reduce the risk of an erroneous deprivation of liberty . . . without incurring some of the drawbacks inherent in recognizing an automatic right to counsel. Those safeguards include (1) notice to the defendant that his "ability to pay" is a critical issue in the contempt proceeding; (2) the use of a form (or the equivalent) to elicit relevant financial information; (3) an opportunity at the hearing for the defendant to respond to statements and questions about his financial status (*e.g.*, those triggered by his responses on the form); and (4) an express finding by the court that the defendant has the ability to pay. . . .

[W]e ultimately believe that the three considerations we have just discussed must carry the day. . . . We consequently hold that the Due Process Clause does not *automatically* require the provision of counsel at civil contempt proceedings to an indigent individual who is subject to a child support order, even if that individual faces incarceration (for up to a year). In particular, that Clause does not require the provision of counsel where the opposing parent or other custodian (to whom support funds are owed) is not represented by counsel and the State provides alternative procedural safeguards equivalent to those we have mentioned (adequate notice of the importance of ability to pay, fair opportunity to present, and to dispute, relevant information, and court findings).

We do not address civil contempt proceedings where the underlying child support payment is owed to the State, for example, for reimbursement of welfare funds paid to the parent with custody. Those proceedings more closely resemble debt-collection proceedings. The government is likely to have counsel or some other competent representative. . . . Neither do we address what due process requires in an unusually complex case where a defendant "can fairly be represented only by a trained advocate." . . .

The record indicates that Turner received neither counsel nor the benefit of alternative procedures like those we have described. He did not receive clear notice that his ability to pay would constitute the critical question in his civil contempt proceeding. No one provided him with a form (or the equivalent) designed to elicit information about his financial circumstances. The court did not find that Turner was able to pay his arrearage, but instead left the relevant "finding" section of the contempt order blank. The court nonetheless found Turner in contempt and ordered him incarcerated. Under these circumstances, Turner's incarceration violated the Due Process Clause. . . .

Notes and Questions

1. **Civil versus criminal contempt.** Delinquent support obligors face incarceration (and/or monetary fines) for contempt of court—that is, the failure to comply with a court's order to make payments specified in a divorce, separation, or paternity decree. While criminal contempt (illustrated by *Oakley*, supra) punishes the contemnor for past misconduct, civil contempt (illustrated by *Turner*) seeks to coerce compliance. Whether the purpose is punitive or remedial determines the criminal versus civil nature of the offense and the applicable procedural safeguards, such as the standard and burden of proof. Hicks ex rel. Feiock v. Feiock, 485 U.S. 624, 631 (1998) ("substance of proceeding and character of relief" determinative). Because compliance purges civil contempt, a civil contemnor "carr[ies] the keys of [his] prison in [his] own pockets," as *Turner* notes.

2. **Inability to pay.** Present inability to pay precludes the use of civil contempt to coerce compliance. Should the alleged contemnor be required to establish inability to pay, or must the petitioner prove ability to pay? See *Hicks*, supra.

What must Turner do to show an inability to pay? What possible sources of funds count? In cases of criminal nonsupport, inability to pay may allow the common law defense of impossibility. People v. Likine, 823 N.W.2d 50 (Mich. 2012).

3. ***Turner's* limits.** When would a contemnor be entitled to appointed counsel under *Turner*? Justice Thomas's omitted dissent (joined by Justice Scalia, and in part by Chief Justice Roberts and Justice Alito) rejects the majority's balancing approach because it "does not account for the interests of the child and custodial parent, who is usually the child's mother. But their interests are the very reason for the child support obligation and the civil contempt proceedings that enforce it." 131 S. Ct. at 2525. How should their interests be protected? If Turner gets an appointed attorney, would fairness compel one for Rogers, too?

Note that the majority distinguishes proceedings brought by the state from those brought by private parties, declining to decide the contemnor's right to counsel in the former. How should lower courts answer that question? Compare Crain v. Crain, 2012 WL 6737836 (Ohio Ct. App. 2012), with State, Department of Family Services v. Currier, 295 P.3d 837 (Wyo. 2013). See also Miller v. Deal, 761 S.E.2d 274, 280 (Ga. 2014) (rejecting categorical right to counsel in such cases). Who initiated the contempt proceeding in *Turner*? On *Turner*'s context and implications, see generally Russell Engler, Turner v. Rogers and the Essential Role of the Courts in Delivering Access to Justice, 7 Harv. L. & Pol'y Rev. 31 (2013).

4. **Effectiveness.** David Chambers's early study of collection rates in Michigan found that "the counties that jailed more did in fact collect more." Despite incarceration's effectiveness, Professor Chambers does not advocate this remedy because he concludes that the probable existence of equally effective but less onerous alternatives makes imprisonment immoral. "It would be immoral in much the same sense that it would be immoral to use a sledgehammer to swat a mosquito on a friend's back. . . ."[66] Do you agree?

NOTE: FROM PRIVATE REMEDIES TO PUBLIC INTERVENTIONS

Government now plays an increasingly visible role in enforcing financial obligations in nonintact families, as *Oakley* and *Turner* illustrate. Although states have long had statutes criminalizing desertion and nonsupport, in the past little help came from direct state intervention because of the limited applications of such laws, prosecutors' heavy caseloads, and reservations about the propriety and effectiveness of punishment.

Instead, under the traditional approach to enforcement as a private concern, an obligor's failure to comply with a court-ordered transfer of property or an award of spousal or child support left the obligee to initiate judicial proceedings for enforcement, a time-consuming process requiring an attorney. Longstanding state remedies include (in addition to contempt citations) imposition of a trust on the obligor's property; reducing past-due payments to money judgments (if accrued installments do not already constitute final judgments), followed by a lien against the obligor's real estate; requiring the obligor to post security or bond; and garnishment or assignment of the obligor's wages or income. Several practical

[66]. Chambers, supra note [64], at 84, 253.

problems made all these civil remedies inefficient and unpredictable, however. Judicial discretion prevailed, and the adversarial nature of enforcement proceedings offered an inhospitable forum for cooperation and compliance. Enforcement of postdivorce obligations to make periodic payments (that is, alimony and child support) proved particularly problematic because they presented such frequent opportunities for noncompliance.

The same problems that prompted Congress in the 1980s to direct the states to use child support guidelines even earlier had focused federal attention on support enforcement: Among data showing rising rates of divorce and out-of-wedlock births, an escalating number of female-headed single-parent families, and an increasing "feminization of poverty,"[67] statistics indicated widespread noncompliance with child support awards. The federal welfare program, as well as state public assistance programs, felt the impact. In several enactments, Congress directed the states to implement new and increasingly aggressive enforcement mechanisms.

Federal involvement began in 1967 when Congress imposed on state welfare agencies responsibility for child support enforcement as a condition for receiving federal funding. Congress directed states to comply with specific federal requirements and adopted a program of federal monitoring.[68]

Today, as *Turner* notes, a "highly complex system" and "elaborate procedural mechanism" created by Congress govern enforcement tools and processes in cases in which states seek reimbursement for public assistance and also in nonwelfare cases. Over the years, states have complied with federal directives by enacting procedures for collecting support by means of income withholding, expedited enforcement (administrative processes for establishing and enforcing support obligations), diversion of state income tax refunds, liens against real and personal property for overdue support, requirements for a bond or security for overdue support, and disclosure of overdue support to consumer reporting agencies. For example, note how, in *Turner*, the family court clerk initiated the contempt proceeding, based on routine review of outstanding child support orders.

Under the current system of block grants, all states must now adopt measures that Congress found successful in particular state experiments or risk their eligibility for such funds. These include strengthened procedures for income withholding, with mandated reporting of new hires by employers to track the employment of delinquent obligors (42 U.S.C. §§653a, 666(b)); tax refund interceptions, automatic seizure of an obligor's assets, and administrative procedures for enforcing support obligations (id. §§664, 666(a)(4), 666(a)(2) & (c)); procedures for reporting delinquencies to credit bureaus (id. §666(a)(7)); and procedures for withholding, suspending, or restricting licenses (including driver's, professional, occupational, and recreational licenses) of obligors owing overdue support (id. §666(a)(16)). Complementing these state measures, federal legislation requires the Secretary of State to deny, revoke, or restrict issuance of passports for nonpayment of child support (id. §652(k)) and requires inclusion in consumer reports of overdue child support (15 U.S.C. §1681s-1). In addition, the Deadbeat Parents Punishment Act of 1998 punishes as a felony the willful failure to pay a support obligation for a

---

[67]. Beller & Graham, supra note [47], at 2-3 (study based on U.S. Census Bureau's Current Population Survey). The data consistently reveal the gendered nature of the problem.

[68]. See generally Marsha Garrison, Child Support and Children's Poverty, 28 Fam. L.Q. 475, 476 (1994). See Garfinkel et al., supra note [56].

child living in another state if the obligation has remained unpaid for more than two years or exceeds $10,000 (18 U.S.C. §228(a)(3)).

All of these measures not only depict the federalization of child support; they also exemplify a larger move away from individually initiated judicial enforcement proceedings in favor of an approach that triggers enforcement automatically, without any action by the obligee.[69] The effort to make enforcement more *public*, however, reveals an increased commitment to *private* support, not government assistance.

Yet, despite more than 40 years of federally orchestrated efforts, child support enforcement remains an intractable problem, as *Oakley* and *Turner* demonstrate. In 2011, almost one-third of parents who were owed child support received only partial payment, and one-quarter received no payment at all. Nonpayment of child support constitutes a major factor contributing to poverty in the United States. More than one-quarter of custodial parents live in poverty, and obligees have been receiving only 62 percent of the $37.9 billion of child support due.[70]

One proposed reform would allow parents relying on a government agency for collection to sue the *agency* for unsatisfactory efforts.[71] Other visions for the future would create universal assured child support benefits,[72] locate responsibility for all children outside the private family while providing supports for caregiving,[73] and make child support enforcement entirely a federal function (for example, by having the I.R.S. enforce all child support orders).[74] These ideas, which conceptualize child support as a national challenge, ensure that controversy about the "federalization" of family policy likely will persist.[75] To the extent that the Supreme Court's 2012 opinion on the ACA allows states to decline to accept new federal conditions without jeopardizing funds they are already receiving, however, Congress's ability to enact new reforms could be limited. See National Fed'n of Indep. Bus. v. Sebelius, 132 S. Ct. 2566 (2012).

---

[69]. States must provide certain expedited procedures for routine cases, but nonwelfare obligees can opt out of enforcement measures made available by the Title IV-D agency. See generally Paul K. Legler, The Impact of Welfare Reform on the Child Support Enforcement System, in Child Support: The Next Frontier 46 (J. Thomas Oldham & Marygold S. Melli, eds., 2000).

[70]. See Grall, supra note [56], at 1, 4, 10.

[71]. See Margaret Ryznar, Two Direct Rights of Action in Child Support Enforcement, 62 Cath. U.L. Rev. 1007, 1028-1031 (2013) (comparing enforcement mechanisms in the United Kingdom).

[72]. Irwin Garfinkel, The Limits of Private Child Support and the Role of an Assured Benefit, in Child Support: The Next Frontier, supra note [69], at 183. See also Tonya L. Brito, Fathers Behind Bars: Rethinking Child Support Policy Toward Low-Income Fathers and Their Families, 15 J. Gender Race & Just. 617, 662 (2012) (proposing public support to complement private support).

[73]. Martha Albertson Fineman, Child Support Is Not the Answer: The Nature of Dependencies and Welfare Reform, in Child Support: The Next Frontier, supra note [69], at 209.

[74]. See Jonathon S. Jemison, Note, Collecting and Enforcing Child Support Orders with the Internal Revenue Service: An Analysis of a Novel Idea, 20 Women's Rts. L. Rep. 137 (1999). Less expansive proposals include the establishment of savings accounts for withheld wages, with access to accounts by custodial parents. See Monica Hof Wallace, Child Support Savings Accounts: An Innovative Approach to Child Support Enforcement, 85 N.C. L. Rev. 1155 (2007).

[75]. See Laura W. Morgan, The Federalization of Child Support, A Shift in the Ruling Paradigm: Child Support as Outside the Contours of "Family Law," 16 J. Am. Acad. Matrimonial Law. 195 (1999).

3. The Challenge of Multistate Cases

A substantial percentage of all child support cases involve parties located in different jurisdictions. What special responses do such cases warrant?

a. Jurisdictional Limitations on Establishing Awards

KULKO v. SUPERIOR COURT

436 U.S. 84 (1978)

Mr. Justice MARSHALL delivered the opinion of the Court. . . .

Appellant Ezra Kulko married appellee Sharon Kulko Horn in 1959, during appellant's three-day stopover in California en route from a military base in Texas to a tour of duty in Korea. At the time of this marriage, both parties were domiciled in and residents of New York State. Immediately following the marriage, Sharon Kulko returned to New York, as did appellant after his tour of duty. [They lived together in New York for 13 years and then separated. Ezra remained in New York with their children, Darwin and Ilsa, and Sharon moved to California. Sharon returned briefly to sign a separation agreement, which provided that the children would live in New York with their father but spend Christmas, Easter, and summer vacations in California with their mother.] Ezra Kulko agreed to pay his wife $3,000 per year in child support for the periods when the children were in her care, custody, and control. Immediately after execution of the separation agreement, Sharon Kulko flew to Haiti and procured a divorce there; the divorce decree incorporated the terms of the agreement. She then returned to California, where she remarried and took the name Horn.

The children resided with appellant during the school year and with their mother on vacations, as provided by the separation agreement, until December 1973. At this time, just before Ilsa was to leave New York to spend Christmas vacation with her mother, she told her father that she wanted to remain in California after her vacation. Appellant bought his daughter a one-way plane ticket, and Ilsa left, taking her clothing with her. Ilsa then commenced living in California with her mother during the school year and spending vacations with her father. In January 1976, appellant's other child, Darwin, called his mother from New York and advised her that he wanted to live with her in California. Unbeknownst to appellant, appellee Horn sent a plane ticket to her son, which he used to fly to California where he took up residence with his mother and sister.

Less than one month after Darwin's arrival in California, appellee Horn commenced this action against appellant in the California Superior Court. She sought to establish the Haitian divorce decree as a California judgment; to modify the judgment so as to award her full custody of the children; and to increase appellant's child-support obligations. Appellant appeared specially and moved to quash service of the summons on the ground that he was not a resident of California and lacked sufficient "minimum contacts" with the State under International Shoe Co. v. Washington, 326 U.S. 310, 316 (1945), to warrant the State's assertion of personal jurisdiction over him.

[The California Supreme Court upheld the lower courts' denial of appellant's motion to quash. It reasoned that California's long-arm statute was meant to reach all bases of in personam jurisdiction consistent with the Constitution, and that jurisdiction over appellant for support of both children was "fair and reasonable" because he purposefully availed himself of the benefits and protections of California law by sending one child, Ilsa, to live there. We reverse.]

The Due Process Clause of the Fourteenth Amendment operates as a limitation on the jurisdiction of state courts to enter judgments affecting rights or interests of nonresident defendants. [T]he constitutional standard for determining whether the State may enter a binding judgment against appellant here is that set forth in this Court's opinion in International Shoe Co. v. Washington, supra: that a defendant "have certain minimum contacts with [the forum State] such that the maintenance of the suit does not offend 'traditional notions of fair play and substantial justice."' 326 U.S., at 316. [A]n essential criterion in all cases is whether the "quality and nature" of the defendant's activity is such that it is "reasonable" and "fair" to require him to conduct his defense in that State. International Shoe Co. v. Washington, [326 U.S.] at 316-317, 319. . . .

In reaching its result, the California Supreme Court did not rely on appellant's glancing presence in the State some 13 years before the events that led to this controversy, nor could it have. Appellant has been in California on only two occasions, once in 1959 for a three-day military stopover on his way to Korea and again in 1960 for a 24-hour stopover on his return from Korean service. To hold such temporary visits to a State a basis for the assertion of in personam jurisdiction over unrelated actions arising in the future would make a mockery of the limitations on state jurisdiction imposed by the Fourteenth Amendment. Nor did the California court rely on the fact that appellant was actually married in California on one of his two brief visits. We agree that where two New York domiciliaries, for reasons of convenience, marry in the State of California and thereafter spend their entire married life in New York, the fact of their California marriage by itself cannot support a California court's exercise of jurisdiction over a spouse who remains a New York resident in an action relating to child support.

Finally, in holding that personal jurisdiction existed, the court below carefully disclaimed reliance on the fact that appellant had agreed at the time of separation to allow his children to live with their mother three months a year and that he had sent them to California each year pursuant to this agreement. [T]o find personal jurisdiction in a State on this basis, merely because the mother was residing there, would discourage parents from entering into reasonable visitation agreements. Moreover, it could arbitrarily subject one parent to suit in any State of the Union where the other parent chose to spend time while having custody of their offspring pursuant to a separation agreement. As we have emphasized: "The unilateral activity of those who claim some relationship with a nonresident defendant cannot satisfy the requirement of contact with the forum State. [I]t is essential in each case that there be some act by which the defendant purposefully avails him[self] of the privilege of conducting activities within the forum State. . . ." Hanson v. Denckla, [357 U.S. 235, 253 (1958)].

The "purposeful act" that the California Supreme Court believed did warrant the exercise of personal jurisdiction over appellant in California was his "actively and fully consent[ing] to Ilsa living in California for the school year . . . and . . . send[ing] her to California for that purpose." [564 P.2d 353, 358 (Cal. 1977).] [Yet, a] father who agrees, in the interests of family harmony and his children's preferences, to allow them to spend more time in California than was required under a separation agreement can hardly be said to have "purposefully availed himself" of the "benefits and protections" of California's laws.[7] . . .

The circumstances in this case clearly render "unreasonable" California's assertion of personal jurisdiction. . . . The cause of action herein asserted arises, not from the defendant's commercial transactions in interstate commerce, but rather from his personal, domestic relations. . . . Furthermore, the controversy between the parties arises from a separation that occurred in the State of New York; appellee Horn seeks modification of a contract that was negotiated in New York and that she flew to New York to sign. [T]he instant action involves an agreement that was entered into with virtually no connection with the forum State.

Finally, basic considerations of fairness point decisively in favor of appellant's State of domicile as the proper forum for adjudication of this case, whatever the merits of appellee's underlying claim. It is appellant who has remained in the State of the marital domicile, whereas it is appellee who has moved across the continent. Appellant has at all times resided in New York State, and, until the separation and appellee's move to California, his entire family resided there as well. As noted above, appellant did no more than acquiesce in the stated preference of one of his children to live with her mother in California. This single act is surely not one that a reasonable parent would expect to result in the substantial financial burden and personal strain of litigating a child-support suit in a forum 3,000 miles away, and we therefore see no basis on which it can be said that appellant could reasonably have anticipated being "haled before a [California] court," Shaffer v. Heitner, 433 U.S. [186, 216 (1977)]. To make jurisdiction in a case such as this turn on whether appellant bought his daughter her ticket or instead unsuccessfully sought to prevent her departure would impose an unreasonable burden on family relations, and one wholly unjustified by the "quality and nature" of appellant's activities in or relating to the State of California. International Shoe Co. v. Washington, 326 U.S., at 319.

In seeking to justify the burden that would be imposed on appellant were the exercise of in personam jurisdiction in California sustained, appellee argues that California has substantial interests in protecting the welfare of its minor residents and in promoting to the fullest extent possible a healthy and supportive family environment in which the children of the State are to be raised. These interests are unquestionably important. But while the presence of the children and one parent in California arguably might favor application of California law in a lawsuit in New York, the fact that California may be the "'center of gravity'" for choice-of-law purposes does not mean that California has personal jurisdiction over the defendant. . . .

7. The court below stated that the presence in California of appellant's daughter gave appellant the benefit of California's "police and fire protection, its school system, its hospital services, its recreational facilities, its libraries and museums. . . ." 564 P.2d, at 356. But, in the circumstances presented here, these services provided by the State were essentially benefits to the child, not the father, and in any event were not benefits that appellant purposefully sought for himself.

Notes and Questions

1. Divisible divorce. Under the doctrine of divisible divorce, due process requires personal jurisdiction over both spouses to resolve the financial incidents of dissolution, although one can get an ex parte dissolution of marriage entitled to full faith and credit. E.g., Estin v. Estin, 334 U.S. 541 (1948); Snider v. Snider, 551 S.E.2d 693 (W. Va. 2001). Applying this doctrine, *Kulko* finds the father's connections with California insufficient to satisfy due process.

Accordingly, Ezra Kulko may remain immune from child support litigation in California, but only until he visits his children there and risks personal service of process. Recall Burnham v. Superior Court, 495 U.S. 604 (1990) (noted in Chapter VI). What impact does this rule have on visitation? Why do benefits provided by California to the children not count as benefits to their father? What alternative jurisdictional rules might avoid these practical and policy-based difficulties? See Monica J. Allen, Child-State Jurisdiction: A Due Process Invitation to Reconsider Some Basic Family Law Assumptions, 26 Fam. L.Q. 293 (1992).

2. Long-arm statutes. With the expansion of personal jurisdiction signaled by International Shoe Co. v. Washington, 326 U.S. 310 (1945), states enacted long-arm statutes designed to reach absent defendants. Some courts construed early "single act" statutes, although they were enacted with other litigation in mind, to apply in family law cases, reasoning that failure to pay support constitutes a "tortious act" in the obligee's domicile or that support rights springing from the marriage contract have financial and business implications. See, e.g., Lozinski v. Lozinski, 408 S.E.2d 310 (W. Va. 1991) (haling husband into court in marital domicile after he moved away).

Under this approach, did Ezra Kulko commit a tortious act in California for purposes of justifying jurisdiction? Any assertion of jurisdiction under single-act statutes must satisfy the Due Process Clause's minimum contacts requirement, explained in *Kulko*. Accordingly, some states followed a second approach, illustrated by California's statute in *Kulko*: long-arm legislation that allows courts to assert jurisdiction whenever due process permits, thus encompassing all the single acts usually listed and any additional jurisdictional bases permitted by the Constitution.

3. Family law long-arm statutes. More recently, states have enacted long-arm statutes explicitly addressing family law cases. For example, Washington's long-arm statute lists several single acts, including "[l]iving in a marital relationship within this state notwithstanding subsequent departure from this state, [as to all proceedings under dissolution of marriage statutes,] so long as the petitioning party has continued to reside in this state or has continued to be a member of the armed forces stationed in this state." Wash. Rev. Code Ann. §4.28.185(1)(f). How should a court construe the marital relationship language of the Washington statute? See State ex rel. Mahoney v. St. John, 964 P.2d 1242 (Wyo. 1998). Will a long absence from a state so weaken the contacts with the defendant's previous home that long-arm jurisdiction becomes improper? See, e.g., Nelson v. Nelson, 891 So. 2d 317 (Ala. Civ. App. 2004).

Some states also allow personal jurisdiction if the activities giving rise to divorce or a related economic claim took place in the state. See, e.g., Cherin v. Cherin, 891 N.E.2d 684 (Mass. App. Ct. 2008). See also C.L. v. W.S., 968 A.2d 211 (N.J. Super. Ct. App. Div. 2009) (conception in state suffices for personal jurisdiction in paternity and child support suits).

Under any of these approaches, should marrying in the state alone suffice? Recall that the Court rejects as a "mockery" this basis for California's jurisdiction over Ezra Kulko. Suppose that a same-sex couple travels to California to enter a domestic partnership, a legal relationship not available or recognized where they live. In a later child support action after their relationship ends, should a court find "purposeful availment" of California's benefits and protections? If so, why? Should marrying in California be treated differently? What is the impact of nationwide marriage equality after Obergefell v. Hodges (Chapter II)?

4. Evolution of UIFSA. Situations like the one in *Kulko* prompted efforts to design multistate solutions, most prominently the Uniform Reciprocal Enforcement of Support Act (URESA), promulgated in 1950 by the National Conference of Commissioners on Uniform State Laws (now called the Uniform Law Commission or ULC), enacted in virtually every state, and substantially revised in 1968. A URESA case required a two-state proceeding, including the filing of a petition in the obligee's state and its transmittal to a court elsewhere with personal jurisdiction over the obligor. The lack of uniformity among the states and the possibility of multiple support orders impaired URESA's success. See generally Laura W. Morgan, Pre-emption or Abdication? Courts Rule Federal Law Trumps State Law in Child Support Jurisdiction, 24 J. Am. Acad. Matrimonial Law. L. 217 (2011).

ULC replaced the earlier models with the Uniform Interstate Family Support Act (UIFSA), approved in 1992 and subsequently amended.[76] See John J. Sampson, Uniform Family Laws and Model Acts, 41 Fam. L.Q. 673, 679-680 (2008). Although based on URESA, UIFSA contains new procedures for establishing, enforcing, and modifying support orders. To assure acceptance by the states, Congress made enactment of UIFSA a condition for federal funding for child support enforcement, in its welfare reform legislation of 1996. 42 U.S.C. §666(f). Like its predecessors, UIFSA covers both spousal and child support, but not property distribution (see §102), and spells out procedures for establishing support orders and enforcing them. UIFSA responds to a number of perceived weaknesses in earlier laws, examined below.

5. Expanding jurisdiction. Critics claim that traditional jurisdictional rules thwart effective support enforcement. In response, a federal commission initially proposed challenging *Kulko* to allow jurisdiction in most support cases in the state of the child's residence. This approach, called "child-state jurisdiction," parallels jurisdiction in the child's home state in custody adjudications under the Uniform Child Custody Jurisdiction and Enforcement Act (UCCJEA) and the Parental Kidnapping Prevention Act (PKPA) (examined in Chapter VIII).

---

[76]. See http://www.uniformlaws.org/shared/docs/interstate%20family%20support/UIFSA_2008_Final_Amended%202015_Revised%20Prefatory%20Note%20and%20Comments.pdf (2008 Act).

UIFSA's drafters rejected the broader "child-state" approach in favor of long-arm statutes. UIFSA's eight bases for jurisdiction over absent obligors (set out in §201) include when the individual resided with the child in the state, the child resides in the state "as the result of acts or directives of the individual," the individual engaged in intercourse in the state and the child may have been conceived therefrom, and there is any other basis consistent with the Constitution for the exercise of personal jurisdiction. This expanded long-arm jurisdiction facilitates a one-state proceeding, in place of the two-state approach under URESA.

Would UIFSA change the result in *Kulko*? Would the "acts or directives" provision apply? Would its application satisfy due process? Why did UIFSA's drafters fail to adopt the more expansive "child-state" approach? See generally Allen, supra. Is it time to rethink *Kulko*'s limitations on jurisdiction? Compare McCaffrey v. Green, 931 P.2d 407 (Alaska 1997), with Ex parte W.C.R., 98 So. 3d 1144 (Ala. Civ. App. 2012).

6. Choice of law. What law should govern in multistate support cases? Note that *Kulko* concedes that California law might govern, even though California lacks jurisdiction. Is it fair to subject Ezra Kulko to California law? UIFSA principally applies the forum's procedural and substantive law (§303).

Problems

1. In *Kulko*, assume that Ezra frequently telephones his children in California, writes to them, provides health insurance for them, pays for their orthodontics, and furnishes them airline tickets so they can visit him in New York. Suppose that Sharon then files a petition to establish a child support award in California (which, if granted, would be the first child support award for this family). Would California have personal jurisdiction over Ezra to order him to pay child support? Why? See In re Marriage of Crew, 549 N.W.2d 527 (Iowa 1996). See also Bergaust v. Flaherty, 703 S.E.2d 248 (Va. Ct. App. 2011).

2. Susan and Reginald became common law spouses in Texas. Throughout the marriage, Reginald, a gang member, abused Susan both mentally and physically. When she attempted to leave him, he had a friend stand on her head while he (Reginald) kicked her in the face. He also abused her daughter from a previous relationship and threatened to kill Susan if she reported him. Susan, pregnant, then left and moved to a friend's trailer. When Reginald continued to threaten and harass her, she fled to her father's home in Colorado. Now, after giving birth, she sues Reginald in Colorado for dissolution of marriage and child support. Reginald, who has never visited Colorado, challenges the court's jurisdiction to order child support. What result in Reginald's jurisdictional challenge and why? Does it matter, in applying *Kulko*'s purposeful availment test, whether Reginald knew where Susan was going when she left Texas? See In re Marriage of Malwitz, 99 P.3d 56 (Colo. 2004); Powers v. District Court, 227 P.3d 1060 (Okla. 2009).

Suppose that Susan seeks a restraining order against Reginald in Colorado. See Caplan v. Donovan, 879 N.E.2d 117 (Mass. 2008). Suppose that she attempts to sue him there for intentional infliction of emotional distress. See Gordon v. Gordon, 887 N.E.2d 35 (Ill. App. Ct. 2008).

b. Modification and Enforcement

DRAPER v. BURKE

881 N.E.2d 122 (Mass. 2008)

GREANEY, J. . . .

The parties grew up in Massachusetts and, in 1980, were married in Amherst, living thereafter in Massachusetts for approximately ten years. During this time, they had two children: a daughter born in 1985, and a son, born in 1987. In 1990, the family moved to New Mexico, and in 1993 to Oregon. The parties were divorced by judgment [in Oregon]. One month before entry of the Oregon judgment, in July, 1997, the wife returned with the children to Massachusetts, and they have continued to live in Massachusetts since that time. Also, in July, 1997, the husband moved to Idaho, where he currently resides.

The Oregon judgment awarded the parties shared legal custody of the children and gave the wife physical custody of the children with reasonable visitation to the husband. The Oregon judgment established the husband's child support obligation at $750 per month, payable to the wife, and provided that the husband's child support obligation would continue "for so long as said child is under the age of eighteen (18) and thereafter for so long as said child is under the age of twenty-one (21) and is a 'child attending school [under Oregon law].'" The issue of college expenses for the children was not addressed in the Oregon judgment, but the parties intended to share those expenses.

In March, 1999, and in December, 2004, the wife filed complaints in the Probate and Family Court [in Massachusetts] to revise and amend the Oregon judgment with respect to the provision of child support, seeking, ultimately, contribution by the husband to the children's college expenses. [The husband moved to dismiss arguing that,] under G.L. c. 209D, §6-611(*a*)(1), of the Legislature's adoption of the 1992 version of the Uniform Interstate Family Support Act (UIFSA), 9 (Part IB) U.L.A. 513 (Master ed. 2005), a Massachusetts court may modify a child support order issued by another State only in circumstances where the person seeking modification is a "nonresident" of the Commonwealth. . . .

[The court below found a material change in circumstances and ordered, inter alia, the husband to reimburse the wife for one-half of the children's college expenses paid to date by the wife and to pay 40 percent of the children's college expenses going forward. The husband appeals, challenging subject matter jurisdiction under UIFSA.]

1. a. The wife does not dispute that the Probate and Family Court lacks subject matter jurisdiction under G.L. c. 209D, §6-611(*a*)(1), to modify the Oregon judgment. In 1995, the Legislature enacted G.L. c. 209D, adopting the original 1992 version of UIFSA [which provides:]

> "(*a*) After a child support order issued in another state has been registered in the commonwealth, the responding tribunal of the commonwealth may modify that order only if . . . it finds that:
>
> "(1) the following requirements are met:

"(i) the child, the individual obligee, and the obligor do not reside in the issuing state;

"(ii) a petitioner who is a nonresident of the commonwealth seeks modification; and

"(iii) the respondent is subject to the personal jurisdiction of the tribunal of the commonwealth."

General Laws c. 209D, §6-611(*a*)(1)(i)-(iii), essentially mirrors that appearing in §611(*a*)(1)(i)-(iii) of the 1992, 1996, and 2001 versions of UIFSA. Here the wife is a resident of Massachusetts and cannot satisfy the second prong of the test in §6-611(*a*)(1), namely, being "a petitioner who is a nonresident of the commonwealth." The comment to the corresponding section of the 1992 UIFSA makes clear that this requirement applies to both an obligee and an obligor, and provides:

> "This [requirement] contemplates . . . that the obligee may seek modification in the obligor's state of residence, or that the obligor may seek a modification in the obligee's state of residence. This restriction attempts to achieve a rough justice between the parties in the majority of cases by preventing a litigant from choosing to seek modification in a local court to the marked disadvantage of the other party."

Comment to UIFSA (1992) §611, supra at 515. The comment to the 2001 UIFSA further states, with an analogy to a sporting event:

> "A colloquial (but easily understood) description of [the] requirement is that the modification movant must 'play an away game on the other party's home field.' This rule applies to either obligor or obligee, depending on which of those parties seeks to modify."

Comment to UIFSA (2001) §611, supra at 256.

b. The husband's proposed resolution of the jurisdiction issue is for the wife to seek modification in Idaho. This option is more convenient practically and economically for him, but the proposal ignores the fact that the wife has no contacts with Idaho and that an Idaho court would not be able to exercise personal jurisdiction over her. The fact that the wife could consent to jurisdiction in Idaho is an option similarly available to the husband in Massachusetts. . . . The Oregon judgment does not address the issue of college expenses and the parties stipulated that they always intended to contribute toward those expenses. In these circumstances, "rough justice" does not require that the wife seek formal modification to ensure that the children receive college expenses. The wife's hand was compelled to seek modification because the children were ready to attend college and the husband had made no contributions toward their college expenses. Because none of the parties or children resides in Oregon, an Oregon court has no subject matter jurisdiction over the modification. See comment to UIFSA (2001) §205, supra at 194 (stating that once obligor, obligee, and child have permanently left issuing State, that State no longer has appropriate nexus with parties or child to exercise continuing, exclusive jurisdiction to modify existing court order, and noting that issuing tribunal has no current information about parties and that taxpayers of State have no reason to expend public funds on adjudication).

2. We come then to the crux of the case—whether, as the wife contends, G.L. c. 209D, §6-611(*a*)(1)(ii), does not bar her complaint for modification because that statutory limitation is preempted by the Full Faith and Credit for Child Support Orders Act, codified at 28 U.S.C. §1738B (2000) (Federal act). See California Fed. Sav. & Loan Ass'n v. Guerra, 479 U.S. 272, 281 (1987) (explaining Federal law may preempt State law where conflict exists between them). . . .

. . . The Federal act was passed in 1994 and was intended "(1) to facilitate the enforcement of child support orders among the States; (2) to discourage continuing interstate controversies over child support in the interest of greater financial stability and secure family relationships for the child; and (3) to avoid jurisdictional competition and conflict among State courts in the establishment of child support orders." Congress expressly found that the lack of uniformity of laws regarding determining authority to establish (and modify) child support orders [encourages noncustodial parents to relocate to avoid jurisdiction; contributes to the pressing problem of relatively low levels of child support payments in interstate cases; encourages disregard of court orders; allows noncustodial parents to avoid payment of support obligations, imposing hardship on children; and leads to excessive relitigation and confusion].

[T]he Federal act obligates States to enforce child support orders issued by another State, and imposes limitations on a State's authority to modify child support orders issued by another State. See 28 U.S.C. §1738B(a). [T]he Federal act provides, in relevant part:

> "A court of a State may modify a child support order issued by a court of another State if—
>
> "(1) the court has jurisdiction to make such a child support order pursuant to subsection (i); and
>
> "(2) (A) the court of the other State no longer has continuing, exclusive jurisdiction of the child support order because that State no longer is the child's State or the residence of any individual contestant. . . ."

Id. §1738B(e). Title 28 U.S.C. §1738B(i), in turn, provides:

> "If there is no individual contestant or child residing in the issuing State, the party or support enforcement agency seeking to modify, or to modify and enforce, a child support order issued in another State shall register that order in a State with jurisdiction over the nonmovant for the purpose of modification."

These provisions of the Federal act confer subject matter jurisdiction in Massachusetts because the issuing State, Oregon, no longer has continuing, exclusive jurisdiction (because the wife, husband, and children no longer reside in Oregon); no other State has modified the Oregon judgment; the parties have not executed written consents to jurisdiction elsewhere; and the Probate and Family Court has personal jurisdiction over the husband.

We reject the husband's arguments to the contrary. Relying on cases from other jurisdictions, [e.g., LeTellier v. LeTellier, 40 S.W.3d 490, 496 (Tenn. 2001),] he suggests that preemption is avoided because the Federal act may be construed in a way to avoid conflict with UIFSA. More particularly, he contends, the term "jurisdiction" in 28 U.S.C. §1738B(i) is ambiguous and may be interpreted to include both personal jurisdiction and subject matter jurisdiction, the latter issue then being governed by G.L. c. 209D, §6-611(*a*)(1). Under such a construction, because a Massachusetts court would not have (pursuant to G.L. c. 209D, §6-611[*a*][1][ii]) subject matter jurisdiction to modify the Oregon judgment, Massachusetts would not have "jurisdiction over the nonmovant for the purpose of modification" under 28 U.S.C. §1738B(i). . . .

The husband's argument overlooks the fact that the term "jurisdiction" cannot be read in isolation and, when read in context, "jurisdiction over the nonmovant" is not ambiguous. . . . The jurisdiction contemplated under 28 U.S.C. §1738B(i) is personal jurisdiction and not subject matter jurisdiction. . . .

Additionally, concern over jurisdictional competition and conflict was not the sole purpose motivating the Federal act [as the congressional language quoted above shows]. . . . When viewed in context with these express purposes and findings, application of the "nonresident" petitioner requirement would create an obstacle to the execution of the objectives of Congress. Preemption is clearly appropriate in these circumstances.

In summary, forcing the wife to litigate in Idaho would unreasonably burden her because her income is substantially less than the husband's and her economic resources most likely have been diminished by paying for college expenses of the children without benefit of contribution by the husband. The Federal act intends to protect the children because they ultimately will suffer (or potentially suffer) the most for the husband's insistence on a jurisdictional measure of convenience. Preemption is required by reason of actual conflict between State and Federal law and to implement the clear objectives of the Federal act. The husband's motion to dismiss was properly denied. [Judgment affirmed.]

Notes and Questions

1. Enforcement under UIFSA. UIFSA uses direct enforcement when an order is sent to an obligor's employer in another state, in turn triggering wage withholding (§501). Alternatively, UIFSA authorizes direct administrative enforcement of an order issued elsewhere by an agency in the obligor's state (§507). UIFSA includes a registration process (§§601-604), allowing courts and agencies in one state to enforce support orders issued in another. Courts have rejected due process challenges to UIFSA's measures that make a foreign order effective and require the obligor to request a hearing (§606). E.g., Schultz v. Butterball, LLC, 402 S.W.3d 61 (Ark. 2012). UIFSA explicitly makes visitation irrelevant (§305(d)).

2. Jurisdiction to modify. In contrast to earlier approaches requiring a two-state procedure with the possibility of multiple and conflicting support orders, UIFSA has a "One-Order, One-Time" rule, limiting modification, as explained by *Draper*. UIFSA's 2001 amendments clarify the distinction between initial jurisdiction and jurisdiction to modify (§201(b)). Suppose that one of the parties in *Draper* had remained in Oregon. Where would jurisdiction to modify lie? UIFSA provides for continuing and exclusive modification jurisdiction in the state issuing the initial award, so long as the obligor, obligee, or the child lives in the state or the parties consent (§205). See, e.g., Castro v. Haugh, 170 Cal. Rptr. 3d 683 (Ct. App. 2014). What would UIFSA's approach mean for the facts of *Kulko*, which—despite its significance for jurisdictional rules generally—concerned a petition to modify child support? (To answer this question, do you need to know whether the initial award was the separation agreement in New York or the Haitian divorce decree?)

3. "Rough justice"? Not only does UIFSA have different jurisdictional rules for initial jurisdiction and modification jurisdiction; it also spells out special rules that govern when the issuing state has lost continuing and exclusive jurisdiction to modify (§611). What is the purpose of these limitations? Do you agree with UIFSA's comments, quoted in *Draper*, that these modification rules achieve a "rough justice" between the litigants? Apart from the conflict that *Draper* finds with the federal statute (discussed below), why does the court conclude that fairness supports Massachusetts as the forum for litigation about the children's college expenses in particular? Should the mother have been required to litigate in Idaho? If the father sought modification, where should he file? Suppose that both parties had moved to the same state. See Pahnke v. Pahnke, 88 A.3d 432, 442 (Vt. 2014).

What does UIFSA's approach mean for *Kulko*? Assuming that the Haitian divorce decree constituted the initial child support award in *Kulko*, would UIFSA's rules disallow Ezra from bringing his modification action in New York, the former marital domicile? Why? How would the *Draper* court answer the question? Recall the Supreme Court's analysis of fairness in *Kulko*. Does the expansion of long-arm jurisdiction for establishing initial awards, plus the requirement of "continuing exclusive jurisdiction" in the issuing state (so long as one party remains there), answer this question? To what extent do UIFSA's limitations address, at least in modification cases, the policy problems posed by rules that subject a parent to personal jurisdiction if service of process is accomplished during a visit with a child who resides out of state?

4. Applicable law in modification cases. With the variation in states' child support guidelines and positions on postmajority support, which state's law applies to modification proceedings in a jurisdiction other than the original forum? Should the law of the state where the child now lives control? See, e.g., In re Edelman and Preston, 38 N.E.3d 50 (Ill. App. Ct. 2015).

5. Enforcement versus modification. Even if all the parties have left the issuing state, so that state lacks jurisdiction to modify, the issuing state retains jurisdiction to enforce its award. E.g., Vaile v. Porsboll, 268 P.3d 1272 (Nev. 2012). Once the issuing state has lost modification jurisdiction, the original order remains in effect there, as well as in other states in which it had been registered, and it can be registered and enforced even in additional states. See In re Marriage of Metz, 69 P.3d 1128, 1132 (Kan. Ct. App. 2003).

6. A national standard: FFCCSOA. Even before the 1996 welfare reform legislation requiring states to adopt UIFSA, Congress enacted measures to facilitate interstate recognition and enforcement of support orders. See 42 U.S.C. §666(a)(9) (requiring state procedures ensuring finality and full faith and credit for all payments or support obligations once due and prohibiting retroactive, as distinguished from prospective, modification everywhere).

Congress subsequently enacted the Full Faith and Credit for Child Support Orders Act (FFCCSOA), 28 U.S.C. §1738B, incorporating many UIFSA concepts. This legislation imposes duties on states to enforce and not modify (except as authorized) child support orders established by other states, consistently with the Act's requirements. It provides for continuing, exclusive jurisdiction by a court that has made an order, so long as the state is the child's state or the residence of any individual contestant, unless a court in another state has modified the order, in accordance with the Act. "Child's state" is defined as "the State in which a child resides." For choice of law, the Act generally dictates application of the forum's law, but specifies the law of the issuing state for interpreting orders. In 1996, Congress amended the legislation in order to make it consistent with UIFSA.

When it required states to adopt UIFSA by 1998 and amended the full faith and credit statute to achieve consistency with UIFSA, Congress was responding to the 1996 version of UIFSA—but since then, the drafters finalized a 2001 version and then amended UIFSA again in 2008 (as discussed below). As a result, states have enacted different versions of this "uniform" law.[77] Do UIFSA and FFCCSOA conflict, as *Draper* concludes? Most courts have followed the argument that the father unsuccessfully advanced in *Draper*, deciding that the statutes can be harmonized and that UIFSA's "rough justice" should control. See, e.g., Pulkkinen v. Pulkkinen, 127 So. 3d 738 (Fla. Dist. Ct. App. 2013); LeTellier v. LeTellier, 40 S.W.3d 490 (Tenn. 2001). Is *Draper*'s contrary analysis persuasive? See Laura W. Morgan, Pre-Emption or Abdication? Courts Rule Federal Law Trumps State Law in Child Support Jurisdiction, 24 J. Am. Acad. Matrimonial Law. 217 (2011) (criticizing *Draper*).

7. Federal parent locator service. *Kulko* and *Draper* concern obligors with known whereabouts. Suppose that an obligor had disappeared to evade support enforcement. Congress responded to this problem by directing the Secretary of Health and Human Services to establish and conduct the "parent locator service." 42 U.S.C. §653. This service relies on Social Security numbers to track absent parents and incorporates the National Directory of New Hires and Federal Case Registry of child support orders. See generally Janet Atkinson, Assisting Children and the Courts: The Federal Parent Locator Service, 83 Judicature 26 (1999).

8. Federal crimes. The Child Support Recovery Act (CSRA), 18 U.S.C. §228, criminalizes the willful failure to pay a past-due support obligation for a child who resides in another state. "Past-due support obligation" means any amount determined by a court order or administrative process to be due for the support and maintenance of a child, or a child and the parent with whom the child is living, if the amount has remained unpaid for more than a year or exceeds $5,000. The CSRA does not create a private right of action for obligees. See, e.g., Salahuddin v. Alaji, 232 F.3d 305 (2d Cir. 2000).

Congress amended the CSRA by enacting the Deadbeat Parents Punishment Act of 1998, 18 U.S.C. §228(a)(3), which makes willful failure to pay a support

[77]. All but six jurisdictions have now enacted the 2008 version of UIFSA. See http://www.uniformlaws.org/Act.aspx?title=Interstate Family Support Act Amendments (2008).

obligation for a child in another state a felony, if the obligation remains unpaid for more than two years or exceeds $10,000. The legislation has survived challenges that it exceeds Congress's authority under the Commerce Clause, on the theory that the payment of a debt constitutes economic activity and the difference in location of obligor and obligee requires satisfaction of the debt by interstate means. E.g., United States v. Kukafka, 478 F.3d 531 (3d Cir. 2007).

9. International support enforcement. Courts split on whether UIFSA applies to cases involving other countries. Compare In re V.L.C., 225 S.W.3d 221 (Tex. App. 2006) (holding Sinaloa, Mexico, is not a "state" under UIFSA), with Arnell v. Arnell, 416 S.W.3d 188 (Tex. Ct. App. 2013) (treating Switzerland as a "state" under UIFSA). The drafters revised UIFSA again in 2008 in response to the Hague Convention on the Recovery of Child Support and Other Forms of Family Maintenance (which the United States signed in 2007). Congress implemented the Convention in enacting the 2014 Preventing Sex Trafficking and Strengthening Families Act. See 42 U.S.C. §652(n).[78] In addition, federal law facilitates international support enforcement by establishing procedures for recognition of "foreign reciprocating countries." 42 U.S.C. §659a.

G. Separation Agreements

Most divorcing parties themselves settle the financial issues incident to dissolution. They then present their agreement to the court for approval.[79] The rules governing property division and spousal and child support thus establish the framework within which such private ordering takes place.[80] This section presents the legal principles applicable to separation agreements (also known as property settlement agreements or marital settlement agreements).

MILES v. MILES

711 S.E.2d 880 (S.C. 2011)

Justice Hearn . . . .

In March 2000, Theodora Miles ("Wife") petitioned for a divorce from James Richard Miles ("Husband") on the ground of adultery and sought custody of the couple['s] two minor children, child support, equitable division of the marital assets, alimony, and attorney's fees. [T]he parties reached an agreement as to many of the issues. . . . The family court approved the agreement, . . . granted Wife a

[78]. States' enactment of the 2008 amendments in 2015 is a condition of continued federal funding for child support programs. See Uniform Law Commission, Why States Should Adopt the Uniform Interstate Family Support Act 2008 Amendments, http://www.uniformlaws.org/shared/docs/interstate%20family%20support/UIFSA%20(2008)%20Why%20States.pdf.

[79]. See ALI Principles, supra note [3], §7.09 cmt. b, reporter's note ("Studies consistently find that approximately 90 percent of divorces are uncontested.").

[80]. Robert H. Mnookin & Lewis Kornhauser, Bargaining in the Shadow of the Law, 88 Yale L.J. 950, 950-952 (1979).

divorce and incorporated the parties' agreement [in its order]. The following language [based on the agreement] is contained in the order:

> 5. [Husband] is hereby ordered to cover [Wife] through his place of employment with health and dental insurance until such time a[s Wife] remarries or obtains employment which provides such coverage to [Wife] as a fringe benefit.
> 6. Alimony is denied to each party.

The agreement contained no language limiting or otherwise restricting modification of its terms.

Six years later, Husband filed this action seeking to modify various aspects of the final order [including] termination of the requirement that he maintain health and dental insurance on Wife due to a substantial change in circumstances. . . . At the time of the proposed modification, Wife did not have insurance coverage through her employer and had not re-married, both of which would terminate Husband's obligation by the terms of the agreement and the court's order. Therefore, the issue before the court was whether the agreement to provide health insurance was a modifiable support obligation or a non-modifiable agreement similar to a property division. . . .

Husband argues the court of appeals erred in affirming the determination [that] his obligation to provide insurance benefits to Wife was unambiguously not a form of support. We agree.

We encourage litigants in family court to reach extrajudicial agreements on marital issues. The interpretation of such agreements is a matter of contract law. . . .

Initially, we note that because the agreement is silent as to the family court's power to modify it, it remained modifiable by the court. *See* Moseley v. Mosier, 306 S.E.2d 624, 627 [(S.C. 1983)] ("[U]nless the agreement unambiguously denies the court jurisdiction, the terms will be modifiable by the court. . . ."). As to whether Husband's obligation is an incident of support, the maintenance of health insurance has the hallmark of spousal support: it provides the receiving spouse a benefit which is normally incident to the marital relationship. Additionally, our courts have previously awarded health insurance as a form of support. Awards of spousal support do not become property divisions, and therefore non-modifiable, absent something more.

Here, the agreement simply states Husband will provide health and dental insurance for Wife. It does not indicate Wife surrendered property rights in exchange for it, nor does the agreement provide any indication that Husband's obligation is anything *other* than support. Additionally, this requirement terminates automatically upon Wife's remarriage or her obtaining employment that provides similar coverage, both instances in which she would be able to obtain this benefit through means other than Husband. The language creating Husband's obligation in the agreement even appears in the same paragraph as the language pertaining to alimony. [A]lthough we agree with the family court and the court of appeals that the agreement is unambiguous, we hold that it unambiguously creates a support obligation.

Wife argues that her decision to waive alimony unambiguously demonstrates the insurance obligation is not an incident of support. However, alimony is not the only form of support available in a divorce. *See* S.C. Code Ann. § 20-3-130 (Supp. 2009) (discussing the different forms of alimony and "[s]uch other form of spousal support . . . as appropriate under the circumstances"). . . . Wife and the family court have placed too much emphasis on the language that the parties "waive[d] alimony." Such semantic distinctions have been abolished in family law. As we said in *Moseley*,

> [t]he parties' intent is rarely revealed from the agreement's words of art. Generally, those terms are used without intending or implying any particular legal consequences. Later, courts impose the consequences upon the unsuspecting parties. Today, we overrule those cases which hold that words of art make a major distinction in the operation of divorce law.

[306 S.E.2d at 627.] The mere fact the parties waived alimony—i.e., permanent and periodic, lump sum, rehabilitative, and reimbursement alimony—does not lead to the inescapable conclusion they accordingly waived all other forms of support [under the common sense approach of] *Moseley*. . . .

Next, it must be determined whether Husband has presented a substantial change in circumstances that would entitle him to a modification of his support obligation. . . . Prior case law has indicated that a party faces a heightened burden when seeking to prove a substantial change in circumstances from a court order approving an agreement. This principle has had the effect of chilling the litigants' desire to resolve their disputes by agreement, which is contrary to this Court's longstanding preference in favor of settlement. Accordingly, we take this opportunity to expressly disavow the line of cases that articulate an even higher burden on the party seeking modification when an agreement is involved. Today, we clarify that . . . the same burden applies whether the family court order in question emanated from an order following a contested hearing or a hearing to approve an agreement.

[Since the 2000 decree, Husband] underwent a triple bypass, tore his rotator cuff, and was diagnosed with colon cancer, all of which required seven operations; as a result of his medical conditions, he is no longer employed and is totally disabled; the income he receives on disability ($1,830 gross per month) is less than half of his former earnings as a police officer; and the insurance premiums he pays pursuant to his child support obligations have increased. Wife does not allege any of these events could have been anticipated at the time of their agreement. Husband further testified the insurance premiums he pays for Wife are approximately $370 per month. As for Wife during this time period, her income has increased from $28,000 per year at the time of the divorce to $45,000 per year.

[W]e find that Husband has demonstrated a substantial change in circumstances that merits a modification in his support obligation to provide health and dental insurance coverage for Wife. However, the record is not complete enough for us to determine the precise extent and mechanics of the modification and [so] a remand is in order. . . .

UNIFORM MARRIAGE AND DIVORCE ACT

§306. [SEPARATION AGREEMENT]

(a) To promote amicable settlement of disputes between parties to a marriage attendant upon their separation or the dissolution of their marriage, the parties may enter into a written separation agreement containing provisions for disposition of any property owned by either of them, maintenance of either of them, and support, custody, and visitation of their children.

(b) In a proceeding for dissolution of marriage or for legal separation, the terms of the separation agreement, except those providing for the support, custody and visitation of children, are binding upon the court unless it finds, after considering the economic circumstances of the parties and any other relevant evidence produced by the parties, on their own motion or on request of the court, that the separation agreement is unconscionable.

(c) If the court finds the separation agreement unconscionable, it may request the parties to submit a revised separation agreement or may make orders for the disposition of property, maintenance, and support.

(d) If the court finds that the separation agreement is not unconscionable as to disposition of property or maintenance, and not unsatisfactory as to support:

(1) unless the separation agreement provides to the contrary, its terms shall be set forth in the decree of dissolution or legal separation and the parties shall be ordered to perform them, or

(2) if the separation agreement provides that its terms shall not be set forth in the decree, the decree shall identify the separation agreement and state that the court has found the terms not unconscionable.

(e) Terms of the agreement set forth in the decree are enforceable by all remedies available for enforcement of a judgment, including contempt, and are enforceable as contract terms.

(f) Except for terms concerning the support, custody, or visitation of children, the decree may expressly preclude or limit modification of terms set forth in the decree if the separation agreement so provides. Otherwise, terms of a separation agreement set forth in the decree are automatically modified by modification of the decree.

Notes and Questions

1. Public policy. At one time, separation agreements were held to violate public policy because they facilitated divorce by removing uncertainty about how a court would resolve the financial incidents. In contrast, UMDA makes the parties' "amicable settlement of disputes" an explicit policy objective.

Why does UMDA reject the traditional disfavor of separation agreements? Does the transition from fault to no-fault divorce explain the change? Does the increasing acceptance of premarital agreements? What are the advantages of private ordering over judicial resolution? See Robert H. Mnookin, Divorce Bargaining: The Limits on Private Ordering, 18 U. Mich. J.L. Reform 1015, 1017-1019 (1985). The disadvantages?

The American Law Institute's Principles of the Law of Family Dissolution also favor private ordering. To encourage settlement, the Principles' formulaic approach (discussed supra) is designed to enhance the predictability of the outcome a court would reach. Accordingly, the Principles' treatment of agreements sets out the requirements for parties to "opt out" of the default rules that would otherwise govern. See ALI Principles §7.02 cmt. a. Chapter 7 covers premarital agreements, postnuptial agreements, separation agreements, and agreements for domestic partnerships and their dissolution. From a public policy perspective, should the law show more or less deference to separation agreements, compared to premarital agreements? Why? See id. §7.09 cmt. b. Does the psychological stress associated with divorce call for greater legal protection of parties entering separation agreements than premarital agreements (discussed in Chapter II)? See Mnookin, supra.

Despite the modern trend in favor of private ordering, what policy-based limitations remain? Suppose that an agreement entered at the time of separation eliminates the use of adultery as a divorce ground or a bar to alimony. See Eason v. Eason, 682 S.E.2d 804 (S.C. 2009). Suppose that one spouse insists on a postnuptial agreement as a condition of continuing the marriage. Should courts in later divorce proceedings accept such terms? See Ansin v. Craven-Ansin, 929 N.E.2d 955 (Mass. 2010). What are the implications for reconciliation agreements of UMDA's timing requirement ("attendant upon" separation or dissolution)? See In re Marriage of Traster, 339 P.3d 778 (Kan. 2014). See also the Uniform Premarital and Marital Agreements Act (examined in Chapter II).

2. **Unconscionability.** How does a court determine whether an agreement is "unconscionable" under UMDA? Does this standard contemplate a substantive evaluation of fairness or only perfunctory judicial review? See, e.g., In re Marriage of Callahan, 984 N.E.2d 531 (Ill. Ct. App. 2013). Some authorities claim that the absence of judicial oversight disproportionately disadvantages women. See, e.g., Penelope Eileen Bryan, The Coercion of Women in Divorce Settlement Negotiations, 74 Denv. U. L. Rev. 931, 937-938 (1997). See also Tess Wilkinson-Ryan & Deborah Small, Negotiating Divorce: Gender and the Behavioral Economics of Divorce Bargaining, 26 Law & Ineq. 109 (2008) (noting, inter alia, the impact on women of the current default rule, awarding no spousal support).

The ALI Principles make presumptively unenforceable agreements that would substantially change the property rights or compensatory spousal payments otherwise due, when enforcement would substantially impair the economic well-being of either a party with custody of the children or a party with substantially fewer economic resources than the other party. ALI Principles §7.09(2). What advantages does this standard have over the "unconscionability" test? What disadvantages? See also id. §7.01 (procedural requirements). See generally Brian H. Bix, The ALI Principles and Agreements: Seeking a Balance Between Status and Contract, in Reconceiving the Family: Critique on the American Law Institute's Principles of the Law of Family Dissolution 372, 387-391 (Robin Fretwell Wilson, ed., 2006).

3. **Attorney's role.** Do the policies favoring the settlement of disputes preclude a malpractice judgment against an attorney who advised a client to sign a separation agreement? Does the client's acceptance of the agreement serve as a malpractice defense? See, e.g., Young v. Grovier & Milone, L.P., 835 N.W.2d 684 (Neb. 2013); Gere v. Louis, 38 A.3d 591 (N.J. 2012). Does the court's approval of the separation agreement as "not unconscionable"?

Although plaintiffs who show professional negligence causing an economic injury can recover for malpractice, the emotional climate of divorce poses risks for attorneys. What should an attorney do when a client asserts that the highest priority is settling the case quickly and asks the attorney to forgo discovery to determine the extent of the marital property? See generally Lewis Becker, Ethical Concerns in Negotiating Family Law Agreements, 30 Fam. L.Q. 587 (1996); Andrew S. Grossman, Avoiding Legal Malpractice in Family Law Cases: The Dangers of Not Engaging in Financial Discovery, 33 Fam. L.Q. 361 (1999).

4. The bargaining process. The conventional wisdom depicts the parties bargaining toward a separation agreement in the "shadow of the law." Under this theory, the outcome that the judge would order if the spouses did not settle significantly influences the settlement that they will reach.[81] In predicting the outcome that adjudication would yield, however, attorneys necessarily consider the high proportion of cases that settle. Further, empirical studies show that judicial review operates primarily as a rubber stamp of the parties' agreements, and that settlements often reflect " 'the best I can get' solution," in turn reflecting a system of "adjudication in the shadow of bargaining."[82]

5. Incorporation and merger. Separation agreements may be "contractual" or "decretal," a distinction with important consequences. Without its incorporation (sometimes called "merger") into a judicial decree, a separation agreement is simply a contract. UMDA §306 creates a presumption of incorporation that parties seeking to avoid must dispel by a clear statement to the contrary.

Enforcement tools depend on the status of the agreement. Contempt of court and possible imprisonment provide remedies for noncompliance with a judicial decree. Such remedies are not available for breach of contract. Grace v. Grace, 655 N.W.2d 595, 600 (Mich. Ct. App. 2002). UMDA §306 makes available all enforcement remedies for "terms of the agreement set forth in the decree." See also ALI Principles §7.10.

Similarly, courts can modify some provisions of a judicial decree if circumstances change (that is, support provisions), as illustrated in *Miles*; courts cannot rewrite the terms of a contract no matter how unfair or inadequate they become. Yet, even in agreements incorporated into judicial decrees, the parties may preclude modification or limit it to certain circumstances. See, e.g., Richardson v. Richardson, 218 S.W.3d 426 (Mo. 2007) (respecting agreement's provision precluding modification, despite allegations that wife would use maintenance funds to hire a "hit man" to kill husband). But see In re Marriage of Cauley, 41 Cal. Rptr. 3d 902 (Ct. App. 2005) (statutory presumption that one convicted of domestic violence cannot receive spousal support trumps nonmodifiability provision, thus permitting termination of support).

6. Tradeoffs. In reaching agreement, the parties resolve several incidents of divorce. The bargaining process may entail purely financial tradeoffs, for example, decreased alimony for a greater share of the marital property. Alternatively, it may entail negotiation of financial and nonfinancial interests, for example, decreased alimony for sole child custody. See, e.g., Scott Altman, Lurking in the Shadow, 68 S. Cal. L. Rev. 493 (1995) (examining custody-property trades in negotiations); Margaret F. Brinig & Michael V. Alexeev, Trading at Divorce: Preferences, Legal

---

[81]. Id. at 951.

[82]. Marygold S. Melli et al., The Process of Negotiation: An Exploratory Investigation in the Context of No-Fault Divorce, 40 Rutgers L. Rev. 1133, 1147, 1159 (1988).

Rules, and Transaction Costs, 8 Ohio St. J. on Disp. Resol. 279 (1993) (theoretical and empirical investigation). According to *Miles*, what weight should the labels in the agreement carry? See also Simpson v. Simpson, 294 P.3d 1212 (Mont. 2013).

Some jurisdictions have special rules for "integrated bargains," that is, agreements in which the consideration exchanged between the parties includes both property rights and support payments. For example, support payments in an integrated bargain incorporated into the divorce decree are not modifiable despite changed circumstances because modification would necessarily alter the property division and upset the parties' carefully crafted quid pro quo. See, e.g., Henderson v. Mogren, 149 So. 3d 629 (Ala. Civ. App. 2014). Further, some agreements use terms or payment structures that leave unclear whether an obligation represents a division of assets, spousal support, or some of both, as in *Miles*. Was the agreement in *Miles* an integrated bargain? Evaluate the court's analysis and result.

7. Vacating the decree. Orders dividing property are final in the sense that a court cannot modify them upon changed circumstances, although they can be reopened if they form part of an agreement procured by fraud or other improper means. Courts follow strict standards for reopening decrees based on marital settlement agreements. E.g., Simkin v. Blank, 968 N.E.2d 459 (N.Y.2012) (refusing to set aside an agreement for mutual mistake despite later discovery that husband's "Madoff accounts" rested on a Ponzi scheme); Esposito v. Esposito, 38 A.3d 1 (R.I. 2012) (refusing to vacate despite husband's failure to disclose the increased value of assets after the agreement was signed but before the judgment was entered).

Should the same standard of unconscionability apply when a party attempts to set aside an agreement after its entry as when the court considers whether to adopt the agreement initially? What would this approach mean for private ordering? Would it invite "judges to patronizingly and paternalistically meddle in the proposed stipulations of presumptively competent divorcing adults"? Crawford v. Crawford, 524 N.W.2d 833, 837 (N.D. 1994) (Neumann, J., dissenting). See also, e.g., Bishopp v. Bishopp, 962 N.Y.S.2d 503 (App. Div. 2013).

The ALI Principles afford the parties a short opportunity to challenge the terms after experiencing the agreement's operation, when a court finds both that the agreement is "tainted" by noncompliance with the procedural or substantive requirements of §7.09 and that "the challenged terms of the decree were substantially less favorable to the moving party than they would have been without the agreement." ALI Principles §7.11.

8. Bargaining with child support. UMDA §306 treats child support, custody, and visitation specially, making the parties' agreement on these issues not binding on the court and preserving the possibility of future modification, despite agreement to contrary. See In re Marriage of Matar & Harake, 300 P.3d 144 (Or. 2013); ALI Principles §§7.06, 7.07, and 7.09. What explains the special treatment of provisions concerning children? What is the difference under UMDA between finding property or maintenance provisions "not unconscionable" and finding (child) support provisions "not unsatisfactory?"

9. Collaborative divorce. Collaborative family law uses a "team approach," in which the parties, their attorneys, and other specialists (such as social workers and accountants) attempt to reach separation agreements, with full transparency and before the filing of a divorce petition. Using techniques similar to mediation, the process seeks not only to avoid the acrimony and expense of litigation but also to help parties reach agreements tailored for the particular family and its members. How might collaborative law have addressed the disputes presented by the cases in this chapter? What ethical problems might it present? (See Chapter VIII.) For a discussion of the history, advantages, and disadvantages, see Luke Salava, Collaborative Divorce: The Unexpectedly Underwhelming Advance of a Promising Solution in Marriage Dissolution, 48 Fam. L.Q. 179 (2014). See also Margaret B. Drew, Collaboration and Coercion, 24 Hastings Women's L.J. 79 (2013) (examining dangers of collaborative law in abuse cases).

Problem

In the property settlement agreement judicially ratified, affirmed, and incorporated by reference in the divorce decree, David agrees to relinquish all his equity in the jointly owned family home (the couple's only asset) in exchange for Marilyn's promise never to request child support. Their agreement explicitly states that Marilyn "has accepted all of David's equity in lieu of requesting child support" and that "should a court ever grant a child support award against David, Marilyn covenants and agrees to pay directly to David any amount of support that he is directed to pay to any party." Pursuant to the agreement, David conveys to Marilyn his equity in the family home, valued at $40,000, where she and the children continue to live. Marilyn alone supports the children.

Six years later, David petitions for definite periods of visitation with the children. Marilyn then petitions for David to pay child support. He counters by moving the court to order Marilyn to reimburse him for any amount of child support the court orders. What result? See Kelley v. Kelley, 449 S.E.2d 55 (Va. 1994). See also Esser v. Esser, 586 S.E.2d 627 (Ga. 2003); Guidash v. Tome, 66 A.3d 122 (Md. Ct. Spec. App. 2013); ALI Principles §3.13.

VIII

Child Custody

Custody disputes arise in many different settings: divorce, guardianship, child abuse and neglect, and adoption.[1] This chapter focuses primarily on the first of these settings. Postdivorce custody law performs a dual function of private dispute resolution and child protection.[2] The resolution of custody disputes thereby reflects the fundamental tension between respect for family autonomy versus the need for state intervention.

When the parents can agree on child custody, the state generally defers to family autonomy. However, in approximately 10 to 20 percent of divorce cases involving children, the parents cannot agree.[3] For these cases, the important question is how these disputes should be resolved. In exploring that issue, this chapter raises questions of substance and process. What standards should govern custody disputes? What factors may courts consider? What role should attorneys, the child, experts, and nonparents (such as grandparents) play in these disputes? By what process should these disputes be resolved? What reforms might improve custody decisionmaking in the context of family dissolution?

---

[1]. For details on these different "strands" of custody law, see Robert H. Mnookin, Child Custody Adjudication: Judicial Functions in the Face of Indeterminacy, 39 Law & Contemp. Probs. 226, 230-246 (1975).

[2]. Id. at 281.

[3]. Eleanor E. Maccoby & Robert H. Mnookin, Dividing the Child: Social and Legal Dilemmas of Custody 134 (1992). See also Daniel Krauss & Bruce Sales, Legal Standards, Expertise, and Experts in the Resolution of Contested Child Custody Cases, 6 Psychol. Pub. Pol'y & L. 843, 843 (2000) (reporting estimates of 6 to 20 percent).

A. Introduction: Effects of Parental Divorce

The following excerpt sheds light on the experience of divorce from the child's perspective:

Elizabeth Marquardt, Between Two Worlds: The Inner Lives of Children of Divorce

21-22, 30-31 (2005)

Dr. Judith Wallerstein (1921-2012), the eminent psychologist who studied the effects of divorce on children

Many people imagine that the hardest time for children of divorce is the moment when their parents first part. That moment *is* hard, but it is only the beginning. The division and restructuring of childhood that immediately follow, and which continue up to and beyond the point the child leaves home, throw into question aspects of childhood that were once taken for granted and keep the divorce very much alive for years to come.

[W]e found that almost two-thirds of children of divorce who stay in contact with both parents say they felt like they grew up in two families, not one. Many changes occur in the wake of divorce. But from the child's point of view, the essential change is this: The child suddenly inherits two distinct worlds in which to grow up.

Growing up in two worlds creates endless and often painful complications for a child. . . . As children of divorce, we became insiders *and* outsiders in each of our parents' worlds. We were outsiders when we looked or acted like our other parent or when we shared experiences in one world that people in the other knew little or nothing about. [W]e were marked as insiders by whatever traits we shared with the family members in one world—physical characteristics, personality, and name—as well as the experiences we shared with that family. . . . Yet because we grew up living in two worlds we never fully belonged in either place. . . .

To outside observers, the children of divorced parents may look no different than the children of intact parents. We ran on the playground, went to school, argued with our siblings, played with blocks, drew pictures in our bedrooms. But we were also vigilant. When Mom came home, we gauged her mood. When we stayed at Dad's, we were often quiet and on good behavior. We paid close attention to the different rules at each parent's home and the conflicts in their expectations of us. We wondered if we looked or acted too much like our father and if that made our mother mad at us. We struggled to remember what we were supposed to say, what secrets or information about one parent we should not share with the other. We adjusted ourselves to each of our parents, shaping our habits and beliefs to mimic theirs when we were around them. We often felt like a different person with each of our parents.

Our parents may no longer have been in conflict, but the conflict between their worlds was still alive. Yet instead of being in the open, visible to outsiders, the conflict between their worlds migrated and took root within us. . . .

The above study reveals that children of divorce are far more likely than those from intact families to admit feeling different with each parent, an outsider in their own home, more mature than their years, lonely, unsafe emotionally, and less likely to seek comfort from their parents.

What are the *long-term* psychological effects of divorce on children? Psychologist Judith Wallerstein's study of 60 postdivorce families finds that the *immediate* effects of divorce vary according to gender, age, and developmental stage: (1) preschoolers manifest regression, aggression, sleep disturbance, and fantasies of abandonment; (2) children aged 5-8 reveal grief, longing for the departed parent, and fantasies of replacement; (3) children aged 8 to 12 evince anxiety, loneliness, and anger; and (4) adolescents act out, suffer depression, have suicidal thoughts, and express anxiety about their having a successful marriage.[4]

Wallerstein's follow-up studies (after 10 and 25 years) find continued negative effects: one-third of the children had psychological problems (e.g., clinical depression), poor academic performance, and difficulties in maintaining intimate interpersonal relationships.[5] A study by psychologist Mavis Hetherington and John Kelly confirms that divorce has long-term consequences for children. However, these authors have considerable more optimism about these effects based on the resiliency of children.[6]

Social psychologist Paul Amato reconciles the divergent findings of Wallerstein and Hetherington. His meta-analysis confirms that (1) children of divorce are more likely to experience psychological problems in adulthood, (2) have more problems in maintaining intimate relationships, and (3) reach adulthood with weaker ties to parents.[7] Nonetheless, he concludes that the long-term effects of divorce are *not as pervasive or as severe* as Wallerstein claims.

Finally, *postdivorce* family experiences have a significant impact on children's adjustment. Experiencing their parents' multiple divorces and remarriages is especially problematic for children.[8]

---

[4]. Judith S. Wallerstein & Joan B. Kelly, Surviving the Breakup: How Children and Parents Cope with Divorce (1996).

[5]. Judith S. Wallerstein & Sandra Blakeslee, Second Chances: Men, Women, and Children a Decade After Divorce (2004); Judith S. Wallerstein et al., The Unexpected Legacy of Divorce: The 25-Year Landmark Study (2001).

[6]. E. Mavis Hetherington & John Kelly, For Better or for Worse: Divorce Reconsidered (2002).

[7]. Paul R. Amato, Reconciling Divergent Perspectives: Judith Wallerstein, Quantitative Family Research, and Children of Divorce, 52 Fam. Relations 334 (2003).

[8]. Judith S. Wallerstein & Julia M. Lewis, Divorced Fathers and Their Adult Offspring: Report from a Twenty-Five Year Longitudinal Study, 42 Fam. L.Q. 695 (2009). For a more recent review of the literature, see Patrick F. Fagan & Aaron Churchill, Family Research Council, The Effects of Divorce on Children (Jan. 11, 2012), www.frc.org/EF/EF12A22.pdf.

As you read though the materials in this chapter, consider the following questions: What should be the impact on policymakers of the effects of divorce on children? Should governmental policy promote marriage? Discourage divorce? Will such policies significantly improve children's well-being?

B. Parental Disputes Concerning Child Custody

1. Standards for Selecting the Custodial Parent: What Should Be the Standard?

a. Presumptions?

(i) Tender Years Presumption

DEVINE v. DEVINE

398 So. 2d 686 (Ala. 1981)

MADDOX, Justice.

[A]ppellant Christopher P. Devine [and] Appellee, Alice Beth Clark Devine were legally and lawfully married on December 17, 1966, . . . and separated in Calhoun County, Alabama, on March 29, 1979. [They have two sons, Matthew, born in 1972, and Timothy, born in 1975.] Since [college] graduation in 1962, Mrs. Devine has taught high school. [I]n 1975, [she] commenced employment with the U.S. Army at Fort McClellan, Alabama, where she was employed continuously through the [trial] as an Educational Specialist. [She] was 38 years of age at the time of [trial]. The Appellant/natural father, Christopher P. Devine [age 41] was a member of the faculty and head of the Guidance and Counseling Department at Jacksonville State University, Jacksonville, Alabama. At the time of the trial, the older son had just completed the first grade at the said University's Elementary Laboratory School and the younger son was enrolled in the said University's Nursery Laboratory School. [The trial court awarded custody of both boys to the mother based on the tender years presumption.]

[T]here exists in Alabama law a presumption that when dealing with children of tender years, the natural mother is presumed, in absence of evidence to the contrary, to be the proper person to be vested with custody of such children. This presumption, while perhaps weaker now than in the past, remains quite viable today. . . .

The sole issue presented for review is whether the trial court's reliance on the tender years presumption deprived the father of his constitutional entitlement to the equal protection of the law. . . .

At common law, it was the father rather than the mother who held a virtual absolute right to the custody of their minor children. This rule of law was fostered, in part, by feudalistic notions concerning the "natural" responsibilities of the husband at common law. The husband was considered the head or master of his family, and, as such, responsible for the care, maintenance, education and religious training of his children. By virtue of these responsibilities, the husband was given a corresponding entitlement to the benefits of his children, i.e., their services and association. It is interesting to note that in many instances these rights and privileges were considered dependent upon the recognized laws of nature and in accordance with the *presumption* that the father could best provide for the necessities of his children. . . .

By contrast, the wife was without any rights to the care and custody of her minor children. By marriage, husband and wife became one person with the legal identity of the woman being totally merged with that of her husband. As a result, her rights were often subordinated to those of her husband and she was laden with numerous marital disabilities. As far as any custodial rights were concerned, Blackstone stated the law to be that the mother was "entitled to no power [over her children], but only to reverence and respect." 1 W. Blackstone, Commentaries on the Law of England 453 (Tucker ed. 1803).

By the middle of the 19th Century, the courts of England began to question and qualify the paternal preference rule. This was due, in part, to the "hardships, not to say cruelty, inflicted upon unoffending mothers by a state of law which took little account of their claims or feelings." W. Forsyth, A Treatise on the Law Relating to the Custody of Infants in Cases of Difference Between Parents or Guardians 66 (1850). Courts reacted by taking a more moderate stance concerning child custody, a stance which conditioned a father's absolute custodial rights upon his fitness as a parent. Ultimately, by a series of statutes culminating with Justice Talfourd's Act, 2 and 3 Vict. c. 54 (1839), Parliament affirmatively extended the rights of mothers, especially as concerned the custody of young children. Justice Talfourd's Act expressly provided that the chancery courts, in cases of divorce and separation, could award the custody of minor children to the mother if the children were less than seven years old. This statute marks the origin of the tender years presumption in England.

In the United States the origin of the tender years presumption is attributed to the 1830 Maryland decision of Helms v. Franciscus, 2 Bl. Ch. (Md.) 544 (1830). In *Helms*, the court, while recognizing the general rights of the father, stated that it would violate the laws of nature to "snatch" an infant from the care of its mother:

> The father is the rightful and legal guardian of all his infant children; and in general, no court can take from him the custody and control of them, thrown upon him by the law, not for his gratification, but on account of his duties, and place them against his will in the hands even of his wife. . . . Yet even a court of common law will not go so far as to hold nature in contempt, and snatch helpless, pulling infancy from the bosom of an affectionate mother, and place it in the coarse hands of the father. The mother is the softest and safest nurse of infancy, and with her it will be left in opposition to this general right of the father.

Thus began a "process of evolution, perhaps reflecting a change in social attitudes, [whereby] the mother came to be the preferred custodian of young children and daughters. . . ." Foster, Life with Father, 11 Fam. L.Q. 327 (1978). . . .

At the present time, the tender years presumption is recognized in Alabama as a rebuttable factual presumption based upon the inherent suitability of the mother to care for and nurture young children. All things being equal, the mother is presumed to be best fitted to guide and care for children of tender years. To rebut this presumption the father must present clear and convincing evidence of the mother's positive unfitness. Thus, the tender years presumption affects the resolution of child custody disputes on both a substantive and procedural level. Substantively, it requires the court to award custody of young children to the mother when the parties, as in the present case, are equally fit parents. Procedurally, it imposes an evidentiary burden on the father to prove the positive unfitness of the mother.

In recent years, the tender years doctrine has been severely criticized by legal commentators as an outmoded means of resolving child custody disputes. . . . In twenty states the doctrine has been expressly abolished by statute or court decision, and in four other states its existence is extremely questionable. . . . In Orr v. Orr, 440 U.S. 268 (1979), the United States Supreme Court held that any statutory scheme which imposes obligations on husbands, but not on wives, establishes a classification based upon sex which is subject to scrutiny under the Fourteenth Amendment. The same must also be true for a legal presumption which imposes evidentiary burdens on fathers, but not on mothers.

[W]e conclude that the tender years presumption represents an unconstitutional gender-based classification which discriminates between fathers and mothers in child custody proceedings solely on the basis of sex.

Notes and Questions

1. Background. Beginning in the mid- to late-nineteenth century, the tender years presumption applied to custody determinations. The presumption (also called the "maternal preference") provided that the biological mother of a young child was entitled to custody unless she was found unfit.

Courts treated the doctrine as (1) a tiebreaker mandating maternal custody if other factors are equal, or (2) a rule placing the burden of persuasion on the father to show that paternal custody serves the child's best interests, or (3) a rule affecting the burden of proof that requires the father, in order to prevail, to prove maternal unfitness. In the 1970s and 1980s, many states (similar to Alabama in *Devine*) declared that the presumption violated either the Equal Protection Clause or state equal rights amendments.

The tender years presumption was introduced, as *Devine* suggests, in an influential nineteenth-century American case that carved out an exception to the paternal preference for infants. Widespread acceptance of the doctrine stemmed from social conditions (industrialization, urbanization, a growing middle class, increasing privatization of the family, the glorification of motherhood, and an intense concern with childrearing). See generally Michael Grossberg, Governing the Hearth: Law and the Family in Nineteenth-Century America 234-285 (1985).

2. Presumptions generally. Consider the advantages and disadvantages of presumptions in custody decisionmaking. Like all presumptions, the tender years doctrine offers relative certainty and thereby avoids the stress of litigation. However, the presumption clearly puts fathers at a disadvantage because they must prove the mother's unfitness before they can gain custody. But might a gender-*neutral* presumption disadvantage the mother? The father? The child? See generally J. Herbie DiFonzo, From the Rule of One to Shared Parenting: Custody Presumptions in Law and Policy, 52 Fam. Ct. Rev. 213 (2014).

3. Best interests standard. The tender years presumption has been replaced by the purportedly gender-neutral "best interests of the child" standard. This highly discretionary standard is based on a list of factors (usually statutory) regarding the child's needs. Some states consider the child's age as one factor in the best interests analysis. See, e.g., Va. Code Ann. §20-124.3; Rosser v. Morris, 135 So. 3d 945 (Miss. Ct. App. 2014) (tender years presumption still exists but is "significantly weakened").

4. ALI Principles. The American Law Institute's Principles of the Law of Family Dissolution prohibit a court from considering the gender of *either* the parent *or* the child in determining custody arrangements. ALI Principles §2.12(1)(b). Should the *child's* gender be relevant in custody decisionmaking? Most courts award custody irrespective of the child's gender. But cf. Copeland v. Copeland, 904 So. 2d 1066 (Miss. 2004) (ruling that gender was a factor favoring father's custody of son). Some evidence suggests, however, that children who are awarded to parents of the same sex are better adjusted and have higher self-esteem. See Robert E. Emery, Marriage, Divorce, and Children's Adjustment 85-86 (1988). Should such findings affect custody decisionmaking?

5. Other presumptions. Most states have abrogated the common law presumption that custody of a nonmarital child vests in the mother. See, e.g., Rosero v. Blake, 581 S.E.2d 41, 49 (N.C. 2003). Does abrogation of this presumption lead to unduly harsh results for single mothers? Or does it marginalize single fathers? See Clare Huntington, Postmarital Family Law: A Legal Structure for Nonmarital Families, 67 Stan. L. Rev. 167, 203-204 (2015).

Some courts rely on other presumptions, such as separation of siblings is not in their best interests (e.g., Moeller v. Moeller, 714 S.E.2d 898, 903 (S.C. Ct. App. 2011)). See generally Jill Elaine Hasday, Siblings in Law, 65 Vand. L. Rev. 897, 914-915 (2012). Another presumption favors biological parents over nonparents (discussed later in this chapter). Still other presumptions bar batterers, murderers, or rapists from obtaining custody. See, e.g., Cal. Fam. Code §3044.

(ii) Primary Caretaker Presumption

The primary caretaker presumption briefly replaced the tender years presumption in a few states. See Pikula v. Pikula, 374 N.W.2d 705 (Minn. 1985); Garska v. McCoy, 278 S.E.2d 357 (W. Va. 1981). According to this presumption, the best interests of the child are served by placing the child with the parent who has taken primary responsibility for the child's care. Today, primary caretaker status serves as one factor in the determination of the child's best interests. See, e.g., Vt. Stat. Ann. tit. 15, §665(b)(6). This doctrine is gender-neutral and offers continuity of care. Critics contend, however, that it overemphasizes caretaking tasks and devalues the father's role. Feminists criticize that, although the doctrine is gender-neutral in theory, it is biased in application (e.g., minimizing some of women's contributions to childcare, such as breastfeeding and emotional caretaking, while maximizing men's smaller contributions).[9]

When West Virginia rejected the presumption, legislators replaced it with the American Law Institute's recommendation[10] that requires the parties to submit a "parenting plan" (a written agreement specifying authority for caretaking, decisionmaking, and the manner of resolution of future disputes). Many states now authorize such parenting plans. According to the ALI Principles, if the parents agree, the court should enforce their agreement unless the agreement is not voluntary or is harmful to the child (§2.06(1)(a), (b)).

If the parents are unable to agree, the ALI Principles provide that the court should award custody based on the allocation of caretaking responsibility prior to the separation (§2.08(1)) (the "approximation standard"). The objective is to replicate the division of responsibility in the former intact family in order to promote stability for the child.[11] Such an outcome defers to the arrangements on which the parties once agreed. The ALI rule may be rebutted by prior parental agreement, the child's preference, the need to keep the siblings together, harm to the child, avoidance of custodial arrangements that would be impractical or interfere with the child's need for stability, and the need to deal with parental relocation (2.08(1)(a) to (g)). Critics fault the recommendation for using a predivorce division of parental responsibilities when divorce necessitates many changes. See generally Katharine T. Bartlett, Prioritizing Past Caretaking in Child-Custody Decisionmaking, 77 Law & Contemp. Probs. 29 (2014).

b. Best Interests of the Child?

(i) Introduction

Robert H. Mnookin, Child-Custody Adjudication: Judicial Functions in the Face of Indeterminacy

39 Law & Contemp. Probs. 226, 233-237, 255-256, 261-264 (1975)

The history of the legal standards governing custody disputes between a child's parents reveals a dramatic movement from rules to a highly discretionary principle. . . . Divorce custody standards now show the overwhelming dominance

[9]. For critical commentary, see Mary E. Becker, Maternal Feelings: Myth, Taboo, and Child Custody, 1 S. Cal. Rev. L. & Women's Stud. 133 (1992); David L. Chambers, Rethinking the Substantive Rules for Custody Disputes in Divorce, 83 Mich. L. Rev. 477 (1984); Martha L. Fineman & Anne Opie, The Uses of Social Science Data in Legal Policymaking: Custody Determinations at Divorce, 1987 Wis. L. Rev. 107.

[10]. The ALI undertook a project to reform family law by clarifying its underlying principles and making policy recommendations. Rejecting the "best interests of the child standard" because of its subjectivity and lack of predictability, the recommendations instead favor parental agreements. See ALI Principles of the Law of Family Dissolution: Analysis and Recommendations §§2.06, 2.11-2.12 (2002) (hereinafter ALI Principles).

[11]. The "approximation standard" was first formulated by Elizabeth Scott, Pluralism, Parental Preference, and Child Custody, 80 Cal. L. Rev. 615 (1992).

of the best-interests principle. [My purpose here] is to expose the inherent indeterminacy of the best-interests standard.

. . . An inquiry about what is best for a child often yields indeterminate results because of the problems of having adequate information, making the necessary predictions, and finding an integrated set of values by which to choose. But some custody cases may still be comparatively easy to decide. While there is no consensus about what is best for a child, there is much consensus about what is very bad (e.g., physical abuse); some short-term predictions about human behavior can be reliably made (e.g., chronic alcoholism or psychosis is difficult quickly to modify). Asking which alternative is in the best interests of a child may have a rather clear-cut answer in situations where one claimant exposes the child to substantial risks of immediate harm and the other claimant already has a substantial personal relationship with the child and poses no such risk. [However, most] custody disputes pose difficult choices. [I]n many private disputes, the court must often choose between parties who each offer advantages and disadvantages, knowing that to deprive the child completely of either relationship will be disruptive. . . .

. . . What are some of the implications of the use of indeterminate standards in custody disputes? Would more precise standards that ask an answerable question be better? [T]he use of an indeterminate standard makes the outcome of litigation difficult to predict. This may encourage more litigation than would a standard that made the outcome of more cases predictable. Because each divorcing parent can often make plausible arguments why a child would be better off with him or her, a best-interests standard probably creates a greater incentive to litigate than would a rule that children should go to the parent of the same sex. . . .

Indeterminate standards also pose an obviously greater risk of violating the fundamental precept that like cases should be decided alike. [W]ith an indeterminate standard, the same case presented to different judges may easily result in different decisions. The use of an indeterminate standard means that state officials may decide on the basis of unarticulated (perhaps even unconscious) predictions and preferences that could be questioned if expressed. . . .

. . . While judges may be ill-equipped to develop and evaluate information about the child, having some other state official decide or making various procedural adjustments (such as giving counsel to the child, providing better staff to courts, or making the proceedings more or less formal) will not cure the root problem. The indeterminacy flows from our inability to predict accurately human behavior and from a lack of social consensus about the values that should inform the decision.

[A]djudication by a more determinate rule would confront the fundamental problems posed by an indeterminate principle. But the choice between indeterminate standards and more precise rules poses a profound dilemma. The absence of rules removes the special burdens of justification and formulation of standards characteristic of adjudication. Unfairness and adverse consequences can result. And yet, rules that relate past events or conduct to legal consequences may themselves create substantial difficulties in the custody area. Our inadequate knowledge about human behavior and our inability to generalize confidently about the relationship between past events or conduct and future behavior

> make the formulation of rules especially problematic. Moreover, the very lack of consensus about values that makes the best-interests standard indeterminate may also make the formulation of rules inappropriate. . . .[12]

Given the shortcomings of the best-interests-of-the-child standard, why has it persisted so long? See Elizabeth S. Scott & Robert Emery, Gender Politics and Child Custody: The Puzzling Persistence of the Best-Interests Standard, 77 Law & Contemp. Probs. 69 (2014). See also Robert Mnookin, Child Custody Revisited, 77 Law & Contemp. Probs. 249 (2014) (contending that his criticisms of the best-interests standard remain relevant today).

UNIFORM MARRIAGE AND DIVORCE ACT (UMDA)

§402. BEST INTEREST OF CHILD

The court shall determine custody in accordance with the best interest of the child. The court shall consider all relevant factors, including:

(1) the wishes of the child's parent or parents as to his custody;

(2) the wishes of the child as to his custodian;

(3) the interaction and interrelationship of the child with his parent or parents, his siblings, and any other person who may significantly affect the child's best interest;

(4) the child's adjustment to his home, school, and community; and

(5) the mental and physical health of all individuals involved.

Courts consider many factors in custody decisions, including the child's preference.

The court shall not consider conduct of a proposed custodian that does not affect his relationship to the child.

The best-interests standard invites courts to consider many factors in custody decisions. Are there some factors that should *not* be determinative? The next case explores this question.

---

[12]. For other criticisms of the best-interests standard, see Katharine T. Bartlett, Preference, Presumption, Predisposition, and Common Sense: From Traditional Custody Doctrines to the American Law Institute's Family Dissolution Project, 36 Fam. L.Q. 11 (2002); Steven N. Peskind, Determining the Undeterminable: The Best Interest of the Child Standard as an Imperfect but Necessary Guidepost to Determine Child Custody, 25 N. Ill. U. L. Rev. 449 (2005).

(ii) Constitutional Factors

(1) Race

PALMORE v. SIDOTI

466 U.S. 429 (1984)

Chief Justice BURGER delivered the opinion of the Court.

We granted certiorari to review a judgment of a state court divesting a natural mother of the custody of her infant child because of her remarriage to a person of a different race.

When petitioner Linda Sidoti Palmore and respondent Anthony J. Sidoti, both Caucasians, were divorced in May 1980 in Florida, the mother was awarded custody of their three-year-old daughter. In September 1981 the father sought custody of the child by filing a petition to modify the prior judgment because of changed conditions. The change was that the child's mother was then cohabiting with a Negro, Clarence Palmore, Jr., whom she married two months later. Additionally, the father made several allegations of instances in which the mother had not properly cared for the child.

After hearing testimony from both parties and considering a court counselor's investigative report, the court noted that the father had made allegations about the child's care, but the court . . . made a finding that "there is no issue as to either party's devotion to the child, adequacy of housing facilities, or respect[a]bility of the new spouse of either parent."

The court then addressed the recommendations of the court counselor, who had made an earlier report "in [another] case coming out of this circuit also involving the social consequences of an interracial marriage. Niles v. Niles, 299 So. 2d 162." From this vague reference to that earlier case, the court turned to the present case and noted the counselor's recommendation for a change in custody because "[t]he wife [petitioner] has chosen for herself and for her child, a life-style unacceptable to her father *and to society*. . . . The child . . . is, or at school age will be, subject to environmental pressures not of choice."

The court then concluded that the best interests of the child would be served by awarding custody to the father. The court's rationale is contained in the following:

> The father's evident resentment of the mother's choice of a black partner is not sufficient to wrest custody from the mother. It is of some significance, however, that the mother did see fit to bring a man into her home and carry on a sexual relationship with him without being married to him. Such action tended to place gratification of her own desires ahead of her concern for the child's future welfare. *This Court feels that despite the strides that have been made in bettering relations between the races in this country, it is inevitable that Melanie will, if allowed to remain in her present situation and attains school age and thus more vulnerable to peer pressures, suffer from the social stigmatization that is sure to come.*

(Emphasis added.)

The Second District Court of Appeal affirmed without opinion, thus denying the Florida Supreme Court jurisdiction to review the case. We granted certiorari, and we reverse.

The judgment of a state court determining or reviewing a child custody decision is not ordinarily a likely candidate for review by this Court. However, the court's opinion, after stating that the "father's evident resentment of the mother's choice of a black partner is not sufficient" to deprive her of custody, then turns to what it regarded as the damaging impact on the child from remaining in a racially-mixed household. This raises important federal concerns arising from the Constitution's commitment to eradicating discrimination based on race.

The Florida court did not focus directly on the parental qualifications of the natural mother or her present husband, or indeed on the father's qualifications to have custody of the child. The court found that "there is no issue as to either party's devotion to the child, adequacy of housing facilities, or respect[a]bility of the new spouse of either parent." This, taken with the absence of any negative finding as to the quality of the care provided by the mother, constitutes a rejection of any claim of petitioner's unfitness to continue the custody of her child.

The court correctly stated that the child's welfare was the controlling factor. But that court was entirely candid and made no effort to place its holding on any ground other than race. Taking the court's findings and rationale at face value, it is clear that the outcome would have been different had petitioner married a Caucasian male of similar respectability.

A core purpose of the Fourteenth Amendment was to do away with all governmentally-imposed discrimination based on race. Classifying persons according to their race is more likely to reflect racial prejudice than legitimate public concerns; the race, not the person, dictates the category. [T]o pass constitutional muster, [racial classifications] must be justified by a compelling governmental interest. . . .

The State, of course, has a duty of the highest order to protect the interests of minor children, particularly those of tender years. In common with most states, Florida law mandates that custody determinations be made in the best interests of the children involved. Fla. Stat. §61.13(2)(b)(1) (1983). The goal of granting custody based on the best interests of the child is indisputably a substantial governmental interest for purposes of the Equal Protection Clause.

It would ignore reality to suggest that racial and ethnic prejudices do not exist or that all manifestations of those prejudices have been eliminated. There is a risk that a child living with a step-parent of a different race may be subject to a variety of pressures and stresses not present if the child were living with parents of the same racial or ethnic origin.

The question, however, is whether the reality of private biases and the possible injury they might inflict are permissible considerations for removal of an infant child from the custody of its natural mother. We have little difficulty concluding that they are not. The Constitution cannot control such prejudices but neither can it tolerate them. Private biases may be outside the reach of the law, but the law cannot, directly or indirectly, give them effect. . . .

. . . The effects of racial prejudice, however real, cannot justify a racial classification removing an infant child from the custody of its natural mother found to be an appropriate person to have such custody. The judgment of the District Court of Appeal is reversed.

Notes and Questions

1. Epilogue. Following the U.S. Supreme Court's decision above, the mother filed a petition in Texas (where the father and child had moved) for a writ of habeas corpus to recover the child and, in Florida, a motion to compel the return of the child (which was opposed there by the father). The Florida court declined jurisdiction in favor of the Texas court. When the mother appealed, the Florida Court of Appeals affirmed, stating:

> The Supreme Court's decision [in *Palmore*] was that the modification of custody could not be predicated upon the mother's association with a black man. Its opinion did not direct a reinstatement of the original custody decree and the immediate return of the child. The Supreme Court did not say that a Florida court could not defer to a Texas court.

472 So. 2d 843, 846 (Fla. Dist. Ct. App. 1985). The court then determined that it would be in the child's best interests to remain in her father's custody given the passage of time and the "substantial upheavals" in the child's life. Id. at 847.

2. Different approaches. Prior to *Palmore*, courts adopted different approaches to the role of race in custody law: (1) race was not relevant to custody, (2) race could be considered as one factor in determining a child's best interests, and (3) race could not be used as the determinative factor. Which view does *Palmore* support?

3. Pretextual reasoning. Professor Katharine Bartlett notes that, in several cases involving white mothers who lost custody after an affair with an African-American man, the court used pretextual rationales for the custody modification (e.g., the mother lied about the affair, her sexual activity displayed poor judgment). Bartlett criticizes that the best interests test is "not a test that compels transparency."[13] How can an appellate court identify race as the unarticulated rationale of a trial court ruling?

4. Promoting racial tolerance. Parents' attitudes of racial tolerance or their willingness to promote their child's biracial identity may influence judicial decision-making. See, e.g., Tipton v. Aaron, 185 S.W.3d 142 (Ark. Ct. App. 2004) (reversing an award of custody to father in favor of mother, whose childrearing philosophy promoted racial tolerance while the father's did not). How much weight *should* courts attach to the need to promote a child's cultural and racial heritage?

5. ALI Principles. The ALI Principles prohibit courts from considering the race or ethnicity of the child, parent, or other member of the household in determining custody arrangements. ALI Principles §2.12(1)(a).

---

[13]. Katharine T. Bartlett, Comparing Race and Sex Discrimination in Custody Cases, 28 Hofstra L. Rev. 877, 884 & n.35 (2000). See also Shani King, The Family Law Canon in a (Post?) Racial Era, 72 Ohio St. L.J. 575, 631 (2011) (contending that the best-interests standard "immunizes racism and perpetuates racial inequality").

Problem

Teri and Richard, a Caucasian couple, have been married for five years. They have a one-year-old son, Dylan. After Teri files for divorce, both parents seek custody of Dylan. At trial, Richard argues that the court should award him custody because Teri, a nurse, is having a relationship with the African-American doctor for whom she works. A family nurse practitioner testifies, when asked if it would be harmful for Dylan to be raised in this environment, that it would be harmful. She adds that interracial relationships are more acceptable in large cities, but that it may be harmful for a child to be raised in such an environment in a small town such as theirs. The trial court finds both parents fit but awards custody to Richard, stating that extramarital affairs interfere with the well-being of the child. It orders no contact between the child and the doctor (an order that Richard did not even request). Teri appeals. What result? See Parker v. Parker, 986 S.W.2d 557 (Tenn. 1999).

(2) Religion

SAGAR v. SAGAR

781 N.E.2d 54 (Mass. App. Ct. 2003)

GRASSO, J.

. . . Sejal Sagar (wife) and Mahendra Sagar (husband) were married in Baroda, India, in 1990 in a traditional religious ceremony. They had known each other for less than a month; the marriage had been arranged by their respective parents. After marriage, the couple moved to the United States, where their only child, a daughter, was born on June 17, 1998. They separated in November, 1998. [In the divorce proceedings, the trial court awarded joint legal custody and granted physical custody to the wife with liberal visitation to the husband.]

During and after marriage, the parties followed substantially the tenets of the Hindu faith. During the wife's pregnancy and after their daughter's birth, the parties engaged in Hindu ceremonies prescribed to mark various transitions in an infant's life, including a religious baby shower, a homecoming ceremony, a naming ceremony, a first visit to the temple, a ceremony for the child's first solid food, and an ear piercing ceremony. The parties attended temple weekly and even had a temple in their home at which they worshiped on a daily basis.

Their relationship was volatile and marred by numerous instances of the husband's physical and mental abuse of the wife. At various times, the husband threw things at the wife, hit her with a rolling pin, pulled her hair, chased her from their house, and burned her with a cigarette. He tore apart a book given her by her brother. The husband was very controlling. He would allow his wife to telephone her relatives only on birthdays and anniversaries; and the contents of the kitchen cabinets had to be arranged as he specified. He threatened to stop paying tuition for the wife's education should she fail to get straight A's. The husband made questionable transfers of marital assets and refused to comply with a court order to hold certain funds in escrow.

[The parties disagree about the performance of a Hindu religious ritual, Chudakarana, upon their young daughter. The ceremony involves shaving of the child's head, placing an auspicious mark on the head, and conferring blessings.] Apart from disagreement over whether the Hindu sacrament of Chudakarana should be performed, the parties are in substantial agreement over the rearing of their daughter, including her religious upbringing. At trial, the husband presented evidence to support his position that a Hindu may not forgo the ritual of Chudakarana. The ceremony, which is believed to contribute to the child's longevity and ward off illness, should be performed before the child is three years old and is a necessary prerequisite to Hindu marriage. If the ceremony is not performed, an elder (here the father) may atone, allowing the ceremony to be performed at a later date. The wife's position was that Chudakarana is not integral to the Hindu faith. Neither she nor her extended family believe in the efficacy or necessity of the ceremony. She did not participate in the ceremony, nor did her brother or cousins. Prior to marriage, the husband never inquired whether she had participated in Chudakarana; neither did she inform him that she had not.

The father claims that the right to insist upon performance of Chudakarana upon his child is protected under both State and Federal Constitutional provisions respecting free exercise of religion. The [trial] judge's decision appears to conclude that the husband's free exercise claim fails because it is not grounded in a sincerely held religious belief. An essential prerequisite to a free exercise claim is a sincerely held religious belief. A court may not examine the truth behind a person's religious beliefs. However, inquiry into the sincerity of a professed belief is constitutionally appropriate under both the First Amendment; and article 2 of the Massachusetts Constitution.

The judge did not question the husband's general devotion to Hinduism. At the same time, he found that "the husband's reasons for his insistence on having the Chudakarana are not purely religious[,] [but] an issue of control." The record supports this determination. We credit, as we must, the judge's finding, based upon his credibility assessment. However, the determination that the husband's motivation is not "purely religious" is different altogether from whether his belief is "sincerely held." We need not, and should not, predicate a decision implicating a parent's free exercise right and his fundamental liberty interest in child rearing upon the tenuous ground that the parents' underlying religious belief is not "sincerely held" because the motivation is not "purely religious."[3]

Although the husband conceptualizes the probate judge's action as a State-imposed limitation on his own free exercise of religion, whether Chudakarana is performed upon the child implicates not only the husband's but also the wife's fundamental rights. These include the right to direct their daughter's upbringing and religious formation.

The due process clause protects certain fundamental rights and liberty interests, including the right of a parent to direct a child's education and upbringing.

3. We also cannot delve into differences between the parties over whether strict adherence to Hindu religious belief requires that Chudakarana be performed. Resolution of that matter clearly would involve assessment of the religion's doctrine. The First Amendment protects sincerely held religious beliefs even when these differ from the established dogma of a religion or are not accepted as dogma by any religion.

For the court to issue an order upholding the husband's fundamental right to direct that the ceremony of Chudakarana be performed upon the child would repudiate permanently the wife's corresponding right to direct that the ceremony not be performed. Conversely, to order that the ceremony not be performed, as the wife would have it, would repudiate the husband's fundamental rights.

A court is justifiably loath to order a restriction on either parent's fundamental rights to free exercise of religion and to determine the child's religious upbringing and is constitutionally limited in doing so unless there is a compelling State interest such as preventing demonstrable physical or psychological harm to the child. . . . Here, the husband failed to demonstrate a compelling State interest for performing the ceremony on the child. Evidence was lacking that failure to perform the ceremony would "cause the child significant harm by adversely affecting the child's health, safety, or welfare." Blixt v. Blixt, 774 N.E.2d 1052, 1060 (Mass. 2002). . . . [Conversely, the wife] did not establish that performing the ceremony would subject the child to physical or psychological harm, a compelling State interest that would support an order restricting the husband's fundamental rights. . . .

. . . [A]bsent proof either way, the order [of the trial court order delaying the ceremony until the child can make that determination, absent the parents' written agreement] is a narrowly tailored accommodation that "intrudes least on the religious inclinations of either parent and . . . is compatible with the health of the child." [Felton v. Felton, 418 N.E.2d 606, 608 (Mass. 1981).] The order neither imposes any limitation upon nor favors either parent's ability to communicate beliefs concerning Chudakarana or to participate in any other beliefs or practices of their shared Hindu faith. The order does not coerce the father to believe as the mother does; nor does it compel him to practice his religion in a particular way. The order leaves open to the parties the opportunity to agree in the future and does not bar future court intervention on this issue should the child be suffering from physical or psychological harm. Finally, the order respects the child's ability to eventually control her own religious destiny while encouraging continued exposure to her parents' religion. . . .

Notes and Questions

1. **Different approaches.** In adjudicating custody disputes about children's religious upbringing, courts generally take one of three approaches: (1) religion may be one, but not the sole, factor in custody decisionmaking; (2) religion may be considered only to the extent that it affects the child's secular well-being, or (3) religion may be considered only for children with ascertainable religious preferences or for whom religion has become an important part of their identity.

2. **Constitutional limitations.** The Constitution constrains judicial consideration of religion. The First Amendment's Free Exercise Clause prohibits courts from interfering with a parent's right to practice his or her religion (or not to practice religion). Under the Establishment Clause (requiring separation between church and state and forbidding excessive government entanglement with religion), a

court may not weigh the relative merits of parents' religions or favor an observant parent over a nonreligious parent.

Critics charge that in practice, courts often disregard First Amendment rights by endorsing one parent's religion over either the other parent's lack of religion or the other's religious upbringing.[14] How can judges adjudicate parental disputes without violating constitutional guarantees? Should courts follow a policy of non-interference? What compelling interest might justify interference? May a court, consistent with constitutional concerns, require a parent to *support* the other parent's religion? See Gerson v. Gerson, 868 N.Y.S.2d 551 (App. Div. 2009).

3. Adverse effect. Although courts cannot favor one parent's religion, courts nonetheless may examine the *effect* of a religious belief or practice on the child. Most courts permit interference with a parent's religious beliefs or practices only when there is evidence of harm to the child. However, courts adhere to different thresholds of harm—(1) actual or substantial harm, or (2) risk of harm.

What test does *Sagar* follow? Will the Sagars' child be harmed if the ceremony is performed? If it is not? Should courts make custody determinations based on the possibility of *future* harm? Does a child's *confusion* resulting from exposure to different religious beliefs constitute sufficient harm? Compare In re Marriage of Minix, 801 N.E.2d 1201 (Ill. Ct. App. 2003), with Holder v. Holder, 872 N.E.2d 1239 (Ohio Ct. App. 2007). Should courts assume that religious disputes always harm children? See Felton v. Felton, 418 N.E.2d 606, 607-608 (Mass. 1981).

4. Premarital agreements. What is the appropriate balance between the parent's constitutional rights and respect for private ordering, for example, when the parents have a premarital agreement about children's religious upbringing? In Zummo v. Zummo, 574 A.2d 1130 (Pa. Super. Ct. 1990), a Jewish mother and Roman Catholic father agreed before their marriage that they would raise their children as Jewish. Upon divorce, the noncustodial father wanted to take the children to Catholic services. Does enforcement of such an agreement constrain the father's free exercise of his religion? If a parent violates the term of a marital agreement about the child's religion, can the parent be held in contempt? See Greene v. Greene, 701 S.E.2d 911 (Ga. Ct. App. 2010).

5. Child's religious preference. What role should the child's own religious preference play in the adjudication of parental disputes? Do you agree that *Sagar* appropriately took into consideration the child's preference? How should a court evaluate whether the child's preference is genuine or the product of parental pressure?

6. Custodial status. How relevant to the outcome in *Sagar* is the parents' custodial status? See Elk Grove Unified Sch. Dist. v. Newdow, 542 U.S. 1 (2004) (determining that a noncustodial father lacks the right to litigate, on daughter's behalf, the constitutionality of the school district's daily recitation of the Pledge of Allegiance).

---

[14]. Eugene Volokh, Parent-Child Speech and Child Custody Speech Restrictions, 81 N.Y.U. L. Rev. 631 (2006); Jennifer Ann Drobac, Note, For the Sake of the Children: Court Consideration of Religion in Child Custody Cases, 50 Stan. L. Rev. 1609, 1611 (1998).

7. **ALI Principles.** The ALI Principles prohibit a court from considering the "religious practices" of either the parent or child in custody decisionmaking except in the following situations: (a) if the religious practices present "severe and almost certain harm" to the child (and then a court may limit the religious practices only to the minimum degree necessary to protect the child), or (b) if necessary to protect the child's ability to practice a religion "that has been a significant part of the child's life." ALI Principles §2.12(1)(c). How does a court determine if the religion has become a "significant part" of the child's life?

Problems

1. When Jeffrey (who is Christian) marries Barbara (who is Jewish), they agree to raise their children as Jews. After the birth of their second child, Jeffrey becomes a member of a fundamentalist Christian faith whose adherents believe that nonmembers are damned to hell. As a result, Jeffrey makes serious efforts to persuade his children to accept his church's teachings. Barbara has recently adopted Orthodox Judaism, and the couple becomes enmeshed in "opposite doctrinal extremes." After the parents file for divorce, both seek custody. Barbara seeks to limit the children's exposure to Jeffrey's religion. The court awards joint legal custody but forbids Jeffrey from exposing the children to religious content that will cause them to feel upset or to worry about themselves or their mother. Barbara appeals the joint custody award, asserting that it is inappropriate because the parents cannot come to any agreement on the children's moral and religious development. What result?

Based on the standard adopted in this jurisdiction, would exposure to the father's religion cause "substantial physical or emotional injury" to the children and have a "similar harmful tendency for the future"? What evidence would suffice to establish substantial harm? Is limiting the children's exposure to Jeffrey's religion appropriate? Is it constitutional? Does the limitation constitute an invasion of privacy? See Kendall v. Kendall, 687 N.E.2d 1228 (Mass. 1997).

2. Shannon and Mathew, the divorced parents of five-year-old Thomas, execute a parenting plan that requires both parents' consent concerning issues of health and education. Shannon is a chiropractor and a proponent of holistic medicine. According to her religious beliefs, "God has provided the human body with an innate immunity system that enables the body to heal itself, and anything introduced into the body to prevent or treat disease violates God's will." For that reason, she opposes vaccinations. Mathew, who is Jewish, prefers their son to receive traditional medical health care, including vaccinations. Thomas is ready to start kindergarten, but his neighborhood public school refuses to admit him unless he is vaccinated. Because Shannon opposes vaccination, she wants to enroll Thomas in a private school that will accommodate her religious beliefs. What result? How should the court assess the element of harm? See Winters v. Brown, 51 So. 3d 656 (Fla. Dist. Ct. App. 2011). See also Cal. Educ. Code §48980.5, Cal. Health & Safety Code §120338 (allowing only medical exemptions for vaccinations and ending the "personal belief exemption").

The parents also disagree about circumcision. Thomas was not circumcised at birth, but Mathew continues to advocate doing so. Mathew argues that he has a constitutionally protected right to circumcise his son and contends that circumcision is medically advisable, independent of the religious reasons for it. He also argues that Thomas himself wants to be circumcised. How should the court rule in this religious dispute? See In re Marriage of Boldt, 176 P.3d 388 (Or. 2008). How should the court assess the element of harm to the child? Suppose that Mathew has Thomas vaccinated or circumcised without Shannon's knowledge or consent. Can the court find him in contempt? See Miller v. Miller, 2013 WL 2382595 (Tenn. Ct. App. 2013).

(iii) Fitness

(1) Sexual Orientation

FULK v. FULK

827 So. 2d 736 (Miss. Ct. App. 2002)

BRIDGES, J., for the court.

This case is before us challenging the [award of] custody of minor child, Jeffery Dustin Fulk, to the biological father, Jeffery A. Fulk. . . . Rhonda and Jeffery were married on September 11, 1999. Their marital bliss ended in separation in September of 2000. One child was born of this union on January 20, 2001. After the birth of the baby, Rhonda briefly returned to the marital home. Further problems ensued, causing Rhonda to take the baby and leave the home permanently. . . . Jeffery filed for divorce on the grounds of "cruel and inhumane treatment," adultery and irreconcilable differences. He also was seeking custody of the child. A temporary hearing was held on February 28, 2001, where Jeffery was granted temporary custody of the child. Rhonda did not appear at this hearing.

[At the subsequent hearing, Rhonda admitted irreconcilable differences between the parties and requested custody. Her request was denied. The judge granted her only limited and supervised visitation.]

The polestar consideration in child custody cases is the best interest and welfare of the child. The *Albright* case [Albright v. Albright, 437 So. 2d 1003 (Miss. 1983)] provided Mississippi courts with guidelines for determining the best placement of the child after custody disputes. These factors include: (1) age, health and sex of the child; (2) determination of the parent that had the continuity of care prior to the separation; (3) which has the best parenting skills and which has the willingness and capacity to provide primary child care; (4) the employment of the parent and responsibilities of that employment; (5) physical and mental health and age of the parents; (6) emotional ties of parent and child; (7) moral fitness of parents; (8) the home, school and community record of the child; (9) the preference by law; (10) stability of home environment and employment of each parent; and (11) other factors relevant to the parent-child relationship. Marital fault should not be used as a sanction in the custody decision, nor should differences in religion, personal values and lifestyles be the sole basis for custody decisions. . . .

Rhonda asserts that the chancellor erred because she failed to consider each and every *Albright* factor thoroughly. . . .

The chancellor determined that all of the factors she examined were in favor of the father. Specifically, that the continuity of care factor favored the father, as the baby had been in his care since the enforcement of the temporary custody order. Furthermore, the court ruled that Jeffery had "done a good job with him." Considering parenting skills, the chancellor found that the father has "good skills" but offers no examples. The father's employment weighed in his favor as the mother had no income at the time of the trial. Concerning the health of the child, the court was under the impression that the father has been administering the baby's medicine properly. The court determined that the mother's affair with an emotionally unstable woman did not speak well of the mother's moral fitness and therefore ruled that moral fitness of the home environment would weigh in the father's favor. The chancellor favored the father's stability of the home over that of the mother's but did not offer an explanation of why.

The chancellor did not discuss the factor of the emotional ties between the child and parent and, more importantly, the age and sex of the child. [A]s the child was very young in age, the chancellor did not need to discuss the community and school record of the child but she failed to disclose this on the record. . . . At the time of this trial, the Fulk baby was only two and a half months old. Although the Mississippi Supreme Court, along with this Court, has significantly weakened the once strong presumption of the "tender years doctrine," it is still a viable consideration which should have been discussed. Furthermore, the chancellor did not offer a valid explanation of how she arrived at the conclusions she did. Simply dictating that the father was favored without explaining *why* he was favored is not enough. Our job, as an appellate court, is to review the chancellor's decision and determine if it was "manifestly erroneous based on a proper analysis of each of the applicable *Albright* factors. This task becomes futile when chancellors fail to consider and discuss each factor when rendering decisions." Powell v. Ayars, 792 So. 2d 240, 244 (Miss. 2001). . . .

Rhonda argues that the chancellor erred by placing too much emphasis on the fact that Rhonda had an adulterous affair with another woman. Jeffery counters that the chancellor was not concerned that the affair was of the lesbian nature but that the person Rhonda had the affair with was a severely emotionally unstable person who testified that she would still be a part of Rhonda's life as a friend and, consequently, be around the baby. Jeffery argues that the chancellor, in determining what was best for the baby, ruled that this unstable person would not be a good influence or provide a good environment for raising a small child.

Albright dictates that "difference in religion, personal values and lifestyles" would not be the sole basis for custody decisions. *Albright,* 437 So. 2d at 1005. Our supreme court addressed a similar issue in [Hollon v. Hollon, 784 So. 2d 943 (Miss. 2001)] and held that too much weight was placed upon the "moral fitness" factor based upon the mother's homosexual affair and reversed the decision of the chancery court. The chancellor in the case at bar stated that although both Rhonda and her female counterpart in the affair testified that the sexual relationship was over, it was her opinion and that of the court, that the sexual relationship was indeed not over. Furthermore, the chancellor found that it was "unacceptable for any child to be around this type of behavior." Apparently, Chancellor Weathersby forgot that the father was the instigator in the triangle relationship, not the mother. . . . Therefore, it was error for the chancellor to have relied so heavily on the affair, as it was not just Rhonda's affair due to Jeffery's willingness to be an eager participant. . . .

The facts in this case are unusual, as skeletons are in both parties' closets. The record indicates that Rhonda and Jeffery's relationship was unsteady during their entire courtship and marriage. . . . Rhonda is a young mother who does not have a source of income. She lives with her parents and a younger sibling. Both of her parents are unemployed and rely on "checks" as means for survival. . . . Jeffery admits to having used drugs and alcohol heavily, although he claims to have now stopped [although Rhonda disputed this assertion].

Two incidents are very disturbing to this Court in our review of the record. Specifically, the time when Jeffery "forgot" his wife was in his home and padlocked her inside the house since it was his habit to padlock the door. At that time, Rhonda was pregnant and trapped inside the home. Her father had to come and take the door off of the hinges to allow his daughter out of the house. Secondly, we view the domestic disturbance call which ended when the police arrested Jeffery for threatening to kill Rhonda and her family with a claw hammer. Jeffery was charged with resisting arrest and domestic violence. Jeffery proceeded to plead guilty to all charges against him and was sentenced to anger management classes. It is not clear from the chancellor's opinion that she considered these incidents. Her bench ruling states, "I find that the father may have done some things in the past he is not proud of, but the Court thinks that the responsibility of fatherhood has matured him. As the Court said before, I view the marital troubles as being part of his violent temper troubles." We are of the opinion these incidents should have been addressed and considered in making the *Albright* findings. It was error for the chancellor to ignore such matters. . . .

The chancellor granted total custody to Jeffery, the father of the baby. Rhonda was granted a minimum of one hour of visitation at a McDonald's on Sunday mornings beginning at 8:00 a.m. . . . Rhonda claims it was error for this restricted visitation to be imposed as it flies in the face of Mississippi's general visitation guidelines. . . . We agree. . . . By restricting Rhonda's visitation with her child of very tender months, not years, to a public restaurant during the early morning hours on a Sunday, the chancellor abused her discretion. . . . [The court reverses and remands.] After appropriate findings are determined, if the chancellor again grants paramount care and custody to the father, it is our opinion that the mother shall be granted overnight and unrestricted visitation, provided no evidence of harm to the child was presented. . . . .

Notes and Questions

1. Epilogue. Rhonda and Jeffery entered into a settlement agreement whereby Jeffery retained custody and Rhonda obtained additional visitation. According to Jeffery's attorney:

> I see the dad and little boy all the time around town. In fact, I just saw both of them the other day in the hardware store. The little boy is very cute and just as

> red-headed as his dad who has a pony-tail down to his waist. You know, when the father got temporary custody, that little boy was only about a few weeks old. The judge said to the father, "Mr. Fulk, how do you know how to take care of such a tiny baby?" The father replied, "I went to the library, ma'am, and read all about it."[15]

Rhonda was represented by Jane E. Tucker, of Phelps Dunbar, Jackson, Mississippi; and by Courtney Joslin, National Center for Lesbian Rights, San Francisco.

2. Sexual conduct generally. A threshold consideration in the determination of the child's best interests is parental fitness. In the fault era, adultery or cohabitation often resulted in a custody denial because courts deemed the "guilty party" unfit. Changes in social mores had an impact on custody law.

Under the modern view, influenced by the Uniform Marriage and Divorce Act (UMDA), sexual conduct is relevant to custody determinations only if the conduct has an adverse effect on the child (the "nexus test"). See UMDA §402. How easy is the test to apply? How does a court separate the effect on the child of a parent's sexual conduct from the effects of the dissolution itself? See, e.g., Gustaves v. Gustaves, 57 P.3d 775 (Idaho 2002) (mother's adultery caused child's regressive behavior). How would *Fulk* be decided under UMDA? Note that gay and lesbian parents have faced the possibility of loss of custody in initial awards and modifications, as well as the loss of visitation rights (discussed later in this chapter).

3. Gender bias.

a. Gender bias against mothers. Does judicial consideration of extramarital sexual conduct in custody decisionmaking reflect gender bias against women? See, e.g., Harrison v. Harrison, 287 S.W.3d 601 (Ark. Ct. App. 2008). See generally Suzanne A. Kim, The Neutered Parent, 24 Yale J.L. & Feminism 1 (2012).

Some courts evaluate sexual conduct (especially the mother's) based on whether the parent has legitimized that conduct (that is, by remarriage). Also, some courts are less tolerant of women who are involved in several intimate relationships. See, e.g., Holmes v. Holmes, 255 S.W.3d 482 (Ark. Ct. App. 2007).

b. Gender bias against fathers. On the other hand, is the legal system biased against fathers? Does the legal system make it difficult, as fathers' rights groups argue, for fathers to obtain sole or joint custody, and thereby "relegat[e] them to the role of economic providers and little else"?[16]

4. Same-sex sexual conduct: Approaches.

a. Traditional approaches. In the past, same-sex sexual conduct was more likely than opposite-sex extramarital sexual conduct to lead to denial (or changes) of custody. Today, significant numbers of gays and lesbians are parents.[17] Prior to

---

[15]. Personal communication, Boyd Atkinson, Law Offices, Cleveland, Miss., Feb. 22, 2006.

[16]. Solangel Maldonado, Beyond Economic Fatherhood: Encouraging Divorced Fathers to Parent, 153 U. Pa. L. Rev. 921, 967 (2005).

[17]. Approximately one-fifth of same-sex couples are raising children. Williams Institute, 700,000 Americans Are Married to a Same-Sex Spouse, Married Same-Sex Couples More Likely to Raise Adopted, Foster Children and Are More Economically Secure, New Reports Show, Mar. 5, 2015, http://williamsinstitute.law.ucla.edu/press/press-releases/married-same-sex-couples-more-likely-to-raise-adopted-foster-children-and-have-more-economic-resources-new-reports-show/#sthash.WtcCtrbr.dpuf.

the 1970s, few gays and lesbians prevailed in custody cases. What are some of the stereotypes that prevented gay and lesbian parents from gaining custody? See Kim H. Pearson, Sexuality in Child Custody Decisions, 50 Fam. Ct. Rev. 280 (2012).

Traditionally, courts have taken one of three approaches to same-sex custody disputes: (1) the parent's sexual orientation constitutes an irrebuttable presumption of unfitness (the per se rule); (2) the parent's sexual orientation evokes a rebuttable presumption of unfitness and requires that the parent prove the absence of harm (absent such proof, the presumption of unfitness applies); (3) the parent's sexual orientation must have, or will have, an adverse impact on the child in order to lead to a denial of custody (the nexus approach). The last approach is the majority rule. See, e.g., Maxwell v. Maxwell, 382 S.W.3d 892 (Ky. Ct. App. 2012).

b. Constitutional issues. Do custody denials to gay and lesbian parents raise constitutional problems? Do *Lawrence* and/or *Obergefell* mandate the view that sexual conduct or sexual orientation should be irrelevant in the best-interests analysis? See generally Michael S. Wald, Adults' Sexual Orientation and State Determinations Regarding Placement of Children, 40 Fam. L.Q. 381 (2006). How can an appellate court identify homophobia as the actual rationale of a trial court ruling when that prejudice is unarticulated or the proffered reasons are pretextual? See, e.g., Holmes v. Holmes, 255 S.W.3d 482 (Ark. Ct. App. 2007).

5. ALI Principles. The ALI Principles of the Law of Family Dissolution prohibit a court from considering either the sexual orientation or the extramarital sexual conduct of a parent except upon a showing that such conduct causes harm to the child. ALI Principles §2.12(1)(d) (sexual orientation) and (e) (extramarital sexual conduct). Which of the foregoing three approaches (in Note 4) does the ALI Principles follow?

6. Harm. What showing of harm suffices under the nexus test? Teasing? Is *potential* harm sufficient? Compare Pulliam v. Smith, 501 S.E.2d 898, 904 (N.C. 1998), with Taylor v. Taylor, 110 S.W.3d 731 (Ark. 2003). Is harm more likely because a parent is "out," or, conversely, "in the closet"? See, e.g., Ex parte J.M.F., 730 So. 2d 1190 (Ala. 1998).

7. Custody denial as a human rights violation. Does a custody denial based on a parent's sexual orientation violate international human rights? See Atala Riffo & Daughters v. Chile, 2012 Inter-Am. Ct. H.R. (ser. C) No. 239 (Feb. 24, 2012) (finding that custody denial violated lesbian mother's right to equal protection under the Inter-American Convention on Human Rights (IACHR)).

Problem

Father and Mother are married and have two children. Six years later, Father files for dissolution. He seeks joint legal custody of the children (now age two and four), and Mother seeks sole custody. He also seeks reasonable visitation. Although conceding that Father should have reasonable visitation, Mother requests that it be supervised. At the hearing, Father testifies that his work and school schedule permit him to spend only one day per week of visitation with the children, and that he is not able to accommodate overnight visits.

He further testifies that he had recently obtained a job after almost a year of unemployment and is planning to move from his one-bedroom apartment to a rental house. Finally, he testifies that he is a transgender individual and that he is receiving counseling and medical care in connection with gender transition issues—issues that he acknowledges caused him emotional difficulties that had affected his family in the time leading up to the separation.

Mother testifies that she lives with the children, her mother, and her grandmother, and that the children have good relationships with all three women. She testifies that the children return from visitation with Father "shivering, cold, hungry, exhausted," unhappy, and, in the case of the younger child, with "massive diaper rash." She further testifies that Father often ignores the children when they try to get his attention. She also expresses concern that the children will be confused by Father's gender transition, and that the confusion is just starting because the person they know as "Daddy" now presents herself as a woman and wishes to be called "Mommy."

The court awards Mother sole legal custody, orders that Father will have four hours of supervised visitation every other week, and appoints a psychological counselor (called a "therapeutic interventionist") to aid in the children's adjustment to Father's gender transition. Father appeals, contending that the court improperly considered his transgender status in denying him joint custody in violation of his equal protection rights, and that the court abused its discretion by restricting his parenting time to supervised visits of four hours once every other week. What result? Tipsword v. Tipsword, 2013 WL 1320444 (Ariz. Ct. App. 2013).

(2) Careers

ROWE v. FRANKLIN

663 N.E.2d 955 (Ohio Ct. App. 1995)

GORMAN, Judge:

Appellant, Kimberly Rowe ("mother"), appeals the trial court's decision designating appellee, Donald J. Franklin ("father"), the residential parent and legal guardian of their then five-year-old son.

[When the parents divorced after four years of marriage, each parent asked for sole custody of the couple's son. While the divorce was pending, the mother moved to Versailles, Kentucky, for her job as a part-time Army pilot. In Kentucky, she applied to law school. She had previously earned a degree in international affairs and business. The father, an ironworker, was unemployed. As part of the divorce proceedings, the trial court ordered that neither parent should remove the child from the state without a court order or parental agreement.]

On September 10, 1993, the mother filed a motion to modify the court's order to allow her to remove the child to Versailles, Kentucky, and to establish his residence there. She had applied to take classes through the University of Kentucky Law School in July and had become pregnant sometime in May by a man whom she had begun seeing in March, and who was married but separated from his wife. In August she enrolled her son in a private school for the times she would attend law school classes. In response to her motion, the father filed an emergency motion for contempt and for return of the child to Ohio. The trial court denied her motion, held the father's contempt motion in abeyance, and allowed the child to remain with the mother until the completion of a previously ordered custody investigation.

Dr. Cynthia Dember completed a psychological evaluation on May 1, 1992. Parenting specialist Jayne Zuberbuhler completed a predecree parenting report on February 18, 1993. . . . Dr. Dember and Ms. Zuberbuhler, while finding both parents adequate, ultimately recommended custody of the child be given to the father. [The trial court awarded custody to the father, and the mother appealed.]

In determining which parent should have custody of a minor child in a divorce proceeding, the trial court is bound to consider the best interests of the child. R.C. §3109.04(F). . . . Concern for a child's well-being or best interests does not, however, provide the court carte blanche to judge the rights and lifestyles of parents by nonstatutory codes of moral or social values. Although a court is not obligated to wear blinders as to a parent's lifestyle and/or morals, including sexual conduct, any state interest in competing lifestyles and accompanying moral values which affect child custody would most equitably be served if limited to a determination of the direct or probable effect of parental conduct on the physical, mental, emotional, and social development of the child, as opposed to a determination of which lifestyle choices made by a parent are "correct." In a society as diverse as the one in which we live, a court is ill-equipped to determine which of such choices are "correct." . . .

We first note that the trial court, using the factors enumerated in R.C. §3109.04(F)(1), concluded that both parents had taken a proper parental interest in the child, that the child was very much attached to both parents, that the child interacted appropriately with both parents, that both parents loved and nurtured the child, and that interference with either relationship could hurt the child. The trial court also determined that the child had bonded with his step-brother, had a good relationship with the mother's male companion, and was doing well in the Kentucky school. Even so, the trial court determined that the child should be removed from the mother and custody granted to the father.

The error in the analysis by which the trial court reached its conclusion, however, is apparent from its comparison of the mother's living situation with the father's. The trial court stated that for the first three years of the child's life,

> [u]ntil Dec. 1991, the child lived in the marital residence which is presently occupied by [father]. He is most familiar with the surroundings, the neighborhood, the people in the neighborhood, etc. [The child] has roots in his home in Cincinnati and but for his mother's move to Kentucky, it appears that his home would be one of stability. He has family here both maternal and paternal. He has friends here. He has friends of both parents who care for him here. The only adjustment necessary for [the child] here is that his mother would not be here.

By contrast, the trial court concluded that the mother and the child did not have substantial roots in the Kentucky community, stating it had not been provided with much information regarding that community. The record, however, belies this contention. Uncontested information was available that: the mother had been working in Kentucky for several years, that she had many friends there that she had met at work, that her son was friendly with and associated with her friends' children, that her son had adapted to the school he attended and had friends there, that the child had friends in the neighborhood with whom he played, and that he attended soccer and karate classes in Kentucky.

The trial court then "thoroughly examine[d]" the child's adjustment to his new home. . . . The record does not support the trial court's finding that the home, the mother's work or her school schedule has required "tremendous" adjustment by the child, nor does it indicate what will necessitate future adjustment. . . .

The trial court stated that it had no concerns about either parent's mental health. It found the father to be stable. . . . In contrast it found that the mother made decisions that caused the court to question her stability. Included in these "questionable" decisions were the many moves she made prior to her current situation, the move to Kentucky, and the sudden and complete relationship with her new male companion and the resulting pregnancy. The trial court deemed that these were not decisions in the best interest of the child and concluded that appellant placed her needs before the child's needs.

The trial court failed to recognize that the moves were precipitated by the father refusing, upon advice of counsel, to move from the marital residence, thus forcing the mother to leave the marital residence with the child, if she desired to terminate the marriage, and to live with the child in a variety of makeshift homes for a short transitional period. It entirely discounted how the father's decision subjected the child to changes in the environment. . . .

In examining the parties' commitment to the child, a nonstatutory factor, the trial court concluded that

> [p]ersonal accomplishments and career goals are obviously worthwhile undertakings. To accomplish what Ms. Rowe has as far as academics is concerned is very commendable. However this court perceives that this child has paid a price. The evidence has shown that Ms. Rowe returned to a full-time law school curriculum when the child was three (3) weeks old. Ms. Rowe returned to her job with the Kentucky National Guard when the child was six (6) weeks old. Ms. Rowe's time to nurture the child has been limited tremendously as she pursues other matters. The Court is cognizant of the time [the child] has spent with babysitters and at child care. In summation, this Court questions the priorities of Ms. Rowe. The *number of poor choices made by Ms. Rowe as to the best interests of [the child] coupled with her personal agenda* indicates to this court that she may not be as committed to [the child's] best interests as she should be.

(Emphasis added.)

The transcript of the mother's law school classes contained in the record indicates that she did not start law school until the fall of 1990 when the child was over two years old. It was at that time that the child received day-care supervision. She had returned to school earlier to continue the coursework necessary to obtain her undergraduate degree the spring semester of 1988 and began taking graduate courses primarily in the evening the following fall. The child was attended to by the parents, family or friends during this period of time. The record shows that the mother did not return to flying until the child was approximately eight months old. . . .

Although pursuing his career and designated as the primary financial support for the family, the father was deemed by the trial court to be dedicated to the well-being of his child and to have a "willingness to be *a good and proper parent.*" (Emphasis added.)

The trial court also considered the mother's relationship with her male companion. [T]he trial court did not like that the mother became sexually involved with a man so soon after the breakup of both of their marriages. . . . There is a total absence of evidence in the record to suggest that the mother's relationship had any unfavorable effect on the child. . . . Although the trial court explicitly stated that the best interest of the child was its primary consideration, the plain meaning of its reasons in reality constitute use of a "reproval of the mother" test. Therefore, we conclude that the trial court abused its discretion by its reliance on an erroneous standard to justify the designation of the residential parent. . . .

Notes and Questions

1. **Career as a factor.** Today, many mothers work outside the home. Maternal employment sometimes plays a role in the application of the best-interests standard. In the past, some courts have denied custody to women lawyers, medical students, architects, and nurses, among others. See Burchard v. Garay, 724 P.2d 486 (Cal. 1986); Prost v. Greene, 652 A.2d 621 (D.C. 1995); Young v. Hector, 740 So. 2d 1153 (Fla. Dist. Ct. App. 1998); Lewis v. Lewis, 219 N.W.2d 910 (Neb. 1974); Fitzsimmons v. Fitzsimmons, 722 P.2d 671 (N.M. Ct. App. 1986).

2. **Gender-based role expectations.** What are the conflicting role expectations for working mothers versus working fathers? What gender stereotypes underlie custody determinations involving working mothers? Why might a working mother be perceived as a "bad mother"? See Amy D. Ronner, Women Who Dance on the Professional Track: Custody and the Red Shoes, 23 Harv. Women's L.J. 173 (2000). Must working mothers be "supermoms" to prevail in custody disputes? Are mothers who work irregular schedules at a particular disadvantage in custody decisionmaking? Compare Kerkhoff v. Kerkhoff, 400 N.W.2d 752 (Minn. Ct. App. 1987), with Bingham v. Bingham, 167 P.3d 14 (Wyo. 2007).

3. **Early attitudes.** Survey data from the 1980s and 1990s reflect gender stereotypes in judges' attitudes toward working women in custody disputes. Beliefs included: "[m]others should be home when their school-age children get home from school"; and, "[a] preschool child is likely to suffer if his/her mother works." Report of the Gender Bias Study of the Supreme Judicial Court, Commonwealth of Massachusetts 63 (1989). To what extent do such attitudes persist?

4. **Day care.** What role should day care arrangements play in custody determinations? How did the trial court in *Rowe* assess this factor? Consideration of day care evokes the following concerns:

a. Gender bias? What gender stereotypes does a parent's reliance on day care evoke? See In re Loyd, 131 Cal. Rptr. 2d 80 (Ct. App. 2003).

b. New spouses. May a court assume that *in-home care* by a *stepparent* (such as the father's new spouse) is preferable in the best interests analysis to the caretaking arrangements of the child's working mother? In-home care by a *prospective* new spouse? See West v. West, 21 P.3d 838 (Alaska 2001); Wellman v. Dutch, 604 N.Y.S.2d 381 (App. Div. 1993).

c. Relatives. Similarly, may a court assume that in-home care by relatives is preferable to the caretaking arrangements of the child's working mother? How should the court weigh the day care contributions of a parent's family members (parent's parents or other relatives) in the best interests analysis? See, e.g., Ireland v. Smith, 542 N.W.2d 344 (Mich. Ct. App. 1995), *aff'd*, 547 N.W.2d 686 (Mich. 1996) (overturning a custody award to a father that was influenced by his choice of his mother as caretaker, compared to the child's mother's choice of institutional day care).

5. Wealth as a factor. What weight, if any, should be given to a parent's superior earning capacity? Generally, the relative wealth of the parties is not decisive unless one parent is unable to provide adequately for the child. Although not a decisive factor, should wealth be a relevant factor? See generally Carolyn J. Frantz, Note, Eliminating Consideration of Parental Wealth in Post-Divorce Child Custody Disputes, 99 Mich. L. Rev. 216 (2000).

6. ALI. The ALI Principles prohibit the court from considering the parents' relative earning capacities or financial circumstances unless the parents' combined financial resources "set practical limits on the custodial arrangements." ALI Principles §2.12(1)(f). Further, the ALI Principles provide that placement in day care does not constitute sufficient changed circumstances to warrant modification. Id. §2.15(3)(c).

7. Time as a factor. Should the amount of time that a parent has available to spend with a child be a relevant factor? Consider the following excerpt.

D. Kelly Weisberg, Professional Women and the Professionalization of Motherhood: Marcia Clark's Double Bind[18]

6 Hastings Women's L.J. 295, 312-319, 321-322 (1995)

There are several problems . . . in utilizing time as a determinative, or even [a] relevant, factor [in the best-interests-of-the-child analysis]. . . . The quantity of time that a parent has available to spend with a child [does not dictate] the quality of that interaction. [Nor does it guarantee] that the available time [will] be spent with the child. . . . Research has also suggested that, at the time of

[18]. The title refers to the case of Marcia Clark (chief prosecutor in O.J. Simpson's murder trial) in which her ex-husband sought custody, contending that her demanding career rendered him a more fit custodian.

Courts' consideration of "time" as a factor in custody decisions creates difficulties for working mothers.

divorce, fathers often overestimate the time they say they want to spend with their children. . . . Research that documents visitation patterns over time supports this finding. . . .

. . . In addition, a focus on the quantity of time that a child spends with a parent may detract from more important considerations. For example, in Renee B. [v. Michael B., No. V5272186 (N.Y. Fam. Ct. May 8, 1992)], a court-appointed expert determined that the unemployed father would be a better custodian than the mother because of his greater availability. In awarding custody to the father, the appellate court gave little weight to the father's character, which had been described by the trial judge as: "cold, pedantic, and humorless, and above all, with a pervasive quality of controlled anger. [E]ven when directly discussing his daughter, there was little sense of the warmth and empathy for her that the mother displayed" [slip op. at 108]. [And, in Prost v. Greene, 652 A.2d 621 (D.C. App. 1995),] by focusing on [the mother's] availability, the trial court minimized allegations of domestic violence by Prost's husband (which had been serious enough to merit a civil protection order). . . .

[Moreover,] societal views have evolved concerning children's need for quantity time. Sociologist Arlie Hochschild writes that in the second half of the nineteenth century, when a woman's place was in the home, child care experts agreed that the child needed a mother's constant care at home. [However, as] women's roles have changed, so has our concept of children's needs: "Nowadays, a child is increasingly imagined to need time with other children, to need 'independence-training,' not to need 'quantity time' with a parent but only a small amount of 'quality time.'"

A second problem regarding consideration of time as a factor in custody decision-making is that a reliance on availability "freezes" the status quo. [That is,] it measures the *present time constraints* of one parent against the *present availability* of the other parent to determine fulfillment of the *present time needs* of a child. Yet, any, or all, of these factors may change significantly over time. . . . Consideration of a parent's current career demands assumes that these constraints are reflective of the career as a whole. [And,] in time, [the noncustodial parent] might be promoted into a more demanding position, accept a different job, [and/or] become involved in a new amorous relationship that would take up more of his time. [Further,] children's demands on a parent's time vary as a function of each developmental stage. For example, once children reach school age, they are absent from home for a large portion of the parent's work day. . . .

A third criticism of reliance on availability as a factor in custody decision-making rests on an unspoken assumption that availability is an objective and easily measurable criteria. [Yet, such assumptions may be] open to challenge. . . . One problem in emphasizing the more visible caretaking activities is that this tends to minimize all the "invisible" work that mothers might perform [e.g.,] arranging for baby-sitting or housekeeper services, scheduling doctors' appointments, scheduling play dates, determining a child's need for new clothes and haircuts, helping with school work, planning domestic chores and events, making grocery lists, paying bills, [and so forth].

. . . A final criticism of reliance on time as a relevant factor in custody decision-making is the subjectivity of the assessment by the parties themselves. Their measurement may be not unbiased, especially given the likelihood of intra-parental conflict and hostility upon divorce. . . .

(3) Domestic Violence

PETERS-RIEMERS v. RIEMERS

644 N.W.2d 197 (N.D. 2002)

NEUMANN, Justice.

. . . Roland met Jenese, a non-U.S. citizen, in Belize in 1995 while vacationing there. . . . In early 1996, at Roland's invitation, Jenese left Belize and moved to North Dakota [to live with Roland]. . . . Jenese became pregnant by Roland, and on June 24, 1997 their son, Johnathan, was born. [O]n March 6, 1999 Roland and Jenese were married. . . . After incurring several instances of physical abuse by Roland, Jenese filed a complaint on March 7, 2000 seeking dissolution of the marriage. [T]he court granted Jenese a decree of divorce from Roland on the grounds of adultery, extreme cruelty, and irreconcilable differences. Upon finding Roland had committed domestic violence, the court awarded physical custody of Johnathan to Jenese and provided Roland "closely supervised" visitation. . . . Roland, acting pro se, has appealed [contending that] the trial court failed to make specific findings in concluding that Roland had perpetrated domestic violence. We disagree.

The trial court made the following specific findings regarding Roland committing domestic violence against Jenese, all of which are supported by the evidence:

In the fall of 1996, Jenese became pregnant with the parties' son. A few months later, in February of 1997, Jenese learned of Roland's physical relationship with [another woman]. A physical argument erupted. During the course of such incident, Roland slapped and punched Jenese. He also kicked her in the stomach. Consequently, Jenese suffered vaginal bleeding and obtained medical treatment. . . .

In October of 1999, Jenese heard Johnathan crying outside. She walked out to discover that Johnathan had fallen down the stairs and had hurt himself. Roland was standing a few yards away from Johnathan, talking on his phone instead of tending to his son. Jenese made an angry comment to Roland about his priorities then went back inside. Roland than came into the kitchen and slapped Jenese in the face.

During the marriage, Roland kept pornographic magazines and videos in the marital residence, sometimes in places where Johnathan would encounter them.

In January of 2000, Jenese destroyed one of Roland's pornographic videos. When Roland discovered his destroyed tape, he came up behind Jenese as she was making a bed and kicked her in the back.

On March 4, 2000, after a verbal argument, Jenese attempted to leave the marital residence with the parties' son, Johnathan. Roland refused to allow her to leave with Johnathan, but attempted to force her out of her home alone. He pinned her left arm behind her back as she held Johnathan tight in her other arm. Jenese escaped long enough to call 911, but Roland hung up the phone. He then punched her in the face, knocking her to the ground. He broke a finger in the process. Jenese was later diagnosed with a fractured bone in her face.

On March 6, 2000, Jenese obtained a Temporary Protection Order against Roland. On March 7, 2000, Roland was charged with felony assault as a result of striking Jenese. A No Contact Order issued as a condition of Roland's Pretrial Release. After a fully contested hearing, [a]n Adult Abuse Protection Order issued against Roland. . . . [Six months later, he pled guilty to a reduced charge of misdemeanor assault.]

Roland's argument that the court did not make specific findings about Roland's abuse of Jenese is without merit. Roland [also] asserts the trial court erred in finding [that] Roland committed domestic violence but Jenese did not. The trial court made the following specific finding:

> Roland committed at least one act of domestic violence which resulted in serious bodily injury to Jenese. During their relationship, there was a pattern of Roland inflicting domestic violence upon Jenese. On occasion, Jenese may have struck, hit, or scratched Roland. However, her actions were largely in self-defense and were of a far less serious nature and degree than Roland's domestic violence.

Under N.D.C.C. §14-09-06.2(j) evidence of domestic violence is a specifically enumerated factor for the court to consider in awarding child custody:

> j. *Evidence of domestic violence.* In awarding custody or granting rights of visitation, the court shall consider evidence of domestic violence. If the court finds credible evidence that domestic violence has occurred, and there exists one incident of domestic violence which resulted in serious bodily injury or involved the use of a dangerous weapon or there exists a pattern of domestic violence within a reasonable time proximate to the proceeding, this combination creates a rebuttable presumption that a parent who has perpetrated domestic violence may not be awarded sole or joint custody of a child. This presumption may be overcome only by clear and convincing evidence that the best interests of the child require that parent's participation as a custodial parent. The court shall cite specific findings of fact to show that the custody or visitation arrangement best protects the child and the parent or other family or household member who is the victim of domestic violence. . . . The fact that the abused parent suffers from the effects of the abuse may not be grounds for denying that parent custody. . . .

Under this statutory provision, a single incident of domestic violence which results in serious bodily injury or a pattern of domestic violence creates a presumption that the perpetrator may not be awarded custody. With regard to the domestic violence factor, the trial court made clear and specific findings. The court found Roland had a pattern of inflicting domestic violence upon Jenese and that in at least one instance that violence resulted in serious bodily injury to her. The court found that although Jenese may have at times acted violently toward Roland, her actions were "largely in self-defense." Acts of domestic violence are mitigated when committed in self-defense. The trial court did not find Jenese's conduct toward Roland rose to a level of violence triggering the presumption against her receiving child custody. We conclude the trial court's findings are supported by the evidence and are not clearly erroneous.

Roland asserts the trial court's finding that Roland inflicted extreme cruelty on Jenese is clearly erroneous. Extreme cruelty is defined under N.D.C.C. §14-05-05 as "the infliction by one party to the marriage of grievous bodily injury or grievous mental suffering upon the other." The trial court awarded Jenese a divorce on the grounds of adultery, extreme cruelty, and irreconcilable differences. Considering the physical violence perpetrated against Jenese by Roland, and his illicit extramarital affairs, there is substantial evidence to support the trial court's conclusion that extreme cruelty, consisting of both grievous bodily injury and grievous mental suffering, was inflicted by Roland upon Jenese during their marriage. The trial court's underlying findings of extramarital conduct and physical abuse are supported by the evidence and are not clearly erroneous. . . .

Notes and Questions

1. **State approaches.** Virtually all states now require courts to consider domestic violence in custody decisions. Some states include domestic violence as a factor in the best-interests analysis. The emerging trend, however, is to provide that evidence of domestic violence creates a rebuttable presumption against awarding custody to the abusive parent.[19]

2. **Written findings.** Some states (like North Dakota in *Peters-Riemers*) require written findings regarding the existence of domestic violence. What explains this requirement?

3. **State variations: Problems of proof.** Statutes with rebuttable presumptions against custody awards to abusers vary in terms of the evidence that triggers the presumption. Some require one severe incident that results in serious bodily injury (e.g., Alaska Stat. §25.24.150(h)). Others require a pattern of abuse (e.g., Ark. Code Ann. §9-13-101(c)(2)); or a criminal conviction (e.g., Fla. Stat. Ann. §61.13). Which is preferable?

What does the statute in *Peters-Riemers* require? Did the plaintiff satisfy the requirement? What additional evidence should trigger the custodial presumption? For example, what should be the relevance of the fact that an abuser is subject to a restraining order?

Statutes also differ regarding the relevance of *past* acts of domestic violence. In *Peters-Riemers*, what was the length of time between the last act of domestic

---

[19]. See Leslie Joan Harris, Failure to Protect from Exposure to Domestic Violence in Private Custody Contests, 44 Fam. L.Q. 169 (2010) (noting that 28 states consider domestic violence as a factor whereas 22 states have presumptions against custody awards to an abusive parent).

violence and the proceedings? Some states require that the violence occur within a reasonable time of any judicial proceeding. See Tulintseff v. Jacobsen, 615 N.W.2d 129 (N.D. 2000). What is the basis for this requirement? How might such a temporal requirement pose problems for victims?

4. **Evidence to rebut the presumption.** What evidence can the abusive parent introduce to rebut the custodial presumption against awards of custody to an abuser? In *Peters-Riemers*, what does the statute require? Some states require evidence that persons who are convicted of crimes of domestic violence undergo treatment programs. Should completion of such programs serve to rebut the presumption? See generally Edward W. Gondolf, Batterer Intervention Systems: Issues, Outcomes, and Recommendations (2002).

5. **Effect of presumption.** When a court finds that the domestic violence presumption is triggered (and not rebutted), what custodial arrangement should a court order? Should application of the presumption preclude sole custody? Joint custody? Joint physical as well as legal custody? What does the statute in *Peters-Riemers* dictate?

6. **Mutual acts of domestic violence.** How should courts deal with *mutual* acts of domestic violence? See ALI Principles §2.11 cmt. c (suggesting courts can impose limits in the custody context on the "primary aggressor but not on the primary victim" in cases in which one parent's abuse is more extreme or dangerous). How does the court in *Peters-Riemers* address this issue?

Some courts respond to mutual acts of domestic violence by issuing mutual protection orders. Such orders have been severely criticized because (1) they are sometimes issued based on insufficient evidence that the violence was mutual, (2) they create enforcement problems for police because they do not indicate which party is the more serious aggressor, and (3) they reflect gender bias on the part of judges.[20] In response to these concerns, some states prohibit mutual protection orders. See, e.g., Fla. Stat. Ann. §741.30(1)(i). Why is the issuance of mutual protection orders especially problematic for victims of domestic violence in the custody context? See, e.g., Alaska Stat. §25.24.150(g).

7. **Gender bias?** Gender bias complicates legal responses to domestic violence in custody decisionmaking. Various studies highlight accounts of lawyers and judges who minimize or discredit reports of domestic violence.[21] Given the increased public attention to the problem of domestic violence, what factors explain the continued judicial skepticism about women's credibility?

8. **Friendly parent provisions.** Some states have "friendly parent provisions" mandating custody awards to the parent who is most likely to maintain the child's relationship with the other parent. How do such provisions pose risks for victims of domestic violence? Should an exception exist to such provisions in the domestic violence context? See, e.g., Alaska Stat. §25.24.150(g).

---

[20]. Thomas L. Hafemeister, If All You Have Is a Hammer: Society's Ineffective Response to Intimate Partner Violence, 60 Cath. U. L. Rev. 919, 990 (2011).

[21]. See Linda D. Elrod & Milfred D. Dale, Paradigm Shifts and Pendulum Swings in Child Custody: The Interests of Children in the Balance, 42 Fam. L.Q. 381, 395 (2008).

9. Failure to protect. Should women be deemed unfit parents for allowing themselves to be abused or for failing to protect their children from abuse? See Nicholson v. Scoppetta, supra Chapter IV. Should state statutes preclude consideration of any effects of domestic violence on the adult *victim* in the determination of the child's best interests? What does the statute in *Peters-Reimer* require?

10. Empirical data. How often do courts grant custody to batterers? Empirical data suggest that trial courts do so with "disturbing" frequency, according to Professor Joan Meier. She notes that, in a significant number of cases, abusers obtain sole or joint custody even in states with rebuttable presumptions.[22] What might explain this fact?

11. Litigation abuse. Legal proceedings (such as hearings for protection orders, divorce, and custody) present abusers with an opportunity to further harass their victims, force contact, exert control, and financially burden them.[23] How can courts address this problem?

12. ALI Principles. UMDA does not address the role of domestic violence in custody decisionmaking. However, the ALI Principles recommend that parents disclose battering in the parenting plan that they submit to the court, and that the court have a process to identify abuse. ALI Principles §§2.06, 2.11. Batterers may not receive custodial responsibility unless the court orders appropriate measures (e.g., completion of a treatment program) to ensure protection of family members. Id. §2.11(2)(i). The Principles suggest that courts be aware that abusers might use custody or visitation rights as harassment. Id. §2.11 cmt. c. Finally, the Principles assert that acts of self-defense do not constitute abuse. Id. Do these provisions provide sufficient protection to victims of domestic violence?

13. Bifurcating domestic violence and custody decisionmaking. Traditionally, courts considered domestic violence in custody determinations only if the violence has been directed at the child. See, e.g., Baker v. Baker, 494 N.W.2d 282 (Minn. 1992). Does this approach make sense? In fact, research reveals the frequency with which child abuse accompanies intimate partner violence (IPV). Batterers are several times more likely than nonbatterers to abuse children physically.[24]

14. Exposure to domestic violence. Even if the child is not physically abused, how harmful is the mere act of *witnessing* domestic violence? Evidence has been mounting in recent years that reveals that the act of witnessing domestic violence (without being a direct victim) is psychologically harmful.[25] The law adopts three

---

[22]. Joan S. Meier, Domestic Violence, Child Custody, and Child Protection: Understanding Judicial Resistance and Imagining the Solutions, 11 Am. U. J. Gender Soc. Pol'y & L. 657, 662 (2003).

[23]. Susan L. Miller & Nicole L. Smolter, Paper Abuse: Documenting New Abuse Tactics, 17 Domestic Violence Rep. 65 (2012); Mary Przekop, Note, One More Battleground: Domestic Violence, Child Custody, and the Batterers' Relentless Pursuit of Their Victims Through the Courts, 9 Seattle J. Soc. Just. 1053, 1060 (2011).

[24]. Lundy Bancroft & Jay G. Silverman, The Batterer as Parent: Addressing the Impact of Domestic Violence on Family Dynamics 42-43 (2002).

[25]. See generally David Finkelhor et al., Children's Exposure to Violence, Crime, and Abuse: An Update, OJJDP Juvenile Justice Bulletin 1, 8 (Sept. 2015) , http://www.ojjdp.gov/publications/index.html.

approaches to children's exposure to domestic violence: (1) the imposition of tort liability on the abuser for intentional infliction of emotional distress (IIED), (2) criminal liability for committing an act of domestic violence in the presence of a child, and (3) treatment of children's exposure to violence as a form of child maltreatment. Children's exposure to domestic violence is explored further in Chapter IV.

Problems

1. Shauna Prewitt's daughter was six months old when Shauna found out that the rapist who had fathered Shauna's child was petitioning for joint custody. According to the state custody law, a court may consider rape as a factor in determining the best interests of a child. Parental custody rights can be awarded, nonetheless, if the rapist-father is not considered a danger to the child. To her surprise, Shauna discovers that rapists enjoy custody rights in many states. In the midst of a two-year custody battle with her rapist, Shauna decides to seek passage of legislation that would terminate rapist-fathers' custody rights while still requiring them to pay child support. Discuss the pros and cons of the proposed legislation. See Rape Survivor Child Custody and Support Act, 23 Pa. Con. Stat. Ann. §5329. See also Nat'l Conf. of State Legislators, Parental Rights and Sexual Assault (Jan. 16, 2015), http://www.ncsl.org/research/human-services/parental-rights-and-sexual-assault.aspx.

In 2015, Congress passed, and President Barack Obama signed, the Rape Survivor Child Custody Act, H.R. 2772, 113th Cong. (2013-2014), as part of the Justice for Victims of Trafficking Act, 42 U.S.C. 14044b. The new law incentivizes states to pass legislation that allows women to petition for the termination of parental rights based on a clear and convincing evidence standard that a child was conceived through rape. See CNN News, Ed Payne and Ted Rowlands, Child Custody Rights for Rapists? Most States Have Them, Aug. 1, 2013, http://www.cnn.com/2013/08/01/us/rapist-child-custody/. Evaluate the new law in terms of its possible benefits, shortcomings, and likely effectiveness.

2. The legislature in the state of Blackacre is considering the following bill on child custody. You are a legislative intern who has been asked to draft a memo evaluating the proposed bill (below). What are its advantages? Its shortcomings? Would you recommend passage of the legislation?

BLACKACRE FAMILY CODE

(1) The court shall determine the allocation of parental responsibilities, including parenting time and decision-making responsibilities, in accordance with the best interests of the child giving paramount consideration to the child's safety and the physical, mental, and emotional conditions and needs of the child as follows:

(a) *Determination of parenting time.* The court may make provisions for parenting time that the court finds are in the child's best interests unless the court finds, after a hearing, that parenting time by the party would endanger the child's physical health or significantly impair the child's emotional development. In addition, in any order imposing or continuing a parenting time restriction, the court shall enumerate the specific factual findings supporting the restriction and may enumerate the conditions that the restricted party could fulfill in order to seek modification in the parenting plan.

(b) *Allocation of decision-making responsibility.* The court shall allocate the decision-making responsibilities between the parties based upon the best interests of the child. When a claim of child abuse or neglect or domestic violence has been made to the court, prior to allocating decisionmaking responsibility, the court shall follow the provision below:

(1) If the court finds that one of the parties has committed child abuse or neglect or domestic violence or has engaged in a pattern of domestic violence or has a history of domestic violence, which factor must be supported by a preponderance of the evidence, then it shall not be in the best interests of the child to allocate mutual decisionmaking with respect to any issue over the objection of the other party, unless the court finds that there is credible evidence of the ability of the parties to make decisions cooperatively in the best interest of the child in a manner that is safe for the abused party and the child. . . .

The above bill was modeled on a new law in Colorado (Colo. Rev. Stat. Ann. §14-10-124). See also Allen M. Bailey, Prioritizing Child Safety as the Prime Best-Interest Factor, 47 Fam. L.Q. 35 (2013).

In thinking about the best-interests-of-the-child determination in custody cases involving domestic violence, consider the following excerpt.

Joan S. Meier, Domestic Violence, Child Custody, and Child Protection: Understanding Judicial Resistance and Imagining the Solutions

11 Am. U. J. Gender Soc. Pol'y & L. 657, 705-707 (2003)

[M]any batterers seek custody, not out of a genuine desire to take care of the children, but to retaliate against or further their control of their partner. The persona of many—though not all—batterers, is inconsistent with the qualities needed to make a good parent. People who need to control and abuse their intimate partners are unlikely to be capable of the loving, nurturing, and self-disciplined behavior that good parenting requires. By definition, a father who abuses the mother has indicated that he cannot put the children's interests first, since their mother's abuse, by undermining her well-being, is inherently harmful to the children. Many batterers expect children to meet their needs, rather than vice versa; this can lead him to expect children to give up their other interests to spend time with him; to demand quiet to an inappropriate degree; to demand physical affection regardless of their feelings; and to become blaming, tearful, or yelling when they fail to meet his needs.

Batterers are often patriarchal, believing in strict gender roles and subordination of females, and can be controlling or authoritarian toward children of both sexes. Batterers "tend to be rigid, authoritarian parents." They tend to expect their will to be obeyed unquestioningly, or to be inflexible in their arrangements, extremely angry at any sign of non-compliance or disrespect, spank more often, and be angry more often than other fathers. In short, they tend to use "power parenting." They are unlikely to possess the empathy that allows parents to treat their children with respect and to validate their feelings, two qualities considered important to raising emotionally healthy, conscientious, caring children.

Many, if not most, batterers both consciously and unconsciously undermine the children's mother and relationships with their mother. Many tell the children that it is their mother's fault that the parents are separated, that they cannot see their father more, that they cannot have certain things, or any other source of sadness in the child's life. Many of my clients' batterers would demean the mother to the children, telling them their mother is a "whore" or "slut," and in at least one case, demanding that the children come out of their rooms to watch him beat her up as punishment for some purported wrong.

Finally, batterers are often manipulative to children as well as partners, denying their own conduct and its effects, blaming the mother, and seeking to persuade the children that they are the "nicer" or "better" parent. Often batterers use the children to further their control over the mother, explicitly or implicitly enlisting the children in his vendetta. . . . In short, it is simply fallacious to assume that past domestic violence is in the past, that it is not directly relevant to future custody, or that it can ever really not impact the children.

NOTE: PHYSICAL DISABILITY

The physical health of the parents is another relevant factor in the best interests determination. All states either mandate or permit consideration of a parent's physical and mental health. See, e.g., UMDA §402(5) (mandating consideration).

Formerly, many trial courts assumed that parents with severe physical disabilities were per se unfit. This presumption manifested itself in different guises according to the specific disability: "deaf parents are thought to be incapable of effectively stimulating language skills, blind parents cannot provide adequate attention or discipline; and parents with spinal cord injuries cannot adequately supervise their children."[26] Courts were especially concerned when the children were not themselves disabled.

In the late 1970s, two cases changed the presumption of unfitness to an emphasis on the *effects* of the parent's disability on the child. See Warnick v.

[26]. Michael Ashley Stein, Mommy Has a Blue Wheelchair: Recognizing the Parental Rights of Individuals with Disabilities, 60 Brook. L. Rev. 1069, 1083 (1994). See also Nat'l Council on Disability, Rocking the Cradle: Ensuring the Rights of Parents with Disabilities and Their Children (2012), https://www.ncd.gov/publications/2012/Sep272012.

Couey, 359 So. 2d 801 (Ala. Civ. App. 1978); In re Marriage of Carney, 598 P.2d 36 (Cal. 1979). In *Carney*, the California Supreme Court refused to change a custody award to a father after he became a quadriplegic as a result of a Jeep accident while serving in the military reserve. The court reasoned that the "essence of parenting"

> lies in the ethical, emotional, and intellectual guidance the parent gives to the child throughout his formative years, and often beyond. The source of this guidance is the adult's own experience of life; its motive power is parental love and concern for the child's well-being; and its teachings deal with such fundamental matters as the child's feelings about himself, his relationships with others, his system of values, his standards of conduct, and his goals and priorities in life. Even if it were true, as the court herein asserted, that William cannot do "anything" for his sons except "talk to them and teach them, be a tutor," that would not only be "enough"—contrary to the court's conclusion—it would be the most valuable service a parent can render. Yet his capacity to do so is entirely unrelated to his physical prowess: however limited his bodily strength may be, a handicapped parent is a whole person to the child who needs his affection, sympathy, and wisdom to deal with the problems of growing up. Indeed, in such matters his handicap may well be an asset: few can pass through the crucible of a severe physical disability without learning enduring lessons in patience and tolerance.

598 P.2d at 44. Some courts still occasionally presume detriment and impose restrictions on disabled parents. Compare Clark v. Madden, 725 N.E.2d 100 (Ind. Ct. App. 2000), with Arneson v. Arneson, 670 N.W.2d 904 (S.D. 2003).

In addition, commentators have documented high removal rates of children from disabled parents. Among the causes of such removals are bias against persons with disabilities, ignorance about disability and adaptive equipment/services, and the lack of appropriate services.[27]

Does the Americans with Disabilities Act of 1996 (ADA), 42 U.S.C. §§12101-12213 (2006), protect disabled parents from the removal of their children? In 2015, the Department of Justice, as well as the Department of Health and Human Services, issued a joint Letter of Findings regarding their investigation of the Massachusetts state welfare department's handling of the case of a 21-year-old mother with a developmental disability. The two departments found that state welfare authorities illegally discriminated against the mother by removing her infant from her care and failing to offer her adequate services, in violation of Title II of the ADA and Section 504 of the Rehabilitation Act of 1973.[28]

---

[27]. Ella Callow et al., Parents with Disabilities in the United States: Prevalence, Perspectives, and a Proposal for Legislative Change to Protect the Right to Family in the Disability Community, 17 Tex. J.C.L.C.R. 9, 15 (2011). See also Margaret Price, Special Needs and Disability in Custody Cases: The Perfect Storm, 46 Fam. L.Q. 177 (2012).

[28]. For a discussion of the case, see Robyn Powell, Federal Agencies Say State Cannot Discriminate Against Parents with Disabilities, 34 No. 3 Child L. Prac. 46 (2015).

c. Joint Custody: Presumption, Preference, or Option?

BELL v. BELL

794 P.2d 97 (Alaska 1990)

MATTHEWS, Chief Justice.

Greg and Debra Bell were married in January 1986. They separated sixteen months later in July 1987. Greg filed for divorce on September 14, 1987. . . . [Here] Greg challenges . . . the trial court's award of legal and physical custody of Scott, the parties' child, to Debra. . . .

Gregory "Scott" Bell was born on August 19, 1986. While married, Greg and Debra shared most child rearing tasks on an equal basis. Since both parents were employed, Sharon Nollman babysat Scott. . . .

When Greg and Debra separated, they agreed to share custody of Scott, alternating physical custody every week or so. Both used Nollman to babysit. They accommodated each other's employment, social, and vacation schedules and shared babysitting expenses. A two-day interim custody hearing was held before Master Andrew Brown on October 15-16, 1987. Based upon the recommendations of an Alaska Court Custody Investigator, Master Brown issued a report recommending that Scott remain in the babysitting care of Nollman and that the parties continue their weekly alternating schedule of shared physical custody of Scott. The court approved the Master's report.

Greg and Debra cooperated in the weekly custody exchanges for another ten and one-half months until trial on August 26 and 29, 1988. However, in early 1988, Debra unilaterally began placing Scott at the Saakaaya Daycare Center during the weeks that she had physical custody. Greg continued to use Nollman during the weeks that he had physical custody of Scott. . . .

Greg and Debra continued to accommodate each other's schedules and to share physical custody of Scott on an alternating basis. They also cooperated in making major decisions about Scott's medical care. . . .

At trial, Ardis Cry, Custody Investigator, Alaska Court System, recommended that shared legal custody continue. She further recommended that Scott have a primary home and that Debra be the primary physical custodian. The trial court awarded legal and physical custody of Scott to Debra. The court also allowed Greg visitation with Scott (1) on alternate weekends from Friday afternoon through Monday morning and on Wednesday evening through Thursday mornings and (2) during four one-week periods spread throughout the year until Scott reaches school age.

Greg contends that the trial court erred by not awarding joint custody to both parents pursuant to AS §25.20.060. AS §25.20.060 states, in part: "The court may award shared custody to both parents if shared custody is determined to be in the best interests of the child." . . .

In reviewing the propriety of the trial court's denial of joint custody, we find it necessary to distinguish between two interrelated aspects of a joint custody arrangement. First, an award of joint custody gives both parents "legal custody" of the child. This means that they "share responsibility in the making of major decisions affecting the child's welfare." Second, an award of joint custody gives both parents "physical custody" of the child. This means that "each is entitled to the companionship of the child over periodic intervals of time." In an act amending AS §25.20.060, the legislature drew this distinction and expressed a policy favoring the award of joint legal custody, regardless of the physical custody arrangement: The legislature finds that . . . it is in the public interest to encourage parents to share the rights and responsibilities of child rearing. While actual physical custody may not be practical or appropriate in all cases, it is the intent of the legislature that both parents have the opportunity to guide and nurture their child and to meet the needs of the child on an equal footing beyond the considerations of support or actual custody. In light of this expression of legislative intent, and because the controlling factual finding underlying the trial court's ruling is clearly erroneous, we reverse the award of sole legal custody to Debra.

The trial court's award was apparently based on its finding that Greg and Debra "are incapable of meaningful communication and/or negotiation regarding the matters that relate to the best interests of [Scott]." . . . Based on our review of the record, however, we hold that this finding is clearly erroneous.

The trial court record and Debra's arguments on appeal indicate only one area of irreconcilable conflict between Greg and Debra—throughout the proceedings below they could not agree on what form of day care would be best for Scott. Greg wanted Scott in Nollman's home, and Debra wanted Scott in Saakaaya Daycare Center.

Given the abundance of contrary evidence indicative of their ability to cooperate in Scott's best interest, however, we think that this one conflict does not warrant the trial court's finding of an "inability" to cooperate. . . . Throughout the 14 months [of their shared custody], they accommodated each other's employment, social, and vacation schedules, and cooperated in making major decisions about Scott's medical care.

Furthermore, after interviewing Greg and Debra, the custody investigator recommended "joint legal custody" because she found that they had the "ability . . . to deal with each other in a civil and mutual manner" and thought that they demonstrated "potential to facilitate cooperation and compromise." Both Greg and Debra also testified to their ability to work cooperatively in Scott's best interest. Moreover, Debra generally agreed with the investigator's recommendations and was willing to settle the custody issue under the terms the investigator recommended. Thus, at trial, both parties agreed that joint legal custody was appropriate.

In light of such evidence, we are left with a firm conviction that the trial court's finding of an inability to cooperate was erroneous. We realize that the disagreement over daycare relates to a fundamental child care issue. But resolution of this issue did not require denial of that which the Alaska legislature recognizes as the favored course; i.e., joint legal custody. We therefore reverse the trial court's denial of joint legal custody and remand with instructions to enter an award of joint legal custody. . . .

Notes and Questions

1. Policy. Joint custody is based on the belief that the child benefits from frequent contact with both parents. The doctrine recognizes that fathers, as well as mothers, have an important role to play in childrearing. A nascent fathers' rights movement spearheaded the passage of joint custody legislation in the late 1970s. Virtually all states now permit some form of joint custody.[29]

2. Definitions. A custody award resolves the dual issues of "legal custody" and "physical custody." Legal custody confers responsibility for major decision-making (that is, the child's upbringing, health, welfare, and education). Physical custody determines the child's residence and confers responsibility for day-to-day decisions regarding physical care. (Compare the ALI Principles' terms of "decisionmaking responsibility" for legal custody and "custodial responsibility" for physical custody.)

In an award of joint legal custody, both parents share responsibility for major childrearing decisions. In such cases, parents may share physical custody or only one parent may be the actual physical custodian. Thus, joint custody is distinguishable from the traditional award of sole custody, which gave one parent (normally the mother) legal control and physical custody, while the other parent (normally the father) had visitation.

3. Presumption, preference, or option. California was the first state to provide for statutory recognition of joint custody awards in 1980. Cal. Fam. Code §3080 (formerly Cal. Civ. Code §4600.5(a)). Currently, states follow three approaches to joint custody. Some states create a presumption of joint custody (although some of these states require parental agreement as a prerequisite). Other states, similar to Alaska in *Bell*, have a preference for joint custody. Third, and most common, some states make joint custody one option in the best-interests determination. Linda D. Elrod & Robert G. Spector, A Review of the Year in Family Law: Numbers of Disputes Increase, 45 Fam. L.Q. 443, 468 (2012) (survey).

4. Constitutional right? Does a parent have a constitutional right to joint custody? See generally David D. Meyer, The Constitutional Rights of Non-Custodial Parents, 34 Hofstra L. Rev. 1461, 1465-1466 (2006). Does a *child* have a constitutional right to have a court award joint custody? See In re A.R.B., 433 S.E.2d 411 (Ga. Ct. App. 1993).

5. Goldstein, Freud, and Solnit. Joint custody signifies a radical departure from conventional psychological wisdom about childrearing. Professors Joseph Goldstein, Anna Freud, and Alfred Solnit propounded the view that stability and minimization of conflict should guide child placement. They said that healthy emotional development requires an "omnipotent" parent on whom the child can rely for all important decisions. To that end, they advocated that custody be awarded only to one parent, who should have power to decide the extent of the

---

[29]. For background on the role of the fathers' rights movement in custody law, see Deborah Dinner, The Divorce Bargain: The Fathers' Rights Movement and Family Inequalities, 101 Va. L. Rev. (forthcoming 2015).

other's contact with the child (even prohibiting it).[30] Do you find their views persuasive?

6. Parental agreement. Should parental agreement be a prerequisite to joint custody awards? Many states mandate such parental agreement. However, other courts award joint custody even if one parent objects. See, e.g., Crider v. Crider, 904 So. 2d 142 (Miss. 2005). Is joint custody to unwilling parents likely to succeed?

7. Considerations. When is an award of joint custody inappropriate? What kind of time sharing is optimal? If courts require equal time, should it be six months with each parent, or nine months with one parent subject to summer vacations with the other, or switching homes every week? Alternating years? See Colvin v. Colvin, 914 So. 2d 662 (La. Ct. App. 2005). Or should courts order the child or children to remain in the family home, with the parents alternating periods there (i.e., "the bird's nest" model)? What other considerations should influence awards of joint custody? Should courts consider the effect on the parent of a *loss* of custody?

8. Parenting plans and parenting coordinators. Many states now provide that parents seeking custody must file a parenting plan (i.e., a written agreement specifying caretaking and decisionmaking authority as well as the manner in which future disputes are to be resolved). A few states mandate them; some states require them only for joint custody; other states give courts discretion to require them. What issues should be included in such agreements?

Some states also authorize appointment of parenting coordinators to investigate issues and help parents resolve disputes. See O'Rourke v. O'Rourke, 2010 WL 4629035 (Tenn. Ct. App. 2010). The Association of Family and Conciliation Courts (AFCC) promulgated guidelines for parenting coordination.[31] Does a requirement that the parents "shall seek the help of a neutral third party" before petitioning the court in the event of future disagreements about parenting violate parents' constitutional rights to due process and access to the courts? See In re Martin, 8 A.3d 60 (N.H. 2010).

9. Parent education. Many states require parent education programs for divorcing parents. Such programs seek to improve postdivorce familial interaction by educating parents about the negative effects of divorce on children and promoting alternative dispute resolution methods for postdivorce disputes. Should states waive the requirement for victims of domestic violence? See, e.g., N.J. Stat. Ann. §2A:34-12.5(e); N.Y. Ct. R. 144.3(e).

10. Joint custody and kidnapping. Can (and should) a parent with joint custody who takes the children without the consent of the other parent be found guilty of kidnapping or liable for custodial interference? See State v. Froland, 936 A.2d 947 (N.J. 2007).

---

[30]. See Joseph Goldstein et al., Beyond the Best Interests of the Child 38 (1973).
[31]. AFCC, Guidelines for Parenting Coordination (2005).

11. Joint custody of pets. Should pet custody cases be decided in the same way as child custody cases? Should divorcing partners be awarded joint custody of pets? Or should pets go where the children go? One commentator describes one unusual case in which the court honored the couple's concerns:

> During a two-hour hearing to determine the placement of their dog, a divorcing couple maintained why they each deserved custody. The wife argued that the dog seemed to enjoy the Bible study she conducted in the home and, therefore, should remain with her. The husband argued that the dog seemed to enjoy riding on the back of his motorcycle and, therefore, should remain with him. Ultimately, the judge ordered joint custody with stipulations that the dog not be forced to wear a helmet while riding on the motorcycle, the dog be allowed to continue to attend the Bible study, no alcoholic beverages be consumed in the dog's presence, and the dog not be allowed to consort with any "ill bred or mongrel type dogs."[32]

12. Criticisms of joint custody. Some states have retreated from joint custody by disavowing joint custody presumptions. In contrast, other states have renewed or reconsidered joint custody presumptions. Although originally touted with great enthusiasm, the practice of joint custody has become increasingly controversial. One commentator identifies several criticisms:

> The push by fathers' rights groups for joint custody . . . has been opposed by women's groups for two reasons: (1) some have seen it as an attempt to reduce the amount of child support by promising a commitment to share the care for the child which is either short-lived or disregarded completely and (2) others have been concerned about the existence of domestic violence.[33]

Some areas evoke special concerns:

a. Joint custody of young children. Some critics question the wisdom of awarding joint custody of infants or toddlers.[34] How well does joint custody serve these children? Should overnights be delayed until children reach the third year of life, as one researcher suggests?[35]

b. Domestic violence and joint custody. Another criticism of joint custody involves its use in cases of domestic violence. Is joint custody, which requires continuing parental communication, appropriate in such cases? Why? See generally Dana Harrington Conner, Back to the Drawing Board: Barriers to Joint Decision-Making in Custody Cases Involving Intimate Partner Violence, 18 Duke J. Gender L. & Pol'y 223 (2011).

---

[32]. Ann Hartwell Britton, Bones of Contention: Custody of Family Pets, 20 J. Am. Acad. Matrimonial Law. 1, 3-4 (2006). See also John DeWitt Gregory, Pet Custody: Distorting Language and the Law, 44 Fam. L.Q. 35 (2010).

[33]. Marygold S. Melli, The American Law Institute Principles of Family Dissolution, the Approximation Rule and Shared-Parenting, 25 N. Ill. U. L. Rev. 347, 352-353 (2005).

[34]. See, e.g., Michael Lamb, Critical Analysis of Research on Parenting Plans and Children's Well-Being, in Parenting Plan Evaluations: Applied Research for the Family Court 214 (K. Kuehnle & L. Drozd eds., 2012); Carol George et al., Divorce in the Nursery: On Infants and Overnight Care, 49 Fam. Ct. Rev. 521 (2011).

[35]. See Marsha Kline Pruett et al., Critical Aspects of Parenting Plans for Young Children, 42 Fam. Ct. Rev. 39, 41 (2004).

13. Empirical research. The advent of joint custody had a significant impact on custody decisions. In a landmark study, Professors Eleanor Maccoby and Robert Mnookin report that in the majority of divorced families in the late 1980s, the divorce decree provided for joint legal custody—even when one parent opposed it. However, the law reform movement failed to influence behavior because within one year of the decree, most children lived with their mothers.[36]

Other studies confirm father disengagement following divorce.[37] What are the policy implications of such disengagement? Finally, a recent study of divorce outcomes after the enactment of a joint custody presumption in one state reports an increase in the amount of child abuse allegations as well as lengthier, more costly, and more contentious custody proceedings.[38] How should policymakers take these findings into account?

The next excerpt elaborates on the implications of joint custody awards generally and also on their implications in the context of domestic violence.

Judith G. Greenberg, Domestic Violence and the Danger of Joint Custody Presumptions

25 N. Ill. U. L. Rev. 403, 407-413 (2005)

. . . One of the most appealing arguments for joint custody, both legal and physical, is that it is in the best interests of the child. . . . [C]ommentators have argued that custodial arrangements that mimic the two-parent family are the most desirable because they produce stability over time in providing continuing contact with both parents. There have been numerous studies of joint custody arrangements and their effects on children. One concludes bluntly that "children in joint custody are better adjusted, across multiple types of measures, than children in sole . . . custody" [citing Robert Bauserman, Child Adjustment in Joint-Custody Versus Sole-Custody Arrangements, 16 J. Fam. Psychol. 91, 97 (2002)].

Nevertheless, there is reason to wonder whether joint custody is really as good for children as this assessment implies. The studies' results are sometimes difficult to interpret. . . . [M]any samples include families that have opted on their own for joint custody in one form or another. The effects of joint custody on children in such families may be radically different from the effects on

---

[36]. Eleanor E. Maccoby & Robert H. Mnookin, Dividing the Child: Social and Legal Dilemmas of Custody 73, 107 (1992).

[37]. See, e.g., Solangel Maldonado, Beyond Economic Fatherhood: Encouraging Divorced Fathers to Parent, 153 U. Pa. L. Rev. 921 (2005); Wallerstein & Lewis, supra note [8].

[38]. Douglas W. Allen & Margaret Brinig, Do Joint Parenting Laws Make Any Difference?, 8 J. Empirical Legal Stud. 304, 307 (2011).

children whose parents did not agree to the joint custody, but for whom joint custody was ordered by a court. . . .

Proponents of a presumption in favor of joint custody also argue that it will equalize the positions of men and women and help to undermine traditional gender roles. Sanford Braver argues that awarding sole custody to a mother with visitation to the father leaves men feeling disenfranchised in terms of their children's lives. . . . The argument is that fathers with joint custody, even if only joint legal custody, are able to participate in the lives of their children more equally with their ex-wives. This furthers sexual equality and would be beneficial to everyone. Once again, however, the data on whether joint custody achieves these goals is contradictory. Sanford Braver, in his study of interviews with divorced fathers and mothers, reports that joint legal custody results in higher rates of father-child visitation. . . . However, other studies have had very different findings as to the effect of joint legal custody on role equalization. One large-scale review of studies of the impact of fathers' visitation found that fathers' involvement affected the children in varying ways depending on the type of involvement, the mother's acceptance of the father's involvement and the degree of conflict between the parents. This hardly indicates that fathers who have joint custody automatically are perceived as taking on a nurturing role. Furthermore, there is evidence that even if the initial custody order provides for joint physical custody, over time the children are likely to end up living in their mothers' custody. . . .

. . . Most commentators recognize that where there has been domestic violence, joint custody is inappropriate. . . . Unfortunately, cases that get to litigation (or even to judicial intervention short of litigation) are exactly those most likely to involve domestic violence. Recent research shows that approximately seventy-five percent of the contested custody cases that require judicial intervention are cases in which there is a history of domestic violence. This means that in situations in which the court sends a case to mediation, orders an evaluation or holds a trial, it is significantly more likely than not that there has been domestic violence. Presumptions in favor of shared custody then do not make sense given that so many of the cases in which the parties cannot resolve the children's custody without judicial intervention are cases involving domestic violence.

Batterers often use any contact afforded them by the court as a means of continuing the abusive relationship with their former partners. Abusive relationships usually involve the batterer establishing control over his victim through a combination of physical, emotional, and financial methods. This is not likely to end with divorce. Indeed, for many targets, the abuse becomes worse at separation. Batterers use any opportunity or contact to perpetuate the abuse in an effort to maintain their control. Some use the continuing connection that comes from joint custody or visitation rights to harass or verbally abuse their victims. Others use it as an opportunity to pressure the victim to return to the batterer. Still others continue their physical abuse during these times. . . .

2. Standards Governing the Noncustodial Parent: Visitation

a. Traditional Rule

Before the rise of joint custody, a court deciding a custody dispute usually determined which of two competing parents should be awarded custody of a child. Custody, under this traditional approach, encompassed both physical and legal custody. A presumption was applicable (although often unarticulated) that reasonable visitation with a noncustodial parent was in the child's best interests. However, that presumption could be overcome by substantial evidence that the noncustodial parent was unfit or that visitation was detrimental to the child's welfare. In the traditional framework, the court usually granted custody to the mother, subject to the father's right of visitation.

Courts have broad discretion in fashioning visitation orders. Thus, courts have authority to specify the time, place, and circumstances of visitation, including the imposition of conditions on visitation by the noncustodial parent. Procedurally, if one parent requests the court to order restrictions on visitation, that parent bears the burden of proof on the need for that restriction.

The model statute below illustrates the traditional rule and its limitations.

UNIFORM MARRIAGE AND DIVORCE ACT (UMDA)

§407. VISITATION

(a) A parent not granted custody of the child is entitled to reasonable visitation rights unless the court finds, after a hearing, that visitation would endanger seriously the child's physical, mental, moral, or emotional health.

(b) The court may modify an order granting or denying visitation rights whenever modification would serve the best interest of the child; but the court shall not restrict a parent's visitation rights unless it finds that the visitation would endanger seriously the child's physical, mental, moral, or emotional health.

b. Restrictions on Visitation

HANKE v. HANKE

615 A.2d 1205 (Md. Ct. Spec. App. 1992)

BELL, Judge.

Appellant, Mary Elizabeth Hanke, brings this appeal, asking us to review an order granting her ex-husband, Dan Wolf Hanke, appellee, overnight visitation with the parties' four-year-old daughter. Ms. Hanke's concern for this child stems, in part, from an incident of sexual abuse by Mr. Hanke of one of Ms. Hanke's daughters (stepchild) from a previous marriage. . . .

On August 1, 1990, Mr. and Ms. Hanke were divorced by a judgment of the Circuit Court for Harford County. Ms. Hanke was granted custody of the parties' child and the issue of Mr. Hanke's visitation privileges was reserved for a later hearing. On March 15, 1991, hearings began to consider visitation. On March 18, 1991, the court ordered unsupervised four-hour visitations on alternate Sunday afternoons from noon until 4:00 P.M. On March 20, 1991, the court ordered Mr. Hanke to submit to a mental health examination by Lawrence Raifman, PhD, J.D. . . . The order of the Harford County judge, who transferred custody to Mr. Hanke, has not been enforced, pending the outcome of the investigation by the Kentucky DSS. [The mother had moved to Kentucky, where her family lived, because she was unable to find employment.]

Mr. Hanke has admitted sexually abusing his 11-year-old stepchild in 1986. This particular instance of sexual abuse was one event, but there is overwhelming evidence that other instances of excessive punishment with sexual overtones had occurred prior to this incident. . . . During a therapy session, Mr. Hanke stated that he was drunk when he sexually molested his stepchild. . . . Mr. Hanke feels that he does not "need any therapy for alcoholism." He did, however, secure therapy for the sexual abuse incident.

At the time of the separation, Ms. Hanke was pregnant with the parties' child who is the subject of this case. The parties separated as soon as Ms. Hanke learned from the 11-year-old child that she had been sexually molested by Mr. Hanke. Criminal charges of sexual molestation were brought against Mr. Hanke for the incident involving his stepchild. As part of the plea bargain entered into by Mr. Hanke for a suspended sentence in the criminal case, he agreed to, among other things, supervised visitation with the parties' child. . . .

The trial judge granted Mr. Hanke unsupervised four-hour weekly visitation periods with the child, beginning in March of 1991. After one of these visits, the parties' child reported to a teenage friend of her stepsister that Mr. Hanke "was touching her where he was not supposed to." Ms. Hanke examined the child and found scarring in the genital area. She immediately reported the matter to the Harford County Department of Social Services (DSS). Based on Ms. Hanke's complaint, DSS had the child examined at Mercy Hospital. The examination was conducted on May 23, 1991, by Dr. Reichel at the Mercy Hospital outpatient clinic. His report states ". . . Prior abuse cannot be excluded." Annetta Bloxham, the DSS caseworker investigating the complaint . . . also testified that she had verified the child's report of sexual molestation . . . by the parents of the teenager, to whom the child had reported the molestation, that the child did indeed report the molestation. This family refused, however, to permit the teenager to testify. . . .

Dr. Raifman, who evaluated Mr. Hanke pursuant to a court order, [concluded] that Mr. Hanke stated that he abused his stepchild to "get at her mother"; that the stepchild had been physically abused by Mr. Hanke for a long time before the incident of sexual abuse; that Mr. Hanke should not be placed in a situation where he is alone with his child; that Mr. Hanke should not continue to use alcohol because he was drunk at the time he sexually abused his stepchild; that Mr. Hanke had not come to terms with his abuse of alcohol as a factor in his abuse of his stepchild. [U]ntil these issues are resolved therapeutically, he is at risk and, therefore, his child is at risk.

Ms. Hanke's attorney, the attorney representing the Harford County DSS, and the attorney representing the child were unanimous in their call for supervised visitation. There was, however, also a small amount of contradictory evidence presented, which the judge seemed to favor, that Ms. Hanke was overreacting to the situation and Mr. Hanke was not a potential danger to their child. On March 18, 1991, the court ordered unsupervised visitation and on August 16, 1991, the court ordered visitation overnight, specifying one of four persons who were close to Mr. Hanke to "be present during visitation periods." The judge refused to protect the child further, and he found that overnight visitation was appropriate.

We have reviewed the findings and holdings in this case, bearing in mind that the ultimate test for custody and visitation is the best interests of the child. In most instances, the decision of the trial judge is accorded great deference, unless it is arbitrary or clearly wrong. We hold that, given the circumstances presented in this case, the decision of the trial judge was clearly wrong.

It is obvious that the trial judge was annoyed because Ms. Hanke moved to Kentucky with the child and was unwilling to allow visitation. Even if the judge were correct that Ms. Hanke was not acting in compliance with the judge's orders, his primary responsibility was to protect this minor child, and not to punish Ms. Hanke by ordering overnight visitation. Then, when he could not enforce the overnight visitation order, the judge next removed the child from her custody with no provisions to protect the child. Where the evidence is such that a parent is justified in believing that the other parent is sexually abusing the child, it is inconceivable that that parent will surrender the child to the abusing parent without stringent safeguards. The fact that the judge does not agree with that parent's fear is immaterial. This is not a case in which there is no basis for the mother's belief. Past behavior is the best predictor of future behavior, and Ms. Hanke, while perhaps incorrect, is not unjustified in her belief that there may be some unresolved problems.

Assuming without deciding that the trial judge was correct in ruling that the child was at no or minimal risk in the overnight visitation, he abused his discretion in failing to provide a specific place for the supervised visitation designed to protect the child fully, with supervisors satisfactory to all parties. He could do no less. . . .

Notes and Questions

1. Traditional approach. Courts can restrict or even deny visitation if the judge believes that the visitation might endanger the child's well-being. Common reasons for visitation restrictions include physical and sexual abuse of a child. In such cases, the judge may order that visitation be supervised in order to protect the child; that is, the alleged abusive parent must spend any time with the child in the presence of a third party who will supervise the visitation. The supervisor may be someone agreed upon by the parents or someone who is appointed by the court.

2. Constitutional right to visitation? Does the abusive parent have a constitutionally protected right to visitation? See Swipies v. Kofka, 419 F.3d 709, 714 (8th Cir. 2005). See also Ayelet Blecher-Prigat, Rethinking Visitation: From a Parental to a Relational Right, 16 Duke J. Gender L. & Pol'y 1, 4 (2009) (some courts treat visitation as protected liberty interest).

3. Supervised visitation programs. Many states now provide supervised visitation *programs* that furnish services to parents in custody disputes involving various forms of abuse and neglect. Services range from close supervision by a constant observer to more minimal supervision. Sometimes, supervision takes place only upon transfer of the child. The location for supervised visits might be at a program center or in another public or private location. What are the advantages and disadvantages of supervision by center staff compared to supervision by a friend or family member?

4. Rebuttable presumption. Some states create a rebuttable presumption against unsupervised visitation if a parent presents credible evidence of physical or sexual abuse. See, e.g., Tex. Fam. Code §153.004. Some courts may even terminate visitation in such cases. If so, is a parent still obligated to support the child? See generally Jason M. Merrill, Note, Falling Through the Cracks: Distinguishing Parental Rights from Parental Obligations in Cases Involving Termination of the Parent-Child Relationship, 11 J.L. & Fam. Stud. 203 (2008).

5. Considerations. Based on courts' wide discretion in fashioning visitation orders, courts may specify the time, place, and circumstances of visitation. Supervised visitation gives rise to a host of difficulties in framing the order. For example, how frequent should visitation be? Should it include overnights? Who should supervise the visitation? Professionals? Relatives? If the supervisor is a relative, should it be a relative of the abuser? Should the relative be required to complete any training in child abuse or domestic violence? See Fla. Stat. Ann. §39.0139(5) (requiring training in child sexual abuse). Should the supervisor be someone the child knows? Should the child's feelings be taken into account in choosing a supervisor? See Matter of Brown v. Erbstoesser, 928 N.Y.S.2d 92 (N.Y. 2011). What role, if any, should cost play as a factor in supervised visitation? If payment for the supervisor is required, who should pay? See Leslie Kaufman, In Custody Rights, a Hurdle for the Poor, N.Y. Times, Apr. 8, 2007, at 125.

6. Unsupervised visitation. When should supervised visitation give way to unsupervised visitation? Suppose that the parent contends that supervised visitation is interfering with the establishment of a good relationship with the child? See Grant v. Grant, 1995 WL 136775 (Ohio Ct. App. 1995). After a suspension of visitation, should visitation be phased in gradually?

7. Treatment conditions. What types of restriction on visitation are enforceable in cases of physical or sexual abuse? Can a court order an abuser to undergo psychological treatment (e.g., for substance abuse, physical abuse, or sexual abuse) as a condition of visitation? See, e.g., Catley v. Sampson, 66 A.3d 834 (R.I. 2013) (suspending visitation until father completed domestic violence counseling and substance abuse treatment). Can a court require that visitation be denied until a therapist recommends otherwise? See Linda R. v. Ari Z., 895 N.Y.S.2d 412 (N.Y. 2010) (finding that delegation of authority to mental health professional was inappropriate).

Should supervised or unsupervised visitation commence only after a parent *seeks* treatment? *Completes* treatment? See, e.g., La. Rev. Stat. Ann. §9:364(C) (requiring completion of treatment for unsupervised visitation). Only after a parent is successfully "rehabilitated"? See, e.g., Mo. Ann. Stat. §452.400 (requiring proof of rehabilitation before unsupervised visitation). If so, who determines "successful" completion of treatment?[39] Can a court order a parent to comply with a treatment program's requirement of admission of guilt? See Wirsching v. Colorado, 360 F.3d 1191, 1205 (10th Cir. 2004).

8. Empirical research. A majority of children who are subject to supervised visitation are victims of parental abuse and neglect, substance abuse, and mental illness.[40] What are the policy implications of this finding?

9. Other conditions. Restrictions on visitation also arise in other contexts, such as the following:

a. Religious exercise. Because visitation often involves weekends, disputes about church attendance may arise. Can a parent be required to present children at a particular religious institution during visitation? Conversely, can a court prohibit a parent from exposing the children to that parent's religion? See, e.g., Franco v. Franco, 2008 WL 4814415 (Ariz. Ct. App. 2008). See generally Joshua Press, The Uses and Abuses of Religion in Child Custody Cases: Parents Outside the Wall of Separation, 84 Ind. L.J. Supplement 47 (2009).

b. Sexual conduct. Courts sometimes restrict a parent's visitation rights based on the parent's sexual conduct (whether heterosexual or same-sex sexual conduct). For example, many courts have disallowed visitation in the presence of a parent's partner if the parties are unmarried. See, e.g., Camp v. McNair, 217 S.W.3d 155 (Ark. Ct. App. 2005); McGriff v. McGriff, 99 P.3d 111 (Idaho 2004).[41] Are such restrictions constitutional after *Lawrence* and *Obergefell*?

c. Substance abuse. Courts also impose conditions on parents who are substance abusers. See Baber v. Baber, 378 S.W.3d 699 (Ark. 2011) (custody modification based on parent's alcohol abuse). See generally David Malleis, Note, The High Price of Parenting High: Medical Marijuana and Its Effects on Child Custody Matters, 33 U. La Verne L. Rev. 357 (2012). What are appropriate restrictions in this context?

d. Firearms possession. Occasionally, a court may order a divorcing parent to store firearms safely during visitation periods for a child's protection. See Matt Pordum, Lawyer, Court Action Could Have Prevented Boy's Fatal Shooting, Evidence Showed Father Left Guns Throughout Home, Las Vegas Sun, Aug. 29, 2005, at A1 (account of 12-year-old boy who died after father violated custody order to lock up guns).

---

[39]. See Peter Jaffe et al., Parenting Arrangements After Domestic Violence, 6 J. Ctr. for Families Child. & Cts. 81, 89 (2005) ("difficulty arises when it is not clear who bears the responsibility for assessing the perpetrator's progress").

[40]. See Janet R. Johnston & Robert B. Straus, Traumatized Children in Supervised Visitation: What Do They Need?, 37 Fam. & Conciliation Cts. Rev. 135, 135 (1999); Jessica Pearson et al., A New Look at an Old Issue: An Evaluation of the State Access and Visitation Grant Program, 43 Fam. Ct. Rev. 371, 376 (2005).

[41]. For criticisms of this approach, see Suzanne A. Kim, The Neutered Parent, 24 Yale J.L. & Feminism 1 (2012); Nancy G. Maxwell & Richard Donner, The Psychological Consequences of Judicially Imposed Closets in Child Custody and Visitation Disputes Involving Gay or Lesbian Parents, 13 Wm. & Mary J. Women & L. 305 (2006).

e. Criminal convictions. Parents may be subject to conditions on visitation if they have been convicted of certain crimes (e.g., child abuse, homicide), or if they are required to register as sex offenders. See generally Dana Harrington Conner, Do No Harm: An Analysis of the Legal and Social Consequences of Child Visitation Determinations for Incarcerated Perpetrators of Extreme Acts of Violence Against Women, 17 Colum. J. Gender & L. 163 (2008).

f. Smoking. Should a parent's smoking lead to conditions on that parent's visitation? See generally William F. Chinnock, No Smoking Around Children: The Family Courts' Mandatory Duty to Restrain Parents and Other Persons from Smoking Around Children, 45 Ariz. L. Rev. 801 (2003).

10. Child's refusal to visit. Can a court condition a noncustodial parent's visits on the *child's* desire to refuse to see that parent?[42] Courts sometimes respond to the *child's* refusal to visit a noncustodial parent by holding the custodial parent in contempt. See, e.g., Woodward v. Woodward, 776 N.W.2d 567 (N.D. 2009). Is this sound policy?

11. Penalty. What should be the penalty if a parent violates the condition on visitation? Temporary suspension of visitation? Denial of visitation? Contempt? Modification of custody? See generally Margaret M. Mahoney, The Enforcement of Child Custody Orders by Contempt Remedies, 68 U. Pitt. L. Rev. 835 (2007).

Problems

1. When Julie and Randy divorce, the court declares Julie to be the sole custodial parent of their two preschool daughters. The trial court rules that Randy's overnight visitation should be supervised by his parents because of Randy's "penchant for pornography." The court orders the restriction because Julie presented evidence that Randy liked to view Internet sites exhibiting sexual material and had placed a personal advertisement on an Internet site in an effort to attract sexual partners. Randy counters that he views Internet material only late at night, after the children are asleep, and that he placed the advertisement out of curiosity. Randy contends that the trial court's restriction on his visitation was an abuse of discretion. What result? See Petty v. Petty, 2005 WL 1183149 (Tenn. Ct. App. 2005).

Suppose that Randy likes to relax and smoke marijuana while he views sexually explicit Internet content. Can the court restrict his marijuana use? Would it make a difference if his state (like Colorado) has legalized the use of medical marijuana, and if he is asserting that he has a medical reason to smoke marijuana (i.e., to relieve his back and knee pain)? See, e.g., In re Marriage of Parr & Lyman, 240 P.3d 509 (Colo. App. 2010).

---

[42]. For a discussion of children's refusal to visit a noncustodial parent, see Steven Friedlander & Marjorie Gans Walters, When a Child Rejects a Parent: Tailoring the Intervention to Fit the Problem, 48 Fam. Ct. Rev. 98 (2010); Janet R. Johnston & Judith Roth Goldman, Outcomes of Family Counseling Interventions with Children Who Resist Visitation: An Addendum to Friedlander and Walters (2010), 48 Fam. Ct. Rev. 112 (2010).

2. Roxie and Jeffrey separate after two years of marriage. Roxie and the couple's baby move in with Roxie's parents. Because Jeffrey performed limited child-care during the marriage and also because of Jeffrey's "unstable lifestyle" (details unspecified), Roxie requests that Jeffrey's contact be limited to supervised visitation at Roxie's home. Jeffrey does not contest the need for supervised visitation. When Jeffrey moves out of state, to New Jersey, he requests a different visitation schedule and proposes as "supervisor" his 21-year-old brother and a friend who lives nearby. At the subsequent divorce proceeding, Roxie is awarded custody. The court awards visitation to Jeffrey on "alternative holidays and during the summer vacation provided he gives twenty-four hours' notice of his intent to visit [and] that one of the individuals [whom he has suggested] be present during said visitation."

Roxie appeals the visitation order, claiming that it is vague and gives no consideration to the qualifications of the visitation supervisors. What result? Would your reasoning change based on the reason for the supervision? Substance abuse? Sexual abuse? Immaturity? If the court does elaborate further, how should it structure the visitation order (based on each of these possibilities)? See Weber v. Weber, 457 S.E.2d 488 (W. Va. 1995).

c. Denial of Visitation

TURNER v. TURNER

919 S.W.2d 340 (Tenn. Ct. App. 1995)

KOCH, J.

This appeal involves an acrimonious postdivorce dispute over child support and visitation. . . . This appeal involves the denial of the father's latest petition for modification and the summary suspension of his visitation for not paying child support. . . .

Rebecca Diane Turner (now Turpin) and Charles Daniel Turner were married in September 1984. They had two children before separating in May 1987. After an unsuccessful attempt at reconciliation, Ms. Turner filed for divorce in June 1989. On August 15, 1990, the trial court entered a final order granting Ms. Turner the divorce and awarding her custody of the parties' children. The trial court also granted Mr. Turner visitation rights and ordered him to pay $704.13 per month in child support and to pay for the children's medical insurance. The trial court later denied Mr. Turner's posttrial motion to alter or amend the child support award but granted him additional visitation.

In early November 1990, Ms. Turner sought to have Mr. Turner held in contempt for being $2,166.52 in arrears in his child support. Mr. Turner responded with a petition admitting that he was delinquent in his child support payments and requesting a reduction in his child support because he was financially unable to comply with the August 1990 order. Thereafter, Mr. Turner paid all the child support due through November 30, 1990, and agreed to pay an additional $475 for the children's medical expenses. Following a hearing in January 1991, the trial court entered an order on February 1, 1991, finding Mr. Turner in contempt for failing to pay child support and to obtain medical insurance for his children. The trial court decided not to act on Mr. Turner's petition to modify his child support because "he comes to the Court with unclean hands." In addition, the trial court directed Mr. Turner to begin paying an additional $177 per month to reimburse Ms. Turner for obtaining medical insurance for the children through her group insurance plan at work.

Ms. Turner filed a second petition in May 1991 seeking to hold Mr. Turner in contempt for inappropriate conduct while he was returning her son from visitation. In December 1993, she filed her third contempt petition complaining that Mr. Turner had harassed and abused her and the children and that he was seriously delinquent in his child support obligations. Following an ex parte hearing, the trial court ordered Mr. Turner's arrest and suspended his visitation rights. Mr. Turner responded, as he had in the past, that he was financially unable to meet his child support obligations and again requested the trial court to reduce his child support.

Following a January 1994 hearing, the trial court filed an order on February 14, 1994, finding Mr. Turner in criminal contempt for violating the orders prohibiting him from harassing and abusing Ms. Turner and the children and also finding him in civil contempt for failing to make his child support payments. The trial court sentenced Mr. Turner to ten days for the criminal contempt to be served consecutively with a six-month sentence for civil contempt but determined that Mr. Turner could purge himself of the civil contempt by paying $40,908.86. The trial court also ordered that Mr. Turner's visitation would be summarily suspended if he did not make prompt and timely support payments.

The trial court summarily suspended Mr. Turner's visitation before he was released from jail because he failed to pay his child support. Mr. Turner filed another petition in July 1994 requesting modification of his child support and reinstatement of his visitation. On December 20, 1994, the trial court filed an order denying Mr. Turner's petition. . . .

Mr. Turner . . . takes issue with the trial court's refusal to permit him to visit his children because he is delinquent in paying his child support. While we are not prepared to say that this sanction is never appropriate, we find that the present facts do not warrant suspending Mr. Turner's visitation rights.

Child custody and visitation decisions should be guided by the best interests of the child. They are not intended to be punitive. Pizzillo v. Pizzillo, 884 S.W.2d 749, 757 (Tenn. Ct. App. 1994); Barnhill v. Barnhill, 826 S.W.2d 443, 453 (Tenn. Ct. App. 1991). As a general rule, the most preferable custody arrangement is one which promotes the children's relationships with both the custodial and noncustodial parent.

Ms. Turner argues in her brief that the children are adversely affected by Mr. Turner's failure to support them, and thus their best interests will be served by cutting off their visitation with their father unless he begins supporting them. This assertion would have some merit if the record contained proof to substantiate it. We find no such proof. The record, however, contains some support for concluding that the children are not going without basic necessities because Ms. Turner is presently able to provide for their needs.

The courts may deny or condition continuing visitation on the grounds of parental neglect. See Mimms v. Mimms, 780 S.W.2d 739, 745 (Tenn. Ct. App. 1989) (parental neglect may be considered in relation to the children's best interests). The denial of visitation is warranted, however, only when the noncustodial parent is financially able to support his or her children but refuses to do so. Since the trial court has not conclusively determined that Mr. Turner is at present willfully refusing to support his children even though he is financially able to do so, we have determined that the order curtailing Mr. Turner's visitation rights should likewise be vacated and that this issue should likewise be addressed and definitively decided on remand. Pending the remand hearing, the trial court should enter an interim order permitting Mr. Turner visitation on whatever terms the trial court determines are just and appropriate. . . .

Notes and Questions

1. **Factors.** Because the Constitution protects the parent-child relationship, courts deny visitation reluctantly. What does *Turner* reveal about whether the failure to pay child support justifies a denial of visitation? What other situations justify a ban on visitation? Physical or sexual abuse? See, e.g., Grossman v. Grossman, 772 N.Y.S.2d 559 (App. Div. 2004). IPV? See, e.g., Beverly v. Bredice, 751 N.Y.S.2d 79 (App. Div. 2002). The risk of child abduction? See, e.g., Damiani v. Damiani, 835 So. 2d 1168 (Fla. Dist. Ct. App. 2002). Substance abuse? See, e.g., Taylor v. Taylor, 646 S.E.2d 238 (Ga. 2007).

2. **Purpose.** What purpose does denial of visitation serve? Protection? Coercion? Punishment? How does *Turner* respond? Is it ever in the child's best interests to deny all contact with a parent?

3. **Rule and exception.** As *Turner* illustrates, visitation normally will not be conditioned upon payment of child support. Nor may support be withheld because an ex-spouse interferes with visitation. Some courts, however, similar to *Turner*, make an exception for willful and intentional failure to pay support which is detrimental to the child. What explains the traditional reluctance to link the two issues?

4. **Defenses.** Should certain actions on the part of the custodial parent that deprive the noncustodial parent of visitation, such as concealment of the child, provide a defense to the failure to pay child support or arrearages during the child's absence? Should it matter if the concealment occurs predivorce or postdivorce? If the child is a minor or an adult at the time that the claim for payment of support arrearages was brought?

5. **Policy.** What are the advantages and disadvantages of disconnecting the issues of support and visitation? Of connecting them? Professor Karen Czapanskiy argues that both approaches limit the custodial parent's need for personal autonomy and reflect gender-based parental roles. She adds that connecting them invites retaliatory withholding of support payments and limitations on the opportunity to spend time with a child.[43]

---

[43]. Karen Czapanskiy, Child Support and Visitation: Rethinking the Connections, 20 Rutgers L.J. 619, 619-620 (1989).

Should the usual rule of independence of support and visitation be "applied in a narrower range of cases," as some commentators urge? For example, should "divorce decrees make suspension of the support obligation the default result during concealment periods, subject to the obligee's demonstrating to the court a justification for the concealment"?[44] If so, what justification would be sufficient?

6. Remedies. If interference with visitation is not a defense to nonpayment of support, should interference be grounds for modification of custody? Compare Vernon v. Vernon, 800 N.E.2d 1085 (N.Y. 2003) (modifying custody), with Bittick v. Bittick, 987 So. 2d 1058 (Miss. Ct. App. 2008) (contra).

What other remedies should address a denial of, or interference with, visitation? Consider the following: (a) compensatory parenting time (e.g., Mich. Comp. Laws §552.642); (b) abatement of the noncustodial parent's past or future support obligation until the custodial parent complies with the visitation order (e.g., Lew v. Sobel, 849 N.Y.S.2d 586 (App. Div. 2007)); (c) payment of attorneys' fees to enforce visitation (e.g., Kolbet v. Kolbet, 760 N.E.2d 1146 (Ind. Ct. App. 2002)); (d) attendance at parenting classes or performance of community service.

7. Coercion. Can or should a parent be compelled to exercise visitation rights? See Daniel Pollack & Susan Mason, Mandatory Visitation: In the Best Interest of the Child, 42 Fam. Ct. Rev. 74 (2004). If the noncustodial parent fails to pick up the child at the scheduled time, what remedies should be available to the custodial parent? See Lederle v. Spivey, 965 A.2d 621 (Conn. Ct. App. 2009).

Does empirical research support the rule that the right to visit and duty to support should not depend on each other? Consider the excerpt below.

Jessica Pearson & Nancy Thoennes, The Denial of Visitation Rights: A Preliminary Look at Its Incidence, Correlates, Antecedents, and Consequences

10 Law & Pol'y 363, 375-379 (1988)

This paper explores the nature and incidence of the denial of visitation rights and the non-payment of child support. [V]isitation denial is a problem with approximately 22 percent of sample mothers reputedly failing to comply with the visitation terms of their divorce decree. . . . [T]hese levels fall far below the reported levels of non-compliance with child support. Only about half of all

[44]. Ira Mark Ellman, Should Visitation Denial Affect the Obligation to Pay Support?, 36 Ariz. St. L.J. 661, 699 (2004). For other commentary on the dependence of visitation and support, compare William V. Fabricius & Sanford L. Braver, Non-Child Support Expenditures on Children by Nonresidential Divorced Fathers, 41 Fam. Ct. Rev. 321 (2003), with Irwin Garfinkel et al., Visitation and Child Support Guidelines, 42 Fam. Ct. Rev. 342 (2004). See also Stacy Brustin & Lisa Vollendorf Martin, Paved with Good Intentions: Unintended Consequences of Federal Proposals to Integrate Child Support and Parenting Time, 48 Ind. L. Rev. 803 (2015) (exploring the risks and benefits of federal proposals to integrate parenting-time provisions in state-initiated child support determinations).

custodial parents owed child support receives the full amount of support owed to them in any given year. Even fewer custodians receive all the payments on time.

[In many cases, noncustodial parents lose contact with their children.] Hetherington, et al. (1978) report that two years following the divorce, 30 percent of the children saw their fathers about once a month or less. . . . Clearly, it is inaccurate to assume that all of these are cases in which custodians encourage sporadic visitation or deny the non-custodian regular access to the children. Indeed in her study, Luepnitz notes that:

> In half of the cases when the non-custodial father visits rarely or never, it is because the children dislike him and have decided not to see him. But in many other cases, custodial mothers report that their ex had split the scene "in order to evade child support payments."

[Deborah A. Luepnitz, Child Custody 34 (1982).]

Further investigation of visitation non-compliance reveals that it rarely stands alone as a postdivorce problem and that such allegations are accompanied by a host of other visitation-related complaints. Moreover, for most parents visitation difficulties appear to become established fairly early on and fail to deviate over time.

Couples with visitation problems are decidedly more embittered than their compliant counterparts and their lack of cooperation, conflict and anger are apparent at the earliest interview, well before the promulgation of a divorce decree and are corroborated by independent interviewer ratings. Although non-payment of child support cases do not always involve a visitation problem, the two phenomena are related and cases with visitation problems are substantially more likely to involve child support non-payment or disputes over support. Both phenomena appear to stem from conflict patterns between the parents, although we were unable to assess causal order in cases that involved both types of non-compliance. . . .

These findings inspire several policy recommendations. Minimally, there is a need for reliable record keeping of both child support and visitation arrears. Without reliable record keeping, violations are difficult to prove, make-up policies are impossible to establish or supervise. . . .

Secondly, these findings underscore the importance of interventions with divorcing couples aimed at enhancing their communication skills and reducing levels of anger and hostility. [A] preliminary assessment of relationships between the non-custodial parent and his children reveals that conflict between divorced parents is a good prediction of both child support payment, visitation and other types of involvement. . . .

A third conclusion of this research is the need to consider child support and visitation issues concurrently. While there is no evidence to suggest that the two issues should be made contingent upon one another so that the denial of one should be a remedy for the withholding of the other, policy should reflect the fact that they co-occur and that grievances in both areas should be jointly aired. This conclusion runs counter to current practice. To date, most court-based mediation services deal with the issues of contested child custody and/or visitation only. . . .

A fourth implication of our research is the need to create and evaluate mechanisms for the enforcement of both child support and visitation orders. [Some states authorize] a make-up visitation policy, including compensatory visitation. Other states have explored the use of fines, tort remedies, etc. Improved visitation enforcement is warranted by the observed incidence of interference, the co-occurrence of visitation and child support problems and equity considerations.

3. Standards Governing Parent Versus Nonparent Disputes

TROXEL v. GRANVILLE

530 U.S. 57 (2000)

Justice O'CONNOR announced the judgment of the Court and delivered an opinion, in which THE CHIEF JUSTICE, Justice GINSBURG, and Justice BREYER join. . . .

Tommie Granville and Brad Troxel shared a relationship that ended in June 1991. The two never married, but they had two daughters, Isabelle and Natalie. Jenifer and Gary Troxel are Brad's parents, and thus the paternal grandparents of Isabelle and Natalie. After Tommie and Brad separated in 1991, Brad lived with his parents and regularly brought his daughters to his parents' home for weekend visitation. Brad committed suicide in May 1993. Although the Troxels at first continued to see Isabelle and Natalie on a regular basis after their son's death, Tommie Granville informed the Troxels in October 1993 that she wished to limit their visitation with her daughters to one short visit per month.

[Two months later, the Troxels filed this petition for visitation.] At trial, the Troxels requested two weekends of overnight visitation per month and two weeks of visitation each summer. Granville did not oppose visitation altogether, but instead asked the court to order one day of visitation per month with no overnight stay. [T]he Superior Court [ordered] visitation one weekend per month, one week during the summer, and four hours on both of the petitioning grandparents' birthdays.

[The Court of Appeals reversed the visitation order based on their statutory interpretation that nonparents lack standing unless a custody action is pending. The state supreme court held that the state statute granting visitation rights to "any parent" at "any time" (Wash. Rev. Code §26.10.160 (3) (1994)) infringed on

Gary and Jenifer Troxel (plaintiffs in Troxel v. Granville) outside the Supreme Court

[handwritten margin notes:] what grandparents wanted (grants) • Superior ct order • ct of Appeals reversed

parents' fundamental right to rear their children. While the appeal was pending, the mother remarried, and her husband adopted the children.]

The demographic changes of the past century make it difficult to speak of an average American family. The composition of families varies greatly from household to household. While many children may have two married parents and grandparents who visit regularly, many other children are raised in single-parent households. In 1996, children living with only one parent accounted for 28 percent of all children under age 18 in the United States. Understandably, in these single-parent households, persons outside the nuclear family are called upon with increasing frequency to assist in the everyday tasks of child rearing. In many cases, grandparents play an important role. For example, in 1998, approximately 4 million children—or 5.6 percent of all children under age 18—lived in the household of their grandparents.

The nationwide enactment of nonparental visitation statutes is assuredly due, in some part, to the States' recognition of these changing realities of the American family. Because grandparents and other relatives undertake duties of a parental nature in many households, States have sought to ensure the welfare of the children therein by protecting the relationships those children form with such third parties. The States' nonparental visitation statutes are further supported by a recognition, which varies from State to State, that children should have the opportunity to benefit from relationships with statutorily specified persons—for example, their grandparents. The extension of statutory rights in this area to persons other than a child's parents, however, comes with an obvious cost. For example, the State's recognition of an independent third-party interest in a child can place a substantial burden on the traditional parent-child relationship. . . .

The liberty interest at issue in this case—the interest of parents in the care, custody, and control of their children—is perhaps the oldest of the fundamental liberty interests recognized by this Court [citing Meyer v. Nebraska, Pierce v. Soc'y of Sisters, and Prince v. Massachusetts]. In light of this extensive precedent, it cannot now be doubted that the Due Process Clause of the Fourteenth Amendment protects the fundamental right of parents to make decisions concerning the care, custody, and control of their children.

Section 26.10.160(3), as applied to Granville and her family in this case, unconstitutionally infringes on that fundamental parental right. The Washington nonparental visitation statute is breathtakingly broad. According to the statute's text, "[*a*]*ny person* may petition the court for visitation rights *at any time*," and the court may grant such visitation rights whenever "visitation may serve *the best interest of the child*." §26.10.160(3) (emphases added). That language effectively permits any third party seeking visitation to subject any decision by a parent concerning visitation of the parent's children to state-court review. Once the visitation petition has been filed in court and the matter is placed before a judge, a parent's decision that visitation would not be in the child's best interest is accorded no deference. Section 26.10.160(3) contains no requirement that a court accord the parent's decision any presumption of validity or any weight whatsoever. Instead, the Washington statute places the best-interest determination solely in the hands of the judge. Should the judge disagree with the parent's estimation of the child's best interests, the judge's view necessarily prevails. Thus, in practical effect, in the

State of Washington a court can disregard and overturn any decision by a fit custodial parent concerning visitation whenever a third party affected by the decision files a visitation petition, based solely on the judge's determination of the child's best interests. . . .

Turning to the facts of this case, the record reveals that the Superior Court's order was based on precisely the type of mere disagreement we have just described and nothing more. The Superior Court's order was not founded on any special factors that might justify the State's interference with Granville's fundamental right to make decisions concerning the rearing of her two daughters. [T]he combination of several factors here compels our conclusion that §26.10.160(3), as applied, exceeded the bounds of the Due Process Clause.

First, the Troxels did not allege, and no court has found, that Granville was an unfit parent. That aspect of the case is important, for there is a presumption that fit parents act in the best interests of their children. [S]o long as a parent adequately cares for his or her children (i.e., is fit), there will normally be no reason for the State to inject itself into the private realm of the family to further question the ability of that parent to make the best decisions concerning the rearing of that parent's children.

The problem here is not that the Washington Superior Court intervened, but that when it did so, it gave no special weight at all to Granville's determination of her daughters' best interests. More importantly, it appears that the Superior Court [adopted "a commonsensical approach [that] it is normally in the best interest of the children to spend quality time with the grandparent" and placed] on Granville, the fit custodial parent, the burden of *disproving* that visitation would be in the best interest of her daughters. . . .

The decisional framework employed by the Superior Court directly contravened the traditional presumption that a fit parent will act in the best interest of his or her child. In that respect, the court's presumption failed to provide any protection for Granville's fundamental constitutional right to make decisions concerning the rearing of her own daughters. In an ideal world, parents might always seek to cultivate the bonds between grandparents and their grandchildren. Needless to say, however, our world is far from perfect, and in it the decision whether such an intergenerational relationship would be beneficial in any specific case is for the parent to make in the first instance. And, if a fit parent's decision of the kind at issue here becomes subject to judicial review, the court must accord at least some special weight to the parent's own determination.

Finally, we note that there is no allegation that Granville ever sought to cut off visitation entirely. Rather, the present dispute originated when Granville informed the Troxels that she would prefer to restrict their visitation with Isabelle and Natalie to one short visit per month and special holidays. . . . The Superior Court gave no weight to Granville's having assented to visitation even before the filing of any visitation petition or subsequent court intervention. . . . Significantly, many other States expressly provide by statute that courts may not award visitation unless a parent has denied (or unreasonably denied) visitation to the concerned third party.

Considered together with the Superior Court's reasons for awarding visitation to the Troxels, the combination of these factors demonstrates that the visitation order in this case was an unconstitutional infringement on Granville's fundamental right to make decisions concerning the care, custody, and control of her two daughters. The Washington Superior Court failed to accord the determination of Granville, a fit custodial parent, any material weight. In fact, the Superior Court made only two formal findings in support of its visitation order. First, the Troxels "are part of a large, central, loving family, all located in this area, and the [Troxels] can provide opportunities for the children in the areas of cousins and music." Second, "[t]he children would be benefitted from spending quality time with the [Troxels], provided that that time is balanced with time with the childrens' [*sic*] nuclear family." These slender findings, in combination with the court's announced presumption in favor of grandparent visitation and its failure to accord significant weight to Granville's already having offered meaningful visitation to the Troxels, show that this case involves nothing more than a simple disagreement between the Washington Superior Court and Granville concerning her children's best interests. The Superior Court's announced reason for ordering one week of visitation in the summer demonstrates our conclusion well: "I look back on some personal experiences. . . . We always spen[t] as kids a week with one set of grandparents and another set of grandparents, [and] it happened to work out in our family that [it] turned out to be an enjoyable experience. Maybe that can, in this family, if that is how it works out." [T]he Due Process Clause does not permit a State to infringe on the fundamental right of parents to make childrearing decisions simply because a state judge believes a "better" decision could be made. [W]e hold that §26.10.160(3), as applied in this case, is unconstitutional. . . .

Because we rest our decision on the sweeping breadth of §26.10.160(3) and the application of that broad, unlimited power in this case, we do not consider the primary constitutional question passed on by the Washington Supreme Court—whether the Due Process Clause requires all nonparental visitation statutes to include a showing of harm or potential harm to the child as a condition precedent to granting visitation. We do not, and need not, define today the precise scope of the parental due process right in the visitation context. [T]he constitutionality of any standard for awarding visitation turns on the specific manner in which that standard is applied. . . . Because much state-court adjudication in this context occurs on a case-by-case basis, we would be hesitant to hold that specific nonparental visitation statutes violate the Due Process Clause as a *per se* matter. . . .

[In separate, omitted, concurring opinions, Justice Souter upheld the state court's determination of the statute's facial unconstitutionality, and Justice Thomas noted that strict scrutiny ought to apply. In separate omitted dissenting opinions, Justice Scalia declined to recognize unenumerated constitutional rights, and Justice Kennedy reasoned that the best interests doctrine is not always an unconstitutional standard in visitation cases.]

Justice STEVENS, dissenting.

. . . While, as the Court recognizes, the Federal Constitution certainly protects the parent-child relationship from arbitrary impairment by the State, we have never held that the parent's liberty interest in this relationship is so inflexible as to establish a rigid constitutional shield, protecting every arbitrary parental decision from any challenge absent a threshold finding of harm. The presumption that parental decisions generally serve the best interests of their children is sound, and clearly in the normal case the parent's interest is paramount. But even a fit parent is capable of treating a child like a mere possession.

Cases like this do not present a bipolar struggle between the parents and the State over who has final authority to determine what is in a child's best interests. There is at a minimum a third individual, whose interests are implicated in every case to which the statute applies—the child. . . .

[Justice Stevens discusses *Lehr* and *Michael H.* to support his argument that limitations to parental liberty interests exist.] A parent's rights with respect to her child have thus never been regarded as absolute, but rather are limited by the existence of an actual, developed relationship with a child, and are tied to the presence or absence of some embodiment of family. These limitations have arisen, not simply out of the definition of parenthood itself, but because of this Court's assumption that a parent's interests in a child must be balanced against the State's long-recognized interests as parens patriae, and, critically, the child's own complementary interest in preserving relationships that serve her welfare and protection.

While this Court has not yet had occasion to elucidate the nature of a child's liberty interests in preserving established familial or family-like bonds, it seems to me extremely likely that, to the extent parents and families have fundamental liberty interests in preserving such intimate relationships, so, too, do children have these interests, and so, too, must their interests be balanced in the equation. At a minimum, our prior cases recognizing that children are, generally speaking, constitutionally protected actors require that this Court reject any suggestion that when it comes to parental rights, children are so much chattel. The constitutional protection against arbitrary state interference with parental rights should not be extended to prevent the States from protecting children against the arbitrary exercise of parental authority that is not in fact motivated by an interest in the welfare of the child.

This is not, of course, to suggest that a child's liberty interest in maintaining contact with a particular individual is to be treated invariably as on a par with that child's parents' contrary interests. Because our substantive due process case law includes a strong presumption that a parent will act in the best interest of her child, it would be necessary, were the state appellate courts actually to confront a challenge to the statute as applied, to consider whether the trial court's assessment of the "best interest of the child" incorporated that presumption. . . . But presumptions notwithstanding, we should recognize that there may be circumstances in which a child has a stronger interest at stake than mere protection from serious harm caused by the termination of visitation by a "person" other than a parent. The almost infinite variety of family relationships that pervade our ever-changing society strongly counsel against the creation by this Court of a constitutional rule that treats a biological parent's liberty interest in the care and supervision of her child as an isolated right that may be exercised arbitrarily. It is indisputably the business of the States, rather than a federal court employing a national standard, to assess in the first instance the relative importance of the conflicting interests that give rise to disputes such as this. . . .

BETHANY v. JONES

378 S.W.3d 731 (Ark. 2011)

CORBIN, J.

The instant matter involves a dispute over child visitation. [Alicia] Bethany and [Emily] Jones were same-sex partners from 2000 until 2008. Then, in 2004, the parties began to take steps toward having a family. A male friend of Jones's agreed to donate sperm. Bethany agreed to carry the child because Jones was experiencing some health issues, including reproductive problems. Through the process of artificial insemination, Bethany became pregnant, and the minor child was born in 2005. The couple chose to give the child Jones's last name and Jones's grandmother's name as the child's middle name. . . .

In 2008, the parties ended their romantic relationship, but at that time agreed to continue co-parenting E.B. However, the situation between Bethany and Jones began to deteriorate. They had a disagreement over Jones keeping E.B. for a twenty-four-hour period, against Bethany's wishes. Bethany, who had entered into a relationship with another woman, decided that it was no longer in E.B.'s best interest to have contact with Jones because she questioned Jones's ability to parent, citing such factors as instability, depression, safety of the child, and truthfulness of Jones. [Bethany denied Jones visitation, and Jones filed the instant action.] Bethany [argues] on the sole basis that nothing in Arkansas law allows her former same-sex partner to seek visitation with the child born to Bethany during their relationship. . . .

Our analysis must begin with the fundamental notion that the Due Process Clause of the Fourteenth Amendment protects the rights of parents to direct and govern the care, custody, and control of their children. See Troxel v. Granville, 530 U.S. 57 (2000) (plurality opinion) (declaring Washington State's grandparent-visitation act unconstitutional as applied). . . . However, this court has distinguished the situation where a grandparent seeks visitation against a parent's wishes, explaining that in a case where a stepparent seeks visitation it is under the theory that he or she stood in loco parentis to the child. . . . We held that the finding of an in loco parentis relationship is different from the grandparent relationships found in *Troxel* . . . because it concerns a person who, in all practical respects, was a parent. Thus, any argument that Jones cannot seek visitation because to do so would interfere with Bethany's right to parent is unavailing. Moreover, our law is well settled that the primary consideration in child-custody cases is the welfare and best interest of the children; all other considerations are secondary.

. . . [T]he doctrine of in loco parentis focuses on the relationship between the child and the person asserting that they stood in loco parentis. Bethany on the other hand seems to argue that because Arkansas does not recognize same-sex marriage or grant domestic-partnership rights, Jones has no legal standing to assert that she stood in loco parentis. In other words, Bethany focuses on her relationship with Jones instead of looking at the relationship between Jones and E.B. There is nothing in our [past decisions] to support Bethany's assertion in this regard. We reiterate that the focus should be on what, if any, bond has formed between the child and the nonparent.

Thus, we must now determine whether the circuit court's finding that Jones stood in loco parentis was clearly erroneous, as we review domestic-relations cases de novo on the record. Considering the ample evidence about the relationship between Jones and E.B., we cannot say that the circuit court clearly erred in finding that she stood in loco parentis to the child. It was undisputed that she was the stay-at-home mom for over three years who took care of E.B. E.B. called her mommy. She thought of Jones's parents as her grandparents and spent holidays with Jones's family. The parties' intentions were always to co-parent, until Bethany unilaterally determined she no longer wanted to allow Jones to have visitation. Taking this all into consideration, we hold that the circuit court correctly determined that Jones was a parent figure to E.B.

Having determined that Jones stood in loco parentis, the question then becomes whether it is in E.B.'s best interest for Jones to have visitation rights, as that is the polestar consideration. . . . For all of the reasons stated above, it is clear that the Plaintiff was [E.B.]'s primary caregiver. A parent-child relationship between [E.B.] and the Plaintiff was deeply established, as were relationships between the child and the Plaintiff's extended family, involving the Plaintiff's mother and father and step-mother and other family members. The Defendant was estranged from her family during most of this time, so the only support provided to the child came from the Plaintiff, the Defendant, and the Plaintiff's extended family.

Finally, the Court questions the Defendant's veracity as to her assertion that [E.B.] has not exhibited any kind of behavior or emotion which would indicate she has been negatively affected by [E.B.]'s abrupt separation from the Plaintiff. Up to this point, [E.B.] has spent most of her life in the Plaintiff's care, and based upon the loving relationship that they formed, shared and enjoyed, it would be in [E.B.]'s best interest to continue to have contact with the Plaintiff.

Clearly, the circuit court weighed the testimony presented and considered the great weight of evidence regarding Jones's care for E.B., the parent-child relationship formed between Jones and the child, and the child's relationships with Jones's family, to determine that it was in E.B.'s best interest to allow Jones's visitation. . . . [W]e cannot say that the circuit court erred in ruling that it was in E.B.'s best interest to have visitation with Jones.

Before leaving this point, we note that Bethany makes several arguments that if we allow the nonbiological parent in this case to stand in loco parentis or to seek any visitation or custody rights to this child, it will open a floodgate that allows any person, i.e., a nanny, a babysitter, a girlfriend or boyfriend to go into court and seek custody of a child. We find this argument unavailing. In fact, the Kentucky Supreme Court in Mullins v. Picklesimer, 317 S.W.3d 569 (Ky. 2010), in a case factually similar to the instant one, rejected any such open-floodgate argument. . . . [T]he Kentucky court concluded that the case was distinguishable from the situation where there is a grandparent, a babysitter, or a boyfriend or girlfriend of the parent, who watched the child for the parent, but who was never intended by the parent to be doing so in the capacity of another parent. . . . Thus, there is no merit to Bethany's contention that this case will open the floodgates to allow anyone to seek visitation with a minor child.

Baker, Justice, dissenting.

There are two competing interests in this appeal: (1) a fit parent's right to exclude a former romantic partner from having any visitation with her minor child after the relationship ended; and (2) a former romantic partner's right to have court-ordered visitation premised upon standing in loco parentis to the minor child during the course of the romantic relationship. The majority focuses on numerous facts regarding the parties' history in this case, seemingly as a basis upon which to craft a new judicial right of visitation for Jones. Yet, the opinion fails to furnish any meaningful analysis of Bethany's right to parent her child as she sees fit. That omission, fostered by the trial court and advanced by the majority, creates the impression that Bethany and Jones have equal legal footing in this dispute; however, they do not.

A parent's Fourteenth Amendment guarantee of due process of law in the right to have and raise children was reaffirmed in Troxel v. Granville, 530 U.S. 57 (2000). . . . Now, any person in Arkansas can petition a court for visitation with a minor child over the objection of the parent. . . . It would be absurd to argue that . . . as against a legal and biological stranger, such as Jones, a parent's decision is entitled to no deference. Today's opinion circumvents the guiding principles that restrict intrusion upon the parent's fundamental right to determine with whom his or her child associates. . . .

Notes and Questions on *Troxel* and *Bethany*

1. Common law rule. At common law, grandparents had no right to visitation with grandchildren in the face of parental objection. All states now have third-party visitation statutes that permit grandparents (and sometimes other persons, as revealed in *Troxel*) to petition for visitation in certain circumstances.

2. Social factors. What societal factors explain the expanding legal recognition of grandparents' rights? Professors Andrew Cherlin and Frank Furstenberg point to several factors:

> All of these trends taken together—changes in mortality, fertility, transportation, communications, the work day, retirement, Social Security, and standards of living—have transformed grandparenthood from its pre-World War II state. More people are living longer to become grandparents and to enjoy a lengthy period of life as grandparents. They can keep in touch more easily with their grandchildren; they have more time to devote to them; they have more money to spend on them; and they are less likely still to be raising their own children.[45]

Custody rights of grandparents take on renewed importance when illness, substance abuse, and economic recession lead biological parents sometimes to ask their own parents for assistance.

3. Approaches prior to *Troxel*. Four types of grandparent visitation statutes existed: (1) those conditioned on the related parent's rights ("derivative rights theory"), (2) those based on family disruption (for example, death of one parent or divorce), (3) those based on best interests theory, and (4) those requiring a

[45]. Andrew J. Cherlin & Frank Furstenberg, Jr., The Modernization of Grandparenthood, in Arlene S. Skolnick ed., The Intimate Environment 131 (6th ed. 1989).

"substantial relationship" between grandparent and child.[46] Some triggering situations (for example, death or divorce) reflect more than one theory. What type was the Washington statute at issue in *Troxel*?

4. Biological parent presumption. A presumption favors biological parents in custody disputes (as opposed to visitation disputes) involving nonparents. That is, courts apply a rebuttable presumption that custody should be awarded to a biological parent absent evidence of unfitness. In a famous grandparents' rights case, a state supreme court refused to follow that presumption. In Painter v. Bannister, 140 N.W.2d 152 (Iowa 1966), a father left his young son with his maternal grandparents when the boy's sister and mother died in an automobile accident. When the father remarried and requested the return of his son, the grandparents refused. The father brought a habeas corpus action. Refusing to apply the parental presumption, the court held that the child's best interests would be served by remaining with the stable, churchgoing, Midwestern grandparents rather than the bohemian writer/father.

5. Right to privacy. Do grandparent visitation statutes unconstitutionally infringe on the right to privacy (that is, parents' constitutional right to make decisions regarding their children)? Prior to *Troxel*, courts were split on that question. How does *Troxel* respond? How influential are Meyer v. Nebraska and Pierce v. Society of Sisters in the Supreme Court's analysis? Do the plurality and dissent (Justice Stevens) treat these precedents differently?

Why do you suppose that Tommie Granville wanted to limit her daughters' visitation with their deceased father's parents? See Ariela R. Dubler, Constructing the Modern American Family: The Stories of Troxel v. Granville, in Family Law Stories 95, 100-101 (Carol Sanger ed., 2008). Should the law be involved in such private dispute resolution?

6. Constitutional issues. In *Troxel*, the plurality held that the Washington statute, as applied to Tommie Granville, violated the Due Process Clause. In what way was the application defective?

By holding the statute unconstitutional as applied, the Court avoided a ruling that the statute was facially unconstitutional. The Court also evaded identifying the appropriate standard of review. What standard of review should apply? Should courts be especially protective of parental interests and apply strict scrutiny? Rational relationship? The undue burden standard (i.e., whether visitation unduly burdens the parents' constitutional rights)?

The Justices also disagreed on what the state must show to justify interference with a parent's decision about third-party visitation. Should the test be the best interests of the child? Harm to the child if visitation is not granted? Compare Bowen v. Bowen, 2012 WL 2406030 (Ark. Ct. App. 2012) (adopting harm test), with Hiller v. Fausey, 904 A.2d 875 (Pa. 2006) (contra). If harm becomes the standard, how substantial must the harm be? See Blixt v. Blixt, 774 N.E.2d 1052, 1060 (Mass. 2002) (significant harm that affects health, safety, or welfare). See generally Jeffrey A. Parness, *Troxel* Revisited: A New Approach to Third-Party Childcare, 18

[46]. Patricia S. Fernandez, Grandparent Access: A Model Statute, 6 Yale L. & Pol'y Rev. 109, 118-124 (1988).

Rich. J.L. & Pub. Int. 227 (2015) (contending that courts should dispense with the need for a showing of harm in third-party disputes if the parents earlier ceded parental authority to the third party).

In the wake of *Troxel*, many jurisdictions revised their statutes to limit the number of persons who may seek visitation and to give deference to a fit parent's wishes. Also, some states moved to a more stringent standard (i.e., harm) rather than the best interests test, or alternatively retained the best interests standard but narrowed it by the inclusion of particular factors.

7. Factors to consider in granting visitation. If you were a legislator or a judge, what factors should be considered in the determination of visitation so as not to infringe on parental rights? For example, in the balance between family privacy and state intervention, should it matter if the dispute involves any of the following?

- An intact family in which both parents object to visitation by the grandparent(s); e.g., Daniels v. Daniels, 885 A.2d 524 (N.J. Super. Ct. App. Div. 2005)
- Married parents who are presently living apart; e.g., *Blixt*, supra
- A family disrupted by the death of a parent; e.g., Lamberts v. Lillig, 670 N.W.2d 129 (Iowa 2003)
- A family disrupted by divorce but with parents who disagree about the grandparent's visitation; e.g., In re Marriage of Harris, 17 Cal. Rptr. 3d 842 (Cal. 2004)
- A child's parents who are not married; e.g., Saul v. Brunetti, 753 So. 2d 26 (Fla. 2000)
- A parent (or parents) who agreed to the visitation at one time; e.g., In re M.M.D., 820 N.E.2d 392 (Ill. 2004)
- A grandparent with a "significant relationship" with the grandchild; e.g., 750 Ill. Comp. Stat. Ann. 5/607(a-5)
- A grandparent who has been "unreasonably" denied visitation (see id.)
- A grandmother seeking visitation with her deceased daughter's child, who had just been adopted by the child's father's new wife; e.g. Jocham v. Sutliff, 26 N.E.3d 82 (Ind. Ct. App. 2015)

8. Stepparents' rights. The rise in divorce contributed to an increasing number of stepparents. Approximately 7.5 percent of children live with stepparents.[47] Traditionally, if a stepparent sought custody over parental objection, the stepparent had to overcome the biological-parent preference. Although stepparents had a legally cognizable relationship with the child *during* the marriage, their parental rights were not recognized at divorce. However, courts have been increasingly willing to grant visitation rights to stepparents, especially given a long-term relationship with a child. Almost two dozen states currently provide visitation rights to stepparents.[48] But cf. In re C.T.C., 339 P.3d 54 (Mont. 2014) (reversing court-ordered visitation with stepmother and remanding to trial court to determine

---

[47]. Rose M. Kreider & Renee Ellis, U.S. Census Bureau, Living Arrangements of Children: 2009, at 4 (June 2011) (according to the most recent available data).

[48]. Compiled from ABA, Chart 6: Third-Party Visitation, 46 Fam. L.Q. 537 (2013).

parental fitness pursuant to *Troxel*). Does an award of stepparent visitation infringe on a biological parent's constitutional rights, based on *Troxel*? See generally Margaret M. Mahoney, Stepparents as Third Parties in Relation to Their Stepchildren, 40 Fam. L.Q. 81 (2006).

9. Psychological parent. Today's families include an increasing number of nonparents who develop close relationships with children and later seek to continue contact, even over parental objections. How far does *Troxel* go in recognizing pluralism in family forms? After *Troxel*, for example, how receptive would the U.S. Supreme Court be in allowing third-party visitation by other relatives and nonrelated persons who are "psychological parents"?

The psychological parent doctrine is derived from an influential book by Joseph Goldstein et al., Beyond the Best Interests of the Child 17-20 (1973). Based on psychoanalytic theory, Goldstein and co-authors Anna Freud and Alfred Solnit point out that a person becomes a psychological parent through daily interaction, companionship, and shared experiences. The concept emphasizes the child's own perspective and experience, rather than legal or formal criteria. The role can be fulfilled by any caring adult.

How far should courts accommodate the parental preference rule and the best-interests standard in disputes involving psychological parents? Should courts limit the doctrine only to visitation (rather than custody)? See, e.g., In re K.H., 773 S.E.2d 20 (W. Va. 2015) (eight-year guardianship of child established grandmother as a "psychological parent" entitled to "liberal" visitation.) Or should courts reject the doctrine and restrict the definition of parent to a biological or adoptive parent? See Cynthia Grant Bowman, The Legal Relationship Between Cohabitants and Their Partners' Children, 13 Theoretical Inquiries L. 127, 136 (2012).

10. Lesbian mother disputes: Traditional approach. In custody determinations involving opposite-sex couples, the mother and father begin on equal footing. In contrast, for lesbian couples, the biological mother traditionally enjoyed a significant advantage over the nonbiological mother because of the biological-parent presumption. See, e.g., Nancy S. v. Michele G., 279 Cal. Rptr. 212 (Ct. App. 1991); Allison D. v. Virginia M., 572 N.E.2d 27 (N.Y. 1991). Why does the court in *Bethany* reject that approach?

11. *Bethany*: Holding. The majority and the dissent in *Bethany* have different readings of *Troxel*. Evaluate these views. For example, does recognition of a second parent's rights infringe on the biological parent's rights, according to *Bethany*? On what basis did the court determine that Emily (the second parent) had standing? How did the court apply the best interests test? Standing tends to be the greatest obstacle for same-sex parents in custody and visitation disputes. Why? See also In re Mullen, 953 N.E.2d 302 (Ohio 2011). The dissent charges that the decision will open a floodgate of litigation. Why? What is the majority's response? Which argument is most persuasive? How might Beth and Emily's marital status, or lack thereof, have affected the outcome?

To date, the trend reflects a greater willingness to recognize the second partner's rights. See In re T.P.S., 978 N.E.2d 1070 (Ill. App. Ct. 2012); Latham v. Schwerdtfeger, 802 N.W.2d 66 (Neb. 2011). Should it make any difference if both mothers have a biological connection to the child—for example, one mother donates an egg, but the other mother gives birth? See, e.g., D.M.T. v. T.M.H., 129 So. 3d 320 (Fla. 2013). What role might Lawrence v. Texas play in custody decisionmaking involving former same-sex partners? What role might *Obergefell* play in future custody disputes between same-sex partners?

12. Written agreement. Should same-sex couples execute written agreements to address issues of custody and visitation? Should they do so regardless of whether they are validly married? If the parents do execute written agreements, will courts recognize such agreements *during* the relationship? *At dissolution*? Compare Morris v. Hawk, 907 N.E.2d 763 (Ohio Ct. App. 2009), with In re LaPiana, 2010 WL 3042394 (Ohio Ct. App. 2010).

13. Law reform: ALI Principles and UPA. The ALI recognizes that biology is not determinative of legal parenthood by recognizing parenthood "by estoppel" and "de facto parents." A parent by estoppel acts as a parent in circumstances that would estop the child's legal parent from denying the claimant's parental status. Parent-by-estoppel status may be created when an individual (1) is obligated for child support, or (2) has lived with the child for at least two years and has a reasonable belief that he is the father, or (3) has had an agreement with the child's legal parent since birth (or for at least two years) to serve as a coparent provided that recognition of parental status would serve the child's best interests. ALI Principles §2.03(1)(b).

A de facto parent is a person, other than a legal parent or parent by estoppel, who has regularly performed an equal or greater share of caretaking, lived with the child for a significant period (not less than two years), and acted as a parent for nonfinancial reasons or as a result of an inability of any legal parent to perform caretaking functions. Id. §2.03(1)(c). De facto parents are not full parents, but they can obtain visitation orders.

The Principles' requirements are more strict regarding de facto parents to avoid intrusion into the parent-child relationship if a legal parent or a parent by estoppel is fit and willing to care for the child (§2.18(1)(a)), or if the custodial allocation would be impractical in light of the number of adults to be allocated custodial responsibility (§2.18(1)(b)). How well do these provisions address situations like those in cases like *Troxel* and *Bethany*? See Robin Fretwell Wilson, Trusting Mothers: A Critique of the American Law Institute's Treatment of De Facto Parents, 38 Hofstra L. Rev. 1103, 1110 (2010). See also LP v. LF, 338 P.3d 908 (Wyo. 2014) (refusing to recognize either de facto parenthood or parenthood by estoppel in the case of a nonbiological father, despite his being listed on the birth certificate and co-parenting the child).

The revised Uniform Parentage Act (UPA), similarly, recognizes that biology is not determinative of legal parenthood. The trend is to apply the UPA's presumed-parent provisions in a gender-neutral manner to same-sex partners (discussed in Chapter V).

14. Child's interests? To what extent does the Constitution protect the *child's* right to retain a relationship with a nonparent? Does *Michael H.* (discussed in Chapter V) shed any light on the matter? Is *Troxel* or *Bethany* concerned with the child's interests? In his dissent in *Troxel*, Justice Stevens is alone in urging that the child's interests should be considered. Do children of same-sex couples have an independent right to maintain relationships with both parents at divorce? See generally

Elizabeth Traylor, Protecting the Rights of Children of Same-Sex Parents in Indiana by Adopting a Version of the Uniform Parentage Act, 48 Ind. L. Rev. 695 (2015).

15. Empirical data: Children's well-being. What is the effect of a parent's sexual orientation on children's development? Research reveals that the children of same-sex parents are similar to those of opposite-sex parents in terms of cognitive abilities, behavior, and self-esteem.[49]

Amici curiae briefs in *Obergefell* (discussed in Chapter II) reported research findings that support the above conclusion. For example, in their brief, the American Sociological Association noted a clear consensus in the social science literature that children of same-sex parents fared as well as children residing in opposite-sex households "over a wide array of well-being measures." In addition, Gary Gates, the research director of the Williams Institute at the University of California, Los Angeles, points out that marriage improves the well-being of children of same-sex couples because marriage reduces the economic vulnerability of these families.[50]

4. The Role of Special Participants

a. The Child's Preference

McMILLEN v. McMILLEN

602 A.2d 845 (Pa. 1992)

LARSEN, Justice.

Appellant Vaughn S. McMillen (father) appeals from an order of the Superior Court vacating the July 22, 1988 child custody order in his favor and reinstating the order of July 31, 1987, which continued primary custody in appellee Carolyn F. Shemo, formerly Carolyn F. McMillen (mother). We reverse.

[The] parties were married on May 2, 1975 and . . . their son Emmett was born on September 30, 1977. The parties were subsequently divorced in . . . Wyoming on September 25, 1981. At the time of the divorce, the Wyoming court awarded primary custody of Emmett to the mother, subject only to the reasonable visitation of the father.

In March of 1982, the father instituted an action in the Court of Common Pleas of Indiana County, Pennsylvania, seeking partial custody of Emmett. On April 27, 1982, the court awarded general custody of Emmett to the mother with the right of visitation in the father. The court limited the father's visitation to

---

[49]. See Abbie E. Goldberg, Lesbian and Gay Parents and Their Children: Research on the Family Life Cycle (2010); Fiona Tasker, Developmental Outcomes for Children Raised by Lesbian and Gay Parents, in What Is Parenthood? Contemporary Debates About the Family 171 (Linda M. McClain & Daniel Cere eds., 2013); Timothy J. Biblarz & Judith Stacey, How Does the Gender of Parents Matter?, 72 J. Marriage & Fam. 3 (2010).

[50]. Brief for American Sociological Association as amicus curiae in support of petitioners, Obergefell v. Hodges, 135 S. Ct. 2584 (2015) (no. 14-556), 2015 WL 2473451; Brief for Gary J. Gates as amicus curiae in support of petitioners, Obergefell v. Hodges, 135 S. Ct. 2584 (2015) (no. 14-556), http://www.scotusblog.com/case-files/cases/obergefell-v-hodges/.

alternating weekends and holidays, one day every other week and two weeks during the summer.

Over the next six years, the father sought modification of the custody order four times and the mother one time. Each time, the Court of Common Pleas significantly expanded the father's visitation rights. From 1986 on, Emmett repeatedly and steadfastly expressed his preference to live with his father. Finally, on July 22, 1988, the Court of Common Pleas awarded general custody of Emmett to the father. . . .

On appeal, the Superior Court vacated the July 22, 1988 custody order and reinstated the previous order of July 31, 1987. In doing so, the Superior Court determined that: 1) the record failed to present any circumstances warranting a change in custody; and 2) the child's best interests would not be served by changing custody merely because the child wished it. . . .

The father argues that the Superior Court, in determining Emmett's best interests, usurped the function of the trial court by ignoring the trial court's factual findings and also failed to give proper weight to Emmett's steadfast desire to live with his father. [A]n appellate court is empowered to determine whether the trial court's incontrovertible factual findings support its factual conclusions, but it may not interfere with those conclusions unless they are unreasonable in view of the trial court's factual findings; and thus, represent a gross abuse of discretion. Having reviewed the previous custody orders in this case, the trial court concluded that both the home of the mother and that of the father were equally acceptable. The trial court, therefore, was forced to look at other factors in making its decision. The only testimony taken at the most recent custody hearing was that of the child, Emmett, who was then almost 11 years old. Emmett testified that he preferred to live with his father.

Although the express wishes of a child are not controlling in custody decisions, such wishes do constitute an important factor that must be carefully considered in determining the child's best interest. The child's preference must be based on good reasons, and the child's maturity and intelligence must be considered. The weight to be given a child's testimony as to his preference can best be determined by the judge before whom the child appears.

Our review of the record shows that Emmett's preference to live with his father is supported by more than sufficient good reasons. Emmett testified that his stepfather frightens, upsets and threatens him, and his mother does nothing to prevent this mistreatment. He testified that he does not get along with either his mother or his stepfather, and that he gets along well with his stepmother. His testimony also revealed that his mother and stepfather leave him alone after school and that, even though his father and stepmother work, he is never left alone when he is at his father's home for the summer. Emmett also stated that his mother interferes with his sporting and farming activities and refuses even to watch him play ball. Thus, we find that Emmett's steadfast wish to live with his father was properly considered, and we find no abuse of discretion in the amount of weight afforded that preference.

Nor do we find an abuse of discretion in the trial court's conclusion that Emmett's best interests would be served more appropriately by placing him in his father's custody. The record supports the trial court's finding that both households were equally suitable. This being so, Emmett's expressed preference to live with his father could not but tip the evidentiary scale in favor of his father. Thus, the trial court's conclusion that it would be in Emmett's best interest to modify the prior custody order by transferring primary custody from the mother to the father is supported by the record, and we find no gross abuse of discretion by the trial court in awarding primary custody to the father.

Notes and Questions

1. Approaches. Is it appropriate to consider a child's custodial preference? If so, when? Most state statutes call for consideration of the child's wishes, at least to some extent. Some states require consideration of a child's wishes (modeled after the UMDA). Other states require consideration of the child's preference after a preliminary finding of maturity. Some states require deference to the wishes of children of a specified age (generally ages 12 to 14). See, e.g., ALI Principles §2.08 cmt. f (recommending ages 11 to 14). Finally, some states give judges complete discretion.

2. Empirical research. Judges' views differ about consideration of children's preferences. Although most judges consider preferences of teenagers as significant, fewer than half accord the same weight to those of children aged 11 to 13 years. Attitudes differ considerably about preschoolers' preferences.[51] Another study reports that most children in contested cases want the opportunity to express their views to a judge and to have those views kept confidential.[52]

3. Reasons. What were Emmett's reasons to change custody in *McMillen*? Should the reasons *underlying* a child's preference influence whether the court considers the child's wishes? For example, should a child's testimony be given *more* weight in cases of substance abuse or domestic violence? See In re Marriage of Sisson, 665 N.W.2d 441 (Iowa Ct. App. 2003). Or if the custodial parent is relocating and the child wants to remain with the noncustodial parent? See Goodhand v. Kildoo, 560 S.E.2d 463 (Va. Ct. App. 2002). How can a court determine if Emmett's reason resulted from his father's coercion?

4. Parental unfitness. Children's preferences are more likely to be considered when both parents are fit (as in *McMillen*) or marginally fit. In such cases, the child's preference may serve as a tiebreaker. Children's preferences may be overridden if the court finds the preferred parent unfit. See, e.g., J.D.V. v. R.M.T., 2004 WL 3245784 (Del. Fam. Ct. 2004) (father's criminal record for sexual abuse).

5. Procedure. What procedural concerns are implicated by consideration of a child's custodial preference?

---

[51]. Barbara A. Atwood, The Child's Voice in Custody Litigation: An Empirical Survey and Suggestions for Reform, 45 Ariz. L. Rev. 629, 634-635 (2003).

[52]. Patrick Parkinson et al., Parents and Children's Views on Talking to Judges in Parenting Disputes in Australia, 21 Int'l J.L. Pol'y & Fam. 84 (2007). See also Jacqueline Clarke, Do I Have a Voice? An Empirical Analysis of Children's Voices in Michigan Custody Litigation, 47 Fam. L.Q. 457 (2013).

a. Who? If it is appropriate to take into account a child's preference, who should do so? The judge? Child's representative? A parent's attorney? A mental health professional?

b. Where? By what procedure should the child's preference be taken into account? Testimony in open court? Other witnesses' testimony in open court? If the parents disagree about whether the child should testify in open court, how should the judge rule? See Addison v. Addison, 463 S.W.3d 755 (Ky. 2015) (upholding court's refusal of wife's request to call her children as witnesses in custody case). See generally Laureen A. D'Ambra, The Importance of Conducting In Camera Testimony of Child Witnesses in Court Proceedings: A Comparative Legal Analysis of Relevant Domestic Relations, Juvenile Justice, and Criminal Cases, 19 Roger Williams U.L. Rev. 323 (2014).

Should a child discuss a custodial preference with a judge in a private interview? One study of state court judges reveals judges' reluctance to conduct in camera interviews of children; one-fourth of the respondents report that they never conduct such interviews, and less than one-fifth conduct such interviews on a regular basis.[53] What do you think explains judges' reluctance?

c. How? Should counsel be present at in camera interviews? See Barrett v. Wright, 897 So. 2d 398 (Ala. Civ. App. 2004) (holding unconstitutional an in camera interview absent counsel or waiver); Hogue v. Hogue, 190 P.3d 1177 (Okla. Civ. App. 2008) (affirming exclusion of counsel based on 15-year-old's wishes). What should be the role of counsel at such interviews? See, e.g., Mo. Rev. Stat. §452.385 (permitting counsel to participate and to be present). If one parent objects, can the interview take place? See KES v. CAT, 107 P.3d 779 (Wyo. 2005) (holding that the court should fashion alternative procedure).

Should interviews be recorded? Compare Molloy v. Molloy, 643 N.W.2d 574 (Mich. 2002) (vacating requirement of recording), with Couch v. Couch, 146 S.W.3d 923 (Ky. 2004) (contra). See also UMDA §404(a) (providing that court may interview child in chambers and permit counsel and recording). Should interviews be limited to determination of the child's preference or encompass any custody matter? Compare In re H.R.C., 781 N.W.2d 105 (Mich. Ct. App. 2009) (interview limited to child's preference), with Thompson v. Thompson, 683 N.W.2d 250 (Mich. Ct. App. 2004) (contra).

Problem

Andrea is the 15-year-old daughter of Jean and David. The parents' marriage has been marked by domestic violence, including severe physical injuries to Jean, police intervention, and orders of protection. After a recent physical altercation, Jean commences divorce proceedings and petitions for custody. David cross-petitions for custody. In an in camera interview, Andrea denies the existence of violence in her parents' marriage and expresses a clear preference for living with her father. Aside from his conduct toward Andrea's mother, David appears to be a model parent who is involved in Andrea's schoolwork and extracurricular

[53]. Atwood, supra note [51], at 636.

activities and who provides her with many material benefits (such as a television set, clothing, a horse, and a trip to Europe). He calls her his "princess" and his "best girl." In contrast, Andrea claims that her mother is not significantly involved in her schoolwork or her extracurricular activities and that she does not enjoy her mother's company or their relationship. What result? Wissink v. Wissink, 749 N.Y.S.2d 550 (App. Div. 2002).

b. Representation for the Child

HOSKINS v HOSKINS

— S.W.3d —, 2015 WL 222177 (Ky. Ct. App. 2015)

THOMPSON, JUDGE:

Cory David Hoskins appeals from an order of the Morgan Circuit Court modifying timesharing with his son. He contends the trial court erroneously considered the report of a guardian *ad litem* (GAL). . . . Based on our Supreme Court's recent clarification of the role of GAL's in domestic child custody and visitation matters, we reverse and remand.

Cory and Melissa Hoskins were divorced on June 26, 2008. [Based on their separation agreement], Cory and Melissa shared joint custody of their son. . . . Melissa was awarded timesharing with the child every Sunday from 6:00 p.m. through the following Wednesday at 6:00 p.m. and Cory was awarded timesharing every Wednesday from 6:00 p.m. until the following Friday at 6:00 p.m. The parties were awarded alternating weekends [and] timesharing on the various traditional holidays.

On March 4, 2013, Melissa filed a motion to modify custody and the parties' parenting schedule, asserting [as the basis that] Cory received a speeding ticket, had remarried and divorced, and moved three times since the parties' divorce. [At the conclusion of the hearing on July 3, 2013, the trial court appointed an attorney as GAL to represent the child's interest and ordered the GAL to file a report with the court.] The GAL reported that the child conveyed that his parents were very active in his life and love him. The GAL also reported [that] the child stated Cory becomes upset when [the parents fight about the custody arrangements]. The GAL recommended [that] the parties refrain from speaking directly to the child or in front of him regarding their personal and legal disputes [and] making derogatory remarks in front of the child. . . .

The trial court entered an order continuing joint custody with the child but ordered that the child reside primarily with Melissa. Cory was awarded timesharing in accordance with the local visitation schedule. Cory appealed.

During the pendency of this appeal, our Supreme Court issued its opinion in Morgan v. Getter, 441 S.W.3d 94 (Ky. 2014) [in which the issue was]: "What is the role of a . . . GAL in a custody, shared parenting, visitation, or support proceeding?" . . . Artfully written, the Court's opinion explains how a hybrid [friend of the court (FOC)/GAL] has emerged in the realm of family law. However, it pointed out that the two are distinct and disavowed the practice of appointing an attorney as counsel for the child and as an investigator and advisor to the court.

The FOC is a creature of statute. The FOC may or may not be an attorney and is appointed as an officer of the court to "investigate the child's and the parents' situations, to file a report summarizing his or her findings, and to make recommendations as to the outcome of the proceeding." . . . [M]ore common in the present-day courts is the appointment of a GAL in vehemently contested domestic custody and visitation matters. However, the GAL is not a replacement for the FOC and has decidedly different roles. The GAL, who is always an attorney, is appointed to "participate actively as legal counsel for the child, to make opening and closing statements, to call and to cross-examine witnesses, to make evidentiary objections and other motions, and to further the child's interest in expeditious, non-acrimonious proceedings."

Despite the distinctions between a FOC and GAL, the Court noted the trial courts have often expected the GAL-appointee to "blur" these roles and "to investigate for the court and to litigate for the child." The Court found it problematic for a GAL appointed to represent the child to also examine records, interview family members and file a report with the court. Its concerns were both ethical and constitutional.

The Court agreed with those commentators and courts that have noted the ethical problems for the attorney and the potential deprivation of due process to a parent when the roles of a FOC and GAL are interchanged. The GAL is subject to the Rules of the Supreme Court (SCR) governing attorneys' conduct including duties of loyalty and confidentiality to his or her client. Additionally, the Court pointed out that SCR 3.130–3.7 prohibits an attorney from being an advocate at a proceeding in which he or she is likely to be a necessary witness. Yet, when ordered by the Court, the GAL is required to submit a report in the very action that he or she is acting as the child's counsel.

These same rules that bind attorneys present constitutional implications for the parent. By definition, a GAL represents the child in the custody or visitation proceeding and, therefore, cannot be a witness. Because the parent cannot cross-examine a GAL as to the basis for any facts or recommendations contained in the GAL's report, there is no opportunity to confront adverse evidence as required by due process. Emphasizing a parent has a protected liberty interest in the care and custody of his or her child, the Court agreed with "the many courts that have held that in these circumstances the party's constitutional due process right trumps the [ethical] rule."

Noting the potential ethical and constitutional implications of the appointment of a hybrid FOC/GAL and the need of our trial courts to have the authority to appoint not only an investigator and advisor to the court but also to appoint an advocate for the child's best interest, the Court asked the rhetorical question: "What is a Court to do?" The Court [in the *Morgan* case] responded to its own question with exceptional clarity [explaining that the court could appoint a FOC to investigate the circumstances on the court's behalf, file a report, and make custodial recommendations. Or, the trial court could appoint a GAL to represent the child's best interests.] The [*Morgan*] Court cautioned that the GAL should not be confused with the FOC.

> The FOC "investigates, reports, and makes custodial recommendations on behalf of the court, and is subject to cross-examination[.]" The GAL "is a lawyer for the child, counseling the child and representing him or her in the course of

> proceedings by, among other things, engaging in discovery, in motion practice, and in presentation of the case at the final hearing." Important to the outcome of this case, the GAL *"neither testifies (by filing a report or otherwise) nor is subject to cross-examination."* (emphasis added).

Here, the circuit court admittedly was without the benefit of the *Morgan* opinion. Nevertheless, it erroneously appointed the GAL to represent the child *and* to conduct an investigation and file a report and, by judicial fiat, created a hybrid FOC/GAL disapproved of in *Morgan*.

[T]he question remains whether the error was harmless. Melissa contends the error was harmless because the trial court relied on other evidence produced at the hearing when modifying timesharing. [But] the only facts recited in the trial court's modification order to support its decision pertain to those stated in the GAL's report. Although the trial court stated its decision was also based on evidence produced at the hearing, its order does not recite what evidence supports its decision to modify timesharing. It is impossible for this Court to determine what admissible evidence supported the trial court's decision. Based on the forgoing, the order of the Morgan Circuit Court is reversed and the case remanded for further proceedings.

Notes and Questions

1. **Background.** The debate over mandatory representation for children in custody and visitation disputes began in the 1960s—sparked by the rising divorce rate, concern about the effects of divorce on children, and recognition of the child's right to counsel in the delinquency context (In re Gault, 387 U.S. 1 (1967)). Should counsel for the child in custody disputes be mandatory? Discretionary? If discretionary, should it be at the court's discretion or the parents'? Does the child have a due process right to counsel in custody disputes?

2. **Discretionary.** Despite considerable support by commentators and practitioners for mandatory counsel, appointment of the child's representative in custody disputes generally remains in the court's discretion. Few states mandate representation for the child in contested custody cases. Wisconsin enacted the first statute requiring guardians ad litem (GALs) in custody disputes in 1971; New Hampshire became the second state in 1979.[54]

3. **Special context: Abuse.** Many jurisdictions provide for representation for the child in custody cases involving allegations of abuse or neglect. Why is representation necessary in such proceedings? Federal law spurred the growth of GAL services by requiring the appointment of GALs for all abused or neglected children in judicial proceedings. See 42 U.S.C. §5106a(b)(2)(A)(xiii) (superseded by 42 U.S.C. §5106(a)(2)(B)(ii)). However, federal law does not require the GAL to be an attorney.

[54]. Richard Ducote, Guardians Ad Litem in Private Custody Litigation: The Case for Abolition, 3 Loy. J. Pub. Int. L. 106, 110 (2002).

4. Factors. When a discretionary standard governs the decision to appoint counsel for children, what factors might influence judicial discretion? Should cost be relevant, for example?

5. Models of representation. As *Hoskins* reveals, considerable debate exists about the appropriate role of the child's representative. Several models exist: (1) a court-designated investigator who makes recommendations, (2) an attorney who represents the child's wishes, (3) an advocate for the children's "best interests," (4) a facilitator/mediator, and (5) some combination.

What roles are most and least invasive of family privacy? If the representative serves as an advocate, should he or she advocate for the child's wishes (regardless of what the attorney believes) or the child's best interests? If the representative ascertains the child's best interests, does this role usurp the authority of the judge? Does the investigator-neutral factfinder's role conflict with the duty to represent a client zealously (Model Code of Professional Responsibility EC 7-1)? What difficulties does each role evoke?

Should the representative's role change based on the type of proceeding (e.g., abuse, delinquency, custody)? Based on the child's age? Abilities? See generally Martin Guggenheim, A Law Guardian by Any Other Name: A Critique of the Report of the Matrimonial Commission, 27 Pace L. Rev. 785 (2007) (criticizing recommendations); Merril Sobie, A Law Guardian by the Same Name: A Response to Professor Guggenheim's Matrimonial Commission Critique, 27 Pace L. Rev. 831 (2007) (rebuttal).

6. State approaches. Jurisdictions differ on the role of the child's representative. Most jurisdictions authorize a GAL who operates as a best-interests attorney; a few jurisdictions appoint a child's attorney. The remaining jurisdictions appoint either a hybrid (best interests attorney and child's attorney) or a combination of representatives depending on the circumstances.[55]

7. Role confusion. Sometimes attorneys characterize their role as either advocate or factfinder but then act inconsistently. Factors that might influence an attorney's perception of roles include: (a) the state law description of the role; (b) instructions given by, or exceptions of, the judge; (c) training that the guardian ad litem received; (d) age of the child and the guardian's understanding of child development, attachment, and permanency planning.[56] What are the risks posed by such role confusion? See, e.g., Kimbrell v. Kimbrell, 331 P.3d 915 (N.M. 2014) (finding that a GAL acting as a "best interests" attorney is shielded by quasi-judicial immunity from tort suits). See generally Dana E. Prescott, Inconvenient Truths: Facts and Frictions in Defense of Guardians Ad Litem for Children, 67 Me. L. Rev. 43 (2014).

8. Attorney as representative? Few jurisdictions require that the child's representative be an attorney. Note, too, that federal child abuse law (discussed above) does not require that the GAL be an attorney. Should a court-appointed

[55]. Annette M. Gonzalez & Linda M. Rio Reichmann, Representing Children in Civil Cases Involving Domestic Violence, 39 Fam. L.Q. 197, 201-202 (2005).

[56]. Howard A. Davidson, The Child's Right to Be Heard and Represented in Judicial Proceedings, 18 Pepp. L. Rev. 255, 263 (1991).

representative be an attorney? See Guggenheim, Critique, supra, at 796-797 (discussing pros and cons).

9. Law reform. Beginning in 2001, several states recommended sweeping changes in the roles of GALs in custody cases. For example, an Ohio task force recommended statewide standards regarding qualifications, fees, training, and responsibilities. A Minnesota task force proposed changes in role definition, training, case load size, supervision, and accountability. The primary criticisms include that GALs occupy roles that are not subject to consistent definitions, have doubtful benefits, undermine fact finding by usurping the judicial role, deprive parents of due process, undermine parental authority and privacy, entail significant costs, are ineffectual in cases of domestic violence, and are unaccountable for their decisions.[57]

10. ABA Standards of Practice. In response to such criticisms, the ABA formulated Standards of Practice for Lawyers Representing Children in Custody Cases. The ABA Standards abolish the name "guardian ad litem" and provide instead for two types of lawyers, each of whom makes evidence-based legal arguments: the child's attorney, who provides independent legal representation in a traditional attorney-client relationship, and the best interests attorney, who independently investigates, assesses, and advocates the child's best interests *as a lawyer*. See Standard II(B) ("Definitions" and cmt.).

Lawyers appointed in either capacity should not "play any other role in the case, and should not testify, file a report, or make recommendations." See Standard III(B) ("Lawyer's Roles"). The Standards also address the problem of role confusion by providing that a lawyer should accept an appointment only with a full understanding of the functions to be performed. If part of the appointment order is confusing or "incompatible with his or her ethical duties," the lawyer should either decline appointment or request clarification or change of the order (or both). See Standards III(A) ("Accepting the Appointment").

11. Uniform Act. In response to the adoption by the ABA of two different sets of standards (Standards for Representation of Children in Abuse, Neglect, and Dependency Cases, adopted in 1995; and Standards of Practice of Lawyers Representing Children in Custody Cases, adopted in 2003), the Uniform Law Commission (ULC) promulgated the Uniform Representation of Children in Abuse, Neglect, and Custody Proceedings Act, adopted in 2006. The purpose of the act is to define the roles/responsibilities of representatives, as well as to address the ethical dimensions of the lawyer-client relationship, access to the child and information relating to the child, and the child's right of action for damages against the representative. Commentators criticize the Uniform Act, as well as the ABA Custody Standards, for the extent of judicial discretion that they vest in the best interests lawyer.[58]

---

[57]. Ducote, supra note [54], at 116.

[58]. See, e.g., Mark Henaghan, What Does a Child's Right to Be Heard in Legal Proceedings Really Mean?, ABA Custody Standards Do Not Go Far Enough, 42 Fam. L.Q. 117 (2008); Jane Spinak, Simon Says Take Three Steps Backwards: The National Conference of Commissioners on Uniform State Laws Recommendations on Child Representation, 6 Nev. L.J. 1385 (2006).

c. Role of Experts

IN RE REBECCA B.

611 N.Y.S.2d 831 (App. Div. 1994)

MEMORANDUM DECISION

[In 1986, after Renee B. and Michael B. had been married for five years, Renee filed for divorce and sole custody of their daughter, Rebecca. The Family Court granted both motions. In 1992, upon discovering that Michael was sleeping in the same bed as Rebecca, Renee petitioned to eliminate Michael's overnight visitation and to require supervised visitation. Michael cross-petitioned for sole custody. The Family Court denied Michael's cross-petition and affirmed the award of sole custody to the mother. The father appealed.]

[The Family Court] Order, dated May 8, 1992, which, inter alia, denied the motion of appellant father for a transfer of the sole legal custody of his daughter from her mother, to him, [is] unanimously modified on the law and the facts, and in the exercise of discretion, to the extent of granting the transfer of the sole legal custody to appellant, with liberal visitation rights to respondent mother, and otherwise, insofar as consistent with such transfer of sole legal custody to appellant, in all respects [is] otherwise affirmed, without costs or disbursements. It is ordered that any further proceedings in the matter in the Family Court be held before another judge.

The Clinical Director of the Family Court's Mental Health Service was qualified to testify as an expert in clinical psychology. He had met with the child on three occasions for a total of three hours and with her and each parent for about forty minutes. He also had met with each parent separately for about seven hours. He concluded that the child's best interests required the transfer of custody to appellant with liberal visitation for the mother noting that appellant was a much less detrimental influence on the child than was the mother, that he was less likely to cause long-term harm to her than was the mother, that the child perceived him as more loving than her mother, and that she had a more profound bond with him. The child made it clear repeatedly to the Clinical Director that she would prefer to live with her father; the mother's spanking, slapping, and locking of the child in her room was difficult for the child to comprehend.

Another psychiatrist, also recommended a change in custody, for the "main reason" that the mother tried so to exclude appellant from the child's life; he believed that appellant as the custodial parent would give better access to the noncustodial parent. From age seven to eight the child had slept with her father on overnight visits, but there had been no suggestion of any improper action by appellant and the practice had ceased. The psychiatrist had found nothing "intrinsically detrimental" in the arrangement. A supervising social worker employed by the Legal Aid Society, also recommended that custody be transferred to appellant.

A psychiatrist retained by the mother testified that custody should be continued with the mother. However, he had spoken only with the mother and with people to whom he was referred by the mother and not to the child or appellant.

The law guardian, believing that appellant was more likely to foster the noncustodial parent's relationship, concluded that the transfer of custody to him was in the best interest of the child.

The trial court denied appellant's motion to transfer custody to him, terming the testimony of the Clinical Director, the first mentioned psychiatrist and the Social Worker not credible. They were, however, the only experts making a recommendation as to custody who had spoken to all three family members, but the trial court repeatedly described their testimony as "flawed." By discounting the testimony of these three witnesses, the trial court essentially left itself without expert testimony on the child's preferences and the quality of her relationships with her parents. Since the mother's psychiatrist had not interviewed the child or appellant, moreover, little weight should be accorded to his recommendation that custody be awarded to the mother. . . .

A determination had been made by Family Court in 1987 that the mother should have custody. The burden was thus on appellant to demonstrate a substantial change of circumstances to justify a change in custody. He did so in 1991 by showing the preference of the child—then seven years of age—to live with him, by showing the bond which had grown between them, by showing petitioner's rather punitive disciplining of the child, which would over time have a deleterious effect on the child, and especially by his showing of petitioner's efforts to exclude him from the child's life.

We must respect the advantage of the trial judge in observing the witnesses, but the authority of this court in matters of custody is as broad as that of the trial court. It always comes down, however, to the best interests of the child and the ability of the parents "to provide for the child's emotional and intellectual development, the quality of the home environment, and the parental guidance provided." The psychiatrist, testifying on behalf of petitioner, said of her: "She is a somewhat temperamental lady who has a temper, and it would be better if she kept her mouth shut more and didn't get into fights with her former husband and her child, but that's normal within the context of this kind of situation." This is not a severe indictment of a person, but it does support other testimony that petitioner tends to be short-tempered and punitive with her daughter and the inference therefrom that the child is being harmed. There has been no showing, on the other hand, that appellant despite his social isolation, tends to be other than helpful, patient, and constructive in his relationship with his daughter.

It has been shown that petitioner attempts to exclude appellant from the child's life. The Clinical Director and the psychiatrist who met with all concerned believe that, if awarded custody, she will continue to do so. Such acts are "so inconsistent with the best interests of the children as to, per se, raise a strong probability that the mother is unfit to act as custodial parent" (Entwistle v. Entwistle, 402 N.Y.S.2d 213 (1978), *appeal dismissed*, 44 N.Y.2d 851 (1978)).

This court finds the testimony of those experts favoring custody of the child to appellant convincing. . . . The trial court's custody award lacked a sound and substantial basis in the record and should not be allowed to stand.

Notes and Questions

1. Different roles. Mental health experts play different roles in custody determinations: (a) conduct evaluations to assess parenting and children's functioning;

(b) gather data (e.g., from schools, medical personnel, social service agencies, etc.); (c) conduct observations of, and interviews with, the parties; and (d) serve as expert witnesses on issues of child development. Most custody evaluators are psychologists, psychiatrists, or social workers. How might their different backgrounds and training influence the performance of their roles? Should courts limit the number of experts who can participate in a given case? Can you identify the various roles of the mental health experts in *Rebecca B.*?

2. Ethical standards. Professionals in custody determinations must observe professional codes of ethics and standards of practice.[59] Stemming from concerns that custody evaluators should be subject to more strict standards, the Association of Family and Conciliation Courts (AFCC) drafted Model Standards for Custody Evaluators in 2006 (available at www.afccnet.org).

3. Trial court findings. The appellate court in *Rebecca B.* reversed two prior rulings in favor of the mother (and an eight-year-long custody arrangement) on the basis that the trial judge erred by rejecting much of the expert testimony. In a lengthy opinion (Renee B. v. Michael B., No. V5272186 (N.Y. Fam. Ct. May 8, 1992)), trial judge George L. Jurow (who has a Ph.D in clinical psychology) explained his reasons for finding certain testimony "not credible" and "flawed":

- The father's expert's objectivity was compromised by his employment as the father's psychiatrist for four years (slip op. at 87); the expert engaged in "collusive interactions" by interviewing the daughter without the mother's knowledge or consent (id. at 88); the expert's conclusion that the mother was alienating the daughter and was responsible for communication difficulties was "factually incorrect and contradicted by other credible evidence" (id. at 89-90) (because the father's confrontations with school officials led them to ban him from the premises, and the father taped all conversations with the wife and daughter); the expert applied a gender-biased standard in recommending paternal custody based on the mother's demanding career as a corporate lawyer (id. at 91-92).
- The supervising social worker (who recommended a custody transfer to the father) adopted "uncritically and without reflection" the opinion of the father's expert without conducting a thorough evaluation (id. at 100).
- The court-appointed expert's evaluation (1) had "important inquiry lapses" (regarding the father's lack of work history and plan to withdraw the daughter from school) (id. at 81); (2) conflicted with that expert's own observations that the father was an "individual who is socially isolated, has no friends, is prone to continued confrontations with people, [and] is 'interpersonally retarded'" (id. at 82); and (3) failed to recognize that the daughter's desire to live with her father was the "product of paternal pressure or an excessive degree of overbearing influence" (id. at 83).

---

[59]. For relevant standards of practice, see American Psychological Ass'n, Ethical Principles of Psychologists and Code of Conduct, 47 Am. Psychol. 1597 (1992); American Psychological Ass'n, Guidelines for Child Custody Evaluations in Divorce Proceedings, 49 Am. Psychol. 677 (1994); Committee on Ethical Guidelines for Forensic Psychologists, Specialty Guidelines for Forensic Psychologists, 15 Law & Hum. Behav. 655 (1991).

Do you agree with the appellate court that the trial court award "lacked a sound and substantial basis" in the record?

4. Parental Alienation Syndrome. The father's expert based his opinion, in part, on evidence of "Parental Alienation Syndrome," a term that he coined to signify a parent's conscious or subconscious attempts to alienate a client from the other parent.[60] Don't many divorcing parents exhibit varying degrees of this syndrome? Although the theory is admissible in court, it has been severely criticized by professionals who claim that it lacks empirical basis, relies on speculations about mothers' purported unconscious desires and their effects on children, and, minimizes abuse and its effects on mothers and children.

5. Criticisms. Some mental health experts make custody recommendations to the court. What problems are posed by this practice?[61] Are mental health professionals capable of determining custodial arrangements in the best interests of children? Does the practice allow professionals to play a dispositive role, give a false aura of reliability, and result from subjective biases and lifestyle preferences?

Do mental health professionals reflect a bias toward joint custody, even in cases when it might be contraindicated? For example, a recent study raises serious concerns about custody evaluators' recommendations in the context of domestic violence. The study reports that many custody evaluators recommend awards to abusers based on the evaluators' denial or minimization of mothers' reports of IPV.[62]

6. Conflict of interest. One expert in *Rebecca B.* was the father's treating psychiatrist. This dual role implicates a potential conflict of interest that many professionals regard as an ethical violation. Can a mental health expert who is treating one of the parties be objective? One commentator has argued:

> It would be very difficult, if not impossible, in most cases for a clinician to "set aside" the attitudes and feelings that constitute the "therapeutic orientation" that has been developed with a given individual or family in exchange for the more detached, skeptical, and objective stance that is necessary for the forensic evaluator.[63]

Is the harm mitigated if the party is a *former* patient?

---

[60]. Richard A. Gardner, The Parental Alienation Syndrome: A Guide for Mental Health and Legal Professionals (1992). For trenchant critiques, see Carol S. Bruch, Parental Alienation Syndrome and Parental Alienation: Getting It Wrong in Child Custody Cases, 35 Fam. L.Q. 527 (2001); Joan S. Meier, Parental Alienation Syndrome and Parental Alienation: A Research Review (Sept. 2013), www.vawnet.org/assoc_files_vawnet/ar_pasupdate.pdf.

[61]. For an analysis of the risks posed by custody evaluators who make recommendations to the court, compare Timothy M. Tippins & Jeffrey P. Wittmann, Empirical and Ethical Problems with Custody Recommendations: A Call for Clinical Humility and Judicial Vigilance, 43 Fam. Ct. Rev. 193 (2005), with Philip M. Stahl, The Benefits and Risks of Child Custody Evaluators Making Recommendations to the Court: A Response to Tippins and Wittman, 43 Fam. Ct. Rev. 260 (2005). See also Lois Weithorn & Thomas Grisso, Psychological Evaluations in Divorce Custody: Problems, Principles, and Procedures, in Psychology and Child Custody Determinations 157, 160 (Lois Weithorn ed., 1987).

[62]. U.S. Dept. of Justice, Child Custody Evaluators' Beliefs About Domestic Abuse Allegations: Their Relationship to Evaluator Demographics, Background, Domestic Violence Knowledge and Custody-Visitation Recommendations 129 (2011).

[63]. Kirk Heilbrun, Child Custody Evaluation: Critically Assessing Mental Health Experts and Psychological Tests, 29 Fam. L.Q. 63, 70-71 (1995).

7. Epilogue. The custody suit cost Renee B. approximately $340,000; the stress resulted in her losing her job.[64] Her subsequent appeal was denied. 645 N.E.2d 1217 (N.Y. 1994). Her ex-husband then attempted to hold her in contempt for failure to pay child support. Having difficulty complying with service of process, he had the process server accompany Rebecca on her visitation with her mother. Rebecca, then 12 years old, read the legal papers and became distraught at the threat of imprisonment of her mother. On her own initiative, Rebecca contacted her court-appointed guardian and refused to return to her father. She subsequently described her life with her father as verging on abuse: her father prohibited her from calling her mother or sending her letters. Rebecca and her guardian petitioned for a change of custody.

The trial court appointed a new expert, awarded the mother temporary custody, and granted the father supervised visitation. On appeal, the court upheld the temporary award of custody to Renee B. The father subsequently moved out of the area. By his choice, he has had no further contact with the daughter, not even telephone calls on her birthday.[65]

Reflections on the Legacy of In re Rebecca B. [66]

by Judge George L. Jurow
Personal communication, May 12, 2015

In almost 30 years as a trial judge on the New York State Family Court bench in Manhattan, *Rebecca B.* was and remains the most notorious custody case I ever tried. The case was the "perfect [bad] storm" of clinical experts. Three of them aligned with the father for very flawed reasons:

The court-appointed "impartial" psychologist severely misdiagnosed the mother, a corporate attorney, as having serious psychiatric pathology, including being "delusional" in her complaints about the father. In a devastating cross-examination, the mother's concerns were all determined to have a solid basis in fact. The psychologist even admitted that the mother had better skills to be the custodial parent, as she had been for the prior eight years. The real, but shadowy, reason for the psychologist's misdiagnosis of the mother was that he, with a very stoic and humorless demeanor, could not relate to the mother, whose temperament was extroverted and sometimes flippant. In my experience, a disconnect in personality styles between an evaluator and a parent, a form of "interview bias," is a common cause of defective forensic reports.

In very biased testimony, Dr. Richard Gardner promoted his controversial theory of Parental Alienation (watering the label down to maternal "exclusionary" behavior). His conflict of interest was substantial, as the father secretly

[64]. Lisa Genasci, Working Mothers at Risk in Custody Disputes: Divorce: Scholars Say Courts Often Hold Women to Higher Parenting Standards Than Their Ex-Spouses, L.A. Times, Mar. 5, 1995, at A8.

[65]. Telephone interview with Bernard H. Clair, Attorney for Renee B. (Clair Greifer LLP, 555 Madison Avenue, 9th Floor, New York City), Aug. 19, 1997, and June 10, 2006.

[66]. Judge George Jurow, J.D., Ph.D., was the trial judge in *Rebecca B.* His doctorate is in clinical psychology. He continues to preside over custody cases, and frequently lectures and writes about forensic custody issues.

brought the child to see Gardner and cultivated his input. This was "hired gun" testimony at its worst. The third aligned expert's testimony, by a clinical social worker, added nothing because it was her first child custody case so she chose to rely on the reports of the former two experts.

The shining star apart from this trio of dysfunctional experts was Dr. Allen Frances, a renowned psychiatrist and diagnostic expert who later chaired the Duke University Department of Psychiatry. He was brought in to refute the psychologist's diagnosis of the mother. He did so, evaluating the mother as having no psychiatric diagnosis or pathology, concluding that she simply was the custodian in a difficult custody dispute that would upset any such similarly situated parent. He also "peer reviewed" the reports by the psychologist and Dr. Gardner, calling them facially "ludicrous." In dismissing Dr. Frances's testimony because he did not interview the father and child, the appellate court misunderstood that his role was to address the mother's misdiagnosis, which did not require him to see the entire family. Nor did Dr. Frances make a custody recommendation as the appellate court misstated.

The erroneous appellate court reversal—no doubt primarily caused by the misleading anomalous line-up of the flawed experts—was met by a critical reaction by the New York matrimonial bar, who publicly objected that too much power was being given to forensic experts. The uproar was heard by the appellate courts who later "clarified" that they did not intend to usurp the role of trial judges in favor of clinicians.

In recent years, New York appellate courts have done a 180-degree turn by expressing major skepticism about the merits of forensic custody experts. In particular, court-appointed experts who were previously blessed with the imprimatur of neutrality are now more scrutinized because of increased attention paid to bias and methodology problems, as foreshadowed by *Rebecca B.*

5. Modification

a. Standard

The paramount concern with child welfare gives courts continuing power to modify custody orders. The standard for modification is higher than for initial awards of custody in order to ensure stability for the child. The emphasis on stability in child placement decisionmaking is a central tenet of the work by Professors Goldstein, Freud, and Solnit, who strongly oppose alteration in child placement based on the child's need for continuity of care. See Joseph Goldstein et al., Beyond the Best Interests of the Child 37 (1973).

Different standards. According to the prevailing standard, the plaintiff has the burden of showing by a preponderance of the evidence that *conditions since the dissolution decree have so materially and substantially changed that the children's best interests require a change of custody*. A few states have a more liberal requirement that modification serve the best interests of the child (regardless of any change in circumstances). Some states adopt an even lower standard when the change pertains to modification of a custodial time allocation rather than a modification of custody. Several states have more stringent rules, influenced by UMDA §409(b) requiring endangerment for nonconsensual changes. Absent serious endangerment, UMDA §409(a) provides for a two-year waiting period following the initial decree.

Do liberal modification standards threaten the constitutionally-based privacy of the postdivorce family? See Joan G. Wexler, Rethinking the Modification of Child Custody Decrees, 94 Yale L.J. 757, 803-818 (1985) (so suggesting). Relying on social science evidence that the custodial parent and child require time for postdivorce adjustment, Wexler supports a type of "serious endangerment" standard, under which the noncustodial parent must prove that modification would outweigh any disruption caused by the change. Further, she argues for a presumption against modification for children under three years of age. What do you think of these suggestions?

Joint custody. Joint custody awards also may be changed if custody arrangements prove unsuccessful or if circumstances change. Some states ease the traditional rule when sole custody is modified to joint, requiring only that the change to joint custody be in the best interests of the child. See, e.g., Alaska Stat. §25.20.110; Mont. Code Ann. §40-4-219.

ALI. The ALI recommends modification upon a showing of (1) a substantial change in the circumstances (relating to the child or one or both parents) on which the parenting plan was based that makes modification necessary for the child's welfare or (2) harm to the child. ALI Principles §2.15(1) & (2). Note that the ALI standard "necessary to the child's welfare" is stricter than that in many state approaches. Changed circumstances must be based on facts "that were not known or have arisen since the entry of the prior order and were not anticipated." Id. §2.15(1). Modification based on a more liberal standard is available for consensual changes, changes in the existing arrangements without objection by the parent opposing the modification, minor modifications to the parenting plan, or the attainment of a specified age for a child who expresses a preference for a custodial change. Id. cmt. a. None of the following justifies modification, absent a showing of harm: a parent's loss of income or employment, remarriage or cohabitation, or use of day care. Id. §2.15(3).

In response to the concern that standards facilitating custody modification do not serve the child's interests, one commentator urges that lawyers encourage clients to use mediation, if possible, and "discourage clients with minor complaints from continually attempting to relitigate custody."[67] In contrast, another commentator suggests that custody arrangements should automatically be reevaluated when children become adolescents, giving special emphasis to children's custodial preferences.[68] Which view do you find more compelling?

---

[67]. Linda D. Elrod, When Should Custody Orders Be Modified? Flexibility versus Stability, 26 Fam. Advoc. 40, 41 (2004).

[68]. Jacqueline Genesio Lux, Growing Pains that Cannot Be Ignored: Automatic Reevaluation of Custody Arrangements at Child's Adolescence, 44 Fam. L.Q. 445, 464 (2010).

Problem

When Roderic and Melinda divorce, they agree to share joint legal custody of their daughter, Geena, who is a preschooler. Melinda has primary physical custody and Roderic has liberal visitation. Four years later, after both Roderick and Melinda have remarried, Roderic files a motion to modify custody. He argues that the circumstances warrant a change to joint physical custody because, in the last four months, Geena's school performance has seriously declined. At the hearing, Geena's elementary schoolteacher, Barbara, testifies that Geena, an exceptionally bright student, performed very well during the first two quarters of the school year, but recently she has failed to complete assignments, forgotten to turn in homework, started talking in class, and earned failing grades. Barbara also testifies that she often discusses Geena's academic performance with Roderic and communicates with him by e-mail because he regularly inquires about Geena's progress. By contrast, Barbara has little contact with Melinda.

Roderic testifies regarding his frequent contacts with Geena's teacher. He also explains that he and his new wife value education and therefore can best assist Geena in her studies. Melinda testifies that she and her new husband also frequently assist Geena with her homework. Melinda attributes the decline in Geena's school performance to the increased conflict from her parents' constant custody disputes. Psychologist Joann Lippert, who conducted a family evaluation report, testifies about Geena's strong attachment to both parents and her desire to maintain a relationship with each. Dr. Lippert recommends that both parents should share physical custody because Geena's best interests would be served if both of her parents were actively involved in their daughter's education. Has there been a substantial change in circumstances affecting Geena's welfare that would warrant modification of custody? In addition, is modification in the child's best interests? What result? Ellis v. Carucci, 161 P.3d 239 (Nev. 2007).

b. Relocation

CIESLUK v. CIESLUK

113 P.3d 135 (Colo. 2005)

Justice Rice delivered the Opinion of the Court.

. . . Mother and Father met and married in Nebraska in 1995. One child, Connor, was born to them on February 27, 1997. In September 2002, the parties amicably divorced. [M]other is the primary residential parent for school residency and other legal residential requirements; Father has parenting time on two weekends and two weekday evenings per month. Mother and Father have joint parental responsibility and decision-making authority.

In February 2003, Mother, a Sprint employee for seven years, was laid off as a result of Sprint's workforce reduction in Colorado. She sought alternative employment in Colorado and in Arizona, where her father, brother, sister-in-law, and nephew reside. Though she was unable to find a comparable job in Colorado,

Sprint interviewed her for a position in Arizona. However, Sprint refused to extend her an offer until she committed to relocating to Arizona.

Consequently, in March 2003, Mother filed a motion to modify parenting time pursuant to [Colo. Rev. Stat. §14-10-129] to allow her to relocate. [After the father opposed the motion, the court appointed a special advocate.] The special advocate concluded that the father's presence in the child's life would be greatly reduced as a result of the relocation and recommended, therefore, that it was in Connor's best interests to stay in close proximity to both Mother and Father. [The trial court denied the mother's motion for modification, stating that "parenthood results in some sacrifice and it is better off for parents to remain in close proximity."] In making this determination, the trial court gave substantial weight to the impact of the move on Connor's relationship with Father and to Mother's failure to establish how the move would "enhance" Connor. Mother appealed.

We first address whether the [custodial presumption test that was articulated in In re Marriage of Francis, 919 P.2d 776 (Colo. 1996) remains viable.] In response to dissatisfaction with *Francis*, the General Assembly amended section 14-10-129, [to require a court to consider not only the normal best-interest factors, but nine special factors, including: reasons why the party wishes to relocate; reasons why the opposing party is objecting; the history and quality of each party's relationship with the child; the educational opportunities for the child at each location; the presence or absence of extended family at each location; any advantages of the child remaining with the primary caregiver; the anticipated impact of the move on the child; whether the court will be able to fashion a new reasonable parenting time schedule; and any other relevant factors bearing on the best interests of the child.] Here, the General Assembly's intent to eliminate the *Francis* presumption is readily apparent on the face of the statute [as well as] the legislative history of the statute. . . .

[W]e turn next to Mother's alternative argument, namely that section 14-10-129, absent a presumption in favor of allowing her to move, discourages her from relocating, and unconstitutionally infringes upon her right to travel. It is well established that a citizen has the right to travel between states. See, e.g., Shapiro v. Thompson, 394 U.S. 618, 629-31 (1969). This right encompasses the right to "migrate, resettle, find a new job, and start a new life." "[I]t makes no difference that the parent who wishes to relocate is not prohibited outright from doing so; a legal rule that operates to chill the exercise of the right, absent a sufficient state interest to do so, is as impermissible as one that bans exercise of the right altogether." Here, though section 14-10-129 does not prohibit outright a majority time parent from relocating, it chills the exercise of that parent's right to travel because, in seeking to relocate, that parent risks losing majority parent status with respect to the minor child.

However, a majority time parent's right to travel is not the sole constitutional right at issue in relocation cases. In addition, a minority time parent has an equally important constitutional right to the care and control of the child. Though consideration of the parents' competing constitutional interests is important in relocation cases, the conflict is not simply between the parents' needs and desires. Rather, the issue in relocation cases is the extent to which the parents' needs and desires are intertwined with the child's best interests. [Although] most courts that have considered this question have acknowledged that the right to travel is implicated when a child's majority time parent seeks to remove the child from the state, these courts cannot agree on how to balance the right to travel with the rights of the minority time parent in a best interests of the child analysis. Instead, three distinct approaches have developed.

The first, Wyoming's, elevates the relocating parent's right to travel over the other competing interests. [Watt v. Watt, 971 P.2d 608 (Wyo. 1999).] The second approach, adopted in Minnesota, eliminates the need to balance the parents' competing constitutional rights in favor of elevating the child's welfare to a compelling state interest. [LaChapelle v. Mitten, 607 N.W.2d 151 (Minn. Ct. App. 2000).] The third approach, New Mexico's, treats all the competing interests as equal, holding that both parents' constitutional interests, as well as the best interests of the child, will be best protected if each parent shares equally in the burden of demonstrating how the child's best interests will be impacted by the proposed relocation. [Jaramillo v. Jaramillo, 823 P.2d 299 (N.M. 1991).] . . . For the reasons set forth below, we adopt the reasoning set forth in *Jaramillo* for relocation disputes in Colorado. . . .

[A] court must begin its analysis with each parent on equal footing; a court may not presume either that a child is better off or disadvantaged by relocating with the majority time parent. Rather, the majority time parent has the duty to present specific, non-speculative information about the child's proposed new living conditions, as well as a concrete plan for modifying parenting time as a result of the move. The minority time parent may choose to contest the relocation in its totality, and thus seek to become the majority time or primary residential parent. Alternatively, the minority time parent may choose not to contest the relocation, but rather object to the revised parenting plan proposed by the majority time parent. In such a circumstance, the minority time parent has the responsibility to propose his or her own parenting plan. Thus, each parent has the burden to persuade the court that the relocation of the child will be in or contrary to the child's best interests, or that the parenting plan he or she proposes should be adopted by the court.

The focus of the court, however, should be the best interests of the child. The court may decide that it is not in the best interests of the child to relocate with the majority time parent. Then, if the majority time parent still wishes to relocate, a new parenting time plan will be necessary. Alternatively, the court may decide that it is in the best interests of the child to relocate with the majority time parent. In that situation, the court must fashion a parenting time plan which protects the constitutional right of the minority time parent to care for and control the child. In either event, the court must thoroughly disclose the reasons for its decision and make specific findings with respect to each of the statutory factors.

[W]e now address the trial court's application of subsection 14-10-129(2)(c) . . . First, the trial court erred when it failed to properly address whether remaining with his primary caregiver would provide Connor any advantages. [The] court reasonably could have concluded that Connor would benefit directly and indirectly by remaining with Mother if she were to relocate to Arizona. As a direct benefit, Connor would enjoy the stability of remaining with his majority time parent. Connor also would benefit from having day-to-day relationships with his grandfather, uncle, aunt, and nephew. Finally, Mother's increased financial stability and family support would undoubtedly increase her own happiness, which would benefit Connor by giving him a more stable home life. This indirect benefit to Connor is not diminished simply because it primarily benefits Mother. . . .

Having failed to discuss advantages to Connor in relocating with Mother, the trial court then proceeded to relate its concern that Mother:

> "continues to believe that whatever is in her best interest is also in Connor's best interest. The Court notes her reasons to relocate. They are all from her point of view and her benefit, job, help from her family which then, I guess, are indirect benefits to Connor but there was nothing directly about how this would *enhance* Connor" (emphasis added).

[R]equiring a parent to show that a move will "enhance the quality of life for the child" is a remnant of the *Francis* test that the General Assembly did not adopt in amending section 14-10-129 Most importantly, the trial court did not impose an equal burden on Father. [A]s a result, Mother was required to carry an unequal share of the burden in demonstrating Connor's best interests.

The trial court aggravated these errors . . . by relying on a general conclusion that parents should remain in close proximity to the child. In reaching this conclusion, the trial court cited an article from the Journal of Family Psychology [citing Sanford L. Braver et al., Relocation of Children after Divorce and Children's Best Interests: New Evidence and Legal Considerations, J. Fam. Psychol., June 2003, at 206]. Though the article's authors stated, "our data cannot establish with certainty that moves cause children substantial harm," the trial court nevertheless interpreted the article as concluding that "a child is generally not benefited by moving away with the custodial parent from a non-custodial parent." Presumably based upon the Braver's article, the court then concluded that "[p]arenthood results in some sacrifice and it is better off for parents to remain in close proximity." [T]he effect of this generalization was to create a presumption in favor of the minority time parent opposing relocation.

Moreover, Braver's article represents only one of many schools of thought on how parenting time affects children. One theory provides that a child's interests are so aligned with the well-being of the majority time parent that that person's decision on behalf of the child should be honored unless there is proof that the decisions are bad ones. [Judith S. Wallerstein & Tony J. Tanke, To Move or Not to Move: Psychological and Legal Considerations in the Relocation of Children Following Divorce, 30 Fam. L.Q. 305, 318 (1996)] Another theory suggests that both parents are entitled to raise the child and that it is extremely important for a child to develop a relationship with both parents. [Joan B. Kelly & Michael E. Lamb, Using Child Development Research to Make Appropriate Custody and Access Decisions for Young Children, 38 Fam. & Conciliation Cts. Rev. 297, 309 (2000).]

A court's duty is not to determine which of these theories is correct. Rather, a court's sole duty in relocation cases is to determine the best interests of a child based upon the facts of each individual case. . . . The trial court in this case failed to perform its duty in accordance with the statute because it imposed an unequal burden on Mother and created a presumption in favor of Father that was potentially contrary to Connor's best interests. [Reversed and remanded with instructions for a new trial.]

Notes and Questions

1. **Frequency of relocation.** Geographic mobility is a fact of life. Within four years after separation or divorce, 75 percent of custodial mothers relocate at least once, and half of these will relocate again.[69] Relocation controversies frequently arise postdivorce when the custodial parent decides to relocate for reasons of remarriage, employment, educational opportunities, or support from relatives.

2. **Good faith and motives.** Many courts consider good faith as a threshold requirement in relocation disputes. How does a court determine its existence? Courts also require that the custodial parent have a legitimate motive. What is the difference between good faith and motive? What motives are legitimate? A desire to be closer to the petitioner's parents? See In re Martin, 8 A.3d 60 (N.H. 2010). Remarriage? See Raffa v. Raffa, 945 N.Y.S.2d 766 (App. Div. 2012). Better employment? Compare Odell v. Odell, 139 So. 3d 1275 (3d Cir. 2014) (hope of opportunity was insufficient to support move), with Newman v. Duffy, 3 N.Y.S.3d 847 (App. Div. 2015) (allowing relocation due to stepfather's transfer). Was Michelle Ciesluk's motive legitimate?

3. **Procedural posture.** Relocation disputes may arise because a decree, statute, or marital settlement agreement requires a custodial parent to seek permission to leave the jurisdiction. Or, the noncustodial parent may petition to enjoin the move and, sometimes, request a custody modification. Absent statutory authority or a settlement agreement, can a trial judge who is making an *initial* custody determination order a parent to live in a specific location? Compare Spahmer v. Gullette, 113 P.3d 158 (Colo. 2005), with Meadows v. Meadows, 3 So. 3d 221 (Ala. Civ. App. 2008).

4. **Burden of proof.** According to *Ciesluk*, what is the burden of proof and which parent should bear it? In relocation disputes, some courts place the burden of proof on the relocating custodial parent to prove that the move is in the child's best interests. Other states place the burden of proof on the noncustodial opposing parent to demonstrate the adverse impact of the relocation. Who do you think should bear the burden of proof?

What should be the burden of proof? That the move is "necessary"? That there is a "compelling reason" for the move? That there are "exceptional circumstances" justifying the move? See Tropea v. Tropea, 642 N.Y.S.2d 575 (N.Y. 1996). That the move will provide a real advantage to the child—or the new family unit? Does a direct benefit in the custodial parent's quality of life translate into a direct benefit to the child? See J.M.R. v. J.M., 1 A.3d 902 (Pa. Super. Ct. 2010). Or conversely, does the noncustodial parent have to show that the move will result in detriment to the child? Does any interference with visitation constitute sufficient detriment? Should the court consider also the possible detriment from disrupting the child's relationship with the custodial parent? See In re Marriage of LaMusga, 88 P.3d 81, 100 (Cal. 2004) (Justice Kennard, dissenting).

---

[69]. Sarah L. Gottfried, Note, Virtual Visitation: The New Wave of Communication Between Children and Non-Custodial Parents in Relocation Cases, 9 Cardozo Women's L.J. 567, 568 (2003) (citing data).

5. Modification. Does relocation automatically constitute a substantial change in circumstances that warrants modification? See Fowler v. Sowers, 151 S.W.3d 357 (Ky. 2003); Arnott v. Arnott, 293 P.3d 440 (Wyo. 2012).

6. Joint custody. Many jurisdictions apply more restrictive relocation rules to parents with joint custody. Why? How should courts resolve such relocation disputes? In these disputes, should courts take into account a parent's *actual* involvement with a child rather than the legal label? See Kawatra v. Kawatra, 182 S.W.3d 800 (Tenn. 2005).

7. Trend and countertrend. Until recently, the trend in relocation cases favored the custodial parent's presumptive right to move. See In re Marriage of Burgess, 913 P.2d 473 (Cal. 1996) (initiating trend). Courts have moved toward a more fact-specific, case-by-case analysis (illustrated by *Ciesluk*).

8. Right to travel. How does *Ciesluk* accommodate the constitutional rights at issue in relocation disputes? Why does it adopt that approach? Which approach do you favor and why? Do the best interests of the child serve as a compelling state interest to overcome the custodial parent's right to travel? See Hood v. Hood, 282 P.3d 671 (Mont. 2012).

Do relocation restrictions infringe on a parent's right to travel or only on a parent's right to travel *with* the child? Should courts consider the noncustodial parent's ability and/or plans to relocate as well? See Quainoo v. Morelon-Quainoo, 87 So. 3d 364 (La. Ct. App. 2012). See generally David V. Chipman & Mindy M. Rush, The Necessity of "Right to Travel" Analysis in Custodial Parent Relocation Cases, 10 Wyo. L. Rev. 267 (2010).

The argument that relocation restrictions violate the right to travel was first advanced over 30 years ago in a classic law review article by a prominent family law professor.[70] By inhibiting custodial parents, but not noncustodial parents, from moving, do relocation restrictions violate equal protection? See, e.g., Fredman v. Fredman, 960 So. 2d 52 (Fla. Dist. Ct. App. 2007). Is requiring a parent to forgo moving in order to retain custody an infringement of parental autonomy and family privacy? See, e.g., Taylor v. Taylor, 849 S.W.2d 319, 329-331 (Tenn. 1993).

9. Gender bias. Do restrictions on a custodial parent's right to relocate reflect gender bias? Do they reinforce traditional gender roles? Consider the following:

> The standard role pattern in marriage was for the husband to predominate in decision making, including the decision of where the family would live, and to provide for the family's financial support. In exchange for this support, the wife was to care for the household and children and follow the husband in his choice of domicile. . . .
>
> [However] in the large number of cases where custodial mothers have remarried and seek to relocate to accompany their spouses, this "child support for child care services" approach creates a paradox. Simply stated, the mother cannot provide services to two husbands at the same time. She cannot fulfill her traditional duty to care for the children and keep them available to both an ex-husband and

---

[70]. Brigitte M. Bodenheimer, Equal Rights, Visitation, and the Right to Move, 1 Fam. Advoc. 18 (1978).

a present husband when the two have chosen geographically distant domiciles. [Restrictions] only serve to create a domiciliary "squatter's rights." The first husband to choose a domicile for the mother is given tremendous leverage . . . to keep the mother caring for his children within his easy access. . . . Yet the custom for the wife to follow her husband in his choice of marital domicile applies as much to the new spouse as it did to the former spouse.[71]

10. Children's interests. Do courts pay sufficient attention to children's interests in relocation disputes? Does *Ciesluk* take into account the child's interests and preferences? See generally Linda D. Elrod, National and International Momentum Builds for More Child Focus in Relocation Disputes, 44 Fam. L.Q. 341 (2010).

11. Intercountry moves. Should the same rules govern interstate and intercountry moves? See In re Marriage of Coulter, 964 N.E.2d 1159 (Ill. App. Ct. 2012); Wiencko v. Takayama, 745 S.E.2d 168 (Va. Ct. App. 2013). May a parent restrict the other parent's right to travel with the children to *certain* countries, particularly where a United States court's jurisdiction over child custody may not be enforced? Several states have statutes that require courts to consider certain abduction factors, such as whether the other country is a signatory to the Hague Convention on the Civil Aspects of International Child Abduction (discussed later in this chapter).

12. Effect of relocation on children. In accommodating interests in relocation disputes, should courts take into account research on the effects of relocation on children? How does *Ciesluk* address the role of social science data in relocation disputes?

Considerable controversy exists on the effects of relocation on children. Psychologist Judith Wallerstein argues that allowing the custodial parent to relocate with the children promotes the latter's best interests because children's postdivorce adjustment is closely entwined with the well-being of the custodial parent.[72] Psychologist Richard Warshak counters that these findings rest on few cases and derive from an earlier era when divorced fathers played a less important role in childrearing.[73] Another study (by Braver, Fabricius, and Ellman, cited in *Ciesluk*) confirms the negative effects of relocation for children who move at least one hour's drive from the noncustodial parent.[74] In rebuttal, sociologist Norval Glenn points out that the effects are not significant regarding the most important areas of psychological well-being (i.e., friendships, dating behavior, substance abuse, and general life satisfaction).[75]

---

[71]. Janet M. Bowermaster, Sympathizing with Solomon: Choosing Between Parents in a Mobile Society, 31 J. Fam. L. 791, 843-845 (1992-1993). See also Julie Hixson-Lambson, Consigning Women to the Immediate Orbit of a Man: How Missouri's Relocation Law Substitutes Judicial Paternalism for Parental Judgment by Forcing Parents to Live Near One Another, 54 St. Louis U. L.J. 1365, 1369 (2010).

[72]. Judith S. Wallerstein & Tony J. Tanke, To Move or Not to Move: Psychological and Legal Considerations in the Relocation of Children Following Divorce, 30 Fam. L.Q. 305, 318 (1996).

[73]. Richard A. Warshak, Social Science and Children's Best Interests in Relocation Cases: *Burgess* Revisited, 34 Fam. L.Q. 83 (2000).

[74]. Sanford L. Braver et al., Relocation of Children after Divorce and Children's Best Interests: New Evidence and Legal Considerations, J. Fam. Psychol., June 2003, at 206.

[75]. Norval Glenn & David Blankenhorn, Does Moving After Divorce Damage Kids? (2003). For another critique, see Carol S. Bruch, Sound Research or Wishful Thinking in Child Custody Cases? Lessons from Relocation Law, 40 Fam. L.Q. 281 (2006).

Should relocation disputes take into account empirical findings that document the gradual *decrease* in divorced fathers' visitation patterns? Sociologists Frank Furstenberg and Andrew Cherlin challenge the importance of children's maintenance of ties with their noncustodial parents. They contend:

> These negative findings about the importance of contact with the father have surprised and puzzled experts in the field. Perhaps the negative findings result from the low levels of contact that most divorced fathers maintain. . . . Although we still advocate strengthening ties to fathers, we believe that public policy should place lower priority on this objective than on [principles that emphasize promoting the effective functioning of custodial parents in order to improve their children's adjustment and to decrease children's exposure to parental conflict].[76]

See also Judith S. Wallerstein & Julia M. Lewis, Divorced Fathers and Their Adult Offspring: Report from a Twenty-Five Year Longitudinal Study, 42 Fam. L.Q. 695 (2009) (pointing out that the relationship between fathers and children at divorce does not predict their postdivorce relationship).

13. Domestic violence. Relocation controversies pose special risks for victims of domestic violence. Why? Can such risks be alleviated? How should courts address requests motivated by this reason? See, e.g., Matter of Eddington v. McCabe, 949 N.Y.S.2d 734 (App. Div. 2012). See generally Catherine F. Klein et al., Border Crossings: Understanding the Civil, Criminal, and Immigration Implications for Battered Women Fleeing Across State Lines with Their Children, 39 Fam. L.Q. 109 (2005).

14. Law reform. The ALI Principles permit a primary parent to relocate with the child if that parent has been exercising a significant majority of custodial responsibility and has a legitimate reason for moving to a location that is reasonable in light of the purpose. Relocation justifies a custody modification only when it "significantly impairs" either parent's ability to exercise custodial responsibilities. ALI Principles §2.17(1). In this event, the court will revise the parenting plan to accommodate the relocation while maintaining the same proportion of residential responsibility.

Two Australian scholars suggested law reforms based on their five-year study of relocation disputes in that country. They recommend that "good faith" should be irrelevant in decisionmaking and children should not be placed in the center of the conflict. They propose that courts resolve relocation disputes based on the following determinations: (1) how close is the nonresidential parent-child relationship and how important is that relationship developmentally to the child, (2) if the relocation is to be permitted, how viable are the proposals for contact with the nonresident parent, and (3) if the nonresidential parent-child relationship is developmentally important to the child and is likely to be diminished if the move is allowed, then (a) what are the viable alternatives to the parents living a long

[76]. Frank F. Furstenberg, Jr. & Andrew J. Cherlin, Divided Families: What Happens to Children When Parents Part 107 (1991).

distance apart? and (b) is a move with the primary caregiver the least detrimental alternative?[77] What do you think of these proposals?

15. Virtual visitation. Some courts and legislatures authorize "virtual visitation," electronic arrangements of visitation and parental sharing of information (regarding health, extracurricular activities, and childcare). Several states (Texas, Utah, Wisconsin, Illinois, North Carolina, and Florida) have enacted laws authorizing courts to order virtual visitation in custody proceedings.[78] What do you think of this solution?

Problem

Mother and Father divorce in Vermont when their daughter is two years old. The divorce order, based on the parties' stipulation, provides that Mother will have sole legal custody. For the next few years until the daughter starts school, the parents share her time roughly equally. Thereafter, Father's contact is reduced to one-third when the daughter starts school. Soon thereafter, Mother notifies Father that she and her fiancé intend to move to Maryland for his employment. Mother, who had lost her teaching job because of budget cuts, plans to look for a teaching position in Maryland. Mother files a motion to modify the parent-child contact schedule that was established in final divorce orders, and Father opposes her motion and seeks sole custody. What result? See Hawkes v. Spence, 878 A.2d 273 (Vt. 2005) (adopting ALI relocation standard). See also Hayes v. Gallacher, 972 P.2d 1138 (Nev. 1999).

6. Jurisdiction and Enforcement

1. UCCJA. Prior to the late 1960s, a state could assert jurisdiction over child custody if it had a "substantial interest" in the case.[79] This interest might stem from the marital domicile or the current residence of either parent or the child. Such a vague standard often led to concurrent assertions of jurisdiction. In addition, because of judicial willingness to reopen custody decisions at the behest of a state resident, decrees were freely modifiable in other states. Supreme Court decisions left unclear whether custody decisions were entitled to the protection of the Full Faith and Credit Clause. The ease with which parents could reopen child custody cases in other states has been described as "a rule of seize-and-run." May v. Anderson, 345 U.S. 528, 542 (1953) (Jackson, J., dissenting).

The Uniform Child Custody Jurisdiction Act (UCCJA) was drafted in 1968 to reduce jurisdictional competition and confusion, as well as to deter parents from forum shopping to relitigate custody. A version of the UCCJA, which applied

[77]. Patrick Parkinson & Judy Cashmore, Reforming Relocation Law: An Evidence-Based Approach, 53 Fam. Ct. Rev. 23 (2015).

[78]. Thomson Reuters, FindLaw, Virtual Visitation (2015), http://family.findlaw.com/child-custody/virtual-visitation.html. See generally Jason LaMarca, Note, Virtually Possible—Using the Internet to Facilitate Custody and Parenting Beyond Relocation, 38 Rutgers Computer & Tech. L.J. 146 (2012).

[79]. Leonard Ratner, Child Custody in a Federal System, 62 Mich. L. Rev. 795, 808 (1964).

to initial custody decisions as well as modifications, was adopted in every state by 1981. The UCCJA identified four alternative bases of jurisdiction (explained below); sought to locate jurisdiction in the forum with access to the most evidence relevant to the custody decision; attempted to ensure that proceedings would occur in one state at a time; and mandated recognition, enforcement, and non-modification of a decree from another state with jurisdiction under the UCCJA.

The four alternative bases for taking jurisdiction included: the child's home state, a significant connection between the state and the parties, emergency jurisdiction when the child is present and the child's welfare is threatened, and the fact that no other state has jurisdiction. "Home state" was defined as the state in which the child lived (immediately preceding the time involved) with a parent or parents for at least six consecutive months.

2. PKPA. In 1980 Congress enacted the Parental Kidnapping Prevention Act (PKPA), 28 U.S.C. §1738A. Despite its title, the PKPA is also relevant in cases involving jurisdiction over child custody. The PKPA was drafted for several reasons. First, it attempted to provide rules that would apply in all states, even those that might never enact the UCCJA. (By the late 1970s, only about half of the states had enacted the UCCJA.) Second, the UCCJA did not obtain the hoped-for uniformity in the treatment of custody disputes because some state legislatures changed the UCCJA provisions, and some state courts interpreted those provisions in different ways.

A principal purpose of the PKPA is to ensure that custody decrees issued by states asserting jurisdiction in conformity with the PKPA receive recognition and enforcement in other states through full faith and credit. The PKPA improved upon the UCCJA in two ways. First, unlike the UCCJA, the PKPA prioritizes the bases of jurisdiction. Specifically, the PKPA gives priority to the "home state" of the child in determining which state may exercise jurisdiction in a custody dispute. Second, the PKPA and UCCJA differ on jurisdiction to modify custody. More than one state might have asserted jurisdiction to modify, under the UCCJA's language. The PKPA provides that once a state has exercised jurisdiction, the initial decree-granting state has "*exclusive* continuing jurisdiction," so long as it remains the residence of the child or any contestant.

3. UCCJEA. Virtually all states have adopted the Uniform Child Custody Jurisdiction and Enforcement Act (UCCJEA), promulgated in 1997 to harmonize some of the differences between the UCCJA and PKPA. The UCCJEA differs from its predecessor UCCJA in several ways. Whereas the UCCJA did not prioritize among the four bases of jurisdiction, the UCCJEA follows the PKPA in giving priority to home state jurisdiction. The UCCJEA also goes beyond the PKPA by eliminating the "best interests" language from the second ("significant connection") basis of jurisdiction and, in addition, severely restricts the use of emergency jurisdiction to the issuance of temporary orders. Like the PKPA, the UCCJEA provides strict requirements for modification: the state that makes the initial custody determination has exclusive continuing jurisdiction so long as a child or parent in the original custody determination remains in that state.

The UCCJEA encompasses all custody and visitation decrees (temporary, permanent, initial, and modifications) and covers those proceedings related to divorce, separation, neglect, abuse, dependency, guardianship, paternity, termination of parental rights, and protection from domestic violence (but not adoptions).

One other improvement in the UCCJEA concerns the law's response in cases of domestic violence. Under the UCCJA and PKPA, temporary emergency jurisdiction arises in extraordinary circumstances where a child is present in a state and subjected to, or threatened with, mistreatment or abuse. However, the UCCJEA §204(a) permits a court to exercise emergency jurisdiction to protect the *child, its siblings, or its parents* (not only the particular child in question).

The UCCJEA provisions regarding initial jurisdiction, exclusive continuing jurisdiction, and modification are set forth below.

UNIFORM CHILD CUSTODY JURISDICTION & ENFORCEMENT ACT

§201. INITIAL CHILD-CUSTODY JURISDICTION

(a) Except as otherwise provided in Section 204 [dealing with emergency jurisdiction over abandoned or abused/neglected children] (below), a court of this State has jurisdiction to make an initial child-custody determination only if:

(1) this State is the home state of the child on the date of the commencement of the proceeding, or was the home State of the child within six months before the commencement of the proceeding and the child is absent from this State but a parent or person acting as a parent continues to live in this State;

(2) a court of another State does not have jurisdiction under paragraph (1), or a court of the home State of the child has declined to exercise jurisdiction on the ground that this State is the more appropriate forum . . . and:

(A) the child and the child's parents, or the child and at least one parent or a person acting as a parent, have a significant connection with this State other than mere physical presence; and

(B) substantial evidence is available in this State concerning the child's care, protection, training, and personal relationships;

(3) all courts having jurisdiction under paragraph (1) or (2) have declined to exercise jurisdiction on the ground that a court of this State is the more appropriate forum to determine the custody of the child . . . or

(4) no court of any other State would have jurisdiction under the criteria specified in paragraph (1), (2), or (3)

(b) Subsection (a) is the exclusive jurisdictional basis for making a child-custody determination by a court of this State.

(c) Physical presence of, or personal jurisdiction over, a party or a child is not necessary or sufficient to make a child-custody determination.

§202. EXCLUSIVE, CONTINUING JURISDICTION

(a) Except as otherwise provided in Section 204 [emergency jurisdiction] (below), a court of this State which has made a child-custody determination consistent with Section 201 or 203 has exclusive, continuing jurisdiction over the determination until:

(1) a court of this State determines that neither the child, the child's parents, and any person acting as a parent do not have a significant connection with this State and that substantial evidence is no longer available in this State concerning the child's care, protection, training, and personal relationships; or

(2) a court of this State or a court of another State determines that the child, the child's parents, and any person acting as a parent do not presently reside in this State.

(b) a court of this State which has made a child-custody determination and does not have exclusive, continuing jurisdiction under this section may modify that determination only if it has jurisdiction to make an initial determination under Section 201.

§203. JURISDICTION TO MODIFY DETERMINATION

(a) Except as otherwise provided in Section 204 [emergency jurisdiction] (below), a court of this State may not modify a child-custody determination made by a court of another State unless a court of this State has jurisdiction to make an initial determination under Section 201(a)(1) or (2) and:

(1) the court of the other State determines it no longer has exclusive, continuing jurisdiction under Section 202 or that a court of this State would be a more convenient forum . . . ; or

(2) a court of this State or a court of the other State determines that the child, the child's parents, and any person acting as a parent do not presently reside in the other State.

§204. TEMPORARY EMERGENCY JURISDICTION

(a) A court of this State has temporary emergency jurisdiction if the child is present in this State and the child has been abandoned or it is necessary in an emergency to protect the child because the child, or a sibling or parent of the child, is subjected to or threatened with mistreatment or abuse. . . .

---

4. Remedies. What remedies are available to contestants who might be awarded conflicting decrees by two states? May they seek resolution in federal court? In Thompson v. Thompson, 484 U.S. 174 (1988), the U.S. Supreme Court held that the PKPA did *not* create an implied cause of action in federal court to determine which of two conflicting state custody decrees is valid, based on the statutory language and legislative history.

The PKPA also assists parents in locating an abducting parent by making the federal parent locator service available to state agencies and applying the Fugitive Felon Act, 18 U.S.C. §1073, to all state felony parental kidnapping cases. The parent locator service was established to assist state welfare departments to locate and force "deadbeat dads" to provide child support. Some proposed to make the service available to private individuals as well as official agencies. However, in the face of resistance by Department of Health and Human Services officials (concerning possible expense and invasions of privacy), the PKPA made the service available only to official agencies.

Additional remedies to enforce custody determinations include civil contempt proceedings and the writ of habeas corpus. Some states also recognize (either by case law or statute) a tort action for custodial interference that may apply to impose liability on a parent for abduction or concealment of a child. See, e.g., Khalifa v. Shannon, 945 A.2d 1244 (Md. 2008). According to the Restatement (Second) of Torts §700 (1977), the tort of interference with the parent-child relationship requires that "[o]ne who, with knowledge that the parent does not consent, abducts or otherwise compels or induces a minor child to leave a parent legally entitled to its custody or not to return to the parent after it has been left him, is subject to liability to the parent." Some states also impose criminal liability for custodial interference. See State v. Froland, 936 A.2d 947 (N.J. 2007). Some states provide exceptions to custodial interference laws for a victim of domestic violence who flees with a child. See, e.g., Fla. Stat. §787.03(2), (4)(b).

NOTE: INTERNATIONAL CHILD ABDUCTION

International parental abductions pose a vexing legal problem. More than 1,000 children are abducted either to or from the United States annually.[80] The rise in international abductions stems from the ease of international transportation as well as the increasing number of binational marriages.[81] The return of these children to the United States depends on the application of the Hague Convention on the Civil Aspects of International Child Abduction. Currently, 93 nations are signatories to this international treaty, including the United States.[82] The United States implemented the Convention by enabling legislation, the International Child Abduction Remedies Act (ICARA), 42 U.S.C. §§9001-9011.

The goal of the Hague Convention is to secure the return of children who are wrongfully removed from or retained in a signatory state and to return them to the country of their "habitual residence" (which must be another contracting nation), where the merits of the custody dispute can be adjudicated. Article 13 of the Convention specifies three affirmative defenses that may be invoked by a taking parent to defeat the child's return: (1) if the taking parent establishes that the child's caretaker was not actually exercising custody rights at the time of removal or retention or had consented to removal or retention; (2) if the taking parent establishes a grave risk that the return would entail physical or psychological harm to the child; and (3) if the court in the forum of the taking parent finds that the child, who has attained an appropriate age and maturity (based on the court's discretion), objects to the return.[83]

The Hague Convention was based on the idea that the likely abductor was a noncustodial father. However, the majority of international parental abductions are carried out by custodial mothers, many of whom are fleeing domestic violence. As a governmental report explains, "the intended beneficiaries of the Convention have become its primary targets."[84] In the past few years, the Supreme Court has heard several important Hague Convention cases.

---

[80]. U.S. Senate Comm. on Foreign Relations, Chairman Menendez Opening Remarks at Hearing on International Parental Child Abduction, http://www.foreign.senate.gov/press/chair/release/chairman-menendez-opening-remarks-at-hearing-on-international-parental-child-abduction.

[81]. Rania Nanos, Note, The Views of a Child: Emerging Interpretation and Significance of the Child's Objection Defense Under the Hague Child Abduction Convention, 22 Brook. J. Int'l L. 437, 437 (1996).

[82]. See Status Table 28: Convention of 25 October 1980 on the Civil Aspects of International Child Abduction, http://hcch.e-vision.nl/index_en.php?act=conventions.status&cid=24.

[83]. Convention on the Civil Aspects of International Child Abduction, Oct. 25, 1980, art. 13, para. 1(a)-(b), T.I.A.S. No. 11,670, at 8, 19 I.L.M. at 1502.

[84]. Nat'l Inst. of Justice, U.S. Dept. of Justice, Multiple Perspectives on Battered Mothers and Their Children Fleeing to the United States for Safety: A Study of Hague Convention Cases 304-305 (2010). See also Goldman School of Public Policy, Recent News: International Child Abduction and Domestic Violence, https://gspp.berkeley.edu/global/the-hague-domestic-violence-project/hague-dv/recent-news ("Although the treaty was created to protect children, the results are often the opposite when domestic violence is involved").

In 2010, the Court held that a common clause in custody decrees that restricts a custodial parent from removing the child from the jurisdiction ("ne exeat order") constitutes a "right of custody" for purposes of the Convention, thereby permitting a father who only had visitation rights to invoke the remedy of return. Abbott v. Abbott, 557 U.S. 933 (2010).

In another case, the Supreme Court ruled on the issue of mootness under the treaty. In Chafin v. Chafin, 133 S. Ct. 1017 (2013), the father accused the mother of domestic violence. However, the mother countered that the father's allegations of abuse were a subterfuge to encourage immigration authorities to deport her to Scotland and thereby deprive her of custody of their child. The mother successfully sought the return of the child under the Hague Convention and then returned to Scotland with the child. The father appealed the ruling, but the Eleventh Circuit Court of Appeals held that his appeal was moot because the child had already returned to a foreign country. The U.S. Supreme Court reversed, finding that the child's return to her home country did not moot the father's appeal.

In the most recent case, Lozano v. Montoya Alvarez, 134 S. Ct. 1224 (2014), a father who had resided with the mother and their child in the United Kingdom petitioned for the child's return more than 16 months after the mother and child had fled domestic violence (rape and battery) to settle in the United States. According to the Hague Convention, if a petition is filed more than one year after a child's removal from the country, a defense is available that the child is now "well settled" in its new environment.

The father argued that the one-year period was subject to equitable tolling whenever the taking parent conceals the child's location. The Court rejected his argument, holding that the well-settled defense is still available even more than a year following the wrongful removal or retention. The Court worried about the effect of wrenching the child again from her environment, effectively punishing her for her parent's flight. The Court reasoned that the Hague Convention is a treaty that is distinguishable from a statute that can be equitably tolled. However, the Court recognized that concealment of a child's location could be a factor to consider when determining if a child is in fact well-settled in the new country.

An effort is currently underway to establish children's exposure to domestic violence as an explicit exception to the automatic return of the child to the country of habitual residence. The Hague Domestic Violence Project was established in 2003 and currently is located at the Goldman School of Public Policy, University of California, Berkeley. The project also provides technical assistance to attorneys representing battered parents who are respondents to Hague petitions in U.S. courts and to judges who are hearing these cases.

Congress has addressed international child abduction with the International Parental Kidnapping Act (IPKA), 18 U.S.C. §1204. IPKA (unlike the Hague Convention) imposes criminal sanctions, making it a federal felony for a parent to wrongfully remove or retain a child outside the United States. IPKA's affirmative defenses differ from those in the Hague Convention. IPKA already has an explicit defense that is available to a parent fleeing domestic violence.

The Uniform Child Abduction Prevention Act (UCAPA) attempts to *prevent* parental abduction by identifying risk factors and establishing various remedies. The Act authorizes courts to impose "abduction prevention measures" either sua sponte or upon the motion of a parent or child welfare agency. Motions must specify risk factors for abduction (such as a party's prior arrest or conviction for a crime of domestic violence or child abuse). The Act has been adopted by 14 states and the District of Columbia.[85]

C. What Process Should Govern Custody Disputes?

1. The Adversary System Versus Mediation Process

Elizabeth S. Scott & Robert Emery, Child Custody Dispute Resolution: The Adversarial System and Divorce Mediation

in Psychology and Child Custody Determinations: Knowledge, Roles and Expertise 23-27, 39-42, 45-51 (Lois A. Weithorn ed., 1987)

The adversary system has been well established in Anglo-American law for hundreds of years. There are two basic characteristics of this dispute resolution model: the decision maker is a neutral party not involved in the dispute (the judge), and the evidence about the dispute that the judge considers is controlled and developed by the disputing parties themselves. These characteristics have several implications for the process. Each litigant, through an attorney, attempts to present all the evidence favorable to his or her side of the case and unfavorable to the opponent's. . . . Adjudication through this process is designed to produce a "winner" and "a loser." . . .

Few other legal confrontations involve the emotional intensity of a custody dispute. In most litigation the adversaries are strangers, business associates, or acquaintances. The divorcing couple's prior intimate relationship exaggerates from the outset the potential for hostility. Because of the prior relationship, each parent may know particularly hurtful and damaging facts about the other. Further, the subject of the dispute, the custody of their child, may be crucially important to each parent. . . . The nature of the inquiry in custody disputes further heightens the tendency to promote hostility. [C]ustody adjudication focuses on the personal qualities of the parent. Each parent's efforts to persuade the judge that he or she is the better custodian may involve presenting evidence about the character, habits, lifestyle, and moral fitness of the former spouse. While in theory only evidence relating to an individual's capacity as a parent is relevant, any character deficiency or behavior that the judge is likely to view negatively often will be exposed. . . .

[85]. Uniform Law Comm'n, Legislative Fact Sheet—Child Abduction Prevention, http://www.uniformlaws.org/LegislativeFactSheet.aspx?title=Child Abduction Prevention.

DIVORCE MEDIATION

Because of the dissatisfaction with the adversary system, there has been an increased interest in developing alternative methods of resolving child custody disputes. In the past several years, divorce mediation has grown dramatically as the major alternative to either litigation or out-of-court negotiation between attorneys. . . .

In divorce mediation the divorcing parties meet with an impartial third party (or parties) to identify, discuss, and one hopes, settle the disputes that result from marital dissolution. While it shares features with some types of marital and family therapy, mediation can be distinguished from many forms of psychotherapy in that it is short term and problem-focused. The process also requires that the mediator be knowledgeable in the legal and economic as well as the social and psychological consequences of divorce. Further, mediation differs from therapy in its objectives, and the exploration of emotional issues is circumscribed by the goal of negotiating a fair and acceptable agreement. Finally, unlike marital therapy, the goal of mediation is *not* reconciliation.

Divorce mediation embraces a model of dispute resolution considerably different from that characterizing the adversary process. Whereas in mediation the parties give up some procedural control in that the mediator directs much of the process, decisional control is not handed over to a third party as it is in adjudication. That the parents retain decisional control also distinguishes mediation from arbitration. Arbitration, like mediation, may encompass less formal procedures than does litigation, but unlike the mediator, the arbitrator is expected to make a decision for the parties if they do not do so themselves. . . .

Some divorce mediators attempt to settle all four of the major issues that must be decided in a divorce: property division, spousal support, custody and visitation, and child support. Almost all mediators, however, [who] work in public court settings [limit] their practice to the issues of custody and visitation. . . . The process by which decisions are reached and the impact it has on the parents' relationship is critical to the integrative decisions regarding child rearing, since both parents are likely to maintain at least some contact with their children after a divorce. . . .

Proponents have argued that mediation will have benefits in areas that have been termed the "four C's." That is, mediation is said to reduce *conflict*, increase *cooperation*, give people more *control* over important decisions in their lives, and achieve these goals at a reduced public or private *cost*. . . .

[A] number of questions remain about the mediation alternative. . . . These questions encompass debates on whether attorneys or mental health professionals are better trained to conduct mediation, whether mediation should be conducted by teams including one member of each profession, or whether a new, distinct profession must be created. . . .

Another set of questions about mediation concerns who should be included or excluded: whether referrals to court-based mediation programs should be mandatory; whether participation in mediation should be completely voluntary; and whether parents should be referred to mediation at individual judges' discretion. These three options now are variously used in jurisdictions throughout the United States. It has also been asked whether certain cases should automatically be excluded from mediation: for example, cases where there are apparently great discrepancies in the parties' relative bargaining power, as where spouse abuse has occurred, or where independent legal findings on matters such as child abuse or neglect must be made.

A third set of questions pertains to the process of mediation itself. Should children be included in mediation sessions? Should grandparents, stepparents, or other interested relatives have a role? What part should mediators play in deciding the content of the negotiated agreement? Should mediators, for example, work toward negotiating joint custody settlements? Moreover, should mediators refuse to be party to agreements they object to on ethical or psychological grounds? . . .

Finally, a set of questions has been raised about what is to happen once mediation ends. What role should attorneys play in regard to a mediated settlement? Can a single attorney review the agreement, should it be reviewed by two attorneys who hold an adversarial perspective, or need it be reviewed by an attorney at all? Perhaps the most controversial debate about the termination of mediation, however, concerns the mediator's role in any subsequent court hearing. Some have argued that when a court hearing is held after mediation fails to produce an agreement, the mediator *should* make a recommendation to the court.

Proponents of this perspective point to the fact that the mediator is already familiar with the family and that such a recommendation will avoid the duplication of efforts inherent in beginning a new custody investigation. Others argue that strict confidentiality is essential to the mediation process. . . . Practice and judicial policy remain unresolved in regard to the important issue of confidentiality. . . .

The following case wrestles with "the most controversial debate" (according to the above excerpt) concerning the mediator's role in making a recommendation to the court.

McLAUGHLIN v. SUPERIOR COURT

189 Cal. Rptr. 479 (Ct. App. 1983)

RATTIGAN, Associate Justice.

Civil Code section 4607 requires prehearing mediation of child custody and visitation disputes in marital dissolution proceedings conducted pursuant to the Family Law Act. The statute also provides that, if the parties fail to agree in the mediation proceedings, the mediator "may, consistent with local court rules, render a recommendation to the court as to the custody or visitation of the child or children" involved. Pursuant to this provision, respondent superior court has adopted a "local court rule," or policy, which (1) requires the mediator to make a recommendation to the court if the parties fail to agree in the mediation proceedings, but (2) prohibits cross-examination of the mediator by the parties. We hold in this original proceeding that the policy is constitutionally invalid in significant respects. . . .

Petitioner Thomas J. McLaughlin and real party in interest Linda Lee McLaughlin were married in 1969. They have three children, whose ages range between 6 and 13 years. [In May 1982, the husband petitioned for dissolution and custody. In response, the wife requested joint legal custody as well as physical custody. Husband then applied for temporary custody with visitation to the wife. The court issued an order to show cause in which the questions of temporary custody and visitation were set for hearing on June 30. The wife filed a declaration in which she requested temporary custody with visitation to the father.]

[At the hearing on the order to show cause,] petitioner's counsel recited his understanding that the pending issues of temporary custody and visitation were to be "referred for mediation." Counsel also stated his view that "the mediation procedure[,] insofar as it allows the mediator to make a recommendation for the Court, and bars the introduction of any testimony from the mediator about what the parties tell him or her[,] is unconstitutional as a denial of the right to cross-examine." On that ground, counsel in effect moved for a "protective order" which would permit mediation proceedings, but which would provide that if they did not result in agreement by the parties, on the issues of temporary custody and visitation, the mediator would be prohibited from making a recommendation to the court unless petitioner were guaranteed the right to cross-examine the mediator. [T]he court denied the motion on the ground that the "protective order" requested would violate a policy the court had adopted pursuant to Civil Code section 4607, subdivision (e).

[An exchange with counsel] included the only available description of respondent court's policy, which has apparently not been memorialized in a written rule. For these reasons, we quote pertinent passages of the exchange in the margin.[3]

[After the court denied petitioner's motion and request for a stay, he appealed to the California Supreme Court. The Supreme Court stayed the hearing and returned the case to the court of appeals for a hearing on the issue of the constitutionality of the practice of mediator recommendations.]

Civil Code section 4607, subdivision (a), clearly requires prehearing mediation of child custody and visitation disputes in marital dissolution proceedings. Subdivision (e) of the statute is also clear to the effect that the mediator "may,

---

3. "The Court [addressing Mr. Brunwasser, petitioner's counsel]: Some counties, as you probably know, do not permit or require a recommendation from the mediator in the event the parties are unable to agree. Some do. This county [i.e., respondent court] does, and therefore, I'm not prepared to give you the protective order you wish. The court feels that in the event the mediator were free to testify as to any of the matters mediated, that is[,] the substance of the matter as gleaned from the mediation session, . . . certainly you would have the right to cross-examine the mediator." However, our instructions as a matter of court policy to the mediators are that they are not to state the basis for their . . . recommendation. . . . In short, the recommendation of the mediator is simply . . . a recommendation to the court without any statement of underlying basis. . . . That's the way we do business here. . . ."

Mr. Brunwasser: . . . I have no objection to mediation. What I have an objection to is a procedure which allows the mediator . . . to communicate with the court and not be subject to defend [sic] his or her opinion by cross-examination.

"The Court: I understand that. I hope you equally understand that it is our policy to require a recommendation if the mediation is unsuccessful. It's a starting point which enables the court . . . [,] in the absence of other evidence, to make an interim order based upon the opinion of the trained counselor, and it's a procedure we opted for when this law was enacted. We're satisfied that the law permits that, and so your motion for a protective order is denied."

consistent with local court rules," make a recommendation to the court on either issue, or both, if the parties fail to reach agreement in the mediation proceedings. Subdivision (e) does not require or authorize disclosure to the parties of a recommendation made by the mediator to the court, nor of the mediator's reasons; it neither requires nor authorizes cross-examination of the mediator by the parties, which would necessarily require or bring about disclosure of the recommendation and the reasons for it; and the statute's express deference to "local court rules" has the effect of making disclosure and cross-examination matters of local option.

As we have seen, respondent court has exercised this option by adopting a policy which requires that the mediator make a recommendation to the court if the parties have failed to agree on child custody or visitation in the mediation proceedings; requires that the mediator not state his or her reasons for the recommendation; and denies the parties the right to cross-examine the mediator on the ground that the reasons have not been disclosed to the court. Amicus curiae has shown us that one large metropolitan superior court follows an entirely different procedure, and that another has adopted a policy which is essentially similar to respondent court's.[7]

The feature of respondent court's policy which prohibits cross-examination of the mediator is consistent with the provision in subdivision (c) of the statute that the mediation proceedings "shall be confidential." The requirement that the mediator not state to the court his or her reasons for the recommendation is consistent with the provision in subdivision (c) which protects the confidentiality of the parties' "communications" to the mediator by making them "official information within the meaning of Section 1040 of the Evidence Code." The facts remain that the policy permits the court to receive a significant recommendation on contested issues but denies the parties the right to cross-examine its source. This combination cannot constitutionally be enforced. . . .

Respondent court contends that the enforcement of its policy prohibiting cross-examination of a mediator who makes a recommendation to it is constitutionally permissible because only "temporary" child custody and visitation are involved and "due process is not required at every stage of a proceeding." . . .

However, the word "temporary" does not appear in Civil Code section 4607. We are not at liberty to interpolate it, by construction. . . . The constitutional infirmities in respondent court's policy are such that it may not be enforced on the theory that only "temporary" custody or visitation are [*sic*] involved. . . .

---

7. Amicus curiae describes the practice of the Los Angeles County Superior Court . . . : Where prehearing mediation proceedings have been conducted . . . , the court (1) neither receives nor permits a recommendation by the mediator and (2) proceeds to hear and determine the contested issue or issues without referring to the unsuccessful mediation process in any way.

Amicus curiae has filed declarations showing the related practice followed in the Superior Court for the City and County of San Francisco. . . . When the initial hearing is called on the same day [as the mediation session], the parties' attorneys communicate the mediator's recommendation to the court. . . . This (appellate) court interprets the [above declaration] to mean that the mediator's reasons for his or her recommendation are not disclosed to the parties, the attorneys, or the court when the recommendation is made in the first instance. This declaration fairly shows that the court makes the initial order on temporary custody or visitation without permitting cross-examination of the mediator. The declaration does not show whether cross-examination of the mediator is permitted at any later hearing.

. . . Our conclusions are consistent with our duty to harmonize the provisions of subdivisions (a) and (e) of the statute without doing violence to its salutary purposes. In addition, it has been shown in the present proceeding that disparities among "local court rules" adopted pursuant to subdivision (e) have had the effect of guaranteeing due process in some superior courts but not in others. Our conclusions will terminate this effect, which the Legislature obviously did not intend.

[The court concluded that the husband was entitled to a writ of mandate which] directs that the court not receive a recommendation from the mediator, as to any contested issue on which agreement is not reached, unless (1) the court has first made a protective order which guarantees the parties the rights to have the mediator testify and to cross-examine him or her concerning the recommendation or (2) the rights have been waived. . . .

Notes and Questions

1. Benefits. Mediation is a form of alternative dispute resolution that respects the parties' autonomy in decisionmaking ("private ordering"). In the adversarial system, the judiciary asserts authority over the financial aspects of dissolution and child custody. Mediation, however, confers broad latitude on the divorcing couple to resolve such matters for themselves. Why do Professors Scott and Emery suggest that mediation is better suited to the resolution of custody disputes? What are the benefits and costs of the adversary system? Of the mediation process?

2. Comparison. How does mediation differ from other forms of alternative dispute resolution (such as arbitration) and from psychotherapy in terms of objectives, process, and the ultimate decisionmaker? See Joan Kelly, Mediation and Psychotherapy: Distinguishing the Differences, 1 Mediation Q. 33 (1983).

3. Historical background. Mediation has longstanding roots in ancient China, Japan, and Africa. In the United States, mediation flourished in the late 1970s, fueled by acceptance of no-fault divorce and dissatisfaction with traditional dispute resolution. In 1981, California became the first state to require mediation (formerly Cal. Civ. Code §4607, now Cal. Fam. Code §3170). California law requires mediation in all cases of contested custody or visitation disputes before the parties can proceed to a hearing.

Many states now provide for mediation, either by encouraging the parties to mediate, providing for discretionary referrals by the court (most common), or mandating mediation.[86] Most statutes provide for court-connected mediation only of custody (rather than spousal support and property issues). What are the advantages and disadvantages of mandatory, as opposed to voluntary, mediation? See Peter Salem, The Emergence of Triage in Family Court Services: The Beginning of the End for Mandatory Mediation?, 47 Fam. Ct. Rev. 371 (2009); Holly A. Streeter-Schaefer, Note, A Look at Court-Mandated Civil Mediation, 49 Drake L.

[86]. Rebecca Hinton, Comment, Giving Children a Right to Be Heard: Suggested Reforms to Provide Louisiana Children a Voice in Child Custody Disputes, 65 La. L. Rev. 1539, 1565 (2005) (pointing out that 13 states make custody mediation mandatory).

Rev. 367 (2001). Does mandatory mediation infringe on the constitutional right of access to the judicial system? See Fuchs v. Martin, 845 N.E.2d 1038 (Ind. 2006).

4. Mediation and domestic violence. Research reveals high rates of domestic violence among couples in divorce mediation.[87] Commentators have noted that mediation poses special dangers for battered women.[88] Such dangers include the risk to victims before and after mediation sessions; agreements that give abusers more access to children than litigated outcomes and thereby provide additional opportunities for abuse; and mediators who are not trained to recognize abusive relationships or to counteract the power imbalance that characterizes the parties' relationship.

Different schools of thought exist about the practice of mediation in domestic violence cases. Some commentators believe that mediation should never be used; others contend that it can be used with adequate safeguards; still others believe that the choice should be left to the victim; and some believe that mediation can always be used even in cases of domestic violence.[89] To which view do you subscribe? See generally Jane C. Murphy & Jana B. Singer, Divorced from Reality (2015) (contending that family dispute resolution must adapt to serve the reality of contemporary families).

Several states have an exception to mandatory mediation in cases of domestic violence. See, e.g., Mont. Code Ann. §40-4-301-2 (prohibiting court from authorizing or continuing mediation if a party has been physically, sexually, or emotionally abused). A few professional organizations require training of and screening by mediators, as well as safeguards for victims, in cases of domestic violence. See Andrew Schepard, An Introduction to the Model Standards of Practice for Family and Divorce Mediation, 35 Fam. L.Q. 1 (2001) (rules adopted by the ABA and Association of Family and Conciliation Courts).

5. Qualifications. Mediation may be provided by publicly funded court services or by mediators in private practice. Currently, statutes often specify qualifications for court-connected mediators. However, until recently, mediators in the private sector were largely unregulated. To address this problem, the ABA Model Standards apply to mediators in public mediation programs as well as in private practice.

6. Role of the mediator. Mental health professionals and lawyers constitute the largest percentage of mediators. How might these different orientations affect the role of the mediator and the practice of mediation?

7. Ethical problems. Ethical problems arose when mediation first became popular. Early questions focused on the proper role of the attorney-mediator. That

[87]. Robin H. Ballard et al., Detecting Intimate Partner Violence in Family and Divorce Mediation: A Randomized Trial of Intimate Partner Violence Screening, 17 Psychol. Pub. Pol'y & L. 241, 243 (2011) (citing rates from 50-85 percent).

[88]. See Jane Murphy & Robert Rubinson, Domestic Violence and Mediation: Responding to the Challenges of Crafting Effective Screens, 39 Fam. L.Q. 53 (2005); Linda C. Neilson, At Cliff's Edge: Judicial Dispute Resolution in Domestic Violence Cases, 52 Fam. Ct. Rev. 529 (2014).

[89]. Susan Landrum, The Ongoing Debate About Mediation in the Context of Domestic Violence: A Call for Empirical Studies of Mediation Effectiveness, 12 Cardozo J. Conflict Resol. 425-426 (2011).

is, did a lawyer-mediator violate the prohibition on representation of conflicting or potentially differing interests or the prohibition of dual representation (of both husband and wife)? State bar ethics committees ruled that a lawyer-mediator could mediate a dispute for the husband and wife so long as the mediator informs the parties that she or he represents neither spouse and will refrain from representing either party if mediation proves unsuccessful, and advises the parties to seek independent legal counsel to review the agreement.[90]

Whether a lawyer-mediator can serve both as a mediator and as the draftsperson of the parties' written settlement agreement poses a recurring ethical dilemma. When a lawyer-mediator drafts a settlement agreement for divorcing spouses, the mediator is acting as an attorney who is representing opposing litigants. Such representation would violate the ethical ban on representing adverse parties in litigation. (Moreover, many jurisdictions specifically prohibit dual representation in divorce cases.) The Utah State Bar's Board of Bar Commissioners issued an opinion prohibiting a lawyer-mediator from representing both spouses in this manner. Utah State Bar Ethics Advisory Op. Comm., Op. 05-03 (2005).

8. Role of attorneys. Attorneys fill a variety of roles in the mediation process. They may serve as mediators; they may also be participant-observers, or reviewers of the mediated agreements. Does the presence of lawyers as participants or reviewers serve to make the system more fair and effective or to undermine the mediation process?

9. Limitations. What limitations should exist on private ordering? Should a mediator draft an agreement that the mediator does not believe is "fair" to one or both parties? Should the mediator defer to the parties' sense of fairness? Mediators differ concerning the extent to which a mediator should intervene in dispute resolution.[91]

10. Children's role. Should children play a role in mediation? What might be the advantages and disadvantages? If children play a role, what should that role consist of? Active participant? Consultant? What factors should influence the nature and extent of children's participation? One study concludes that when children are consulted in the divorce mediation process, re-litigation rates decrease.[92]

11. Confidentiality. Confidentiality is central to the mediation process. As *McLaughlin* explains, some locales permit the mediator to make a recommendation to the court if mediation proves unsuccessful. What is the practical effect of this policy? Consider the following:

> The power to make a recommendation to the court gives the mediator considerable authority. Although the court is not bound to follow the mediator's

---

[90]. Linda J. Silberman, Professional Responsibility Problems of Divorce Mediation, 16 Fam. L.Q. 107, 110-119 (1982).

[91]. Joseph P. Folger & Sydney E. Bernard, Divorce Mediation: When Mediators Challenge the Divorcing Parties, 10 Mediation Q. 5, 19 (1985) (approximately 25 percent of mediators adopt a highly interventionist stance to achieve fairness and protect weaker parties).

[92]. Jennifer E. McIntosh et al., Child-Focused and Child-Inclusive Divorce Mediation: Comparative Outcomes from a Prospective Study of Postseparation Adjustment, 46 Fam. Ct. Rev. 105 (2008).

recommendation, such a recommendation will probably influence a judge's decision. The mediator has spent more time with the parties than the judge, and the mediator has seen the parties interact. The mediator may have interviewed the children and other significant people. The mediator's education and experience adds credibility to his or her assessment of the case. Based on the collective weight of these factors, there is a high likelihood that the judge will "rubber stamp" the mediator's recommendation.[93]

The requirement of confidentiality raises an other issue. For example, the statute at issue in *McLaughlin* requires that "[m]ediation proceedings shall be held in private and shall be confidential, and all communications, verbal or written, from the parties to the mediator . . . shall be [privileged]." Once a mediator makes a recommendation and is subject to cross-examination, the mediator may have to divulge confidential communications that were elicited during mediation. Might warning the parties of this possibility interfere with the creation of trust?

McLaughlin requires that the policy of confidentiality yield to due process concerns. Is this an optimum accommodation of these competing interests? One commentator responds as follows:

> Permitting the mediator to make a recommendation undermines the neutrality of the mediator's role. The purpose of the mediation is to encourage the parties to create their own agreement. The mediator's opinion should not matter. . . . When the mediator is given the power to choose between the parties, his role is elevated to that of a judge. The best way to guarantee the parties their due process rights and ensure the confidentiality of the mediation sessions is to prohibit the mediator from making a recommendation at all.[94]

McLaughlin also has implications for battered women. The policy of permitting mediators to make recommendations (even if the mediators are subject to cross-examination) permits the disclosure of private information that the victim has chosen to reveal in the mediation. Stemming from concerns that this may lead to risks for the victim, some statutes provide exceptions to the confidentiality privilege for mediators in cases of child abuse or elder abuse. See, e.g., Me. R. Evid. 514(c).

12. Collaborative law. Collaborative law is an innovative form of alternative dispute resolution in which the parties and their attorneys agree to use cooperative techniques without resorting to judicial intervention except for court approval of the agreement. If the parties fail to reach an agreement through collaborative law, their attorneys must withdraw from representation. In 2001, Texas became the first state to provide for resolution of certain family matters by collaborative law. See Tex. Fam. Code §153.0072 (superseded by §§15.001-15.116). The Uniform Collaborative Law Act (UCLA) clarifies issues of informed consent, disqualification, party disclosure of information, and evidentiary privileges. Uniform Law Comm., Collaborative Law Act, http://www.uniformlaws.org/Act.aspx?title=Collaborative+Law+Act.

---

[93]. Susan Kuhn, Comment Mandatory Mediation: California Civil Code Section 4607, 33 Emory L.J. 733, 770-771 (1984).

[94]. Id. at 776.

Critics argue that collaborative law is incompatible with the duty to represent clients zealously; fails to meet the standards of full disclosure and informed consent regarding limited scope representation; creates problems regarding attorney-client confidentiality and conflicts of interest; and is not appropriate in many cases (e.g., domestic violence, substance abuse, and mental illness). Advocates point to the benefit from the saving of cost and time, and the diminution in emotional toll.[95] What is your view?

The most controversial aspect of collaborative law is the disqualification agreement. The Colorado Bar Association Ethics Committee declares that collaborative law is per se unethical, reasoning that the disqualification agreement creates an insurmountable conflict of interest impairing the lawyer's independent judgment about the need for litigation. Colorado Bar Association, Ethics Op. 115, Ethical Considerations in the Collaborative and Cooperative Law Contexts (Feb. 24, 2007). In contrast, the ABA's ethics committee asserts that collaborative law is consistent with professional conduct rules. ABA Standing Comm. on Ethics and Prof'l Responsibility, Formal Op. 07-447 (2007). Which view do you find most compelling?

Problem

Diane and Michael have been married for nine years. They have four children. Diane was the primary caregiver of the children during most of the marriage. She files for divorce after she begins a relationship with another man, Sam, who is a previously convicted sex offender. The court-appointed GAL recommends that Michael be given sole legal and physical custody because he is "the more stable parent," "more cooperative to work with," and the children are "calmer and more stable" when they are with him. In contrast, according to the GAL, Diane's home is more "chaotic and disorganized."

After the parties are unable to reach an agreement, the judge awards sole legal and physical custody of the oldest child to Michael, with custody of the remaining children to Diane. The court restricts the mother's custody by requiring that her contact with the children may occur only in the absence of Sam. Further, the parties' settlement agreement is merged and incorporated into their divorce decree. Their agreement contains the following provision (required by the judge): "[i]f the parties are unable to reach an agreement about parenting, the parties shall engage the services of a mediator before either may file an action in court. The costs associated with mediation shall be shared equally by the parties, unless otherwise reallocated by the mediator." Michael appeals the court order to mediate at the parties' expense, claiming that the judge's order violates his state constitutional right of free access to the courts. What result? Ventrice v. Ventrice, 26 N.E.3d 1128 (Mass. App. Ct. 2015).

---

[95]. Compare Diana M. Comes, Note, Meet Me in the Middle: The Time Is Ripe for Tennessee to Adopt the Uniform Collaborative Law Act, 41 U. Mem. L. Rev. 551, 562-569 (2011), with Marsha B. Freeman, Collaborative Law: Recognizing the Need for a New Default Method of Family Law Resolution, 17 Barry L. Rev. 15, 27 (2011).

2. Coin Flipping

Robert H. Mnookin, Child-Custody Adjudication: Judicial Functions in the Face of Indeterminacy

39 Law & Contemp. Probs. 226, 289-291 (1975)

RANDOM SELECTION

[Would] a random process of decision be fairer and more efficient than adjudication under a best-interests principle? Individualized adjudication means that the result will often turn on a largely intuitive evaluation based on unspoken values and unproven predictions. We would more frankly acknowledge both our ignorance and the presumed equality of the natural parents were we to flip a coin. Whether one had a separate flip for each child or one flip for all the children, the process would certainly be cheaper and quicker. It would avoid the pain associated with an adversary proceeding that requires an open exploration of the intimate aspects of family life and an ultimate judgment that one parent is preferable to the other. And it might have beneficial effects on private negotiations.

Resolving a custody dispute by state-administered coin-flip would probably be viewed as unacceptable by most in our society. Perhaps this reaction reflects an abiding faith, despite the absence of an empirical basis for it, that letting a judge choose produces better results for the child. Alternatively, flipping a coin might be unacceptable for some because it represents an abdication of the search for wisdom. . . .

[A] coin-flip would be a government affirmation of the equality of the parents. In a custody case, however, a coin-flip also symbolically abdicates government responsibility for the child and symbolically denies the importance of human differences and distinctiveness. Moreover, flipping a coin would deprive the parents of a process and a forum where their anger and aspirations might be expressed. In all, these symbolic and participatory values of adjudication would be lost by a random process. . . .

IX

Parentage: Formation, Consequences, and Limits of the Parent-Child Relationship

Law traditionally identified a child's parents based on biology, marriage to the child's mother, and adoption. Now, such familiar connections provide only a starting point for more expansive and often more contested approaches that look to behaviors, functions, and intentions to determine parentage. These new approaches also defy conventional assumptions reflected in gendered terms such as "mother" and "father" and the numerical norm of two. Despite temptation to think of the parent-child relationship as natural and privately created, family law chooses which bonds between adults and children to recognize, which ones to ignore, and what consequences follow. In constructing the parent-child relationship, the state thus plays a determinative (if not always visible) role.

This chapter explores the following questions: Who is a child's parent under the law? Why does parentage matter? What are the limits of the parent-child relationship, including the principles governing its termination?

A. Identifying Who Is a Parent

1. Means of Conception

a. Sexual Conception Versus Alternative Insemination

IN RE M.F.

938 N.E.2d 1256 (Ind. Ct. App. 2010)

FRIEDLANDER, Judge. . . .

[This is an appeal in a suit against W.M. (Father) to establish his paternity of two children, M.F. and C.F., born to J.F. (Mother). The suit arose from the following facts:] [I]n 1996, Mother was cohabiting and in a committed, long-term relationship with a woman we shall refer to henceforth as Life Partner. They wanted a child, so Mother and Father, who was a friend of Mother's, agreed that he would provide sperm with which to impregnate Mother. After [M.F.] was conceived but a few weeks before M.F. was born, the parties signed an agreement (the Donor Agreement) prepared by counsel for Mother [which] contained the following provisions:

> 6. Waiver and Release by Mother. Mother hereby waives all rights to child support and financial assistance from Donor. . . .
>
> 7. Waiver and Release by Donor. Donor hereby waives all rights to custody of or visitation with such child. . . .
>
> 8. Mutual Covenant Not to Sue. Mother and Donor mutually agree to forever refrain from initiating, pressing, or in any way aiding or proceeding upon an action to establish legal paternity of the child due to be born on or about September 19, 1996.

[After conception with help again from Father,] C.F. was born to [M]other seven years later, in 2003. Mother and Life Partner were still together at the time.

Mother and Life Partner's relationship ended sometime around 2008, when the [two] children were approximately twelve and five years old, respectively. [Mother sought public assistance, so the county prosecutor filed, on Mother's behalf, a petition to establish Father's paternity, for purposes of obtaining child support from him. Father cited the Donor Agreement as his defense. Despite DNA evidence of his genetic paternity, the trial court denied the petition to establish paternity, based on contract grounds. This appeal followed.]

[Despite the presence of all elements of an otherwise valid contract, we have here] a specific kind of contract, i.e., one between sperm donor and recipient regarding the conception of a child. . . . Our Supreme Court discussed contracts of this particular variety at some length in Straub v. B.M.T. by Todd, 645 N.E.2d 597 (Ind. 1994). [*Straub*] noted that other jurisdictions that have addressed support issues arising from situations involving artificial fertilization have done so via the adoption of statutes based on the Uniform Parentage Act (UPA) and the Uniform Status of Children of Assisted Conception Act (USCACA). [*Straub* also noted] that "[t]he majority of states adopting [similar] legislation . . . hold that the donor of semen . . . provided to a licensed physician for use in the artificial fertilization of a woman, is treated under the law as if he . . . were not the natural parent of the child thereby conceived." [*Straub*,] 645 N.E.2d at 600 [(citing Jhordan v. Mary K., 224 Cal. Rptr. 530 (Ct. App. 1986)).]

[Although *Straub* explicitly addressed "the emerging contract principles surrounding reproductive technology," the parties in *Straub* had not used alternative insemination or other technologies, but rather sexual intercourse. Thus, on] the critical question of the enforceability of assisted conception contracts in Indiana, [*Straub*] held that the agreement [in that case] failed on several counts, including: (1) insemination was achieved via intercourse ("there is no such thing as 'artificial insemination by intercourse'", [645 N.E.2d] at 601); (2) the agreement appeared "for all the world as a rather traditional attempt to forego this child's right to support from [the donor]", *id.*; and (3) the agreement contained "none of the formalities and protections which the legislatures and courts of other jurisdictions have thought necessary to address when enabling childless individuals to bear children." *Id.* Notably, however, the Court in *Straub* appears to have signaled that assisted conception contracts might be enforceable in Indiana in certain circumstances. . . . *Straub* may be fairly read as endorsing the view that such contracts may be valid if they comport with [certain legal] requirements. . . .

[B]oth Mother and Father appear to concede that the viability of the Donor Agreement in the instant case depends upon the manner in which insemination occurred. Per *Straub*, if insemination occurred via intercourse, the Donor Agreement would be unenforceable as against public policy. . . . Thus, an apparently complicated issue can be boiled down to simple legal question—who bore the burden of proof [on the method of conception]?

In this case, the parties entered into a facially valid contract whereby Mother agreed that she would not seek to establish paternity of M.F. in Father. Mother seeks to invalidate that Donor Agreement on the ground that the manner of insemination renders the Donor Agreement void as against public policy. As such, she seeks to avoid the contract. We conclude that this case is governed by the rule providing that a party that seeks to avoid a contract bears the burden of proof on matters of avoidance. . . . Thus, Mother bore the burden of proving that [conception occurred by intercourse, not alternative insemination, in turn rendering] the Donor Agreement unenforceable.

We . . . can find no indication of the manner in which Mother was inseminated with respect to the first pregnancy. . . . Therefore, Mother failed to prove that insemination [occurred] in such a way as to render the Donor Agreement unenforceable and void as against public policy. [Hence,] the trial court did not err in denying her petition to establish paternity with respect to M.F.

We pause at this point to make several observations about [an] area of concern expressed by the dissent, i.e., the formalities of the contract itself. Specifically, we address our colleague's concern that our holding today might enable parties to easily escape the responsibility of supporting one's biological child [by] concocting an informal, spur-of-the-moment written instrument whereby the biological mother and father agree that the father is absolved of any responsibility in connection with the child. Two aspects of our ruling prevent this possibility. First, . . . we hold today that a physician must be involved in the process of artificial insemination. At a minimum, this involvement includes the requirement that the semen first be provided to the physician. . . .

Second, we do not mean to sanction the view that a writing consisting of a few lines scribbled on the back of a scrap of paper found lying about will suffice in this kind of case. To the contrary, the instrument in question must reflect the parties' careful consideration of the implications of such an agreement and a thorough understanding of its meaning and import. The Donor Agreement in the instant case easily meets these requirements. . . . In fact, Paragraph 21 provides, "Donor specifically acknowledges that the Agreement was drafted by counsel retained by Mother, and that he has been provided full opportunity to review this Agreement with counsel of his own choosing before executing this Agreement." The structure and sophistication of the document leaves little doubt about the veracity of this paragraph.

The Donor Agreement itself is a six-page, twenty-four-paragraph document that covers in detail matters such as acknowledgment of rights and obligations, waiver, mutual consent not to sue, a consent to adopt, a hold-harmless clause, mediation and arbitration, penalties for failure to comply, amending the agreement, severability, a four-corners clause, and a choice-of-laws provision. [Although] we are reluctant to set forth specific requirements with respect to such a contract's form and content, . . . parties who execute a contract less formal and thorough than this one do so at their own peril.

Although we have affirmed the trial court's order with respect to M.F., we address sua sponte an issue not separately presented by the parties, i.e., the correctness of the order denying the petition to establish paternity with respect to the second child, C.F. In its order, the trial court found: "Shortly before the birth of the first child, the mother and Respondent entered into a written agreement stating that the Respondent would not be responsible for the child *and any further children which might result from the Respondent's donated sperm.*" The highlighted language reflects the trial court's determination that the Donor Agreement applied to C.F. as well as M.F. We conclude this construction of the Donor Agreement is erroneous.

The Donor Agreement provided as follows:

> 2. Donor has provided his semen to Mother for the purpose of inseminating Mother, and as a result, Mother has become pregnant and is expected to give birth on or about September 19, 1996. . . .

Throughout the remainder of the Donor Agreement, the product of insemination, i.e., the subject of the Donor Agreement, is referred to as either "the child" or "such child" . . . . [The contract] cannot be construed to apply to future children conceived as a result of artificial insemination involving Mother and Father. Therefore, the trial court erred in holding that a valid, enforceable contract existed that would prohibit an action to establish paternity of C.F. in Father. In view of the fact that DNA testing established, and Father concedes, that he is the biological father of C.F., this cause is remanded with instructions to grant Mother's petition to establish paternity with respect to C.F. . . .

CRONE, Judge, concurring in part and dissenting in part:

. . . Because the core of this dispute falls squarely within the province of family law . . . and because our default position in Indiana is that a parent is legally obligated to support his biological child, I would hold that Father must bear the burden of proving that the terms of the Donor Agreement are consistent with public policy and/or that the Donor Agreement was performed consistent with public policy. In other words, as the party seeking to avoid his support obligation, Father should bear the burden of proving the validity of an exception to a well-established rule.

I agree with the majority that our supreme court in *Straub* "appears to have signaled that assisted conception contracts might be enforceable in Indiana in certain circumstances." I would hold that those circumstances must be extremely limited. . . . At the very least, an assisted conception contract should provide that a donor's semen must be given to a licensed physician and that the artificial insemination must be performed by (or at least under the supervision of) the physician. Such a provision would both impress upon the parties the seriousness of their endeavor and safeguard the health of everyone involved. [Physician involvement can also create a formal, documented structure for the donor-recipient relationship, preventing misunderstandings between the parties.] I believe that such prerequisites to finding a valid exception to the general obligation to support would be consistent with *Straub* and a natural extension of its reasoning. . . .

Notes and Questions

1. Rationale. The parties and the court all agree that W.M. is the *genetic* father of both children. Why does the court conclude he is the legal father only of the younger sibling? The U.S. Supreme Court has emphasized the equal treatment of children, regardless of the circumstances of their birth, in striking down legal disadvantages once imposed on nonmarital children. Such "illegitimacy" cases often cite children's inability to control the circumstances of their birth. See Clark v. Jeter (Chapter V). To what extent does the outcome in *M.F.* depart from these precedents—because one sibling has two parents and sources of child support while the other has only one? (Obviously, children cannot control the circumstances of their conception.)

2. Sexual conception. Why should the means of conception matter in determining whether legal parentage follows from genetic parentage? Why is "there is no such thing as 'artificial insemination by intercourse,'" as the court observes? But see In re Parental Responsibilities of A.R.L., 318 P.3d 581 (Colo. Ct. App. 2013) (allowing mother's female partner to petition for recognition as child's second parent and excluding "donor" from consideration, despite sexual conception).

Consistent with the dominant approach, the *M.F.* court recognizes the genetic father as the legal father of the younger sibling, following the rule for sexual conception exemplified by Wallis v. Smith (Chapter V). Many cases like *Wallis* suggest that the benefits to the child of additional child support trump the man's interest in avoiding unwanted fatherhood, even when he can establish a case of misrepresentation leading to conception. See, e.g., Dubay v. Wells, 506 F.3d 422 (6th Cir. 2007). Reinforced by welfare reform measures emphasizing "personal responsibility," such case law signals that one central purpose of the family is ensuring private sources of support for economically dependent members of society—often called the privatization of dependency. See, e.g., 42 U.S.C. §§601 et seq.; Melissa Murray,

Family Law's Doctrines, 163 U. Pa. L. Rev. 1985 (2015); Laura A. Rosenbury, Federal Visions of Private Family Support, 67 Vand. L. Rev. 1835 (2014).

3. Alternative insemination.

a. Background: Married women. When courts and legislatures first confronted alternative insemination by donor (often called artificial insemination or AID), the typical scenario involved a married woman and her infertile husband. Rejecting early analogies to adultery and using doctrines such as the presumption of legitimacy and equitable estoppel, courts recognized the husband as the legal father. See, e.g., In re Adoption of Anonymous, 345 N.Y.S.2d 430 (Sur. Ct. 1973). Eighteen states followed §5 of the original UPA, which recognizes as the father a husband who consents in writing to AID performed by a licensed physician and, as noted in *M.F.*, states that the "donor of semen provided to a licensed physician for artificial insemination of a woman other than the donor's wife is treated in law as if he were not the natural father. . . ." The new UPA, promulgated in 2000 (amended in 2002), reaches similar results, stating that a donor is not a parent (§702) and recognizing the husband as the father even without express consent, if he and the woman live together with the child during the first two years and openly hold out the child as their own (§704). These provisions, however, do not apply to children conceived sexually (§701). On the history of donor insemination, see Kara W. Swanson, Banking on the Body: The Market in Blood, Milk, and Sperm in Modern America (2014).

b. Marriage equality. With the advent of marriage equality, courts have applied the principles summarized above to children conceived by lesbian couples using AID. See, e.g., Roe v. Patton, 2015 WL 4476734 (D. Utah 2015) (granting order to treat the mother's wife as the second legal parent, naming her on the child's birth certificate); Adoption of a Minor, 29 N.E.3d 830 (Mass. 2015) (determining that a known sperm donor is not a parent entitled to notice of adoption by a married lesbian couple). Does the different treatment of sexual conception versus conception by alternative insemination unfairly disadvantage gay men seeking fatherhood? See Elizabeth J. Levy, Virgin Fathers: Paternity Law, Assisted Reproductive Technology, and the Legal Bias Against Gay Dads, 22 Am. U. J. Gender Soc. Pol'y & L. 893 (2014).

c. Single women and donor insemination. Consistent with *M.F.*'s conclusions about the older sibling, several jurisdictions recognize a single mother as the sole legal parent of children conceived by donor insemination. For example, in In re K.M.H., 169 P.3d 1025 (Kan. 2007), the majority rejected the paternity claim of the genetic father, who wanted to exercise visitation and provide support, because his failure to "opt in" to fatherhood via written agreement, required by Kansas statute, made him a donor, with no legal status; the court also upheld the constitutionality of the statute. In Ferguson v. McKiernan, 940 A.2d 1236 (Pa. 2007), the woman unsuccessfully sought child support from the genetic father, notwithstanding an agreement that he would have no parental responsibilities if he would donate sperm to her, with the majority upholding the contract. What interests and policies explain such results?

While protecting donors and facilitating choices by prospective mothers, do such results undermine the interests of children? Compare id. at 1248 (noting that these children would not have been born, absent agreement), with Marsha Garrison, Law Making for Baby Making: An Interpretive Approach to the Determination of Legal Parentage, 113 Harv. L. Rev. 835, 906 (2000) ("our legal system grants no parent, male or female, the right to be a sole parent").

If the privatization of dependency helps explain cases like *Wallis* and *Dubay*, supra, why does such reasoning apply only in cases of sexual conception? Indeed, in *M.F.*, both children need support despite their different origins. See Susan Frelich Appleton, Illegitimacy and Sex, Old and New, 20 Am U. J. Gender Soc. Pol'y & L. 347, 372 (2012).

d. Women in nonmarital relationships. Why did the court not consider the mother's former "life partner" as the children's second parent? See, e.g., Elisa B. v. Superior Ct., 117 P.3d 660 (Cal. 2005) (noted infra p. 864).

e. Physician's participation. Does the traditional understanding of AID as a medical treatment for infertility explain why *M.F.* requires physician assistance in order to "cut off" the donor's parental status? See also Bruce v. Boardwine, 770 S.E.2d 774 (Va. Ct. App. 2015). Although the original UPA (cited in *M.F.*) required physician participation, the new UPA abandons this requirement. UPA §702 (cmt). Why?

f. Gender. Despite physician-participation requirements, women have long performed alternative insemination themselves, without medical assistance. What are the consequences for attempts to restrict and regulate the practice? Judge Posner observes:

> Artificial insemination . . . is rich with social implications. [A]s a practical matter, it places lesbian custody of children beyond the reach of governmental regulation. Beyond that, it allows women to escape having to share parental rights with men, since the sperm donor, whether provided through the woman's physician or through a sperm bank, is anonymous. It therefore accelerates the shift of economic power from men to women. . . .[1]

See generally Courtney Megan Cahill, Regulating at the Margins: Non-Traditional Kinship and the Legal Regulation of Intimate and Family Life, 54 Ariz. L. Rev. 43 (2012).

g. Commodification. Although the couple in *M.F.* turned to a friend, many women and couples who pursue alternative insemination obtain semen from a sperm bank. In such transactions, according to Martha Ertman, alternative insemination works as a free, open, and largely unregulated market in which sperm donors, sperm banks, and recipients sell and buy goods and information pursuant to principles of supply and demand. Professor Ertman continues:

> Alternative insemination generally involves at least two separate transactions. The sperm bank first purchases sperm from a donor and subsequently sells the sperm to a woman who uses it to become a mother. . . . While the transactions differ in important respects, both transactions commodify gametes, and in doing so commodify parental rights and responsibilities. . . .[2]

---

[1]. Richard A. Posner, Sex and Reason 421 (1992).

[2]. Martha M. Ertman, What's Wrong with a Parenthood Market? A New and Improved Theory of Commodification, 82 N.C. L. Rev. 1, 14-16 (2003).

Ertman proceeds to highlight both the negative implications of such commodification and its benefits, including the facilitation of new family forms. Would you recommend new legal restrictions? New means to foster this market? See also Swanson, supra.

h. Medical regulation. What role should government play in screening and checking the medical histories of semen donors? What records should be kept? What risks follow from inadequate donor screening and recordkeeping? See Naomi Cahn, Test Tube Families: Why the Fertility Market Needs Regulation 194-200 (2009).

The Food and Drug Administration (FDA) first began regulating donated reproductive tissue in May 2005. These donor eligibility rules require testing for specific diseases, including HIV and hepatitis. 21 C.F.R. §§1271.45-1271.90. In accompanying nonbinding recommendations, the FDA now makes ineligible, based on increased risk, any man who has had sex with another man in the preceding five years, effectively precluding gay men from donating semen.[3] For critiques of this policy, see John G. Culhane, Bad Science, Worse Policy: The Exclusion of Gay Males from Donor Pools, 24 St. Louis U. Pub. L. Rev. 129 (2005).

On the issue of regulation designed to give donor-conceived children access to information about their genetic relatives, see infra p. 897.

Problem

A "free sperm" movement challenges the FDA's health-based regulatory regime (see supra, Note 3h). Seeking to legitimize the practice of using informal arrangements between donors and recipients (often initiated online) without government oversight, a California woman sues the FDA, contending that its screening requirements for donor insemination are expensive and burdensome and unconstitutionally interfere with privacy, sexual liberty, and procreative autonomy. She also asserts equal protection violations because the FDA regulates alternative insemination but not natural insemination, in turn driving some donors and recipients simply to use natural insemination instead. How should the court decide the case? Why? See Doe v. Hamburg, 2013 WL 3783749 (N.D. Cal. 2013); Susan Frelich Appleton, Between the Binaries: Exploring the Legal Boundaries of Nonanonymous Sperm Donation, 49 Fam. L.Q. 93, 109-115 (2015).

---

[3]. See Center for Biologics & Research, U.S. Dept. of Health & Human Servs., Guidance for Industry: Eligibility Determination for Donors of Human Cells, Tissues, and Cellular and Tissue-Based Products (HCT/Ps) (Aug. 2007), http://www.fda.gov/downloads/BiologicsBloodVaccines/GuidanceComplianceRegulatoryInformation/Guidances/Tissue/ucm091345.pdf.

b. Posthumous Conception

ASTRUE v. CAPATO

132 S. Ct. 2021 (2012)

Justice GINSBURG delivered the opinion of the Court.

Karen and Robert Capato married in 1999. Robert died of cancer less than three years later. With the help of in vitro fertilization, Karen gave birth to twins 18 months after her husband's death [using sperm that he froze before undergoing chemotherapy]. Karen's application for Social Security survivors benefits for the twins, which the Social Security Administration (SSA) denied, prompted this litigation. The technology that made the twins' conception and birth possible, it is safe to say, was not contemplated by Congress when the relevant provisions of the Social Security Act (Act) originated (1939) or were amended to read as they now do (1965).

[The Capatos, who lived in Florida, had a son before Robert died. Robert's will made no provision for children conceived after his death, although the couple had asked their lawyer to place future offspring on a par with existing children. In seeking survivors benefits for the twins,] Karen Capato, respondent here, relies on the Act's initial definition of "child" in 42 U.S.C. §416(e): "'[C]hild' means . . . the child or legally adopted child of an [insured] individual." Robert was an insured individual, and the twins, it is uncontested, are the biological children of Karen and Robert. That satisfies the Act's terms, and no further inquiry is in order, Karen maintains. The SSA, however, identifies subsequent provisions, §§416(h)(2) and (h)(3)(C), as critical, and reads them to entitle biological children to benefits only if they qualify for inheritance from the decedent under state intestacy law, or satisfy one of the statutory alternatives to that requirement.

. . . We conclude that the SSA's reading is better attuned to the statute's text and its design to benefit primarily those supported by the deceased wage earner in his or her lifetime. And even if the SSA's longstanding interpretation is not the only reasonable one, it is at least a permissible construction that garners the Court's respect under [principles of administrative law].

Congress amended the Social Security Act in 1939 to provide a monthly benefit for designated surviving family members of a deceased insured wage earner. "Child's insurance benefits" are among the Act's family-protective measures. [W]e must decide whether the Capato twins rank as "child[ren]" under the Act's definitional provisions. . . . Under the heading "Determination of family status," §416(h)(2)(A) provides: "In determining whether an applicant is the child or parent of [an] insured individual for purposes of this subchapter, the Commissioner of Social Security shall apply [the intestacy law of the insured individual's domiciliary State]." . . .

. . . As the SSA reads the statute, 42 U.S.C. §416(h) governs the meaning of "child" in §416(e)(1). In other words, §416(h) is a gateway through which all applicants for insurance benefits as a "child" must pass. . . . [Citing biology and marriage,] Karen Capato argues, and the Third Circuit held, that §416(h), far from supplying the governing law, is irrelevant in this case. Instead, the Court of Appeals determined, §416(e) alone is dispositive of the controversy. 631 F. 3d, at 630-631. . . . Section 416(h) comes into play, the court reasoned, only when "a claimant's status as a deceased wage-earner's child is in doubt." *Id.*, at 631. That limitation, the court suggested, is evident from §416(h)'s caption: "Determination of family status." Here, "there is no family status to determine," the court said, *id.*, at 630, so §416(h) has no role to play. . . .

Nothing in §416(e)'s tautological definition ("'child' means . . . the child . . . of an individual") suggests that Congress understood the word "child" to refer only to the children of married parents. . . . Nor does §416(e) indicate that Congress intended "biological" parentage to be prerequisite to "child" status under that provision. As the SSA points out, "[i]n 1939, there was no such thing as a scientifically proven biological relationship between a child and a father, which is . . . part of the reason that the word 'biological' appears nowhere in the Act." Moreover, laws directly addressing use of today's assisted reproduction technology do not make biological parentage a universally determinative criterion [citing donor insemination statutes from California and Massachusetts]. We note, in addition, that marriage does not ever and always make the parentage of a child certain, nor does the absence of marriage necessarily mean that a child's parentage is uncertain. An unmarried couple can agree that a child is theirs, while the parentage of a child born during a marriage may be uncertain.

Finally, it is far from obvious that Karen Capato's proposed definition—"biological child of married parents,"—would cover the posthumously conceived Capato twins. Under Florida law, a marriage ends upon the death of a spouse. If that law applies, rather than a court-declared preemptive federal law, the Capato twins, conceived *after* the death of their father, would not qualify as "marital" children. . . .

[T]he SSA finds a key textual cue in §416(h)(2)(A)'s opening instruction: "In determining whether an applicant is the child . . . of [an] insured individual *for purposes of this subchapter*," the Commissioner shall apply state intestacy law. (Emphasis added.) . . . The Act commonly refers to state law [of the domicile] on matters of family status. . . . Time limits also qualify the statutes of several States that accord inheritance rights to posthumously conceived children [citing statutes from various states]. See also Uniform Probate Code §2-120(k), 8 U.L.A. 58 (Supp. 2011) (treating a posthumously conceived child as "in gestation at the individual's death," but only if specified time limits are met). No time constraints attend the Third Circuit's ruling in this case, under which the biological child of married parents is eligible for survivors benefits, no matter the length of time between the father's death and the child's conception and birth.

The paths to receipt of benefits laid out in the Act and regulations, we must not forget, proceed from Congress' perception of the core purpose of the legislation. The aim was not to create a program "generally benefiting needy persons"; it was, more particularly, to "provide . . . dependent members of [a wage earner's] family with protection against the hardship occasioned by [the] loss of [the insured's] earnings." . . .

The SSA's construction of the Act, respondent charges, raises serious constitutional concerns under the equal protection component of the Due Process Clause.

She alleges: "Under the government's interpretation . . . , posthumously conceived children are treated as an inferior subset of natural children who are ineligible for government benefits simply because of their date of birth and method of conception."

. . . We have applied an intermediate level of scrutiny to laws "burden[ing] illegitimate children for the sake of punishing the illicit relations of their parents, because 'visiting this condemnation on the head of an infant is illogical and unjust.'" Clark v. Jeter, 486 U.S. 456, 461, (1988) (quoting Weber v. Aetna Casualty & Surety Co., 406 U.S. 164, 175 (1972)). No showing has been made that posthumously conceived children share the characteristics that prompted our skepticism of classifications disadvantaging children of unwed parents. We therefore need not decide whether heightened scrutiny would be appropriate were that the case.[10] Under rational-basis review, the regime Congress adopted easily passes inspection [because] that regime is "reasonably related to the government's twin interests in [reserving] benefits [for] those children who have lost a parent's support, and in using reasonable presumptions to minimize the administrative burden of proving dependency on a case-by-case basis." . . .

Tragic circumstances—Robert Capato's death before he and his wife could raise a family—gave rise to this case. But the law Congress enacted calls for resolution of Karen Capato's application for child's insurance benefits by reference to state intestacy law. We cannot replace that reference by creating a uniform federal rule the statute's text scarcely supports. . . .

Notes and Questions

1. **Background.** A posthumous child traditionally was a child conceived before a parent's death but born thereafter. A common law presumption, now codified in many states, legitimates a child born within nine months after the death of the mother's husband. Assisted reproductive technologies (ARTs), including cryopreservation of genetic material, have made possible the birth of children *conceived or implanted after* a parent's death. Frozen semen, for example, can be thawed for insemination or fertilization of ova in vitro, as in the principal case. Embryos and even ova can also be preserved for future use. And physicians can now extract semen from men after death. See Lori B. Andrews, The Clone Age: Adventures in the New World of Reproductive Technology 222-236 (2000) ("the sperminator").

10. Ironically, while drawing an analogy to the "illogical and unjust" discrimination [that] children born out of wedlock encounter, see Weber v. Aetna Casualty & Surety Co., 406 U. S. 164, 175-176 (1972), respondent asks us to differentiate between children whose parents were married and children whose parents' liaisons were not blessed by clergy or the State. She would eliminate the intestacy test only for biological children of *married parents*.

Posthumous conception raises several intertwined legal issues, including the interests of the deceased gamete providers, the parentage of the resulting children, and their treatment by inheritance law.[4] To what extent should the resolution of these issues determine eligibility for the federal benefits at stake in *Capato*? Consider the following:

2. Progenitors' and children's interests. Is posthumous conception a protected right of the deceased? See John A. Robertson, Posthumous Reproduction, 69 Ind. L.J. 1027 (1994). Does the surviving spouse have a right to procreate the deceased's genetic offspring? Do the children-to-be have interests at stake justifying state restrictions on access to posthumous reproduction? Cf. John A. Robertson, Gay and Lesbian Access to Assisted Reproductive Technology, 55 Case W. Res. L. Rev. 323, 347 (2004) (noting "nonidentity problem" in attempts to justify restrictions to protect children because "the children sought to be protected by banning . . . access to ARTs will not then be born").

3. Posthumous parentage. Why did the Court reject the arguments that the twins are Robert's children? Is Robert the twins' father? Do they have no father? See Arianne Renan Barzilay, You're on Your Own, Baby: Reflections on *Capato*'s Legacy, 46 Ind. L. Rev. 557 (2013) (reading case and statute to reflect a concept of family dominated by a male breadwinner).

The UPA (§707) recognizes the decedent as a parent when assisted reproduction is used after death only if the decedent consented in a record to such posthumous use. Accord American Bar Association (ABA) Model Act Governing Assisted Reproduction §501.3(f) (Feb. 2008);[5] Human Fertilisation and Embryology Act of 2008, ch. 22, §39 (U.K.). If enacted by states in the United States, would such laws provide a better reference point than state intestacy law? The Uniform Probate Code takes a more expansive approach, making intent controlling and allowing proof thereof through means other than written consent. See Kristine S. Knaplund, Children of Assisted Reproduction, 45 U. Mich. J.L. Reform 899 (2012).

4. Inheritance. State law varies on the inheritance rights of posthumously conceived children. Some statutes grant rights to such children if the deceased parent gave consent during his lifetime. However, the nature of the required consent varies. Compare La. Rev. Stat. Ann. §9:391.1(A) (requiring deceased's specific, written authorization for spouse to use his gametes), with Tex. Fam. Code Ann. §160.707 (requiring that deceased spouse "consented in a record kept by a licensed physician that if assisted reproduction were to occur after death the deceased spouse would be a parent of the child"). See In re Certified Question from the United States District Court for the Western District of Michigan, 825 N.W.2d 566, 571-572 (Mich. 2012) (categorizing states' positions).

What should state law require for a posthumously conceived child to inherit from this parent's intestate estate? Under Massachusetts law, the surviving parent

---

[4]. Browne Lewis, Graveside Birthday Parties: The Legal Consequences of Forming Families Posthumously, 60 Case W. Res. L. Rev. 1159 (2010).

[5]. See http://www.abanet.org/family/.committees/artmodelact.pdf.

must establish in a timely manner the deceased's genetic relationship and affirmative consent both to conceive posthumously and to support the child. Woodward v. Commissioner of Soc. Sec., 760 N.E.2d 257, 269 (Mass. 2002). How should the parent manifest consent? Should a presumption of a child's entitlement arise merely from the existence of a parent's cryopreserved reproductive material? Cf. Vernoff v. Astrue, 568 F.3d 1102 (9th Cir. 2009). Should a signed agreement leaving the frozen semen to the deceased's wife suffice? See Burns v. Astrue, 289 P.3d 551 (Utah 2012). See generally Jennifer Matystik, Posthumously Conceived Children: Why States Should Update Their Intestacy Laws After Astrue v. Capato, 28 Berkeley J. Gender L. & Just. 269 (2013).

Given that genetic material can be frozen and brought to term years after the deaths of both biological parents, should states require children's claims for inheritance or benefits to commence within a certain time after the parent's death? What period of time would you propose? See La. Rev. Stat. Ann. §9:391.1(A) (requiring birth within three years of the decedent's death). Do short time periods provide adequate opportunity for the surviving parent to grieve the other's death and to prepare to rear a child alone? See Kristen M. Benvenuti Pytel, Left Out No Longer: A Call for Advancement in Legislation for Posthumously Conceived Children, 11 J.L. Soc'y 70, 105-107 (2009/2010) (reviewing timing requirements in Restatement (Third) of Property and Uniform Probate Code).

5. Contrary rulings. Because the Social Security Act looks to state intestacy law, some posthumously conceived children have succeeded in receiving the benefits sought on behalf of the Capato twins. For example, in Gillett-Netting v. Barnhart, 371 F.3d 593 (9th Cir. 2004), the court concluded that, because the twins in that case were "legitimate children under Arizona law, they [were conclusively] deemed dependent under §402(d)(3) and [needed] not demonstrate actual dependency nor deemed dependency under the provisions of §416(h)." Id. at 599. Does this analysis remain good law after *Capato*? How would one show "actual dependency" when the child is conceived after the insured's death?

6. Inheritance of genetic material. Is genetic material property that one owns? Does one have a right to bequeath sperm or embryos for use in posthumous reproduction? For a will contest between the decedent's adult children from a prior marriage and his girlfriend, to whom he had bequeathed frozen sperm before his suicide, see Hecht v. Superior Court, 20 Cal. Rptr. 2d 275 (Ct. App. 1993), 59 Cal. Rptr. 2d 222, 228 (Ct. App. 1996). Cf. Hall v. Fertility Inst. of New Orleans, 647 So. 2d 1348 (La. Ct. App. 1994). Suppose that a widow claims the sperm, even though her late husband did not express the intent to conceive posthumously. See In re Estate of Kievernagel, 83 Cal. Rptr. 3d 311 (Ct. App. 2008). See also Kurchner v. State Farm Fire & Cas. Co., 858 So. 2d 1220 (Fla. Dist. Ct. App. 2003) (treating frozen semen as personal property, so insurance policy for bodily injury does not cover destruction); Speranza v. Repro Lab, Inc., 875 N.Y.S.2d 449 (App. Div. 2009) (denying deceased man's parents his frozen semen as part of his estate). On progenitors' disputes about the disposition of frozen embryos, see Szafranski v. Dunston, infra.

2. Parentage by Adoption

Stephen B. Presser, The Historical Background of the American Law of Adoption

11 J. Fam. L. 443, 446-489 (1971)

We can document the practice of adoption among the ancient Babylonians, Egyptians, and Hebrews, as well as the Greeks, but the most advanced early law on adoption which we have is from the Romans. In contrast with current adoption law, which has as its purpose the "best interests" of the child, it appears that ancient adoption law, and particularly the Roman example, was clearly designed to benefit the *adopter*, and any benefits to the adoptee were secondary. There were two broad purposes that Roman adoption law served: (1) to avoid extinction of the family, and (2) to perpetuate rites of family religious worship. . . .

[Adoption was not known at common law.] The usual explanation for the absence of a legal recognition of adoption in the English common law is the inordinately high regard for blood lineage of the English. [Another possible reason was xenophobia.]

The purpose of the American adoption statutes passed in the middle of the nineteenth century was to provide for the welfare of dependent children, a purpose quite different from that of the old Roman laws. [On the other hand, in England] there were mechanisms for the care of children, dependent and otherwise, that made adoption for social welfare purposes unnecessary. These mechanisms, which were instituted early and which were very well developed by the seventeenth century, were the institutions of "putting out" and "apprenticeship." In a very real sense, these institutions were a form of "adoption," although the purpose was neither inheritance nor the perpetuation of the adopter's family, but the temporary training of the child. [T]he customs of "apprenticeship" and "service" were brought to America by the New England Puritans. . . .

The first comprehensive adoption statute was passed in 1851 in Massachusetts. Among its key provisions were requirements 1) that written consent be given by the natural parents . . . ; 2) that the child himself must consent if he is fourteen years of age or older; 3) that the adopter's [spouse] must join in the petition for adoption; 4) that the probate judge . . . must be satisfied that the petitioner(s) were "of sufficient ability to bring up the child . . . and that it is fit and proper that such adoption should take effect" . . . ; 5) that once the adoption was approved by the probate court, the adopted child would become "to all intents and purposes" the legal child of the petitioner(s); [and] 6) that the natural parents would be deprived by the decree of adoption of all legal rights and obligations respecting the adopted child. . . .

[The purpose of the Massachusetts law and others like it remains unclear. One theory says that an increase in adoptions arranged by foundling societies prompted these statutes.] It is naive to attribute the passage of adoption statutes in so many states solely to the activities of "foundling societies." The activity of these societies *is* demonstrative of a larger movement for child welfare of which the passage of the adoption statutes also represents a part. This movement came about as a result of the economic changes which made the stop-gap institutions of apprenticeship, service, and indenture quite unable to cope with the great numbers of children who had been neglected by their families and also were neglected, until about the middle of the nineteenth century in most cases, by the society and the state. In order to understand better the motives that lay behind the passage of the adoption statutes, it is important to understand some of these other developments in child welfare work. . . .

[F]rom philanthropic motives most probably inspired by the continuing plight of dependent children in the hands of public authorities, private agencies for the care of such children were founded. . . . In the first half of the nineteenth century, at least seventy-seven such agencies were founded. . . . After 1850 the increase in the number of such agencies was even more rapid. . . . Before 1850, the private agencies sought to teach their charges to read and write. . . . Prior to the establishment of the public school systems and compulsory attendance, the agencies felt their primary service should be to give to their children the rudiments of an education before they were placed out in indenture or service.

Around 1850, however, private agencies began to be founded with the avowed purpose of placing younger children in a suitable family atmosphere. The work of some of the "infant's hospitals," "foundling asylums," and "maternity hospitals" in New York and Boston stands out in this regard, as does the work of the Children's Aid Societies started in those cities in 1853 and 1865, respectively. . . . The Children's Aid Societies made efforts to place children in suitable homes, usually homes far from the city, in the expanding states and territories of the West. [T]he Children's Aid Society of New York [ ] placed over twenty thousand children in homes out of New York City in the twenty years after it was founded. . . .

[Many of] the children placed by such agencies as the New York Children's Aid Society found themselves in situations which not only resembled "adoption" as we know it today but which was called by the same name. As the phenomenon of children in adopted homes became more common, there was increased pressure not only to pass laws regulating and insuring the legal relations between adopted children and their natural and adoptive parents, but to guarantee that some benefits of heirship were conferred on the adopted child. This pressure, which originated with the activities of the charitable associations working in child welfare, led to passage of the general adoption statutes in the third quarter of the nineteenth century. . . .

ADOPTIVE COUPLE v. BABY GIRL

133 S. Ct. 2552 (2013)

Justice Alito delivered the opinion of the Court.

This case is about a little girl (Baby Girl) who is classified as an Indian because she is 1.2% (3/256) Cherokee. Because Baby Girl is classified in this way, the South Carolina Supreme Court held that certain provisions of the federal Indian Child

Welfare Act of 1978 required her to be taken, at the age of 27 months, from the only parents she had ever known and handed over to her biological father, who had attempted to relinquish his parental rights and who had no prior contact with the child. The provisions of the federal statute at issue here do not demand this result. . . .

"The Indian Child Welfare Act of 1978 (ICWA), 25 U.S.C. §§1901–1963, was the product of rising concern in the mid-1970's over the consequences to Indian children, Indian families, and Indian tribes of abusive child welfare practices that resulted in the separation of large numbers of Indian children from their families and tribes through adoption or foster care placement, usually in non-Indian homes." Mississippi Band of Choctaw Indians v. Holyfield, 490 U.S. 30, 32 (1989). Congress found that "an alarmingly high percentage of Indian families [were being] broken up by the removal, often unwarranted, of their children from them by nontribal public and private agencies." §1901(4). This "wholesale removal of Indian children from their homes" prompted Congress to enact the ICWA, which establishes federal standards that govern state-court child custody proceedings involving Indian children [including proceedings for termination of parental rights and adoption].

In this case, Birth Mother (who is predominantly Hispanic) and Biological Father (who is a member of the Cherokee Nation) became engaged in December 2008. One month later, [after] learning of [Birth Mother's] pregnancy, Biological Father asked Birth Mother to move up the date of the wedding. He also refused to provide any financial support until after the two had married. The couple's relationship deteriorated, and Birth Mother broke off the engagement in May 2009. In June, Birth Mother sent Biological Father a text message asking if he would rather pay child support or relinquish his parental rights. Biological Father responded via text message that he relinquished his rights.

Adoptive Couple, Melanie and Matt Capobianco, at a news conference

Birth Mother then decided to put Baby Girl up for adoption. [Her attorney contacted the Cherokee Nation to determine whether Biological Father was formally enrolled, but misspelled his name and provided an incorrect birth date, so Biological Father's membership in the tribal records could not be verified.]

Working through a private adoption agency, Birth Mother selected Adoptive Couple, non-Indians living in South Carolina, to adopt Baby Girl. Adoptive Couple supported Birth Mother both emotionally and financially throughout her pregnancy. Adoptive Couple was present at Baby Girl's birth in Oklahoma on September 15, 2009, and Adoptive Father even cut the umbilical cord. The next morning, Birth Mother signed forms relinquishing her parental rights and consenting to the adoption. Adoptive Couple initiated adoption proceedings in South Carolina a few days later, and returned there with Baby Girl. After returning to South Carolina, Adoptive Couple allowed Birth Mother to visit and communicate with Baby Girl. . . .

. . . Biological Father [received notice and] signed papers stating that he accepted service and that he was "not contesting the adoption." But [he later testified that] he thought that he was relinquishing his rights to Birth Mother, not to Adoptive Couple. Biological Father contacted a lawyer the day after signing the papers, and subsequently requested a stay of the adoption proceedings. [The Cherokee Nation identified Biological Father as a registered member and intervened in the litigation.] In the adoption proceedings, Biological Father sought custody and stated that he did not consent to Baby Girl's adoption. . . .

[After a trial, the South Carolina Family Court denied the adoption petition on the ground that Adoptive Couple had not shown compliance with applicable ICWA provisions. Biological Father was awarded custody, and Baby Girl, age 27 months, was handed over to him. He terminated contact with Adoptive Couple and has made no attempt to contact Birth Mother. The South Carolina Supreme Court affirmed, and we granted certiorari.] It is undisputed that, had Baby Girl not been 3/256 Cherokee, Biological Father would have had no right to object to her adoption under South Carolina law. . . . [The Court considers the ICWA provisions applied by the courts below.]

Baby Girl (Baby Veronica) with Dusten Brown, her biological father

Section 1912(f) [of the ICWA] provides that "[n]o termination of parental rights may be ordered in such proceeding in the absence of a determination, supported by evidence beyond a reasonable doubt, . . . that the *continued custody* of the child by the parent or Indian custodian is likely to result in serious emotional or physical damage to the child." (Emphasis added.) . . . . The adjective "continued" plainly refers to a pre-existing state [and does not apply to an Indian parent who never had custody of the child.] [T]he primary mischief the ICWA was designed to counteract was the unwarranted *removal* of Indian children from Indian families due to the cultural insensitivity and biases of social workers and state courts. . . . [W]hen, as here, the adoption of an Indian child is voluntarily and lawfully initiated by a non-Indian parent with sole custodial rights, the ICWA's primary goal of preventing the unwarranted removal of Indian children and the dissolution of Indian families is not implicated. . . .

Section 1912(d) provides that "[a]ny party" seeking to terminate parental rights to an Indian child under state law "shall satisfy the court that active efforts have been made to provide remedial services and rehabilitative programs designed *to prevent the breakup of the Indian family* and that these efforts have proved unsuccessful." (Emphasis added.) . . . Section 1912(d) is a sensible requirement when applied to state social workers who might otherwise be too quick to remove Indian children from their Indian families. It would, however, be unusual to apply §1912(d) in the context of an Indian parent who abandoned a child prior to birth and who never had custody of the child. . . .

In the decision below, the South Carolina Supreme Court suggested that if it had terminated Biological Father's rights, then §1915(a)'s preferences for the adoptive placement of an Indian child would have been applicable. . . . Section 1915(a) provides that "[i]n any adoptive placement of an Indian child under State law, a preference shall be given, in the absence of good cause to the contrary, to a placement with (1) a member of the child's extended family; (2) other members of the Indian child's tribe; or (3) other Indian families." Contrary to the South Carolina Supreme Court's suggestion, §1915(a)'s preferences are inapplicable in cases where no alternative party has formally sought to adopt the child. This is because there simply is no "preference" to apply if no alternative party that is eligible to be preferred under §1915(a) has come forward. [No adoption petition was filed by the Biological Father, the paternal grandparents, or other members of the Tribe.]

The Indian Child Welfare Act was enacted to help preserve the cultural identity and heritage of Indian tribes, but under the State Supreme Court's reading, the Act would put certain vulnerable children at a great disadvantage solely because an ancestor—even a remote one—was an Indian. [A] biological Indian father could abandon his child *in utero* and refuse any support for the birth mother—perhaps contributing to the mother's decision to put the child up for adoption—and then could play his ICWA trump card at the eleventh hour to override the mother's decision and the child's best interests. If this were possible, many prospective adoptive parents would surely pause before adopting any child who might possibly qualify as an Indian under the ICWA. Such an interpretation would raise equal protection concerns, but [the ICWA provisions used below do not apply here.] We therefore reverse the judgment of the South Carolina Supreme Court and remand the case for further proceedings not inconsistent with this opinion. . . .

Justice SCALIA, dissenting.

. . . The Court's opinion, it seems to me, needlessly demeans the rights of parenthood. It has been the constant practice of the common law to respect the entitlement of those who bring a child into the world to raise that child. We do not inquire whether leaving a child with his parents is "in the best interest of the child." It sometimes is not; he would be better off raised by someone else. But parents have their rights, no less than children do. This father wants to raise his daughter, and the statute amply protects his right to do so. There is no reason in law or policy to dilute that protection.

Justice SOTOMAYOR, with whom Justice GINSBURG and Justice KAGAN join, and with whom Justice SCALIA joins in part, dissenting.

A casual reader of the Court's opinion could be forgiven for thinking this an easy case, one in which the text of the applicable statute clearly points the way to the only sensible result. In truth, however, the path from the text of the Indian Child Welfare Act of 1978 (ICWA) to the result the Court reaches is anything but clear, and its result anything but right. . . .

Better to start at the beginning and consider the operation of the statute as a whole. ICWA commences with express findings. Congress recognized that "there is no resource that is more vital to the continued existence and integrity of Indian tribes than their children," 25 U.S.C. §1901(3), and it found that this resource was threatened. State authorities insufficiently sensitive to "the essential tribal relations of Indian people and the cultural and social standards prevailing in Indian communities and families" were breaking up Indian families and moving Indian children to non-Indian homes and institutions. . . . Consistent with these findings,

Congress declared its purpose "to protect the best interests of Indian children and to promote the stability and security of Indian tribes and families by the establishment of minimum Federal standards" applicable to child custody proceedings involving Indian children. . . .

First, ICWA defines the term "parent" broadly to mean "any biological parent . . . of an Indian child or any Indian person who has lawfully adopted an Indian child." §1903(9). . . . [I]t is clear that Birth Father has a federally recognized status as Baby Girl's "parent" and that his "parent-child relationship" with her is subject to the protections of the Act [based on the Act's comprehensive definition of "child custody proceeding"]. . . .

The majority . . . asserts baldly that "when an Indian parent abandons an Indian child prior to birth and that child has never been in the Indian parent's legal or physical custody, there is no 'relationship' that would be 'discontinu[ed]' . . . by the termination of the Indian parent's rights." Says who? Certainly not the statute. Section 1903 recognizes Birth Father as Baby Girl's "parent," and, in conjunction with ICWA's other provisions, it further establishes that their "parent-child relationship" is protected under federal law. . . .

The entire foundation of the majority's argument that subsection (f) does not apply is the lonely phrase "continued custody." It simply cannot bear the interpretive weight the majority would place on it. . . . A court applying §1912(f) where the parent does not have pre-existing custody should, as Birth Father argues, determine whether the party seeking termination of parental rights has established that the continuation of the parent-child relationship will result in "serious emotional or physical damage to the child." . . .

The majority's textually strained and illogical reading of the statute might be explicable, if not justified, if there were reason to believe that it avoided anomalous results or furthered a clear congressional policy. . . . With respect to §1912(d), [there] is nothing "bizarre" about placing on the party seeking to terminate a father's parental rights the burden of showing that the step is necessary as well as justified. . . . In any event, the question is a nonissue in this case given the family court's finding that Birth Father is "a fit and proper person to have custody of his child" who "has demonstrated [his] ability to parent effectively" and who possesses "unwavering love for this child." Petitioners cannot show that rehabilitative efforts have "proved unsuccessful," 25 U.S.C. §1912(d), because Birth Father is not in need of rehabilitation.[11] . . .

On a more general level, the majority intimates that ICWA grants Birth Father an undeserved windfall: in the majority's words, an "ICWA trump card" he can "play . . . at the eleventh hour to override the mother's decision and the child's best interests." The implicit argument is that Congress could not possibly have intended to recognize a parent-child relationship between Birth Father and Baby Girl that would have to be legally terminated (either by valid consent or involuntary termination) before the adoption could proceed.

---

11. The majority's concerns about what might happen if no state or tribal authority stepped in to provide remedial services are therefore irrelevant here. But as a general matter, if a parent has rights that are an obstacle to an adoption, the state- and federal-law safeguards of those rights must be honored, irrespective of prospective adoptive parents' understandable and valid desire to see the adoption finalized. "We must remember that the purpose of an adoption is to provide a home for a child, not a child for a home." In re Petition of Doe, [638 N.E.2d 181, 190 (Ill. 1994)] (Heiple, J., supplemental opinion supporting denial of rehearing).

But this supposed anomaly is illusory. In fact, the law of at least 15 States did precisely that at the time ICWA was passed [citations to state statutes omitted]. And the law of a number of States still does so [citing authorities that require notice of adoption to all potential fathers or consent in the absence of termination of parental rights for parental fault].

Without doubt, laws protecting biological fathers' parental rights can lead—even outside the context of ICWA—to outcomes that are painful and distressing for both would-be adoptive families, who lose a much wanted child, and children who must make a difficult transition [citing cases]. Balancing the legitimate interests of unwed biological fathers against the need for stability in a child's family situation is difficult, to be sure, and States have, over the years, taken different approaches to the problem. Some States, like South Carolina, have opted to hew to the constitutional baseline established by this Court's precedents and do not require a biological father's consent to adoption unless he has provided financial support during pregnancy. See Quilloin v. Walcott, 434 U.S. 246, 254–256 (1978); [Lehr v. Robertson, 463 U.S. 248, 261 (1983)]. Other States, however, have decided to give the rights of biological fathers more robust protection and to afford them consent rights on the basis of their biological link to the child. At the time that ICWA was passed, as noted, over one-fourth of States did so. ICWA, on a straightforward reading of the statute, is consistent with the law of those States that protected, and protect, birth fathers' rights more vigorously. . . .

The majority also protests that a contrary result to the one it reaches would interfere with the adoption of Indian children. This claim is the most perplexing of all. A central purpose of ICWA is to "promote the stability and security of Indian . . . families," 25 U.S.C. §1902, in part by countering the trend of placing "an alarmingly high percentage of [Indian] children . . . in non-Indian foster and adoptive homes and institutions." §1901(4). . . . ICWA does not interfere with the adoption of Indian children except to the extent that it attempts to avert the necessity of adoptive placement and makes adoptions of Indian children by non-Indian families less likely. The majority may consider this scheme unwise. But no principle of construction licenses a court to interpret a statute with a view to averting the very consequences Congress expressly stated it was trying to bring about. . . .

The majority casts Birth Father as responsible for the painful circumstances in this case, suggesting that he intervened "at the eleventh hour to override the mother's decision and the child's best interests." I have no wish to minimize the trauma of removing a 27-month-old child from her adoptive family. It bears remembering, however, that Birth Father took action to assert his parental rights when Baby Girl was four months old, as soon as he learned of the impending adoption. . . . Baby Girl has now resided with her father for 18 months. However difficult it must have been for her to leave Adoptive Couple's home when she was just over 2 years old, it will be equally devastating now if, at the age of 3 1/2, she is again removed from her home and sent to live halfway across the country. Such a fate is not foreordained, of course. But it can be said with certainty that the anguish this case has caused will only be compounded by today's decision. . . .

Notes and Questions

1. Background. Adoption, unknown at common law, is a purely statutory institution. Although many statutes enacted in the mid-nineteenth century reflected the old civil law of adoption, the Massachusetts statute (described by Professor Presser) transformed the earlier understanding by making adoption "a legal procedure" and "creat[ing] a means of establishing an artificial bond between a parent and child that closely approximated the legal ideal of republican domestic relations."[6]

As the dispute in *Adoptive Couple* illustrates, adoption "cuts off" the adoptee's legal connections to his or her original family, replacing those with ties to the new family. Following an adoption, the state typically seals the adoptee's original birth certificate and issues a new one, as if the adoptee had been born to the adoptive parents. See generally Elizabeth J. Samuels, The Idea of Adoption: An Inquiry into the History of Adult Adoptee Access to Birth Records, 53 Rutgers L. Rev. 367 (2001).

2. Paths to adoption proceedings. In the United States, children subject to adoption proceedings include (a) children for whom the state has terminated parental rights, (b) children surrendered for adoption by their birth parents (as the mother did in *Adoptive Couple*), (c) children adopted by a stepparent or a parent's partner, and (d) children brought from abroad through the process of intercountry adoption. (See Note: Intercountry Adoption, infra.)[7]

3. "Biology plus" in adoption. On what basis did *Adoptive Couple* determine that the ICWA did not apply? Did the majority conclude that Biological Father was not a "parent" under the ICWA or that he was a "parent" whose rights could be terminated? What difference does this distinction make? As Justice Sotomayor's dissent notes, South Carolina (which supplies the governing law if the ICWA does not apply) does not require a genetic father's consent to adoption if he has not provided financial support during pregnancy. The Constitution permits such state action under the "biology plus" test that emerged in the wake of Stanley v. Illinois (Chapter V). Why does genetic paternity of sexually conceived children alone suffice for legal paternity in cases like *M.F.*, supra, but not here? See generally Shreya A. Fadia, Note, Adopting "Biology Plus" in Federal Indian Law: Adoptive Couple v. Baby Girl's Refashioning of ICWA's Framework, 114 Colum. L. Rev. 2007 (2014). (For additional examination of unmarried birth fathers in the adoption context, see Note: Adoption and Unmarried Birth Fathers, infra.) After remand in *Adoptive Couple*, the adoption was finalized over the birth father's objection. 746 S.E.2d 346 (S.C. 2013).

---

[6]. Michael Grossberg, Governing the Hearth: Law and the Family in Nineteenth-Century America 271 (1985).

[7]. Census data from 2010 show that, of the 64.8 million children under 18 living with a householder, two percent are adopted children. Rose M. Kreider & Daphne A. Lofquist, U.S. Census Bureau, Adopted Children and Stepchildren: 2010, at 4 (Apr. 2014), https://www.census.gov/prod/2014pubs/p20-572.pdf. See also Paul J. Placek, National Adoption Data Assembled by the National Council on Adoption, in Adoption Factbook V 3, 4 (National Council for Adoption 2011) (citing data from 2007).

4. Adoptive placement.

a. Matching. Adoption flourished during the Progressive Era as a "child rescue" project that would find new homes for children suffering from poverty, neglect, and abuse. See generally Stephen O'Connor, Orphan Trains: The Story of Charles Loring Brace and the Children He Saved and Failed (2001). As social workers began to exercise jurisdiction over this domain, they asserted expertise in "matching" children with new families so that adoption would imitate nature. See, e.g., Crump v. Montgomery, 154 A.2d 802 (Md. 1959) (removing child from prospective adoptive family because he was "overplaced," based on presumed intelligence).

Congress responded to a longstanding practice of racial matching by legislating in 1996 the "removal of barriers to interethnic adoption," providing that no state or other entity in a state receiving federal funds can "deny to any individual the opportunity to become an adoptive or a foster parent, on the basis of the race, color, or national origin of the individual, or of the child, involved." 42 U.S.C. §1996b (amending the earlier, and less restrictive, federal Multi-Ethnic Placement Act). How might race-matching of adoptees of color serve their best interests? See, e.g., Twila L. Perry, Race, Color, and the Adoption of Biracial Children, 17 J. Gender Race & Just. 73 (2014).

As *Adoptive Couple* notes, §1915(a) of the ICWA lists placement preferences for children of Native American heritage. Critics of *Adoptive Couple* claim that the majority erroneously treated the ICWA's preferences as disfavored race-matching measures and substituted its own preference for a color-blind approach. See Bethany R. Berger, In the Name of the Child: Race, Gender, and Economics in Adoptive Couple v. Baby Girl, 67 Fla. L. Rev. 295, 327-329 (2015). How do the ICWA's preferences differ from race-matching measures? Put differently, how can you reconcile Congress's disapproval of race matching in adoption and the placement preferences included in the ICWA? Does *Adoptive Couple* portend the demise of the ICWA? See Ashby Jones, Adoptive Parents Fight Tribal Hurdles, Wall St. J., Oct. 17-18, 2015, at A3.

Despite the rejection of official race matching, may the state honor prospective adopters' own race-based preferences? See R. Richard Banks, The Color of Desire: Fulfilling Adoptive Parents' Racial Preferences Through Discriminatory State Action, 107 Yale L.J. 875 (1998). Note that, in independent placements, like that in *Adoptive Couple*, birth parents typically select placements according to their own preferences. What constraints, if any, should limit their choices?

b. Screening. The adoption process usually includes a close evaluation of the prospective adopters, often called a "home study" or a "preplacement investigation." See, e.g., Iowa Code §600.8; 23 Pa. Cons. Stat. §2530. Under the Uniform Adoption Act (UAA), all placements require an individualized evaluation before the adoption becomes final (§§3-601 to 3-603). Do you agree with the criticism that such regulation of adoption, in comparison to the "privacy" that shields sexual reproduction, reflects a preference for biological relationships and signals distrust of those who would raise a "child born to another" or who seek to parent "someone else's child"?[8]

c. Fees and expenses. Payment of the birth parents' medical and other expenses by the adoptive parents has long been permissible, notwithstanding prohibitions

---

[8]. Elizabeth Bartholet, Family Bonds: Adoption, Infertility, and the New World of Child Production 69 (rev. ed. 1999). See id. at 34, 93.

against child selling and trafficking, which apply to parents as well as to attorneys and others. See, e.g., N.Y. Soc. Serv. Law §374(6) (listing reimbursable expenses).

5. Beyond matching. In the late twentieth century, the idea that adoption should imitate nature faced challenges on several fronts. The decriminalization of abortion and the decreased stigma of unmarried motherhood meant that fewer highly desired white infants were available for prospective adopters, increasing transracial adoptions of children of color. In the meantime, state intervention based on abuse and neglect increased the number of children in foster care, often older children and minorities. In the Adoption and Safe Families Act of 1997 (ASFA), Congress directed states to pursue adoption for children who could not be quickly returned to their homes. See 42 U.S.C. §675(5) (requiring states to seek terminations of parental rights after a limited period of foster care); id. §673b (providing financial incentives for states to increase adoptions of children in foster care). See generally Dorothy Roberts, Shattered Bonds: The Color of Child Welfare 165-172 (2002) (critiquing ASFA's biased assumptions and impact). In addition, as gays and lesbians became more open about their relationships and sought to form families, they often pursued adoption, with data showing that such adults tend to adopt children with "special needs" and of other races.[9] How do you explain this pattern?

6. LGBT adoptions.

a. Florida's ban. A Florida screening statute excluded all gays and lesbians, providing that no otherwise eligible person may adopt "if that person is a homosexual." After several unsuccessful constitutional challenges (e.g., Lofton v. Secretary of Department of Children & Family Services, 358 F.3d 804 (11th Cir. 2004)), Florida's ban fell in 2010. In Florida Department of Children & Families v. Adoption of X.X.G., 45 So. 3d 79 (Fla. Dist. Ct. App. 2010), F.G., a gay man had successfully served as a foster parent for two children with serious health problems, previously removed from their birth families because of abandonment and neglect. When the children became eligible for adoption, F.G. applied, but the department recommended against his application solely on the basis of the statute, while conceding that he otherwise met all adoption criteria. After a trial, the court granted F.G's adoption petition and found the statute unconstitutional. On the department's appeal, the court held the statute irrational and in violation of equal protection, given the individualized evaluation that each petition for adoption triggers, the eligibility of gays and lesbians to serve as foster parents and guardians, and the absence of empirical evidence that parental sexual orientation affects child well-being.

b. Adoption rights? Do adults like F.G. have a "right to adopt"? A right to be free from discrimination in adoption? See generally Carlos A. Ball, The Right to Be Parents: LGBT Families and the Transformation of Parenthood 169-180 (2012). In contrast to the law in Florida, several states have laws prohibiting discrimination

[9]. Adoption advocates have argued that allowing nontraditional families to adopt will increase the likelihood of permanent homes for parentless children. See David M. Brodzinsky, Expanding Resources for Children III: Research-Based Practices in Adoption by Gays and Lesbians 16 (Evan B. Donaldson Adoption Inst., 2011), http://adoptioninstitute.org/old/publications/2011_10_Expanding_Resources_BestPractices.pdf.

based on sexual orientation in adoption. In a case like *X.X.G.*, what constitutional rights might the children have at stake? See Tanya Washington, Suffer Not the Little Children: Prioritizing Children's Rights in Constitutional Challenges to "Same-Sex Adoption Bans," 39 Cap. U. L. Rev. 231, 235 (2011).

c. Social science evidence. *X.X.G.* relied in part on social science evidence to hold Florida's law irrational. What risks does judicial reliance on such evidence pose? See Libby Adler, Just the Facts: The Perils of Expert Testimony and Findings of Fact in Gay Rights Litigation, 7 Unbound: Harv. J. Legal Left 1 (2011); Susan Frelich Appleton, Gender and Parentage: Family Law's Equality Project in Our Empirical Age, in What Is Parenthood? Contemporary Debates About the Family 237 (Linda McClain & Daniel Cere eds., 2013).

d. Religious objections. In Massachusetts, in the wake of marriage equality, Catholic Charities, which had managed adoption cases, mostly involving children with special needs, halted these services once a ban on discrimination against gays and lesbians became a condition for retaining the necessary state license. Should all state legislatures create a special exemption from antidiscrimination laws for religious adoption agencies, as some states have done? E.g., Conn. Gen. Stat. §46b-35b (covering religious organizations that do not receive public funds); Mich. Comp. Laws Ann. §710.23g (prohibiting adverse government action for agencies declining to provide adoption services because of religious beliefs). Compare Douglas NeJaime, Marriage Inequality: Same-Sex Relationships, Religious Exemptions, and the Production of Sexual Orientation Discrimination, 100 Cal. L. Rev. 1169 (2012) (criticizing such exemptions, as part of the larger movement for conscience protection in the face of gay rights), with Robin Fretwell Wilson, A Matter of Conviction: Moral Clashes over Same-Sex Adoption, 22 BYU J. Pub. L. 475 (2008) (recommending conscience clauses like those developed in the abortion context to resolve moral clashes over same-sex adoption).

7. Stepparent and second-parent adoption. State adoption statutes have long included provisions for stepparent adoptions, in which one parent's spouse adopts the children after termination of the other parent's rights. Such statutes traditionally assumed that each child may have no more than one male and one female parent. In the 1990s, several courts began to permit second-parent adoptions in families headed by same-sex couples, interpreting and applying statutes that had not contemplated such families to allow a biological or adoptive parent's same-sex partner to become a second parent by adoption, without terminating the former's parental rights under the traditional cut-off rule. For example, in Adoption of Tammy, 619 N.E.2d 315 (Mass. 1993), Massachusetts's highest court permitted Helen Cooksey, the partner of renowned physician Susan Love, to adopt the child born to Susan (after donor insemination from Helen's cousin). It reached this result by construing the Massachusetts statute's authorization of "a person" to petition for adoption to cover two unmarried individuals who file a joint petition. Further, the court read the usual cut-off provision inapplicable when, as here, the parent is a party to the adoption petition. Throughout the opinion, the court emphasized why the second-parent adoption would serve the child's best interests. See also, e.g., In re Adoption of Doe, 326 P.3d 347 (Idaho 2014).

Other courts have compared such adoptions explicitly to stepparent adoptions. Compare In re Adoptions of B.L.V.B. & E.L.V.B., 628 A.2d 1271 (Vt. 1993) (permitting second-parent adoptions to come within statutory exception for stepparents), with S.J.L.S. v. T.L.S., 265 S.W.3d 804, 822-828 (Ky. Ct. App. 2008) (rejecting concept of "'stepparent-like' adoption" as inconsistent with state adoption laws). See also Boseman v. Jarrell, 704 S.E.2d 494 (N.C. 2010). Several states now authorize second-parent adoptions by statute, permitting one partner to adopt the other's child or permitting them both to adopt together a child not related to either. E.g., Cal. Fam. Code §9000(b) (second-parent adoption for domestic partners).

Does nationwide marriage equality compel all states to apply stepparent adoption laws and procedures to same-sex couples? Note that the two Michigan plaintiffs before the Supreme Court in Obergefell v. Hodges (Chapter II), nurses April DeBoer and Jayne Rowse, were committed partners, each of whom had adopted two children with "special needs." The women's inability to marry prevented DeBoer from adopting Rowse's children under Michigan law and vice versa, leaving the children at risk of becoming parentless if the legal mother died. See 135 S. Ct. 2584, 2595 (2015); Julie Bosman, One Couple's Unanticipated Journey to Center of Landmark Gay Rights Case, N.Y. Times, Jan. 25, 2015, at A14. On the challenge to Mississippi's law after *Obergefell*, see Tamar Lewin, Mississippi Ban on Adoptions by Same-Sex Couples Is Challenged, N.Y. Times, Aug. 13, 2015, at A9.

April DeBoer, Jayne Rowse, and their children

8. Full faith and credit to adoption decrees. Before nationwide marriage equality, some states declined to recognize adoption decrees issued to same-sex couples in other states. See, e.g., Okla. Stat. Ann. tit. 10, §7502-1.4(A). Most courts held that full faith and credit compels respect in a second forum for a judicial decree validly issued in the first forum, regardless of the second forum's public policy. See Finstuen v. Crutcher, 496 F.3d 1139 (10th Cir. 2007) (invalidating Oklahoma statute). A minority view, however, distinguished *recognition* of out-of-state adoption decrees from *enforcement* thereof. Under this reasoning, the second forum cannot question the adoption itself but has no obligation to issue a new birth certificate. See Adar v. Smith, 639 F.3d 146 (5th Cir.), *cert. denied*, 132 S. Ct. 400 (2011). See generally Steve Sanders, Interstate Recognition of Parent-Child Relationships: The Limits of the State Interests Paradigm and the Role of Due Process, 2011 U. Chi. Legal F. 233.

What is the impact of *Obergefell* on the recognition of same-sex couples' *out-of-state* adoption decrees? Recall that *Obergefell* found the issue of *marriage recognition* unnecessary to address. Recall also that United States v. Windsor (Chapter II) struck down the definitional section of the Defense of Marriage Act (DOMA) but did not address the section permitting states to refuse recognition to same-sex marriages celebrated in other states. See generally Tara Siegel Bernard, Same-Sex Parents' Rights May Be Unresolved After Justices' Ruling, N.Y. Times, June 15, 2015, at B1.

Problem

Pamela V. and Michael J. have filed a petition to adopt Garrett. Pamela is Garrett's birth mother, and Michael is Pamela's brother. Pamela and Michael reside together and plan to rear Garrett together. Garrett's birth father, Chad, from whom Pamela is now divorced, has consented to the adoption. The state's statutes have been construed to permit second-parent adoptions by a parent's same-sex partner. Should the court grant the petition? Why? See In re Adoption of Garrett, 841 N.Y.S.2d 731 (Sur. Ct. 2007). But see In re Adoption of G., 978 N.Y.S.2d 622 (Sur. Ct. 2013); Jessica R. Feinberg, Friends as Co-Parents, 43 U.S.F. L. Rev. 799 (2009); Cynthia R. Mabry, Joint and Shared Parenting: Valuing All Families and All Children in the Adoption Process with an Expanded Notion of Family, 17 Am. U. J. Gender Soc. Pol'y & L. 659 (2009).

Suppose now that Michael is Pamela's father (and Garrett's grandfather), who does not reside in the same household but spends time with Garrett three or four times each week. Should the court grant Michael's petition to adopt Garrett, while leaving Pamela's parental rights intact? Why? See In re Adoption of A.M., 930 N.E.2d 613 (Ind. Ct. App. 2010). See also In re A., 893 N.Y.S.2d 751 (Fam. Ct. 2010) (considering joint adoption petition of child's grandmother and aunt).

3. Parentage Based on Formalities, Function, and Intent

a. Traditional Doctrines: Legitimacy and Estoppel

MICHAEL H. v. GERALD D.

491 U.S. 110 (1989)

Review the above case, reprinted in Chapter V.

K.E.M. v. P.C.S.

38 A.3d 798 (Pa. 2012)

Mr. Justice Saylor. . . .

[Appellant, a married mother, sued Appellee for child support of G.L.M., whom they conceived in an extramarital affair. Appellant had discussed the affair and the child's conception with her husband, H.M.M., who submitted to genetic testing, which excluded him as a possible father. At his request, his name was not entered on the birth certificate. Appellee declined to have genetic testing, but acknowledged G.L.M. as his son and periodically spent time with him and gave him gifts. G.L.M. referred to both men as "Daddy." Appellee ended his relationship with Appellant, and contemporaneously, she and H.M.M. separated, but they did not divorce. The trial court recognized H.M.M. as the legal father on two alternative bases: First, the marital presumption of paternity (which makes the husband the legal father of the mother's child) should apply because the couple remained married and there was no evidence of irretrievable marital breakdown. Alternatively, H.M.M. should be regarded as G.L.M.'s father under paternity by estoppel—based on his holding himself out as a parent even after learning he was not the biological father, at the child's baptism, on tax returns, and to the general public. The appellate court affirmed, relying on paternity by estoppel while rejecting the marital presumption, which it said does not apply when the husband has full knowledge that he is not the biological father. This appeal to the state supreme court followed.]

Appellate ct ruling

[First,] we clarify what is, and is not, before the Court. [This case] squarely concerns paternity by estoppel, not the presumption of paternity. While it would be ideal if a comprehensive scheme for paternity determinations and attendant support obligations were set out in one place, this simply is not the nature of common law judicial decision making.[4] As to the presumption of paternity, we note only that recent Pennsylvania decisions have relegated it to a substantially more limited role, by narrowing its application to situations in which the underlying policies will be advanced (centrally, where there is an intact marriage to be protected). [T]his does increase the relative importance of paternity by estoppel in the support arena.

Second, . . . an enhanced role for genetic testing may have more limited relevance in the paternity by estoppel setting (as contrasted with the presumption of paternity). In the estoppel cases, a legal determination is being made that it is in the best interests of the child to continue to recognize the husband as the father. . . .

Third, we believe there remains a role for paternity by estoppel in the Pennsylvania common law, in the absence of definitive legislative involvement.[6] We recognize the intransigent difficulties in this area of the law involving social, moral, and very personal interests[:]

> Absent any overriding equities in favor of the putative father, such as fraud, the law cannot permit a party to renounce even an assumed duty of parentage when by doing so, the innocent child would be victimized. Relying upon the representation

4. . . . Unlike the legislative process, the adjudicatory process is structured to cast a narrow focus on matters framed by litigants before the Court. . . . [Although developing a comprehensive paternity scheme is a legislative prerogative, various model statutes] provide a platform for discussion, at the very least. See, e.g., Nat'l Conference on Uniform State Laws, Uniform Parentage Act (2002); ALI, Principles of the Law of Family Dissolution: Analysis and Recommendations (2002).

6. Notably, the American Law Institute's Principles of Family Dissolution endorses the application of paternity by estoppel to a person who has "lived with the child since the child's birth, holding out and accepting full and permanent responsibilities as parent, as part of a prior co-parenting arrangement with the child's legal parent . . . to raise a child together each with full parental rights and responsibilities, when the court finds that recognition of the individual as a parent is in the child's best interests. . . ." ALI, Principles of the Law of Family Dissolution: Analysis and Recommendations §2.03(1)(b)(iii) (2002).

> of the parental relationship, a child naturally and normally extends his love and affection to the putative parent. The representation of parentage inevitably obscures the identity and whereabouts of the natural father, so that the child will be denied the love, affection and support of the natural father. As time wears on, the fiction of parentage reduces the likelihood that the child will ever have the opportunity of knowing or receiving the love of his natural father. While the law cannot prohibit the putative father from informing the child of their true relationship, it can prohibit him from employing the sanctions of the law to avoid the obligations which their assumed relationship would otherwise impose.

this standard

Commonwealth ex rel. Gonzalez v. Andreas, 369 A.2d 416, 419 ([Pa. Super. Ct.] 1976). The operative language of this passage centers on the best interests of the child, and we are of the firm belief—in terms of common law decisionmaking—that this remains the proper, overarching litmus, at least in the wider range of cases. . . . Even in the landscape of modern science, Pennsylvania courts have remained reluctant to abandon wholesale the common law presumptions and dictates, as they reflect ideals, aspirations, and mandates in furtherance of the best-interests objective. . . .

[I]t is our considered view that the determination of paternity by estoppel should be better informed according to the actual best interests of the child, rather than by rote pronouncements grounded merely on the longevity of abstractly portrayed (and perhaps largely ostensible) parental relationships. . . . [T]he present record . . . is very sparse in terms of G.L.M.'s best interests. The record offers very little feel for the closeness of G.L.M.'s relationship with H.M.M. [W]e have no sense for the harm that would befall G.L.M. if H.M.M.'s parental status were to be disestablished, either fully or, as some intermediate court decisions are now suggesting is permissible, partially (i.e., for purposes of support). But see Michael H. v. Gerald D., 491 U.S. 110, 118 (1989) (plurality) (indicating that the law of one state "like nature itself, makes no provision for dual fatherhood").

Implementation of a common law scheme encompassing paternity by estoppel vindicating the best interests of children in paternity disputes on an individualized basis will obviously require development through multiple cases as different fact patterns arise. In terms of guidance, however, absent undue hardship or impossibility, we do not believe a court should dismiss a support claim against a purported biological father based on an estoppel theory vesting legal parenthood in another man without the latter being brought before the court at least as a witness. Moreover, certainly, the [trial] court has the authority to appoint a guardian ad litem to advocate the child's best interests in concrete terms.

The legal fictions perpetuated through the years (including the proposition that genetic testing is irrelevant in certain paternity-related matters) retain their greatest force where there is truly an intact family attempting to defend itself against third-party intervention. In cases involving separation and divorce, we direct that the Uniform Act on Blood Tests to Determine Paternity is now to be applied on its terms insofar as it authorizes testing. At the very least, the identification of G.L.M.'s biological father is a relevant fact for purposes of determining who should pay for the services of a guardian ad litem to vindicate G.L.M.'s best interests. A biological father can do at least this much.

Additionally, recognizing the [trial] court's good intentions in attempting to incentivize reconciliation between Appellant and H.M.M., the parties were separated as of the time of the support, and with apparent good reason. The abstract possibility that the marital unit might be saved, in these circumstances, is not, in our view, a strong reason supporting the dismissal of the claim for support from Appellee.

[W]e realize that there will be children of broken marriages who may never enjoy the supportive relationship with either "psychological" or biological fathers. All things being equal in this regard, we conclude that the responsibility for fatherhood should lie with the biological father. To the degree the equities come into play (after consideration of the child's best interests), continuing deception potentially relevant to a husband's continuance in a marriage may be a relevant factor. . . .

In summary, paternity by estoppel continues to pertain in Pennsylvania, but it will apply only where it can be shown, on a developed record, that it is in the best interests of the involved child. The dismissal of the support claim in this case will not be sustained in the absence of a closer assessment. . . .

[Mr. Justice BAER, dissenting, joined by Mr. Justice MCCAFFERY:]

. . . I would abrogate [paternity by estoppel] in its entirety, with the limited exception of where its invocation would preserve the status of a husband who chooses to parent a non-biological child born into an existing marriage. [I]n most cases, applying the doctrine of paternity by estoppel simply does not protect the child. Adults in today's world will discover who the biological father is. When that happens, the child will generally be told as soon as he is old enough to understand. Thus, the law should encourage the mother's husband to try to maintain the intact marriage and amalgamate the child by a different father into the family home. If this fails, the mother's husband's efforts should be recognized, and paternity by estoppel should be invoked if he desires to maintain the parental relationship. Otherwise, mother's husband should not be punished for "doing the right thing." In such circumstances, the mother should be required to turn to the biological father, who, being able to father the child, should also be required to support him. . . .

Notes and Questions on *Michael H.* and *K.E.M.*

1. Parentage presumptions, old and new. Just as law sometimes makes genetic parentage insufficient or irrelevant for legal parentage, it also identifies nonbiological connections that trigger parental status. The classic example is the marital presumption or presumption of legitimacy, unsuccessfully challenged in *Michael H.*, which makes the formality of marriage the basis of "one of the strongest [presumptions] known to law": the paternity of the mother's husband. See, e.g., Duckett v. Goforth, 649 S.E.2d 72, 81 (S.C. Ct. App. 2007). As *K.E.M.* indicates, the availability of genetic testing has weakened this presumption in some jurisdictions.

What is the status of the presumption of legitimacy in Pennsylvania after *K.E.M.*? According to the case, what is the relationship between this presumption and "paternity by estoppel"? The court indicates that the legislature should develop a comprehensive parentage scheme (footnote 4). What should that scheme provide? Evaluate the UPA provisions reprinted in Chapter V.

2. Estoppel. Under the principal case, what triggers "paternity by estoppel"? As noted in footnote 6 of *K.E.M.*, the ALI Principles recognize "parents by estoppel." They have the same rights and responsibilities as legal parents, but parental status by estoppel arises only in the context of dissolution of the family relationship. ALI Principles §2.03. Evaluate the criteria listed in footnote 6. In addition, parentage by estoppel can arise when one is ordered to pay child support. Id. §203(b)(i). But see, e.g., LP v. LF, 338 P.3d 908 (Wyo. 2014) (rejecting parentage by estoppel).

3. A "new illegitimacy"? Given the Supreme Court's rulings invalidating most discrimination against nonmarital children (e.g., Clark v. Jeter, Chapter V), does the traditional legitimacy presumption threaten the goal of children's equality reflected in those cases? What role should this presumption play today? The drafters of the original 1973 UPA sought to treat marital and nonmarital children equally by supplementing the traditional presumption of legitimacy with a network of conduct-based presumptions, most notably a presumption of paternity arising from a man's receiving a child into his home and holding the child out as his own. A revised UPA, first promulgated in 2000, attempting to respond to improved genetic tests, retained the presumption based on marriage but initially eliminated the "holding out" presumption, on the theory that genetic testing would identify the fathers of children born outside marriage. In 2002, the drafters restored the "holding out" provision, albeit with a new durational requirement that such conduct occur during the first two years of the child's life. Why did the drafters make this change? See UPA §204 & cmt.

Despite the apparently waning importance of marriage in parentage law, scholars discern a "new illegitimacy," because some courts recognize a mother's same-sex partner as the child's second parent only when the couple has married or when they would have done so if possible. See In re Madrone, 350 P.3d 495 (Or. Ct. App. 2015); Nancy D. Polikoff, The New "Illegitimacy": Winning Backward in the Protection of the Children of Lesbian Couples, 20 Am. U. J. Gender Soc. Pol'y & L. 721 (2012). Other jurisdictions take more inclusive approaches, illustrated by Chatterjee v. King (Chapter V). Will the advent of nationwide marriage equality further marginalize nonmarital families and children? Several scholars would abolish the presumption of legitimacy because of its role in exacerbating inequalities among families and the undue power that they say it gives to the biological mother. See June Carbone & Naomi Cahn, Marriage Markets: How Inequality Is Remaking the American Family 134 (2014): Clare Huntington, Postmarital Family Law: A Legal Structure for Nonmarital Families, 67 Stan. L. Rev. 167, 225 (2015). What should take its place? Expanded use of parentage by estoppel? Parentage based on genetics?

4. Case-by-case approach. Evaluate *K.E.M.*'s decision to consider the facts of each case to determine whether to base paternity on genetic evidence. What are the advantages of this approach? The disadvantages? What should "best interests" entail in this context? See, e.g., In re Nicholas H., 46 P.3d 932 (Cal. 2002); Department of Soc. Servs. ex rel. Byer v. Wright, 678 N.W.2d 586 (S.D. 2004). But see B.E.B. v. R.L.B., 979 P.2d 514 (Alaska 1999) (application of paternity by estoppel rests only on risk of financial harm, not emotional harm, to child). How might the child's age be relevant? See D.W. v. R.W., 52 A.3d 1043 (N.J. 2012); V.E. v. W.M., 54 A.3d 368 (Pa. Super. Ct. 2012).

5. Which father(s)? An omitted part of the *K.E.M.* opinion explains that Appellant sued Appellee and opposed application of paternity by estoppel because she assumed that, otherwise, the child would be "left fatherless," with no father responsible for support. The court replies in a footnote: "Appellant's argument, in this respect, does not account for the possibility of her asserting paternity by estoppel in a support action against H.M.M." Under the court's analysis, are both men candidates for paternity by estoppel? Must the court choose just one? California now statutorily allows recognition of more than two parents if recognizing only two would be detrimental to the child. Cal. Fam. Code §7612 (amended by A.B. 1049). On recognizing more than two parents in child support cases, see infra p. 865.

6. Legal fictions? What is "real" parentage? What evidence do you see suggesting that *K.E.M.* assumes that biology creates "real" parentage? In quoting an earlier case, Brinkley v. King, 701 A.2d 176, 180 (Pa. 1997), *K.E.M.* characterizes Pennsylvania's parentage doctrines as follows: "The presumption of paternity and the doctrine of estoppel . . . embody the two great fictions of the law of paternity: the presumption of paternity embodies the fiction that regardless of biology, the married people to whom the child was born are the parents; and the doctrine of estoppel embodies the fiction that, regardless of biology, in the absence of a marriage, the person who has cared for the child is the parent." Adoption also has been described as a legal fiction. How would you challenge such understandings?

b. Modern Reproductive Collaborations: The Rise of Parentage by Intent

NOTE: TRADITIONAL SURROGACY AND THE *BABY M* CASE

In the 1970s, some married couples unable to procreate because of the wife's infertility, her genetic disease, or her disability turned to alternative insemination, arranging to use the husband's semen with a willing woman who, after conception and in exchange for compensation, would carry her pregnancy to term for the couple. Then, she would terminate her parental rights to the resulting child so that the biological father's wife could complete adoption proceedings. Pioneered by Michigan attorney Noel Keane, who drafted the first such formal agreement in 1976, these arrangements became known as "surrogate-mother arrangements" or simply "surrogacy arrangements." See generally Lori B. Andrews, Between Strangers: Surrogate Mothers, Expectant Fathers, and Brave New Babies (1989); Carol Sanger, Developing Markets in Baby-Making: In the Matter of Baby M, 30 Harv. J.L. & Gender 67 (2007).

Surrogacy commanded the national limelight in 1986 when one so-called surrogate mother, Mary Beth Whitehead, gave birth to a baby girl but refused to relinquish her to the commissioning couple, William and Elizabeth Stern, who had agreed to pay $10,000 to her and $7,500 to the Infertility Center of New York (ICNY), one of Keane's agencies. Although the Sterns prevailed in the trial

Elizabeth and William Stern arrive to testify in the Baby *M* case.

Mary Beth Whitehead testifies at a hearing about whether to outlaw surrogacy.

court, they lost their suit to enforce the surrogacy contract before the New Jersey Supreme Court in the famous case In re Baby M, 537 A.2d 1227 (N.J. 1988). Specifically, the state supreme court held that the surrogacy contract conflicts with principles of adoption law, including the prohibition on the use of money in adoptions. Id. at 1240. The court also emphasized the agreement's inconsistency with public policies that attempt to keep together children and "both of their natural parents." Id. at 1247. While leaving room for unpaid surrogacy by willing parties, the court refused to terminate Whitehead's parental rights over her objection; it recognized William Stern (not Whitehead's husband) as the child's father; and it found that nonenforcement of the contract worked no violation of the Sterns' constitutional rights. Based on the testimony of 11 experts, the court determined that custody with the Sterns would serve the child's best interests. Although the relationship between Whitehead and the Sterns stemmed solely from the agreement they signed at the ICNY, they would henceforth share the rearing of a daughter because, on remand, Whitehead won a gradually increasing visitation schedule. See 14 Fam. L. Rep. (BNA) 1276 (Apr. 12, 1988).[10]

While data showed that the parties perform most surrogacy contracts without resort to litigation, the failed surrogacy arrangement in *Baby M* sparked enormous controversy. Feminists divided, with some advocating a complete ban on surrogacy on the grounds that it commodifies and exploits women and children,[11] reduces women to "baby machines,"[12] subjects them to the patriarchal control of the medical profession,[13] and resembles slavery[14] and prostitution.[15] These critics questioned the very term "surrogate mother," arguing that a woman who gestates a pregnancy

---

[10]. When "Baby M" turned 18, she initiated proceedings to terminate Mary Beth Whitehead's parental rights, and Elizabeth Stern then adopted her. See Mike Kelly, 25 Years After Baby M, Surrogacy Questions Remain Unanswered, NorthJersey.com, Mar. 30, 2012, http://www.northjersey.com/news/kelly-25-years-after-baby-m-surrogacy-questions-remain-unanswered-1.745725?page=all.

[11]. See, e.g., Anita L. Allen, Privacy, Surrogacy, and the *Baby M Case,* 76 Geo. L.J. 1759, 1783, 1791 (1988); Cass R. Sunstein, Neutrality in Constitutional Law (with Special Reference to Pornography, Abortion, and Surrogacy), 92 Colum. L. Rev. 1, 47 (1992).

[12]. See, e.g., Gena Corea, Junk Liberty, in Reconstructing Babylon: Essays on Women and Technology 142, 153-156 (H. Patricia Hynes ed., 1991).

[13]. See, e.g., Gena Corea, The Mother Machine: Reproductive Technologies from Artificial Insemination to Artificial Wombs (1985).

[14]. Professor Anita L. Allen observes that slavery "had the effect of causing black women to become surrogate mothers on behalf of slave owners." Anita L. Allen, Surrogacy, Slavery and the Ownership of Life, 13 Harv. J.L. & Pub. Pol'y 132, 140 (1990).

[15]. E.g., Carole Pateman, The Sexual Contract 209-218 (1988); Margaret Jane Radin, Contested Commodities 131-153 (1996).

and gives birth is simply a mother, without qualification.[16] Others condemned surrogacy's underlying racist and eugenic motivations, pursued at the expense of existing children who need homes.[17] Still others, however, argued that surrogacy restrictions constitute unwarranted intrusion into reproductive autonomy, reflecting gender stereotypes and paternalism.[18] In particular, Professor Marjorie Shultz, urging deference to the intent of the parties, saw in surrogacy a unique opportunity for gender-neutral parentage laws:

> . . . To say that the factual issues are "the same" as if Whitehead and William Stern had simply had a child out of wedlock ignores the centrally important fact that modern reproductive techniques allow the separation of personal and sexual intimacy from procreation. . . . It ignores that the father here differs in important ways from stereotypical unwed fathers. In particular, it ignores that the child in question exists only because of its progenitors' individual intentions, their reciprocal decisions, and their behavior and expectations in the wake of such decisions. . . .
>
> . . . Unlike biologically-based variables, the capacity to form and express intentions is gender-neutral. [H]aving rejected any role for intention, the court fell back on gender stereotypes to resolve the issues. . . . The court's decision reinforced stereotypes regarding the desirability of segregating women from the market, the unpredictability of women's intentions and decisions, and the givenness of women's biological destiny. Perhaps worst of all, it acted to lock in existing gender-based spheres of influence in our society, refusing to recognize fragile, emergent male efforts to claim a meaningful role in access to and nurture of children. . . .[19]

Consistent with the *Baby M* opinion, many lawmakers and commentators called for legislation, despite deep disagreement about whether such enactments should criminalize, regulate, or protect surrogacy and whether the law of adoption, alternative insemination, or reproductive privacy should provide the governing principles. Even efforts to draft a uniform law for the United States, the Uniform Status of Children of Assisted Conception Act (USCACA), produced two alternatives, with one framework banning surrogacy and the other regulating it. About half the states enacted surrogacy statutes. Some outlaw the practice, others allow but regulate it, and still others have no governing law at all. See, e.g., Peter Nicolas, Straddling the Columbia: A Constitutional Law Professor's Musings on Circumventing Washington State's Criminal Prohibition on Compensated Surrogacy, 89 Wash. L. Rev. 1235, 1239-1245 (2014) (identifying six categories of state surrogacy laws). Other countries also developed legal responses, such as England's Surrogacy Arrangements Act of 1985 and its later refinements, including

---

[16]. E.g., Barbara Katz Rothman, Recreating Motherhood 168-172 (2000).

[17]. Elizabeth S. Anderson, Is Women's Labor a Commodity?, 19 Phil. & Pub. Aff. 71, 91 (1990).

[18]. See, e.g., Debra Satz, Markets in Women's Reproductive Labor, 21 Phil. & Pub. Aff. 107, 117 (1992) ("dilemma for those who wish to use the mother-fetus bond to condemn [surrogacy] contracts while endorsing [privacy] right to choose abortion"); Carmel Shalev, Birth Power 9-10 (1989) ("[A]mid the serious debate on the morality of [all varieties of] medical reproduction, only surrogacy has been addressed in terms of criminal norms. It occurred to me that the reason for this was the untraditional role that women play in these arrangements.").

[19]. Marjorie Maguire Shultz, Reproductive Technology and Intent-Based Parenthood: An Opportunity for Gender-Neutrality, 1990 Wis. L. Rev. 297, 376-379. But see Pamela Laufer-Ukeles, Essay, Approaching Surrogate Motherhood: Reconsidering Difference, 26 Vt. L. Rev. 407, 436 (2002) (arguing that surrogacy reveals the need for "an asymmetrical notion of [gender] equality").

the 2008 version of the Act. See, e.g., Human Fertilisation and Embryology Act of 2008, ch. 22, §54 (U.K.).[20]

Today, the "traditional surrogacy arrangement" exemplified in *Baby M*, in which one woman provides both genes and gestation, has largely given way to more technologically sophisticated collaborations made possible by in vitro fertilization (IVF). "Gestational surrogacy arrangements" use ova extracted from the intended mother (i.e., Elizabeth Stern in *Baby M*) or from a donor, but not from the woman who will gestate the pregnancy. Although more costly than traditional surrogacy, gestational surrogacy evokes a more favorable legal response in some jurisdictions. Compare Johnson v. Calvert, 851 P.2d 776 (Cal. 1993) (enforcing gestational surrogacy arrangement), and 750 Ill. Comp. Stat. Ann. 47/10 (authorizing enforceable surrogacy arrangements, when the "gestational surrogate has made no genetic contribution" to the intended child), with In re Baby, 447 S.W.3d 807 (Tenn. 2014) (holding enforceable some portions of traditional surrogacy agreement but not provision terminating parental rights), and In re F.T.R., 833 N.W.2d 634 (Wis. 2013) (same). As a result, infertility clinics now routinely use gestational surrogacy, as reflected in a new UPA that supersedes USCACA. See UPA prefatory note & UPA art. 8 prefatory cmt.

Medical advances like IVF also permit reproductive collaborations that have sparked controversies like those in the following cases:

ST. MARY v. DAMON

309 P.3d 1027 (Nev. 2013)

By the Court, SAITTA . . .

Approximately one year after entering into a romantic relationship with each other, [Sha'Kayla] St. Mary and [Veronica Lynn] Damon moved in together. They planned to have a child, deciding that Damon would have her egg fertilized by a sperm donor, and St. Mary would carry the fertilized egg and give birth to the child. In October 2007, Damon's eggs were implanted into St. Mary. Around the same time, Damon drafted a co-parenting agreement, which she and St. Mary signed. The agreement indicated that Damon and St. Mary sought to "jointly and equally share parental responsibility, with both of [them] providing support and guidance." In it, they stated that they would "make every effort to jointly share the responsibilities of raising [their] child," including paying for expenses and making major child-related decisions. The agreement provided that if their relationship ended, they would each work to ensure that the other maintained a close relationship with the child, share the duties of raising the child, and make a "good-faith effort to jointly make all major decisions affecting" the child.

St. Mary gave birth to a child in June 2008. The hospital birth confirmation report and certificate of live birth listed only St. Mary as the child's mother. The child was given both parties' last names, however, in the hyphenated form of St. Mary-Damon.

---

[20]. In 2015, regulations on mitochondrial donations were enacted. See The Human Fertilisation and Embryology (Mitochondrial Donation) Regulations of 2015, http://www.legislation.gov.uk/uksi/2015/572/contents/made.

For several months, St. Mary primarily stayed home caring for the child during the day while Damon worked. But, nearly one year after the child's birth, their romantic relationship ended, St. Mary moved out of the home, and St. Mary and Damon disagreed about how to share their time with the child. St. Mary signed an affidavit declaring that Damon was the biological mother of the child, and in 2009, Damon filed an ex parte petition with the district court to establish maternity, seeking to have the child's birth certificate amended to add Damon as a mother. The district court issued an order stating that St. Mary gave birth to the child and that Damon "is the biological and legal mother of said child." The 2009 order also directed that the birth certificate be amended to add Damon's name as a mother.

Thereafter, St. Mary instituted the underlying case by filing a complaint and motion, in a separate district court case, to establish custody, visitation, and child support. In response, Damon contended that, due to her biological connection, she was entitled to sole custody of the child. Damon attached the 2009 order to her opposition. . . .

[Based on] the 2009 birth certificate order and believing that Damon's status as the sole legal and biological mother had already been determined, the [district] court decided that it would only consider the issue of third-party visitation [and] barred consideration of St. Mary's assertion of custody rights. . . . [After a hearing,] the district court issued an order providing that St. Mary was entitled to third-party visitation but not custody. The court reiterated that the scope of the evidentiary hearing had been limited to the issue of third-party visitation and noted that St. Mary could not be awarded custody of the child because previous orders determined that she "has no biological or legal rights whatsoever under Nevada law." Relying on NRS 126.045, which was repealed by the 2013 Legislature, the court also concluded that the co-parenting agreement was null and void because under that statute "a surrogate agreement is only for married couples, which only include one man and one woman." See Nev. Stat., ch. 213, § 36, at 813 (repealing NRS 126.045). The 2011 order further provided that although St. Mary gave birth to the child, she "was simply a carrier for [the child]," and that she must "realize that [Damon] is the mother." As a result, St. Mary was granted third-party visitation rights and denied any rights as a legal mother. This appeal from the 2011 order followed. . . .

St. Mary may be the child's legal mother

To determine parentage in Nevada, courts must look to the Nevada Parentage Act, which is modeled after the Uniform Parentage Act (UPA). . . . In Nevada, all of the "rights, privileges, duties and obligations" accompanying parenthood are conferred on those persons who are deemed to have a parent-child relationship with the child, regardless of the parents' marital status. Surrogates who bear a child conceived through assisted conception for another, on the other hand, are often not entitled to claim parental rights. See NRS 126.045 (2009) (defining "[s]urrogate" as "an adult woman who enters into an agreement to bear a child conceived through assisted conception for the intended parents," who are treated as the natural parents); 2013 Nev. Stat., ch. 213, §§ 10, 23, 27 at 807–08, 810–11 (replacing the term "surrogate" with "[g]estational carrier" and defining such as a woman "who is not an intended parent and who enters into a gestational agreement," wherein she gives up "legal and physical custody" of the child to the intended parent or parents and may "relinquish all rights and duties as the parent [ ] of a child conceived through assisted reproduction"); Black's Law Dictionary 1036 (8th ed.2004) (defining surrogate as "[a] woman who carries out the gestational function and gives birth to a child for another"). Accordingly, whether St. Mary is treated as someone other than a legal mother, such as a surrogate, is of the upmost significance.

The multiple ways to prove maternity

[T]he Nevada Parentage Act provides several ways to determine a child's legal mother [including proof of a woman's giving birth and through application of paternity statutes] "[i]nsofar as practicable." Paternity may be established in a variety of ways, including through presumptions based on marriage and cohabitation, NRS 126.051(1)(a)-(c), presumptions based on receiving the child into the home and openly holding oneself out as a parent, NRS 126.051(1)(d), genetic testing, NRS 126.051(2), and voluntary acknowledgment, NRS 126.053. Hence, a determination of parentage rests upon a wide array of considerations rather than genetics alone.

This case presents a situation where two women proffered evidence that could establish or generate a conclusive presumption of maternity to either woman. . . . By dividing the reproductive roles of conceiving a child, St. Mary and Damon each assumed functions traditionally used to evidence a legal maternal relationship. Hence, this matter raises the issue of whether the Nevada Parentage Act and its policies preclude a child from having two legal mothers where two women split the genetic and physical functions of creating a child.

The law does not preclude a child from having two legal mothers

[In relying on the 2009 birth certificate order and refusing to consider St. Mary's assertions of maternity or custody, the district court] impliedly operated on the premise that a child, created by artificial insemination through an anonymous sperm donor, may not have two mothers under the law. However, contrary to this premise, the Nevada Parentage Act and its policies do not preclude such a child from having two legal mothers.

Although NRS 126.051(3) contains procedures for rebutting paternity presumptions by clear and convincing evidence or "a court decree establishing *paternity* . . . by another *man*" (emphases added), and while NRS 126.051(3) arguably applies in maternity cases, we decline to read this provision of the statute as conveying clear legislative intent to deprive a child conceived by artificial insemination of the emotional, financial, and physical support of an intended mother who "actively assisted in the decision and process of bringing [the child] into this world." In Nevada, as in other states, the best interest of the child is the paramount concern in determining the custody and care of children. Both the Legislature and this court have acknowledged that, generally, a child's best interest is served by maintaining two actively involved parents. . . .

Of the jurisdictions that have addressed the issue of maternity between two women who created a child through assisted reproduction, California is highly instructive. . . . California's precedent is highly persuasive because it pertains to a statutory scheme that is substantially similar to Nevada's and advances the policies that underlie the Nevada Parentage Act—preventing children from "becom[ing] wards of the state," minding a child's best interest, and serving a child's best interest with the support of two parents. . . . Hence, there is no legal or policy-based barrier to the establishment under NRS Chapter 126, as it existed at the time of the district court's determinations and as it exists now, of a legal parent and child relationship with both St. Mary and Damon. . . .

. . . Although St. Mary's parentage can be established by virtue of her having given birth to the child, the parties dispute whether they intended for St. Mary to be the child's parent or simply a surrogate or gestational carrier who lacked a legal parent-child relationship to the child. Therefore, upon remand, the district court must hold an evidentiary hearing to determine whether St. Mary is the child's legal mother or if she is someone without a legal relationship to the child, during which the court may consider any relevant evidence for establishing maternity under the Nevada Parentage Act.

The co-parenting agreement was not a surrogacy agreement and was consistent with Nevada's public policy

St. Mary asserts that the co-parenting agreement demonstrates the parties' intent regarding parentage and custody of the child and that the district court erred in determining that the co-parenting agreement was an unenforceable surrogacy agreement under NRS 126.045. Damon responds that, because the agreement was between an unmarried intended parent and a surrogate and purported to resolve issues of parentage and child custody, the district court correctly deemed that the co-parenting agreement was prohibited by NRS 126.045 (2009).

. . . Here, St. Mary and Damon's co-parenting agreement was not within the scope of NRS 126.045. The agreement lacked any language intimating that St. Mary acted as a surrogate, such as language indicating that she surrendered custody of the child or relinquished her rights as a mother to the child. Rather, the agreement expressed that St. Mary would share the parental duties of raising the child and would jointly make major parenting decisions with Damon.

"Parties are free to contract, and the courts will enforce their contracts if they are not unconscionable, illegal, or in violation of public policy." It is presumed that fit parents act in the best interest of their children. Troxel v. Granville, 530 U.S. 57, 68 (2000). Thus, public policy favors fit parents entering agreements to resolve issues pertaining to their minor child's "custody, care, and visitation."

When a child has the opportunity to be supported by two loving and fit parents pursuant to a co-parenting agreement, this opportunity is to be given due consideration and must not be foreclosed on account of the parents being of the same sex. . . . St. Mary and Damon's co-parenting agreement was aligned with Nevada's policy of allowing parents to agree on how to best provide for their child. Within their co-parenting agreement, St. Mary and Damon sought to provide for their child's best interest by agreeing to share the responsibilities of raising the child, even if the relationship between St. Mary and Damon ended. The agreement's language provides the indicia of an effort by St. Mary and Damon to make the child's best interest their priority. Thus, in the event that St. Mary is found to be a legal mother, the district court must consider the parties' co-parenting agreement in making its child custody determination. [Reversed and remanded.]

JASON P. v. DANIELLE S.

171 Cal. Rptr. 3d 789 (Ct. App.), *review denied,* 2014 Cal. LEXIS 5345 (Cal. 2014)

WILLHITE, J.

Family Code section 7613, subdivision (b) (hereafter, section 7613(b)) currently provides: "The donor of semen provided to a licensed physician and surgeon or to a licensed sperm bank for use in assisted reproduction of a woman other than the donor's spouse is treated in law as if he were not the natural parent of a child thereby conceived, unless otherwise agreed to in a writing signed by the donor and the woman prior to the conception of the child." In Steven S. v. Deborah D., [25 Cal.Rptr.3d 482 (Ct. App. 2005)] (*Steven S.*), we reversed a finding of paternity in favor of a donor of semen provided to a licensed physician, rejecting the sperm donor's argument "that we should look beyond the words of the statute to find legislative intent for a public policy favoring a finding of paternity where, as here, the mother was in an intimate relationship with a known donor and also attempted to conceive naturally, albeit unsuccessfully." In rejecting the donor's argument, we employed broad and categorical language. We declared: "There can be no paternity claim from a sperm donor who is not married to the woman who becomes pregnant with the donated semen, so long as it was provided to a licensed physician."

We should not have been so categorical, because we were not faced with a donor seeking to establish paternity under section 7611, the presumed parentage statute, and therefore had no occasion to consider whether section 7613(b) precludes any such attempt. We do so now, and conclude that section 7613(b) does not preclude a donor from establishing that he is a presumed father under section 7611. . . .

The parties agreed upon the following facts at the start of the trial. Jason and Danielle cohabitated for many years, but they never married. Gus was conceived through in vitro fertilization (IVF). Jason provided to a licensed fertility clinic the sperm used in the IVF procedure. Jason is not listed on Gus's birth certificate, and there is no voluntary declaration of paternity. Gus has no other natural, presumed, or potential biological father.

In addition to the agreed-upon facts, Jason presented evidence that he and Danielle tried to have a baby naturally beginning in 2006. Although Danielle became pregnant in December 2006, the pregnancy was not viable after six and a half weeks. In 2007, Danielle had two intrauterine insemination (IUI) procedures using Jason's sperm, but neither resulted in a pregnancy. In October 2007, after being advised that their inability to conceive might be due to issues regarding Jason's sperm count, Jason had a surgical procedure to address that problem. She and Jason also began to look into having an IVF procedure.

In May 2008, Danielle moved out of Jason's home and bought a home nearby. The following month, she purchased sperm of an anonymous donor from a sperm bank and told Jason she was going to pursue motherhood as a single mother. At some point in the fall of 2008, she looked at a Web site for "single mothers by choice" to learn about her rights; she learned that in California, a man who gives his sperm for artificial insemination is never treated in the law as though he is the father. In September 2008, she moved back into Jason's house while the house she bought was being remodeled.

In November 2008 or January 2009, Jason gave Danielle a letter in which he wrote that he was not ready to be a father, but if Danielle wanted to use his sperm to conceive, she had his blessing as long as she did not tell others. Danielle chose to use Jason's sperm rather than the anonymous donor's sperm she had purchased.

After having an unsuccessful IUI procedure in January 2009 using Jason's sperm, Danielle decided to try an IVF procedure. Before the procedure, Danielle and Jason both signed a series of informed consent forms provided by California Fertility Partners. On each form, Danielle filled in both her name and Jason's name in the spaces designated for the "Intended Parent." On March 9, 2009, Jason took Danielle to California Fertility Partners for the IVF procedure. The procedure was successful, and Gus was born in December 2009.

At trial, Jason presented evidence regarding his relationship with Gus and Danielle over the next two and a half years. For example, he presented evidence that Danielle referred to Jason as "Dada" when speaking to Gus, and Gus called Jason "Dada." When Jason was working in New York for six months, Danielle and Gus flew there several times and stayed with Jason at his apartment. When Danielle and Gus were not in New York with Jason, Jason communicated with Gus over the Internet by Skype. Jason continued to maintain contact with Gus until the middle of 2012, when Danielle terminated her relationship with Jason.

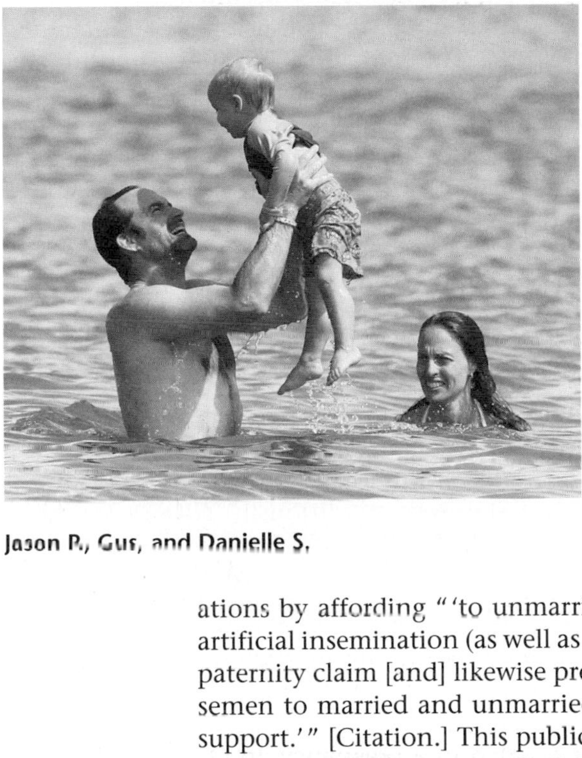

Jason P., Gus, and Danielle S.

[In Jason's suit to establish a parental relationship, the trial court granted Danielle's motion for a nonsuit, relying on *Steven S.* and rejecting Jason's arguments based on estoppel and section 7611(d).] Finally, the trial court found that application of section 7613(b) to Jason is not unconstitutional. The court noted that "the Legislature has weighed competing public policies regarding paternity and sperm donors, and has reconciled those considerations by affording "'to unmarried women a statutory right to bear children by artificial insemination (as well as a right of men to donate semen) without fear of a paternity claim [and] likewise provided men with a statutory vehicle for donating semen to married and unmarried women alike without fear of liability for child support.'" [Citation.] This public policy determination is within the Legislature's authority, and does not make § 7613(b) unconstitutional."

Having found that Jason did not have a parent and child relationship with Gus, the trial court found Jason was not entitled to custody of, or visitation with, Gus . . . Judgment was entered in favor of Danielle, from which Jason appeals. . . .

[O]ur categorical statement [in *Steven S.*] appears to have been undermined by an observation the California Supreme Court made in a case decided a few months after our decision in *Steven S.* In K.M. v. E.G., [117 P.3d 673 (Cal. 2005)], the Supreme Court examined section 7613(b) in the context of a lesbian couple, where one of the women, K.M., provided ova to her partner, E.G., for use in an IVF procedure. After the relationship ended, K.M. filed an action to establish a parental relationship with the twin girls born to E.G. as a result of the

IVF procedure. The trial court granted E.G.'s motion to dismiss, finding, among other things, that K.M.'s position was analogous to that of a sperm donor under section 7613(b).

The Supreme Court reversed, finding that the facts "[did] not present a 'true "egg donation"' situation" because the couple lived together and intended to bring the child into their joint home, and therefore section 7613(b), assuming it applied to women who donate ova, did not apply. The court . . . noted that, while the Model UPA "'restricts application of the nonpaternity provision of [section 7613(b)] to a "*married* woman other than the donor's wife[,]" . . . in California, [section 7613(b)] applies to all women, married or not. Thus, the California Legislature has afforded unmarried as well as married women a statutory vehicle for obtaining semen for artificial insemination without fear that the donor may claim paternity and has likewise provided men with a statutory vehicle for donating semen to married and unmarried women alike without fear of liability for child support.'" The court concluded: "It is clear, therefore, that California intended to expand the protection of the model act to include unmarried women so that unmarried women could avail themselves of artificial insemination. But there is nothing to indicate that California intended to expand the reach of this provision so far that it would apply if a man provided semen to be used to impregnate his unmarried partner in order to produce a child that would be raised in their joint home. It would be surprising, to say the least, to conclude that the Legislature intended such a result." The Supreme Court did not address the applicability of section 7611(d) in sperm or ova donation cases in K.M. v. E.G. . . .

[We] hold that section 7613(b) should be interpreted only to preclude a sperm donor from establishing paternity based upon his biological connection to the child, and does not preclude him from establishing that he is a presumed parent under section 7611(d) based upon postbirth conduct. We reach this conclusion because we must construe section 7613(b) [in the context of the entire statutory scheme.] Section 7613(b) and section 7611 both are part of the UPA. Section 7611 provides that "[a] person is presumed to be the natural parent of a child if the person meets [certain statutory conditions.]" Those conditions [include several related to marriage or attempted marriage to the child's mother as well as "holding out" as when] the presumed parent receives the child into his or her home and openly holds out the child as his or her natural child (§ 7611, subd. (d)). . . .

"'The paternity presumptions are driven by state interest in preserving the integrity of the family and legitimate concern for the welfare of the child. The state has an "'interest in preserving and protecting the developed parent-child . . . relationships which give young children social and emotional strength and stability.'"'" (*In re* Nicholas H., [46 P.3d 932 (Cal. 2002)].) . . . "The statutory purpose [of section 7611] is to distinguish between those fathers who have entered into some familial relationship with the mother and child and those who have not." A biological connection to the child is not necessary for the presumption of paternity to arise. Nor is it necessary for the person seeking presumed parent status to have entered into the familial relationship from the time of conception or birth. "[T]he premise behind the category of presumed father is that an individual who has demonstrated a commitment to the child and the child's welfare—regardless of whether he is biologically the father—is entitled to the elevated status of presumed fatherhood." Thus, a sperm donor who has established a familial relationship with the child, and has demonstrated a commitment to the child and the child's welfare, can be found to be a presumed parent even though he could not establish paternity based upon his biological connection to the child.

By interpreting section 7613(b) only to preclude a sperm donor from establishing paternity based upon his biological connection to the child, while allowing him to establish that he is a presumed parent under section 7611 based upon a demonstrated familial relationship, we allow both statutes to retain effectiveness and promote the purpose of each. . . .

Our holding that a sperm donor is not precluded from establishing presumed parentage does not mean that a mother who conceives through assisted reproduction and allows the sperm donor to have some kind of relationship with the child necessarily loses her right to be the sole parent. First, section 7611 requires a *familial* relationship. . . . A mother wishing to retain her *sole* right to parent her child conceived through assisted reproduction can limit the kind of contact she allows the sperm donor to have with her child to ensure that the relationship does not rise to the level of presumed parent and child.

Second, the presumption of parentage under section 7611 is, with certain exceptions, a *rebuttable* presumption. (§ 7612, subd. (a).) Thus, even if a sperm donor can establish that he received the child into his home and openly held out the child as his natural child, the trial court nevertheless may conclude based on other evidence that the presumption has been rebutted and the sperm donor is not the child's natural father.

In this case, Jason was denied the opportunity to present evidence to show that he is Gus's presumed father under section 7611(d). Therefore, the judgment must be reversed and the matter remanded for further proceedings. [The court rejected Jason's arguments based on estoppel and the informed consent forms for the medical procedures, and it found his constitutional challenge moot.]

Notes and Questions on *St. Mary* and *Jason P.*

1. Collaborative reproduction. IVF makes possible several forms of "collaborative reproduction." For example, an intended mother can gestate a fetus conceived with a donor's egg and the sperm of her husband/partner. See, e.g., In re C.K.G., 173 S.W.3d 714 (Tenn. 2005). Or, the intended parents can hire a "gestational surrogate" (often called a "gestational carrier") after creating a pre-embryo with their own genetic material. See, e.g., Johnson v. Calvert, 851 P.2d 776 (Cal. 1993); Nolan v. LaBree, 52 A.3d 923 (Me. 2012). Sometimes a gestational surrogate carries donated genetic material (a donated embryo or an embryo created with a donor egg or donor sperm or both) so that one or both intended parents have no biological tie to the resulting child. See, e.g., In re Marriage of Buzzanca, 72 Cal. Rptr. 2d 280 (Ct. App. 1998); cf. Sieglein v. Schmidt, 120 A.3d 790 (Md. Ct. Spec. App. 2015). And, as in *St. Mary,* lesbian couples can divide genetic and gestational contributions (sometimes called "reciprocal IVF"), giving each woman a biological tie to the child. Mitochondrial contributions, permitted in United

Kingdom and designed to avoid passing on genetic diseases, allow what some dub "three-parent IVF." See I. Glenn Cohen et al., Transatlantic Lessons in Regulation of Mitochondrial Replacement Therapy, 348 Science, Apr. 2015, at 178.

All of these developments raise questions about legal parentage of the resulting children. See generally, e.g., Lynda Wray Black, The Birth of a Parent: Defining Parentage for Lenders of Genetic Material, 92 Neb. L. Rev. 799 (2014). Further, by allowing reproduction in settings where it was not previously possible, they transform understandings of family, sex, and gender. See Kimberly M. Mutcherson, Transformative Reproduction, 16 J. Gender Race & Just. 187 (2013); Darren Rosenblum, Unsex Mothering: Toward a New Culture of Parenting, 35 Harv. J. L. & Gender 57 (2012).

2. Intent-based parentage. What role does intent play in *St. Mary*? California case law pioneered parentage based on intent, following a theory originally proposed by Professor Marjorie Shultz, who wrote "[w]ithin the context of artificial reproductive techniques, intentions that are voluntarily chosen, deliberate, express and bargained-for ought presumptively to determine legal parenthood."[21] The California Supreme Court first applied the test in *Johnson*, supra, to recognize as parents the commissioning couple who provided the genetic material and intended to rear the child, rather than the gestational surrogate who decided during the pregnancy not to relinquish the child upon birth. Given the conflicting indicia of maternity under California parentage statutes (gestation and genetics), the court broke the "tie" based on the parties' intent and causation (but for the agreement, the child would not exist). Thereafter, *Buzzanca*, supra, invoked intent to rule that divorcing spouses were both the legal parents of a child who was created from a frozen embryo that they obtained from a fertility clinic and who was born to a gestational surrogate whom they hired; as a result, John Buzzanca could not avoid paying child support. Despite these precedents, California courts have not used intent to resolve disputes in traditional surrogacy cases (in which the gestational surrogate bears her genetic child, as in *Baby M*, supra). Why?

What are the advantages of intent-based parentage? The disadvantages? See Mary Patricia Byrn & Lisa Giddings, An Empirical Analysis of the Use of the Intent Test to Determine Parentage in Assisted Reproductive Technology Cases, 50 Hous. L. Rev. 1295, 1324 (2013) (finding judges apply the intent test in over 20 percent of cases). How should a court determine the parties' intent when they offer conflicting testimony, as in *St. Mary*? In a dispute with facts similar to those in *St. Mary*, K.M. v. E.G., 117 P.3d 673 (Cal. 2005) (described in *Jason P.* and cited in an omitted portion of *St. Mary*), the California Supreme Court tweaked the intent test. Instead of considering exclusively who the parties intended would be the child's parents at the time of conception or pregnancy, the court placed weight on the parties' intent that the resulting child would be raised in their joint home. Does this change improve the test?

What happens to intent-based parentage in *Jason P.*? Does the opinion indicate that subsequent behavior can show that the parties' original intent changed over time? Or is the court using an alternative test for parentage? See generally Susan Frelich Appleton, Between the Binaries: Exploring the Legal Boundaries of Nonanonymous Sperm Donation, 49 Fam. L.Q. 93 (2015).

---

[21]. Shultz, supra note [19], at 323.

3. Alternatives to intent.

a. Uniform Parentage Act of 1973. The 1973 version of the UPA, which California enacted, indicates that genetic parentage establishes legal parentage. UPA §11 (blood tests). See also *Nolan,* supra. As applied in an egg donation case, however, this principle would require issuance of a birth certificate identifying the genetic mother as the legal mother and a subsequent adoption by the intended mother. Given the legal treatment of donor insemination, does this approach violate equal protection? See generally D.M.T. v. T.M.H., 129 So. 3d 320 (Fla. 2013). As a practical matter, should the state require genetic testing of each child at birth to determine parentage?

b. New Uniform Parentage Act. The UPA of 2000 (amended in 2002) responds to technological advances in genetics and reproductive medicine. This model statute generally treats egg donors as sperm donors, with no legal status, and makes the intended mother the legal mother without government intervention. See UPA §702 (cmt.). The model act explicitly applies to couples without regard to marital status. UPA §202. As *St. Mary* illustrates, several states enacting the UPA have opted for a gender-neutral reading of its provisions to allow application to same-sex couples. See, e.g., *D.M.T.,* supra. But see, e.g., Dubose v. North, 332 P.3d 311 (Okla. Civ. App. 2014). More broadly, this model recognizes as the legal mother the woman giving birth, with her husband (or wife or partner), rather than the "donor," as the presumed second parent. See UPA §201(a). See also, e.g., *C.K.G.,* supra (recognizing gestational, intended mother). This Act, however, goes on to provide for "gestational agreements," as follows:

§801. GESTATIONAL AGREEMENT AUTHORIZED

(a) A prospective gestational mother, her husband if she is married, a donor or the donors, and the intended parents may enter into a written agreement providing that:

(1) the prospective gestational mother agrees to pregnancy by means of assisted reproduction;

(2) the prospective gestational mother, her husband if she is married, and the donors relinquish all rights and duties as the parents of a child conceived through assisted reproduction; and

(3) the intended parents become the parents of the child.

(b) The man and the woman who are the intended parents must both be parties to the gestational agreement.

(c) A gestational agreement is enforceable only if validated as provided in Section 803.

(d) A gestational agreement does not apply to the birth of a child conceived by means of sexual intercourse.

(e) A gestational agreement may provide for payment of consideration.

(f) A gestational agreement may not limit the right of the gestational mother to make decisions to safeguard her health or that of the embryos or fetus.

Validation of a gestational agreement requires procedures tantamount to a preconception adoption, including a home study and judicial approval, and makes the intended parents the child's legal parents. The parties can terminate a validated gestational agreement only before the pregnancy begins, or a court can do so for good cause. A gestational agreement without validation is not enforceable, but the intended parents may be liable for support. See UPA §§806-809.[22] Why did the court decide that St. Mary might not be a surrogate under the Nevada statute?

Must the UPA's surrogacy provisions apply to a single man who intends to become a parent via surrogacy? See In re Roberto d.B., 923 A.2d 115 (Md. 2007). To gay male couples? Do the Supreme Court's marriage-equality cases compel states to allow compensated surrogacy for gay couples? See Martha A. Field, Compensated Surrogacy, 89 Wash. L. Rev. 1155 (2014) (no). But see Douglas NeJaime, *Griswold*'s Progeny: Assisted Reproduction, Procreative Liberty, and Sexual Orientation Equality, 124 Yale L. J. Forum 340 (2015).

c. Functional approaches. Several contemporary authorities emphasize conduct and lived familial relationships in determining parentage. E.g., J. Herbie DiFonzo & Ruth C. Stern, Breaking the Mold and Picking up the Pieces: Rights of Parenthood and Parentage in Nontraditional Families, 51 Fam. Ct. Rev. 104 (2013). To what extent does intent-based parentage resemble the functional approach? See Richard F. Storrow, Parenthood by Pure Intention: Reproduction and the Functional Approach to Assisted Parentage, 53 Hastings L.J. 597 (2002). Whose interests does a functional approach serve?

Does *Jason P.* rely on a functional approach? Note how the court must ignore Jason P.'s genetic paternity, given his status as a donor. What differences between intent-based parentage and a functional approach emerge from *Jason P.*? Should the limited function that Jason P. has played in the child's life accord him a limited parental role, falling short of the full parentage that Danielle S. exercises? See Pamela Laufer-Ukeles & Ayelet Blecher-Prigat, Between Function and Form: Towards a Differentiated Model of Functional Parenthood, 20 Geo. Mason L. Rev. 419 (2013).What facts should prove relevant on remand? According to news reports, Jason P. prevailed.[23]

4. Constitutional claims. What liberty interests are at stake in *St. Mary* and *Jason P.*? Does Stanley v. Illinois (Chapter V) give each petitioner a constitutional right to a continued relationship with the child? On what basis? Jason P.'s constitutional arguments were deemed moot, given the court's reading of the statute. Cf. L.F. v. Breit, 736 S.E.2d 711, 722 (Va. 2013) (holding that absolutely foreclosing parentage "solely by virtue of [a man's] status as an unmarried donor" would violate due process). See also *D.M.T.*, supra. How will *Jason P.* influence the conduct

---

[22]. Eleven states have enacted the new UPA (Alabama, Delaware, Illinois, Maine, New Mexico, North Dakota, Oklahoma, Texas, Utah, Washington, and Wyoming). See http://www.uniformlaws.org/LegislativeFactSheet.aspx?title=Parentage Act. However, not all have included the sections on gestational agreements. See, e.g., Ala. Code §26-17-801 (reserving section); Wyo. Sta. Ann. §§14-2-401 et seq. (omitting this chapter). The Family Law Section of the American Bar Association (ABA) has proposed a model act governing assisted reproduction; while comprehensively addressing the issues, the drafters indicate that this model's provisions are not designed to conflict with or supersede the UPA's treatment of a number of topics, e.g., the status of resulting children and gestational agreements. See American Bar Association Model Act Governing Assisted Reproduction, arts. 6 & 7 (Feb. 2008), http://apps.americanbar.org/family/committees/artmodelact.pdf.

[23]. See Jason Patric Huge Victory Declared Legal Parent, TMZ, Nov. 3, 2014, http://www.tmz.com/2014/11/03/jason-patric-legal-parent-father-court-baby-mama/. For the parties' contrasting perspectives, compare Vanessa Grigoriadis, Tempest in a Test Tube: Jason Patric's Brutal Custody Battle, Rolling Stone, July 15, 2014, http://www.rollingstone.com/culture/news/tempest-in-a-test-tube-jason-patrics-brutal-custody-battle-20140715, with Jason Patric's Lawyer Responds to RS Custody Battle Story, Rolling Stone, July 15, 2014, http://www.rollingstone.com/culture/news/jason-patrics-lawyer-responds-to-rs-custody-battle-story-20140715.

of parents like Danielle S., who wish to prevent a known donor from acquiring parental status?

5. Default rules and departures. Most of the rules surveyed above attempt to articulate default rules that determine parentage in the absence of affirmative steps to achieve a different allocation of rights and responsibilities (for example, a termination of parental rights and adoption, steps that entail considerable state intervention). Even with a rule based on intent, however, when must the parties take action to memorialize their plans and prevent future challenges?

a. Agreements. How would the court have decided *St. Mary* without the co-parenting agreement? Other courts have recognized the importance of contracts in determining parentage. E.g., Frazier v. Goudschaal, 295 P.3d 542 (Kan. 2013). How can you reconcile judicial reliance on such agreements with the usual rule that parents cannot bargain away their children's rights and the traditional disfavor of "parentage by contract"? E.g., T.F. v. B.L., 813 N.E.2d 1244, 1251 (Mass. 2004). See generally Deborah Zalesne, The Contractual Family: The Role of the Market in Shaping Family Formations and Rights, 36 Cardozo L. Rev. 1027 (2015).

b. Adoption. When should the law make adoption necessary? Should St. Mary or Damon (or both) have needed to adopt the child to be recognized as a legal mother? Cf. Nancy D. Polikoff, A Mother Should Not Have to Adopt Her Own Child: Parentage Laws for Children of Lesbian Couples in the Twenty-First Century, 5 Stan. J. C.R. & C.L. 201 (2009). Why do several states require adoption by the intended mother in traditional surrogacy cases, while allowing intent alone to suffice in gestational surrogacy cases? In recognizing the commissioning couple as the parents in *Buzzanca*, supra, the court expressly rejected an "adoption default" model for most collaborative reproductive arrangements. 72 Cal. Rptr. 2d at 289. But see In re T.J.S., 54 A.3d 263 (N.J. 2012). On what basis should couples like the Buzzancas be able to avoid adoption procedures in order to become the parents of a child with no genetic or gestational tie to either of them? Evaluate the approach of the new UPA, supra, which requires, in effect, a preimplantation adoption procedure whenever the intended mother is not the woman giving birth.

When should the law disallow adoption because the individual is already presumed to be a parent? A New York court denied the adoption petition of a mother's wife on the theory that the presumption of legitimacy already secures her parental status, as it would if she were the mother's husband. The couple worried that, if the family moved to a state that then did not recognize same-sex marriage, only an adoption could protect her relationship with the mother's child. Matter of Seb C-M, X 2013-21 (N.Y. Sur. Ct. 2014) (summarized 40 Fam. L. Rep. (BNA) 1159 (Feb. 11, 2014)).

c. Birth certificates. Default rules also determine the parentage information entered on the child's birth certificate. Generally, the woman giving birth is listed as the mother. E.g., In re M.M.M., 428 S.W.3d 389 (Tex. App. 2014). In some cases, however, the parties have gone to court before the child is born to litigate the content of the anticipated birth certificate. In Culliton v. Beth Israel Deaconess Medical Ctr., 756 N.E.2d 1133 (Mass. 2001), a gestational surrogacy case, the genetic and intended parents successfully petitioned to be named as parents on the original birth certificate. But see *T.J.S.*, supra (rejecting arguments for entering the intended mother's name on the birth certificate and requiring her to adopt the child, as decided by an evenly divided court); Doe v. N.Y. City Bd. of Health, 782 N.Y.S.2d 180 (Sup. Ct. 2004) (ordering two sets of birth certificates, with the first, naming the gestational mother, to be sealed). Suppose that an unmarried man arranges to have a child by means of a gestational surrogate using an ovum donated by another woman. Neither woman seeks to be the mother of the child or to participate in rearing. May the birth certificate list only the father? See *In re Roberto d.B.*, supra (yes). May the birth certificate list two fathers and no mother? See Raftapol v. Ramey, 12 A.3d 783 (Conn. 2010) (yes). Anecdotal evidence indicates that many surrogates prefer to work with such couples. See, e.g., Ginia Bellafante, Surrogate Mothers' New Niche: Bearing Babies for Gay Couples, N.Y. Times, May 27, 2005, at A1. What reasons might explain this preference?

d. Prebirth stipulations and judgments. Some intended parents, especially same-sex couples, go to court to obtain a prebirth order of parentage for children of assisted reproduction. See Howard Fink & June Carbone, Between Private Ordering and Public Fiat: A New Paradigm for Family Law Decision-making, 5 J.L. Fam. Stud. 1, 45 (2003). Does a prebirth judgment foreclose a later change of mind? If not, what good is it? If so, what limits should apply? See generally Dara E. Purvis, Intended Parents and the Problem of Perspective, 24 Yale J.L. & Feminism 210, 244-253 (2012) (recommending such orders). Should an adoption follow after the child is born?

e. Registration. Under Illinois's Gestational Surrogacy Act, enacted in 2004, the intended parents are the legal parents upon the child's birth, based on the prior certification of a surrogacy agreement by parties who meet statutory eligibility requirements and the filing of completed forms with the Department of Public Health. These requirements include previous childbearing by the surrogate (who cannot be the genetic mother of the child), consultation with independent counsel and mental health evaluations for the surrogate and the intended parents, a medical justification for the procedure, compensation placed in escrow, and the contribution of at least one of the gametes by an intended parent. 750 Ill. Comp. Stat. 47/1-47/75. To what extent would reliance on voluntary acknowledgments, increasingly used to establish paternity, suffice for same-sex couples and others using assisted reproduction? See Leslie Joan Harris, Voluntary Acknowledgments of Parentage for Same-Sex Couples, 20 Am. U. J. Gender Soc. Pol'y & L. 467 (2012).

f. Other consequences. Fixing parental status before or at the time of birth (either through a default rule or a prebirth procedure) can have other important consequences, such as authority to consent to the infant's medical treatment and insurance coverage for neonatal intensive care. See Mid-South Ins. Co. v. Doe, 274 F. Supp. 2d 757 (D.S.C. 2003).

6. "Embryo adoption." Families that create embryos (from their own genetic material or that donated by others) often have many left over. Some donate them for research, while others make them available to other families. See, e.g., Tamar Lewin, Industry's Growth Leads to Leftover Embryos, and Painful Choices, N.Y. Times, June 18, 2015, at A1. The choice of terminology for the latter disposition—"embryo adoption" versus "embryo donation"—evokes abortion politics. See Jessica R. Hoffman, You Say Adoption, I Say Objection: Why the Word War over Embryo Disposition Is More Than Just Semantics, 46 Fam. L.Q. 397 (2012).

How does the terminology affect our understanding of adoption, with its traditional emphasis on child welfare? Despite conventional wisdom claiming that facilitating assisted reproduction decreases adoption (by creating children who will take the place of adoptees in families), empirical studies fail to find such effects. See I. Glenn Cohen & Daniel L. Chen, Trading-off Reproductive Technology and Adoption: Does Subsidizing IVF Decrease Adoption Rates and Should It Matter?, 95 Minn. L. Rev. 485 (2010).

Alternatively, does the use of the term "adoption" in this new context reinforce adoption's stigma, suggesting "there is something deeply suspect" about parenting someone else's child?[24]

7. Race and class. Might a preference for white babies explain why some infertile families choose "embryo adoption" over conventional adoption? In *Johnson,* supra, the gestational surrogate was part African-American; the genetic, intended mother was Filipina; and the genetic, intended father was white. To what extent did the race of the parties influence the determination of parentage? Will gestational surrogacy produce a new class of poor and minority women (here and abroad) who provide care prenatally for the children of wealthy whites? See, e.g., Khiara M. Bridges, *Windsor,* Surrogacy, and Race, 89 Wash. L. Rev. 1125 (2014). Do parents suffer a compensable injury when a clinic mistakenly uses genetic material of the "wrong race"? See, e.g., Christy Gutowski, Sperm Donation Lawsuit to be Decided in DuPage; Racial Aspects of Donor Mix-up Led to National Debate, Chi. Trib., Apr. 4, 2015, 2015 WLNR 9885989 (reporting damages suit by white lesbian couple after the birth of biracial daughter). On the role of intermediaries in matching intended parents with genetic material, see Dov Fox, Race Sorting in Family Formation, 49 Fam. L.Q. 55 (2015).

8. Limitations.

a. Medical regulation. A laissez-faire approach to assisted reproduction prevails in the United States, with limits left up to the market and its participants — health care providers, fertility clinics, and patients exploring every possible route to procreation. See generally Naomi Cahn, Test Tube Families: Why the Fertility Market Needs Regulation (2009). But see Jody Lyneé Madeira, Woman Scorned?: Resurrecting Infertile Women's Decision-Making Autonomy, 71 Md. L. Rev. 339 (2012). Multifetal pregnancies pose a significant risk in fertility treatment. See Urska Velikonja, The Costs of Multiple Gestation Pregnancies in Assisted Reproduction, 32 Harv. J.L. & Gender 463 (2009). In the one notable exception to self-regulation, federal legislation (designed in part to develop "informed consumers") requires fertility programs to report their pregnancy rates to the Department of Health and Human Services for annual publication and distribution to the public. 42 U.S.C. §§263a-1 to 263a-7. What other information should fertility clinics be required to disclose? See Jim Hawkins, Selling ART: An Empirical Assessment of Advertising on Fertility Clinics' Websites, 88 Ind. L.J. 1147, 1174-1177 (2013).

b. Pricing. What limits would you recommend on payment for egg "donation"? Many college newspapers publish advertisements for young, white donors with high SAT scores. See Kenneth Baum, Golden Eggs: Towards the Rational

---

[24]. Bartholet, supra note [8], at 69.

Regulation of Oocyte Donation, 2001 BYU L. Rev. 107; Julia D. Mahoney, The Market for Human Tissue, 86 Va. L. Rev. 163 (2000). Some fertility clinics have oocyte-sharing programs, allowing patients to receive treatment for reduced fees in exchange for donating some of their eggs to other patients. What is the proper way to balance autonomy, protection from exploitation, and fair compensation for hormonal therapy and surgery that entail some risks? See Ethics Comm. of the Am. Soc'y for Reprod. Med., Financial Incentives in Recruitment of Oocyte Donors, 88 Fertility & Sterility 305 (2007) (more than $5,000 requires justification, more than $10,000 is inappropriate, and sharing programs need clear and fair policies); Hillary B. Alberta, et al., Risk Disclosure and the Recruitment of Oocyte Donors: Are Advertisers Telling the Full Story?, 42 J.L. Med. & Ethics 232 (2014). See also Tamar Lewin, Egg Donors Want to Name Their Price, N.Y. Times, Oct. 17, 2015, at A1 (reporting federal class action).

With respect to rules allowing or prohibiting payments, should the law treat sperm, eggs, and embryos alike? Why? While conceding the existing commerce in sperm and eggs, the President's Council on Bioethics called for interim legislation prohibiting the purchase and sale of human embryos. Why? See The President's Council on Bioethics, Reproduction and Responsibility: The Regulation of New Biotechnologies 226-227 (2004). Nonetheless, a California company has been creating embryos for sale in an effort to lower the price of fertility treatments. See Lewin, Industry's Growth Leads to Leftover Embryos, supra. How would you evaluate this practice?

What is the appropriate fee for gestational services? What legal approach would appropriately reflect the dual character of surrogacy arrangements, which are both intimate and commercial? See Pamela Laufer-Ukeles, Mothering for Money: Regulating Commercial Intimacy, 88 Ind. L.J. 1223 (2013). On how the "moral panic" about commodification sparked by *Baby M*, supra, dissipated over time, see Elizabeth S. Scott, Surrogacy and the Politics of Commodification, 72 Law & Contemp. Probs. 109 (Summer 2009).

c. Screening. Should the state screen intended parents who use assisted reproduction, as adoption law requires? Should the law condition surrogacy on the intended mother's infertility? Is access to surrogacy a "right" to which those who cannot otherwise procreate are entitled? The Israeli Supreme Court has answered in the negative, refusing to recognize as a parent a woman with muscular dystrophy, who commissioned a child through a surrogacy arrangement using donor egg and sperm. The court reasoned that approval of such agreements, when the intended parent has no genetic connection to the child, could result in child trafficking. See Israel Faxx, Supreme Court: Quadriplegic Woman Cannot Raise Child, 2015 WLNR 10281377 (Apr. 9, 2015).

What limits, if any, on family form should control? The 2009 birth in California of IVF octuplets to an unemployed single mother of six other IVF children focused attention on the absence of regulation, medical and otherwise. E.g., Radhika Rao, How (Not) to Regulate Assisted Reproductive Technology: Lessons from "Octomom," 49 Fam. L.Q. 135 (2015).

d. Age. In response to pregnancies achieved by postmenopausal women using donor eggs ("granny births"), some countries have enacted restrictions. Would similar legislation in the United States survive constitutional challenge? Does "old" parenthood pose harm to children? Parents? Society? Should similar restrictions apply to alternative insemination to deter old fatherhood? Such questions regularly surface with news reports of births to women in their sixties using donor eggs.[25]

e. Eugenics. Assisted reproduction allows recipients to select genetic material. For example, sperm banks provide elaborate profiles of donors' characteristics, including physical characteristics, educational backgrounds, skills, interests, and talents. Despite the perils of eugenics, why shouldn't those using donor insemination be informed and demanding consumers? Instead, should medical personnel make the selection? The state? On genetic engineering, see Girard Kelly, Comment, Choosing the Genetics of Our Children: Options for Framing Public Policy, 30 Santa Clara High Tech. L.J. 303 (2014).

9. Other countries. Israel legalized surrogacy in 1996 with the passage of the Surrogate Motherhood Agreements Law, 1996, S.H. 1577. See D. Kelly Weisberg, The Birth of Surrogacy in Israel 197-200 (2005). The law in the United Kingdom generally recognizes the woman carrying the pregnancy as the mother, but authorizes a court order treating the "applicants" as a child's parents. Applicants must be a couple—either married, civil partners, or a pair "who are living as partners in an enduring family relationship and are not within prohibited degrees" for intimate relationships; further, the child must be conceived with the gametes of one of the applicants. Single persons remain ineligible for parental orders. Human Fertilisation and Embryology Act of 2008, ch. 22, §§33, 54 (U.K.).[26] Several European countries impose stricter medical regulations on assisted reproduction. See Velikonja, supra.

10. Reproductive tourism. The legal variations, both at home and abroad, raise many classic conflict-of-laws issues when participants (including brokers) seek the most hospitable parentage regimes. What sort of connections with a jurisdiction should trigger the application of its laws? Compare Hodas v. Morin, 814 N.E.2d 320 (Mass. 2004), with In re Infants H., 904 N.E.2d 203 (Ind. 2009). See generally Susan Frelich Appleton, Surrogacy Arrangements and the Conflict of Laws, 1990 Wis. L. Rev. 399. In addition to favorable laws, economic conditions might draw intended parents away from home (for example, with surrogacy in countries such as India costing far less than in the United States). What problems might such practices pose? How, if at all, should such reproductive tourism be regulated? See generally Charles P. Kindregan & Danielle White, International Fertility Tourism: The Potential for Stateless Children in Cross-Border Commercial Surrogacy Arrangements, 36 Suffolk Transnat'l L. Rev. 527 (2013); Nida Najar, India: Government Seeks to End Surrogacy for Foreign Couples, N.Y. Times, Oct. 29, 2015, at A12.

Problems

1. Robert and his wife, Denise, arranged to have Denise bear a child conceived from embryos created for them with Robert's sperm and eggs from an anonymous

[25]. E.g., Lindsay Kimble, 65-Year-Old German Schoolteacher Gives Birth to Quadruplets, Is Now Mother of 17: Reports, People Magazine, May 23, 2015, http://www.people.com/article/65-year-old-woman-gives-birth-quadruplets.

[26]. Human Fertilisation and Embryology Act 2008: Explanatory Notes 32, http://www.opsi.gov.uk/acts/acts2008/en/ukpgaen_20080022_en.pdf.

donor. Clinic doctors transferred some of the embryos not only to Denise, but also to Susan, an unmarried woman who arranged to become a single mother with an embryo from anonymous donors. Denise gave birth to a girl and Susan a boy—genetic siblings. After the clinic disclosed the error, Robert and Denise sue for parental rights to the boy, while Susan asserts that she is his sole legal parent. Whom should the court recognize as the parents? Why? Can intent-based parentage resolve this dispute? Should the court give both families some access to the child? See Robert B. v. Susan B., 135 Cal. Rptr. 2d 785 (Ct. App. 2003); Marjorie M. Shultz, Taking Account of ARTs in Determining Parenthood: A Troubling Dispute in California, 19 Wash. U. J.L. & Pol'y 77 (2005).

If the mix-up had resulted in one woman giving birth to twin boys, one of whom was genetically hers and her husband's and the other the genetic child of a second married couple, would your answers change? Suppose that the error were disclosed before the twins' birth. Suppose that the second couple's own efforts to have a child had failed—so the twin in question was their only chance for genetic offspring. Suppose that the first couple and their genetic son are Caucasian and the second couple and the second twin are African-American. See Perry-Rogers v. Fasano, 715 N.Y.S.2d 19 (App. Div. 2000); Leslie Bender, Genes, Parents, and Assisted Reproductive Technologies: ARTs, Mistakes, Sex, Race, & Law, 12 Colum. J. Gender & L. 1 (2003). Suppose that the mix-up in either case resulted not from negligence, but from the clinic's deliberate misuse of genetic material—misuse revealed only years after the children were born. See Prato-Morrison v. Doe, 126 Cal. Rptr. 2d 509 (Ct. App. 2002) (suit from theft of embryos at U.C. Irvine); Alice M. Noble-Allgire, Switched at the Fertility Clinic: Determining Maternal Rights When a Child Is Born from Stolen or Misdelivered Genetic Material, 64 Mo. L. Rev. 517 (1999).

2. Child was conceived through sexual intercourse between Birth Mother and Husband, who at all relevant times was married to Wife. Husband and Wife assert that they arranged with Birth Mother to act as a surrogate and that, as part of their unwritten agreement, they attended all of Birth Mother's medical appointments and paid for all expenses related to Child's birth. They further state that they have been Child's sole caregivers since his birth. Birth Mother asserts that Child's conception resulted from her intimate personal relationship with Husband. She denies the existence of any surrogacy agreement and states that she participated in Child's care for the first two years of his life, until Husband severed her contact with Child.

Wife seeks to establish her maternity by invoking a gender-neutral reading of the state's paternity presumptions, which follow the UPA (without the gestational agreement sections), based on (1) her marriage to Husband and (2) her holding out Child as her own. Birth Mother argues that, as a matter of law, she is Child's "natural mother" within the meaning of the UPA because she undisputedly is the biological parent and she gave birth. Who should prevail? Why? See In re S.N.V., 284 P.3d 147 (Colo. Ct. App. 2011). Cf. In re Parental Responsibilities of A.R.L., 318 P.3d 581 (Colo. Ct. App. 2013); In re T.J.S., 54 A.3d 263, 269 (N.J. 2012) (Albin, J., dissenting).

c. Precommitment Versus Contemporaneous Consent: Frozen Embryo Disputes

SZAFRANSKI v. DUNSTON

34 N.E.3d 1132 (Ill. App. Ct. 2015)

Justice Liu delivered the judgment of the court, with opinion:

[Jacob, a firefighter and paramedic, and Karla, a physician, had a dating relationship that neither thought had long-term prospects. Following a diagnosis of non-Hodgkins lymphoma and a recommendation for chemotherapy, Karla was devastated to learn of the loss of fertility that could result. Despite a painful tumor, she delayed treatment to explore IVF. After considering using anonymously donated sperm to create embryos to freeze, Karla asked Jacob if he would help her, and he agreed. Working with physicians at Northwestern Medical Faculty Foundation (NMFF), Jacob deposited his sperm, and he and Karla signed a 21-page informed consent form on March 25, 2010. The form explained Northwestern's legal rights and obligations and provided:]

> Embryos are understood to be your property, with rights of survivorship. No use can be made of these embryos without the consent of both partners (if applicable).
>
> a) In the event of divorce or dissolution of the marriage or partnership, NMFF will abide by the terms of the court decree or settlement agreement regarding the ownership and/or other rights to the embryos.
>
> b) In the event of the death or legal incapacitation of one partner, the other partner will retain decision-making authority regarding the embryos.
>
> c) In the event both partners die or are legally incapacitated, or if a surviving partner dies or is legally incapacitated while the embryos are still stored at NMFF, the embryos shall become the sole and exclusive property of NMFF. In this event, I/we elect to: (please select and initial your choice). Note: both the patient and the partner must agree on disposition; as with other decisions relating to IVF, you are encouraged to discuss this issue

Below this paragraph, Karla and Jacob initialed the space next to the option to "[d]onate the embryos to another couple." [Another paragraph advised them to consult an attorney, given uncertainties in the law.]

Later that day, following their appointment at Northwestern, Jacob and Karla met with Nidhi Desai, an attorney, to discuss the IVF procedure and their options for the pre-embryos. Desai presented the couple with two possible arrangements: a co-parenting agreement or a sperm donor agreement. Desai explained that, under a co-parenting agreement, Jacob would be involved in any resulting child's life as a co-parent, including sharing financial responsibility. She also explained that, under a sperm donor agreement, Jacob would have no obligations and would be waiving his parental rights. Desai informed the parties that if they wanted to use a sperm donor agreement, each party would require independent legal representation and they would have to hire an additional attorney for this purpose. [Karla notified her that they would use the co-parenting agreement, but the parties never signed it.]

[On April 6, ova were retrieved from Karla, three were successfully fertilized with Jacob's sperm, and Karla began chemotherapy.] In May, after Karla's second chemotherapy cycle, Jacob ended their relationship in a text message. Karla responded with an inquiry about the pre-embryos, but received no response.

On June 14, 2010, Jacob sent Karla an e-mail for the first time after ending their relationship. [He] admitted in the e-mail that he had concealed from her his true feelings and reservations about their relationship while simultaneously seeking a way to end it that would leave her "in a position to move on intact despite the loss of [their] relationship." In a paragraph describing his concerns about their separation and their pre-embryos, he wrote:

> "When you asked me if I would be the donor for your emergent egg harvesting I still have no reservations in my answer. If you desired to have the possibility of having 'a' child in the future and I could be of help to you, I'd do it all over again. But now that we've already gone through with everything I wonder if you in asking me were doing so out of a longing to have 'my' child instead. The two are very different things, things neither you nor I were clear upon, because we never discussed our thoughts and feelings when given such choices. Karla, I rather desired you to have a child of your own in the future with the return of your health, not for us to have a child when that time comes. I know now that there isn't a possibility of a future for us together and that our relationship has faltered. I wonder if you would've rather gone with a random donor in knowing this, a question that my indecision has robbed you of, even in spite of my assumed generosity and caring actions. I'm sorry for this and I hope you can forgive me even after everything I've put you through. Now in the after math [*sic*] of that decision, I'm faced with even more compounding issues all stemming from my fear of the truth. Karla, do you still wish to keep the embryo's [*sic*] after all of this? Do you desire the potential to have 'a' child in the future or 'my' child, because if your choice is the ladder [*sic*] I won't be there? I had no intention of being there. I ask myself, would you have asked someone instead of me if I had said no, or would you have even gone through with it at all? It's far too late to be saying this, but you and I both know we never had the needed time to make such a decision and rather hastily went about things due to your health."

Jacob also expressed concern about the [negative] reaction he had received from his friends and family when discussing the fact that he had participated in the IVF process with Karla. . . . Finally, he acknowledged a fear of being rebuked or rejected for having helped Karla:

> ". . . I just wonder if my future happiness in life will be tethered to the women [*sic*] I cared for years ago and the child I never knew."

On September 6, 2010, Jacob sent Karla another e-mail, announcing that he could not let her use the pre-embryos and that he wanted them to be donated to science or research. In her email back to Jacob that same day, Karla responded: "Those embryos mean everything to me and I will fight this to the bitter end." [Jacob indicated he would sign a sperm donor agreement; after rejecting documents drafted by an attorney, Jacob prepared his own agreement, which gave Karla full custody.] Karla testified that she would have signed Jacob's proposed agreement, but Northwestern indicated that it would not abide by its terms. [Jacob then sued Karla, Karla prevailed, and Jacob appealed. A two-day trial followed after remand, Karla prevailed again, and Jacob appealed again.]

An oral agreement is binding where there is an offer, an acceptance, and a meeting of the minds as to the terms of the agreement. . . . [S]everal facts are not in dispute. Significantly, Jacob does not challenge the finding that an oral contract was created on March 24 when Karla asked him if he would be willing to donate his sperm to create pre-embryos with her, and he manifested his acceptance of Karla's offer by responding "yes." . . . Both parties further acknowledged, through trial testimony, that the purpose of the oral contract was for Jacob to provide his sperm to fertilize Karla's eggs so that she could preserve her ability to have a biologically related child of her own in the future, after her chemotherapy treatment ended. Finally, it is undisputed that the parties knew that the pre-embryos would have to be cryopreserved for later use and that they would not be transferred to Karla for implantation, at the earliest, until after she finished her chemotherapy treatment. . . . [The circuit] court concluded that Jacob had agreed to donate sperm specifically for the purpose of allowing Karla to later have a child of her own and that the parties intended for Karla to use any resulting pre-embryos without Jacob's consent. . . .

. . . Jacob argues that, at the time the contract was formed, he agreed only to donate sperm for Karla's IVF procedure so that she could attempt to have a biologically related child later, no more and no less. He maintains that he and Karla "never even discussed or contemplated" the issue of how the pre-embryos would be used or disposed of following the IVF and cryopreservation. In sum, he argues that "[c]onsent to create pre-embryos is not consent to their possible use at some unknown time in the future." . . .

The record reveals several instances where Jacob could have voiced his alleged desire about wanting a right to consent to Karla's use of the pre-embryos and, nevertheless, remained silent on the issue. . . . [E]ven in the midst of their dispute over the pre-embryos, Jacob indicated, in his June 14 e-mail to Karla, that his consent to her use was unconditional. . . .

. . . After considering the testimony and evidence presented at trial, the circuit court concluded that the parties understood that the purpose of creating the pre-embryos was to preserve Karla's ostensibly last opportunity to have a biological child in the future, without conditions. . . . We further find that the relief Jacob seeks—essentially, incorporating a limitation into the oral contract—would change the fundamental essence of the parties' oral contract. . . .

The next issue is the legal effect of the Informed Consent that the parties signed on March 25. [The court determines that that, absent evidence of any other agreement between the parties, the March 24 contract is controlling and that] the terms of the Informed Consent in this case neither modified nor contradicted the parties' oral agreement of March 24. . . .

[We have] emphasized the importance of honoring advance agreements between IVF participants. Central to [this position is] the idea that advance agreements allow parties to settle their rights and obligations *before* an issue over rights or obligations arise. Here, the parties have reached a binding oral contract concerning the use of pre-embryos that, unless modified or contradicted, remained in full force and effect . . .

. . . Jacob urges this court to construe the consent provision as an expression of the parties' intent that neither of them could use the pre-embryos without the other's consent in the event of separation. Under his proposed reading, the preprinted boilerplate inserted by Northwestern into the consent provision would govern the disposition of the pre-embryos such that Jacob could withhold his consent to Karla's use at any time. This interpretation would run directly contrary to the language giving Jacob and Karla—not Northwestern—the right to decide the fate of their pre-embryos. Contrary to Jacob's argument, the lack of any dispositional option in this provision is not evidence of an advance agreement to "reserve" his consent to the future use of the pre-embryos. Instead, it is evidence of the *absence* of any agreement in the Informed Consent regarding disposition upon the couple's separation.

Jacob's proposed reading of the consent provision also fails to consider that Northwestern has not specified what will happen in the event an unmarried couple separates. Northwestern specifically addressed how the couple's pre-embryos will be disposed of in three different situations—divorce, death of one partner, and death of both partners—but, significantly, it did not address how their pre-embryos would be treated in the event that they separated. . . . Under the circumstances, we can only interpret this as a purposeful omission.

Finally, Jacob's interpretation of the consent provision is inconsistent with the language of the consent provision itself. The consent provision begins with a statement written in the passive voice: "Embryos are understood to be your property, with rights of survivorship." From the start, it is clear that the provision is phrased to state Northwestern's policy with respect to its patients; that is, Northwestern understands that the embryos are "your," *i.e.,* Jacob and Karla's, property. . . . If this provision was intended to be an expression of the parties' dispositional intent, it would contain language more reflective of a choice . . . .

. . . However, even assuming *arguendo* that the document is ambiguous, we find that the extrinsic evidence also supports our interpretation that the parties never intended to be bound to a particular disposition in signing the document. . . . Here, the evidence suggested that the parties were told that they would both need to consent to any use of the pre-embryos because they were not married. Jacob, however, agreed that [the physician] did not ask Karla or him what should happen to the pre-embryos in the event of their separation [and] encouraged them to consult with an attorney to resolve that particular issue. . . . Ultimately, neither the plain language of the Informed Consent nor the related extrinsic evidence suggests that the parties agreed upon a particular disposition in the event of their separation. . . .

We [also] agree with the circuit court's conclusion that Karla is entitled to control of the pre-embryos under [the balancing of interests test, which rests entirely on factual evidence]. . . . [W]e cannot say the circuit court's ruling, that Karla's interest in using the pre-embryos outweighs any interest Jacob has in preventing their use, was against the manifest weight of the evidence. At the heart of the evidence is an irrefutable fact: the sole purpose for using Jacob's sperm to fertilize Karla's last viable eggs was to preserve her ability to have a biological child in the future at some point after her chemotherapy treatment ended. The parties both recognized this when they agreed to create the pre-embryos together.

We concur in the circuit court's ruling that Karla's interest in using the pre-embryos is paramount given her inability to have a biological child by any other means. . . . Although Karla has other options for becoming a parent, there is no evidence that she could have a biological child other than by using the pre-embryos. We decline to make a judicial determination that alternative methods of parenthood offer Karla an acceptable substitute to biological parenthood.

We also find no reason to disturb the circuit court's determination that Jacob's concern about not finding love in the future is "speculative." Moreover, his privacy concern is largely moot now as a result of the very public nature of this case. . . . Our opinion should not be read to minimize Jacob's concerns about becoming the biological father of a child born under these circumstances. We recognize the far-reaching consequences of the decision that Jacob made, in a short amount of time and under exigent circumstances, when he agreed to assist Karla in her IVF procedure. Jacob's lack of hesitation in agreeing to help her create the pre-embryos was noteworthy and uncommonly selfless. . . . Jacob's interests in not using the pre-embryos and keeping them frozen, indefinitely, are valid and not insubstantial. Under the unique circumstances in this case, however, Karla's interests in using the pre-embryos to have a biologically related child—given her ovarian failure and inability to create any more pre-embryos with her own eggs, prevail over Jacob's interests in not using them.

Finally, we must acknowledge the remaining elephant in the room—Jacob's concern that he could be financially responsible for any child resulting from the pre-embryos. . . . We note only that this decision should not be construed as a ruling on Jacob's legal status under any applicable parentage or child support statutes. We see no basis in the record why Jacob would be precluded from seeking a legal declaration of his parental status. See 750 ILCS 40/3(b) (West 2012) ("The donor of semen provided to a licensed physician for use in artificial insemination of a woman other than the donor's wife shall be treated in law as if he were not the natural father of a child thereby conceived."). . . .

Jacob has renewed his arguments . . . that he has a right not to be a parent under both the United States and Illinois Constitutions. . . . Jacob maintains that "[t]he placement of the pre-embryo inside the woman's body is equivalent to the act of intercourse." He argues that while "IVF and pre-embryo cryopreservation are scientific and technological marvels[,] * * * their splendor should not bedazzle the courts into overlooking th[is] basic equivalence." We . . . reaffirm our prior ruling that there is "no constitutional obstacle to honoring an agreement regarding the disposition of pre-embryos, and where there has been no advance agreement regarding the disposition of pre-embryos, then to balance the parties' interests in the event of a dispute." . . . [Affirmed.]

Notes and Questions

1. Timing of intent. Cryopreservation allows embryos created at Time A to be used later, at Time B. Disputes arise when, at Time B, one party no longer wants to abide by the "precommitment" made at Time A. In upholding the oral agreement, *Szafranski* determines that the parties should be bound by the intent expressed at Time A. What are the advantages of this approach? See John A. Robertson, Precommitment Strategies for Disposition of Frozen Embryos, 50 Emory L.J. 989, 1038-1041 (2001). What additional procedural safeguards, if any, would you require to enforce the oral agreement in *Szafranski*? See Deborah L. Forman, Embryo Disposition, Divorce, & Family Law Contracting: A Model for Enforceability, 24 Colum. J. Gender & L. 378 (2013).

Under this approach, what weight should be accorded to consent forms provided by the fertility clinic and signed by the parties at Time A? See, e.g., Fla. Stat. Ann. §742.17 (calling for written agreements between the commissioning couple and the treating physician about embryo disposition in "unforeseen circumstance[s]" and spelling out default rules for particular situations). Did the signed form in *Szafranski* reflect the same intent as the oral agreement? Based on empirical investigation, a significant majority of fertility patients report that they read and understood clinic consent forms. Jody Lyneé Madeira, The Art of Informed Consent: Assessing Patient Perceptions, Behaviors, and Lived Experience of IVF and Embryo Disposition Informed Consent Processes, 49 Fam. L.Q. 7, 9 (2015).

2. "Forced parenthood"? *Szafranski* departs from several prominent cases that resolved the dispute in favor of the party wishing to avoid procreation at Time B, regardless of intent at Time A. E.g., J.B. v. M.B., 783 A.2d 707 (N.J. 2001); Davis v. Davis, 842 S.W.2d 588, 604 (Tenn. 1992). As the Massachusetts Supreme Court explained, citing constitutional cases and authorities rejecting suits for breach of promise to marry: "[P]rior agreements to enter into familial relationships (marriage or parenthood) should not be enforced against individuals who subsequently reconsider their decisions. This enhances the 'freedom of personal choice in matters of marriage and family life.'" A.Z. v. B.Z., 725 N.E.2d 1051, 1059 (Mass. 2000).

Commentators read such cases to articulate a principle against forcing parenthood on an unwilling party. See Susan B. Apel, Cryopreserved Embryos: A Response to "Forced Parenthood" and the Role of Intent, 39 Fam. L.Q. 663 (2005). What does the notion of "forced parenthood" entail? Would an agreement to relieve the unwilling party of parental duties fully address the problem? Would (should) such agreements be enforceable? What does *Szafranski* suggest? See also Yehezkel Margalit, To Be or Not to Be (a Parent)?—Not Precisely the Question: The Frozen Embryo Dispute, 18 Cardozo J.L. & Gender 355 (2012). Or is something more at stake beyond financial obligations? In *Davis*, supra, the court rejected the wife's plan to donate the embryos to other families. Why? To what extent did Roe v. Wade (Chapter I) address the burdens of forced genetic parenthood, apart from the burdens of forced pregnancy? See generally Mary Ziegler, Abortion and the Constitutional Right (Not) to Procreate, 48 U. Rich. L. Rev. 1263 (2014) (considering ARTs disputes in context of spousal consent requirements for abortion).

3. Contemporaneous mutual consent. Cases like *A.Z.*, supra, require contemporaneous mutual consent at Time B for the use of genetic material. Why? See Carl H. Coleman, Procreative Liberty and Contemporaneous Choice: An Inalienable Rights Approach to Frozen Embryo Disputes, 84 Minn. L. Rev. 55 (1999). But see Kaiponanea T. Matsumura, Binding Future Selves, 75 La. L. Rev. 71 (2014) (critiquing theory of different selves at Time A and Time B).

What implications does contemporaneous mutual consent have for the private-ordering trend in family law? Do you agree with arguments that contemporaneous mutual consent safeguards reproductive autonomy and that family law more generally supports those who wish to reconsider their decisions to enter personal relationships? Why? See generally Susan Frelich Appleton, Reproduction and Regret, 23 Yale J.L. & Feminism 255 (2011). What would be the implication of requiring contemporaneous mutual consent for posthumous reproduction (see Astrue v. Capato, supra)?

4. Alternative approaches. *Szafranski* also uses a "balancing of interests" test that some courts have applied in the absence of a controlling agreement. See, e.g., Reber v. Reiss, 42 A.3d 1131 (Pa. Super. Ct. 2012). Do you agree that Karla's interests trump Jacob's? Why? The court's analysis reflects reliance on whether use of the embryos constitutes a party's "last procreative chance." Professor Robertson points out the gendered significance of this consideration because, "[a]lthough there will be few men who will become infertile during the IVF and embryo storage process, many women might," with advancing age.[27] Nonetheless, some courts have noted that adoption represents another route to parenthood or have ruled that the interests of the party opposing procreation at Time B should always prevail, regardless of "last procreative chance." E.g., Evans v. United Kingdom, App. No. 6339/05, [2007] 1 F.L.R. 1990 (Eur. Ct. H.R. Grand Chamber) (based on U.K. legislation requiring contemporaneous mutual consent). Will the still-developing technology of freezing unfertilized ova eliminate such problems?

5. The legal status of embryos.

a. Background. Early disputes sought to classify frozen pre-embryos. In Del Zio v. Presbyterian Hospital, 1978 U.S. Dist. LEXIS 14450 (S.D.N.Y. 1978), a couple won $50,000 for the deliberate destruction of a culture containing their eggs and sperm by health care providers who questioned the safety of this then-untried procedure. The jury based its award on plaintiffs' claims for emotional distress, while rejecting their claims for conversion of property. Are embryos property? Compare York v. Jones, 717 F. Supp. 421 (E.D. Va. 1989) (property), with *Davis*, 842 S.W.2d at 594-597 (intermediate category between "persons" and "property"). See also Miller v. American Infertility Group of Ill., S.C., 897 N.E.2d 837 (Ill. App. Ct. 2008) (rejecting wrongful-death claim for an embryo not yet implanted); cf. J.C.M. v. A.N.A., [2012] B.C.J. No. 802 (treating purchased sperm as property to be divided upon dissolution of Canadian female couple's relationship).

b. Embryonic "personhood." Louisiana has a statutory scheme defining the "in vitro fertilized human ovum" as both a "juridical person" until implanted and a "biological human being" and entitling "such ovum to sue or be sued." La. Rev. Stat. Ann. §§9:121-9:126. The law prohibits intentional destruction of "viable" fertilized ova, explaining that "[a]n in vitro fertilized human ovum that fails to develop further over a thirty-six hour period except when the embryo is in a state of cryopreservation, is considered non-viable and is not a juridical person." Id. §9:129. The statute makes available for "adoptive implantation" those fertilized ova for which the IVF patients have renounced their own parental rights for in utero implantation. Id. §9:130. The law precludes inheritance rights for an ovum unless live birth occurs. Id. §9:133. Louisiana applies the "best interest of the in vitro fertilized ovum" test in any disputes. Id. §9:131. Does this test mean that the party seeking implantation must prevail? The trial court in *Davis* so ruled. See 842 S.W.2d at 594. See also Nick Loeb, Sofía Vergara's Ex-Fiancé: Our Frozen Embryos Have a Right to Live, N.Y. Times, Apr. 30, 2015, at A31.

Recently, antiabortion advocates have petitioned for state ballot measures defining "person" "to include every human being from the moment of fertilization, cloning, or the equivalent thereof." Such initiatives have failed to win approval, following campaigns emphasizing how they might threaten contraception and IVF. E.g., Denise Grady, Medical Nuances Drove "No" Vote in Mississippi, N.Y. Times, Nov. 15, 2011, at D1.

6. Destruction. What legal rules should govern the storage of the growing number of unused cryopreserved pre-embryos? Under a model law proposed by

---

[27]. John A. Robertson, Precommitment Strategies for Disposition of Frozen Embryos, 50 Emory L.J. 989, 1014 (2001).

the ABA, absent a contrary agreement, embryos are deemed abandoned after five years and an unsuccessful search to find the interested participants; disposal of abandoned embryos must follow the most recent recorded agreement between the participants and the storage facility, with a court order for disposition required in the absence of such agreement.[28] For the emotional and ethical difficulties that the disposition of unused embryos often poses for the progenitors, see Tamar Lewin, Industry's Growth Leads to Leftover Embryos, and Painful Choices, N.Y. Times, June 18, 2015, at A1. See generally June Carbone & Naomi Cahn, Embryo Fundamentalism, 18 Wm. & Mary Bill Rts. J. 1015 (2010). On "embryo adoption," see supra pp. 842-843.

7. **Factual variations.** Suppose that the pre-embryos in *Szafranski* had been created from donated eggs. Could the court's rationale apply to a commissioning adult who used another's genetic material? Suppose that Karla does not plan to gestate the pre-embryos but intends to parent the resulting child. Would she still prevail? See Litowitz v. Litowitz, 48 P.3d 261 (Wash. 2002).

How would the court have treated the dispute if Karla and Jacob had been a divorcing couple? What sort of bargains might divorcing parties demand for their reproductive futures? See Katelin Eastman, Note, "Alimony for Your Eggs": Fertility Compensation in Divorce Proceedings, 42 Pepp. L. Rev. 293 (2015).

B. Consequences of Parentage: Parental Rights and Responsibilities

Why does parentage matter? Law ordinarily draws sharp distinctions between parents and nonparents, with parents alone assigned what is usually an indivisible bundle of rights and responsibilities, as the following materials show.

1. Parental Autonomy: Family Privacy Revisited

MEYER v. NEBRASKA

262 U.S. 390 (1923)

Review the above case, reprinted in Chapter I.

[28]. American Bar Association Model Act Governing Assisted Reproduction §504 (Feb. 2008), http://www.abanet.org/family/committees/artmodelact.pdf.

PIERCE v. SOCIETY OF SISTERS

268 U.S. 510 (1925)

Review the above case, reprinted in Chapter I.

PRINCE v. MASSACHUSETTS

321 U.S. 158 (1944)

Mr. Justice RUTLEDGE delivered the opinion of the Court.

The case brings for review another episode in the conflict between Jehovah's Witnesses and state authority. This time Sarah Prince appeals from convictions for violating Massachusetts' child labor laws, by acts said to be a rightful exercise of her religious convictions. . . .

. . . Mrs. Prince, living in Brockton, is the mother of two young sons. She also has legal custody of Betty Simmons [her niece, age nine,] who lives with them. The children too are Jehovah's Witnesses and both Mrs. Prince and Betty testified they were ordained ministers. The former was accustomed to go each week on the streets of Brockton to distribute "Watchtower" and "Consolation," according to the usual plan. She had permitted the children to engage in this activity previously, and had been warned against doing so by the school attendance officer, Mr. Perkins. But, until December 18, 1941, she generally did not take them with her at night.

That evening, as Mrs. Prince was preparing to leave her home, the children asked to go. She at first refused. Childlike, they resorted to tears and, motherlike, she yielded. Arriving downtown, Mrs. Prince permitted the children "to engage in the preaching work with her upon the sidewalks." That is, with specific reference to Betty, she and Mrs. Prince took positions about twenty feet apart near a street intersection. Betty held up in her hand, for passersby to see, copies of "WatchTower" and "Consolation." From her shoulder hung the usual canvas magazine bag, on which was printed "Watchtower and Consolation 5 cents per copy." No one accepted a copy from Betty that evening and she received no money. Nor did her aunt. But on other occasions, Betty had received funds and given out copies. . . .

[Appellant argues] squarely on freedom of religion under the First Amendment, applied by the Fourteenth to the states. She buttresses this foundation, however, with a claim of parental right as secured by the due process clause of the latter Amendment. Cf. Meyer v. Nebraska, 262 U.S. 390 [(1923)]. Thus, two claimed liberties are at stake. One is the parent's, to bring up the child in the way he should go, which for appellant means to teach him the tenets and the practices of their faith. The other freedom is the child's, to observe these; and among them is "to preach the gospel . . . by public distribution" of "Watchtower" and "Consolation," in conformity with the scripture: "A little child shall lead them." . . .

To make accommodation between these freedoms and an exercise of state authority always is delicate. . . . It is cardinal with us that the custody, care and nurture of the child reside first in the parents, whose primary function and freedom include preparation for obligations the state can neither supply nor hinder [citing *Pierce*]. And it is in recognition of this that these decisions have respected the private realm of family life which the state cannot enter.

But the family itself is not beyond regulation in the public interest, as against a claim of religious liberty. Reynolds v. United States, 98 U.S. 145 [(1878)]; Davis v. Beason, 133 U.S. 333 [(1890)]. And neither rights of religion nor rights of parenthood are beyond limitation. Acting to guard the general interest in youth's well being, the state as parens patriae may restrict the parent's control by requiring school attendance, regulating or prohibiting the child's labor, and in many other ways. Its authority is not nullified merely because the parent grounds his claim to control the child's course of conduct on religion or conscience. . . .

But it is said the state cannot do so here. . . . The child's presence on the street, with her guardian, distributing or offering to distribute the magazines, it is urged, was in no way harmful to her, nor in any event more so than the presence of many other children at the same time and place, engaged in shopping and other activities not prohibited. . . .

[The] state's authority over children's activities is broader than over like actions of adults. This is peculiarly true of public activities and in matters of employment. A democratic society rests, for its continuance, upon the healthy, well-rounded growth of young people into full maturity as citizens, with all that implies. . . . Among evils most appropriate for [protective] action are the crippling effects of child employment, more especially in public places, and the possible harms arising from other activities subject to all the diverse influences of the street. . . .

. . . The case reduces itself therefore to the question whether the presence of the child's guardian puts a limit to the state's power. . . . Parents may be free to become martyrs themselves. But it does not follow they are free, in identical circumstances, to make martyrs of their children before they have reached the age of full and legal discretion when they can make that choice for themselves. Massachusetts has determined that an absolute prohibition, though one limited to streets and public places and to the incidental uses proscribed, is necessary to accomplish its legitimate objectives. . . . [Affirmed.]

TROXEL v. GRANVILLE

530 U.S. 57 (2000)

Review the above case, reprinted in Chapter VIII.

Notes and Questions on *Meyer, Pierce, Prince,* and *Troxel*

1. Parental autonomy. *Meyer* and *Pierce* establish the foundation for the right to privacy. These cases interpret the liberty protected by the Due Process Clause to encompass parental autonomy, the right to rear a child as the parent sees fit.

2. Children as property. Although revered as "liberal icons" that protect privacy and promote pluralism, *Meyer* and *Pierce* express a conservative attachment to the patriarchal family and a view of children as property owned by their parents, according to Professor Barbara Bennett Woodhouse. After examining the historical context of the cases, she concludes:

> . . . By constitutionalizing a patriarchal notion of parental rights, *Meyer* and *Pierce* interrupted the trend of family law moving toward children's rights and revitalized the notion of rights of possession. . . . Patriarchal notions of ownership do not lend themselves to a child-centered theory of custody or parenthood. . . .
>
> [O]ur legal system fails to respect children. Children are often used as instruments, as in *Meyer* and *Pierce*. The child is denied her own voice and identity and becomes a conduit for the parents' religious expression, cultural identity, and class aspirations. The parents' authority to speak for and through the child is explicit in *Meyer*'s "right of control" and *Pierce*'s "high duty" of the parent to direct his child's destiny. . . .[29]

See also Dara E. Purvis, The Origin of Parental Rights: Labor, Intent, and Fathers, 41 Fla. St. U. L. Rev. 645 (2014) (invoking labor-based theory of property).

If property ownership provides the wrong legal model for the parent-child relationship, what alternative understandings might prove more helpful? Parenting as creative expression, protected by the First Amendment?[30] Caregiving as preparation of children for democratic citizenship?[31] Parents as stewards or fiduciaries?[32] For additional legal analogies, see Susan Frelich Appleton, Restating Childhood, 79 Brook. L. Rev. 525, 542-549 (2014).

3. *Prince* and its precedents. Based on *Meyer* and *Pierce*, how should the Court have decided *Prince*? Is *Prince* a stronger or weaker case for parental autonomy than *Meyer* or *Pierce*, given that Sarah Prince's parental autonomy claim rested more squarely on her asserted freedom of religion and Betty's own beliefs were put in evidence? In light of the outcome in *Prince*, what does the Court mean by "a private realm of family life which the state cannot enter"?

4. Harm? *Prince* reveals that the state's interest (as parens patriae) in protecting children from harm circumscribes parental autonomy. What harm threatened nine-year-old Betty? Was she actually harmed or merely exposed to the risk of harm? Should the mere risk of harm justify state intervention in the family? Who decides what constitutes harm to a child? Does *Prince* identify the scope of state power to restrict parental freedom in the interest of child protection?

To what extent does *Troxel* depart from *Prince*'s harm standard? What do the different Justices say about this standard in *Troxel*? Do the *Troxel* opinions go beyond the context of third-party visitation to raise questions about other state incursions on parental autonomy that cannot be justified as necessary to protect a child from harm or potential harm?

---

[29]. Barbara Bennett Woodhouse, "Who Owns the Child?": *Meyer* and *Pierce* and the Child as Property, 33 Wm. & Mary L. Rev. 995, 996, 1113-1114 (1992).

[30]. Merry Jean Chan, Note, The Authorial Parent: An Intellectual Property Model of Parental Rights, 78 N.Y.U. L. Rev. 1186 (2003).

[31]. Anne C. Dailey, Developing Citizens, 91 Iowa L. Rev. 431 (2006).

[32]. Kevin Noble Maillard, Rethinking Children as Property: The Transitive Family, 32 Cardozo L. Rev. 225 (2010); Elizabeth S. Scott & Robert E. Scott, Parents as Fiduciaries, 81 Va. L. Rev. 2401 (1995).

5. Educational prerogatives.

a. The* Yoder *case. Constitutional parental autonomy received a boost when Amish parents successfully challenged a compulsory school attendance law, as it applied to their children after the eighth grade. Wisconsin v. Yoder, 406 U.S. 205 (1972). As the Court explained, compulsory school attendance laws grew out of the same concerns that produced the child labor restrictions in *Prince*. Using a "balancing process," *Yoder* emphasized Amish opposition to exposure to worldly activities, the law-abiding nature of the Amish population, and the work on the family farm to be undertaken in place of continued schooling—suggesting a limited, if not unique, ruling.

b. Children's interests. In his famous partial dissent in *Yoder*, Justice Douglas focused on the children's rights. He would canvass them before deciding whether or not they should be exempted from school attendance. Id. at 242 (Douglas, J., dissenting in part). Under the *Prince* harm standard, what is the risk of harm to the Amish child? Are the *Yoder* parents making "martyrs" of their children, despite *Prince*'s admonition? Cf. Jeffrey Shulman, The Parent as (Mere) Educational Trustee: Whose Education Is It, Anyway?, 89 Neb. L. Rev. 290 (2010).

If, when asked, an Amish child expressed a preference to stay in school, would he or she continue to live at home? Receive parental support? What other consequences might follow? Alternatively, should the issue be what serves the children's best interests, rather than what the children say they want? Should the law presume that parents can better identify such interests? Or the state? Compare, e.g., Martin Guggenheim, What's Wrong with Children's Rights (2005), and Emily Buss, Essay, "Parental" Rights, 88 Va. L. Rev. 635 (2002) (preferring parents), with James G. Dwyer, Religious Schools v. Children's Rights (1998) (preferring state). Would "canvassing" the child's view also make sense in the context of schooling choices, as in *Pierce*, or third-party visitation disputes, as in *Troxel*?

c. Home schooling. Does *Yoder* protect a parent's choice of home schooling, which every U.S. jurisdiction now makes legal? If *Yoder* protects home schooling, does it undervalue the state's interest in exposing minors to relationships with diverse peers and the interests of the students themselves? See Emily Buss, The Adolescent's Stake in the Allocation of Educational Control Between Parent and State, 67 U. Chi. L. Rev. 1233 (2000); Carmen Green, Note, Educational Empowerment: A Child's Right to Attend Public School, 103 Geo. L.J. 1089 (2015).

To what extent may the state regulate home schooling without violating parental autonomy? See Tanya K. Dumas et al., Evidence for Homeschooling: Constitutional Analysis in Light of Social Science Research, 16 Widener L. Rev. 63 (2010). Alternatively, does the Constitution *compel* state regulation of home schooling? Why? See Kimberly A. Yuracko, Education off the Grid: Constitutional Constraints on Homeschooling, 96 Cal. L. Rev. 123 (2008).

d. Vouchers. In Zelman v. Simmons-Harris, 536 U.S. 639 (2002), the Court upheld an Ohio school voucher program that included parochial schools against a challenge claiming a violation of the First Amendment's Establishment Clause. The majority emphasized that the program did not have the prohibited effect of advancing religion because individual parental choices about how to use the state assistance, not government action itself, directed the funds to religious schools. Would vouchers make available the private school option protected in *Pierce*, regardless of a family's economic status? At what cost? See, e.g., Osamudia R. James, Opt-Out Education: School Choice as Racial Subordination, 99 Iowa L. Rev. 1083 (2014).

e. Curricular controversies. Do parents have a right to "opt out" of sex education for their children? See generally Noa Ben-Asher, The Lawmaking Family, 90 Wash. U. L. Rev. 363 (2012). Suppose that parents object to schools' efforts to promote respect for LGBT individuals and couples. See Parker v. Hurley, 514 F.3d 87 (1st Cir. 2008); Douglas NeJaime, Inclusion, Accommodation, and Recognition: Accounting for Differences Based on Religion and Sexual Orientation, 32 Harv. J.L. & Gender 303 (2009). How does nationwide marriage equality affect the analysis? Do students themselves have a right to comprehensive sex education? See Kelly E. Mannion, Steubenville and Beyond: The Constitutional Case for Comprehensive Sex Education, 20 Cardozo J.L. & Gender 307 (2014).

6. Medical prerogatives.

a. Basic principles. In Parham v. J.R., 442 U.S. 584 (1979), the Court upheld Georgia's system allowing parents to commit their children to state mental institutions, over the child's objection and without an adversary hearing. Rejecting arguments that procedural due process requires safeguards beyond those provided by Georgia, the Court emphasized the traditional understanding that parents speak for their children regarding medical treatment:

> Our jurisprudence historically has reflected Western civilization concepts of the family as a unit with broad parental authority over minor children. . . . Surely, this [authority] includes a "high duty" to recognize symptoms of illness and to seek and follow medical advice. The law's concept of the family rests on a presumption that parents possess what a child lacks in maturity, experience, and capacity for judgment required for making life's difficult decisions. More important, historically it has recognized that natural bonds of affection lead parents to act in the best interests of their children. 1 W. Blackstone, Commentaries *447; 2 J. Kent, Commentaries on American Law *190. . . .
>
> . . . Simply because the decision of a parent is not agreeable to a child or because it involves risks does not automatically transfer the power to make that decision from the parents to some agency or officer of the state. The same characterizations can be made for a tonsillectomy, appendectomy, or other medical procedure. Most children, even in adolescence, simply are not able to make sound judgments concerning many decisions, including their need for medical care or treatment. Parents can and must make those judgments. . . . The fact that a child may balk at hospitalization or complain about a parental refusal to provide cosmetic surgery does not diminish the parents' authority to decide what is best for the child. Neither state officials nor federal courts are equipped to review such parental decisions. . . .

442 U.S. at 602-604. Indeed, the commitment decisions in question were treated as "voluntary," despite the child's opposition, because they were initiated by parents. To what extent does *Parham* leave room to recognize a child's right to choose or reject medical treatment? See B. Jessie Hill, Constituting Children's Bodily Integrity, 64 Duke L.J. 1295 (2015).

b. Minors' abortions. Recall Cincinnati Women's Services v. Taft (Chapter I). Can you reconcile the procedures the Court has required in the minors' abortion cases with its more deferential approach in *Parham*? Why does the Court show more skepticism about parental decisions regarding children's medical treatment in the abortion cases than in *Parham*? Do judges have greater competence in deciding the issues posed in judicial bypasses for minors seeking abortions than in conflicts concerning "voluntary commitments" of minors by their parents?

c. Sterilization. What safeguards, if any, are required when parents of an adult child with developmental disabilities seek to have her sterilized, as recommended by physicians, before she moves to a group home? See, e.g., In re Wirsing, 573 N.W.2d 51 (Mich. 1998); In re Grady, 426 A.2d 467 (N.J. 1981). See generally Norman L. Cantor, Making Medical Decisions for the Profoundly Mentally Disabled (2005). Is the surgery "voluntary" because the parents have requested it?

d. Circumcision. Federal law criminalizes female genital mutilation, including female circumcision. 18 U.S.C. §116. Congress has not criminalized male circumcision, which flourishes as both a religious tradition and a secular practice, usually performed on infants. In 2011, when San Francisco sought to ban male circumcision as a child-protective measure, California enacted a statute to protect parental authority to have sons circumcised. Cal. Health & Safety Code §125850. Germany enacted similar protective legislation, following a court ruling equating male circumcision with bodily injury.[33] How do you explain the different legal treatment of male and female circumcision? Why does parental autonomy protect one but not the other? How might the *Prince* harm standard apply here?

e. Treatment for intersex and transgender minors. Per conventional protocols, parents of infants born with ambiguous genitalia or other indicia of intersex were asked to consent to early surgery to achieve promptly improved conformity to a traditional sexual category. The American Academy of Pediatrics reconsidered this approach in 2006, and many authorities now urge that parents rear the child in one gender or the other, while delaying any irreversible intervention until the child is sufficiently mature to participate in the decision. See, e.g., Alison Davidian, Beyond the Locker Room: Changing Narratives on Early Surgery for Intersex Children, 26 Wis. J.L. Gender & Soc'y 1 (2011). What role should law play when a very young child exhibits gender dysphoria and parents must decide whether to permit hormonal treatment so that the child will not confront puberty in the "wrong body"? Does parental consent suffice for such treatment? Alternatively, may minors gain access to such treatment without parental consent? Popular culture is increasingly bringing such issues into the public discourse. See, e.g., Alexandra Alter, Transgender Children's Books Fill a Void and Break a Taboo, N.Y. Times, June 7, 2015, at A1.

f. Vaccinations. Exemptions to vaccination requirements are raising issues of parental autonomy, children's interests, and public health. What exemptions

---

[33]. Melissa Eddy, German Lawmakers Vote to Protect Right to Circumcision, N.Y. Times, Dec. 13, 2012, at A14.

would you allow? See generally Dorit Rubinstein Reiss, Thou Shalt Not Take the Name of the Lord Thy God in Vain: Use and Abuse of Religious Exemptions from School Immunization Requirements, 65 Hastings L.J. 1551 (2014).

Problems

1. The school board in New York City adopts a condom distribution program for high school students. Designed to curb both the increasing rate of adolescent HIV infection and the rising number of teenage pregnancies, the program allows any high school student who so wishes to obtain condoms without parental notification or consent. Parents challenge the program, claiming that it infringes their due process rights to rear their children as they see fit. They assert that the Constitution requires that the program have a parental "opt-out" provision, to honor their freedom to promote the value of sexual abstinence to their children. The school board asserts that such a provision would leave the children of parents who "opt out" vulnerable to HIV and pregnancy, if those children were sexually active without parental knowledge. What result and why? Compare Alfonso v. Fernandez, 606 N.Y.S.2d 259 (App. Div. 1993), with Curtis v. School Comm. of Falmouth, 652 N.E.2d 580 (Mass. 1995). Is the dispute one between parents and the school board alone? What interests do the students have at stake? How should such interests be taken into account?[34]

2. Zach, age 16, recently told his parents that he is gay. In response, his parents enrolled him in a fundamentalist Christian "boot camp" program promising "reparative therapy" to make him straight. See Alex Williams, Gay Teenager Stirs a Storm, N.Y. Times, July 17, 2005, §9, at 1 (reporting story of Zach and describing program of "Love in Action"). If Zach, depressed and anxious, opposes his parents' decision, what procedural or substantive recourse does he have? See John Alan Cohan, Parental Duties and the Right of Homosexual Minors to Refuse "Reparative" Therapy, 11 Buff. Women's L.J. 67 (2002/2003). If Zach's public school, rather than Zach himself, had disclosed his sexual orientation to his parents, would the school have violated his right to privacy? See C.N. v. Wolf, 410 F. Supp. 2d 894 (C.D. Cal. 2005).

In 2012, California became the first state to ban "therapy" intended to change a minor's sexual orientation. Cal. Bus. & Prof. Code §865.1. Do such laws unconstitutionally infringe parental autonomy? The right of minors to receive information? See Doe ex rel. Doe v. Governor of New Jersey, 783 F.3d 150 (3d Cir. 2015).

---

[34]. Today, Congress provides two funding streams for sex education: one for states that choose abstinence-only teaching and another for states that choose "personal responsibility education." See 42 U.S.C. §§710, 713.

2. Parental Obligations

STACY M. v. JASON M.

858 N.W.2d 852 (Neb. 2015)

STEPHAN, J. . . .

Jason and Stacy M.'s marriage was dissolved by a decree [that] required Jason to pay child support for three minor children. . . . Jason suspected during the marriage that he was not the biological father of the youngest child, but he did not raise the issue of paternity in the dissolution proceedings. In 2013, Jason obtained genetic testing which established he was not the father of the child. Through counsel, he subsequently filed a pleading entitled "Action in Equity to Suspend Child Support." He alleged Stacy knew the identity of the youngest child's biological father but refused to obtain child support from him. . . .

Jason and Stacy testified at [two evidentiary] hearings. Jason acknowledged that since the dissolution of the marriage, he has always exercised his visitation rights with the child and enjoys an "[e]xcellent" relationship with him. They celebrate holidays together, attend church together, go hunting and fishing, and enjoy other sporting activities. He wants the relationship to continue. His position in this case is aptly summarized by the following excerpt from his testimony:

> [J]ust for the record, I would like you, the judge, to know and Stacy to know that I would continue and will always love [the child] as my son until I die. He is considered my son. I just feel that it's not my responsibility to pay child support for [a child] that is not biologically mine. . . .

Stacy testified she did not know that Jason was not the biological father of the child until learning of the genetic testing results. She testified that at the relevant time, she was drinking at a bar with friends and thought she had been "drugged" and then "taken advantage of sexually" by a man whose identity she did not know. She did not report this incident because she was ashamed. She has never attempted to determine the identity of the child's biological father. She agreed that Jason had a very good relationship with the child which she wants to continue. She stated that the child "thinks the world" of Jason [who is the only father the child has known] and that she has not told the child that Jason is not his biological father, because "it would crush him." Stacy testified that she used the child support paid by Jason to support the child and that termination of the child support obligation or the paternal relationship would not be in the child's best interests. The district court denied the relief sought by Jason[, who appeals.]

There is compelling evidence that Jason is not the biological father of the child in question. But . . . a finding that an individual is not a biological father is not the equivalent of a finding that an individual is not the legal father. Under Nebraska common law, later embodied in Neb.Rev.Stat. § 42–377 (Reissue 2008), legitimacy of children born during wedlock is presumed. This presumption may be rebutted only by clear, satisfactory, and convincing evidence. . . .

The parentage of a child born during a marriage is traditionally contested, if at all, in dissolution proceedings. The marital presumption of paternity can be rebutted at that time. . . . When the parties fail to submit evidence at the dissolution proceeding rebutting the presumption of paternity, the dissolution court can find paternity based on the presumption alone. The trial court necessarily makes such a finding when it orders child support, because the trial court could not order child support without finding that the presumed father was the father of the child. Thus, a dissolution decree which orders child support is a legal determination of paternity. As a result, any dissolution decree that orders child support is res judicata on the issue of paternity. Under common law, the issue cannot be relitigated except under very limited circumstances through a motion to vacate or modify the decree. [Alisha C. v. Jeremy C., 808 N.W.2d 875 (Neb. 2012).]

However, in 2008, the Legislature enacted § 43–1412.01, which overrides res judicata principles and allows, in limited circumstances, an adjudicated father to disestablish a prior, final paternity determination based on genetic evidence that the adjudicated father is not the biological father. Section 43–1412.01 gives the court discretion to determine whether disestablishment of paternity is appropriate in light of both the adjudicated father's interests and the best interests of the child.

During both the proceedings below and in this appeal, Jason unequivocally stated he is *not* seeking disestablishment of paternity pursuant to § 43–1412.01. Despite this, he argues that the language of the statute supports the equitable remedy he pursues by providing "a court with the authority to suspend a child support order without necessarily disestablishing paternity." The first sentence of § 43.1412.01 authorizes an individual to ask a court to "set aside a final judgment, court order, administrative order, obligation to pay child support, or any other legal determination of paternity" based on the results of genetic testing. Jason argues that the use of the word "or" distinguishes an "obligation to pay child support" from a "legal determination of paternity," thus authorizing a court to suspend the former without affecting the latter.

But this argument ignores the use of the word "other" in the same sentence. As we have noted, a decree of dissolution which orders a man to pay child support is an implicit determination of paternity, even if the issue of paternity was not contested. Clearly, this sentence of the statute lists an "obligation to pay child support" as one of several forms of a "legal determination of paternity" which may be challenged through genetic test results. This plain meaning is underscored by the fourth sentence of the statute, which provides: "A court that sets aside a determination of paternity in accordance with this section shall order completion of a new birth record and may order any other appropriate relief, including setting aside an obligation to pay child support." In short, the language of the statute does not provide any support for the equitable relief which Jason seeks. Rather, it permits but does not require a court to set aside a child support obligation when paternity has been disestablished. It does not authorize any change in child support without such disestablishment.

Section 43–1412.01 provides Jason with a remedy at law to seek disestablishment of paternity and elimination of his child support obligation. But he has elected not to utilize that remedy, because he does not wish to disestablish paternity and thereby terminate the parental relationship. It is commendable that Jason has maintained a loving relationship with the child after learning that he is not the biological father. However, the parental relationship is not one which can be bifurcated in the manner Jason urges. . . . The obligation of support is a duty of a legally determined parent. . . . The district court did not err in denying the requested relief. [Affirmed.]

Notes and Questions

1. Rationale. *Stacy M.* holds that parentage necessarily entails child support obligations. It thus complements the point suggested in *M.F.*, supra, that establishing parentage or recognizing an individual as a legal parent is a prerequisite to imposing a child support obligation.

What theory makes *parents* financially responsible for their children? See Ira Mark Ellman & Tara O'Toole Ellman, The Theory of Child Support, 45 Harv. J. on Legis. 107, 129 (2008) (articulating "principle of the primacy of the parents' support obligation"). To the extent that children constitute community assets, the next generation of citizens, why shouldn't taxpayers assume responsibility, as they do for public education, for example? See, e.g., Anne Alstott, Private Tragedies: Family Law as Social Insurance, 4 Harv. L. & Pol'y Rev. 3 (2010); Scott Altman, A Theory of Child Support, 17 Int'l J.L. Pol'y & Fam. 173 (2003). Recall that the litigation in *M.F.*, supra, began when the children's mother sought public assistance.

Some theorists trace to Blackstone an "exchange view" of parenthood that treats parental obligations as the moral basis of parental rights. See Katharine T. Bartlett, Re-Expressing Parenthood, 98 Yale L.J. 293, 297-298 (1988); Harry D. Krause, Child Support Reassessed: Limits of Private Responsibility and the Public Interest, in Divorce Reform at the Crossroads 166, 178-179 (Stephen D. Sugarman & Herma Hill Kay eds., 1990). Does that help explain the rejection of Jason's claim for relief in *Stacy M.*?

2. Estoppel. To what extent does the court's reasoning suggest an approach similar to "paternity by estoppel," examined in *K.E.M.*, supra? Under the ALI Principles (§2.03), an individual required to pay child support is a parent by estoppel, with full parental status. Why should parentage follow from support duties? See A.H. v. M.P., 857 N.E.2d 1061, 1072-1075 (Mass. 2006) (rejecting this basis for parentage).

3. Gender. The principle demonstrated by *Stacy M.* applies without regard to gender. Thus, for example, in a then-landmark California case, the state supreme court recognized Elisa B. as the second mother of twins conceived by anonymous donor insemination and born to her partner, Emily, as a prerequisite to Elisa's support obligation after the county sought to collect reimbursement for the public assistance provided to Emily. Elisa B. v. Superior Ct., 117 P.3d 660 (Cal. 2005). The court used a gender-neutral reading of the UPA based on Elisa's receiving the twins into her home (which she had shared with Emily) and holding them out as her own. Now, several other jurisdictions have applied such paternity laws in a gender-neutral fashion, and nationwide marriage equality is sure to strengthen this trend. Why did *M.F.*, supra, fail to look to the mother's partner as a second parent, and thus a source of child support, instead of pursuing the sperm donor?

Should mothers and fathers have identical support duties? In contrast to the norm of equal responsibility now imposed on mothers and fathers to provide child support, Professor Martha Fineman articulates a different vision: The state should provide financial support for mothers so that they can care for their children, because childcare is work that ought to be valued. See generally Martha Albertson Fineman, The Autonomy Myth: A Theory of Dependency (2004). This approach rejects current "welfare reform" measures requiring custodial mothers of young children to work outside the home. See 42 U.S.C. §607(b)(5) (permitting state option). Evaluate Fineman's proposal.

4. All-or-nothing parentage. Law has long regarded parentage as exclusive and complete—the position reflected in *Stacy M.*'s statement that "the parental relationship is not one which can be bifurcated in the manner Jason urges." See Katharine T. Barlett, Rethinking Parenthood as an Exclusive Status: The Need for Legal Alternatives When the Premise of the Nuclear Family Has Failed, 70 Va. L. Rev. 879, 883 (1984). Whose interests does this doctrine serve? What advantages might "bifurcation" offer? Suppose that men in Jason's situation disestablish paternity as the only way to obtain relief from child support and the legal parents deny them access to the child. See Tex. Fam. Code Ann. §161.005 (facilitating termination of parental rights by "duped dads"); Ruth Padawer, Losing Fatherhood, N.Y. Times, Nov. 22, 2009, at MM38.

5. More than two parents? If child support obligations form a key objective of determining parentage, wouldn't recognizing more than two parents further advance the goal? See Melanie B. Jacobs, More Parents, More Money: Reflections on the Financial Implications of Multiple Parentage, 16 Cardozo J.L. & Gender 217 (2010). In Jacob v. Shultz-Jacob, 923 A.2d 473 (Pa. Super. Ct. 2007), the court determined that, for child-support purposes, a mother, her former partner (another woman), and the friend who donated sperm and remained involved in the children's lives were all legal parents. See also State Department of Children & Family Services ex rel. A.L. v. Lowrie, 167 So. 3d 573 (La. 2015) (holding biological father and mother's ex-husband should share child support obligation under Louisiana's dual-paternity doctrine). What disadvantages might follow from recognition of multiple parents? See generally Susan Frelich Appleton, Parents by the Numbers, 37 Hofstra L. Rev. 11 (2008). What is the allure of a two-parent model? See Katharine K. Baker, Bionormativity and the Construction of Parenthood, 42 Ga. L. Rev. 649 (2008).

6. Obligations without rights? If parental obligations must accompany parental rights, what about the reverse—obligations without rights? Why? What actions enable one to extricate oneself from parental financial responsibility? Should a voluntary agreement to relinquish all parental rights suffice? See In re Carr, 938 A.2d 89 (N.H. 2007) (imposing support duties notwithstanding such agreement). The state's termination of parental rights? Jurisdictions are split. Compare In re C.N., 839 N.W.2d 841 (N.D. 2013), with Guardianship of Anthony J., 980 A.2d 1250 (Me. 2009).

7. Other responsibilities? What other obligations does parentage entail? Must an *unwilling* parent spend time with a child or participate in childrearing decisions? Family law traditionally has not compelled such involvement. See, e.g., James G. Dwyer, A Taxonomy of Children's Existing Rights in State Decision Making About Their Relationships, 11 Wm. & Mary Bill Rts. J. 845, 858 (2003). Under what circumstances should parents be held responsible for damages when their children cause harm to the person or property of another? See Restatement (Third) of the Law of Torts: Liability for Physical Harm §41 (2012). To what extent do parents (and the state) have obligations to meet children's educational needs? See Emily Buss, The Gap in Law Between Developmental Expectations and Educational Obligations, 79 U. Chi. L. Rev. 59 (2012).

C. Limits: Ending and Curtailing Parental Rights and Duties

1. Termination of Parental Rights

a. The Child Welfare System

SANTOSKY v. KRAMER

455 U.S. 745 (1982)

Justice BLACKMUN delivered the opinion of the Court. . . .

Under New York law, the State may terminate, over parental objection, the rights of parents in their natural child upon a finding that the child is "permanently neglected." The New York Family Court Act §622 requires that only a "fair preponderance of the evidence" support that finding. Thus, in New York, the factual certainty required to extinguish the parent-child relationship is no greater than that necessary to award money damages in an ordinary civil action. . . . The question here is whether New York's "fair preponderance of the evidence" standard is constitutionally sufficient.

Petitioners John Santosky II and Annie Santosky are the natural parents of Tina and John III. In November 1973, after incidents reflecting parental neglect, respondent Kramer, Commissioner of the Ulster County Department of Social Services, initiated a neglect proceeding under Fam. Ct. Act §1022 and removed Tina from her natural home. About 10 months later, he removed John III and placed him with foster parents. On the day John was taken, Annie Santosky gave birth to a third child, Jed. When Jed was only three days old, respondent transferred him to a foster home on the ground that immediate removal was necessary to avoid imminent danger to his life or health.

In October 1978, respondent petitioned the Ulster County Family Court to terminate petitioners' parental rights in the three children. [When petitioners challenged the "preponderance" standard, the] Family Court Judge rejected this constitutional challenge, and weighed the evidence under the statutory standard. While acknowledging that the Santoskys had maintained contact with their children, the judge found those visits "at best superficial and devoid of any real emotional content." After deciding that the agency had made "'diligent efforts' to encourage and strengthen the parental relationship," he concluded that the Santoskys were incapable, even with public assistance, of planning for the future of their children. The judge later held a dispositional hearing and ruled that the best interests of the three children required permanent termination of the Santoskys' custody. [Petitioners unsuccessfully appealed.]

Last Term in Lassiter v. Department of Social Services, 452 U.S. 18 (1981), this Court [held] that the Fourteenth Amendment's Due Process Clause does not require the appointment of counsel for indigent parents in every parental status termination proceeding. The case casts light, however, on the two central questions here—whether process is constitutionally due a natural parent at a State's parental rights termination proceeding, and, if so, what process is due. . . .

The fundamental liberty interest of natural parents in the care, custody, and management of their child does not evaporate simply because they have not been model parents or have lost temporary custody of their child to the State. Even when blood relationships are strained, parents retain a vital interest in preventing the irretrievable destruction of their family life. If anything, persons faced with forced dissolution of their parental rights have a more critical need for procedural protections than do those resisting state intervention into ongoing family affairs. When the State moves to destroy weakened familial bonds, it must provide the parents with fundamentally fair procedures.

In *Lassiter*, the Court and three dissenters agreed that the nature of the process due in parental rights termination proceedings turns on a balancing of the "three distinct factors" specified in Mathews v. Eldridge, 424 U.S. 319, 335 (1976): the private interests affected by the proceeding; the risk of error created by the State's chosen procedure; and the countervailing governmental interest supporting use of the challenged procedure. . . . Evaluation of the three *Eldridge* factors compels the conclusion that use of a "fair preponderance of the evidence" standard in [termination] proceedings is inconsistent with due process.

"The extent to which procedural due process must be afforded the recipient is influenced by the extent to which he may be 'condemned to suffer grievous loss.' " . . . *Lassiter* declared it "plain beyond the need for multiple citation" that a natural parent's "desire for and right to 'the companionship, care, custody, and management of his or her children' " is an interest far more precious than any property right. 452 U.S., at 27 quoting Stanley v. Illinois, 405 U.S., at 651. When the State initiates a parental rights termination proceeding, it seeks not merely to infringe that fundamental liberty interest, but to end it. . . . Thus, the first *Eldridge* factor—the private interest affected—weighs heavily against use of the preponderance standard at a state-initiated permanent neglect proceeding. . . .

[T]the factfinding hearing pits the State directly against the parents. The State alleges that the natural parents are at fault. The questions disputed and decided are what the State did—"made diligent efforts,"—and what the natural parents did not do—"maintain contact with or plan for the future of the child." The State marshals an array of public resources to prove its case and disprove the parents' case. Victory by the State not only makes termination of parental rights possible; it entails a judicial determination that the parents are unfit to raise their own children.[10]

---

10. The Family Court judge in the present case expressly refused to terminate petitioners' parental rights on a "non-statutory, no-fault basis." Nor is it clear that the State constitutionally could terminate a parent's rights without showing parental unfitness. See Quilloin v. Walcott, 434 U.S. 246, 255 (1978) ("We have little doubt that the Due Process Clause would be offended '[i]f a State were to attempt to force the breakup of a natural family, over the objections of the parents and their children, without some showing of unfitness and for the sole reason that to do so was thought to be in the children's best interest,' " quoting Smith v. Organization of Foster Families, 431 U.S. 816, 862-863 (1977) (Stewart, J., concurring in judgment)).

[U]ntil the State proves parental unfitness, the child and his parents share a vital interest in preventing erroneous termination of their natural relationship. Thus, at the factfinding, the interests of the child and his natural parents coincide to favor use of error-reducing procedures. . . .

Under Mathews v. Eldridge, we next must consider both the risk of erroneous deprivation of private interests resulting from use of a "fair preponderance" standard and the likelihood that a higher evidentiary standard would reduce that risk. . . . In New York, the factfinding stage of a state-initiated permanent neglect proceeding bears many of the indicia of a criminal trial. . . . The State, the parents, and the child are all represented by counsel. The State seeks to establish a series of historical facts about the intensity of its agency's efforts to reunite the family, the infrequency and insubstantiality of the parents' contacts with their child, and the parents' inability or unwillingness to formulate a plan for the child's future. The attorneys submit documentary evidence, and call witnesses who are subject to cross-examination. [T]he judge then determines whether the State has proved the statutory elements of permanent neglect by a fair preponderance of the evidence.

At such a proceeding, numerous factors combine to magnify the risk of erroneous factfinding. Permanent neglect proceedings employ imprecise substantive standards that leave determinations unusually open to the subjective values of the judge. [T]he court possesses unusual discretion to underweigh probative facts that might favor the parent. Because parents subject to termination proceedings are often poor, uneducated, or members of minority groups, such proceedings are often vulnerable to judgments based on cultural or class bias.

The State's ability to assemble its case almost inevitably dwarfs the parents' ability to mount a defense. No predetermined limits restrict the sums an agency may spend in prosecuting a given termination proceeding. The State's attorney usually will be expert on the issues contested and the procedures employed at the factfinding hearing, and enjoys full access to all public records concerning the family. The State may call on experts in family relations, psychology, and medicine to bolster its case. Furthermore, the primary witnesses at the hearing will be the agency's own professional caseworkers whom the State has empowered both to investigate the family situation and to testify against the parents. Indeed, because the child is already in agency custody, the State even has the power to shape the historical events that form the basis for termination.[13]

The disparity between the adversaries' litigation resources is matched by a striking asymmetry in their litigation options. Unlike criminal defendants, natural parents have no "double jeopardy" defense against repeated state termination efforts. If the State initially fails to win termination, as New York did here, it always can try once again to cut off the parents' rights after gathering more or better evidence. Yet even when the parents have attained the level of fitness required by the State, they have no similar means by which they can forestall future termination efforts.

---

13. In this case, for example, the parents claim that the State sought court orders denying them the right to visit their children, which would have prevented them from maintaining the contact required by Fam. Ct. Act §614.1(d). The parents further claim that the State cited their rejection of social services they found offensive or superfluous as proof of the agency's "diligent efforts" and their own "failure to plan" for the children's future. . . .

Coupled with a "fair preponderance of the evidence" standard, these factors create a significant prospect of erroneous termination. A standard of proof that by its very terms demands consideration of the quantity, rather than the quality, of the evidence may misdirect the factfinder in the marginal case. . . .

Raising the standard of proof would have both practical and symbolic consequences. . . . An elevated standard of proof in a parental rights termination proceeding would alleviate "the possible risk that a factfinder might decide to [deprive] an individual based solely on a few isolated instances of unusual conduct [or] . . . idiosyncratic behavior." Addington v. Texas, 441 U.S., at 427. "Increasing the burden of proof is one way to impress the factfinder with the importance of the decision and thereby perhaps to reduce the chances that inappropriate" terminations will be ordered. Ibid.

The Appellate Division approved New York's preponderance standard on the ground that it properly "balanced rights possessed by the child . . . with those of the natural parents. . . . " 427 N.Y.S.2d, at 320. By so saying, the court suggested that a preponderance standard properly allocates the risk of error between the parents and the child. That view is fundamentally mistaken.

The court's theory assumes that termination of the natural parents' rights invariably will benefit the child.[15] Yet we have noted above that the parents and the child share an interest in avoiding erroneous termination. Even accepting the court's assumption, we cannot agree with its conclusion that a preponderance standard fairly distributes the risk of error between parent and child. Use of that standard reflects the judgment that society is nearly neutral between erroneous termination of parental rights and erroneous failure to terminate those rights. For the child, the likely consequence of an erroneous failure to terminate is preservation of an uneasy status quo. For the natural parents, however, the consequence of an erroneous termination is the unnecessary destruction of their natural family. A standard that allocates the risk of error nearly equally between those two outcomes does not reflect properly their relative severity.

Two state interests are at stake in parental rights termination proceedings—a parens patriae interest in preserving and promoting the welfare of the child and a fiscal and administrative interest in reducing the cost and burden of such proceedings. A standard of proof more strict than preponderance of the evidence is consistent with both interests.

. . . As parens patriae, the State's goal is to provide the child with a permanent home. Yet while there is still reason to believe that positive, nurturing parent-child relationships exist, the parens patriae interest favors preservation, not severance, of natural familial bonds. . . . We cannot believe that it would burden the State unduly to require that its factfinders have the same factual certainty when terminating the parent-child relationship as they must have to suspend a driver's

---

15. This is a hazardous assumption at best. Even when a child's natural home is imperfect, permanent removal from that home will not necessarily improve his welfare. See, e.g., Wald, State Intervention on Behalf of "Neglected" Children: A Search for Realistic Standards, 27 Stan. L. Rev. 985, 993 (1975) ("In fact, under current practice, coercive intervention frequently results in placing a child in a more detrimental situation than he would be in without intervention").

Nor does termination of parental rights necessarily ensure adoption. Even when a child eventually finds an adoptive family, he may spend years moving between state institutions and "temporary" foster placements after his ties to his natural parents have been severed.

license. [Without deciding the outcome under a constitutionally proper standard,] we vacate the judgment of the Appellate Division and remand the case for further proceedings not inconsistent with this opinion. . . .

Justice REHNQUIST, with whom THE CHIEF JUSTICE, Justice WHITE, and Justice O'CONNOR join, dissenting.

. . . New York has created an exhaustive program to assist parents in regaining the custody of their children and to protect parents from the unfair deprivation of their parental rights. And yet the majority's myopic scrutiny of the standard of proof blinds it to the very considerations and procedures which make the New York scheme "fundamentally fair." . . .

The three children to which this case relates were removed from petitioners' custody [pursuant to New York's procedures] and in response to what can only be described as shockingly abusive treatment.[10]

[P]etitioners received training by a mother's aide, a nutritional aide, and a public health nurse, and counseling at a family planning clinic. In addition, the plan provided psychiatric treatment and vocational training for the father, and counseling at a family service center for the mother. Between early 1976 and the final termination decision in April 1979, the State spent more than $15,000 in these efforts to rehabilitate petitioners as parents.

Petitioners' response to the State's effort was marginal at best. They wholly disregarded some of the available services and participated only sporadically in the others. As a result, and out of growing concern over the length of the children's stay in foster care, the Department petitioned in September 1976 for permanent termination of petitioners' parental rights so that the children could be adopted by other families. Although the Family Court recognized that petitioners' reaction to the State's efforts was generally "non-responsive, even hostile," the fact that they were "at least superficially cooperative" led it to conclude that there was yet hope of further improvement and an eventual reuniting of the family. Accordingly, the petition for permanent termination was dismissed. [In October 1978, the agency again filed a termination proceeding because petitioners had made few efforts to take advantage of Social Services or to visit their children.]

[T]he State's extraordinary 4-year effort to reunite petitioners' family was not just unsuccessful, it was altogether rebuffed by parents unwilling to improve their circumstances sufficiently to permit a return of their children. At every step of this protracted process petitioners were accorded those procedures and protections which traditionally have been required by due process of law. . . . It is inconceivable to me that these procedures were "fundamentally unfair" to petitioners. . . .

---

10. Tina Apel, the oldest of petitioners' five children, was removed from their custody by court order in November 1973 when she was two years old. Removal proceedings were commenced in response to complaints by neighbors and reports from a local hospital that Tina had suffered injuries in petitioners' home including a fractured left femur, treated with a home-made splint; bruises on the upper arms, forehead, flank, and spine; and abrasions of the upper leg. The following summer, John Santosky III, petitioners' second oldest child, was also removed from petitioner's custody. John, who was less than one year old at the time, was admitted to the hospital suffering malnutrition, bruises on the eye and forehead, cuts on the foot, blisters on the hand, and multiple pin pricks on the back. Jed Santosky, the third oldest of petitioners' children, was removed from his parents' custody when only three days old as a result of the abusive treatment of the two older children.

The interests at stake in this case demonstrate that New York has selected a constitutionally permissible standard of proof.

On one side is the interest of parents in a continuation of the family unit and the raising of their own children. The importance of this interest cannot easily be overstated. Few consequences of judicial action are so grave as the severance of natural family ties. . . . On the other side of the termination proceeding are the often countervailing interests of the child. A stable, loving homelife is essential to a child's physical, emotional, and spiritual well-being. . . .

In addition to the child's interest in a normal homelife, "the State has an urgent interest in the welfare of the child." Lassiter v. Department of Social Services, 452 U.S., at 27. Few could doubt that the most valuable resource of a self-governing society is its population of children who will one day become adults and themselves assume the responsibility of self-governance. . . .

When, in the context of a permanent neglect termination proceeding, the interests of the child and the State in a stable, nurturing homelife are balanced against the interests of the parents in the rearing of their child, it cannot be said that either set of interests is so clearly paramount as to require that the risk of error be allocated to one side or the other. Accordingly, a State constitutionally may conclude that the risk of error should be borne in roughly equal fashion by use of the preponderance-of-the-evidence standard of proof. . . .

Notes and Questions

1. **Background.** Based on the harm standard articulated in *Prince*, supra, the state may intervene in the family to protect children. Termination of parental rights (TPR) proceedings represent the culmination of such interventions, generally evolving over several stages. Initially, state child welfare workers ask a family court or juvenile court to assert jurisdiction over the child. (In an emergency, the state might use summary seizure to remove the child from the home, followed by a jurisdictional proceeding.) For the state to be able to exercise its authority, the court must find by a preponderance of the evidence that the child meets statutory criteria, which typically provide for jurisdiction over abused, neglected, and dependent children. Because of the constitutional status of family integrity as a fundamental right, some authorities require such initial intervention to meet the requirements of strict scrutiny (especially if temporary custody of the child is to follow). See, e.g., In re Juvenile Appeal (83-CD), 455 A.2d 1313, 1318-1322 (Conn. 1983). See generally John Thomas Halloran, Families First: Reframing Parental Rights as Familial Rights in Termination of Parental Rights Proceedings, 18 U.C. Davis J. Juv. L. & Pol'y 51 (2014). Assuming satisfaction of this jurisdictional threshold, the court then selects a disposition. Dispositional alternatives include, inter alia, educational sessions for parents, ongoing home visits, or placement of the child in foster care, with efforts to address the problem and reunify the family as the preferred solution. The *Santosky* dissent discusses several of these options.

As *Santosky* explains, if the problem requiring removal of the child from home persists, the state may seek TPR. Such proceedings, in turn, entail an initial stage at which the court makes a determination of unfitness (the "unfitness stage") and a subsequent stage at which the court determines whether TPR would serve the child's best interests (sometimes called "the best-interests stage"). (*Santosky* refers somewhat differently to the stages of a child neglect proceeding, pursuant to New York statute, as "the fact-finding hearing," at which the state is required to prove permanent neglect, and "the dispositional hearing," at which the court determines which placement serves the child's best interests.) These stages may occur in a single hearing.

All of these decisions take place against a backdrop of laws designed to be expansive in the name of child protection, thus inviting value judgments about proper parenting that might well reflect bias based on race, culture, and class. See Shani King, The Family Law Canon in a (Post?) Racial Era, 72 Ohio St. L.J. 575 (2011); Janet L. Wallace & Lisa R. Pruitt, Judging Parents, Judging Place: Poverty, Rurality, and Termination of Parental Rights, 77 Mo. L. Rev. 95 (2012).

2. Standard. What do the various participants in TPR proceedings have at stake in the distribution of the risk of error? Why does the majority reject neutrality as the appropriate balance between erroneous terminations of parental rights and erroneous failures to terminate those rights? What are the consequences of each type of erroneous decision? Does the clear-and-convincing-evidence standard, required in *Santosky*, adequately protect family integrity and parental autonomy? Adequately protect the interests of children? Increase the likelihood that children spend lengthy periods in foster care? See Sharon B. Hershkowitz, Due Process and the Termination of Parental Rights, 19 Fam. L.Q. 245, 292-295 (1985). Some laws require a higher standard still. See In re KMO, 280 P.3d 1203, 1214 (Wyo. 2012) (noting the requirement of proof beyond a reasonable doubt for Native American parents under ICWA). Should they do so?

Although *Santosky* requires the clear-and-convincing-evidence standard before TPR, several states reason that *Santosky* applies only to the determination of unfitness, with a lower standard of proof governing the best-interests stage. Compare In re B.H., 348 S.W.3d 770 (Mo. 2011), with KC v. State, 351 P.3d 236 (Wyo. 2015). See also Josh Gupta-Kagan, Filling the Due Process Donut Hole: Abuse and Neglect Cases Between Disposition and Permanency, 10 Conn. Pub. Int. L.J. 13, 14 (2010) (criticizing absence of safeguards "in the middle of abuse and neglect cases"). What implications does *Santosky* have for such matters?

3. Establishing parentage compared. Should the same standard govern termination of parental rights and the establishment of parentage? How does the risk of error cut in the latter context? In Rivera v. Minnich, 483 U.S. 574 (1987), Jean Marie Minnich, an unmarried woman, sought child support for her three-week-old son, alleging that Gregory Rivera was the father. Rivera argued that due process required clear and convincing evidence, relying on *Santosky*. Rejecting the higher standard, the Court held that due process requires only a preponderance of the evidence to meet the standard of proof in paternity proceedings. The Court distinguished the state's *imposition* of parent-child obligations from *termination* because of the latter's severe consequences (the elimination of preexisting rights). Justice Brennan, dissenting, argued that paternity proceedings result in "the imposition of a lifelong relationship with significant financial, legal, and moral dimensions." Id. at 583. Is neutrality with respect to erroneous decisions more appropriate for establishing paternity than for terminating parental rights? Is it more problematic for the "wrong" father to be recognized or for no father at all to meet the test?

For whom? Cf. Hodge v. Craig, 382 S.W.3d 325 (Tenn. 2012). What of concerns about "forced parenthood," supra p. 852? To what extent is child support the key issue? Recall that, in some states, TPR does not end child support obligations. See supra p. 865.

4. Substantive implications. Although *Santosky* resolves an issue of procedural due process, what implications does it have for constitutionally required substantive standards? Would a law that based TPR exclusively on a showing of the child's best interests survive constitutional review? Why? What inferences do you draw from the majority's footnote 10? In an omitted passage, the dissent responds:

> By holding that due process requires proof by clear and convincing evidence the majority surely cannot mean that any state scheme passes constitutional muster so long as it applies that standard of proof. A state law permitting termination of parental rights upon a showing of neglect by clear and convincing evidence certainly would not be acceptable to the majority if it provided no procedures other than one 30-minute hearing. Similarly, the majority probably would balk at a state scheme that permitted termination of parental rights on a clear and convincing showing merely that such action would be in the best interests of the child.

455 U.S. at 772-773 (Rehnquist, J., dissenting). Does the Constitution permit "no-fault" terminations if they serve the child's interests? See, e.g., J.H. v. Indiana Dept. of Child Servs., 934 N.E.2d 1127 (Ind. 2010); In re Adoption/Guardianship of Alonza D., 987 A.2d 536 (Md. 2010).

5. ASFA. In response to criticisms that children were too often languishing in foster care because of an overemphasis on parents' rights, Congress in 1997 enacted the Adoption and Safe Families Act (ASFA), Pub. L. No. 105-89, 111 Stat. 2115 (codified as amended in scattered sections of 42 U.S.C.). ASFA eliminates the requirement that the state undertake reasonable efforts to reunify the family in certain severe cases (i.e., torture, sexual abuse, a parent's murder of another child, or a parent's loss of parental rights to a sibling) (42 U.S.C. §671(a)(15)(D)). In addition, ASFA aims to facilitate adoption by reducing the amount of time that children spend in foster care. ASFA shortens the period triggering permanency hearings to no later than 12 months after the child's entry into foster care and also requires states to seek termination of parental rights for children who have been in foster care for 15 of the last 22 months (id. §675(5)(E)). States need not file such petitions if (a) a relative cares for the child, (b) a state agency believes that termination would not be in the best interests of the child, or (c) a state agency has failed to provide the family with reunification services.

Critics claim that these reforms undervalue minority families and encourage transfer of African-American children to white families—serving the needs of adopters rather than children. See Dorothy Roberts, Shattered Bonds: The Color of Child Welfare 165-172 (2002); Cynthia Godsoe, Parsing Parenthood, 17 Lewis & Clark L. Rev. 113 (2013).

Under ASFA, the child welfare system (including foster care and TPR) produces large numbers of children to be adopted, with data from 2008 showing 463,000 children in foster care, of whom 123,000 were awaiting adoption, and 285,000 children exiting foster care, of whom 19 percent were adopted.[35]

6. Right to counsel. Is *Santosky* consistent with Lassiter v. Department of Social Services, 452 U.S. 18 (1981), discussed in *Santosky*? Which procedural protection, a right to counsel or a heightened standard of proof, is more valuable to parents fighting terminations? Which offers better protection of children's interests? Which imposes greater costs on the state? Despite the Supreme Court's holding in *Lassiter*, many states guarantee indigent parents the right to counsel in TPR proceedings. E.g., J.B. v. Florida Department of Children & Families, 170 So. 3d 780 (Fla. 2015) (requiring effective assistance of counsel).

What is a child's standing in TPR cases? See In re Z.H., 2015 WL 4755282 (Ohio Ct. App. 2015) (recognizing standing to appeal TPR). Should the child have legal representation in TPR proceedings? See In re Christina M., 908 A.2d 1073 (Conn. 2006); In re Dependency of MSR, 271 P.3d 234, 245 (Wash. 2012). A guardian ad litem? See Farthing v. McGee, 158 So. 3d 1223 (Miss. Ct. App. 2015). See also Barbara Atwood, Representing Children Who Can't or Won't Direct Counsel: Best Interests Lawyering or No Lawyer at All?, 53 Ariz. L. Rev. 381 (2011).

7. Alternatives to TPR. Even if the state decides that parents are unfit to rear their children, must TPR follow? Long-term foster care, guardianship without TPR, or open adoption (discussed infra) offer alternatives permitting the retention of ties with biological families. What are the advantages of each? The disadvantages? See, e.g., Sacha Coupet, Swimming Upstream Against the Great Adoption Tide: Making the Case for "Impermanence," 34 Cap. U. L. Rev. 405 (2005); Josh Gupta-Kagan, The New Permanency, 19 U.C. Davis J. Juv. L. & Pol'y 1 (2015).

b. Adoption Surrender

SCARPETTA v. SPENCE-CHAPIN ADOPTION SERVICE

269 N.E.2d 787 (N.Y. 1971)

JASEN, J.

This appeal involves the return of an out-of-wedlock infant to its natural mother after she had executed a purported surrender of the child to an authorized adoption agency. . . .

The infant child was born on May 18, 1970, to Olga Scarpetta, who was unmarried and 32 years old. She had become pregnant in her native Colombia by a married Colombian in the summer of 1969. Seeking to minimize the shame of an out-of-wedlock child to herself and her family, Miss Scarpetta came to New York for the purpose of having her child. She was well acquainted with this country and its language. She had had her early schooling in New Jersey and her college education in California. Indeed, she had been trained in the social sciences.

---

[35]. Elisa Rosman et al., Finding Permanence for Kids: NCFA Recommendations for Immediate Improvement to the Foster Care System, in Adoption Factbook V, supra note [7], at 199.

Four days after the birth of the child, she placed the infant for boarding care with Spence-Chapin Adoption Service, an agency authorized by statute to receive children for adoption. Ten days later, a surrender document was executed by Miss Scarpetta to the agency, and on June 18, 1970, the baby was placed with a family for adoption. Five days later, on June 23, 1970, the mother repented her actions and requested that the child be returned to her.

After several unsuccessful attempts to regain her child from the agency, the mother commenced this habeas corpus proceeding. Before the surrender, the mother had had a number of interviews with representatives of the adoption agency. On the other hand, shortly before or after the birth of the child, her family in Colombia, well-to-do, and devout in their religion, were shocked that she should put out her child for adoption by strangers. They assured her of their support and backing and urged her to raise her own child. [The courts below ruled in favor of Scarpetta. This court affirms.]

The resolution of the issue of whether or not a mother, who has surrendered her child to an authorized adoption agency, may regain the child's custody, has received various treatment by the legislatures and courts in the United States. At one extreme, several jurisdictions adhere to the rule that the parent has an absolute right to regain custody of her child prior to the final adoption decree. On the other hand, some jurisdictions adhere to the rule that the parent's surrender is final, absent fraud or duress. The majority of the jurisdictions, however, place the parent's right to regain custody within the discretion of the court—the position which, of course, our Legislature has taken. The discretionary rule allows the court leeway to approve a revocation of the surrender when the facts of the individual case warrant it and avoids the obvious dangers posed by the rigidity of the extreme positions.

In New York, a surrender executed by a mother, in which she voluntarily consents to a change of guardianship and custody to an authorized agency for the purpose of adoption, is expressly sanctioned by law. (Social Services Law, §384.) The statute nowhere endows a surrender with irrevocability foreclosing a mother from applying to the court to restore custody of the child to her. In fact, the legislation is clear that, until there has been an actual adoption, or the agency has met the requirements of the Social Services Law [requiring agency or court approval of surrender following notice], the surrender remains under, and subject to, judicial supervision.

Inherent to judicial supervision of surrenders is the recognition that documents of surrender are unilateral, not contracts or deeds, and are almost always executed under circumstances which may cast doubt upon their voluntariness or on understanding of the consequences of their execution. . . . Of necessity, therefore, there is always an issue about the fact of surrender, document or no document. On the other hand, the courts have the strongest obligation not to permit surrenders to be undone except for the weightiest reasons. . . .

Having the power to direct a change of custody from the agency back to the natural parent, notwithstanding the document of surrender, the court should exercise it only when it determines "that the interest of such child will be promoted thereby and that such parent is fit, competent and able to duly maintain, support and educate such child." (Social Services Law, §383, subd. 1.) . . . It has repeatedly been determined, insofar as the best interests of the child are concerned, that "[the] mother or father has a right to the care and custody of a child, superior to that of all others, unless he or she has abandoned that right or is proved unfit to assume the duties and privileges of parenthood." [Citations omitted.]

The primacy of status thus accorded the natural parent is not materially altered or diminished by the mere fact of surrender under the statute, although it is a factor to be considered by the court. To hold, as the agency suggests—that a surrender to an authorized adoption agency constitutes, as a matter of law, an abandonment—would frustrate the policy underlying our legislation, which allows a mother to regain custody of her child, notwithstanding the surrender to the agency, provided, of course, that there is some showing of improvidence in the making of the surrender, that the interest of such child will be promoted and "that such parent is fit, competent, and able to duly maintain, support, and educate such child." . . .

In no case, however, may a contest between a parent and nonparent resolve itself into a simple factual issue as to which affords the better surroundings, or as to which party is better equipped to raise the child. It may well be that the prospective adoptive parents would afford a child some material advantages over and beyond what the natural mother may be able to furnish, but these advantages, passing and transient as they are, cannot outweigh a mother's tender care and love unless it is clearly established that she is unfit to assume the duties and privileges of parenthood.

We conclude that the record before us supports the finding by the courts below that the surrender was improvident and that the child's best interests—moral and temporal—will be best served by its return to the natural mother.

Within 23 days after the child had been given over to the agency, and only 5 days after the prospective adoptive parents had gained provisional custody of the child, the mother sought its return. If the matter had been resolved at that time, much heartache and distress would have been avoided. . . .

[The court rejects the prospective adoptive parents' petition to intervene on the ground that intervention would necessarily lead to disclosure of the names of the natural parents and prospective adoptive parents to each other, in violation of the policy of secrecy, which relies on the adoption agency to serve as the intermediary.] Similarly, we find no merit to the contention that the failure to allow the prospective adoptive parents to intervene in the instant proceeding deprived them of due process of law so as to render the court's determination awarding custody of the child to the mother, constitutionally invalid. The prospective adoptive parents do not have legal custody of the baby. Spence-Chapin, the adoption agency, by virtue of the mother's surrender, was vested with legal custody. The agency, in turn, had placed the baby with the prospective adoptive parents pursuant to an arrangement reached between them, for the purpose of prospective adoption of the child. This arrangement is, of course, subject to our adoption statutes, and in no way conveys any vested rights in the child to the prospective adoptive parents. . . .

Notes and Questions

1. **Epilogue.** After the court's decision, the adoptive family (the DiMartinos) fled with "Baby Lenore" to Florida. Scarpetta filed a habeas corpus action there,

claiming full faith and credit for the New York decision. The DiMartinos successfully argued that they should not be bound by litigation in which they were not permitted to participate. At the ensuing trial, the court focused on the child's best interests. Experts testified on her development with the DiMartinos and the trauma that separation from them would cause. The Florida court ruled that the DiMartinos should retain custody. The U.S. Supreme Court denied certiorari, DiMartino v. Scarpetta, 404 U.S. 805 (1971). See Henry H. Foster, Jr., Adoption and Child Custody: Best Interests of the Child?, 22 Buff. L. Rev. 1, 8 (1972).

In response to the case, New York amended the statute to provide that in contested revocation cases, parents who consented "have no right to the custody of the child superior to that of the adoptive parents" and custody "shall be awarded solely on the basis of the best interests of the child," with no presumption favoring any particular disposition. N.Y. Dom. Rel. Law §115-b(6)(d)(v).

2. Agency versus independent placement. The adoption process can begin, as *Scarpetta* illustrates, when the birth parent voluntarily relinquishes (or "surrenders") the child to a state-licensed or state-operated agency. The agency takes legal custody and selects a placement following an evaluation of the prospective adopters, often called a "home study" or a "preplacement investigation." See, e.g., Iowa Code Ann. §600.8; 23 Pa. Cons. Stat. Ann. §2530. After a residential period under the agency's supervision, a court issues an adoption decree. Traditionally, neither the birth parents nor the adopters learn the others' identities. Moreover, if the placement fails during the trial period, the child returns to the agency's care, not to the birth parent, whose rights are terminated by the relinquishment. By contrast, in independent adoptions, the birth parent typically selects the adopters, often with assistance from an intermediary. Today, public agencies process far more adoptions than do private agencies, such as the one in *Scarpetta*, with independent adoptions accounting for a smaller but still substantial number.[36] See generally L. Jean Emery, Agency versus Independent Adoption: The Case for Agency Adoption, The Future of Children, Spring 1993, at 139; Mark T. McDermott, Agency versus Independent Adoption: The Case for Independent Adoption, The Future of Children, supra, at 146.

3. Surrender. According to the principal case, why did Olga Scarpetta surrender her child? Why did she change her mind?

Scarpetta exemplifies surrender during an era (between World War II until the Supreme Court's Roe v. Wade ruling in 1973) when white unmarried mothers faced enormous pressure to surrender upon birth because adoption practice treated them as deviant and unfit to parent, yet able to provide valuable resources (babies) to married infertile couples. The stories of some of these women reflect parental coercion, stigma, shame, and lifelong emotional scars, despite experts' contentions that surrender would help these women reconstitute their lives in a healthy way. See Ann Fessler, The Girls Who Went Away: The Hidden History of Women Who Surrendered Children for Adoption in the Decades Before Roe v. Wade (2006). Such information has prompted historian Rickie Solinger to

---

[36]. Of the 76,489 domestic adoptions of nonrelatives in 2007, 42,978 were processed by public agencies, 20,254 by private agencies, and 13,257 by private individuals, usually attorneys. Placek, supra note [7], at 4.

conclude that "adoption is rarely about mothers' choices; it is, instead, about the abject choicelessness of some resourceless women."[37]

Now, most unmarried women rear their children.[38] What social constraints influence surrender today?

4. Revocation of consent. Of the different approaches to revocation surveyed by *Scarpetta*, which is most sound? What can states do to improve the consent process and minimize attempted revocations? See Elizabeth J. Samuels, Time to Decide? The Laws Governing Mothers' Consents to the Adoption of Their Newborn Infants, 72 Tenn. L. Rev. 509 (2005). To what extent should the concern about regret expressed in the abortion context in Gonzales v. Carhart (Chapter I) apply to adoption revocations? With what legal effect? See Susan Frelich Appleton, Reproduction and Regret, 23 Yale J.L. & Feminism 255 (2011). Jurisdictions regulate consent and revocation in various ways:

a. Time period. One approach makes determinative the timing of consent or revocation. For example, Illinois law provides that consent may be signed no sooner than 72 hours after the child's birth and that actions to revoke consent, when permitted, must commence within 12 months. 750 Ill. Comp. Stat. Ann. 50/9; id. 50/11. In some jurisdictions, consent is effective immediately. See, e.g., McCann v. Doe, 660 S.E.2d 500, 506 (S.C. 2008). Another approach allows withdrawal of consent anytime before the final decree of termination of parental rights or adoption. E.g., 25 U.S.C. §1913(c) (Indian Child Welfare Act). Should prebirth consents be permitted? See In re Adoption of N.J.G., 891 N.E.2d 60 (Ind. Ct. App. 2008). How much time for revocation ought to be allowed?

b. Fraud, duress, or immaturity. Many states invalidate consent procured by fraud or coercion, although courts read such terms narrowly in adoption cases. See, e.g., In re S.K.L. H., 204 P.3d 320, 327 (Alaska 2009) (confusion, mistake, and change of heart do not suffice). What procedures are required for birth parents with mental disabilities? See In re Welfare of H.Q., 330 P.3d 195 (Wash. Ct. App. 2014). Can minors validly consent to adoption? See Ohio Rev. Code Ann. §3107.084(a) (making consent not voidable by reason of minor's age). Some jurisdictions address this problem by requiring, in addition, the consent of the minor birth parent's parents. See, e.g., Minn. Stat. Ann. §259.24 subdiv. 2. Can a minor birth parent who subsequently seeks to revoke consent be bound by her own parents' consent? Should the law require that minor birth parents have the advice of counsel? See In re Adoption of A.L.O., 132 P.3d 543 (Mont. 2006). For comparisons of the legal treatment of minors' decisionmaking in the adoption and abortion contexts, see Maya Manian, Minors, Parents, and Minor Parents, 80 Mo. L. Rev. (forthcoming 2016); Malinda L. Seymore, Sixteen and Pregnant: Minors' Consent in Abortion and Adoption, 25 Yale J.L. & Feminism 99 (2013).

5. Consent substitutes. Can a state constitutionally grant an adoption *without* valid parental consent? Involuntary TPR comporting with all procedural and substantive requirements dispenses with the need for parental consent, as shown by

---

[37]. Rickie Solinger, Beggars and Choosers: How the Politics of Choice Shapes Adoption, Abortion, and Welfare in the United States 67 (2001). See id. at 69-70.

[38]. Placek, supra note [7], at 7 (reporting 10.3 adoptions per 1,000 nonmarital births).

Santosky, supra. Given that abandonment suffices, should a parent's incarceration constitute abandonment or otherwise be considered determinative? Compare In re Adoption of C.M., 414 S.W.3d 622 (Mo. Ct. App. 2013), with In re K.J.B., 339 P.3d 824 (Mont. 2014). Can a state replace consent or the usual grounds for TPR with a showing that adoption serves the child's best interests? See, e.g., Mass. Gen. Laws Ann. ch. 210, §3(a)(ii) (so permitting); In re Adoption of Ta'Niya C., 8 A.3d 745 (Md. 2010). What considerations should (or must) a best-interests analysis include? See In re J.C.F., 73 A.3d 1007 (D.C. 2013); Copeland v. Todd, 715 S.E.2d 11 (Va. 2011). Will a statutory time period in foster care meet the constitutional test? Compare In re H.G., 757 N.E.2d 864 (Ill. 2001), with Doe v. Roe, 578 S.E.2d 733 (S.C. Ct. App. 2003).

6. Safe haven laws. In response to publicized cases of infanticide and abandonment, states enacted laws promising immunity and anonymity to mothers who leave babies at designated sites ("safe havens"), thus making these babies available for adoption. See Carol Sanger, Infant Safe Haven Laws: Legislating in the Culture of Life, 106 Colum. L. Rev. 753 (2006). Nebraska's statute did not specify an age range, prompting parents from other states to leave children, including teenagers, with severe mental health problems at Nebraska safe havens until the legislature modified the law to cover only infants. See Laury Oaks, Giving Up Baby: Safe Haven Laws, Motherhood, and Reproductive Justice 150-161 (2015).

NOTE: ADOPTION AND UNMARRIED BIRTH FATHERS

Traditionally, most states made only the consent of the mother necessary before the adoption of a nonmarital child. The Supreme Court's recognition of the parental rights of some unmarried birth fathers in 1972 in Stanley v. Illinois (Chapter V) prompted reconsideration of this practice, in an effort to protect adoptive placements from subsequent constitutional challenge by fathers excluded from the process. Yet the Court's emphasis on the ongoing relationship between Peter Stanley and his children and the suggestion that biology alone does not trigger protected parental status left unclear the application of the principle to newborns who had yet to spend time with their birth fathers, especially when the birth mothers purposely sought to prevent the fathers from becoming involved with (or even knowing about) the children. The term "thwarted father" emerged to describe such cases. In Lehr v. Robertson, 463 U.S. 248 (1983), the Court rejected an unmarried father's constitutional challenge to a stepparent adoption because he had failed to enter his name in a paternity registry, despite some evidence that he was a thwarted father. See id. at 268-269 (White, J., dissenting). Whether a similar result would follow when the birth mother seeks to surrender her own rights to the child remained unclear. That was the scenario in Adoptive Couple v. Baby Girl, supra, although the father agreed to relinquish his rights (even if unaware of the mother's adoption plan) and the case centered on the application of the ICWA.

The Supreme Court precedents invite different readings. According to Dean David Meyer, under the "child-centered" view, only an actual parent-child relationship matters, not the efforts of a father whom the mother successfully thwarts. Under a second reading, the Court is concerned not with the existence of the relationship, but also with "the strength of the father's moral claim [that is,] whether the claimant has acted in a way deserving of protection."[39] The second view raises several additional questions: How does a father show that he is deserving? Does an *offer* to provide support for the mother suffice? Can the father's prebirth conduct be determinative? Suppose that the father does not know about the conception or birth. See, e.g., In re Adoption of Anderson, 624 S.E.2d 626 (N.C. 2006); In re Marquette S., 734 N.W.2d 81 (Wis. 2007). If there are several possible fathers, must they all take affirmative steps to preserve their rights? Does criminal conduct prevent a finding that a father is "deserving"? For example, suppose that the child is conceived as the result of a sexual assault. Compare Adoption of Kelsey S., 823 P.2d 1216, 1237 n.14 (Cal. 1992), with LeClair v. Reed, 939 A.2d 466 (Vt. 2007). Suppose that the mother purposely deceived the father to prevent his knowledge (say, by falsely claiming a miscarriage or falsely promising she would not place the child for adoption). Compare In re Adoption of Baby Girl P., 242 P.3d 1168 (Kan. 2010), with In re Adoption of B.Y., 356 P.3d 1215 (Utah 2015). More generally, the underlying question posed by these cases concerns the appropriate balance of power between unmarried birth mothers and fathers, especially when they have different plans for the child's future. See Michael J. Higdon, Marginalized Fathers and Demonized Mothers: A Feminist Look at the Reproductive Freedom of Unmarried Men, 66 Ala. L. Rev. 507 (2015).

In the wake of such questions, states have developed several approaches for addressing the rights of unmarried birth fathers in the adoption process. Consider the following variations:

a. Expanded definitions. In the wake of high-profile challenges to adoptive placements by thwarted fathers, several states expanded the grounds for terminating parental rights, broadening definitions of "abandonment" and "unfitness." Most of these laws, however, have not been interpreted to allow "no-fault" terminations.[40]

b. Registries. Several states use "putative father registries," which eliminate the need for adoption notification or consent for a man who failed to take the initiative by registering. The Supreme Court approved reliance on a registry system in *Lehr*, supra. A model appears in the new UPA. According to the drafters, the UPA's approach facilitates and expedites infant adoptions, in which "time is of the essence," while requiring notification to fathers of older children and exempting fathers of infants who initiate timely proceedings to establish paternity. See UPA (cmt. on Art. 4); see also UPA §402 (requiring registration no later than 30 days after birth or commencement of paternity proceedings before termination of parental rights). These laws leave several issues unaddressed: Must the risk-averse man register even without knowledge of a pregnancy because the sexual relationship itself puts him on notice? See In re S.D.W., 758 S.E.2d 374 (N.C. 2014). Where must he register if he is not certain of the woman's location? See In re Baby Boy B., 394 S.W.3d 837 (Ark. 2012); Nevares v. M.L.S., 345 P.3d 719 (Utah 2015). What should be the consequences of substantial, but less than complete, compliance? See In re Adoption of J.S., 2014 WL 5573353 (Utah 2014) (finding no constitutional violation in proceeding over the objections of birth father who registered,

---

[39]. David D. Meyer, Family Ties: Solving the Constitutional Dilemma of the Faultless Father, 41 Ariz. L. Rev. 753, 764 (1999).

[40]. See id. at 770-792.

but failed to file the required affidavit), *cert. denied*, 2015 WL 1133360 (U.S. 2015). Do adoption agencies have a duty to check such registries? See Kramer v. Catholic Charities of Diocese of Fort Wayne-South Bend Inc., 32 N.E.3d 227 (Ind. 2015).

c. Publication. Another approach entails notifying unidentified fathers by posting or publication. Often, such publications exclude the mother's name to protect her privacy, thus compromising their ability to convey information to a putative father. See Alison S. Pally, Father by Newspaper Ad: The Impact of In re the Adoption of a Minor Child on the Definition of Fatherhood, 13 Colum. J. Gender & L. 169 (2004) (critiquing a former Florida statute compelling disclosure of the mother's name and all places where conception might have occurred).

d. Demonstrating full commitment. Some states have developed rules that require notice of adoption to unwed fathers who promptly come forward and demonstrate a full commitment to exercising parental responsibilities, even if prevented by the mother from establishing a relationship. In California, these men are called "*Kelsey S.* fathers," named after the case in which the state supreme court developed the doctrine. See *Kelsey S.*, supra; V.S. v. M.L., 166 Cal. Rptr.3d 376 (Ct. App. 2014). (The first Problem below seeks to apply this doctrine.)

Problems

1. Mark (then 20) asks Stephanie (then 15) to marry after a short acquaintance. She declines. A few months later they learn that Stephanie is pregnant. They decide on adoption. Stephanie then leaves Arizona to visit California. After meeting John and Margaret there, she chooses them to adopt the baby.

On her return to Arizona, Stephanie's relationship with Mark deteriorates. Stephanie excludes him from birthing classes. Following two violent outbursts, Mark attempts suicide and enters drug rehabilitation therapy. He then informs Stephanie he no longer favors adoption.

Stephanie returns to California, gives birth, places the child with John and Margaret, and consents to their adoption. Mark, when he learns of the birth a week later, immediately consults an attorney, sends out birth announcements, and purchases baby supplies. Thereafter, he consistently expresses his desire to take full parental responsibilities.

John and Margaret seek to terminate Mark's parental rights in California, citing Adoption of Kelsey S., 823 P.2d 1216 (Cal. 1992). They claim that *Kelsey S.* gives Mark no veto over the adoption because he failed to demonstrate full commitment to parental responsibilities throughout the pregnancy. Mark also invokes *Kelsey S.*, counterarguing that he attempted to maintain a relationship with Stephanie during the pregnancy and that, since birth, he has done everything possible to assume full parental responsibility. He also claims that John and Margaret's interpretation of *Kelsey S.* discriminates by allowing mothers to decide after birth to withhold consent for adoption, while requiring fathers to decide early in the pregnancy.

What result and why? What policy issues does each reading of *Kelsey S.* raise? See Adoption of Michael H., 898 P.2d 891 (Cal. 1995); Carol A. Gorenberg, Fathers' Rights vs. Children's Best Interests: Establishing a Predictable Standard for California Adoption Disputes, 31 Fam. L.Q. 169 (1997).

2. T.W. gives birth to twin daughters in Missouri. While her premature twins are hospitalized, T.W. brings them breast milk. Because T.W. is rearing three other children, she explores the possibility of placing the twins for adoption. Seeking an open adoption (which Missouri does not permit), she chooses a California couple whom she locates with help from an adoption professional and the Internet. Later, within the permissible time period for revocation, she reclaims the twins because she concludes that the couple would not respect her preference for continuing contact. Next, she chooses a British couple, and an Arkansas court issues the adoption decrees. After British social service workers find this couple unfit and the Arkansas adoption is set aside for lack of jurisdiction, the twins are placed in foster care in Missouri. T.W., who by then changes her mind about adoption, seeks the twins' return to her custody.

The Missouri family court terminates T.W.'s parental rights on the ground that she abandoned the twins and emotionally abused them by relinquishing them twice for adoption. T.W. appeals, contending that she neither abandoned nor abused the twins and asserting that no other permissible basis for termination exists. What result and why? See In re K.A.W., 133 S.W.3d 1 (Mo. 2004). Cf. In re Adoption of D.N.T., 843 So. 2d 690, 706-707 (Miss. 2003). Of what relevance is T.W.'s use of the Internet to find a placement? See Michelle M. Hughes, Internet Promises, Scares, and Surprises: New Realities of Adoption, 41 Cap. U. L. Rev. 279 (2013). If the foster parents now wish to adopt the children, *should* the court resolve the dispute by deciding whether adoption or their return to T.W. will serve their best interests? See Moore v. Asente, 110 S.W.3d 336 (Ky. 2003). *Can* the court decide on the basis of the twins' best interests? Cf. In re R.C., 745 N.E.2d 1233 (Ill. 2001).

c. Adoption Disruption and Dissolution

IN RE ADOPTION OF M.S.

103 Cal. Rptr. 3d 715 (Ct. App. 2010)

SIMS, J.

This is a tragic case in which there can be no good ending for anyone. Appellants Eleanor P. and Martin S. appeal from an order denying their petition to set aside their Ukrainian adoption of a Ukrainian girl, M.S. The petition was opposed by the State Department of Social Services (the Department or DSS). Appellants contend the trial court erred in construing Family Code section 9100,[1]

---

1. Undesignated statutory references are to the Family Code. Section 9100 provides:

(a) If a child adopted pursuant to the law of this state shows evidence of a developmental disability or mental illness as a result of conditions existing before the adoption to an extent that the child cannot be relinquished to an adoption agency on the grounds that the child is considered unadoptable, and of which conditions the adoptive parents or parent had no knowledge or notice before the entry of the order of adoption, a petition setting forth those facts may be filed by the adoptive parents or parent with the court that granted the adoption petition. If these facts are proved to the satisfaction of the court, it may make an order setting aside the order of adoption.

(b) The petition shall be filed within five years after the entry of the order of adoption.

(c) The court clerk shall immediately notify the department at Sacramento of the petition. Within 60 days after the notice, the department shall file a full report with the court and shall appear before the court for the purpose of representing the adopted child.

which authorizes the court to vacate adoptions, as inapplicable to an "intercountry adoption" completed in Ukraine.[2]

In early 2003, appellants began the process to adopt a foreign-born child. Appellants engaged a California lawyer and a private California adoption agency, Heartsent Adoptions, Inc. (Heartsent), which was licensed by the Department to provide noncustodial intercountry adoption services. [Appellants traveled to Ukraine, where they adopted three-year-old M.S. pursuant to a Ukrainian court decree that stated in part:] "It was found out from the case documents that the child's [biological] mother is mentally sick. She left the child at the hospital and never visited her. The place of father's residence was not identified. Since February 2002 the child has been made the ward of the government. The medical history of the girl says that she is almost healthy though psychologically delayed." A hospital record says the mother has epilepsy. [Appellants claimed they were not aware of this information.]

Appellants brought M.S. to live in their Davis home. They did not "readopt" M.S. in California, as authorized by section 8919.[4]

In California, various evaluations were performed due to M.S.'s low level of functioning. Health care professionals diagnosed her with spastic cerebral palsy, reactive attachment disorder, oppositional defiance disorder, moderate mental retardation, global developmental delay, ataxia, fetal alcohol syndrome or effect, microcephaly, and posttraumatic stress disorder. Appellants assert M.S. cannot live in a normal home environment, is unadoptable, and has been living in intensive foster care placement in Arizona since 2005. . . .

Appellants cite no legal authority for undoing the Ukraine adoption except section 9100 [which] authorizes the superior court to vacate an adoption of a child "adopted pursuant to the law of this state." . . . However, the language of section 9100 itself, plus the language of a companion statute—section 9101—clearly show that section 9100 is limited to undoing adoptions that were granted by California state courts. [T]he California Legislature surely did not intend to legislate court filings in a Ukrainian court. We therefore infer [that] "the court that granted the adoption petition" in section 9100 must be a California state court.

2. An "intercountry adoption" is "the adoption of a foreign-born child for whom federal law makes a special immigration visa available. Intercountry adoption includes completion of the adoption in the child's native country or completion of the adoption in this state." (§8527.)

4. Section 8919 provides:

> (a) Each state resident who adopts a child through an intercountry adoption that is finalized in a foreign country shall readopt the child in this state if it is required by the Department of Homeland Security. Except as provided in subdivision (c), the readoption shall include, but is not limited to, at least one postplacement in-home visit, the filing of the adoption petition, the intercountry adoption court report, accounting reports, the home study report, and the final adoption order. . . .
>
> (b) Each state resident who adopts a child through an intercountry adoption that is finalized in a foreign country may readopt the child in this state. Except as provided in subdivision (c), the readoption shall meet the standards described in subdivision (a).
>
> (c)(1) A state resident who adopts a child through an intercountry adoption that is finalized in a foreign country with adoption standards that meet or exceed those of this state, as certified by the State Department of Social Services, may readopt the child in this state according to this subdivision. The readoption shall include one postplacement in-home visit and the final adoption order. . . .

. . . In the event an adoption is vacated under section 9100, section 9101 places responsibility for the support of the now unadopted child on "[t]he county in which the proceeding for adoption was had." In this case, there is no such county in California, and the California Legislature obviously has no power to order a Ukrainian county (if such even exists) to support the child. . . .

Appellants offer two main arguments against our conclusion [that they cannot vacate the adoption here].

First, they say that where section 9100 provides that a petition "may be filed . . . with the court that granted the adoption petition," the word "may" is permissive, not mandatory. . . . In this sentence, the word "may" is used in the permissive sense of giving a parent or parents discretion whether to file a petition under section 9100. This is in stark contrast to section 8919, which *requires* a readoption of a child adopted in a foreign country "if it is required by the Department of Homeland Security." . . .

[O]nce the decision is made to file a petition, the petition must be filed "with the court that granted the adoption petition." This is the only construction that makes sense. No other court is designated as the proper place for the filing of a petition. If the petition could be filed in *any* court, then reference to "the court that granted the adoption petition" would be unnecessary. Moreover, since the petition seeks to unadopt a child, it is only reasonable to require the petition to be filed in the court that has the records of the original adoption. Thus, if a petition under section 9100 is filed, it *must* be filed "with the court that granted the adoption petition." [Here, that forum is in Ukraine.]

[The California court also rejects Appellants' second argument, urging a liberal construction of section 9100.] [W]e conclude that section 9100 applies only to adoptions granted by a California state court. . . .

Sarah Kershaw, In Some Adoptions, Love Doesn't Conquer All

N.Y. Times, Apr. 18, 2010, at ST1

At times, Kelly Lytle Baehr wondered how they would all get through it. Two years ago, she and her husband adopted three boys from Ukraine—two of them 8, the other 16—and brought them back to their home in Omaha. She knew assimilation into a family life would not be easy; all had come from troubled backgrounds, including one who had spent the first five years of his life in a prison orphanage back in Ukraine, and had a mother who drank while she was pregnant.

She was often tested by the strains of raising these three new sons. The youngest of them, Ian (born Igor) had rummaged in garbage dumps in Ukraine for toys, with [hubcaps] and discarded car parts his only possessions. At the Baehrs's home in Nebraska, he soon became a wild, uncontrollable kleptomaniac, she said. The other 8-year-old, Erik, struggled to attach to her—kicking, screaming, biting and yelling, "I hate you." Only the oldest son, Viktor, seemed to welcome his new life quickly, blending easily into the family and eventually making the honor roll at his high school.

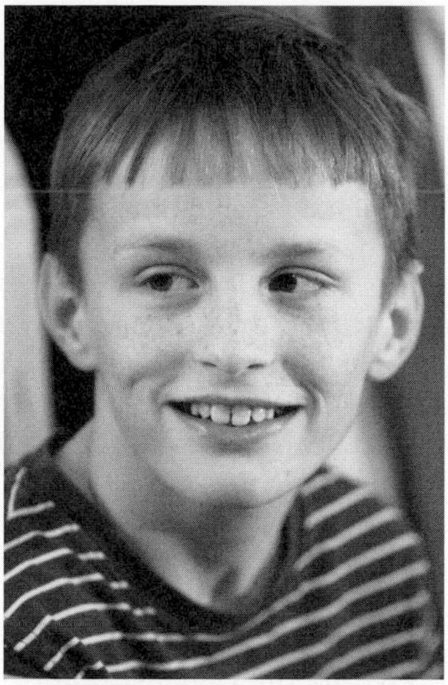

Artyom Savelyev (formerly Justin Hansen) returned alone to his native Russia, sent back by his American adoptive mother.

When Ms. Lytle Baehr, who is going through a divorce and has custody of her children, heard the news break two weeks ago about Torry Ann Hansen shipping her 7-year-old adopted son [Justin] back to Russia on a plane, unaccompanied, with just a note to the authorities, she felt something approaching sympathy. "When it boils down to it, I'm really similar to the woman in Tennessee," Ms. Lytle Baehr said in a telephone interview this week. "We've all been there." . . .

"Most of these parents are grossly, grossly ill-prepared," said Ronald S. Federici, a developmental neuropsychologist. "Agencies saying they do all this training and support—that's a bunch of junk. Some do, most don't. A lot of families are uneducated at huge levels about the psychological trauma of being deprived and neglected, of under-socialized children who have had profound developmental failures."

Russia is the third largest source of adoptions to the United States, after China and Ethiopia, with about 1,600 adoptions in 2009, according to State Department figures. About 3,500 Russian children and 3,000 American families were in some stage of the adoption process when the country reportedly halted adoptions. Russia has been a popular choice because the process can be much faster than in countries like China, and because there are often more boys available. . . .

The majority of both international and domestic adoptions turn out well, but the Hansen case has shined a spotlight on those that are problematic and the need for more postadoption services for struggling families, adoption experts say. Some agencies, including the one Ms. Hansen used, offer extensive training and preparation and continuing support services, training parents on issues like fetal alcohol syndrome and the psychological and neurological effects of institutionalization on children. Studies show, for example, that for every month in an orphanage a child's I.Q. drops one point. . . .

[Ellen McDaniels] took her daughter, whom she adopted from Russia in 2001 at the age of 8, to therapists for years. The child spent her first five years in an orphanage and was later adopted by two families who ended the adoptions before Ms. McDaniels, who lives in western Massachusetts, and her husband adopted her. Ms. McDaniels, 52, said she later discovered [that] the child had a history of being sexually abused and was sent to the orphanage when she was 18 months old, after her mother, an alcoholic, died of tuberculosis. A psychiatrist diagnosed severe reactive attachment disorder and posttraumatic stress disorder, and an inability to understand or have remorse for her actions. . . .

[T]wo months ago, after what Ms. McDaniels described as nine years of frightening, exhausting and heartbreaking efforts to cope with her daughter's behavioral problems—including, she said, her sexually abusing and threatening other children, threatening to burn down the house, hiding knives in her trundle bed, refusing to take medication and running away—she terminated her parental rights. (When parents end an adoption, legally terminating their parental rights, it is known as a disruption. Parents turn their child over to the custody of the state, through a children's agency, or, more likely, contact their adoption agency for guidance on how to end the adoption. The adoption agency can then try to find the child another home.) . . .

The decision to end the adoption, even after so many awful years, was heartbreaking, Ms. McDaniels said, and she was wracked with shame and guilt.

"I felt that I was a failure and that I condemned her to a life of hopelessness," she said. "I knew I couldn't help her, but I knew I didn't want to throw her away. But sometimes as a parent you feel like you have a lot more power than you do. You say to yourself, 'Can I make a difference in this child's life?' And if the answer is no, you need to walk away."

"I don't agree with what Torry Hansen did," she said. "But I almost think there's a certain little part of me that says, 'You just saved yourselves nine years of torment.' Knowing what I know now, I would have given up sooner because a lot of people got hurt." . . .

[S]ome advocates for adoptive families—who note that the majority of domestic and international adoptions are successful—say parents should feel less ashamed of considering the option of disruption. It could have been better for Ms. Hansen's son, Justin, who might have found another family, they said, although the Associated Press reported that three Russian families had come forward offering to adopt Justin. . . .

Typically parents must sign a waiver with their adoption agencies, who say they cannot be held liable for problems with a child that were not previously disclosed to the agency, and advocates say that reputable agencies make clear the risks associated with international adoption, because often children are abandoned at birth or orphanages do not keep complete medical records.

Earlier this week, all seemed fine at the Baehr home, with Ms. Lytle Baehr posting this status update on her Facebook page: "Enjoyed dinner with the boys at a fairly questionable Mexican restaurant. Followed it up with some rocking Black Eyed Peas at home and a family dance party! Whoo hoo!"

But the past is never far away. During a telephone interview, Ian was talking about how he liked living in the United States because it was "more peaceful." . . . When he turned 9 and received his birthday presents, he told his adoptive mother, "I wish I could take what I have now and give it to myself when I was little."

NOTE: INTERCOUNTRY ADOPTION

Only 7,092 children born abroad joined U.S. families in 2013, continuing a recent decline.[41] Authorities attribute interest in intercountry adoption to the

[41]. Intercountry Adoption Statistics, Bureau of Consular Affairs, U.S. Dept. of State, http://travel.state.gov/content/adoptionsabroad/en/about-us/statistics.html. Between 2009 and 2012, the top three countries placing children for adoption in the United States were China, Ethiopia, and Russia. Id. The number of adoptions of children born outside the United States began to decline in 2004, after years on the rise. Rose M. Kreider, Internationally Adopted Children in the U.S.: 2008, in Adoption Factbook V, supra note [7], at 81.

domestic shortage of "highly desirable" adoptees, agency restrictions on adopters, and a belief that intercountry adoptions are less vulnerable to postplacement challenges because of defective birth-parent consent.[42] Poverty and natural disasters abroad, as well as religious imperatives, also have moved some prospective adopters.[43]

Several bodies of law might ordinarily apply to international adoptions: federal immigration laws, state adoption standards, and the foreign country's relinquishment requirements. As *M.S.* indicates, two adoptions might be routinely required—the first in the country of origin, to enable the child to travel to the United States, and the second in the adoptive parents' state, given the absence of full faith and credit for decrees from foreign countries.

Significant developments have occurred in recent years. For example, federal immigration law, which limits entry to foreign adoptees who are "orphans," expanded the definition of the term to include not only children whose parents both have died, but also those whose parents both have disappeared, have abandoned or deserted them, or have become separated or lost from them, as well as children for whom the sole surviving parent cannot provide care and has irrevocably released the child for adoption and emigration. 8 U.S.C. §1101(b)(1)(F). In addition, some jurisdictions stopped requiring a full state proceeding if a foreign adoption has been completed. See, e.g., In re Adoption of Doe, 923 N.E.2d 1129 (N.Y. 2010) (according comity to Cambodian adoption). Moreover, federal legislation now provides for automatic U.S. citizenship for many children adopted abroad by U.S. citizens. 8 U.S.C. §1431(b). This Child Citizenship Act thus treats children adopted abroad by U.S. citizens the same as those born abroad to U.S. citizens. See also id. §1101(b)(1)(F) (immediate relative classification for such children); In re C.G.H., 75 A.3d 166 (D.C. 2013) (interpreting federal statute).

The Hague Convention on Protection of Children and Cooperation in Respect of Intercountry Adoption has ushered in even more notable reforms.[44] This Convention, which applies only when both countries involved are Convention parties, is designed to regularize international adoptions by requiring a finding that the child is adoptable and a determination that the adoption would serve the child's best interests. The Convention also establishes supervisory central authorities to impose minimum norms and procedures and mandates recognition of such adoptions in other signatory countries. The Convention has met with both praise and criticism. Observers predict that this regime will facilitate U.S. citizens' intercountry adoptions by removing procedural hurdles, such as the need for readoption in the parents' domicile, while also creating new barriers and increasing expenses.[45] Further, concern persists that the U.S. regulations issued pursuant

[42]. See, e.g., In re B.G.C., 496 N.W.2d 239 (Iowa 1992); Deleith Duke Gossett, If Charity Begins at Home, Why Do We Go Searching Abroad? Why the Federal Adoption Tax Credit Should Not Subsidize International Adoptions, 17 Lewis & Clark L. Rev. 839 (2013).

[43]. See, e.g., Megan Lindsey, Examining Intercountry Adoption After the Earthquake in Haiti, in Adoption Factbook V, supra note [7], at 345; David M. Smolin, The Corrupting Influence of the United States on a Vulnerable Intercountry Adoption System: A Guide for Stakeholders, Hague and Non-Hague Nations, NGOs, and Concerned Parties, 15 J.L. & Fam. Stud. 81 (2013).

[44]. In 2000, the United States enacted implementing legislation for this Convention, 42 U.S.C. §§14901-14954, but ratification here did not occur until 2007, with the Convention entering into force in this country on April 1, 2008. See Anne Laquer Estin, Families Across Borders: The Hague Children's Conventions and the Case for International Family Law in the United States, 62 Fla. L. Rev. 47, 80-84 (2010).

[45]. See Estin, supra note [44], at 85-90.

to the Convention fail to address payments to birth parents and might increase child trafficking.[46]

Intercountry adoption laws can reflect other political controversies. For example, Russia has now banned adoptions of Russian children by American citizens, a move that observers attribute to retaliation for U.S. laws protecting human rights.[47]

Against this background, intercountry adoption remains controversial. Supporters contend that such adoptions represent humanitarian and empathetic responses to the plight of children living in institutions or on the streets in other countries—indeed, a compelling matter of international human rights.[48] Some critics, however, point out the underlying colonialism reflected by the practice, while others emphasize the similarity to baby selling, given the predominance of market behavior.[49] Finally, LGBT adopters face multiple obstacles, including prohibitions in several of the top sending countries.[50]

Notes and Questions

1. Adoption failure. Adoption failure occurs either when the child is removed before the adoption is final (disruption) or when a final adoption is abrogated or annulled (dissolution). Dissolutions are difficult to track, but studies place the current rate of disruption at between 10 and 25 percent.[51] The adoption failure rate increased with the growing number of placements of special needs children (including older children) and children from foster care.

Adoption failure attracted public attention through news stories of parents who, frustrated by the difficulties experienced by some adopted children, have "rehomed" them—sending them to live with others without state scrutiny. In one case, an Arkansas legislator, Justin Harris, sent his adopted daughters to live with a man who sexually abused one of them. Harris contends that the state failed to provide the services necessary to support the family's care of troubled

---

[46]. See Trish Maskew, The Failure of Promise: The U.S. Regulations on Intercountry Adoption Under the Hague Convention, 60 Admin. L. Rev. 487 (2008).

[47]. See Marie A. Failinger, Moving Toward Human Rights Principles for Intercountry Adoption, 39 N.C. J. Int'l L. & Com. Reg. 523, 523-524 (2014).

[48]. Id. See, e.g., Elizabeth Bartholet, International Adoption: A Way Forward, 55 N.Y.L. Sch. L. Rev. 687 (2010/2011); James G. Dwyer, Inter-Country Adoption and the Special Rights Fallacy, 35 U. Pa. J. Int'l L. 189 (2013).

[49]. Regarding colonialism, see generally Shani King, Challenging MonoHumanism: An Argument for Changing the Way We Think About Intercountry Adoption, 30 Mich. J. Int'l L. 413 (2009); Twila L. Perry, Transracial and International Adoption: Mothers, Hierarchy, Race, and Feminist Legal Theory, 10 Yale J.L. & Feminism 101, 130-137 (1998). Regarding trafficking, see generally Patricia Meier, Note, Small Commodities: How Child Traffickers Exploit Children and Families in Intercountry Adoption and What the United States Must Do to Stop Them, 12 J. Gender Race & Just. 185 (2008); David M. Smolin, Child Laundering as Exploitation: Applying Anti-Trafficking Norms to Intercountry Adoption Under the Coming Hague Regime, 32 Vt. L. Rev. 1 (2007).

[50]. Jennifer B. Mertus, Barriers, Hurdles, and Discrimination: The Current Status of LGBT Intercountry Adoption and Why Changes Must Be Made to Effectuate the Best Interests of the Child, 39 Cap. U. L. Rev. 271 (2011).

[51]. Paula St. John, Happy and Whole: Preventing Disruption by Building Healthy Families, in Adoption Factbook V, supra note [7], at 157 n.2. See generally Lita Linzer Schwartz, When Adoptions Go Wrong: Psychological and Legal Issues of Adoption Disruption (2006); Jennifer F. Coakley & Jill D. Berrick, Research Review, In a Rush to Permanency: Preventing Adoption Disruption, 13 Child & Fam. Soc. Work 101, 102, 107 (2007).

children. See Abby Phillip, The Story of an Arkansas Politician Who Gave Away His Adopted Child, and the Tragedy That Followed, Wash. Post, Mar. 13, 2015, 2015 WLNR 7569390. On rehoming children adopted from abroad, see Destinee Roman, Comment, Please Confirm Your Online Order: One Child Adopted from Overseas at No Cost, 52 Hous. L. Rev. 1007 (2015).

2. Standards. What criteria must be met to dissolve an adoption? Should adoptive parents who seek to end their relationship to a child be limited to the same avenues available to biological parents—voluntary or involuntary termination of parental rights, with consideration of best interests? See Margaret M. Mahoney, Permanence and Parenthood: The Case for Abolishing the Adoption Annulment Doctrine, 42 Ind. L. Rev. 639 (2009). Should cases be decided by courts based on equitable discretion or legislative criteria? Consider the criteria in the California statute (footnote 1 in *M.S.*). See also Ky. Rev. Stat. Ann. §199.540(1) (different "ethnological ancestry"). Who may petition? What time limits, if any, should control? See, e.g., Mich. Comp. Laws Ann. §710.64(1) (21 days); Neb. Rev. Stat. §43-116 (2008). Does dissolution infringe the adoptee's constitutional rights? See In re Adoption of Kay C., 278 Cal. Rptr. 907 (Ct. App. 1991) (no).

Did you find convincing the *M.S.* court's conclusion that it lacked jurisdiction? Why might the appellants have failed to readopt the child in California? Why did the court reject the liberal construction of the statute that they urged? Who benefits from the court's strict approach? What additional insights does the *New York Times* story offer? As a matter of policy, should courts be more or less willing to permit the voluntary severance of legal ties when parentage is based on adoption, rather than procreation? Why? For critical analysis condemning the absence of a state-supervised procedure for dissolving adoption, in light of the "new reality" of adoption, see Andrea B. Carroll, Breaking Forever Families, 76 Ohio St. L.J. 259, 261 (2015).

3. Wrongful adoption. As an alternative to dissolving an adoption, some parents have successfully sued adoption agencies for fraud or the tort of "wrongful adoption," based on the defendant's intentional or negligent concealment of the child's medical condition. See, e.g., Jackson v. State, 956 P.2d 35 (Mont. 1998); Mallette v. Children's Friend & Serv., 661 A.2d 67 (R.I. 1995). What public policy issues do such negligence suits raise? Compare Richard P. v. Vista Del Mar Child Care Serv., 165 Cal. Rptr. 370, 374 (Ct. App. 1980), with M.H. v. Caritas Family Servs., 488 N.W.2d 282, 288 (Minn. 1992).

The case law raises a host of questions: Must plaintiffs prove that they would not have adopted but for the misrepresentation? See McKinney v. State, 950 P.2d 461 (Wash. 1998) (jury must find proximate cause). Can plaintiffs recover punitive damages? See Ross v. Louise Wise Servs., Inc., 868 N.E.2d 189 (N.Y. 2007) (no). Can they recover for emotional distress? Compare Price v. State, 57 P.3d 639 (Wash. 2002) (permitting recovery), with Rowey v. Children's Friend & Servs., 2003 WL 23196347 (R.I. Super. Ct. 2003) (only when supported by medical evidence). Can agencies obtain valid waivers of disclosure? See Ferenc v. World Child, Inc., 977 F. Supp. 56 (D.D.C. 1997), *aff'd*, 172 F.3d 919 (D.C. Cir. 1998) (yes). Does the adopted child have a claim? See Dresser v. Cradle of Hope Adoption Ctr., Inc., 358 F. Supp. 2d 620, 640-642 (E.D. Mich. 2005) (agency owes duty to child to provide medical information so adopters can obtain proper treatment). But see *Rowey*, supra.

4. Disclosure laws. Several modern statutes require full disclosure to prospective adoptive parents of the child's medical history, e.g., Ariz. Rev. Stat. Ann. §8-129(A); Cal. Fam. Code §8706. Despite requirements in the Hague Convention, supra, for the collection and preservation of an adoptee's medical and social history, U.S. implementation fails to address specifically certain important types of information, such as genetic conditions, a family history of mental illness, and sexual or child abuse.[52]

5. Reforms to minimize disruptions.

a. Adoption as a process. Experts emphasize that adoption is a process, not a single act. Successful adoptions, particularly of older children who have spent time in foster care, require education and ongoing work. For example, recent studies highlight specific challenges confronting transracial adoptees, such as coping with difference and discrimination and constructing a positive racial or ethnic identity; thus, advocates contend, race should be considered as one factor in the effort to select adopters who can best serve a child's needs and to provide the particular support required for the placement to succeed. See J. Savannah Lengsfelder, Who Is a "Suitable" Adoptive Parent?, 5 Harv. L. & Pol'y Rev. 433 (2011) (advocating broad approach to suitability, emphasizing preparation and education).[53] For additional recommendations, based on an empirical study in New York, see Dawn J. Post & Brian Zimmerman, The Revolving Doors of Family Court: Confronting Broken Adoptions, 40 Cap. U. L. Rev. 437 (2012).

b. More disclosure? Should preadoptive genetic testing for medical problems become a part of the placement process? Would such tests violate privacy rights? See Jessica Ann Schlee, Notes & Comments, Genetic Testing: Technology That Is Changing the Adoption Process, 18 N.Y.L. Sch. J. Hum. Rts. 133 (2001). What about general adoption information, including rates of disability and mental illness among adoptees? See Ellen Wertheimer, Of Apples and Trees: Adoption and Informed Consent, 25 Quinnipiac L. Rev. 601 (2007) (so advocating).

Do biological parents have a duty of full disclosure in relinquishing their children? To the extent that such laws impose disclosure duties on birth parents upon relinquishment, should these duties include updating the information in the event of subsequent familial health problems? See R. Scott Smith, Disclosure of Post-Adoption Family Medical Information: A Continuing Birth Parent Duty, 35 Fam. L.Q. 553 (2001).

---

[52]. D. Marianne Brower Blair, Admonitions or Accountability?: U.S. Implementation of the Hague Adoption Convention Requirements for the Collection and Disclosure of Medical and Social History of Transnationally Adopted Children, 40 Cap. U. L. Rev. 325 (2012).

[53]. Evan B. Donaldson Adoption Inst., Finding Families for African American Children: The Role of Race & Law in Adoption from Foster Care—Policy & Practice Perspective 5-6 (2008), http://66.227.70.18/advocacy/findingfamilies.pdf. Meanwhile, the foster care system includes a disproportionate number of African-American children (32 percent, although African-American children constitute 15 percent of the U.S. child population), and such children take longer to achieve permanency than other foster children. Id. at 11-12. See generally Jennifer Ludden, Helping Foster Kids Even After Adoption (National Public Radio broadcast, Aug. 28, 2012).

Problem

Barbara gives birth to a child and surrenders him to the Children's Home Society (CHS), a state-licensed private adoption agency, which places the baby in an adoptive family. As part of the relinquishment process, CHS provides counseling for Barbara. It also obtains detailed health and background information from her. Ten years later, Barbara marries and has two children, a daughter and a son. When this son dies in infancy, Barbara learns she carries a genetic defect that afflicts male offspring. Barbara contacts CHS to determine the health of her first son and learns from CHS that he, too, suffers from the genetic disease.

Barbara sues CHS for wrongful death, negligent and intentional infliction of emotional distress, and fraud. In essence, she claims that CHS had a duty to inform her of the genetic disease of the son whom she surrendered, so that she could make informed choices about future childbearing. What result? See Olson v. Children's Home Soc'y, 252 Cal. Rptr. 11 (Ct. App. 1988). But cf. Molloy v. Meier, 679 N.W.2d 711 (Minn. 2004).

2. Shared Rights and Responsibilities: The Challenge of "Community Parenting"[54]

Traditional doctrine makes parentage all-encompassing and exclusive. This section examines modern practices that challenge this conventional "all or nothing" view, such as open adoption, access to gamete donors, foster care, and guardianship. In these contexts, the lines between parents and nonparents become less distinct, with multiple parties sharing parental functions.

GROVES v. CLARK

982 P.2d 446 (Mont. 1999)

Justice William E. Hunt, Sr. delivered the Opinion of the Court. . . .

This is the second appeal filed in this case concerning postadoption visitation between Groves and L.C. A more detailed account of the facts of this case can be found in Groves v. Clark, 920 P.2d 981 [(Mont. 1996)]. To summarize, in January 1994, when L.C. was three years old, Groves signed a document terminating her parental rights to L.C., relinquishing custody of L.C. to Lutheran Social Services (LSS), and consenting to adoption. Groves and the Clarks signed a written visitation agreement which provided the following: Groves would have unrestricted visitation with L.C. so long as she gave the Clarks two days notice; Groves would have unrestricted telephone contact with L.C.; and Groves would have the right to take L.C. out of school in the event she had to "go to Butte for some emergency." This agreement was drafted by the LSS and neither party consulted an

[54]. This phrase comes from Laura T. Kessler, Community Parenting, 24 Wash. U. J.L. & Pol'y 47 (2007). Although Professor Kessler focuses on the advantages of recognizing more than two parents for a given child, "community parenting" also suggests other doctrines and practices that require sharing the usual bundle of parental rights and responsibilities.

attorney before signing it. In February 1994, the District Court entered an order terminating Groves' parental rights to L.C. and awarding custody of L.C. to LSS. In September 1994, the Clarks legally adopted L.C.

Groves and the Clarks abided by the terms of the visitation agreement until June 5, 1995, when Groves notified the Clarks that she wanted to take L.C. to Butte for the weekend and the Clarks refused. The Clarks told Groves that she was welcome to visit L.C. in their home, but could not take L.C. on extended out-of-town trips. [Groves then sought specific performance of the visitation agreement, and the Clarks objected, moving for summary judgment. The District Court denied Groves's petition for specific performance on the ground that the postadoption visitation agreement was void and unenforceable. Groves appealed to this Court, which reversed, holding:]

> Birth parents and prospective adoptive parents are free to contract for postadoption visitation and . . . trial courts must give effect to such contracts when continued visitation is in the best interest of the child.

We remanded the case to the District Court for a hearing on whether enforcement of the parties' visitation agreement would be in the best interest of L.C.

Based on the evidence produced at trial, the [District Court] found that a bond existed between Groves and L.C. and that it was highly likely L.C. would suffer from issues of abandonment, identity, and grieving unless appropriate visitation with Groves was granted. Ultimately, the court found that continued visitation between Groves and L.C. was in L.C.'s best interest. . . . Specifically, the court granted Groves unsupervised monthly weekend visitation with L.C. and required the parties to share equally in the transportation costs. Additionally, the court granted Groves telephone contact with L.C. at least once per week. The court recommended that the parties seek adoption counseling and attempt to agree upon future visitation modifications that may be appropriate as L.C. matures.

[On appeal,] the Clarks assert that the adoptive parents' wishes are paramount in deciding whether a postadoption visitation agreement should be enforced. The Clarks cite several cases from other jurisdictions purportedly holding that adoptive parents have the right to determine whether it is in the best interest of the adopted child to maintain contact with the birth mother. [Citations omitted.] The Clarks also cite cases from other jurisdictions purportedly holding that the mere fact that the adoptive parents oppose visitation provides a sufficient basis for finding that visitation is not in the best interest of the child. [Citations omitted.]

We reject the Clarks' assertions. . . . The law in Montana, which also happens to be the law of this case, is clear: whether a postadoption visitation agreement is enforceable shall be decided by the District Court pursuant to a "best interests" analysis. The adoptive parents' wishes is but one factor among many to be considered by the District Court.

Next, the Clarks argue that the court did not adequately consider and evaluate the evidence when applying the "best interests" standard. [The Clarks] testified that visitation adversely affected L.C. in that afterward she would evidence insecurity about her adoption status, would be moody and difficult to discipline. On the other hand, the court heard the testimony of the Petitioner's [Groves's] experts including Kathy Gerhke [an adoptive parenting instructor] and Debbie O'Brien [a family counselor] which explained this as a normal occurrence. Based on their testimony, this court finds that it is highly likely L.C. will suffer from issues of abandonment, identity, and grieving unless appropriate visitation is granted. L.C. lived with her mother for over three years. The evidence, including from a visitation facilitator, was that visitation was a happy experience for L.C. . . .

[T]he Clarks assert that visitation with Groves is not in L.C.'s best interests because the Clarks do not know the details of the visitation such as where L.C. will be, what L.C. will be doing, and with whom L.C. will be associating. The Clarks have expressed concern over L.C.'s sleeping arrangements at Groves's residence. The Clarks disapprove of L.C. snowmobiling and riding in a car without wearing a seatbelt. . . . These concerns were not presented to the District Court at trial. . . .

[W]e determine that the court's finding that visitation between Groves and L.C. was in the best interest of L.C. was not clearly erroneous. . . . We [also] agree with the District Court that modification of the parties' original visitation agreement was within its discretion in accordance with determining the best interests of L.C. . . . It would be incongruous for a court to hold that visitation is in the best interest of a child and then enforce a visitation agreement that was not in the best interest of the child. For these reasons, we determine that the District Court did not abuse its discretion in modifying the parties' postadoption visitation agreement. . . .

Colton Wooten, A Father's Day Plea to Sperm Donors

N.Y. Times, June 19, 2011, at WK9 (op ed)

WHEN I was 5, my mother revealed to me that I had been conceived through artificial insemination. . . . Because my understanding of conventional conception was so thin, my mom remained vague about the details of my conception—in all its complexity—until I got older.

When that time came, I learned how my mother, closing in on her 40s, found herself unmarried and childless. She had finished graduate school and established a career, but regretted not having a family. And so she decided to take the business of having a baby into her own capable hands [with the help of the University of North Carolina fertility clinic's sperm bank]. Artificial insemination seemed like a smart idea, perhaps the only idea. . . .

My mom's decision intrigued many people. Some saw it as a triumph of female self-sufficiency. But others, particularly her close friends and family, were shocked. "You can't have a baby without a man!" they would gasp.

It turns out, of course, you can, and pretty easily. The harder part, at least for that baby as he grows older, is the mystery of who that man was. Or is.

I didn't think much about that until 2006, when I was in eighth grade and my teacher assigned my class a genealogy project. We were supposed to research our family history and create a family tree to share with the class. In the past, whenever questioned about my father's absence by friends or teachers, I wove intricate alibis: he was a doctor on call; he was away on business in Russia; he had died, prematurely, of a heart attack. In my head, I'd always dismissed him as my "biological father," with that distant, medical phrase.

But the assignment made me think about him in a new way. I decided to call the U.N.C. fertility center, hoping at least to learn my father's name, his age or any minutiae of his existence that the clinic would be willing to divulge. But I was told that no files were saved for anonymous donors, so there was no information they could give me.

In the early days of in vitro fertilization, single women and sterile couples often overlooked a child's eventual desire to know where he came from. Even today, despite recent movies like "The Kids Are All Right," there is too little substantial debate on the subject. The emotional and developmental deficits that stem from an ignorance of one's origins are still largely ignored.

I understand why fertility centers chose to keep sperm donation anonymous. They were attempting to prevent extra chaos, like custody battles, intrusion upon happy families (on either party's side), mothers showing up on donors' doorsteps with homely, misbegotten children with runny noses and untied shoelaces to beg for child support. It's entirely reasonable, and yet the void that many children and young adults born from artificial insemination experience from simply not knowing transcends reason.

I don't resent my mom; she did the best thing she knew how to do at the time, and found a way to make a child under the circumstances. But babies born of the procedure in the future should have the right to know who their donors are, and even have some contact with them. Sperm donors need to realize that they are fathers. When I was doing college interviews, one of the interviewers told me that he didn't have any children, but that he had donated sperm while in college because he needed the money. He didn't realize that he probably is someone's father, regardless of whether he knows his child.

I'm one of those children, and I want to know who my father is. There are some programs like the Donor Sibling Registry that try to connect those conceived through sperm and egg donation with lost half-siblings and sometimes even parents. But I don't have much hope that I'll ever find him.

For my eighth grade project, I settled on fabricating the unknown side of my family tree, and not much has changed since then. I'm 18 now, today is Father's Day, and I still hardly know anything about my biological father, just a few vague details that my mother remembers from reading his profile so many years ago. I know that he was a medical student at U.N.C. the year I was born. I know that he had olive skin and brown hair. I know that his mother was Italian and his father Irish.

I call myself an only child, but I could very well be one of many siblings. I could even be predisposed to some potentially devastating disease. Because I do not know what my father looks like, I could never recognize him in a crowd of people. I am sometimes overwhelmed by the infinite possibilities, by the reality that my father could be anywhere: in the neighboring lane of traffic on a Friday during rush hour, behind me in line at the bank or the pharmacy, or even changing the oil in my car after many weeks of mechanical neglect.

I am sometimes at such a petrifying loss for words or emotions that make sense that I can only feel astonished by the fact that he could be anyone.

Notes and Questions

1. Background.

a. Secrecy in adoption. Since World War II, secrecy shrouded the adoption process in most states. The reasons included the stigma associated with nonmarital births, the fear that birth parents would intrude in adoptive families, and the belief that adoptive families should imitate biological families. To maintain this secrecy, statutes provide for the issuance of a new birth certificate when a child is adopted, changing the name of the adoptee to that of the adoptive parents. (The original birth certificate is then sealed.) Courts have rejected adult adoptees' constitutional challenges to sealed-record laws, concluding that the right to privacy does not include a fundamental "right to know" one's biological parents and that adoptees do not constitute a suspect class for equal protection purposes. The laws survive rational basis review as protection for the interests of all parties. See, e.g., In re Roger B., 418 N.E.2d 751 (Ill. 1981). But see, e.g., Jessica R. Caterina, Glorious Bastards: The Legal and Civil Birthright of Adoptees to Access Their Medical Records in Search of Genetic Identity, 61 Syracuse L. Rev. 145 (2010).

b. Law reform. Modern legislative reforms facilitate adult adoptees' access to such information through the creation of registries for willing parties and contact-veto protocols. E.g., Mich. Comp. Laws §710.68(7); N.Y. Pub. Health Law §4138-c. Voluntary connections over the Internet, without state assistance, have diminished the importance of such laws, however. See Mary Kate Kearney & Arrielle Millstein, Meeting the Challenges of Adoption in an Internet Age, 41 Cap. U. L. Rev. 237 (2013).

c. Open adoption. In contrast to law reform measures making information available to an adoptee upon reaching adulthood, open adoption focuses on young adoptees. The rise of open or cooperative adoption emerged from several developments: First, an increasing number of older children, with established bonds to their birth families, have become available for adoption. Second, because of the decreased availability of the most sought-after infants for adoption following the legalization of abortion, birth parents can demand enhanced conditions in placement, including open-adoption arrangements. Finally, experts claim that an open system avoids the damaging psychological effects of anonymity for adoptees, birth parents, and adopters. See Cynthia R. Mabry, The Psychological and Emotional Ties That Bind Biological and Adoptive Families: Whether Court-Ordered Postadoption Contact Is in an Adoptive Child's Best Interest, 42 Cap. U. L. Rev. 285 (2014). See also Malinda L. Seymore, Openness in International Adoption, 46 Colum. Hum. Rts. L. Rev. 163 (2015) (noting that interest in openness seen in domestic adoptions is just beginning in intercountry adoptions).

2. Enforcement. Several states allow voluntary open adoption but permit the adoptive parents to determine whether to abide by such agreements. *Groves* cites cases from Arizona, Colorado, Maryland, and Pennsylvania taking this position. Alternatively, some states authorize judicial approval of such agreements upon a finding of best interests and then enforcement of agreements so approved. E.g., Minn. Stat. Ann. §259.58; Birth Mother v. Adoptive Parents, 59 P.3d 1233, 1236 (Nev. 2002). Some states allow open adoption of children adopted by foster parents, but not children placed privately. Why? See Monty S. v. Jason W., 863 N.W.2d 484 (Neb. 2015). See generally Carol Sanger, Bargaining for Motherhood: Postadoption Visitation Agreements, 41 Hofstra L. Rev. 309 (2012).

3. Parental rights. Why does *Groves* go beyond voluntary arrangements, allowing courts to fashion arrangements that the parties have not chosen? Does *Groves* make adoptive parents "second-class parents"? Should adoptive parents have the same rights as other parents to determine the extent of their children's visitation, if any, with other persons? See Troxel v. Granville (Chapter VIII). In *Groves*, who should resolve the asserted disputes about snowmobiling and seatbelts? Does open adoption conflict with the very concept of adoption, as some older cases held? E.g., Hill v. Moorman, 525 So. 2d 681 (La. Ct. App. 1988). Even when all parties are committed to postadoption contact, the relationships often pose emotional challenges. E.g., Amy Seek, God and Jetfire: Confessions of a Birth Mother (2015). Nonetheless, empirical data show that openness produces greater satisfaction with the adoption process for birth parents and adoptive parents than traditional closed adoptions.[55]

4. Adoptees' interests. To what extent does *Groves* (correctly) frame the issue as one of the child's interests instead of parental rights? Some advocates of a child-centered analysis propose recognition of children's relationship rights in adoption and other contexts.[56] The insights animating the open-adoption movement suggest additional reforms, including a more gradual transition from one family to another so that placement would become a process rather than an event.[57] See also Assemb. B. 3298, 238th Leg. Sess. (N.Y. 2015) (proposing "bill of adoptee rights").

6. Grandparent visitation. Some states have special rules authorizing postadoption visitation by grandparents. E.g., Tex. Fam. Code §161.206(c). Do such laws rest on the interests of grandparents, children, or both? Why not rely on the general best-interests test for such cases? To what extent does *Troxel*, supra, make these laws constitutionally vulnerable? See In re Visitation of M. L. B., 983 N.E.2d 583 (Ind. 2013); In re Hunter H., 744 S.E.2d 228 (W.Va. 2013).

7. Sibling visitation. Are special rules warranted for postadoption visitation by biological siblings? Why? Do siblings have a fundamental right to family integrity requiring them to be placed together for adoption? See In re Meridian H., 798 N.W.2d 96 (Neb. 2011). What standard should courts use when adoptive parents oppose visitation with biological siblings? See In re D.C., 4 A.3d 1004 (N.J. 2010). See generally Rebecca L. Scharf, Separated at Adoption: Addressing the Challenges of Maintaining Sibling-of-Origin Bonds in Post-Adoption Families, 19 U.C. Davis J. Juv. L. & Poly 84 (2015).

---

[55]. David M. Martin et al., Toward a Greater Understanding of Openness: A Report from the Early Growth and Development Study, in Adoption Factbook V, supra note [7], at 471, 474.

[56]. James G. Dwyer, The Relationship Rights of Children (2006); Ayelet Blecher-Prigat, Rethinking Visitation: From a Parental to a Relationship Right, 16 Duke J. Gender L. & Pol'y 1 (2009).

[57]. Barbara L. Atwell, Nature and Nurture: Revisiting the Infant Adoption Process, 18 Wm. & Mary J. Women & L. 201 (2012).

8. Secrecy versus disclosure in assisted reproduction. The 1973 UPA (§5) explicitly provided for sealed records concerning donor insemination. Do the same considerations that have prompted access to original birth certificates and open adoption apply to collaborative reproduction? Traditionally, one advantage of ARTs over adoption for prospective parents has been the ability for the family to "pass" as one created without assistance. For example, no one needed to know that a husband was not the genetic father of the child to whom the wife gave birth with help from donor insemination. See, e.g., Harnicher v. University of Utah Med. Ctr., 962 P.2d 67 (Utah 1998) (unsuccessful suit to recover for emotional distress after clinic used wrong donor's sperm, resulting in triplets whose hair color revealed the absence of genetic connection to the husband). How should law balance such parental concerns with the "need to know" asserted by those like Colton Wooten in his op-ed piece?

Today, parents often openly discuss their children's origins, sperm banks facilitate donor-child meetings when the donor has agreed to such contact, and children can register on a website designed to introduce them to others conceived by the same donor.[58] Some foreign countries, including the United Kingdom, now make available both health and identifying information. Human Fertilisation and Embryology Act of 2008, ch. 22, §24 (U.K.) (§§31ZA-31ZE, amending the 1990 Act). Is it unconstitutional to require preservation of adoption records so that adoptees may have access to information about their origins without doing the same for those conceived by donor insemination? A Canadian provincial court so held. Pratten v. British Columbia (Attorney General), [2011] B.C.J. No. 931.

What law reforms would you recommend in the United States? To what extent should the law support the establishment of relationships among genetically connected individuals living in separate families? See Naomi Cahn, The New Kinship: Constructing Donor-Conceived Families (2013). See also Mary Patricia Byrn & Rebecca Ireland, Anonymously Provided Sperm and the Constitution, 23 Colum. J. Gender & L. 1 (2012) (arguing that requiring identifying information about donors infringes the constitutional rights of those who conceive with ARTs); I. Glenn Cohen, Response: Rethinking Sperm-Donor Anonymity: Of Changed Selves, Nonidentity, and One-Night Stands, 100 Geo. L.J. 431 (2012) (challenging recommendations to abandon anonymity).

NOTE: FOSTER CARE AND GUARDIANSHIP

When the state removes children from their homes to protect them from abuse and neglect, it often places them in foster families. This arrangement, which divides rights and responsibilities among parents, the state, and foster parents, is often justified by its ability to offer the advantages of a nurturing setting for children in need while maintaining state supervision and promoting reunification with the family of origin. See Smith v. Organization of Foster Families for Equality & Reform, 431 U.S. 816, 826 (1977) (noting New York's division of parental functions among parents, the child welfare agency, and foster parents). Although traditionally understood as a transitional arrangement, foster families might develop strong emotional bonds and wish to remain together. See id. Today, foster care

---

[58]. Sometimes such registries disclose unexpected information. See Jacqueline Mroz, From One Sperm Donor, 150 Children, N.Y. Times, Sept. 6, 2011, at D1.

retains inherent ambiguities, sometimes providing a path to reunification; sometimes leading to TPR and adoption, either by the foster family or others; and sometimes lasting until the child "ages out" by reaching majority. See 42 U.S.C. §675.

Foster parents receive payment from the state for their services. As a result, some expansive approaches to parentage exclude foster parents for this reason alone. For example, the ALI Principles explicitly require that someone who lived with the child and performed substantial caretaking do so "for reasons primarily other than financial compensation" in order to qualify as a "de facto parent." ALI Principles §2.03(1)(c). Presumably, paid nannies would be disqualified for similar reasons, regardless of the child's emotional bond. The result is that, under Troxel v. Granville (Chapter VIII), after reunification a parent can prevent the child's continued contact with a foster parent. But see In re Custody of A.F.J., 314 P.3d 373 (Wash. 2013).

Critics have noted that this restrictive approach to paid caregivers reflects class bias and subordinates a child's emotional bonds to other factors. See, e.g., Pamela Laufer-Ukeles, Money, Caregiving, and Kinship: Should Paid Caregivers Be Allowed to Obtain De Facto Parental Status?, 74 Mo. L. Rev. 25 (2009); Dorothy E. Roberts, Spiritual and Menial Housework, 9 Yale J.L. & Feminism 51 (1997). Nonetheless, subsidies to adults who adopt children with special needs have not raised questions about the adopters' parental status. See, e.g., 42 U.S.C. §673b.

Like foster care, guardianship defies the traditional understanding of parentage as complete and exclusive. See Katharine T. Bartlett, Rethinking Parenthood as an Exclusive Status: The Need for Legal Alternatives When the Premise of the Nuclear Family Has Failed, 70 Va. L. Rev. 879 (1984). Guardianship has emerged as especially important in the context of kinship care, when relatives often choose not to pursue adoption in order to maintain the official status of the child's "parent," regardless of who is performing day-to-day parental functions. E.g., Freedom C. v. Brian D., 280 P.3d 909 (N.M. 2012). Alternative proposals would allow adoption without the termination of parental rights. See Josh Gupta-Kagan, Non-Exclusive Adoption and Child Welfare, 66 Ala. L. Rev. 715 (2015).[59]

Traditionally, parents serve as a child's "natural guardians," but courts appoint a guardian for a minor (or incompetent) when parental care is unavailable or inadequate to serve a particular need of the child. For example, absence for military service might prompt a parent to name a guardian. E.g., Lebo v. Lebo, 886 So. 2d 491 (La. Ct. App. 2004). Most courts hold that, even after seeking a guardianship, a fit parent enjoys the constitutionally based presumption that he or she acts in the child's best interest, including when petitioning to terminate the guardianship. E.g., Matter of Guardianship of W.L., 467 S.W.3d 129 (Ark. 2015).

Contemporary arrangements include standby guardianship, which emerged from the HIV/AIDS epidemic to enable parents suffering from terminal illness to plan for the future of their children before death or incapacitation takes place. This approach responds to the particular situation of ill single mothers by allowing for a "backup" guardian without requiring the mother to relinquish parental rights. See, e.g., Va. Code Ann. §§16.1-349 to 16.1-355. But see In re Richard P., 708 S.E.2d 479 (W. Va. 2010) (healthy parent cannot name friend as co-guardian).

---

[59]. Although the preference for "permanence" under ASFA (see supra pp. 873-874) and related state laws often made ineligible for subsidies kinship foster parents, who want neither to adopt nor to allow non-family members to adopt the child, such support became available under reforms enacted in 2008. See 42 U.S.C. §5106(a)(4); id. §5113(b)(6); Fostering Connections to Success and Increasing Adoptions Act of 2008, Pub. L. No. 110-351, 122 Stat. 3949.

3. Emancipation

When may a child's own conduct limit parental authority and duties?

STATE v. C.R. & R.R.

797 P.2d 459 (Utah Ct. App. 1990)

JACKSON, J. . . .

In October 1984, R.R., nearly fifteen, left his parents' home and lived with various relatives. In the spring of 1985, a petition was filed with the juvenile court alleging that R.R. was a dependent child. See Utah Code Ann. §78-3a-16(1)(c) (1987); Utah Code Ann. §78-3a-2(20) (1987). When R.R.'s mother admitted the allegations in July 1985, the juvenile court found R.R. to be dependent within the meaning of the statute and temporarily awarded legal custody of R.R. to the Utah Department of Family Services (DFS). . . . In October 1986, the temporary order terminated and custody of R.R. was awarded to his parents, to be supervised by DFS until June 1987.

The State filed a petition against R.R.'s parents in the fall of 1988 . . . , seeking reimbursement of $1,159.06 in support for R.R. expended by the State during the period of January 1985 through October 10, 1986. Relying on the common law doctrine of emancipation, R.R.'s parents contested the petition and claimed that their duty to support R.R. was terminated in October 1984 when he voluntarily left their home to live elsewhere and live a lifestyle of which they disapproved. According to the parents' unrefuted testimony, they never ordered R.R. to leave. They were willing to support him in their own home along with his younger siblings if he would agree to abide by their rules. R.R. left to reside elsewhere, they testified, because he refused to accept their condition that he give up his homosexual lifestyle. In response, the State argued that R.R.'s parents had not met their burden of proving emancipation because there was no evidence R.R. was financially independent or that he was able to provide his own residence. The State also argued that R.R. had not left home voluntarily because his parents had forced him to leave the household.

. . . The basic issue presented . . . is whether the juvenile court erroneously concluded that the doctrine of emancipation is not a part of the law in Utah. . . . In American law, judicial emancipation refers to the nonstatutory termination of certain rights and obligations of the parent-child relationship during the child's minority. Katz, Schroeder, & Sidman, Emancipating Our Children—Coming of Legal Age in America, 7 Fam. L.Q. 211, 214 (1973) (hereinafter Katz).

As a result of statutory and common law developments, the American parent is generally held responsible for his child's financial support, health, education, morality, and for instilling in him respect for people and authority. To facilitate the performance of these obligations, the parent is vested with the custody and control of the child, including the requisite disciplinary authority. And, under a heritage of the past, the parent is also entitled to the child's services, and, by derivation, to his or her earnings. When a child is adjudicated a fully emancipated minor, these reciprocal rights and responsibilities are extinguished and are no longer legally enforceable: the emancipated child is thus legally treated as an adult. Although apparently undeveloped at English common law, the doctrine of emancipation has been described as a "basic tenet of family law" in this country, applied by American courts since the early nineteenth century. . . . In several nineteenth century decisions, the fact that a minor voluntarily abandoned the parent's home to pursue a life free from parental control was alone considered sufficient to support a finding of emancipation that terminated the parent's duty of support. As a result, third parties who subsequently furnished necessaries to the minor could not recover from the parent, even in the absence of evidence that the minor was either capable of self-support or had actually supported himself.

[T]he doctrine of emancipation continues to be an accepted part of the common law in this country. [On remand, the trial court should articulate the factors relevant to showing emancipation, determine whether the parents established that their sons were emancipated, and decide whether application of the doctrine would conflict with any Utah law, such as those providing parental support duties.]

Notes and Questions

1. Common law emancipation. The doctrine of emancipation ends certain disabilities of minority. Correlatively, it releases parents from certain obligations to their minor children. Thus, it allows minors to free themselves from parental control before adulthood. Emancipation arises frequently in postdivorce litigation over child support.

Longstanding common law principles of family privacy and parental authority undergird emancipation, highlighting the traditional reciprocity of the parent's duty of support and the child's duty of obedience. See Katharine T. Bartlett, Re-Expressing Parenthood, 98 Yale L.J. 293, 297-298 (1988). For example, in the classic case Roe v. Doe, 272 N.E.2d 567 (N.Y. 1971), the court applied to the parent-child relationship in the intact family the same rule of nonintervention that McGuire v. McGuire (Chapter III) had invoked for married couples. Declining to allow judicial interference with a father's decision to withhold support from his daughter unless she lived in a college dormitory instead of an apartment, the court said:

> The father has the right, in the absence of caprice, misconduct or neglect, to require that the daughter conform to his reasonable demands. Should she disagree, and at her age [20, when the age of majority was 21,] that is surely her prerogative, she may elect not to comply; but in so doing, she subjects herself to her father's lawful wrath. Where, as here, she abandons her home, she forfeits her right to support.

Id. at 570. Does the court suggest that it would reach a different result had it deemed the father's demands "unreasonable"? Who decides reasonableness? How would this approach apply to the facts in *C.R.*?

2. Parental role. Who must initiate the child's departure from home for emancipation to occur? In some states, the child must initiate the departure because otherwise parents could "'divorce their children' and avoid paying child support simply by sending their children away to live with a third party or, worse yet, just throwing the child out of the house." Dunson v. Dunson, 769 N.E.2d 1120, 1124 (Ind. 2002). Who decides whether the parent or child caused the "breakdown"? On remand in *C.R.*, must the court determine who initiated R.R.'s departure from home? Other authorities recognize multiple paths to emancipation:

> Emancipation can be accomplished in one of three ways: (1) by express parental consent; (2) by implied parental consent; or (3) by a change of the child's status in the eyes of society. The third method is usually shown by the child entering the military or marriage; however, it can also be shown when a child, who is able to care for his [*sic*] or herself, voluntarily chooses to leave the parental home and attempts to "fight the battle of life on [his or her] own account."

Scruggs v. Scruggs, 161 S.W.3d 383, 390 (Mo. Ct. App. 2005).

The family conflict precipitating R.R.'s departure from home in the principal case is not uncommon. Empirical studies of homeless youth show a disproportionate number of LGBT minors rejected by their families.[60]

3. Criteria. What factors trigger emancipation? Courts often consider financial independence; living away, especially with parental consent; and the creation of new relationships inconsistent with a subordinate role in the parents' family, such as marriage or military enlistment. Compare Purdy v. Purdy, 578 S.E.2d 30 (S.C. Ct. App. 2003) (pregnancy, cohabitation, and employment are insufficient if minor is not self-supporting), with Caldwell v. Caldwell, 823 So. 2d 1216, 1221 (Miss. Ct. App. 2002) (child's "adult decisions," such as becoming pregnant, help show emancipation). Is imprisonment a self-emancipating event? See In re Marriage of Baumgartner, 912 N.E.2d 783 (Ill. App. Ct. 2009). Suppose that the minor depends on public assistance for support. Compare Dowell v. Dowell, 73 S.W.3d 709 (Mo. Ct. App. 2002), with Oneida County Comm'r of Soc. Servs. v. S., 659 N.Y.S.2d 606 (App. Div. 1997).

A majority of states (including Utah) have now codified the criteria for emancipation. Under California's Emancipation of Minors Act, for example, marriage, active duty in the armed forces, or a judicial declaration emancipates a person under age 18. Cal. Fam. Code §7002. To obtain a judicial declaration of emancipation, a minor must petition the court, setting forth that he or she is at least 14 years old, is willingly living apart from parents with their acquiescence, is managing his or her own financial affairs (shown by an attached declaration of income and expenses), and has no income derived from criminal activity. Id. §7120(b). The court must grant the petition if it finds the minor has met these requirements "and that emancipation would not be contrary to the minor's best interest." Id. §7122(a). Why does California specify the age of 14? Cf., e.g., Kan. Stat. Ann. §§38-108 to 38-109 (specifying no age); Va. Code Ann. §16.1-331 (sixteenth birthday).

---

[60]. See Andrew Cray, et al., Seeking Shelter: The Experiences and Unmet Needs of LGBT Homeless Youth 4 (Center for Am. Progress 2013), https://www.americanprogress.org/wp-content/uploads/2013/09/LGBTHomelessYouth.pdf (stating that "between 9 percent and 45 percent of [homeless] youth are LGBT" and that LGBT youth are "more likely to be homeless than their peers.").

4. Consequences. Notwithstanding emancipation, some prerogatives (for example, driver's license and voting) come only with the attainment of a certain age. Why? Given that the maturity deemed necessary for different adult activities might vary, should law recognize partial or limited emancipation? See, e.g., Diamond v. Diamond, 283 P.3d 260 (N.M. 2012). Cf. Hillary Rodham, Children Under the Law, 43 Harv. Educ. Rev. 487, 507 (1973) (advocating "abolition of the general status of minority and adoption of an area-by-area approach (as has already been done . . . in the motor vehicle statutes)"); Jonathan Todres, Maturity, 48 Hous. L. Rev. 1107 (2012). Should emancipation be permanent, or may it be temporary? See, e.g., Thomas v. Campbell, 960 So. 2d 694 (Ala. Civ. App. 2006).

5. Teen parents. At common law, becoming a parent emancipates a minor. Should that rule prevail today? See LaBrecque v. Parsons, 910 N.E.2d 947 (Mass. App. Ct. 2009). Should states establish a minimum age for parenting or otherwise regulate parenting by minors? Why? See Emily Buss, The Parental Rights of Minors, 48 Buff. L. Rev. 785 (2000); Kendra Huard Fershee, A Parent Is a Parent, No Matter How Small, 18 Wm. & Mary J. Women & L. 425 (2012).

Under federal welfare law, teenage parents must live with their parents or in other adult-supervised settings to qualify for assistance. 42 U.S.C. §608(a)(5). Another provision, designed to deter teen pregnancy, gives the states the option of enforcing support orders against the grandparents of children whose parents are minors receiving welfare; the provision explicitly refers to the "parents of the noncustodial parent." 42 U.S.C. §666(a)(18). What are the implications for parental autonomy? For the ability of children to escape parental authority?

6. The mature minor rule. The mature minor rule, followed in many jurisdictions, is a species of limited or partial emancipation. Under this exception to the common law rule requiring parental consent for medical treatment of a minor, a child near majority can give effective consent if capable of appreciating the nature, extent, and consequences of the treatment. See, e.g., Cardwell v. Bechtol, 724 S.W.2d 739 (Tenn. 1987). See also Barbara L. Atwell, The Modern Age of Informed Consent, 40 U. Rich. L. Rev. 591, 592 (2006) (examining convergence of medical innovations and delay in "fully realized adulthood").

Many states statutorily adopted a mature minor rule specifically for medical care related to drug abuse, venereal disease, and pregnancy, excluding abortion. See, e.g., Mo. Rev. Stat. §431.061(4). Why do such statutes cover these particular situations? Is a lesser degree of maturity necessary for the medical care specified by these statutes than for other treatment? Or do such statutes reflect altogether different concerns? See Martin Guggenheim, What's Wrong with Children's Rights 236 (2005) (all agree that treatment is the only appropriate result). What explains the requirement of parental or judicial involvement for abortion and the absence of similar requirements for medical treatment incident to childbirth? See Planned Parenthood of Cent. N.J. v. Farmer, 762 A.2d 620 (N.J. 2000). (On minors' abortions, see Cincinnati Women's Services v. Taft (Chapter I)).

Should mature minors be able to refuse life-sustaining treatment? Compare In re E.G., 549 N.E.2d 322 (Ill. 1989), with O.G. v. Baum, 790 S.W.2d 839, 842 (Tex. Ct. App. 1990). See Commonwealth v. Nixon, 761 A.2d 1151 (Pa. 2000).

7. Children's autonomy?

a. Children's rights. The United States is one of just two United Nations (UN) member countries (with Somalia) that have not ratified the UN Convention on the Rights of the Child (CRC). See, e.g., Elizabeth Bartholet, Ratification by the United States of the Convention on the Rights of the Child: Pros and Cons from a Child's Rights Perspective, 633 Annals Am. Acad. Pol. & Soc. Sci. 80, 80 (2011). Opposition stems from perceived threats to parental rights. See, e.g., Senate Proceedings on the Hague Convention on International Recovery of Child Support and Family Maintenance, Sept. 29, 2010 (emphasizing commitment to parental rights and reaffirming the U.S. nonratification of CRC). To what extent does the Constitution protect children's rights? See Anne C. Dailey, Children's Constitutional Rights, 95 Minn. L. Rev. 2099 (2011). See generally Joanna L. Grossman & Lawrence M. Friedman, Inside the Castle: Law and the Family in 20th Century America 279-285 (2011).

b. A right of exit? Do emancipation and state intervention (including TPR) provide sufficient "exit rights" for children, given the privacy surrounding the family? Professor Barbara Bennett Woodhouse observes:

> Most fictive entities recognized by the state, from corporations to marriages, are created through voluntary acts and offer various rights of participation as well as a right of exit. The caretaking unit, composed . . . by persons who are inherently and essentially in positions of inequality, is uniquely dangerous and more open, rather than less open, to abuse if completely privatized. This is especially true because children have few, if any, exit options. The right of exit was integral to the message of *McGuire* [Chapter III]. Compare the situation of children whose parents fail to live up to their duties. Children have limited exit options, they cannot file for divorce, no matter how badly their parent has treated them.[61]

See Laura M. Purdy, Boundaries of Authority: Should Children Be Able to Divorce Their Parents?, in Having and Raising Children: Unconventional Families, Hard Choices, and the Social Good 153 (Uma Narayan & Julia J. Bartkowiak, eds., 1999). Children's efforts to "divorce" their parents have not fared well in terms of recognizing the child's own right to sue. See, e.g., Kingsley v. Kingsley, 623 So. 2d 780 (Fla. Dist. Ct. App. 1993); Ryan v. Ryan, 677 N.W.2d 899 (Mich. Ct. App. 2004). But cf. In re Snyder, 532 P.2d 278 (Wash. 1975) (allowing minor to file her own dependency petition, so that she need not return home). What reforms, if any, would you recommend?

c. Recognizing children's experiences on their own terms. To what extent has law assumed that children spend their time only at home or in school? What role do class and race play in prevailing assumptions? How might family law take into account children's lives today, namely that "[m]uch of childhood takes place in spaces between home and school: in playgrounds, parks, child care centers, churches, community gyms, sporting fields, dance studios, music room, after-school clubs, and cyberspace"?[62] What challenges to the standard legal treatment of children emerge from "the reality [that] millions of children today . . . are

---

[61]. Barbara Bennett Woodhouse, The Dark Side of Family Privacy, 67 Geo. Wash. L. Rev. 1247, 1253 (1999).

[62]. Laura A. Rosenbury, Between Home and School, 155 U. Pa. L. Rev. 833, 834 (2006).

spending significant portions of their childhood apart from, or independent of, the traditional family environment and the care of an adult"?[63]

Problems

1. Five-year-old Elian Gonzalez used an inner tube to survive a hazardous boat trip from Cuba to Florida, although his mother perished in the same attempt to come to the United States (before the recent reestablishment of diplomatic relations between the two countries). In Miami, Elian was placed temporarily in the custody of his great-uncle, Lazaro Gonzalez, and his family. Elian's father, who had separated from his mother but had maintained an ongoing relationship with the boy, asked the Miami relatives to return him to Cuba, where Elian would live with his father, his wife, and their child. The Miami relatives decline and now file a petition for asylum on behalf of Elian. Assuming that the federal asylum statute applies to a child, who should decide whether Elian applies for asylum or returns to Cuba? Elian? His father? The Miami relatives who now have custody? Federal immigration officials? A family court? If so, should the decision be made in Miami or Cuba? Of what relevance is the fact that Elian's custodial parent, his mother, had decided to move with him to the United States? See Gonzalez v. Reno, 212 F.3d 1338 (11th Cir. 2000). Cf. Reno v. Flores, 507 U.S. 292, 302-303 (1993); Julia Preston, Young and Alone, Facing Court and Deportation, N.Y. Times, Aug. 26, 2012, at A1.

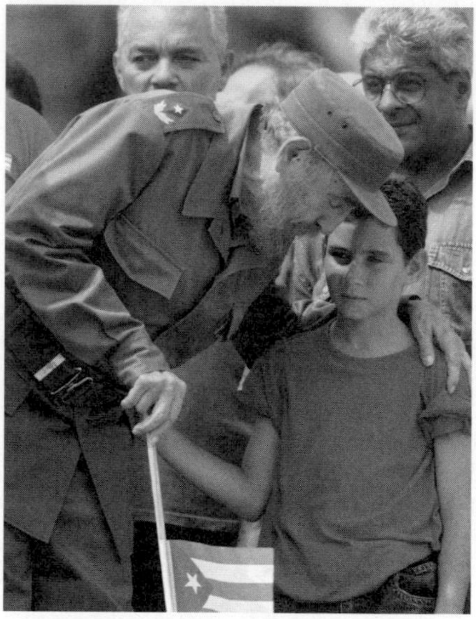

President Fidel Castro (left) and Elian Gonzalez at the May Day parade in Havana after the latter's return to Cuba

Instead, now assume that Elian arrived in the United States at age 12, not 5. He firmly expressed his desire to stay with his Miami relatives instead of returning to Cuba to live with his father, stepmother, and half-brother. Six months after Elian's arrival, his father seeks the assistance of the family court in Miami in returning Elian to his custody; the Department of Children and Family Services asks this court to adjudge Elian a minor in need of supervision and a ward of the state (so that he can remain in the United States); and Elian seeks a declaration of emancipation. What result and why?

This latter scenario is based on the case of Walter Polovchak, who came to the United States with his parents from the then–Ukrainian Soviet Socialist Republic and refused to accompany them when they returned. See In re Polovchak, 454 N.E.2d 258 (Ill. 1983), *cert. denied*, 465 U.S. 1065 (1984). See also Polovchak v.

[63]. See Jonathan Todres, Independent Children and the Legal Construction of Childhood, 23 S. Cal. Interdisc. L.J. 261, 261 (2014).

Meese, 774 F.2d 731 (7th Cir. 1985); Leslie A. Fithian, Note, Forcible Repatriation of Minors: The Competing Rights of Parent and Child, 37 Stan. L. Rev. 187 (1984). Walter tells his own story in Walter Polovchak with Kevin Klose, Freedom's Child: A Courageous Teenager's Story of Fleeing His Parents, and the Soviet Union, to Live in America (1988).

2. Ernest and Regina Twigg sought discovery to determine the paternity of Kimberly Mays. They alleged that Kimberly, who was reared by Robert Mays and his wife (now deceased), was actually the Twiggs' daughter, who had been switched at birth at the hospital. (The daughter reared by the Twiggs, born on the same date at the same hospital, had died of a heart ailment; during the course of her medical treatment, the Twiggs first learned that she was not their biological daughter.) After stipulated blood tests corroborated the Twiggs' claim and the Twiggs sued for custody, Kimberly (age 15) sues for termination of their parental rights so that she can remain with Mays. What result and why? See Twigg v. Mays, 1993 WL 330624 (Fla. Cir. Ct. 1993). Alternatively, suppose that Kimberly sues to terminate Robert Mays's parental rights because she prefers to live with the Twiggs. See Kim Mays Happy with Family, St. Petersburg Times, Nov. 15, 1994, at 5B. See generally Cynthia R. Mabry, The Tragic and Chaotic Aftermath of a Baby Switch: Should Policy and Common Law, Blood Ties, or Psychological Bonds Prevail?, 6 Wm. & Mary J. Women & L. 1 (1999).

■ TABLE OF CASES

Principal cases are indicated by italics.

■ INDEX